THE GOLDEN BOUGH

A HISTORY OF MYTH AND RELIGION

SIR JAMES FRAZER

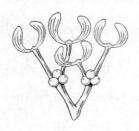

CHANCELLOR
PRESS

The Golden Bough was first published in
two volumes 1890; three volumes, 1900; twelve volumes 1911-15

This abridged volume first published in 1922 by
Macmillan & Co. Limited

1994 by Chancellor Press
an imprint of Reed Consumer Books Limited
Michelin House
81 Fulham Road
London SW3 6RB
and Auckland, Melbourne, Singapore and Toronto

A CIP catalogue record for this title is available
at the British Library

ISBN 1 85152 586 6

Printed in Great Britain by The Bath Press

PREFACE

THE primary aim of this book is to explain the remarkable rule which regulated the succession to the priesthood of Diana at Aricia. When I first set myself to solve the problem more than thirty years ago, I thought that the solution could be propounded very briefly, but I soon found that to render it probable or even intelligible it was necessary to discuss certain more general questions, some of which had hardly been broached before. In successive editions the discussion of these and kindred topics has occupied more and more space, the enquiry has branched out in more and more directions, until the two volumes of the original work have expanded into twelve. Meantime a wish has often been expressed that the book should be issued in a more compendious form. This abridgment is an attempt to meet the wish and thereby to bring the work within the range of a wider circle of readers. While the bulk of the book has been greatly reduced, I have endeavoured to retain its leading principles, together with an amount of evidence sufficient to illustrate them clearly. The language of the original has also for the most part been preserved, though here and there the exposition has been somewhat condensed. In order to keep as much of the text as possible I have sacrificed all the notes, and with them all exact references to my authorities. Readers who desire to ascertain the source of any particular statement must therefore consult the larger work, which is fully documented and provided with a complete bibliography.

In the abridgment I have neither added new matter nor altered the views expressed in the last edition ; for the evidence which has come to my knowledge in the meantime has on the whole served either to confirm my former conclusions or to furnish fresh illustrations of old principles. Thus, for example, on the crucial question of the practice of putting kings to death either at the end of a fixed period or whenever their health and strength began to fail, the body of evidence which points to the wide prevalence of such a custom has been considerably augmented in the interval. A striking instance of a limited monarchy of this sort is furnished by the powerful mediaeval kingdom of the Khazars in Southern Russia, where the kings were liable to be put to death either on the expiry of a set term or whenever some public calamity, such as drought, dearth, or defeat in war, seemed to indicate a failure of their natural powers. The evidence for the systematic killing of the Khazar kings, drawn from the accounts of old Arab travellers, has been collected by me elsewhere.[1] Africa, again, has supplied several fresh examples of a similar practice of regicide. Among them the most notable perhaps is the custom formerly observed in Bunyoro of choosing every year from a particular clan a mock king, who was supposed to incarnate the late king, co-habited with his widows at his temple-tomb, and after reigning for a week was strangled.[2] The custom presents a close parallel to the ancient Babylonian festival of the Sacaea, at which a mock king was dressed in the royal robes, allowed to enjoy the real king's concubines, and after reigning for five days was stripped, scourged, and put to death. That festival in its turn has lately received fresh light from certain Assyrian inscriptions,[3] which seem to confirm the interpretation which I formerly gave of the festival as a New Year celebration and the parent of the Jewish festival of Purim.[4] Other recently discovered parallels to the priestly kings of Aricia are African priests and kings who used to be put to death at the end of seven or of two years, after being liable in the interval to be attacked and killed by a strong man, who there-upon succeeded to the priesthood or the kingdom.[5]

With these and other instances of like customs before us it is no longer possible to regard the rule of succession to the priesthood of Diana at Aricia as exceptional; it clearly exemplifies a widespread institution, of which the most numerous and the most similar cases have thus far been found in Africa. How far the facts point to an early influence of Africa on Italy, or even to the existence of an African population in Southern Europe, I do not presume to say. The pre-

[1] J. G. Frazer, "The Killing of the Khazar Kings," *Folk-lore*, xxviii. (1917) pp. 382-407.

[2] Rev. J. Roscoe, *The Soul of Central Africa* (London, 1922), p. 200. Compare J. G. Frazer, "The Mackie Ethnological Expedition to Central Africa," *Man*, xx. (1920) p. 181.

[3] H. Zimmern, *Zum babylonischen Neujahrsfest* (Leipzig, 1918). Compare A. H. Sayce, in *Journal of the Royal Asiatic Society*, July 1921, pp. 440-442.

[4] *The Golden Bough*, Part VI. *The Scapegoat*, pp. 354 *sqq.*, 412 *sqq.*

[5] P. Amaury Talbot, in *Journal of the African Society*, July 1916, pp. 309 *sq.*; *id.*, in *Folk-lore*, xxvi. (1916) pp. 79 *sq.*; H. R. Palmer, in *Journal of the African Society*, July 1912, pp. 403, 407 *sq.*

historic relations between the two continents are still obscure and still under investigation.

Whether the explanation which I have offered of the institution is correct or not must be left to the future to determine. I shall always be ready to abandon it if a better can be suggested. Meantime in committing the book in its new form to the judgment of the public I desire to guard against a misapprehension of its scope which appears to be still rife, though I have sought to correct it before now. If in the present work I have dwelt at some length on the worship of trees, it is not, I trust, because I exaggerate its importance in the history of religion, still less because I would deduce from it a whole system of mythology ; it is simply because I could not ignore the subject in attempting to explain the significance of a priest who bore the title of King of the Wood, and one of whose titles to office was the plucking of a bough—the Golden Bough—from a tree in the sacred grove. But I am so far from regarding the reverence for trees as of supreme importance for the evolution of religion that I consider it to have been altogether subordinate to other factors, and in particular to the fear of the human dead, which, on the whole, I believe to have been probably the most powerful force in the making of primitive religion. I hope that after this explicit disclaimer I shall no longer be taxed with embracing a system of mythology which I look upon not merely as false but as preposterous and absurd. But I am too familiar with the hydra of error to expect that by lopping off one of the monster's heads I can prevent another, or even the same, from sprouting again. I can only trust to the candour and intelligence of my readers to rectify this serious misconception of my views by a comparison with my own express declaration.

J. G. FRAZER.

1 Brick Court, Temple,
  London, *June* 1922.

Longior undecimi nobis decimique libelli
  Artatus labor est et breve rasit opus.
Plura legant vacui.

MARTIAL, xii. 5.

CONTENTS

ix

CONTENTS

CHAPTER 1

THE KING OF THE WOOD

§ 1. *Diana and Virbius.*—Who does not know Turner's picture of the Golden Bough ? The scene, suffused with the golden glow of imagination in which the divine mind of Turner steeped and transfigured even the fairest natural landscape, is a dream-like vision of the little woodland lake of Nemi—" Diana's Mirror," as it was called by the ancients. No one who has seen that calm water, lapped in a green hollow of the Alban hills, can ever forget it. The two characteristic Italian villages which slumber on its banks, and the equally Italian palace whose terraced gardens descend steeply to the lake, hardly break the stillness and even the solitariness of the scene. Dian herself might still linger by this lonely shore, still haunt these woodlands wild.

In antiquity this sylvan landscape was the scene of a strange and recurring tragedy. On the northern shore of the lake, right under the precipitous cliffs on which the modern village of Nemi is perched, stood the sacred grove and sanctuary of Diana Nemorensis, or Diana of the Wood. The lake and the grove were sometimes known as the lake and grove of Aricia. But the town of Aricia (the modern La Riccia) was situated about three miles off, at the foot of the Alban Mount, and separated by a steep descent from the lake, which lies in a small crater-like hollow on the mountain side. In this sacred grove there grew a certain tree round which at any time of the day, and probably far into the night, a grim figure might be seen to prowl. In his hand he carried a drawn sword, and he kept peering warily about him as if at every instant he expected to be set upon by an enemy. He was a priest and a murderer ; and the man for whom he looked was sooner or later to murder him and hold the priesthood in his stead. Such was the rule of the sanctuary. A candidate for the priesthood could only succeed to office by slaying the priest, and having slain him, he retained office till he was himself slain by a stronger or a craftier.

The post which he held by this precarious tenure carried with it the title of king ; but surely no crowned head ever lay uneasier, or was visited by more evil dreams, than his. For year in year out, in summer and winter, in fair weather and in foul, he had to keep his lonely watch, and whenever he snatched a troubled slumber it was at the peril of his life. The least relaxation of his vigilance, the smallest abatement of his strength of limb or skill of fence, put him in jeopardy ; grey hairs might seal his death-warrant. To gentle and pious pilgrims at the shrine the sight of him might well seem to darken the fair landscape, as when a cloud suddenly blots the sun on a bright day. The

B

dreamy blue of Italian skies, the dappled shade of summer woods, and the sparkle of waves in the sun, can have accorded but ill with that stern and sinister figure. Rather we picture to ourselves the scene as it may have been witnessed by a belated wayfarer on one of those wild autumn nights when the dead leaves are falling thick, and the winds seem to sing the dirge of the dying year. It is a sombre picture, set to melancholy music—the background of forest showing black and jagged against a lowering and stormy sky, the sighing of the wind in the branches, the rustle of the withered leaves under foot, the lapping of the cold water on the shore, and in the foreground, pacing to and fro, now in twilight and now in gloom, a dark figure with a glitter of steel at the shoulder whenever the pale moon, riding clear of the cloud-rack, peers down at him through the matted boughs.

The strange rule of this priesthood has no parallel in classical antiquity, and cannot be explained from it. To find an explanation we must go farther afield. No one will probably deny that such a custom savours of a barbarous age, and, surviving into imperial times, stands out in striking isolation from the polished Italian society of the day, like a primaeval rock rising from a smooth-shaven lawn. It is the very rudeness and barbarity of the custom which allow us a hope of explaining it. For recent researches into the early history of man have revealed the essential similarity with which, under many superficial differences, the human mind has elaborated its first crude philosophy of life. Accordingly, if we can show that a barbarous custom, like that of the priesthood of Nemi, has existed elsewhere ; if we can detect the motives which led to its institution ; if we can prove that these motives have operated widely, perhaps universally, in human society, producing in varied circumstances a variety of institutions specifically different but generically alike ; if we can show, lastly, that these very motives, with some of their derivative institutions, were actually at work in classical antiquity ; then we may fairly infer that at a remoter age the same motives gave birth to the priesthood of Nemi. Such an inference, in default of direct evidence as to how the priesthood did actually arise, can never amount to demonstration. But it will be more or less probable according to the degree of completeness with which it fulfils the conditions I have indicated. The object of this book is, by meeting these conditions, to offer a fairly probable explanation of the priesthood of Nemi.

I begin by setting forth the few facts and legends which have come down to us on the subject. According to one story the worship of Diana at Nemi was instituted by Orestes, who, after killing Thoas, king of the Tauric Chersonese (the Crimea), fled with his sister to Italy, bringing with him the image of the Tauric Diana hidden in a faggot of sticks. After his death his bones were transported from Aricia to Rome and buried in front of the temple of Saturn, on the Capitoline slope, beside the temple of Concord. The bloody ritual which legend ascribed to the Tauric Diana is familiar to classical readers ; it is said that every stranger who landed on the shore was sacrificed on her altar. But transported to Italy, the rite assumed a milder form. Within the sanctuary at Nemi grew a certain tree of which no branch might be broken. Only a runaway slave was allowed to break off, if he could, one of its boughs. Success in the attempt entitled him to fight the priest in single combat, and if he slew him he reigned in his stead with the title of King of the Wood (*Rex Nemorensis*). According to the public opinion of the ancients the fateful branch was that Golden Bough which, at the Sibyl's bidding, Aeneas plucked before he essayed the perilous journey to the world of the dead. The flight of the slave represented, it was said, the flight of Orestes ; his combat with the priest was a reminiscence of the human sacrifices once offered to the Tauric Diana. This rule of succession by the sword was observed down to imperial times ; for amongst his other freaks Caligula, thinking that the priest of Nemi had held office too long, hired a more stalwart ruffian to slay him ; and a Greek traveller, who visited Italy in the age of the Antonines, remarks that down to his time the priesthood was still the prize of victory in a single combat.

Of the worship of Diana at Nemi some leading features can still be made out. From the votive offerings which have been found on the site, it appears that she was conceived of especially as a huntress, and further as blessing men and women with offspring, and granting expectant mothers an easy delivery. Again, fire seems to have played a foremost part in her ritual. For during her annual festival, held on the thirteenth of August, at the hottest time of the year, her grove shone with a multitude of torches, whose ruddy glare was reflected by the lake ; and throughout the length and breadth of Italy the day was kept with holy rites at every domestic hearth. Bronze statuettes found in her precinct represent the goddess herself holding a torch in her raised right hand ; and women whose prayers had been heard by her came crowned with wreaths and bearing lighted torches to the sanctuary in fulfilment of their vows. Some one unknown dedicated a perpetually burning lamp in a little shrine at Nemi for the safety of the Emperor Claudius and his family. The terra-cotta lamps which have been discovered in the grove may perhaps have served a like purpose for humbler persons. If so, the analogy of the custom to the Catholic practice of dedicating holy candles in churches would be obvious. Further, the title of Vesta borne by Diana at Nemi points clearly to the maintenance of a perpetual holy fire in her sanctuary. A large circular basement at the north-east corner of the temple, raised on three steps and bearing traces of a mosaic pavement, probably supported a round temple of Diana in her character of Vesta, like the round temple of Vesta in the Roman Forum. Here the sacred fire would seem to have been tended by Vestal Virgins, for the head of a Vestal in terra-cotta was found on the spot, and the worship of a perpetual fire, cared for by holy maidens, appears to have been common in Latium from the earliest to the latest times. Further, at the annual festival of the goddess, hunting dogs were crowned and wild beasts were not molested ; young people went through a purificatory ceremony in her honour; wine was brought forth, and the feast consisted of a kid, cakes served piping hot on plates of leaves, and apples still hanging in clusters on the boughs.

But Diana did not reign alone in her grove at Nemi. Two lesser divinities shared her forest sanctuary. One was Egeria, the nymph of the clear water which, bubbling from the basaltic rocks, used to fall in graceful cascades into the lake at the place called Le Mole, because here were established the mills of the modern village of Nemi. The purling of the stream as it ran over the pebbles is mentioned by Ovid, who tells us that he had often drunk of its water. Women with child used to sacrifice to Egeria, because she was believed, like Diana, to be able to grant them an easy delivery. Tradition ran that the nymph had been the wife or mistress of the wise king Numa, that he had consorted with her in the secrecy of the sacred grove, and that the laws which he gave the Romans had been inspired by communion with her divinity. Plutarch compares the legend with other tales of the loves of goddesses for mortal men, such as the love of Cybele and the Moon for the fair youths Attis and Endymion. According to some, the trysting-place of the lovers was not in the woods of Nemi but in a grove outside the dripping Porta Capena at Rome, where another sacred spring of Egeria gushed from a dark cavern. Every day the Roman Vestals fetched water from this spring to wash the temple of Vesta, carrying it in earthenware pitchers on their heads. In Juvenal's time the natural rock had been encased in marble, and the hallowed spot was profaned by gangs of poor Jews, who were suffered to squat, like gypsies, in the grove. We may suppose that the spring which fell into the lake of Nemi was the true original Egeria, and that when the first settlers moved down from the Alban hills to the banks of the Tiber they brought the nymph with them and found a new home for her in a grove outside the gates. The remains of baths which have been discovered within the sacred precinct, together with many terra-cotta models of various parts of the human body, suggest that the waters of Egeria were used to heal the sick, who may have signified their hopes or testified their gratitude by dedicating likenesses of the diseased members to the goddess, in accordance with a custom which is still observed in many parts of Europe. To this day it would seem that the spring retains medicinal virtues.

The other of the minor deities at Nemi was Virbius. Legend had it that Virbius was the young Greek hero Hippolytus, chaste and fair, who learned the art of venery from the centaur Chiron, and spent all his days in the greenwood chasing wild beasts with the virgin huntress Artemis (the Greek counterpart of Diana) for his only comrade. Proud of her divine society, he spurned the love of women, and this proved his bane. For Aphrodite, stung by his scorn, inspired his stepmother Phaedra with love of him; and when he disdained her wicked advances she falsely accused him to his father Theseus. The slander was believed, and Theseus prayed to his sire Poseidon to avenge the imagined wrong. So while Hippolytus drove in a chariot by the shore of the Saronic Gulf, the sea-god sent a fierce bull forth from the waves. The terrified horses bolted, threw Hippolytus from the chariot, and dragged him at their hoofs to death. But Diana, for the love she bore Hippolytus, persuaded the leech Aesculapius to bring her fair young hunter back to life by his simples. Jupiter, indignant that a mortal man should return from the gates of death, thrust down the meddling leech himself to Hades. But Diana hid her favourite from the angry god in a thick cloud, disguised his features by adding years to his life, and then bore him far away to the dells of Nemi, where she entrusted him to the nymph Egeria, to live there, unknown and solitary, under the name of Virbius, in the depth of the Italian forest. There he reigned a king, and there he dedicated a precinct to Diana. He had a comely son, Virbius, who, undaunted by his father's fate, drove a team of fiery steeds to join the Latins in the war against Aeneas and the Trojans. Virbius was worshipped as a god not only at Nemi but elsewhere ; for in Campania we hear of a special priest devoted to his service. Horses were excluded from the Arician grove and sanctuary because horses had killed Hippolytus. It was unlawful to touch his image. Some thought that he was the sun. " But the truth is," says Servius, " that he is a deity associated with Diana, as Attis is associated with the Mother of the Gods, and Erichthonius with Minerva, and Adonis with Venus." What the nature of that association was we shall enquire presently. Here it is worth observing that in his long and chequered career this mythical personage has displayed a remarkable tenacity of life. For we can hardly doubt that the Saint Hippolytus of the Roman calendar, who was dragged by horses to death on the thirteenth of August, Diana's own day, is no other than the Greek hero of the same name, who, after dying twice over as a heathen sinner, has been happily resuscitated as a Christian saint.

It needs no elaborate demonstration to convince us that the stories told to account for Diana's worship at Nemi are unhistorical. Clearly they belong to that large class of myths which are made up to explain the origin of a religious ritual and have no other foundation than the resemblance, real or imaginary, which may be traced between it and some foreign ritual. The incongruity of these Nemi myths is indeed transparent, since the foundation of the worship is traced now to Orestes and now to Hippolytus, according as this or that feature of the ritual has to be accounted for. The real value of such tales is that they serve to illustrate the nature of the worship by providing a standard with which to compare it ; and further, that they bear witness indirectly to its venerable age by showing that the true origin was lost in the mists of a fabulous antiquity. In the latter respect these Nemi legends are probably more to be trusted than the apparently historical tradition, vouched for by Cato the Elder, that the sacred grove was dedicated to Diana by a certain Egerius Baebius or Laevius of Tusculum, a Latin dictator, on behalf of the peoples of Tusculum, Aricia, Lanuvium, Laurentum, Cora, Tibur, Pometia, and Ardea.

This tradition indeed speaks for the great age of the sanctuary, since it seems to date its foundation sometime before 495 B.C., the year in which Pometia was sacked by the Romans and disappears from history. But we cannot suppose that so barbarous a rule as that of the Arician priesthood was deliberately instituted by a league of civilised communities, such as the Latin cities undoubtedly were. It must have been handed down from a time beyond the memory of man, when Italy was still in a far ruder state than any known to us in the historical period. The credit of the tradition is rather shaken than confirmed by another story which ascribes the foundation of the sanctuary to a certain Manius Egerius, who gave rise to the saying, " There are many Manii at Aricia." This proverb some explained by alleging that Manius Egerius was the ancestor of a long and distinguished line, whereas others thought it meant that there were many ugly and deformed people at Aricia, and they derived the name Manius from *Mania*, a bogy or bugbear to frighten children. A Roman satirist uses the name Manius as typical of the beggars who lay in wait for pilgrims on the Arician slopes. These differences of opinion, together with the discrepancy between Manius Egerius of Aricia and Egerius Laevius of Tusculum, as well as the resemblance of both names to the mythical Egeria, excite our suspicion. Yet the tradition recorded by Cato seems too circumstantial, and its sponsor too respectable, to allow us to dismiss it as an idle fiction. Rather we may suppose that it refers to some ancient restoration or reconstruction of the sanctuary, which was actually carried out by the confederate states. At any rate it testifies to a belief that the grove had been from early times a common place of worship for many of the oldest cities of the country, if not for the whole Latin confederacy.

§ 2. *Artemis and Hippolytus.*—I have said that the Arician legends of Orestes and Hippolytus, though worthless as history, have a certain value in so far as they may help us to understand the worship at Nemi better by comparing it with the ritual and myths of other sanctuaries. We must ask ourselves, Why did the authors of these legends pitch upon Orestes and Hippolytus in order to explain Virbius and the King of the Wood ? In regard to Orestes, the answer is obvious. He and the image of the Tauric Diana, which could only be appeased with human blood, were dragged in to render intelligible the murderous rule of succession to the Arician priesthood. In regard to Hippolytus the case is not so plain. The manner of his death suggests readily enough a reason for the exclusion of horses from the grove ; but this by itself seems hardly enough to account for the identification. We must try to probe deeper by examining the worship as well as the legend or myth of Hippolytus.

He had a famous sanctuary at his ancestral home of Troezen, situated on that beautiful, almost landlocked bay, where groves of oranges and lemons, with tall cypresses soaring like dark spires above the garden of the Hesperides, now clothe the strip of fertile shore at the foot of the rugged mountains. Across the blue water of the

tranquil bay, which it shelters from the open sea, rises Poseidon's
sacred island, its peaks veiled in the sombre green of the pines.   On
this fair coast Hippolytus was worshipped.   Within his sanctuary
stood a temple with an ancient image.   His service was performed
by a priest who held office for life : every year a sacrificial festival
was held in his honour ; and his untimely fate was yearly mourned,
with weeping and doleful chants, by unwedded maids.   Youths and
maidens dedicated locks of their hair in his temple before marriage.
His grave existed at Troezen, though the people would not show it.
It has been suggested, with great plausibility, that in the handsome
Hippolytus, beloved of Artemis, cut off in his youthful prime, and
yearly mourned by damsels, we have one of those mortal lovers of
a goddess who appear so often in ancient religion, and of whom Adonis
is the most familiar type.   The rivalry of Artemis and Phaedra for
the affection of Hippolytus reproduces, it is said, under different
names, the rivalry of Aphrodite and Proserpine for the love of Adonis,
for Phaedra is merely a double of Aphrodite.   The theory probably
does no injustice either to Hippolytus or to Artemis.   For Artemis was
originally a great goddess of fertility, and, on the principles of early
religion, she who fertilises nature must herself be fertile, and to be that
she must necessarily have a male consort.   On this view, Hippolytus was
the consort of Artemis at Troezen, and the shorn tresses offered to him
by the Troezenian youths and maidens before marriage were designed
to strengthen his union with the goddess, and so to promote the fruitfulness of the earth, of cattle, and of mankind.   It is some confirmation of this view that within the precinct of Hippolytus at Troezen
there were worshipped two female powers named Damia and Auxesia,
whose connexion with the fertility of the ground is unquestionable.
When Epidaurus suffered from a dearth, the people, in obedience to
an oracle, carved images of Damia and Auxesia out of sacred olive-
wood, and no sooner had they done so and set them up than the earth
bore fruit again.   Moreover, at Troezen itself, and apparently within
the precinct of Hippolytus, a curious festival of stone-throwing was
held in honour of these maidens, as the Troezenians called them ;
and it is easy to show that similar customs have been practised in
many lands for the express purpose of ensuring good crops.   In the
story of the tragic death of the youthful Hippolytus we may discern
an analogy with similar tales of other fair but mortal youths who paid
with their lives for the brief rapture of the love of an immortal goddess.
These hapless lovers were probably not always mere myths, and the
legends which traced their spilt blood in the purple bloom of the violet,
the scarlet stain of the anemone, or the crimson flush of the rose were
no idle poetic emblems of youth and beauty fleeting as the summer
flowers.   Such fables contain a deeper philosophy of the relation of
the life of man to the life of nature—a sad philosophy which gave
birth to a tragic practice.   What that philosophy and that practice
were, we shall learn later on.

§ 3. *Recapitulation.*—We can now perhaps understand why the ancients identified Hippolytus, the consort of Artemis, with Virbius, who, according to Servius, stood to Diana as Adonis to Venus, or Attis to the Mother of the Gods. For Diana, like Artemis, was a goddess of fertility in general, and of childbirth in particular. As such she, like her Greek counterpart, needed a male partner. That partner, if Servius is right, was Virbius. In his character of the founder of the sacred grove and first king of Nemi, Virbius is clearly the mythical predecessor or archetype of the line of priests who served Diana under the title of Kings of the Wood, and who came, like him, one after the other, to a violent end. It is natural, therefore, to conjecture that they stood to the goddess of the grove in the same relation in which Virbius stood to her ; in short, that the mortal King of the Wood had for his queen the woodland Diana herself. If the sacred tree which he guarded with his life was supposed, as seems probable, to be her special embodiment, her priest may not only have worshipped it as his goddess but embraced it as his wife. There is at least nothing absurd in the supposition, since even in the time of Pliny a noble Roman used thus to treat a beautiful beech-tree in another sacred grove of Diana on the Alban hills. He embraced it, he kissed it, he lay under its shadow, he poured wine on its trunk. Apparently he took the tree for the goddess. The custom of physically marrying men and women to trees is still practised in India and other parts of the East. Why should it not have obtained in ancient Latium ?

Reviewing the evidence as a whole, we may conclude that the worship of Diana in her sacred grove at Nemi was of great importance and immemorial antiquity ; that she was revered as the goddess of woodlands and of wild creatures, probably also of domestic cattle and of the fruits of the earth ; that she was believed to bless men and women with offspring and to aid mothers in childbed ; that her holy fire, tended by chaste virgins, burned perpetually in a round temple within the precinct ; that associated with her was a water-nymph Egeria who discharged one of Diana's own functions by succouring women in travail, and who was popularly supposed to have mated with an old Roman king in the sacred grove ; further, that Diana of the Wood herself had a male companion Virbius by name, who was to her what Adonis was to Venus, or Attis to Cybele ; and, lastly, that this mythical Virbius was represented in historical times by a line of priests known as Kings of the Wood, who regularly perished by the swords of their successors, and whose lives were in a manner bound up with a certain tree in the grove, because so long as that tree was uninjured they were safe from attack.

Clearly these conclusions do not of themselves suffice to explain the peculiar rule of succession to the priesthood. But perhaps the survey of a wider field may lead us to think that they contain in germ the solution of the problem. To that wider survey we must now address ourselves. It will be long and laborious, but may possess something of the interest and charm of a voyage of discovery, in which we shall visit many strange foreign lands, with strange foreign peoples, and still stranger customs. The wind is in the shrouds : we shake out our sails to it, and leave the coast of Italy behind us for a time.

CHAPTER II

PRIESTLY KINGS

THE questions which we have set ourselves to answer are mainly two : first, why had Diana's priest at Nemi, the King of the Wood, to slay his predecessor ? second, why before doing so had he to pluck the branch of a certain tree which the public opinion of the ancients identified with Virgil's Golden Bough ?

The first point on which we fasten is the priest's title. Why was he called the King of the Wood ? Why was his office spoken of as a kingdom ?

The union of a royal title with priestly duties was common in ancient Italy and Greece. At Rome and in other cities of Latium there was a priest called the Sacrificial King or King of the Sacred Rites, and his wife bore the title of Queen of the Sacred Rites. In republican Athens the second annual magistrate of the state was called the King, and his wife the Queen ; the functions of both were religious. Many other Greek democracies had titular kings, whose duties, so far as they are known, seem to have been priestly, and to have centred round the Common Hearth of the state. Some Greek states had several of these titular kings, who held office simultaneously. At Rome the tradition was that the Sacrificial King had been appointed after the abolition of the monarchy in order to offer the sacrifices which before had been offered by the kings. A similar view as to the origin of the priestly kings appears to have prevailed in Greece. In itself the opinion is not improbable, and it is borne out by the example of Sparta, almost the only purely Greek state which retained the kingly form of government in historical times. For in Sparta all state sacrifices were offered by the kings as descendants of the god. One of the two Spartan kings held the priesthood of Zeus Lacedaemon, the other the priesthood of Heavenly Zeus.

This combination of priestly functions with royal authority is familiar to every one. Asia Minor, for example, was the seat of various great religious capitals peopled by thousands of sacred slaves, and ruled by pontiffs who wielded at once temporal and spiritual authority, like the popes of mediaeval Rome. Such priest-ridden cities were Zela and Pessinus. Teutonic kings, again, in the old heathen days seem to have stood in the position, and to have exercised the powers, of high priests. The Emperors of China offered public sacrifices, the details of which were regulated by the ritual books. The King of Madagascar was high-priest of the realm. At the great festival of the new year, when a bullock was sacrificed for the good of the kingdom, the king stood over the sacrifice to offer prayer and thanksgiving, while his attendants slaughtered the animal.   In the monarchical states which still maintain their independence among the Gallas of Eastern Africa, the king sacrifices on the mountain tops and regulates the immolation of human victims ; and the dim light of tradition reveals a similar union of temporal and spiritual power, of royal and priestly duties, in the kings of that delightful region of Central America whose ancient capital, now buried under the rank growth of the tropical forest, is marked by the stately and mysterious ruins of Palenque.

When we have said that the ancient kings were commonly priests also, we are far from having exhausted the religious aspect of their office.   In those days the divinity that hedges a king was no empty form of speech, but the expression of a sober belief.   Kings were revered, in many cases not merely as priests, that is, as intercessors between man and god, but as themselves gods, able to bestow upon their subjects and worshippers those blessings which are commonly supposed to be beyond the reach of mortals, and are sought, if at all, only by prayer and sacrifice offered to superhuman and invisible beings.   Thus kings are often expected to give rain and sunshine in due season, to make the crops grow, and so on.   Strange as this expectation appears to us, it is quite of a piece with early modes of thought.   A savage hardly conceives the distinction commonly drawn by more advanced peoples between the natural and the supernatural. To him the world is to a great extent worked by supernatural agents, that is, by personal beings acting on impulses and motives like his own, liable like him to be moved by appeals to their pity, their hopes, and their fears.   In a world so conceived he sees no limit to his power of influencing the course of nature to his own advantage.   Prayers, promises, or threats may secure him fine weather and an abundant crop from the gods ; and if a god should happen, as he sometimes believes, to become incarnate in his own person, then he need appeal to no higher being ; he, the savage, possesses in himself all the powers necessary to further his own well-being and that of his fellow-men.

This is one way in which the idea of a man-god is reached.   But there is another.   Along with the view of the world as pervaded by spiritual forces, savage man has a different, and probably still older, conception in which we may detect a germ of the modern notion of natural law or the view of nature as a series of events occurring in an invariable order without the intervention of personal agency.   The germ of which I speak is involved in that sympathetic magic, as it may be called, which plays a large part in most systems of superstition. In early society the king is frequently a magician as well as a priest ; indeed he appears to have often attained to power by virtue of his supposed proficiency in the black or white art.   Hence in order to understand the evolution of the kingship and the sacred character with which the office has commonly been invested in the eyes of savage or barbarous peoples, it is essential to have some acquaintance with the principles of magic and to form some conception of the extraordinary hold which that ancient system of superstition has had on the human mind in all ages and all countries. Accordingly I propose to consider the subject in some detail.

CHAPTER III

SYMPATHETIC MAGIC

§ 1. *The Principles of Magic.*——If we analyse the principles of thought on which magic is based, they will probably be found to resolve themselves into two : first, that like produces like, or that an effect resembles its cause ; and, second, that things which have once been in contact with each other continue to act on each other at a distance after the physical contact has been severed. The former principle may be called the Law of Similarity, the latter the Law of Contact or Contagion. From the first of these principles, namely the Law of Similarity, the magician infers that he can produce any effect he desires merely by imitating it : from the second he infers that whatever he does to a material object will affect equally the person with whom the object was once in contact, whether it formed part of his body or not. Charms based on the Law of Similarity may be called Homoeopathic or Imitative Magic. Charms based on the Law of Contact or Contagion may be called Contagious Magic. To denote the first of these branches of magic the term Homoeopathic is perhaps preferable, for the alternative term Imitative or Mimetic suggests, if it does not imply, a conscious agent who imitates, thereby limiting the scope of magic too narrowly. For the same principles which the magician applies in the practice of his art are implicitly believed by him to regulate the operations of inanimate nature ; in other words, he tacitly assumes that the Laws of Similarity and Contact are of universal application and are not limited to human actions. In short, magic is a spurious system of natural law as well as a fallacious guide of conduct ; it is a false science as well as an abortive art. Regarded as a system of natural law, that is, as a statement of the rules which determine the sequence of events throughout the world, it may be called Theoretical Magic : regarded as a set of precepts which human beings observe in order to compass their ends, it may be called Practical Magic. At the same time it is to be borne in mind that the primitive magician knows magic only on its practical side ; he never analyses the mental processes on which his practice is based, never reflects on the abstract principles involved in his actions. With him, as with the vast majority of men, logic is implicit, not explicit : he reasons just as he digests his food in complete ignorance of the intellectual and physiological processes which are essential to the one operation and to the other. In short, to him magic is always an art, never a science ; the very idea of science is lacking in his undeveloped mind. It is for the philosophic student to trace the train of thought which underlies the magician's practice ; to draw out the few simple threads of which the tangled skein is composed ; to disengage the abstract principles from their concrete applications ; in short, to discern the spurious science behind the bastard art.

If my analysis of the magician's logic is correct, its two great principles turn out to be merely two different misapplications of the association of ideas. Homoeopathic magic is founded on the association of ideas by similarity : contagious magic is founded on the association of ideas by contiguity. Homoeopathic magic commits the mistake of assuming that things which resemble each other are the same : contagious magic commits the mistake of assuming that things which have once been in contact with each other are always in contact. But in practice the two branches are often combined ; or, to be more exact, while homoeopathic or imitative magic may be practised by itself, contagious magic will generally be found to involve an application of the homoeopathic or imitative principle. Thus generally stated the two things may be a little difficult to grasp, but they will readily become intelligible when they are illustrated by particular examples. Both trains of thought are in fact extremely simple and elementary. It could hardly be otherwise, since they are familiar in the concrete, though certainly not in the abstract, to the crude intelligence not only of the savage, but of ignorant and dull-witted people everywhere. Both branches of magic, the homoeopathic and the contagious, may conveniently be comprehended under the general name of Sympathetic Magic, since both assume that things act on each other at a distance through a secret sympathy, the impulse being transmitted from one to the other by means of what we may conceive as a kind of invisible ether, not unlike that which is postulated by modern science for a precisely similar purpose, namely, to explain how things can physically affect each other through a space which appears to be empty.

It may be convenient to tabulate as follows the branches of magic according to the laws of thought which underlie them :

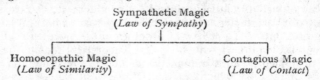

Sympathetic Magic
(*Law of Sympathy*)

Homoeopathic Magic   Contagious Magic
(*Law of Similarity*)   (*Law of Contact*)

I will now illustrate these two great branches of sympathetic magic by examples, beginning with homoeopathic magic.

§ 2. *Homoeopathic or Imitative Magic.*—Perhaps the most familiar application of the principle that like produces like is the attempt which has been made by many peoples in many ages to injure or destroy an enemy by injuring or destroying an image of him, in the belief that, just as the image suffers, so does the man, and that when it perishes

he must die.   A few instances out of many may be given to prove at
once the wide diffusion of the practice over the world and its remarkable persistence through the ages.   For thousands of years ago it was
known to the sorcerers of ancient India, Babylon, and Egypt, as well
as of Greece and Rome, and at this day it is still resorted to by cunning
and malignant savages in Australia, Africa, and Scotland.   Thus the
North American Indians, we are told, believe that by drawing the
figure of a person in sand, ashes, or clay, or by considering any object
as his body, and then pricking it with a sharp stick or doing it any
other injury, they inflict a corresponding injury on the person represented.   For example, when an Ojebway Indian desires to work evil
on any one, he makes a little wooden image of his enemy and runs a
needle into its head or heart, or he shoots an arrow into it, believing
that wherever the needle pierces or the arrow strikes the image, his
foe will the same instant be seized with a sharp pain in the corresponding part of his body ; but if he intends to kill the person outright, he
burns or buries the puppet, uttering certain magic words as he does
so.   The Peruvian Indians moulded images of fat mixed with grain to
imitate the persons whom they disliked or feared, and then burned the
effigy on the road where the intended victim was to pass.   This they
called burning his soul.

A Malay charm of the same sort is as follows.   Take parings of
nails, hair, eyebrows, spittle, and so forth of your intended victim,
enough to represent every part of his person, and then make them
up into his likeness with wax from a deserted bees' comb.   Scorch
the figure slowly by holding it over a lamp every night for seven nights,
and say :

> " *It is not wax that I am scorching,*
> *It is the liver, heart, and spleen of So-and-so that I scorch.*"

After the seventh time burn the figure, and your victim will die.
This charm obviously combines the principles of homoeopathic and
contagious magic ; since the image which is made in the likeness of
an enemy contains things which once were in contact with him, namely,
his nails, hair, and spittle.   Another form of the Malay charm, which
resembles the Ojebway practice still more closely, is to make a corpse
of wax from an empty bees' comb and of the length of a footstep ;
then pierce the eye of the image, and your enemy is blind ; pierce the
stomach, and he is sick ; pierce the head, and his head aches ; pierce
the breast, and his breast will suffer.   If you would kill him outright,
transfix the image from the head downwards ; enshroud it as you
would a corpse ; pray over it as if you were praying over the dead ;
then bury it in the middle of a path where your victim will be sure to
step over it.   In order that his blood may not be on your head, you
should say :

> " *It is not I who am burying him,*
> *It is Gabriel who is burying him.*"

Thus the guilt of the murder will be laid on the shoulders of the archangel Gabriel, who is a great deal better able to bear it than you are.

If homoeopathic or imitative magic, working by means of images, has commonly been practised for the spiteful purpose of putting obnoxious people out of the world, it has also, though far more rarely, been employed with the benevolent intention of helping others into it. In other words, it has been used to facilitate childbirth and to procure offspring for barren women. Thus among the Bataks of Sumatra a barren woman, who would become a mother, will make a wooden image of a child and hold it in her lap, believing that this will lead to the fulfilment of her wish. In the Babar Archipelago, when a woman desires to have a child, she invites a man who is himself the father of a large family to pray on her behalf to Upulero, the spirit of the sun. A doll is made of red cotton, which the woman clasps in her arms, as if she would suckle it. Then the father of many children takes a fowl and holds it by the legs to the woman's head, saying, " O Upulero, make use of the fowl ; let fall, let descend a child, I beseech you, I entreat you, let a child fall and descend into my hands and on my lap." Then he asks the woman, " Has the child come ? " and she answers, " Yes, it is sucking already." After that the man holds the fowl on the husband's head, and mumbles some form of words. Lastly, the bird is killed and laid, together with some betel, on the domestic place of sacrifice. When the ceremony is over, word goes about in the village that the woman has been brought to bed, and her friends come and congratulate her. Here the pretence that a child has been born is a purely magical rite designed to secure, by means of imitation or mimicry, that a child really shall be born ; but an attempt is made to add to the efficacy of the rite by means of prayer and sacrifice. To put it otherwise, magic is here blent with and reinforced by religion.

Among some of the Dyaks of Borneo, when a woman is in hard labour, a wizard is called in, who essays to facilitate the delivery in a rational manner by manipulating the body of the sufferer. Meantime another wizard outside the room exerts himself to attain the same end by means which we should regard as wholly irrational. He, in fact, pretends to be the expectant mother ; a large stone attached to his stomach by a cloth wrapt round his body represents the child in the womb, and, following the directions shouted to him by his colleague on the real scene of operations, he moves this make-believe baby about on his body in exact imitation of the movements of the real baby till the infant is born.

The same principle of make-believe, so dear to children, has led other peoples to employ a simulation of birth as a form of adoption, and even as a mode of restoring a supposed dead person to life. If you pretend to give birth to a boy, or even to a great bearded man who has not a drop of your blood in his veins, then, in the eyes of primitive law and philosophy, that boy or man is really your son to all intents and purposes. Thus Diodorus tells us that when Zeus persuaded his jealous wife Hera to adopt Hercules, the goddess got into bed, and clasping the burly hero to her bosom, pushed him through

her robes and let him fall to the ground in imitation of a real birth ;
and the historian adds that in his own day the same mode of adopting
children was practised by the barbarians. At the present time it is
said to be still in use in Bulgaria and among the Bosnian Turks. A
woman will take a boy whom she intends to adopt and push or pull
him through her clothes ; ever afterwards he is regarded as her very
son, and inherits the whole property of his adoptive parents. Among
the Berawans of Sarawak, when a woman desires to adopt a grown-
up man or woman, a great many people assemble and have a feast.
The adopting mother, seated in public on a raised and covered seat,
allows the adopted person to crawl from behind between her legs.
As soon as he appears in front he is stroked with the sweet-scented
blossoms of the areca palm, and tied to the woman.   Then the adopting
mother and the adopted son or daughter, thus bound together, waddle
to the end of the house and back again in front of all the spectators.
The tie established between the two by this graphic imitation of
childbirth is very strict ; an offence committed against an adopted
child is reckoned more heinous than one committed against a real
child.   In ancient Greece any man who had been supposed
to be dead, and for whom in his absence funeral rites had been performed, was treated as dead to society till he had gone through the
form of being born again. He was passed through a woman's lap,
then washed, dressed in swaddling-clothes, and put out to nurse.
Not until this ceremony had been punctually performed might he
mix freely with living folk. In ancient India, under similar circumstances, the supposed dead man had to pass the first night after his
return in a tub filled with a mixture of fat and water ; there he sat
with doubled-up fists and without uttering a syllable, like a child in
the womb, while over him were performed all the sacraments that
were wont to be celebrated over a pregnant woman. Next morning
he got out of the tub and went through once more all the other sacraments he had formerly partaken of from his youth up ; in particular,
he married a wife or espoused his old one over again with due solemnity.

Another beneficent use of homoeopathic magic is to heal or prevent
sickness. The ancient Hindoos performed an elaborate ceremony,
based on homoeopathic magic, for the cure of jaundice. Its main
drift was to banish the yellow colour to yellow creatures and yellow
things, such as the sun, to which it properly belongs, and to procure
for the patient a healthy red colour from a living, vigorous source,
namely a red bull. With this intention, a priest recited the following
spell : " Up to the sun shall go thy heart-ache and thy jaundice :
in the colour of the red bull do we envelop thee ! We envelop thee
in red tints, unto long life. May this person go unscathed and be
free of yellow colour ! The cows whose divinity is Rohini, they who,
moreover, are themselves red (*rohinih*)—in their every form and
every strength we do envelop thee.   Into the parrots, into the thrush,
do we put thy jaundice, and, furthermore, into the yellow wagtail
do we put thy jaundice." While he uttered these words, the priest,

in order to infuse the rosy hue of health into the sallow patient, gave him water to sip which was mixed with the hair of a red bull ; he poured water over the animal's back and made the sick man drink it ; he seated him on the skin of a red bull and tied a piece of the skin to him. Then in order to improve his colour by thoroughly eradicating the yellow taint, he proceeded thus. He first daubed him from head to foot with a yellow porridge made of turmeric or curcuma (a yellow plant), set him on a bed, tied three yellow birds, to wit a parrot, a thrush, and a yellow wagtail, by means of a yellow string to the foot of the bed ; then pouring water over the patient, he washed off the yellow porridge, and with it no doubt the jaundice, from him to the birds. After that, by way of giving a final bloom to his complexion, he took some hairs of a red bull, wrapt them in gold leaf, and glued them to the patient's skin. The ancients held that if a person suffering from jaundice looked sharply at a stone-curlew, and the bird looked steadily at him, he was cured of the disease. " Such is the nature," says Plutarch, "and such the temperament of the creature that it draws out and receives the malady which issues, like a stream, through the eyesight." So well recognised among bird-fanciers was this valuable property of the stone-curlew that when they had one of these birds for sale they kept it carefully covered, lest a jaundiced person should look at it and be cured for nothing. The virtue of the bird lay not in its colour but in its large golden eye, which naturally drew out the yellow jaundice. Pliny tells of another, or perhaps the same, bird, to which the Greeks gave their name for jaundice, because if a jaundiced man saw it, the disease left him and slew the bird. He mentions also a stone which was supposed to cure jaundice because its hue resembled that of a jaundiced skin.

One of the great merits of homoeopathic magic is that it enables the cure to be performed on the person of the doctor instead of on that of his victim, who is thus relieved of all trouble and inconvenience, while he sees his medical man writhe in anguish before him. For example, the peasants of Perche, in France, labour under the impression that a prolonged fit of vomiting is brought about by the patient's stomach becoming unhooked, as they call it, and so falling down. Accordingly, a practitioner is called in to restore the organ to its proper place. After hearing the symptoms he at once throws himself into the most horrible contortions, for the purpose of unhooking his own stomach. Having succeeded in the effort, he next hooks it up again in another series of contortions and grimaces, while the patient experiences a corresponding relief. Fee five francs. In like manner a Dyak medicine-man, who has been fetched in a case of illness, will lie down and pretend to be dead. He is accordingly treated like a corpse, is bound up in mats, taken out of the house, and deposited on the ground. After about an hour the other medicine-men loose the pretended dead man and bring him to life ; and as he recovers, the sick person is supposed to recover too. A cure for a tumour, based on the principle of homoeopathic magic, is prescribed by Marcellus of Bordeaux, court physician to Theodosius the First, in his curious work on medicine. It is as follows. Take a root of vervain, cut it across, and hang one end of it round the patient's neck, and the other in the smoke of the fire. As the vervain dries up in the smoke, so the tumour will also dry up and disappear. If the patient should afterwards prove ungrateful to the good physician, the man of skill can avenge himself very easily by throwing the vervain into water : for as the root absorbs the moisture once more, the tumour will return. The same sapient writer recommends you, if you are troubled with pimples, to watch for a falling star, and then instantly, while the star is still shooting from the sky, to wipe the pimples with a cloth or anything that comes to hand. Just as the star falls from the sky, so the pimples will fall from your body ; only you must be very careful not to wipe them with your bare hand, or the pimples will be transferred to it.

Further, homoeopathic and in general sympathetic magic plays a great part in the measures taken by the rude hunter or fisherman to secure an abundant supply of food. On the principle that like produces like, many things are done by him and his friends in deliberate imitation of the result which he seeks to attain ; and, on the other hand, many things are scrupulously avoided because they bear some more or less fanciful resemblance to others which would really be disastrous.

Nowhere is the theory of sympathetic magic more systematically carried into practice for the maintenance of the food supply than in the barren regions of Central Australia. Here the tribes are divided into a number of totem clans, each of which is charged with the duty of multiplying their totem for the good of the community by means of magical ceremonies. Most of the totems are edible animals and plants, and the general result supposed to be accomplished by these ceremonies is that of supplying the tribe with food and other necessaries. Often the rites consist of an imitation of the effect which the people desire to produce ; in other words, their magic is homoeopathic or imitative. Thus among the Warramunga the headman of the white cockatoo totem seeks to multiply white cockatoos by holding an effigy of the bird and mimicking its harsh cry. Among the Arunta the men of the witchetty grub totem perform ceremonies for multiplying the grub which the other members of the tribe use as food. One of the ceremonies is a pantomime representing the fully developed insect in the act of emerging from the chrysalis. A long narrow structure of branches is set up to imitate the chrysalis case of the grub. In this structure a number of men, who have the grub for their totem, sit and sing of the creature in its various stages. Then they shuffle out of it in a squatting posture, and as they do so they sing of the insect emerging from the chrysalis. This is supposed to multiply the numbers of the grubs. Again, in order to multiply emus, which are an important article of food, the men of the emu totem paint on the ground the sacred design of their totem, especially the parts of the emu which they like best to eat, namely, the fat and the eggs. Round this painting the men sit and sing. Afterwards performers, wearing head-dresses to represent the long neck and small head of the emu, mimic the appearance of the bird as it stands aimlessly peering about in all directions.

The Indians of British Columbia live largely upon the fish which abound in their seas and rivers. If the fish do not come in due season, and the Indians are hungry, a Nootka wizard will make an image of a swimming fish and put it into the water in the direction from which the fish generally appear. This ceremony, accompanied by a prayer to the fish to come, will cause them to arrive at once. The islanders of Torres Straits use models of dugong and turtles to charm dugong and turtle to their destruction. The Toradjas of Central Celebes believe that things of the same sort attract each other by means of their indwelling spirits or vital ether. Hence they hang up the jaw-bones of deer and wild pigs in their houses, in order that the spirits which animate these bones may draw the living creatures of the same kind into the path of the hunter. In the island of Nias, when a wild pig has fallen into the pit prepared for it, the animal is taken out and its back is rubbed with nine fallen leaves, in the belief that this will make nine more wild pigs fall into the pit, just as the nine leaves fell from the tree. In the East Indian islands of Saparoea, Haroekoe, and Noessa Laut, when a fisherman is about to set a trap for fish in the sea, he looks out for a tree, of which the fruit has been much pecked at by birds. From such a tree he cuts a stout branch and makes of it the principal post in his fish-trap; for he believes that, just as the tree lured many birds to its fruit, so the branch cut from that tree will lure many fish to the trap.

The western tribes of British New Guinea employ a charm to aid the hunter in spearing dugong or turtle. A small beetle, which haunts coco-nut trees, is placed in the hole of the spear-haft into which the spear-head fits. This is supposed to make the spear-head stick fast in the dugong or turtle, just as the beetle sticks fast to a man's skin when it bites him. When a Cambodian hunter has set his nets and taken nothing, he strips himself naked, goes some way off, then strolls up to the net as if he did not see it, lets himself be caught in it, and cries, " Hillo ! what's this ? I'm afraid I'm caught." After that the net is sure to catch game. A pantomime of the same sort has been acted within living memory in our Scottish Highlands. The Rev. James Macdonald, now of Reay in Caithness, tells us that in his boy-hood when he was fishing with companions about Loch Aline and they had had no bites for a long time, they used to make a pretence of throwing one of their fellows overboard and hauling him out of the water, as if he were a fish; after that the trout or silloch would begin to nibble, according as the boat was on fresh or salt water. Before a Carrier Indian goes out to snare martens, he sleeps by himself for about ten nights beside the fire with a little stick pressed down on his neck. This naturally causes the fall-stick of his trap to drop down on the neck of the marten. Among the Galelareese, who inhabit a district in the northern part of Halmahera, a large island to the west of New Guinea, it is a maxim that when you are loading your gun to go out shooting, you should always put the bullet in your mouth before you insert it in the gun ; for by so doing you practically eat the game that is to be hit by the bullet, which therefore cannot possibly miss the mark. A Malay who has baited a trap for crocodiles, and is awaiting results, is careful in eating his curry always to begin by swallowing three lumps of rice successively ; for this helps the bait to slide more easily down the crocodile's throat. He is equally scrupulous not to take any bones out of his curry ; for, if he did, it seems clear that the sharp-pointed stick on which the bait is skewered would similarly work itself loose, and the crocodile would get off with the bait. Hence in these circumstances it is prudent for the hunter, before he begins his meal, to get somebody else to take the bones out of his curry, otherwise he may at any moment have to choose between swallowing a bone and losing the crocodile.

This last rule is an instance of the things which the hunter abstains from doing lest, on the principle that like produces like, they should spoil his luck. For it is to be observed that the system of sympathetic magic is not merely composed of positive precepts ; it comprises a very large number of negative precepts, that is, prohibitions. It tells you not merely what to do, but also what to leave undone. The positive precepts are charms : the negative precepts are taboos. In fact the whole doctrine of taboo, or at all events a large part of it, would seem to be only a special application of sympathetic magic, with its two great laws of similarity and contact. Though these laws are certainly not formulated in so many words nor even conceived in the abstract by the savage, they are nevertheless implicitly believed by him to regulate the course of nature quite independently of human will. He thinks that if he acts in a certain way, certain consequences will inevitably follow in virtue of one or other of these laws ; and if the consequences of a particular act appear to him likely to prove disagreeable or dangerous, he is naturally careful not to act in that way lest he should incur them. In other words, he abstains from doing that which, in accordance with his mistaken notions of cause and effect, he falsely believes would injure him ; in short, he subjects himself to a taboo. Thus taboo is so far a negative application of practical magic. Positive magic or sorcery says, " Do this in order that so and so may happen." Negative magic or taboo says, " Do not do this, lest so and so should happen." The aim of positive magic or sorcery is to produce a desired event ; the aim of negative magic or taboo is to avoid an undesirable one. But both consequences, the desirable and the undesirable, are supposed to be brought about in accordance with the laws of similarity and contact. And just as the desired consequence is not really effected by the observance of a magical ceremony, so the dreaded consequence does not really result from the violation of a taboo. If the supposed evil necessarily followed a breach of taboo, the taboo would not be a taboo but a precept of morality or common sense.   It is not a taboo to say, " Do not put your hand in the fire " ; it is a rule of common sense, because the forbidden action entails a real, not an imaginary evil.   In short, those negative precepts which we call taboo are just as vain and futile as those positive precepts which we call sorcery.   The two things are merely opposite sides or poles of one great disastrous fallacy, a mistaken conception of the association of ideas.   Of that fallacy, sorcery is the positive, and taboo the negative pole.   If we give the general name of magic to the whole erroneous system, both theoretical and practical, then taboo may be defined as the negative side of practical magic.   To put this in tabular form :

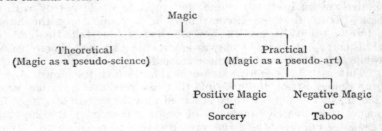

I have made these remarks on taboo and its relations to magic because I am about to give some instances of taboos observed by hunters, fishermen, and others, and I wished to show that they fall under the head of Sympathetic Magic, being only particular applications of that general theory.   Thus, among the Esquimaux boys are forbidden to play cat's cradle, because if they did so their fingers might in later life become entangled in the harpoon-line.   Here the taboo is obviously an application of the law of similarity, which is the basis of homoeopathic magic : as the child's fingers are entangled by the string in playing cat's cradle, so they will be entangled by the harpoon-line when he is a man and hunts whales.   Again, among the Huzuls of the Carpathian Mountains the wife of a hunter may not spin while her husband is eating, or the game will turn and wind like the spindle, and the hunter will be unable to hit it.   Here again the taboo is clearly derived from the law of similarity.   So, too, in most parts of ancient Italy women were forbidden by law to spin on the highroads as they walked, or even to carry their spindles openly, because any such action was believed to injure the crops.   Probably the notion was that the twirling of the spindle would twirl the corn-stalks and prevent them from growing straight.   So, too, among the Ainos of Saghalien a pregnant woman may not spin nor twist ropes for two months before her delivery, because they think that if she did so the child's guts might be entangled like the thread.   For a like reason in Bilaspore, a district of India, when the chief men of a village meet in council, no one present should twirl a spindle ; for they think that if such a thing were to happen, the discussion, like the spindle, would move in a circle and never be wound up.   In some of the East Indian islands any one who comes to the house of a hunter must walk straight in ; he may not loiter at the door, for were he to do so, the game would in like manner stop in front of the hunter's snares and then turn back, instead of being caught in the trap.   For a similar reason it is a rule with the Toradjas of Central Celebes that no one may stand or loiter on the ladder of a house where there is a pregnant woman, for such delay would retard the birth of the child ; and in various parts of Sumatra the woman herself in these circumstances is forbidden to stand at the door or on the top rung of the house-ladder under pain of suffering hard labour for her imprudence in neglecting so elementary a precaution.   Malays engaged in the search for camphor eat their food dry and take care not to pound their salt fine.   The reason is that the camphor occurs in the form of small grains deposited in the cracks of the trunk of the camphor-tree.   Accordingly it seems plain to the Malay that if, while seeking for camphor, he were to eat his salt finely ground, the camphor would be found also in fine grains ; whereas by eating his salt coarse he ensures that the grains of the camphor will also be large.   Camphor hunters in Borneo use the leathery sheath of the leaf-stalk of the Penang palm as a plate for food, and during the whole of the expedition they will never wash the plate, for fear that the camphor might dissolve and disappear from the crevices of the tree. Apparently they think that to wash their plates would be to wash out the camphor crystals from the trees in which they are imbedded.   The chief product of some parts of Laos, a province of Siam, is lac.   This is a resinous gum exuded by a red insect on the young branches of trees, to which the little creatures have to be attached by hand.   All who engage in the business of gathering the gum abstain from washing themselves and especially from cleansing their heads, lest by removing the parasites from their hair they should detach the other insects from the boughs. Again, a Blackfoot Indian who has set a trap for eagles, and is watching it, would not eat rosebuds on any account ; for he argues that if he did so, and an eagle alighted near the trap, the rosebuds in his own stomach would make the bird itch, with the result that instead of swallowing the bait the eagle would merely sit and scratch himself. Following this train of thought the eagle hunter also refrains from using an awl when he is looking after his snares ; for surely if he were to scratch with an awl, the eagles would scratch him.   The same disastrous consequence would follow if his wives and children at home used an awl while he is out after eagles, and accordingly they are forbidden to handle the tool in his absence for fear of putting him in bodily danger.

Among the taboos observed by savages none perhaps are more numerous or important than the prohibitions to eat certain foods, and of such prohibitions many are demonstrably derived from the law of similarity and are accordingly examples of negative magic. Just as the savage eats many animals or plants in order to acquire certain desirable qualities with which he believes them to be endowed, so he avoids eating many other animals and plants lest he should acquire certain undesirable qualities with which he believes them to be infected. In eating the former he practises positive magic ; in abstaining from the latter he practises negative magic. Many examples of such positive magic will meet us later on ; here I will give a few instances of such negative magic or taboo. For example, in Madagascar soldiers are forbidden to eat a number of foods lest on the principle of homoeopathic magic they should be tainted by certain dangerous or undesirable properties which are supposed to inhere in these particular viands. Thus they may not taste hedgehog, " as it is feared that this animal, from its propensity of coiling up into a ball when alarmed, will impart a timid shrinking disposition to those who partake of it." Again, no soldier should eat an ox's knee, lest like an ox he should become weak in the knees and unable to march. Further, the warrior should be careful to avoid partaking of a cock that has died fighting or anything that has been speared to death ; and no male animal may on any account be killed in his house while he is away at the wars. For it seems obvious that if he were to eat a cock that had died fighting, he would himself be slain on the field of battle ; if he were to partake of an animal that had been speared, he would be speared himself ; if a male animal were killed in his house during his absence, he would himself be killed in like manner and perhaps at the same instant. Further, the Malagasy soldier must eschew kidneys, because in the Malagasy language the word for kidney is the same as that for " shot " ; so shot he would certainly be if he ate a kidney.

The reader may have observed that in some of the foregoing examples of taboos the magical influence is supposed to operate at considerable distances ; thus among the Blackfoot Indians the wives and children of an eagle hunter are forbidden to use an awl during his absence, lest the eagles should scratch the distant husband and father ; and again no male animal may be killed in the house of a Malagasy soldier while he is away at the wars, lest the killing of the animal should entail the killing of the man. This belief in the sympathetic influence exerted on each other by persons or things at a distance is of the essence of magic. Whatever doubts science may entertain as to the possibility of action at a distance, magic has none ; faith in telepathy is one of its first principles. A modern advocate of the influence of mind upon mind at a distance would have no difficulty in convincing a savage ; the savage believed in it long ago, and what is more, he acted on his belief with a logical consistency such as his civilised brother in the faith has not yet, so far as I am aware, exhibited in his conduct. For the savage is convinced not only that magical ceremonies affect persons and things afar off, but that the simplest acts of daily life may do so too. Hence on important occasions the behaviour of friends and relations at a distance is often regulated by a more or less elaborate code of rules, the neglect of which by the one set of persons would, it is supposed, entail misfortune or even death on the absent ones. In particular when a party of men are out hunting or fighting, their kinsfolk at home are often expected to do certain things or to abstain from doing certain others, for the sake of ensuring the safety and success of the distant hunters or warriors. I will now give some instances of this magical telepathy both in its positive and in its negative aspect.

In Laos when an elephant hunter is starting for the chase, he warns his wife not to cut her hair or oil her body in his absence ; for if she cut her hair the elephant would burst the toils, if she oiled herself it would slip through them. When a Dyak village has turned out to hunt wild pigs in the jungle, the people who stay at home may not touch oil or water with their hands during the absence of their friends ; for if they did so, the hunters would all be " butter-fingered " and the prey would slip through their hands.

Elephant-hunters in East Africa believe that, if their wives prove unfaithful in their absence, this gives the elephant power over his pursuer, who will accordingly be killed or severely wounded. Hence if a hunter hears of his wife's misconduct, he abandons the chase and returns home. If a Wagogo hunter is unsuccessful, or is attacked by a lion, he attributes it to his wife's misbehaviour at home, and returns to her in great wrath. While he is away hunting, she may not let any one pass behind her or stand in front of her as she sits ; and she must lie on her face in bed. The Moxos Indians of Bolivia thought that if a hunter's wife was unfaithful to him in his absence he would be bitten by a serpent or a jaguar. Accordingly, if such an accident happened to him, it was sure to entail the punishment, and often the death, of the woman, whether she was innocent or guilty. An Aleutian hunter of sea-otters thinks that he cannot kill a single animal if during his absence from home his wife should be unfaithful or his sister unchaste.

The Huichol Indians of Mexico treat as a demi-god a species of cactus which throws the eater into a state of ecstasy. The plant does not grow in their country, and has to be fetched every year by men who make a journey of forty-three days for the purpose. Meanwhile the wives at home contribute to the safety of their absent husbands by never walking fast, much less running, while the men are on the road. They also do their best to ensure the benefits which, in the shape of rain, good crops, and so forth, are expected to flow from the sacred mission. With this intention they subject themselves to severe restrictions like those imposed upon their husbands. During the whole of the time which elapses till the festival of the cactus is held, neither party washes except on certain occasions, and then only with water brought from the distant country where the holy plant grows. They also fast much, eat no salt, and are bound to strict continence. Any one who breaks this law is punished with illness, and, moreover, jeopardises the result which all are striving for. Health, luck, and life are to be gained by gathering the cactus, the gourd of the God of Fire ; but inasmuch as the pure fire cannot benefit the impure, men and women must not only

remain chaste for the time being, but must also purge themselves
from the taint of past sin.   Hence four days after the men have started
the women gather and confess to Grandfather Fire with what men
they have been in love from childhood till now.   They may not omit
a single one, for if they did so the men would not find a single cactus.
So to refresh their memories each one prepares a string with as many
knots as she has had lovers.   This she brings to the temple, and,
standing before the fire, she mentions aloud all the men she has scored
on her string, name after name.   Having ended her confession, she
throws the string into the fire, and when the god has consumed it in
his pure flame, her sins are forgiven her and she departs in peace.
From now on the women are averse even to letting men pass near
them.   The cactus-seekers themselves make in like manner a clean
breast of all their frailties.   For every peccadillo they tie a knot on a
string, and after they have " talked to all the five winds " they deliver
the rosary of their sins to the leader, who burns it in the fire.

   Many of the indigenous tribes of Sarawak are firmly persuaded
that were the wives to commit adultery while their husbands are
searching for camphor in the jungle, the camphor obtained by the
men would evaporate.   Husbands can discover, by certain knots in
the tree, when their wives are unfaithful ; and it is said that in former
days many women were killed by jealous husbands on no better
evidence than that of these knots.   Further, the wives dare not
touch a comb while their husbands are away collecting the camphor ;
for if they did so, the interstices between the fibres of the tree, instead
of being filled with the precious crystals, would be empty like the
spaces between the teeth of a comb.   In the Kei Islands, to the south-
west of New Guinea, as soon as a vessel that is about to sail for a
distant port has been launched, the part of the beach on which it
lay is covered as speedily as possible with palm branches, and becomes
sacred.   No one may thenceforth cross that spot till the ship comes
home.   To cross it sooner would cause the vessel to perish.   Moreover, all the time that the voyage lasts three or four young girls,
specially chosen for the duty, are supposed to remain in sympathetic
connexion with the mariners and to contribute by their behaviour
to the safety and success of the voyage.   On no account, except for
the most necessary purpose, may they quit the room that has been
assigned to them.   More than that, so long as the vessel is believed
to be at sea they must remain absolutely motionless, crouched on
their mats with their hands clasped between their knees.   They may
not turn their heads to the left or to the right or make any other
movement whatsoever.   If they did, it would cause the boat to pitch
and toss ; and they may not eat any sticky stuff, such as rice boiled
in coco-nut milk, for the stickiness of the food would clog the passage
of the boat through the water.   When the sailors are supposed to
have reached their destination, the strictness of these rules is somewhat relaxed ; but during the whole time that the voyage lasts the
girls are forbidden to eat fish which have sharp bones or stings, such

as the sting-ray, lest their friends at sea should be involved in sharp, stinging trouble.

Where beliefs like these prevail as to the sympathetic connexion between friends at a distance, we need not wonder that above everything else war, with its stern yet stirring appeal to some of the deepest and tenderest of human emotions, should quicken in the anxious relations left behind a desire to turn the sympathetic bond to the utmost account for the benefit of the dear ones who may at any moment be fighting and dying far away. Hence, to secure an end so natural and laudable, friends at home are apt to resort to devices which will strike us as pathetic or ludicrous, according as we consider their object or the means adopted to effect it. Thus in some districts of Borneo, when a Dyak is out head-hunting, his wife or, if he is unmarried, his sister must wear a sword day and night in order that he may always be thinking of his weapons; and she may not sleep during the day nor go to bed before two in the morning, lest her husband or brother should thereby be surprised in his sleep by an enemy. Among the Sea Dyaks of Banting in Sarawak the women strictly observe an elaborate code of rules while the men are away fighting. Some of the rules are negative and some are positive, but all alike are based on the principles of magical homoeopathy and telepathy. Amongst them are the following. The women must wake very early in the morning and open the windows as soon as it is light; otherwise their absent husbands will oversleep themselves. The women may not oil their hair, or the men will slip. The women may neither sleep nor doze by day, or the men will be drowsy on the march. The women must cook and scatter popcorn on the verandah every morning; so will the men be agile in their movements. The rooms must be kept very tidy, all boxes being placed near the walls; for if any one were to stumble over them, the absent husbands would fall and be at the mercy of the foe. At every meal a little rice must be left in the pot and put aside; so will the men far away always have something to eat and need never go hungry. On no account may the women sit at the loom till their legs grow cramped, otherwise their husbands will likewise be stiff in their joints and unable to rise up quickly or to run away from the foe. So in order to keep their husbands' joints supple the women often vary their labours at the loom by walking up and down the verandah. Further, they may not cover up their faces, or the men would not be able to find their way through the tall grass or jungle. Again, the women may not sew with a needle, or the men will tread on the sharp spikes set by the enemy in the path. Should a wife prove unfaithful while her husband is away, he will lose his life in the enemy's country. Some years ago all these rules and more were observed by the women of Banting, while their husbands were fighting for the English against rebels. But alas! these tender precautions availed them little; for many a man, whose faithful wife was keeping watch and ward for him at home, found a soldier's grave.

In the island of Timor, while war is being waged, the high-priest never quits the temple ; his food is brought to him or cooked inside ; day and night he must keep the fire burning, for if he were to let it die out, disaster would befall the warriors and would continue so long as the hearth was cold. Moreover, he must drink only hot water during the time the army is absent ; for every draught of cold water would damp the spirits of the people, so that they could not vanquish the enemy. In the Kei Islands, when the warriors have departed, the women return indoors and bring out certain baskets containing fruits and stones. These fruits and stones they anoint and place on a board, murmuring as they do so, " O lord sun, moon, let the bullets rebound from our husbands, brothers, betrothed, and other relations, just as raindrops rebound from these objects which are smeared with oil." As soon as the first shot is heard, the baskets are put aside, and the women, seizing their fans, rush out of the houses. Then, waving their fans in the direction of the enemy, they run through the village, while they sing, " O golden fans ! let our bullets hit, and those of the enemy miss." In this custom the ceremony of anointing stones, in order that the bullets may recoil from the men like raindrops from the stones, is a piece of pure homoeopathic or imitative magic ; but the prayer to the sun, that he will be pleased to give effect to the charm, is a religious and perhaps later addition. The waving of the fans seems to be a charm to direct the bullets towards or away from their mark, according as they are discharged from the guns of friends or foes.

An old historian of Madagascar informs us that " while the men are at the wars, and until their return, the women and girls cease not day and night to dance, and neither lie down nor take food in their own houses. And although they are very voluptuously inclined, they would not for anything in the world have an intrigue with another man while their husband is at the war, believing firmly that if that happened, their husband would be either killed or wounded. They believe that by dancing they impart strength, courage, and good fortune to their husbands ; accordingly during such times they give themselves no rest, and this custom they observe very religiously."

Among the Tshi-speaking peoples of the Gold Coast the wives of men who are away with the army paint themselves white, and adorn their persons with beads and charms. On the day when a battle is expected to take place, they run about armed with guns, or sticks carved to look like guns, and taking green paw-paws (fruits shaped somewhat like a melon), they hack them with knives, as if they were chopping off the heads of the foe. The pantomime is no doubt merely an imitative charm, to enable the men to do to the enemy as the women do to the paw-paws. In the West African town of Framin, while the Ashantee war was raging some years ago, Mr. Fitzgerald Marriott saw a dance performed by women whose husbands had gone as carriers to the war. They were painted white and wore nothing but a short petticoat. At their head was a shrivelled old sorceress in a very short white petticoat, her black hair arranged in a sort of long projecting horn, and her black face, breasts, arms, and legs profusely adorned with white circles and crescents. All carried long white brushes made of buffalo or horse tails, and as they danced they sang, " Our husbands have gone to Ashanteeland ; may they sweep their enemies off the face of the earth ! "

Among the Thompson Indians of British Columbia, when the men were on the war-path, the women performed dances at frequent intervals. These dances were believed to ensure the success of the expedition. The dancers flourished their knives, threw long sharp-pointed sticks forward, or drew sticks with hooked ends repeatedly backward and forward. Throwing the sticks forward was symbolic of piercing or warding off the enemy, and drawing them back was symbolic of drawing their own men from danger. The hook at the end of the stick was particularly well adapted to serve the purpose of a life-saving apparatus. The women always pointed their weapons towards the enemy's country. They painted their faces red and sang as they danced, and they prayed to the weapons to preserve their husbands and help them to kill many foes. Some had eagle-down stuck on the points of their sticks. When the dance was over, these weapons were hidden. If a woman whose husband was at the war thought she saw hair or a piece of a scalp on the weapon when she took it out, she knew that her husband had killed an enemy. But if she saw a stain of blood on it, she knew he was wounded or dead. When the men of the Yuki tribe in California were away fighting, the women at home did not sleep ; they danced continually in a circle, chanting and waving leafy wands. For they said that if they danced all the time, their husbands would not grow tired. Among the Haida Indians of the Queen Charlotte Islands, when the men had gone to war, the women at home would get up very early in the morning and pretend to make war by falling upon their children and feigning to take them for slaves. This was supposed to help their husbands to go and do likewise. If a wife were unfaithful to her husband while he was away on the war-path, he would probably be killed. For ten nights all the women at home lay with their heads towards the point of the compass to which the war-canoes had paddled away. Then they changed about, for the warriors were supposed to be coming home across the sea. At Masset the Haida women danced and sang war-songs all the time their husbands were away at the wars, and they had to keep everything about them in a certain order. It was thought that a wife might kill her husband by not observing these customs. When a band of Carib Indians of the Orinoco had gone on the war-path, their friends left in the village used to calculate as nearly as they could the exact moment when the absent warriors would be advancing to attack the enemy. Then they took two lads, laid them down on a bench, and inflicted a most severe scourging on their bare backs. This the youths submitted to without a murmur, supported in their sufferings by the firm conviction, in which they had been bred from childhood, that on the constancy and fortitude with which they bore the cruel ordeal depended the valour and success of their comrades in the battle.

Among the many beneficent uses to which a mistaken ingenuity has applied the principle of homoeopathic or imitative magic, is that of causing trees and plants to bear fruit in due season. In Thüringen the man who sows flax carries the seed in a long bag which reaches from his shoulders to his knees, and he walks with long strides, so that the bag sways to and fro on his back. It is believed that this will cause the flax to wave in the wind. In the interior of Sumatra rice is sown by women who, in sowing, let their hair hang loose down their back, in order that the rice may grow luxuriantly and have long stalks. Similarly, in ancient Mexico a festival was held in honour of the goddess of maize, or " the long-haired mother," as she was called. It began at the time " when the plant had attained its full growth, and fibres shooting forth from the top of the green ear indicated that the grain was fully formed. During this festival the women wore their long hair unbound, shaking and tossing it in the dances which were the chief feature in the ceremonial, in order that the tassel of the maize might grow in like profusion, that the grain might be correspondingly large and flat, and that the people might have abundance." In many parts of Europe dancing or leaping high in the air are approved homoeo- pathic modes of making the crops grow high. Thus in Franche-Comtê they say that you should dance at the Carnival in order to make the hemp grow tall.

The notion that a person can influence a plant homoeopathically by his act or condition comes out clearly in a remark made by a Malay woman. Being asked why she stripped the upper part of her body naked in reaping the rice, she explained that she did it to make the rice-husks thinner, as she was tired of pounding thick-husked rice. Clearly, she thought that the less clothing she wore the less husk there would be on the rice. The magic virtue of a pregnant woman to communicate fertility is known to Bavarian and Austrian peasants, who think that if you give the first fruit of a tree to a woman with child to eat, the tree will bring forth abundantly next year. On the other hand, the Baganda believe that a barren wife infects her husband's garden with her own sterility and prevents the trees from bearing fruit ; hence a childless woman is generally divorced. The Greeks and Romans sacrificed pregnant victims to the goddesses of the corn and of the earth, doubtless in order that the earth might teem and the corn swell in the ear. When a Catholic priest remonstrated with the Indians of the Orinoco on allowing their women to sow the fields in the blazing sun, with infants at their breasts, the men answered, " Father, you don't understand these things, and that is why they vex you. You know that women are accustomed to bear children, and that we men are not. When the women sow, the stalk of the maize bears two or three ears, the root of the yucca yields two or three basketfuls, and everything multiplies in proportion. Now why is that ? Simply because the women know how to bring forth, and know how to make the seed which they sow bring forth also. Let them sow, then ; we men don't know as much about it as they do."

Thus on the theory of homoeopathic magic a person can influence vegetation either for good or for evil according to the good or the bad character of his acts or states : for example, a fruitful woman makes plants fruitful, a barren woman makes them barren. Hence this belief in the noxious and infectious nature of certain personal qualities or accidents has given rise to a number of prohibitions or rules of avoidance : people abstain from doing certain things lest they should homoeo-pathically infect the fruits of the earth with their own undesirable state or condition. All such customs of abstention or rules of avoidance are examples of negative magic or taboo. Thus, for example, arguing from what may be called the infectiousness of personal acts or states, the Galelareese say that you ought not to shoot with a bow and arrows under a fruit-tree, or the tree will cast its fruit even as the arrows fall to the ground ; and that when you are eating water-melon you ought not to mix the pips which you spit out of your mouth with the pips which you have put aside to serve as seed ; for if you do, though the pips you spat out may certainly spring up and blossom, yet the blossoms will keep falling off just as the pips fell from your mouth, and thus these pips will never bear fruit. Precisely the same train of thought leads the Bavarian peasant to believe that if he allows the graft of a fruit-tree to fall on the ground, the tree that springs from that graft will let its fruit fall untimely. When the Chams of Cochinchina are sowing their dry ricefields and desire that no shower should fall, they eat their rice dry in order to prevent rain from spoiling the crop.

In the foregoing cases a person is supposed to influence vegetation homoeopathically. He infects trees or plants with qualities or accidents, good or bad, resembling and derived from his own. But on the principle of homoeopathic magic the influence is mutual : the plant can infect the man just as much as the man can infect the plant. In magic, as I believe in physics, action and reaction are equal and opposite. The Cherokee Indians are adepts in practical botany of the homoeopathic sort. Thus wiry roots of the catgut plant are so tough that they can almost stop a ploughshare in the furrow. Hence Cherokee women wash their heads with a decoction of the roots to make the hair strong, and Cherokee ball-players wash themselves with it to toughen their muscles. It is a Galelareese belief that if you eat a fruit which has fallen to the ground, you will yourself contract a disposition to stumble and fall ; and that if you partake of something which has been forgotten (such as a sweet potato left in the pot or a banana in the fire), you will become forgetful. The Galelareese are also of opinion that if a woman were to consume two bananas growing from a single head she would give birth to twins. The Guarani Indians of South America thought that a woman would become a mother of twins if she ate a double grain of millet. In Vedic times a curious application of this principle supplied a charm by which a banished prince might be restored to his kingdom.

He had to eat food cooked on a fire which was fed with wood which had grown out of the stump of a tree which had been cut down. The recuperative power manifested by such a tree would in due course be communicated through the fire to the food, and so to the prince, who ate the food which was cooked on the fire which was fed with the wood which grew out of the tree. The Sundanese think that if a house is built of the wood of thorny trees, the life of the people who dwell in that house will likewise be thorny and full of trouble.

There is a fruitful branch of homoeopathic magic which works by means of the dead ; for just as the dead can neither see nor hear nor speak, so you may on homoeopathic principles render people blind, deaf, and dumb by the use of dead men's bones or anything else that is tainted by the infection of death. Thus among the Galelareese, when a young man goes a-wooing at night, he takes a little earth from a grave and strews it on the roof of his sweetheart's house just above the place where her parents sleep. This, he fancies, will prevent them from waking while he converses with his beloved, since the earth from the grave will make them sleep as sound as the dead. Burglars in all ages and many lands have been patrons of this species of magic, which is very useful to them in the exercise of their profession. Thus a South Slavonian housebreaker sometimes begins operations by throwing a dead man's bone over the house, saying, with pungent sarcasm, " As this bone may waken, so may these people waken " ; after that not a soul in the house can keep his or her eyes open. Similarly, in Java the burglar takes earth from a grave and sprinkles it round the house which he intends to rob ; this throws the inmates into a deep sleep. With the same intention a Hindoo will strew ashes from a pyre at the door of the house ; Indians of Peru scatter the dust of dead men's bones ; and Ruthenian burglars remove the marrow from a human shin-bone, pour tallow into it, and having kindled the tallow, march thrice round the house with this candle burning, which causes the inmates to sleep a death-like sleep. Or the Ruthenian will make a flute out of a human leg-bone and play upon it ; whereupon all persons within hearing are overcome with drowsiness. The Indians of Mexico employed for this maleficent purpose the left fore-arm of a woman who had died in giving birth to her first child ; but the arm had to be stolen. With it they beat the ground before they entered the house which they designed to plunder ; this caused every one in the house to lose all power of speech and motion ; they were as dead, hearing and seeing everything, but perfectly powerless ; some of them, however, really slept and even snored. In Europe similar properties were ascribed to the Hand of Glory, which was the dried and pickled hand of a man who had been hanged. If a candle made of the fat of a malefactor who had also died on the gallows was lighted and placed in the Hand of Glory as in a candlestick, it rendered motionless all persons to whom it was presented ; they could not stir a finger any more than if they were dead. Sometimes the dead man's hand is itself the candle, or rather bunch of candles, all its withered fingers being set on fire ; but should any member of the household be awake, one of the fingers will not kindle. Such nefarious lights can only be extinguished with milk. Often it is prescribed that the thief's candle should be made of the finger of a new-born or, still better, unborn child ; sometimes it is thought needful that the thief should have one such candle for every person in the house, for if he has one candle too little somebody in the house will wake and catch him. Once these tapers begin to burn, there is nothing but milk that will put them out. In the seventeenth century robbers used to murder pregnant women in order thus to extract candles from their wombs. An ancient Greek robber or burglar thought he could silence and put to flight the fiercest watchdogs by carrying with him a brand plucked from a funeral pyre. Again, Servian and Bulgarian women who chafe at the restraints of domestic life will take the copper coins from the eyes of a corpse, wash them in wine or water, and give the liquid to their husbands to drink. After swallowing it, the husband will be as blind to his wife's peccadilloes as the dead man was on whose eyes the coins were laid.

Further, animals are often conceived to possess qualities or properties which might be useful to man, and homoeopathic or imitative magic seeks to communicate these properties to human beings in various ways. Thus some Bechuanas wear a ferret as a charm, because, being very tenacious of life, it will make them difficult to kill. Others wear a certain insect, mutilated, but living, for a similar purpose. Yet other Bechuana warriors wear the hair of a hornless ox among their own hair, and the skin of a frog on their mantle, because a frog is slippery, and the ox, having no horns, is hard to catch ; so the man who is provided with these charms believes that he will be as hard to hold as the ox and the frog. Again, it seems plain that a South African warrior who twists tufts of rats' hair among his own curly black locks will have just as many chances of avoiding the enemy's spear as the nimble rat has of avoiding things thrown at it ; hence in these regions rats' hair is in great demand when war is expected. One of the ancient books of India prescribes that when a sacrifice is offered for victory, the earth out of which the altar is to be made should be taken from a place where a boar has been wallowing, since the strength of the boar will be in that earth. When you are playing the one-stringed lute, and your fingers are stiff, the thing to do is to catch some long-legged field spiders and roast them, and then rub your fingers with the ashes ; that will make your fingers as lithe and nimble as the spiders' legs— at least so think the Galelareese. To bring back a runaway slave an Arab will trace a magic-circle on the ground, stick a nail in the middle of it, and attach a beetle by a thread to the nail, taking care that the sex of the beetle is that of the fugitive. As the beetle crawls round and round, it will coil the thread about the nail, thus shortening its tether and drawing nearer to the centre at every circuit. So by virtue of homoeopathic magic the runaway slave will be drawn back to his master.

Among the western tribes of British New Guinea, a man who has

killed a snake will burn it and smear his legs with the ashes when he
goes into the forest ; for no snake will bite him for some days afterwards.   If a South Slavonian has a mind to pilfer and steal at market,
he has nothing to do but to burn a blind cat, and then throw a pinch
of its ashes over the person with whom he is higgling ; after that he
can take what he likes from the booth, and the owner will not be a bit
the wiser, having become as blind as the deceased cat with whose
ashes he has been sprinkled.   The thief may even ask boldly, " Did
I pay for it ? " and the deluded huckster will reply, " Why, certainly."
Equally simple and effectual is the expedient adopted by natives of
Central Australia who desire to cultivate their beards.   They prick
the chin all over with a pointed bone, and then stroke it carefully with
a magic stick or stone, which represents a kind of rat that has very
long whiskers.   The virtue of these whiskers naturally passes into the
representative stick or stone, and thence by an easy transition to the
chin, which, consequently, is soon adorned with a rich growth of
beard.   The ancient Greeks thought that to eat the flesh of the wakeful
nightingale would prevent a man from sleeping ; that to smear the
eyes of a blear-sighted person with the gall of an eagle would give him
the eagle's vision ; and that a raven's eggs would restore the blackness
of the raven to silvery hair.   Only the person who adopted this last
mode of concealing the ravages of time had to be most careful to keep
his mouth full of oil all the time he applied the eggs to his venerable
locks, else his teeth as well as his hair would be dyed raven black, and
no amount of scrubbing and scouring would avail to whiten them
again.   The hair-restorer was in fact a shade too powerful, and in
applying it you might get more than you bargained for.

The Huichol Indians admire the beautiful markings on the backs
of serpents.   Hence when a Huichol woman is about to weave or
embroider, her husband catches a large serpent and holds it in a cleft
stick, while the woman strokes the reptile with one hand down the
whole length of its back ; then she passes the same hand over her
forehead and eyes, that she may be able to work as beautiful patterns
in the web as the markings on the back of the serpent.

On the principle of homoeopathic magic, inanimate things, as well
as plants and animals, may diffuse blessing or bane around them,
according to their own intrinsic nature and the skill of the wizard to
tap or dam, as the case may be, the stream of weal or woe.   In Samarcand women give a baby sugar-candy to suck and put glue in the palm
of its hand, in order that, when the child grows up, his words may be
sweet and precious things may stick to his hands as if they were glued.
The Greeks thought that a garment made from the fleece of a sheep
that had been torn by a wolf would hurt the wearer, setting up an itch
or irritation in his skin.   They were also of opinion that if a stone
which had been bitten by a dog were dropped in wine, it would make
all who drank of that wine to fall out among themselves.   Among
the Arabs of Moab a childless woman often borrows the robe of a
woman who has had many children, hoping with the robe to acquire

the fruitfulness of its owner. The Caffres of Sofala, in East Africa, had a great dread of being struck with anything hollow, such as a reed or a straw, and greatly preferred being thrashed with a good thick cudgel or an iron bar, even though it hurt very much. For they thought that if a man were beaten with anything hollow, his inside would waste away till he died. In Eastern seas there is a large shell which the Buginese of Celebes call the " old man " (*kadjâwo*). On Fridays they turn these " old men " upside down and place them on the thresholds of their houses, believing that whoever then steps over the threshold of the house will live to be old. At initiation a Brahman boy is made to tread with his right foot on a stone, while the words are repeated, " Tread on this stone ; like a stone be firm " ; and the same ceremony is performed, with the same words, by a Brahman bride at her marriage. In Madagascar a mode of counteracting the levity of fortune is to bury a stone at the foot of the heavy house-post. The common custom of swearing upon a stone may be based partly on a belief that the strength and stability of the stone lend confirmation to an oath. Thus the old Danish historian Saxo Grammaticus tells us that " the ancients, when they were to choose a king, were wont to stand on stones planted in the ground, and to proclaim their votes, in order to foreshadow from the steadfastness of the stones that the deed would be lasting."

But while a general magical efficacy may be supposed to reside in all stones by reason of their common properties of weight and solidity, special magical virtues are attributed to particular stones, or kinds of stone, in accordance with their individual or specific qualities of shape and colour. For example, the Indians of Peru employed certain stones for the increase of maize, others for the increase of potatoes, and others again for the increase of cattle. The stones used to make maize grow were fashioned in the likeness of cobs of maize, and the stones destined to multiply cattle had the shape of sheep.

In some parts of Melanesia a like belief prevails that certain sacred stones are endowed with miraculous powers which correspond in their nature to the shape of the stone. Thus a piece of water-worn coral on the beach often bears a surprising likeness to a bread-fruit. Hence in the Banks Islands a man who finds such a coral will lay it at the root of one of his bread-fruit trees in the expectation that it will make the tree bear well. If the result answers his expectation, he will then, for a proper remuneration, take stones of less marked character from other men and let them lie near his, in order to imbue them with the magic virtue which resides in it. Similarly, a stone with little discs upon it is good to bring in money ; and if a man found a large stone with a number of small ones under it, like a sow among her litter, he was sure that to offer money upon it would bring him pigs. In these and similar cases the Melanesians ascribe the marvellous power, not to the stone itself, but to its indwelling spirit ; and sometimes, as we have just seen, a man endeavours to propitiate the spirit by laying down offerings on the stone. But the conception of spirits that must be propitiated lies outside the sphere of magic, and within that of religion. Where such a conception is found, as here, in conjunction with purely magical ideas and practices, the latter may generally be assumed to be the original stock on which the religious conception has been at some later time engrafted. For there are strong grounds for thinking that, in the evolution of thought, magic has preceded religion. But to this point we shall return presently.

The ancients set great store on the magical qualities of precious stones ; indeed it has been maintained, with great show of reason, that such stones were used as amulets long before they were worn as mere ornaments. Thus the Greeks gave the name of tree-agate to a stone which exhibits tree-like markings, and they thought that if two of these gems were tied to the horns or necks of oxen at the plough, the crop would be sure to be plentiful. Again, they recognised a milk-stone which produced an abundant supply of milk in women if only they drank it dissolved in honey-mead. Milk-stones are used for the same purpose by Greek women in Crete and Melos at the present day ; in Albania nursing mothers wear the stones in order to ensure an abundant flow of milk. Again, the Greeks believed in a stone which cured snake-bites, and hence was named the snake-stone ; to test its efficacy you had only to grind the stone to powder and sprinkle the powder on the wound. The wine-coloured amethyst received its name, which means " not drunken," because it was supposed to keep the wearer of it sober ; and two brothers who desired to live at unity were advised to carry magnets about with them, which, by drawing the twain together, would clearly prevent them from falling out.

The ancient books of the Hindoos lay down a rule that after sunset on his marriage night a man should sit silent with his wife till the stars begin to twinkle in the sky. When the pole-star appears, he should point it out to her, and, addressing the star, say, " Firm art thou ; I see thee, the firm one. Firm be thou with me, O thriving one ! " Then, turning to his wife, he should say, " To me Brihaspati has given thee ; obtaining offspring through me, thy husband, live with me a hundred autumns." The intention of the ceremony is plainly to guard against the fickleness of fortune and the instability of earthly bliss by the steadfast influence of the constant star. It is the wish expressed in Keats's last sonnet :

" Bright star ! would I were steadfast as thou art—
Not in lone splendour hung aloft the night."

Dwellers by the sea cannot fail to be impressed by the sight of its ceaseless ebb and flow, and are apt, on the principles of that rude philosophy of sympathy and resemblance which here engages our attention, to trace a subtle relation, a secret harmony, between its tides and the life of man, of animals, and of plants. In the flowing tide they see not merely a symbol, but a cause of exuberance, of prosperity, and of life, while in the ebbing tide they discern a real agent as well as a melancholy emblem of failure, of weakness, and of death.

The Breton peasant fancies that clover sown when the tide is coming in will grow well, but that if the plant be sown at low water or when the tide is going out, it will never reach maturity, and that the cows which feed on it will burst.   His wife believes that the best butter is made when the tide has just turned and is beginning to flow, that milk which foams in the churn will go on foaming till the hour of high water is past, and that water drawn from the well or milk extracted from the cow while the tide is rising will boil up in the pot or saucepan and overflow into the fire.   According to some of the ancients, the skins of seals, even after they had been parted from their bodies, remained in secret sympathy with the sea, and were observed to ruffle when the tide was on the ebb.   Another ancient belief, attributed to Aristotle, was that no creature can die except at ebb tide.   The belief, if we can trust Pliny, was confirmed by experience, so far as regards human beings, on the coast of France.   Philostratus also assures us that at Cadiz dying people never yielded up the ghost while the water was high.   A like fancy still lingers in some parts of Europe.   On the Cantabrian coast they think that persons who die of chronic or acute disease expire at the moment when the tide begins to recede.   In Portugal, all along the coast of Wales, and on some parts of the coast of Brittany, a belief is said to prevail that people are born when the tide comes in, and die when it goes out.   Dickens attests the existence of the same superstition in England.   " People can't die, along the coast," said Mr. Peggotty, " except when the tide's pretty nigh out. They can't be born, unless it's pretty nigh in—not properly born till flood."   The belief that most deaths happen at ebb tide is said to be held along the east coast of England from Northumberland to Kent. Shakespeare must have been familiar with it, for he makes Falstaff die " even just between twelve and one, e'en at the turning o' the tide." We meet the belief again on the Pacific coast of North America among the Haidas.   Whenever a good Haida is about to die he sees a canoe manned by some of his dead friends, who come with the tide to bid him welcome to the spirit land.   " Come with us now," they say, " for the tide is about to ebb and we must depart."   At Port Stephens, in New South Wales, the natives always buried their dead at flood tide, never at ebb, lest the retiring water should bear the soul of the departed to some distant country.

To ensure a long life the Chinese have recourse to certain complicated charms, which concentrate in themselves the magical essence emanating, on homoeopathic principles, from times and seasons, from persons and from things.   The vehicles employed to transmit these happy influences are no other than grave-clothes.   These are provided by many Chinese in their lifetime, and most people have them cut out and sewn by an unmarried girl or a very young woman, wisely calculating that, since such a person is likely to live a great many years to come, a part of her capacity to live long must surely pass into the clothes, and thus stave off for many years the time when they shall be put to their proper use.   Further, the garments are made by preference in a year which has an intercalary month ; for to the Chinese mind it seems plain that grave-clothes made in a year which is unusually long will possess the capacity of prolonging life in an unusually high degree. Amongst the clothes there is one robe in particular on which special pains have been lavished to imbue it with this priceless quality. It is a long silken gown of the deepest blue colour, with the word " longevity " embroidered all over it in thread of gold. To present an aged parent with one of these costly and splendid mantles, known as " longevity garments," is esteemed by the Chinese an act of filial piety and a delicate mark of attention. As the garment purports to prolong the life of its owner, he often wears it, especially on festive occasions, in order to allow the influence of longevity, created by the many golden letters with which it is bespangled, to work their full effect upon his person. On his birthday, above all, he hardly ever fails to don it, for in China common sense bids a man lay in a large stock of vital energy on his birthday, to be expended in the form of health and vigour during the rest of the year. Attired in the gorgeous pall, and absorbing its blessed influence at every pore, the happy owner receives complacently the congratulations of friends and relations, who warmly express their admiration of these magnificent cerements, and of the filial piety which prompted the children to bestow so beautiful and useful a present on the author of their being.

Another application of the maxim that like produces like is seen in the Chinese belief that the fortunes of a town are deeply affected by its shape, and that they must vary according to the character of the thing which that shape most nearly resembles. Thus it is related that long ago the town of Tsuen-cheu-fu, the outlines of which are like those of a carp, frequently fell a prey to the depredations of the neighbouring city of Yung-chun, which is shaped like a fishing-net, until the inhabitants of the former town conceived the plan of erecting two tall pagodas in their midst. These pagodas, which still tower above the city of Tsuen-cheu-fu, have ever since exercised the happiest influence over its destiny by intercepting the imaginary net before it could descend and entangle in its meshes the imaginary carp. Some forty years ago the wise men of Shanghai were much exercised to discover the cause of a local rebellion. On careful enquiry they ascertained that the rebellion was due to the shape of a large new temple which had most unfortunately been built in the shape of a tortoise, an animal of the very worst character. The difficulty was serious, the danger was pressing ; for to pull down the temple would have been impious, and to let it stand as it was would be to court a succession of similar or worse disasters. However, the genius of the local professors of geomancy, rising to the occasion, triumphantly surmounted the difficulty and obviated the danger. By filling up two wells, which represented the eyes of the tortoise, they at once blinded that disreputable animal and rendered him incapable of doing further mischief.

Sometimes homoeopathic or imitative magic is called in to annul an evil omen by accomplishing it in mimicry. The effect is to circumvent destiny by substituting a mock calamity for a real one. In Madagascar this mode of cheating the fates is reduced to a regular system. Here every man's fortune is determined by the day or hour of his birth, and if that happens to be an unlucky one his fate is sealed, unless the mischief can be extracted, as the phrase goes, by means of a substitute. The ways of extracting the mischief are various. For example, if a man is born on the first day of the second month (February), his house will be burnt down when he comes of age. To take time by the forelock and avoid this catastrophe, the friends of the infant will set up a shed in a field or in the cattle-fold and burn it. If the ceremony is to be really effective, the child and his mother should be placed in the shed and only plucked, like brands, from the burning hut before it is too late. Again, dripping November is the month of tears, and he who is born in it is born to sorrow. But in order to disperse the clouds that thus gather over his future, he has nothing to do but to take the lid off a boiling pot and wave it about. The drops that fall from it will accomplish his destiny and so prevent the tears from trickling from his eyes. Again, if fate has decreed that a young girl, still unwed, should see her children, still unborn, descend before her with sorrow to the grave, she can avert the calamity as follows. She kills a grasshopper, wraps it in a rag to represent a shroud, and mourns over it like Rachel weeping for her children and refusing to be comforted. Moreover, she takes a dozen or more other grasshoppers, and having removed some of their superfluous legs and wings she lays them about their dead and shrouded fellow. The buzz of the tortured insects and the agitated motions of their mutilated limbs represent the shrieks and contortions of the mourners at a funeral. After burying the deceased grasshopper she leaves the rest to continue their mourning till death releases them from their pain ; and having bound up her dishevelled hair she retires from the grave with the step and carriage of a person plunged in grief. Thenceforth she looks cheerfully forward to seeing her children survive her ; for it cannot be that she should mourn and bury them twice over. Once more, if fortune has frowned on a man at his birth and penury has marked him for her own, he can easily erase the mark in question by purchasing a couple of cheap pearls, price three halfpence, and burying them. For who but the rich of this world can thus afford to fling pearls away ?

§ 3. *Contagious Magic.*—Thus far we have been considering chiefly that branch of sympathetic magic which may be called homoeopathic or imitative. Its leading principle, as we have seen, is that like produces like, or, in other words, that an effect resembles its cause. The other great branch of sympathetic magic, which I have called Contagious Magic, proceeds upon the notion that things which have once been conjoined must remain ever afterwards, even when quite dissevered from each other, in such a sympathetic relation that whatever is done to the one must similarly affect the other. Thus the logical basis of Contagious Magic, like that of Homoeopathic Magic, is a mistaken association of ideas ; its physical basis, if we may speak of such a thing, like the physical basis of Homoeopathic Magic, is a material medium of some sort which, like the ether of modern physics, is assumed to unite distant objects and to convey impressions from one to the other. The most familiar example of Contagious Magic is the magical sympathy which is supposed to exist between a man and any severed portion of his person, as his hair or nails ; so that whoever gets possession of human hair or nails may work his will, at any distance, upon the person from whom they were cut. This superstition is world-wide ; instances of it in regard to hair and nails will be noticed later on in this work.

Among the Australian tribes it was a common practice to knock out one or more of a boy's front teeth at those ceremonies of initiation to which every male member had to submit before he could enjoy the rights and privileges of a full-grown man. The reason of the practice is obscure ; all that concerns us here is the belief that a sympathetic relation continued to exist between the lad and his teeth after the latter had been extracted from his gums. Thus among some of the tribes about the River Darling, in New South Wales, the extracted tooth was placed under the bark of a tree near a river or water-hole ; if the bark grew over the tooth, or if the tooth fell into the water, all was well ; but if it were exposed and the ants ran over it, the natives believed that the boy would suffer from a disease of the mouth. Among the Murring and other tribes of New South Wales the extracted tooth was at first taken care of by an old man, and then passed from one headman to another, until it had gone all round the community, when it came back to the lad's father, and finally to the lad himself. But however it was thus conveyed from hand to hand, it might on no account be placed in a bag containing magical substances, for to do so would, they believed, put the owner of the tooth in great danger. The late Dr. Howitt once acted as custodian of the teeth which had been extracted from some novices at a ceremony of initiation, and the old men earnestly besought him not to carry them in a bag in which they knew that he had some quartz crystals. They declared that if he did so the magic of the crystals would pass into the teeth, and so injure the boys. Nearly a year after Dr. Howitt's return from the ceremony he was visited by one of the principal men of the Murring tribe, who had travelled some two hundred and fifty miles from his home to fetch back the teeth. This man explained that he had been sent for them because one of the boys had fallen into ill health, and it was believed that the teeth had received some injury which had affected him. He was assured that the teeth had been kept in a box apart from any substances, like quartz crystals, which could influence them ; and he returned home bearing the teeth with him carefully wrapt up and concealed.

The Basutos are careful to conceal their extracted teeth, lest these should fall into the hands of certain mythical beings who haunt graves, and who could harm the owner of the tooth by working magic on it. In Sussex some fifty years ago a maid-servant remonstrated strongly against the throwing away of children's cast teeth, affirming that should they be found and gnawed by any animal, the child's new tooth would be, for all the world, like the teeth of the animal that had bitten the old one. In proof of this she named old Master Simmons, who had a very large pig's tooth in his upper jaw, a personal defect that he always averred was caused by his mother, who threw away one of his cast teeth by accident into the hog's trough. A similar belief has led to practices intended, on the principles of homoeopathic magic, to replace old teeth by new and better ones. Thus in many parts of the world it is customary to put extracted teeth in some place where they will be found by a mouse or a rat, in the hope that, through the sympathy which continues to subsist between them and their former owner, his other teeth may acquire the same firmness and excellence as the teeth of these rodents. For example, in Germany it is said to be an almost universal maxim among the people that when you have had a tooth taken out you should insert it in a mouse's hole. To do so with a child's milk-tooth which has fallen out will prevent the child from having toothache. Or you should go behind the stove and throw your tooth backwards over your head, saying, " Mouse, give me your iron tooth ; I will give you my bone tooth." After that your other teeth will remain good. Far away from Europe, at Raratonga, in the Pacific, when a child's tooth was extracted, the following prayer used to be recited :

" Big rat ! little rat !
Here is my old tooth.
Pray give me a new one."

Then the tooth was thrown on the thatch of the house, because rats make their nests in the decayed thatch. The reason assigned for invoking the rats on these occasions was that rats' teeth were the strongest known to the natives.

Other parts which are commonly believed to remain in a sympathetic union with the body, after the physical connexion has been severed, are the navel-string and the afterbirth, including the placenta. So intimate, indeed, is the union conceived to be, that the fortunes of the individual for good or evil throughout life are often supposed to be bound up with one or other of these portions of his person, so that if his navel-string or afterbirth is preserved and properly treated, he will be prosperous ; whereas if it be injured or lost, he will suffer accordingly. Thus certain tribes of Western Australia believe that a man swims well or ill, according as his mother at his birth threw the navel-string into water or not. Among the natives on the Pennefather River in Queensland it is believed that a part of the child's spirit (cho-i) stays in the afterbirth. Hence the grandmother takes the afterbirth away and buries it in the sand. She marks the spot by a number of twigs which she sticks in the ground in a circle, tying their tops together so that the structure resembles a cone. When Anjea, the being who causes conception in women by putting mud babies into their wombs, comes along and sees the place, he takes out the spirit and carries it away to one of his haunts, such as a tree, a hole in a rock, or a lagoon, where it may remain for years. But some time or other he will put the spirit again into a baby, and it will be born once more into the world. In Ponape, one of the Caroline Islands, the navel-string is placed in a shell and then disposed of in such a way as shall best adapt the child for the career which the parents have chosen for him ; for example, if they wish to make him a good climber, they will hang the navel-string on a tree. The Kei islanders regard the navel-string as the brother or sister of the child, according to the sex of the infant. They put it in a pot with ashes, and set it in the branches of a tree, that it may keep a watchful eye on the fortunes of its comrade. Among the Bataks of Sumatra, as among many other peoples of the Indian Archipelago, the placenta passes for the child's younger brother or sister, the sex being determined by the sex of the child, and it is buried under the house. According to the Bataks it is bound up with the child's welfare, and seems, in fact, to be the seat of the transferable soul, of which we shall hear something later on. The Karo Bataks even affirm that of a man's two souls it is the true soul that lives with the placenta under the house ; that is the soul, they say, which begets children.

The Baganda believe that every person is born with a double, and this double they identify with the afterbirth, which they regard as a second child. The mother buries the afterbirth at the root of a plantain tree, which then becomes sacred until the fruit has ripened, when it is plucked to furnish a sacred feast for the family. Among the Cherokees the navel-string of a girl is buried under a corn-mortar, in order that the girl may grow up to be a good baker ; but the navel-string of a boy is hung up on a tree in the woods, in order that he may be a hunter. The Incas of Peru preserved the navel-string with the greatest care, and gave it to the child to suck whenever it fell ill. In ancient Mexico they used to give a boy's navel-string to soldiers, to be buried by them on a field of battle, in order that the boy might thus acquire a passion for war. But the navel-string of a girl was buried beside the domestic hearth, because this was believed to inspire her with a love of home and a taste for cooking and baking.

Even in Europe many people still believe that a person's destiny is more or less bound up with that of his navel-string or afterbirth. Thus in Rhenish Bavaria the navel-string is kept for a while wrapt up in a piece of old linen, and then cut or pricked to pieces according as the child is a boy or a girl, in order that he or she may grow up to be a skilful workman or a good sempstress. In Berlin the midwife commonly delivers the dried navel-string to the father with a strict injunction to preserve it carefully, for so long as it is kept the child will live and thrive and be free from sickness. In Beauce and Perche the people are careful to throw the navel-string neither into water nor into fire, believing that if that were done the child would be drowned or burned.

Thus in many parts of the world the navel-string, or more commonly the afterbirth, is regarded as a living being, the brother or sister of the infant, or as the material object in which the guardian spirit of the child or part of its soul resides. Further, the sympathetic connexion supposed to exist between a person and his afterbirth or navel-string comes out very clearly in the widespread custom of treating the afterbirth or navel-string in ways which are supposed to influence for life the character and career of the person, making him, if it is a man, a nimble climber, a strong swimmer, a skilful hunter, or a brave soldier, and making her, if it is a woman, a cunning sempstress, a good baker, and so forth. Thus the beliefs and usages concerned with the afterbirth or placenta, and to a less extent with the navel-string, present a remarkable parallel to the widespread doctrine of the transferable or external soul and the customs founded on it. Hence it is hardly rash to conjecture that the resemblance is no mere chance coincidence, but that in the afterbirth or placenta we have a physical basis (not necessarily the only one) for the theory and practice of the external soul. The consideration of that subject is reserved for a later part of this work.

A curious application of the doctrine of contagious magic is the relation commonly believed to exist between a wounded man and the agent of the wound, so that whatever is subsequently done by or to the agent must correspondingly affect the patient either for good or evil. Thus Pliny tells us that if you have wounded a man and are sorry for it, you have only to spit on the hand that gave the wound, and the pain of the sufferer will be instantly alleviated. In Melanesia, if a man's friends get possession of the arrow which wounded him, they keep it in a damp place or in cool leaves, for then the inflammation will be trifling and will soon subside. Meantime the enemy who shot the arrow is hard at work to aggravate the wound by all the means in his power. For this purpose he and his friends drink hot and burning juices and chew irritating leaves, for this will clearly inflame and irritate the wound. Further, they keep the bow near the fire to make the wound which it has inflicted hot ; and for the same reason they put the arrow-head, if it has been recovered, into the fire. Moreover, they are careful to keep the bow-string taut and to twang it occasionally, for this will cause the wounded man to suffer from tension of the nerves and spasms of tetanus. " It is constantly received and avouched," says Bacon, " that the anointing of the weapon that maketh the wound will heal the wound itself. In this experiment, upon the relation of men of credit (though myself, as yet, am not fully inclined to believe it), you shall note the points following : first, the ointment wherewith this is done is made of divers ingredients, whereof the strangest and hardest to come by are the moss upon the skull of a dead man unburied, and the fats of a boar and a bear killed in the act of generation." The precious ointment compounded out of these and other ingredients was applied, as the philosopher explains, not to the wound but to the weapon, and that even though the injured man was at a great distance and knew nothing about it. The experiment, he tells us, had been tried of wiping the ointment off the weapon without the knowledge of the person hurt, with the result that he was presently in a great rage of pain until the weapon was anointed again. Moreover, " it is affirmed that if you cannot get the weapon, yet if you put an instrument of iron or wood resembling the weapon into the wound, whereby it bleedeth, the anointing of that instrument will serve and work the effect." Remedies of the sort which Bacon deemed worthy of his attention are still in vogue in the eastern counties of England. Thus in Suffolk if a man cuts himself with a bill-hook or a scythe he always takes care to keep the weapon bright, and oils it to prevent the wound from festering. If he runs a thorn or, as he calls it, a bush into his hand, he oils or greases the extracted thorn. A man came to a doctor with an inflamed hand, having run a thorn into it while he was hedging. On being told that the hand was festering, he remarked, " That didn't ought to, for I greased the bush well arter I pulled it out." If a horse wounds its foot by treading on a nail, a Suffolk groom will invariably preserve the nail, clean it, and grease it every day, to prevent the foot from festering. Similarly Cambridgeshire labourers think that if a horse has run a nail into its foot, it is necessary to grease the nail with lard or oil and put it away in some safe place, or the horse will not recover. A few years ago a veterinary surgeon was sent for to attend a horse which had ripped its side open on the hinge of a farm gatepost. On arriving at the farm he found that nothing had been done to the wounded horse, but that a man was busy trying to pry the hinge out of the gatepost in order that it might be greased and put away, which, in the opinion of the Cambridge wiseacres, would conduce to the recovery of the animal. Similarly Essex rustics opine that, if a man has been stabbed with a knife, it is essential to his recovery that the knife should be greased and laid across the bed on which the sufferer is lying. So in Bavaria you are directed to anoint a linen rag with grease and tie it on the edge of the axe that cut you, taking care to keep the sharp edge upwards. As the grease on the axe dries, your wound heals. Similarly in the Harz Mountains they say that if you cut yourself, you ought to smear the knife or the scissors with fat and put the instrument away in a dry place in the name of the Father, of the Son, and of the Holy Ghost. As the knife dries, the wound heals. Other people, however, in Germany say that you should stick the knife in some damp place in the ground, and that your hurt will heal as the knife rusts. Others again, in Bavaria, recommend you to smear the axe or whatever it is with blood and put it under the eaves.

The train of reasoning which thus commends itself to English and German rustics, in common with the savages of Melanesia and America, is carried a step farther by the aborigines of Central Australia, who conceive that under certain circumstances the near relations of a wounded man must grease themselves, restrict their diet, and regulate their behaviour in other ways in order to ensure his recovery. Thus when a lad has been circumcised and the wound is not yet healed, his mother may not eat opossum, or a certain kind of lizard, or carpet snake, or any kind of fat, for otherwise she would retard the healing of the boy's wound. Every day she greases her digging-sticks and never lets them out of her sight ; at night she sleeps with them close to her head. No one is allowed to touch them. Every day also she rubs her body all over with grease, as in some way this is believed to help her son's recovery. Another refinement of the same principle is due to the ingenuity of the German peasant. It is said that when one of his pigs or sheep breaks its leg, a farmer of Rhenish Bavaria or Hesse will bind up the leg of a chair with bandages and splints in due form. For some days thereafter no one may sit on that chair, move it, or knock up against it ; for to do so would pain the injured pig or sheep and hinder the cure. In this last case it is clear that we have passed wholly out of the region of contagious magic and into the region of homoeopathic or imitative magic ; the chair-leg, which is treated instead of the beast's leg, in no sense belongs to the animal, and the application of bandages to it is a mere simulation of the treatment which a more rational surgery would bestow on the real patient.

The sympathetic connexion supposed to exist between a man and the weapon which has wounded him is probably founded on the notion that the blood on the weapon continues to feel with the blood in his body. For a like reason the Papuans of Tumleo, an island off New Guinea, are careful to throw into the sea the bloody bandages with which their wounds have been dressed, for they fear that if these rags fell into the hands of an enemy he might injure them magically thereby. Once when a man with a wound in his mouth, which bled constantly, came to the missionaries to be treated, his faithful wife took great pains to collect all the blood and cast it into the sea. Strained and unnatural as this idea may seem to us, it is perhaps less so than the belief that magic sympathy is maintained between a person and his clothes, so that whatever is done to the clothes will be felt by the man himself, even though he may be far away at the time. In the Wotjobaluk tribe of Victoria a wizard would sometimes get hold of a man's opossum rug and roast it slowly in the fire, and as he did so the owner of the rug would fall sick. If the wizard consented to undo the charm, he would give the rug back to the sick man's friends, bidding them put it in water, " so as to wash the fire out." When that happened, the sufferer would feel a refreshing coolness and probably recover. In Tanna, one of the New Hebrides, a man who had a grudge at another and desired his death would try to get possession of a cloth which had touched the sweat of his enemy's body. If he succeeded, he rubbed the cloth carefully over with the leaves and twigs of a certain tree, rolled and bound cloth, twigs, and leaves into a long sausage-shaped bundle, and burned it slowly in the fire. As the bundle was consumed, the victim fell ill, and when it was reduced to ashes, he died. In this last form of enchantment, however, the magical sympathy may be supposed to exist not so much between the man and the cloth as between the man and the sweat which issued from his body. But in other cases of the same sort it seems that the garment by itself is enough to give the sorcerer a hold upon his victim. The witch in Theocritus, while she melted an image or lump of wax in order that her faithless lover might melt with love of her, did not forget to throw into the fire a shred of his cloak which he had dropped in her house. In Prussia they say that if you cannot catch a thief, the next best thing you can do is to get hold of a garment which he may have shed in his flight ; for if you beat it soundly, the thief will fall sick. This belief is firmly rooted in the popular mind. Some eighty or ninety years ago, in the neighbourhood of Berend, a man was detected trying to steal honey, and fled, leaving his coat behind him. When he heard that the enraged owner of the honey was mauling his lost coat, he was so alarmed that he took to his bed and died.

Again, magic may be wrought on a man sympathetically, not only through his clothes and severed parts of himself, but also through the impressions left by his body in sand or earth. In particular, it is a world-wide superstition that by injuring footprints you injure the feet that made them. Thus the natives of South-eastern Australia think that they can lame a man by placing sharp pieces of quartz, glass, bone, or charcoal in his footprints. Rheumatic pains are often attributed by them to this cause. Seeing a Tatungolung man very lame, Mr. Howitt asked him what was the matter. He said, " Some fellow has put *bottle* in my foot." He was suffering from rheumatism, but believed that an enemy had found his foot-track and had buried in it a piece of broken bottle, the magical influence of which had entered his foot.

Similar practices prevail in various parts of Europe. Thus in Mecklenburg it is thought that if you drive a nail into a man's footprint he will fall lame ; sometimes it is required that the nail should be taken from a coffin. A like mode of injuring an enemy is resorted to in some parts of France. It is said that there was an old woman who used to frequent Stow in Suffolk, and she was a witch. If, while she walked, any one went after her and stuck a nail or a knife into her footprint in the dust, the dame could not stir a step till it was withdrawn. Among the South Slavs a girl will dig up the earth from the footprints of the man she loves and put it in a flower-pot. Then she plants in the pot a marigold, a flower that is thought to be fadeless. And as its golden blossom grows and blooms and never fades, so shall her sweetheart's love grow and bloom, and never, never fade. Thus the love-spell acts on the man through the earth he trod on. An old Danish mode of concluding a treaty was based on the same idea of the sympathetic connexion between a man and his footprints : the covenanting parties sprinkled each other's footprints with their own blood, thus giving a pledge of fidelity. In ancient Greece superstitions of the same sort seem to have been current, for it was thought that if a horse stepped on the track of a wolf he was seized with numbness ; and a maxim ascribed to Pythagoras forbade people to pierce a man's footprints with a nail or a knife.

The same superstition is turned to account by hunters in many

parts of the world for the purpose of running down the game. Thus a German huntsman will stick a nail taken from a coffin into the fresh spoor of the quarry, believing that this will hinder the animal from escaping. The aborigines of Victoria put hot embers in the tracks of the animals they were pursuing. Hottentot hunters throw into the air a handful of sand taken from the footprints of the game, believing that this will bring the animal down. Thompson Indians used to lay charms on the tracks of wounded deer ; after that they deemed it superfluous to pursue the animal any farther that day, for being thus charmed it could not travel far and would soon die. Similarly, Ojebway Indians placed " medicine " on the track of the first deer or bear they met with, supposing that this would soon bring the animal into sight, even if it were two or three days' journey off ; for this charm had power to compress a journey of several days into a few hours. Ewe hunters of West Africa stab the footprints of game with a sharp-pointed stick in order to maim the quarry and allow them to come up with it.

But though the footprint is the most obvious it is not the only impression made by the body through which magic may be wrought on a man. The aborigines of South-eastern Australia believe that a man may be injured by burying sharp fragments of quartz, glass, and so forth in the mark made by his reclining body ; the magical virtue of these sharp things enters his body and causes those acute pains which the ignorant European puts down to rheumatism. We can now understand why it was a maxim with the Pythagoreans that in rising from bed you should smooth away the impression left by your body on the bed-clothes. The rule was simply an old precaution against magic, forming part of a whole code of superstitious maxims which antiquity fathered on Pythagoras, though doubtless they were familiar to the barbarous forefathers of the Greeks long before the time of that philosopher.

§ 4. *The Magician's Progress.*—We have now concluded our examination of the general principles of sympathetic magic. The examples by which I have illustrated them have been drawn for the most part from what may be called private magic, that is from magical rites and incantations practised for the benefit or the injury of individuals. But in savage society there is commonly to be found in addition what we may call public magic, that is, sorcery practised for the benefit of the whole community. Wherever ceremonies of this sort are observed for the common good, it is obvious that the magician ceases to be merely a private practitioner and becomes to some extent a public functionary. The development of such a class of functionaries is of great importance for the political as well as the religious evolution of society. For when the welfare of the tribe is supposed to depend on the performance of these magical rites, the magician rises into a position of much influence and repute, and may readily acquire the rank and authority of a chief or king. The profession accordingly draws into its ranks some of the ablest and most ambitious men of the tribe, because it holds out to them a prospect of honour, wealth, and power such as hardly any other

career could offer. The acuter minds perceive how easy it is to dupe
their weaker brother and to play on his superstition for their own
advantage. Not that the sorcerer is always a knave and impostor ;
he is often sincerely convinced that he really possesses those wonderful
powers which the credulity of his fellows ascribes to him. But the
more sagacious he is, the more likely he is to see through the fallacies
which impose on duller wits. Thus the ablest members of the profession must tend to be more or less conscious deceivers ; and it is
just these men who in virtue of their superior ability will generally
come to the top and win for themselves positions of the highest dignity
and the most commanding authority. The pitfalls which beset the
path of the professional sorcerer are many, and as a rule only the man
of coolest head and sharpest wit will be able to steer his way through
them safely. For it must always be remembered that every single
profession and claim put forward by the magician as such is false ;
not one of them can be maintained without deception, conscious or
unconscious. Accordingly the sorcerer who sincerely believes in his
own extravagant pretensions is in far greater peril and is much more
likely to be cut short in his career than the deliberate impostor. The
honest wizard always expects that his charms and incantations will
produce their supposed effect ; and when they fail, not only really, as
they always do, but conspicuously and disastrously, as they often do,
he is taken aback : he is not, like his knavish colleague, ready with
a plausible excuse to account for the failure, and before he can find
one he may be knocked on the head by his disappointed and angry
employers.

The general result is that at this stage of social evolution the
supreme power tends to fall into the hands of men of the keenest
intelligence and the most unscrupulous character. If we could balance
the harm they do by their knavery against the benefits they confer
by their superior sagacity, it might well be found that the good greatly
outweighed the evil. For more mischief has probably been wrought
in the world by honest fools in high places than by intelligent rascals.
Once your shrewd rogue has attained the height of his ambition, and
has no longer any selfish end to further, he may, and often does, turn
his talents, his experience, his resources, to the service of the public.
Many men who have been least scrupulous in the acquisition of power
have been most beneficent in the use of it, whether the power they
aimed at and won was that of wealth, political authority, or what not.
In the field of politics the wily intriguer, the ruthless victor, may end by
being a wise and magnanimous ruler, blessed in his lifetime, lamented
at his death, admired and applauded by posterity. Such men, to
take two of the most conspicuous instances, were Julius Caesar and
Augustus. But once a fool always a fool, and the greater the power
in his hands the more disastrous is likely to be the use he makes of it.
The heaviest calamity in English history, the breach with America,
might never have occurred if George the Third had not been an
honest dullard.

Thus, so far as the public profession of magic affected the constitution of savage society, it tended to place the control of affairs in the hands of the ablest man : it shifted the balance of power from the many to the one : it substituted a monarchy for a democracy, or rather for an oligarchy of old men ; for in general the savage community is ruled, not by the whole body of adult males, but by a council of elders. The change, by whatever causes produced, and whatever the character of the early rulers, was on the whole very beneficial. For the rise of monarchy appears to be an essential condition of the emergence of mankind from savagery. No human being is so hidebound by custom and tradition as your democratic savage ; in no state of society consequently is progress so slow and difficult. The old notion that the savage is the freest of mankind is the reverse of the truth. He is a slave, not indeed to a visible master, but to the past, to the spirits of his dead forefathers, who haunt his steps from birth to death, and rule him with a rod of iron. What they did is the pattern of right, the unwritten law to which he yields a blind unquestioning obedience. The least possible scope is thus afforded to superior talent to change old customs for the better. The ablest man is dragged down by the weakest and dullest, who necessarily sets the standard, since he cannot rise, while the other can fall. The surface of such a society presents a uniform dead level, so far as it is humanly possible to reduce the natural inequalities, the immeasurable real differences of inborn capacity and temper, to a false superficial appearance of equality. From this low and stagnant condition of affairs, which demagogues and dreamers in later times have lauded as the ideal state, the Golden Age, of humanity, everything that helps to raise society by opening a career to talent and proportioning the degrees of authority to men's natural abilities, deserves to be welcomed by all who have the real good of their fellows at heart. Once these elevating influences have begun to operate—and they cannot be for ever suppressed—the progress of civilisation becomes comparatively rapid. The rise of one man to supreme power enables him to carry through changes in a single lifetime which previously many generations might not have sufficed to effect ; and if, as will often happen, he is a man of intellect and energy above the common, he will readily avail himself of the opportunity. Even the whims and caprices of a tyrant may be of service in breaking the chain of custom which lies so heavy on the savage. And as soon as the tribe ceases to be swayed by the timid and divided counsels of the elders, and yields to the direction of a single strong and resolute mind, it becomes formidable to its neighbours and enters on a career of aggrandisement, which at an early stage of history is often highly favourable to social, industrial, and intellectual progress. For extending its sway, partly by force of arms, partly by the voluntary submission of weaker tribes, the community soon acquires wealth and slaves, both of which, by relieving some classes from the perpetual struggle for a bare subsistence, afford them an opportunity of devoting themselves to that disinterested pursuit of knowledge which is the noblest and most powerful instrument to ameliorate the lot of man.

Intellectual progress, which reveals itself in the growth of art and science and the spread of more liberal views, cannot be dissociated from industrial or economic progress, and that in its turn receives an immense impulse from conquest and empire. It is no mere accident that the most vehement outbursts of activity of the human mind have followed close on the heels of victory, and that the great conquering races of the world have commonly done most to advance and spread civilisation, thus healing in peace the wounds they inflicted in war. The Babylonians, the Greeks, the Romans, the Arabs are our witnesses in the past : we may yet live to see a similar outburst in Japan. Nor, to remount the stream of history to its sources, is it an accident that all the first great strides towards civilisation have been made under despotic and theocratic governments, like those of Egypt, Babylon, and Peru, where the supreme ruler claimed and received the servile allegiance of his subjects in the double character of a king and a god. It is hardly too much to say that at this early epoch despotism is the best friend of humanity and, paradoxical as it may sound, of liberty. For after all there is more liberty in the best sense—liberty to think our own thoughts and to fashion our own destinies—under the most absolute despotism, the most grinding tyranny, than under the apparent freedom of savage life, where the individual's lot is cast from the cradle to the grave in the iron mould of hereditary custom.

So far, therefore, as the public profession of magic has been one of the roads by which the ablest men have passed to supreme power, it has contributed to emancipate mankind from the thraldom of tradition and to elevate them into a larger, freer life, with a broader outlook on the world. This is no small service rendered to humanity. And when we remember further that in another direction magic has paved the way for science, we are forced to admit that if the black art has done much evil, it has also been the source of much good ; that if it is the child of error, it has yet been the mother of freedom and truth.

CHAPTER IV

MAGIC AND RELIGION

THE examples collected in the last chapter may suffice to illustrate the general principles of sympathetic magic in its two branches, to which we have given the names of Homoeopathic and Contagious respectively. In some cases of magic which have come before us we have seen that the operation of spirits is assumed, and that an attempt is made to win their favour by prayer and sacrifice. But these cases are on the whole exceptional ; they exhibit magic tinged and alloyed with religion. Wherever sympathetic magic occurs in its pure unadulterated form, it assumes that in nature one event follows another necessarily and invariably without the intervention of any spiritual or personal agency. Thus its fundamental conception is identical with that of modern science; underlying the whole system is a faith, implicit but real and firm, in the order and uniformity of nature. The magician does not doubt that the same causes will always produce the same effects, that the performance of the proper ceremony, accompanied by the appropriate spell, will inevitably be attended by the desired result, unless, indeed, his incantations should chance to be thwarted and foiled by the more potent charms of another sorcerer. He supplicates no higher power : he sues the favour of no fickle and wayward being : he abases himself before no awful deity. Yet his power, great as he believes it to be, is by no means arbitrary and unlimited. He can wield it only so long as he strictly conforms to the rules of his art, or to what may be called the laws of nature as conceived by him. To neglect these rules, to break these laws in the smallest particular, is to incur failure, and may even expose the unskilful practitioner himself to the utmost peril. If he claims a sovereignty over nature, it is a constitutional sovereignty rigorously limited in its scope and exercised in exact conformity with ancient usage. Thus the analogy between the magical and the scientific conceptions of the world is close. In both of them the succession of events is assumed to be perfectly regular and certain, being determined by immutable laws, the operation of which can be foreseen and calculated precisely ; the elements of caprice, of chance, and of accident are banished from the course of nature. Both of them open up a seemingly boundless vista of possibilities to him who knows the causes of things and can touch the secret springs that set in motion the vast and intricate mechanism of the world. Hence the strong attraction which magic and science alike have exercised on the human mind ; hence the powerful stimulus that both have given to the pursuit of knowledge. They lure the weary enquirer, the footsore seeker, on through the wilderness of disappointment in the present by their endless promises of the future : they take him up to the top of an exceeding high mountain and show him, beyond the dark clouds and rolling mists at his feet, a vision of the celestial city, far off, it may be, but radiant with unearthly splendour, bathed in the light of dreams.

The fatal flaw of magic lies not in its general assumption of a sequence of events determined by law, but in its total misconception of the nature of the particular laws which govern that sequence. If we analyse the various cases of sympathetic magic which have been passed in review in the preceding pages, and which may be taken as fair samples of the bulk, we shall find, as I have already indicated, that they are all mistaken applications of one or other of two great fundamental laws of thought, namely, the association of ideas by similarity and the association of ideas by contiguity in space or time. A mistaken association of similar ideas produces homoeopathic or imitative magic : a mistaken association of contiguous ideas produces contagious magic. The principles of association are excellent in

E

themselves, and indeed absolutely essential to the working of the human mind.   Legitimately applied they yield science ; illegitimately applied they yield magic, the bastard sister of science.   It is therefore a truism, almost a tautology, to say that all magic is necessarily false and barren ; for were it ever to become true and fruitful, it would no longer be magic but science.   From the earliest times man has been engaged in a search for general rules whereby to turn the order of natural phenomena to his own advantage, and in the long search he has scraped together a great hoard of such maxims, some of them golden and some of them mere dross.   The true or golden rules constitute the body of applied science which we call the arts ; the false are magic.

If magic is thus next of kin to science, we have still to enquire how it stands related to religion.   But the view we take of that relation will necessarily be coloured by the idea which we have formed of the nature of religion itself ; hence a writer may reasonably be expected to define his conception of religion before he proceeds to investigate its relation to magic.   There is probably no subject in the world about which opinions differ so much as the nature of religion, and to frame a definition of it which would satisfy every one must obviously be impossible.   All that a writer can do is, first, to say clearly what he means by religion, and afterwards to employ the word consistently in that sense throughout his work.   By religion, then, I understand a propitiation or conciliation of powers superior to man which are believed to direct and control the course of nature and of human life. Thus defined, religion consists of two elements, a theoretical and a practical, namely, a belief in powers higher than man and an attempt to propitiate or please them.   Of the two, belief clearly comes first, since we must believe in the existence of a divine being before we can attempt to please him.   But unless the belief leads to a corresponding practice, it is not a religion but merely a theology ; in the language of St. James, " faith, if it hath not works, is dead, being alone."   In other words, no man is religious who does not govern his conduct in some measure by the fear or love of God.   On the other hand, mere practice, divested of all religious belief, is also not religion.   Two men may behave in exactly the same way, and yet one of them may be religious and the other not.   If the one acts from the love or fear of God, he is religious ; if the other acts from the love or fear of man, he is moral or immoral according as his behaviour comports or conflicts with the general good.   Hence belief and practice or, in theological language, faith and works are equally essential to religion, which cannot exist without both of them.   But it is not necessary that religious practice should always take the form of a ritual ; that is, it need not consist in the offering of sacrifice, the recitation of prayers, and other outward ceremonies.   Its aim is to please the deity, and if the deity is one who delights in charity and mercy and purity more than in oblations of blood, the chanting of hymns, and the fumes of incense, his worshippers will best please him, not by prostrating themselves before him, by intoning his praises, and by filling his temples with costly gifts, but by being pure and merciful and charitable towards men, for in so doing they will imitate, so far as human infirmity allows, the perfections of the divine nature. It was this ethical side of religion which the Hebrew prophets, inspired with a noble ideal of God's goodness and holiness, were never weary of inculcating. Thus Micah says : " He hath shewed thee, O man, what is good ; and what doth the Lord require of thee, but to do justly, and to love mercy, and to walk humbly with thy God ? " And at a later time much of the force by which Christianity conquered the world was drawn from the same high conception of God's moral nature and the duty laid on men of conforming themselves to it. " Pure religion and undefiled," says St. James, " before God and the Father is this, To visit the fatherless and widows in their affliction, and to keep himself unspotted from the world."

But if religion involves, first, a belief in superhuman beings who rule the world, and, second, an attempt to win their favour, it clearly assumes that the course of nature is to some extent elastic or variable, and that we can persuade or induce the mighty beings who control it to deflect, for our benefit, the current of events from the channel in which they would otherwise flow. Now this implied elasticity or variability of nature is directly opposed to the principles of magic as well as of science, both of which assume that the processes of nature are rigid and invariable in their operation, and that they can as little be turned from their course by persuasion and entreaty as by threats and intimidation. The distinction between the two conflicting views of the universe turns on their answer to the crucial question, Are the forces which govern the world conscious and personal, or unconscious and impersonal ? Religion, as a conciliation of the superhuman powers, assumes the former member of the alternative. For all conciliation implies that the being conciliated is a conscious or personal agent, that his conduct is in some measure uncertain, and that he can be prevailed upon to vary it in the desired direction by a judicious appeal to his interests, his appetites, or his emotions. Conciliation is never employed towards things which are regarded as inanimate, nor towards persons whose behaviour in the particular circumstances is known to be determined with absolute certainty. Thus in so far as religion assumes the world to be directed by conscious agents who may be turned from their purpose by persuasion, it stands in fundamental antagonism to magic as well as to science, both of which take for granted that the course of nature is determined, not by the passions or caprice of personal beings, but by the operation of immutable laws acting mechanically. In magic, indeed, the assumption is only implicit, but in science it is explicit. It is true that magic often deals with spirits, which are personal agents of the kind assumed by religion ; but whenever it does so in its proper form, it treats them exactly in the same fashion as it treats inanimate agents, that is, it constrains or coerces instead of conciliating or propitiating them as religion would do. Thus it assumes that all personal beings, whether human or divine, are in the last resort subject to those impersonal forces which control all things, but which nevertheless can be turned to account by any one who knows how to manipulate them by the appropriate ceremonies and spells. In ancient Egypt, for example, the magicians claimed the power of compelling even the highest gods to do their bidding, and actually threatened them with destruction in case of disobedience. Sometimes, without going quite so far as that, the wizard declared that he would scatter the bones of Osiris or reveal his sacred legend, if the god proved contumacious. Similarly in India at the present day the great Hindoo trinity itself of Brahma, Vishnu, and Siva is subject to the sorcerers, who, by means of their spells, exercise such an ascendancy over the mightiest deities, that these are bound submissively to execute on earth below, or in heaven above, whatever commands their masters the magicians may please to issue. There is a saying everywhere current in India : " The whole universe is subject to the gods ; the gods are subject to the spells (*mantras*) ; the spells to the Brahmans ; therefore the Brahmans are our gods."

This radical conflict of principle between magic and religion sufficiently explains the relentless hostility with which in history the priest has often pursued the magician. The haughty self-sufficiency of the magician, his arrogant demeanour towards the higher powers, and his unabashed claim to exercise a sway like theirs could not but revolt the priest, to whom, with his awful sense of the divine majesty, and his humble prostration in presence of it, such claims and such a demeanour must have appeared an impious and blasphemous usurpation of prerogatives that belong to God alone. And sometimes, we may suspect, lower motives concurred to whet the edge of the priest's hostility. He professed to be the proper medium, the true intercessor between God and man, and no doubt his interests as well as his feelings were often injured by a rival practitioner, who preached a surer and smoother road to fortune than the rugged and slippery path of divine favour.

Yet this antagonism, familiar as it is to us, seems to have made its appearance comparatively late in the history of religion. At an earlier stage the functions of priest and sorcerer were often combined or, to speak perhaps more correctly, were not yet differentiated from each other. To serve his purpose man wooed the good-will of gods or spirits by prayer and sacrifice, while at the same time he had recourse to ceremonies and forms of words which he hoped would of themselves bring about the desired result without the help of god or devil. In short, he performed religious and magical rites simultaneously ; he uttered prayers and incantations almost in the same breath, knowing or recking little of the theoretical inconsistency of his behaviour, so long as by hook or crook he contrived to get what he wanted. Instances of this fusion or confusion of magic with religion have already met us in the practices of Melanesians and of other peoples.

The same confusion of magic and religion has survived among peoples that have risen to higher levels of culture. It was rife in ancient India and ancient Egypt ; it is by no means extinct among European peasantry at the present day. With regard to ancient India we are told by an eminent Sanscrit scholar that " the sacrificial ritual at the earliest period of which we have detailed information is pervaded with practices that breathe the spirit of the most primitive magic." Speaking of the importance of magic in the East, and especially in Egypt, Professor Maspero remarks that " we ought not to attach to the word magic the degrading idea which it almost inevitably calls up in the mind of a modern. Ancient magic was the very foundation of religion. The faithful who desired to obtain some favour from a god had no chance of succeeding except by laying hands on the deity, and this arrest could only be effected by means of a certain number of rites, sacrifices, prayers, and chants, which the god himself had revealed, and which obliged him to do what was demanded of him."

Among the ignorant classes of modern Europe the same confusion of ideas, the same mixture of religion and magic, crops up in various forms. Thus we are told that in France " the majority of the peasants still believe that the priest possesses a secret and irresistible power over the elements. By reciting certain prayers which he alone knows and has the right to utter, yet for the utterance of which he must afterwards demand absolution, he can, on an occasion of pressing danger, arrest or reverse for a moment the action of the eternal laws of the physical world. The winds, the storms, the hail, and the rain are at his command and obey his will. The fire also is subject to him, and the flames of a conflagration are extinguished at his word." For example, French peasants used to be, perhaps are still, persuaded that the priests could celebrate, with certain special rites, a Mass of the Holy Spirit, of which the efficacy was so miraculous that it never met with any opposition from the divine will ; God was forced to grant whatever was asked of Him in this form, however rash and importunate might be the petition. No idea of impiety or irreverence attached to the rite in the minds of those who, in some of the great extremities of life, sought by this singular means to take the kingdom of heaven by storm. The secular priests generally refused to say the Mass of the Holy Spirit ; but the monks, especially the Capuchin friars, had the reputation of yielding with less scruple to the entreaties of the anxious and distressed. In the constraint thus supposed by Catholic peasantry to be laid by the priest upon the deity we seem to have an exact counterpart of the power which the ancient Egyptians ascribed to their magicians. Again, to take another example, in many villages of Provence the priest is still reputed to possess the faculty of averting storms. It is not every priest who enjoys this reputation ; and in some villages, when a change of pastors takes place, the parishioners are eager to learn whether the new incumbent has the power (*pouder*), as they call it. At the first sign of a heavy storm they put him to the proof by inviting him to exorcise the threatening clouds ; and if the result answers to their hopes, the new shepherd is assured of the sympathy and respect of his flock. In some parishes, where the reputation of the curate in this respect stood higher than that of his rector, the relations between the two have been so strained in consequence that the bishop has had to translate the rector to another benefice. Again, Gascon peasants believe that to revenge themselves on their enemies bad men will sometimes induce a priest to say a mass called the Mass of Saint Sécaire. Very few priests know this mass, and three-fourths of those who do know it would not say it for love or money. None but wicked priests dare to perform the gruesome ceremony, and you may be quite sure that they will have a very heavy account to render for it at the last day. No curate or bishop, not even the archbishop of Auch, can pardon them ; that right belongs to the pope of Rome alone. The Mass of Saint Sécaire may be said only in a ruined or deserted church, where owls mope and hoot, where bats flit in the gloaming, where gypsies lodge of nights, and where toads squat under the desecrated altar. Thither the bad priest comes by night with his light o' love, and at the first stroke of eleven he begins to mumble the mass backwards, and ends just as the clocks are knelling the midnight hour. His leman acts as clerk. The host he blesses is black and has three points ; he consecrates no wine, but instead he drinks the water of a well into which the body of an unbaptized infant has been flung. He makes the sign of the cross, but it is on the ground and with his left foot. And many other things he does which no good Christian could look upon without being struck blind and deaf and dumb for the rest of his life. But the man for whom the mass is said withers away little by little, and nobody can say what is the matter with him ; even the doctors can make nothing of it. They do not know that he is slowly dying of the Mass of Saint Sécaire.

Yet though magic is thus found to fuse and amalgamate with religion in many ages and in many lands, there are some grounds for thinking that this fusion is not primitive, and that there was a time when man trusted to magic alone for the satisfaction of such wants as transcended his immediate animal cravings. In the first place a consideration of the fundamental notions of magic and religion may incline us to surmise that magic is older than religion in the history of humanity. We have seen that on the one hand magic is nothing but a mistaken application of the very simplest and most elementary processes of the mind, namely the association of ideas by virtue of resemblance or contiguity ; and that on the other hand religion assumes the operation of conscious or personal agents, superior to man, behind the visible screen of nature. Obviously the conception of personal agents is more complex than a simple recognition of the similarity or contiguity of ideas ; and a theory which assumes that the course of nature is determined by conscious agents is more abstruse and recondite, and requires for its apprehension a far higher degree of intelligence and reflection, than the view that things succeed each other simply by reason of their contiguity or resemblance. The very beasts associate the ideas of things that are like each other or that have been found together in their experience ; and they could hardly survive for a day if they ceased to do so. But who attributes to the animals a belief that the phenomena of nature are worked by a multitude of invisible animals or by one enormous and prodigiously strong animal behind the scenes? It is probably no injustice to the brutes to assume that the honour of devising a theory of this latter sort must be reserved for human reason. Thus, if magic be deduced immediately from elementary processes of reasoning, and be, in fact, an error into which the mind falls almost spontaneously, while religion rests on conceptions which the merely animal intelligence can hardly be supposed to have yet attained to, it becomes probable that magic arose before religion in the evolution of our race, and that man essayed to bend nature to his wishes by the sheer force of spells and enchantments before he strove to coax and mollify a coy, capricious, or irascible deity by the soft insinuation of prayer and sacrifice.

The conclusion which we have thus reached deductively from a consideration of the fundamental ideas of magic and religion is confirmed inductively by the observation that among the aborigines of Australia, the rudest savages as to whom we possess accurate information, magic is universally practised, whereas religion in the sense of a propitiation or conciliation of the higher powers seems to be nearly unknown. Roughly speaking, all men in Australia are magicians, but not one is a priest; everybody fancies he can influence his fellows or the course of nature by sympathetic magic, but nobody dreams of propitiating gods by prayer and sacrifice.

But if in the most backward state of human society now known to us we find magic thus conspicuously present and religion conspicuously absent, may we not reasonably conjecture that the civilised races of the world have also at some period of their history passed through a similar intellectual phase, that they attempted to force the great powers of nature to do their pleasure before they thought of courting their favour by offerings and prayer—in short that, just as on the material side of human culture there has everywhere been an Age of Stone, so on the intellectual side there has everywhere been an Age of Magic? There are reasons for answering this question in the affirmative. When we survey the existing races of mankind from Greenland to Tierra del Fuego, or from Scotland to Singapore, we observe that they are distinguished one from the other by a great variety of religions, and that these distinctions are not, so to speak, merely coterminous with the broad distinctions of race, but descend into the minuter subdivisions of states and commonwealths, nay, that they honeycomb the town, the village, and even the family, so that the surface of society all over the world is cracked and seamed, sapped and mined with rents and fissures and yawning crevasses opened up by the disintegrating influence of religious dissension. Yet when we have penetrated through these differences, which affect mainly the intelligent and thoughtful part of the community, we shall find underlying them all a solid stratum of intellectual agreement among the dull, the weak, the ignorant, and the superstitious, who constitute, unfortunately, the vast majority of mankind. One of the great achievements of the nineteenth century was to run shafts down into this low mental stratum in many parts of the world, and thus to discover its substantial identity everywhere. It is beneath our feet—and not very far beneath them—here in Europe at the present day, and it crops up on the surface in the heart of the Australian wilderness and wherever the advent of a higher civilisation has not crushed it underground. This universal faith, this truly Catholic creed, is a belief in the efficacy of magic. While religious systems differ not only in different countries, but in the same country in different ages, the system of sympathetic magic remains everywhere and at all times substantially alike in its principles and practice. Among the ignorant and superstitious classes of modern Europe it is very much what it was thousands of years ago in Egypt and India, and what it now is among the lowest savages surviving in the remotest corners of the world. If the test of truth lay in a show of hands or a counting of heads, the system of magic might appeal, with far more reason than the Catholic Church, to the proud motto, " *Quod semper, quod ubique, quod ab omnibus*," as the sure and certain credential of its own infallibility.

It is not our business here to consider what bearing the permanent existence of such a solid layer of savagery beneath the surface of society, and unaffected by the superficial changes of religion and culture, has upon the future of humanity. The dispassionate observer, whose studies have led him to plumb its depths, can hardly regard it otherwise than as a standing menace to civilisation. We seem to move on a thin crust which may at any moment be rent by the subterranean forces slumbering below. From time to time a hollow murmur underground or a sudden spirt of flame into the air tells of what is going on beneath our feet. Now and then the polite world is startled by a paragraph in a newspaper which tells how in Scotland an image has been found stuck full of pins for the purpose of killing an obnoxious laird or minister, how a woman has been slowly roasted to death as a witch in Ireland, or how a girl has been murdered and chopped up in Russia to make those candles of human tallow by whose light thieves hope to pursue their midnight trade unseen. But whether the influences that make for further progress, or those that threaten to undo what has already been accomplished, will ultimately prevail ; whether the impulsive energy of the minority or the dead weight of the majority of mankind will prove the stronger force to carry us up to higher heights or to sink us into lower depths, are questions rather for the sage, the moralist, and the statesman, whose eagle vision scans the future, than for the humble student of the present and the past. Here we are only concerned to ask how far the uniformity, the universality, and the permanence of a belief in magic, compared with the endless variety and the shifting character of religious creeds, raises a presumption that the former represents a ruder and earlier phase of the human mind, through which all the races of mankind have passed or are passing on their way to religion and science.

If an Age of Religion has thus everywhere, as I venture to surmise, been preceded by an Age of Magic, it is natural that we should enquire what causes have led mankind, or rather a portion of them, to abandon magic as a principle of faith and practice and to betake themselves to religion instead. When we reflect upon the multitude, the variety, and the complexity of the facts to be explained, and the scantiness of our information regarding them, we shall be ready to acknowledge that a full and satisfactory solution of so profound a problem is hardly to be hoped for, and that the most we can do in the present state of our knowledge is to hazard a more or less plausible conjecture. With all due diffidence, then, I would suggest that a tardy recognition of the inherent falsehood and barrenness of magic set the more thoughtful part of mankind to cast about for a truer theory of nature and a more fruitful method of turning her resources to account. The shrewder intelligences must in time have come to perceive that magical ceremonies and incantations did not really effect the results which they were designed to produce, and which the majority of their simpler fellows still believed that they did actually produce. This great discovery of the inefficacy of magic must have wrought a radical though probably slow revolution in the minds of those who had the sagacity to make it. The discovery amounted to this, that men for the first time recognised their inability to manipulate at pleasure certain natural forces which hitherto they had believed to be completely within their control. It was a confession of human ignorance and weakness. Man saw that he had taken for causes what were no causes, and that all his efforts to work by means of these imaginary causes had been vain. His painful toil had been wasted, his curious ingenuity had been squandered to no purpose. He had been pulling at strings to which nothing was attached ; he had been marching, as he thought, straight to the goal, while in reality he had only been treading in a narrow circle. Not that the effects which he had striven so hard to produce did not continue to manifest themselves. They were still produced, but not by him. The rain still fell on the thirsty ground : the sun still pursued his daily, and the moon her nightly journey across the sky : the silent procession of the seasons still moved in light and shadow, in cloud and sunshine across the earth : men were still born to labour and sorrow, and still, after a brief sojourn here, were gathered to their fathers in the long home hereafter. All things indeed went on as before, yet all seemed different to him from whose eyes the old scales had fallen. For he could no longer cherish the pleasing illusion that it was he who guided the earth and the heaven in their courses, and that they would cease to perform their great revolutions were he to take his feeble hand from the wheel. In the death of his enemies and his friends he no longer saw a proof of the resistless potency of his own or of hostile enchantments ; he now knew that friends and foes alike had succumbed to a force stronger than any that he could wield, and in obedience to a destiny which he was powerless to control.

Thus cut adrift from his ancient moorings and left to toss on a troubled sea of doubt and uncertainty, his old happy confidence in himself and his powers rudely shaken, our primitive philosopher must have been sadly perplexed and agitated till he came to rest, as in a quiet haven after a tempestuous voyage, in a new system of faith and practice, which seemed to offer a solution of his harassing doubts and a substitute, however precarious, for that sovereignty over nature which he had reluctantly abdicated. If the great world went on its way without the help of him or his fellows, it must surely be because there were other beings, like himself, but far stronger, who, unseen themselves, directed its course and brought about all the varied series of events which he had hitherto believed to be dependent on his own magic. It was they, as he now believed, and not he himself, who made the stormy wind to blow, the lightning to flash, and the thunder to roll ; who had laid the foundations of the solid earth and set bounds to the restless sea that it might not pass ; who caused all the glorious lights of heaven to shine ; who gave the fowls of the air their meat and the wild beasts of the desert their prey ; who bade the fruitful land to bring forth in abundance, the high hills to be clothed with forests, the bubbling springs to rise under the rocks in the valleys, and green pastures to grow by still waters ; who breathed into man's nostrils and made him live, or turned him to destruction by famine and pestilence and war. To these mighty beings, whose handiwork he traced in all the gorgeous and varied pageantry of nature, man now addressed himself, humbly confessing his dependence on their invisible power, and beseeching them of their mercy to furnish him with all good things, to defend him from the perils and dangers by which our mortal life is compassed about on every hand, and finally to bring his immortal spirit, freed from the burden of the body, to some happier world, beyond the reach of pain and sorrow, where he might rest with them and with the spirits of good men in joy and felicity for ever.

In this, or some such way as this, the deeper minds may be conceived to have made the great transition from magic to religion. But even in them the change can hardly ever have been sudden ; probably it proceeded very slowly, and required long ages for its more or less perfect accomplishment. For the recognition of man's powerlessness to influence the course of nature on a grand scale must have been gradual ; he cannot have been shorn of the whole of his fancied dominion at a blow. Step by step he must have been driven back from his proud position ; foot by foot he must have yielded, with a sigh, the ground which he had once viewed as his own. Now it would be the wind, now the rain, now the sunshine, now the thunder, that he confessed himself unable to wield at will ; and as province after province of nature thus fell from his grasp, till what had once seemed a kingdom threatened to shrink into a prison, man must have been more and more profoundly impressed with a sense of his own helplessness and the might of the invisible beings by whom he believed himself to be surrounded. Thus religion, beginning as a slight and partial acknowledgment of powers superior to man, tends with the growth of knowledge to deepen into a confession of man's entire and absolute dependence on the divine ; his old free bearing is exchanged for an attitude of lowliest prostration before the mysterious powers of the unseen, and his highest virtue is to submit his will to theirs : *In la sua volontade è nostra pace.*   But this deepening sense of religion, this more perfect submission to the divine will in all things, affects only those higher intelligences who have breadth of view enough to comprehend the vastness of the universe and the littleness of man.   Small minds cannot grasp great ideas ; to their narrow comprehension, their purblind vision, nothing seems really great and important but themselves.   Such minds hardly rise into religion at all.   They are, indeed, drilled by their betters into an outward conformity with its precepts and a verbal profession of its tenets ; but at heart they cling to their old magical superstitions, which may be discountenanced and forbidden, but cannot be eradicated by religion, so long as they have their roots deep down in the mental framework and constitution of the great majority of mankind.

The reader may well be tempted to ask, How was it that intelligent men did not sooner detect the fallacy of magic ?   How could they continue to cherish expectations that were invariably doomed to disappointment ?   With what heart persist in playing venerable antics that led to nothing, and mumbling solemn balderdash that remained without effect ?   Why cling to beliefs which were so flatly contradicted by experience ?   How dare to repeat experiments that had failed so often ?   The answer seems to be that the fallacy was far from easy to detect, the failure by no means obvious, since in many, perhaps in most, cases the desired event did actually follow, at a longer or shorter interval, the performance of the rite which was designed to bring it about ; and a mind of more than common acuteness was needed to perceive that, even in these cases, the rite was not necessarily the cause of the event.   A ceremony intended to make the wind blow or the rain fall, or to work the death of an enemy, will always be followed, sooner or later, by the occurrence it is meant to bring to pass ; and primitive man may be excused for regarding the occurrence as a direct result of the ceremony, and the best possible proof of its efficacy.   Similarly, rites observed in the morning to help the sun to rise, and in spring to wake the dreaming earth from her winter sleep, will invariably appear to be crowned with success, at least within the temperate zones ; for in these regions the sun lights his golden lamp in the east every morning, and year by year the vernal earth decks herself afresh with a rich mantle of green.   Hence the practical savage, with his conservative instincts, might well turn a deaf ear to the subtleties of the theoretical doubter, the philosophic radical, who presumed to hint that sunrise and spring might not, after all, be direct consequences of the punctual performance of certain daily or yearly ceremonies, and that the sun might perhaps continue to rise and trees to blossom though the ceremonies were occasionally intermitted, or even discontinued altogether.   These sceptical doubts would naturally be repelled by the other with scorn and indignation as airy reveries subversive of the faith and manifestly contradicted by experience. " Can anything be plainer," he might say, " than that I light my twopenny candle on earth and that the sun then kindles his great fire in heaven ? I should be glad to know whether, when I have put on my green robe in spring, the trees do not afterwards do the same ? These are facts patent to everybody, and on them I take my stand. I am a plain practical man, not one of your theorists and splitters of hairs and choppers of logic. Theories and speculation and all that may be very well in their way, and I have not the least objection to your indulging in them, provided, of course, you do not put them in practice. But give me leave to stick to facts ; then I know where I am." The fallacy of this reasoning is obvious to us, because it happens to deal with facts about which we have long made up our minds. But let an argument of precisely the same calibre be applied to matters which are still under debate, and it may be questioned whether a British audience would not applaud it as sound, and esteem the speaker who used it a safe man—not brilliant or showy, perhaps, but thoroughly sensible and hard-headed. If such reasonings could pass muster among ourselves, need we wonder that they long escaped detection by the savage ?

CHAPTER V

THE MAGICAL CONTROL OF THE WEATHER

§ 1. *The Public Magician.*—The reader may remember that we were led to plunge into the labyrinth of magic by a consideration of two different types of man-god. This is the clue which has guided our devious steps through the maze, and brought us out at last on higher ground, whence, resting a little by the way, we can look back over the path we have already traversed and forward to the longer and steeper road we have still to climb.

As a result of the foregoing discussion, the two types of human gods may conveniently be distinguished as the religious and the magical man-god respectively. In the former, a being of an order different from and superior to man is supposed to become incarnate, for a longer or a shorter time, in a human body, manifesting his super-human power and knowledge by miracles wrought and prophecies uttered through the medium of the fleshly tabernacle in which he has deigned to take up his abode. This may also appropriately be called the inspired or incarnate type of man-god. In it the human body is merely a frail earthly vessel filled with a divine and immortal spirit. On the other hand, a man-god of the magical sort is nothing but a man who possesses in an unusually high degree powers which most of his fellows arrogate to themselves on a smaller scale ; for in rude society there is hardly a person who does not dabble in magic. Thus, whereas a man-god of the former or inspired type derives his divinity from a deity who has stooped to hide his heavenly radiance behind a dull mask of earthly mould, a man-god of the latter type draws his extraordinary power from a certain physical sympathy with nature. He is not merely the receptacle of a divine spirit.   His whole being, body and soul, is so delicately attuned to the harmony of the world that a touch of his hand or a turn of his head may send a thrill vibrating through the universal framework of things ; and conversely his divine organism is acutely sensitive to such slight changes of environment as would leave ordinary mortals wholly unaffected.   But the line between these two types of man-god, however sharply we may draw it in theory, is seldom to be traced with precision in practice, and in what follows I shall not insist on it.

We have seen that in practice the magic art may be employed for the benefit either of individuals or of the whole community, and that according as it is directed to one or other of these two objects it may be called private or public magic.   Further, I pointed out that the public magician occupies a position of great influence, from which, if he is a prudent and able man, he may advance step by step to the rank of a chief or king.   Thus an examination of public magic conduces to an understanding of the early kingship, since in savage and barbarous society many chiefs and kings appear to owe their authority in great measure to their reputation as magicians.

Among the objects of public utility which magic may be employed to secure, the most essential is an adequate supply of food.   The examples cited in preceding pages prove that the purveyors of food— the hunter, the fisher, the farmer—all resort to magical practices in the pursuit of their various callings ; but they do so as private individuals for the benefit of themselves and their families, rather than as public functionaries acting in the interest of the whole people.   It is otherwise when the rites are performed, not by the hunters, the fishers, the farmers themselves, but by professional magicians on their behalf.   In primitive society, where uniformity of occupation is the rule, and the distribution of the community into various classes of workers has hardly begun, every man is more or less his own magician ; he practises charms and incantations for his own good and the injury of his enemies.   But a great step in advance has been taken when a special class of magicians has been instituted ; when, in other words, a number of men have been set apart for the express purpose of benefiting the whole community by their skill, whether that skill be directed to the healing of diseases, the forecasting of the future, the regulation of the weather, or any other object of general utility.   The impotence of the means adopted by most of these practitioners to accomplish their ends ought not to blind us to the immense importance of the institution itself.   Here is a body of men relieved, at least in the higher stages of savagery, from the need of earning their livelihood by hard manual toil, and allowed, nay, expected and encouraged, to prosecute researches into the secret ways of nature.   It was at once their duty and their interest to know more than their fellows, to acquaint themselves with everything that could aid man in his arduous struggle with nature, everything that could mitigate his sufferings and prolong his life. The properties of drugs and minerals, the causes of rain and drought, of thunder and lightning, the changes of the seasons, the phases of the moon, the daily and yearly journeys of the sun, the motions of the stars, the mystery of life, and the mystery of death, all these things must have excited the wonder of these early philosophers, and stimulated them to find solutions of problems that were doubtless often thrust on their attention in the most practical form by the importunate demands of their clients, who expected them not merely to understand but to regulate the great processes of nature for the good of man. That their first shots fell very far wide of the mark could hardly be helped. The slow, the never-ending approach to truth consists in perpetually forming and testing hypotheses, accepting those which at the time seem to fit the facts and rejecting the others. The views of natural causation embraced by the savage magician no doubt appear to us manifestly false and absurd ; yet in their day they were legitimate hypotheses, though they have not stood the test of experience. Ridicule and blame are the just meed, not of those who devised these crude theories, but of those who obstinately adhered to them after better had been propounded. Certainly no men ever had stronger incentives in the pursuit of truth than these savage sorcerers. To maintain at least a show of knowledge was absolutely necessary ; a single mistake detected might cost them their life. This no doubt led them to practise imposture for the purpose of concealing their ignorance ; but it also supplied them with the most powerful motive for substituting a real for a sham knowledge, since, if you would appear to know anything, by far the best way is actually to know it. Thus, however justly we may reject the extravagant pretensions of magicians and condemn the deceptions which they have practised on mankind, the original institution of this class of men has, take it all in all, been productive of incalculable good to humanity. They were the direct predecessors, not merely of our physicians and surgeons, but of our investigators and discoverers in every branch of natural science. They began the work which has since been carried to such glorious and beneficent issues by their successors in after ages ; and if the beginning was poor and feeble, this is to be imputed to the inevitable difficulties which beset the path of knowledge rather than to the natural incapacity or wilful fraud of the men themselves.

§ 2. *The Magical Control of Rain.*—Of the things which the public magician sets himself to do for the good of the tribe, one of the chief is to control the weather and especially to ensure an adequate fall of rain. Water is an essential of life, and in most countries the supply of it depends upon showers. Without rain vegetation withers, animals and men languish and die. Hence in savage communities the rain-maker is a very important personage ; and often a special class of magicians exists for the purpose of regulating the heavenly water-supply. The methods by which they attempt to discharge the duties of their office are commonly, though not always, based on the principle of homoeopathic or imitative magic. If they wish to make rain they simulate it by sprinkling water or mimicking clouds : if their object is to stop rain and cause drought, they avoid water and resort to warmth and fire for the sake of drying up the too abundant moisture. Such attempts are by no means confined, as the cultivated reader might imagine, to the naked inhabitants of those sultry lands like Central Australia and some parts of Eastern and Southern Africa, where often for months together the pitiless sun beats down out of a blue and cloudless sky on the parched and gaping earth. They are, or used to be, common enough among outwardly civilised folk in the moister climate of Europe. I will now illustrate them by instances drawn from the practice both of public and private magic.

Thus, for example, in a village near Dorpat, in Russia, when rain was much wanted, three men used to climb up the fir-trees of an old sacred grove. One of them drummed with a hammer on a kettle or small cask to imitate thunder ; the second knocked two fire-brands together and made the sparks fly, to imitate lightning ; and the third, who was called " the rain-maker," had a bunch of twigs with which he sprinkled water from a vessel on all sides. To put an end to drought and bring down rain, women and girls of the village of Ploska are wont to go naked by night to the boundaries of the village and there pour water on the ground. In Halmahera, or Gilolo, a large island to the west of New Guinea, a wizard makes rain by dipping a branch of a particular kind of tree in water and then scattering the moisture from the dripping bough over the ground. In New Britain the rain-maker wraps some leaves of a red and green striped creeper in a banana-leaf, moistens the bundle with water, and buries it in the ground ; then he imitates with his mouth the plashing of rain. Amongst the Omaha Indians of North America, when the corn is withering for want of rain, the members of the sacred Buffalo Society fill a large vessel with water and dance four times round it. One of them drinks some of the water and spirts it into the air, making a fine spray in imitation of a mist or drizzling rain. Then he upsets the vessel, spilling the water on the ground ; whereupon the dancers fall down and drink up the water, getting mud all over their faces. Lastly, they squirt the water into the air, making a fine mist. This saves the corn. In spring-time the Natchez of North America used to club together to purchase favourable weather for their crops from the wizards. If rain was needed, the wizards fasted and danced with pipes full of water in their mouths. The pipes were perforated like the nozzle of a watering-can, and through the holes the rain-maker blew the water towards that part of the sky where the clouds hung heaviest. But if fine weather was wanted, he mounted the roof of his hut, and with extended arms, blowing with all his might, he beckoned to the clouds to pass by. When the rains do not come in due season the people of Central Angoniland repair to what is called the rain-temple.   Here they clear away the grass, and the leader pours beer into a pot which is buried in the ground, while he says, "Master *Chauta*, you have hardened your heart towards us, what would you have us do?   We must perish indeed.   Give your children the rains, there is the beer we have given you."   Then they all partake of the beer that is left over, even the children being made to sip it.   Next they take branches of trees and dance and sing for rain. When they return to the village they find a vessel of water set at the doorway by an old woman ; so they dip their branches in it and wave them aloft, so as to scatter the drops.   After that the rain is sure to come driving up in heavy clouds.   In these practices we see a combination of religion with magic ; for while the scattering of the water-drops by means of branches is a purely magical ceremony, the prayer for rain and the offering of beer are purely religious rites.   In the Mara tribe of Northern Australia the rain-maker goes to a pool and sings over it his magic song.   Then he takes some of the water in his hands, drinks it, and spits it out in various directions.   After that he throws water all over himself, scatters it about, and returns quietly to the camp.   Rain is supposed to follow.   The Arab historian Makrizi describes a method of stopping rain which is said to have been resorted to by a tribe of nomads called Alqamar in Hadramaut.   They cut a branch from a certain tree in the desert, set it on fire, and then sprinkled the burning brand with water.   After that the vehemence of the rain abated, just as the water vanished when it fell on the glowing brand. Some of the Eastern Angamis of Manipur are said to perform a somewhat similar ceremony for the opposite purpose, in order, namely, to produce rain.   The head of the village puts a burning brand on the grave of a man who has died of burns, and quenches the brand with water, while he prays that rain may fall.   Here the putting out the fire with water, which is an imitation of rain, is reinforced by the influence of the dead man, who, having been burnt to death, will naturally be anxious for the descent of rain to cool his scorched body and assuage his pangs.

Other people besides the Arabs have used fire as a means of stopping rain.   Thus the Sulka of New Britain heat stones red hot in the fire and then put them out in the rain, or they throw hot ashes in the air. They think that the rain will soon cease to fall, for it does not like to be burned by the hot stones or ashes.   The Telugus send a little girl out naked into the rain with a burning piece of wood in her hand, which she has to show to the rain.   That is supposed to stop the downpour.   At Port Stephens in New South Wales the medicine-men used to drive away rain by throwing fire-sticks into the air, while at the same time they puffed and shouted.   Any man of the Anula tribe in Northern Australia can stop rain by simply warming a green stick in the fire, and then striking it against the wind.

In time of severe drought the Dieri of Central Australia, loudly lamenting the impoverished state of the country and their own half-starved condition, call upon the spirits of their remote predecessors,

whom they call Mura-muras, to grant them power to make a heavy rainfall.   For they believe that the clouds are bodies in which rain is generated
by their own ceremonies or those of neighbouring tribes, through the
influence of the Mura-muras.   The way in which they set about drawing
rain from the clouds is this.   A hole is dug about twelve feet long and
eight or ten broad, and over this hole a conical hut of logs and branches
is made.   Two wizards, supposed to have received a special inspiration
from the Mura-muras, are bled by an old and influential man with a
sharp flint ;   and the blood, drawn from their arms below the elbow,
is made to flow on the other men of the tribe, who sit huddled together
in the hut.   At the same time the two bleeding men throw handfuls
of down about, some of which adheres to the blood-stained bodies of
their comrades, while the rest floats in the air.   The blood is thought
to represent the rain, and the down the clouds.   During the ceremony
two large stones are placed in the middle of the hut ;   they stand for
gathering clouds and presage rain.   Then the wizards who were bled
carry away the two stones for about ten or fifteen miles, and place
them as high as they can in the tallest tree.   Meanwhile the other
men gather gypsum, pound it fine, and throw it into a water-hole.
This the Mura-muras see, and at once they cause clouds to appear in
the sky.   Lastly, the men, young and old, surround the hut, and,
stooping down, butt at it with their heads, like so many rams.   Thus
they force their way through it and reappear on the other side, repeating the process till the hut is wrecked.   In doing this they are
forbidden to use their hands or arms ;   but when the heavy logs alone
remain, they are allowed to pull them out with their hands.   " The
piercing of the hut with their heads symbolises the piercing of the
clouds ;   the fall of the hut, the fall of the rain."   Obviously, too, the
act of placing high up in trees the two stones, which stand for clouds,
is a way of making the real clouds to mount up in the sky.   The Dieri
also imagine that the foreskins taken from lads at circumcision have
a great power of producing rain.   Hence the Great Council of the tribe
always keeps a small stock of foreskins ready for use.   They are carefully concealed, being wrapt up in feathers with the fat of the wild
dog and of the carpet snake.   A woman may not see such a parcel
opened on any account.   When the ceremony is over, the foreskin is
buried, its virtue being exhausted.   After the rains have fallen, some
of the tribe always undergo a surgical operation, which consists in
cutting the skin of their chest and arms with a sharp flint.   The wound
is then tapped with a flat stick to increase the flow of blood, and red
ochre is rubbed into it.   Raised scars are thus produced.   The reason
alleged by the natives for this practice is that they are pleased with the
rain, and that there is a connexion between the rain and the scars.
Apparently the operation is not very painful, for the patient laughs
and jokes while it is going on.   Indeed, little children have been seen
to crowd round the operator and patiently take their turn ;   then after
being operated on, they ran away, expanding their little chests and
singing for the rain to beat upon them.   However, they were not so

F

well pleased next day, when they felt their wounds stiff and sore.   In Java, when rain is wanted, two men will sometimes thrash each other with supple rods till the blood flows down their backs ; the streaming blood represents the rain, and no doubt is supposed to make it fall on the ground.   The people of Egghiou, a district of Abyssinia, used to engage in sanguinary conflicts with each other, village against village, for a week together every January for the purpose of procuring rain. Some years ago the emperor Menelik forbade the custom.   However, the following year the rain was deficient, and the popular outcry so great that the emperor yielded to it, and allowed the murderous fights to be resumed, but for two days a year only.   The writer who mentions the custom regards the blood shed on these occasions as a propitiatory sacrifice offered to spirits who control the showers ; but perhaps, as in the Australian and Javanese ceremonies, it is an imitation of rain. The prophets of Baal, who sought to procure rain by cutting themselves with knives till the blood gushed out, may have acted on the same principle.

There is a widespread belief that twin children possess magical powers over nature, especially over rain and the weather.   This curious superstition prevails among some of the Indian tribes of British Columbia, and has led them often to impose certain singular restrictions or taboos on the parents of twins, though the exact meaning of these restrictions is generally obscure.   Thus the Tsimshian Indians of British Columbia believe that twins control the weather ; therefore they pray to wind and rain, " Calm down, breath of the twins." Further, they think that the wishes of twins are always fulfilled ; hence twins are feared, because they can harm the man they hate. They can also call the salmon and the olachen or candle-fish, and so they are known by a name which means " making plentiful."   In the opinion of the Kwakiutl Indians of British Columbia twins are trans- formed salmon ; hence they may not go near water, lest they should be changed back again into the fish.   In their childhood they can summon any wind by motions of their hands, and they can make fair or foul weather, and also cure diseases by swinging a large wooden rattle.   The Nootka Indians of British Columbia also believe that twins are somehow related to salmon.   Hence among them twins may not catch salmon, and they may not eat or even handle the fresh fish. They can make fair or foul weather, and can cause rain to fall by painting their faces black and then washing them, which may represent the rain dripping from the dark clouds.   The Shuswap Indians, like the Thompson Indians, associate twins with the grizzly bear, for they call them " young grizzly bears."   According to them, twins remain throughout life endowed with supernatural powers.   In particular they can make good or bad weather.   They produce rain by spilling water from a basket in the air ; they make fine weather by shaking a small flat piece of wood attached to a stick by a string ; they raise storms by strewing down on the ends of spruce branches.

The same power of influencing the weather is attributed to twins by the Baronga, a tribe of Bantu negroes who inhabit the shores of Delagoa Bay in South-eastern Africa. They bestow the name of *Tilo*— that is, the sky—on a woman who has given birth to twins, and the infants themselves are called the children of the sky. Now when the storms which generally burst in the months of September and October have been looked for in vain, when a drought with its prospect of famine is threatening, and all nature, scorched and burnt up by a sun that has shone for six months from a cloudless sky, is panting for the beneficent showers of the South African spring, the women perform ceremonies to bring down the longed-for rain on the parched earth. Stripping themselves of all their garments, they assume in their stead girdles and head-dresses of grass, or short petticoats made of the leaves of a particular sort of creeper. Thus attired, uttering peculiar cries and singing ribald songs, they go about from well to well, cleansing them of the mud and impurities which have accumulated in them. The wells, it may be said, are merely holes in the sand where a little turbid unwholesome water stagnates. Further, the women must repair to the house of one of their gossips who has given birth to twins, and must drench her with water, which they carry in little pitchers. Having done so they go on their way, shrieking out their loose songs and dancing immodest dances. No man may see these leaf-clad women going their rounds. If they meet a man, they maul him and tnrust him aside. When they have cleansed the wells, they must go and pour water on the graves of their ancestors in the sacred grove. It often happens, too, that at the bidding of the wizard they go and pour water on the graves of twins. For they think that the grave of a twin ought always to be moist, for which reason twins are regularly buried near a lake. If all their efforts to procure rain prove abortive, they will remember that such and such a twin was buried in a dry place on the side of a hill. " No wonder," says the wizard in such a case, " that the sky is fiery. Take up his body and dig him a grave on the shore of the lake." His orders are at once obeyed, for this is supposed to be the only means of bringing down the rain.

Some of the foregoing facts strongly support an interpretation which Professor Oldenberg has given of the rules to be observed by a Brahman who would learn a particular hymn of the ancient Indian collection known as the Samaveda. The hymn, which bears the name of the Ṣakvarī song, was believed to embody the might of Indra's weapon, the thunderbolt ; and hence, on account of the dreadful and dangerous potency with which it was thus charged, the bold student who essayed to master it had to be isolated from his fellow-men, and to retire from the village into the forest. Here for a space of time, which might vary, according to different doctors of the law, from one to twelve years, he had to observe certain rules of life, among which were the following. Thrice a day he had to touch water ; he must wear black garments and eat black food ; when it rained, he might not seek the shelter of a roof, but had to sit in the rain and say, " Water is the Sakvarī song " ; when the lightning flashed, he said, " That is

like the Sakvarī song "; when the thunder pealed, he said, " The Great
One is making a great noise." He might never cross a running stream
without touching water ; he might never set foot on a ship unless his
life were in danger, and even then he must be sure to touch water when
he went on board ; " for in water," so ran the saying, " lies the virtue
of the Ṣakvarī song.' When at last he was allowed to learn the song
itself, he had to dip his hands in a vessel of water in which plants of all
sorts had been placed. If a man walked in the way of all these precepts,
the rain-god Parjanya, it was said, would send rain at the wish of that
man. It is clear, as Professor Oldenberg well points out, that " all
these rules are intended to bring the Brahman into union with water,
to make him, as it were, an ally of the water powers, and to guard him
against their hostility. The black garments and the black food have
the same significance ; no one will doubt that they refer to the rain-
clouds when he remembers that a black victim is sacrificed to procure
rain ; ' it is black, for such is the nature of rain.' In respect of another
rain-charm it is said plainly, ' He puts on a black garment edged with
black, for such is the nature of rain.' We may therefore assume that
here in the circle of ideas and ordinances of the Vedic schools there have
been preserved magical practices of the most remote antiquity, which
were intended to prepare the rain-maker for his office and dedicate
him to it."

It is interesting to observe that where an opposite result is desired,
primitive logic enjoins the weather-doctor to observe precisely opposite
rules of conduct. In the tropical island of Java, where the rich vegetation attests the abundance of the rainfall, ceremonies for the making
of rain are rare, but ceremonies for the prevention of it are not uncommon. When a man is about to give a great feast in the rainy
season and has invited many people, he goes to a weather-doctor and
asks him to " prop up the clouds that may be lowering." If the doctor
consents to exert his professional powers, he begins to regulate his
behaviour by certain rules as soon as his customer has departed. He
must observe a fast, and may neither drink nor bathe ; what little he
eats must be eaten dry, and in no case may he touch water. The host,
on his side, and his servants, both male and female, must neither wash
clothes nor bathe so long as the feast lasts, and they have all during its
continuance to observe strict chastity. The doctor seats himself on a
new mat in his bedroom, and before a small oil-lamp he murmurs,
shortly before the feast takes place, the following prayer or incantation :
" Grandfather and Grandmother Sroekoel " (the name seems to be taken
at random ; others are sometimes used), " return to your country.
Akkemat is your country. Put down your water-cask, close it properly,
that not a drop may fall out." While he utters this prayer the sorcerer
looks upwards, burning incense the while. So among the Toradjas the
rain-doctor, whose special business it is to drive away rain, takes care
not to touch water before, during, or after the discharge of his professional duties. He does not bathe, he eats with unwashed hands,
he drinks nothing but palm wine, and if he has to cross a stream he is

careful not to step in the water.   Having thus prepared himself for his task he has a small hut built for himself outside of the village in a rice-field, and in this hut he keeps up a little fire, which on no account may be suffered to go out.   In the fire he burns various kinds of wood, which are supposed to possess the property of driving off rain ; and he puffs in the direction from which the rain threatens to come, holding in his hand a packet of leaves and bark which derive a similar cloud-compelling virtue, not from their chemical composition, but from their names, which happen to signify something dry or volatile.   If clouds should appear in the sky while he is at work, he takes lime in the hollow of his hand and blows it towards them.   The lime, being so very dry, is obviously well adapted to disperse the damp clouds.   Should rain afterwards be wanted, he has only to pour water on his fire, and immediately the rain will descend in sheets.

The reader will observe how exactly the Javanese and Toradja observances, which are intended to prevent rain, form the antithesis of the Indian observances, which aim at producing it.   The Indian sage is commanded to touch water thrice a day regularly as well as on various special occasions ; the Javanese and Toradja wizards may not touch it at all.   The Indian lives out in the forest, and even when it rains he may not take shelter ; the Javanese and the Toradja sit in a house or a hut.   The one signifies his sympathy with water by receiving the rain on his person and speaking of it respectfully ; the others light a lamp or a fire and do their best to drive the rain away.   Yet the principle on which all three act is the same ; each of them, by a sort of childish make-believe, identifies himself with the phenomenon which he desires to produce.   It is the old fallacy that the effect resembles its cause : if you would make wet weather, you must be wet ; if you would make dry weather, you must be dry.

In South-eastern Europe at the present day ceremonies are observed for the purpose of making rain which not only rest on the same general train of thought as the preceding, but even in their details resemble the ceremonies practised with the same intention by the Baronga of Delagoa Bay.   Among the Greeks of Thessaly and Macedonia, when a drought has lasted a long time, it is customary to send a procession of children round to all the wells and springs of the neighbourhood.   At the head of the procession walks a girl adorned with flowers, whom her companions drench with water at every halting-place, while they sing an invocation, of which the following is part :

" *Perperia, all fresh bedewed,*   *Send thou us a still, small rain ;*
Freshen all the neighbourhood ;   *That the fields may fruitful be,*
By the woods, on the highway,   *And vines in blossom we may see ;*
As thou goest, to God now pray :   *That the grain be full and sound,*
O my God, upon the plain,   *And wealthy grow the folks around."*

In time of drought the Serbians strip a girl to her skin and clothe her from head to foot in grass, herbs, and flowers, even her face being hidden behind a veil of living green.   Thus disguised she is called the Dodola, and goes through the village with a troop of girls. They stop before every house ; the Dodola keeps turning herself round and dancing, while the other girls form a ring about her singing one of the Dodola songs, and the housewife pours a pail of water over her. One of the songs they sing runs thus :

"We go through the village ; *Faster go the clouds ;*
The clouds go in the sky ; *They have overtaken us,*
We go faster, *And wetted the corn and the vine."*

At Poona in India, when rain is needed, the boys dress up one of their number in nothing but leaves and call him King of Rain. Then they go round to every house in the village, where the householder or his wife sprinkles the Rain King with water, and gives the party food of various kinds. When they have thus visited all the houses, they strip the Rain King of his leafy robes and feast upon what they have gathered.

Bathing is practised as a rain-charm in some parts of Southern and Western Russia. Sometimes after service in church the priest in his robes has been thrown down on the ground and drenched with water by his parishioners. Sometimes it is the women who, without stripping off their clothes, bathe in crowds on the day of St. John the Baptist, while they dip in the water a figure made of branches, grass, and herbs, which is supposed to represent the saint. In Kursk, a province of Southern Russia, when rain is much wanted, the women seize a passing stranger and throw him into the river, or souse him from head to foot. Later on we shall see that a passing stranger is often taken for a deity or the personification of some natural power. It is recorded in official documents that during a drought in 1790 the peasants of Scheroutz and Werboutz collected all the women and compelled them to bathe, in order that rain might fall. An Armenian rain-charm is to throw the wife of a priest into the water and drench her. The Arabs of North Africa fling a holy man, willy-nilly, into a spring as a remedy for drought. In Minahassa, a province of North Celebes, the priest bathes as a rain-charm. In Central Celebes when there has been no rain for a long time and the rice-stalks begin to shrivel up, many of the villagers, especially the young folk, go to a neighbouring brook and splash each other with water, shouting noisily, or squirt water on one another through bamboo tubes. Sometimes they imitate the plump of rain by smacking the surface of the water with their hands, or by placing an inverted gourd on it and drumming on the gourd with their fingers.

Women are sometimes supposed to be able to make rain by ploughing, or pretending to plough. Thus the Pshaws and Chewsurs of the Caucasus have a ceremony called " ploughing the rain," which they observe in time of drought. Girls yoke themselves to a plough and drag it into a river, wading in the water up to their girdles. In the same circumstances Armenian girls and women do the same. The oldest woman, or the priest's wife, wears the priest's dress, while the others, dressed as men, drag the plough through the water against the stream.

In the Caucasian province of Georgia, when a drought has lasted long, marriageable girls are yoked in couples with an ox-yoke on their shoulders, a priest holds the reins, and thus harnessed they wade through rivers, puddles, and marshes, praying, screaming, weeping, and laughing. In a district of Transylvania, when the ground is parched with drought, some girls strip themselves naked, and, led by an older woman, who is also naked, they steal a harrow and carry it across the fields to a brook, where they set it afloat. Next they sit on the harrow and keep a tiny flame burning on each corner of it for an hour. Then they leave the harrow in the water and go home. A similar rain-charm is resorted to in some parts of India ; naked women drag a plough across a field by night, while the men keep carefully out of the way, for their presence would break the spell.

Sometimes the rain-charm operates through the dead. Thus in New Caledonia the rain-makers blackened themselves all over, dug up a dead body, took the bones to a cave, jointed them, and hung the skeleton over some taro leaves. Water was poured over the skeleton to run down on the leaves. They believed that the soul of the deceased took up the water, converted it into rain, and showered it down again. In Russia, if common report may be believed, it is not long since the peasants of any district that chanced to be afflicted with drought used to dig up the corpse of some one who had drunk himself to death and sink it in the nearest swamp or lake, fully persuaded that this would ensure the fall of the needed rain. In 1868 the prospect of a bad harvest, caused by a prolonged drought, induced the inhabitants of a village in the Tarashchansk district to dig up the body of a Raskolnik, or Dissenter, who had died in the preceding December. Some of the party beat the corpse, or what was left of it, about the head, exclaiming, " Give us rain ! " while others poured water on it through a sieve. Here the pouring of water through a sieve seems plainly an imitation of a shower, and reminds us of the manner in which Strepsiades in Aristophanes imagined that rain was made by Zeus. Sometimes, in order to procure rain, the Toradjas make an appeal to the pity of the dead. Thus, in the village of Kalingooa there is the grave of a famous chief, the grandfather of the present ruler. When the land suffers from unseasonable drought, the people go to this grave, pour water on it, and say, " O grandfather, have pity on us ; if it is your will that this year we should eat, then give rain." After that they hang a bamboo full of water over the grave ; there is a small hole in the lower end of the bamboo, so that the water drips from it continually. The bamboo is always refilled with water until rain drenches the ground. Here, as in New Caledonia, we find religion blent with magic, for the prayer to the dead chief, which is purely religious, is eked out with a magical imitation of rain at his grave. We have seen that the Baronga of Delagoa Bay drench the tombs of their ancestors, especially the tombs of twins, as a rain-charm. Among some of the Indian tribes in the region of the Orinoco it was customary for the relations of a deceased person to disinter his bones a year after burial, burn them, and scatter the ashes to the winds, because they believed that the ashes were changed into rain, which the dead man sent in return for his obsequies. The Chinese are convinced that when human bodies remain unburied, the souls of their late owners feel the discomfort of rain, just as living men would do if they were exposed without shelter to the inclemency of the weather. These wretched souls, therefore, do all in their power to prevent the rain from falling, and often their efforts are only too successful. Then drought ensues, the most dreaded of all calamities in China, because bad harvests, dearth, and famine follow in its train. Hence it has been a common practice of the Chinese authorities in time of drought to inter the dry bones of the unburied dead for the purpose of putting an end to the scourge and conjuring down the rain.

Animals, again, often play an important part in these weather-charms. The Anula tribe of Northern Australia associate the dollar-bird with rain, and call it the rain-bird. A man who has the bird for his totem can make rain at a certain pool. He catches a snake, puts it alive into the pool, and after holding it under water for a time takes it out, kills it, and lays it down by the side of the creek. Then he makes an arched bundle of grass stalks in imitation of a rainbow, and sets it up over the snake. After that all he does is to sing over the snake and the mimic rainbow ; sooner or later the rain will fall. They explain this procedure by saying that long ago the dollar-bird had as a mate at this spot a snake, who lived in the pool and used to make rain by spitting up into the sky till a rainbow and clouds appeared and rain fell. A common way of making rain in many parts of Java is to bathe a cat or two cats, a male and a female ; sometimes the animals are carried in procession with music. Even in Batavia you may from time to time see children going about with a cat for this purpose ; when they have ducked it in a pool, they let it go.

Among the Wambugwe of East Africa, when the sorcerer desires to make rain, he takes a black sheep and a black calf in bright sunshine, and has them placed on the roof of the common hut in which the people live together. Then he slits the stomachs of the animals and scatters their contents in all directions. After that he pours water and medicine into a vessel ; if the charm has succeeded, the water boils up and rain follows. On the other hand, if the sorcerer wishes to prevent rain from falling, he withdraws into the interior of the hut, and there heats a rock-crystal in a calabash. In order to procure rain the Wagogo sacrifice black fowls, black sheep, and black cattle at the graves of dead ancestors, and the rain-maker wears black clothes during the rainy season. Among the Matabele the rain-charm employed by sorcerers was made from the blood and gall of a black ox. In a district of Sumatra, in order to procure rain, all the women of the village, scantily clad, go to the river, wade into it, and splash each other with the water. A black cat is thrown into the stream and made to swim about for a while, then allowed to escape to the bank, pursued by the splashing of the women. The Garos of Assam offer a black goat on the top of a very high mountain in time of drought. In all these cases the colour of the animal is part of the charm ; being black, it will darken the sky with rain-clouds. So the Bechuanas burn the stomach of an ox at evening, because they say, " The black smoke will gather the clouds and cause the rain to come." The Timorese sacrifice a black pig to the Earth-goddess for rain, a white or red one to the Sun-god for sunshine. The Angoni sacrifice a black ox for rain and a white one for fine weather. Among the high mountains of Japan there is a district in which, if rain has not fallen for a long time, a party of villagers goes in procession to the bed of a mountain torrent, headed by a priest, who leads a black dog. At the chosen spot they tether the beast to a stone, and make it a target for their bullets and arrows. When its life-blood bespatters the rocks, the peasants throw down their weapons and lift up their voices in supplication to the dragon divinity of the stream, exhorting him to send down forthwith a shower to cleanse the spot from its defilement. Custom has prescribed that on these occasions the colour of the victim shall be black, as an emblem of the wished-for rain-clouds. But if fine weather is wanted, the victim must be white, without a spot.

The intimate association of frogs and toads with water has earned for these creatures a widespread reputation as custodians of rain ; and hence they often play a part in charms designed to draw needed showers from the sky. Some of the Indians of the Orinoco held the toad to be the god or lord of the waters, and for that reason feared to kill the creature. They have been known to keep frogs under a pot and to beat them with rods when there was a drought. It is said that the Aymara Indians often make little images of frogs and other aquatic animals and place them on the tops of the hills as a means of bringing down rain. The Thompson Indians of British Columbia and some people in Europe think that to kill a frog will cause rain to fall. In order to procure rain people of low caste in the Central Provinces of India will tie a frog to a rod covered with green leaves and branches of the *nîm* tree (*Azadirachta Indica*) and carry it from door to door singing :

> " *Send soon, O frog, the jewel of water !*
> *And ripen the wheat and millet in the field.*"

The Kapus or Reddis are a large caste of cultivators and landowners in the Madras Presidency. When rain fails, women of the caste will catch a frog and tie it alive to a new winnowing fan made of bamboo. On this fan they spread a few margosa leaves and go from door to door singing, " Lady frog must have her bath. O rain-god, give a little water for her at least." While the Kapu women sing this song, the woman of the house pours water over the frog and gives an alms, convinced that by so doing she will soon bring rain down in torrents.

Sometimes, when a drought has lasted a long time, people drop the usual hocus-pocus of imitative magic altogether, and being far too angry to waste their breath in prayer they seek by threats and curses or even downright physical force to extort the waters of heaven from the supernatural being who has, so to say, cut them off at the main. In a Japanese village, when the guardian divinity had long been deaf to the peasants' prayers for rain, they at last threw down his image and, with curses loud and long, hurled it head foremost into a stinking rice-field. "There," they said, " you may stay yourself for a while, to see how *you* will feel after a few days' scorching in this broiling sun that is burning the life from our cracking fields." In the like circumstances the Feloupes of Senegambia cast down their fetishes and drag them about the fields, cursing them till rain falls.

The Chinese are adepts in the art of taking the kingdom of heaven by storm. Thus, when rain is wanted they make a huge dragon of paper or wood to represent the rain-god, and carry it about in procession ; but if no rain follows, the mock-dragon is execrated and torn to pieces. At other times they threaten and beat the god if he does not give rain ; sometimes they publicly depose him from the rank of deity. On the other hand, if the wished-for rain falls, the god is promoted to a higher rank by an imperial decree. In April 1888 the mandarins of Canton prayed to the god Lung-wong to stop the incessant downpour of rain ; and when he turned a deaf ear to their petitions they put him in a lock-up for five days. This had a salutary effect. The rain ceased and the god was restored to liberty. Some years before, in time of drought, the same deity had been chained and exposed to the sun for days in the courtyard of his temple in order that he might feel for himself the urgent need of rain. So when the Siamese need rain, they set out their idols in the blazing sun ; but if they want dry weather, they unroof the temples and let the rain pour down on the idols. They think that the inconvenience to which the gods are thus subjected will induce them to grant the wishes of their worshippers.

The reader may smile at the meteorology of the Far East ; but precisely similar modes of procuring rain have been resorted to in Christian Europe within our own lifetime. By the end of April 1893 there was great distress in Sicily for lack of water. The drought had lasted six months. Every day the sun rose and set in a sky of cloudless blue. The gardens of the Conca d' Oro, which surround Palermo with a magnificent belt of verdure, were withering. Food was becoming scarce. The people were in great alarm. All the most approved methods of procuring rain had been tried without effect. Processions had traversed the streets and the fields. Men, women, and children, telling their beads, had lain whole nights before the holy images. Consecrated candles had burned day and night in the churches. Palm branches, blessed on Palm Sunday, had been hung on the trees. At Solaparuta, in accordance with a very old custom, the dust swept from the churches on Palm Sunday had been spread on the fields. In ordinary years these holy sweepings preserve the crops ; but that year, if you will believe me, they had no effect whatever. At Nicosia the inhabitants, bare-headed and bare-foot, carried the crucifixes through all the wards of the town and scourged each other with iron whips. It was all in vain. Even the great St. Francis of Paolo himself, who annually performs the miracle of rain and is carried every spring through the market-gardens, either could not or would not help. Masses, vespers, concerts, illuminations, fire-works— nothing could move him. At last the peasants began to lose patience. Most of the saints were banished. At Palermo they dumped St. Joseph in a garden to see the state of things for himself, and they swore to leave him there in the sun till rain fell. Other saints were turned, like naughty children, with their faces to the wall. Others again, stripped of their beautiful robes, were exiled far from their parishes, threatened, grossly insulted, ducked in horse-ponds. At Caltanisetta the golden wings of St. Michael the Archangel were torn from his shoulders and replaced with wings of pasteboard ; his purple mantle was taken away and a clout wrapt about him instead. At Licata the patron saint, St. Angelo, fared even worse, for he was left without any garments at all ; he was reviled, he was put in irons, he was threatened with drowning or hanging. " Rain or the rope ! " roared the angry people at him, as they shook their fists in his face.

Sometimes an appeal is made to the pity of the gods. When their corn is being burnt up by the sun, the Zulus look out for a " heaven bird," kill it, and throw it into a pool. Then the heaven melts with tenderness for the death of the bird ; " it wails for it by raining, wailing a funeral wail." In Zululand women sometimes bury their children up to the neck in the ground, and then retiring to a distance keep up a dismal howl for a long time. The sky is sup- posed to melt with pity at the sight. Then the women dig the children out and feel sure that rain will soon follow. They say that they call to " the lord above " and ask him to send rain. If it comes they declare that " Usondo rains." In times of drought the Guanches of Teneriffe led their sheep to sacred ground, and there they separated the lambs from their dams, that their plaintive bleating might touch the heart of the god. In Kumaon a way of stopping rain is to pour hot oil in the left ear of a dog. The animal howls with pain, his howls are heard by Indra, and out of pity for the beast's sufferings the god stops the rain. Sometimes the Toradjas attempt to procure rain as follows. They place the stalks of certain plants in water, saying, " Go and ask for rain, and so long as no rain falls I will not plant you again, but there shall you die." Also they string some fresh-water snails on a cord, and hang the cord on a tree, and say to the snails, " Go and ask for rain, and so long as no rain comes, I will not take you back to the water." Then the snails go and weep, and the gods take pity and send rain. However, the foregoing cere- monies are religious rather than magical, since they involve an appeal to the compassion of higher powers.

Stones are often supposed to possess the property of bringing on rain, provided they be dipped in water or sprinkled with it, or treated in some other appropriate manner. In a Samoan village a certain stone was carefully housed as the representative of the rain-making god, and in time of drought his priests carried the stone in procession and dipped it in a stream. Among the Ta-ta-thi tribe of New South Wales the rain-maker breaks off a piece of quartz-crystal and spits it towards the sky ; the rest of the crystal he wraps in emu feathers, soaks both crystal and feathers in water, and carefully hides them. In the Keramin tribe of New South Wales the wizard retires to the bed of a creek, drops water on a round flat stone, then covers up and conceals it. Among some tribes of North-western Australia the rain-maker repairs to a piece of ground which is set apart for the purpose of rain-making. There he builds a heap of stones or sand, places on the top of it his magic stone, and walks or dances round the pile chanting his incantations for hours, till sheer exhaustion obliges him to desist, when his place is taken by his assistant. Water is sprinkled on the stone and huge fires are kindled. No layman may approach the sacred spot while the mystic ceremony is being performed. When the Sulka of New Britain wish to procure rain they blacken stones with the ashes of certain fruits and set them out, along with certain other plants and buds, in the sun. Then a handful of twigs is dipped in water and weighted with stones, while a spell is chanted. After that rain should follow. In Manipur, on a lofty hill to the east of the capital, there is a stone which the popular imagination likens to an umbrella. When rain is wanted, the rajah fetches water from a spring below and sprinkles it on the stone. At Sagami in Japan there is a stone which draws down rain whenever water is poured on it. When the Wakondyo, a tribe of Central Africa, desire rain, they send to the Wawamba, who dwell at the foot of snowy mountains, and are the happy possessors of a " rain-stone." In consideration of a proper payment, the Wawamba wash the precious stone, anoint it with oil, and put it in a pot full of water. After that the rain cannot fail to come. In the arid wastes of Arizona and New Mexico the Apaches sought to make rain by carrying water from a certain spring and throwing it on a particular point high up on a rock ; after that they imagined that the clouds would soon gather, and that rain would begin to fall.

But customs of this sort are not confined to the wilds of Africa and Asia or the torrid deserts of Australia and the New World. They have been practised in the cool air and under the grey skies of Europe. There is a fountain called Barenton, of romantic fame, in those " wild woods of Broceliande," where, if legend be true, the wizard Merlin still sleeps his magic slumber in the hawthorn shade. Thither the Breton peasants used to resort when they needed rain. They caught some of the water in a tankard and threw it on a slab near the spring. On Snowdon there is a lonely tarn called Dulyn, or the Black Lake, lying " in a dismal dingle surrounded by high and dangerous rocks." A row of stepping-stones runs out into the lake, and if any one steps on the stones and throws water so as to wet the farthest stone, which is called the Red Altar, " it is but a chance that you do not get rain before night, even when it is hot weather." In these cases it appears probable that, as in Samoa, the stone is regarded as more or less divine. This appears from the custom sometimes observed of dipping a cross in the Fountain of Barenton to procure rain, for this is plainly a Christian substitute for the old pagan way of throwing water on the stone. At various places in France it is, or used till lately to be, the practice to dip the image of a saint in water as a means of procuring rain. Thus, beside the old priory of Commagny there is a spring of St. Gervais, whither the inhabitants go in procession to obtain rain or fine weather according to the needs of the crops. In times of great drought they throw into the basin of the fountain an ancient stone image of the saint that stands in a sort of niche from which the fountain flows. At Collobrières and Carpentras a similar practice was observed with the images of St. Pons and St. Gens respectively. In several villages of Navarre prayers for rain used to be offered to St. Peter, and by way of enforcing them the villagers carried the image of the saint in procession to the river, where they thrice invited him to reconsider his resolution and to grant their prayers ; then, if he was still obstinate, they plunged him in the water, despite the remonstrances of the clergy, who pleaded with as much truth as piety that a simple caution or admonition administered to the image would produce an equally good effect. After this the rain was sure to fall within twenty-four hours. Catholic countries do not enjoy a monopoly of making rain by ducking holy images in water. In Mingrelia, when the crops are suffering from want of rain, they take a particularly holy image and dip it in water every day till a shower falls ; and in the Far East the Shans drench the images of Buddha with water when the rice is perishing of drought. In all such cases the practice is probably at bottom a sympathetic charm, however it may be disguised under the appearance of a punishment or a threat.

Like other peoples, the Greeks and Romans sought to obtain rain by magic, when prayers and processions had proved ineffectual. For example, in Arcadia, when the corn and trees were parched with drought, the priest of Zeus dipped an oak branch into a certain spring on Mount Lycaeus. Thus troubled, the water sent up a misty cloud, from which rain soon fell upon the land. A similar mode of making rain is still practised, as we have seen, in Halmahera near New Guinea. The people of Crannon in Thessaly had a bronze chariot which they kept in a temple. When they desired a shower they shook the chariot and the shower fell. Probably the rattling of the chariot was meant to imitate thunder ; we have already seen that mock thunder and lightning form part of a rain-charm in Russia and Japan. The legendary Salmoneus, King of Elis, made mock thunder by dragging bronze kettles behind his chariot, or by driving over a bronze bridge, while he hurled blazing torches in imitation of lightning. It was his impious wish to mimic the thundering car of Zeus as it rolled across the vault of heaven. Indeed he declared that he was actually Zeus, and caused sacrifices to be offered to himself as such. Near a temple of Mars, outside the walls of Rome, there was kept a certain stone known as the *lapis manalis.* In time of drought the stone was dragged into Rome, and this was supposed to bring down rain immediately.

§ 3. *The Magical Control of the Sun.*—As the magician thinks he can make rain, so he fancies he can cause the sun to shine, and can hasten or stay its going down. At an eclipse the Ojebways used to imagine that the sun was being extinguished. So they shot fire-tipped arrows in the air, hoping thus to rekindle his expiring light. The Sencis of Peru also shot burning arrows at the sun during an eclipse, but apparently they did this not so much to relight his lamp as to drive away a savage beast with which they supposed him to be struggling. Conversely during an eclipse of the moon some tribes of the Orinoco used to bury lighted brands in the ground ; because, said they, if the moon were to be extinguished, all fire on earth would be extinguished with her, except such as was hidden from her sight. During an eclipse of the sun the Kamtchatkans were wont to bring out fire from their huts and pray the great luminary to shine as before. But the prayer addressed to the sun shows that this ceremony was religious rather than magical. Purely magical, on the other hand, was the ceremony observed on similar occasions by the Chilcotin Indians. Men and women tucked up their robes, as they do in travelling, and then leaning on staves, as if they were heavy laden, they continued to walk in a circle till the eclipse was over. Apparently they thought thus to support the failing steps of the sun as he trod his weary round in the sky. Similarly in ancient Egypt the king, as the representative of the sun, walked solemnly round the walls of a temple in order to ensure that the sun should perform his daily journey round the sky without the interruption of an eclipse or other mishap. And after the autumnal equinox the ancient Egyptians held a festival called " the nativity of the sun's walking-stick," because, as the luminary declined daily in the sky, and his light and heat diminished, he was supposed to need a staff on which to lean. In New Caledonia, when a wizard desires to make sunshine he takes some plants and corals to the burial-ground and fashions them into a bundle, adding two locks of hair cut from a living child of his family, also two teeth or an entire jawbone from the skeleton of an ancestor. He then climbs a mountain whose top catches the first rays of the morning sun. Here he deposits three sorts of plants on a flat stone, places a branch of dry coral beside them, and hangs the bundle of charms over the stone. Next morning he returns to the spot and sets fire to the bundle at the moment when the sun rises from the sea. As the smoke curls up, he rubs the stone with the dry coral, invokes his ancestors, and says : " Sun ! I do this that you may be burning hot, and eat up all the clouds in the sky." The same ceremony is repeated at sunset. The New Caledonians also make a drought by means of a disc-shaped stone with a hole in it. At the moment when the sun rises, the wizard holds the stone in his hand and passes a burning brand repeatedly into the hole, while he says : " I kindle the sun, in order that he may eat up the clouds and dry up our land, so that it may produce nothing." The Banks Islanders make sunshine by means of a mock sun. They take a very round stone, called a *vat loa* or sunstone, wind red braid about it, and stick it with owls' feathers to represent rays, singing the proper spell in a low voice. Then they hang it on some high tree, such as a banyan or a casuarina, in a sacred place.

The offering made by the Brahman in the morning is supposed to produce the sun, and we are told that " assuredly it would not rise, were he not to make that offering." The ancient Mexicans conceived the sun as the source of all vital force ; hence they named him Ipalnemohuani, " He by whom men live." But if he bestowed life on the world, he needed also to receive life from it. And as the heart is the seat and symbol of life, bleeding hearts of men and animals were presented to the sun to maintain him in vigour and enable him to run his course across the sky. Thus the Mexican sacrifices to the sun were magical rather than religious, being designed, not so much to please and propitiate him, as physically to renew his energies of heat, light, and motion. The constant demand for human victims to feed the solar fire was met by waging war every year on the neighbouring tribes and bringing back troops of captives to be sacrificed on the altar. Thus the ceaseless wars of the Mexicans and their cruel system of human sacrifices, the most monstrous on record, sprang in great measure from a mistaken theory of the solar system. No more striking illustration could be given of the disastrous consequences that may flow in practice from a purely speculative error. The ancient Greeks believed that the sun drove in a chariot across the sky ; hence the Rhodians, who worshipped the sun as their chief deity, annually dedicated a chariot and four horses to him, and flung them into the sea for his use. Doubtless they thought that after a year's work his old horses and chariot would be worn out. From a like motive, probably, the idolatrous kings of Judah dedicated chariots and horses to the sun, and the Spartans, Persians, and Massagetae sacrificed horses to him. The Spartans performed the sacrifice on the top of Mount Taygetus, the beautiful range behind which they saw the great luminary set every night. It was as natural for the inhabitants of the valley of Sparta to do this as it was for the islanders of Rhodes to throw the chariot and horses into the sea, into which the sun seemed to them to sink at evening. For thus, whether on the mountain or in the sea, the fresh horses stood ready for the weary god where they would be most welcome, at the end of his day's journey.

As some people think they can light up the sun or speed him on his way, so others fancy they can retard or stop him. In a pass of the Peruvian Andes stand two ruined towers on opposite hills. Iron hooks are clamped into their walls for the purpose of stretching a net from one tower to the other. The net is intended to catch the sun. Stories of men who have caught the sun in a noose are widely spread. When the sun is going southward in the autumn, and sinking lower and lower in the Arctic sky, the Esquimaux of Iglulik play the game of cat's cradle in order to catch him in the meshes of the string and so prevent his disappearance. On the contrary, when the sun is moving northward in the spring, they play the game of cup-and-ball to hasten his return. When an Australian blackfellow wishes to stay the sun from going down till he gets home, he puts a sod in the fork of a tree, exactly facing the setting sun. On the other hand, to make it go down faster, the Australians throw sand into the air and blow with their mouths towards the sun, perhaps to waft the lingering orb westward and bury it under the sands into which it appears to sink at night.

As some people imagine they can hasten the sun, so others fancy they can jog the tardy moon. The natives of New Guinea reckon months by the moon, and some of them have been known to throw stones and spears at the moon, in order to accelerate its progress and so to hasten the return of their friends, who were away from home for twelve months working on a tobacco plantation. The Malays think that a bright glow at sunset may throw a weak person into a fever. Hence they attempt to extinguish the glow by spitting out water and throwing ashes at it. The Shuswap Indians believe that they can bring on cold weather by burning the wood of a tree that has been struck by lightning. The belief may be based on the observation that in their country cold follows a thunder-storm. Hence in spring, when these Indians are travelling over the snow on high ground, they burn splinters of such wood in the fire in order that the crust of the snow may not melt.

§ 4. *The Magical Control of the Wind.*—Once more, the savage thinks he can make the wind to blow or to be still. When the day is hot and a Yakut has a long way to go, he takes a stone which he has chanced to find in an animal or fish, winds a horse-hair several times round it, and ties it to a stick. He then waves the stick about, uttering a spell. Soon a cool breeze begins to blow. In order to procure a cool wind for nine days the stone should first be dipped in the blood of a bird or beast and then presented to the sun, while the sorcerer makes three turns contrary to the course of the luminary. If a Hottentot desires the wind to drop, he takes one of his fattest skins and hangs it on the end of a pole, in the belief that by blowing the skin down the wind will lose all its force and must itself fall. Fuegian wizards throw shells against the wind to make it drop. The natives of the island of Bibili, off New Guinea, are reputed to make wind by blowing with their mouths. In stormy weather the Bogadjim people say, " The Bibili folk are at it again, blowing away." Another way of making wind which is practised in New Guinea is to strike a " wind-stone " lightly with a stick ; to strike it hard would bring on a hurricane. So in Scotland witches used to raise the wind by dipping a rag in water and beating it thrice on a stone, saying :

> " I knok this rag upone this stane
> To raise the wind in the divellis name,
> It sall not lye till I please againe."

In Greenland a woman in child-bed and for some time after delivery is supposed to possess the power of laying a storm. She has only to go out of doors, fill her mouth with air, and coming back into the house blow it out again. In antiquity there was a family at Corinth which enjoyed the reputation of being able to still the raging wind ; but we do not know in what manner its members exercised a useful function, which probably earned for them a more solid recompense than mere repute among the seafaring population of the isthmus. Even in Christian times, under the reign of Constantine, a certain Sopater suffered death at Constantinople on a charge of binding the winds by magic, because it happened that the corn-ships of Egypt and Syria were detained afar off by calms or head-winds, to the rage and disappointment of the hungry Byzantine rabble. Finnish wizards used to sell wind to storm-stayed mariners. The wind was enclosed in three knots ; if they undid the first knot, a moderate wind sprang up ; if the second, it blew half a gale ; if the third, a hurricane. Indeed the Esthonians, whose country is divided from Finland only by an arm of the sea, still believe in the magical powers of their northern neighbours. The bitter winds that blow in spring from the north and north-east, bringing ague and rheumatic inflammations in their train, are set down by the simple Esthonian peasantry to the machinations of the Finnish wizards and witches. In particular they regard with special dread three days in spring to which they give the name of Days of the Cross ; one of them falls on the Eve of Ascension Day. The people in the neighbourhood of Fellin fear to go out on these days lest the cruel winds from Lappland should smite them dead. A popular Esthonian song runs :

> " Wind of the Cross ! rushing and mighty !
> Heavy the blow of thy wings sweeping past !
> Wild wailing wind of misfortune and sorrow,
> Wizards of Finland ride by on the blast."

It is said, too, that sailors, beating up against the wind in the Gulf of Finland, sometimes see a strange sail heave in sight astern and overhaul them hand over hand. On she comes with a cloud of canvas —all her studding-sails out—right in the teeth of the wind, forging her way through the foaming billows, dashing back the spray in sheets from her cutwater, every sail swollen to bursting, every rope strained to cracking. Then the sailors know that she hails from Finland.

The art of tying up the wind in three knots, so that the more knots are loosed the stronger will blow the wind, has been attributed to wizards in Lappland and to witches in Shetland, Lewis, and the Isle of Man. Shetland seamen still buy winds in the shape of knotted handkerchiefs or threads from old women who claim to rule the storms. There are said to be ancient crones in Lerwick now who live by selling wind. Ulysses received the winds in a leathern bag from Aeolus, King of the Winds. The Motumotu in New Guinea think that storms are sent by an Oiabu sorcerer ; for each wind he has a bamboo which he opens at pleasure. On the top of Mount Agu in Togo, a district of West Africa, resides a fetish called Bagba, who is supposed to control the wind and the rain. His priest is said to keep the winds shut up in great pots.

G

Often the stormy wind is regarded as an evil being who may be intimidated, driven away, or killed. When storms and bad weather have lasted long and food is scarce with the Central Esquimaux, they endeavour to conjure the tempest by making a long whip of seaweed, armed with which they go down to the beach and strike out in the direction of the wind, crying, " *Taba* (it is enough) ! " Once when north-westerly winds had kept the ice long on the coast and food was becoming scarce, the Esquimaux performed a ceremony to make a calm. A fire was kindled on the shore, and the men gathered round it and chanted. An old man then stepped up to the fire and in a coaxing voice invited the demon of the wind to come under the fire and warm himself. When he was supposed to have arrived, a vessel of water, to which each man present had contributed, was thrown on the flames by an old man, and immediately a flight of arrows sped towards the spot where the fire had been. They thought that the demon would not stay where he had been so badly treated. To complete the effect, guns were discharged in various directions, and the captain of a European vessel was invited to fire on the wind with cannon. On the twenty-first of February 1883 a similar ceremony was performed by the Esquimaux of Point Barrow, Alaska, with the intention of killing the spirit of the wind. Women drove the demon from their houses with clubs and knives, with which they made passes in the air ; and the men, gathering round a fire, shot him with their rifles and crushed him under a heavy stone the moment that steam rose in a cloud from the smouldering embers, on which a tub of water had just been thrown.

The Lengua Indians of the Gran Chaco ascribe the rush of a whirl-wind to the passage of a spirit and they fling sticks at it to frighten it away. When the wind blows down their huts, the Payaguas of South America snatch up firebrands and run against the wind, menacing it with the blazing brands, while others beat the air with their fists to frighten the storm. When the Guaycurus are threatened by a severe storm, the men go out armed, and the women and children scream their loudest to intimidate the demon. During a tempest the inhabitants of a Batak village in Sumatra have been seen to rush from their houses armed with sword and lance. The rajah placed himself at their head, and with shouts and yells they hewed and hacked at the invisible foe. An old woman was observed to be speci-ally active in the defence of her house, slashing the air right and left with a long sabre. In a violent thunderstorm, the peals sounding very near, the Kayans of Borneo have been seen to draw their swords threateningly half out of their scabbards, as if to frighten away the demons of the storm. In Australia the huge columns of red sand that move rapidly across a desert tract are thought by the natives to be spirits passing along. Once an athletic young black ran after one of these moving columns to kill it with boomerangs. He was away two or three hours, and came back very weary, saying he had killed Koochee (the demon), but that Koochee had growled at him and he must die. Of the Bedouins of Eastern Africa it is said that " no whirl-wind ever sweeps across the path without being pursued by a dozen savages with drawn creeses, who stab into the centre of the dusty column in order to drive away the evil spirit that is believed to be riding on the blast."

In the light of these examples a story told by Herodotus, which his modern critics have treated as a fable, is perfectly credible. He says, without however vouching for the truth of the tale, that once in the land of the Psylli, the modern Tripoli, the wind blowing from the Sahara had dried up all the water-tanks. So the people took counsel and marched in a body to make war on the south wind. But when they entered the desert the simoom swept down on them and buried them to a man. The story may well have been told by one who watched them disappearing, in battle array, with drums and cymbals beating, into the red cloud of whirling sand.

CHAPTER VI

MAGICIANS AS KINGS

THE foregoing evidence may satisfy us that in many lands and many races magic has claimed to control the great forces of nature for the good of man. If that has been so, the practitioners of the art must necessarily be personages of importance and influence in any society which puts faith in their extravagant pretensions, and it would be no matter for surprise if, by virtue of the reputation which they enjoy and of the awe which they inspire, some of them should attain to the highest position of authority over their credulous fellows. In point of fact magicians appear to have often developed into chiefs and kings.

Let us begin by looking at the lowest race of men as to whom we possess comparatively full and accurate information, the aborigines of Australia. These savages are ruled neither by chiefs nor kings. So far as their tribes can be said to have a political constitution, it is a democracy or rather an oligarchy of old and influential men, who meet in council and decide on all measures of importance to the practical exclusion of the younger men. Their deliberative assembly answers to the senate of later times : if we had to coin a word for such a government of elders we might call it a *gerontocracy*. The elders who in aboriginal Australia thus meet and direct the affairs of their tribe appear to be for the most part the headmen of their respective totem clans. Now in Central Australia, where the desert nature of the country and the almost complete isolation from foreign influences have retarded progress and preserved the natives on the whole in their most primitive state, the headmen of the various totem clans are charged with the important task of performing magical ceremonies for the multiplication of the totems, and as the great majority of the totems are edible animals or plants, it follows that these men are commonly expected to provide the people with food by means of magic.   Others have to make the rain to fall or to render other services to the community.   In short, among the tribes of Central Australia the headmen are public magicians.   Further, their most important function is to take charge of the sacred storehouse, usually a cleft in the rocks or a hole in the ground, where are kept the holy stones and sticks (*churinga*) with which the souls of all the people, both living and dead, are apparently supposed to be in a manner bound up.   Thus while the headmen have certainly to perform what we should call civil duties, such as to inflict punishment for breaches of tribal custom, their principal functions are sacred or magical.

When we pass from Australia to New Guinea we find that, though the natives stand at a far higher level of culture than the Australian aborigines, the constitution of society among them is still essentially democratic or oligarchic, and chieftainship exists only in embryo. Thus Sir William MacGregor tells us that in British New Guinea no one has ever arisen wise enough, bold enough, and strong enough to become the despot even of a single district.   " The nearest approach to this has been the very distant one of some person becoming a renowned wizard ; but that has only resulted in levying a certain amount of blackmail."

According to a native account, the origin of the power of Melanesian chiefs lies entirely in the belief that they have communication with mighty ghosts, and wield that supernatural power whereby they can bring the influence of the ghosts to bear.   If a chief imposed a fine, it was paid because the people universally dreaded his ghostly power, and firmly believed that he could inflict calamity and sickness upon such as resisted him.   As soon as any considerable number of his people began to disbelieve in his influence with the ghosts, his power to levy fines was shaken.   Again, Dr. George Brown tells us that in New Britain " a ruling chief was always supposed to exercise priestly functions, that is, he professed to be in constant communication with the *tebarans* (spirits), and through their influence he was enabled to bring rain or sunshine, fair winds or foul ones, sickness or health, success or disaster in war, and generally to procure any blessing or curse for which the applicant was willing to pay a sufficient price."

Still rising in the scale of culture we come to Africa, where both the chieftainship and the kingship are fully developed ; and here the evidence for the evolution of the chief out of the magician, and especially out of the rainmaker, is comparatively plentiful.   Thus among the Wambugwe, a Bantu people of East Africa, the original form of government was a family republic, but the enormous power of the sorcerers, transmitted by inheritance, soon raised them to the rank of petty lords or chiefs.   Of the three chiefs living in the country in 1894 two were much dreaded as magicians, and the wealth of cattle they possessed came to them almost wholly in the shape of presents bestowed for their services in that capacity. Their principal art was that of rain-making. The chiefs of the Watataru, another people of East Africa, are said to be nothing but sorcerers destitute of any direct political influence. Again, among the Wagogo of East Africa the main power of the chiefs, we are told, is derived from their art of rain-making. If a chief cannot make rain himself, he must procure it from some one who can.

Again, among the tribes of the Upper Nile the medicine-men are generally the chiefs. Their authority rests above all upon their supposed power of making rain, for " rain is the one thing which matters to the people in those districts, as if it does not come down at the right time it means untold hardships for the community. It is therefore small wonder that men more cunning than their fellows should arrogate to themselves the power of producing it, or that having gained such a reputation, they should trade on the credulity of their simpler neighbours." Hence " most of the chiefs of these tribes are rain-makers, and enjoy a popularity in proportion to their powers to give rain to their people at the proper season. . . . Rain-making chiefs always build their villages on the slopes of a fairly high hill, as they no doubt know that the hills attract the clouds, and that they are, therefore, fairly safe in their weather forecasts." Each of these rain-makers has a number of rain-stones, such as rock-crystal, aventurine, and amethyst, which he keeps in a pot. When he wishes to produce rain he plunges the stones in water, and taking in his hand a peeled cane, which is split at the top, he beckons with it to the clouds to come or waves them away in the way they should go, muttering an incantation the while. Or he pours water and the entrails of a sheep or goat into a hollow in a stone and then sprinkles the water towards the sky. Though the chief acquires wealth by the exercise of his supposed magical powers, he often, perhaps generally, comes to a violent end ; for in time of drought the angry people assemble and kill him, believing that it is he who prevents the rain from falling. Yet the office is usually hereditary and passes from father to son. Among the tribes which cherish these beliefs and observe these customs are the Latuka, Bari, Laluba, and Lokoiya.

In Central Africa, again, the Lendu tribe, to the west of Lake Albert, firmly believe that certain people possess the power of making rain. Among them the rain-maker either is a chief or almost invariably becomes one. The Banyoro also have a great respect for the dispensers of rain, whom they load with a profusion of gifts. The great dispenser, he who has absolute and uncontrollable power over the rain, is the king ; but he can depute his power to other persons, so that the benefit may be distributed and the heavenly water laid on over the various parts of the kingdom.

In Western as well as in Eastern and Central Africa we meet with the same union of chiefly with magical functions. Thus in the Fan tribe the strict distinction between chief and medicine-man does not exist. The chief is also a medicine-man and a smith to boot ; for the Fans esteem the smith's craft sacred, and none but chiefs may meddle with it.

As to the relation between the offices of chief and rain-maker in South Africa a well-informed writer observes : " In very old days the chief was the great Rain-maker of the tribe. Some chiefs allowed no one else to compete with them, lest a successful Rain-maker should be chosen as chief. There was also another reason : the Rain-maker was sure to become a rich man if he gained a great reputation, and it would manifestly never do for the chief to allow any one to be too rich. The Rain-maker exerts tremendous control over the people, and so it would be most important to keep this function connected with royalty. Tradition always places the power of making rain as the fundamental glory of ancient chiefs and heroes, and it seems probable that it may have been the origin of chieftainship. The man who made the rain would naturally become the chief. In the same way Chaka [the famous Zulu despot] used to declare that he was the only diviner in the country, for if he allowed rivals his life would be insecure." Similarly speaking of the South African tribes in general, Dr. Moffat says that " the rain-maker is in the estimation of the people no mean personage, possessing an influence over the minds of the people superior even to that of the king, who is likewise compelled to yield to the dictates of this arch-official."

The foregoing evidence renders it probable that in Africa the king has often been developed out of the public magician, and especially out of the rain-maker. The unbounded fear which the magician inspires and the wealth which he amasses in the exercise of his profession may both be supposed to have contributed to his promotion. But if the career of a magician and especially of a rain-maker offers great rewards to the successful practitioner of the art, it is beset with many pitfalls into which the unskilful or unlucky artist may fall. The position of the public sorcerer is indeed a very precarious one ; for where the people firmly believe that he has it in his power to make the rain to fall, the sun to shine, and the fruits of the earth to grow, they naturally impute drought and dearth to his culpable negligence or wilful obstinacy, and they punish him accordingly. Hence in Africa the chief who fails to procure rain is often exiled or killed. Thus, in some parts of West Africa, when prayers and offerings presented to the king have failed to procure rain, his subjects bind him with ropes and take him by force to the grave of his forefathers that he may obtain from them the needed rain. The Banjars in West Africa ascribe to their king the power of causing rain or fine weather. So long as the weather is fine they load him with presents of grain and cattle. But if long drought or rain threatens to spoil the crops, they insult and beat him till the weather changes. When the harvest fails or the surf on the coast is too heavy to allow of fishing, the people of Loango accuse their king of a " bad heart " and depose him. On the Grain Coast the high priest or fetish king, who bears the title of Bodio, is responsible for the health of the community, the fertility of the earth, and the abundance of fish in the sea and rivers ; and if the country suffers in any of these respects the Bodio is deposed from his office. In Ussukuma, a great district on the southern bank of the Victoria Nyanza, " the rain and locust question is part and parcel of the Sultan's government. He, too, must know how to make rain and drive away the locusts. If he and his medicine-men are unable to accomplish this, his whole existence is at stake in times of distress. On a certain occasion, when the rain so greatly desired by the people did not come, the Sultan was simply driven out (in Ututwa, near Nassa). The people, in fact, hold that rulers must have power over Nature and her phenomena." Again, we are told of the natives of the Nyanza region generally that " they are persuaded that rain only falls as a result of magic, and the important duty of causing it to descend devolves on the chief of the tribe. If rain does not come at the proper time, everybody complains. More than one petty king has been banished his country because of drought." Among the Latuka of the Upper Nile, when the crops are withering, and all the efforts of the chief to draw down rain have proved fruitless, the people commonly attack him by night, rob him of all he possesses, and drive him away. But often they kill him.

In many other parts of the world kings have been expected to regulate the course of nature for the good of their people and have been punished if they failed to do so. It appears that the Scythians, when food was scarce, used to put their king in bonds. In ancient Egypt the sacred kings were blamed for the failure of the crops, but the sacred beasts were also held responsible for the course of nature. When pestilence and other calamities had fallen on the land, in consequence of a long and severe drought, the priests took the animals by night and threatened them, but if the evil did not abate they slew the beasts. On the coral island of Niuē or Savage Island, in the South Pacific, there formerly reigned a line of kings. But as the kings were also high priests, and were supposed to make the food grow, the people became angry with them in times of scarcity and killed them ; till at last, as one after another was killed, no one would be king, and the monarchy came to an end. Ancient Chinese writers inform us that in Corea the blame was laid on the king whenever too much or too little rain fell and the crops did not ripen. Some said that he must be deposed, others that he must be slain.

Among the American Indians the furthest advance towards civilisation was made under the monarchical and theocratic governments of Mexico and Peru ; but we know too little of the early history of these countries to say whether the predecessors of their deified kings were medicine-men or not. Perhaps a trace of such a succession may be detected in the oath which the Mexican kings, when they mounted the throne, swore that they would make the sun to shine, the clouds to give rain, the rivers to flow, and the earth to bring forth fruits in abundance. Certainly, in aboriginal America the sorcerer or medicine-man, surrounded by a halo of mystery and an atmosphere of awe, was a personage of great influence and importance, and he may well have developed into a chief or king in many tribes, though positive evidence of such a development appears to be lacking.   Thus Catlin tells us that in North America the medicine-men " are valued as dignitaries in the tribe, and the greatest respect is paid to them by the whole community ; not only for their skill in their *materia medica*, but more especially for their tact in magic and mysteries, in which they all deal to a very great extent. . . . In all tribes their doctors are conjurers—are magicians—are sooth-sayers, and I had like to have said high-priests, inasmuch as they superintend and conduct all their religious ceremonies ; they are looked upon by all as oracles of the nation.   In all councils of war and peace, they have a seat with the chiefs, are regularly consulted before any public step is taken, and the greatest deference and respect is paid to their opinions."   Similarly in California " the shaman was, and still is, perhaps the most important individual among the Maidu.   In the absence of any definite system of government, the word of a shaman has great weight : as a class they are regarded with much awe, and as a rule are obeyed much more than the chief."

In South America also the magicians or medicine-men seem to have been on the highroad to chieftainship or kingship.   One of the earliest settlers on the coast of Brazil, the Frenchman Thevet, reports that the Indians " hold these *pages* (or medicine-men) in such honour and reverence that they adore, or rather idolise them.   You may see the common folk go to meet them, prostrate themselves, and pray to them, saying, ' Grant that I be not ill, that I do not die, neither I nor my children,' or some such request.   And he answers, ' You shall not die, you shall not be ill,' and such like replies.   But sometimes if it happens that these *pages* do not tell the truth, and things turn out otherwise than they predicted, the people make no scruple of killing them as unworthy of the title and dignity of *pages*."   Among the Lengua Indians of the Gran Chaco every clan has its cazique or chief, but he possesses little authority.   In virtue of his office he has to make many presents, so he seldom grows rich and is generally more shabbily clad than any of his subjects.   " As a matter of fact the magician is the man who has most power in his hands, and he is accustomed to receive presents instead of to give them."   It is the magician's duty to bring down misfortune and plagues on the enemies of his tribe, and to guard his own people against hostile magic.   For these services he is well paid, and by them he acquires a position of great influence and authority.

Throughout the Malay region the rajah or king is commonly regarded with superstitious veneration as the possessor of supernatural powers, and there are grounds for thinking that he too, like apparently so many African chiefs, has been developed out of a simple magician. At the present day the Malays firmly believe that the king possesses a personal influence over the works of nature, such as the growth of the crops and the bearing of fruit-trees.   The same prolific virtue is supposed to reside, though in a lesser degree, in his delegates, and even in the persons of Europeans who chance to have charge of districts. Thus in Selangor, one of the native states of the Malay Peninsula, the success or failure of the rice crops is often attributed to a change of district officers. The Toorateyas of Southern Celebes hold that the prosperity of the rice depends on the behaviour of their princes, and that bad government, by which they mean a government which does not conform to ancient custom, will result in a failure of the crops.

The Dyaks of Sarawak believed that their famous English ruler, Rajah Brooke, was endowed with a certain magical virtue which, if properly applied, could render the rice-crops abundant. Hence when he visited a tribe, they used to bring him the seed which they intended to sow next year, and he fertilised it by shaking over it the women's necklaces, which had been previously dipped in a special mixture. And when he entered a village, the women would wash and bathe his feet, first with water, and then with the milk of a young coco-nut, and lastly with water again, and all this water which had touched his person they preserved for the purpose of distributing it on their farms, believing that it ensured an abundant harvest. Tribes which were too far off for him to visit used to send him a small piece of white cloth and a little gold or silver, and when these things had been impregnated by his generative virtue they buried them in their fields, and confidently expected a heavy crop. Once when a European remarked that the rice-crops of the Samban tribe were thin, the chief immediately replied that they could not be otherwise, since Rajah Brooke had never visited them, and he begged that Mr. Brooke might be induced to visit his tribe and remove the sterility of their land.

The belief that kings possess magical or supernatural powers by virtue of which they can fertilise the earth and confer other benefits on their subjects would seem to have been shared by the ancestors of all the Aryan races from India to Ireland, and it has left clear traces of itself in our own country down to modern times. Thus the ancient Hindoo law-book called *The Laws of Manu* describes as follows the effects of a good king's reign : " In that country where the king avoids taking the property of mortal sinners, men are born in due time and are long-lived. And the crops of the husbandmen spring up, each as it was sown, and the children die not, and no misshaped offspring is born." In Homeric Greece kings and chiefs were spoken of as sacred or divine ; their houses, too, were divine and their chariots sacred ; and it was thought that the reign of a good king caused the black earth to bring forth wheat and barley, the trees to be loaded with fruit, the flocks to multiply, and the sea to yield fish. In the Middle Ages, when Waldemar I., King of Denmark, travelled in Germany, mothers brought their infants and husbandmen their seed for him to lay his hands on, thinking that children would both thrive the better for the royal touch, and for a like reason farmers asked him to throw the seed for them. It was the belief of the ancient Irish that when their kings observed the customs of their ancestors, the seasons were mild, the crops plentiful, the cattle fruitful, the waters abounded with fish, and the fruit trees had to be propped up on account of the weight of their produce. A canon attributed to St. Patrick enumerates among the blessings that attend the reign of a just king " fine weather, calm seas, crops abundant, and trees laden with fruit." On the other hand, dearth, dryness of cows, blight of fruit, and scarcity of corn were regarded as infallible proofs that the reigning king was bad.

Perhaps the last relic of such superstitions which lingered about our English kings was the notion that they could heal scrofula by their touch. The disease was accordingly known as the King's Evil. Queen Elizabeth often exercised this miraculous gift of healing. On Mid-summer Day 1633, Charles the First cured a hundred patients at one swoop in the chapel royal at Holyrood. But it was under his son Charles the Second that the practice seems to have attained its highest vogue. It is said that in the course of his reign Charles the Second touched near a hundred thousand persons for scrofula. The press to get near him was sometimes terrific. On one occasion six or seven of those who came to be healed were trampled to death. The cool-headed William the Third contemptuously refused to lend himself to the hocus-pocus ; and when his palace was besieged by the usual unsavoury crowd, he ordered them to be turned away with a dole. On the only occasion when he was importuned into laying his hand on a patient, he said to him, " God give you better health and more sense." How-ever, the practice was continued, as might have been expected, by the dull bigot James the Second and his dull daughter Queen Anne.

The kings of France also claimed to possess the same gift of healing by touch, which they are said to have derived from Clovis or from St. Louis, while our English kings inherited it from Edward the Con-fessor. Similarly the savage chiefs of Tonga were believed to heal scrofula and cases of indurated liver by the touch of their feet ; and the cure was strictly homoeopathic, for the disease as well as the cure was thought to be caused by contact with the royal person or with anything that belonged to it.

On the whole, then, we seem to be justified in inferring that in many parts of the world the king is the lineal successor of the old magician or medicine-man. When once a special class of sorcerers has been segregated from the community and entrusted by it with the discharge of duties on which the public safety and welfare are believed to depend, these men gradually rise to wealth and power, till their leaders blossom out into sacred kings. But the great social revolution which thus begins with democracy and ends in despotism is attended by an intellectual revolution which affects both the conception and the functions of royalty. For as time goes on, the fallacy of magic becomes more and more apparent to the acuter minds and is slowly displaced by religion ; in other words, the magician gives way to the priest, who renouncing the attempt to control directly the processes of nature for the good of man, seeks to attain the same end indirectly by appealing to the gods to do for him what he no longer fancies he can do for himself.

Hence the king, starting as a magician, tends gradually to exchange the practice of magic for the priestly functions of prayer and sacrifice. And while the distinction between the human and the divine is still imperfectly drawn, it is often imagined that men may themselves attain to godhead, not merely after their death, but in their lifetime, through the temporary or permanent possession of their whole nature by a great and powerful spirit. No class of the community has benefited so much as kings by this belief in the possible incarnation of a god in human form. The doctrine of that incarnation, and with it the theory of the divinity of kings in the strict sense of the word, will form the subject of the following chapter.

CHAPTER VII

INCARNATE HUMAN GODS

THE instances which in the preceding chapters I have drawn from the beliefs and practices of rude peoples all over the world, may suffice to prove that the savage fails to recognise those limitations to his power over nature which seem so obvious to us. In a society where every man is supposed to be endowed more or less with powers which we should call supernatural, it is plain that the distinction between gods and men is somewhat blurred, or rather has scarcely emerged. The conception of gods as superhuman beings endowed with powers to which man possesses nothing comparable in degree and hardly even in kind, has been slowly evolved in the course of history. By primitive peoples the supernatural agents are not regarded as greatly, if at all, superior to man ; for they may be frightened and coerced by him into doing his will. At this stage of thought the world is viewed as a great democracy ; all beings in it, whether natural or supernatural, are supposed to stand on a footing of tolerable equality. But with the growth of his knowledge man learns to realise more clearly the vastness of nature and his own littleness and feebleness in presence of it. The recognition of his helplessness does not, however, carry with it a corresponding belief in the impotence of those supernatural beings with which his imagination peoples the universe. On the contrary, it enhances his conception of their power. For the idea of the world as a system of impersonal forces acting in accordance with fixed and invariable laws has not yet fully dawned or darkened upon him. The germ of the idea he certainly has, and he acts upon it, not only in magic art, but in much of the business of daily life. But the idea remains undeveloped, and so far as he attempts to explain the world he lives in, he pictures it as the manifestation of conscious will and personal agency. If then he feels himself to be so frail and slight, how vast and powerful must he deem the beings who control the gigantic machinery of nature ! Thus as his old sense of equality with the gods slowly vanishes, he resigns at the same time the hope of directing the course of nature by his own unaided resources, that is, by magic, and looks more and more to the gods as the sole repositories of those supernatural powers which he once claimed to share with them. With the advance of knowledge, therefore, prayer and sacrifice assume the leading place in religious ritual ; and magic, which once ranked with them as a legitimate equal, is gradually relegated to the background and sinks to the level of a black art. It is now regarded as an encroachment, at once vain and impious, on the domain of the gods, and as such encounters the steady opposition of the priests, whose reputation and influence rise or fall with those of their gods. Hence, when at a late period the distinction between religion and superstition has emerged, we find that sacrifice and prayer are the resource of the pious and enlightened portion of the community, while magic is the refuge of the superstitious and ignorant. But when, still later, the conception of the elemental forces as personal agents is giving way to the recognition of natural law ; then magic, based as it implicitly is on the idea of a necessary and invariable sequence of cause and effect, independent of personal will, reappears from the obscurity and discredit into which it had fallen, and by investigating the causal sequences in nature, directly prepares the way for science. Alchemy leads up to chemistry.

The notion of a man-god, or of a human being endowed with divine or supernatural powers, belongs essentially to that earlier period of religious history in which gods and men are still viewed as beings of much the same order, and before they are divided by the impassable gulf which, to later thought, opens out between them. Strange, therefore, as may seem to us the idea of a god incarnate in human form, it has nothing very startling for early man, who sees in a man-god or a god-man only a higher degree of the same supernatural powers which he arrogates in perfect good faith to himself. Nor does he draw any very sharp distinction between a god and a powerful sorcerer. His gods are often merely invisible magicians who behind the veil of nature work the same sort of charms and incantations which the human magician works in a visible and bodily form among his fellows. And as the gods are commonly believed to exhibit themselves in the likeness of men to their worshippers, it is easy for the magician, with his supposed miraculous powers, to acquire the reputation of being an incarnate deity. Thus beginning as little more than a simple conjurer, the medicine-man or magician tends to blossom out into a full-blown god and king in one. Only in speaking of him as a god we must beware of importing into the savage conception of deity those very abstract and complex ideas which we attach to the term. Our ideas on this profound subject are the fruit of a long intellectual and moral evolution, and they are so far from being shared by the savage that he cannot even understand them when they are explained to him. Much of the controversy which has raged as to the religion of the lower races has sprung merely from a mutual misunderstanding. The savage does not understand the thoughts of the civilised man, and few civilised men understand the thoughts of the savage. When the savage uses his word for god, he has in his mind a

being of a certain sort : when the civilised man uses his word for god.
he has in his mind a being of a very different sort ; and if, as commonly
happens, the two men are equally unable to place themselves at the
other's point of view, nothing but confusion and mistakes can result
from their discussions.   If we civilised men insist on limiting the name
of God to that particular conception of the divine nature which we
ourselves have formed, then we must confess that the savage has no
god at all.   But we shall adhere more closely to the facts of history if
we allow most of the higher savages at least to possess a rudimentary
notion of certain supernatural beings who may fittingly be called gods,
though not in the full sense in which we use the word.   That rudimentary notion represents in all probability the germ out of which the
civilised peoples have gradually evolved their own high conceptions of
deity ; and if we could trace the whole course of religious development,
we might find that the chain which links our idea of the Godhead with
that of the savage is one and unbroken.

With these explanations and cautions I will now adduce some
examples of gods who have been believed by their worshippers to be
incarnate in living human beings, whether men or women.   The persons
in whom a deity is thought to reveal himself are by no means always
kings or descendants of kings ; the supposed incarnation may take
place even in men of the humblest rank.   In India, for example, one
human god started in life as a cotton-bleacher and another as the son
of a carpenter.   I shall therefore not draw my examples exclusively
from royal personages, as I wish to illustrate the general principle of the
deification of living men, in other words, the incarnation of a deity in
human form.   Such incarnate gods are common in rude society.   The
incarnation may be temporary or permanent.   In the former case, the
incarnation—commonly known as inspiration or possession—reveals
itself in supernatural knowledge rather than in supernatural power.   In
other words, its usual manifestations are divination and prophecy rather
than miracles.   On the other hand, when the incarnation is not merely
temporary, when the divine spirit has permanently taken up its abode
in a human body, the god-man is usually expected to vindicate his
character by working miracles.   Only we have to remember that by
men at this stage of thought miracles are not considered as breaches of
natural law.   Not conceiving the existence of natural law, primitive
man cannot conceive a breach of it.   A miracle is to him merely an
unusually striking manifestation of a common power.

The belief in temporary incarnation or inspiration is world-wide.
Certain persons are supposed to be possessed from time to time by a
spirit or deity ; while the possession lasts, their own personality lies in
abeyance, the presence of the spirit is revealed by convulsive shiverings
and shakings of the man's whole body, by wild gestures and excited
looks, all of which are referred, not to the man himself, but to the
spirit which has entered into him ; and in this abnormal state all his
utterances are accepted as the voice of the god or spirit dwelling in
him and speaking through him.   Thus, for example, in the Sandwich

Islands, the king, personating the god, uttered the responses of the oracle from his concealment in a frame of wicker-work. But in the southern islands of the Pacific the god " frequently entered the priest, who, inflated as it were with the divinity, ceased to act or speak as a voluntary agent, but moved and spoke as entirely under supernatural influence. In this respect there was a striking resemblance between the rude oracles of the Polynesians, and those of the celebrated nations of ancient Greece. As soon as the god was supposed to have entered the priest, the latter became violently agitated, and worked himself up to the highest pitch of apparent frenzy, the muscles of the limbs seemed convulsed, the body swelled, the countenance became terrific, the features distorted, and the eyes wild and strained. In this state he often rolled on the earth, foaming at the mouth, as if labouring under the influence of the divinity by whom he was possessed, and, in shrill cries, and violent and often indistinct sounds, revealed the will of the god. The priests, who were attending, and versed in the mysteries, received, and reported to the people, the declarations which had been thus received. When the priest had uttered the response of the oracle, the violent paroxysm gradually subsided, and comparative composure ensued. The god did not, however, always leave him as soon as the communication had been made. Sometimes the same *taura*, or priest, continued for two or three days possessed by the spirit or deity ; a piece of a native cloth, of a peculiar kind, worn round one arm, was an indication of inspiration, or of the indwelling of the god with the individual who wore it. The acts of the man during this period were considered as those of the god, and hence the greatest attention was paid to his expressions, and the whole of his deportment. . . . When *uruhia*, (under the inspiration of the spirit,) the priest was always considered as sacred as the god, and was called, during this period, *atua*, god, though at other times only denominated *taura* or priest."

But examples of such temporary inspiration are so common in every part of the world and are now so familiar through books on ethnology that it is needless to multiply illustrations of the general principle. It may be well, however, to refer to two particular modes of producing temporary inspiration, because they are perhaps less known than some others, and because we shall have occasion to refer to them later on. One of these modes of producing inspiration is by sucking the fresh blood of a sacrificed victim. In the temple of Apollo Diradiotes at Argos, a lamb was sacrificed by night once a month ; a woman, who had to observe a rule of chastity, tasted the blood of the lamb, and thus being inspired by the god she prophesied or divined. At Aegira in Achaia the priestess of Earth drank the fresh blood of a bull before she descended into the cave to prophesy. Similarly among the Kuruvikkarans, a class of bird-catchers and beggars in Southern India, the goddess Kali is believed to descend upon the priest, and he gives oracular replies after sucking the blood which streams from the cut throat of a goat. At a festival of the Alfoors of Minahassa, in Northern Celebes, after a pig has been killed, the priest rushes furiously at it, thrusts his head into the carcase, and drinks of the blood. Then he is dragged away from it by force and set on a chair, whereupon he begins to prophesy how the rice-crop will turn out that year. A second time he runs at the carcase and drinks of the blood ; a second time he is forced into the chair and continues his predictions. It is thought that there is a spirit in him which possesses the power of prophecy.

The other mode of producing temporary inspiration, to which I shall here refer, consists in the use of a sacred tree or plant. Thus in the Hindoo Koosh a fire is kindled with twigs of the sacred cedar ; and the Dainyal or sibyl, with a cloth over her head, inhales the thick pungent smoke till she is seized with convulsions and falls senseless to the ground. Soon she rises and raises a shrill chant, which is caught up and loudly repeated by her audience. So Apollo's prophetess ate the sacred laurel and was fumigated with it before she prophesied. The Bacchanals ate ivy, and their inspired fury was by some believed to be due to the exciting and intoxicating properties of the plant. In Uganda the priest, in order to be inspired by his god, smokes a pipe of tobacco fiercely till he works himself into a frenzy ; the loud excited tones in which he then talks are recognised as the voice of the god speaking through him. In Madura, an island off the north coast of Java, each spirit has its regular medium, who is oftener a woman than a man. To prepare herself for the reception of the spirit she inhales the fumes of incense, sitting with her head over a smoking censer. Gradually she falls into a sort of trance accompanied by shrieks, grimaces, and violent spasms. The spirit is now supposed to have entered into her, and when she grows calmer her words are regarded as oracular, being the utterances of the indwelling spirit, while her own soul is temporarily absent.

The person temporarily inspired is believed to acquire, not merely divine knowledge, but also, at least occasionally, divine power. In Cambodia, when an epidemic breaks out, the inhabitants of several villages unite and go with a band of music at their head to look for the man whom the local god is supposed to have chosen for his temporary incarnation. When found, the man is conducted to the altar of the god, where the mystery of incarnation takes place. Then the man becomes an object of veneration to his fellows, who implore him to protect the village against the plague. A certain image of Apollo, which stood in a sacred cave at Hylae near Magnesia, was thought to impart superhuman strength. Sacred men, inspired by it, leaped down precipices, tore up huge trees by the roots, and carried them on their backs along the narrowest defiles. The feats performed by inspired dervishes belong to the same class.

Thus far we have seen that the savage, failing to discern the limits of his ability to control nature, ascribes to himself and to all men certain powers which we should now call supernatural. Further, we have seen that, over and above this general supernaturalism, some persons are supposed to be inspired for short periods by a divine spirit, and thus temporarily to enjoy the knowledge and power of the indwelling deity. From beliefs like these it is an easy step to the conviction that certain men are permanently possessed by a deity, or in some other undefined way are endued with so high a degree of supernatural power as to be ranked as gods and to receive the homage of prayer and sacrifice. Sometimes these human gods are restricted to purely supernatural or spiritual functions. Sometimes they exercise supreme political power in addition. In the latter case they are kings as well as gods, and the government is a theocracy. Thus in the Marquesas or Washington Islands there was a class of men who were deified in their lifetime. They were supposed to wield a supernatural power over the elements : they could give abundant harvests or smite the ground with barrenness ; and they could inflict disease or death. Human sacrifices were offered to them to avert their wrath. There were not many of them, at the most one or two in each island. They lived in mystic seclusion. Their powers were sometimes, but not always, hereditary. A missionary has described one of these human gods from personal observation. The god was a very old man who lived in a large house within an enclosure. In the house was a kind of altar, and on the beams of the house and on the trees round it were hung human skeletons, head down. No one entered the enclosure except the persons dedicated to the service of the god ; only on days when human victims were sacrificed might ordinary people penetrate into the precinct. This human god received more sacrifices than all the other gods ; often he would sit on a sort of scaffold in front of his house and call for two or three human victims at a time. They were always brought, for the terror he inspired was extreme. He was invoked all over the island, and offerings were sent to him from every side. Again, of the South Sea Islands in general we are told that each island had a man who represented or personified the divinity. Such men were called gods, and their substance was confounded with that of the deity. The man-god was sometimes the king himself ; oftener he was a priest or subordinate chief.

The ancient Egyptians, far from restricting their adoration to cats and dogs and such small deer, very liberally extended it to men. One of these human deities resided at the village of Anabis, and burnt sacrifices were offered to him on the altars ; after which, says Porphyry, he would eat his dinner just as if he were an ordinary mortal. In classical antiquity the Sicilian philosopher Empedocles gave himself out to be not merely a wizard but a god. Addressing his fellow-citizens in verse he said :

" *O friends, in this great city that climbs the yellow slope*
Of Agrigentum's citadel, who make good works your scope,
Who offer to the stranger a haven quiet and fair,
All hail ! Among you honoured I walk with lofty air.
With garlands, blooming garlands you crown my noble brow.
A mortal man no longer, a deathless godhead now.

Where e'er I go, the people crowd round and worship pay,
And thousands follow seeking to learn the better way.
Some crave prophetic visions, some smit with anguish sore
Would fain hear words of comfort and suffer pain no more."

He asserted that he could teach his disciples how to make the wind to blow or be still, the rain to fall and the sun to shine, how to banish sickness and old age and to raise the dead. When Demetrius Poliorcetes restored the Athenian democracy in 307 B.C., the Athenians decreed divine honours to him and his father Antigonus, both of them being then alive, under the title of the Saviour Gods. Altars were set up to the Saviours, and a priest appointed to attend to their worship. The people went forth to meet their deliverer with hymns and dances, with garlands and incense and libations ; they lined the streets and sang that he was the only true god, for the other gods slept, or dwelt far away, or were not. In the words of a contemporary poet, which were chanted in public and sung in private :

" Of all the gods the greatest and the dearest
To the city are come.
For Demeter and Demetrius
Together time has brought.
She comes to hold the Maiden's awful rites,
And he joyous and fair and laughing,
As befits a god.
A glorious sight, with all his friends about him,
He in their midst,
They like to stars, and he the sun.
Son of Poseidon the mighty, Aphrodite's son,
All hail !
The other gods dwell far away,
Or have no ears,
Or are not, or pay us no heed.
But thee we present see,
No god of wood or stone, but godhead true.
Therefore to thee we pray."

The ancient Germans believed that there was something holy in women, and accordingly consulted them as oracles. Their sacred women, we are told, looked on the eddying rivers and listened to the murmur or the roar of the water, and from the sight and sound foretold what would come to pass. But often the veneration of the men went further, and they worshipped women as true and living goddesses. For example, in the reign of Vespasian a certain Veleda, of the tribe of the Bructeri, was commonly held to be a deity, and in that character reigned over her people, her sway being acknowledged far and wide. She lived in a tower on the river Lippe, a tributary of the Rhine. When the people of Cologne sent to make a treaty with her, the ambassadors were not admitted to her presence ; the negotiations were conducted through a minister, who acted as the mouthpiece of her divinity and reported her oracular utterances. The example shows how easily among our rude forefathers the ideas of divinity and royalty coalesced. It is said that among the Getae down to the beginning of our era there was always a man who personified a god and was called God by the people. He dwelt on a sacred mountain and acted as adviser to the king.

According to the early Portuguese historian, Dos Santos, the Zimbas, or Muzimbas, a people of South-eastern Africa, " do not adore idols or recognise any god, but instead they venerate and honour their king, whom they regard as a divinity, and they say he is the greatest and best in the world. And the said king says of himself that he alone is god of the earth, for which reason if it rains when he does not wish it to do so, or is too hot, he shoots arrows at the sky for not obeying him." The Mashona of Southern Africa informed their bishop that they had once had a god, but that the Matabeles had driven him away. " This last was in reference to a curious custom in some villages of keeping a man they called their god. He seemed to be consulted by the people and had presents given to him. There was one at a village belonging to a chief Magondi, in the old days. We were asked not to fire off any guns near the village, or we should frighten him away." This Mashona god was formerly bound to render an annual tribute to the king of the Matabele in the shape of four black oxen and one dance. A missionary has seen and described the deity discharging the latter part of his duty in front of the royal hut. For three mortal hours, without a break, to the banging of a tambourine, the click of castanettes, and the drone of a monotonous song, the swarthy god engaged in a frenzied dance, crouching on his hams like a tailor, sweating like a pig, and bounding about with an agility which testified to the strength and elasticity of his divine legs.

The Baganda of Central Africa believed in a god of Lake Nyanza, who sometimes took up his abode in a man or woman. The incarnate god was much feared by all the people, including the king and the chiefs. When the mystery of incarnation had taken place, the man, or rather the god, removed about a mile and a half from the margin of the lake, and there awaited the appearance of the new moon before he engaged in his sacred duties. From the moment that the crescent moon appeared faintly in the sky, the king and all his subjects were at the command of the divine man, or *Lubare* (god), as he was called, who reigned supreme not only in matters of faith and ritual, but also in questions of war and state policy. He was consulted as an oracle ; by his word he could inflict or heal sickness, withhold rain, and cause famine. Large presents were made him when his advice was sought. The chief of Urua, a large region to the west of Lake Tanganyika, " arrogates to himself divine honours and power and pretends to abstain from food for days without feeling its necessity ; and, indeed, declares that as a god he is altogether above requiring food and only eats, drinks, and smokes for the pleasure it affords him." Among the Gallas, when a woman grows tired of the cares of housekeeping, she begins to talk incoherently and to demean herself extravagantly. This is a sign of the descent of the holy spirit Callo upon her. Immediately her husband prostrates himself and adores her ; she ceases to bear the humble title of wife and is called " Lord " ; domestic duties have no further claim on her, and her will is a divine law.

The king of Loango is honoured by his people " as though he were a god ; and he is called Sambee and Pango, which mean god. They believe that he can let them have rain when he likes ; and once a year,

in December, which is the time they want rain, the people come to
beg of him to grant it to them." On this occasion the king, standing
on his throne, shoots an arrow into the air, which is supposed to bring
on rain. Much the same is said of the king of Mombasa. Down to a
few years ago, when his spiritual reign on earth was brought to an
abrupt end by the carnal weapons of English marines and bluejackets,
the king of Benin was the chief object of worship in his dominions.
" He occupies a higher post here than the Pope does in Catholic Europe ;
for he is not only God's vicegerent upon earth, but a god himself, whose
subjects both obey and adore him as such, although I believe their
adoration to arise rather from fear than love." The king of Iddah
told the English officers of the Niger Expedition, " God made me
after his own image ; I am all the same as God ; and he appointed me
a king."

A peculiarly bloodthirsty monarch of Burma, by name Badonsachen, whose very countenance reflected the inbred ferocity of his
nature, and under whose reign more victims perished by the executioner
than by the common enemy, conceived the notion that he was something more than mortal, and that this high distinction had been granted
him as a reward for his numerous good works. Accordingly he laid
aside the title of king and aimed at making himself a god. With this
view, and in imitation of Buddha, who, before being advanced to the
rank of a divinity, had quitted his royal palace and seraglio and retired
from the world, Badonsachen withdrew from his palace to an immense
pagoda, the largest in the empire, which he had been engaged in con-
structing for many years. Here he held conferences with the most
learned monks, in which he sought to persuade them that the five
thousand years assigned for the observance of the law of Buddha were
now elapsed, and that he himself was the god who was destined to
appear after that period, and to abolish the old law by substituting
his own. But to his great mortification many of the monks undertook to demonstrate the contrary ; and this disappointment, combined with his love of power and his impatience under the restraints of
an ascetic life, quickly disabused him of his imaginary godhead, and
drove him back to his palace and his harem. The king of Siam " is
venerated equally with a divinity. His subjects ought not to look
him in the face ; they prostrate themselves before him when he passes,
and appear before him on their knees, their elbows resting on the
ground." There is a special language devoted to his sacred person
and attributes, and it must be used by all who speak to or of him.
Even the natives have difficulty in mastering this peculiar vocabulary.
The hairs of the monarch's head, the soles of his feet, the breath of his
body, indeed every single detail of his person, both outward and inward, have particular names. When he eats or drinks, sleeps or walks,
a special word indicates that these acts are being performed by the
sovereign, and such words cannot possibly be applied to the acts of any
other person whatever. There is no word in the Siamese language
by which any creature of higher rank or greater dignity than a monarch

can be described ; and the missionaries, when they speak of God, are forced to use the native word for king.

But perhaps no country in the world has been so prolific of human gods as India ; nowhere has the divine grace been poured out in a more liberal measure on all classes of society from kings down to milkmen. Thus amongst the Todas, a pastoral people of the Neilgherry Hills of Southern India, the dairy is a sanctuary, and the milkman who attends to it has been described as a god. On being asked whether the Todas salute the sun, one of these divine milkmen replied, " Those poor fellows do so, but I," tapping his chest, " I, a god ! why should I salute the sun ? " Every one, even his own father, prostrates himself before the milkman, and no one would dare to refuse him anything. No human being, except another milkman, may touch him ; and he gives oracles to all who consult him, speaking with the voice of a god.

Further, in India " every king is regarded as little short of a present god." The Hindoo law-book of Manu goes farther and says that " even an infant king must not be despised from an idea that he is a mere mortal ; for he is a great deity in human form." There is said to have been a sect in Orissa some years ago who worshipped the late Queen Victoria in her lifetime as their chief divinity. And to this day in India all living persons remarkable for great strength or valour or for supposed miraculous powers run the risk of being worshipped as gods. Thus, a sect in the Punjaub worshipped a deity whom they called Nikkal Sen. This Nikkal Sen was no other than the redoubted General Nicholson, and nothing that the general could do or say damped the ardour of his adorers. The more he punished them, the greater grew the religious awe with which they worshipped him. At Benares not many years ago a celebrated deity was incarnate in the person of a Hindoo gentleman who rejoiced in the euphonious name of Swami Bhaskaranandaji Saraswati, and looked uncommonly like the late Cardinal Manning, only more ingenuous. His eyes beamed with kindly human interest, and he took what is described as an innocent pleasure in the divine honours paid him by his confiding worshippers.

At Chinchvad, a small town about ten miles from Poona in Western India, there lives a family of whom one in each generation is believed by a large proportion of the Mahrattas to be an incarnation of the elephant-headed god Gunputty. That celebrated deity was first made flesh about the year 1640 in the person of a Brahman of Poona, by name Mooraba Gosseyn, who sought to work out his salvation by abstinence, mortification, and prayer. His piety had its reward. The god himself appeared to him in a vision of the night and promised that a portion of his, that is, of Gunputty's holy spirit should abide with him and with his seed after him even to the seventh generation. The divine promise was fulfilled. Seven successive incarnations, transmitted from father to son, manifested the light of Gunputty to a dark world. The last of the direct line, a heavy-looking god with very weak eyes, died in the year 1810. But the cause of truth was too sacred, and the value of the church property too considerable, to allow the Brahmans

to contemplate with equanimity the unspeakable loss that would be
sustained by a world which knew not Gunputty. Accordingly they
sought and found a holy vessel in whom the divine spirit of the master
had revealed itself anew, and the revelation has been happily continued
in an unbroken succession of vessels from that time to this. But a
mysterious law of spiritual economy, whose operation in the history of
religion we may deplore though we cannot alter, has decreed that the
miracles wrought by the god-man in these degenerate days cannot
compare with those which were wrought by his predecessors in days
gone by ; and it is even reported that the only sign vouchsafed by him
to the present generation of vipers is the miracle of feeding the multitude
whom he annually entertains to dinner at Chinchvad.

A Hindoo sect, which has many representatives in Bombay and
Central India, holds that its spiritual chiefs or Maharajas, as they are
called, are representatives or even actual incarnations on earth of the
god Krishna. And as Krishna looks down from heaven with most
favour on such as minister to the wants of his successors and vicars on
earth, a peculiar rite called Self-devotion has been instituted, whereby
his faithful worshippers make over their bodies, their souls, and,
what is perhaps still more important, their worldly substance to his
adorable incarnations ; and women are taught to believe that the
highest bliss for themselves and their families is to be attained by
yielding themselves to the embraces of those beings in whom the
divine nature mysteriously coexists with the form and even the appetites
of true humanity.

Christianity itself has not uniformly escaped the taint of these unhappy delusions ; indeed it has often been sullied by the extravagances
of vain pretenders to a divinity equal to or even surpassing that of its
great Founder. In the second century Montanus the Phrygian claimed
to be the incarnate Trinity, uniting in his single person God the
Father, God the Son, and God the Holy Ghost. Nor is this an isolated
case, the exorbitant pretension of a single ill-balanced mind. From
the earliest times down to the present day many sects have believed
that Christ, nay God himself, is incarnate in every fully initiated
Christian, and they have carried this belief to its logical conclusion by
adoring each other. Tertullian records that this was done by his
fellow-Christians at Carthage in the second century ; the disciples of
St. Columba worshipped him as an embodiment of Christ ; and in the
eighth century Elipandus of Toledo spoke of Christ as " a god among
gods," meaning that all believers were gods just as truly as Jesus
himself. The adoration of each other was customary among the
Albigenses, and is noticed hundreds of times in the records of the
Inquisition at Toulouse in the early part of the fourteenth century.

In the thirteenth century there arose a sect called the Brethren
and Sisters of the Free Spirit, who held that by long and assiduous
contemplation any man might be united to the deity in an ineffable
manner and become one with the source and parent of all things, and
that he who had thus ascended to God and been absorbed in his beatific

essence, actually formed part of the Godhead, was the Son of God in the same sense and manner with Christ himself, and enjoyed thereby a glorious immunity from the trammels of all laws human and divine. Inwardly transported by this blissful persuasion, though outwardly presenting in their aspect and manners a shocking air of lunacy and distraction, the sectaries roamed from place to place, attired in the most fantastic apparel and begging their bread with wild shouts and clamour, spurning indignantly every kind of honest labour and industry as an obstacle to divine contemplation and to the ascent of the soul towards the Father of spirits. In all their excursions they were followed by women with whom they lived on terms of the closest familiarity. Those of them who conceived they had made the greatest proficiency in the higher spiritual life dispensed with the use of clothes altogether in their assemblies, looking upon decency and modesty as marks of inward corruption, characteristics of a soul that still grovelled under the dominion of the flesh and had not yet been elevated into communion with the divine spirit, its centre and source. Sometimes their progress towards this mystic communion was accelerated by the Inquisition, and they expired in the flames, not merely with unclouded serenity, but with the most triumphant feelings of cheerfulness and joy.

About the year 1830 there appeared, in one of the States of the American Union bordering on Kentucky, an impostor who declared that he was the Son of God, the Saviour of mankind, and that he had reappeared on earth to recall the impious, the unbelieving, and sinners to their duty. He protested that if they did not mend their ways within a certain time, he would give the signal, and in a moment the world would crumble to ruins. These extravagant pretensions were received with favour even by persons of wealth and position in society. At last a German humbly besought the new Messiah to announce the dreadful catastrophe to his fellow-countrymen in the German language, as they did not understand English, and it seemed a pity that they should be damned merely on that account. The would-be Saviour in reply confessed with great candour that he did not know German. " What ! " retorted the German, " you the Son of God, and don't speak all languages, and don't even know German ? Come, come ; you are a knave, a hypocrite, and a madman. Bedlam is the place for you." The spectators laughed, and went away ashamed of their credulity.

Sometimes, at the death of the human incarnation, the divine spirit transmigrates into another man. The Buddhist Tartars believe in a great number of living Buddhas, who officiate as Grand Lamas at the head of the most important monasteries. When one of these Grand Lamas dies his disciples do not sorrow, for they know that he will soon reappear, being born in the form of an infant. Their only anxiety is to discover the place of his birth. If at this time they see a rainbow they take it as a sign sent them by the departed Lama to guide them to his cradle. Sometimes the divine infant himself reveals his identity. " I am the Grand Lama," he says, " the living Buddha of such and such a temple. Take me to my old monastery. I am its immortal head." In whatever way the birthplace of the Buddha is revealed, whether by the Buddha's own avowal or by the sign in the sky, tents are struck, and the joyful pilgrims, often headed by the king or one of the most illustrious of the royal family, set forth to find and bring home the infant god. Generally he is born in Tibet, the holy land, and to reach him the caravan has often to traverse the most frightful deserts. When at last they find the child they fall down and worship him. Before, however, he is acknowledged as the Grand Lama whom they seek he must satisfy them of his identity. He is asked the name of the monastery of which he claims to be the head, how far off it is, and how many monks live in it ; he must also describe the habits of the deceased Grand Lama and the manner of his death. Then various articles, as prayer-books, tea-pots, and cups, are placed before him, and he has to point out those used by himself in his previous life. If he does so without a mistake his claims are admitted, and he is conducted in triumph to the monastery. At the head of all the Lamas is the Dalai Lama of Lhasa, the Rome of Tibet. He is regarded as a living god, and at death his divine and immortal spirit is born again in a child. According to some accounts the mode of discovering the Dalai Lama is similar to the method, already described, of discovering an ordinary Grand Lama. Other accounts speak of an election by drawing lots from a golden jar. Wherever he is born, the trees and plants put forth green leaves : at his bidding flowers bloom and springs of water rise ; and his presence diffuses heavenly blessings.

But he is by no means the only man who poses as a god in these regions. A register of all the incarnate gods in the Chinese empire is kept in the *Li fan yüan* or Colonial Office at Peking. The number of gods who have thus taken out a licence is one hundred and sixty. Tibet is blessed with thirty of them, Northern Mongolia rejoices in nineteen, and Southern Mongolia basks in the sunshine of no less than fifty-seven. The Chinese government, with a paternal solicitude for the welfare of its subjects, forbids the gods on the register to be reborn anywhere but in Tibet. They fear lest the birth of a god in Mongolia should have serious political consequences by stirring the dormant patriotism and warlike spirit of the Mongols, who might rally round an ambitious native deity of royal lineage and seek to win for him, at the point of the sword, a temporal as well as a spiritual kingdom. But besides these public or licensed gods there are a great many little private gods, or unlicensed practitioners of divinity, who work miracles and bless their people in holes and corners ; and of late years the Chinese government has winked at the rebirth of these pettifogging deities outside of Tibet. However, once they are born, the government keeps its eye on them as well as on the regular practitioners, and if any of them misbehaves he is promptly degraded, banished to a distant monastery, and strictly forbidden ever to be born again in the flesh.

From our survey of the religious position occupied by the king in rude societies we may infer that the claim to divine and supernatural powers put forward by the monarchs of great historical empires like those of Egypt, Mexico, and Peru, was not the simple outcome of inflated vanity or the empty expression of a grovelling adulation ; it was merely a survival and extension of the old savage apotheosis of living kings. Thus, for example, as children of the Sun the Incas of Peru were revered like gods ; they could do no wrong, and no one dreamed of offending against the person, honour, or property of the monarch or of any of the royal race. Hence, too, the Incas did not, like most people, look on sickness as an evil. They considered it a messenger sent from their father the Sun to call them to come and rest with him in heaven. Therefore the usual words in which an Inca announced his approaching end were these : " My father calls me to come and rest with him." They would not oppose their father's will by offering sacrifice for recovery, but openly declared that he had called them to his rest. Issuing from the sultry valleys upon the lofty tableland of the Colombian Andes, the Spanish conquerors were astonished to find, in contrast to the savage hordes they had left in the sweltering jungles below, a people enjoying a fair degree of civilisation, practising agriculture, and living under a government which Humboldt has compared to the theocracies of Tibet and Japan. These were the Chibchas, Muyscas, or Mozcas, divided into two kingdoms, with capitals at Bogota and Tunja, but united apparently in spiritual allegiance to the high pontiff of Sogamozo or Iraca. By a long and ascetic novitiate, this ghostly ruler was reputed to have acquired such sanctity that the waters and the rain obeyed him, and the weather depended on his will. The Mexican kings at their accession, as we have seen, took an oath that they would make the sun to shine, the clouds to give rain, the rivers to flow, and the earth to bring forth fruits in abundance. We are told that Montezuma, the last king of Mexico, was worshipped by his people as a god.

The early Babylonian kings, from the time of Sargon I. till the fourth dynasty of Ur or later, claimed to be gods in their lifetime. The monarchs of the fourth dynasty of Ur in particular had temples built in their honour ; they set up their statues in various sanctuaries and commanded the people to sacrifice to them ; the eighth month was especially dedicated to the kings, and sacrifices were offered to them at the new moon and on the fifteenth of each month. Again, the Parthian monarchs of the Arsacid house styled themselves brothers of the sun and moon and were worshipped as deities. It was esteemed sacrilege to strike even a private member of the Arsacid family in a brawl.

The kings of Egypt were deified in their lifetime, sacrifices were offered to them, and their worship was celebrated in special temples and by special priests. Indeed the worship of the kings sometimes cast that of the gods into the shade. Thus in the reign of Merenra a high official declared that he had built many holy places in order that the spirits of the king, the ever-living Merenra, might be invoked

" more than all the gods." " It has never been doubted that the king claimed actual divinity ; he was the ' great god,' the ' golden Horus,' and son of Ra. He claimed authority not only over Egypt, but over ' all lands and nations,' ' the whole world in its length and its breadth, the east and the west,' ' the entire compass of the great circuit of the sun,' ' the sky and what is in it, the earth and all that is upon it,' ' every creature that walks upon two or upon four legs, all that fly or flutter, the whole world offers her productions to him.' Whatever in fact might be asserted of the Sun-god, was dogmatically predicable of the king of Egypt. His titles were directly derived from those of the Sun-god." " In the course of his existence," we are told, " the king of Egypt exhausted all the possible conceptions of divinity which the Egyptians had framed for themselves. A superhuman god by his birth and by his royal office, he became the deified man after his death. Thus all that was known of the divine was summed up in him."

We have now completed our sketch, for it is no more than a sketch, of the evolution of that sacred kingship which attained its highest form, its most absolute expression, in the monarchies of Peru and Egypt. Historically, the institution appears to have originated in the order of public magicians or medicine-men ; logically it rests on a mistaken deduction from the association of ideas. Men mistook the order of their ideas for the order of nature, and hence imagined that the control which they have, or seem to have, over their thoughts, permitted them to exercise a corresponding control over things. The men who for one reason or another, because of the strength or the weakness of their natural parts, were supposed to possess these magical powers in the highest degree, were gradually marked off from their fellows and became a separate class, who were destined to exercise a most far-reaching influence on the political, religious, and intellectual evolution of mankind. Social progress, as we know, consists mainly in a successive differentiation of functions, or, in simpler language, a division of labour. The work which in primitive society is done by all alike and by all equally ill, or nearly so, is gradually distributed among different classes of workers and executed more and more per- fectly ; and so far as the products, material or immaterial, of this specialised labour are shared by all, the whole community benefits by the increasing specialisation. Now magicians or medicine-men appear to constitute the oldest artificial or professional class in the evolution of society. For sorcerers are found in every savage tribe known to us ; and among the lowest savages, such as the Australian aborigines, they are the only professional class that exists. As time goes on, and the process of differentiation continues, the order of medicine-men is itself subdivided into such classes as the healers of disease, the makers of rain, and so forth ; while the most powerful member of the order wins for himself a position as chief and gradually develops into a sacred king, his old magical functions falling more and more into the back- ground and being exchanged for priestly or even divine duties, in proportion as magic is slowly ousted by religion. Still later, a partition is effected between the civil and the religious aspect of the kingship, the temporal power being committed to one man and the spiritual to another. Meanwhile the magicians, who may be repressed but cannot be extirpated by the predominance of religion, still addict themselves to their old occult arts in preference to the newer ritual of sacrifice and prayer ; and in time the more sagacious of their number perceive the fallacy of magic and hit upon a more effectual mode of manipulating the forces of nature for the good of man ; in short, they abandon sorcery for science. I am far from affirming that the course of development has everywhere rigidly followed these lines : it has doubtless varied greatly in different societies. I merely mean to indicate in the broadest outline what I conceive to have been its general trend. Regarded from the industrial point of view the evolution has been from uniformity to diversity of function : regarded from the political point of view, it has been from democracy to despotism. With the later history of monarchy, especially with the decay of despotism and its displacement by forms of government better adapted to the higher needs of humanity, we are not concerned in this enquiry : our theme is the growth, not the decay, of a great and, in its time, beneficent institution.

CHAPTER VIII

DEPARTMENTAL KINGS OF NATURE

THE preceding investigation has proved that the same union of sacred functions with a royal title which meets us in the King of the Wood at Nemi, the Sacrificial King at Rome, and the magistrate called the King at Athens, occurs frequently outside the limits of classical antiquity and is a common feature of societies at all stages from barbarism to civilisation. Further, it appears that the royal priest is often a king, not only in name but in fact, swaying the sceptre as well as the crosier. All this confirms the traditional view of the origin of the titular and priestly kings in the republics of ancient Greece and Italy. At least by showing that the combination of spiritual and temporal power, of which Graeco-Italian tradition preserved the memory, has actually existed in many places, we have obviated any suspicion of improbability that might have attached to the tradition. Therefore we may now fairly ask, May not the King of the Wood have had an origin like that which a probable tradition assigns to the Sacrificial King of Rome and the titular King of Athens ? In other words, may not his predecessors in office have been a line of kings whom a republican revolution stripped of their political power, leaving them only their religious functions and the shadow of a crown ? There are at least two reasons for answering this question in the negative. One reason is drawn from the abode of the priest of Nemi ; the other from his title, the King of the Wood. If his predecessors had been kings in the ordinary sense, he would surely have been found residing, like the fallen kings of Rome and Athens, in the city of which the sceptre had passed from him.   This city must have been Aricia, for there was none nearer.   But Aricia was three miles off from his forest sanctuary by the lake shore.   If he reigned, it was not in the city, but in the greenwood.   Again his title, King of the Wood, hardly allows us to suppose that he had ever been a king in the common sense of the word. More likely he was a king of nature, and of a special side of nature, namely, the woods from which he took his title.   If we could find instances of what we may call departmental kings of nature, that is of persons supposed to rule over particular elements or aspects of nature, they would probably present a closer analogy to the King of the Wood than the divine kings we have been hitherto considering, whose control of nature is general rather than special.   Instances of such departmental kings are not wanting.

On a hill at Bomma near the mouth of the Congo dwells Namvulu Vumu, King of the Rain and Storm.   Of some of the tribes on the Upper Nile we are told that they have no kings in the common sense ; the only persons whom they acknowledge as such are the Kings of the Rain, *Mata Kodou*, who are credited with the power of giving rain at the proper time, that is, in the rainy season.   Before the rains begin to fall at the end of March the country is a parched and arid desert ; and the cattle, which form the people's chief wealth, perish for lack of grass.   So, when the end of March draws on, each householder betakes himself to the King of the Rain and offers him a cow that he may make the blessed waters of heaven to drip on the brown and withered pastures. If no shower falls, the people assemble and demand that the king shall give them rain ; and if the sky still continues cloudless, they rip up his belly, in which he is believed to keep the storms.   Amongst the Bari tribe one of these Rain Kings made rain by sprinkling water on the ground out of a handbell.

Among tribes on the outskirts of Abyssinia a similar office exists and has been thus described by an observer : " The priesthood of the Alfai, as he is called by the Barea and Kunama, is a remarkable one ; he is believed to be able to make rain.   This office formerly existed among the Algeds and appears to be still common to the Nuba negroes.   The Alfai of the Barea, who is also consulted by the northern Kunama, lives near Tembadere on a mountain alone with his family. The people bring him tribute in the form of clothes and fruits, and cultivate for him a large field of his own.   He is a kind of king, and his office passes by inheritance to his brother or sister's son.   He is supposed to conjure down rain and to drive away the locusts.   But if he disappoints the people's expectation and a great drought arises in the land, the Alfai is stoned to death, and his nearest relations are obliged to cast the first stone at him.   When we passed through the country, the office of Alfai was still held by an old man ; but I heard that rainmaking had proved too dangerous for him and that he had renounced his office."

In the backwoods of Cambodia live two mysterious sovereigns known as the King of the Fire and the King of the Water. Their fame is spread all over the south of the great Indo-Chinese peninsula ; but only a faint echo of it has reached the West. Down to a few years ago no European, so far as is known, had ever seen either of them ; and their very existence might have passed for a fable, were it not that till lately communications were regularly maintained between them and the King of Cambodia, who year by year exchanged presents with them. Their royal functions are of a purely mystic or spiritual order ; they have no political authority ; they are simple peasants, living by the sweat of their brow and the offerings of the faithful. According to one account they live in absolute solitude, never meeting each other and never seeing a human face. They inhabit successively seven towers perched upon seven mountains, and every year they pass from one tower to another. People come furtively and cast within their reach what is needful for their subsistence. The kingship lasts seven years, the time necessary to inhabit all the towers successively ; but many die before their time is out. The offices are hereditary in one or (according to others) two royal families, who enjoy high consideration, have revenues assigned to them, and are exempt from the necessity of tilling the ground. But naturally the dignity is not coveted, and when a vacancy occurs, all eligible men (they must be strong and have children) flee and hide themselves. Another account, admitting the reluctance of the hereditary candidates to accept the crown, does not countenance the report of their hermit-like seclusion in the seven towers. For it represents the people as prostrating themselves before the mystic kings whenever they appear in public, it being thought that a terrible hurricane would burst over the country if this mark of homage were omitted. Like many other sacred kings, of whom we shall read in the sequel, the Kings of Fire and Water are not allowed to die a natural death, for that would lower their reputation. Accordingly when one of them is seriously ill, the elders hold a consultation and if they think he cannot recover they stab him to death. His body is burned and the ashes are piously collected and publicly honoured for five years. Part of them is given to the widow, and she keeps them in an urn, which she must carry on her back when she goes to weep on her husband's grave.

We are told that the Fire King, the more important of the two, whose supernatural powers have never been questioned, officiates at marriages, festivals, and sacrifices in honour of the *Yan* or spirit. On these occasions a special place is set apart for him ; and the path by which he approaches is spread with white cotton cloths. A reason for confining the royal dignity to the same family is that this family is in possession of certain famous talismans which would lose their virtue or disappear if they passed out of the family. These talismans are three : the fruit of a creeper called *Cui*, gathered ages ago at the time of the last deluge, but still fresh and green ; a rattan, also very old but bearing flowers that never fade ; and lastly, a sword containing a *Yan* or spirit, who guards it constantly and works miracles with it. The spirit is said to be that of a slave, whose blood chanced to fall upon the blade while it was being forged, and who died a voluntary death to expiate his involuntary offence.   By means of the two former talismans the Water King can raise a flood that would drown the whole earth.   If the Fire King draws the magic sword a few inches from its sheath, the sun is hidden and men and beasts fall into a profound sleep ; were he to draw it quite out of the scabbard, the world would come to an end.   To this wondrous brand sacrifices of buffaloes, pigs, fowls, and ducks are offered for rain.   It is kept swathed in cotton and silk ; and amongst the annual presents sent by the King of Cambodia were rich stuffs to wrap the sacred sword.

Contrary to the common usage of the country, which is to bury the dead, the bodies of both these mystic monarchs are burnt, but their nails and some of their teeth and bones are religiously preserved as amulets.   It is while the corpse is being consumed on the pyre that the kinsmen of the deceased magician flee to the forest and hide themselves, for fear of being elevated to the invidious dignity which he has just vacated.   The people go and search for them, and the first whose lurking place they discover is made King of Fire or Water.

These, then, are examples of what I have called departmental kings of nature.   But it is a far cry to Italy from the forests of Cambodia and the sources of the Nile.   And though Kings of Rain, Water, and Fire have been found, we have still to discover a King of the Wood to match the Arician priest who bore that title.   Perhaps we shall find him nearer home.

CHAPTER IX

THE WORSHIP OF TREES

§ 1. *Tree-spirits.*—In the religious history of the Aryan race in Europe the worship of trees has played an important part.   Nothing could be more natural.   For at the dawn of history Europe was covered with immense primaeval forests, in which the scattered clearings must have appeared like islets in an ocean of green.   Down to the first century before our era the Hercynian forest stretched eastward from the Rhine for a distance at once vast and unknown ; Germans whom Caesar questioned had travelled for two months through it without reaching the end.   Four centuries later it was visited by the Emperor Julian, and the solitude, the gloom, the silence of the forest appear to have made a deep impression on his sensitive nature.   He declared that he knew nothing like it in the Roman empire.   In our own country the wealds of Kent, Surrey, and Sussex are remnants of the great forest of Anderida, which once clothed the whole of the south-eastern portion of the island.   Westward it seems to have stretched till it joined another forest that extended from Hampshire to Devon.   In the reign of Henry II. the citizens of London still hunted the wild bull and the boar in the woods of Hampstead.   Even under the later Plantagenets the royal forests were sixty-eight in number.   In the forest of Arden it was said that down to modern times a squirrel might leap from tree to tree for nearly the whole length of Warwickshire.   The excavation of ancient pile-villages in the valley of the Po has shown that long before the rise and probably the foundation of Rome the north of Italy was covered with dense woods of elms, chestnuts, and especially of oaks.   Archaeology is here confirmed by history ; for classical writers contain many references to Italian forests which have now disappeared.   As late as the fourth century before our era Rome was divided from central Etruria by the dreaded Ciminian forest, which Livy compares to the woods of Germany.   No merchant, if we may trust the Roman historian, had ever penetrated its pathless solitudes : and it was deemed a most daring feat when a Roman general, after sending two scouts to explore its intricacies, led his army into the forest and, making his way to a ridge of the wooded mountains, looked down on the rich Etrurian fields spread out below.   In Greece beautiful woods of pine, oak, and other trees still linger on the slopes of the high Arcadian mountains, still adorn with their verdure the deep gorge through which the Ladon hurries to join the sacred Alpheus, and were still, down to a few years ago, mirrored in the dark blue waters of the lonely lake of Pheneus ; but they are mere fragments of the forests which clothed great tracts in antiquity, and which at a more remote epoch may have spanned the Greek peninsula from sea to sea.

From an examination of the Teutonic words for " temple " Grimm has made it probable that amongst the Germans the oldest sanctuaries were natural woods.   However that may be, tree-worship is well attested for all the great European families of the Aryan stock. Amongst the Celts the oak-worship of the Druids is familiar to every one, and their old word for a sanctuary seems to be identical in origin and meaning with the Latin *nemus*, a grove or woodland glade, which still survives in the name of Nemi.   Sacred groves were common among the ancient Germans, and tree-worship is hardly extinct amongst their descendants at the present day.   How serious that worship was in former times may be gathered from the ferocious penalty appointed by the old German laws for such as dared to peel the bark of a standing tree.   The culprit's navel was to be cut out and nailed to the part of the tree which he had peeled, and he was to be driven round and round the tree till all his guts were wound about its trunk.   The intention of the punishment clearly was to replace the dead bark by a living substitute taken from the culprit ; it was a life for a life, the life of a man for the life of a tree.   At Upsala, the old religious capital of Sweden, there was a sacred grove in which every tree was regarded as divine.   The heathen Slavs worshipped trees and groves.   The Lithuanians were not converted to Christianity till towards the close of the fourteenth century, and amongst them at the date of their conversion the worship of trees was prominent.   Some of them revered remarkable oaks and other great shady trees, from which they received oracular responses.   Some maintained holy groves about their villages or houses, where even to break a twig would have been a sin. They thought that he who cut a bough in such a grove either died suddenly or was crippled in one of his limbs. Proofs of the prevalence of tree-worship in ancient Greece and Italy are abundant. In the sanctuary of Aesculapius at Cos, for example, it was forbidden to cut down the cypress-trees under a penalty of a thousand drachms. But nowhere, perhaps, in the ancient world was this antique form of religion better preserved than in the heart of the great metropolis itself. In the Forum, the busy centre of Roman life, the sacred fig-tree of Romulus was worshipped down to the days of the empire, and the withering of its trunk was enough to spread consternation through the city. Again, on the slope of the Palatine Hill grew a cornel-tree which was esteemed one of the most sacred objects in Rome. Whenever the tree appeared to a passer-by to be drooping, he set up a hue and cry which was echoed by the people in the street, and soon a crowd might be seen running helter-skelter from all sides with buckets of water, as if (says Plutarch) they were hastening to put out a fire.

Among the tribes of the Finnish-Ugrian stock in Europe the heathen worship was performed for the most part in sacred groves, which were always enclosed with a fence. Such a grove often consisted merely of a glade or clearing with a few trees dotted about, upon which in former times the skins of the sacrificial victims were hung. The central point of the grove, at least among the tribes of the Volga, was the sacred tree, beside which everything else sank into insignificance. Before it the worshippers assembled and the priest offered his prayers, at its roots the victim was sacrificed, and its boughs sometimes served as a pulpit. No wood might be hewn and no branch broken in the grove, and women were generally forbidden to enter it.

But it is necessary to examine in some detail the notions on which the worship of trees and plants is based. To the savage the world in general is animate, and trees and plants are no exception to the rule. He thinks that they have souls like his own, and he treats them accordingly. "They say," writes the ancient vegetarian Porphyry, "that primitive men led an unhappy life, for their superstition did not stop at animals but extended even to plants. For why should the slaughter of an ox or a sheep be a greater wrong than the felling of a fir or an oak, seeing that a soul is implanted in these trees also?" Similarly, the Hidatsa Indians of North America believe that every natural object has its spirit, or to speak more properly, its shade. To these shades some consideration or respect is due, but not equally to all. For example, the shade of the cottonwood, the greatest tree in the valley of the Upper Missouri, is supposed to possess an intelligence which, if properly approached, may help the Indians in certain undertakings; but the shades of shrubs and grasses are of little account. When the Missouri, swollen by a freshet in spring, carries away part of its banks and sweeps some tall tree into its current, it is said that the spirit of the tree cries, while the roots still cling to the land and until the trunk falls with a splash into the stream.

Formerly the Indians considered it wrong to fell one of these giants, and when large logs were needed they made use only of trees which had fallen of themselves. Till lately some of the more credulous old men declared that many of the misfortunes of their people were caused by this modern disregard for the rights of the living cottonwood. The Iroquois believed that each species of tree, shrub, plant, and herb had its own spirit, and to these spirits it was their custom to return thanks. The Wanika of Eastern Africa fancy that every tree, and especially every coco-nut tree, has its spirit ; " the destruction of a cocoa-nut tree is regarded as equivalent to matricide, because that tree gives them life and nourishment, as a mother does her child." Siamese monks, believing that there are souls everywhere, and that to destroy anything whatever is forcibly to dispossess a soul, will not break a branch of a tree, " as they will not break the arm of an innocent person." These monks, of course, are Buddhists. But Buddhist animism is not a philosophical theory. It is simply a common savage dogma incorporated in the system of an historical religion. To suppose, with Benfey and others, that the theories of animism and transmigration current among rude peoples of Asia are derived from Buddhism, is to reverse the facts.

Sometimes it is only particular sorts of trees that are supposed to be tenanted by spirits. At Grbalj in Dalmatia it is said that among great beeches, oaks, and other trees there are some that are endowed with shades or souls, and whoever fells one of them must die on the spot, or at least live an invalid for the rest of his days. If a woodman fears that a tree which he has felled is one of this sort, he must cut off the head of a live hen on the stump of the tree with the very same axe with which he cut down the tree. This will protect him from all harm, even if the tree be one of the animated kind. The silk-cotton trees, which rear their enormous trunks to a stupendous height, far out-topping all the other trees of the forest, are regarded with reverence throughout West Africa, from the Senegal to the Niger, and are believed to be the abode of a god or spirit. Among the Ewe-speaking peoples of the Slave Coast the indwelling god of this giant of the forest goes by the name of Huntin. Trees in which he specially dwells—for it is not every silk-cotton tree that he thus honours—are surrounded by a girdle of palm-leaves ; and sacrifices of fowls, and occasionally of human beings, are fastened to the trunk or laid against the foot of the tree. A tree distinguished by a girdle of palm-leaves may not be cut down or injured in any way ; and even silk-cotton trees which are not supposed to be animated by Huntin may not be felled unless the woodman first offers a sacrifice of fowls and palm-oil to purge himself of the proposed sacrilege. To omit the sacrifice is an offence which may be punished with death. Among the Kangra mountains of the Punjaub a girl used to be annually sacrificed to an old cedar-tree, the families of the village taking it in turn to supply the victim. The tree was cut down not very many years ago.

If trees are animate, they are necessarily sensitive and the cutting of them down becomes a delicate surgical operation, which must be performed with as tender a regard as possible for the feelings of the sufferers, who otherwise may turn and rend the careless or bungling operator. When an oak is being felled " it gives a kind of shriekes or groanes, that may be heard a mile off, as if it were the genius of the oake lamenting. E. Wyld, Esq., hath heard it severall times." The Ojebways " very seldom cut down green or living trees, from the idea that it puts them to pain, and some of their medicine-men profess to have heard the wailing of the trees under the axe." Trees that bleed and utter cries of pain or indignation when they are hacked or burned occur very often in Chinese books, even in Standard Histories. Old peasants in some parts of Austria still believe that forest-trees are animate, and will not allow an incision to be made in the bark without special cause ; they have heard from their fathers that the tree feels the cut not less than a wounded man his hurt. In felling a tree they beg its pardon. It is said that in the Upper Palatinate also old woodmen still secretly ask a fine, sound tree to forgive them before they cut it down. So in Jarkino the woodman craves pardon of the tree he fells. Before the Ilocanes of Luzon cut down trees in the virgin forest or on the mountains, they recite some verses to the following effect : " Be not uneasy, my friend, though we fell what we have been ordered to fell." This they do in order not to draw down on themselves the hatred of the spirits who live in the trees, and who are apt to avenge themselves by visiting with grievous sickness such as injure them wantonly. The Basoga of Central Africa think that, when a tree is cut down, the angry spirit which inhabits it may cause the death of the chief and his family. To prevent this disaster they consult a medicine-man before they fell a tree. If the man of skill gives leave to proceed, the woodman first offers a fowl and a goat to the tree ; then as soon as he has given the first blow with the axe, he applies his mouth to the cut and sucks some of the sap. In this way he forms a brotherhood with the tree, just as two men become blood-brothers by sucking each other's blood. After that he can cut down his tree-brother with impunity.

But the spirits of vegetation are not always treated with deference and respect. If fair words and kind treatment do not move them, stronger measures are sometimes resorted to. The durian-tree of the East Indies, whose smooth stem often shoots up to a height of eighty or ninety feet without sending out a branch, bears a fruit of the most delicious flavour and the most disgusting stench. The Malays cultivate the tree for the sake of its fruit, and have been known to resort to a peculiar ceremony for the purpose of stimulating its fertility. Near Jugra in Selangor there is a small grove of durian-trees, and on a specially chosen day the villagers used to assemble in it. Thereupon one of the local sorcerers would take a hatchet and deliver several shrewd blows on the trunk of the most barren of the trees, saying, " Will you now bear fruit or not ? If you do not, I shall fell you." To this the tree replied through the mouth of another man

I

who had climbed a mangostin-tree hard by (the durian-tree being unclimbable), " Yes, I will now bear fruit ; I beg you not to fell me." So in Japan to make trees bear fruit two men go into an orchard. One of them climbs up a tree and the other stands at the foot with an axe. The man with the axe asks the tree whether it will yield a good crop next year and threatens to cut it down if it does not. To this the man among the branches replies on behalf of the tree that it will bear abundantly. Odd as this mode of horticulture may seem to us, it has its exact parallels in Europe. On Christmas Eve many a South Slavonian and Bulgarian peasant swings an axe threateningly against a barren fruit-tree, while another man standing by intercedes for the menaced tree, saying, " Do not cut it down ; it will soon bear fruit." Thrice the axe is swung, and thrice the impending blow is arrested at the entreaty of the intercessor. After that the frightened tree will certainly bear fruit next year.

The conception of trees and plants as animated beings naturally results in treating them as male and female, who can be married to each other in a real, and not merely a figurative or poetical, sense of the word. The notion is not purely fanciful, for plants like animals have their sexes and reproduce their kind by the union of the male and female elements. But whereas in all the higher animals the organs of the two sexes are regularly separated between different individuals, in most plants they exist together in every individual of the species. This rule, however, is by no means universal, and in many species the male plant is distinct from the female. The distinction appears to have been observed by some savages, for we are told that the Maoris " are acquainted with the sex of trees, etc., and have distinct names for the male and female of some trees." The ancients knew the difference between the male and the female date-palm, and fertilised them artificially by shaking the pollen of the male tree over the flowers of the female. The fertilisation took place in spring. Among the heathen of Harran the month during which the palms were fertilised bore the name of the Date Month, and at this time they celebrated the marriage festival of all the gods and goddesses. Different from this true and fruitful marriage of the palm are the false and barren marriages of plants which play a part in Hindoo superstition. For example, if a Hindoo has planted a grove of mangos, neither he nor his wife may taste of the fruit until he has formally married one of the trees, as a bridegroom, to a tree of a different sort, commonly a tamarind-tree, which grows near it in the grove. If there is no tamarind to act as bride, a jasmine will serve the turn. The expenses of such a marriage are often considerable, for the more Brahmans are feasted at it, the greater the glory of the owner of the grove. A family has been known to sell its golden and silver trinkets and to borrow all the money they could in order to marry a mango-tree to a jasmine with due pomp and ceremony. On Christmas Eve German peasants used to tie fruit-trees together with straw ropes to make them bear fruit, saying that the trees were thus married.

In the Moluccas, when the clove-trees are in blossom, they are treated like pregnant women. No noise may be made near them ; no light or fire may be carried past them at night ; no one may approach them with his hat on, all must uncover in their presence. These precautions are observed lest the tree should be alarmed and bear no fruit, or should drop its fruit too soon, like the untimely delivery of a woman who has been frightened in her pregnancy. So in the East the growing rice-crop is often treated with the same considerate regard as a breeding woman. Thus in Amboyna, when the rice is in bloom, the people say that it is pregnant and fire no guns and make no other noises near the field, for fear lest, if the rice were thus disturbed, it would miscarry, and the crop would be all straw and no grain.

Sometimes it is the souls of the dead which are believed to animate trees. The Dieri tribe of Central Australia regard as very sacred certain trees which are supposed to be their fathers transformed ; hence they speak with reverence of these trees, and are careful that they shall not be cut down or burned. If the settlers require them to hew down the trees, they earnestly protest against it, asserting that were they to do so they would have no luck, and might be punished for not protecting their ancestors. Some of the Philippine Islanders believe that the souls of their ancestors are in certain trees, which they therefore spare. If they are obliged to fell one of these trees, they excuse themselves to it by saying that it was the priest who made them do it. The spirits take up their abode, by preference, in tall and stately trees with great spreading branches. When the wind rustles the leaves, the natives fancy it is the voice of the spirit ; and they never pass near one of these trees without bowing respectfully and asking pardon of the spirit for disturbing his repose. Among the Ignorrotes, every village has its sacred tree, in which the souls of the dead forefathers of the hamlet reside. Offerings are made to the tree, and any injury done to it is believed to entail some misfortune on the village. Were the tree cut down, the village and all its inhabitants would inevitably perish.

In Corea the souls of people who die of the plague or by the road-side, and of women who expire in childbed, invariably take up their abode in trees. To such spirits offerings of cake, wine, and pork are made on heaps of stones piled under the trees. In China it has been customary from time immemorial to plant trees on graves in order thereby to strengthen the soul of the deceased and thus to save his body from corruption ; and as the evergreen cypress and pine are deemed to be fuller of vitality than other trees, they have been chosen by preference for this purpose. Hence the trees that grow on graves are sometimes identified with the souls of the departed. Among the Miao-Kia, an aboriginal race of Southern and Western China, a sacred tree stands at the entrance of every village, and the inhabitants believe that it is tenanted by the soul of their first ancestor and that it rules their destiny. Sometimes there is a sacred grove near a village, where the trees are suffered to rot and die on the spot. Their fallen branches cumber the ground, and no one may remove them unless he has first asked leave of the spirit of the tree and offered him a sacrifice. Among the Maraves of Southern Africa the burial-ground is always regarded as a holy place where neither a tree may be felled nor a beast killed, because everything there is supposed to be tenanted by the souls of the dead.

In most, if not all, of these cases the spirit is viewed as incorporate in the tree ; it animates the tree and must suffer and die with it. But, according to another and probably later opinion, the tree is not the body, but merely the abode of the tree-spirit, which can quit it and return to it at pleasure. The inhabitants of Siaoo, an East Indian island, believe in certain sylvan spirits who dwell in forests or in great solitary trees. At full moon the spirit comes forth from his lurking-place and roams about. He has a big head, very long arms and legs, and a ponderous body. In order to propitiate the wood-spirits people bring offerings of food, fowls, goats, and so forth to the places which they are supposed to haunt. The people of Nias think that, when a tree dies, its liberated spirit becomes a demon, which can kill a coco-nut palm by merely lighting on its branches, and can cause the death of all the children in a house by perching on one of the posts that support it. Further, they are of opinion that certain trees are at all times inhabited by roving demons who, if the trees were damaged, would be set free to go about on errands of mischief. Hence the people respect these trees, and are careful not to cut them down.

Not a few ceremonies observed at cutting down haunted trees are based on the belief that the spirits have it in their power to quit the trees at pleasure or in case of need. Thus when the Pelew Islanders are felling a tree, they conjure the spirit of the tree to leave it and settle on another. The wily negro of the Slave Coast, who wishes to fell an *ashorin* tree, but knows that he cannot do it so long as the spirit remains in the tree, places a little palm-oil on the ground as a bait, and then, when the unsuspecting spirit has quitted the tree to partake of this dainty, hastens to cut down its late abode. When the Toboong-koos of Celebes are about to clear a piece of forest in order to plant rice, they build a tiny house and furnish it with tiny clothes and some food and gold. Then they call together all the spirits of the wood, offer them the little house with its contents, and beseech them to quit the spot. After that they may safely cut down the wood without fear-ing to wound themselves in so doing. Before the Tomori, another tribe of Celebes, fell a tall tree they lay a quid of betel at its foot, and invite the spirit who dwells in the tree to change his lodging ; moreover, they set a little ladder against the trunk to enable him to descend with safety and comfort. The Mandelings of Sumatra endeavour to lay the blame of all such misdeeds at the door of the Dutch authorities. Thus when a man is cutting a road through a forest and has to fell a tall tree which blocks the way, he will not begin to ply his axe until he has said : " Spirit who lodgest in this tree, take it not ill that I cut down thy dwelling, for it is done at no wish of mine but by order of the Controller." And when he wishes to clear a piece of forest-land for cultivation, it is necessary that he should come to a satisfactory understanding with the woodland spirits who live there before he lays low their leafy dwellings. For this purpose he goes to the middle of the plot of ground, stoops down, and pretends to pick up a letter. Then unfolding a bit of paper he reads aloud an imaginary letter from the Dutch Government, in which he is strictly enjoined to set about clearing the land without delay. Having done so, he says : " You hear that, spirits. I must begin clearing at once, or I shall be hanged."

Even when a tree has been felled, sawn into planks, and used to build a house, it is possible that the woodland spirit may still be lurking in the timber, and accordingly some people seek to propitiate him before or after they occupy the new house. Hence, when a new dwelling is ready the Toradjas of Celebes kill a goat, a pig, or a buffalo, and smear all the woodwork with its blood. If the building is a *lobo* or spirit-house, a fowl or a dog is killed on the ridge of the roof, and its blood allowed to flow down on both sides. The ruder Tonapoo in such a case sacrifice a human being on the roof. This sacrifice on the roof of a *lobo* or temple serves the same purpose as the smearing of blood on the woodwork of an ordinary house. The intention is to propitiate the forest-spirits who may still be in the timber ; they are thus put in good humour and will do the inmates of the house no harm. For a like reason people in Celebes and the Moluccas are much afraid of planting a post upside down at the building of a house ; for the forest-spirit, who might still be in the timber, would very naturally resent the indignity and visit the inmates with sickness. The Kayans of Borneo are of opinion that tree-spirits stand very stiffly on the point of honour and visit men with their displeasure for any injury done to them. Hence after building a house, whereby they have been forced to ill-treat many trees, these people observe a period of penance for a year, during which they must abstain from many things, such as the killing of bears, tiger-cats, and serpents.

§ 2. *Beneficent Powers of Tree-Spirits.*—When a tree comes to be viewed, no longer as the body of the tree-spirit, but simply as its abode which it can quit at pleasure, an important advance has been made in religious thought. Animism is passing into polytheism. In other words, instead of regarding each tree as a living and conscious being, man now sees in it merely a lifeless, inert mass, tenanted for a longer or shorter time by a supernatural being who, as he can pass freely from tree to tree, thereby enjoys a certain right of possession or lordship over the trees, and, ceasing to be a tree-soul, becomes a forest god. As soon as the tree-spirit is thus in a measure disengaged from each particular tree, he begins to change his shape and assume the body of a man, in virtue of a general tendency of early thought to clothe all abstract spiritual beings in concrete human form. Hence in classical art the sylvan deities are depicted in human shape, their woodland character being denoted by a branch or some equally obvious symbol. But this change of shape does not affect the essential character of the tree-spirit. The powers which he exercised as a tree-soul incorporate in a tree, he still continues to wield as a god of trees. This I shall now attempt to prove in detail. I shall show, first, that trees considered as animate beings are credited with the power of making the rain to fall, the sun to shine, flocks and herds to multiply, and women to bring forth easily ; and, second, that the very same powers are attributed to tree-gods conceived as anthropomorphic beings or as actually incarnate in living men.

First, then, trees or tree-spirits are believed to give rain and sunshine. When the missionary Jerome of Prague was persuading the heathen Lithuanians to fell their sacred groves, a multitude of women besought the Prince of Lithuania to stop him, saying that with the woods he was destroying the house of god from which they had been wont to get rain and sunshine. The Mundaris in Assam think that if a tree in the sacred grove is felled the sylvan gods evince their displeasure by withholding rain. In order to procure rain the inhabitants of Monyo, a village in the Sagaing district of Upper Burma, chose the largest tamarind-tree near the village and named it the haunt of the spirit (*nat*) who controls the rain. Then they offered bread, coconuts, plantains, and fowls to the guardian spirit of the village and to the spirit who gives rain, and they prayed, " O Lord *nat* have pity on us poor mortals, and stay not the rain. Inasmuch as our offering is given ungrudgingly, let the rain fall day and night." Afterwards libations were made in honour of the spirit of the tamarind-tree ; and still later three elderly women, dressed in fine clothes and wearing necklaces and earrings, sang the Rain Song.

Again, tree-spirits make the crops to grow. Amongst the Mundaris every village has its sacred grove, and " the grove deities are held responsible for the crops, and are especially honoured at all the great agricultural festivals." The negroes of the Gold Coast are in the habit of sacrificing at the foot of certain tall trees, and they think that if one of these were felled all the fruits of the earth would perish. The Gallas dance in couples round sacred trees, praying for a good harvest. Every couple consists of a man and woman, who are linked together by a stick, of which each holds one end. Under their arms they carry green corn or grass. Swedish peasants stick a leafy branch in each furrow of their corn-fields, believing that this will ensure an abundant crop. The same idea comes out in the German and French custom of the Harvest-May. This is a large branch or a whole tree, which is decked with ears of corn, brought home on the last waggon from the harvest-field, and fastened on the roof of the farmhouse or of the barn, where it remains for a year. Mannhardt has proved that this branch or tree embodies the tree-spirit conceived as the spirit of vegetation in general, whose vivifying and fructifying influence is thus brought to bear upon the corn in particular. Hence in Swabia the Harvest-May is fastened amongst the last stalks of corn left standing on the field ; in other places it is planted on the corn-field and the last sheaf cut is attached to its trunk.

Again, the tree-spirit makes the herds to multiply and blesses women with offspring.   In Northern India the *Emblica officinalis* is a sacred tree.   On the eleventh of the month Phalgun (February) libations are poured at the foot of the tree, a red or yellow string is bound about the trunk, and prayers are offered to it for the fruitfulness of women, animals, and crops.   Again, in Northern India the coco-nut is esteemed one of the most sacred fruits, and is called Sriphala, or the fruit of Sri, the goddess of prosperity.   It is the symbol of fertility, and all through Upper India is kept in shrines and presented by the priests to women who desire to become mothers.   In the town of Qua, near Old Calabar, there used to grow a palm-tree which ensured con-ception to any barren woman who ate a nut from its branches.   In Europe the May-tree or May-pole is apparently supposed to possess similar powers over both women and cattle.   Thus in some parts of Germany on the first of May the peasants set up May-trees or May-bushes at the doors of stables and byres, one for each horse and cow ; this is thought to make the cows yield much milk.   Of the Irish we are told that " they fancy a green bough of a tree, fastened on May-day against the house, will produce plenty of milk that summer."

On the second of July some of the Wends used to set up an oak-tree in the middle of the village with an iron cock fastened to its top ; then they danced round it, and drove the cattle round it to make them thrive.   The Circassians regard the pear-tree as the protector of cattle. So they cut down a young pear-tree in the forest, branch it, and carry it home, where it is adored as a divinity.   Almost every house has one such pear-tree.   In autumn, on the day of the festival, the tree is carried into the house with great ceremony to the sound of music and amid the joyous cries of all the inmates, who compliment it on its fortunate arrival.   It is covered with candles, and a cheese is fastened to its top.   Round about it they eat, drink, and sing.   Then they bid the tree good-bye and take it back to the courtyard, where it remains for the rest of the year, set up against the wall, without receiving any mark of respect.

In the Tuhoe tribe of Maoris " the power of making women fruitful is ascribed to trees.   These trees are associated with the navel-strings of definite mythical ancestors, as indeed the navel-strings of all children used to be hung upon them down to quite recent times.   A barren woman had to embrace such a tree with her arms, and she received a male or a female child according as she embraced the east or the west side."   The common European custom of placing a green bush on May Day before or on the house of a beloved maiden probably originated in the belief of the fertilising power of the tree-spirit.   In some parts of Bavaria such bushes are set up also at the houses of newly-married pairs, and the practice is only omitted if the wife is near her confinement ; for in that case they say that the husband has " set up a May-bush for himself."   Among the South Slavonians a barren woman, who desires to have a child, places a new chemise upon a fruitful tree on the eve of St. George's Day.   Next morning before sunrise she examines the garment, and if she finds that some living creature has crept on it, she hopes that her wish will be fulfilled within the year. Then she puts on the chemise, confident that she will be as fruitful as the tree on which the garment has passed the night. Among the Kara-Kirghiz barren women roll themselves on the ground under a solitary apple-tree in order to obtain offspring. Lastly, the power of granting to women an easy delivery at child-birth is ascribed to trees both in Sweden and Africa. In some districts of Sweden there was formerly a *bårdträd* or guardian-tree (lime, ash, or elm) in the neighbourhood of every farm. No one would pluck a single leaf of the sacred tree, any injury to which was punished by ill-luck or sickness. Pregnant women used to clasp the tree in their arms in order to ensure an easy delivery. In some negro tribes of the Congo region pregnant women make themselves garments out of the bark of a certain sacred tree, because they believe that this tree delivers them from the dangers that attend child-bearing. The story that Leto clasped a palm-tree and an olive-tree or two laurel-trees, when she was about to give birth to the divine twins Apollo and Artemis, perhaps points to a similar Greek belief in the efficacy of certain trees to facilitate delivery.

CHAPTER X

RELICS OF TREE-WORSHIP IN MODERN EUROPE

FROM the foregoing review of the beneficent qualities commonly ascribed to tree-spirits, it is easy to understand why customs like the May-tree or May-pole have prevailed so widely and figured so prominently in the popular festivals of European peasants. In spring or early summer or even on Midsummer Day, it was and still is in many parts of Europe the custom to go out to the woods, cut down a tree and bring it into the village, where it is set up amid general rejoicings, or the people cut branches in the woods, and fasten them on every house. The intention of these customs is to bring home to the village, and to each house, the blessings which the tree-spirit has in its power to bestow. Hence the custom in some places of planting a May-tree before every house, or of carrying the village May-tree from door to door, that every household may receive its share of the blessing. Out of the mass of evidence on this subject a few examples may be selected.

Sir Henry Piers, in his *Description of Westmeath*, writing in 1682 says : " On May-eve, every family sets up before their door a green bush, strewed over with yellow flowers, which the meadows yield plentifully. In countries where timber is plentiful, they erect tall slender trees, which stand high, and they continue almost the whole year ; so as a stranger would go nigh to imagine that they were all signs of ale-sellers, and that all houses were ale-houses." In Northampton-shire a young tree ten or twelve feet high used to be planted before each house on May Day so as to appear growing ; flowers were thrown over it and strewn about the door. "Among ancient customs still retained by the Cornish, may be reckoned that of decking their doors and porches on the first of May with green boughs of sycamore and hawthorn, and of planting trees, or rather stumps of trees, before their houses." In the north of England it was formerly the custom for young people to rise a little after midnight on the morning of the first of May, and go out with music and the blowing of horns into the woods, where they broke branches and adorned them with nosegays and crowns of flowers. This done, they returned about sunrise and fastened the flower-decked branches over the doors and windows of their houses. At Abingdon in Berkshire young people formerly went about in groups on May morning, singing a carol of which the following are two of the verses :

" We've been rambling all the night,   *A garland gay we bring you here ;*
   And sometime of this day ;   *And at your door we stand ;*
And now returning back again,   *It is a sprout well budded out,*
   We bring a garland gay.   *The work of our Lord's hand."*

At the towns of Saffron Walden and Debden in Essex on the first of May little girls go about in parties from door to door singing a song almost identical with the above and carrying garlands ; a doll dressed in white is usually placed in the middle of each garland. Similar customs have been and indeed are still observed in various parts of England. The garlands are generally in the form of hoops intersecting each other at right angles. It appears that a hoop wreathed with rowan and marsh marigold, and bearing suspended within it two balls, is still carried on May Day by villagers in some parts of Ireland. The balls, which are sometimes covered with gold and silver paper, are said to have originally represented the sun and moon.

In some villages of the Vosges Mountains on the first Sunday of May young girls go in bands from house to house, singing a song in praise of May, in which mention is made of the " bread and meal that come in May." If money is given them, they fasten a green bough to the door ; if it is refused, they wish the family many children and no bread to feed them. In the French department of Mayenne, boys who bore the name of *Maillotins* used to go about from farm to farm on the first of May singing carols, for which they received money or a drink ; they planted a small tree or a branch of a tree. Near Saverne in Alsace bands of people go about carrying May-trees. Amongst them is a man dressed in a white shirt with his face blackened ; in front of him is carried a large May-tree, but each member of the band also carries a smaller one. One of the company bears a huge basket, in which he collects eggs, bacon, and so forth.

On the Thursday before Whitsunday the Russian villagers " go out into the woods, sing songs, weave garlands, and cut down a young birch-tree, which they dress up in woman's clothes, or adorn with many-coloured shreds and ribbons. After that comes a feast, at the end of which they take the dressed-up birch-tree, carry it home to their village with joyful dance and song, and set it up in one of the houses, where it remains as an honoured guest till Whitsunday. On the two intervening days they pay visits to the house where their ' guest ' is ; but on the third day, Whitsunday, they take her to a stream and fling her into its waters," throwing their garlands after her. In this Russian custom the dressing of the birch in woman's clothes shows how clearly the tree is personified ; and the throwing it into a stream is most probably a rain-charm.

In some parts of Sweden on the eve of May Day lads go about carrying each a bunch of fresh birch twigs wholly or partly in leaf. With the village fiddler at their head, they make the round of the houses singing May songs ; the burden of their songs is a prayer for fine weather, a plentiful harvest, and worldly and spiritual blessings. One of them carries a basket in which he collects gifts of eggs and the like. If they are well received, they stick a leafy twig in the roof over the cottage door. But in Sweden midsummer is the season when these ceremonies are chiefly observed. On the Eve of St. John (the twenty-third of June) the houses are thoroughly cleansed and garnished with green boughs and flowers. Young fir-trees are raised at the doorway and elsewhere about the homestead ; and very often small umbrageous arbours are constructed in the garden. In Stockholm on this day a leaf-market is held at which thousands of May-poles (*Maj Stänger*), from six inches to twelve feet high, decorated with leaves, flowers, slips of coloured paper, gilt egg-shells strung on reeds, and so on, are exposed for sale. Bonfires are lit on the hills, and the people dance round them and jump over them. But the chief event of the day is setting up the May-pole. This consists of a straight and tall spruce-pine tree, stripped of its branches. " At times hoops and at others pieces of wood, placed crosswise, are attached to it at intervals ; whilst at others it is provided with bows, representing, so to say, a man with his arms akimbo. From top to bottom not only the ' Maj Stäng ' (May-pole) itself, but the hoops, bows, etc., are orna-mented with leaves, flowers, slips of various cloth, gilt egg-shells, etc. ; and on the top of it is a large vane, or it may be a flag." The raising of the May-pole, the decoration of which is done by the village maidens, is an affair of much ceremony ; the people flock to it from all quarters, and dance round it in a great ring. Midsummer customs of the same sort used to be observed in some parts of Germany. Thus in the towns of the Upper Harz Mountains tall fir-trees, with the bark peeled off their lower trunks, were set up in open places and decked with flowers and eggs, which were painted yellow and red. Round these trees the young folk danced by day and the old folk in the evening. In some parts of Bohemia also a May-pole or midsummer-tree is erected on St. John's Eve. The lads fetch a tall fir or pine from the wood and set it up on a height, where the girls deck it with nosegays, garlands, and red ribbons. It is afterwards burned.

It would be needless to illustrate at length the custom, which has prevailed in various parts of Europe, such as England, France, and Germany, of setting up a village May-tree or May-pole on May Day. A few examples will suffice.   The puritanical writer Phillip Stubbes in his *Anatomie of Abuses*, first published at London in 1583, has described with manifest disgust how they used to bring in the May-pole in the days of good Queen Bess.   His description affords us a vivid glimpse of merry England in the olden time.   " Against May, Whitsonday, or other time, all the yung men and maides, olde men and wives, run gadding over night to the woods, groves, hils, and mountains, where they spend all the night in plesant pastimes ; and in the morning they return, bringing with them birch and branches of trees, to deck their assemblies withall.   And no mervaile, for there is a great Lord present amongst them, as superintendent and Lord over their pastimes and sportes, namely, Sathan, prince of hel.   But the chiefest jewel they bring from thence is their May-pole, which they bring home with great veneration, as thus.   They have twentie or fortie yoke of oxen, every oxe having a sweet nose-gay of flouers placed on the tip of his hornes, and these oxen drawe home this May-pole (this stinkyng ydol, rather), which is covered all over with floures and hearbs, bound round about with strings, from the top to the bottome, and sometime painted with variable colours, with two or three hundred men, women and children following it with great devotion.   And thus beeing reared up, with handkercheefs and flags hovering on the top, they straw the ground rounde about, binde green boughes about it, set up sommer haules, bowers, and arbors hard by it.   And then fall they to daunce about it, like as the heathen people did at the dedication of the Idols, whereof this is a perfect pattern, or rather the thing itself.   I have heard it credibly reported (and that *viva voce*) by men of great gravitie and reputation, that of fortie, threescore, or a hundred maides going to the wood over night, there have scaresly the third part of them returned home againe undefiled."

In Swabia on the first of May a tall fir-tree used to be fetched into the village, where it was decked with ribbons and set up ; then the people danced round it merrily to music.   The tree stood on the village green the whole year through, until a fresh tree was brought in next May Day.   In Saxony " people were not content with bringing the summer symbolically (as king or queen) into the village ; they brought the fresh green itself from the woods even into the houses : that is the May or Whitsuntide trees, which are mentioned in documents from the thirteenth century onwards.   The fetching in of the May-tree was also a festival.   The people went out into the woods to seek the May (*majum quaerere*), brought young trees, especially firs and birches, to the village and set them up before the doors of the houses or of the cattle-stalls or in the rooms.   Young fellows erected such May-trees, as we have already said, before the chambers of their sweethearts.   Besides these household Mays, a great May-tree or May-pole, which had also been brought in solemn procession to the village, was set up in the middle of the village or in the market-place of the town.   It had been chosen by the whole community, who watched over it most carefully. Generally the tree was stripped of its branches and leaves, nothing but the crown being left, on which were displayed, in addition to many-coloured ribbons and cloths, a variety of victuals such as sausages, cakes, and eggs. The young folk exerted themselves to obtain these prizes. In the greasy poles which are still to be seen at our fairs we have a relic of these old May-poles. Not uncommonly there was a race on foot or on horseback to the May-tree—a Whitsunday pastime which in course of time has been divested of its goal and survives as a popular custom to this day in many parts of Germany." At Bordeaux on the first of May the boys of each street used to erect in it a May-pole, which they adorned with garlands and a great crown ; and every evening during the whole of the month the young people of both sexes danced singing about the pole. Down to the present day May-trees decked with flowers and ribbons are set up on May Day in every village and hamlet of gay Provence. Under them the young folk make merry and the old folk rest.

In all these cases, apparently, the custom is or was to bring in a new May-tree each year. However, in England the village May-pole seems as a rule, at least in later times, to have been permanent, not renewed annually. Villages of Upper Bavaria renew their May-pole once every three, four, or five years. It is a fir-tree fetched from the forest, and amid all the wreaths, flags, and inscriptions with which it is bedecked, an essential part is the bunch of dark green foliage left at the top " as a memento that in it we have to do, not with a dead pole, but with a living tree from the greenwood." We can hardly doubt that originally the practice everywhere was to set up a new May-tree every year. As the object of the custom was to bring in the fructifying spirit of vegetation, newly awakened in spring, the end would have been defeated if, instead of a living tree, green and sappy, an old withered one had been erected year after year or allowed to stand permanently. When, however, the meaning of the custom had been forgotten, and the May-tree was regarded simply as a centre for holiday merry-making, people saw no reason for felling a fresh tree every year, and preferred to let the same tree stand permanently, only decking it with fresh flowers on May Day. But even when the May-pole had thus become a fixture, the need of giving it the appearance of being a green tree, not a dead pole, was sometimes felt. Thus at Weverham in Cheshire " are two May-poles, which are decorated on this day (May Day) with all due attention to the ancient solemnity ; the sides are hung with garlands, and the top terminated by a birch or other tall slender tree with its leaves on ; the bark being peeled, and the stem spliced to the pole, so as to give the appearance of one tree from the summit." Thus the renewal of the May-tree is like the renewal of the Harvest-May ; each is intended to secure a fresh portion of the fertilising spirit of vegetation, and to preserve it throughout the year. But whereas the efficacy of the Harvest-May is restricted to promoting the growth of the crops, that of the May-tree or May-branch extends also, as we have seen, to women

and cattle.   Lastly, it is worth noting that the old May-tree is sometimes burned at the end of the year.   Thus in the district of Prague
young people break pieces of the public May-tree and place them behind
the holy pictures in their rooms, where they remain till next May Day,
and are then burned on the hearth.   In Würtemberg the bushes which
are set up on the houses on Palm Sunday are sometimes left there for a
year and then burnt.

So much for the tree-spirit conceived as incorporate or immanent
in the tree.   We have now to show that the tree-spirit is often conceived and represented as detached from the tree and clothed in human
form, and even as embodied in living men or women.   The evidence
for this anthropomorphic representation of the tree-spirit is largely
to be found in the popular customs of European peasantry.

There is an instructive class of cases in which the tree-spirit is
represented simultaneously in vegetable form and in human form,
which are set side by side as if for the express purpose of explaining
each other.   In these cases the human representative of the tree-
spirit is sometimes a doll or puppet, sometimes a living person, but
whether a puppet or a person, it is placed beside a tree or bough ; so
that together the person or puppet, and the tree or bough, form a
sort of bilingual inscription, the one being, so to speak, a translation
of the other.   Here, therefore, there is no room left for doubt that
the spirit of the tree is actually represented in human form.   Thus in
Bohemia, on the fourth Sunday in Lent, young people throw a puppet
called Death into the water ;   then the girls go into the wood, cut
down a young tree, and fasten to it a puppet dressed in white clothes
to look like a woman ; with this tree and puppet they go from house
to house collecting gratuities and singing songs with the refrain :

> " We carry Death out of the village,
> We bring Summer into the village."

Here, as we shall see later on, the " Summer " is the spirit of vegetation returning or reviving in spring.   In some parts of our own country
children go about asking for pence with some small imitations of
May-poles, and with a finely-dressed doll which they call the Lady
of the May.   In these cases the tree and the puppet are obviously
regarded as equivalent.

At Thann, in Alsace, a girl called the Little May Rose, dressed in
white, carries a small May-tree, which is gay with garlands and ribbons.
Her companions collect gifts from door to door, singing a song :

> " Little May Rose turn round three times,
> Let us look at you round and round !
> Rose of the May, come to the greenwood away,
> We will be merry all.
> So we go from the May to the roses."

In the course of the song a wish is expressed that those who give nothing
may lose their fowls by the marten, that their vine may bear no clusters,

their tree no nuts, their field no corn ; the produce of the year is supposed to depend on the gifts offered to these May singers. Here and in the cases mentioned above, where children go about with green boughs or garlands on May Day singing and collecting money, the meaning is that with the spirit of vegetation they bring plenty and good luck to the house, and they expect to be paid for the service. In Russian Lithuania, on the first of May, they used to set up a green tree before the village. Then the rustic swains chose the prettiest girl, crowned her, swathed her in birch branches and set her beside the May-tree, where they danced, sang, and shouted " O May ! O May ! " In Brie (Isle de France) a May-tree is erected in the midst of the village ; its top is crowned with flowers ; lower down it is twined with leaves and twigs, still lower with huge green branches. The girls dance round it, and at the same time a lad wrapt in leaves and called Father May is led about. In the small towns of the Franken Wald mountains in Northern Bavaria, on the second of May, a *Walber* tree is erected before a tavern, and a man dances round it, enveloped in straw from head to foot in such a way that the ears of corn unite above his head to form a crown. He is called the *Walber*, and used to be led in procession through the streets, which were adorned with sprigs of birch.

Amongst the Slavs of Carinthia, on St. George's Day (the twenty-third of April), the young people deck with flowers and garlands a tree which has been felled on the eve of the festival. The tree is then carried in procession, accompanied with music and joyful acclamations, the chief figure in the procession being the Green George, a young fellow clad from head to foot in green birch branches. At the close of the ceremonies the Green George, that is an effigy of him, is thrown into the water. It is the aim of the lad who acts Green George to step out of his leafy envelope and substitute the effigy so adroitly that no one shall perceive the change. In many places, however, the lad himself who plays the part of Green George is ducked in a river or pond, with the express intention of thus ensuring rain to make the fields and meadows green in summer. In some places the cattle are crowned and driven from their stalls to the accompaniment of a song :

> " *Green George we bring,*
> *Green George we accompany,*
> *May he feed our herds well.*
> *If not, to the water with him.* "

Here we see that the same powers of making rain and fostering the cattle, which are ascribed to the tree-spirit regarded as incorporate in the tree, are also attributed to the tree-spirit represented by a living man.

Among the gypsies of Transylvania and Roumania the festival of Green George is the chief celebration of spring. Some of them keep it on Easter Monday, others on St. George's Day (the twenty-third of April). On the eve of the festival a young willow tree is cut down, adorned with garlands and leaves, and set up in the ground. Women with child place one of their garments under the tree, and leave it there over night ; if next morning they find a leaf of the tree lying on the garment, they know that their delivery will be easy. Sick and old people go to the tree in the evening, spit on it thrice, and say, " You will soon die, but let us live." Next morning the gypsies gather about the willow. The chief figure of the festival is Green George, a lad who is concealed from top to toe in green leaves and blossoms. He throws a few handfuls of grass to the beasts of the tribe, in order that they may have no lack of fodder throughout the year. Then he takes three iron nails, which have lain for three days and nights in water, and knocks them into the willow ; after which he pulls them out and flings them into a running stream to propitiate the water-spirits. Finally, a pretence is made of throwing Green George into the water, but in fact it is only a puppet made of branches and leaves which is ducked in the stream. In this version of the custom the powers of granting an easy delivery to women and of communicating vital energy to the sick and old are clearly ascribed to the willow ; while Green George, the human double of the tree, bestows food on the cattle, and further ensures the favour of the water-spirits by putting them in indirect communication with the tree.

Without citing more examples to the same effect, we may sum up the results of the preceding pages in the words of Mannhardt : " The customs quoted suffice to establish with certainty the conclusion that in these spring processions the spirit of vegetation is often represented both by the May-tree and in addition by a man dressed in green leaves or flowers or by a girl similarly adorned. It is the same spirit which animates the tree and is active in the inferior plants and which we have recognised in the May-tree and the Harvest-May. Quite consistently the spirit is also supposed to manifest his presence in the first flower of spring and reveals himself both in a girl representing a May-rose, and also, as giver of harvest, in the person of the *Walber*. The procession with this representative of the divinity was supposed to produce the same beneficial effects on the fowls, the fruit-trees, and the crops as the presence of the deity himself. In other words, the mummer was regarded not as an image but as an actual representative of the spirit of vegetation ; hence the wish expressed by the attendants on the May-rose and the May-tree that those who refuse them gifts of eggs, bacon, and so forth, may have no share in the blessings which it is in the power of the itinerant spirit to bestow. We may conclude that these begging processions with May-trees or May-boughs from door to door (' bringing the May or the summer ') had everywhere originally a serious and, so to speak, sacramental significance ; people really believed that the god of growth was present unseen in the bough ; by the procession he was brought to each house to bestow his blessing. The names May, Father May, May Lady, Queen of the May, by which the anthropomorphic spirit of vegetation is often denoted, show that the idea of the spirit of vegetation is blent with a personification of the season at which his powers are most strikingly manifested."

So far we have seen that the tree-spirit or the spirit of vegetation in general is represented either in vegetable form alone, as by a tree, bough, or flower ; or in vegetable and human form simultaneously, as by a tree, bough, or flower in combination with a puppet or a living person. It remains to show that the representation of him by a tree, bough, or flower is sometimes entirely dropped, while the representation of him by a living person remains. In this case the representative character of the person is generally marked by dressing him or her in leaves or flowers ; sometimes, too, it is indicated by the name he or she bears.

Thus in some parts of Russia on St. George's Day (the twenty-third of April) a youth is dressed out, like our Jack-in-the-Green, with leaves and flowers. The Slovenes call him the Green George. Holding a lighted torch in one hand and a pie in the other, he goes out to the corn-fields, followed by girls singing appropriate songs. A circle of brushwood is next lighted, in the middle of which is set the pie. All who take part in the ceremony then sit down around the fire and divide the pie among them. In this custom the Green George dressed in leaves and flowers is plainly identical with the similarly disguised Green George who is associated with a tree in the Carinthian, Transylvanian, and Roumanian customs observed on the same day. Again, we saw that in Russia at Whitsuntide a birch-tree is dressed in woman's clothes and set up in the house. Clearly equivalent to this is the custom observed on Whit-Monday by Russian girls in the district of Pinsk. They choose the prettiest of their number, envelop her in a mass of foliage taken from the birch-trees and maples, and carry her about through the village.

In Ruhla as soon as the trees begin to grow green in spring, the children assemble on a Sunday and go out into the woods, where they choose one of their playmates to be the Little Leaf Man. They break branches from the trees and twine them about the child till only his shoes peep out from the leafy mantle. Holes are made in it for him to see through, and two of the children lead the Little Leaf Man that he may not stumble or fall. Singing and dancing they take him from house to house, asking for gifts of food such as eggs, cream, sausages, and cakes. Lastly, they sprinkle the Leaf Man with water and feast on the food they have collected. In the Fricktal, Switzerland, at Whitsuntide boys go out into a wood and swathe one of their number in leafy boughs. He is called the Whitsuntide-lout, and being mounted on horseback with a green branch in his hand he is led back into the village. At the village-well a halt is called and the leaf-clad lout is dismounted and ducked in the trough. Thereby he acquires the right of sprinkling water on everybody, and he exercises the right specially on girls and street urchins. The urchins march before him in bands begging him to give them a Whitsuntide wetting.

In England the best-known example of these leaf-clad mummers is the Jack-in-the-Green, a chimney-sweeper who walks encased in a pyramidal framework of wickerwork, which is covered with holly and ivy, and surmounted by a crown of flowers and ribbons.   Thus arrayed he dances on May Day at the head of a troop of chimney-sweeps, who collect pence.   In Fricktal a similar frame of basketwork is called the Whitsuntide Basket.   As soon as the trees begin to bud, a spot is chosen in the wood, and here the village lads make the frame with all secrecy, lest others should forestall them.   Leafy branches are twined round two hoops, one of which rests on the shoulders of the wearer, the other encircles his calves ; holes are made for his eyes and mouth ; and a large nosegay crowns the whole.   In this guise he appears suddenly in the village at the hour of vespers, preceded by three boys blowing on horns made of willow bark.   The great object of his supporters is to set up the Whitsuntide Basket on the village well, and to keep it and him there, despite the efforts of the lads from neighbouring villages, who seek to carry off the Whitsuntide Basket and set it up on their own well.

In the class of cases of which the foregoing are specimens it is obvious that the leaf-clad person who is led about is equivalent to the May-tree, May-bough, or May-doll, which is carried from house to house by children begging.   Both are representatives of the beneficent spirit of vegetation, whose visit to the house is recompensed by a present of money or food.

Often the leaf-clad person who represents the spirit of vegetation is known as the king or the queen ; thus, for example, he or she is called the May King, Whitsuntide King, Queen of May, and so on.   These titles, as Mannhardt observes, imply that the spirit incorporate in vegetation is a ruler, whose creative power extends far and wide.

In a village near Salzwedel a May-tree is set up at Whitsuntide and the boys race to it ; he who reaches it first is king ; a garland of flowers is put round his neck and in his hand he carries a May-bush, with which, as the procession moves along, he sweeps away the dew.   At each house they sing a song, wishing the inmates good luck, referring to the " black cow in the stall milking white milk, black hen on the nest laying white eggs," and begging a gift of eggs, bacon, and so on.   At the village of Ellgoth in Silesia a ceremony called the King's Race is observed at Whitsuntide.   A pole with a cloth tied to it is set up in a meadow, and the young men ride past it on horseback, each trying to snatch away the cloth as he gallops by.   The one who succeeds in carrying it off and dipping it in the neighbouring Oder is proclaimed King.   Here the pole is clearly a substitute for a May-tree.   In some villages of Brunswick at Whitsuntide a May King is completely enveloped in a May-bush.   In some parts of Thüringen also they have a May King at Whitsuntide, but he is dressed up rather differently.   A frame of wood is made in which a man can stand ; it is completely covered with birch boughs and is surmounted by a crown of birch and flowers, in which a bell is fastened.   This frame is placed in the wood

K

and the May King gets into it. The rest go out and look for him, and when they have found him they lead him back into the village to the magistrate, the clergyman, and others, who have to guess who is in the verdurous frame. If they guess wrong, the May King rings his bell by shaking his head, and a forfeit of beer or the like must be paid by the unsuccessful guesser. At Wahrstedt the boys at Whitsuntide choose by lot a king and a high-steward. The latter is completely concealed in a May-bush, wears a wooden crown wreathed with flowers, and carries a wooden sword. The king, on the other hand, is only distinguished by a nosegay in his cap, and a reed, with a red ribbon tied to it, in his hand. They beg for eggs from house to house, threatening that, where none are given, none will be laid by the hens throughout the year. In this custom the high-steward appears, for some reason, to have usurped the insignia of the king. At Hildesheim five or six young fellows go about on the afternoon of Whit-Monday cracking long whips in measured time and collecting eggs from the houses. The chief person of the band is the Leaf King, a lad swathed so completely in birchen twigs that nothing of him can be seen but his feet. A huge head-dress of birchen twigs adds to his apparent stature. In his hand he carries a long crook, with which he tries to catch stray dogs and children. In some parts of Bohemia on Whit-Monday the young fellows disguise themselves in tall caps of birch bark adorned with flowers. One of them is dressed as a king and dragged on a sledge to the village green, and if on the way they pass a pool the sledge is always overturned into it. Arrived at the green they gather round the king ; the crier jumps on a stone or climbs up a tree and recites lampoons about each house and its inmates. Afterwards the disguises of bark are stripped off and they go about the village in holiday attire, carrying a May-tree and begging. Cakes, eggs, and corn are sometimes given them. At Grossvargula, near Langensalza, in the eighteenth century a Grass King used to be led about in procession at Whitsuntide. He was encased in a pyramid of poplar branches, the top of which was adorned with a royal crown of branches and flowers. He rode on horseback with the leafy pyramid over him, so that its lower end touched the ground, and an opening was left in it only for his face. Surrounded by a cavalcade of young fellows, he rode in procession to the town hall, the parsonage, and so on, where they all got a drink of beer. Then under the seven lindens of the neighbouring Sommerberg, the Grass King was stripped of his green casing ; the crown was handed to the Mayor, and the branches were stuck in the flax fields in order to make the flax grow tall. In this last trait the fertilising influence ascribed to the representative of the tree-spirit comes out clearly. In the neighbourhood of Pilsen (Bohemia) a conical hut of green branches, without any door, is erected at Whitsuntide in the midst of the village. To this hut rides a troop of village lads with a king at their head. He wears a sword at his side and a sugar-loaf hat of rushes on his head. In his train are a judge, a crier, and a personage called the Frog-flayer or Hangman. This last is a sort of ragged merryandrew, wearing a rusty old sword and bestriding a sorry hack. On reaching the hut the crier dismounts and goes round it looking for a door. Finding none, he says, " Ah, this is perhaps an enchanted castle ; the witches creep through the leaves and need no door." At last he draws his sword and hews his way into the hut, where there is a chair, on which he seats himself and proceeds to criticise in rhyme the girls, farmers, and farm-servants of the neighbourhood. When this is over, the Frog-flayer steps forward and, after exhibiting a cage with frogs in it, sets up a gallows on which he hangs the frogs in a row. In the neighbour-hood of Plas the ceremony differs in some points. The king and his soldiers are completely clad in bark, adorned with flowers and ribbons ; they all carry swords and ride horses, which are gay with green branches and flowers. While the village dames and girls are being criticised at the arbour, a frog is secretly pinched and poked by the crier till it quacks. Sentence of death is passed on the frog by the king ; the hangman beheads it and flings the bleeding body among the spectators. Lastly, the king is driven from the hut and pursued by the soldiers. The pinching and beheading of the frog are doubtless, as Mannhardt observes, a rain-charm. We have seen that some Indians of the Orinoco beat frogs for the express purpose of producing rain, and that killing a frog is a European rain-charm.

Often the spirit of vegetation in spring is represented by a queen instead of a king. In the neighbourhood of Libchowic (Bohemia), on the fourth Sunday in Lent, girls dressed in white and wearing the first spring flowers, as violets and daisies, in their hair, lead about the village a girl who is called the Queen and is crowned with flowers. During the procession, which is conducted with great solemnity, none of the girls may stand still, but must keep whirling round continually and singing. In every house the Queen announces the arrival of spring and wishes the inmates good luck and blessings, for which she receives presents. In German Hungary the girls choose the prettiest girl to be their Whitsuntide Queen, fasten a towering wreath on her brow, and carry her singing through the streets. At every house they stop, sing old ballads, and receive presents. In the south-east of Ireland on May Day the prettiest girl used to be chosen Queen of the district for twelve months. She was crowned with wild flowers ; feasting, dancing, and rustic sports followed, and were closed by a grand procession in the evening. During her year of office she presided over rural gather-ings of young people at dances and merry-makings. If she married before next May Day, her authority was at an end, but her successor was not elected till that day came round. The May Queen is common in France and familiar in England.

Again the spirit of vegetation is sometimes represented by a king and queen, a lord and lady, or a bridegroom and bride. Here again the parallelism holds between the anthropomorphic and the vegetable representation of the tree-spirit, for we have seen above that trees are sometimes married to each other. At Halford in south Warwickshire the children go from house to house on May Day, walking two and two in procession and headed by a King and Queen. Two boys carry a May-pole some six or seven feet high, which is covered with flowers and greenery. Fastened to it near the top are two cross-bars at right angles to each other. These are also decked with flowers, and from the ends of the bars hang hoops similarly adorned. At the houses the children sing May songs and receive money, which is used to provide tea for them at the schoolhouse in the afternoon. In a Bohemian village near Königgrätz on Whit-Monday the children play the king's game, at which a king and queen march about under a canopy, the queen wearing a garland, and the youngest girl carrying two wreaths on a plate behind them. They are attended by boys and girls called groomsmen and bridesmaids, and they go from house to house collecting gifts. A regular feature in the popular celebration of Whitsuntide in Silesia used to be, and to some extent still is, the contest for the king-ship. This contest took various forms, but the mark or goal was generally the May-tree or May-pole. Sometimes the youth who suc-ceeded in climbing the smooth pole and bringing down the prize was proclaimed the Whitsuntide King and his sweetheart the Whitsuntide Bride. Afterwards the king, carrying the May-bush, repaired with the rest of the company to the alehouse, where a dance and a feast ended the merry-making. Often the young farmers and labourers raced on horseback to the May-pole, which was adorned with flowers, ribbons, and a crown. He who first reached the pole was the Whitsun-tide King, and the rest had to obey his orders for that day. The worst rider became the clown. At the May-tree all dismounted and hoisted the king on their shoulders. He nimbly swarmed up the pole and brought down the May-bush and the crown, which had been fastened to the top. Meantime the clown hurried to the alehouse and proceeded to bolt thirty rolls of bread and to swig four quart bottles of brandy with the utmost possible despatch. He was followed by the king, who bore the May-bush and crown at the head of the company. If on their arrival the clown had already disposed of the rolls and the brandy, and greeted the king with a speech and a glass of beer, his score was paid by the king ; otherwise he had to settle it himself. After church time the stately procession wound through the village. At the head of it rode the king, decked with flowers and carrying the May-bush. Next came the clown with his clothes turned inside out, a great flaxen beard on his chin, and the Whitsuntide crown on his head. Two riders disguised as guards followed. The procession drew up before every farmyard ; the two guards dismounted, shut the clown into the house, and claimed a contribution from the housewife to buy soap with which to wash the clown's beard. Custom allowed them to carry off any victuals which were not under lock and key. Last of all they came to the house in which the king's sweetheart lived. She was greeted as Whitsuntide Queen and received suitable presents—to wit, a many-coloured sash, a cloth, and an apron. The king got as a prize, a vest, a neckcloth, and so forth, and had the right of setting up the May-bush or Whitsuntide-tree before his master's yard, where it remained as an honourable token till the same day next year. Finally the procession took its way to the tavern, where the king and queen opened the dance. Sometimes the Whitsuntide King and Queen succeeded to office in a different way. A man of straw, as large as life and crowned with a red cap, was conveyed in a cart, between two men armed and disguised as guards, to a place where a mock court was waiting to try him. A great crowd followed the cart. After a formal trial the straw man was condemned to death and fastened to a stake on the execution ground. The young men with bandaged eyes tried to stab him with a spear. He who succeeded became king and his sweetheart queen. The straw man was known as the Goliath.

In a parish of Denmark it used to be the custom at Whitsuntide to dress up a little girl as the Whitsun-bride and a little boy as her groom. She was decked in all the finery of a grown-up bride, and wore a crown of the freshest flowers of spring on her head. Her groom was as gay as flowers, ribbons, and knots could make him. The other children adorned themselves as best they could with the yellow flowers of the trollius and caltha. Then they went in great state from farmhouse to farmhouse, two little girls walking at the head of the procession as bridesmaids, and six or eight outriders galloping ahead on hobby-horses to announce their coming. Contributions of eggs, butter, loaves, cream, coffee, sugar, and tallow-candles were received and conveyed away in baskets. When they had made the round of the farms, some of the farmers' wives helped to arrange the wedding feast, and the children danced merrily in clogs on the stamped clay floor till the sun rose and the birds began to sing. All this is now a thing of the past. Only the old folks still remember the little Whitsun-bride and her mimic pomp.

We have seen that in Sweden the ceremonies associated elsewhere with May Day or Whitsuntide commonly take place at Midsummer. Accordingly we find that in some parts of the Swedish province of Blekinge they still choose a Midsummer's Bride, to whom the " church coronet " is occasionally lent. The girl selects for herself a Bride-groom, and a collection is made for the pair, who for the time being are looked on as man and wife. The other youths also choose each his bride. A similar ceremony seems to be still kept up in Norway.

In the neighbourhood of Briançon (Dauphiné) on May Day the lads wrap up in green leaves a young fellow whose sweetheart has deserted him or married another. He lies down on the ground and feigns to be asleep. Then a girl who likes him, and would marry him, comes and wakes him, and raising him up offers him her arm and a flag. So they go to the alehouse, where the pair lead off the dancing. But they must marry within the year, or they are treated as old bachelor and old maid, and are debarred the company of the young folk. The lad is called the Bridegroom of the month of May. In the alehouse he puts off his garment of leaves, out of which, mixed with flowers, his partner in the dance makes a nosegay, and wears it at her breast next day, when he leads her again to the alehouse. Like this is a Russian custom

observed in the district of Nerechta on the Thursday before Whitsunday. The girls go out into a birch-wood, wind a girdle or band
round a stately birch, twist its lower branches into a wreath, and kiss
each other in pairs through the wreath. The girls who kiss through
the wreath call each other gossips. Then one of the girls steps forward,
and mimicking a drunken man, flings herself on the ground, rolls on
the grass, and feigns to fall fast asleep. Another girl wakens the
pretended sleeper and kisses him ; then the whole bevy trips singing
through the wood to twine garlands, which they throw into the water.
In the fate of the garlands floating on the stream they read their own.
Here the part of the sleeper was probably at one time played by a lad.
In these French and Russian customs we have a forsaken bridegroom,
in the following a forsaken bride. On Shrove Tuesday the Slovenes
of Oberkrain drag a straw puppet with joyous cries up and down the
village ; then they throw it into the water or burn it, and from the
height of the flames they judge of the abundance of the next harvest.
The noisy crew is followed by a female masker, who drags a great
board by a string and gives out that she is a forsaken bride.

Viewed in the light of what has gone before, the awakening of the
forsaken sleeper in these ceremonies probably represents the revival
of vegetation in spring. But it is not easy to assign their respective
parts to the forsaken bridegroom and to the girl who wakes him from
his slumber. Is the sleeper the leafless forest or the bare earth of
winter ? Is the girl who wakens him the fresh verdure or the genial
sunshine of spring ? It is hardly possible, on the evidence before us,
to answer these questions.

In the Highlands of Scotland the revival of vegetation in spring
used to be graphically represented on St. Bride's Day, the first of
February. Thus in the Hebrides " the mistress and servants of each
family take a sheaf of oats, and dress it up in women's apparel, put
it in a large basket, and lay a wooden club by it, and this they call
Briid's bed ; and then the mistress and servants cry three times,
' Briid is come, Briid is welcome.' This they do just before going to
bed, and when they rise in the morning they look among the ashes,
expecting to see the impression of Briid's club there ; which if they do,
they reckon it a true presage of a good crop and prosperous year, and
the contrary they take as an ill omen." The same custom is described
by another witness thus : " Upon the night before Candlemas it is
usual to make a bed with corn and hay, over which some blankets are
laid, in a part of the house, near the door. When it is ready, a person
goes out and repeats three times, . . . ' Bridget, Bridget, come in ;
thy bed is ready.' One or more candles are left burning near it all
night." Similarly in the Isle of Man " on the eve of the first of
February, a festival was formerly kept, called, in the Manks language,
Laa'l Breeshey, in honour of the Irish lady who went over to the Isle
of Man to receive the veil from St. Maughold. The custom was to
gather a bundle of green rushes, and standing with them in the hand
on the threshold of the door, to invite the holy Saint Bridget to come

and lodge with them that night.   In the Manks language, the invitation ran thus : ' *Brede, Brede, tar gys my thie tar dyn thie ayms noght. Foshil jee yn dorrys da Brede, as lhig da Brede e heet staigh.*'   In English : ' Bridget, Bridget, come to my house, come to my house to-night. Open the door for Bridget, and let Bridget come in.'   After these words were repeated, the rushes were strewn on the floor by way of a carpet or bed for St. Bridget.   A custom very similar to this was also observed in some of the Out-Isles of the ancient kingdom of Man." In these Manx and Highland ceremonies it is obvious that St. Bride, or St. Bridget, is an old heathen goddess of fertility, disguised in a thread-bare Christian cloak.   Probably she is no other than Brigit, the Celtic goddess of fire and apparently of the crops.

Often the marriage of the spirit of vegetation in spring, though not directly represented, is implied by naming the human representative of the spirit, " the Bride," and dressing her in wedding attire.   Thus in some villages of Altmark at Whitsuntide, while the boys go about carrying a May-tree or leading a boy enveloped in leaves and flowers, the girls lead about the May Bride, a girl dressed as a bride with a great nosegay in her hair.   They go from house to house, the May Bride singing a song in which she asks for a present, and tells the inmates of each house that if they give her something they will themselves have something the whole year through ; but if they give her nothing they will themselves have nothing.   In some parts of Westphalia two girls lead a flower-crowned girl called the Whitsuntide Bride from door to door, singing a song in which they ask for eggs.

CHAPTER XI

THE INFLUENCE OF THE SEXES ON VEGETATION

FROM the preceding examination of the spring and summer festivals of Europe we may infer that our rude forefathers personified the powers of vegetation as male and female, and attempted, on the principle of homoeopathic or imitative magic, to quicken the growth of trees and plants by representing the marriage of the sylvan deities in the persons of a King and Queen of May, a Whitsun Bridegroom and Bride, and so forth.   Such representations were accordingly no mere symbolic or allegorical dramas, pastoral plays designed to amuse or instruct a rustic audience.   They were charms intended to make the woods to grow green, the fresh grass to sprout, the corn to shoot, and the flowers to blow.   And it was natural to suppose that the more closely the mock marriage of the leaf-clad or flower-decked mummers aped the real marriage of the woodland sprites, the more effective would be the charm.   Accordingly we may assume with a high degree of probability that the profligacy which notoriously attended these ceremonies was at one time not an accidental excess but an essential part of the rites, and that in the opinion of those who performed them the marriage of trees and plants could not be fertile without the real union of the human sexes. At the present day it might perhaps be vain to look in civilised Europe for customs of this sort observed for the explicit purpose of promoting the growth of vegetation. But ruder races in other parts of the world have consciously employed the intercourse of the sexes as a means to ensure the fruitfulness of the earth ; and some rites which are still, or were till lately, kept up in Europe can be reasonably explained only as stunted relics of a similar practice. The following facts will make this plain.

For four days before they committed the seed to the earth the Pipiles of Central America kept apart from their wives " in order that on the night before planting they might indulge their passions to the fullest extent ; certain persons are even said to have been appointed to perform the sexual act at the very moment when the first seeds were deposited in the ground." The use of their wives at that time was indeed enjoined upon the people by the priests as a religious duty, in default of which it was not lawful to sow the seed. The only possible explanation of this custom seems to be that the Indians confused the process by which human beings reproduce their kind with the process by which plants discharge the same function, and fancied that by resorting to the former they were simultaneously forwarding the latter. In some parts of Java, at the season when the bloom will soon be on the rice, the husbandman and his wife visit their fields by night and there engage in sexual intercourse for the purpose of promoting the growth of the crop. In the Leti, Sarmata, and some other groups of islands which lie between the western end of New Guinea and the northern part of Australia, the heathen population regard the sun as the male principle by whom the earth or female principle is fertilised. They call him Upu-lera or Mr. Sun, and represent him under the form of a lamp made of coco-nut leaves, which may be seen hanging everywhere in their houses and in the sacred fig-tree. Under the tree lies a large flat stone, which serves as a sacrificial table. On it the heads of slain foes were and are still placed in some of the islands. Once a year, at the beginning of the rainy season, Mr. Sun comes down into the holy fig-tree to fertilise the earth, and to facilitate his descent a ladder with seven rungs is considerately placed at his disposal. It is set up under the tree and is adorned with carved figures of the birds whose shrill clarion heralds the approach of the sun in the East. On this occasion pigs and dogs are sacrificed in profusion ; men and women alike indulge in a saturnalia ; and the mystic union of the sun and the earth is dramatically represented in public, amid song and dance, by the real union of the sexes under the tree. The object of the festival, we are told, is to procure rain, plenty of food and drink, abundance of cattle and children and riches from Grandfather Sun. They pray that he may make every she-goat to cast two or three young, the people to multiply, the dead pigs to be replaced by living pigs, the empty rice-baskets to be filled, and so on. And to induce him to grant their requests they offer him pork and rice and liquor, and invite him to fall to. In the Babar

Islands a special flag is hoisted at this festival as a symbol of the creative energy of the sun ; it is of white cotton, about nine feet high, and consists of the figure of a man in an appropriate attitude. It would be unjust to treat these orgies as a mere outburst of unbridled passion ; no doubt they are deliberately and solemnly organised as essential to the fertility of the earth and the welfare of man.

The same means which are thus adopted to stimulate the growth of the crops are naturally employed to ensure the fruitfulness of trees. In some parts of Amboyna, when the state of the clove plantation indicates that the crop is likely to be scanty, the men go naked to the plantations by night, and there seek to fertilise the trees precisely as they would impregnate women, while at the same time they call out for " More cloves ! " This is supposed to make the trees bear fruit more abundantly.

The Baganda of Central Africa believe so strongly in the intimate relation between the intercourse of the sexes and the fertility of the ground that among them a barren wife is generally sent away, because she is supposed to prevent her husband's garden from bearing fruit. On the contrary, a couple who have given proof of extraordinary fertility by becoming the parents of twins are believed by the Baganda to be endowed with a corresponding power of increasing the fruitfulness of the plantain-trees, which furnish them with their staple food. Some little time after the birth of the twins a ceremony is performed, the object of which clearly is to transmit the reproductive virtue of the parents to the plantains. The mother lies down on her back in the thick grass near the house and places a flower of the plantain between her legs ; then her husband comes and knocks the flower away with his genital member. Further, the parents go through the country, performing dances in the gardens of favoured friends, apparently for the purpose of causing the plantain-trees to bear fruit more abundantly.

In various parts of Europe customs have prevailed both at spring and harvest which are clearly based on the same crude notion that the relation of the human sexes to each other can be so used as to quicken the growth of plants. For example, in the Ukraine on St. George's Day (the twenty-third of April) the priest in his robes, attended by his acolytes, goes out to the fields of the village, where the crops are beginning to show green above the ground, and blesses them. After that the young married people lie down in couples on the sown fields and roll several times over on them, in the belief that this will promote the growth of the crops. In some parts of Russia the priest himself is rolled by women over the sprouting crop, and that without regard to the mud and holes which he may encounter in his beneficent progress. If the shepherd resists or remonstrates, his flock murmurs, " Little Father, you do not really wish us well, you do not wish us to have corn, although you do wish to live on our corn." In some parts of Germany at harvest the men and women, who have reaped the corn, roll together on the field. This again is probably a mitigation of an older and ruder custom designed to impart fertility to the fields by methods like those resorted to by the Pipiles of Central America long ago and by the cultivators of rice in Java at the present time.

To the student who cares to track the devious course of the human mind in its gropings after truth, it is of some interest to observe that the same theoretical belief in the sympathetic influence of the sexes on vegetation, which has led some peoples to indulge their passions as a means of fertilising the earth, has led others to seek the same end by directly opposite means. From the moment that they sowed the maize till the time that they reaped it, the Indians of Nicaragua lived chastely, keeping apart from their wives and sleeping in a separate place. They ate no salt, and drank neither cocoa nor *chicha*, the fermented liquor made from maize ; in short the season was for them, as the Spanish historian observes, a time of abstinence. To this day some of the Indian tribes of Central America practise continence for the purpose of thereby promoting the growth of the crops. Thus we are told that before sowing the maize the Kekchi Indians sleep apart from their wives, and eat no flesh for five days, while among the Lanquineros and Cajaboneros the period of abstinence from these carnal pleasures extends to thirteen days. So amongst some of the Germans of Transylvania it is a rule that no man may sleep with his wife during the whole of the time that he is engaged in sowing his fields. The same rule is observed at Kalotaszeg in Hungary ; the people think that if the custom were not observed the corn would be mildewed. Similarly a Central Australian headman of the Kaitish tribe strictly abstains from marital relations with his wife all the time that he is performing magical ceremonies to make the grass grow ; for he believes that a breach of this rule would prevent the grass seed from sprouting properly. In some of the Melanesian islands, when the yam vines are being trained, the men sleep near the gardens and never approach their wives ; should they enter the garden after breaking this rule of continence the fruits of the garden would be spoilt.

If we ask why it is that similar beliefs should logically lead, among different peoples, to such opposite modes of conduct as strict chastity and more or less open debauchery, the reason, as it presents itself to the primitive mind, is perhaps not very far to seek. If rude man identifies himself, in a manner, with nature ; if he fails to distinguish the impulses and processes in himself from the methods which nature adopts to ensure the reproduction of plants and animals, he may leap to one of two conclusions. Either he may infer that by yielding to his appetites he will thereby assist in the multiplication of plants and animals ; or he may imagine that the vigour which he refuses to expend in reproducing his own kind, will form as it were a store of energy whereby other creatures, whether vegetable or animal, will somehow benefit in propagating their species. Thus from the same crude philosophy, the same primitive notions of nature and life, the savage may derive by different channels a rule either of profligacy or of asceticism.

To readers bred in a religion which is saturated with the ascetic idealism of the East, the explanation which I have given of the rule of continence observed under certain circumstances by rude or savage peoples may seem far-fetched and improbable. They may think that moral purity, which is so intimately associated in their minds with the observance of such a rule, furnishes a sufficient explanation of it ; they may hold with Milton that chastity in itself is a noble virtue, and that the restraint which it imposes on one of the strongest impulses of our animal nature marks out those who can submit to it as men raised above the common herd, and therefore worthy to receive the seal of the divine approbation. However natural this mode of thought may seem to us, it is utterly foreign and indeed incomprehensible to the savage. If he resists on occasion the sexual instinct, it is from no high idealism, no ethereal aspiration after moral purity, but for the sake of some ulterior yet perfectly definite and concrete object, to gain which he is prepared to sacrifice the immediate gratification. of his senses. That this is or may be so, the examples I have cited are amply sufficient to prove. They show that where the instinct of self-preservation, which manifests itself chiefly in the search for food, conflicts or appears to conflict with the instinct which conduces to the propagation of the species, the former instinct, as the primary and more fundamental, is capable of overmastering the latter. In short, the savage is willing to restrain his sexual propensity for the sake of food. Another object for the sake of which he consents to exercise the same self-restraint is victory in war. Not only the warrior in the field but his friends at home will often bridle their sensual appetites from a belief that by so doing they will the more easily overcome their enemies. The fallacy of such a belief, like the belief that the chastity of the sower conduces to the growth of the seed, is plain enough to us ; yet perhaps the self-restraint which these and the like beliefs, vain and false as they are, have imposed on mankind, has not been without its utility in bracing and strengthening the breed. For strength of character in the race as in the individual consists mainly in the power of sacrificing the present to the future, of disregarding the immediate temptations of ephemeral pleasure for more distant and lasting sources of satisfaction. The more the powe¬ is exercised the higher and stronger becomes the character ; till the height of heroism is reached in men who renounce the pleasures of life and even life itself for the sake of keeping or winning for others, perhaps in distant ages, the blessings of freedom and truth.

CHAPTER XII

THE SACRED MARRIAGE

§ 1. *Diana as a Goddess of Fertility.*—We have seen that according to a widespread belief, which is not without a foundation in fact, plants reproduce their kinds through the sexual union of male and female elements, and that on the principle of homoeopathic or imitative magic this reproduction is supposed to be stimulated by the real or mock marriage of men and women, who masquerade for the time being as spirits of vegetation. Such magical dramas have played a great part in the popular festivals of Europe, and based as they are on a very crude conception of natural law, it is clear that they must have been handed down from a remote antiquity. We shall hardly, therefore, err in assuming that they date from a time when the forefathers of the civilised nations of Europe were still barbarians, herding their cattle and cultivating patches of corn in the clearings of the vast forests, which then covered the greater part of the continent, from the Mediterranean to the Arctic Ocean. But if these old spells and enchantments for the growth of leaves and blossoms, of grass and flowers and fruit, have lingered down to our own time in the shape of pastoral plays and popular merry-makings, is it not reasonable to suppose that they survived in less attenuated forms some two thousand years ago among the civilised peoples of antiquity? Or, to put it otherwise, is it not likely that in certain festivals of the ancients we may be able to detect the equivalents of our May Day, Whitsuntide, and Midsummer celebrations, with this difference, that in those days the ceremonies had not yet dwindled into mere shows and pageants, but were still religious or magical rites, in which the actors consciously supported the high parts of gods and goddesses? Now in the first chapter of this book we found reason to believe that the priest who bore the title of King of the Wood at Nemi had for his mate the goddess of the grove, Diana herself. May not he and she, as King and Queen of the Wood, have been serious counterparts of the merry mummers who play the King and Queen of May, the Whitsuntide Bridegroom and Bride in modern Europe? and may not their union have been yearly celebrated in a *theogamy* or divine marriage? Such dramatic weddings of gods and goddesses, as we shall see presently, were carried out as solemn religious rites in many parts of the ancient world; hence there is no intrinsic improbability in the supposition that the sacred grove at Nemi may have been the scene of an annual ceremony of this sort. Direct evidence that it was so there is none, but analogy pleads in favour of the view, as I shall now endeavour to show.

Diana was essentially a goddess of the woodlands, as Ceres was a goddess of the corn and Bacchus a god of the vine. Her sanctuaries were commonly in groves, indeed every grove was sacred to her, and she is often associated with the forest god Silvanus in dedications. But whatever her origin may have been, Diana was not always a mere goddess of trees. Like her Greek sister Artemis, she appears to have developed into a personification of the teeming life of nature, both animal and vegetable. As mistress of the greenwood she would naturally be thought to own the beasts, whether wild or tame, that ranged through it, lurking for their prey in its gloomy depths, munching the fresh leaves and shoots among the boughs, or cropping the herbage in the open glades and dells. Thus she might come to be the patron goddess both of hunters and herdsmen, just as Silvanus was the god not only of woods, but of cattle. Similarly in Finland the wild beasts of the forest were regarded as the herds of the woodland God Tapio and of his stately and beautiful wife. No man might slay one of these animals without the gracious permission of their divine owners. Hence the hunter prayed to the sylvan deities, and vowed rich offerings to them if they would drive the game across his path. And cattle also seem to have enjoyed the protection of those spirits of the woods, both when they were in their stalls and while they strayed in the forest. Before the Gayos of Sumatra hunt deer, wild goats, or wild pigs with hounds in the woods, they deem it necessary to obtain the leave of the unseen Lord of the forest. This is done according to a prescribed form by a man who has special skill in woodcraft. He lays down a quid of betel before a stake which is cut in a particular way to represent the Lord of the Wood, and having done so he prays to the spirit to signify his consent or refusal. In his treatise on hunting, Arrian tells us that the Celts used to offer an annual sacrifice to Artemis on her birth-day, purchasing the sacrificial victim with the fines which they had paid into her treasury for every fox, hare, and roe that they had killed in the course of the year. The custom clearly implied that the wild beasts belonged to the goddess, and that she must be compensated for their slaughter.

But Diana was not merely a patroness of wild beasts, a mistress of woods and hills, of lonely glades and sounding rivers ; conceived as the moon, and especially, it would seem, as the yellow harvest moon, she filled the farmer's grange with goodly fruits, and heard the prayers of women in travail. In her sacred grove at Nemi, as we have seen, she was especially worshipped as a goddess of childbirth, who bestowed offspring on men and women. Thus Diana, like the Greek Artemis, with whom she was constantly identified, may be described as a goddess of nature in general and of fertility in particular. We need not wonder, therefore, that in her sanctuary on the Aventine she was represented by an image copied from the many-breasted idol of the Ephesian Artemis, with all its crowded emblems of exuberant fecundity. Hence too we can understand why an ancient Roman law, attributed to King Tullus Hostilius, prescribed that, when incest had been committed, an expiatory sacrifice should be offered by the pontiffs in the grove of Diana. For we know that the crime of incest is commonly supposed to cause a dearth ; hence it would be meet that atonement for the offence should be made to the goddess of fertility.

Now on the principle that the goddess of fertility must herself be fertile, it behoved Diana to have a male partner. Her mate, if the testimony of Servius may be trusted, was that Virbius who had his representative, or perhaps rather his embodiment, in the King of the Wood at Nemi. The aim of their union would be to promote the fruitfulness of the earth, of animals, and of mankind ; and it might naturally be thought that this object would be more surely attained

if the sacred nuptials were celebrated every year, the parts of the
divine bride and bridegroom being played either by their images or
by living persons.   No ancient writer mentions that this was done in
the grove at Nemi ; but our knowledge of the Arician ritual is so scanty
that the want of information on this head can hardly count as a fatal
objection to the theory.   That theory, in the absence of direct evidence,
must necessarily be based on the analogy of similar customs practised
elsewhere.   Some modern examples of such customs, more or less
degenerate, were described in the last chapter.   Here we shall consider
their ancient counterparts.

§ 2. *The Marriage of the Gods.*—At Babylon the imposing sanctuary
of Bel rose like a pyramid above the city in a series of eight towers or
stories, planted one on the top of the other.   On the highest tower,
reached by an ascent which wound about all the rest, there stood a
spacious temple, and in the temple a great bed, magnificently draped
and cushioned, with a golden table beside it.   In the temple no image
was to be seen, and no human being passed the night there, save a
single woman, whom, according to the Chaldean priests, the god chose
from among all the women of Babylon.   They said that the deity himself came into the temple at night and slept in the great bed ; and the
woman, as a consort of the god, might have no intercourse with mortal
man.

At Thebes in Egypt a woman slept in the temple of Ammon as the
consort of the god, and, like the human wife of Bel at Babylon, she was
said to have no commerce with a man.   In Egyptian texts she is often
mentioned as " the divine consort," and usually she was no less a
personage than the Queen of Egypt herself.   For, according to the
Egyptians, their monarchs were actually begotten by the god Ammon,
who assumed for the time being the form of the reigning king, and in
that disguise had intercourse with the queen.   The divine procreation
is carved and painted in great detail on the walls of two of the oldest
temples in Egypt, those of Deir el Bahari and Luxor ; and the inscriptions attached to the paintings leave no doubt as to the meaning of
the scenes.

At Athens the god of the vine, Dionysus, was annually married to
the Queen, and it appears that the consummation of the divine union,
as well as the espousals, was enacted at the ceremony ; but whether
the part of the god was played by a man or an image we do not know.
We learn from Aristotle that the ceremony took place in the old official
residence of the King, known as the Cattle-stall, which stood near the
Prytaneum or Town-hall on the north-eastern slope of the Acropolis.
The object of the marriage can hardly have been any other than that
of ensuring the fertility of the vines and other fruit-trees, of which
Dionysus was the god.   Thus both in form and in meaning the
ceremony would answer to the nuptials of the King and Queen of May.

In the great mysteries solemnised at Eleusis in the month of
September the union of the sky-god Zeus with the corn-goddess
Demeter appears to have been represented by the union of the hiero-

phant with the priestess of Demeter, who acted the parts of god and goddess. But their intercourse was only dramatic or symbolical, for the hierophant had temporarily deprived himself of his virility by an application of hemlock. The torches having been extinguished, the pair descended into a murky place, while the throng of worshippers awaited in anxious suspense the result of the mystic congress, on which they believed their own salvation to depend. After a time the hiero- phant reappeared, and in a blaze of light silently exhibited to the assembly a reaped ear of corn, the fruit of the divine marriage. Then in a loud voice he proclaimed, " Queen Brimo has brought forth a sacred boy Brimos," by which he meant, " The Mighty One has brought forth the Mighty." The corn-mother in fact had given birth to her child, the corn, and her travail-pangs were enacted in the sacred drama. This revelation of the reaped corn appears to have been the crowning act of the mysteries. Thus through the glamour shed round these rites by the poetry and philosophy of later ages there still looms, like a distant landscape through a sunlit haze, a simple rustic festival designed to cover the wide Eleusinian plain with a plenteous harvest by wedding the goddess of the corn to the sky-god, who fertilised the bare earth with genial showers. Every few years the people of Plataea, in Boeotia, held a festival called the Little Daedala, at which they felled an oak-tree in an ancient oak forest. Out of the tree they carved an image, and having dressed it as a bride, they set it on a bullock-cart with a bridesmaid beside it. The image seems then to have been drawn to the bank of the river Asopus and back to the town, attended by a piping and dancing crowd. Every sixty years the festival of the Great Daedala was celebrated by all the people of Boeotia ; and at it all the images, fourteen in number, which had accumulated at the lesser festivals, were dragged on wains in pro- cession to the river Asopus and then to the top of Mount Cithaeron, where they were burnt on a great pyre. The story told to explain the festivals suggests that they celebrated the marriage of Zeus to Hera, represented by the oaken image in bridal array. In Sweden every year a life-size image of Frey, the god of fertility, both animal and vegetable, was drawn about the country in a waggon attended by a beautiful girl who was called the god's wife. She acted also as his priestess in his great temple at Upsala. Wherever the waggon came with the image of the god and his blooming young bride, the people crowded to meet them and offered sacrifices for a fruitful year.

Thus the custom of marrying gods either to images or to human beings was widespread among the nations of antiquity. The ideas on which such a custom is based are too crude to allow us to doubt that the civilised Babylonians, Egyptians, and Greeks inherited it from their barbarous or savage forefathers. This presumption is strengthened when we find rites of a similar kind in vogue among the lower races. Thus, for example, we are told that once upon a time the Wotyaks of the Malmyz district in Russia were distressed by a series of bad harvests. They did not know what to do, but at last concluded that their powerful but mischievous god Keremet must be angry at being unmarried. So a deputation of elders visited the Wotyaks of Cura and came to an understanding with them on the subject. Then they returned home, laid in a large stock of brandy, and having made ready a gaily decked waggon and horses, they drove in procession with bells ringing, as they do when they are fetching home a bride, to the sacred grove at Cura. There they ate and drank merrily all night, and next morning they cut a square piece of turf in the grove and took it home with them. After that, though it fared well with the people of Malmyz, it fared ill with the people of Cura ; for in Malmyz the bread was good, but in Cura it was bad. Hence the men of Cura who had consented to the marriage were blamed and roughly handled by their indignant fellow-villagers. "What they meant by this marriage ceremony," says the writer who reports it, " it is not easy to imagine. Perhaps, as Bechterew thinks, they meant to marry Keremet to the kindly and fruitful Mukylćin, the Earth-wife, in order that she might influence him for good." When wells are dug in Bengal, a wooden image of a god is made and married to the goddess of water.

Often the bride destined for the god is not a log or a clod, but a living woman of flesh and blood. The Indians of a village in Peru have been known to marry a beautiful girl, about fourteen years of age, to a stone shaped like a human being, which they regarded as a god (*huaca*). All the villagers took part in the marriage ceremony, which lasted three days, and was attended with much revelry. The girl thereafter remained a virgin and sacrificed to the idol for the people. They showed her the utmost reverence and deemed her divine. Every year about the middle of March, when the season for fishing with the drag-net began, the Algonquins and Hurons married their nets to two young girls, aged six or seven. At the wedding feast the net was placed between the two maidens, and was exhorted to take courage and catch many fish. The reason for choosing the brides so young was to make sure that they were virgins. The origin of the custom is said to have been this. One year, when the fishing season came round, the Algonquins cast their nets as usual, but took nothing. Surprised at their want of success, they did not know what to make of it, till the soul or genius (*oki*) of the net appeared to them in the likeness of a tall well-built man, who said to them in a great passion, " I have lost my wife and I cannot find one who has known no other man but me ; that is why you do not succeed, and why you never will succeed till you give me satisfaction on this head." So the Algonquins held a council and resolved to appease the spirit of the net by marrying him to two such very young girls that he could have no ground of complaint on that score for the future. They did so, and the fishing turned out all that could be wished. The thing got wind among their neighbours the Hurons, and they adopted the custom. A share of the catch was always given to the families of the two girls who acted as brides of the net for the year.

The Oraons of Bengal worship the Earth as a goddess, and annually

celebrate her marriage with the Sun-god Dharmē at the time when the
sāl tree is in blossom.   The ceremony is as follows.   All bathe, then the
men repair to the sacred grove (*sarnā*), while the women assemble at the
house of the village priest.   After sacrificing some fowls to the Sun-god
and the demon of the grove, the men eat and drink.   " The priest is
then carried back to the village on the shoulders of a strong man.
Near the village the women meet the men and wash their feet.   With
beating of drums and singing, dancing, and jumping, all proceed to the
priest's house, which has been decorated with leaves and flowers.   Then
the usual form of marriage is performed between the priest and his wife,
symbolising the supposed union between Sun and Earth.   After the
ceremony all eat and drink and make merry ;   they dance and sing
obscene songs, and finally indulge in the vilest orgies.   The object is to
move the mother earth to become fruitful."   Thus the Sacred Marriage
of the Sun and Earth, personated by the priest and his wife, is celebrated
as a charm to ensure the fertility of the ground ;   and for the same
purpose, on the principle of homoeopathic magic, the people indulge in
a licentious orgy.

It deserves to be remarked that the supernatural being to whom
women are married is often a god or spirit of water.   Thus Mukasa,
the god of the Victoria Nyanza lake, who was propitiated by the
Baganda every time they undertook a long voyage, had virgins provided for him to serve as his wives.   Like the Vestals they were bound
to chastity, but unlike the Vestals they seem to have been often
unfaithful.   The custom lasted until Mwanga was converted to Christianity.   The Akikuyu of British East Africa worship the snake of a
certain river, and at intervals of several years they marry the snake-god
to women, but especially to young girls.   For this purpose huts are
built by order of the medicine-men, who there consummate the sacred
marriage with the credulous female devotees.   If the girls do not repair
to the huts of their own accord in sufficient numbers, they are seized
and dragged thither to the embraces of the deity.   The offspring of
these mystic unions appears to be fathered on God (*Ngai*) ;   certainly
there are children among the Akikuyu who pass for children of God.
It is said that once, when the inhabitants of Cayeli in Buru—an East
Indian island—were threatened with destruction by a swarm of
crocodiles, they ascribed the misfortune to a passion which the prince
of the crocodiles had conceived for a certain girl.   Accordingly, they
compelled the damsel's father to dress her in bridal array and deliver
her over to the clutches of her crocodile lover.

A usage of the same sort is reported to have prevailed in the Maldive
Islands before the conversion of the inhabitants to Islam.   The famous
Arab traveller Ibn Batutah has described the custom and the manner
in which it came to an end.   He was assured by several trustworthy
natives, whose names he gives, that when the people of the islands were
idolaters there appeared to them every month an evil spirit among the
jinn, who came from across the sea in the likeness of a ship full of
burning lamps.   The wont of the inhabitants, as soon as they perceived

him, was to take a young virgin, and, having adorned her, to lead her to a heathen temple that stood on the shore, with a window looking out to sea. There they left the damsel for the night, and when they came back in the morning they found her a maid no more, and dead. Every month they drew lots, and he upon whom the lot fell gave up his daughter to the jinnee of the sea. The last of the maidens thus offered to the demon was rescued by a pious Berber, who by reciting the Koran succeeded in driving the jinnee back into the sea.

Ibn Batutah's narrative of the demon lover and his mortal brides closely resembles a well-known type of folk-tale, of which versions have been found from Japan and Annam in the East to Senegambia, Scandinavia, and Scotland in the West. The story varies in details from people to people, but as commonly told it runs thus. A certain country is infested by a many-headed serpent, dragon, or other monster, which would destroy the whole people if a human victim, generally a virgin, were not delivered up to him periodically. Many victims have perished, and at last it has fallen to the lot of the king's own daughter to be sacrificed. She is exposed to the monster, but the hero of the tale, generally a young man of humble birth, interposes in her behalf, slays the monster, and receives the hand of the princess as his reward. In many of the tales the monster, who is sometimes described as a serpent, inhabits the water of a sea, a lake, or a fountain. In other versions he is a serpent or dragon who takes possession of the springs of water, and only allows the water to flow or the people to make use of it on condition of receiving a human victim.

It would probably be a mistake to dismiss all these tales as pure inventions of the story-teller. Rather we may suppose that they reflect a real custom of sacrificing girls or women to be the wives of water-spirits, who are very often conceived as great serpents or dragons.

CHAPTER XIII

THE KINGS OF ROME AND ALBA

§ 1. *Numa and Egeria.*—From the foregoing survey of custom and legend we may infer that the sacred marriage of the powers both of vegetation and of water has been celebrated by many peoples for the sake of promoting the fertility of the earth, on which the life of animals and men ultimately depends, and that in such rites the part of the divine bridegroom or bride is often sustained by a man or woman. The evidence may, therefore, lend some countenance to the conjecture that in the sacred grove at Nemi, where the powers of vegetation and of water manifested themselves in the fair forms of shady woods, tumbling cascades, and glassy lake, a marriage like that of our King and Queen of May was annually celebrated between the mortal King of the Wood and the immortal Queen of the Wood, Diana. In this connexion an important figure in the grove was the water-nymph Egeria, who was worshipped by pregnant women because she, like Diana, could grant them an easy delivery. From this it seems fairly safe to conclude that, like many other springs, the water of Egeria was credited with a power of facilitating conception as well as delivery. The votive offerings found on the spot, which clearly refer to the begetting of children, may possibly have been dedicated to Egeria rather than to Diana, or perhaps we should rather say that the water-nymph Egeria is only another form of the great nature-goddess Diana herself, the mistress of sounding rivers as well as of umbrageous woods, who had her home by the lake and her mirror in its calm waters, and whose Greek counterpart Artemis loved to haunt meres and springs. The identification of Egeria with Diana is confirmed by a statement of Plutarch that Egeria was one of the oak-nymphs whom the Romans believed to preside over every green oak-grove ; for, while Diana was a goddess of the woodlands in general, she appears to have been intimately associated with oaks in particular, especially at her sacred grove of Nemi. Perhaps, then, Egeria was the fairy of a spring that flowed from the roots of a sacred oak. Such a spring is said to have gushed from the foot of the great oak at Dodona, and from its murmurous flow the priestess drew oracles. Among the Greeks a draught of water from certain sacred springs or wells was supposed to confer prophetic powers. This would explain the more than mortal wisdom with which, according to tradition, Egeria inspired her royal husband or lover Numa. When we remember how very often in early society the king is held responsible for the fall of rain and the fruitfulness of the earth, it seems hardly rash to conjecture that in the legend of the nuptials of Numa and Egeria we have a reminiscence of a sacred marriage which the old Roman kings regularly contracted with a goddess of vegetation and water for the purpose of enabling him to discharge his divine or magical functions. In such a rite the part of the goddess might be played either by an image or a woman, and if by a woman, probably by the Queen. If there is any truth in this conjecture, we may suppose that the King and Queen of Rome masqueraded as god and goddess at their marriage, exactly as the King and Queen of Egypt appear to have done. The legend of Numa and Egeria points to a sacred grove rather than to a house as the scene of the nuptial union, which, like the marriage of the King and Queen of May, or of the vine-god and the Queen of Athens, may have been annually celebrated as a charm to ensure the fertility not only of the earth but of man and beast. Now, according to some accounts, the scene of the marriage was no other than the sacred grove of Nemi, and on quite independent grounds we have been led to suppose that in that same grove the King of the Wood was wedded to Diana. The convergence of the two distinct lines of enquiry suggests that the legendary union of the Roman king with Egeria may have been a reflection or duplicate of the union of the King of the Wood with Egeria or her double Diana. This does not imply that the Roman kings ever served as Kings of the Wood in the Arician grove, but only that they may originally have been invested with a sacred character of the same general kind, and may have held office on similar terms. To be more explicit, it is possible that they reigned, not by right of birth, but in virtue of their supposed divinity as representatives or embodiments of a god, and that as such they mated with a goddess, and had to prove their fitness from time to time to discharge their divine functions by engaging in a severe bodily struggle, which may often have proved fatal to them, leaving the crown to their victorious adversary. Our knowledge of the Roman kingship is far too scanty to allow us to affirm any one of these propositions with confidence; but at least there are some scattered hints or indications of a similarity in all these respects between the priests of Nemi and the kings of Rome, or perhaps rather between their remote predecessors in the dark ages which preceded the dawn of legend.

§ 2. *The King as Jupiter.*—In the first place, then, it would seem that the Roman king personated no less a deity than Jupiter himself. For down to imperial times victorious generals celebrating a triumph, and magistrates presiding at the games in the Circus, wore the costume of Jupiter, which was borrowed for the occasion from his great temple on the Capitol; and it has been held with a high degree of probability both by ancients and moderns that in so doing they copied the traditionary attire and insignia of the Roman kings. They rode a chariot drawn by four laurel-crowned horses through the city, where every one else went on foot: they wore purple robes embroidered or spangled with gold: in the right hand they bore a branch of laurel, and in the left hand an ivory sceptre topped with an eagle: a wreath of laurel crowned their brows: their face was reddened with vermilion; and over their head a slave held a heavy crown of massy gold fashioned in the likeness of oak leaves. In this attire the assimilation of the man to the god comes out above all in the eagle-topped sceptre, the oaken crown, and the reddened face. For the eagle was the bird of Jove, the oak was his sacred tree, and the face of his image standing in his four-horse chariot on the Capitol was in like manner regularly dyed red on festivals; indeed, so important was it deemed to keep the divine features properly rouged that one of the first duties of the censors was to contract for having this done. As the triumphal procession always ended in the temple of Jupiter on the Capitol, it was peculiarly appropriate that the head of the victor should be graced by a crown of oak leaves, for not only was every oak consecrated to Jupiter, but the Capitoline temple of the god was said to have been built by Romulus beside a sacred oak, venerated by shepherds, to which the king attached the spoils won by him from the enemy's general in battle. We are expressly told that the oak crown was sacred to Capitoline Jupiter; a passage of Ovid proves that it was regarded as the god's special emblem.

According to a tradition which we have no reason to reject, Rome was founded by settlers from Alba Longa, a city situated on the slope of the Alban hills, overlooking the lake and the Campagna. Hence if the Roman kings claimed to be representatives or embodiments of

Jupiter, the god of the sky, of the thunder, and of the oak, it is natural to suppose that the kings of Alba, from whom the founder of Rome traced his descent, may have set up the same claim before them. Now the Alban dynasty bore the name of Silvii or Wood, and it can hardly be without significance that in the vision of the historic glories of Rome revealed to Aeneas in the underworld, Virgil, an antiquary as well as a poet, should represent all the line of Silvii as crowned with oak. A chaplet of oak leaves would thus seem to have been part of the insignia of the old kings of Alba Longa as of their successors the kings of Rome ; in both cases it marked the monarch as the human representative of the oak-god. The Roman annals record that one of the kings of Alba, Romulus, Remulus, or Amulius Silvius by name, set up for being a god in his own person, the equal or superior of Jupiter. To support his pretensions and overawe his subjects, he constructed machines whereby he mimicked the clap of thunder and the flash of lightning. Diodorus relates that in the season of fruitage, when thunder is loud and frequent, the king commanded his soldiers to drown the roar of heaven's artillery by clashing their swords against their shields. But he paid the penalty of his impiety, for he perished, he and his house, struck by a thunderbolt in the midst of a dreadful storm. Swollen by the rain, the Alban lake rose in flood and drowned his palace. But still, says an ancient historian, when the water is low and the surface unruffled by a breeze, you may see the ruins of the palace at the bottom of the clear lake. Taken along with the similar story of Salmoneus, king of Elis, this legend points to a real custom observed by the early kings of Greece and Italy, who, like their fellows in Africa down to modern times, may have been expected to produce rain and thunder for the good of the crops. The priestly king Numa passed for an adept in the art of drawing down lightning from the sky. Mock thunder, we know, has been made by various peoples as a rain-charm in modern times ; why should it not have been made by kings in antiquity ?

Thus, if the kings of Alba and Rome imitated Jupiter as god of the oak by wearing a crown of oak leaves, they seem also to have copied him in his character of a weather-god by pretending to make thunder and lightning. And if they did so, it is probable that, like Jupiter in heaven and many kings on earth, they also acted as public rain-makers, wringing showers from the dark sky by their enchantments whenever the parched earth cried out for the refreshing moisture. At Rome the sluices of heaven were opened by means of a sacred stone, and the ceremony appears to have formed part of the ritual of Jupiter Elicius, the god who elicits from the clouds the flashing lightning and the dripping rain. And who so well fitted to perform the ceremony as the king, the living representative of the sky-god ?

If the kings of Rome aped Capitoline Jove, their predecessors the kings of Alba probably laid themselves out to mimic the great Latian Jupiter, who had his seat above the city on the summit of the Alban Mountain. Latinus, the legendary ancestor of the dynasty, was said to have been changed into Latian Jupiter after vanishing from the world in the mysterious fashion characteristic of the old Latin kings. The sanctuary of the god on the top of the mountain was the religious centre of the Latin League, as Alba was its political capital till Rome wrested the supremacy from its ancient rival.   Apparently no temple, in our sense of the word, was ever erected to Jupiter on this his holy mountain ; as god of the sky and thunder he appropriately received the homage of his worshippers in the open air.   The massive wall, of which some remains still enclose the old garden of the Passionist monastery, seems to have been part of the sacred precinct which Tarquin the Proud, the last king of Rome, marked out for the solemn annual assembly of the Latin League.   The god's oldest sanctuary on this airy mountain-top was a grove ; and bearing in mind not merely the special consecration of the oak to Jupiter, but also the traditional oak crown of the Alban kings and the analogy of the Capitoline Jupiter at Rome, we may suppose that the trees in the grove were oaks.   We know that in antiquity Mount Algidus, an outlying group of the Alban hills, was covered with dark forests of oak ; and among the tribes who belonged to the Latin League in the earliest days, and were entitled to share the flesh of the white bull sacrificed on the Alban Mount, there was one whose members styled themselves the Men of the Oak, doubt-less on account of the woods among which they dwelt.

But we should err if we pictured to ourselves the country as covered in historical times with an unbroken forest of oaks.   Theophrastus has left us a description of the woods of Latium as they were in the fourth century before Christ.   He says : " The land of the Latins is all moist.   The plains produce laurels, myrtles, and wonderful beeches ; for they fell trees of such a size that a single stem suffices for the keel of a Tyrrhenian ship.   Pines and firs grow in the mountains.   What they call the land of Circe is a lofty headland thickly wooded with oak, myrtle, and luxuriant laurels.   The natives say that Circe dwelt there, and they show the grave of Elpenor, from which grow myrtles such as wreaths are made of, whereas the other myrtle-trees are tall." Thus the prospect from the top of the Alban Mount in the early days of Rome must have been very different in some respects from what it is to-day.   The purple Apennines, indeed, in their eternal calm on the one hand, and the shining Mediterranean in its eternal unrest on the other, no doubt looked then much as they look now, whether bathed in sunshine or chequered by the fleeting shadows of clouds ; but instead of the desolate brown expanse of the fever-stricken Campagna, spanned by its long lines of ruined aqueducts, like the broken arches of the bridge in the vision of Mirza, the eye must have ranged over woodlands that stretched away, mile after mile, on all sides, till their varied hues of green or autumnal scarlet and gold melted insensibly into the blue of the distant mountains and sea.

But Jupiter did not reign alone on the top of his holy mountain. He had his consort with him, the goddess Juno, who was worshipped here under the same title, Moneta, as on the Capitol at Rome.   As the oak crown was sacred to Jupiter and Juno on the Capitol, so we may suppose it was on the Alban Mount, from which the Capitoline worship was derived. Thus the oak-god would have his oak-goddess in the sacred oak grove. So at Dodona the oak-god Zeus was coupled with Dione, whose very name is only a dialectically different form of Juno; and so on the top of Mount Cithaeron, as we have seen, he appears to have been periodically wedded to an oaken image of Hera. It is probable, though it cannot be positively proved, that the sacred marriage of Jupiter and Juno was annually celebrated by all the peoples of the Latin stock in the month which they named after the goddess, the midsummer month of June.

If at any time of the year the Romans celebrated the sacred marriage of Jupiter and Juno, as the Greeks commonly celebrated the corresponding marriage of Zeus and Hera, we may suppose that under the Republic the ceremony was either performed over images of the divine pair or acted by the Flamen Dialis and his wife the Flaminica. For the Flamen Dialis was the priest of Jove; indeed, ancient and modern writers have regarded him, with much probability, as a living image of Jupiter, a human embodiment of the sky-god. In earlier times the Roman king, as representative of Jupiter, would naturally play the part of the heavenly bridegroom at the sacred marriage, while his queen would figure as the heavenly bride, just as in Egypt the king and queen masqueraded in the character of deities, and as at Athens the queen annually wedded the vine-god Dionysus. That the Roman king and queen should act the parts of Jupiter and Juno would seem all the more natural because these deities themselves bore the title of King and Queen.

Whether that was so or not, the legend of Numa and Egeria appears to embody a reminiscence of a time when the priestly king himself played the part of the divine bridegroom; and as we have seen reason to suppose that the Roman kings personated the oak-god, while Egeria is expressly said to have been an oak-nymph, the story of their union in the sacred grove raises a presumption that at Rome in the regal period a ceremony was periodically performed exactly analogous to that which was annually celebrated at Athens down to the time of Aristotle. The marriage of the King of Rome to the oak-goddess, like the wedding of the vine-god to the Queen of Athens, must have been intended to quicken the growth of vegetation by homoeopathic magic. Of the two forms of the rite we can hardly doubt that the Roman was the older, and that long before the northern invaders met with the vine on the shores of the Mediterranean their forefathers had married the tree-god to the tree-goddess in the vast oak forests of Central and Northern Europe. In the England of our day the forests have mostly disappeared, yet still on many a village green and in many a country lane a faded image of the sacred marriage lingers in the rustic pageantry of May Day.

CHAPTER XIV

THE SUCCESSION TO THE KINGDOM IN ANCIENT LATIUM

In regard to the Roman king, whose priestly functions were inherited by his successor the King of the Sacred Rites, the foregoing discussion has led us to the following conclusions. He represented and indeed personated Jupiter, the great god of the sky, the thunder, and the oak, and in that character made rain, thunder, and lightning for the good of his subjects, like many more kings of the weather in other parts of the world. Further, he not only mimicked the oak-god by wearing an oak wreath and other insignia of divinity, but he was married to an oak-nymph Egeria, who appears to have been merely a local form of Diana in her character of a goddess of woods, of waters, and of childbirth. All these conclusions, which we have reached mainly by a considera-tion of the Roman evidence, may with great probability be applied to the other Latin communities. They too probably had of old their divine or priestly kings, who transmitted their religious functions, without their civil powers, to their successors the Kings of the Sacred Rites.

But we have still to ask, What was the rule of succession to the kingdom among the old Latin tribes? According to tradition, there were in all eight kings of Rome, and with regard to the five last of them, at all events, we can hardly doubt that they actually sat on the throne, and that the traditional history of their reigns is, in its main outlines, correct. Now it is very remarkable that though the first king of Rome, Romulus, is said to have been descended from the royal house of Alba, in which the kingship is represented as hereditary in the male line, not one of the Roman kings was immediately succeeded by his son on the throne. Yet several left sons or grandsons behind them. On the other hand, one of them was descended from a former king through his mother, not through his father, and three of the kings, namely Tatius, the elder Tarquin, and Servius Tullius, were succeeded by their sons-in-law, who were all either foreigners or of foreign descent. This suggests that the right to the kingship was transmitted in the female line, and was actually exercised by foreigners who married the royal princesses. To put it in technical language, the succession to the kingship at Rome and probably in Latium generally would seem to have been determined by certain rules which have moulded early society in many parts of the world, namely exogamy, *beena* marriage, and female kinship or mother-kin. Exogamy is the rule which obliges a man to marry a woman of a different clan from his own: *beena* marriage is the rule that he must leave the home of his birth and live with his wife's people; and female kinship or mother-kin is the system of tracing relationship and transmitting the family name through women instead of through men. If these principles regulated descent of the kingship among the ancient Latins, the state of things in this respect would be somewhat as follows. The political and religious centre of each community would be the perpetual fire on the king's hearth tended by Vestal Virgins of the royal clan.   The king would be a man of another clan, perhaps of another town or even of another race, who had married a daughter of his predecessor and received the kingdom with her.   The children whom he had by her would inherit their mother's name, not his ; the daughters would remain at home ; the sons, when they grew up, would go away into the world, marry, and settle in their wives' country, whether as kings or commoners. Of the daughters who stayed at home, some or all would be dedicated as Vestal Virgins for a longer or shorter time to the service of the fire on the hearth, and one of them would in time become the consort of her father's successor.

This hypothesis has the advantage of explaining in a simple and natural way some obscure features in the traditional history of the Latin kingship.   Thus the legends which tell how Latin kings were born of virgin mothers and divine fathers become at least more intelligible.   For, stripped of their fabulous element, tales of this sort mean no more than that a woman has been gotten with child by a man unknown ; and this uncertainty as to fatherhood is more easily compatible with a system of kinship which ignores paternity than with one which makes it all-important.   If at the birth of the Latin kings their fathers were really unknown, the fact points either to a general looseness of life in the royal family or to a special relaxation of moral rules on certain occasions, when men and women reverted for a season to the licence of an earlier age.   Such Saturnalias are not uncommon at some stages of social evolution.   In our own country traces of them long survived in the practices of May Day and Whitsuntide, if not of Christmas.   Children born of the more or less promiscuous intercourse which characterises festivals of this kind would naturally be fathered on the god to whom the particular festival was dedicated.

In this connexion it may be significant that a festival of jollity and drunkenness was celebrated by the plebeians and slaves at Rome on Midsummer Day, and that the festival was specially associated with the fireborn King Servius Tullius, being held in honour of Fortuna, the goddess who loved Servius as Egeria loved Numa.   The popular merrymakings at this season included foot-races and boat-races ; the Tiber was gay with flower-wreathed boats, in which young folk sat quaffing wine.   The festival appears to have been a sort of Midsummer Saturnalia answering to the real Saturnalia which fell at Midwinter. In modern Europe, as we shall learn later on, the great Midsummer festival has been above all a festival of lovers and of fire ; one of its principal features is the pairing of sweethearts, who leap over the bonfires hand in hand or throw flowers across the flames to each other. And many omens of love and marriage are drawn from the flowers which bloom at this mystic season.   It is the time of the roses and of love.   Yet the innocence and beauty of such festivals in modern times ought not to blind us to the likelihood that in earlier days they were marked by coarser features, which were probably of the essence of the rites. Indeed, among the rude Esthonian peasantry these features seem to have lingered down to our own generation, if not to the present day. One other feature in the Roman celebration of Midsummer deserves to be specially noticed. The custom of rowing in flower-decked boats on the river on this day proves that it was to some extent a water festival ; and water has always, down to modern times, played a conspicuous part in the rites of Midsummer Day, which explains why the Church, in throwing its cloak over the old heathen festival, chose to dedicate it to St. John the Baptist.

The hypothesis that the Latin kings may have been begotten at an annual festival of love is necessarily a mere conjecture, though the traditional birth of Numa at the festival of the Parilia, when shepherds leaped across the spring bonfires, as lovers leap across the Midsummer fires, may perhaps be thought to lend it a faint colour of probability. But it is quite possible that the uncertainty as to their fathers may not have arisen till long after the death of the kings, when their figures began to melt away into the cloudland of fable, assuming fantastic shapes and gorgeous colouring as they passed from earth to heaven. If they were alien immigrants, strangers and pilgrims in the land they ruled over, it would be natural enough that the people should forget their lineage, and forgetting it should provide them with another, which made up in lustre what it lacked in truth. The final apotheosis, which represented the kings not merely as sprung from gods but as themselves deities incarnate, would be much facilitated if in their lifetime, as we have seen reason to think, they had actually laid claim to divinity.

If among the Latins the women of royal blood always stayed at home and received as their consorts men of another stock, and often of another country, who reigned as kings in virtue of their marriage with a native princess, we can understand not only why foreigners wore the crown at Rome, but also why foreign names occur in the list of the Alban kings. In a state of society where nobility is reckoned only through women—in other words, where descent through the mother is everything, and descent through the father is nothing—no objection will be felt to uniting girls of the highest rank to men of humble birth, even to aliens or slaves, provided that in themselves the men appear to be suitable mates. What really matters is that the royal stock, on which the prosperity and even the existence of the people is supposed to depend, should be perpetuated in a vigorous and efficient form, and for this purpose it is necessary that the women of the royal family should bear children to men who are physically and mentally fit, according to the standard of early society, to discharge the important duty of procreation. Thus the personal qualities of the kings at this stage of social evolution are deemed of vital importance. If they, like their consorts, are of royal and divine descent, so much the better ; but it is not essential that they should be so.

At Athens, as at Rome, we find traces of succession to the throne by marriage with a royal princess; for two of the most ancient kings of Athens, namely Cecrops and Amphictyon, are said to have married the daughters of their predecessors. This tradition is to a certain extent confirmed by evidence, pointing to the conclusion that at Athens male kinship was preceded by female kinship.

Further, if I am right in supposing that in ancient Latium the royal families kept their daughters at home and sent forth their sons to marry princesses and reign among their wives' people, it will follow that the male descendants would reign in successive generations over different kingdoms. Now this seems to have happened both in ancient Greece and in ancient Sweden; from which we may legitimately infer that it was a custom practised by more than one branch of the Aryan stock in Europe. Many Greek traditions relate how a prince left his native land, and going to a far country married the king's daughter and succeeded to the kingdom. Various reasons are assigned by ancient Greek writers for these migrations of the princes. A common one is that the king's son had been banished for murder. This would explain very well why he fled his own land, but it is no reason at all why he should become king of another. We may suspect that such reasons are afterthoughts devised by writers, who, accustomed to the rule that a son should succeed to his father's property and kingdom, were hard put to it to account for so many traditions of kings' sons who quitted the land of their birth to reign over a foreign kingdom. In Scandinavian tradition we meet with traces of similar customs. For we read of daughters' husbands who received a share of the kingdoms of their royal fathers-in-law, even when these fathers-in-law had sons of their own; in particular, during the five generations which preceded Harold the Fair-haired, male members of the Ynglingar family, which is said to have come from Sweden, are reported in the *Heimskringla* or *Sagas of the Norwegian Kings* to have obtained at least six provinces in Norway by marriage with the daughters of the local kings.

Thus it would seem that among some Aryan peoples, at a certain stage of their social evolution, it has been customary to regard women and not men as the channels in which royal blood flows, and to bestow the kingdom in each successive generation on a man of another family, and often of another country, who marries one of the princesses and reigns over his wife's people. A common type of popular tale, which relates how an adventurer, coming to a strange land, wins the hand of the king's daughter and with her the half or the whole of the kingdom, may well be a reminiscence of a real custom.

Where usages and ideas of this sort prevail, it is obvious that the kingship is merely an appanage of marriage with a woman of the blood royal. The old Danish historian Saxo Grammaticus puts this view of the kingship very clearly in the mouth of Hermutrude, a legendary queen of Scotland. "Indeed she was a queen," says Hermutrude, "and but that her sex gainsaid it, might be deemed a king; nay (and this is yet truer), whomsoever she thought worthy of her bed was at once a king, and she yielded her kingdom with herself. Thus her sceptre and her hand went together." The statement is all the more significant because it appears to reflect the actual practice of the Pictish kings. We know from the testimony of Bede that, whenever a doubt arose as to the succession, the Picts chose their kings from the female rather than the male line.

The personal qualities which recommended a man for a royal alliance and succession to the throne would naturally vary according to the popular ideas of the time and the character of the king or his substitute, but it is reasonable to suppose that among them in early society physical strength and beauty would hold a prominent place.

Sometimes apparently the right to the hand of the princess and to the throne has been determined by a race. The Alitemnian Libyans awarded the kingdom to the fleetest runner. Amongst the old Prussians, candidates for nobility raced on horseback to the king, and the one who reached him first was ennobled. According to tradition the earliest games at Olympia were held by Endymion, who set his sons to run a race for the kingdom. His tomb was said to be at the point of the racecourse from which the runners started. The famous story of Pelops and Hippodamia is perhaps only another version of the legend that the first races at Olympia were run for no less a prize than a kingdom.

These traditions may very well reflect a real custom of racing for a bride, for such a custom appears to have prevailed among various peoples, though in practice it has degenerated into a mere form or pretence. Thus " there is one race, called the ' Love Chase,' which may be considered a part of the form of marriage among the Kirghiz. In this the bride, armed with a formidable whip, mounts a fleet horse, and is pursued by all the young men who make any pretensions to her hand. She will be given as a prize to the one who catches her, but she has the right, besides urging on her horse to the utmost, to use her whip, often with no mean force, to keep off those lovers who are unwelcome to her, and she will probably favour the one whom she has already chosen in her heart." The race for the bride is found also among the Koryaks of North-eastern Asia. It takes place in a large tent, round which many separate compartments called *pologs* are arranged in a continuous circle. The girl gets a start and is clear of the marriage if she can run through all the compartments without being caught by the bridegroom. The women of the encampment place every obstacle in the man's way, tripping him up, belabouring him with switches, and so forth, so that he has little chance of succeeding unless the girl wishes it and waits for him. Similar customs appear to have been practised by all the Teutonic peoples ; for the German, Anglo-Saxon, and Norse languages possess in common a word for marriage which means simply bride-race. Moreover, traces of the custom survived into modern times.

Thus it appears that the right to marry a girl, and especially a princess, has often been conferred as a prize in an athletic contest. There would be no reason, therefore, for surprise if the Roman kings, before bestowing their daughters in marriage, should have resorted to this ancient mode of testing the personal qualities of their future sons-in-law and successors.   If my theory is correct, the Roman king and queen personated Jupiter and his divine consort, and in the character of these divinities went through the annual ceremony of a sacred marriage for the purpose of causing the crops to grow and men and cattle to be fruitful and multiply.   Thus they did what in more northern lands we may suppose the King and Queen of May were believed to do in days of old.   Now we have seen that the right to play the part of the King of May and to wed the Queen of May has sometimes been determined by an athletic contest, particularly by a race.   This may have been a relic of an old marriage custom of the sort we have examined, a custom designed to test the fitness of a candidate for matrimony.   Such a test might reasonably be applied with peculiar rigour to the king in order to ensure that no personal defect should incapacitate him for the performance of those sacred rites and cere-monies on which, even more than on the despatch of his civil and military duties, the safety and prosperity of the community were believed to depend.   And it would be natural to require of him that from time to time he should submit himself afresh to the same ordeal for the sake of publicly demonstrating that he was still equal to the discharge of his high calling.   A relic of that test perhaps survived in the ceremony known as the Flight of the King (*regifugium*), which continued to be annually observed at Rome down to imperial times. On the twenty-fourth day of February a sacrifice used to be offered in the Comitium, and when it was over the King of the Sacred Rites fled from the Forum.   We may conjecture that the Flight of the King was originally a race for an annual kingship, which may have been awarded as a prize to the fleetest runner.   At the end of the year the king might run again for a second term of office ; and so on, until he was defeated and deposed or perhaps slain.   In this way what had once been a race would tend to assume the character of a flight and a pursuit.   The king would be given a start ; he ran and his competitors ran after him, and if he were overtaken he had to yield the crown and perhaps his life to the lightest of foot among them.   In time a man of masterful character might succeed in seating himself permanently on the throne and reducing the annual race or flight to the empty form which it seems always to have been within historical times.   The rite was sometimes interpreted as a commemoration of the expulsion of the kings from Rome ; but this appears to have been a mere afterthought devised to explain a ceremony of which the old meaning was forgotten.   It is far more likely that in acting thus the King of the Sacred Rites was merely keeping up an ancient custom which in the regal period had been annually observed by his predecessors the kings.   What the original intention of the rite may have been must probably always remain more or less a matter of conjecture.   The present explanation is suggested with a full sense of the difficulty and obscurity in which the subject is involved.

Thus, if my theory is correct, the yearly flight of the Roman king was a relic of a time when the kingship was an annual office awarded, along with the hand of a princess, to the victorious athlete or gladiator, who thereafter figured along with his bride as a god and goddess at a sacred marriage designed to ensure the fertility of the earth by homoeopathic magic.   If I am right in supposing that in very early times the old Latin kings personated a god and were regularly put to death in that character, we can better understand the mysterious or violent ends to which so many of them are said to have come.   We have seen that, according to tradition, one of the kings of Alba was killed by a thunderbolt for impiously mimicking the thunder of Jupiter. Romulus is said to have vanished mysteriously like Aeneas, or to have been cut to pieces by the patricians whom he had offended, and the seventh of July, the day on which he perished, was a festival which bore some resemblance to the Saturnalia.   For on that day the female slaves were allowed to take certain remarkable liberties.   They dressed up as free women in the attire of matrons and maids, and in this guise they went forth from the city, scoffed and jeered at all whom they met, and engaged among themselves in a fight, striking and throwing stones at each other.   Another Roman king who perished by violence was Tatius, the Sabine colleague of Romulus.   It is said that he was at Lavinium offering a public sacrifice to the ancestral gods, when some men, to whom he had given umbrage, despatched him with the sacrificial knives and spits which they had snatched from the altar.   The occasion and the manner of his death suggest that the slaughter may have been a sacrifice rather than an assassination.   Again, Tullus Hostilius, the successor of Numa, was commonly said to have been killed by lightning, but many held that he was murdered at the instigation of Ancus Marcius, who reigned after him.   Speaking of the more or less mythical Numa, the type of the priestly king, Plutarch observes that " his fame was enhanced by the fortunes of the later kings.   For of the five who reigned after him the last was deposed and ended his life in exile, and of the remaining four not one died a natural death ; for three of them were assassinated and Tullus Hostilius was consumed by thunderbolts."

These legends of the violent ends of the Roman kings suggest that the contest by which they gained the throne may sometimes have been a mortal combat rather than a race.   If that were so, the analogy which we have traced between Rome and Nemi would be still closer. At both places the sacred kings, the living representatives of the godhead, would thus be liable to suffer deposition and death at the hand of any resolute man who could prove his divine right to the holy office by the strong arm and the sharp sword.   It would not be surprising if among the early Latins the claim to the kingdom should often have been settled by single combat ; for down to historical times the Umbrians regularly submitted their private disputes to the ordeal of battle, and he who cut his adversary's throat was thought thereby to have proved the justice of his cause beyond the reach of cavil.

CHAPTER XV

THE WORSHIP OF THE OAK

THE worship of the oak tree or of the oak god appears to have been shared by all the branches of the Aryan stock in Europe. Both Greeks and Italians associated the tree with their highest god, Zeus or Jupiter, the divinity of the sky, the rain, and the thunder. Perhaps the oldest and certainly one of the most famous sanctuaries in Greece was that of Dodona, where Zeus was revered in the oracular oak. The thunder-storms which are said to rage at Dodona more frequently than any-where else in Europe, would render the spot a fitting home for the god whose voice was heard alike in the rustling of the oak leaves and in the crash of thunder. Perhaps the bronze gongs which kept up a humming in the wind round the sanctuary were meant to mimic the thunder that might so often be heard rolling and rumbling in the coombs of the stern and barren mountains which shut in the gloomy valley. In Boeotia, as we have seen, the sacred marriage of Zeus and Hera, the oak god and the oak goddess, appears to have been celebrated with much pomp by a religious federation of states. And on Mount Lycaeus in Arcadia the character of Zeus as god both of the oak and of the rain comes out clearly in the rain charm practised by the priest of Zeus, who dipped an oak branch in a sacred spring. In his latter capacity Zeus was the god to whom the Greeks regularly prayed for rain. Nothing could be more natural; for often, though not always, he had his seat on the mountains where the clouds gather and the oaks grow. On the acropolis at Athens there was an image of Earth praying to Zeus for rain. And in time of drought the Athenians themselves prayed, "Rain, rain, O dear Zeus, on the cornland of the Athenians and on the plains."

Again, Zeus wielded the thunder and lightning as well as the rain. At Olympia and elsewhere he was worshipped under the surname of Thunderbolt; and at Athens there was a sacrificial hearth of Lightning Zeus on the city wall, where some priestly officials watched for lightning over Mount Parnes at certain seasons of the year. Further, spots which had been struck by lightning were regularly fenced in by the Greeks and consecrated to Zeus the Descender, that is, to the god who came down in the flash from heaven. Altars were set up within these enclosures and sacrifices offered on them. Several such places are known from inscriptions to have existed in Athens.

Thus when ancient Greek kings claimed to be descended from Zeus, and even to bear his name, we may reasonably suppose that they also attempted to exercise his divine functions by making thunder and rain for the good of their people or the terror and confusion of their foes. In this respect the legend of Salmoneus probably reflects the pretensions of a whole class of petty sovereigns who reigned of old, each over his little canton, in the oak-clad highlands of Greece.

Like their kinsmen the Irish kings, they were expected to be a source of fertility to the land and of fecundity to the cattle ; and how could they fulfil these expectations better than by acting the part of their kinsman Zeus, the great god of the oak, the thunder, and the rain ? They personified him, apparently, just as the Italian kings personified Jupiter.

In ancient Italy every oak was sacred to Jupiter, the Italian counterpart of Zeus ; and on the Capitol at Rome the god was worshipped as the deity not merely of the oak, but of the rain and the thunder. Contrasting the piety of the good old times with the scepticism of an age when nobody thought that heaven was heaven, or cared a fig for Jupiter, a Roman writer tells us that in former days noble matrons used to go with bare feet, streaming hair, and pure minds, up the long Capitoline slope, praying to Jupiter for rain. And straightway, he goes on, it rained bucketsful, then or never, and everybody returned dripping like drowned rats. " But nowadays," says he, " we are no longer religious, so the fields lie baking."

When we pass from southern to central Europe we still meet with the great god of the oak and the thunder among the barbarous Aryans who dwelt in the vast primaeval forests. Thus among the Celts of Gaul the Druids esteemed nothing more sacred than the mistletoe and the oak on which it grew ; they chose groves of oaks for the scene of their solemn service, and they performed none of their rites without oak leaves. " The Celts," says a Greek writer, " worship Zeus, and the Celtic image of Zeus is a tall oak." The Celtic conquerors, who settled in Asia in the third century before our era, appear to have carried the worship of the oak with them to their new home ; for in the heart of Asia Minor the Galatian senate met in a place which bore the pure Celtic name of Drynemetum, " the sacred oak grove " or " the temple of the oak." Indeed the very name of Druids is believed by good authorities to mean no more than " oak men."

In the religion of the ancient Germans the veneration for sacred groves seems to have held the foremost place, and according to Grimm the chief of their holy trees was the oak. It appears to have been especially dedicated to the god of thunder, Donar or Thunar, the equivalent of the Norse Thor ; for a sacred oak near Geismar, in Hesse, which Boniface cut down in the eighth century, went among the heathen by the name of Jupiter's oak (*robur Jovis*), which in old German would be *Donares eih*, " the oak of Donar." That the Teutonic thunder god Donar, Thunar, Thor was identified with the Italian thunder god Jupiter appears from our word Thursday, Thunar's day, which is merely a rendering of the Latin *dies Jovis*. Thus among the ancient Teutons, as among the Greeks and Italians, the god of the oak was also the god of the thunder. Moreover, he was regarded as the great fertilising power, who sent rain and caused the earth to bear fruit ; for Adam of Bremen tells us that " Thor presides in the air ; he it is who rules thunder and lightning, wind and rains, fine weather and crops." In these respects, therefore, the Teutonic thunder god again resembled his southern counterparts Zeus and Jupiter.

Amongst the Slavs also the oak appears to have been the sacred tree of the thunder god Perun, the counterpart of Zeus and Jupiter. It is said that at Novgorod there used to stand an image of Perun in the likeness of a man with a thunder-stone in his hand. A fire of oak wood burned day and night in his honour ; and if ever it went out the attendants paid for their negligence with their lives. Perun seems, like Zeus and Jupiter, to have been the chief god of his people ; for Procopius tells us that the Slavs " believe that one god, the maker of lightning, is alone lord of all things, and they sacrifice to him oxen and every victim."

The chief deity of the Lithuanians was Perkunas or Perkuns, the god of thunder and lightning, whose resemblance to Zeus and Jupiter has often been pointed out. Oaks were sacred to him, and when they were cut down by the Christian missionaries, the people loudly complained that their sylvan deities were destroyed. Perpetual fires, kindled with the wood of certain oak-trees, were kept up in honour of Perkunas ; if such a fire went out, it was lighted again by friction of the sacred wood. Men sacrificed to oak-trees for good crops, while women did the same to lime-trees ; from which we may infer that they regarded oaks as male and lime-trees as female. And in time of drought, when they wanted rain, they used to sacrifice a black heifer, a black he-goat, and a black cock to the thunder god in the depths of the woods. On such occasions the people assembled in great numbers from the country round about, ate and drank, and called upon Perkunas. They carried a bowl of beer thrice round the fire, then poured the liquor on the flames, while they prayed to the god to send showers. Thus the chief Lithuanian deity presents a close resemblance to Zeus and Jupiter, since he was the god of the oak, the thunder, and the rain.

From the foregoing survey it appears that a god of the oak, the thunder, and the rain was worshipped of old by all the main branches of the Aryan stock in Europe, and was indeed the chief deity of their pantheon.

CHAPTER XVI

DIANUS AND DIANA

In this chapter I propose to recapitulate the conclusions to which the enquiry has thus far led us, and drawing together the scattered rays of light, to turn them on the dark figure of the priest of Nemi.

We have found that at an early stage of society men, ignorant of the secret processes of nature and of the narrow limits within which it is in our power to control and direct them, have commonly arrogated to themselves functions which in the present state of knowledge we

should deem superhuman or divine. The illusion has been fostered
and maintained by the same causes which begot it, namely, the
marvellous order and uniformity with which nature conducts her
operations, the wheels of her great machine revolving with a smooth-
ness and precision which enable the patient observer to anticipate in
general the season, if not the very hour, when they will bring round the
fulfilment of his hopes or the accomplishment of his fears. The
regularly recurring events of this great cycle, or rather series of cycles,
soon stamp themselves even on the dull mind of the savage. He
foresees them, and foreseeing them mistakes the desired recurrence
for an effect of his own will, and the dreaded recurrence for an effect
of the will of his enemies.   Thus the springs which set the vast machine
in motion, though they lie far beyond our ken, shrouded in a mystery
which we can never hope to penetrate, appear to ignorant man to lie
within his reach : he fancies he can touch them and so work by magic
art all manner of good to himself and evil to his foes.   In time the
fallacy of this belief becomes apparent to him : he discovers that there
are things he cannot do, pleasures which he is unable of himself to
procure, pains which even the most potent magician is powerless to
avoid. The unattainable good, the inevitable ill, are now ascribed
by him to the action of invisible powers, whose favour is joy and life,
whose anger is misery and death. Thus magic tends to be displaced
by religion, and the sorcerer by the priest.   At this stage of thought
the ultimate causes of things are conceived to be personal beings, many
in number and often discordant in character, who partake of the nature
and even of the frailty of man, though their might is greater than his,
and their life far exceeds the span of his ephemeral existence. Their
sharply-marked individualities, their clear-cut outlines have not yet
begun, under the powerful solvent of philosophy, to melt and coalesce
into that single unknown substratum of phenomena which, according
to the qualities with which our imagination invests it, goes by one or
other of the high-sounding names which the wit of man has devised
to hide his ignorance.   Accordingly, so long as men look on their gods
as beings akin to themselves and not raised to an unapproachable
height above them, they believe it to be possible for those of their
own number who surpass their fellows to attain to the divine rank
after death or even in life.   Incarnate human deities of this latter
sort may be said to halt midway between the age of magic and the
age of religion. If they bear the names and display the pomp of
deities, the powers which they are supposed to wield are commonly
those of their predecessor the magician.   Like him, they are expected to
guard their people against hostile enchantments, to heal them in
sickness, to bless them with offspring, and to provide them with an
abundant supply of food by regulating the weather and performing
the other ceremonies which are deemed necessary to ensure the fertility
of the earth and the multiplication of animals. Men who are credited
with powers so lofty and far-reaching naturally hold the highest place
in the land, and while the rift between the spiritual and the temporal

spheres has not yet widened too far, they are supreme in civil as well as religious matters : in a word, they are kings as well as gods. Thus the divinity which hedges a king has its roots deep down in human history, and long ages pass before these are sapped by a profounder view of nature and man.

In the classical period of Greek and Latin antiquity the reign of kings was for the most part a thing of the past ; yet the stories of their lineage, titles, and pretensions suffice to prove that they too claimed to rule by divine right and to exercise superhuman powers. Hence we may without undue temerity assume that the King of the Wood at Nemi, though shorn in later times of his glory and fallen on evil days, represented a long line of sacred kings who had once received not only the homage but the adoration of their subjects in return for the manifold blessings which they were supposed to dispense. What little we know of the functions of Diana in the Arician grove seems to prove that she was here conceived as a goddess of fertility, and particularly as a divinity of childbirth. It is reasonable, therefore, to suppose that in the discharge of these important duties she was assisted by her priest, the two figuring as King and Queen of the Wood in a solemn marriage, which was intended to make the earth gay with the blossoms of spring and the fruits of autumn, and to gladden the hearts of men and women with healthful offspring.

If the priest of Nemi posed not merely as a king, but as a god of the grove, we have still to ask, What deity in particular did he personate ? The answer of antiquity is that he represented Virbius, the consort or lover of Diana. But this does not help us much, for of Virbius we know little more than the name. A clue to the mystery is perhaps supplied by the Vestal fire which burned in the grove. For the perpetual holy fires of the Aryans in Europe appear to have been commonly kindled and fed with oak wood, and in Rome itself, not many miles from Nemi, the fuel of the Vestal fire consisted of oaken sticks or logs, as has been proved by a microscopic analysis of the charred embers of the Vestal fire, which were discovered by Commendatore G. Boni in the course of the memorable excavations which he conducted in the Roman forum at the end of the nineteenth century. But the ritual of the various Latin towns seems to have been marked by great uniformity ; hence it is reasonable to conclude that wherever in Latium a Vestal fire was maintained, it was fed, as at Rome, with wood of the sacred oak. If this was so at Nemi, it becomes probable that the hallowed grove there consisted of a natural oak-wood, and that therefore the tree which the King of the Wood had to guard at the peril of his life was itself an oak ; indeed, it was from an evergreen oak, according to Virgil, that Aeneas plucked the Golden Bough. Now the oak was the sacred tree of Jupiter, the supreme god of the Latins. Hence it follows that the King of the Wood, whose life was bound up in a fashion with an oak, personated no less a deity than Jupiter himself. At least the evidence, slight as it is, seems to point to this conclusion. The old Alban dynasty of the Silvii or Woods, with their crown of oak leaves, apparently aped the style and emulated the powers of Latian Jupiter, who dwelt on the top of the Alban Mount. It is not impossible that the King of the Wood, who guarded the sacred oak a little lower down the mountain, was the lawful successor and representative of this ancient line of the Silvii or Woods. At all events, if I am right in supposing that he passed for a human Jupiter, it would appear that Virbius, with whom legend identified him, was nothing but a local form of Jupiter, considered perhaps in his original aspect as a god of the greenwood.

The hypothesis that in later times at all events the King of the Wood played the part of the oak-god Jupiter, is confirmed by an examination of his divine partner Diana. For two distinct lines of argument converge to show that if Diana was a queen of the woods in general, she was at Nemi a goddess of the oak in particular. In the first place, she bore the title of Vesta, and as such presided over a perpetual fire, which we have seen reason to believe was fed with oak wood. But a goddess of fire is not far removed from a goddess of the fuel which burns in the fire ; primitive thought perhaps drew no sharp line of distinction between the blaze and the wood that blazes. In the second place, the nymph Egeria at Nemi appears to have been merely a form of Diana, and Egeria is definitely said to have been a Dryad, a nymph of the oak. Elsewhere in Italy the goddess had her home on oak-clad mountains. Thus Mount Algidus, a spur of the Alban hills, was covered in antiquity with dark forests of oak, both of the evergreen and the deciduous sort. In winter the snow lay long on these cold hills, and their gloomy oak-woods were believed to be a favourite haunt of Diana, as they have been of brigands in modern times. Again, Mount Tifata, the long abrupt ridge of the Apennines which looks down on the Campanian plain behind Capua, was wooded of old with evergreen oaks, among which Diana had a temple. Here Sulla thanked the goddess for his victory over the Marians in the plain below, attesting his gratitude by inscriptions which were long after-wards to be seen in the temple. On the whole, then, we conclude that at Nemi the King of the Wood personated the oak-god Jupiter and mated with the oak-goddess Diana in the sacred grove. An echo of their mystic union has come down to us in the legend of the loves of Numa and Egeria, who according to some had their trysting-place in these holy woods.

To this theory it may naturally be objected that the divine consort of Jupiter was not Diana but Juno, and that if Diana had a mate at all he might be expected to bear the name not of Jupiter, but of Dianus or Janus, the latter of these forms being merely a corruption of the former. All this is true, but the objection may be parried by observing that the two pairs of deities, Jupiter and Juno on the one side, and Dianus and Diana, or Janus and Jana, on the other side, are merely duplicates of each other, their names and their functions being in substance and origin identical. With regard to their names, all four of them come from the same Aryan root DI, meaning " bright," which

occurs in the names of the corresponding Greek deities, Zeus and his
old female consort Dione.   In regard to their functions, Juno and
Diana were both goddesses of fecundity and childbirth, and both were
sooner or later identified with the moon.   As to the true nature and
functions of Janus the ancients themselves were puzzled ; and where
they hesitated, it is not for us confidently to decide.   But the view
mentioned by Varro that Janus was the god of the sky is supported not
only by the etymological identity of his name with that of the sky-god
Jupiter, but also by the relation in which he appears to have stood to
Jupiter's two mates, Juno and Juturna.   For the epithet Junonian
bestowed on Janus points to a marriage union between the two deities ;
and according to one account Janus was the husband of the water-
nymph Juturna, who according to others was beloved by Jupiter.
Moreover, Janus, like Jove, was regularly invoked, and commonly
spoken of, under the title of Father.   Indeed, he was identified with
Jupiter not merely by the logic of the learned St. Augustine, but by the
piety of a pagan worshipper who dedicated an offering to Jupiter
Dianus.   A trace of his relation to the oak may be found in the oak-
woods of the Janiculum, the hill on the right bank of the Tiber, where
Janus is said to have reigned as a king in the remotest ages of Italian
history.

Thus, if I am right, the same ancient pair of deities was variously
known among the Greek and Italian peoples as Zeus and Dione, Jupiter
and Juno, or Dianus (Janus) and Diana (Jana), the names of the
divinities being identical in substance, though varying in form with
the dialect of the particular tribe which worshiped them.   At first,
when the peoples dwelt near each other, the difference between the
deities would be hardly more than one of name ; in other words,
it would be almost purely dialectical.   But the gradual dispersion
of the tribes, and their consequent isolation from each other, would
favour the growth of divergent modes of conceiving and worshipping
the gods whom they had carried with them from their old home, so
that in time discrepancies of myth and ritual would tend to spring up
and thereby to convert a nominal into a real distinction between the
divinities.   Accordingly when, with the slow progress of culture, the
long period of barbarism and separation was passing away, and the
rising political power of a single strong community had begun to draw
or hammer its weaker neighbours into a nation, the confluent peoples
would throw their gods, like their dialects, into a common stock ;
and thus it might come about that the same ancient deities, which their
forefathers had worshipped together before the dispersion, would now
be so disguised by the accumulated effect of dialectical and religious
divergencies that their original identity might fail to be recognised,
and they would take their places side by side as independent divinities
in the national pantheon.

This duplication of deities, the result of the final fusion of kindred
tribes who had long lived apart, would account for the appearance of
Janus beside Jupiter, and of Diana or Jana beside Juno in the Roman

religion. At least this appears to be a more probable theory than the
opinion, which has found favour with some modern scholars, that
Janus was originally nothing but the god of doors. That a deity of
his dignity and importance, whom the Romans revered as a god
of gods and the father of his people, should have started in life
as a humble, though doubtless respectable, doorkeeper appears very
unlikely. So lofty an end hardly consorts with so lowly a beginning. It is more probable that the door (*janua*) got its name from
Janus than that he got his name from it. This view is strengthened
by a consideration of the word *janua* itself. The regular word for door
is the same in all the languages of the Aryan family from India to Ireland. It is *dur* in Sanscrit, *thura* in Greek, *tür* in German, *door* in
English, *dorus* in old Irish, and *foris* in Latin. Yet besides this ordinary
name for door, which the Latins shared with all their Aryan brethren,
they had also the name *janua*, to which there is no corresponding term
in any Indo-European speech. The word has the appearance of being
an adjectival form derived from the noun *Janus*. I conjecture that
it may have been customary to set up an image or symbol of Janus at
the principal door of the house in order to place the entrance under the
protection of the great god. A door thus guarded might be known as
a *janua foris*, that is, a Januan door, and the phrase might in time be
abridged into *janua*, the noun *foris* being understood but not expressed.
From this to the use of *janua* to designate a door in general, whether
guarded by an image of Janus or not, would be an easy and natural
transition.

If there is any truth in this conjecture, it may explain very simply
the origin of the double head of Janus, which has so long exercised the
ingenuity of mythologists. When it had become customary to guard
the entrance of houses and towns by an image of Janus, it might well
be deemed necessary to make the sentinel god look both ways, before
and behind, at the same time, in order that nothing should escape his
vigilant eye. For if the divine watchman always faced in one direction, it is easy to imagine what mischief might have been wrought
with impunity behind his back. This explanation of the double-
headed Janus at Rome is confirmed by the double-headed idol which
the Bush negroes in the interior of Surinam regularly set up as a
guardian at the entrance of a village. The idol consists of a block of
wood with a human face rudely carved on each side ; it stands under
a gateway composed of two uprights and a cross-bar. Beside the
idol generally lies a white rag intended to keep off the devil ; and
sometimes there is also a stick which seems to represent a bludgeon
or weapon of some sort. Further, from the cross-bar hangs a small
log which serves the useful purpose of knocking on the head any evil
spirit who might attempt to pass through the gateway. Clearly
this double-headed fetish at the gateway of the negro villages in
Surinam bears a close resemblance to the double-headed images of
Janus which, grasping a stick in one hand and a key in the other, stood
sentinel at Roman gates and doorways ; and we can hardly doubt that

in both cases the heads facing two ways are to be similarly explained as expressive of the vigilance of the guardian god, who kept his eye on spiritual foes behind and before, and stood ready to bludgeon them on the spot. We may, therefore, dispense with the tedious and unsatisfactory explanations with which, if we may trust Ovid, the wily Janus himself fobbed off an anxious Roman enquirer.

To apply these conclusions to the priest of Nemi, we may suppose that as the mate of Diana he represented originally Dianus or Janus rather than Jupiter, but that the difference between these deities was of old merely superficial, going little deeper than the names, and leaving practically unaffected the essential functions of the god as a power of the sky, the thunder, and the oak. It was fitting, therefore, that his human representative at Nemi should dwell, as we have seen reason to believe he did, in an oak grove. His title of King of the Wood clearly indicates the sylvan character of the deity whom he served ; and since he could only be assailed by him who had plucked the bough of a certain tree in the grove, his own life might be said to be bound up with that of the sacred tree. Thus he not only served but embodied the great Aryan god of the oak ; and as an oak-god he would mate with the oak-goddess, whether she went by the name of Egeria or Diana. Their union, however consummated, would be deemed essential to the fertility of the earth and the fecundity of man and beast. Further, as the oak-god was also a god of the sky, the thunder, and the rain, so his human representative would be required, like many other divine kings, to cause the clouds to gather, the thunder to peal, and the rain to descend in due season, that the fields and orchards might bear fruit and the pastures be covered with luxuriant herbage. The reputed possessor of powers so exalted must have been a very important personage ; and the remains of buildings and of votive offerings which have been found on the site of the sanctuary combine with the testimony of classical writers to prove that in later times it was one of the greatest and most popular shrines in Italy. Even in the old days, when the champaign country around was still parcelled out among the petty tribes who composed the Latin League, the sacred grove is known to have been an object of their common reverence and care. And just as the kings of Cambodia used to send offerings to the mystic kings of Fire and Water far in the dim depths of the tropical forest, so, we may well believe, from all sides of the broad Latian plain the eyes and footsteps of Italian pilgrims turned to the quarter where, standing sharply out against the faint blue line of the Apennines or the deeper blue of the distant sea, the Alban Mountain rose before them, the home of the mysterious priest of Nemi, the King of the Wood. There, among the green woods and beside the still waters of the lonely hills, the ancient Aryan worship of the god of the oak, the thunder, and the dripping sky lingered in its early, almost Druidical form, long after a great political and intellectual revolution had shifted the capital of Latin religion from the forest to the city, from Nemi to Rome.

CHAPTER XVII

THE BURDEN OF ROYALTY

§ 1. *Royal and Priestly Taboos.*—At a certain stage of early society the king or priest is often thought to be endowed with supernatural powers or to be an incarnation of a deity, and consistently with this belief the course of nature is supposed to be more or less under his control, and he is held responsible for bad weather, failure of the crops, and similar calamities. To some extent it appears to be assumed that the king's power over nature, like that over his subjects and slaves, is exerted through definite acts of will; and therefore if drought, famine, pestilence, or storms arise, the people attribute the misfortune to the negligence or guilt of their king, and punish him accordingly with stripes and bonds, or, if he remains obdurate, with deposition and death. Sometimes, however, the course of nature, while regarded as dependent on the king, is supposed to be partly independent of his will. His person is considered, if we may express it so, as the dynamical centre of the universe, from which lines of force radiate to all quarters of the heaven; so that any motion of his—the turning of his head, the lifting of his hand—instantaneously affects and may seriously disturb some part of nature. He is the point of support on which hangs the balance of the world, and the slightest irregularity on his part may overthrow the delicate equipoise. The greatest care must, therefore, be taken both by and of him; and his whole life, down to its minutest details, must be so regulated that no act of his, voluntary or involuntary, may disarrange or upset the established order of nature. Of this class of monarchs the Mikado or Dairi, the spiritual emperor of Japan, is or rather used to be a typical example. He is an incarnation of the sun goddess, the deity who rules the universe, gods and men included; once a year all the gods wait upon him and spend a month at his court. During that month, the name of which means "without gods," no one frequents the temples, for they are believed to be deserted. The Mikado receives from his people and assumes in his official proclamations and decrees the title of "manifest or incarnate deity," and he claims a general authority over the gods of Japan. For example, in an official decree of the year 646 the emperor is described as "the incarnate god who governs the universe."

The following description of the Mikado's mode of life was written about two hundred years ago:

"Even to this day the princes descended of this family, more particularly those who sit on the throne, are looked upon as persons most holy in themselves, and as Popes by birth. And, in order to preserve these advantageous notions in the minds of their subjects, they are obliged to take an uncommon care of their sacred persons, and to do such things, which, examined according to the customs of other nations, would be thought ridiculous and impertinent. It will not be improper to give a few instances of it. He thinks that it would be very prejudicial to his dignity and holiness to touch the ground with his feet ; for this reason, when he intends to go anywhere, he must be carried thither on men's shoulders. Much less will they suffer that he should expose his sacred person to the open air, and the sun is not thought worthy to shine on his head. There is such a holiness ascribed to all the parts of his body that he dares to cut off neither his hair, nor his beard, nor his nails. However, lest he should grow too dirty, they may clean him in the night when he is asleep ; because, they say, that which is taken from his body at that time, hath been stolen from him, and that such a theft doth not prejudice his holiness or dignity. In ancient times, he was obliged to sit on the throne for some hours every morning, with the imperial crown on his head, but to sit altogether like a statue, without stirring either hands or feet, head or eyes, nor indeed any part of his body, because, by this means, it was thought that he could preserve peace and tranquillity in his empire ; for if, unfortunately, he turned himself on one side or the other, or if he looked a good while towards any part of his dominions, it was apprehended that war, famine, fire, or some other great misfortune was near at hand to desolate the country. But it having been afterwards discovered, that the imperial crown was the palladium, which by its immobility could preserve peace in the empire, it was thought expedient to deliver his imperial person, consecrated only to idleness and pleasures, from this burthensome duty, and therefore the crown is at present placed on the throne for some hours every morning. His victuals must be dressed every time in new pots, and served at table in new dishes : both are very clean and neat, but made only of common clay ; that without any considerable expense they may be laid aside, or broke, after they have served once. They are generally broke, for fear they should come into the hands of laymen for they believe religiously, that if any layman should presume to eat his food out of these sacred dishes, it would swell and inflame his mouth and throat. The like ill effect is dreaded from the Dairi's sacred habits ; for they believe that if a layman should wear them, without the Emperor's express leave or command, they would occasion swellings and pains in all parts of his body." To the same effect an earlier account of the Mikado says : " It was considered as a shameful degradation for him even to touch the ground with his foot. The sun and moon were not even permitted to shine upon his head. None of the superfluities of the body were ever taken from him, neither his hair, his beard, nor his nails were cut. Whatever he eat was dressed in new vessels."

Similar priestly or rather divine kings are found, at a lower level of barbarism, on the west coast of Africa. At Shark Point near Cape Padron, in Lower Guinea, lives the priestly king Kukulu, alone in a wood. He may not touch a woman nor leave his house ; indeed he may not even quit his chair, in which he is obliged to sleep sitting, for if he lay down no wind would arise and navigation would be stopped. He regulates storms, and in general maintains a wholesome and equable state of the atmosphere. On Mount Agu in Togo there lives a fetish or spirit called Bagba, who is of great importance for the whole of the surrounding country. The power of giving or withholding rain is ascribed to him, and he is lord of the winds, including the Harmattan, the dry, hot wind which blows from the interior. His priest dwells in a house on the highest peak of the mountain, where he keeps the winds bottled up in huge jars. Applications for rain, too, are made to him, and he does a good business in amulets, which consist of the teeth and claws of leopards. Yet though his power is great and he is indeed the real chief of the land, the rule of the fetish forbids him ever to leave the mountain, and he must spend the whole of his life on its summit. Only once a year may he come down to make purchases in the market ; but even then he may not set foot in the hut of any mortal man, and must return to his place of exile the same day. The business of government in the villages is conducted by subordinate chiefs, who are appointed by him. In the West African kingdom of Congo there was a supreme pontiff called Chitomé or Chitombé, whom the negroes regarded as a god on earth and all-powerful in heaven. Hence before they would taste the new crops they offered him the first-fruits, fearing that manifold misfortunes would befall them if they broke this rule. When he left his residence to visit other places within his jurisdiction, all married people had to observe strict continence the whole time he was out ; for it was supposed that any act of incontinence would prove fatal to him. And if he were to die a natural death, they thought that the world would perish, and the earth, which he alone sustained by his power and merit, would immediately be annihilated. Amongst the semi-barbarous nations of the New World, at the date of the Spanish conquest, there were found hierarchies or theocracies like those of Japan ; in particular, the high pontiff of the Zapotecs appears to have presented a close parallel to the Mikado. A powerful rival to the king himself, this spiritual lord governed Yopaa, one of the chief cities of the kingdom, with absolute dominion. It is impossible, we are told, to overrate the reverence in which he was held. He was looked on as a god whom the earth was not worthy to hold nor the sun to shine upon. He profaned his sanctity if he even touched the ground with his foot. The officers who bore his palanquin on their shoulders were members of the highest families : he hardly deigned to look on anything around him ; and all who met him fell with their faces to the earth, fearing that death would overtake them if they saw even his shadow. A rule of continence was regularly imposed on the Zapotec priests, especially upon the high pontiff ; but " on certain days in each year, which were generally celebrated with feasts and dances, it was customary for the high priest to become drunk. While in this state, seeming to belong neither to heaven nor to earth, one of the most beautiful of the virgins consecrated to the service of the gods was brought to him." If the child she bore him was a son, he was brought up as a prince of the blood, and the eldest son succeeded his father on the pontifical throne. The supernatural powers attributed to this pontiff are not specified, but probably they resembled those of the Mikado and Chitomé.

Wherever, as in Japan and West Africa, it is supposed that the order of nature, and even the existence of the world, is bound up with the life of the king or priest, it is clear that he must be regarded by his subjects as a source both of infinite blessing and of infinite danger.   On the one hand, the people have to thank him for the rain and sunshine which foster the fruits of the earth, for the wind which brings ships to their coasts, and even for the solid ground beneath their feet.   But what he gives he can refuse ; and so close is the dependence of nature on his person, so delicate the balance of the system of forces whereof he is the centre, that the least irregularity on his part may set up a tremor which shall shake the earth to its foundations.   And if nature may be disturbed by the slightest involuntary act of the king, it is easy to conceive the convulsion which his death might provoke.   The natural death of the Chitomé, as we have seen, was thought to entail the destruction of all things.   Clearly, therefore, out of a regard for their own safety, which might be imperilled by any rash act of the king, and still more by his death, the people will exact of their king or priest a strict conformity to those rules, the observance of which is deemed necessary for his own preservation, and consequently for the preservation of his people and the world.   The idea that early kingdoms are despotisms in which the people exist only for the sovereign, is wholly inapplicable to the monarchies we are considering.   On the contrary, the sovereign in them exists only for his subjects ; his life is only valuable so long as he discharges the duties of his position by ordering the course of nature for his people's benefit.   So soon as he fails to do so, the care, the devotion, the religious homage which they had hitherto lavished on him cease and are changed into hatred and contempt ; he is dismissed ignominiously, and may be thankful if he escapes with his life. Worshipped as a god one day, he is killed as a criminal the next.   But in this changed behaviour of the people there is nothing capricious or inconsistent.   On the contrary, their conduct is entirely of a piece.   If their king is their god, he is or should be also their preserver ; and if he will not preserve them, he must make room for another who will.   So long, however, as he answers their expectations, there is no limit to the care which they take of him, and which they compel him to take of himself.   A king of this sort lives hedged in by a ceremonious etiquette, a network of prohibitions and observances, of which the intention is not to contribute to his dignity, much less to his comfort, but to restrain him from conduct which, by disturbing the harmony of nature, might involve himself, his people, and the universe in one common catastrophe.   Far from adding to his comfort, these observances, by trammelling his every act, annihilate his freedom and often render the very life, which it is their object to preserve, a burden and sorrow to him.

Of the supernaturally endowed kings of Loango it is said that the more powerful a king is, the more taboos is he bound to observe ; they regulate all his actions, his walking and his standing, his eating and drinking, his sleeping and waking.   To these restraints the heir to the throne is subject from infancy ; but as he advances in life the number of abstinences and ceremonies which he must observe increases, " until at the moment that he ascends the throne he is lost in the ocean of rites and taboos."   In the crater of an extinct volcano, enclosed on all sides by grassy slopes, lie the scattered huts and yam-fields of Riabba, the capital of the native king of Fernando Po.   This mysterious being lives in the lowest depths of the crater, surrounded by a harem of forty women, and covered, it is said, with old silver coins.   Naked savage as he is, he yet exercises far more influence in the island than the Spanish governor at Santa Isabel.   In him the conservative spirit of the Boobies or aboriginal inhabitants of the island is, as it were, incorporate.   He has never seen a white man and, according to the firm conviction of all the Boobies, the sight of a pale face would cause his instant death.   He cannot bear to look upon the sea ; indeed it is said that he may never see it even in the distance, and that therefore he wears away his life with shackles on his legs in the dim twilight of his hut.   Certain it is that he has never set foot on the beach.   With the exception of his musket and knife, he uses nothing that comes from the whites ; European cloth never touches his person, and he scorns tobacco, rum, and even salt.

Among the Ewe-speaking peoples of the Slave Coast " the king is at the same time high priest.   In this quality he was, particularly in former times, unapproachable by his subjects.   Only by night was he allowed to quit his dwelling in order to bathe and so forth.   None but his representative, the so-called ' visible king,' with three chosen elders might converse with him, and even they had to sit on an ox-hide with their backs turned to him.   He might not see any European nor any horse, nor might he look upon the sea, for which reason he was not allowed to quit his capital even for a few moments.   These rules have been disregarded in recent times."   The king of Dahomey himself is subject to the prohibition of beholding the sea, and so are the kings of Loango and Great Ardra in Guinea.   The sea is the fetish of the Eyeos, to the north-west of Dahomey, and they and their king are threatened with death by their priests if ever they dare to look on it. It is believed that the king of Cayor in Senegal would infallibly die within the year if he were to cross a river or an arm of the sea.   In Mashonaland down to recent times the chiefs would not cross certain rivers, particularly the Rurikwi and the Nyadiri ; and the custom was still strictly observed by at least one chief within recent years. " On no account will the chief cross the river.   If it is absolutely necessary for him to do so, he is blindfolded and carried across with shouting and singing.   Should he walk across, he will go blind or die and certainly lose the chieftainship."   So among the Mahafalys and Sakalavas in the south of Madagascar some kings are forbidden to sail on the sea or to cross certain rivers.   Among the Sakalavas the chief is regarded as a sacred being, but " he is held in leash by a crowd of restrictions, which regulate his behaviour like that of the emperor of China.   He can undertake nothing whatever unless the sorcerers have declared the omens favourable : he may not eat warm food : on certain days he may not quit his hut ; and so on." Among some of the hill tribes of Assam both the headman and his wife have to observe many taboos in respect of food ; thus they may not eat buffalo, pork, dog, fowl, or tomatoes. The headman must be chaste, the husband of one wife, and he must separate himself from her on the eve of a general or public observance of taboo. In one group of tribes the headman is forbidden to eat in a strange village, and under no provocation whatever may he utter a word of abuse. Apparently the people imagine that the violation of any of these taboos by a headman would bring down misfortune on the whole village.

The ancient kings of Ireland, as well as the kings of the four provinces of Leinster, Munster, Connaught, and Ulster, were subject to certain quaint prohibitions or taboos, on the due observance of which the prosperity of the people and the country, as well as their own, was supposed to depend. Thus, for example, the sun might not rise on the king of Ireland in his bed at Tara, the old capital of Erin ; he was forbidden to alight on Wednesday at Magh Breagh, to traverse Magh Cuillinn after sunset, to incite his horse at Fan-Chomair, to go in a ship upon the water the Monday after Bealltaine (May Day), and to leave the track of his army upon Ath Maighne the Tuesday after All-Hallows. The king of Leinster might not go round Tuath Laighean left-hand-wise on Wednesday, nor sleep between the Dothair (Dodder) and the Duibhlinn with his head inclining to one side, nor encamp for nine days on the plains of Cualann, nor travel the road of Duibhlinn on Monday, nor ride a dirty black-heeled horse across Magh Maistean. The king of Munster was prohibited from enjoying the feast of Loch Lein from one Monday to another ; from banqueting by night in the beginning of harvest before Geim at Leitreacha ; from encamping for nine days upon the Siuir ; and from holding a border meeting at Gabhran. The king of Connaught might not conclude a treaty respecting his ancient palace of Cruachan after making peace on All-Hallows Day, nor go in a speckled garment on a grey speckled steed to the heath of Dal Chais, nor repair to an assembly of women at Seaghais, nor sit in autumn on the sepulchral mounds of the wife of Maine, nor contend in running with the rider of a grey one-eyed horse at Ath Gallta between two posts. The king of Ulster was forbidden to attend the horse fair at Rath Line among the youths of Dal Araidhe, to listen to the fluttering of the flocks of birds of Linn Saileach after sunset, to celebrate the feast of the bull of Daire-mic-Daire, to go into Magh Cobha in the month of March, and to drink of the water of Bo Neimhidh between two darknesses. If the kings of Ireland strictly observed these and many other customs, which were enjoined by immemorial usage, it was believed that they would never meet with mischance or misfortune, and ·would live for ninety years without experiencing the decay of old age ; that no epidemic or mortality would occur during their reigns ; and that the seasons would be favourable and the earth yield its fruit in abundance ; whereas, if they set the ancient usages at naught, the country would be visited with plague, famine, and bad weather.

The kings of Egypt were worshipped as gods, and the routine of their daily life was regulated in every detail by precise and unvarying rules. " The life of the kings of Egypt," says Diodorus, " was not like that of other monarchs who are irresponsible and may do just what they choose ; on the contrary, everything was fixed for them by law, not only their official duties, but even the details of their daily life. . . . The hours both of day and night were arranged at which the king had to do, not what he pleased, but what was prescribed for him. . . . For not only were the times appointed at which he should transact public business or sit in judgment ; but the very hours for his walking and bathing and sleeping with his wife, and, in short, performing every act of life were all settled. Custom enjoined a simple diet ; the only flesh he might eat was veal and goose, and he might only drink a prescribed quantity of wine." However, there is reason to think that these rules were observed, not by the ancient Pharaohs, but by the priestly kings who reigned at Thebes and in Ethiopia at the close of the twentieth dynasty.

Of the taboos imposed on priests we may see a striking example in the rules of life prescribed for the Flamen Dialis at Rome, who has been interpreted as a living image of Jupiter, or a human embodiment of the sky-spirit. They were such as the following : The Flamen Dialis might not ride or even touch a horse, nor see an army under arms, nor wear a ring which was not broken, nor have a knot on any part of his garments ; no fire except a sacred fire might be taken out of his house ; he might not touch wheaten flour or leavened bread ; he might not touch or even name a goat, a dog, raw meat, beans, and ivy ; he might not walk under a vine ; the feet of his bed had to be daubed with mud ; his hair could be cut only by a free man and with a bronze knife, and his hair and nails when cut had to be buried under a lucky tree ; he might not touch a dead body nor enter a place where one was burned ; he might not see work being done on holy days ; he might not be uncovered in the open air ; if a man in bonds were taken into his house, the captive had to be unbound and the cords had to be drawn up through a hole in the roof and so let down into the street. His wife, the Flaminica, had to observe nearly the same rules, and others of her own besides. She might not ascend more than three steps of the kind of staircase called Greek ; at a certain festival she might not comb her hair ; the leather of her shoes might not be made from a beast that had died a natural death, but only from one that had been slain or sacrificed ; if she heard thunder she was tabooed till she had offered an expiatory sacrifice.

Among the Grebo people of Sierra Leone there is a pontiff who bears the title of Bodia and has been compared, on somewhat slender grounds, to the high priest of the Jews. He is appointed in accordance with the behest of an oracle. At an elaborate ceremony of installation he is anointed, a ring is put on his ankle as a badge of office, and the door-posts of his house are sprinkled with the blood of a sacrificed goat. He has charge of the public talismans and idols, which he feeds with rice and oil every new moon ; and he sacrifices on behalf of the town to the dead and to demons. Nominally his power is very great, but in practice it is very limited ; for he dare not defy public opinion, and he is held responsible, even with his life, for any adversity that befalls the country. It is expected of him that he should cause the earth to bring forth abundantly, the people to be healthy, war to be driven far away, and witchcraft to be kept in abeyance. His life is trammelled by the observance of certain restrictions or taboos. Thus he may not sleep in any house but his own official residence, which is called the " anointed house " with reference to the ceremony of anointing him at inauguration. He may not drink water on the highway. He may not eat while a corpse is in the town, and he may not mourn for the dead. If he dies while in office, he must be buried at dead of night ; few may hear of his burial, and none may mourn for him when his death is made public. Should he have fallen a victim to the poison ordeal by drinking a decoction of sassywood, as it is called, he must be buried under a running stream of water.

Among the Todas of Southern India the holy milkman, who acts as priest of the sacred dairy, is subject to a variety of irksome and burdensome restrictions during the whole time of his incumbency, which may last many years. Thus he must live at the sacred dairy and may never visit his home or any ordinary village. He must be celibate ; if he is married he must leave his wife. On no account may any ordinary person touch the holy milkman or the holy dairy ; such a touch would so defile his holiness that he would forfeit his office. It is only on two days a week, namely Mondays and Thursdays, that a mere layman may even approach the milkman ; on other days, if he has any business with him, he must stand at a distance (some say a quarter of a mile) and shout his message across the intervening space. Further, the holy milkman never cuts his hair or pares his nails so long as he holds office ; he never crosses a river by a bridge, but wades through a ford and only certain fords ; if a death occurs in his clan, he may not attend any of the funeral ceremonies, unless he first resigns his office and descends from the exalted rank of milkman to that of a mere common mortal. Indeed it appears that in old days he had to resign the seals, or rather the pails, of office whenever any member of his clan departed this life. However, these heavy restraints are laid in their entirety only on milkmen of the very highest class.

§ 2. *Divorce of the Spiritual from the Temporal Power.*—The burdensome observances attached to the royal or priestly office produced their natural effect. Either men refused to accept the office, which hence tended to fall into abeyance ; or accepting it, they sank under its weight into spiritless creatures, cloistered recluses, from whose nerveless fingers the reins of government slipped into the firmer grasp of men who were often content to wield the reality of sovereignty without its name. In some countries this rift in the supreme power deepened into a total and permanent separation of the spiritual and temporal powers, the old royal house retaining their purely religious functions, while the civil government passed into the hands of a younger and more vigorous race.

To take examples. In a previous part of this work we saw that in Cambodia it is often necessary to force the kingships of Fire and Water upon the reluctant successors, and that in Savage Island the monarchy actually came to an end because at last no one could be induced to accept the dangerous distinction. In some parts of West Africa, when the king dies, a family council is secretly held to determine his successor. He on whom the choice falls is suddenly seized, bound, and thrown into the fetish-house, where he is kept in durance till he consents to accept the crown. Sometimes the heir finds means of evading the honour which it is sought to thrust upon him ; a ferocious chief has been known to go about constantly armed, resolute to resist by force any attempt to set him on the throne. The savage Timmes of Sierra Leone, who elect their king, reserve to themselves the right of beating him on the eve of his coronation ; and they avail themselves of this constitutional privilege with such hearty goodwill that sometimes the unhappy monarch does not long survive his elevation to the throne. Hence when the leading chiefs have a spite at a man and wish to rid themselves of him, they elect him king. Formerly, before a man was proclaimed king of Sierra Leone, it used to be the custom to load him with chains and thrash him. Then the fetters were knocked off, the kingly robe was placed on him, and he received in his hands the symbol of royal dignity, which was nothing but the axe of the executioner. It is not therefore surprising to read that in Sierra Leone, where such customs have prevailed, "except among the Mandingoes and Suzees, few kings are natives of the countries they govern. So different are their ideas from ours, that very few are solicitous of the honour, and competition is very seldom heard of."

The Mikados of Japan seem early to have resorted to the expedient of transferring the honours and burdens of supreme power to their infant children ; and the rise of the Tycoons, long the temporal sovereigns of the country, is traced to the abdication of a certain Mikado in favour of his three-year-old son. The sovereignty having been wrested by a usurper from the infant prince, the cause of the Mikado was championed by Yoritomo, a man of spirit and conduct, who overthrew the usurper and restored to the Mikado the shadow, while he retained for himself the substance, of power. He bequeathed to his descendants the dignity he had won, and thus became the founder of the line of Tycoons. Down to the latter half of the sixteenth century the Tycoons were active and efficient rulers ; but the same fate overtook them which had befallen the Mikados. Immeshed in the same inextricable web of custom and law, they degenerated into mere puppets, hardly stirring from their palaces and occupied in a perpetual round of empty ceremonies, while the real business of

government was managed by the council of state. In Tonquin the
monarchy ran a similar course. Living like his predecessors in
effeminacy and sloth, the king was driven from the throne by an
ambitious adventurer named Mack, who from a fisherman had risen
to be Grand Mandarin. But the king's brother Tring put down the
usurper and restored the king, retaining, however, for himself and
his descendants the dignity of general of all the forces. Thenceforward
the kings, though invested with the title and pomp of sovereignty,
ceased to govern. While they lived secluded in their palaces, all
real political power was wielded by the hereditary generals.

In Mangaia, a Polynesian island, religious and civil authority were
lodged in separate hands, spiritual functions being discharged by a line
of hereditary kings, while the temporal government was entrusted from
time to time to a victorious war-chief, whose investiture, however,
had to be completed by the king. Similarly in Tonga, besides the
civil king whose right to the throne was partly hereditary and partly
derived from his warlike reputation and the number of his fighting
men, there was a great divine chief who ranked above the king and
the other chiefs in virtue of his supposed descent from one of the
chief gods. Once a year the first-fruits of the ground were offered
to him at a solemn ceremony, and it was believed that if these offerings were not made the vengeance of the gods would fall in a
signal manner on the people. Peculiar forms of speech, such as
were applied to no one else, were used in speaking of him, and everything that he chanced to touch became sacred or tabooed. When
he and the king met, the monarch had to sit down on the ground in
token of respect until his holiness had passed by. Yet though he
enjoyed the highest veneration by reason of his divine origin, this
sacred personage possessed no political authority, and if he ventured
to meddle with affairs of state it was at the risk of receiving a rebuff
from the king, to whom the real power belonged, and who finally
succeeded in ridding himself of his spiritual rival.

In some parts of Western Africa two kings reign side by side, a
fetish or religious king and a civil king, but the fetish king is really
supreme. He controls the weather and so forth, and can put a stop
to everything. When he lays his red staff on the ground, no one may
pass that way. This division of power between a sacred and a secular
ruler is to be met with wherever the true negro culture has been left
unmolested, but where the negro form of society has been disturbed,
as in Dahomey and Ashantee, there is a tendency to consolidate the
two powers in a single king.

In some parts of the East Indian island of Timor we meet with a
partition of power like that which is represented by the civil king
and the fetish king of Western Africa. Some of the Timorese tribes
recognise two rajahs, the ordinary or civil rajah, who governs the
people, and the fetish or taboo rajah, who is charged with the control
of everything that concerns the earth and its products. This latter
ruler has the right of declaring anything taboo ; his permission must

be obtained before new land may be brought under cultivation, and he must perform certain necessary ceremonies when the work is being carried out. If drought or blight threatens the crops, his help is invoked to save them. Though he ranks below the civil rajah, he exercises a momentous influence on the course of events, for his secular colleague is bound to consult him in all important matters. In some of the neighbouring islands, such as Rotti and eastern Flores, a spiritual ruler of the same sort is recognised under various native names, which all mean "lord of the ground." Similarly in the Mekeo district of British New Guinea there is a double chieftainship. The people are divided into two groups according to families, and each of the groups has its chief. One of the two is the war chief, the other is the taboo chief. The office of the latter is hereditary; his duty is to impose a taboo on any of the crops, such as the coco-nuts and areca nuts, whenever he thinks it desirable to prohibit their use. In his office we may perhaps detect the beginning of a priestly dynasty, but as yet his functions appear to be more magical than religious, being concerned with the control of the harvests rather than with the pro- pitiation of higher powers.

CHAPTER XVIII

THE PERILS OF THE SOUL

§ 1. *The Soul as a Mannikin.*—The foregoing examples have taught us that the office of a sacred king or priest is often hedged in by a series of burdensome restrictions or taboos, of which a principal purpose appears to be to preserve the life of the divine man for the good of his people. But if the object of the taboos is to save his life, the question arises, How is their observance supposed to effect this end? To understand this we must know the nature of the danger which threatens the king's life, and which it is the intention of these curious restrictions to guard against. We must, therefore, ask: What does early man understand by death? To what causes does he attribute it? And how does he think it may be guarded against?

As the savage commonly explains the processes of inanimate nature by supposing that they are produced by living beings working in or behind the phenomena, so he explains the phenomena of life itself. If an animal lives and moves, it can only be, he thinks, because there is a little animal inside which moves it : if a man lives and moves, it can only be because he has a little man or animal inside who moves him. The animal inside the animal, the man inside the man, is the soul. And as the activity of an animal or man is explained by the presence of the soul, so the repose of sleep or death is explained by its absence ; sleep or trance being the temporary, death being the permanent absence of the soul. Hence if death be the permanent absence of the soul, the way to guard against it is either to prevent the soul from leaving the body, or, if it does depart, to ensure that it shall return. The precautions adopted by savages to secure one or other of these ends take the form of certain prohibitions or taboos, which are nothing but rules intended to ensure either the continued presence or the return of the soul. In short, they are life-preservers or life-guards. These general statements will now be illustrated by examples.

Addressing some Australian blacks, a European missionary said, " I am not one, as you think, but two." Upon this they laughed. " You may laugh as much as you like," continued the missionary, " I tell you that I am two in one ; this great body that you see is one ; within that there is another little one which is not visible. The great body dies, and is buried, but the little body flies away when the great one dies." To this some of the blacks replied, " Yes, yes. We also are two, we also have a little body within the breast." On being asked where the little body went after death, some said it went behind the bush, others said it went into the sea, and some said they did not know. The Hurons thought that the soul had a head and body, arms and legs ; in short, that it was a complete little model of the man himself. The Esquimaux believe that " the soul exhibits the same shape as the body it belongs to, but is of a more subtle and ethereal nature." According to the Nootkas the soul has the shape of a tiny man ; its seat is the crown of the head. So long as it stands erect, its owner is hale and hearty ; but when from any cause it loses its upright position, he loses his senses. Among the Indian tribes of the Lower Fraser River, man is held to have four souls, of which the principal one has the form of a mannikin, while the other three are shadows of it. The Malays conceive the human soul as a little man, mostly invisible and of the bigness of a thumb, who corresponds exactly in shape, proportion, and even in complexion to the man in whose body he resides. This mannikin is of a thin unsubstantial nature, though not so impalpable but that it may cause displacement on entering a physical object, and it can flit quickly from place to place ; it is temporarily absent from the body in sleep, trance, and disease, and permanently absent after death.

So exact is the resemblance of the mannikin to the man, in other words, of the soul to the body, that, as there are fat bodies and thin bodies, so there are fat souls and thin souls ; as there are heavy bodies and light bodies, long bodies and short bodies, so there are heavy souls and light souls, long souls and short souls. The people of Nias think that every man, before he is born, is asked how long or how heavy a soul he would like, and a soul of the desired weight or length is measured out to him. The heaviest soul ever given out weighs about ten grammes. The length of a man's life is proportioned to the length of his soul ; children who die young had short souls. The Fijian conception of the soul as a tiny human being comes clearly out in the customs observed at the death of a chief among the Nakelo tribe. When a chief dies, certain men, who are the hereditary undertakers, call him, as he lies, oiled and ornamented, on fine mats, saying, " Rise, sir, the chief, and let us be going. The day has come over the land." Then they conduct him to the river side, where the ghostly ferryman comes to ferry Nakelo ghosts across the stream. As they thus attend the chief on his last journey, they hold their great fans close to the ground to shelter him, because, as one of them explained to a mission- ary, " His soul is only a little child." People in the Punjaub who tattoo themselves believe that at death the soul, " the little entire man or woman " inside the mortal frame, will go to heaven blazoned with the same tattoo patterns which adorned the body in life. Some- times, however, as we shall see, the human soul is conceived not in human but in animal form.

§ 2. *Absence and Recall of the Soul.*—The soul is commonly supposed to escape by the natural openings of the body, especially the mouth and nostrils. Hence in Celebes they sometimes fasten fish-hooks to a sick man's nose, navel, and feet, so that if his soul should try to escape it may be hooked and held fast. A Turik on the Baram River, in Borneo, refused to part with some hook-like stones, because they, as it were, hooked his soul to his body, and so prevented the spiritual portion of him from becoming detached from the material. When a Sea Dyak sorcerer or medicine-man is initiated, his fingers are supposed to be furnished with fish-hooks, with which he will thereafter clutch the human soul in the act of flying away, and restore it to the body of the sufferer. But hooks, it is plain, may be used to catch the souls of enemies as well as of friends. Acting on this principle head-hunters in Borneo hang wooden hooks beside the skulls of their slain enemies in the belief that this helps them on their forays to hook in fresh heads. One of the implements of a Haida medicine-man is a hollow bone, in which he bottles up departing souls, and so restores them to their owners. When any one yawns in their presence the Hindoos always snap their thumbs, believing that this will hinder the soul from issuing through the open mouth. The Marquesans used to hold the mouth and nose of a dying man, in order to keep him in life by prevent- ing his soul from escaping ; the same custom is reported of the New Caledonians ; and with the like intention the Bagobos of the Philippine Islands put rings of brass wire on the wrists or ankles of their sick. On the other hand, the Itonamas of South America seal up the eyes, nose, and mouth of a dying person, in case his ghost should get out and carry off others ; and for a similar reason the people of Nias, who fear the spirits of the recently deceased and identify them with the breath, seek to confine the vagrant soul in its earthly tabernacle by bunging up the nose or tying up the jaws of the corpse. Before leaving a corpse the Wakelbura of Australia used to place hot coals in its ears in order to keep the ghost in the body, until they had got such a good start that he could not overtake them. In Southern Celebes, to hinder the escape of a woman's soul in childbed, the nurse ties a band as tightly as possible round the body of the expectant mother. The Minangkabauers of Sumatra observe a similar custom ; a skein of thread or a string is sometimes fastened round the wrist or loins of a woman in childbed, so that when her soul seeks to depart in her hour of travail it may find the egress barred.   And lest the soul of a babe should escape and be lost as soon as it is born, the Alfoors of Celebes, when a birth is about to take place, are careful to close every opening in the house, even the keyhole ; and they stop up every chink and cranny in the walls.   Also they tie up the mouths of all animals inside and outside the house, for fear one of them might swallow the child's soul.   For a similar reason all persons present in the house, even the mother herself, are obliged to keep their mouths shut the whole time the birth is taking place.   When the question was put, Why they did not hold their noses also, lest the child's soul should get into one of them ? the answer was that breath being exhaled as well as inhaled through the nostrils, the soul would be expelled before it could have time to settle down.   Popular expressions in the language of civilised peoples, such as to have one's heart in one's mouth, or the soul on the lips or in the nose, show how natural is the idea that the life or soul may escape by the mouth or nostrils.

Often the soul is conceived as a bird ready to take flight.   This conception has probably left traces in most languages, and it lingers as a metaphor in poetry.   The Malays carry out the conception of the bird-soul in a number of odd ways.   If the soul is a bird on the wing, it may be attracted by rice, and so either prevented from flying away or lured back again from its perilous flight.   Thus in Java when a child is placed on the ground for the first time (a moment which uncultured people seem to regard as especially dangerous), it is put in a hen-coop and the mother makes a clucking sound, as if she were calling hens.   And in Sintang, a district of Borneo, when a person, whether man, woman, or child, has fallen out of a house or off a tree, and has been brought home, his wife or other kinswoman goes as speedily as possible to the spot where the accident happened, and there strews rice, which has been coloured yellow, while she utters the words, " Cluck ! cluck ! soul !   So-and-so is in his house again.   Cluck ! cluck ! soul ! "   Then she gathers up the rice in a basket, carries it to the sufferer, and drops the grains from her hand on his head, saying again, " Cluck ! cluck ! soul ! "   Here the intention clearly is to decoy back the loitering bird-soul and replace it in the head of its owner.

The soul of a sleeper is supposed to wander away from his body and actually to visit the places, to see the persons, and to perform the acts of which he dreams.   For example, when an Indian of Brazil or Guiana wakes up from a sound sleep, he is firmly convinced that his soul has really been away hunting, fishing, felling trees, or whatever else he has dreamed of doing, while all the time his body has been lying motionless in his hammock.   A whole Bororo village has been thrown into a panic and nearly deserted because somebody had dreamed that he saw enemies stealthily approaching it.   A Macusi Indian in weak health, who dreamed that his employer had made him haul the canoe up a series of difficult cataracts, bitterly reproached his master next morning for his want of consideration in thus making a poor invalid go out and toil during the night. The Indians of the Gran Chaco are often heard to relate the most incredible stories as things which they have themselves seen and heard ; hence strangers who do not know them intimately say in their haste that these Indians are liars. In point of fact the Indians are firmly convinced of the truth of what they relate ; for these wonderful adventures are simply their dreams, which they do not distinguish from waking realities.

Now the absence of the soul in sleep has its dangers, for if from any cause the soul should be permanently detained away from the body, the person thus deprived of the vital principle must die. There is a German belief that the soul escapes from a sleeper's mouth in the form of a white mouse or a little bird, and that to prevent the return of the bird or animal would be fatal to the sleeper. Hence in Transylvania they say that you should not let a child sleep with its mouth open, or its soul will slip out in the shape of a mouse, and the child will never wake. Many causes may detain the sleeper's soul. Thus, his soul may meet the soul of another sleeper and the two souls may fight ; if a Guinea negro wakens with sore bones in the morning, he thinks that his soul has been thrashed by another soul in sleep. Or it may meet the soul of a person just deceased and be carried off by it ; hence in the Aru Islands the inmates of a house will not sleep the night after a death has taken place in it, because the soul of the deceased is supposed to be still in the house and they fear to meet it in a dream. Again, the soul of the sleeper may be prevented by an accident or by physical force from returning to his body. When a Dyak dreams of falling into the water, he supposes that this accident has really befallen his spirit, and he sends for a wizard, who fishes for the spirit with a hand-net in a basin of water till he catches it and restores it to its owner. The Santals tell how a man fell asleep, and growing very thirsty, his soul, in the form of a lizard, left his body and entered a pitcher of water to drink. Just then the owner of the pitcher happened to cover it ; so the soul could not return to the body and the man died. While his friends were preparing to burn the body some one uncovered the pitcher to get water. The lizard thus escaped and returned to the body, which immediately revived ; so the man rose up and asked his friends why they were weeping. They told him they thought he was dead and were about to burn his body. He said he had been down a well to get water, but had found it hard to get out and had just returned. So they saw it all.

It is a common rule with primitive people not to waken a sleeper, because his soul is away and might not have time to get back ; so if the man wakened without his soul, he would fall sick. If it is absolutely necessary to rouse a sleeper, it must be done very gradually, to allow the soul time to return. A Fijian in Matuku, suddenly wakened from a nap by somebody treading on his foot, has been heard bawling after his soul and imploring it to return. He had just been dreaming that he was far away in Tonga, and great was his alarm on suddenly wakening to find his body in Matuku.   Death stared him in the face unless his soul could be induced to speed at once across the sea and reanimate its deserted tenement.   The man would probably have died of fright if a missionary had not been at hand to allay his terror.

Still more dangerous is it in the opinion of primitive man to move a sleeper or alter his appearance, for if this were done the soul on its return might not be able to find or recognise its body, and so the person would die.   The Minangkabauers deem it highly improper to blacken or dirty the face of a sleeper, lest the absent soul should shrink from re-entering a body thus disfigured.   Patani Malays fancy that if a person's face be painted while he sleeps, the soul which has gone out of him will not recognise him, and he will sleep on till his face is washed.   In Bombay it is thought equivalent to murder to change the aspect of a sleeper, as by painting his face in fantastic colours or giving moustaches to a sleeping woman.   For when the soul returns it will not know its own body, and the person will die.

But in order that a man's soul should quit his body, it is not necessary that he should be asleep.   It may quit him in his waking hours, and then sickness, insanity, or death will be the result.   Thus a man of the Wurunjeri tribe in Australia lay at his last gasp because his spirit had departed from him.   A medicine-man went in pursuit and caught the spirit by the middle just as it was about to plunge into the sunset glow, which is the light cast by the souls of the dead as they pass in and out of the under-world, where the sun goes to rest.   Having captured the vagrant spirit, the doctor brought it back under his opossum rug, laid himself down on the dying man, and put the soul back into him, so that after a time he revived.   The Karens of Burma are perpetually anxious about their souls, lest these should go roving from their bodies, leaving the owners to die.   When a man has reason to fear that his soul is about to take this fatal step, a ceremony is performed to retain or recall it, in which the whole family must take part.   A meal is prepared consisting of a cock and hen, a special kind of rice, and a bunch of bananas.   Then the head of the family takes the bowl which is used to skim rice, and knocking with it thrice on the top of the house-ladder says : " *Prrrroo!* Come back, soul, do not tarry outside ! If it rains, you will be wet.   If the sun shines, you will be hot.   The gnats will sting you, the leeches will bite you, the tigers will devour you, the thunder will crush you. *Prrrroo!* Come back, soul !   Here it will be well with you.   You shall want for nothing.   Come and eat under shelter from the wind and the storm."   After that the family partakes of the meal, and the ceremony ends with everybody tying their right wrist with a string which has been charmed by a sorcerer. Similarly the Lolos of South-western China believe that the soul leaves the body in chronic illness.   In that case they read a sort of elaborate litany, calling on the soul by name and beseeching it to return from the hills, the vales, the rivers, the forests, the fields, or from wherever it may be straying.   At the same time cups of water, wine, and rice are set at the door for the refreshment of the weary wandering spirit. When the ceremony is over, they tie a red cord round the arm of the sick man to tether the soul, and this cord is worn by him until it decays and drops off.

Some of the Congo tribes believe that when a man is ill, his soul has left his body and is wandering at large. The aid of the sorcerer is then called in to capture the vagrant spirit and restore it to the invalid. Generally the physician declares that he has successfully chased the soul into the branch of a tree. The whole town thereupon turns out and accompanies the doctor to the tree, where the strongest men are deputed to break off the branch in which the soul of the sick man is supposed to be lodged. This they do and carry the branch back to the town, insinuating by their gestures that the burden is heavy and hard to bear. When the branch has been brought to the sick man's hut, he is placed in an upright position by its side, and the sorcerer performs the enchantments by which the soul is believed to be restored to its owner.

Pining, sickness, great fright, and death are ascribed by the Bataks of Sumatra to the absence of the soul from the body. At first they try to beckon the wanderer back, and to lure him, like a fowl, by strewing rice. Then the following form of words is commonly repeated : " Come back, O soul, whether thou art lingering in the wood, or on the hills, or in the dale. See, I call thee with a *toemba bras*, with an egg of the fowl Rajah *moelija*, with the eleven healing leaves. Detain it not, let it come straight here, detain it not, neither in the wood, nor on the hill, nor in the dale. That may not be. O come straight home ! " Once when a popular traveller was leaving a Kayan village, the mothers, fearing that their children's souls might follow him on his journey, brought him the boards on which they carry their infants and begged him to pray that the souls of the little ones would return to the familiar boards and not go away with him into the far country. To each board was fastened a looped string for the purpose of tethering the vagrant spirits, and through the loop each baby was made to pass a chubby finger to make sure that its tiny soul would not wander away.

In an Indian story a king conveys his soul into the dead body of a Brahman, and a hunchback conveys his soul into the deserted body of the king. The hunchback is now king and the king is a Brahman. However, the hunchback is induced to show his skill by transferring his soul to the dead body of a parrot, and the king seizes the opportunity to regain possession of his own body. A tale of the same type, with variations of detail, reappears among the Malays. A king has incautiously transferred his soul to an ape, upon which the vizier adroitly inserts his own soul into the king's body and so takes possession of the queen and the kingdom, while the true king languishes at court in the outward semblance of an ape. But one day the false king, who played for high stakes, was watching a combat of rams, and it happened that the animal on which he had laid his money fell down dead. All efforts to restore animation proved unavailing till the false king, with the instinct of a true sportsman, transferred his own soul to the body of the deceased ram, and thus renewed the fray. The real king in the body of the ape saw his chance, and with great presence of mind darted back into his own body, which the vizier had rashly vacated. So he came to his own again, and the usurper in the ram's body met with the fate he richly deserved. Similarly the Greeks told how the soul of Hermotimus of Clazomenae used to quit his body and roam far and wide, bringing back intelligence of what he had seen on his rambles to his friends at home ; until one day, when his spirit was abroad, his enemies contrived to seize his deserted body and committed it to the flames.

The departure of the soul is not always voluntary. It may be extracted from the body against its will by ghosts, demons, or sorcerers. Hence, when a funeral is passing the house, the Karens tie their children with a special kind of string to a particular part of the house, lest the souls of the children should leave their bodies and go into the corpse which is passing. The children are kept tied in this way until the corpse is out of sight. And after the corpse has been laid in the grave, but before the earth has been shovelled in, the mourners and friends range themselves round the grave, each with a bamboo split lengthwise in one hand and a little stick in the other ; each man thrusts his bamboo into the grave, and drawing the stick along the groove of the bamboo points out to his soul that in this way it may easily climb up out of the tomb. While the earth is being shovelled in, the bamboos are kept out of the way, lest the souls should be in them, and so should be inadvertently buried with the earth as it is being thrown into the grave ; and when the people leave the spot they carry away the bamboos, begging their souls to come with them. Further, on returning from the grave each Karen provides himself with three little hooks made of branches of trees, and calling his spirit to follow him, at short intervals, as he returns, he makes a motion as if hooking it, and then thrusts the hook into the ground. This is done to prevent the soul of the living from staying behind with the soul of the dead. When the Karo-Bataks have buried somebody and are filling in the grave, a sorceress runs about beating the air with a stick. This she does in order to drive away the souls of the survivors, for if one of these souls happened to slip into the grave and to be covered up with earth, its owner would die.

In Uea, one of the Loyalty Islands, the souls of the dead seem to have been credited with the power of stealing the souls of the living. For when a man was sick the soul-doctor would go with a large troop of men and women to the graveyard. Here the men played on flutes and the women whistled softly to lure the soul home. After this had gone on for some time they formed in procession and moved homewards, the flutes playing and the women whistling all the way, while they led back the wandering soul and drove it gently along with open palms. On entering the patient's dwelling they commanded the soul in a loud voice to enter his body.

Often the abduction of a man's soul is set down to demons. Thus fits and convulsions are generally ascribed by the Chinese to the agency of certain mischievous spirits who love to draw men's souls out of their bodies. At Amoy the spirits who serve babies and children in this way rejoice in the high-sounding titles of " celestial agencies bestriding galloping horses " and " literary graduates residing half-way up in the sky." When an infant is writhing in convulsions, the frightened mother hastens to the roof of the house, and, waving about a bamboo pole to which one of the child's garments is attached, cries out several times, " My child So-and-so, come back, return home ! " Meantime, another inmate of the house bangs away at a gong in the hope of attracting the attention of the strayed soul, which is supposed to recognise the familiar garment and to slip into it. The garment containing the soul is then placed on or beside the child, and if the child does not die recovery is sure to follow, sooner or later. Similarly some Indians catch a man's lost soul in his boots and restore it to his body by putting his feet into them.

In the Moluccas when a man is unwell it is thought that some devil has carried away his soul to the tree, mountain, or hill where he (the devil) resides. A sorcerer having pointed out the devil's abode, the friends of the patient carry thither cooked rice, fruit, fish, raw eggs, a hen, a chicken, a silken robe, gold, armlets, and so forth. Having set out the food in order they pray, saying : " We come to offer to you, O devil, this offering of food, clothes, gold, and so on ; take it and release the soul of the patient for whom we pray. Let it return to his body, and he who now is sick shall be made whole." Then they eat a little and let the hen loose as a ransom for the soul of the patient ; also they put down the raw eggs ; but the silken robe, the gold, and the armlets they take home with them. As soon as they are come to the house they place a flat bowl containing the offerings which have been brought back at the sick man's head, and say to him : " Now is your soul released, and you shall fare well and live to grey hairs on the earth."

Demons are especially feared by persons who have just entered a new house. Hence at a house-warming among the Alfoors of Mina-hassa in Celebes the priest performs a ceremony for the purpose of restoring their souls to the inmates. He hangs up a bag at the place of sacrifice and then goes through a list of the gods. There are so many of them that this takes him the whole night through without stopping. In the morning he offers the gods an egg and some rice. By this time the souls of the household are supposed to be gathered in the bag. So the priest takes the bag, and holding it on the head of the master of the house, says, " Here you have your soul ; go (soul) to-morrow away again." He then does the same, saying the same words, to the housewife and all the other members of the family. Amongst the same Alfoors one way of recovering a sick man's soul is to let down a bowl by a belt out of a window and fish for the soul till it is caught in the bowl and hauled up. And among the same people, when a priest is bringing back a sick man's soul which he has caught in a cloth, he is preceded by a girl holding the large leaf of a certain palm over his head as an umbrella to keep him and the soul from getting wet, in case it should rain ; and he is followed by a man brandishing a sword to deter other souls from any attempt at rescuing the captured spirit.

Sometimes the lost soul is brought back in a visible shape. The Salish or Flathead Indians of Oregon believe that a man's soul may be separated for a time from his body without causing death and without the man being aware of his loss. It is necessary, however, that the lost soul should be soon found and restored to its owner or he will die. The name of the man who has lost his soul is revealed in a dream to the medicine-man, who hastens to inform the sufferer of his loss. Generally a number of men have sustained a like loss at the same time ; all their names are revealed to the medicine-man, and all employ him to recover their souls. The whole night long these soulless men go about the village from lodge to lodge, dancing and singing. Towards daybreak they go into a separate lodge, which is closed up so as to be totally dark. A small hole is then made in the roof, through which the medicine-man, with a bunch of feathers, brushes in the souls, in the shape of bits of bone and the like, which he receives on a piece of matting. A fire is next kindled, by the light of which the medicine-man sorts out the souls. First he puts aside the souls of dead people, of which there are usually several ; for if he were to give the soul of a dead person to a living man, the man would die instantly. Next he picks out the souls of all the persons present, and making them all to sit down before him, he takes the soul of each, in the shape of a splinter of bone, wood, or shell, and placing it on the owner's head, pats it with many prayers and contortions till it descends into the heart and so resumes its proper place.

Again, souls may be extracted from their bodies or detained on their wanderings not only by ghosts and demons but also by men, especially by sorcerers. In Fiji, if a criminal refused 'to confess, the chief sent for a scarf with which " to catch away the soul of the rogue." At the sight or even at the mention of the scarf the culprit generally made a clean breast. For if he did not, the scarf would be waved over his head till his soul was caught in it, when it would be carefully folded up and nailed to the end of a chief's canoe ; and for want of his soul the criminal would pine and die. The sorcerers of Danger Island used to set snares for souls. The snares were made of stout cinet, about fifteen to thirty feet long, with loops on either side of different sizes, to suit the different sizes of souls ; for fat souls there were large loops, for thin souls there were small ones. When a man was sick against whom the sorcerers had a grudge, they set up these soul-snares near his house and watched for the flight of his soul. If in the shape of a bird or an insect it was caught in the snare, the man would infallibly die. In some parts of West Africa, indeed, wizards are continually setting traps to catch souls that wander from their bodies in sleep ; and when they have caught one, they tie it up over the fire, and as it shrivels in the heat the owner sickens. This is done, not out of any grudge towards the sufferer, but purely as a matter of business. The wizard does not care whose soul he has captured, and will readily restore it to its owner, if only he is paid for doing so. Some sorcerers keep regular asylums for strayed souls, and anybody who has lost or mislaid his own soul can always have another one from the asylum on payment of the usual fee. No blame whatever attaches to men who keep these private asylums or set traps for passing souls ; it is their profession, and in the exercise of it they are actuated by no harsh or unkindly feelings. But there are also wretches who from pure spite or for the sake of lucre set and bait traps with the deliberate purpose of catching the soul of a particular man ; and in the bottom of the pot, hidden by the bait, are knives and sharp hooks which tear and rend the poor soul, either killing it outright or mauling it so as to impair the health of its owner when it succeeds in escaping and returning to him. Miss Kingsley knew a Kruman who became very anxious about his soul, because for several nights he had smelt in his dreams the savoury smell of smoked crawfish seasoned with red pepper. Clearly some ill-wisher had set a trap baited with this dainty for his dream-soul, intending to do him grievous bodily, or rather spiritual, harm ; and for the next few nights great pains were taken to keep his soul from straying abroad in his sleep. In the sweltering heat of the tropical night he lay sweating and snorting under a blanket, his nose and mouth tied up with a handkerchief to prevent the escape of his precious soul. In Hawaii there were sorcerers who caught souls of living people, shut them up in calabashes, and gave them to people to eat. By squeezing a captured soul in their hands they discovered the place where people had been secretly buried.

Nowhere perhaps is the art of abducting human souls more carefully cultivated or carried to higher perfection than in the Malay Peninsula. Here the methods by which the wizard works his will are various, and so too are his motives. Sometimes he desires to destroy an enemy, sometimes to win the love of a cold or bashful beauty. Thus, to take an instance of the latter sort of charm, the following are the directions given for securing the soul of one whom you wish to render distraught. When the moon, just risen, looks red above the eastern horizon, go out, and standing in the moonlight, with the big toe of your right foot on the big toe of your left, make a speaking-trumpet of your right hand and recite through it the following words :

> " OM.   I loose my shaft, I loose it and the moon clouds over,
> I loose it, and the sun is extinguished.
> I loose it, and the stars burn dim.
> But it is not the sun, moon, and stars that I shoot at,
> It is the stalk of the heart of that child of the congregation,
> So-and-so.
>
> Cluck ! cluck ! soul of So-and-so, come and walk with me,
> Come and sit with me,
> Come and sleep and share my pillow.
> Cluck ! cluck ! soul."

Repeat this thrice and after every repetition blow through your hollow fist. Or you may catch the soul in your turban, thus. Go out on the night of the full moon and the two succeeding nights ; sit down on an ant-hill facing the moon, burn incense, and recite the following incantation :

" I bring you a betel leaf to chew,
Dab the lime on to it, Prince Ferocious,
For Somebody, Prince Distraction's
*   daughter, to chew.*
Somebody at sunrise be distraught for
*   love of me,*
Somebody at sunset be distraught for
*   love of me.*
As you remember your parents,
*   remember me ;*
As you remember your house and
*   house-ladder, remember me ;*
When thunder rumbles, remember me ;
When wind whistles, remember me ;

When the heavens rain, remember me ;
When cocks crow, remember me :
When the dial-bird tells its tales,
*   remember me ;*
When you look up at the sun, remember
*   me ;*
When you look up at the moon,
*   remember me,*
For in that self-same moon I am there.
Cluck ! cluck ! soul of Somebody come
*   hither to me.*
I do not mean to let you have my soul,
Let your soul come hither to mine."

Now wave the end of your turban towards the moon seven times each night. Go home and put it under your pillow, and if you want to wear it in the daytime, burn incense and say, " It is not a turban that I carry in my girdle, but the soul of Somebody."

The Indians of the Nass River, in British Columbia, are impressed with a belief that a physician may swallow his patient's soul by mistake. A doctor who is believed to have done so is made by the other members of the faculty to stand over the patient, while one of them thrusts his fingers down the doctor's throat, another kneads him in the stomach with his knuckles, and a third slaps him on the back. If the soul is not in him after all, and if the same process has been repeated upon all the medical men without success, it is concluded that the soul must be in the head-doctor's box. A party of doctors, therefore, waits upon him at his house and requests him to produce his box. When he has done so and arranged its contents on a new mat, they take the votary of Aesculapius and hold him up by the heels with his head in a hole in the floor. In this position they wash his head, and " any water remaining from the ablution is taken and poured upon the sick man's head." No doubt the lost soul is in the water.

§ 3. *The Soul as a Shadow and a Reflection.*—But the spiritual dangers I have enumerated are not the only ones which beset the savage. Often he regards his shadow or reflection as his soul, or at all events as a vital part of himself, and as such it is necessarily a source of danger to him. For if it is trampled upon, struck, or stabbed, he will feel the injury as if it were done to his person ; and if it is detached from him entirely (as he believes that it may be) he will die. In the island of Wetar there are magicians who can make a man ill by stabbing his shadow with a pike or hacking it with a sword. After Sankara had destroyed the Buddhists in India, it is said that he journeyed to Nepaul, where he had some difference of opinion with the Grand Lama. To prove his supernatural powers, he soared into the air. But as he mounted up, the Grand Lama, perceiving his shadow swaying and wavering on the ground, struck his knife into it and down fell Sankara and broke his neck.

In the Banks Islands there are some stones of a remarkably long shape which go by the name of " eating ghosts," because certain powerful and dangerous ghosts are believed to lodge in them. If a man's shadow falls on one of these stones, the ghost will draw his soul out from him, so that he will die. Such stones, therefore, are set in a house to guard it ; and a messenger sent to a house by the absent owner will call out the name of the sender, lest the watchful ghost in the stone should fancy that he came with evil intent and should do him a mischief. At a funeral in China, when the lid is about to be placed on the coffin, most of the bystanders, with the exception of the nearest kin, retire a few steps or even retreat to another room, for a person's health is believed to be endangered by allowing his shadow to be enclosed in a coffin. And when the coffin is about to be lowered into the grave most of the spectators recoil to a little distance lest their shadows should fall into the grave and harm should thus be done to their persons. The geomancer and his assistants stand on the side of the grave which is turned away from the sun ; and the grave-diggers and coffin-bearers attach their shadows firmly to their persons by tying a strip of cloth tightly round their waists. Nor is it human beings alone who are thus liable to be injured by means of their shadows. Animals are to some extent in the same predicament. A small snail, which frequents the neighbourhood of the limestone hills in Perak, is believed to suck the blood of cattle through their shadows ; hence the beasts grow lean and sometimes die from loss of blood. The ancients supposed that in Arabia, if a hyaena trod on a man's shadow, it deprived him of the power of speech and motion ; and that if a dog, standing on a roof in the moonlight, cast a shadow on the ground and a hyaena trod on it, the dog would fall down as if dragged with a rope. Clearly in these cases the shadow, if not equivalent to the soul, is at least regarded as a living part of the man or the animal, so that injury done to the shadow is felt by the person or animal as if it were done to his body.

Conversely, if the shadow is a vital part of a man or an animal, it may under certain circumstances be as hazardous to be touched by it as it would be to come into contact with the person or animal. Hence the savage makes it a rule to shun the shadow of certain persons whom for various reasons he regards as sources of dangerous influence. Amongst the dangerous classes he commonly ranks mourners and women in general, but especially his mother-in-law. The Shuswap Indians think that the shadow of a mourner falling upon a person would make him sick. Amongst the Kurnai of Victoria novices at initiation were cautioned not to let a woman's shadow fall across them, as this would make them thin, lazy, and stupid. An Australian native is said to have once nearly died of fright because the shadow of his mother-in-law fell on his legs as he lay asleep under a tree. The awe and dread with which the untutored savage contemplates his mother-

in-law are amongst the most familiar facts of anthropology. In the
Yuin tribes of New South Wales the rule which forbade a man to
hold any communication with his wife's mother was very strict. He
might not look at her or even in her direction. It was a ground of
divorce if his shadow happened to fall on his mother-in-law : in that
case he had to leave his wife, and she returned to her parents. In
New Britain the native imagination fails to conceive the extent and
nature of the calamities which would result from a man's accidentally
speaking to his wife's mother ; suicide of one or both would probably
be the only course open to them. The most solemn form of oath a
New Briton can take is, " Sir, if I am not telling the truth, I hope I
may shake hands with my mother-in-law."

Where the shadow is regarded as so intimately bound up with the
life of the man that its loss entails debility or death, it is natural to
expect that its diminution should be regarded with solicitude and
apprehension, as betokening a corresponding decrease in the vital
energy of its owner. In Amboyna and Uliase, two islands near
the equator, where necessarily there is little or no shadow cast at
noon, the people make it a rule not to go out of the house at mid-
day, because they fancy that by doing so a man may lose the shadow
of his soul. The Mangaians tell of a mighty warrior, Tukaitawa,
whose strength waxed and waned with the length of his shadow. In
the morning, when his shadow fell longest, his strength was greatest ;
but as the shadow shortened towards noon his strength ebbed with
it, till exactly at noon it reached its lowest point ; then, as the shadow
stretched out in the afternoon, his strength returned. A certain hero
discovered the secret of Tukaitawa's strength and slew him at noon.
The savage Besisis of the Malay Peninsula fear to bury their dead at
noon, because they fancy that the shortness of their shadows at that
hour would sympathetically shorten their own lives.

Nowhere, perhaps, does the equivalence of the shadow to the life
or soul come out more clearly than in some customs practised to this
day in South-eastern Europe. In modern Greece, when the foundation
of a new building is being laid, it is the custom to kill a cock, a ram,
or a lamb, and to let its blood flow on the foundation-stone, under
which the animal is afterwards buried. The object of the sacrifice
is to give strength and stability to the building. But sometimes,
instead of killing an animal, the builder entices a man to the foundation-
stone, secretly measures his body, or a part of it, or his shadow, and
buries the measure under the foundation-stone ; or he lays the foundation-stone upon the man's shadow. It is believed that the man will
die within the year. The Roumanians of Transylvania think that he
whose shadow is thus immured will die within forty days ; so persons
passing by a building which is in course of erection may hear a warning
cry, " Beware lest they take thy shadow ! " Not long ago there were
still shadow-traders whose business it was to provide architects with
the shadows necessary for securing their walls. In these cases the
measure of the shadow is looked on as equivalent to the shadow itself,

and to bury it is to bury the life or soul of the man, who, deprived of it, must die. Thus the custom is a substitute for the old practice of immuring a living person in the walls, or crushing him under the foundation-stone of a new building, in order to give strength and durability to the structure, or more definitely in order that the angry ghost may haunt the place and guard it against the intrusion of enemies.

As some peoples believe a man's soul to be in his shadow, so other (or the same) peoples believe it to be in his reflection in water or a mirror. Thus " the Andamanese do not regard their shadows but their reflections (in any mirror) as their souls." When the Motumotu of New Guinea first saw their likenesses in a looking-glass, they thought that their reflections were their souls. In New Caledonia the old men are of opinion that a person's reflection in water or a mirror is his soul ; but the younger men, taught by the Catholic priests, maintain that it is a reflection and nothing more, just like the reflection of palm-trees in the water. The reflection-soul, being external to the man, is exposed to much the same dangers as the shadow-soul. The Zulus will not look into a dark pool because they think there is a beast in it which will take away their reflections, so that they die. The Basutos say that crocodiles have the power of thus killing a man by dragging his reflection under water. When one of them dies suddenly and from no apparent cause, his relatives will allege that a crocodile must have taken his shadow some time when he crossed a stream. In Saddle Island, Melanesia, there is a pool "into which if any one looks he dies ; the malignant spirit takes hold upon his life by means of his reflection on the water."

We can now understand why it was a maxim both in ancient India and ancient Greece not to look at one's reflection in water, and why the Greeks regarded it as an omen of death if a man dreamed of seeing himself so reflected. They feared that the water-spirits would drag the person's reflection or soul under water, leaving him soulless to perish. This was probably the origin of the classical story of the beautiful Narcissus, who languished and died through seeing his reflection in the water.

Further, we can now explain the widespread custom of covering up mirrors or turning them to the wall after a death has taken place in the house. It is feared that the soul, projected out of the person in the shape of his reflection in the mirror, may be carried off by the ghost of the departed, which is commonly supposed to linger about the house till the burial. The custom is thus exactly parallel to the Aru custom of not sleeping in a house after a death for fear that the soul, projected out of the body in a dream, may meet the ghost and be carried off by it. The reason why sick people should not see themselves in a mirror, and why the mirror in a sick-room is therefore covered up, is also plain ; in time of sickness, when the soul might take flight so easily, it is particularly dangerous to project it out of the body by means of the reflection in a mirror. The rule is therefore precisely parallel to the rule observed by some peoples of not allowing sick people to sleep ; for in sleep the soul is projected out of the body, and there is always a risk that it may not return.

As with shadows and reflections, so with portraits ; they are often believed to contain the soul of the person portrayed. People who hold this belief are naturally loth to have their likenesses taken ; for if the portrait is the soul, or at least a vital part of the person portrayed, whoever possesses the portrait will be able to exercise a fatal influence over the original of it. Thus the Esquimaux of Bering Strait believe that persons dealing in witchcraft have the power of stealing a person's shade, so that without it he will pine away and die. Once at a village on the lower Yukon River an explorer had set up his camera to get a picture of the people as they were moving about among their houses. While he was focussing the instrument, the headman of the village came up and insisted on peeping under the cloth. Being allowed to do so, he gazed intently for a minute at the moving figures on the ground glass, then suddenly withdrew his head and bawled at the top of his voice to the people, " He has all of your shades in this box." A panic ensued among the group, and in an instant they disappeared helter-skelter into their houses. The Tepehuanes of Mexico stood in mortal terror of the camera, and five days' persuasion was necessary to induce them to pose for it. When at last they consented, they looked like criminals about to be executed. They believed that by photographing people the artist could carry off their souls and devour them at his leisure moments. They said that, when the pictures reached his country, they would die or some other evil would befall them. When Dr. Catat and some companions were exploring the Bara country on the west coast of Madagascar, the people suddenly became hostile. The day before the travellers, not without difficulty, had photographed the royal family, and now found themselves accused of taking the souls of the natives for the purpose of selling them when they returned to France. Denial was vain ; in compliance with the custom of the country they were obliged to catch the souls, which were then put into a basket and ordered by Dr. Catat to return to their respective owners.

Some villagers in Sikhim betrayed a lively horror and hid away whenever the lens of a camera, or " the evil eye of the box " as they called it, was turned on them. They thought it took away their souls with their pictures, and so put it in the power of the owner of the pictures to cast spells on them, and they alleged that a photograph of the scenery blighted the landscape. Until the reign of the late King of Siam no Siamese coins were ever stamped with the image of the king, " for at that time there was a strong prejudice against the making of portraits in any medium. Europeans who travel into the jungle have, even at the present time, only to point a camera at a crowd to procure its instant dispersion. When a copy of the face of a person is made and taken away from him, a portion of his life goes with the picture. Unless the sovereign had been blessed with the years of a Methusaleh he could scarcely have permitted his life to be distributed in small pieces together with the coins of the realm."

Beliefs of the same sort still linger in various parts of Europe. Not very many years ago some old women in the Greek island of Carpathus were very angry at having their likenesses drawn, thinking that in consequence they would pine and die. There are persons in the West of Scotland "who refuse to have their likenesses taken lest it prove unlucky; and give as instances the cases of several of their friends who never had a day's health after being photographed."

CHAPTER XIX

TABOOED ACTS

§ 1. *Taboos on Intercourse with Strangers.*—So much for the primitive conceptions of the soul and the dangers to which it is exposed. These conceptions are not limited to one people or country; with variations of detail they are found all over the world, and survive, as we have seen, in modern Europe. Beliefs so deep-seated and so widespread must necessarily have contributed to shape the mould in which the early kingship was cast. For if every person was at such pains to save his own soul from the perils which threatened it on so many sides, how much more carefully must *he* have been guarded upon whose life hung the welfare and even the existence of the whole people, and whom therefore it was the common interest of all to preserve? Therefore we should expect to find the king's life protected by a system of pre-cautions or safeguards still more numerous and minute than those which in primitive society every man adopts for the safety of his own soul. Now in point of fact the life of the early kings is regulated, as we have seen and shall see more fully presently, by a very exact code of rules. May we not then conjecture that these rules are in fact the very safeguards which we should expect to find adopted for the pro-tection of the king's life? An examination of the rules themselves confirms this conjecture. For from this it appears that some of the rules observed by the kings are identical with those observed by private persons out of regard for the safety of their souls; and even of those which seem peculiar to the king, many, if not all, are most readily explained on the hypothesis that they are nothing but safeguards or lifeguards of the king. I will now enumerate some of these royal rules or taboos, offering on each of them such comments and explanations as may serve to set the original intention of the rule in its proper light.

As the object of the royal taboos is to isolate the king from all sources of danger, their general effect is to compel him to live in a state of seclusion, more or less complete, according to the number and stringency of the rules he observes. Now of all sources of danger none are more dreaded by the savage than magic and witchcraft, and he suspects all strangers of practising these black arts. To guard against the baneful influence exerted voluntarily or involuntarily by strangers is therefore an elementary dictate of savage prudence. Hence before strangers are allowed to enter a district, or at least before they are permitted to mingle freely with the inhabitants, certain ceremonies are often performed by the natives of the country for the purpose of disarming the strangers of their magical powers, of counteracting the baneful influence which is believed to emanate from them, or of disinfecting, so to speak, the tainted atmosphere by which they are supposed to be surrounded. Thus, when the ambassadors sent by Justin II., Emperor of the East, to conclude a peace with the Turks had reached their destination, they were received by shamans, who subjected them to a ceremonial purification for the purpose of exorcising all harmful influence. Having deposited the goods brought by the ambassadors in an open place, these wizards carried burning branches of incense round them, while they rang a bell and beat on a tambourine, snorting and falling into a state of frenzy in their efforts to dispel the powers of evil. Afterwards they purified the ambassadors themselves by leading them through the flames. In the island of Nanumea (South Pacific) strangers from ships or from other islands were not allowed to communicate with the people until they all, or a few as representatives of the rest, had been taken to each of the four temples in the island, and prayers offered that the god would avert any disease or treachery which these strangers might have brought with them. Meat offerings were also laid upon the altars, accompanied by songs and dances in honour of the god. While these ceremonies were going on, all the people except the priests and their attendants kept out of sight. Amongst the Ot Danoms of Borneo it is the custom that strangers entering the territory should pay to the natives a certain sum, which is spent in the sacrifice of buffaloes or pigs to the spirits of the land and water, in order to reconcile them to the presence of the strangers, and to induce them not to withdraw their favour from the people of the country, but to bless the rice-harvest, and so forth. The men of a certain district in Borneo, fearing to look upon a European traveller lest he should make them ill, warned their wives and children not to go near him. Those who could not restrain their curiosity killed fowls to appease the evil spirits and smeared themselves with the blood. "More dreaded," says a traveller in Central Borneo, "than the evil spirits of the neighbourhood are the evil spirits from a distance which accompany travellers. When a company from the middle Mahakam river visited me among the Blu-u Kayans in the year 1897, no woman showed herself outside her house without a burning bundle of *plehiding* bark, the stinking smoke of which drives away evil spirits."

When Crevaux was travelling in South America he entered a village of the Apalai Indians. A few moments after his arrival some of the Indians brought him a number of large black ants, of a species whose bite is painful, fastened on palm leaves. Then all the people of the village, without distinction of age or sex, presented themselves to him, and he had to sting them all with the ants on their faces, thighs, and other parts of their bodies. Sometimes, when he applied the ants too tenderly, they called out "More! more!" and were not satisfied till

their skin was thickly studded with tiny swellings like what might
have been produced by whipping them with nettles. The object of
this ceremony is made plain by the custom observed in Amboyna and
Uliase of sprinkling sick people with pungent spices, such as ginger
and cloves, chewed fine, in order by the prickling sensation to drive
away the demon of disease which may be clinging to their persons.
In Java a popular cure for gout or rheumatism is to rub Spanish pepper
into the nails of the fingers and toes of the sufferer ; the pungency of
the pepper is supposed to be too much for the gout or rheumatism,
who accordingly departs in haste. So on the Slave Coast the mother
of a sick child sometimes believes that an evil spirit has taken possession
of the child's body, and in order to drive him out, she makes small cuts
in the body of the little sufferer and inserts green peppers or spices in
the wounds, believing that she will thereby hurt the evil spirit and
force him to be gone. The poor child naturally screams with pain,
but the mother hardens her heart in the belief that the demon is
suffering equally.

It is probable that the same dread of strangers, rather than any
desire to do them honour, is the motive of certain ceremonies which
are sometimes observed at their reception, but of which the intention
is not directly stated. In the Ongtong Java Islands, which are inhabited by Polynesians, the priests or sorcerers seem to wield great
influence. Their main business is to summon or exorcise spirits for
the purpose of averting or dispelling sickness, and of procuring favourable winds, a good catch of fish, and so on. When strangers land on
the islands, they are first of all received by the sorcerers, sprinkled
with water, anointed with oil, and girt with dried pandanus leaves.
At the same time sand and water are freely thrown about in all directions, and the newcomer and his boat are wiped with green leaves.
After this ceremony the strangers are introduced by the sorcerers to
the chief. In Afghanistan and in some parts of Persia the traveller,
before he enters a village, is frequently received with a sacrifice of
animal life or food, or of fire and incense. The Afghan Boundary
Mission, in passing by villages in Afghanistan, was often met with
fire and incense. Sometimes a tray of lighted embers is thrown under
the hoofs of the traveller's horse, with the words, " You are welcome."
On entering a village in Central Africa Emin Pasha was received with
the sacrifice of two goats ; their blood was sprinkled on the path and
the chief stepped over the blood to greet Emin. Sometimes the dread
of strangers and their magic is too great to allow of their reception on
any terms. Thus when Speke arrived at a certain village, the natives
shut their doors against him, " because they had never before seen a
white man nor the tin boxes that the men were carrying : ' Who
knows,' they said, ' but that these very boxes are the plundering
Watuta transformed and come to kill us ? You cannot be admitted.'
No persuasion could avail with them, and the party had to proceed to
the next village."

The fear thus entertained of alien visitors is often mutual. Entering a strange land the savage feels that he is treading enchanted ground, and he takes steps to guard against the demons that haunt it and the magical arts of its inhabitants. Thus on going to a strange land the Maoris performed certain ceremonies to make it " common," lest it might have been previously " sacred." When Baron Miklucho-Maclay was approaching a village on the Maclay Coast of New Guinea, one of the natives who accompanied him broke a branch from a tree and going aside whispered to it for a while ; then stepping up to each member of the party, one after another, he spat something upon his back and gave him some blows with the branch. Lastly, he went into the forest and buried the branch under withered leaves in the thickest part of the jungle. This ceremony was believed to protect the party against all treachery and danger in the village they were approaching. The idea probably was that the malignant influences were drawn off from the persons into the branch and buried with it in the depths of the forest. In Australia, when a strange tribe has been invited into a district and is approaching the encampment of the tribe which owns the land, " the strangers carry lighted bark or burning sticks in their hands, for the purpose, they say, of clearing and purifying the air." When the Toradjas are on a head-hunting expedition and have entered the enemy's country, they may not eat any fruits which the foe has planted nor any animal which he has reared until they have first committed an act of hostility, as by burning a house or killing a man. They think that if they broke this rule they would receive something of the soul or spiritual essence of the enemy into themselves, which would destroy the mystic virtue of their talismans.

Again, it is believed that a man who has been on a journey may have contracted some magic evil from the strangers with whom he has associated. Hence, on returning home, before he is re-admitted to the society of his tribe and friends, he has to undergo certain purificatory ceremonies. Thus the Bechuanas " cleanse or purify themselves after journeys by shaving their heads, etc., lest they should have contracted from strangers some evil by witchcraft or sorcery." In some parts of western Africa, when a man returns home after a long absence, before he is allowed to visit his wife, he must wash his person with a particular fluid, and receive from the sorcerer a certain mark on his forehead, in order to counteract any magic spell which a stranger woman may have cast on him in his absence, and which might be communicated through him to the women of his village. Two Hindoo ambassadors, who had been sent to England by a native prince and had returned to India, were considered to have so polluted themselves by contact with strangers that nothing but being born again could restore them to purity. " For the purpose of regeneration it is directed to make an image of pure gold of the female power of nature, in the shape either of a woman or of a cow. In this statue the person to be regenerated is enclosed, and dragged through the usual channel. As a statue of pure gold and of proper dimensions would be too expensive, it is sufficient to make an image of the sacred *Yoni*, through which the person to be regenerated is to pass." Such an image of pure gold was made at the prince's command, and his ambassadors were born again by being dragged through it.

When precautions like these are taken on behalf of the people in general against the malignant influence supposed to be exercised by strangers, it is no wonder that special measures are adopted to protect the king from the same insidious danger. In the middle ages the envoys who visited a Tartar Khan were obliged to pass between two fires before they were admitted to his presence, and the gifts they brought were also carried between the fires. The reason assigned for the custom was that the fire purged away any magic influence which the strangers might mean to exercise over the Khan. When subject chiefs come with their retinues to visit Kalamba (the most powerful chief of the Bashilange in the Congo Basin) for the first time or after being rebellious, they have to bathe, men and women together, in two brooks on two successive days, passing the nights under the open sky in the market-place. After the second bath they proceed, entirely naked, to the house of Kalamba, who makes a long white mark on the breast and forehead of each of them. Then they return to the market-place and dress, after which they undergo the pepper ordeal. Pepper is dropped into the eyes of each of them, and while this is being done the sufferer has to make a confession of all his sins, to answer all questions that may be put to him, and to take certain vows. This ends the ceremony, and the strangers are now free to take up their quarters in the town for as long as they choose to remain.

§ 2. *Taboos on Eating and Drinking.*—In the opinion of savages the acts of eating and drinking are attended with special danger ; for at these times the soul may escape from the mouth, or be extracted by the magic arts of an enemy present. Among the Ewe-speaking peoples of the Slave Coast " the common belief seems to be that the indwelling spirit leaves the body and returns to it through the mouth ; hence, should it have gone out, it behoves a man to be careful about opening his mouth, lest a homeless spirit should take advantage of the opportunity and enter his body. This, it appears, is considered most likely to take place while the man is eating." Precautions are therefore adopted to guard against these dangers. Thus of the Bataks it is said that " since the soul can leave the body, they always take care to prevent their soul from straying on occasions when they have most need of it. But it is only possible to prevent the soul from straying when one is in the house. At feasts one may find the whole house shut up, in order that the soul may stay and enjoy the good things set before it." The Zafimanelo in Madagascar lock their doors when they eat, and hardly any one ever sees them eating. The Warua will not allow any one to see them eating and drinking, being doubly particular that no person of the opposite sex shall see them doing so. " I had to pay a man to let me see him drink ; I could not make a man let a woman see him drink." When offered a drink they often ask that a cloth may be held up to hide them whilst drinking.

If these are the ordinary precautions taken by common people, the precautions taken by kings are extraordinary. The king of Loango may not be seen eating or drinking by man or beast under pain of death. A favourite dog having broken into the room where the king was dining, the king ordered it to be killed on the spot. Once the king's own son, a boy of twelve years old, inadvertently saw the king drink. Immediately the king ordered him to be finely apparelled and feasted, after which he commanded him to be cut in quarters, and carried about the city with a proclamation that he had seen the king drink. " When the king has a mind to drink, he has a cup of wine brought ; he that brings it has a bell in his hand, and as soon as he has delivered the cup to the king, he turns his face from him and rings the bell, on which all present fall down with their faces to the ground, and continue so till the king has drunk. . . . His eating is much in the same style, for which he has a house on purpose, where his victuals are set upon a bensa or table : which he goes to, and shuts the door : when he has done, he knocks and comes out. So that none ever see the king eat or drink. For it is believed that if any one should, the king shall immediately die." The remnants of his food are buried, doubtless to prevent them from falling into the hands of sorcerers, who by means of these fragments might cast a fatal spell over the monarch. The rules observed by the neighbouring king of Cacongo were similar ; it was thought that the king would die if any of his subjects were to see him drink. It is a capital offence to see the king of Dahomey at his meals. When he drinks in public, as he does on extraordinary occasions, he hides himself behind a curtain, or hand-kerchiefs are held up round his head, and all the people throw themselves with their faces to the earth. When the king of Bunyoro in Central Africa went to drink milk in the dairy, every man must leave the royal enclosure and all the women had to cover their heads till the king returned. No one might see him drink. One wife accompanied him to the dairy and handed him the milk-pot, but she turned away her face while he drained it.

§ 3. *Taboos on showing the Face.*—In some of the preceding cases the intention of eating and drinking in strict seclusion may perhaps be to hinder evil influences from entering the body rather than to prevent the escape of the soul. This certainly is the motive of some drinking customs observed by natives of the Congo region. Thus we are told of these people that " there is hardly a native who would dare to swallow a liquid without first conjuring the spirits. One of them rings a bell all the time he is drinking ; another crouches down and places his left hand on the earth ; another veils his head ; another puts a stalk of grass or a leaf in his hair, or marks his forehead with a line of clay. This fetish custom assumes very varied forms. To explain them, the black is satisfied to say that they are an energetic mode of conjuring spirits." In this part of the world a chief will commonly ring a bell at each draught of beer which he swallows, and at the same moment a lad stationed in front of him brandishes a spear " to keep at bay the spirits which might try to sneak into the old chief's body by the same road as the beer." The same motive of warding off evil spirits probably explains the custom observed by some African sultans of veiling their faces. The Sultan of Darfur wraps up his face with a piece of white muslin, which goes round his head several times, covering his mouth and nose first, and then his forehead, so that only his eyes are visible. The same custom of veiling the face as a mark of sovereignty is said to be observed in other parts of Central Africa. The Sultan of Wadai always speaks from behind a curtain ; no one sees his face except his intimates and a few favoured persons.

§ 4. *Taboos on quitting the House.*—By an extension of the like precaution kings are sometimes forbidden ever to leave their palaces ; or, if they are allowed to do so, their subjects are forbidden to see them abroad. The fetish king of Benin, who was worshipped as a deity by his subjects, might not quit his palace. After his coronation the king of Loango is confined to his palace, which he may not leave. The king of Onitsha " does not step out of his house into the town unless a human sacrifice is made to propitiate the gods : on this account he never goes out beyond the precincts of his premises." Indeed we are told that he may not quit his palace under pain of death or of giving up one or more slaves to be executed in his presence. As the wealth of the country is measured in slaves, the king takes good care not to infringe the law. Yet once a year at the Feast of Yams the king is allowed, and even required by custom, to dance before his people outside the high mud wall of the palace. In dancing he carries a great weight, generally a sack of earth, on his back to prove that he is still able to support the burden and cares of state. Were he unable to discharge this duty, he would be immediately deposed and perhaps stoned. The kings of Ethiopia were worshipped as gods, but were mostly kept shut up in their palaces. On the mountainous coast of Pontus there dwelt in antiquity a rude and warlike people named the Mosyni or Mosynoeci, through whose rugged country the Ten Thousand marched on their famous retreat from Asia to Europe. These barbarians kept their king in close custody at the top of a high tower, from which after his election he was never more allowed to descend. Here he dispensed justice to his people ; but if he offended them, they punished him by stopping his rations for a whole day, or even starving him to death. The kings of Sabaea or Sheba, the spice country of Arabia, were not allowed to go out of their palaces ; if they did so, the mob stoned them to death. But at the top of the palace there was a window with a chain attached to it. If any man deemed he had suffered wrong, he pulled the chain, and the king perceived him and called him in and gave judgment.

§ 5. *Taboos on leaving Food over.*—Again, magic mischief may be wrought upon a man through the remains of the food he has partaken of, or the dishes out of which he has eaten. On the principles of sympathetic magic a real connexion continues to subsist between the food which a man has in his stomach and the refuse of it which he has left untouched, and hence by injuring the refuse you can simultaneously injure the eater. Among the Narrinyeri of South Australia every adult is constantly on the look-out for bones of beasts, birds, or fish, of which the flesh has been eaten by somebody, in order to construct a deadly charm out of them. Every one is therefore careful to burn the bones of the animals which he has eaten, lest they should fall into the hands of a sorcerer. Too often, however, the sorcerer succeeds in getting hold of such a bone, and when he does so he believes that he has the power of life and death over the man, woman, or child who ate the flesh of the animal. To put the charm in operation he makes a paste of red ochre and fish oil, inserts in it the eye of a cod and a small piece of the flesh of a corpse, and having rolled the compound into a ball sticks it on the top of the bone. After being left for some time in the bosom of a dead body, in order that it may derive a deadly potency by contact with corruption, the magical implement is set up in the ground near the fire, and as the ball melts, so the person against whom the charm is directed wastes with disease ; if the ball is melted quite away, the victim will die. When the bewitched man learns of the spell that is being cast upon him, he endeavours to buy the bone from the sorcerer, and if he obtains it he breaks the charm by throwing the bone into a river or lake. In Tana, one of the New Hebrides, people bury or throw into the sea the leavings of their food, lest these should fall into the hands of the disease-makers. For if a disease-maker finds the remnants of a meal, say the skin of a banana, he picks it up and burns it slowly in the fire. As it burns, the person who ate the banana falls ill and sends to the disease-maker, offering him presents if he will stop burning the banana skin. In New Guinea the natives take the utmost care to destroy or conceal the husks and other remains of their food, lest these should be found by their enemies and used by them for the injury or destruction of the eaters. Hence they burn their leavings, throw them into the sea, or otherwise put them out of harm's way.

From a like fear, no doubt, of sorcery, no one may touch the food which the king of Loango leaves upon his plate ; it is buried in a hole in the ground. And no one may drink out of the king's vessel. In antiquity the Romans used immediately to break the shells of eggs and of snails which they had eaten, in order to prevent enemies from making magic with them. The common practice, still observed among us, of breaking egg-shells after the eggs have been eaten may very well have originated in the same superstition.

The superstitious fear of the magic that may be wrought on a man through the leavings of his food has had the beneficial effect of inducing many savages to destroy refuse which, if left to rot, might through its corruption have proved a real, not a merely imaginary, source of disease and death. Nor is it only the sanitary condition of a tribe which has benefited by this superstition ; curiously enough the same baseless dread, the same false notion of causation, has indirectly strengthened the moral bonds of hospitality, honour, and good faith among men who entertain it. For it is obvious that no one who intends to harm a man by working magic on the refuse of his food will himself partake of that food, because if he did so he would, on the principles of sympathetic magic, suffer equally with his enemy from any injury done to the refuse. This is the idea which in primitive society lends sanctity to the bond produced by eating together ; by participation in the same food two men give, as it were, hostages for their good behaviour ; each guarantees the other that he will devise no mischief against him, since, being physically united with him by the common food in their stomachs, any harm he might do to his fellow would recoil on his own head with precisely the same force with which it fell on the head of his victim. In strict logic, however, the sympathetic bond lasts only so long as the food is in the stomach of each of the parties. Hence the covenant formed by eating together is less solemn and durable than the covenant formed by transfusing the blood of the covenanting parties into each other's veins, for this transfusion seems to knit them together for life.

CHAPTER XX

TABOOED PERSONS

§ 1. *Chiefs and Kings tabooed.*—We have seen that the Mikado's food was cooked every day in new pots and served up in new dishes ; both pots and dishes were of common clay, in order that they might be broken or laid aside after they had been once used. They were generally broken, for it was believed that if any one else ate his food out of these sacred dishes, his mouth and throat would become swollen and inflamed. The same ill effect was thought to be experienced by any one who should wear the Mikado's clothes without his leave ; he would have swellings and pains all over his body. In Fiji there is a special name (*kana lama*) for the disease supposed to be caused by eating out of a chief's dishes or wearing his clothes. " The throat and body swell, and the impious person dies. I had a fine mat given to me by a man who durst not use it because Thakombau's eldest son had sat upon it. There was always a family or clan of commoners who were exempt from this danger. I was talking about this once to Thakombau. ' Oh yes,' said he. ' Here, So-and-so ! come and scratch my back.' The man scratched ; he was one of those who could do it with impunity." The name of the men thus highly privileged was *Na nduka ni*, or the dirt of the chief.

In the evil effects thus supposed to follow upon the use of the vessels or clothes of the Mikado and a Fijian chief we see that other side of the god-man's character to which attention has been already called. The divine person is a source of danger as well as of blessing ; he must not only be guarded, he must also be guarded against. His sacred organism, so delicate that a touch may disorder it, is also, as it were,

electrically charged with a powerful magical or spiritual force which
may discharge itself with fatal effect on whatever comes in contact
with it.   Accordingly the isolation of the man-god is quite as necessary
for the safety of others as for his own.   His magical virtue is in the
strictest sense of the word contagious : his divinity is a fire, which,
under proper restraints, confers endless blessings, but, if rashly touched
or allowed to break bounds, burns and destroys what it touches.
Hence the disastrous effects supposed to attend a breach of taboo ; the
offender has thrust his hand into the divine fire, which shrivels up and
consumes him on the spot.

The Nubas, for example, who inhabit the wooded and fertile range
of Jebel Nuba in Eastern Africa, believe that they would die if they
entered the house of their priestly king ; however, they can evade the
penalty of their intrusion by baring the left shoulder and getting
the king to lay his hand on it.   And were any man to sit on a stone
which the king has consecrated to his own use, the transgressor
would die within the year.   The Cazembes of Angola regard their king
as so holy that no one can touch him without being killed by the
magical power which pervades his sacred person.   But since contact
with him is sometimes unavoidable, they have devised a means whereby
the sinner can escape with his life.   Kneeling down before the king he
touches the back of the royal hand with the back of his own, then snaps
his fingers ; afterwards he lays the palm of his hand on the palm of the
king's hand, then snaps his fingers again.   This ceremony is repeated
four or five times, and averts the imminent danger of death.   In
Tonga it was believed that if any one fed himself with his own hands
after touching the sacred person of a superior chief or anything that
belonged to him, he would swell up and die ; the sanctity of the chief,
like a virulent poison, infected the hands of his inferior, and, being
communicated through them to the food, proved fatal to the eater.
A commoner who had incurred this danger could disinfect himself
by performing a certain ceremony, which consisted in touching the
sole of a chief's foot with the palm and back of each of his hands,
and afterwards rinsing his hands in water.   If there was no water
near, he rubbed his hands with the juicy stem of a plantain or banana.
After that he was free to feed himself with his own hands without
danger of being attacked by the malady which would otherwise follow
from eating with tabooed or sanctified hands.   But until the ceremony
of expiation or disinfection had been performed, if he wished to eat,
he had either to get some one to feed him, or else to go down on his
knees and pick up the food from the ground with his mouth like a
beast.   He might not even use a toothpick himself, but might guide
the hand of another person holding the toothpick.   The Tongans were
subject to induration of the liver and certain forms of scrofula, which
they often attributed to a failure to perform the requisite expiation
after having inadvertently touched a chief or his belongings.   Hence
they often went through the ceremony as a precaution, without knowing that they had done anything to call for it.   The king of Tonga

could not refuse to play his part in the rite by presenting his foot to such as desired to touch it, even when they applied to him at an inconvenient time. A fat unwieldy king, who perceived his subjects approaching with this intention, while he chanced to be taking his walks abroad, has been sometimes seen to waddle as fast as his legs could carry him out of their way, in order to escape the importunate and not wholly disinterested expression of their homage. If any one fancied he might have already unwittingly eaten with tabooed hands, he sat down before the chief, and, taking the chief's foot, pressed it against his own stomach, that the food in his belly might not injure him, and that he might not swell up and die. Since scrofula was regarded by the Tongans as a result of eating with tabooed hands, we may conjecture that persons who suffered from it among them often resorted to the touch or pressure of the king's foot as a cure for their malady. The analogy of the custom with the old English practice of bringing scrofulous patients to the king to be healed by his touch is sufficiently obvious, and suggests, as I have already pointed out elsewhere, that among our own remote ancestors scrofula may have obtained its name of the King's Evil from a belief, like that of the Tongans, that it was caused as well as cured by contact with the divine majesty of kings.

In New Zealand the dread of the sanctity of chiefs was at least as great as in Tonga. Their ghostly power, derived from an ancestral spirit, diffused itself by contagion over everything they touched, and could strike dead all who rashly or unwittingly meddled with it. For instance, it once happened that a New Zealand chief of high rank and great sanctity had left the remains of his dinner by the wayside. A slave, a stout, hungry fellow, coming up after the chief had gone, saw the unfinished dinner, and ate it up without asking questions. Hardly had he finished when he was informed by a horror-stricken spectator that the food of which he had eaten was the chief's. " I knew the unfortunate delinquent well. He was remarkable for courage, and had signalised himself in the wars of the tribe," but " no sooner did he hear the fatal news than he was seized by the most extraordinary convulsions and cramp in the stomach, which never ceased till he died, about sundown the same day. He was a strong man, in the prime of life, and if any pakeha [European] freethinker should have said he was not killed by the *tapu* of the chief, which had been communicated to the food by contact, he would have been listened to with feelings of contempt for his ignorance and inability to understand plain and direct evidence." This is not a solitary case. A Maori woman having eaten of some fruit, and being afterwards told that the fruit had been taken from a tabooed place, exclaimed that the spirit of the chief, whose sanctity had been thus profaned, would kill her. This was in the afternoon, and next day by twelve o'clock she was dead. A Maori chief's tinder-box was once the means of killing several persons ; for, having been lost by him, and found by some men who used it to light their pipes, they died of fright on learning to whom it had belonged.

So, too, the garments of a high New Zealand chief will kill any one else who wears them. A chief was observed by a missionary to throw down a precipice a blanket which he found too heavy to carry. Being asked by the missionary why he did not leave it on a tree for the use of a future traveller, the chief replied that " it was the fear of its being taken by another which caused him to throw it where he did, for if it were worn, his tapu " (that is, his spiritual power communicated by contact to the blanket and through the blanket to the man) " would kill the person." For a similar reason a Maori chief would not blow a fire with his mouth ; for his sacred breath would communicate its sanctity to the fire, which would pass it on to the pot on the fire, which would pass it on to the meat in the pot, which would pass it on to the man who ate the meat, which was in the pot, which stood on the fire, which was breathed on by the chief ; so that the eater, infected by the chief's breath conveyed through these intermediaries, would surely die.

Thus in the Polynesian race, to which the Maoris belong, superstition erected round the persons of sacred chiefs a real, though at the same time purely imaginary barrier, to transgress which actually entailed the death of the transgressor whenever he became aware of what he had done. This fatal power of the imagination working through superstitious terrors is by no means confined to one race ; it appears to be common among savages. For example, among the aborigines of Australia a native will die after the infliction of even the most superficial wound, if only he believes that the weapon which inflicted the wound had been sung over and thus endowed with magical virtue. He simply lies down, refuses food, and pines away. Similarly among some of the Indian tribes of Brazil, if the medicine-man predicted the death of any one who had offended him, " the wretch took to his hammock instantly in such full expectation of dying, that he would neither eat nor drink, and the prediction was a sentence which faith effectually executed."

§ 2. *Mourners tabooed.*—Thus regarding his sacred chiefs and kings as charged with a mysterious spiritual force which so to say explodes at contact, the savage naturally ranks them among the dangerous classes of society, and imposes upon them the same sort of restraints that he lays on manslayers, menstruous women, and other persons whom he looks upon with a certain fear and horror. For example, sacred kings and priests in Polynesia were not allowed to touch food with their hands, and had therefore to be fed by others ; and as we have just seen, their vessels, garments, and other property might not be used by others on pain of disease and death. Now precisely the same observances are exacted by some savages from girls at their first menstruation, women after childbirth, homicides, mourners, and all persons who have come into contact with the dead. Thus, for example, to begin with the last class of persons, among the Maoris any one who had handled a corpse, helped to convey it to the grave, or touched a dead man's bones, was cut off from all intercourse and almost all communication with mankind. He could not enter any house, or come into contact with any person or thing, without utterly bedevilling them. He might not even touch food with his hands, which had become so frightfully tabooed or unclean as to be quite useless. Food would be set for him on the ground, and he would then sit or kneel down, and, with his hands carefully held behind his back, would gnaw at it as best he could. In some cases he would be fed by another person, who with outstretched arm contrived to do it without touching the tabooed man ; but the feeder was himself subjected to many severe restrictions, little less onerous than those which were imposed upon the other. In almost every populous village there lived a degraded wretch, the lowest of the low, who earned a sorry pittance by thus waiting upon the defiled. Clad in rags, daubed from head to foot with red ochre and stinking shark oil, always solitary and silent, generally old, haggard, and wizened, often half crazed, he might be seen sitting motionless all day apart from the common path or thoroughfare of the village, gazing with lack-lustre eyes on the busy doings in which he might never take a part. Twice a day a dole of food would be thrown on the ground before him to munch as well as he could without the use of his hands ; and at night, huddling his greasy tatters about him, he would crawl into some miserable lair of leaves and refuse, where, dirty, cold, and hungry, he passed, in broken ghost-haunted slumbers, a wretched night as a prelude to another wretched day. Such was the only human being deemed fit to associate at arm's length with one who had paid the last offices of respect and friendship to the dead. And when, the dismal term of his seclusion being over, the mourner was about to mix with his fellows once more, all the dishes he had used in his seclusion were diligently smashed, and all the garments he had worn were carefully thrown away, lest they should spread the contagion of his defilement among others, just as the vessels and clothes of sacred kings and chiefs are destroyed or cast away for a similar reason. So complete in these respects is the analogy which the savage traces between the spiritual influences that emanate from divinities and from the dead, between the odour of sanctity and the stench of corruption.

The rule which forbids persons who have been in contact with the dead to touch food with their hands would seem to have been universal in Polynesia. Thus in Samoa " those who attended the deceased were most careful not to handle food, and for days were fed by others as if they were helpless infants. Baldness and the loss of teeth were supposed to be the punishment inflicted by the household god if they violated the rule." Again, in Tonga, " no person can touch a dead chief without being taboo'd for ten lunar months, except chiefs, who are only taboo'd for three, four, or five months, according to the superiority of the dead chief ; except again it be the body of Tooitonga [the great divine chief], and then even the greatest chief would be taboo'd ten months. . . . During the time a man is taboo'd he must not feed himself with his own hands, but must be fed by somebody else :

he must not even use a toothpick himself, but must guide another person's hand holding the toothpick. If he is hungry and there is no one to feed him, he must go down upon his hands and knees, and pick up his victuals with his mouth : and if he infringes upon any of these rules, it is firmly expected that he will swell up and die."

Among the Shuswap of British Columbia widows and widowers in mourning are secluded and forbidden to touch their own head or body ; the cups and cooking-vessels which they use may be used by no one else. They must build a sweat-house beside a creek, sweat there all night and bathe regularly, after which they must rub their bodies with branches of spruce. The branches may not be used more than once, and when they have served their purpose they are stuck into the ground all round the hut. No hunter would come near such mourners, for their presence is unlucky. If their shadow were to fall on any one, he would be taken ill at once. They employ thorn bushes for bed and pillow, in order to keep away the ghost of the deceased ; and thorn bushes are also laid all around their beds. This last precaution shows clearly what the spiritual danger is which leads to the exclusion of such persons from ordinary society ; it is simply a fear of the ghost who is supposed to be hovering near them. In the Mekeo district of British New Guinea a widower loses all his civil rights and becomes a social outcast, an object of fear and horror, shunned by all. He may not cultivate a garden, nor show himself in public, nor traverse the village, nor walk on the roads and paths. Like a wild beast he must skulk in the long grass and the bushes ; and if he sees or hears any one coming, especially a woman, he must hide behind a tree or a thicket. If he wishes to fish or hunt, he must do it alone and at night. If he would consult any one, even the missionary, he does so by stealth and at night ; he seems to have lost his voice and speaks only in whispers. Were he to join a party of fishers or hunters, his presence would bring misfortune on them ; the ghost of his dead wife would frighten away the fish or the game. He goes about everywhere and at all times armed with a tomahawk to defend himself, not only against wild boars in the jungle, but against the dreaded spirit of his departed spouse, who would do him an ill turn if she could ; for all the souls of the dead are malignant and their only delight is to harm the living.

§ 3. *Women tabooed at Menstruation and Childbirth.*—In general, we may say that the prohibition to use the vessels, garments, and so forth of certain persons, and the effects supposed to follow an infraction of the rule, are exactly the same whether the persons to whom the things belong are sacred or what we might call unclean and polluted. As the garments which have been touched by a sacred chief kill those who handle them, so do the things which have been touched by a menstruous woman. An Australian black-fellow, who discovered that his wife had lain on his blanket at her menstrual period, killed her and died of terror himself within a fortnight. Hence Australian women at these times are forbidden under pain of death to touch anything that men use, or even to walk on a path that any man frequents. They are also secluded at childbirth, and all vessels used by them during their seclusion are burned. In Uganda the pots which a woman touches, while the impurity of childbirth or of menstruation is on her, should be destroyed ; spears and shields defiled by her touch are not destroyed but only purified. "Among all the Déné and most other American tribes, hardly any other being was the object of so much dread as a menstruating woman. As soon as signs of that condition made themselves apparent in a young girl she was carefully segregated from all but female company, and had to live by herself in a small hut away from the gaze of the villagers or of the male members of the roving band. While in that awful state, she had to abstain from touching anything belonging to man, or the spoils of any venison or other animal, lest she would thereby pollute the same, and condemn the hunters to failure, owing to the anger of the game thus slighted. Dried fish formed her diet, and cold water, absorbed through a drinking tube, was her only beverage. Moreover, as the very sight of her was dangerous to society, a special skin bonnet, with fringes falling over her face down to her breast, hid her from the public gaze, even some time after she had recovered her normal state." Among the Bribri Indians of Costa Rica a menstruous woman is regarded as unclean. The only plates she may use for her food are banana leaves, which, when she has done with them, she throws away in some sequestered spot ; for were a cow to find them and eat them, the animal would waste away and perish. And she drinks out of a special vessel for a like reason ; because if any one drank out of the same cup after her, he would surely die.

Among many peoples similar restrictions are imposed on women in childbed and apparently for similar reasons ; at such periods women are supposed to be in a dangerous condition which would infect any person or thing they might touch ; hence they are put into quarantine until, with the recovery of their health and strength, the imaginary danger has passed away. Thus, in Tahiti a woman after childbirth was secluded for a fortnight or three weeks in a temporary hut erected on sacred ground ; during the time of her seclusion she was debarred from touching provisions, and had to be fed by another. Further, if any one else touched the child at this period, he was subjected to the same restrictions as the mother until the ceremony of her purification had been performed. Similarly in the island of Kadiak, off Alaska, a woman about to be delivered retires to a miserable low hovel built of reeds, where she must remain for twenty days after the birth of her child, whatever the season may be, and she is considered so unclean that no one will touch her, and food is reached to her on sticks. The Bribri Indians regard the pollution of childbed as much more dangerous even than that of menstruation. When a woman feels her time approaching, she informs her husband, who makes haste to build a hut for her in a lonely spot. There she must live alone, holding no converse with anybody save her mother or another woman. After her delivery the medicine-man purifies her by breathing on her and laying an animal, it matters not what, upon her. But even this ceremony only mitigates her uncleanness into a state considered to be equivalent to that of a menstruous woman ; and for a full lunar month she must live apart from her housemates, observing the same rules with regard to eating and drinking as at her monthly periods. The case is still worse, the pollution is still more deadly, if she has had a miscarriage or has been delivered of a stillborn child. In that case she may not go near a living soul : the mere contact with things she has used is exceedingly dangerous : her food is handed to her at the end of a long stick. This lasts generally for three weeks, after which she may go home, subject only to the restrictions incident to an ordinary confinement.

Some Bantu tribes entertain even more exaggerated notions of the virulent infection spread by a woman who has had a miscarriage and has concealed it. An experienced observer of these people tells us that the blood of childbirth " appears to the eyes of the South Africans to be tainted with a pollution still more dangerous than that of the menstrual fluid. The husband is excluded from the hut for eight days of the lying-in period, chiefly from fear that he might be contaminated by this secretion. He dare not take his child in his arms for the three first months after the birth. But the secretion of childbed is particularly terrible when it is the product of a miscarriage, especially *a concealed miscarriage.* In this case it is not merely the man who is threatened or killed, it is the whole country, it is the sky itself which suffers. By a curious association of ideas a physiological fact causes cosmic troubles ! " As for the disastrous effect which a miscarriage may have on the whole country I will quote the words of a medicine-man and rain-maker of the Ba-Pedi tribe : " When a woman has had a miscarriage, when she has allowed her blood to flow, and has hidden the child, it is enough to cause the burning winds to blow and to parch the country with heat. The rain no longer falls, for the country is no longer in order. When the rain approaches the place where the blood is, it will not dare to approach. It will fear and remain at a distance. That woman has committed a great fault. She has spoiled the country of the chief, for she has hidden blood which had not yet been well congealed to fashion a man. That blood is taboo. It should never drip on the road ! The chief will assemble his men and say to them, ' Are you in order in your villages ? ' Some one will answer, ' Such and such a woman was pregnant and we have not yet seen the child which she has given birth to.' Then they go and arrest the woman. They say to her, ' Show us where you have hidden it.' They go and dig at the spot, they sprinkle the hole with a decoction of two sorts of roots prepared in a special pot. They take a little of the earth of this grave, they throw it into the river, then they bring back water from the river and sprinkle it where she shed her blood. She herself must wash every day with the medicine. Then the country will be moistened again (by rain). Further, we (medicine-men) summon the women of the country ; we tell them to prepare a ball of the earth which contains

P

the blood. They bring it to us one morning. If we wish to prepare medicine with which to sprinkle the whole country, we crumble this earth to powder ; at the end of five days we send little boys and little girls, girls that yet know nothing of women's affairs and have not yet had relations with men. We put the medicine in the horns of oxen, and these children go to all the fords, to all the entrances of the country. A little girl turns up the soil with her mattock, the others dip a branch in the horn and sprinkle the inside of the hole saying, ' Rain ! rain ! ' So we remove the misfortune which the women have brought on the roads ; the rain will be able to come. The country is purified ! "

§ 4. *Warriors tabooed.*—Once more, warriors are conceived by the savage to move, so to say, in an atmosphere of spiritual danger which constrains them to practise a variety of superstitious observances quite different in their nature from those rational precautions which, as a matter of course, they adopt against foes of flesh and blood. The general effect of these observances is to place the warrior, both before and after victory, in the same state of seclusion or spiritual quarantine in which, for his own safety, primitive man puts his human gods and other dangerous characters. Thus when the Maoris went out on the war-path they were sacred or taboo in the highest degree, and they and their friends at home had to observe strictly many curious customs over and above the numerous taboos of ordinary life. They became, in the irreverent language of Europeans who knew them in the old fighting days, " tabooed an inch thick " ; and as for the leader of the expedition, he was quite unapproachable. Similarly, when the Israelites marched forth to war they were bound by certain rules of ceremonial purity identical with rules observed by Maoris and Australian black-fellows on the war-path. The vessels they used were sacred, and they had to practise continence and a custom of personal cleanliness of which the original motive, if we may judge from the avowed motive of savages who conform to the same custom, was a fear lest the enemy should obtain the refuse of their persons, and thus be enabled to work their destruction by magic. Among some Indian tribes of North America a young warrior in his first campaign had to conform to certain customs, of which two were identical with the observances imposed by the same Indians on girls at their first menstruation : the vessels he ate and drank out of might be touched by no other person, and he was forbidden to scratch his head or any other part of his body with his fingers ; if he could not help scratching himself, he had to do it with a stick. The latter rule, like the one which forbids a tabooed person to feed himself with his own fingers, seems to rest on the supposed sanctity or pollution, whichever we choose to call it, of the tabooed hands. Moreover, among these Indian tribes the men on the war-path had always to sleep at night with their faces turned towards their own country ; however uneasy the posture, they might not change it. They might not sit upon the bare ground, nor wet their feet, nor walk on a beaten path if they could help it ; when they had no choice but to walk on a path, they sought to counteract the ill effect of doing so by doctoring their legs with certain medicines or charms which they carried with them for the purpose. No member of the party was permitted to step over the legs, hands, or body of any other member who chanced to be sitting or lying on the ground ; and it was equally forbidden to step over his blanket, gun, tomahawk, or anything that belonged to him. If this rule was inadvertently broken, it became the duty of the member whose person or property had been stepped over to knock the other member down, and it was similarly the duty of that other to be knocked down peaceably and without resistance. The vessels out of which the warriors ate their food were commonly small bowls of wood or birch bark, with marks to distinguish the two sides ; in marching from home the Indians invariably drank out of one side of the bowl, and in returning they drank out of the other. When on their way home they came within a day's march of the village, they hung up all their bowls on trees, or threw them away on the prairie, doubtless to prevent their sanctity or defilement from being communicated with disastrous effects to their friends, just as we have seen that the vessels and clothes of the sacred Mikado, of women at childbirth and menstruation, and of persons defiled by contact with the dead are destroyed or laid aside for a similar reason. The first four times that an Apache Indian goes out on the war-path, he is bound to refrain from scratching his head with his fingers and from letting water touch his lips. Hence he scratches his head with a stick, and drinks through a hollow reed or cane. Stick and reed are attached to the warrior's belt and to each other by a leathern thong. The rule not to scratch their heads with their fingers, but to use a stick for the purpose instead, was regularly observed by Ojebways on the war-path.

With regard to the Creek Indians and kindred tribes we are told they " will not cohabit with women while they are out at war ; they religiously abstain from every kind of intercourse even with their own wives, for the space of three days and nights before they go to war, and so after they return home, because they are to sanctify themselves." Among the Ba-Pedi and Ba-Thonga tribes of South Africa not only have the warriors to abstain from women, but the people left behind in the villages are also bound to continence ; they think that any incontinence on their part would cause thorns to grow on the ground traversed by the warriors, and that success would not attend the expedition.

Why exactly many savages have made it a rule to refrain from women in time of war, we cannot say for certain, but we may conjecture that their motive was a superstitious fear lest, on the principles of sympathetic magic, close contact with women should infect them with feminine weakness and cowardice. Similarly some savages imagine that contact with a woman in childbed enervates warriors and enfeebles their weapons. Indeed the Kayans of Central Borneo go so far as to hold that to touch a loom or women's clothes would so weaken a man that he would have no success in hunting, fishing, and war. Hence it is not merely sexual intercourse with women that the savage warrior sometimes shuns ; he is careful to avoid the sex altogether. Thus among the hill tribes of Assam, not only are men forbidden to cohabit with their wives during or after a raid, but they may not eat food cooked by a woman ; nay, they should not address a word even to their own wives. Once a woman, who unwittingly broke the rule by speaking to her husband while he was under the war taboo, sickened and died when she learned the awful crime she had committed.

§ 5. *Manslayers tabooed.*—If the reader still doubts whether the rules of conduct which we have just been considering are based on superstitious fears or dictated by a rational prudence, his doubts will probably be dissipated when he learns that rules of the same sort are often imposed even more stringently on warriors after the victory has been won and when all fear of the living corporeal foe is at an end. In such cases one motive for the inconvenient restrictions laid on the victors in their hour of triumph is probably a dread of the angry ghosts of the slain ; and that the fear of the vengeful ghosts does influence the behaviour of the slayers is often expressly affirmed. The general effect of the taboos laid on sacred chiefs, mourners, women at child-birth, men on the war-path, and so on, is to seclude or isolate the tabooed persons from ordinary society, this effect being attained by a variety of rules, which oblige the men or women to live in separate huts or in the open air, to shun the commerce of the sexes, to avoid the use of vessels employed by others, and so forth. Now the same effect is produced by similar means in the case of victorious warriors, particularly such as have actually shed the blood of their enemies. In the island of Timor, when a warlike expedition has returned in triumph bringing the heads of the vanquished foe, the leader of the expedition is forbidden by religion and custom to return at once to his own house. A special hut is prepared for him, in which he has to reside for two months, undergoing bodily and spiritual purification. During this time he may not go to his wife nor feed himself ; the food must be put into his mouth by another person. That these observances are dictated by fear of the ghosts of the slain seems certain ; for from another account of the ceremonies performed on the return of a successful head-hunter in the same island we learn that sacrifices are offered on this occasion to appease the soul of the man whose head has been taken ; the people think that some misfortune would befall the victor were such offerings omitted. Moreover, a part of the ceremony consists of a dance accompanied by a song, in which the death of the slain man is lamented and his forgiveness is entreated. " Be not angry," they say, " because your head is here with us ; had we been less lucky, our heads might now have been exposed in your village. We have offered the sacrifice to appease you. Your spirit may now rest and leave us at peace. Why were you our enemy ? Would it not have been better that we should remain friends ? Then your blood would not have been spilt and your head would not have been cut off." The people of Paloo in Central Celebes take the heads of their enemies in war and afterwards propitiate the souls of the slain in the temple.

Among the tribes at the mouth of the Wanigela River, in New Guinea, " a man who has taken life is considered to be impure until he has undergone certain ceremonies : as soon as possible after the deed he cleanses himself and his weapon. This satisfactorily accomplished, he repairs to his village and seats himself on the logs of sacrificial staging. No one approaches him or takes any notice whatever of him. A house is prepared for him which is put in charge of two or three small boys as servants. He may eat only toasted bananas, and only the centre portion of them—the ends being thrown away. On the third day of his seclusion a small feast is prepared by his friends, who also fashion some new perineal bands for him. This is called *ivi poro*. The next day the man dons all his best ornaments and badges for taking life, and sallies forth fully armed and parades the village. The next day a hunt is organised, and a kangaroo selected from the game captured. It is cut open and the spleen and liver rubbed over the back of the man. He then walks solemnly down to the nearest water, and standing straddle-legs in it washes himself. All the young untried warriors swim between his legs. This is supposed to impart courage and, strength to them. The following day, at early dawn, he dashes out of his house, fully armed, and calls aloud the name of his victim. Having satisfied himself that he has thoroughly scared the ghost of the dead man, he returns to his house. The beating of flooring-boards and the lighting of fires is also a certain method of scaring the ghost. A day later his purification is finished. He can then enter his wife's house."

In Windessi, Dutch New Guinea, when a party of head-hunters has been successful, and they are nearing home, they announce their approach and success by blowing on triton shells. Their canoes are also decked with branches. The faces of the men who have taken a head are blackened with charcoal. If several have taken part in killing the same victim, his head is divided among them. They always time their arrival so as to reach home in the early morning. They come rowing to the village with a great noise, and the women stand ready to dance in the verandahs of the houses. The canoes row past the *room sram* or house where the young men live ; and as they pass, the murderers throw as many pointed sticks or bamboos at the wall or the roof as there were enemies killed. The day is spent very quietly. Now and then they drum or blow on the conch ; at other times they beat the walls of the houses with loud shouts to drive away the ghosts of the slain. So the Yabim of New Guinea believe that the spirit of a murdered man pursues his murderer and seeks to do him a mischief. Hence they drive away the spirit with shouts and the beating of drums. When the Fijians had buried a man alive, as they often did, they used at nightfall to make a great uproar by means of bamboos, trumpet-shells, and so forth, for the purpose of frightening away his ghost, lest he should attempt to return to his old home. And to render his house unattractive to him they dismantled it and clothed it with everything that to their ideas seemed most repulsive. On the evening of the day on which they had tortured a prisoner to death, the American Indians were wont to run through the village with hideous yells, beating with sticks on the furniture, the walls, and the roofs of the huts to prevent the angry ghost of their victim from settling there and taking vengeance for the torments that his body had endured at their hands. "Once," says a traveller, "on approaching in the night a village of Ottawas, I found all the inhabitants in confusion : they were all busily engaged in raising noises of the loudest and most inharmonious kind. Upon inquiry, I found that a battle had been lately fought between the Ottawas and the Kickapoos, and that the object of all this noise was to prevent the ghosts of the departed combatants from entering the village."

Among the Basutos "ablution is specially performed on return from battle. It is absolutely necessary that the warriors should rid themselves, as soon as possible, of the blood they have shed, or the shades of their victims would pursue them incessantly, and disturb their slumbers. They go in a procession, and in full armour, to the nearest stream. At the moment they enter the water a diviner, placed higher up, throws some purifying substances into the current. This is, however, not strictly necessary. The javelins and battle-axes also undergo the process of washing." Among the Bageshu of East Africa a man who has killed another may not return to his own house on the same day, though he may enter the village and spend the night in a friend's house. He kills a sheep and smears his chest, his right arm, and his head with the contents of the animal's stomach. His children are brought to him and he smears them in like manner. Then he smears each side of the doorway with the tripe and entrails, and finally throws the rest of the stomach on the roof of his house. For a whole day he may not touch food with his hands, but picks it up with two sticks and so conveys it to his mouth. His wife is not under any such restrictions. She may even go to mourn for the man whom her husband has killed, if she wishes to do so. Among the Angoni, to the north of the Zambesi, warriors who have slain foes on an expedition smear their bodies and faces with ashes, hang garments of their victims on their persons, and tie bark ropes round their necks, so that the ends hang down over their shoulders or breasts. This costume they wear for three days after their return, and rising at break of day they run through the village uttering frightful yells to drive away the ghosts of the slain, which, if they were not thus banished from the houses, might bring sickness and misfortune on the inmates.

In some of these accounts nothing is said of an enforced seclusion, at least after the ceremonial cleansing, but some South African tribes certainly require the slayer of a very gallant foe in war to keep apart from his wife and family for ten days after he has washed his body in running water. He also receives from the tribal doctor a medicine which he chews with his food. When a Nandi of East Africa has killed a member of another tribe, he paints one side of his body, spear, and sword red, and the other side white. For four days after the slaughter he is considered unclean and may not go home. He has to build a small shelter by a river and live there ; he may not associate with his wife or sweetheart, and he may eat nothing but porridge, beef, and goat's flesh. At the end of the fourth day he must purify himself by taking a strong purge made from the bark of the *segetet* tree and by drinking goat's milk mixed with blood. Among the Bantu tribes of Kavirondo, when a man has killed an enemy in warfare he shaves his head on his return home, and his friends rub a medicine, which generally consists of goat's dung, over his body to prevent the spirit of the slain man from troubling him. Exactly the same custom is practised for the same reason by the Wageia of East Africa. With the Ja-Luo of Kavirondo the custom is somewhat different. Three days after his return from the fight the warrior shaves his head. But before he may enter his village he has to hang a live fowl, head uppermost, round his neck ; then the bird is decapitated and its head left hanging round his neck. Soon after his return a feast is made for the slain man, in order that his ghost may not haunt his slayer. In the Pelew Islands, when the men return from a warlike expedition in which they have taken a life, the young warriors who have been out fighting for the first time, and all who handled the slain, are shut up in the large council-house and become tabooed. They may not quit the edifice, nor bathe, nor touch a woman, nor eat fish ; their food is limited to coco-nuts and syrup. They rub themselves with charmed leaves and chew charmed betel. After three days they go together to bathe as near as possible to the spot where the man was killed.

Among the Natchez Indians of North America young braves who had taken their first scalps were obliged to observe certain rules of abstinence for six months. They might not sleep with their wives nor eat flesh ; their only food was fish and hasty-pudding. If they broke these rules, they believed that the soul of the man they had killed would work their death by magic, that they would gain no more successes over the enemy, and that the least wound inflicted on them would prove mortal. When a Choctaw had killed an enemy and taken his scalp, he went into mourning for a month, during which he might not comb his hair, and if his head itched he might not scratch it except with a little stick which he wore fastened to his wrist for the purpose. This ceremonial mourning for the enemies they had slain was not uncommon among the North American Indians.

Thus we see that warriors who have taken the life of a foe in battle are temporarily cut off from free intercourse with their fellows, and especially with their wives, and must undergo certain rites of purification before they are readmitted to society. Now if the purpose of their seclusion and of the expiatory rites which they have to perform is, as we have been led to believe, no other than to shake off, frighten, or appease the angry spirit of the slain man, we may safely conjecture that the similar purification of homicides and murderers, who have imbrued their hands in the blood of a fellow-tribesman, had at first the same significance, and that the idea of a moral or spiritual regeneration symbolised by the washing, the fasting, and so on, was merely a later interpretation put upon the old custom by men who had outgrown the primitive modes of thought in which the custom originated. The conjecture will be confirmed if we can show that savages have actually imposed certain restrictions on the murderer of a fellow-tribesman from a definite fear that he is haunted by the ghost of his victim. This we can do with regard to the Omahas of North America. Among these Indians the kinsmen of a murdered man had the right to put the murderer to death, but sometimes they waived their right in consideration of presents which they consented to accept. When the life of the murderer was spared, he had to observe certain stringent rules for a period which varied from two to four years. He must walk barefoot, and he might eat no warm food, nor raise his voice, nor look around. He was compelled to pull his robe about him and to have it tied at the neck even in hot weather ; he might not let it hang loose or fly open. He might not move his hands about, but had to keep them close to his body. He might not comb his hair, and it might not be blown about by the wind. When the tribe went out hunting, he was obliged to pitch his tent about a quarter of a mile from the rest of the people " lest the ghost of his victim should raise a high wind, which might cause damage." Only one of his kindred was allowed to remain with him at his tent. No one wished to eat with him, for they said, " If we eat with him whom Wakanda hates, Wakanda will hate us." Sometimes he wandered at night crying and lamenting his offence. At the end of his long isolation the kinsmen of the murdered man heard his crying and said, " It is enough. Begone, and walk among the crowd. Put on moccasins and wear a good robe." Here the reason alleged for keeping the murderer at a considerable distance from the hunters gives the clue to all the other restrictions laid on him : he was haunted and therefore dangerous. The ancient Greeks believed that the soul of a man who had just been killed was wroth with his slayer and troubled him ; wherefore it was needful even for the involuntary homicide to depart from his country for a year until the anger of the dead man had cooled down ; nor might the slayer return until sacrifice had been offered and ceremonies of purification performed. If his victim chanced to be a foreigner, the homicide had to shun the native country of the dead man as well as his own. The legend of the matricide Orestes, how he roamed from place to place pursued by the Furies of his murdered mother, and none would sit at meat with him, or take him in, till he had been purified, reflects faithfully the real Greek dread of such as were still haunted by an angry ghost.

§ 6. *Hunters and Fishers tabooed.*—In savage society the hunter and the fisherman have often to observe rules of abstinence and to submit to ceremonies of purification of the same sort as those which are obligatory on the warrior and the manslayer ; and though we cannot in all cases perceive the exact purpose which these rules and ceremonies are supposed to serve, we may with some probability assume that, just as the dread of the spirits of his enemies is the main motive for the seclusion and purification of the warrior who hopes to take or has already taken their lives, so the huntsman or fisherman who complies with similar customs is principally actuated by a fear of the spirits of the beasts, birds, or fish which he has killed or intends to kill.   For the savage commonly conceives animals to be endowed with souls and intelligences like his own, and hence he naturally treats them with similar respect.   Just as he attempts to appease the ghosts of the men he has slain, so he essays to propitiate the spirits of the animals he has killed.   These ceremonies of propitiation will be described later on in this work ; here we have to deal, first, with the taboos observed by the hunter and the fisherman before or during the hunting and fishing seasons, and, second, with the ceremonies of purification which have to be practised by these men on returning with their booty from a successful chase.

While the savage respects, more or less, the souls of all animals, he treats with particular deference the spirits of such as are either especially useful to him or formidable on account of their size, strength, or ferocity.   Accordingly the hunting and killing of these valuable or dangerous beasts are subject to more elaborate rules and ceremonies than the slaughter of comparatively useless and insignificant creatures. Thus the Indians of Nootka Sound prepared themselves for catching whales by observing a fast for a week, during which they ate very little, bathed in the water several times a day, sang, and rubbed their bodies, limbs, and faces with shells and bushes till they looked as if they had been severely torn with briars.   They were likewise required to abstain from any commerce with their women for the like period, this last condition being considered indispensable to their success.   A chief who failed to catch a whale has been known to attribute his failure to a breach of chastity on the part of his men.   It should be remarked that the conduct thus prescribed as a preparation for whaling is precisely that which in the same tribe of Indians was required of men about to go on the war-path.   Rules of the same sort are, or were formerly, observed by Malagasy whalers.   For eight days before they went to sea the crew of a whaler used to fast, abstaining from women and liquor, and confessing their most secret faults to each other ; and if any man was found to have sinned deeply, he was forbidden to share in the expedition.   In the island of Mabuiag continence was imposed on the people both before they went to hunt the dugong and while the turtles were pairing.   The turtle-season lasts during parts of October and November ; and if at that time unmarried persons had sexual intercourse with each other, it was believed that when the canoe approached the floating turtle, the male would separate from the female and both would dive down in different directions.   So at Mowat in New Guinea men have no relation with women when the turtle are coupling, though there is considerable laxity of morals at other times.

In the island of Uap, one of the Caroline group, every fisherman plying his craft lies under a most strict taboo during the whole of the fishing season, which lasts for six or eight weeks. Whenever he is on shore he must spend all his time in the men's clubhouse, and under no pretext whatever may he visit his own house or so much as look upon the faces of his wife and womenkind. Were he but to steal a glance at them, they think that flying fish must inevitably bore out his eyes at night. If his wife, mother, or daughter brings any gift for him or wishes to talk with him, she must stand down towards the shore with her back turned to the men's clubhouse. Then the fisherman may go out and speak to her, or with his back turned to her he may receive what she has brought him; after which he must return at once to his rigorous confinement. Indeed the fishermen may not even join in dance and song with the other men of the clubhouse in the evening; they must keep to themselves and be silent. In Mirzapur, when the seed of the silkworm is brought into the house, the Kol or Bhuiyar puts it in a place which has been carefully plastered with holy cow-dung to bring good luck. From that time the owner must be careful to avoid ceremonial impurity. He must give up cohabitation with his wife; he may not sleep on a bed, nor shave himself, nor cut his nails, nor anoint himself with oil, nor eat food cooked with butter, nor tell lies, nor do anything else that he deems wrong. He vows to Singarmati Devi that, if the worms are duly born, he will make her an offering. When the cocoons open and the worms appear, he assembles the women of the house and they sing the same song as at the birth of a baby, and red lead is smeared on the parting of the hair of all the married women of the neighbourhood. When the worms pair, re-joicings are made as at a marriage. Thus the silkworms are treated as far as possible like human beings. Hence the custom which prohibits the commerce of the sexes while the worms are hatching may be only an extension, by analogy, of the rule which is observed by many races, that the husband may not cohabit with his wife during pregnancy and lactation.

In the island of Nias the hunters sometimes dig pits, cover them lightly over with twigs, grass, and leaves, and then drive the game into them. While they are engaged in digging the pits, they have to observe a number of taboos. They may not spit, or the game would turn back in disgust from the pits. They may not laugh, or the sides of the pit would fall in. They may eat no salt, prepare no fodder for swine, and in the pit they may not scratch themselves, for if they did, the earth would be loosened and would collapse. And the night after digging the pit they may have no intercourse with a woman, or all their labour would be in vain.

This practice of observing strict chastity as a condition of success in hunting and fishing is very common among rude races; and the instances of it which have been cited render it probable that the rule is always based on a superstition rather than on a consideration of the temporary weakness which a breach of the custom may entail on the hunter or fisherman. In general it appears to be supposed that the evil effect of incontinence is not so much that it weakens him, as that, for some reason or other, it offends the animals, who in consequence will not suffer themselves to be caught. A Carrier Indian of British Columbia used to separate from his wife for a full month before he set traps for bears, and during this time he might not drink from the same vessel as his wife, but had to use a special cup made of birch bark. The neglect of these precautions would cause the game to escape after it had been snared. But when he was about to snare martens, the period of continence was cut down to ten days.

An examination of all the many cases in which the savage bridles his passions and remains chaste from motives of superstition, would be instructive, but I cannot attempt it now. I will only add a few miscellaneous examples of the custom before passing to the ceremonies of purification which are observed by the hunter and fisherman after the chase and the fishing are over. The workers in the salt-pans near Siphoum, in Laos, must abstain from all sexual relations at the place where they are at work ; and they may not cover their heads nor shelter themselves under an umbrella from the burning rays of the sun. Among the Kachins of Burma the ferment used in making beer is prepared by two women, chosen by lot, who during the three days that the process lasts may eat nothing acid and may have no conjugal relations with their husbands ; otherwise it is supposed that the beer would be sour. Among the Masai honey-wine is brewed by a man and a woman who live in a hut set apart for them till the wine is ready for drinking. But they are strictly forbidden to have sexual intercourse with each other during this time ; it is deemed essential that they should be chaste for two days before they begin to brew and for the whole of the six days that the brewing lasts. The Masai believe that were the couple to commit a breach of chastity, not only would the wine be undrinkable but the bees which made the honey would fly away. Similarly they require that a man who is making poison should sleep alone and observe other taboos which render him almost an outcast. The Wandorobbo, a tribe of the same region as the Masai, believe that the mere presence of a woman in the neighbourhood of a man who is brewing poison would deprive the poison of its venom, and that the same thing would happen if the wife of the poison-maker were to commit adultery while her husband was brewing the poison. In this last case it is obvious that a rationalistic explanation of the taboo is impossible. How could the loss of virtue in the poison be a physical consequence of the loss of virtue in the poison-maker's wife ? Clearly the effect which the wife's adultery is supposed to have on the poison is a case of sympathetic magic ; her misconduct sympathetically affects her husband and his work at a distance. We may, accordingly, infer with some confidence that the rule of continence imposed on the poison-maker himself is also a simple case of sympathetic magic, and not, as a civilised reader might be disposed to conjecture, a wise precaution designed to prevent him from accidentally poisoning his wife.

Among the Ba-Pedi and Ba-thonga tribes of South Africa, when the site of a new village has been chosen and the houses are building, all the married people are forbidden to have conjugal relations with each other. If it were discovered that any couple had broken this rule, the work of building would immediately be stopped, and another site chosen for the village. For they think that a breach of chastity would spoil the village which was growing up, that the chief would grow lean and perhaps die, and that the guilty woman would never bear another child. Among the Chams of Cochin-China, when a dam is made or repaired on a river for the sake of irrigation, the chief who offers the traditional sacrifices and implores the protection of the deities on the work, has to stay all the time in a wretched hovel of straw, taking no part in the labour, and observing the strictest continence ; for the people believe that a breach of his chastity would entail a breach of the dam. Here, it is plain, there can be no idea of maintaining the mere bodily vigour of the chief for the accomplishment of a task in which he does not even bear a hand.

If the taboos or abstinences observed by hunters and fishermen before and during the chase are dictated, as we have seen reason to believe, by superstitious motives, and chiefly by a dread of offending or frightening the spirits of the creatures whom it is proposed to kill, we may expect that the restraints imposed after the slaughter has been perpetrated will be at least as stringent, the slayer and his friends having now the added fear of the angry ghosts of his victims before their eyes. Whereas on the hypothesis that the abstinences in question, including those from food, drink, and sleep, are merely salutary precautions for maintaining the men in health and strength to do their work, it is obvious that the observance of these abstinences or taboos after the work is done, that is, when the game is killed and the fish caught, must be wholly superfluous, absurd, and inexplicable. But as I shall now show, these taboos often continue to be enforced or even increased in stringency after the death of the animals, in other words, after the hunter or fisher has accomplished his object by making his bag or landing his fish. The rationalistic theory of them therefore breaks down entirely ; the hypothesis of superstition is clearly the only one open to us.

Among the Inuit or Esquimaux of Bering Strait "the dead bodies of various animals must be treated very carefully by the hunter who obtains them, so that their shades may not be offended and bring bad luck or even death upon him or his people." Hence the Unalit hunter who has had a hand in the killing of a white whale, or even has helped to take one from the net, is not allowed to do any work for the next four days, that being the time during which the shade or ghost of the whale is supposed to stay with its body. At the same time no one in the village may use any sharp or pointed instrument for fear of wounding the whale's shade, which is believed to be hovering invisible in the neighbourhood ; and no loud noise may be made lest it should frighten or offend the ghost. Whoever cuts a whale's body with an iron axe will die. Indeed the use of all iron instruments is forbidden in the village during these four days.

These same Esquimaux celebrate a great annual festival in December, when the bladders of all the seals, whales, walrus, and white bears that have been killed in the year are taken into the assembly-house of the village. They remain there for several days, and so long as they do so the hunters avoid all intercourse with women, saying that if they failed in that respect the shades of the dead animals would be offended. Similarly among the Aleuts of Alaska the hunter who had struck a whale with a charmed spear would not throw again, but returned at once to his home and separated himself from his people in a hut specially constructed for the purpose, where he stayed for three days without food or drink, and without touching or looking upon a woman. During this time of seclusion he snorted occasionally in imitation of the wounded and dying whale, in order to prevent the whale which he had struck from leaving the coast. On the fourth day he emerged from his seclusion and bathed in the sea, shrieking in a hoarse voice and beating the water with his hands. Then, taking with him a companion, he repaired to that part of the shore where he expected to find the whale stranded. If the beast was dead, he at once cut out the place where the death-wound had been inflicted. If the whale was not dead, he again returned to his home and continued washing himself until the whale died. Here the hunter's imitation of the wounded whale is probably intended by means of homoeopathic magic to make the beast die in earnest. Once more the soul of the grim polar bear is offended if the taboos which concern him are not observed. His soul tarries for three days near the spot where it left his body, and during these days the Esquimaux are particularly careful to conform rigidly to the laws of taboo, because they believe that punishment overtakes the transgressor who sins against the soul of a bear far more speedily than him who sins against the souls of the sea-beasts.

When the Kayans have shot one of the dreaded Bornean panthers, they are very anxious about the safety of their souls, for they think that the soul of a panther is almost more powerful than their own. Hence they step eight times over the carcase of the dead beast reciting the spell, " Panther, thy soul under my soul." On returning home they smear themselves, their dogs, and their weapons with the blood of fowls in order to calm their souls and hinder them from fleeing away ; for, being themselves fond of the flesh of fowls, they ascribe the same taste to their souls. For eight days afterwards they must bathe by day and by night before going out again to the chase. Among the Hottentots, when a man has killed a lion, leopard, elephant, or rhinoceros, he is esteemed a great hero, but he has to remain at home quite idle for three days, during which his wife may not come near him ; she is also enjoined to restrict herself to a poor diet and to eat no more than is barely necessary to keep her in health. Similarly the Lapps deem it the height of glory to kill a bear, which they consider the king of beasts.   Nevertheless, all the men who take part in the slaughter are regarded as unclean, and must live by themselves for three days in a hut or tent made specially for them, where they cut up and cook the bear's carcase.   The reindeer which brought in the carcase on a sledge may not be driven by a woman for a whole year ; indeed, according to one account, it may not be used by anybody for that period.   Before the men go into the tent where they are to be secluded, they strip themselves of the garments they had worn in killing the bear, and their wives spit the red juice of alder bark in their faces.   They enter the tent not by the ordinary door but by an opening at the back.   When the bear's flesh has been cooked, a portion of it is sent by the hands of two men to the women, who may not approach the men's tent while the cooking is going on.   The men who convey the flesh to the women pretend to be strangers bringing presents from a foreign land ; the women keep up the pretence and promise to tie red threads round the legs of the strangers.   The bear's flesh may not be passed in to the women through the door of their tent, but must be thrust in at a special opening made by lifting up the hem of the tent-cover.   When the three days' seclusion is over and the men are at liberty to return to their wives, they run, one after the other, round the fire, holding the chain by which pots are suspended over it.   This is regarded as a form of purification ; they may now leave the tent by the ordinary door and rejoin the women.   But the leader of the party must still abstain from cohabitation with his wife for two days more.

Again, the Caffres are said to dread greatly the boa-constrictor or an enormous serpent resembling it ; " and being influenced by certain superstitious notions they even fear to kill it.   The man who happened to put it to death, whether in self-defence or otherwise, was formerly required to lie in a running stream of water during the day for several weeks together ; and no beast whatever was allowed to be slaughtered at the hamlet to which he belonged, until this duty had been fully performed.   The body of the snake was then taken and carefully buried in a trench, dug close to the cattle-fold, where its remains, like those of a chief, were henceforward kept perfectly undisturbed. The period of penance, as in the case of mourning for the dead, is now happily reduced to a few days."   In Madras it is considered a great sin to kill a cobra.   When this has happened, the people generally burn the body of the serpent, just as they burn the bodies of human beings.   The murderer deems himself polluted for three days.   On the second day milk is poured on the remains of the cobra.   On the third day the guilty wretch is free from pollution.

In these last cases the animal whose slaughter has to be atoned for is sacred, that is, it is one whose life is commonly spared from motives of superstition.   Yet the treatment of the sacrilegious slayer seems to resemble so closely the treatment of hunters and fishermen who have killed animals for food in the ordinary course of business, that the ideas on which both sets of customs are based may be assumed to be substantially the same. Those ideas, if I am right, are the respect which the savage feels for the souls of beasts, especially valuable or formidable beasts, and the dread which he entertains of their vengeful ghosts. Some confirmation of this view may be drawn from the ceremonies observed by fishermen of Annam when the carcase of a whale is washed ashore. These fisherfolk, we are told, worship the whale on account of the benefits they derive from it. There is hardly a village on the sea-shore which has not its small pagoda, containing the bones, more or less authentic, of a whale. When a dead whale is washed ashore, the people accord it a solemn burial. The man who first caught sight of it acts as chief mourner, performing the rites which as chief mourner and heir he would perform for a human kinsman. He puts on all the garb of woe, the straw hat, the white robe with long sleeves turned inside out, and the other paraphernalia of full mourning. As next of kin to the deceased he presides over the funeral rites. Perfumes are burned, sticks of incense kindled, leaves of gold and silver scattered, crackers let off. When the flesh has been cut off and the oil extracted, the remains of the carcase are buried in the sand. Afterwards a shed is set up and offerings are made in it. Usually some time after the burial the spirit of the dead whale takes possession of some person in the village and declares by his mouth whether he is a male or a female.

CHAPTER XXI

TABOOED THINGS

§ 1. *The Meaning of Taboo.* — Thus in primitive society the rules of ceremonial purity observed by divine kings, chiefs, and priests agree in many respects with the rules observed by homicides, mourners, women in childbed, girls at puberty, hunters and fishermen, and so on. To us these various classes of persons appear to differ totally in character and condition ; some of them we should call holy, others we might pronounce unclean and polluted. But the savage makes no such moral distinction between them ; the conceptions of holiness and pollution are not yet differentiated in his mind. To him the common feature of all these persons is that they are dangerous and in danger, and the danger in which they stand and to which they expose others is what we should call spiritual or ghostly, and therefore imaginary. The danger, however, is not less real because it is imaginary ; imagination acts upon man as really as does gravitation, and may kill him as certainly as a dose of prussic acid. To seclude these persons from the rest of the world so that the dreaded spiritual danger shall neither reach them nor spread from them, is the object of the taboos which they have to observe. These taboos act, so to say, as electrical insulators to preserve the spiritual force with which these persons are charged from suffering or inflicting harm by contact with the outer world.

To the illustrations of these general principles which have been already given I shall now add some more, drawing my examples, first, from the class of tabooed things, and, second, from the class of tabooed words ; for in the opinion of the savage both things and words may, like persons, be charged or electrified, either temporarily or permanently, with the mysterious virtue of taboo, and may therefore require to be banished for a longer or shorter time from the familiar usage of common life. And the examples will be chosen with special reference to those sacred chiefs, kings and priests, who, more than anybody else, live fenced about by taboo as by a wall. Tabooed things will be illustrated in the present chapter, and tabooed words in the next.

§ 2. *Iron tabooed.*—In the first place we may observe that the awful sanctity of kings naturally leads to a prohibition to touch their sacred persons. Thus it was unlawful to lay hands on the person of a Spartan king : no one might touch the body of the king or queen of Tahiti : it is forbidden to touch the person of the king of Siam under pain of death ; and no one may touch the king of Cambodia, for any purpose whatever, without his express command. In July 1874 the king was thrown from his carriage and lay insensible on the ground, but not one of his suite dared to touch him ; a European coming to the spot carried the injured monarch to his palace. Formerly no one might touch the king of Corea ; and if he deigned to touch a subject, the spot touched became sacred, and the person thus honoured had to wear a visible mark (generally a cord of red silk) for the rest of his life. Above all, no iron might touch the king's body. In 1800 King Tieng-tsong-tai-oang died of a tumour in the back, no one dreaming of employing the lancet, which would probably have saved his life. It is said that one king suffered terribly from an abscess in the lip, till his physician called in a jester, whose pranks made the king laugh heartily, and so the abscess burst. Roman and Sabine priests might not be shaved with iron but only with bronze razors or shears ; and whenever an iron graving-tool was brought into the sacred grove of the Arval Brothers at Rome for the purpose of cutting an inscription in stone, an expiatory sacrifice of a lamb and a pig must be offered, which was repeated when the graving-tool was removed from the grove. As a general rule iron might not be brought into Greek sanctuaries. In Crete sacrifices were offered to Menedemus without the use of iron, because the legend ran that Menedemus had been killed by an iron weapon in the Trojan war. The Archon of Plataea might not touch iron ; but once a year, at the annual commemoration of the men who fell at the battle of Plataea, he was allowed to carry a sword wherewith to sacrifice a bull. To this day a Hottentot priest never uses an iron knife, but always a sharp splint of quartz, in sacrificing an animal or circumcising a lad. Among the Ovambo of South-west Africa custom requires that lads should be circumcised with a sharp flint ; if none is to hand, the operation may be performed with iron, but the iron must afterwards be buried.   Amongst the Moquis of Arizona stone knives, hatchets, and so on have passed out of common use, but are retained in religious ceremonies.   After the Pawnees had ceased to use stone arrow-heads for ordinary purposes, they still employed them to slay the sacrifices, whether human captives or buffalo and deer.   Amongst the Jews no iron tool was used in building the Temple at Jerusalem or in making an altar.   The old wooden bridge (*Pons Sublicius*) at Rome, which was considered sacred, was made and had to be kept in repair without the use of iron or bronze.   It was expressly provided by law that the temple of Jupiter Liber at Furfo might be repaired with iron tools.   The council chamber at Cyzicus was constructed of wood without any iron nails, the beams being so arranged that they could be taken out and replaced.

This superstitious objection to iron perhaps dates from that early time in the history of society when iron was still a novelty, and as such was viewed by many with suspicion and dislike.   For everything new is apt to excite the awe and dread of the savage. " It is a curious superstition," says a pioneer in Borneo, " this of the Dusuns, to attribute anything—whether good or bad, lucky or unlucky—that happens to them to something novel which has arrived in their country.   For instance, my living in Kindram has caused the intensely hot weather we have experienced of late."   The unusually heavy rains which happened to follow the English survey of the Nicobar Islands in the winter of 1886–1887 were imputed by the alarmed natives to the wrath of the spirits at the theodolites, dumpy-levellers, and other strange instruments which had been set up in so many of their favourite haunts ; and some of them proposed to soothe the anger of the spirits by sacrificing a pig.   In the seventeenth century a succession of bad seasons excited a revolt among the Esthonian peasantry, who traced the origin of the evil to a watermill, which put a stream to some inconvenience by checking its flow. The first introduction of iron ploughshares into Poland having been followed by a succession of bad harvests, the farmers attributed the badness of the crops to the iron ploughshares, and discarded them for the old wooden ones.   To this day the primitive Baduwis of Java, who live chiefly by husbandry, will use no iron tools in tilling their fields.

The general dislike of innovation, which always makes itself strongly felt in the sphere of religion, is sufficient by itself to account for the superstitious aversion to iron entertained by kings and priests and attributed by them to the gods ; possibly this aversion may have been intensified in places by some such accidental cause as the series of bad seasons which cast discredit on iron ploughshares in Poland.   But the disfavour in which iron is held by the gods and their ministers has another side.   Their antipathy to the metal furnishes men with a weapon which may be turned against the spirits when occasion serves.   As their dislike of iron is supposed to be so great that they will not approach persons and things protected by

the obnoxious metal, iron may obviously be employed as a charm
for banning ghosts and other dangerous spirits. And often it is so
used. Thus in the Highlands of Scotland the great safeguard against
the elfin race is iron, or, better yet, steel. The metal in any form,
whether as a sword, a knife, a gun-barrel, or what not, is all-powerful
for this purpose. Whenever you enter a fairy dwelling you should
always remember to stick a piece of steel, such as a knife, a needle,
or a fish-hook, in the door; for then the elves will not be able to
shut the door till you come out again. So too when you have shot
a deer and are bringing it home at night, be sure to thrust a knife
into the carcase, for that keeps the fairies from laying their weight
on it. A knife or a nail in your pocket is quite enough to prevent
the fairies from lifting you up at night. Nails in the front of a bed
ward off elves from women " in the straw " and from their babes;
but to make quite sure it is better to put the smoothing-iron under
the bed, and the reaping-hook in the window. If a bull has fallen
over a rock and been killed, a nail stuck into it will preserve the
flesh from the fairies. Music discoursed on a Jew's harp keeps
the elfin women away from the hunter, because the tongue of the
instrument is of steel. In Morocco iron is considered a great
protection against demons; hence it is usual to place a knife or
dagger under a sick man's pillow. The Singhalese believe that
they are constantly surrounded by evil spirits, who lie in wait to
do them harm. A peasant would not dare to carry good food, such
as cakes or roast meat, from one place to another without putting
an iron nail on it to prevent a demon from taking possession of the
viands and so making the eater ill. No sick person, whether man
or woman, would venture out of the house without a bunch of keys
or a knife in his hand, for without such a talisman he would fear that
some devil might take advantage of his weak state to slip into his
body. And if a man has a large sore on his body he tries to keep a
morsel of iron on it as a protection against demons. On the Slave Coast
when a mother sees her child gradually wasting away, she concludes
that a demon has entered into the child, and takes her measures
accordingly. To lure the demon out of the body of her offspring,
she offers a sacrifice of food; and while the devil is bolting it, she
attaches iron rings and small bells to her child's ankles and hangs
iron chains round his neck. The jingling of the iron and the tinkling
of the bells are supposed to prevent the demon, when he has concluded
his repast, from entering again into the body of the little sufferer.
Hence many children may be seen in this part of Africa weighed down
with iron ornaments.

§ 3. *Sharp Weapons tabooed.*—There is a priestly king to the north
of Zengwih in Burma, revered by the Sotih as the highest spiritual and
temporal authority, into whose house no weapon or cutting instrument
may be brought. This rule may perhaps be explained by a custom
observed by various peoples after a death; they refrain from the use of
sharp instruments so long as the ghost of the deceased is supposed to be

near, lest they should wound it.   Thus among the Esquimaux of Bering
Strait " during the day on which a person dies in the village no one is
permitted to work, and the relatives must perform no labour during the
three following days.   It is especially forbidden during this period to
cut with any edged instrument, such as a knife or an axe ; and the
use of pointed instruments, like needles or bodkins, is also forbidden.
This is said to be done to avoid cutting or injuring the shade, which
may be present at any time during this period, and, if accidentally
injured by any of these things, it would become very angry and bring
sickness or death to the people.   The relatives must also be very
careful at this time not to make any loud or harsh noises that may
startle or anger the shade."   We have seen that in like manner after
killing a white whale these Esquimaux abstain from the use of cutting
or pointed instruments for four days, lest they should unwittingly cut
or stab the whale's ghost.   The same taboo is sometimes observed by
them when there is a sick person in the village, probably from a fear of
injuring his shade which may be hovering outside of his body.   After
a death the Roumanians of Transylvania are careful not to leave a knife
lying with the sharp edge uppermost so long as the corpse remains in
the house, " or else the soul will be forced to ride on the blade."   For
seven days after a death, the corpse being still in the house, the Chinese
abstain from the use of knives and needles, and even of chopsticks,
eating their food with their fingers.   On the third, sixth, ninth, and
fortieth days after the funeral the old Prussians and Lithuanians used
to prepare a meal, to which, standing at the door, they invited the
soul of the deceased.   At these meals they sat silent round the table
and used no knives, and the women who served up the food were also
without knives.   If any morsels fell from the table they were left lying
there for the lonely souls that had no living relations or friends to feed
them.   When the meal was over the priest took a broom and swept
the souls out of the house, saying, " Dear souls, ye have eaten and
drunk.   Go forth, go forth."   We can now understand why no cutting
instrument may be taken into the house of the Burmese pontiff.   Like
so many priestly kings, he is probably regarded as divine, and it is
therefore right that his sacred spirit should not be exposed to the risk
of being cut or wounded whenever it quits his body to hover invisible
in the air or to fly on some distant mission.

§ 4. *Blood tabooed.*—We have seen that the Flamen Dialis was
forbidden to touch or even name raw flesh.   At certain times a
Brahman teacher is enjoined not to look on raw flesh, blood, or persons
whose hands have been cut off.   In Uganda the father of twins is in
a state of taboo for some time after the birth ; among other rules he
is forbidden to kill anything or to see blood.   In the Pelew Islands
when a raid has been made on a village and a head carried off, the
relations of the slain man are tabooed and have to submit to certain
observances in order to escape the wrath of his ghost.   They are shut
up in the house, touch no raw flesh, and chew betel over which an
incantation has been uttered by the exorcist.   After this the ghost

of the slaughtered man goes away to the enemy's country in pursuit
of his murderer. The taboo is probably based on the common belief
that the soul or spirit of the animal is in the blood. As tabooed
persons are believed to be in a perilous state—for example, the relations
of the slain man are liable to the attacks of his indignant ghost—it
is especially necessary to isolate them from contact with spirits ;
hence the prohibition to touch raw meat. But as usual the taboo is
only the special enforcement of a general precept ; in other words, its
observance is particularly enjoined in circumstances which seem
urgently to call for its application, but apart from such circumstances
the prohibition is also observed, though less strictly, as a common
rule of life. Thus some of the Esthonians will not taste blood because
they believe that it contains the animal's soul, which would enter the
body of the person who tasted the blood. Some Indian tribes of
North America, " through a strong principle of religion, abstain in
the strictest manner from eating the blood of any animal, as it contains
the life and spirit of the beast." Jewish hunters poured out the
blood of the game they had killed and covered it up with dust. They
would not taste the blood, believing that the soul or life of the animal
was in the blood, or actually was the blood.

It is a common rule that royal blood may not be shed upon the
ground. Hence when a king or one of his family is to be put to death
a mode of execution is devised by which the royal blood shall not be
spilt upon the earth. About the year 1688 the generalissimo of the
army rebelled against the king of Siam and put him to death " after
the manner of royal criminals, or as princes of the blood are treated
when convicted of capital crimes, which is by putting them into a
large iron caldron, and pounding them to pieces with wooden pestles,
because none of their royal blood must be spilt on the ground, it being,
by their religion, thought great impiety to contaminate the divine blood
by mixing it with earth." When Kublai Khan defeated and took his
uncle Nayan, who had rebelled against him, he caused Nayan to be
put to death by being wrapt in a carpet and tossed to and fro till he
died, " because he would not have the blood of his Line Imperial spilt
upon the ground or exposed in the eye of Heaven and before the Sun."
" Friar Ricold mentions the Tartar maxim : ' One Khan will put
another to death to get possession of the throne, but he takes great
care that the blood be not spilt. For they say that it is highly improper that the blood of the Great Khan should be spilt upon the
ground ; so they cause the victim to be smothered somehow or other.'
The like feeling prevails at the court of Burma, where a peculiar mode
of execution without bloodshed is reserved for princes of the blood."

The reluctance to spill royal blood seems to be only a particular
case of a general unwillingness to shed blood or at least to allow it to
fall on the ground. Marco Polo tells us that in his day persons caught
in the streets of Cambaluc (Peking) at unseasonable hours were arrested,
and if found guilty of a misdemeanour were beaten with a stick.
" Under this punishment people sometimes die, but they adopt it in

order to eschew bloodshed, for their *Bacsis* say that it is an evil thing
to shed man's blood." In West Sussex people believe that the ground
on which human blood has been shed is accursed and will remain barren
for ever. Among some primitive peoples, when the blood of a tribesman has to be spilt it is not suffered to fall upon the ground, but is
received upon the bodies of his fellow-tribesmen. Thus in some
Australian tribes boys who are being circumcised are laid on a platform,
formed by the living bodies of the tribesmen ; and when a boy's tooth
is knocked out as an initiatory ceremony, he is seated on the shoulders
of a man, on whose breast the blood flows and may not be wiped away.
" Also the Gauls used to drink their enemies' blood and paint themselves therewith. So also they write that the old Irish were wont ;
and so have I seen some of the Irish do, but not their enemies' but
friends' blood, as, namely, at the execution of a notable traitor at
Limerick, called Murrogh O'Brien, I saw an old woman, which was his
foster-mother, take up his head whilst he was quartered and suck up
all the blood that ran thereout, saying that the earth was not worthy
to drink it, and therewith also steeped her face and breast and tore her
hair, crying out and shrieking most terribly." Among the Latuka of
Central Africa the earth on which a drop of blood has fallen at childbirth is carefully scraped up with an iron shovel, put into a pot along
with the water used in washing the mother, and buried tolerably deep
outside the house on the left-hand side. In West Africa, if a drop of
your blood has fallen on the ground, you must carefully cover it up,
rub and stamp it into the soil ; if it has fallen on the side of a canoe
or a tree, the place is cut out and the chip destroyed. One motive of
these African customs may be a wish to prevent the blood from falling
into the hands of magicians, who might make an evil use of it. That
is admittedly the reason why people in West Africa stamp out any
blood of theirs which has dropped on the ground or cut out any wood
that has been soaked with it. From a like dread of sorcery natives of
New Guinea are careful to burn any sticks, leaves, or rags which are
stained with their blood ; and if the blood has dripped on the ground
they turn up the soil and if possible light a fire on the spot. The same
fear explains the curious duties discharged by a class of men called
ramanga or " blue blood " among the Betsileo of Madagascar. It is
their business to eat all the nail-parings and to lick up all the spilt
blood of the nobles. When the nobles pare their nails, the parings are
collected to the last scrap and swallowed by these *ramanga*. If the
parings are too large, they are minced small and so gulped down.
Again, should a nobleman wound himself, say in cutting his nails or
treading on something, the *ramanga* lick up the blood as fast as possible.
Nobles of high rank hardly go anywhere without these humble attendants ; but if it should happen that there are none of them present, the
cut nails and the spilt blood are carefully collected to be afterwards
swallowed by the *ramanga*. There is scarcely a nobleman of any
pretensions who does not strictly observe this custom, the intention
of which probably is to prevent these parts of his person from falling

into the hands of sorcerers, who on the principles of contagious magic could work him harm thereby.

The general explanation of the reluctance to shed blood on the ground is probably to be found in the belief that the soul is in the blood, and that therefore any ground on which it may fall necessarily becomes taboo or sacred. In New Zealand anything upon which even a drop of a high chief's blood chances to fall becomes taboo or sacred to him. For instance, a party of natives having come to visit a chief in a fine new canoe, the chief got into it, but in doing so a splinter entered his foot, and the blood trickled on the canoe, which at once became sacred to him. The owner jumped out, dragged the canoe ashore opposite the chief's house, and left it there. Again, a chief in entering a missionary's house knocked his head against a beam, and the blood flowed. The natives said that in former times the house would have belonged to the chief. As usually happens with taboos of universal application, the prohibition to spill the blood of a tribesman on the ground applies with peculiar stringency to chiefs and kings, and is observed in their case long after it has ceased to be observed in the case of others.

§ 5. *The Head tabooed.*—Many peoples regard the head as peculiarly sacred ; the special sanctity attributed to it is sometimes explained by a belief that it contains a spirit which is very sensitive to injury or disrespect. Thus the Yorubas hold that every man has three spiritual inmates, of whom the first, called Olori, dwells in the head and is the man's protector, guardian, and guide. Offerings are made to this spirit, chiefly of fowls, and some of the blood mixed with palm-oil is rubbed on the forehead. The Karens suppose that a being called the *tso* resides in the upper part of the head, and while it retains its seat no harm can befall the person from the efforts of the seven *Kelahs*, or personified passions. " But if the *tso* becomes heedless or weak certain evil to the person is the result. Hence the head is carefully attended to, and all possible pains are taken to provide such dress and attire as will be pleasing to the *tso.*" The Siamese think that a spirit called *khuan* or *kwun* dwells in the human head, of which it is the guardian spirit. The spirit must be carefully protected from injury of every kind ; hence the act of shaving or cutting the hair is accompanied with many ceremonies. The *kwun* is very sensitive on points of honour, and would feel mortally insulted if the head in which he resides were touched by the hand of a stranger. The Cambodians esteem it a grave offence to touch a man's head ; some of them will not enter a place where anything whatever is suspended over their heads ; and the meanest Cambodian would never consent to live under an inhabited room. Hence the houses are built of one story only ; and even the Government respects the prejudice by never placing a prisoner in the stocks under the floor of a house, though the houses are raised high above the ground. The same superstition exists amongst the Malays ; for an early traveller reports that in Java people " wear nothing on their heads, and say that nothing must be on their heads . . . and if any person were to put his hand upon their head they would kill him ; and they do not build houses with storeys, in order that they may not walk over each other's heads."

The same superstition as to the head is found in full force throughout Polynesia. Thus of Gattanewa, a Marquesan chief, it is said that " to touch the top of his head, or anything which had been on his head, was sacrilege. To pass over his head was an indignity never to be forgotten." The son of a Marquesan high priest has been seen to roll on the ground in an agony of rage and despair, begging for death, because some one had desecrated his head and deprived him of his divinity by sprinkling a few drops of water on his hair. But it was not the Marquesan chiefs only whose heads were sacred. The head of every Marquesan was taboo, and might neither be touched nor stepped over by another ; even a father might not step over the head of his sleeping child ; women were forbidden to carry or touch anything that had been in contact with, or had merely hung over, the head of their husband or father. No one was allowed to be over the head of the king of Tonga. In Tahiti any one who stood over the king or queen, or passed his hand over their heads, might be put to death. Until certain rites were performed over it, a Tahitian infant was especially taboo ; whatever touched the child's head, while it was in this state, became sacred and was deposited in a consecrated place railed in for the purpose at the child's house. If a branch of a tree touched the child's head, the tree was cut down ; and if in its fall it injured another tree so as to penetrate the bark, that tree also was cut down as unclean and unfit for use. After the rites were performed these special taboos ceased ; but the head of a Tahitian was always sacred, he never carried anything on it, and to touch it was an offence. So sacred was the head of a Maori chief that " if he only touched it with his fingers, he was obliged immediately to apply them to his nose, and snuff up the sanctity which they had acquired by the touch, and thus restore it to the part from whence it was taken." On account of the sacredness of his head a Maori chief " could not blow the fire with his mouth, for the breath being sacred, communicated his sanctity to it, and a brand might be taken by a slave, or a man of another tribe, or the fire might be used for other purposes, such as cooking, and so cause his death."

§ 6. *Hair tabooed.*—When the head was considered so sacred that it might not even be touched without grave offence, it is obvious that the cutting of the hair must have been a delicate and difficult operation. The difficulties and dangers which, on the primitive view, beset the operation are of two kinds. There is first the danger of disturbing the spirit of the head, which may be injured in the process and may revenge itself upon the person who molests him. Secondly, there is the difficulty of disposing of the shorn locks. For the savage believes that the sympathetic connexion which exists between himself and every part of his body continues to exist even after the physical connexion has been broken, and that therefore he will suffer from any harm that may befall the severed parts of his body, such as the clippings of his hair or the parings of his nails. Accordingly he takes care that these severed portions of himself shall not be left in places where they might either be exposed to accidental injury or fall into the hands of malicious persons who might work magic on them to his detriment or death. Such dangers are common to all, but sacred persons have more to fear from them than ordinary people, so the precautions taken by them are proportionately stringent. The simplest way of evading the peril is not to cut the hair at all; and this is the expedient adopted where the risk is thought to be more than usually great. The Frankish kings were never allowed to crop their hair; from their childhood upwards they had to keep it unshorn. To poll the long locks that floated on their shoulders would have been to renounce their right to the throne. When the wicked brothers Clotaire and Childebert coveted the kingdom of their dead brother Clodomir, they inveigled into their power their little nephews, the two sons of Clodomir; and having done so, they sent a messenger bearing scissors and a naked sword to the children's grandmother, Queen Clotilde, at Paris. The envoy showed the scissors and the sword to Clotilde, and bade her choose whether the children should be shorn and live or remain unshorn and die. The proud queen replied that if her grandchildren were not to come to the throne she would rather see them dead than shorn. And murdered they were by their ruthless uncle Clotaire with his own hand. The king of Ponape, one of the Caroline Islands, must wear his hair long, and so must his grandees. Among the Hos, a negro tribe of West Africa, " there are priests on whose head no razor may come during the whole of their lives. The god who dwells in the man forbids the cutting of his hair on pain of death. If the hair is at last too long, the owner must pray to his god to allow him at least to clip the tips of it. The hair is in fact conceived as the seat and lodging-place of his god, so that were it shorn the god would lose his abode in the priest." The members of a Masai clan, who are believed to possess the art of making rain, may not pluck out their beards, because the loss of their beards would, it is supposed, entail the loss of their rain-making powers. The head chief and the sorcerers of the Masai observe the same rule for a like reason: they think that were they to pull out their beards, their supernatural gifts would desert them.

Again, men who have taken a vow of vengeance sometimes keep their hair unshorn till they have fulfilled their vow. Thus of the Marquesans we are told that " occasionally they have their head entirely shaved, except one lock on the crown, which is worn loose or put up in a knot. But the latter mode of wearing the hair is only adopted by them when they have a solemn vow, as to revenge the death of some near relation, etc. In such case the lock is never cut off until they have fulfilled their promise." A similar custom was sometimes observed by the ancient Germans; among the Chatti the young warriors never clipped their hair or their beard till they had slain an enemy. Among the Toradjas, when a child's hair is cut to rid it of vermin, some locks are allowed to remain on the crown of the

head as a refuge for one of the child's souls.   Otherwise the soul would
have no place in which to settle, and the child would sicken.   The
Karo-Bataks are much afraid of frightening away the soul of a child ;
hence when they cut its hair, they always leave a patch unshorn, to
which the soul can retreat before the shears.   Usually this lock remains
unshorn all through life, or at least up till manhood.

§ 7. *Ceremonies at Hair-cutting.*—But when it becomes necessary
to crop the hair, measures are taken to lessen the dangers which are
supposed to attend the operation.   The chief of Namosi in Fiji always
ate a man by way of precaution when he had had his hair cut.   " There
was a certain clan that had to provide the victim, and they used to sit
in solemn council among themselves to choose him.   It was a sacrificial
feast to avert evil from the chief."   Amongst the Maoris many spells
were uttered at hair-cutting ; one, for example, was spoken to consecrate the obsidian knife with which the hair was cut ; another was
pronounced to avert the thunder and lightning which hair-cutting was
believed to cause.   " He who has had his hair cut is in immediate
charge of the Atua (spirit) ; he is removed from the contact and society
of his family and his tribe ; he dare not touch his food himself ; it is
put into his mouth by another person ; nor can he for some days
resume his accustomed occupations or associate with his fellow-men."
The person who cuts the hair is also tabooed ; his hands having been
in contact with a sacred head, he may not touch food with them or
engage in any other employment ; he is fed by another person with
food cooked over a sacred fire.   He cannot be released from the taboo
before the following day, when he rubs his hands with potato or fern
root which has been cooked on a sacred fire ; and this food having
been taken to the head of the family in the female line and eaten by
her, his hands are freed from the taboo.   In some parts of New Zealand
the most sacred day of the year was that appointed for hair-cutting ;
the people assembled in large numbers on that day from all the neighbourhood.

§ 8. *Disposal of Cut Hair and Nails.*—But even when the hair and
nails have been safely cut, there remains the difficulty of disposing of
them, for their owner believes himself liable to suffer from any harm
that may befall them.   The notion that a man may be bewitched by
means of the clippings of his hair, the parings of his nails, or any other
severed portion of his person is almost world-wide, and attested by
evidence too ample, too familiar, and too tedious in its uniformity to
be here analysed at length.   The general idea on which the superstition
rests is that of the sympathetic connexion supposed to persist between
a person and everything that has once been part of his body or in any
way closely related to him.   A very few examples must suffice.   They
belong to that branch of sympathetic magic which may be called
contagious.   Dread of sorcery, we are told, formed one of the most
salient characteristics of the Marquesan islanders in the old days.   The
sorcerer took some of the hair, spittle, or other bodily refuse of the man
he wished to injure, wrapped it up in a leaf, and placed the packet in

a bag woven of threads or fibres, which were knotted in an intricate way. The whole was then buried with certain rites, and thereupon the victim wasted away of a languishing sickness which lasted twenty days. His life, however, might be saved by discovering and digging up the buried hair, spittle, or what not ; for as soon as this was done the power of the charm ceased. A Maori sorcerer intent on bewitching somebody sought to get a tress of his victim's hair, the parings of his nails, some of his spittle, or a shred of his garment. Having obtained the object, whatever it was, he chanted certain spells and curses over it in a falsetto voice and buried it in the ground. As the thing decayed, the person to whom it had belonged was supposed to waste away. When an Australian blackfellow wishes to get rid of his wife, he cuts off a lock of her hair in her sleep, ties it to his spear-thrower, and goes with it to a neighbouring tribe, where he gives it to a friend. His friend sticks the spear-thrower up every night before the camp fire, and when it falls down it is a sign that the wife is dead. The way in which the charm operates was explained to Dr. Howitt by a Wirajuri man. " You see," he said, " when a blackfellow doctor gets hold of something belonging to a man and roasts it with things, and sings over it, the fire catches hold of the smell of the man, and that settles the poor fellow."

The Huzuls of the Carpathians imagine that if mice get a person's shorn hair and make a nest of it, the person will suffer from headache or even become idiotic. Similarly in Germany it is a common notion that if birds find a person's cut hair, and build their nests with it, the person will suffer from headache ; sometimes it is thought that he will have an eruption on the head. The same superstition prevails, or used to prevail, in West Sussex.

Again it is thought that cut or combed-out hair may disturb the weather by producing rain and hail, thunder and lightning. We have seen that in New Zealand a spell was uttered at hair-cutting to avert thunder and lightning. In the Tyrol, witches are supposed to use cut or combed-out hair to make hailstones or thunderstorms with. Thlinkeet Indians have been known to attribute stormy weather to the rash act of a girl who had combed her hair outside of the house. The Romans seem to have held similar views, for it was a maxim with them that no one on shipboard should cut his hair or nails except in a storm, that is, when the mischief was already done. In the Highlands of Scotland it is said that no sister should comb her hair at night if she have a brother at sea. In West Africa, when the Mani of Chitombe or Jumba died, the people used to run in crowds to the corpse and tear out his hair, teeth, and nails, which they kept as a rain-charm, believing that otherwise no rain would fall. The Makoko of the Anzikos begged the missionaries to give him half their beards as a rain-charm.

If cut hair and nails remain in sympathetic connexion with the person from whose body they have been severed, it is clear that they can be used as hostages for his good behaviour by any one who may chance to possess them ; for on the principles of contagious magic he has only to injure the hair or nails in order to hurt simultaneously their original owner. Hence when the Nandi have taken a prisoner they shave his head and keep the shorn hair as a surety that he will not attempt to escape ; but when the captive is ransomed, they return his shorn hair with him to his own people.

To preserve the cut hair and nails from injury and from the dangerous uses to which they may be put by sorcerers, it is necessary to deposit them in some safe place. The shorn locks of a Maori chief were gathered with much care and placed in an adjoining cemetery. The Tahitians buried the cuttings of their hair at the temples. In the streets of Soku a modern traveller observed cairns of large stones piled against walls with tufts of human hair inserted in the crevices. On asking the meaning of this, he was told that when any native of the place polled his hair he carefully gathered up the clippings and deposited them in one of these cairns, all of which were sacred to the fetish and therefore inviolable. These cairns of sacred stones, he further learned, were simply a precaution against witchcraft, for if a man were not thus careful in disposing of his hair, some of it might fall into the hands of his enemies, who would, by means of it, be able to cast spells over him and so compass his destruction. When the top-knot of a Siamese child has been cut with great ceremony, the short hairs are put into a little vessel made of plantain leaves and set adrift on the nearest river or canal. As they float away, all that was wrong or harmful in the child's disposition is believed to depart with them. The long hairs are kept till the child makes a pilgrimage to the holy Footprint of Buddha on the sacred hill at Prabat. They are then presented to the priests, who are supposed to make them into brushes with which they sweep the Footprint ; but in fact so much hair is thus offered every year that the priests cannot use it all, so they quietly burn the superfluity as soon as the pilgrims' backs are turned. The cut hair and nails of the Flamen Dialis were buried under a lucky tree. The shorn tresses of the Vestal Virgins were hung on an ancient lotus-tree.

Often the clipped hair and nails are stowed away in any secret place, not necessarily in a temple or cemetery or at a tree, as in the cases already mentioned. Thus in Swabia you are recommended to deposit your clipped hair in some spot where neither sun nor moon can shine on it, for example in the earth or under a stone. In Danzig it is buried in a bag under the threshold. In Ugi, one of the Solomon Islands, men bury their hair lest it should fall into the hands of an enemy, who would make magic with it and so bring sickness or calamity on them. The same fear seems to be general in Melanesia, and has led to a regular practice of hiding cut hair and nails. The same practice prevails among many tribes of South Africa, from a fear lest wizards should get hold of the severed particles and work evil with them. The Caffres carry still further this dread of allowing any portion of themselves to fall into the hands of an enemy ; for not only do they bury their cut hair and nails in a secret spot, but when one of them cleans the head of another he preserves the vermin which he catches, " carefully delivering them to the person to whom they originally appertained, supposing, according to their theory, that as they derived their support from the blood of the man from whom they were taken, should they be killed by another, the blood of his neighbour would be in his possession, thus placing in his hands the power of some super-human influence."

Sometimes the severed hair and nails are preserved, not to prevent them from falling into the hands of a magician, but that the owner may have them at the resurrection of the body, to which some races look forward. Thus the Incas of Peru " took extreme care to preserve the nail-parings and the hairs that were shorn off or torn out with a comb ; placing them in holes or niches in the walls ; and if they fell out, any other Indian that saw them picked them up and put them in their places again. I very often asked different Indians, at various times, why they did this, in order to see what they would say, and they all replied in the same words saying, ' Know that all persons who are born must return to life ' (they have no word to express resuscitation), ' and the souls must rise out of their tombs with all that belonged to their bodies. We, therefore, in order that we may not have to search for our hair and nails at a time when there will be much hurry and confusion, place them in one place, that they may be brought together more conveniently, and, whenever it is possible, we are also careful to spit in one place.' " Similarly the Turks never throw away the parings of their nails, but carefully stow them in cracks of the walls or of the boards, in the belief that they will be needed at the resurrection. The Armenians do not throw away their cut hair and nails and extracted teeth, but hide them in places that are esteemed holy, such as a crack in the church wall, a pillar of the house, or a hollow tree. They think that all these severed portions of themselves will be wanted at the resurrection, and that he who has not stowed them away in a safe place will have to hunt about for them on the great day. In the village of Drumconrath in Ireland there used to be some old women who, having ascertained from Scripture that the hairs of their heads were all numbered by the Almighty, expected to have to account for them at the day of judgment. In order to be able to do so they stuffed the severed hair away in the thatch of their cottages.

Some people burn their loose hair to save it from falling into the hands of sorcerers. This is done by the Patagonians and some of the Victorian tribes. In the Upper Vosges they say that you should never leave the clippings of your hair and nails lying about, but burn them to hinder the sorcerers from using them against you. For the same reason Italian women either burn their loose hairs or throw them into a place where no one is likely to look for them. The almost universal dread of witchcraft induces the West African negroes, the Makololo of South Africa, and the Tahitians to burn or bury their shorn hair. In the Tyrol many people burn their hair lest the witches should use it to raise thunderstorms ; others burn or bury it to prevent the birds from lining their nests with it, which would cause the heads from which the hair came to ache.

This destruction of the hair and nails plainly involves an inconsistency of thought. The object of the destruction is avowedly to prevent these severed portions of the body from being used by sorcerers. But the possibility of their being so used depends upon the supposed sympathetic connexion between them and the man from whom they were severed. And if this sympathetic connexion still exists, clearly these severed portions cannot be destroyed without injury to the man.

§ 9. *Spittle tabooed.*—The same fear of witchcraft which has led so many people to hide or destroy their loose hair and nails has induced other or the same people to treat their spittle in a like fashion. For on the principles of sympathetic magic the spittle is part of the man, and whatever is done to it will have a corresponding effect on him. A Chilote Indian, who has gathered up the spittle of an enemy, will put it in a potato, and hang the potato in the smoke, uttering certain spells as he does so in the belief that his foe will waste away as the potato dries in the smoke. Or he will put the spittle in a frog and throw the animal into an inaccessible, unnavigable river, which will make the victim quake and shake with ague. The natives of Urewera, a district of New Zealand, enjoyed a high reputation for their skill in magic. It was said that they made use of people's spittle to bewitch them. Hence visitors were careful to conceal their spittle, lest they should furnish these wizards with a handle for working them harm. Similarly among some tribes of South Africa no man will spit when an enemy is near, lest his foe should find the spittle and give it to a wizard, who would then mix it with magical ingredients so as to injure the person from whom it fell. Even in a man's own house his saliva is carefully swept away and obliterated for a similar reason.

If common folk are thus cautious, it is natural that kings and chiefs should be doubly so. In the Sandwich Islands chiefs were attended by a confidential servant bearing a portable spittoon, and the deposit was carefully buried every morning to put it out of the reach of sorcerers. On the Slave Coast, for the same reason, whenever a king or chief expectorates, the saliva is scrupulously gathered up and hidden or buried. The same precautions are taken for the same reason with the spittle of the chief of Tabali in Southern Nigeria.

The magical use to which spittle may be put marks it out, like blood or nail-parings, as a suitable material basis for a covenant, since by exchanging their saliva the covenanting parties give each other a guarantee of good faith. If either of them afterwards forswears himself, the other can punish his perfidy by a magical treatment of the perjurer's spittle which he has in his custody. Thus when the Wajagga of East Africa desire to make a covenant, the two parties will sometimes sit down with a bowl of milk or beer between them, and after uttering an incantation over the beverage they each take a mouthful of the milk or beer and spit it into the other's mouth. In urgent cases, when there is no time to spend on ceremony, the two will simply spit into each other's mouth, which seals the covenant just as well.

§ 10. *Foods tabooed.*—As might have been expected, the super-stitions of the savage cluster thick about the subject of food ; and he abstains from eating many animals and plants, wholesome enough in themselves, which for one reason or another he fancies would prove dangerous or fatal to the eater. Examples of such abstinence are too familiar and far too numerous to quote. But if the ordinary man is thus deterred by superstitious fear from partaking of various foods, the restraints of this kind which are laid upon sacred or tabooed persons, such as kings and priests, are still more numerous and stringent. We have already seen that the Flamen Dialis was forbidden to eat or even name several plants and animals, and that the flesh diet of Egyptian kings was restricted to veal and goose. In antiquity many priests and many kings of barbarous peoples abstained wholly from a flesh diet. The *Gangas* or fetish priests of the Loango Coast are forbidden to eat or even see a variety of animals and fish, in con-sequence of which their flesh diet is extremely limited ; often they live only on herbs and roots, though they may drink fresh blood. The heir to the throne of Loango is forbidden from infancy to eat pork ; from early childhood he is interdicted the use of the *cola* fruit in company ; at puberty he is taught by a priest not to partake of fowls except such as he has himself killed and cooked ; and so the number of taboos goes on increasing with his years. In Fernando Po the king after installation is forbidden to eat *cocco* (*arum acaule*), deer, and porcupine, which are the ordinary foods of the people. The head chief of the Masai may eat nothing but milk, honey, and the roasted livers of goats ; for if he partook of any other food he would lose his power of soothsaying and of compounding charms.

§ 11. *Knots and Rings tabooed.*—We have seen that among the many taboos which the Flamen Dialis at Rome had to observe, there was one that forbade him to have a knot on any part of his garments, and another that obliged him to wear no ring unless it were broken. In like manner Moslem pilgrims to Mecca are in a state of sanctity or taboo and may wear on their persons neither knots nor rings. These rules are probably of kindred significance, and may conveniently be considered together. To begin with knots, many people in different parts of the world entertain a strong objection to having any knot about their person at certain critical seasons, particularly childbirth, marriage, and death. Thus among the Saxons of Transylvania, when a woman is in travail all knots on her garments are untied, because it is believed that this will facilitate her delivery, and with the same intention all the locks in the house, whether on doors or boxes, are unlocked. The Lapps think that a lying-in woman should have no knot on her garments, because a knot would have the effect of making the delivery difficult and painful. In the East Indies this superstition is extended to the whole time of pregnancy ; the people believe that if a pregnant woman were to tie knots, or braid, or make anything fast, the child would thereby be constricted or the woman would herself be " tied up " when her time came. Nay, some of them enforce the observance of the rule on the father as well as the mother of the unborn child. Among the Sea Dyaks neither of the parents may bind up anything with string or make anything fast during the wife's pregnancy. In the Toumbuluh tribe of North Celebes a ceremony is performed in the fourth or fifth month of a woman's pregnancy, and after it her husband is forbidden, among many other things, to tie any fast knots and to sit with his legs crossed over each other.

In all these cases the idea seems to be that the tying of a knot would, as they say in the East Indies, " tie up " the woman, in other words, impede and perhaps prevent her delivery, or delay her convalescence after the birth. On the principles of homoeopathic or imitative magic the physical obstacle or impediment of a knot on a cord would create a corresponding obstacle or impediment in the body of the woman. That this is really the explanation of the rule appears from a custom observed by the Hos of West Africa at a difficult birth. When a woman is in hard labour and cannot bring forth, they call in a magician to her aid. He looks at her and says, " The child is bound in the womb, that is why she cannot be delivered." On the entreaties of her female relations he then promises to loose the bond so that she may bring forth. For that purpose he orders them to fetch a tough creeper from the forest, and with it he binds the hands and feet of the sufferer on her back. Then he takes a knife and calls out the woman's name, and when she answers he cuts through the creeper with a knife, saying, " I cut through to-day thy bonds and thy child's bonds." After that he chops up the creeper small, puts the bits in a vessel of water, and bathes the woman with the water. Here the cutting of the creeper with which the woman's hands and feet are bound is a simple piece of homoeopathic or imitative magic : by releasing her limbs from their bonds the magician imagines that he simultaneously releases the child in her womb from the trammels which impede its birth. The same train of thought underlies a practice observed by some peoples of opening all locks, doors, and so on, while a birth is taking place in the house. We have seen that at such a time the Germans of Transylvania open all the locks, and the same thing is done also in Voigtland and Mecklenburg. In north-western Argyllshire superstitious people used to open every lock in the house at childbirth. In the island of Salsette near Bombay, when a woman is in hard labour, all locks of doors or drawers are opened with a key to facilitate her delivery. Among the Mandelings of Sumatra the lids of all chests, boxes, pans, and so forth are opened ; and if this does not produce the desired effect, the anxious husband has to strike the projecting ends of some of the house-beams in order to loosen them ; for they think that " everything must be open and loose to facilitate the delivery." In Chittagong, when a woman·cannot bring her child to the birth, the midwife gives orders to throw all doors and windows wide open, to uncork all bottles, to remove the bungs from all casks, to unloose the cows in the stall, the horses in the stable, the watchdog in his kennel, to set free sheep, fowls, ducks, and so forth. This universal liberty accorded to the animals and even to inanimate things is, according to the people, an infallible means of ensuring the woman's delivery and allowing the babe to be born. In the island of Saghalien, when a woman is in labour, her husband undoes everything that can be undone. He loosens the plaits of his hair and the laces of his shoes. Then he unties whatever is tied in the house or its vicinity. In the courtyard he takes the axe out of the log in which it is stuck; he unfastens the boat, if it is moored to a tree, he withdraws the cartridges from his gun, and the arrows from his crossbow.

Again, we have seen that a Toumbuluh man abstains not only from tying knots, but also from sitting with crossed legs during his wife's pregnancy. The train of thought is the same in both cases. Whether you cross threads in tying a knot, or only cross your legs in sitting at your ease, you are equally, on the principles of homoeopathic magic, crossing or thwarting the free course of things, and your action cannot but check and impede whatever may be going forward in your neighbourhood. Of this important truth the Romans were fully aware. To sit beside a pregnant woman or a patient under medical treatment with clasped hands, says the grave Pliny, is to cast a malignant spell over the person, and it is worse still if you nurse your leg or legs with your clasped hands, or lay one leg over the other. Such postures were regarded by the old Romans as a let and hindrance to business of every sort, and at a council of war or a meeting of magistrates, at prayers and sacrifices, no man was suffered to cross his legs or clasp his hands. The stock instance of the dreadful consequences that might flow from doing one or the other was that of Alcmena, who travailed with Hercules for seven days and seven nights, because the goddess Lucina sat in front of the house with clasped hands and crossed legs, and the child could not be born until the goddess had been beguiled into changing her attitude. It is a Bulgarian superstition that if a pregnant woman is in the habit of sitting with crossed legs, she will suffer much in childbed. In some parts of Bavaria, when conversation comes to a standstill and silence ensues, they say, " Surely somebody has crossed his legs."

The magical effect of knots in trammelling and obstructing human activity was believed to be manifested at marriage not less than at birth. During the Middle Ages, and down to the eighteenth century, it seems to have been commonly held in Europe that the consummation of marriage could be prevented by any one who, while the wedding ceremony was taking place, either locked a lock or tied a knot in a cord, and then threw the lock or the cord away. The lock or the knotted cord had to be flung into water; and until it had been found and unlocked, or untied, no real union of the married pair was possible. Hence it was a grave offence, not only to cast such a spell, but also to steal or make away with the material instrument of it, whether lock or knotted cord. In the year 1718 the parliament of Bordeaux sentenced some one to be burned alive for having spread desolation through a whole family by means of knotted cords; and in 1705 two persons were condemned to death in Scotland for stealing certain charmed knots which a woman had made, in order thereby to mar the wedded happiness of Spalding of Ashintilly. The belief in the efficacy of these charms appears to have lingered in the Highlands of Perthshire down to the end of the eighteenth century, for at that time it was still customary in the beautiful parish of Logierait, between the river Tummel and the river Tay, to unloose carefully every knot in the clothes of the bride and bridegroom before the celebration of the marriage ceremony. We meet with the same superstition and the same custom at the present day in Syria. The persons who help a Syrian bridegroom to don his wedding garments take care that no knot is tied on them and no button buttoned, for they believe that a button buttoned or a knot tied would put it within the power of his enemies to deprive him of his nuptial rights by magical means. The fear of such charms is diffused all over North Africa at the present day. To render a bridegroom impotent the enchanter has only to tie a knot in a handkerchief which he had previously placed quietly on some part of the bridegroom's body when he was mounted on horseback ready to fetch his bride : so long as the knot in the handkerchief remains tied, so long will the bridegroom remain powerless to consummate the marriage.

The maleficent power of knots may also be manifested in the infliction of sickness, disease, and all kinds of misfortune. Thus among the Hos of West Africa a sorcerer will sometimes curse his enemy and tie a knot in a stalk of grass, saying, " I have tied up So-and-so in this knot. May all evil light upon him ! When he goes into the field, may a snake sting him ! When he goes to the chase, may a ravening beast attack him ! And when he steps into a river, may the water sweep him away ! When it rains, may the lightning strike him ! May evil nights be his ! " It is believed that in the knot the sorcerer has bound up the life of his enemy. In the Koran there is an allusion to the mischief of " those who puff into the knots," and an Arab commentator on the passage explains that the words refer to women who practise magic by tying knots in cords, and then blowing and spitting upon them. He goes on to relate how, once upon a time, a wicked Jew bewitched the prophet Mohammed himself by tying nine knots on a string, which he then hid in a well. So the prophet fell ill, and nobody knows what might have happened if the archangel Gabriel had not opportunely revealed to the holy man the place where the knotted cord was concealed. The trusty Ali soon fetched the baleful thing from the well ; and the prophet recited over it certain charms, which were specially revealed to him for the purpose. At every verse of the charms a knot untied itself, and the prophet experienced a certain relief.

R

If knots are supposed to kill, they are also supposed to cure. This follows from the belief that to undo the knots which are causing sickness will bring the sufferer relief. But apart from this negative virtue of maleficent knots, there are certain beneficent knots to which a positive power of healing is ascribed. Pliny tells us that some folk cured diseases of the groin by taking a thread from a web, tying seven or nine knots on it, and then fastening it to the patient's groin; but to make the cure effectual it was necessary to name some widow as each knot was tied. O'Donovan describes a remedy for fever employed among the Turcomans. The enchanter takes some camel hair and spins it into a stout thread, droning a spell the while. Next he ties seven knots on the thread, blowing on each knot before he pulls it tight. This knotted thread is then worn as a bracelet on his wrist by the patient. Every day one of the knots is untied and blown upon, and when the seventh knot is undone the whole thread is rolled up into a ball and thrown into a river, bearing away (as they imagine) the fever with it.

Again knots may be used by an enchantress to win a lover and attach him firmly to herself. Thus the love-sick maid in Virgil seeks to draw Daphnis to her from the city by spells and by tying three knots on each of three strings of different colours. So an Arab maiden, who had lost her heart to a certain man, tried to gain his love and bind him to herself by tying knots in his whip; but her jealous rival undid the knots. On the same principle magic knots may be employed to stop a runaway. In Swazieland you may often see grass tied in knots at the side of the footpaths. Every one of these knots tells of a domestic tragedy. A wife has run away from her husband, and he and his friends have gone in pursuit, binding up the paths, as they call it, in this fashion to prevent the fugitive from doubling back over them. A net, from its affluence of knots, has always been considered in Russia very efficacious against sorcerers; hence in some places, when a bride is being dressed in her wedding attire, a fishing-net is flung over her to keep her out of harm's way. For a similar purpose the bridegroom and his companions are often girt with pieces of net, or at least with tight-drawn girdles, for before a wizard can begin to injure them he must undo all the knots in the net, or take off the girdles. But often a Russian amulet is merely a knotted thread. A skein of red wool wound about the arms and legs is thought to ward off agues and fevers; and nine skeins, fastened round a child's neck, are deemed a preservative against scarlatina. In the Tver Government a bag of a special kind is tied to the neck of the cow which walks before the rest of a herd, in order to keep off wolves; its force binds the maw of the ravening beast. On the same principle, a padlock is carried thrice round a herd of horses before they go afield in the spring, and the bearer locks and unlocks it as he goes, saying, " I lock from my herd the mouths of the grey wolves with this steel lock."

Knots and locks may serve to avert not only wizards and

wolves but death itself.   When they brought a woman to the stake
at St. Andrews in 1572 to burn her alive for a witch, they found
on her a white cloth like a collar, with strings and many knots on
the strings.   They took it from her, sorely against her will, for she
seemed to think that she could not die in the fire, if only the cloth
with the knotted strings was on her.   When it was taken away, she
said, " Now I have no hope of myself."   In many parts of England it
is thought that a person cannot die so long as any locks are locked or
bolts shot in the house.   It is therefore a very common practice to
undo all locks and bolts when the sufferer is plainly near his end, in
order that his agony may not be unduly prolonged.   For example, in
the year 1863, at Taunton, a child lay sick of scarlatina and death
seemed inevitable.   " A jury of matrons was, as it were, empanelled,
and to prevent the child ' dying hard ' all the doors in the house, all the
drawers, all the boxes, all the cupboards were thrown wide open, the
keys taken out, and the body of the child placed under a beam,
whereby a sure, certain, and easy passage into eternity could be
secured."   Strange to say, the child declined to avail itself of the
facilities for dying so obligingly placed at its disposal by the sagacity
and experience of the British matrons of Taunton ; it preferred to
live rather than give up the ghost just then.

The rule which prescribes that at certain magical and religious
ceremonies the hair should hang loose and the feet should be bare is
probably based on the same fear of trammelling and impeding the
action in hand, whatever it may be, by the presence of any knot or
constriction, whether on the head or on the feet of the performer.   A
similar power to bind and hamper spiritual as well as bodily activities
is ascribed by some people to rings.   Thus in the island of Carpathus
people never button the clothes they put upon a dead body and they
are careful to remove all rings from it ; " for the spirit, they say, can
even be detained in the little finger, and cannot rest."   Here it is
plain that even if the soul is not definitely supposed to issue at death
from the finger-tips, yet the ring is conceived to exercise a certain
constrictive influence which detains and imprisons the immortal spirit
in spite of its efforts to escape from the tabernacle of clay ; in short
the ring, like the knot, acts as a spiritual fetter.   This may have been
the reason of an ancient Greek maxim, attributed to Pythagoras,
which forbade people to wear rings.   Nobody might enter the ancient
Arcadian sanctuary of the Mistress at Lycosura with a ring on his or
her finger.   Persons who consulted the oracle of Faunus had to be
chaste, to eat no flesh, and to wear no rings.

On the other hand, the same constriction which hinders the egress
of the soul may prevent the entrance of evil spirits ; hence we find
rings used as amulets against demons, witches, and ghosts.   In the
Tyrol it is said that a woman in childbed should never take off her
wedding-ring, or spirits and witches will have power over her.   Among
the Lapps, the person who is about to place a corpse in the coffin
receives from the husband, wife, or children of the deceased a brass

ring, which he must wear fastened to his right arm until the corpse is safely deposited in the grave. The ring is believed to serve the person as an amulet against any harm which the ghost might do to him. How far the custom of wearing finger-rings may have been influenced by, or even have sprung from, a belief in their efficacy as amulets to keep the soul in the body, or demons out of it, is a question which seems worth considering. Here we are only concerned with the belief in so far as it seems to throw light on the rule that the Flamen Dialis might not wear a ring unless it were broken. Taken in conjunction with the rule which forbade him to have a knot on his garments, it points to a fear that the powerful spirit embodied in him might be trammelled and hampered in its goings-out and comings-in by such corporeal and spiritual fetters as rings and knots.

CHAPTER XXII

TABOOED WORDS

§ 1. *Personal Names tabooed.*—Unable to discriminate clearly between words and things, the savage commonly fancies that the link between a name and the person or thing denominated by it is not a mere arbitrary and ideal association, but a real and substantial bond which unites the two in such a way that magic may be wrought on a man just as easily through his name as through his hair, his nails, or any other material part of his person. In fact, primitive man regards his name as a vital portion of himself and takes care of it accordingly. Thus, for example, the North American Indian " regards his name, not as a mere label, but as a distinct part of his personality, just as much as are his eyes or his teeth, and believes that injury will result as surely from the malicious handling of his name as from a wound inflicted on any part of his physical organism. This belief was found among the various tribes from the Atlantic to the Pacific, and has occasioned a number of curious regulations in regard to the concealment and change of names." Some Esquimaux take new names when they are old, hoping thereby to get a new lease of life. The Tolampoos of Celebes believe that if you write a man's name down you can carry off his soul along with it. Many savages at the present day regard their names as vital parts of themselves, and therefore take great pains to conceal their real names, lest these should give to evil-disposed persons a handle by which to injure their owners.

Thus, to begin with the savages who rank at the bottom of the social scale, we are told that the secrecy with which among the Australian aborigines personal names are often kept from general knowledge " arises in great measure from the belief that an enemy, who knows your name, has in it something which he can use magically to your detriment." " An Australian black," says another writer,

" is always very unwilling to tell his real name, and there is no doubt that this reluctance is due to the fear that through his name he may be injured by sorcerers." Amongst the tribes of Central Australia every man, woman, and child has, besides a personal name which is in common use, a secret or sacred name which is bestowed by the older men upon him or her soon after birth, and which is known to none but the fully initiated members of the group. This secret name is never mentioned except upon the most solemn occasions ; to utter it in the hearing of women or of men of another group would be a most serious breach of tribal custom, as serious as the most flagrant case of sacrilege among ourselves. When mentioned at all, the name is spoken only in a whisper, and not until the most elaborate precautions have been taken that it shall be heard by no one but members of the group. " The native thinks that a stranger knowing his secret name would have special power to work him ill by means of magic."

The same fear seems to have led to a custom of the same sort amongst the ancient Egyptians, whose comparatively high civilisation was strangely dashed and chequered with relics of the lowest savagery. Every Egyptian received two names, which were known respectively as the true name and the good name, or the great name and the little name ; and while the good or little name was made public, the true or great name appears to have been carefully concealed. A Brahman child receives two names, one for common use, the other a secret name which none but his father and mother should know. The latter is only used at ceremonies such as marriage. The custom is intended to protect the person against magic, since a charm only becomes effectual in combination with the real name. Similarly, the natives of Nias believe that harm may be done to a person by the demons who hear his name pronounced. Hence the names of infants, who are especially exposed to the assaults of evil spirits, are never spoken ; and often in haunted spots, such as the gloomy depths of the forest, the banks of a river, or beside a bubbling spring, men will abstain from calling each other by their names for a like reason.

The Indians of Chiloe keep their names secret and do not like to have them uttered aloud ; for they say that there are fairies or imps on the mainland or neighbouring islands who, if they knew folk's names, would do them an injury : but so long as they do not know the names, these mischievous sprites are powerless. The Araucanians will hardly ever tell a stranger their names because they fear that he would thereby acquire some supernatural power over themselves. Asked his name by a stranger, who is ignorant of their superstitions, an Araucanian will answer, " I have none." When an Ojebway is asked his name, he will look at some bystander and ask him to answer. " This reluctance arises from an impression they receive when young, that if they repeat their own names it will prevent their growth, and they will be small in stature. On account of this unwillingness to tell their names, many strangers have fancied that they either have no names or have forgotten them."

In this last case no scruple seems to be felt about communicating a man's name to strangers, and no ill effects appear to be dreaded as a consequence of divulging it ; harm is only done when a name is spoken by its owner. Why is this ? and why in particular should a man be thought to stunt his growth by uttering his own name ? We may conjecture that to savages who act and think thus a person's name only seems to be a part of himself when it is uttered with his own breath ; uttered by the breath of others it has no vital connexion with him, and no harm can come to him through it. Whereas, so these primitive philosophers may have argued, when a man lets his own name pass his lips, he is parting with a living piece of himself, and if he persists in so reckless a course he must certainly end by dissipating his energy and shattering his constitution. Many a broken-down debauchee, many a feeble frame wasted with disease, may have been pointed out by these simple moralists to their awe-struck disciples as a fearful example of the fate that must sooner or later overtake the profligate who indulges immoderately in the seductive habit of mentioning his own name.

However we may explain it, the fact is certain that many a savage evinces the strongest reluctance to pronounce his own name, while at the same time he makes no objection at all to other people pronouncing it, and will even invite them to do so for him in order to satisfy the curiosity of an inquisitive stranger. Thus in some parts of Madagascar it is taboo for a person to tell his own name, but a slave or attendant will answer for him. The same curious inconsistency, as it may seem to us, is recorded of some tribes of American Indians. Thus we are told that " the name of an American Indian is a sacred thing, not to be divulged by the owner himself without due consideration. One may ask a warrior of any tribe to give his name, and the question will be met with either a point-blank refusal or the more diplomatic evasion that he cannot understand what is wanted of him. The moment a friend approaches, the warrior first interrogated will whisper what is wanted, and the friend can tell the name, receiving a reciprocation of the courtesy from the other." This general statement applies, for example, to the Indian tribes of British Columbia, as to whom it is said that " one of their strangest prejudices, which appears to pervade all tribes alike, is a dislike to telling their names—thus you never get a man's right name from himself ; but they will tell each other's names without hesitation." In the whole of the East Indian Archipelago the etiquette is the same. As a general rule no one will utter his own name. To enquire, " What is your name ? " is a very indelicate question in native society. When in the course of administrative or judicial business a native is asked his name, instead of replying he will look at his comrade to indicate that he is to answer for him, or he will say straight out, " Ask him." The superstition is current all over the East Indies without exception, and it is found also among the Motu and Motumotu tribes, the Papuans of Finsch Haven in North New Guinea, the Nufoors of Dutch New Guinea, and the Melanesians of the

Bismarck Archipelago.   Among many tribes of South Africa men and women never mention their names if they can get any one else to do it for them, but they do not absolutely refuse when it cannot be avoided.

Sometimes the embargo laid on personal names is not permanent ; it is conditional on circumstances, and when these change it ceases to operate.   Thus when the Nandi men are away on a foray, nobody at home may pronounce the names of the absent warriors ; they must be referred to as birds.   Should a child so far forget itself as to mention one of the distant ones by name, the mother would rebuke it, saying, " Don't talk of the birds who are in the heavens."   Among the Bangala of the Upper Congo, while a man is fishing and when he returns with his catch, his proper name is in abeyance and nobody may mention it. Whatever the fisherman's real name may be, he is called *mwele* without distinction.   The reason is that the river is full of spirits, who, if they heard the fisherman's real name, might so work against him that he would catch little or nothing.   Even when he has caught his fish and landed with them, the buyer must still not address him by his proper name, but must only call him *mwele* ; for even then, if the spirits were to hear his proper name, they would either bear it in mind and serve him out another day, or they might so mar the fish he had caught that he would get very little for them.   Hence the fisherman can extract heavy damages from anybody who mentions his name, or can compel the thoughtless speaker to relieve him of the fish at a good price so as to restore his luck.   When the Sulka of New Britain are near the territory of their enemies the Gaktei, they take care not to mention them by their proper name, believing that were they to do so, their foes would attack and slay them.   Hence in these circumstances they speak of the Gaktei as *o lapsiek*, that is, " the rotten tree-trunks," and they imagine that by calling them that they make the limbs of their dreaded enemies ponderous and clumsy like logs.   This example illustrates the extremely materialistic view which these savages take of the nature of words ; they suppose that the mere utterance of an expression signifying clumsiness will homoeopathically affect with clumsiness the limbs of their distant foemen.   Another illustration of this curious misconception is furnished by a Caffre superstition that the character of a young thief can be reformed by shouting his name over a boiling kettle of medicated water, then clapping a lid on the kettle and leaving the name to steep in the water for several days.   It is not in the least necessary that the thief should be aware of the use that is being made of his name behind his back ; the moral reformation will be effected without his knowledge.

When it is deemed necessary that a man's real name should be kept secret, it is often customary, as we have seen, to call him by a surname or nickname.   As distinguished from the real or primary names, these secondary names are apparently held to be no part of the man himself, so that they may be freely used and divulged to everybody without endangering his safety thereby.   Sometimes in order to avoid the use of his own name a man will be called after his child. Thus we are informed that "the Gippsland blacks objected strongly to let any one outside the tribe know their names, lest their enemies, learning them, should make them vehicles of incantation, and so charm their lives away. As children were not thought to have enemies, they used to speak of a man as ' the father, uncle, or cousin of So-and-so,' naming a child ; but on all occasions abstained from mentioning the name of a grown-up person." The Alfoors of Poso in Celebes will not pronounce their own names. Among them, accordingly, if you wish to ascertain a person's name, you ought not to ask the man himself, but should enquire of others. But if this is impossible, for example, when there is no one else near, you should ask him his child's name, and then address him as the " Father of So-and-so." Nay, these Alfoors are shy of uttering the names even of children ; so when a boy or girl has a nephew or niece, he or she is addressed as " Uncle of So-and-so," or " Aunt of So-and-so." In pure Malay society, we are told, a man is never asked his name, and the custom of naming parents after their children is adopted only as a means of avoiding the use of the parents' own names. The writer who makes this statement adds in confirmation of it that childless persons are named after their younger brothers. Among the land Dyaks children as they grow up are called, according to their sex, the father or mother of a child of their father's or mother's younger brother or sister, that is, they are called the father or mother of what we should call their first cousin. The Caffres used to think it discourteous to call a bride by her own name, so they would call her " the Mother of So-and-so," even when she was only betrothed, far less a wife and a mother. Among the Kukis and Zemis or Kacha Nagas of Assam parents drop their names after the birth of a child and are named Father and Mother of So-and-so. Childless couples go by the name of " the childless father," " the childless mother," " the father of no child," " the mother of no child." The widespread custom of naming a father after his child has sometimes been supposed to spring from a desire on the father's part to assert his paternity, apparently as a means of obtaining those rights over his children which had previously, under a system of mother-kin, been possessed by the mother. But this explanation does not account for the parallel custom of naming the mother after her child, which seems commonly to coexist with the practice of naming the father after the child. Still less, if possible, does it apply to the customs of calling childless couples the father and mother of children which do not exist, of naming people after their younger brothers, and of designating children as the uncles and aunts of So-and-so, or as the fathers and mothers of their first cousins. But all these practices are explained in a simple and natural way if we suppose that they originate in a reluctance to utter the real names of persons addressed or directly referred to. That reluctance is probably based partly on a fear of attracting the notice of evil spirits, partly on a dread of revealing the name to sorcerers, who would thereby obtain a handle for injuring the owner of the name.

§ 2. *Names of Relations tabooed.*—It might naturally be expected that the reserve so commonly maintained with regard to personal names would be dropped or at least relaxed among relations and friends. But the reverse of this is often the case. It is precisely the persons most intimately connected by blood and especially by marriage to whom the rule applies with the greatest stringency. Such people are often forbidden, not only to pronounce each other's names, but even to utter ordinary words which resemble or have a single syllable in common with these names. The persons who are thus mutually debarred from mentioning each other's names are especially husbands and wives, a man and his wife's parents, and a woman and her husband's father. For example, among the Caffres a woman may not publicly pronounce the birth-name of her husband or of any of his brothers, nor may she use the interdicted word in its ordinary sense. If her husband, for instance, be called u-Mpaka, from *impaka*, a small feline animal, she must speak of that beast by some other name. Further, a Caffre wife is forbidden to pronounce even mentally the names of her father-in-law and of all her husband's male relations in the ascending line ; and whenever the emphatic syllable of any of their names occurs in another word, she must avoid it by substituting either an entirely new word, or, at least, another syllable in its place. Hence this custom has given rise to an almost distinct language among the women, which the Caffres call " women's speech." The interpretation of this " women's speech " is naturally very difficult, " for no definite rules can be given for the formation of these substituted words, nor is it possible to form a dictionary of them, their number being so great— since there may be many women, even in the same tribe, who would be no more at liberty to use the substitutes employed by some others, than they are to use the original words themselves." A Caffre man, on his side, may not mention the name of his mother-in-law, nor may she pronounce his ; but he is free to utter words in which the emphatic syllable of her name occurs. A Kirghiz woman dares not pronounce the names of the older relations of her husband, nor even use words which resemble them in sound. For example, if one of these relations is called Shepherd, she may not speak of sheep, but must call them " the bleating ones " ; if his name is Lamb, she must refer to lambs as " the young bleating ones." In Southern India wives believe that to tell their husband's name or to pronounce it even in a dream would bring him to an untimely end. Among the Sea Dyaks a man may not pronounce the name of his father-in-law or mother-in-law without incurring the wrath of the spirits. And since he reckons as his father-in-law and mother-in-law not only the father and mother of his own wife, but also the fathers and mothers of his brothers' wives and sisters' husbands, and likewise the fathers and mothers of all his cousins, the number of tabooed names may be very considerable and the opportunities of error correspondingly numerous. To make confusion worse confounded, the names of persons are often the names of common things, such as moon, bridge, barley, cobra, leopard ; so that when any of a man's many fathers-in-law and mothers-in-law are called by such names, these common words may not pass his lips. Among the Alfoors of Minahassa, in Celebes, the custom is carried still further so as to forbid the use even of words which merely resemble the personal names in sound. It is especially the name of a father-in-law which is thus laid under an interdict. If he, for example, is called Kalala, his son-in-law may not speak of a horse by its common name *kawalo* ; he must call it a " riding-beast " (*sasakajan*). So among the Alfoors of the island of Buru it is taboo to mention the names of parents and parents-in-law, or even to speak of common objects by words which resemble these names in sound. Thus, if your mother-in-law is called Dalu, which means " betel," you may not ask for betel by its ordinary name, you must ask for " red mouth " ; if you want betel-leaf, you may not say betel-leaf (*dalu 'mun*), you must say *karon fenna*. In the same island it is also taboo to mention the name of an elder brother in his presence. Transgressions of these rules are punished with fines. In Sunda it is thought that a particular crop would be spoilt if a man were to mention the names of his father and mother.

Among the Nufoors of Dutch New Guinea persons who are related to each other by marriage are forbidden to mention each other's names. Among the connexions whose names are thus tabooed are wife, mother-in-law, father-in-law, your wife's uncles and aunts and also her grand-uncles and grand-aunts, and the whole of your wife's or your husband's family in the same generation as yourself, except that men may mention the names of their brothers-in-law, though women may not. The taboo comes into operation as soon as the betrothal has taken place and before the marriage has been celebrated. Families thus connected by the betrothal of two of their members are not only forbidden to pronounce each other's names ; they may not even look at each other, and the rule gives rise to the most comical scenes when they happen to meet unexpectedly. And not merely the names themselves, but any words that sound like them are scrupulously avoided and other words used in their place. If it should chance that a person has inadvertently uttered a forbidden name, he must at once throw himself on the floor and say, " I have mentioned a wrong name. I throw it through the chinks of the floor in order that I may eat well."

In the western islands of Torres Straits a man never mentioned the personal names of his father-in-law, mother-in-law, brother-in-law, and sister-in-law ; and a woman was subject to the same restrictions. A brother-in-law might be spoken of as the husband or brother of some one whose name it was lawful to mention ; and similarly a sister-in-law might be called the wife of So-and-so. If a man by chance used the personal name of his brother-in-law, he was ashamed and hung his head. His shame was only relieved when he had made a present as compensation to the man whose name he had taken in vain. The same compensation was made to a sister-in-law, a father-in-law, and a mother-in-law for the accidental mention of their names.

Among the natives who inhabit the coast of the Gazelle Peninsula in
New Britain to mention the name of a brother-in-law is the grossest
possible affront you can offer to him ; it is a crime punishable with
death.   In the Banks' Islands, Melanesia, the taboos laid on the names
of persons connected by marriage are very strict.   A man will not
mention the name of his father-in-law, much less the name of his
mother-in-law, nor may he name his wife's brother ; but he may
name his wife's sister—she is nothing to him.   A woman may not
name her father-in-law, nor on any account her son-in-law.   Two
people whose children have intermarried are also debarred from
mentioning each other's names.   And not only are all these persons
forbidden to utter each other's names ; they may not even pronounce
ordinary words which chance to be either identical with these names
or to have any syllables in common with them.   Thus we hear of a
native of these islands who might not use the common words for
" pig " and " to die," because these words occurred in the polysyllabic
name of his son-in-law ; and we are told of another unfortunate who
might not pronounce the everyday words for " hand " and " hot "
on account of his wife's brother's name, and who was even debarred
from mentioning the number " one," because the word for " one "
formed part of the name of his wife's cousin.

The reluctance to mention the names or even syllables of the names
of persons connected with the speaker by marriage can hardly be
separated from the reluctance evinced by so many people to utter
their own names or the names of the dead or of chiefs and kings ;
and if the reticence as to these latter names springs mainly from
superstition, we may infer that the reticence as to the former has no
better foundation.   That the savage's unwillingness to mention his
own name is based, at least in part, on a superstitious fear of the ill
use that might be made of it by his foes, whether human or spiritual,
has already been shown.   It remains to examine the similar usage in
regard to the names of the dead and of royal personages.

§ 3. *Names of the Dead tabooed.*—The custom of abstaining from all
mention of the names of the dead was observed in antiquity by the
Albanians of the Caucasus, and at the present day it is in full force
among many savage tribes.   Thus we are told that one of the customs
most rigidly observed and enforced amongst the Australian aborigines
is never to mention the name of a deceased person, whether male or
female ; to name aloud one who has departed this life would be a gross
violation of their most sacred prejudices, and they carefully abstain
from it.   The chief motive for this abstinence appears to be a fear of
evoking the ghost, although the natural unwillingness to revive past
sorrows undoubtedly operates also to draw the veil of oblivion over
the names of the dead.   Once Mr. Oldfield so terrified a native by
shouting out the name of a deceased person, that the man fairly took
to his heels and did not venture to show himself again for several days.
At their next meeting he bitterly reproached the rash white man for
his indiscretion ; " nor could I," adds Mr. Oldfield, " induce him by

any means to utter the awful sound of a dead man's name, for by so doing he would have placed himself in the power of the malign spirits." Among the aborigines of Victoria the dead were very rarely spoken of, and then never by their names ; they were referred to in a subdued voice as " the lost one " or " the poor fellow that is no more." To speak of them by name would, it was supposed, excite the malignity of Couit-gil, the spirit of the departed, which hovers on earth for a time before it departs for ever towards the setting sun. Of the tribes on the Lower Murray River we are told that when a person dies " they carefully avoid mentioning his name ; but if compelled to do so, they pronounce it in a very low whisper, so faint that they imagine the spirit cannot hear their voice." Amongst the tribes of Central Australia no one may utter the name of the deceased during the period of mourning, unless it is absolutely necessary to do so, and then it is only done in a whisper for fear of disturbing and annoying the man's spirit which is walking about in ghostly form. If the ghost hears his name mentioned he concludes that his kinsfolk are not mourning for him properly ; if their grief were genuine they could not bear to bandy his name about. Touched to the quick by their hard-hearted indifference, the indignant ghost will come and trouble them in dreams.

The same reluctance to utter the names of the dead appears to prevail among all the Indian tribes of America from Hudson's Bay Territory to Patagonia. Among the Goajiros of Colombia to mention the dead before his kinsmen is a dreadful offence, which is often punished with death ; for if it happen on the *rancho* of the deceased, in presence of his nephew or uncle, they will assuredly kill the offender on the spot if they can. But if he escapes, the penalty resolves itself into a heavy fine, usually of two or more oxen.

A similar reluctance to mention the names of the dead is reported of peoples so widely separated from each other as the Samoyeds of Siberia and the Todas of Southern India ; the Mongols of Tartary and the Tuaregs of the Sahara ; the Ainos of Japan and the Akamba and Nandi of Eastern Africa ; the Tinguianes of the Philippines and the inhabitants of the Nicobar Islands, of Borneo, of Madagascar, and of Tasmania. In all cases, even where it is not expressly stated, the fundamental reason for this avoidance is probably the fear of the ghost. That this is the real motive with the Tuaregs we are positively informed. They dread the return of the dead man's spirit, and do all they can to avoid it by shifting their camp after a death, ceasing for ever to pronounce the name of the departed, and eschewing everything that might be regarded as an evocation or recall of his soul. Hence they do not, like the Arabs, designate individuals by adding to their personal names the names of their fathers ; they never speak of So-and-so, son of So-and-so ; they give to every man a name which will live and die with him. So among some of the Victorian tribes in Australia personal names were rarely perpetuated, because the natives believed that any one who adopted the name of a deceased person would not live long ; probably his ghostly namesake was supposed to come and fetch him away to the spirit-land.

The same fear of the ghost, which moves people to suppress his old name, naturally leads all persons who bear a similar name to exchange it for another, lest its utterance should attract the attention of the ghost, who cannot reasonably be expected to discriminate between all the different applications of the same name. Thus we are told that in the Adelaide and Encounter Bay tribes of South Australia the repugnance to mentioning the names of those who have died lately is carried so far, that persons who bear the same name as the deceased abandon it, and either adopt temporary names or are known by any others that happen to belong to them. A similar custom prevails among some of the Queensland tribes; but the prohibition to use the names of the dead is not permanent, though it may last for many years. In some Australian tribes the change of name thus brought about is permanent; the old name is laid aside for ever, and the man is known by his new name for the rest of his life, or at least until he is obliged to change it again for a like reason. Among the North American Indians all persons, whether men or women, who bore the name of one who had just died were obliged to abandon it and to adopt other names, which was formally done at the first ceremony of mourning for the dead. In some tribes to the east of the Rocky Mountains this change of name lasted only during the season of mourning, but in other tribes on the Pacific Coast of North America it seems to have been permanent.

Sometimes by an extension of the same reasoning all the near relations of the deceased change their names, whatever they may happen to be, doubtless from a fear that the sound of the familiar names might lure back the vagrant spirit to its old home. Thus in some Victorian tribes the ordinary names of all the next of kin were disused during the period of mourning, and certain general terms, prescribed by custom, were substituted for them. To call a mourner by his own name was considered an insult to the departed, and often led to fighting and bloodshed. Among Indian tribes of North-western America near relations of the deceased often change their names " under an impression that spirits will be attracted back to earth if they hear familiar names often repeated." Among the Kiowa Indians the name of the dead is never spoken in the presence of the relatives, and on the death of any member of a family all the others take new names. This custom was noted by Raleigh's colonists on Roanoke Island more than three centuries ago. Among the Lengua Indians not only is a dead man's name never mentioned, but all the survivors change their names also. They say that Death has been among them and has carried off a list of the living, and that he will soon come back for more victims; hence in order to defeat his fell purpose they change their names, believing that on his return Death, though he has got them all on his list, will not be able to identify them under their new names, and will depart to pursue the search elsewhere. Nicobarese mourners take new names in order to escape the unwelcome attentions of the ghost ; and for the same purpose they disguise themselves by shaving their heads so that the ghost is unable to recognise them.

Further, when the name of the deceased happens to be that of some common object, such as an animal, or plant, or fire, or water, it is sometimes considered necessary to drop that word in ordinary speech and replace it by another. A custom of this sort, it is plain, may easily be a potent agent of change in language ; for where it prevails to any considerable extent many words must constantly become obsolete and new ones spring up. And this tendency has been re-marked by observers who have recorded the custom in Australia, America, and elsewhere. For example, with regard to the Australian aborigines it has been noted that " the dialects change with almost every tribe. Some tribes name their children after natural objects ; and when the person so named dies, the word is never again mentioned ; another word has therefore to be invented for the object after which the child was called." The writer gives as an instance the case of a man whose name Karla signified " fire " ; when Karla died, a new word for fire had to be introduced. " Hence," adds the writer, " the language is always changing." Again, in the Encounter Bay tribe of South Australia, if a man of the name of Ngnke, which means " water," were to die, the whole tribe would be obliged to use some other word to express water for a considerable time after his decease. The writer who records this custom surmises that it may explain the presence of a number of synonyms in the language of the tribe. This conjecture is confirmed by what we know of some Victorian tribes whose speech comprised a regular set of synonyms to be used instead of the common terms by all members of a tribe in times of mourning. For instance, if a man called Waa (" crow ") departed this life, during the period of mourning for him nobody might call a crow a *waa* ; everybody had to speak of the bird as a *narrapart*. When a person who rejoiced in the title of Ringtail Opossum (*weearn*) had gone the way of all flesh, his sorrowing relations and the tribe at large were bound for a time to refer to ringtail opossums by the more sonorous name of *manuungkuurt*. If the community were plunged in grief for the loss of a respected female who bore the honourable name of Turkey Bustard, the proper name for turkey bustards, which was *barrim barrim*, went out, and *tillit tilliitsh* came in. And so *mutatis mutandis* with the names of Black Cockatoo, Grey Duck, Gigantic Crane, Kangaroo, Eagle, Dingo, and the rest.

A similar custom used to be constantly transforming the language of the Abipones of Paraguay, amongst whom, however, a word once abolished seems never to have been revived. New words, says the missionary Dobrizhoffer, sprang up every year like mushrooms in a night, because all words that resembled the names of the dead were abolished by proclamation and others coined in their place. The mint of words was in the hands of the old women of the tribe, and whatever term they stamped with their approval and put in circulation was immediately accepted without a murmur by high and low alike, and spread like wildfire through every camp and settlement of the tribe. You would be astonished, says the same missionary, to see how meekly the whole nation acquiesces in the decision of a withered old hag, and how completely the old familiar words fall instantly out of use and are never repeated either through force of habit or forgetfulness. In the seven years that Dobrizhoffer spent among these Indians the native word for jaguar was changed thrice, and the words for crocodile, thorn, and the slaughter of cattle underwent similar though less varied vicissitudes. As a result of this habit, the vocabularies of the missionaries teemed with erasures, old words having constantly to be struck out as obsolete and new ones inserted in their place. In many tribes of British New Guinea the names of persons are also the names of common things. The people believe that if the name of a deceased person is pronounced, his spirit will return, and as they have no wish to see it back among them the mention of his name is tabooed and a new word is created to take its place, whenever the name happens to be a common term of the language. Consequently many words are permanently lost or revived with modified or new meanings. In the Nicobar Islands a similar practice has similarly affected the speech of the natives. "A most singular custom," says Mr. de Roepstorff, "prevails among them which one would suppose must most effectually hinder the 'making of history,' or, at any rate, the transmission of historical narrative. By a strict rule, which has all the sanction of Nicobar superstition, no man's name may be mentioned after his death ! To such a length is this carried that when, as very frequently happens, the man rejoiced in the name of 'Fowl,' 'Hat,' 'Fire,' 'Road,' etc., in its Nicobarese equivalent, the use of these words is carefully eschewed for the future, not only as being the personal designation of the deceased, but even as the names of the common things they represent ; the words die out of the language, and either new vocables are coined to express the thing intended, or a substitute for the disused word is found in other Nicobarese dialects or in some foreign tongue. This extraordinary custom not only adds an element of instability to the language, but destroys the continuity of political life, and renders the record of past events precarious and vague, if not impossible."

That a superstition which suppresses the names of the dead must cut at the very root of historical tradition has been remarked by other workers in this field. "The Klamath people," observes Mr. A. S. Gatschet, "possess no historic traditions going further back in time than a century, for the simple reason that there was a strict law prohibiting the mention of the person or acts of a deceased individual by *using his name*. This law was rigidly observed among the Californians no less than among the Oregonians, and on its transgression the death penalty could be inflicted. This is certainly enough to suppress all historical knowledge within a people. How can history be written without names ? "

In many tribes, however, the power of this superstition to blot out the memory of the past is to some extent weakened and impaired by a natural tendency of the human mind. Time, which wears out the deepest impressions, inevitably dulls, if it does not wholly efface, the print left on the savage mind by the mystery and horror of death. Sooner or later, as the memory of his loved ones fades slowly away, he becomes more willing to speak of them, and thus their rude names may sometimes be rescued by the philosophic enquirer before they have vanished, like autumn leaves or winter snows, into the vast undistinguished limbo of the past. In some of the Victorian tribes the prohibition to mention the names of the dead remained in force only during the period of mourning ; in the Port Lincoln tribe of South Australia it lasted many years. Among the Chinook Indians of North America " custom forbids the mention of a dead man's name, at least till many years have elapsed after the bereavement." Among the Puyallup Indians the observance of the taboo is relaxed after several years, when the mourners have forgotten their grief ; and if the deceased was a famous warrior, one of his descendants, for instance a great-grandson, may be named after him. In this tribe the taboo is not much observed at any time except by the relations of the dead. Similarly the Jesuit missionary Lafitau tells us that the name of the departed and the similar names of the survivors were, so to say, buried with the corpse until, the poignancy of their grief being abated, it pleased the relations to " lift up the tree and raise the dead." By raising the dead they meant bestowing the name of the departed upon some one else, who thus became to all intents and purposes a reincarnation of the deceased, since on the principles of savage philosophy the name is a vital part, if not the soul, of the man.

Among the Lapps, when a woman was with child and near the time of her delivery, a deceased ancestor or relation used to appear to her in a dream and inform her what dead person was to be born again in her infant, and whose name the child was therefore to bear. If the woman had no such dream, it fell to the father or the relatives to determine the name by divination or by consulting a wizard. Among the Khonds a birth is celebrated on the seventh day after the event by a feast given to the priest and to the whole village. To determine the child's name the priest drops grains of rice into a cup of water, naming with each grain a deceased ancestor. From the movements of the seed in the water, and from observations made on the person of the infant, he pronounces which of his progenitors has reappeared in him, and the child generally, at least among the northern tribes, receives the name of that ancestor. Among the Yorubas, soon after a child has been born, a priest of Ifa, the god of divination, appears on the scene to ascertain what ancestral soul has been reborn in the infant. As soon as this has been decided, the parents are told that the child must conform in all respects to the manner of life of the ancestor who now animates him or her, and if, as often happens, they profess ignorance, the priest supplies the necessary information. The child usually receives the name of the ancestor who has been born again in him.

§ 4. *Names of Kings and other Sacred Persons tabooed.*—When we see that in primitive society the names of mere commoners, whether alive or dead, are matters of such anxious care, we need not be surprised that great precautions should be taken to guard from harm the names of sacred kings and priests. Thus the name of the king of Dahomey is always kept secret, lest the knowledge of it should enable some evil-minded person to do him a mischief. The appellations by which the different kings of Dahomey have been known to Europeans are not their true names, but mere titles, or what the natives call " strong names." The natives seem to think that no harm comes of such titles being known, since they are not, like the birth-names, vitally connected with their owners. In the Galla kingdom of Ghera the birth-name of the sovereign may not be pronounced by a subject under pain of death, and common words which resemble it in sound are changed for others. Among the Bahima of Central Africa, when the king dies, his name is abolished from the language, and if his name was that of an animal, a new appellation must be found for the creature at once. For example, the king is often called a lion ; hence at the death of a king named Lion a new name for lions in general has to be coined. In Siam it used to be difficult to ascertain the king's real name, since it was carefully kept secret from fear of sorcery ; any one who mentioned it was clapped into gaol. The king might only be referred to under certain high-sounding titles, such as " the august," " the perfect," " the supreme," " the great emperor," " descendant of the angels," and so on. In Burma it was accounted an impiety of the deepest dye to mention the name of the reigning sovereign ; Burmese subjects, even when they were far from their country, could not be prevailed upon to do so ; after his accession to the throne the king was known by his royal titles only.

Among the Zulus no man will mention the name of the chief of his tribe or the names of the progenitors of the chief, so far as he can remember them ; nor will he utter common words which coincide with or merely resemble in sound tabooed names. In the tribe of the Dwandwes there was a chief called Langa, which means the sun ; hence the name of the sun was changed from *langa* to *gala*, and so remains to this day, though Langa died more than a hundred years ago. Again, in the Xnumayo tribe the word meaning " to herd cattle " was changed from *alusa* or *ayusa* to *kagesa*, because u-Mayusi was the name of the chief. Besides these taboos, which were observed by each tribe separately, all the Zulu tribes united in tabooing the name of the king who reigned over the whole nation. Hence, for example, when Panda was king of Zululand, the word for " a root of a tree," which is *impando*, was changed to *nxabo*. Again, the word for " lies " or " slander " was altered from *amacebo* to *amakwata*, because *amacebo* contains a syllable of the name of the famous King Cetchwayo. These substitutions are not, however, carried so far by the men as by the women, who omit every sound even remotely resembling one that occurs in a tabooed name. At the king's kraal, indeed, it is sometimes difficult to understand the speech of the royal wives, as they treat in this fashion the names not only of the king and his forefathers, but even of his and their brothers back for generations. When to these tribal and national taboos we add those family taboos on the names of connexions by marriage which have been already described, we can easily understand how it comes about that in Zululand every tribe has words peculiar to itself, and that the women have a considerable vocabulary of their own. Members, too, of one family may be debarred from using words employed by those of another. The women of one kraal, for instance, may call a hyaena by its ordinary name ; those of the next may use the common substitute ; while in a third the substitute may also be unlawful and another term may have to be invented to supply its place. Hence the Zulu language at the present day almost presents the appearance of being a double one ; indeed, for multitudes of things it possesses three or four synonyms, which through the blending of tribes are known all over Zululand.

In Madagascar a similar custom everywhere prevails and has resulted, as among the Zulus, in producing certain dialectic differences in the speech of the various tribes. There are no family names in Madagascar, and almost every personal name is drawn from the language of daily life and signifies some common object or action or quality, such as a bird, a beast, a tree, a plant, a colour, and so on. Now, whenever one of these common words forms the name or part of the name of the chief of the tribe, it becomes sacred and may no longer be used in its ordinary signification as the name of a tree, an insect, or what not. Hence a new name for the object must be invented to replace the one which has been discarded. It is easy to conceive what confusion and uncertainty may thus be introduced into a language when it is spoken by many little local tribes each ruled by a petty chief with his own sacred name. Yet there are tribes and people who submit to this tyranny of words as their fathers did before them from time immemorial. The inconvenient results of the custom are especially marked on the western coast of the island, where, on account of the large number of independent chieftains, the names of things, places, and rivers have suffered so many changes that confusion often arises, for when once common words have been banned by the chiefs the natives will not acknowledge to have ever known them in their old sense.

But it is not merely the names of living kings and chiefs which are tabooed in Madagascar ; the names of dead sovereigns are equally under a ban, at least in some parts of the island. Thus among the Sakalavas, when a king has died, the nobles and people meet in council round the dead body and solemnly choose a new name by which the deceased monarch shall be henceforth known. After the new name has been adopted, the old name by which the king was known during his life becomes sacred and may not be pronounced under pain of death. Further, words in the common language which bear any resemblance to the forbidden name also become sacred and have to be replaced by others. Persons who uttered these forbidden words were looked on not only as grossly rude, but even as felons ; they had committed a capital crime. However, these changes of vocabulary are confined to the district over which the deceased king reigned ; in the neighbouring districts the old words continue to be employed in the old sense.

The sanctity attributed to the persons of chiefs in Polynesia naturally extended also to their names, which on the primitive view are hardly separable from the personality of their owners. Hence in Polynesia we find the same systematic prohibition to utter the names of chiefs or of common words resembling them which we have already met with in Zululand and Madagascar. Thus in New Zealand the name of a chief is held so sacred that, when it happens to be a common word, it may not be used in the language, and another has to be found to replace it. For example, a chief to the southward of East Cape bore the name of Maripi, which signified a knife, hence a new word (*nekra*) for knife was introduced, and the old one became obsolete. Elsewhere the word for water (*wai*) had to be changed, because it chanced to be the name of the chief, and would have been desecrated by being applied to the vulgar fluid as well as to his sacred person. This taboo naturally produced a plentiful crop of synonyms in the Maori language, and travellers newly arrived in the country were sometimes puzzled at finding the same things called by quite different names in neighbouring tribes. When a king comes to the throne in Tahiti, any words in the language that resemble his name in sound must be changed for others. In former times, if any man were so rash as to disregard this custom and to use the forbidden words, not only he but all his relations were immediately put to death. But the changes thus introduced were only temporary ; on the death of the king the new words fell into disuse, and the original ones were revived.

In ancient Greece the names of the priests and other high officials who had to do with the performance of the Eleusinian mysteries might not be uttered in their lifetime. To pronounce them was a legal offence. The pedant in Lucian tells how he fell in with these august personages haling along to the police court a ribald fellow who had dared to name them, though well he knew that ever since their consecration it was unlawful to do so, because they had become anonymous, having lost their old names and acquired new and sacred titles. From two inscriptions found at Eleusis it appears that the names of the priests were committed to the depths of the sea ; probably they were engraved on tablets of bronze or lead, which were then thrown into deep water in the Gulf of Salamis. The intention doubtless was to keep the names a profound secret ; and how could that be done more surely than by sinking them in the sea ? what human vision could spy them glimmering far down in the dim depths of the green water ? A clearer illustration of the confusion between the incorporeal and the corporeal, between the name and its material embodiment, could hardly be found than in this practice of civilised Greece.

§ 5. *Names of Gods tabooed.*—Primitive man creates his gods in his own image. Xenophanes remarked long ago that the complexion of negro gods was black and their noses flat ; that Thracian gods were ruddy and blue-eyed ; and that if horses, oxen, and lions only believed in gods and had hands wherewith to portray them, they would doubtless fashion their deities in the form of horses, and oxen, and lions. Hence just as the furtive savage conceals his real name because he fears that sorcerers might make an evil use of it, so he fancies that his gods must likewise keep their true names secret, lest other gods or even men should learn the mystic sounds and thus be able to conjure with them. Nowhere was this crude conception of the secrecy and magical virtue of the divine name more firmly held or more fully developed than in ancient Egypt, where the superstitions of a dateless past were embalmed in the hearts of the people hardly less effectually than the bodies of cats and crocodiles and the rest of the divine menagerie in their rock-cut tombs. The conception is well illustrated by a story which tells how the subtle Isis wormed his secret name from Ra, the great Egyptian god of the sun. Isis, so runs the tale, was a woman mighty in words, and she was weary of the world of men, and yearned after the world of the gods. And she meditated in her heart, saying, " Cannot I by virtue of the great name of Ra make myself a goddess and reign like him in heaven and earth ? " For Ra had many names, but the great name which gave him all power over gods and men was known to none but himself. Now the god was by this time grown old ; he slobbered at the mouth and his spittle fell upon the ground. So Isis gathered up the spittle and the earth with it, and kneaded thereof a serpent and laid it in the path where the great god passed every day to his double kingdom after his heart's desire. And when he came forth according to his wont, attended by all his company of gods, the sacred serpent stung him, and the god opened his mouth and cried, and his cry went up to heaven. And the company of gods cried, " What aileth thee ? " and the gods shouted, " Lo and behold ! " But he could not answer ; his jaws rattled, his limbs shook, the poison ran through his flesh as the Nile floweth over the land. When the great god had stilled his heart, he cried to his followers, " Come to me, O my children, offspring of my body. I am a prince, the son of a prince, the divine seed of a god. My father devised my name ; my father and my mother gave me my name, and it remained hidden in my body since my birth, that no magician might have magic power over me. I went out to behold that which I have made, I walked in the two lands which I have created, and lo ! something stung me. What it was, I know not. Was it fire ? was it water ? My heart is on fire, my flesh trembleth, all my limbs do quake. Bring me the children of the gods with healing words and understanding lips, whose power reacheth to heaven." Then came to him the children of the gods, and they were very sorrowful. And Isis came with her craft, whose mouth is full of the breath of life, whose spells chase pain away, whose word maketh the dead to live. She said, " What is it, divine Father ? what is it ? " The holy god opened his mouth, he spake and said, " I went upon my way, I walked after my heart's desire in the two regions which I have made to behold that which I have created, and lo ! a serpent that I saw not stung me. Is it fire ? is it water ? I am colder than water, I am hotter than fire, all my limbs sweat, I tremble, mine eye is not steadfast, I behold not the sky, the moisture bedeweth my face as in summer-time." Then spake Isis, " Tell me thy name, divine Father, for the man shall live who is called by his name." Then answered Ra, " I created the heavens and the earth, I ordered the mountains, I made the great and wide sea, I stretched out the two horizons like a curtain. I am he who openeth his eyes and it is light, and who shutteth them and it is dark. At his command the Nile riseth, but the gods know not his name. I am Khepera in the morning, I am Ra at noon, I am Tum at eve." But the poison was not taken away from him ; it pierced deeper, and the great god could no longer walk. Then said Isis to him, " That was not thy name that thou spakest unto me. Oh tell it me, that the poison may depart ; for he shall live whose name is named." Now the poison burned like fire, it was hotter than the flame of fire. The god said, " I consent that Isis shall search into me, and that my name shall pass from my breast into hers." Then the god hid himself from the gods, and his place in the ship of eternity was empty. Thus was the name of the great god taken from him, and Isis, the witch, spake, " Flow away poison, depart from Ra. It is I, even I, who overcome the poison and cast it to the earth ; for the name of the great god hath been taken away from him. Let Ra live and let the poison die." Thus spake great Isis, the queen of the gods, she who knows Ra and his true name."

From this story it appears that the real name of the god, with which his power was inextricably bound up, was supposed to be lodged, in an almost physical sense, somewhere in his breast, from which Isis extracted it by a sort of surgical operation and transferred with all its supernatural powers to herself. In Egypt attempts like that of Isis to appropriate the power of a high god by possessing herself of his name were not mere legends told of the mythical beings of a remote past ; every Egyptian magician aspired to wield like powers by similar means. For it was believed that he who possessed the true name possessed the very being of god or man, and could force even a deity to obey him as a slave obeys his master. Thus the art of the magician consisted in obtaining from the gods a revelation of their sacred names, and he left no stone unturned to accomplish his end. When once a god in a moment of weakness or forgetfulness had imparted to the wizard the wondrous lore, the deity had no choice but to submit humbly to the man or pay the penalty of his contumacy.

The belief in the magic virtue of divine names was shared by the Romans. When they sat down before a city, the priests addressed the guardian deity of the place in a set form of prayer or incantation, inviting him to abandon the beleaguered city and come over to the Romans, who would treat him as well as or better than he had ever been treated in his old home. Hence the name of the guardian deity of Rome was kept a profound secret, lest the enemies of the republic might lure him away, even as the Romans themselves had induced many gods to desert, like rats, the falling fortunes of cities that had sheltered them in happier days. Nay, the real name, not merely of its guardian deity, but of the city itself, was wrapt in mystery and might never be uttered, not even in the sacred rites. A certain Valerius Soranus, who dared to divulge the priceless secret, was put to death or came to a bad end. In like manner, it seems, the ancient Assyrians were forbidden to mention the mystic names of their cities ; and down to modern times the Cheremiss of the Caucasus keep the names of their communal villages secret from motives of superstition.

If the reader has had the patience to follow this examination of the superstitions attaching to personal names, he will probably agree that the mystery in which the names of royal personages are so often shrouded is no isolated phenomenon, no arbitrary expression of courtly servility and adulation, but merely the particular application of a general law of primitive thought, which includes within its scope common folk and gods as well as kings and priests.

CHAPTER XXIII

OUR DEBT TO THE SAVAGE

It would be easy to extend the list of royal and priestly taboos, but the instances collected in the preceding pages may suffice as specimens. To conclude this part of our subject it only remains to state summarily the general conclusions to which our enquiries have thus far conducted us. We have seen that in savage or barbarous society there are often found men to whom the superstition of their fellows ascribes a controlling influence over the general course of nature. Such men are accordingly adored and treated as gods. Whether these human divinities also hold temporal sway over the lives and fortunes of their adorers, or whether their functions are purely spiritual and supernatural, in other words, whether they are kings as well as gods or only the latter, is a distinction which hardly concerns us here. Their supposed divinity is the essential fact with which we have to deal. In virtue of it they are a pledge and guarantee to their worshippers of the continuance and orderly succession of those physical phenomena upon which mankind depends for subsistence. Naturally, therefore, the life and health of such a god-man are matters of anxious concern to the people whose welfare and even existence are bound up with his ; naturally he is constrained by them to conform to such rules as the wit of early man has devised for averting the ills to which flesh is heir, including the last ill, death. These rules, as an examination of them has shown, are nothing but the maxims with which, on the primitive view, every man of common prudence must comply if he would live long in the land. But while in the case of ordinary men the observance of the rules is left to the choice of the individual, in the case of the god-man it is enforced under penalty of dismissal from his high station, or even of death. For his worshippers have far too great a stake in his life to allow him to play fast and loose with it. Therefore all the quaint superstitions, the old-world maxims, the venerable saws which the ingenuity of savage philosophers elaborated long ago, and which old women at chimney corners still impart as treasures of great price to their descendants gathered round the cottage fire on winter evenings—all these antique fancies clustered, all these cobwebs of the brain were spun about the path of the old king, the human god, who, immeshed in them like a fly in the toils of a spider, could hardly stir a limb for the threads of custom, " light as air but strong as links of iron," that crossing and recrossing each other in an endless maze bound him fast within a network of observances from which death or deposition alone could release him.

Thus to students of the past the life of the old kings and priests teems with instruction. In it was summed up all that passed for wisdom when the world was young. It was the perfect pattern after which every man strove to shape his life ; a faultless model constructed with rigorous accuracy upon the lines laid down by a barbarous philosophy. Crude and false as that philosophy may seem to us, it would be unjust to deny it the merit of logical consistency. Starting from a conception of the vital principle as a tiny being or soul existing in, but distinct and separable from, the living being, it deduces for the practical guidance of life a system of rules which in general hangs well together and forms a fairly complete and harmonious whole. The flaw—and it is a fatal one—of the system lies not in its reasoning, but in its premises ; in its conception of the nature of life, not in any irrelevancy of the conclusions which it draws from that conception. But to stigmatise these premises as ridiculous because we can easily detect their falseness, would be ungrateful as well as unphilosophical. We stand upon the foundation reared by the generations that have gone before, and we can but dimly realise the painful and prolonged efforts which it has cost humanity to struggle up to the point, no very exalted one after all, which we have reached. Our gratitude is due to the nameless and forgotten toilers, whose patient thought and active exertions have largely made us what we are. The amount of new knowledge which one age, certainly which one man, can add to the common store is small, and it argues stupidity or dishonesty, besides ingratitude, to ignore the heap while vaunting the few grains which it may have been our privilege to add to it. There is indeed little danger at present of undervaluing the contributions which modern times and even classical antiquity have made to the general advancement of our race. But when we pass these limits, the case is different. Contempt and ridicule or abhorrence and denunciation are too often the only recognition vouchsafed to the savage and his ways. Yet of the benefactors whom we are bound thankfully to commemorate, many, perhaps most, were savages. For when all is said and done our resemblances to the savage are still far more numerous than our differences from him ; and what we have in common with him, and deliberately retain as true and useful, we owe to our savage forefathers who slowly acquired by experience and transmitted to us by inheritance those seemingly fundamental ideas which we are apt to regard as original and intuitive. We are like heirs to a fortune which has been handed down for so many ages that the memory of those who built it up is lost, and its possessors for the time being regard it as having been an original and unalterable possession of their race since the beginning of the world. But reflection and enquiry should satisfy us that to our predecessors we are indebted for much of what we thought most our own, and that their errors were not wilful extravagances or the ravings of insanity, but simply hypotheses, justifiable as such at the time when they were propounded, but which a fuller experience has proved to be inadequate. It is only by the successive testing of hypotheses and rejection of the false that truth is at last elicited. After all, what we call truth is only the hypothesis which is found to work best. Therefore in reviewing the opinions and practices of rude1 ages and races we shall do well to look with leniency upon their errors as inevitable slips made in the search for truth, and to give them the benefit of that indulgence which we ourselves may one day stand in need of : *cum excusatione itaque veteres audiendi sunt.*

CHAPTER XXIV

THE KILLING OF THE DIVINE KING

§ 1. *The Mortality of the Gods.*—Man has created gods in his own likeness and being himself mortal he has naturally supposed his creatures to be in the same sad predicament. Thus the Greenlanders believed that a wind could kill their most powerful god, and that he would certainly die if he touched a dog. When they heard of the Christian God, they kept asking if he never died, and being informed that he did not, they were much surprised, and said that he must be a very great god indeed. In answer to the enquiries of Colonel Dodge, a North American Indian stated that the world was made by the Great Spirit. Being asked which Great Spirit he meant, the good one or the bad one, " Oh, neither of *them*," replied he, " the Great Spirit that made the world is dead long ago. He could not possibly have lived as long as this." A tribe in the Philippine Islands told the Spanish conquerors that the grave of the Creator was upon the top of Mount Cabunian. Heitsi-eibib, a god or divine hero of the Hottentots, died several times and came to life again. His graves are generally to be met with in narrow defiles between mountains.   When the Hottentots pass one of them, they throw a stone on it for good luck, sometimes muttering " Give us plenty of cattle."   The grave of Zeus, the great god of Greece, was shown to visitors in Crete as late as about the beginning of our era.   The body of Dionysus was buried at Delphi beside the golden statue of Apollo, and his tomb bore the inscription, " Here lies Dionysus dead, the son of Semele."   According to one account, Apollo himself was buried at Delphi ; for Pythagoras is said to have carved an inscription on his tomb, setting forth how the god had been killed by the python and buried under the tripod.

The great gods of Egypt themselves were not exempt from the common lot.   They too grew old and died.   But when at a later time the discovery of the art of embalming gave a new lease of life to the souls of the dead by preserving their bodies for an indefinite time from corruption, the deities were permitted to share the benefit of an in- vention which held out to gods as well as to men a reasonable hope of immortality.   Every province then had the tomb and mummy of its dead god.   The mummy of Osiris was to be seen at Mendes ; Thinis boasted of the mummy of Anhouri ; and Heliopolis rejoiced in the possession of that of Toumou.   The high gods of Babylon also, though they appeared to their worshippers only in dreams and visions, were conceived to be human in their bodily shape, human in their passions, and human in their fate ; for like men they were born into the world, and like men they loved and fought and died.

§ 2. *Kings killed when their Strength fails.*—If the high gods, who dwell remote from the fret and fever of this earthly life, are yet believed to die at last, it is not to be expected that a god who lodges in a frail tabernacle of flesh should escape the same fate, though we hear of African kings who have imagined themselves immortal by virtue of their sorceries.   Now primitive peoples, as we have seen, sometimes believe that their safety and even that of the world is bound up with the life of one of these god-men or human incarnations of the divinity. Naturally, therefore, they take the utmost care of his life, out of a regard for their own.   But no amount of care and precaution will prevent the man-god from growing old and feeble and at last dying. His worshippers have to lay their account with this sad necessity and to meet it as best they can.   The danger is a formidable one ; for if the course of nature is dependent on the man-god's life, what cata- strophes may not be expected from the gradual enfeeblement of his powers and their final extinction in death ?   There is only one way of averting these dangers.   The man-god must be killed as soon as he shows symptoms that his powers are beginning to fail, and his soul must be transferred to a vigorous successor before it has been seriously impaired by the threatened decay.   The advantages of thus putting the man-god to death instead of allowing him to die of old age and disease are, to the savage, obvious enough.   For if the man-god dies what we call a natural death, it means, according to the savage, that his soul has either voluntarily departed from his body and refuses to return, or more commonly that it has been extracted, or at least detained in its wanderings, by a demon or sorcerer. In any of these cases the soul of the man-god is lost to his worshippers, and with it their prosperity is gone and their very existence endangered. Even if they could arrange to catch the soul of the dying god as it left his lips or his nostrils and so transfer it to a successor, this would not effect their purpose ; for, dying of disease, his soul would necessarily leave his body in the last stage of weakness and exhaustion, and so enfeebled it would continue to drag out a languid, inert existence in any body to which it might be transferred. Whereas by slaying him his worshippers could, in the first place, make sure of catching his soul as it escaped and transferring it to a suitable successor ; and, in the second place, by putting him to death before his natural force was abated, they would secure that the world should not fall into decay with the decay of the man-god. Every purpose, therefore, was answered, and all dangers averted by thus killing the man-god and transferring his soul, while yet at its prime, to a vigorous successor.

The mystic kings of Fire and Water in Cambodia are not allowed to die a natural death. Hence when one of them is seriously ill and the elders think that he cannot recover, they stab him to death. The people of Congo believed, as we have seen, that if their pontiff the Chitomé were to die a natural death, the world would perish, and the earth, which he alone sustained by his power and merit, would immediately be annihilated. Accordingly when he fell ill and seemed likely to die, the man who was destined to be his successor entered the pontiff's house with a rope or a club and strangled or clubbed him to death. The Ethiopian kings of Meroe were worshipped as gods ; but whenever the priests chose, they sent a messenger to the king, ordering him to die, and alleging an oracle of the gods as their authority for the command. This command the kings always obeyed down to the reign of Ergamenes, a contemporary of Ptolemy II., King of Egypt. Having received a Greek education which emancipated him from the superstitions of his countrymen, Ergamenes ventured to disregard the command of the priests, and, entering the Golden Temple with a body of soldiers, put the priests to the sword.

Customs of the same sort appear to have prevailed in this part of Africa down to modern times. In some tribes of Fazoql the king had to administer justice daily under a certain tree. If from sickness or any other cause he was unable to discharge this duty for three whole days, he was hanged on the tree in a noose, which contained two razors so arranged that when the noose was drawn tight by the weight of the king's body they cut his throat.

A custom of putting their divine kings to death at the first symptoms of infirmity or old age prevailed until lately, if indeed it is even now extinct and not merely dormant, among the Shilluk of the White Nile, and in recent years it has been carefully investigated by Dr. C. G. Seligman. The reverence which the Shilluk pay to their king appears to arise chiefly from the conviction that he is a reincarnation of the spirit of Nyakang, the semi-divine hero who founded the dynasty and settled the tribe in their present territory. It is a fundamental article of the Shilluk creed that the spirit of the divine or semi-divine Nyakang is incarnate in the reigning king, who is accordingly himself invested to some extent with the character of a divinity. But while the Shilluk hold their kings in high, indeed religious reverence and take every precaution against their accidental death, nevertheless they cherish " the conviction that the king must not be allowed to become ill or senile, lest with his diminishing vigour the cattle should sicken and fail to bear their increase, the crops should rot in the fields, and man, stricken with disease, should die in ever-increasing numbers." To prevent these calamities it used to be the regular custom with the Shilluk to put the king to death whenever he showed signs of ill-health or failing strength. One of the fatal symptoms of decay was taken to be an incapacity to satisfy the sexual passions of his wives, of whom he has very many, distributed in a large number of houses at Fashoda. When this ominous weakness manifested itself, the wives reported it to the chiefs, who are popularly said to have intimated to the king his doom by spreading a white cloth over his face and knees as he lay slumbering in the heat of the sultry afternoon. Execution soon followed the sentence of death. A hut was specially built for the occasion : the king was led into it and lay down with his head resting on the lap of a nubile virgin : the door of the hut was then walled up ; and the couple were left without food, water, or fire to die of hunger and suffocation. This was the old custom, but it was abolished some five generations ago on account of the excessive sufferings of one of the kings who perished in this way. It is said that the chiefs announce his fate to the king, and that afterwards he is strangled in a hut which has been specially built for the occasion.

From Dr. Seligman's enquiries it appears that not only was the Shilluk king liable to be killed with due ceremony at the first symptoms of incipient decay, but even while he was yet in the prime of health and strength he might be attacked at any time by a rival and have to defend his crown in a combat to the death. According to the common Shilluk tradition any son of a king had the right thus to fight the king in possession and, if he succeeded in killing him, to reign in his stead. As every king had a large harem and many sons, the number of possible candidates for the throne at any time may well have been not inconsiderable, and the reigning monarch must have carried his life in his hand. But the attack on him could only take place with any prospect of success at night ; for during the day the king surrounded himself with his friends and bodyguards, and an aspirant to the throne could hardly hope to cut his way through them and strike home. It was otherwise at night. For then the guards were dismissed and the king was alone in his enclosure with his favourite wives, and there was no man near to defend him except a few herdsmen, whose huts stood a little way off. The hours of darkness were therefore the season of peril for the king. It is said that he used to pass them in constant watchfulness, prowling round his huts fully armed, peering into the blackest shadows, or himself standing silent and alert, like a sentinel on duty, in some dark corner. When at last his rival appeared, the fight would take place in grim silence, broken only by the clash of spears and shields, for it was a point of honour with the king not to call the herdsmen to his assistance.

Like Nyakang himself, their founder, each of the Shilluk kings after death is worshipped at a shrine, which is erected over his grave, and the grave of a king is always in the village where he was born. The tomb-shrine of a king resembles the shrine of Nyakang, consisting of a few huts enclosed by a fence ; one of the huts is built over the king's grave, the others are occupied by the guardians of the shrine. Indeed the shrines of Nyakang and the shrines of the kings are scarcely to be distinguished from each other, and the religious rituals observed at all of them are identical in form and vary only in matters of detail, the variations being due apparently to the far greater sanctity attributed to the shrines of Nyakang. The grave-shrines of the kings are tended by certain old men or women, who correspond to the guardians of the shrines of Nyakang. They are usually widows or old men-servants of the deceased king, and when they die they are succeeded in their office by their descendants. Moreover, cattle are dedicated to the grave-shrines of the kings and sacrifices are offered at them just as at the shrines of Nyakang.

In general the principal element in the religion of the Shilluk would seem to be the worship which they pay to their sacred or divine kings, whether dead or alive. These are believed to be animated by a single divine spirit, which has been transmitted from the semi-mythical, but probably in substance historical, founder of the dynasty through all his successors to the present day. Hence, regarding their kings as incarnate divinities on whom the welfare of men, of cattle, and of the corn implicitly depends, the Shilluk naturally pay them the greatest respect and take every care of them ; and however strange it may seem to us, their custom of putting the divine king to death as soon as he shows signs of ill-health or failing strength springs directly from their profound veneration for him and from their anxiety to preserve him, or rather the divine spirit by which he is animated, in the most perfect state of efficiency : nay, we may go further and say that their practice of regicide is the best proof they can give of the high regard in which they hold their kings. For they believe, as we have seen, that the king's life or spirit is so sympathetic-ally bound up with the prosperity of the whole country, that if he fell ill or grew senile the cattle would sicken and cease to multiply, the crops would rot in the fields, and men would perish of widespread disease. Hence, in their opinion, the only way of averting these calamities is to put the king to death while he is still hale and hearty, in order that the divine spirit which he has inherited from his pre-decessors may be transmitted in turn by him to his successor while it is still in full vigour and has not yet been impaired by the weakness of disease and old age. In this connexion the particular symptom which is commonly said to seal the king's death-warrant is highly significant; when he can no longer satisfy the passions of his numerous wives, in other words, when he has ceased, whether partially or wholly, to be able to reproduce his kind, it is time for him to die and to make room for a more vigorous successor. Taken along with the other reasons which are alleged for putting the king to death, this one suggests that the fertility of men, of cattle, and of the crops is believed to depend sympathetically on the generative power of the king, so that the complete failure of that power in him would involve a corresponding failure in men, animals, and plants, and would thereby entail at no distant date the entire extinction of all life, whether human, animal, or vegetable. No wonder, that with such a danger before their eyes the Shilluk should be most careful not to let the king die what we should call a natural death of sickness or old age. It is characteristic of their attitude towards the death of the kings that they refrain from speaking of it as death : they do not say that a king has died but simply that he has " gone away " like his divine ancestors Nyakang and Dag, the two first kings of the dynasty, both of whom are reported not to have died but to have disappeared. The similar legends of the mysterious disappearance of early kings in other lands, for example at Rome and in Uganda, may well point to a similar custom of putting them to death for the purpose of preserving their life.

On the whole the theory and practice of the divine kings of the Shilluk correspond very nearly to the theory and practice of the priests of Nemi, the Kings of the Wood, if my view of the latter is correct. In both we see a series of divine kings on whose life the fertility of men, of cattle, and of vegetation is believed to depend, and who are put to death, whether in single combat or otherwise, in order that their divine spirit may be transmitted to their successors in full vigour, uncontaminated by the weakness and decay of sickness or old age, because any such degeneration on the part of the king would, in the opinion of his worshippers, entail a corresponding degeneration on mankind, on cattle, and on the crops. Some points in this explanation of the custom of putting divine kings to death, particularly the method of transmitting their divine souls to their successors, will be dealt with more fully in the sequel. Meantime we pass to other examples of the general practice.

The Dinka are a congeries of independent tribes in the valley of the White Nile. They are essentially a pastoral people, passionately devoted to the care of their numerous herds of oxen, though they also keep sheep and goats, and the women cultivate small quantities of millet and sesame. For their crops and above all for their pastures they depend on the regularity of the rains : in seasons of prolonged drought they are said to be reduced to great extremities. Hence the rain-maker is a very important personage among them to this day; indeed the men in authority whom travellers dub chiefs or sheikhs are in fact the actual or potential rain-makers of the tribe or community. Each of them is believed to be animated by the spirit of a great rain-maker, which has come down to him through a succession of rain-makers; and in virtue of this inspiration a successful rain-maker enjoys very great power and is consulted on all important matters. Yet in spite, or rather in virtue, of the high honour in which he is held, no Dinka rain-maker is allowed to die a natural death of sickness or old age; for the Dinka believe that if such an untoward event were to happen, the tribe would suffer from disease and famine, and the herds would not yield their increase. So when a rain-maker feels that he is growing old and infirm, he tells his children that he wishes to die. Among the Agar Dinka a large grave is dug and the rain-maker lies down in it, surrounded by his friends and relatives. From time to time he speaks to the people, recalling the past history of the tribe, reminding them how he has ruled and advised them, and instructing them how they are to act in the future. Then, when he has concluded his admonition, he bids them cover him up. So the earth is thrown down on him as he lies in the grave, and he soon dies of suffocation. Such, with minor variations, appears to be the regular end of the honourable career of a rain-maker in all the Dinka tribes. The Khor-Adar Dinka told Dr. Seligman that when they have dug the grave for their rain-maker they strangle him in his house. The father and paternal uncle of one of Dr. Seligman's informants had both been rain-makers and both had been killed in the most regular and orthodox fashion. Even if a rain-maker is quite young he will be put to death should he seem likely to perish of disease. Further, every precaution is taken to prevent a rain-maker from dying an accidental death, for such an end, though not nearly so serious a matter as death from illness or old age, would be sure to entail sickness on the tribe. As soon as a rain-maker is killed, his valuable spirit is supposed to pass to a suitable successor, whether a son or other near blood relation.

In the Central African kingdom of Bunyoro down to recent years custom required that as soon as the king fell seriously ill or began to break up from age, he should die by his own hand; for, according to an old prophecy, the throne would pass away from the dynasty if ever the king were to die a natural death. He killed himself by draining a poisoned cup. If he faltered or were too ill to ask for the cup, it was his wife's duty to administer the poison. When the king of Kibanga, on the Upper Congo, seems near his end, the sorcerers put a rope round his neck, which they draw gradually tighter till he dies. If the king of Gingiro happens to be wounded in war, he is put to death by his comrades, or, if they fail to kill him, by his kinsfolk, however hard he may beg for mercy. They say they do it that he may not die by the hands of his enemies. The Jukos are a heathen tribe of the Benue river, a great tributary of the Niger. In their country " the town of Gatri is ruled by a king who is elected by the

big men of the town as follows. When in the opinion of the big
men the king has reigned long enough, they give out that ' the king
is sick '—a formula understood by all to mean that they are going to
kill him, though the intention is never put more plainly. They then
decide who is to be the next king. How long he is to reign is settled
by the influential men at a meeting ; the question is put and answered
by each man throwing on the ground a little piece of stick for each
year he thinks the new king should rule. The king is then told, and
a great feast prepared, at which the king gets drunk on guinea-corn
beer. After that he is speared, and the man who was chosen becomes
king. Thus each Juko king knows that he cannot have very many
more years to live, and that he is certain of his predecessor's fate.
This, however, does not seem to frighten candidates. The same
custom of king-killing is said to prevail at Quonde and Wukari as
well as at Gatri." In the three Hausa kingdoms of Gobir, Katsina,
and Daura, in Northern Nigeria, as soon as a king showed signs of
failing health or growing infirmity, an official who bore the title of
Killer of the Elephant appeared and throttled him.

The Matiamvo is a great king or emperor in the interior of Angola.
One of the inferior kings of the country, by name Challa, gave to a
Portuguese expedition the following account of the manner in which
the Matiamvo comes by his end. " It has been customary," he said,
" for our Matiamvos to die either in war or by a violent death, and
the present Matiamvo must meet this last fate, as, in consequence
of his great exactions, he has lived long enough. When we come to
this understanding, and decide that he should be killed, we invite
him to make war with our enemies, on which occasion we all accompany
him and his family to the war, when we lose some of our people. If
he escapes unhurt, we return to the war again and fight for three or
four days. We then suddenly abandon him and his family to their
fate, leaving him in the enemy's hands. Seeing himself thus deserted,
he causes his throne to be erected, and, sitting down, calls his family
around him. He then orders his mother to approach ; she kneels
at his feet ; he first cuts off her head, then decapitates his sons in
succession, next his wives and relatives, and, last of all, his most
beloved wife, called Anacullo. This slaughter being accomplished,
the Matiamvo, dressed in all his pomp, awaits his own death, which
immediately follows, by an officer sent by the powerful neighbouring
chiefs, Caniquinha and Canica. This officer first cuts off his legs
and arms at the joints, and lastly he cuts off his head ; after which
the head of the officer is struck off. All the potentates retire from the
encampment, in order not to witness his death. It is my duty to
remain and witness his death, and to mark the place where the head
and arms have been deposited by the two great chiefs, the enemies
of the Matiamvo. They also take possession of all the property
belonging to the deceased monarch and his family, which they convey
to their own residence. I then provide for the funeral of the mutilated
remains of the late Matiamvo, after which I retire to his capital and

proclaim the new government. I then return to where the head, legs, and arms have been deposited, and, for forty slaves, I ransom them, together with the merchandise and other property belonging to the deceased, which I give up to the new Matiamvo, who has been proclaimed. This is what has happened to many Matiamvos, and what must happen to the present one."

It appears to have been a Zulu custom to put the king to death as soon as he began to have wrinkles or grey hairs. At least this seems implied in the following passage written by one who resided for some time at the court of the notorious Zulu tyrant Chaka, in the early part of the nineteenth century : " The extraordinary violence of the king's rage with me was mainly occasioned by that absurd nostrum, the hair oil, with the notion of which Mr. Farewell had impressed him as being a specific for removing all indications of age. From the first moment of his having heard that such a preparation was attainable, he evinced a solicitude to procure it, and on every occasion never forgot to remind us of his anxiety respecting it ; more especially on our departure on the mission his injunctions were particularly directed to this object. It will be seen that it is one of the barbarous customs of the Zoolas in their choice or election of their kings that he must neither have wrinkles nor grey hairs, as they are both distinguishing marks of disqualification for becoming a monarch of a warlike people. It is also equally indispensable that their king should never exhibit those proofs of having become unfit and incompetent to reign ; it is therefore important that they should conceal these indications so long as they possibly can. Chaka had become greatly apprehensive of the approach of grey hairs ; which would at once be the signal for him to prepare to make his exit from this sublunary world, it being always followed by the death of the monarch." The writer to whom we are indebted for this instructive anecdote of the hair oil omits to specify the mode in which a grey-haired and wrinkled Zulu chief used " to make his exit from this sublunary world " ; but on analogy we may conjecture that he was killed.

The custom of putting kings to death as soon as they suffered from any personal defect prevailed two centuries ago in the Caffre kingdom of Sofala. We have seen that these kings of Sofala were regarded as gods by their people, being entreated to give rain or sunshine, according as each might be wanted. Nevertheless a slight bodily blemish, such as the loss of a tooth, was considered a sufficient cause for putting one of these god-men to death, as we learn from the following passage of an old Portuguese historian : " It was formerly the custom of the kings of this land to commit suicide by taking poison when any disaster or natural physical defect fell upon them, such as impotence, infectious disease, the loss of their front teeth, by which they were disfigured, or any other deformity or affliction. To put an end to such defects they killed themselves, saying that the king should be free from any blemish, and if not, it was better for his honour that he should die and seek another life where he would be made whole, for there everything was perfect.   But the Quiteve (king) who reigned when I was in those parts would not imitate his predecessors in this, being discreet and dreaded as he was ; for having lost a front tooth he caused it to be proclaimed throughout the kingdom that all should be aware that he had lost a tooth and should recognise him when they saw him without it, and if his predecessors killed themselves for such things they were very foolish, and he would not do so ; on the contrary, he would be very sorry when the time came for him to die a natural death, for his life was very necessary to preserve his kingdom and defend it from his enemies ; and he recommended his successors to follow his example."

The king of Sofala who dared to survive the loss of his front tooth was thus a bold reformer like Ergamenes, king of Ethiopia.   We may conjecture that the ground for putting the Ethiopian kings to death was, as in the case of the Zulu and Sofala kings, the appearance on their person of any bodily defect or sign of decay ; and that the oracle which the priests alleged as the authority for the royal execution was to the effect that great calamities would result from the reign of a king who had any blemish on his body ; just as an oracle warned Sparta against a " lame reign," that is, the reign of a lame king.   It is some confirmation of this conjecture that the kings of Ethiopia were chosen for their size, strength, and beauty long before the custom of killing them was abolished.   To this day the Sultan of Wadai must have no obvious bodily defect, and the king of Angoy cannot be crowned if he has a single blemish, such as a broken or a filed tooth or the scar of an old wound.   According to the Book of Acaill and many other authorities no king who was afflicted with a personal blemish might reign over Ireland at Tara.   Hence, when the great King Cormac Mac Art lost one eye by an accident, he at once abdicated.

Many days' journey to the north-east of Abomey, the old capital of Dahomey, lies the kingdom of Eyeo.   "The Eyeos are governed by a king, no less absolute than the king of Dahomey, yet subject to a regulation of state, at once humiliating and extraordinary.   When the people have conceived an opinion of his ill-government, which is sometimes insidiously infused into them by the artifice of his discontented ministers, they send a deputation to him with a present of parrots' eggs, as a mark of its authenticity, to represent to him that the burden of government must have so far fatigued him that they consider it full time for him to repose from his cares and indulge himself with a little sleep.   He thanks his subjects for their attention to his ease, retires to his own apartment as if to sleep, and there gives directions to his women to strangle him.   This is immediately executed, and his son quietly ascends the throne upon the usual terms of holding the reins of government no longer than whilst he merits the approbation of the people."   About the year 1774, a king of Eyeo, whom his ministers attempted to remove in the customary manner, positively refused to accept the proffered parrots' eggs at their hands, telling

T

them that he had no mind to take a nap, but on the contrary was resolved to watch for the benefit of his subjects. The ministers, surprised and indignant at his recalcitrancy, raised a rebellion, but were defeated with great slaughter, and thus by his spirited conduct the king freed himself from the tyranny of his councillors and established a new precedent for the guidance of his successors. However, the old custom seems to have revived and persisted until late in the nineteenth century, for a Catholic missionary, writing in 1884, speaks of the practice as if it were still in vogue. Another missionary, writing in 1881, thus describes the usage of the Egbas and the Yorubas of West Africa : " Among the customs of the country one of the most curious is unquestionably that of judging and punishing the king. Should he have earned the hatred of his people by exceeding his rights, one of his councillors, on whom the heavy duty is laid, requires of the prince that he shall ' go to sleep,' which means simply ' take poison and die.' If his courage fails him at the supreme moment, a friend renders him this last service, and quietly, without betraying the secret, they prepare the people for the news of the king's death. In Yoruba the thing is managed a little differently. When a son is born to the king of Oyo, they make a model of the infant's right foot in clay and keep it in the house of the elders (*ogboni*). If the king fails to observe the customs of the country, a messenger, without speaking a word, shows him his child's foot. The king knows what that means. He takes poison and goes to sleep." The old Prussians acknowledged as their supreme lord a ruler who governed them in the name of the gods, and was known as " God's Mouth." When he felt himself weak and ill, if he wished to leave a good name behind him, he had a great heap made of thorn-bushes and straw, on which he mounted and delivered a long sermon to the people, exhorting them to serve the gods and promising to go to the gods and speak for the people. Then he took some of the perpetual fire which burned in front of the holy oak-tree, and lighting the pile with it burned himself to death.

§ 3. *Kings killed at the End of a Fixed Term.*—In the cases hitherto described, the divine king or priest is suffered by his people to retain office until some outward defect, some visible symptom of failing health or advancing age, warns them that he is no longer equal to the discharge of his divine duties ; but not until such symptoms have made their appearance is he put to death. Some peoples, however, appear to have thought it unsafe to wait for even the slightest symptom of decay and have preferred to kill the king while he was still in the full vigour of life. Accordingly, they have fixed a term beyond which he might not reign, and at the close of which he must die, the term fixed upon being short enough to exclude the probability of his degenerating physically in the interval. In some parts of Southern India the period fixed was twelve years. Thus, according to an old traveller, in the province of Quilacare, " there is a Gentile house of prayer, in which there is an idol which they hold in great account, and every twelve years they celebrate a great feast to it, whither all the Gentiles go as to a jubilee. This temple possesses many lands and much revenue : it is a very great affair. This province has a king over it, who has not more than twelve years to reign from jubilee to jubilee. His manner of living is in this wise, that is to say : when the twelve years are completed, on the day of this feast there assemble together innumerable people, and much money is spent in giving food to Bramans. The king has a wooden scaffolding made, spread over with silken hangings : and on that day he goes to bathe at a tank with great ceremonies and sound of music, after that he comes to the idol and prays to it, and mounts on to the scaffolding, and there before all the people he takes some very sharp knives, and begins to cut off his nose, and then his ears, and his lips, and all his members, and as much flesh off himself as he can ; and he throws it away very hurriedly until so much of his blood is spilled that he begins to faint, and then he cuts his throat himself. And he performs this sacrifice to the idol, and whoever desires to reign other twelve years and under-take this martyrdom for love of the idol, has to be present looking on at this : and from that place they raise him up as king."

The king of Calicut, on the Malabar coast, bears the title of Samorin or Samory. He " pretends to be of a higher rank than the Brahmans, and to be inferior only to the invisible gods ; a pretention that was acknowledged by his subjects, but which is held as absurd and abomin-able by the Brahmans, by whom he is only treated as a Sudra." Formerly the Samorin had to cut his throat in public at the end of a twelve years' reign. But towards the end of the seventeenth century the rule had been modified as follows : " Many strange customs were observed in this country in former times, and some very odd ones are still continued. It was an ancient custom for the Samorin to reign but twelve years, and no longer. If he died before his term was expired, it saved him a troublesome ceremony of cutting his own throat, on a publick scaffold erected for the purpose. He first made a feast for all his nobility and gentry, who are very numerous. After the feast he saluted his guests, and went on the scaffold, and very decently cut his own throat in the view of the assembly, and his body was, a little while after, burned with great pomp and ceremony, and the grandees elected a new Samorin. Whether that custom was a religious or a civil ceremony, I know not, but it is now laid aside. And a new custom is followed by the modern Samorins, that jubilee is proclaimed throughout his dominions, at the end of twelve years, and a tent is pitched for him in a spacious plain, and a great feast is celebrated for ten or twelve days, with mirth and jollity, guns firing night and day, so at the end of the feast any four of the guests that have a mind to gain a crown by a desperate action, in fighting their way through 30 or 40,000 of his guards, and kill the Samorin in his tent, he that kills him succeeds him in his empire. In anno 1695, one of those jubilees happened, and the tent pitched near Pennany, a seaport of his, about fifteen leagues to the southward of Calicut. There were but three men that would venture on that desperate action, who fell in, with sword and target, among the guard, and, after they had killed and wounded many, were themselves killed. One of the desperados had a nephew of fifteen or sixteen years of age, that kept close by his uncle in the attack on the guards, and, when he saw him fall, the youth got through the guards into the tent, and made a stroke at his Majesty's head, and had certainly despatched him if a large brass lamp which was burning over his head had not marred the blow ; but, before he could make another, he was killed by the guards ; and, I believe, the same Samorin reigns yet. I chanced to come that time along the coast and heard the guns for two or three days and nights successively."

The English traveller, whose account I have quoted, did not himself witness the festival he describes, though he heard the sound of the firing in the distance. Fortunately, exact records of these festivals and of the number of men who perished at them have been preserved in the archives of the royal family at Calicut. In the latter part of the nineteenth century they were examined by Mr. W. Logan, with the personal assistance of the reigning king, and from his work it is possible to gain an accurate conception both of the tragedy and of the scene where it was periodically enacted down to 1743, when the ceremony took place for the last time.

The festival at which the king of Calicut staked his crown and his life on the issue of battle was known as the " Great Sacrifice." It fell every twelfth year, when the planet Jupiter was in retrograde motion in the sign of the Crab, and it lasted twenty-eight days, culminating at the time of the eighth lunar asterism in the month of Makaram. As the date of the festival was determined by the position of Jupiter in the sky, and the interval between two festivals was twelve years, which is roughly Jupiter's period of revolution round the sun, we may conjecture that the splendid planet was supposed to be in a special sense the king's star and to rule his destiny, the period of its revolution in heaven corresponding to the period of his reign on earth. However that may be, the ceremony was observed with great pomp at the Tirunavayi temple, on the north bank of the Ponnani River. The spot is close to the present railway line. As the train rushes by, you can just catch a glimpse of the temple, almost hidden behind a clump of trees on the river bank. From the western gateway of the temple a perfectly straight road, hardly raised above the level of the surrounding rice-fields and shaded by a fine avenue, runs for half a mile to a high ridge with a precipitous bank, on which the outlines of three or four terraces can still be traced. On the topmost of these terraces the king took his stand on the eventful day. The view which it commands is a fine one. Across the flat expanse of the rice-fields, with the broad placid river winding through them, the eye ranges eastward to high tablelands, their lower slopes embowered in woods, while afar off looms the great chain of the western Ghauts, and in the furthest distance the Neilgherries or Blue Mountains, hardly distinguishable from the azure of the sky above.

But it was not to the distant prospect that the king's eyes naturally turned at this crisis of his fate. His attention was arrested by a spectacle nearer at hand. For all the plain below was alive with troops, their banners waving gaily in the sun, the white tents of their many camps standing sharply out against the green and gold of the rice-fields. Forty thousand fighting men or more were gathered there to defend the king. But if the plain swarmed with soldiers, the road that cuts across it from the temple to the king's stand was clear of them. Not a soul was stirring on it. Each side of the way was barred by palisades, and from the palisades on either hand a long hedge of spears, held by strong arms, projected into the empty road, their blades meeting in the middle and forming a glittering arch of steel. All was now ready. The king waved his sword. At the same moment a great chain of massy gold, enriched with bosses, was placed on an elephant at his side. That was the signal. On the instant a stir might be seen half a mile away at the gate of the temple. A group of swordsmen, decked with flowers and smeared with ashes, has stepped out from the crowd. They have just partaken of their last meal on earth, and they now receive the last blessings and farewells of their friends. A moment more and they are coming down the lane of spears, hewing and stabbing right and left at the spearmen, winding and turning and writhing among the blades as if they had no bones in their bodies. It is all in vain. One after the other they fall, some nearer the king, some farther off, content to die, not for the shadow of a crown, but for the mere sake of approving their dauntless valour and swordsman-ship to the world. On the last days of the festival the same magnificent display of gallantry, the same useless sacrifice of life was repeated again and again. Yet perhaps no sacrifice is wholly useless which proves that there are men who prefer honour to life.

" It is a singular custom in Bengal," says an old native historian of India, " that there is little of hereditary descent in succession to the sovereignty. . . . Whoever kills the king, and succeeds in placing him-self on that throne, is immediately acknowledged as king ; all the *amirs*, *wazirs*, soldiers, and peasants instantly obey and submit to him, and consider him as being as much their sovereign as they did their former prince, and obey his orders implicitly. The people of Bengal say, ' We are faithful to the throne ; whoever fills the throne we are obedient and true to it.' " A custom of the same sort formerly prevailed in the little kingdom of Passier, on the northern coast of Sumatra. The old Portuguese historian De Barros, who informs us of it, remarks with surprise that no wise man would wish to be king of Passier, since the monarch was not allowed by his subjects to live long. From time to time a sort of fury seized the people, and they marched through the streets of the city chanting with loud voices the fatal words, " The king must die ! " When the king heard that song of death he knew that his hour had come. The man who struck the fatal blow was of the royal lineage, and as soon as he had done the deed of blood and seated himself on the throne he was regarded as the legitimate king, provided that he contrived to maintain his seat peaceably for a single day. This, however, the regicide did not always succeed in doing. When Fernão Peres d'Andrade, on a voyage to China, put in at Passier for a cargo of spices, two kings were massacred, and that in the most peaceable and orderly manner, without the smallest sign of tumult or sedition in the city, where everything went on in its usual course, as if the murder or execution of a king were a matter of everyday occurrence. Indeed, on one occasion three kings were raised to the dangerous elevation and followed each other on the dusty road of death in a single day. The people defended the custom, which they esteemed very laudable and even of divine institution, by saying that God would never allow so high and mighty a being as a king, who reigned as his vicegerent on earth, to perish by violence unless for his sins he thoroughly deserved it. Far away from the tropical island of Sumatra a rule of the same sort appears to have obtained among the old Slavs. When the captives Gunn and Jarmerik contrived to slay the king and queen of the Slavs and made their escape, they were pursued by the barbarians, who shouted after them that if they would only come back they would reign instead of the murdered monarch, since by a public statute of the ancients the succession to the throne fell to the king's assassin. But the flying regicides turned a deaf ear to promises which they regarded as mere baits to lure them back to destruction ; they continued their flight, and the shouts and clamour of the barbarians gradually died away in the distance.

When kings were bound to suffer death, whether at their own hands or at the hands of others, on the expiration of a fixed term of years, it was natural that they should seek to delegate the painful duty, along with some of the privileges of sovereignty, to a substitute who should suffer vicariously in their stead. This expedient appears to have been resorted to by some of the princes of Malabar. Thus we are informed by a native authority on that country that " in some places all powers both executive and judicial were delegated for a fixed period to natives by the sovereign. This institution was styled *Thalavettiparothiam* or authority obtained by decapitation. . . . It was an office tenable for five years during which its bearer was invested with supreme despotic powers within his jurisdiction. On the expiry of the five years the man's head was cut off and thrown up in the air amongst a large concourse of villagers, each of whom vied with the other in trying to catch it in its course down. He who succeeded was nominated to the post for the next five years."

When once kings, who had hitherto been bound to die a violent death at the end of a term of years, conceived the happy thought of dying by deputy in the persons of others, they would very naturally put it in practice ; and accordingly we need not wonder at finding so popular an expedient, or traces of it, in many lands. Scandinavian traditions contain some hints that of old the Swedish kings reigned only for periods of nine years, after which they were put to death or had to find a substitute to die in their stead. Thus Aun or On, king of Sweden, is said to have sacrificed to Odin for length of days and to

have been answered by the god that he should live so long as he sacrificed one of his sons every ninth year.   He sacrificed nine of them in
this manner, and would have sacrificed the tenth and last, but the
Swedes would not allow him.   So he died and was buried in a mound
at Upsala.   Another indication of a similar tenure of the crown occurs
in a curious legend of the deposition and banishment of Odin.   Offended
at his misdeeds, the other gods outlawed and exiled him, but set up
in his place a substitute, Oller by name, a cunning wizard, to whom
they accorded the symbols both of royalty and of godhead.   The
deputy bore the name of Odin, and reigned for nearly ten years, when
he was driven from the throne, while the real Odin came to his own
again.   His discomfited rival retired to Sweden and was afterwards
slain in an attempt to repair his shattered fortunes.   As gods are often
merely men who loom large through the mists of tradition, we may
conjecture that this Norse legend preserves a confused reminiscence
of ancient Swedish kings who reigned for nine or ten years together,
then abdicated, delegating to others the privilege of dying for their
country.   The great festival which was held at Upsala every nine
years may have been the occasion on which the king or his deputy was
put to death.   We know that human sacrifices formed part of the rites.

There are some grounds for believing that the reign of many
ancient Greek kings was limited to eight years, or at least that at the
end of every period of eight years a new consecration, a fresh out-
pouring of the divine grace, was regarded as necessary in order to enable
them to discharge their civil and religious duties.   Thus it was a rule
of the Spartan constitution that every eighth year the ephors should
choose a clear and moonless night and sitting down observe the sky in
silence.   If during their vigil they saw a meteor or shooting star, they
inferred that the king had sinned against the deity, and they suspended
him from his functions until the Delphic or Olympic oracle should
reinstate him in them.   This custom, which has all the air of great
antiquity, was not suffered to remain a dead letter even in the last
period of the Spartan monarchy ; for in the third century before our
era a king, who had rendered himself obnoxious to the reforming
party, was actually deposed on various trumped-up charges, among
which the allegation that the ominous sign had been seen in the sky
took a prominent place.

If the tenure of the regal office was formerly limited among the
Spartans to eight years, we may naturally ask, why was that precise
period selected as the measure of a king's reign ?   The reason is
probably to be found in those astronomical considerations which
determined the early Greek calendar.   The difficulty of reconciling
lunar with solar time is one of the standing puzzles which has taxed
the ingenuity of men who are emerging from barbarism.   Now an
octennial cycle is the shortest period at the end of which sun and
moon really mark time together after overlapping, so to say, throughout the whole of the interval.   Thus, for example, it is only once in
every eight years that the full moon coincides with the longest or

shortest day ; and as this coincidence can be observed with the aid of a simple dial, the observation is naturally one of the first to furnish a base for a calendar which shall bring lunar and solar times into tolerable, though not exact, harmony. But in early days the proper adjustment of the calendar is a matter of religious concern, since on it depends a knowledge of the right seasons for propitiating the deities whose favour is indispensable to the welfare of the community. No wonder, therefore, that the king, as the chief priest of the state, or as himself a god, should be liable to deposition or death at the end of an astronomical period. When the great luminaries had run their course on high, and were about to renew the heavenly race, it might well be thought that the king should renew his divine energies, or prove them unabated, under pain of making room for a more vigorous successor. In Southern India, as we have seen, the king's reign and life terminated with the revolution of the planet Jupiter round the sun. In Greece, on the other hand, the king's fate seems to have hung in the balance at the end of every eight years, ready to fly up and kick the beam as soon as the opposite scale was loaded with a falling star.

Whatever its origin may have been, the cycle of eight years appears to have coincided with the normal length of the king's reign in other parts of Greece besides Sparta. Thus Minos, king of Cnossus in Crete, whose great palace has been unearthed in recent years, is said to have held office for periods of eight years together. At the end of each period he retired for a season to the oracular cave on Mount Ida, and there communed with his divine father Zeus, giving him an account of his kingship in the years that were past, and receiving from him instructions for his guidance in those which were to come. The tradition plainly implies that at the end of every eight years the king's sacred powers needed to be renewed by intercourse with the godhead, and that without such a renewal he would have forfeited his right to the throne.

Without being unduly rash we may surmise that the tribute of seven youths and seven maidens whom the Athenians were bound to send to Minos every eight years had some connexion with the renewal of the king's power for another octennial cycle. Traditions varied as to the fate which awaited the lads and damsels on their arrival in Crete ; but the common view appears to have been that they were shut up in the labyrinth, there to be devoured by the Minotaur, or at least to be imprisoned for life. Perhaps they were sacrificed by being roasted alive in a bronze image of a bull, or of a bull-headed man, in order to renew the strength of the king and of the sun, whom he personated. This at all events is suggested by the legend of Talos, a bronze man who clutched people to his breast and leaped with them into the fire, so that they were roasted alive. He is said to have been given by Zeus to Europa, or by Hephaestus to Minos, to guard the island of Crete, which he patrolled thrice daily. According to one account he was a bull, according to another he was the sun. Probably he was identical with the Minotaur, and stripped of his mythical features was nothing but a bronze image of the sun represented as a man with a bull's head. In order to renew the solar fires, human victims may have been sacrificed to the idol by being roasted in its hollow body or placed on its sloping hands and allowed to roll into a pit of fire. It was in the latter fashion that the Carthaginians sacrificed their offspring to Moloch. The children were laid on the hands of a calf-headed image of bronze, from which they slid into a fiery oven, while the people danced to the music of flutes and timbrels to drown the shrieks of the burning victims. The resemblance which the Cretan traditions bear to the Carthaginian practice suggests that the worship associated with the names of Minos and the Minotaur may have been powerfully influenced by that of a Semitic Baal. In the tradition of Phalaris, tyrant of Agrigentum, and his brazen bull we may have an echo of similar rites in Sicily, where the Carthaginian power struck deep roots.

In the province of Lagos the Ijebu tribe of the Yoruba race is divided into two branches, which are known respectively as the Ijebu Ode and the Ijebu Remon. The Ode branch of the tribe is ruled by a chief who bears the title of Awujale and is surrounded by a great deal of mystery. Down to recent times his face might not be seen even by his own subjects, and if circumstances obliged him to communicate with them he did so through a screen which hid him from view. The other or Remon branch of the Ijebu tribe is governed by a chief, who ranks below the Awujale. Mr. John Parkinson was informed that in former times this subordinate chief used to be killed with ceremony after a rule of three years. As the country is now under British protection the custom of putting the chief to death at the end of a three years' reign has long been abolished, and Mr. Parkinson was unable to ascertain any particulars on the subject.

At Babylon, within historical times, the tenure of the kingly office was in practice lifelong, yet in theory it would seem to have been merely annual. For every year at the festival of Zagmuk the king had to renew his power by seizing the hands of the image of Marduk in his great temple of Esagil at Babylon. Even when Babylon passed under the power of Assyria, the monarchs of that country were expected to legalise their claim to the throne every year by coming to Babylon and performing the ancient ceremony at the New Year festival, and some of them found the obligation so burdensome that rather than discharge it they renounced the title of king altogether and contented themselves with the humbler one of Governor. Further, it would appear that in remote times, though not within the historical period, the kings of Babylon or their barbarous predecessors forfeited not merely their crown but their life at the end of a year's tenure of office. At least this is the conclusion to which the following evidence seems to point. According to the historian Berosus, who as a Babylonian priest spoke with ample knowledge, there was annually celebrated in Babylon a festival called the Sacaea. It began on the sixteenth day of the month Lous, and lasted for five days, during which masters and servants changed places, the servants giving orders and the masters obeying them. A prisoner condemned to death was dressed in the king's robes, seated on the king's throne, allowed to issue whatever commands he pleased, to eat, drink, and enjoy himself, and to lie with the king's concubines. But at the end of the five days he was stripped of his royal robes, scourged, and hanged or impaled. During his brief term of office he bore the title of Zoganes. This custom might perhaps have been explained as merely a grim jest perpetrated in a season of jollity at the expense of an unhappy criminal. But one circumstance—the leave given to the mock king to enjoy the king's concubines—is decisive against this interpretation. Considering the jealous seclusion of an oriental despot's harem we may be quite certain that permission to invade it would never have been granted by the despot, least of all to a condemned criminal, except for the very gravest cause. This cause could hardly be other than that the condemned man was about to die in the king's stead, and that to make the substitution perfect it was necessary he should enjoy the full rights of royalty during his brief reign. There is nothing surprising in this substitution. The rule that the king must be put to death either on the appearance of any symptom of bodily decay or at the end of a fixed period is certainly one which, sooner or later, the kings would seek to abolish or modify. We have seen that in Ethiopia, Sofala, and Eyeo the rule was boldly set aside by enlightened monarchs ; and that in Calicut the old custom of killing the king at the end of twelve years was changed into a permission granted to any one at the end of the twelve years' period to attack the king, and, in the event of killing him, to reign in his stead ; though, as the king took care at these times to be surrounded by his guards, the permission was little more than a form. Another way of modifying the stern old rule is seen in the Babylonian custom just described. When the time drew near for the king to be put to death (in Babylon this appears to have been at the end of a single year's reign) he abdicated for a few days, during which a temporary king reigned and suffered in his stead. At first the temporary king may have been an innocent person, possibly a member of the king's own family ; but with the growth of civilisation the sacrifice of an innocent person would be revolting to the public sentiment, and accordingly a condemned criminal would be invested with the brief and fatal sovereignty. In the sequel we shall find other examples of a dying criminal representing a dying god. For we must not forget that, as the case of the Shilluk kings clearly shows, the king is slain in his character of a god or a demigod, his death and resurrection, as the only means of perpetuating the divine life unimpaired, being deemed necessary for the salvation of his people and the world.

A vestige of a practice of putting the king to death at the end of a year's reign appears to have survived in the festival called Macahity, which used to be celebrated in Hawaii during the last month of the year. About a hundred years ago a Russian voyager described the custom as follows : " The taboo Macahity is not unlike to our festival of Christmas. It continues a whole month, during which the people amuse themselves with dances, plays, and sham-fights of every kind. The king must open this festival wherever he is. On this occasion his majesty dresses himself in his richest cloak and helmet, and is paddled in a canoe along the shore, followed sometimes by many of his subjects. He embarks early, and must finish his excursion at sunrise. The strongest and most expert of the warriors is chosen to receive him on his landing. This warrior watches the canoe along the beach ; and as soon as the king lands, and has thrown off his cloak, he darts his spear at him, from a distance of about thirty paces, and the king must either catch the spear in his hand, or suffer from it : there is no jesting in the business. Having caught it, he carries it under his arm, with the sharp end downwards, into the temple or *heavoo*. On his entrance, the assembled multitude begin their sham-fights, and immediately the air is obscured by clouds of spears, made for the occasion with blunted ends. Hamamea [the king] has been frequently advised to abolish this ridiculous ceremony, in which he risks his life every year ; but to no effect. His answer always is, that he is as able to catch a spear as any one on the island is to throw it at him. During the Macahity, all punishments are remitted throughout the country ; and no person can leave the place in which he commences these holidays, let the affair be ever so important."

That a king should regularly have been put to death at the close of a year's reign will hardly appear improbable when we learn that to this day there is still a kingdom in which the reign and the life of the sovereign are limited to a single day. In Ngoio, a province of the ancient kingdom of Congo, the rule obtains that the chief who assumes the cap of sovereignty is always killed on the night after his coronation. The right of succession lies with the chief of the Musurongo ; but we need not wonder that he does not exercise it, and that the throne stands vacant. " No one likes to lose his life for a few hours' glory on the Ngoio throne."

CHAPTER XXV

TEMPORARY KINGS

In some places the modified form of the old custom of regicide which appears to have prevailed at Babylon has been further softened down. The king still abdicates annually for a short time and his place is filled by a more or less nominal sovereign ; but at the close of his short reign the latter is no longer killed, though sometimes a mock execution still survives as a memorial of the time when he was actually put to death. To take examples. In the month of Méac (February) the king of Cambodia annually abdicated for three days. During this time he performed no act of authority, he did not touch the seals, he did not even receive the revenues which fell due. In his stead there reigned a temporary king called Sdach Méac, that is, King February. The office of temporary king was hereditary in a family distantly connected with the royal house, the sons succeeding the fathers and the younger brothers the elder brothers just as in the succession to the real sovereignty. On a favourable day fixed by the astrologers the temporary king was conducted by the mandarins in triumphal procession. He rode one of the royal elephants, seated in the royal palanquin, and escorted by soldiers who, dressed in appropriate costumes, represented the neighbouring peoples of Siam, Annam, Laos, and so on. In place of the golden crown he wore a peaked white cap, and his regalia, instead of being of gold encrusted with diamonds, were of rough wood. After paying homage to the real king, from whom he received the sovereignty for three days, together with all the revenues accruing during that time (though this last custom has been omitted for some time), he moved in procession round the palace and through the streets of the capital. On the third day, after the usual procession, the temporary king gave orders that the elephants should trample under foot the "mountain of rice," which was a scaffold of bamboo surrounded by sheaves of rice. The people gathered up the rice, each man taking home a little with him to secure a good harvest. Some of it was also taken to the king, who had it cooked and presented to the monks.

In Siam on the sixth day of the moon in the sixth month (the end of April) a temporary king is appointed, who for three days enjoys the royal prerogatives, the real king remaining shut up in his palace. This temporary king sends his numerous satellites in all directions to seize and confiscate whatever they can find in the bazaar and open shops ; even the ships and junks which arrive in harbour during the three days are forfeited to him and must be redeemed. He goes to a field in the middle of the city, whither they bring a gilded plough drawn by gaily-decked oxen. After the plough has been anointed and the oxen rubbed with incense, the mock king traces nine furrows with the plough, followed by aged dames of the palace scattering the first seed of the season. As soon as the nine furrows are drawn, the crowd of spectators rushes in and scrambles for the seed which has just been sown, believing that, mixed with the seed-rice, it will ensure a plentiful crop. Then the oxen are unyoked, and rice, maize, sesame, sago, bananas, sugar-cane, melons, and so on, are set before them ; whatever they eat first will, it is thought, be dear in the year following, though some people interpret the omen in the opposite sense. During this time the temporary king stands leaning against a tree with his right foot resting on his left knee. From standing thus on one foot he is popularly known as King Hop ; but his official title is Phaya Phollathep, " Lord of the Heavenly Hosts." He is a sort of Minister of Agriculture ; all disputes about fields, rice, and so forth, are referred to him. There is moreover another ceremony in which he personates the king. It takes place in the second month (which falls in the cold season) and lasts three days. He is conducted in procession to an open place opposite the Temple of the Brahmans, where there are a number of poles dressed like May-poles, upon which the Brahmans swing. All the while that they swing and dance, the Lord of the Heavenly Hosts has to stand on one foot upon a seat which is made of bricks plastered over, covered with a white cloth, and hung with tapestry. He is supported by a wooden frame with a gilt canopy, and two Brahmans stand one on each side of him. The dancing Brahmans carry buffalo horns with which they draw water from a large copper caldron and sprinkle it on the spectators; this is supposed to bring good luck, causing the people to dwell in peace and quiet, health and prosperity. The time during which the Lord of the Heavenly Hosts has to stand on one foot is about three hours. This is thought " to prove the dispositions of the Devattas and spirits." If he lets his foot down " he is liable to forfeit his property and have his family enslaved by the king; as it is believed to be a bad omen, portending destruction to the state, and instability to the throne. But if he stand firm he is believed to have gained a victory over evil spirits, and he has moreover the privilege, ostensibly at least, of seizing any ship which may enter the harbour during these three days, and taking its contents, and also of entering any open shop in the town and carrying away what he chooses."

Such were the duties and privileges of the Siamese King Hop down to about the middle of the nineteenth century or later. Under the reign of the late enlightened monarch this quaint personage was to some extent both shorn of the glories and relieved of the burden of his office. He still watches, as of old, the Brahmans rushing through the air in a swing suspended between two tall masts, each some ninety feet high; but he is allowed to sit instead of stand, and, although public opinion still expects him to keep his right foot on his left knee during the whole of the ceremony, he would incur no legal penalty were he, to the great chagrin of the people, to put his weary foot to the ground. Other signs, too, tell of the invasion of the East by the ideas and civilisation of the West. The thoroughfares that lead to the scene of the performance are blocked with carriages: lamp-posts and telegraph posts, to which eager spectators cling like monkeys, rise above the dense crowd; and, while a tatterdemalion band of the old style, in gaudy garb of vermilion and yellow, bangs and tootles away on drums and trumpets of an antique pattern, the procession of bare-footed soldiers in brilliant uniforms steps briskly along to the lively strains of a modern military band playing " Marching through Georgia."

On the first day of the sixth month, which was regarded as the beginning of the year, the king and people of Samarcand used to put on new clothes and cut their hair and beards. Then they repaired to a forest near the capital where they shot arrows on horseback for seven days. On the last day the target was a gold coin, and he who hit it had the right to be king for one day. In Upper Egypt on the first day of the solar year by Coptic reckoning, that is, on the tenth of September, when the Nile has generally reached its highest point, the regular government is suspended for three days and every town chooses its own ruler. This temporary lord wears a sort of tall fool's cap and a long flaxen beard, and is enveloped in a strange mantle. With a wand of office in his hand and attended by men disguised as scribes, executioners, and so forth, he proceeds to the Governor's house. The latter allows himself to be deposed ; and the mock king, mounting the throne, holds a tribunal, to the decisions of which even the governor and his officials must bow. After three days the mock king is condemned to death ; the envelope or shell in which he was encased is committed to the flames, and from its ashes the Fellah creeps forth. The custom perhaps points to an old practice of burning a real king in grim earnest. In Uganda the brothers of the king used to be burned, because it was not lawful to shed the royal blood.

The Mohammedan students of Fez, in Morocco, are allowed to appoint a sultan of their own, who reigns for a few weeks, and is known as *Sultan t-tulba*, " the Sultan of the Scribes." This brief authority is put up for auction and knocked down to the highest bidder. It brings some substantial privileges with it, for the holder is freed from taxes thenceforward, and he has the right of asking a favour from the real sultan. That favour is seldom refused ; it usually consists in the release of a prisoner. Moreover, the agents of the student-sultan levy fines on the shopkeepers and householders, against whom they trump up various humorous charges. The temporary sultan is surrounded with the pomp of a real court, and parades the streets in state with music and shouting, while a royal umbrella is held over his head. With the so-called fines and free-will offerings, to which the real sultan adds a liberal supply of provisions, the students have enough to furnish forth a magnificent banquet ; and altogether they enjoy themselves thoroughly, indulging in all kinds of games and amusements. For the first seven days the mock sultan remains in the college ; then he goes about a mile out of the town and encamps on the bank of the river, attended by the students and not a few of the citizens. On the seventh day of his stay outside the town he is visited by the real sultan, who grants him his request and gives him seven more days to reign, so that the reign of " the Sultan of the Scribes " nominally lasts three weeks. But when six days of the last week have passed the mock sultan runs back to the town by night. This temporary sultanship always falls in spring, about the beginning of April. Its origin is said to have been as follows. When Mulai Rasheed II. was fighting for the throne in 1664 or 1665, a certain Jew usurped the royal authority at Taza. But the rebellion was soon suppressed through the loyalty and devotion of the students. To effect their purpose they resorted to an ingenious stratagem. Forty of them caused themselves to be packed in chests which were sent as a present to the usurper. In the dead of night, while the unsuspecting Jew was slumbering peacefully among the packing-cases, the lids were stealthily raised, the brave forty crept forth, slew the usurper, and took possession of the city in the name of the real sultan, who, to mark his gratitude for the help thus rendered·him in time of need, conferred on the students the right of annually appointing a sultan of their own. The narrative has all the air of a fiction devised to explain an old custom, of which the real meaning and origin had been forgotten.

A custom of annually appointing a mock king for a single day was observed at Lostwithiel in Cornwall down to the sixteenth century. On " little Easter Sunday " the freeholders of the town and manor assembled together, either in person or by their deputies, and one among them, as it fell to his lot by turn, gaily attired and gallantly mounted, with a crown on his head, a sceptre in his hand, and a sword borne before him, rode through the principal street to the church, dutifully attended by all the rest on horseback. The clergyman in his best robes received him at the churchyard stile and conducted him to hear divine service. On leaving the church he repaired, with the same pomp, to a house provided for his reception. Here a feast awaited him and his suite, and being set at the head of the table he was served on bended knees, with all the rites due to the estate of a prince. The ceremony ended with the dinner, and every man returned home.

Sometimes the temporary king occupies the throne, not annually, but once for all at the beginning of each reign. Thus in the kingdom of Jambi in Sumatra it is the custom that at the beginning of a new reign a man of the people should occupy the throne and exercise the royal prerogatives for a single day. The origin of the custom is explained by a tradition that there were once five royal brothers, the four elder of whom all declined the throne on the ground of various bodily defects, leaving it to their youngest brother. But the eldest occupied the throne for one day, and reserved for his descendants a similar privilege at the beginning of every reign. Thus the office of temporary king is hereditary in a family akin to the royal house. In Bilaspur it seems to be the custom, after the death of a Rajah, for a Brahman to eat rice out of the dead Rajah's hand, and then to occupy the throne for a year. At the end of the year the Brahman receives presents and is dismissed from the territory, being forbidden apparently to return. " The idea seems to be that the spirit of the Rájá enters into the Bráhman who eats the *khir* (rice and milk) out of his hand when he is dead, as the Brahman is apparently carefully watched during the whole year, and not allowed to go away." The same or a similar custom is believed to obtain among the hill states about Kangra. The custom of banishing the Brahman who represents the king may be a substitute for putting him to death. At the installation of a prince of Carinthia a peasant, in whose family the office was hereditary, ascended a marble stone which stood surrounded by meadows in a spacious valley ; on his right stood a black mother-cow, on his left a lean ugly mare. A rustic crowd gathered about him. Then the future prince, dressed as a peasant and carrying a shepherd's staff, drew near, attended by courtiers and magistrates. On perceiving him the peasant called out, " Who is this whom I see coming so proudly along ? " The people answered, " The prince of the land." The peasant was then prevailed on to surrender the marble seat to the prince on condition of receiving sixty pence, the cow and mare, and exemption from taxes. But before yielding his place he gave the prince a light blow on the cheek.

Some points about these temporary kings deserve to be specially noticed before we pass to the next branch of the evidence. In the first place, the Cambodian and Siamese examples show clearly that it is especially the divine or magical functions of the king which are transferred to his temporary substitute. This appears from the belief that by keeping up his foot the temporary king of Siam gained a victory over the evil spirits, whereas by letting it down he imperilled the existence of the state. Again, the Cambodian ceremony of trampling down the " mountain of rice," and the Siamese ceremony of opening the ploughing and sowing, are charms to produce a plentiful harvest, as appears from the belief that those who carry home some of the trampled rice, or of the seed sown, will thereby secure a good crop. Moreover, when the Siamese representative of the king is guiding the plough, the people watch him anxiously, not to see whether he drives a straight furrow, but to mark the exact point on his leg to which the skirt of his silken robe reaches ; for on that is supposed to hang the state of the weather and the crops during the ensuing season. If the Lord of the Heavenly Hosts hitches up his garment above his knee, the weather will be wet and heavy rains will spoil the harvest. If he lets it trail to his ankle, a drought will be the consequence. But fine weather and heavy crops will follow if the hem of his robe hangs exactly half-way down the calf of his leg. So closely is the course of nature, and with it the weal or woe of the people, dependent on the minutest act or gesture of the king's representative. But the task of making the crops grow, thus deputed to the temporary kings, is one of the magical functions regularly supposed to be discharged by kings in primitive society. The rule that the mock king must stand on one foot upon a raised seat in the rice-field was perhaps originally meant as a charm to make the crop grow high ; at least this was the object of a similar ceremony observed by the old Prussians. The tallest girl, standing on one foot upon a seat, with her lap full of cakes, a cup of brandy in her right hand and a piece of elm-bark or linden-bark in her left, prayed to the god Waizganthos that the flax might grow as high as she was standing. Then, after draining the cup, she had it refilled, and poured the brandy on the ground as an offering to Waizganthos, and threw down the cakes for his attendant sprites. If she remained steady on one foot throughout the ceremony, it was an omen that the flax crop would be good ; but if she let her foot down, it was feared that the crop might fail. The same significance perhaps attaches to the swinging of the Brahmans, which the Lord of the Heavenly Hosts had formerly to witness standing on one foot. On the principles of

homoeopathic or imitative magic it might be thought that the higher
the priests swing the higher will grow the rice. For the ceremony is
described as a harvest festival, and swinging is practised by the Letts
of Russia with the avowed intention of influencing the growth of the
crops. In the spring and early summer, between Easter and St. John's
Day (the summer solstice), every Lettish peasant is said to devote his
leisure hours to swinging diligently ; for the higher he rises in the air
the higher will his flax grow that season.

In the foregoing cases the temporary king is appointed annually
in accordance with a regular custom. But in other cases the appointment is made only to meet a special emergency, such as to relieve the
real king from some actual or threatened evil by diverting it to a
substitute, who takes his place on the throne for a short time. The
history of Persia furnishes instances of such occasional substitutes for
the Shah. Thus Shah Abbas the Great, being warned by his astrologers
in the year 1591 that a serious danger impended over him, attempted
to avert the omen by abdicating the throne and appointing a certain
unbeliever named Yusoofee, probably a Christian, to reign in his stead.
The substitute was accordingly crowned, and for three days, if we may
trust the Persian historians, he enjoyed not only the name and the
state but the power of the king. At the end of his brief reign he was
put to death : the decree of the stars was fulfilled by this sacrifice ;
and Abbas, who reascended his throne in a most propitious hour, was
promised by his astrologers a long and glorious reign.

CHAPTER XXVI

SACRIFICE OF THE KING'S SON

A point to notice about the temporary kings described in the foregoing chapter is that in two places (Cambodia and Jambi) they come
of a stock which is believed to be akin to the royal family. If the
view here taken of the origin of these temporary kingships is correct,
we can easily understand why the king's substitute should sometimes
be of the same race as the king. When the king first succeeded in
getting the life of another accepted as a sacrifice instead of his own,
he would have to show that the death of that other would serve the
purpose quite as well as his own would have done. Now it was as a
god or demigod that the king had to die ; therefore the substitute who
died for him had to be invested, at least for the occasion, with the
divine attributes of the king. This, as we have just seen, was certainly
the case with the temporary kings of Siam and Cambodia ; they were
invested with the supernatural functions, which in an earlier stage of
society were the special attributes of the king. But no one could so
well represent the king in his divine character as his son, who might
be supposed to share the divine afflatus of his father. No one, therefore,

U

could so appropriately die for the king and, through him, for the whole people, as the king's son.

We have seen that according to tradition, Aun or On, King of Sweden, sacrificed nine of his sons to Odin at Upsala in order that his own life might be spared. After he had sacrificed his second son he received from the god an answer that he should live so long as he gave him one of his sons every ninth year. When he had sacrificed his seventh son, he still lived, but was so feeble that he could not walk but had to be carried in a chair. Then he offered up his eighth son, and lived nine years more, lying in his bed. After that he sacrificed his ninth son, and lived another nine years, but so that he drank out of a horn like a weaned child. He now wished to sacrifice his only remaining son to Odin, but the Swedes would not allow him. So he died and was buried in a mound at Upsala.

In ancient Greece there seems to have been at least one kingly house of great antiquity of which the eldest sons were always liable to be sacrificed in room of their royal sires. When Xerxes was marching through Thessaly at the head of his mighty host to attack the Spartans at Thermopylae, he came to the town of Alus. Here he was shown the sanctuary of Laphystian Zeus, about which his guides told him a strange tale. It ran somewhat as follows. Once upon a time the king of the country, by name Athamas, married a wife Nephele, and had by her a son called Phrixus and a daughter named Helle. Afterwards he took to himself a second wife called Ino, by whom he had two sons, Learchus and Melicertes. But his second wife was jealous of her step-children, Phrixus and Helle, and plotted their death. She went about very cunningly to compass her bad end. First of all she persuaded the women of the country to roast the seed corn secretly before it was committed to the ground. So next year no crops came up and the people died of famine. Then the king sent messengers to the oracle at Delphi to enquire the cause of the dearth. But the wicked step-mother bribed the messenger to give out as the answer of the god that the dearth would never cease till the children of Athamas by his first wife had been sacrificed to Zeus. When Athamas heard that, he sent for the children, who were with the sheep. But a ram with a fleece of gold opened his lips, and speaking with the voice of a man warned the children of their danger. So they mounted the ram and fled with him over land and sea. As they flew over the sea, the girl slipped from the animal's back, and falling into water was drowned. But her brother Phrixus was brought safe to the land of Colchis, where reigned a child of the Sun. Phrixus married the king's daughter, and she bore him a son Cytisorus. And there he sacrificed the ram with the golden fleece to Zeus the God of Flight ; but some will have it that he sacrificed the animal to Laphystian Zeus. The golden fleece itself he gave to his wife's father, who nailed it to an oak tree, guarded by a sleepless dragon in a sacred grove of Ares. Meanwhile at home an oracle had commanded that King Athamas himself should be sacrificed as an expiatory offering for the whole country. So the people

decked him with garlands like a victim and led him to the altar, where
they were just about to sacrifice him when he was rescued either by
his grandson Cytisorus, who arrived in the nick of time from Colchis,
or by Hercules, who brought tidings that the king's son Phrixus was
yet alive.   Thus Athamas was saved, but afterwards he went mad,
and mistaking his son Learchus for a wild beast shot him dead.   Next
he attempted the life of his remaining son Melicertes, but the child
was rescued by his mother Ino, who ran and threw herself and him
from a high rock into the sea.   Mother and son were changed into
marine divinities, and the son received special homage in the isle of
Tenedos, where babes were sacrificed to him.   Thus bereft of wife
and children the unhappy Athamas quitted his country, and on
enquiring of the oracle where he should dwell was told to take up his
abode wherever he should be entertained by wild beasts.   He fell in
with a pack of wolves devouring sheep, and when they saw him they
fled and left him the bleeding remnants of their prey.   In this way
the oracle was fulfilled.   But because King Athamas had not been
sacrificed as a sin-offering for the whole country, it was divinely decreed
that the eldest male scion of his family in each generation should be
sacrificed without fail, if ever he set foot in the town-hall, where the
offerings were made to Laphystian Zeus by one of the house of Athamas.
Many of the family, Xerxes was informed, had fled to foreign lands to
escape this doom ; but some of them had returned long afterwards,
and being caught by the sentinels in the act of entering the town-hall
were wreathed as victims, led forth in procession, and sacrificed.
These instances appear to have been notorious, if not frequent ; for
the writer of a dialogue attributed to Plato, after speaking of the
immolation of human victims by the Carthaginians, adds that such
practices were not unknown among the Greeks, and he refers with
horror to the sacrifices offered on Mount Lycaeus and by the descendants of Athamas.

The suspicion that this barbarous custom by no means fell into
disuse even in later days is strengthened by a case of human sacrifice
which occurred in Plutarch's time at Orchomenus, a very ancient city
of Boeotia, distant only a few miles across the plain from the historian's
birthplace.   Here dwelt a family of which the men went by the name
of Psoloeis or " Sooty," and the women by the name of Oleae or
" Destructive."   Every year at the festival of the Agrionia the priest
of Dionysus pursued these women with a drawn sword, and if he overtook one of them he had the right to slay her.   In Plutarch's lifetime
the right was actually exercised by a priest Zoilus.   The family thus
liable to furnish at least one human victim every year was of royal
descent, for they traced their lineage to Minyas, the famous old king
of Orchomenus, the monarch of fabulous wealth, whose stately treasury,
as it is called, still stands in ruins at the point where the long rocky
hill of Orchomenus melts into the vast level expanse of the Copaic
plain.   Tradition ran that the king's three daughters long despised
the other women of the country for yielding to the Bacchic frenzy,

and sat at home in the king's house scornfully plying the distaff and the loom, while the rest, wreathed with flowers, their dishevelled locks streaming to the wind, roamed in ecstasy the barren mountains that rise above Orchomenus, making the solitude of the hills to echo to the wild music of cymbals and tambourines. But in time the divine fury infected even the royal damsels in their quiet chamber ; they were seized with a fierce longing to partake of human flesh, and cast lots among themselves which should give up her child to furnish a cannibal feast. The lot fell on Leucippe, and she surrendered her son Hippasus, who was torn limb from limb by the three. From these misguided women sprang the Oleae and the Psoloeis, of whom the men were said to be so called because they wore sad-coloured raiment in token of their mourning and grief.

Now this practice of taking human victims from a family of royal descent at Orchomenus is all the more significant because Athamas himself is said to have reigned in the land of Orchomenus even before the time of Minyas, and because over against the city there rises Mount Laphystius, on which, as at Alus in Thessaly, there was a sanctuary of Laphystian Zeus, where, according to tradition, Athamas purposed to sacrifice his two children Phrixus and Helle. On the whole, comparing the traditions about Athamas with the custom that obtained with regard to his descendants in historical times, we may fairly infer that in Thessaly and probably in Boeotia there reigned of old a dynasty of which the kings were liable to be sacrificed for the good of the country to the god called Laphystian Zeus, but that they contrived to shift the fatal responsibility to their offspring, of whom the eldest son was regularly destined to the altar. As time went on, the cruel custom was so far mitigated that a ram was accepted as a vicarious sacrifice in room of the royal victim, provided always that the prince abstained from setting foot in the town-hall where the sacrifices were offered to Laphystian Zeus by one of his kinsmen. But if he were rash enough to enter the place of doom, to thrust himself wilfully, as it were, on the notice of the god who had good-naturedly winked at the substitution of a ram, the ancient obligation which had been suffered to lie in abeyance recovered all its force, and there was no help for it but he must die. The tradition which associated the sacrifice of the king or his children with a great dearth points clearly to the belief, so common among primitive folk, that the king is responsible for the weather and the crops, and that he may justly pay with his life for the inclemency of the one or the failure of the other. Athamas and his line, in short, appear to have united divine or magical with royal functions ; and this view is strongly supported by the claims to divinity which Salmoneus, the brother of Athamas, is said to have set up. We have seen that this presumptuous mortal professed to be no other than Zeus himself, and to wield the thunder and lightning, of which he made a trumpery imitation by the help of tinkling kettles and blazing torches. If we may judge from analogy, his mock thunder and lightning were no mere scenic exhibition designed to deceive and impress the beholders; they were enchantments practised by the royal magician for the purpose of bringing about the celestial phenomena which they feebly mimicked.

Among the Semites of Western Asia the king, in a time of national danger, sometimes gave his own son to die as a sacrifice for the people. Thus Philo of Byblus, in his work on the Jews, says: " It was an ancient custom in a crisis of great danger that the ruler of a city or nation should give his beloved son to die for the whole people, as a ransom offered to the avenging demons; and the children thus offered were slain with mystic rites. So Cronus, whom the Phoenicians call Israel, being king of the land and having an only-begotten son called Jeoud (for in the Phoenician tongue Jeoud signifies 'only-begotten'), dressed him in royal robes and sacrificed him upon an altar in a time of war, when the country was in great danger from the enemy." When the king of Moab was besieged by the Israelites and hard beset, he took his eldest son, who should have reigned in his stead, and offered him for a burnt offering on the wall.

CHAPTER XXVII

SUCCESSION TO THE SOUL

To the view that in early times, and among barbarous races, kings have frequently been put to death at the end of a short reign, it may be objected that such a custom would tend to the extinction of the royal family. The objection may be met by observing, first, that the kingship is often not confined to one family, but may be shared in turn by several; second, that the office is frequently not hereditary, but is open to men of any family, even to foreigners, who may fulfil the requisite conditions, such as marrying a princess or vanquishing the king in battle; and, third, that even if the custom did tend to the extinction of a dynasty, that is not a consideration which would prevent its observance among people less provident of the future and less heedful of human life than ourselves. Many races, like many individuals, have indulged in practices which must in the end destroy them. The Polynesians seem regularly to have killed two-thirds of their children. In some parts of East Africa the proportion of infants massacred at birth is said to be the same. Only children born in certain presentations are allowed to live. The Jagas, a conquering tribe in Angola, are reported to have put to death all their children, without exception, in order that the women might not be cumbered with babies on the march. They recruited their numbers by adopting boys and girls of thirteen or fourteen years of age, whose parents they had killed and eaten. Among the Mbaya Indians of South America the women used to murder all their children except the last, or the one they believed to be the last. If one of them had another child afterwards, she killed it. We need not wonder that this practice entirely destroyed a branch of the Mbaya nation, who had been for many years the most formidable enemies of the Spaniards. Among the Lengua Indians of the Gran Chaco, the missionaries discovered what they describe as " a carefully planned system of racial suicide, by the practice of infanticide by abortion, and other methods." Nor is infanticide the only mode in which a savage tribe commits suicide. A lavish use of the poison ordeal may be equally effective. Some time ago a small tribe named Uwet came down from the hill country, and settled on the left branch of the Calabar river in West Africa. When the missionaries first visited the place, they found the population considerable, distributed into three villages. Since then the constant use of the poison ordeal has almost extinguished the tribe. On one occasion the whole population took poison to prove their innocence. About half perished on the spot, and the remnant, we are told, still continuing their superstitious practice, must soon become extinct. With such examples before us we need not hesitate to believe that many tribes have felt no scruple or delicacy in observing a custom which tends to wipe out a single family. To attribute such scruples to them is to commit the common, the perpetually repeated mistake of judging the savage by the standard of European civilisation. If any of my readers set out with the notion that all races of men think and act much in the same way as educated Englishmen, the evidence of superstitious belief and custom collected in this work should suffice to disabuse him of so erroneous a prepossession.

The explanation here given of the custom of killing divine persons assumes, or at least is readily combined with, the idea that the soul of the slain divinity is transmitted to his successor. Of this transmission I have no direct proof except in the case of the Shilluk, among whom the practice of killing the divine king prevails in a typical form, and with whom it is a fundamental article of faith that the soul of the divine founder of the dynasty is immanent in every one of his slain successors. But if this is the only actual example of such a belief which I can adduce, analogy seems to render it probable that a similar succession to the soul of the slain god has been supposed to take place in other instances, though direct evidence of it is wanting. For it has been already shown that the soul of the incarnate deity is often supposed to transmigrate at death into another incarnation ; and if this takes place when the death is a natural one, there seems no reason why it should not take place when the death has been brought about by violence. Certainly the idea that the soul of a dying person may be transmitted to his successor is perfectly familiar to primitive peoples. In Nias the eldest son usually succeeds his father in the chieftainship. But if from any bodily or mental defect the eldest son is disqualified for ruling, the father determines in his lifetime which of his sons shall succeed him. In order, however, to establish his right of succession, it is necessary that the son upon whom his father's choice falls shall catch in his mouth or in a bag the last breath, and with it the soul, of the dying chief. For whoever catches his last breath is chief equally with the appointed successor. Hence the other brothers, and sometimes also strangers, crowd round the dying man to catch his soul as it passes. The houses in Nias are raised above the ground on posts, and it has happened that when the dying man lay with his face on the floor, one of the candidates has bored a hole in the floor and sucked in the chief's last breath through a bamboo tube. When the chief has no son, his soul is caught in a bag, which is fastened to an image made to represent the deceased ; the soul is then believed to pass into the image.

Sometimes it would appear that the spiritual link between a king and the souls of his predecessors is formed by the possession of some part of their persons. In Southern Celebes the regalia often consist of corporeal portions of deceased rajahs, which are treasured as sacred relics and confer the right to the throne. Similarly among the Saka-lavas of Southern Madagascar a vertebra of the neck, a nail, and a lock of hair of a deceased king are placed in a crocodile's tooth and carefully kept along with the similar relics of his predecessors in a house set apart for the purpose. The possession of these relics constitutes the right to the throne. A legitimate heir who should be deprived of them would lose all his authority over the people, and on the contrary a usurper who should make himself master of the relics would be acknowledged king without dispute. When the Alake or king of Abeokuta in West Africa dies, the principal men decapitate his body, and placing the head in a large earthen vessel deliver it to the new sovereign ; it becomes his fetish and he is bound to pay it honours. Sometimes, in order apparently that the new sovereign may inherit more surely the magical and other virtues of the royal line, he is required to eat a piece of his dead predecessor. Thus at Abeokuta not only was the head of the late king presented to his successor, but the tongue was cut out and given him to eat. Hence, when the natives wish to signify that the sovereign reigns, they say, " He has eaten the king." A custom of the same sort is still practised at Ibadan, a large town in the interior of Lagos, West Africa. When the king dies his head is cut off and sent to his nominal suzerain, the Alafin of Oyo, the paramount king of Yoruba land ; but his heart is eaten by his successor. This ceremony was performed not very many years ago at the accession of a new king of Ibadan.

Taking the whole of the preceding evidence into account, we may fairly suppose that when the divine king or priest is put to death his spirit is believed to pass into his successor. In point of fact, among the Shilluk of the White Nile, who regularly kill their divine kings, every king on his accession has to perform a ceremony which appears designed to convey to him the same sacred and worshipful spirit which animated all his predecessors, one after the other, on the throne.

CHAPTER XXVIII

THE KILLING OF THE TREE-SPIRIT

§ 1. *The Whitsuntide Mummers.*—It remains to ask what light the custom of killing the divine king or priest sheds upon the special subject of our enquiry. In an earlier part of this work we saw reason to suppose that the King of the Wood at Nemi was regarded as an incarnation of a tree-spirit or of the spirit of vegetation, and that as such he would be endowed, in the belief of his worshippers, with a magical power of making the trees to bear fruit, the crops to grow, and so on. His life must therefore have been held very precious by his worshippers, and was probably hedged in by a system of elaborate precautions or taboos like those by which, in so many places, the life of the man-god has been guarded against the malignant influence of demons and sorcerers. But we have seen that the very value attached to the life of the man-god necessitates his violent death as the only means of preserving it from the inevitable decay of age. The same reasoning would apply to the King of the Wood ; he, too, had to be killed in order that the divine spirit, incarnate in him, might be trans-ferred in its integrity to his successor. The rule that he held office till a stronger should slay him might be supposed to secure both the preservation of his divine life in full vigour and its transference to a suitable successor as soon as that vigour began to be impaired. For so long as he could maintain his position by the strong hand, it might be inferred that his natural force was not abated ; whereas his defeat and death at the hands of another proved that his strength was begin-ning to fail and that it was time his divine life should be lodged in a less dilapidated tabernacle. This explanation of the rule that the King of the Wood had to be slain by his successor at least renders that rule perfectly intelligible. It is strongly supported by the theory and practice of the Shilluk, who put their divine king to death at the first signs of failing health, lest his decrepitude should entail a corre-sponding failure of vital energy on the corn, the cattle, and men. Moreover, it is countenanced by the analogy of the Chitomé, upon whose life the existence of the world was supposed to hang, and who was therefore slain by his successor as soon as he showed signs of breaking up. Again, the terms on which in later times the King of Calicut held office are identical with those attached to the office of King of the Wood, except that whereas the former might be assailed by a candidate at any time, the King of Calicut might only be attacked once every twelve years. But as the leave granted to the King of Calicut to reign so long as he could defend himself against all comers was a mitigation of the old rule which set a fixed term to his life, so we may conjecture that the similar permission granted to the King of the Wood was a mitigation of an older custom of putting him to death at the end of a definite period. In both cases the new rule gave to the god-man at least a chance for his life, which under the old rule was denied him ; and people probably reconciled themselves to the change by reflecting that so long as the god-man could maintain himself by the sword against all assaults, there was no reason to apprehend that the fatal decay had set in.

The conjecture that the King of the Wood was formerly put to death at the expiry of a fixed term, without being allowed a chance for his life, will be confirmed if evidence can be adduced of a custom of periodically killing his counterparts, the human representatives of the tree-spirit, in Northern Europe. Now in point of fact such a custom has left unmistakable traces of itself in the rural festivals of the peasantry. To take examples.

At Niederpöring, in Lower Bavaria, the Whitsuntide representative of the tree-spirit—the *Pfingstl* as he was called—was clad from top to toe in leaves and flowers. On his head he wore a high pointed cap, the ends of which rested on his shoulders, only two holes being left in it for his eyes. The cap was covered with water-flowers and surmounted with a nosegay of peonies. The sleeves of his coat were also made of water-plants, and the rest of his body was enveloped in alder and hazel leaves. On each side of him marched a boy holding up one of the *Pfingstl's* arms. These two boys carried drawn swords, and so did most of the others who formed the procession. They stopped at every house where they hoped to receive a present ; and the people, in hiding, soused the leaf-clad boy with water. All rejoiced when he was well drenched. Finally he waded into the brook up to his middle ; whereupon one of the boys, standing on the bridge, pretended to cut off his head. At Wurmlingen, in Swabia, a score of young fellows dress themselves on Whit-Monday in white shirts and white trousers, with red scarves round their waists and swords hanging from the scarves. They ride on horseback into the wood, led by two trumpeters blowing their trumpets. In the wood they cut down leafy oak branches, in which they envelop from head to foot him who was the last of their number to ride out of the village. His legs, however, are encased separately, so that he may be able to mount his horse again. Further, they give him a long artificial neck, with an artificial head and a false face on the top of it. Then a May-tree is cut, generally an aspen or beech about ten feet high ; and being decked with coloured handkerchiefs and ribbons it is entrusted to a special "May-bearer." The cavalcade then returns with music and song to the village. Amongst the personages who figure in the procession are a Moorish king with a sooty face and a crown on his head, a Dr. Iron-Beard, a corporal, and an executioner. They halt on the village green, and each of the characters makes a speech in rhyme. The executioner announces that the leaf-clad man has been condemned to death, and cuts off his false head. Then the riders race to the May-tree, which has been set up a little way off. The first man who succeeds in wrenching it from the ground as he gallops past keeps it with all its decorations. The ceremony is observed every second or third year.

In Saxony and Thüringen there is a Whitsuntide ceremony called
" chasing the Wild Man out of the bush," or " fetching the Wild Man
out of the wood." A young fellow is enveloped in leaves or moss and
called the Wild Man. He hides in the wood and the other lads of the
village go out to seek him. They find him, lead him captive out of
the wood, and fire at him with blank muskets. He falls like dead to
the ground, but a lad dressed as a doctor bleeds him, and he comes
to life again. At this they rejoice, and, binding him fast on a waggon,
take him to the village, where they tell all the people how they have
caught the Wild Man. At every house they receive a gift. In the
Erzgebirge the following custom was annually observed at Shrovetide
about the beginning of the seventeenth century. Two men disguised
as Wild Men, the one in brushwood and moss, the other in straw,
were led about the streets, and at last taken to the market-place, where
they were chased up and down, shot and stabbed. Before falling they
reeled about with strange gestures and spirted blood on the people
from bladders which they carried. When they were down, the hunts-
men placed them on boards and carried them to the ale-house, the
miners marching beside them and winding blasts on their mining
tools as if they had taken a noble head of game. A very similar Shrovetide custom is still observed near Schluckenau in Bohemia. A man
dressed up as a Wild Man is chased through several streets till he
comes to a narrow lane across which a cord is stretched. He stumbles
over the cord and, falling to the ground, is overtaken and caught by
his pursuers. The executioner runs up and stabs with his sword a
bladder filled with blood which the Wild Man wears round his body ;
so the Wild Man dies, while a stream of blood reddens the ground.
Next day a straw-man, made up to look like the Wild Man, is placed
on a litter, and, accompanied by a great crowd, is taken to a pool
into which it is thrown by the executioner. The ceremony is called
" burying the Carnival."

In Semic (Bohemia) the custom of beheading the King is observed
on Whit-Monday. A troop of young people disguise themselves ;
each is girt with a girdle of bark and carries a wooden sword and a
trumpet of willow-bark. The King wears a robe of tree-bark adorned
with flowers, on his head is a crown of bark decked with flowers and
branches, his feet are wound about with ferns, a mask hides his face,
and for a sceptre he has a hawthorn switch in his hand. A lad leads
him through the village by a rope fastened to his foot, while the rest
dance about, blow their trumpets, and whistle. In every farmhouse
the King is chased round the room, and one of the troop, amid much
noise and outcry, strikes with his sword a blow on the King's robe of
bark till it rings again. Then a gratuity is demanded. The ceremony
of decapitation, which is here somewhat slurred over, is carried out
with a greater semblance of reality in other parts of Bohemia. Thus
in some villages of the Königgrätz district on Whit-Monday the girls
assemble under one lime-tree and the young men under another, all
dressed in their best and tricked out with ribbons. The young men

twine a garland for the Queen, and the girls another for the King. When they have chosen the King and Queen they all go in procession two and two, to the ale-house, from the balcony of which the crier proclaims the names of the King and Queen. Both are then invested with the insignia of their office and are crowned with the garlands, while the music plays up. Then some one gets on a bench and accuses the King of various offences, such as ill-treating the cattle. The King appeals to witnesses and a trial ensues, at the close of which the judge, who carries a white wand as his badge of office, pronounces a verdict of " Guilty " or " Not guilty." If the verdict is " Guilty," the judge breaks his wand, the King kneels on a white cloth, all heads are bared, and a soldier sets three or four hats, one above the other, on his Majesty's head. The judge then pronounces the word " Guilty " thrice in a loud voice, and orders the crier to behead the King. The crier obeys by striking off the King's hats with his wooden sword.

But perhaps, for our purpose, the most instructive of these mimic executions is the following Bohemian one. In some places of the Pilsen district (Bohemia) on Whit-Monday the King is dressed in bark, ornamented with flowers and ribbons ; he wears a crown of gilt paper and rides a horse, which is also decked with flowers. Attended by a judge, an executioner, and other characters, and followed by a train of soldiers, all mounted, he rides to the village square, where a hut or arbour of green boughs has been erected under the May-trees, which are firs, freshly cut, peeled to the top, and dressed with flowers and ribbons. After the dames and maidens of the village have been criticised and a frog beheaded, the cavalcade rides to a place previously determined upon, in a straight, broad street. Here they draw up in two lines and the King takes to flight. He is given a short start and rides off at full speed, pursued by the whole troop. If they fail to catch him he remains King for another year, and his companions must pay his score at the ale-house in the evening. But if they overtake and catch him he is scourged with hazel rods or beaten with the wooden swords and compelled to dismount. Then the executioner asks, " Shall I behead this King ? " The answer is given, " Behead him " ; the executioner brandishes his axe, and with the words, " One, two, three, let the King headless be ! " he strikes off the King's crown. Amid the loud cries of the bystanders the King sinks to the ground ; then he is laid on a bier and carried to the nearest farmhouse.

In most of the personages who are thus slain in mimicry it is impossible not to recognise representatives of the tree-spirit or spirit of vegetation, as he is supposed to manifest himself in spring. The bark, leaves, and flowers in which the actors are dressed, and the season of the year at which they appear, show that they belong to the same class as the Grass King, King of the May, Jack-in-the-Green, and other representatives of the vernal spirit of vegetation which we examined in an earlier part of this work. As if to remove any possible doubt on this head, we find that in two cases these slain men are brought into direct connexion with May-trees, which are the impersonal, as the May King, Grass King, and so forth, are the personal representatives of the tree-spirit. The drenching of the *Pfingstl* with water and his wading up to the middle into the brook are, therefore, no doubt rain-charms like those which have been already described.

But if these personages represent, as they certainly do, the spirit of vegetation in spring, the question arises, Why kill them ? What is the object of slaying the spirit of vegetation at any time and above all in spring, when his services are most wanted ? The only probable answer to this question seems to be given in the explanation already proposed of the custom of killing the divine king or priest. The divine life, incarnate in a material and mortal body, is liable to be tainted and corrupted by the weakness of the frail medium in which it is for a time enshrined ; and if it is to be saved from the increasing enfeeblement which it must necessarily share with its human incarnation as he advances in years, it must be detached from him before, or at least as soon as, he exhibits signs of decay, in order to be transferred to a vigorous successor. This is done by killing the old representative of the god and conveying the divine spirit from him to a new incarnation. The killing of the god, that is, of his human incarnation, is therefore merely a necessary step to his revival or resurrection in a better form. Far from being an extinction of the divine spirit, it is only the beginning of a purer and stronger manifestation of it. If this explanation holds good of the custom of killing divine kings and priests in general, it is still more obviously applicable to the custom of annually killing the representative of the tree-spirit or spirit of vegetation in spring. For the decay of plant life in winter is readily interpreted by primitive man as an enfeeblement of the spirit of vegetation ; the spirit has, he thinks, grown old and weak and must therefore be renovated by being slain and brought to life in a younger and fresher form. Thus the killing of the representative of the tree-spirit in spring is regarded as a means to promote and quicken the growth of vegetation. For the killing of the tree-spirit is associated always (we must suppose) implicitly, and sometimes explicitly also, with a revival or resurrection of him in a more youthful and vigorous form. So in the Saxon and Thüringen custom, after the Wild Man has been shot he is brought to life again by a doctor ; and in the Wurmlingen ceremony there figures a Dr. Iron-Beard, who probably once played a similar part ; certainly in another spring ceremony, which will be described presently, Dr. Iron-Beard pretends to restore a dead man to life. But of this revival or resurrection of the god we shall have more to say anon.

The points of similarity between these North European personages and the subject of our enquiry—the King of the Wood or priest of Nemi—are sufficiently striking. In these northern maskers we see kings, whose dress of bark and leaves along with the hut of green boughs and the fir-trees, under which they hold their court, proclaim them unmistakably as, like their Italian counterpart, Kings of the Wood. Like him they die a violent death, but like him they may escape from it for a time by their bodily strength and agility ; for in several of these northern customs the flight and pursuit of the king is a prominent part of the ceremony, and in one case at least if the king can outrun his pursuers he retains his life and his office for another year.   In this last case the king in fact holds office on condition of running for his life once a year, just as the King of Calicut in later times held office on condition of defending his life against all comers once every twelve years, and just as the priest of Nemi held office on condition of defending himself against any assault at any time.   In every one of these instances the life of the god-man is prolonged on condition of his showing, in a severe physical contest of fight or flight, that his bodily strength is not decayed, and that, therefore, the violent death, which sooner or later is inevitable, may for the present be postponed.   With regard to flight it is noticeable that flight figured conspicuously both in the legend and in the practice of the King of the Wood.   He had to be a runaway slave in memory of the flight of Orestes, the traditional founder of the worship ; hence the Kings of the Wood are described by an ancient writer as " both strong of hand and fleet of foot."   Perhaps if we knew the ritual of the Arician grove fully we might find that the king was allowed a chance for his life by flight, like his Bohemian brother.   I have already conjectured that the annual flight of the priestly king at Rome (*regifugium*) was at first a flight of the same kind ; in other words, that he was originally one of those divine kings who are either put to death after a fixed period or allowed to prove by the strong hand or the fleet foot that their divinity is vigorous and unimpaired.   One more point of resemblance may be noted between the Italian King of the Wood and his northern counterparts.   In Saxony and Thüringen the representative of the tree-spirit, after being killed, is brought to life again by a doctor.   This is exactly what legend affirmed to have happened to the first King of the Wood at Nemi, Hippolytus or Virbius, who after he had been killed by his horses was restored to life by the physician Aesculapius.   Such a legend tallies well with the theory that the slaying of the King of the Wood was only a step to his revival or resurrection in his successor.

§ 2. *Burying the Carnival.*—Thus far I have offered an explanation of the rule which required that the priest of Nemi should be slain by his successor.   The explanation claims to be no more than probable ; our scanty knowledge of the custom and of its history forbids it to be more.   But its probability will be augmented in proportion to the extent to which the motives and modes of thought which it assumes can be proved to have operated in primitive society.   Hitherto the god with whose death and resurrection we have been chiefly concerned has been the tree-god.   But if I can show that the custom of killing the god and the belief in his resurrection originated, or at least existed, in the hunting and pastoral stage of society, when the slain god was an animal, and that it survived into the agricultural stage, when the slain god was the corn or a human being representing the corn, the probability of my explanation will have been considerably increased.

This I shall attempt to do in the sequel, and in the course of the discussion I hope to clear up some obscurities which still remain, and to answer some objections which may have suggested themselves to the reader.

We start from the point at which we left off—the spring customs of European peasantry. Besides the ceremonies already described there are two kindred sets of observances in which the simulated death of a divine or supernatural being is a conspicuous feature. In one of them the being whose death is dramatically represented is a personification of the Carnival; in the other it is Death himself. The former ceremony falls naturally at the end of the Carnival, either on the last day of that merry season, namely Shrove Tuesday, or on the first day of Lent, namely Ash Wednesday. The date of the other ceremony—the Carrying or Driving out of Death, as it is commonly called—is not so uniformly fixed. Generally it is the fourth Sunday in Lent, which hence goes by the name of Dead Sunday; but in some places the celebration falls a week earlier, in others, as among the Czechs of Bohemia, a week later, while in certain German villages of Moravia it is held on the first Sunday after Easter. Perhaps, as has been suggested, the date may originally have been variable, depending on the appearance of the first swallow or some other herald of the spring. Some writers regard the ceremony as Slavonic in its origin. Grimm thought it was a festival of the New Year with the old Slavs, who began their year in March. We shall first take examples of the mimic death of the Carnival, which always falls before the other in the calendar.

At Frosinone, in Latium, about half-way between Rome and Naples, the dull monotony of life in a provincial Italian town is agreeably broken on the last day of the Carnival by the ancient festival known as the *Radica*. About four o'clock in the afternoon the town band, playing lively tunes and followed by a great crowd, proceeds to the Piazza del Plebiscito, where is the Sub-Prefecture as well as the rest of the Government buildings. Here, in the middle of the square, the eyes of the expectant multitude are greeted by the sight of an immense car decked with many-coloured festoons and drawn by four horses. Mounted on the car is a huge chair, on which sits enthroned the majestic figure of the Carnival, a man of stucco about nine feet high with a rubicund and smiling countenance. Enormous boots, a tin helmet like those which grace the heads of officers of the Italian marine, and a coat of many colours embellished with strange devices, adorn the outward man of this stately personage. His left hand rests on the arm of the chair, while with his right he gracefully salutes the crowd, being moved to this act of civility by a string which is pulled by a man who modestly shrinks from publicity under the mercy-seat. And now the crowd, surging excitedly round the car, gives vent to its feelings in wild cries of joy, gentle and simple being mixed up together and all dancing furiously the *Saltarello*. A special feature of the festival is that every one must carry in his hand what is called a *radica* (" root "), by which is meant a huge leaf of the aloe or rather the agave.   Any one who ventured into the crowd without such a leaf would be unceremoniously hustled out of it, unless indeed he bore as a substitute a large cabbage at the end of a long stick or a bunch of grass curiously plaited.   When the multitude, after a short turn, has escorted the slow-moving car to the gate of the Sub-Prefecture, they halt, and the car, jolting over the uneven ground, rumbles into the courtyard.   A hush now falls on the crowd, their subdued voices sounding, according to the description of one who has heard them, like the murmur of a troubled sea.   All eyes are turned anxiously to the door from which the Sub-Prefect himself and the other representatives of the majesty of the law are expected to issue and pay their homage to the hero of the hour.   A few moments of suspense and then a storm of cheers and hand-clapping salutes the appearance of the dignitaries, as they file out and, descending the staircase, take their place in the procession.   The hymn of the Carnival is now thundered out, after which, amid a deafening roar, aloe leaves and cabbages are whirled aloft and descend impartially on the heads of the just and the unjust, who lend fresh zest to the proceedings by engaging in a free fight.   When these preliminaries have been concluded to the satisfaction of all concerned, the procession gets under weigh.   The rear is brought up by a cart laden with barrels of wine and policemen, the latter engaged in the congenial task of serving out wine to all who ask for it, while a most internecine struggle, accompanied by a copious discharge of yells, blows, and blasphemy, goes on among the surging crowd at the cart's tail in their anxiety not to miss the glorious opportunity of intoxicating themselves at the public expense.   Finally, after the procession has paraded the principal streets in this majestic manner, the effigy of Carnival is taken to the middle of a public square, stripped of his finery, laid on a pile of wood, and burnt amid the cries of the multitude, who thundering out once more the song of the Carnival fling their so-called " roots " on the pyre and give themselves up without restraint to the pleasures of the dance.

In the Abruzzi a pasteboard figure of the Carnival is carried by four grave-diggers with pipes in their mouths and bottles of wine slung at their shoulder-belts.   In front walks the wife of the Carnival, dressed in mourning and dissolved in tears.   From time to time the company halts, and while the wife addresses the sympathising public, the grave-diggers refresh the inner man with a pull at the bottle.   In the open square the mimic corpse is laid on a pyre, and to the roll of drums, the shrill screams of the women, and the gruffer cries of the men a light is set to it.   While the figure burns, chestnuts are thrown about among the crowd.   Sometimes the Carnival is represented by a straw-man at the top of a pole which is borne through the town by a troop of mummers in the course of the afternoon.   When evening comes on, four of the mummers hold out a quilt or sheet by the corners, and the figure of the Carnival is made to tumble into it.   The procession is then resumed, the performers weeping crocodile tears and emphasising the poignancy of their grief by the help of saucepans and dinner bells. Sometimes, again, in the Abruzzi the dead Carnival is personified by a living man who lies in a coffin, attended by another who acts the priest and dispenses holy water in great profusion from a bathing tub.

At Lerida, in Catalonia, the funeral of the Carnival was witnessed by an English traveller in 1877. On the last Sunday of the Carnival a grand procession of infantry, cavalry, and maskers of many sorts, some on horseback and some in carriages, escorted the grand car of His Grace Pau Pi, as the effigy was called, in triumph through the principal streets. For three days the revelry ran high, and then at midnight on the last day of the Carnival the same procession again wound through the streets, but under a different aspect and for a different end. The triumphal car was exchanged for a hearse, in which reposed the effigy of his dead Grace : a troop of maskers, who in the first procession had played the part of Students of Folly with many a merry quip and jest, now, robed as priests and bishops, paced slowly along holding aloft huge lighted tapers and singing a dirge. All the mummers wore crape, and all the horsemen carried blazing flambeaux. Down the high street, between the lofty, many-storeyed and balconied houses, where every window, every balcony, every housetop was crammed with a dense mass of spectators, all dressed and masked in fantastic gorgeousness, the procession took its melancholy way. Over the scene flashed and played the shifting cross-lights and shadows from the moving torches : red and blue Bengal lights flared up and died out again ; and above the trampling of the horses and the measured tread of the marching multitude rose the voices of the priests chanting the requiem, while the military bands struck in with the solemn roll of the muffled drums. On reaching the principal square the procession halted, a burlesque funeral oration was pronounced over the defunct Pau Pi, and the lights were extinguished. Immediately the devil and his angels darted from the crowd, seized the body and fled away with it, hotly pursued by the whole multitude, yelling, screaming, and cheering. Naturally the fiends were overtaken and dispersed ; and the sham corpse, rescued from their clutches, was laid in a grave that had been made ready for its reception. Thus the Carnival of 1877 at Lerida died and was buried.

A ceremony of the same sort is observed in Provence on Ash Wednesday. An effigy called Caramantran, whimsically attired, is drawn in a chariot or borne on a litter, accompanied by the populace in grotesque costumes, who carry gourds full of wine and drain them with all the marks, real or affected, of intoxication. At the head of the procession are some men disguised as judges and barristers, and a tall gaunt personage who masquerades as Lent ; behind them follow young people mounted on miserable hacks and attired as mourners who pretend to bewail the fate that is in store for Caramantran. In the principal square the procession halts, the tribunal is constituted,

and Caramantran placed at the bar.   After a formal trial he is sentenced
to death amid the groans of the mob : the barrister who defended
him embraces his client for the last time : the officers of justice do
their duty : the condemned is set with his back to a wall and hurried
into eternity under a shower of stones.   The sea or a river receives
his mangled remains.   Throughout nearly the whole of the Ardennes
it was and still is customary on Ash Wednesday to burn an effigy
which is supposed to represent the Carnival, while appropriate verses
are sung round about the blazing figure.   Very often an attempt is
made to fashion the effigy in the likeness of the husband who is reputed
to be least faithful to his wife of any in the village.   As might
perhaps have been anticipated, the distinction of being selected for
portraiture under these painful circumstances has a slight tendency
to breed domestic jars, especially when the portrait is burnt in front
of the house of the gay deceiver whom it represents, while a powerful
chorus of caterwauls, groans, and other melodious sounds bears public
testimony to the opinion which his friends and neighbours entertain
of his private virtues.   In some villages of the Ardennes a young man
of flesh and blood, dressed up in hay and straw, used to act the part
of Shrove Tuesday (*Mardi Gras*), as the personification of the Carnival
is often called in France after the last day of the period which he
personates.   He was brought before a mock tribunal, and being condemned to death was placed with his back to a wall, like a soldier at
a military execution, and fired at with blank cartridges.   At Vrigne-
aux-Bois one of these harmless buffoons, named Thierry, was accidentally killed by a wad that had been left in a musket of the firing-party.
When poor Shrove Tuesday dropped under the fire, the applause
was loud and long, he did it so naturally ; but when he did not get
up again, they ran to him and found him a corpse.   Since then there
have been no more of these mock executions in the Ardennes.

In Normandy on the evening of Ash Wednesday it used to be the
custom to hold a celebration called the Burial of Shrove Tuesday.
A squalid effigy scantily clothed in rags, a battered old hat crushed
down on his dirty face, his great round paunch stuffed with straw,
represented the disreputable old rake who, after a long course of
dissipation, was now about to suffer for his sins.   Hoisted on the
shoulders of a sturdy fellow, who pretended to stagger under the
burden, this popular personification of the Carnival promenaded
the streets for the last time in a manner the reverse of triumphal.
Preceded by a drummer and accompanied by a jeering rabble, among
whom the urchins and all the tag-rag and bobtail of the town mustered
in great force, the figure was carried about by the flickering light of
torches to the discordant din of shovels and tongs, pots and pans,
horns and kettles, mingled with hootings, groans, and hisses.   From
time to time the procession halted, and a champion of morality
accused the broken-down old sinner of all the excesses he had committed and for which he was now about to be burned alive.   The
culprit, having nothing to urge in his own defence, was thrown on a

heap of straw, a torch was put to it, and a great blaze shot up, to the delight of the children who frisked round it screaming out some old popular verses about the death of the Carnival. Sometimes the effigy was rolled down the slope of a hill before being burnt. At Saint-Lô the ragged effigy of Shrove Tuesday was followed by his widow, a big burly lout dressed as a woman with a crape veil, who emitted sounds of lamentation and woe in a stentorian voice. After being carried about the streets on a litter attended by a crowd of maskers, the figure was thrown into the River Vire. The final scene has been graphically described by Madame Octave Feuillet as she witnessed it in her childhood some sixty years ago. " My parents invited friends to see, from the top of the tower of Jeanne Couillard, the funeral procession passing. It was there that, quaffing lemonade—the only refreshment allowed because of the fast—we witnessed at nightfall a spectacle of which I shall always preserve a lively recollection. At our feet flowed the Vire under its old stone bridge. On the middle of the bridge lay the figure of Shrove Tuesday on a litter of leaves, surrounded by scores of maskers dancing, singing, and carrying torches. Some of them in their motley costumes ran along the parapet like fiends. The rest, worn out with their revels, sat on the posts and dozed. Soon the dancing stopped, and some of the troop, seizing a torch, set fire to the effigy, after which they flung it into the river with redoubled shouts and clamour. The man of straw, soaked with resin, floated away burning down the stream of the Vire, lighting up with its funeral fires the woods on the bank and the battlements of the old castle in which Louis XI. and Francis I. had slept. When the last glimmer of the blazing phantom had vanished, like a falling star, at the end of the valley, every one withdrew, crowd and maskers alike, and we quitted the ramparts with our guests."

In the neighbourhood of Tübingen on Shrove Tuesday a straw-man, called the Shrovetide Bear, is made up ; he is dressed in a pair of old trousers, and a fresh black-pudding or two squirts filled with blood are inserted in his neck. After a formal condemnation he is beheaded, laid in a coffin, and on Ash Wednesday is buried in the churchyard. This is called " Burying the Carnival." Amongst some of the Saxons of Transylvania the Carnival is hanged. Thus at Braller on Ash Wednesday or Shrove Tuesday two white and two chestnut horses draw a sledge on which is placed a straw-man swathed in a white cloth ; beside him is a cart-wheel which is kept turning round. Two lads disguised as old men follow the sledge lamenting. The rest of the village lads, mounted on horseback and decked with ribbons, accompany the procession, which is headed by two girls crowned with evergreen and drawn in a waggon or sledge. A trial is held under a tree, at which lads disguised as soldiers pronounce sentence of death. The two old men try to rescue the straw-man and to fly with him, but to no purpose ; he is caught by the two girls and handed over to the executioner, who hangs him on a tree. In vain the old men try to climb up the tree and take him down ; they always tumble down, and at last in despair they throw themselves on the ground and weep and howl for the hanged man. An official then makes a speech in which he declares that the Carnival was condemned to death because he had done them harm, by wearing out their shoes and making them tired and sleepy. At the " Burial of Carnival " in Lechrain, a man dressed as a woman in black clothes is carried on a litter or bier by four men ; he is lamented over by men disguised as women in black clothes, then thrown down before the village dung-heap, drenched with water, buried in the dung-heap, and covered with straw. On the evening of Shrove Tuesday the Esthonians make a straw figure called *metsik* or " wood-spirit " ; one year it is dressed with a man's coat and hat, next year with a hood and a petticoat. This figure is stuck on a long pole, carried across the boundary of the village with loud cries of joy, and fastened to the top of a tree in the wood. The ceremony is believed to be a protection against all kinds of misfortune.

Sometimes at these Shrovetide or Lenten ceremonies the resurrection of the pretended dead person is enacted. Thus, in some parts of Swabia on Shrove Tuesday Dr. Iron-Beard professes to bleed a sick man, who thereupon falls as dead to the ground ; but the doctor at last restores him to life by blowing air into him through a tube. In the Harz Mountains, when Carnival is over, a man is laid on a baking-trough and carried with dirges to a grave ; but in the grave a glass of brandy is buried instead of the man. A speech is delivered and then the people return to the village-green or meeting-place, where they smoke the long clay pipes which are distributed at funerals. On the morning of Shrove Tuesday in the following year the brandy is dug up and the festival begins by every one tasting the spirit which, as the phrase goes, has come to life again.

§ 3. *Carrying out Death.*—The ceremony of " Carrying out Death " presents much the same features as " Burying the Carnival " ; except that the carrying out of Death is generally followed by a ceremony, or at least accompanied by a profession, of bringing in Summer, Spring, or Life. Thus in Middle Franken, a province of Bavaria, on the fourth Sunday in Lent, the village urchins used to make a straw effigy of Death, which they carried about with burlesque pomp through the streets, and afterwards burned with loud cries beyond the bounds. The Frankish custom is thus described by a writer of the sixteenth century : " At Mid-Lent, the season when the church bids us rejoice, the young people of my native country make a straw image of Death, and fastening it to a pole carry it with shouts to the neighbouring villages. By some they are kindly received, and after being refreshed with milk, peas, and dried pears, the usual food of that season, are sent home again. Others, however, treat them with anything but hospitality ; for, looking on them as harbingers of misfortune, to wit of death, they drive them from their boundaries with weapons and insults." In the villages near Erlangen, when the fourth Sunday in Lent came round, the peasant girls used to dress themselves in all their finery with flowers in their hair. Thus attired they repaired to the neighbouring town, carrying puppets which were adorned with leaves and covered with white cloths. These they took from house to house in pairs, stopping at every door where they expected to receive something, and singing a few lines in which they announced that it was Mid-Lent and that they were about to throw Death into the water. When they had collected some trifling gratuities they went to the River Regnitz and flung the puppets representing Death into the stream. This was done to ensure a fruitful and prosperous year; further, it was considered a safeguard against pestilence and sudden death. At Nuremberg girls of seven to eighteen years of age go through the streets bearing a little open coffin, in which is a doll hidden under a shroud. Others carry a beech branch, with an apple fastened to it for a head, in an open box. They sing, " We carry Death into the water, it is well," or " We carry Death into the water, carry him in and out again." In some parts of Bavaria down to 1780 it was believed that a fatal epidemic would ensue if the custom of " Carrying out Death " were not observed.

In some villages of Thüringen, on the fourth Sunday of Lent, the children used to carry a puppet of birchen twigs through the village, and then threw it into a pool, while they sang, " We carry the old Death out behind the herdsman's old house ; we have got Summer, and Kroden's (?) power is destroyed." At Debschwitz or Dobschwitz, near Gera, the ceremony of " Driving out Death " is or was annually observed on the first of March. The young people make up a figure of straw or the like materials, dress it in old clothes, which they have begged from houses in the village, and carry it out and throw it into the river. On returning to the village they break the good news to the people, and receive eggs and other victuals as a reward. The ceremony is or was supposed to purify the village and to protect the inhabitants from sickness and plague. In other villages of Thüringen, in which the population was originally Slavonic, the carrying out of the puppet is accompanied with the singing of a song, which begins, " Now we carry Death out of the village and Spring into the village." At the end of the seventeenth and beginning of the eighteenth century the custom was observed in Thüringen as follows. The boys and girls made an effigy of straw or the like materials, but the shape of the figure varied from year to year. In one year it would represent an old man, in the next an old woman, in the third a young man, and in the fourth a maiden, and the dress of the figure varied with the character it personated. There used to be a sharp contest as to where the effigy was to be made, for the people thought that the house from which it was carried forth would not be visited with death that year. Having been made, the puppet was fastened to a pole and carried by a girl if it represented an old man, but by a boy if it represented an old woman. Thus it was borne in procession, the young people holding sticks in their hands and singing that they were driving out Death. When they came to water they threw the effigy into it and ran hastily back, fearing that it might jump on their shoulders and wring their necks. They also took care not to touch it, lest it should dry them up. On their return they beat the cattle with the sticks, believing that this would make the animals fat or fruitful. Afterwards they visited the house or houses from which they had carried the image of Death, where they received a dole of half-boiled peas. The custom of " Carrying out Death " was practised also in Saxony. At Leipsic the bastards and public women used to make a straw effigy of Death every year at Mid-Lent. This they carried through all the streets with songs and showed it to the young married women. Finally they threw it into the River Parthe. By this ceremony they professed to make the young wives fruitful, to purify the city, and to protect the inhabitants for that year from plague and other epidemics.

Ceremonies of the same sort are observed at Mid-Lent in Silesia. Thus in many places the grown girls with the help of the young men dress up a straw figure with women's clothes and carry it out of the village towards the setting sun. At the boundary they strip it of its clothes, tear it in pieces, and scatter the fragments about the fields. This is called "Burying Death." As they carry the image out, they sing that they are about to bury Death under an oak, that he may depart from the people. Sometimes the song runs that they are bearing Death over hill and dale to return no more. In the Polish neighbourhood of Gross-Strehlitz the puppet is called Goik. It is carried on horseback and thrown into the nearest water. The people think that the ceremony protects them from sickness of every sort in the coming year. In the districts of Wohlau and Guhrau the image of Death used to be thrown over the boundary of the next village. But as the neighbours feared to receive the ill-omened figure, they were on the look-out to repel it, and hard knocks were often exchanged between the two parties. In some Polish parts of Upper Silesia the effigy, representing an old woman, goes by the name of Marzana, the goddess of death. It is made in the house where the last death occurred, and is carried on a pole to the boundary of the village, where it is thrown into a pond or burnt. At Polkwitz the custom of " Carrying out Death " fell into abeyance ; but an outbreak of fatal sickness which followed the intermission of the ceremony induced the people to resume it.

In Bohemia the children go out with a straw-man, representing Death, to the end of the village, where they burn it, singing—

" Now carry we Death out of the village,   Welcome, dear Summer,
The new Summer into the village,   Green little corn."

At Tabor in Bohemia the figure of Death is carried out of the town and flung from a high rock into the water, while they sing—

" Death swims on the water,   And do thou, O holy Marketa,
Summer will soon be here,   Give us a good year
We carried Death away for you,   For wheat and for rye."
We brought the Summer.

In other parts of Bohemia they carry Death to the end of the village, singing—

" *We carry Death out of the village,*   *Dear Spring, we bid you welcome,*
And the New Year into the village.   *Green grass, we bid you welcome.*"

Behind the village they erect a pyre, on which they burn the straw figure, reviling and scoffing at it the while.   Then they return, singing—

" *We have carried away Death,*   *He has taken up his quarters in the village,*
And brought Life back.   *Therefore sing joyous songs.*"

In some German villages of Moravia, as in Jassnitz and Seitendorf, the young folk assemble on the third Sunday in Lent and fashion a straw-man, who is generally adorned with a fur cap and a pair of old leathern hose, if such are to be had.   The effigy is then hoisted on a pole and carried by the lads and lasses out into the open fields.   On the way they sing a song, in which it is said that they are carrying Death away and bringing dear Summer into the house, and with Summer the May and the flowers.   On reaching an appointed place they dance in a circle round the effigy with loud shouts and screams, then suddenly rush at it and tear it to pieces with their hands.   Lastly, the pieces are thrown together in a heap, the pole is broken, and fire is set to the whole.   While it burns the troop dances merrily round it, rejoicing at the victory won by Spring ; and when the fire has nearly died out they go to the householders to beg for a present of eggs wherewith to hold a feast, taking care to give as a reason for the request that they have carried Death out and away.

The preceding evidence shows that the effigy of Death is often regarded with fear and treated with marks of hatred and abhorrence. Thus the anxiety of the villagers to transfer the figure from their own to their neighbours' land, and the reluctance of the latter to receive the ominous guest, are proof enough of the dread which it inspires. Further, in Lusatia and Silesia the puppet is sometimes made to look in at the window of a house, and it is believed that some one in the house will die within the year unless his life is redeemed by the payment of money.   Again, after throwing the effigy away, the bearers sometimes run home lest Death should follow them, and if one of them falls in running, it is believed that he will die within the year.   At Chrudim, in Bohemia, the figure of Death is made out of a cross, with a head and mask stuck at the top, and a shirt stretched out on it.   On the fifth Sunday in Lent the boys take this effigy to the nearest brook or pool, and standing in a line throw it into the water.   Then they all plunge in after it ; but as soon as it is caught no one more may enter the water.   The boy who did not enter the water or entered it last will die within the year, and he is obliged to carry the Death back to the village.   The effigy is then burned.   On the other hand, it is believed that no one will die within the year in the house out of which the figure of Death has been carried ; and the village out of which Death has been driven is sometimes supposed to be protected against sickness and plague. In some villages of Austrian Silesia on the Saturday before Dead Sunday an effigy is made of old clothes, hay, and straw, for the purpose of driving Death out of the village. On Sunday the people, armed with sticks and straps, assemble before the house where the figure is lodged. Four lads then draw the effigy by cords through the village amid exultant shouts, while all the others beat it with their sticks and straps. On reaching a field which belongs to a neighbouring village they lay down the figure, cudgel it soundly, and scatter the fragments over the field. The people believe that the village from which Death has been thus carried out will be safe from any infectious disease for the whole year.

§ 4. *Bringing in Summer.*—In the preceding ceremonies the return of Spring, Summer, or Life, as a sequel to the expulsion of Death, is only implied or at most announced. In the following ceremonies it is plainly enacted. Thus in some parts of Bohemia the effigy of Death is drowned by being thrown into the water at sunset ; then the girls go out into the wood and cut down a young tree with a green crown, hang a doll dressed as a woman on it, deck the whole with green, red, and white ribbons, and march in procession with their *Lito* (Summer) into the village, collecting gifts and singing—

> " *Death swims in the water,*   *With yellow pancakes.*
> *Spring comes to visit us,*   *We carried Death out of the village,*
> *With eggs that are red,*   *We are carrying Summer into the village.*"

In many Silesian villages the figure of Death, after being treated with respect, is stript of its clothes and flung with curses into the water, or torn to pieces in a field. Then the young folk repair to a wood, cut down a small fir-tree, peel the trunk, and deck it with festoons of evergreens, paper roses, painted egg-shells, motley bits of cloth, and so forth. The tree thus adorned is called Summer or May. Boys carry it from house to house singing appropriate songs and begging for presents. Among their songs is the following :

> " *We have carried Death out,*   *The Summer and the May,*
> *We are bringing the dear Summer back,*   *And all the flowers gay.*"

Sometimes they also bring back from the wood a prettily adorned figure, which goes by the name of Summer, May, or the Bride ; in the Polish districts it is called Dziewanna, the goddess of spring.

At Eisenach on the fourth Sunday in Lent young people used to fasten a straw-man, representing Death, to a wheel, which they trundled to the top of a hill. Then setting fire to the figure they allowed it and the wheel to roll down the slope. Next they cut a tall fir-tree, tricked it out with ribbons, and set it up in the plain. The men then climbed the tree to fetch down the ribbons. In Upper Lusatia the figure of Death, made of straw and rags, is dressed in a veil furnished by the last bride and a shirt provided by the house in which the last death took place. Thus arrayed the figure is stuck on the end of a long pole and carried at full speed by the tallest and strongest girl, while the rest

pelt the effigy with sticks and stones. Whoever hits it will be sure
to live through the year. In this way Death is carried out of the
village and thrown into the water or over the boundary of the next
village. On their way home each one breaks a green branch and
carries it gaily with him till he reaches the village, when he throws it
away. Sometimes the young people of the next village, upon whose
land the figure has been thrown, run after them and hurl it back, not
wishing to have Death among them. Hence the two parties occasionally come to blows.

In these cases Death is represented by the puppet which is thrown
away, Summer or Life by the branches or trees which are brought
back. But sometimes a new potency of life seems to be attributed
to the image of Death itself, and by a kind of resurrection it becomes
the instrument of the general revival. Thus in some parts of Lusatia
women alone are concerned in carrying out Death, and suffer no male
to meddle with it. Attired in mourning, which they wear the whole
day, they make a puppet of straw, clothe it in a white shirt, and
give it a broom in one hand and a scythe in the other. Singing songs
and pursued by urchins throwing stones, they carry the puppet to the
village boundary, where they tear it in pieces. Then they cut down
a fine tree, hang the shirt on it, and carry it home singing. On the
Feast of Ascension the Saxons of Braller, a village of Transylvania,
not far from Hermannstadt, observe the ceremony of " Carrying out
Death " in the following manner. After morning service all the
school-girls repair to the house of one of their number, and there dress
up the Death. This is done by tying a threshed-out sheaf of corn into
a rough semblance of a head and body, while the arms are simulated
by a broomstick thrust through it horizontally. The figure is dressed
in the holiday attire of a young peasant woman, with a red hood, silver
brooches, and a profusion of ribbons at the arms and breast. The
girls bustle at their work, for soon the bells will be ringing to vespers,
and the Death must be ready in time to be placed at the open window,
that all the people may see it on their way to church. When vespers
are over, the longed-for moment has come for the first procession
with the Death to begin ; it is a privilege that belongs to the school-
girls alone. Two of the older girls seize the figure by the arms and
walk in front : all the rest follow two and two. Boys may take no
part in the procession, but they troop after it gazing with open-mouthed
admiration at the " beautiful Death." So the procession goes through
all the streets of the village, the girls singing the old hymn that begins—

> " Gott mein Vater, deine Liebe
> Reicht so weit der Himmel ist,"

to a tune that differs from the ordinary one. When the procession
has wound its way through every street, the girls go to another house,
and having shut the door against the eager prying crowd of boys who
follow at their heels, they strip the Death and pass the naked truss of
straw out of the window to the boys, who pounce on it, run out of the

village with it without singing, and fling the dilapidated effigy into the neighbouring brook. This done, the second scene of the little drama begins. While the boys were carrying away the Death out of the village, the girls remained in the house, and one of them is now dressed in all the finery which had been worn by the effigy. Thus arrayed she is led in procession through all the streets to the singing of the same hymn as before. When the procession is over they all betake themselves to the house of the girl who played the leading part. Here a feast awaits them from which also the boys are excluded. It is a popular belief that the children may safely begin to eat gooseberries and other fruit after the day on which Death has thus been carried out ; for Death, which up to that time lurked especially in gooseberries, is now destroyed. Further, they may now bathe with impunity out of doors. Very similar is the ceremony which, down to recent years, was observed in some of the German villages of Moravia. Boys and girls met on the afternoon of the first Sunday after Easter, and together fashioned a puppet of straw to represent Death. Decked with bright-coloured ribbons and cloths, and fastened to the top of a long pole, the effigy was then borne with singing and clamour to the nearest height, where it was stript of its gay attire and thrown or rolled down the slope. One of the girls was next dressed in the gauds taken from the effigy of Death, and with her at its head the procession moved back to the village. In some villages the practice is to bury the effigy in the place that has the most evil reputation of all the country-side : others throw it into running water.

In the Lusatian ceremony described above, the tree which is brought home after the destruction of the figure of Death is plainly equivalent to the trees or branches which, in the preceding customs, were brought back as representatives of Summer or Life, after Death had been thrown away or destroyed. But the transference of the shirt worn by the effigy of Death to the tree clearly indicates that the tree is a kind of revivification, in a new form, of the destroyed effigy. This comes out also in the Transylvanian and Moravian customs : the dressing of a girl in the clothes worn by the Death, and the leading her about the village to the same song which had been sung when the Death was being carried about, show that she is intended to be a kind of resuscitation of the being whose effigy has just been destroyed. These examples therefore suggest that the Death whose demolition is represented in these ceremonies cannot be regarded as the purely destructive agent which we understand by Death. If the tree which is brought back as an embodiment of the reviving vegetation of spring is clothed in the shirt worn by the Death which has just been destroyed, the object certainly cannot be to check and counteract the revival of vegetation : it can only be to foster and promote it. Therefore the being which has just been destroyed—the so-called Death—must be supposed to be endowed with a vivifying and quickening influence, which it can communicate to the vegetable and even the animal world. This ascription of a life-giving virtue to the figure of Death is put beyond a doubt by the custom, observed in some places, of taking pieces of the straw effigy of Death and placing them in the fields to make the crops grow, or in the manger to make the cattle thrive. Thus in Spachendorf, a village of Austrian Silesia, the figure of Death, made of straw, brushwood, and rags, is carried with wild songs to an open place outside the village and there burned, and while it is burning a general struggle takes place for the pieces, which are pulled out of the flames with bare hands. Each one who secures a fragment of the effigy ties it to a branch of the largest tree in his garden, or buries it in his field, in the belief that this causes the crops to grow better. In the Troppau district of Austrian Silesia the straw figure which the boys make on the fourth Sunday in Lent is dressed by the girls in woman's clothes and hung with ribbons, necklace, and garlands. Attached to a long pole it is carried out of the village, followed by a troop of young people of both sexes, who alternately frolic, lament, and sing songs. Arrived at its destination—a field outside the village —the figure is stripped of its clothes and ornaments ; then the crowd rushes at it and tears it to bits, scuffling for the fragments. Every one tries to get a wisp of the straw of which the effigy was made, because such a wisp, placed in the manger, is believed to make the cattle thrive. Or the straw is put in the hens' nest, it being supposed that this prevents the hens from carrying away their eggs, and makes them brood much better. The same attribution of a fertilising power to the figure of Death appears in the belief that if the bearers of the figure, after throwing it away, beat cattle with their sticks, this will render the beasts fat or prolific. Perhaps the sticks had been previously used to beat the Death, and so had acquired the fertilising power ascribed to the effigy. We have seen, too, that at Leipsic a straw effigy of Death was shown to young wives to make them fruitful.

It seems hardly possible to separate from the May-trees the trees or branches which are brought into the village after the destruction of the Death. The bearers who bring them in profess to be bringing in the Summer, therefore the trees obviously represent the Summer ; indeed in Silesia they are commonly called the Summer or the May, and the doll which is sometimes attached to the Summer-tree is a duplicate representative of the Summer, just as the May is sometimes represented at the same time by a May-tree and a May Lady. Further, the Summer-trees are adorned like May-trees with ribbons and so on ; like May-trees, when large, they are planted in the ground and climbed up ; and like May-trees, when small, they are carried from door to door by boys or girls singing songs and collecting money. And as if to demonstrate the identity of the two sets of customs the bearers of the Summer-tree sometimes announce that they are bringing in the Summer and the May. The customs, therefore, of bringing in the May and bringing in the Summer are essentially the same ; and the Summer-tree is merely another form of the May-tree, the only dis- tinction (besides that of name) being in the time at which they are respectively brought in ; for while the May-tree is usually fetched in on the first of May or at Whitsuntide, the Summer-tree is fetched in on the fourth Sunday in Lent. Therefore, if the May-tree is an embodiment of the tree-spirit or spirit of vegetation, the Summer-tree must likewise be an embodiment of the tree-spirit or spirit of vegetation. But we have seen that the Summer-tree is in some cases a revivification of the effigy of Death. It follows, therefore, that in these cases the effigy called Death must be an embodiment of the tree-spirit or spirit of vegetation. This inference is confirmed, first, by the vivifying and fertilising influence which the fragments of the effigy of Death are believed to exercise both on vegetable and on animal life ; for this influence, as we saw in an earlier part of this work, is supposed to be a special attribute of the tree-spirit. It is confirmed, secondly, by observing that the effigy of Death is sometimes decked with leaves or made of twigs, branches, hemp, or a threshed-out sheaf of corn ; and that sometimes it is hung on a little tree and so carried about by girls collecting money, just as is done with the May-tree and the May Lady, and with the Summer-tree and the doll attached to it. In short, we are driven to regard the expulsion of Death and the bringing in of Summer as, in some cases at least, merely another form of that death and revival of the spirit of vegetation in spring which we saw enacted in the killing and resurrection of the Wild Man. The burial and resurrection of the Carnival is probably another way of expressing the same idea. The interment of the representative of the Carnival under a dung-heap is natural, if he is supposed to possess a quickening and fertilising influence like that ascribed to the effigy of Death. The Esthonians, indeed, who carry the straw figure out of the village in the usual way on Shrove Tuesday, do not call it the Carnival, but the Wood-spirit (*Metsik*), and they clearly indicate the identity of the effigy with the wood-spirit by fixing it to the top of a tree in the wood, where it remains for a year, and is besought almost daily with prayers and offerings to protect the herds ; for like a true wood-spirit the *Metsik* is a patron of cattle. Sometimes the *Metsik* is made of sheaves of corn.

Thus we may fairly conjecture that the names Carnival, Death, and Summer are comparatively late and inadequate expressions for the beings personified or embodied in the customs with which we have been dealing. The very abstractness of the names bespeaks a modern origin ; for the personification of times and seasons like the Carnival and Summer, or of an abstract notion like death, is not primitive. But the ceremonies themselves bear the stamp of a dateless antiquity ; therefore we can hardly help supposing that in their origin the ideas which they embodied were of a more simple and concrete order. The notion of a tree, perhaps of a particular kind of tree (for some savages have no word for tree in general), or even of an individual tree, is sufficiently concrete to supply a basis from which by a gradual process of generalisation the wider idea of a spirit of vegetation might be reached. But this general idea of vegetation would readily be confounded with the season in which it manifests itself ; hence the substitution of Spring, Summer, or May for the tree-spirit or spirit of vegetation would be easy and natural. Again, the concrete notion of the dying tree or dying vegetation would by a similar process of generalisation glide into a notion of death in general ; so that the practice of carrying out the dying or dead vegetation in spring, as a preliminary to its revival, would in time widen out into an attempt to banish Death in general from the village or district. The view that in these spring ceremonies Death meant originally the dying or dead vegetation of winter has the high support of W. Mannhardt ; and he confirms it by the analogy of the name Death as applied to the spirit of the ripe corn. Commonly the spirit of the ripe corn is conceived, not as dead, but as old, and hence it goes by the name of the Old Man or the Old Woman. But in some places the last sheaf cut at harvest, which is generally believed to be the seat of the corn spirit, is called " the Dead One " : children are warned against entering the corn-fields because Death sits in the corn ; and, in a game played by Saxon children in Transylvania at the maize harvest, Death is represented by a child completely covered with maize leaves.

§ 5. *Battle of Summer and Winter.* — Sometimes in the popular customs of the peasantry the contrast between the dormant powers of vegetation in winter and their awakening vitality in spring takes the form of a dramatic contest between actors who play the parts respectively of Winter and Summer. Thus in the towns of Sweden on May Day two troops of young men on horseback used to meet as if for mortal combat. One of them was led by a representative of Winter clad in furs, who threw snowballs and ice in order to prolong the cold weather. The other troop was commanded by a representative of Summer covered with fresh leaves and flowers. In the sham fight which followed the party of Summer came off victorious, and the ceremony ended with a feast. Again, in the region of the middle Rhine, a representative of Summer clad in ivy combats a representative of Winter clad in straw or moss and finally gains a victory over him. The vanquished foe is thrown to the ground and stripped of his casing of straw, which is torn to pieces and scattered about, while the youthful comrades of the two champions sing a song to commemorate the defeat of Winter by Summer. Afterwards they carry about a summer garland or branch and collect gifts of eggs and bacon from house to house. Sometimes the champion who acts the part of Summer is dressed in leaves and flowers and wears a chaplet of flowers on his head. In the Palatinate this mimic conflict takes place on the fourth Sunday in Lent. All over Bavaria the same drama used to be acted on the same day, and it was still kept up in some places down to the middle of the nineteenth century or later. While Summer appeared clad all in green, decked with fluttering ribbons, and carrying a branch in blossom or a little tree hung with apples and pears, Winter was muffled up in cap and mantle of fur and bore in his hand a snow-shovel or a flail. Accompanied by their respective retinues dressed in corresponding attire, they went through all the streets of the village, halting before the houses and singing staves of old songs, for which they received presents of bread, eggs, and fruit. Finally, after a short struggle, Winter was beaten by Summer and ducked in the village well or driven out of the village with shouts and laughter into the forest.

At Goepfritz in Lower Austria, two men personating Summer and Winter used to go from house to house on Shrove Tuesday, and were everywhere welcomed by the children with great delight. The representative of Summer was clad in white and bore a sickle ; his comrade, who played the part of Winter, had a fur cap on his head, his arms and legs were swathed in straw, and he carried a flail. In every house they sang verses alternately. At Drömling in Brunswick, down to the present time, the contest between Summer and Winter is acted every year at Whitsuntide by a troop of boys and a troop of girls. The boys rush singing, shouting, and ringing bells from house to house to drive Winter away ; after them come the girls singing softly and led by a May Bride, all in bright dresses and decked with flowers and garlands to represent the genial advent of spring. Formerly the part of Winter was played by a straw-man which the boys carried with them ; now it is acted by a real man in disguise.

Among the central Esquimaux of North America the contest between representatives of summer and winter, which in Europe has long degenerated into a mere dramatic performance, is still kept up as a magical ceremony of which the avowed intention is to influence the weather. In autumn, when storms announce the approach of the dismal Arctic winter, the Esquimaux divide themselves into two parties called respectively the ptarmigans and the ducks, the ptarmigans comprising all persons born in winter, and the ducks all persons born in summer. A long rope of sealskin is then stretched out, and each party laying hold of one end of it seeks by tugging with might and main to drag the other party over to its side. If the ptarmigans get the worst of it, then summer has won the game and fine weather may be expected to prevail through the winter.

§ 6. *Death and Resurrection of Kostrubonko.*—In Russia funeral ceremonies like those of " Burying the Carnival " and " Carrying out Death " are celebrated under the names, not of Death or the Carnival, but of certain mythic figures, Kostrubonko, Kostroma, Kupalo, Lada, and Yarilo. These Russian ceremonies are observed both in spring and at midsummer. Thus " in Little Russia it used to be the custom at Eastertide to celebrate the funeral of a being called Kostrubonko, the deity of the spring. A circle was formed of singers who moved slowly around a girl who lay on the ground as if dead, and as they went they sang :

> ' Dead, dead is our Kostrubonko !
> Dead, dead is our dear one ! '

until the girl suddenly sprang up, on which the chorus joyfully exclaimed :

> ' Come to life, come to life has our Kostrubonko !
> Come to life, come to life has our dear one ! ' "

On the Eve of St. John (Midsummer Eve) a figure of Kupalo is made of straw and " is dressed in woman's clothes, with a necklace and a floral crown. Then a tree is felled, and, after being decked with ribbons, is set up on some chosen spot. Near this tree, to which they give the name of Marena [Winter or Death], the straw figure is placed, together with a table, on which stand spirits and viands. Afterwards a bonfire is lit, and the young men and maidens jump over it in couples, carrying the figure with them. On the next day they strip the tree and the figure of their ornaments, and throw them both into a stream." On St. Peter's Day, the twenty-ninth of June, or on the following Sunday, " the Funeral of Kostroma " or of Lada or of Yarilo is celebrated in Russia. In the Governments of Penza and Simbirsk the funeral used to be represented as follows. A bonfire was kindled on the twenty-eighth of June, and on the next day the maidens chose one of their number to play the part of Kostroma. Her companions saluted her with deep obeisances, placed her on a board, and carried her to the bank of a stream. There they bathed her in the water, while the oldest girl made a basket of lime-tree bark and beat it like a drum. Then they returned to the village and ended the day with processions, games, and dances. In the Murom district Kostroma was represented by a straw figure dressed in woman's clothes and flowers. This was laid in a trough and carried with songs to the bank of a lake or river. Here the crowd divided into two sides, of which the one attacked and the other defended the figure. At last the assailants gained the day, stripped the figure of its dress and ornaments, tore it in pieces, trod the straw of which it was made under foot, and flung it into the stream ; while the defenders of the figure hid their faces in their hands and pretended to bewail the death of Kostroma. In the district of Kostroma the burial of Yarilo was celebrated on the twenty-ninth or thirtieth of June. The people chose an old man and gave him a small coffin containing a Priapus-like figure representing Yarilo. This he carried out of the town, followed by women chanting dirges and expressing by their gestures grief and despair. In the open fields a grave was dug, and into it the figure was lowered amid weeping and wailing, after which games and dances were begun, " calling to mind the funeral games celebrated in old times by the pagan Slavonians." In Little Russia the figure of Yarilo was laid in a coffin and carried through the streets after sunset surrounded by drunken women, who kept repeating mournfully, " He is dead ! he is dead ! " The men lifted and shook the figure as if they were trying to recall the dead man to life. Then they said to the women, " Women, weep not. I know what is sweeter than honey." But the women continued to lament and chant, as they do at funerals. " Of what was he guilty ? He was so good. He will arise no more. O how shall we part from thee ? What is life without thee ? Arise, if only for a brief hour. But he rises not, he rises not." At last the Yarilo was buried in a grave.

§ 7. *Death and Revival of Vegetation.*—These Russian customs are plainly of the same nature as those which in Austria and Germany are known as " Carrying out Death." Therefore if the interpretation here adopted of the latter is right, the Russian Kostrubonko, Yarilo, and the rest must also have been originally embodiments of the spirit of vegetation, and their death must have been regarded as a necessary preliminary to their revival. The revival as a sequel to the death is enacted in the first of the ceremonies described, the death and resurrection of Kostrubonko. The reason why in some of these Russian ceremonies the death of the spirit of vegetation is celebrated at midsummer may be that the decline of summer is dated from Midsummer Day, after which the days begin to shorten, and the sun sets out on his downward journey :

> *" To the darksome hollows*
> *Where the frosts of winter lie."*

Such a turning-point of the year, when vegetation might be thought to share the incipient though still almost imperceptible decay of summer, might very well be chosen by primitive man as a fit moment for resorting to those magic rites by which he hopes to stay the decline, or at least to ensure the revival, of plant life.

But while the death of vegetation appears to have been represented in all, and its revival in some, of these spring and midsummer ceremonies, there are features in some of them which can hardly be explained on this hypothesis alone. The solemn funeral, the lamentations, and the mourning attire, which often characterise these rites, are indeed appropriate at the death of the beneficent spirit of vegetation. But what shall we say of the glee with which the effigy is often carried out, of the sticks and stones with which it is assailed, and the taunts and curses which are hurled at it ? What shall we say of the dread of the effigy evinced by the haste with which the bearers scamper home as soon as they have thrown it away, and by the belief that some one must soon die in any house into which it has looked ? This dread might perhaps be explained by a belief that there is a certain infectiousness in the dead spirit of vegetation which renders its approach dangerous. But this explanation, besides being rather strained, does not cover the rejoicings which often attend the carrying out of Death. We must therefore recognise two distinct and seemingly opposite features in these ceremonies : on the one hand, sorrow for the death, and affection and respect for the dead ; on the other hand, fear and hatred of the dead, and rejoicings at his death. How the former of these features is to be explained I have attempted to show : how the latter came to be so closely associated with the former is a question which I shall try to answer in the sequel.

§ 8. *Analogous Rites in India.*—In the Kanagra district of India there is a custom observed by young girls in spring which closely resembles some of the European spring ceremonies just described. It is called the *Ralî Ka melâ*, or fair of Ralî, the *Ralî* being a small painted earthen image of Siva or Pârvatî. The custom is in vogue all over the

Kanagra district, and its celebration, which is entirely confined to young girls, lasts through most of Chet (March-April) up to the Sankrânt of Baisâkh (April). On a morning in March all the young girls of the village take small baskets of *dûb* grass and flowers to an appointed place, where they throw them in a heap. Round this heap they stand in a circle and sing. This goes on every day for ten days, till the heap of grass and flowers has reached a fair height. Then they cut in the jungle two branches, each with three prongs at one end, and place them, prongs downwards, over the heap of flowers, so as to make two tripods or pyramids. On the single uppermost points of these branches they get an image-maker to construct two clay images, one to represent Siva, and the other Pârvatî. The girls then divide themselves into two parties, one for Siva and one for Pârvatî, and marry the images in the usual way, leaving out no part of the ceremony. After the marriage they have a feast, the cost of which is defrayed by contributions solicited from their parents. Then at the next Sankrânt (Baisâkh) they all go together to the river-side, throw the images into a deep pool, and weep over the place, as though they were performing funeral obsequies. The boys of the neighbourhood often tease them by diving after the images, bringing them up, and waving them about while the girls are crying over them. The object of the fair is said to be to secure a good husband.

That in this Indian ceremony the deities Siva and Pârvatî are conceived as spirits of vegetation seems to be proved by the placing of their images on branches over a heap of grass and flowers. Here, as often in European folk-custom, the divinities of vegetation are represented in duplicate, by plants and by puppets. The marriage of these Indian deities in spring corresponds to the European ceremonies in which the marriage of the vernal spirits of vegetation is represented by the King and Queen of May, the May Bride, Bridegroom of the May, and so forth. The throwing of the images into the water, and the mourning for them, are the equivalents of the European customs of throwing the dead spirit of vegetation under the name of Death, Yarilo, Kostroma, and the rest, into the water and lamenting over it. Again, in India, as often in Europe, the rite is performed exclusively by females. The notion that the ceremony helps to procure husbands for the girls can be explained by the quickening and fertilising influence which the spirit of vegetation is believed to exert upon the life of man as well as of plants.

§ 9. *The Magic Spring.*—The general explanation which we have been led to adopt of these and many similar ceremonies is that they are, or were in their origin, magical rites intended to ensure the revival of nature in spring. The means by which they were supposed to effect this end were imitation and sympathy. Led astray by his ignorance of the true causes of things, primitive man believed that in order to produce the great phenomena of nature on which his life depended he had only to imitate them, and that immediately by a secret sympathy or mystic influence the little drama which he acted in forest glade or mountain dell, on desert plain or wind-swept shore, would be taken up and repeated by mightier actors on a vaster stage. He fancied that by masquerading in leaves and flowers he helped the bare earth to clothe herself with verdure, and that by playing the death and burial of winter he drove that gloomy season away, and made smooth the path for the footsteps of returning spring. If we find it hard to throw ourselves even in fancy into a mental condition in which such things seem possible, we can more easily picture to ourselves the anxiety which the savage, when he first began to lift his thoughts above the satisfaction of his merely animal wants, and to meditate on the causes of things, may have felt as to the continued operation of what we now call the laws of nature. To us, familiar as we are with the conception of the uniformity and regularity with which the great cosmic phenomena succeed each other, there seems little ground for apprehension that the causes which produce these effects will cease to operate, at least within the near future. But this confidence in the stability of nature is bred only by the experience which comes of wide observation and long tradition ; and the savage, with his narrow sphere of observation and his short-lived tradition, lacks the very elements of that experience which alone could set his mind at rest in face of the ever-changing and often menacing aspects of nature. No wonder, therefore, that he is thrown into a panic by an eclipse, and thinks that the sun or the moon would surely perish, if he did not raise a clamour and shoot his puny shafts into the air to defend the luminaries from the monster who threatens to devour them. No wonder he is terrified when in the darkness of night a streak of sky is suddenly illumined by the flash of a meteor, or the whole expanse of the celestial arch glows with the fitful light of the Northern Streamers. Even phenomena which recur at fixed and uniform intervals may be viewed by him with apprehension, before he has come to recognise the orderliness of their recurrence. The speed or slowness of his recognition of such periodic or cyclic changes in nature will depend largely on the length of the particular cycle. The cycle, for example, of day and night is every-where, except in the polar regions, so short and hence so frequent that men probably soon ceased to discompose themselves seriously as to the chance of its failing to recur, though the ancient Egyptians, as we have seen, daily wrought enchantments to bring back to the east in the morning the fiery orb which had sunk at evening in the crimson west. But it was far otherwise with the annual cycle of the seasons. To any man a year is a considerable period, seeing that the number of our years is but few at the best. To the primitive savage, with his short memory and imperfect means of marking the flight of time, a year may well have been so long that he failed to recognise it as a cycle at all, and watched the changing aspects of earth and heaven with a perpetual wonder, alternately delighted and alarmed, elated and cast down, according as the vicissitudes of light and heat, of plant and animal life, ministered to his comfort or threatened his existence. In autumn when the withered leaves were whirled about the forest by

Y

the nipping blast, and he looked up at the bare boughs, could he feel sure that they would ever be green again ? As day by day the sun sank lower and lower in the sky, could he be certain that the luminary would ever retrace his heavenly road ?   Even the waning moon, whose pale sickle rose thinner and thinner every night over the rim of the eastern horizon, may have excited in his mind a fear lest, when it had wholly vanished, there should be moons no more.

These and a thousand such misgivings may have thronged the fancy and troubled the peace of the man who first began to reflect on the mysteries of the world he lived in, and to take thought for a more distant future than the morrow. It was natural, therefore, that with such thoughts and fears he should have done all that in him lay to bring back the faded blossom to the bough, to swing the low sun of winter up to his old place in the summer sky, and to restore its orbed fulness to the silver lamp of the waning moon. We may smile at his vain endeavours if we please, but it was only by making a long series of experiments, of which some were almost inevitably doomed to failure, that man learned from experience the futility of some of his attempted methods and the fruitfulness of others. After all, magical ceremonies are nothing but experiments which have failed and which continue to be repeated merely because, for reasons which have already been indicated, the operator is unaware of their failure. With the advance of knowledge these ceremonies either cease to be performed altogether or are kept up from force of habit long after the intention with which they were instituted has been forgotten. Thus fallen from their high estate, no longer regarded as solemn rites on the punctual performance of which the welfare and even the life of the community depend, they sink gradually to the level of simple pageants, mummeries, and pastimes, till in the final stage of degeneration they are wholly abandoned by older people, and, from having once been the most serious occupation of the sage, become at last the idle sport of children. It is in this final stage of decay that most of the old magical rites of our European forefathers linger on at the present day, and even from this their last retreat they are fast being swept away by the rising tide of those multitudinous forces, moral, intellectual, and social, which are bearing mankind onward to a new and unknown goal. We may feel some natural regret at the disappearance of quaint customs and picturesque ceremonies, which have preserved to an age often deemed dull and prosaic something of the flavour and freshness of the olden time, some breath of the springtime of the world ; yet our regret will be lessened when we remember that these pretty pageants, these now innocent diversions, had their origin in ignorance and superstition ; that if they are a record of human endeavour, they are also a monument of fruitless ingenuity, of wasted labour, and of blighted hopes ; and that for all their gay trappings—their flowers, their ribbons, and their music—they partake far more of tragedy than of farce.

The interpretation which, following in the footsteps of W. Mannhardt, I have attempted to give of these ceremonies has been not a little confirmed by the discovery, made since this book was first written, that the natives of Central Australia regularly practise magical ceremonies for the purpose of awakening the dormant energies of nature at the approach of what may be called the Australian spring. Nowhere apparently are the alternations of the seasons more sudden and the contrasts between them more striking than in the deserts of Central Australia, where at the end of a long period of drought the sandy and stony wilderness, over which the silence and desolation of death appear to brood, is suddenly, after a few days of torrential rain, transformed into a landscape smiling with verdure and peopled with teeming multitudes of insects and lizards, of frogs and birds. The marvellous change which passes over the face of nature at such times has been compared even by European observers to the effect of magic ; no wonder, then, that the savage should regard it as such in very deed. Now it is just when there is promise of the approach of a good season that the natives of Central Australia are wont especially to perform those magical ceremonies of which the avowed intention is to multiply the plants and animals they use as food. These ceremonies, therefore, present a close analogy to the spring customs of our European peasantry not only in the time of their celebration, but also in their aim ; for we can hardly doubt that in instituting rites designed to assist the revival of plant life in spring our primitive forefathers were moved, not by any sentimental wish to smell at early violets, or pluck the rathe primrose, or watch yellow daffodils dancing in the breeze, but by the very practical consideration, certainly not formulated in abstract terms, that the life of man is inextricably bound up with that of plants, and that if they were to perish he could not survive. And as the faith of the Australian savage in the efficacy of his magic rites is confirmed by observing that their performance is invariably followed, sooner or later, by that increase of vegetable and animal life which it is their object to produce, so, we may suppose, it was with European savages in the olden time. The sight of the fresh green in brake and thicket, of vernal flowers blowing on mossy banks, of swallows arriving from the south, and of the sun mounting daily higher in the sky, would be welcomed by them as so many visible signs that their enchantments were indeed taking effect, and would inspire them with a cheerful confidence that all was well with a world which they could thus mould to suit their wishes. Only in autumn days, as summer slowly faded, would their confidence again be dashed by doubts and misgivings at symptoms of decay, which told how vain were all their efforts to stave off for ever the approach of winter and of death.

CHAPTER XXIX

THE MYTH OF ADONIS

THE spectacle of the great changes which annually pass over the face of the earth has powerfully impressed the minds of men in all ages, and stirred them to meditate on the causes of transformations so vast and wonderful.   Their curiosity has not been purely dis-interested ; for even the savage cannot fail to perceive how intimately his own life is bound up with the life of nature, and how the same processes which freeze the stream and strip the earth of vegetation menace him with extinction.   At a certain stage of development men seem to have imagined that the means of averting the threatened calamity were in their own hands, and that they could hasten or retard the flight of the seasons by magic art.   Accordingly they per-formed ceremonies and recited spells to make the rain to fall, the sun to shine, animals to multiply, and the fruits of the earth to grow.   In course of time the slow advance of knowledge, which has dispelled so many cherished illusions, convinced at least the more thoughtful portion of mankind that the alternations of summer and winter, of spring and autumn, were not merely the result of their own magical rites, but that some deeper cause, some mightier power, was at work behind the shifting scenes of nature.   They now pictured to themselves the growth and decay of vegetation, the birth and death of living creatures, as effects of the waxing or waning strength of divine beings, of gods and goddesses, who were born and died, who married and begot children, on the pattern of human life.

Thus the old magical theory of the seasons was displaced, or rather supplemented, by a religious theory.   For although men now attributed the annual cycle of change primarily to corresponding changes in their deities, they still thought that by performing certain magical rites they could aid the god, who was the principle of life, in his struggle with the opposing principle of death.   They imagined that they could recruit his failing energies and even raise him from the dead.   The ceremonies which they observed for this purpose were in substance a dramatic representation of the natural processes which they wished to facilitate ; for it is a familiar tenet of magic that you can produce any desired effect by merely imitating it.   And as they now explained the fluctuations of growth and decay, of reproduction and dissolution, by the marriage, the death, and the rebirth or revival of the gods, their religious or rather magical dramas turned in great measure on these themes.   They set forth the fruitful union of the powers of fertility, the sad death of one at least of the divine partners, and his joyful resurrection.   Thus a religious theory was blended with a magical practice.   The combination is familiar in history.   Indeed, few religions have ever succeeded in wholly extricating themselves from the old trammels of magic.   The inconsistency of acting on two opposite principles, however it may vex the soul of the philosopher, rarely troubles the common man ; indeed he is seldom even aware of it. His affair is to act, not to analyse the motives of his action. If mankind had always been logical and wise, history would not be a long chronicle of folly and crime.

Of the changes which the seasons bring with them, the most striking within the temperate zone are those which affect vegetation. The influence of the seasons on animals, though great, is not nearly so manifest. Hence it is natural that in the magical dramas designed to dispel winter and bring back spring the emphasis should be laid on vegetation, and that trees and plants should figure in them more prominently than beasts and birds. Yet the two sides of life, the vegetable and the animal, were not dissociated in the minds of those who observed the ceremonies. Indeed they commonly believed that the tie between the animal and the vegetable world was even closer than it really is ; hence they often combined the dramatic representation of reviving plants with a real or a dramatic union of the sexes for the purpose of furthering at the same time and by the same act the multiplication of fruits, of animals, and of men. To them the principle of life and fertility, whether animal or vegetable, was one and indivisible. To live and to cause to live, to eat food and to beget children, these were the primary wants of men in the past, and they will be the primary wants of men in the future so long as the world lasts. Other things may be added to enrich and beautify human life, but unless these wants are first satisfied, humanity itself must cease to exist. These two things, therefore, food and children, were what men chiefly sought to procure by the performance of magical rites for the regulation of the seasons.

Nowhere, apparently, have these rites been more widely and solemnly celebrated than in the lands which border the eastern Mediterranean. Under the names of Osiris, Tammuz, Adonis, and Attis, the peoples of Egypt and Western Asia represented the yearly decay and revival of life, especially of vegetable life, which they personified as a god who annually died and rose again from the dead. In name and detail the rites varied from place to place : in substance they were the same. The supposed death and resurrection of this oriental deity, a god of many names but of essentially one nature, is now to be examined. We begin with Tammuz or Adonis.

The worship of Adonis was practised by the Semitic peoples of Babylonia and Syria, and the Greeks borrowed it from them as early as the seventh century before Christ. The true name of the deity was Tammuz : the appellation of Adonis is merely the Semitic *Adon*, "lord," a title of honour by which his worshippers addressed him. But the Greeks through a misunderstanding converted the title of honour into a proper name. In the religious literature of Babylonia Tammuz appears as the youthful spouse or lover of Ishtar, the great mother goddess, the embodiment of the reproductive energies of nature. The references to their connexion with each other in myth and ritual are both fragmentary and obscure, but we gather from them that every year Tammuz was believed to die, passing away from the cheerful earth to the gloomy subterranean world, and that every year his divine mistress journeyed in quest of him " to the land from which there is no returning, to the house of darkness, where dust lies on door and bolt." During her absence the passion of love ceased to operate : men and beasts alike forgot to reproduce their kinds : all life was threatened with extinction. So intimately bound up with the goddess were the sexual functions of the whole animal kingdom that without her presence they could not be discharged. A messenger of the great god Ea was accordingly despatched to rescue the goddess on whom so much depended. The stern queen of the infernal regions, Allatu or Eresh-Kigal by name, reluctantly allowed Ishtar to be sprinkled with the Water of Life and to depart, in company probably with her lover Tammuz, that the two might return together to the upper world, and that with their return all nature might revive.

Laments for the departed Tammuz are contained in several Babylonian hymns, which liken him to plants that quickly fade. He is

> " *A tamarisk that in the garden has drunk no water,*
>   *Whose crown in the field has brought forth no blossom.*
> *A willow that rejoiced not by the watercourse,*
>   *A willow whose roots were torn up.*
> *A herb that in the garden had drunk no water.*"

His death appears to have been annually mourned, to the shrill music of flutes, by men and women about midsummer in the month named after him, the month of Tammuz. The dirges were seemingly chanted over an effigy of the dead god, which was washed with pure water, anointed with oil, and clad in a red robe, while the fumes of incense rose into the air, as if to stir his dormant senses by their pungent fragrance and wake him from the sleep of death. In one of these dirges, inscribed *Lament of the Flutes for Tammuz*, we seem still to hear the voices of the singers chanting the sad refrain and to catch, like far-away music, the wailing notes of the flutes :

> " *At his vanishing away she lifts up a lament,*
>   ' *Oh my child !* ' *at his vanishing away she lifts up a lament ;*
> ' *My Damu !* ' *at his vanishing away she lifts up a lament.*
>   ' *My enchanter and priest !* ' *at his vanishing away she lifts up a lament,*
> *At the shining cedar, rooted in a spacious place,*
>   *In Eanna, above and below, she lifts up a lament.*
> *Like the lament that a house lifts up for its master, lifts she up a lament,*
>   *Like the lament that a city lifts up for its lord, lifts she up a lament.*
> *Her lament is the lament for a herb that grows not in the bed,*
>   *Her lament is the lament for the corn that grows not in the ear.*
> *Her chamber is a possession that brings not forth a possession,*
>   *A weary woman, a weary child, forspent.*
> *Her lament is for a great river, where no willows grow,*
>   *Her lament is for a field, where corn and herbs grow not.*
> *Her lament is for a pool, where fishes grow not.*
>   *Her lament is for a thicket of reeds, where no reeds grow.*

Her lament is for woods, where tamarisks grow not.
   Her lament is for a wilderness where no cypresses (?) grow.
Her lament is for the depth of a garden of trees, where honey and wine grow not.
   Her lament is for meadows, where no plants grow.
Her lament is for a palace, where length of life grows not."

The tragical story and the melancholy rites of Adonis are better known to us from the descriptions of Greek writers than from the fragments of Babylonian literature or the brief reference of the prophet Ezekiel, who saw the women of Jerusalem weeping for Tammuz at the north gate of the temple. Mirrored in the glass of Greek mythology, the oriental deity appears as a comely youth beloved by Aphrodite. In his infancy the goddess hid him in a chest, which she gave in charge to Persephone, queen of the nether world. But when Persephone opened the chest and beheld the beauty of the babe, she refused to give him back to Aphrodite, though the goddess of love went down herself to hell to ransom her dear one from the power of the grave. The dispute between the two goddesses of love and death was settled by Zeus, who decreed that Adonis should abide with Persephone in the under world for one part of the year, and with Aphrodite in the upper world for another part. At last the fair youth was killed in hunting by a wild boar, or by the jealous Ares, who turned himself into the likeness of a boar in order to compass the death of his rival. Bitterly did Aphrodite lament her loved and lost Adonis. In this form of the myth, the contest between Aphrodite and Persephone for the possession of Adonis clearly reflects the struggle between Ishtar and Allatu in the land of the dead, while the decision of Zeus that Adonis is to spend one part of the year under ground and another part above ground is merely a Greek version of the annual disappearance and reappearance of Tammuz.

CHAPTER XXX

ADONIS IN SYRIA

The myth of Adonis was localised and his rites celebrated with much solemnity at two places in Western Asia. One of these was Byblus on the coast of Syria, the other was Paphos in Cyprus. Both were great seats of the worship of Aphrodite, or rather of her Semitic counterpart, Astarte ; and of both, if we accept the legends, Cinyras, the father of Adonis, was king. Of the two cities Byblus was the more ancient ; indeed it claimed to be the oldest city in Phoenicia, and to have been founded in the early ages of the world by the great god El, whom Greeks and Romans identified with Cronus and Saturn respectively. However that may have been, in historical times it ranked as a holy place, the religious capital of the country, the Mecca or Jerusalem of the Phoenicians. The city stood on a height beside the sea, and contained a great sanctuary of Astarte, where in the midst of a spacious open court, surrounded by cloisters and approached from below by staircases, rose a tall cone or obelisk, the holy image of the goddess. In this sanctuary the rites of Adonis were celebrated. Indeed the whole city was sacred to him, and the River Nahr Ibrahim, which falls into the sea a little to the south of Byblus, bore in antiquity the name of Adonis. This was the kingdom of Cinyras. From the earliest to the latest times the city appears to have been ruled by kings, assisted perhaps by a senate or council of elders.

The last king of Byblus bore the ancient name of Cinyras, and was beheaded by Pompey the Great for his tyrannous excesses. His legendary namesake Cinyras is said to have founded a sanctuary of Aphrodite, that is, of Astarte, at a place on Mount Lebanon, distant a day's journey from the capital. The spot was probably Aphaca, at the source of the River Adonis, half-way between Byblus and Baalbec ; for at Aphaca there was a famous grove and sanctuary of Astarte which Constantine destroyed on account of the flagitious character of the worship. The site of the temple has been discovered by modern travellers near the miserable village which still bears the name of Afka at the head of the wild, romantic, wooded gorge of the Adonis. The hamlet stands among groves of noble walnut-trees on the brink of the lyn. A little way off the river rushes from a cavern at the foot of a mighty amphitheatre of towering cliffs to plunge in a series of cascades into the awful depths of the glen. The deeper it descends, the ranker and denser grows the vegetation, which, sprouting from the crannies and fissures of the rocks, spreads a green veil over the roaring or murmuring stream in the tremendous chasm below. There is something delicious, almost intoxicating, in the freshness of these tumbling waters, in the sweetness and purity of the mountain air, in the vivid green of the vegetation. The temple, of which some massive hewn blocks and a fine column of Syenite granite still mark the site, occupied a terrace facing the source of the river and commanding a magnificent prospect. Across the foam and the roar of the waterfalls you look up to the cavern and away to the top of the sublime precipices above. So lofty is the cliff that the goats which creep along its ledges to browse on the bushes appear like ants to the spectator hundreds of feet below. Seaward the view is especially impressive when the sun floods the profound gorge with golden light, revealing all the fantastic buttresses and rounded towers of its mountain rampart, and falling softly on the varied green of the woods which clothe its depths. It was here that, according to the legend, Adonis met Aphrodite for the first or the last time, and here his mangled body was buried. A fairer scene could hardly be imagined for a story of tragic love and death. Yet, sequestered as the valley is and must always have been, it is not wholly deserted. A convent or a village may be observed here and there standing out against the sky on the top of some beetling crag, or clinging to the face of a nearly perpendicular cliff high above the foam and the din of the river ; and at evening the lights that

twinkle through the gloom betray the presence of human habitations
on slopes which might seem inaccessible to man. In antiquity the
whole of the lovely vale appears to have been dedicated to Adonis,
and to this day it is haunted by his memory ; for the heights which
shut it in are crested at various points by ruined monuments of his
worship, some of them overhanging dreadful abysses, down which it
turns the head dizzy to look and see the eagles wheeling about their
nests far below. One such monument exists at Ghineh. The face
of a great rock, above a roughly hewn recess, is here carved with
figures of Adonis and Aphrodite. He is portrayed with spear in rest,
awaiting the attack of a bear, while she is seated in an attitude of
sorrow. Her grief-stricken figure may well be the mourning Aphrodite of the Lebanon described by Macrobius, and the recess in the
rock is perhaps her lover's tomb. Every year, in the belief of his
worshippers, Adonis was wounded to death on the mountains, and
every year the face of nature itself was dyed with his sacred blood.
So year by year the Syrian damsels lamented his untimely fate, while
the red anemone, his flower, bloomed among the cedars of Lebanon,
and the river ran red to the sea, fringing the winding shores of the
blue Mediterranean, whenever the wind set inshore, with a sinuous
band of crimson.

CHAPTER XXXI

ADONIS IN CYPRUS

The island of Cyprus lies but one day's sail from the coast of Syria.
Indeed, on fine summer evenings its mountains may be descried loom-
ing low and dark against the red fires of sunset. With its rich mines
of copper and its forests of firs and stately cedars, the island naturally
attracted a commercial and maritime people like the Phoenicians ;
while the abundance of its corn, its wine, and its oil must have rendered
it in their eyes a Land of Promise by comparison with the niggardly
nature of their own rugged coast, hemmed in between the mountains
and the sea. Accordingly they settled in Cyprus at a very early date
and remained there long after the Greeks had also established themselves on its shores ; for we know from inscriptions and coins that
Phoenician kings reigned at Citium, the Chittim of the Hebrews, down
to the time of Alexander the Great. Naturally the Semitic colonists
brought their gods with them from the mother-land. They worshipped
Baal of the Lebanon, who may well have been Adonis, and at Amathus
on the south coast they instituted the rites of Adonis and Aphrodite,
or rather Astarte. Here, as at Byblus, these rites resembled the
Egyptian worship of Osiris so closely that some people even identified
the Adonis of Amathus with Osiris.

But the great seat of the worship of Aphrodite and Adonis in
Cyprus was Paphos on the south-western side of the island. Among

the petty kingdoms into which Cyprus was divided from the earliest times until the end of the fourth century before our era Paphos must have ranked with the best. It is a land of hills and billowy ridges, diversified by fields and vineyards and intersected by rivers, which in the course of ages have carved for themselves beds of such tremendous depth that travelling in the interior is difficult and tedious. The lofty range of Mount Olympus (the modern Troodos), capped with snow the greater part of the year, screens Paphos from the northerly and easterly winds and cuts it off from the rest of the island. On the slopes of the range the last pine-woods of Cyprus linger, sheltering here and there monasteries in scenery not unworthy of the Apennines. The old city of Paphos occupied the summit of a hill about a mile from the sea ; the newer city sprang up at the harbour some ten miles off. The sanctuary of Aphrodite at Old Paphos (the modern Kuklia) was one of the most celebrated shrines in the ancient world. According to Herodotus, it was founded by Phoenician colonists from Ascalon ; but it is possible that a native goddess of fertility was worshipped on the spot before the arrival of the Phoenicians, and that the newcomers identified her with their own Baalath or Astarte, whom she may have closely resembled. If two deities were thus fused in one, we may suppose that they were both varieties of that great goddess of motherhood and fertility whose worship appears to have been spread all over Western Asia from a very early time. The supposition is confirmed as well by the archaic shape of her image as by the licentious character of her rites ; for both that shape and those rites were shared by her with other Asiatic deities. Her image was simply a white cone or pyramid. In like manner, a cone was the emblem of Astarte at Byblus, of the native goddess whom the Greeks called Artemis at Perga in Pamphylia, and of the sun-god Heliogabalus at Emesa in Syria. Conical stones, which apparently served as idols, have also been found at Golgi in Cyprus, and in the Phoenician temples of Malta ; and cones of sandstone came to light at the shrine of the " Mistress of Torquoise " among the barren hills and frowning precipices of Sinai.

In Cyprus it appears that before marriage all women were formerly obliged by custom to prostitute themselves to strangers at the sanctuary of the goddess, whether she went by the name of Aphrodite, Astarte, or what not. Similar customs prevailed in many parts of Western Asia. Whatever its motive, the practice was clearly regarded, not as an orgy of lust, but as a solemn religious duty performed in the service of that great Mother Goddess of Western Asia whose name varied, while her type remained constant, from place to place. Thus at Babylon every woman, whether rich or poor, had once in her life to submit to the embraces of a stranger at the temple of Mylitta, that is, of Ishtar or Astarte, and to dedicate to the goddess the wages earned by this sanctified harlotry. The sacred precinct was crowded with women waiting to observe the custom. Some of them had to wait there for years. At Heliopolis or Baalbec in Syria, famous for the imposing grandeur of its ruined temples, the custom of the country required that every maiden should prostitute herself to a stranger at the temple of Astarte, and matrons as well as maids testified their devotion to the goddess in the same manner. The emperor Constantine abolished the custom, destroyed the temple, and built a church in its stead. In Phoenician temples women prostituted themselves for hire in the service of religion, believing that by this conduct they propitiated the goddess and won her favour. " It was a law of the Amorites, that she who was about to marry should sit in fornication seven days by the gate." At Byblus the people shaved their heads in the annual mourning for Adonis. Women who refused to sacrifice their hair had to give themselves up to strangers on a certain day of the festival, and the money which they thus earned was devoted to the goddess. A Greek inscription found at Tralles in Lydia proves that the practice of religious prostitution survived in that country as late as the second century of our era. It records of a certain woman, Aurelia Aemilia by name, not only that she herself served the god in the capacity of a harlot at his express command, but that her mother and other female ancestors had done the same before her ; and the publicity of the record, engraved on a marble column which supported a votive offering, shows that no stain attached to such a life and such a parentage. In Armenia the noblest families dedicated their daughters to the service of the goddess Anaitis in her temple at Acilisena, where the damsels acted as prostitutes for a long time before they were given in marriage. Nobody scrupled to take one of these girls to wife when her period of service was over. Again, the goddess Ma was served by a multitude of sacred harlots at Comana in Pontus, and crowds of men and women flocked to her sanctuary from the neighbouring cities and country to attend the biennial festivals or to pay their vows to the goddess.

If we survey the whole of the evidence on this subject, some of which has still to be laid before the reader, we may conclude that a great Mother Goddess, the personification of all the reproductive energies of nature, was worshipped under different names but with a substantial similarity of myth and ritual by many peoples of Western Asia ; that associated with her was a lover, or rather series of lovers, divine yet mortal, with whom she mated year by year, their commerce being deemed essential to the propagation of animals and plants, each in their several kind ; and further, that the fabulous union of the divine pair was simulated and, as it were, multiplied on earth by the real, though temporary, union of the human sexes at the sanctuary of the goddess for the sake of thereby ensuring the fruitfulness of the ground and the increase of man and beast.

At Paphos the custom of religious prostitution is said to have been instituted by King Cinyras, and to have been practised by his daughters, the sisters of Adonis, who, having incurred the wrath of Aphrodite, mated with strangers and ended their days in Egypt. In this form of the tradition the wrath of Aphrodite is probably a feature added by a later authority, who could only regard conduct which shocked his own moral sense as a punishment inflicted by the goddess instead of as a sacrifice regularly enjoined by her on all her devotees. At all events the story indicates that the princesses of Paphos had to conform to the custom as well as women of humble birth.

Among the stories which were told of Cinyras, the ancestor of the priestly kings of Paphos and the father of Adonis, there are some that deserve our attention. In the first place, he is said to have begotten his son Adonis in incestuous intercourse with his daughter Myrrha at a festival of the corn-goddess, at which women robed in white were wont to offer corn-wreaths as first-fruits of the harvest and to observe strict chastity for nine days. Similar cases of incest with a daughter are reported of many ancient kings. It seems unlikely that such reports are without foundation, and perhaps equally improbable that they refer to mere fortuitous outbursts of unnatural lust. We may suspect that they are based on a practice actually observed for a definite reason in certain special circumstances. Now in countries where the royal blood was traced through women only, and where consequently the king held office merely in virtue of his marriage with an hereditary princess, who was the real sovereign, it appears to have often happened that a prince married his own sister, the princess royal, in order to obtain with her hand the crown which otherwise would have gone to another man, perhaps to a stranger. May not the same rule of descent have furnished a motive for incest with a daughter ? For it seems a natural corollary from such a rule that the king was bound to vacate the throne on the death of his wife, the queen, since he occupied it only by virtue of his marriage with her. When that marriage terminated, his right to the throne terminated with it and passed at once to his daughter's husband. Hence if the king desired to reign after his wife's death, the only way in which he could legitimately continue to do so was by marrying his daughter, and thus prolonging through her the title which had formerly been his through her mother.

Cinyras is said to have been famed for his exquisite beauty and to have been wooed by Aphrodite herself. Thus it would appear, as scholars have already observed, that Cinyras was in a sense a duplicate of his handsome son Adonis, to whom the inflammable goddess also lost her heart. Further, these stories of the love of Aphrodite for two members of the royal house of Paphos can hardly be dissociated from the corresponding legend told of Pygmalion, a Phoenician king of Cyprus, who is said to have fallen in love with an image of Aphrodite and taken it to his bed. When we consider that Pygmalion was the father-in-law of Cinyras, that the son of Cinyras was Adonis, and that all three, in successive generations, are said to have been concerned in a love-intrigue with Aphrodite, we can hardly help concluding that the early Phoenician kings of Paphos, or their sons, regularly claimed to be not merely the priests of the goddess but also her lovers, in other words, that in their official capacity they personated Adonis. At all events Adonis is said to have reigned in Cyprus, and it appears to be certain that the title of Adonis was regularly borne by the sons of all

the Phoenician kings of the island. It is true that the title strictly
signified no more than " lord " ; yet the legends which connect these
Cyprian princes with the goddess of love make it probable that they
claimed the divine nature as well as the human dignity of Adonis.
The story of Pygmalion points to a ceremony of a sacred marriage
in which the king wedded the image of Aphrodite, or rather of Astarte.
If that was so, the tale was in a sense true, not of a single man only,
but of a whole series of men, and it would be all the more likely to be
told of Pygmalion, if that was a common name of Semitic kings in
general, and of Cyprian kings in particular. Pygmalion, at all events,
is known as the name of the famous king of Tyre from whom his sister
Dido fled ; and a king of Citium and Idalium in Cyprus, who reigned
in the time of Alexander the Great, was also called Pygmalion, or
rather Pumiyathon, the Phoenician name which the Greeks corrupted
into Pygmalion. Further, it deserves to be noted that the names
Pygmalion and Astarte occur together in a Punic inscription on a
gold medallion which was found in a grave at Carthage ; the characters
of the inscription are of the earliest type. As the custom of religious
prostitution at Paphos is said to have been founded by King Cinyras
and observed by his daughters, we may surmise that the kings of
Paphos played the part of the divine bridegroom in a less innocent
rite than the form of marriage with a statue ; in fact, that at certain
festivals each of them had to mate with one or more of the sacred
harlots of the temple, who played Astarte to his Adonis. If that was
so, there is more truth than has commonly been supposed in the
reproach cast by the Christian fathers that the Aphrodite worshipped
by Cinyras was a common whore. The fruit of their union would
rank as sons and daughters of the deity, and would in time become
the parents of gods and goddesses, like their fathers and mothers
before them. In this manner Paphos, and perhaps all sanctuaries of
the great Asiatic goddess where sacred prostitution was practised,
might be well stocked with human deities, the offspring of the divine
king by his wives, concubines, and temple harlots. Any one of these
might probably succeed his father on the throne or be sacrificed in his
stead whenever stress of war or other grave junctures called, as they
sometimes did, for the death of a royal victim. Such a tax, levied
occasionally on the king's numerous progeny for the good of the
country, would neither extinguish the divine stock nor break the
father's heart, who divided his paternal affection among so many.
At all events, if, as there seems reason to believe, Semitic kings were
often regarded at the same time as hereditary deities, it is easy to
understand the frequency of Semitic personal names which imply
that the bearers of them were the sons or daughters, the brothers or
sisters, the fathers or mothers of a god, and we need not resort to the
shifts employed by some scholars to evade the plain sense of the
words. This interpretation is confirmed by a parallel Egyptian usage :
for in Egypt, where the kings were worshipped as divine, the queen
was called " the wife of the god " or " the mother of the god," and

the title " father of the god " was borne not only by the king's real father but also by his father-in-law. Similarly, perhaps, among the Semites any man who sent his daughter to swell the royal harem may have been allowed to call himself " the father of the god."

If we may judge by his name, the Semitic king who bore the name of Cinyras was, like King David, a harper ; for the name of Cinyras is clearly connected with the Greek *cinyra*, " a lyre," which in its turn comes from the Semitic *kinnor*, " a lyre," the very word applied to the instrument on which David played before Saul. We shall probably not err in assuming that at Paphos as at Jerusalem the music of the lyre or harp was not a mere pastime designed to while away an idle hour, but formed part of the service of religion, the moving influence of its melodies being perhaps set down, like the effect of wine, to the direct inspiration of a deity. Certainly at Jerusalem the regular clergy of the temple prophesied to the music of harps, of psalteries, and of cymbals ; and it appears that the irregular clergy also, as we may call the prophets, depended on some such stimulus for inducing the ecstatic state which they took for immediate converse with the divinity. Thus we read of a band of prophets coming down from a high place with a psaltery, a timbrel, a pipe, and a harp before them, and prophesying as they went. Again, when the united forces of Judah and Ephraim were traversing the wilderness of Moab in pursuit of the enemy, they could find no water for three days, and were like to die of thirst, they and the beasts of burden. In this emergency the prophet Elisha, who was with the army, called for a minstrel and bade him play. Under the influence of the music he ordered the soldiers to dig trenches in the sandy bed of the waterless waddy through which lay the line of march. They did so, and next morning the trenches were full of the water that had drained down into them underground from the desolate, forbidding mountains on either hand. The prophet's success in striking water in the wilderness resembles the reported success of modern dowsers, though his mode of procedure was different. Incidentally he rendered another service to his countrymen. For the skulking Moabites from their lairs among the rocks saw the red sun of the desert reflected in the water, and taking it for the blood, or perhaps rather for an omen of the blood, of their enemies, they plucked up heart to attack the camp and were defeated with great slaughter.

Again, just as the cloud of melancholy which from time to time darkened the moody mind of Saul was viewed as an evil spirit from the Lord vexing him, so on the other hand the solemn strains of the harp, which soothed and composed his troubled thoughts, may well have seemed to the hag-ridden king the very voice of God or of his good angel whispering peace. Even in our own day a great religious writer, himself deeply sensitive to the witchery of music, has said that musical notes, with all their power to fire the blood and melt the heart, cannot be mere empty sounds and nothing more ; no, they have escaped from some higher sphere, they are outpourings of eternal

harmony, the voice of angels, the Magnificat of saints. It is thus
that the rude imaginings of primitive man are transfigured and his
feeble lispings echoed with a rolling reverberation in the musical prose
of Newman.   Indeed the influence of music on the development of
religion is a subject which would repay a sympathetic study.   For
we cannot doubt that this, the most intimate and affecting of all the
arts, has done much to create as well as to express the religious
emotions, thus modifying more or less deeply the fabric of belief to
which at first sight it seems only to minister.   The musician has done
his part as well as the prophet and the thinker in the making of religion.
Every faith has its appropriate music, and the difference between the
creeds might almost be expressed in musical notation.   The interval,
for example, which divides the wild revels of Cybele from the stately
ritual of the Catholic Church is measured by the gulf which severs the
dissonant clash of cymbals and tambourines from the grave harmonies
of Palestrina and Handel.   A different spirit breathes in the difference
of the music.

CHAPTER XXXII

THE RITUAL OF ADONIS

AT the festivals of Adonis, which were held in Western Asia and in
Greek lands, the death of the god was annually mourned, with a bitter
wailing, chiefly by women ; images of him, dressed to resemble corpses,
were carried out as to burial and then thrown into the sea or into
springs ; and in some places his revival was celebrated on the following
day.   But at different places the ceremonies varied somewhat in the
manner and apparently also in the season of their celebration.   At
Alexandria images of Aphrodite and Adonis were displayed on two
couches ; beside them were set ripe fruits of all kinds, cakes, plants
growing in flower-pots, and green bowers twined with anise.   The
marriage of the lovers was celebrated one day, and on the morrow
women attired as mourners, with streaming hair and bared breasts,
bore the image of the dead Adonis to the sea-shore and committed it
to the waves.   Yet they sorrowed not without hope, for they sang
that the lost one would come back again.   The date at which this
Alexandrian ceremony was observed is not expressly stated ; but
from the mention of the ripe fruits it has been inferred that it took
place in late summer.   In the great Phoenician sanctuary of Astarte
at Byblus the death of Adonis was annually mourned, to the shrill
wailing notes of the flute, with weeping, lamentation, and beating of
the breast ; but next day he was believed to come to life again and
ascend up to heaven in the presence of his worshippers.   The disconsolate believers, left behind on earth, shaved their heads as the
Egyptians did on the death of the divine bull Apis ; women who
could not bring themselves to sacrifice their beautiful tresses had to

give themselves up to strangers on a certain day of the festival, and to dedicate to Astarte the wages of their shame.

This Phoenician festival appears to have been a vernal one, for its date was determined by the discoloration of the River Adonis, and this has been observed by modern travellers to occur in spring. At that season the red earth washed down from the mountains by the rain tinges the water of the river, and even the sea, for a great way with a blood-red hue, and the crimson stain was believed to be the blood of Adonis, annually wounded to death by the boar on Mount Lebanon. Again, the scarlet anemone is said to have sprung from the blood of Adonis, or to have been stained by it ; and as the anemone blooms in Syria about Easter, this may be thought to show that the festival of Adonis, or at least one of his festivals, was held in spring. The name of the flower is probably derived from Naaman (" darling "), which seems to have been an epithet of Adonis. The Arabs still call the anemone " wounds of the Naaman." The red rose also was said to owe its hue to the same sad occasion ; for Aphrodite, hastening to her wounded lover, trod on a bush of white roses ; the cruel thorns tore her tender flesh, and her sacred blood dyed the white roses for ever red. It would be idle, perhaps, to lay much weight on evidence drawn from the calendar of flowers, and in particular to press an argument so fragile as the bloom of the rose. Yet so far as it counts at all, the tale which links the damask rose with the death of Adonis points to a summer rather than to a spring celebration of his passion. In Attica, certainly, the festival fell at the height of summer. For the fleet which Athens fitted out against Syracuse, and by the destruction of which her power was permanently crippled, sailed at mid summer, and by an ominous coincidence the sombre rites of Adonis were being celebrated at the very time. As the troops marched down to the harbour to embark, the streets through which they passed were lined with coffins and corpse-like effigies, and the air was rent with the noise of women wailing for the dead Adonis. The circumstance cast a gloom over the sailing of the most splendid armament that Athens ever sent to sea. Many ages afterwards, when the Emperor Julian made his first entry into Antioch, he found in like manner the gay, the luxurious capital of the East plunged in mimic grief for the annual death of Adonis ; and if he had any presentiment of coming evil, the voices of lamentation which struck upon his ear must have seemed to sound his knell.

The resemblance of these ceremonies to the Indian and European ceremonies which I have described elsewhere is obvious. In particular, apart from the somewhat doubtful date of its celebration, the Alexandrian ceremony is almost identical with the Indian. In both of them the marriage of two divine beings, whose affinity with vegetation seems indicated by the fresh plants with which they are surrounded, is celebrated in effigy, and the effigies are afterwards mourned over and thrown into the water. From the similarity of these customs to each other and to the spring and midsummer customs of modern Europe we should naturally expect that they all admit of a common explanation. Hence, if the explanation which I have adopted of the latter is correct, the ceremony of the death and resurrection of Adonis must also have been a dramatic representation of the decay and revival of plant life. The inference thus based on the resemblance of the customs is confirmed by the following features in the legend and ritual of Adonis. His affinity with vegetation comes out at once in the common story of his birth. He was said to have been born from a myrrh-tree, the bark of which bursting, after a ten months' gestation, allowed the lovely infant to come forth. According to some, a boar rent the bark with his tusk and so opened a passage for the babe. A faint rationalistic colour was given to the legend by saying that his mother was a woman named Myrrh, who had been turned into a myrrh-tree soon after she had conceived the child. The use of myrrh as incense at the festival of Adonis may have given rise to the fable. We have seen that incense was burnt at the corresponding Babylonian rites, just as it was burnt by the idolatrous Hebrews in honour of the Queen of Heaven, who was no other than Astarte. Again, the story that Adonis spent half, or according to others a third, of the year in the lower world and the rest of it in the upper world, is explained most simply and naturally by supposing that he represented vegetation, especially the corn, which lies buried in the earth half the year and reappears above ground the other half. Certainly of the annual phenomena of nature there is none which suggests so obviously the idea of death and resurrection as the disappearance and reappearance of vegetation in autumn and spring. Adonis has been taken for the sun ; but there is nothing in the sun's annual course within the temperate and tropical zones to suggest that he is dead for half or a third of the year and alive for the other half or two-thirds. He might, indeed, be conceived as weakened in winter, but dead he could not be thought to be ; his daily reappearance contradicts the supposition. Within the Arctic Circle, where the sun annually disappears for a continuous period which varies from twenty-four hours to six months according to the latitude, his yearly death and resurrection would certainly be an obvious idea ; but no one except the unfortunate astronomer Bailly has maintained that the Adonis worship came from the Arctic regions. On the other hand, the annual death and revival of vegetation is a conception which readily presents itself to men in every stage of savagery and civilisation ; and the vastness of the scale on which this ever-recurring decay and regeneration takes place, together with man's intimate dependence on it for subsistence, combine to render it the most impressive annual occurrence in nature, at least within the temperate zones. It is no wonder that a phenomenon so important, so striking, and so universal should, by suggesting similar ideas, have given rise to similar rites in many lands. We may, therefore, accept as probable an explanation of the Adonis worship which accords so well with the facts of nature and with the analogy of similar rites in other lands. Moreover, the explanation is countenanced by a considerable body of opinion amongst the ancients themselves, who again and again interpreted the dying and reviving god as the reaped and sprouting grain.

The character of Tammuz or Adonis as a corn-spirit comes out plainly in an account of his festival given by an Arabic writer of the tenth century. In describing the rites and sacrifices observed at the different seasons of the year by the heathen Syrians of Harran, he says : " Tammuz (July). In the middle of this month is the festival of el-Bûgât, that is, of the weeping women, and this is the Tâ-uz festival, which is celebrated in honour of the god Tâ-uz. The women bewail him, because his lord slew him so cruelly, ground his bones in a mill, and then scattered them to the wind. The women (during this festival) eat nothing which has been ground in a mill, but limit their diet to steeped wheat, sweet vetches, dates, raisins, and the like." Tâ-uz, who is no other than Tammuz, is here like Burns's John Barleycorn :

" *They wasted o'er a scorching flame*   *But a miller us'd him worst of all,*
  The marrow of his bones ;   *For he crush'd him between two stones.*"

This concentration, so to say, of the nature of Adonis upon the cereal crops is characteristic of the stage of culture reached by his worshippers in historical times. They had left the nomadic life of the wandering hunter and herdsman far behind them ; for ages they had been settled on the land, and had depended for their subsistence mainly on the products of tillage. The berries and roots of the wilderness, the grass of the pastures, which had been matters of vital importance to their ruder forefathers, were now of little moment to them : more and more their thoughts and energies were engrossed by the staple of their life, the corn ; more and more accordingly the propitiation of the deities of fertility in general and of the corn-spirit in particular tended to become the central feature of their religion. The aim they set before themselves in celebrating the rites was thoroughly practical. It was no vague poetical sentiment which prompted them to hail with joy the rebirth of vegetation and to mourn its decline. Hunger, felt or feared, was the mainspring of the worship of Adonis.

It has been suggested by Father Lagrange that the mourning for Adonis was essentially a harvest rite designed to propitiate the corn-god, who was then either perishing under the sickles of the reapers or being trodden to death under the hoofs of the oxen on the threshing-floor. While the men slew him, the women wept crocodile tears at home to appease his natural indignation by a show of grief for his death. The theory fits in well with the dates of the festivals, which fell in spring or summer ; for spring and summer, not autumn, are the seasons of the barley and wheat harvests in the lands which worshipped Adonis. Further, the hypothesis is confirmed by the practice of the Egyptian reapers, who lamented, calling upon Isis, when they cut the first corn ; and it is recommended by the analogous customs of many hunting tribes, who testify great respect for the animals which they kill and eat.

Thus interpreted the death of Adonis is not the natural decay of vegetation in general under the summer heat or the winter cold ; it is the violent destruction of the corn by man, who cuts it down on the field, stamps it to pieces on the threshing-floor, and grinds it to powder in the mill. That this was indeed the principal aspect in which Adonis presented himself in later times to the agricultural peoples of the Levant, may be admitted ; but whether from the beginning he had been the corn and nothing but the corn, may be doubted. At an earlier period he may have been to the herdsman, above all, the tender herbage which sprouts after rain, offering rich pasture to the lean and hungry cattle. Earlier still he may have embodied the spirit of the nuts and berries which the autumn woods yield to the savage hunter and his squaw. And just as the husband-man must propitiate the spirit of the corn which he consumes, so the herdsman must appease the spirit of the grass and leaves which his cattle munch, and the hunter must soothe the spirit of the roots which he digs, and of the fruits which he gathers from the bough. In all cases the propitiation of the injured and angry sprite would naturally comprise elaborate excuses and apologies, accompanied by loud lamentations at his decease whenever, through some deplorable accident or necessity, he happened to be murdered as well as robbed. Only we must bear in mind that the savage hunter and herdsman of those early days had probably not yet attained to the abstract idea of vegetation in general ; and that accordingly, so far as Adonis existed for them at all, he must have been the *Adon* or lord of each individual tree and plant rather than a personification of vegetable life as a whole. Thus there would be as many Adonises as there were trees and shrubs and each of them might expect to receive satisfaction for any damage done to his person or property. And year by year, when the trees were deciduous, every Adonis would seem to bleed to death with the red leaves of autumn and to come to life again with the fresh green of spring.

There is some reason to think that in early times Adonis was sometimes personated by a living man who died a violent death in the character of the god. Further, there is evidence which goes to show that among the agricultural peoples of the Eastern Mediter-ranean, the corn-spirit, by whatever name he was known, was often represented, year by year, by human victims slain on the harvest-field. If that was so, it seems likely that the propitiation of the corn-spirit would tend to fuse to some extent with the worship of the dead. For the spirits of these victims might be thought to return to life in the ears which they had fattened with their blood, and to die a second death at the reaping of the corn. Now the ghosts of those who have perished by violence are surly and apt to wreak their vengeance on their slayers whenever an opportunity offers. Hence the attempt to appease the souls of the slaughtered victims would naturally blend, at least in the popular conception, with the attempt to pacify the slain corn-spirit. And as the dead came back in the sprouting corn, so they might be thought to return in the spring flowers, waked from their long sleep by the soft vernal airs. They had been laid to their rest under the sod. What more natural than to imagine that the violets and the hyacinths, the roses and the anemones, sprang from their dust, were empurpled or incarnadined by their blood, and contained some portion of their spirit ?

> " *I sometimes think that never blows so red*
> *The Rose as where some buried Caesar bled ;*
> *That every Hyacinth the Garden wears*
> *Dropt in her Lap from some once lovely Head.*
>
> " *And this reviving Herb whose tender Green*
> *Fledges the River-Lip on which we lean—*
> *Ah, lean upon it lightly, for who knows*
> *From what once lovely Lip it springs unseen ? "*

In the summer after the battle of Landen, the most sanguinary battle of the seventeenth century in Europe, the earth, saturated with the blood of twenty thousand slain, broke forth into millions of poppies, and the traveller who passed that vast sheet of scarlet might well fancy that the earth had indeed given up her dead. At Athens the great Commemoration of the Dead fell in spring about the middle of March, when the early flowers are in bloom. Then the dead were believed to rise from their graves and go about the streets, vainly endeavouring to enter the temples and dwellings, which were barred against these perturbed spirits with ropes, buckthorn, and pitch. The name of the festival, according to the most obvious and natural interpretation, means the Festival of Flowers, and the title would fit well with the substance of the ceremonies if at that season the poor ghosts were indeed thought to creep from the narrow house with the opening flowers. There may therefore be a measure of truth in the theory of Renan, who saw in the Adonis worship a dreamy voluptuous cult of death, conceived not as the King of Terrors, but as an insidious enchanter who lures his victims to himself and lulls them into an eternal sleep. The infinite charm of nature in the Lebanon, he thought, lends itself to religious emotions of this sensuous, visionary sort, hovering vaguely between pain and pleasure, between slumber and tears. It would doubtless be a mistake to attribute to Syrian peasants the worship of a conception so purely abstract as that of death in general. Yet it may be true that in their simple minds the thought of the reviving spirit of vegetation was blent with the very concrete notion of the ghosts of the dead, who come to life again in spring days with the early flowers, with the tender green of the corn and the many-tinted blossoms of the trees. Thus their views of the death and resurrection of nature would be coloured by their views of the death and resurrection of man, by their personal sorrows and hopes and fears. In like manner we cannot doubt that Renan's theory of Adonis was itself deeply tinged by passionate memories, memories of the slumber akin to death which sealed his own eyes on the slopes of the Lebanon, memories of the sister who sleeps in the land of Adonis never again to wake with the anemones and the roses.

CHAPTER XXXIII

THE GARDENS OF ADONIS

PERHAPS the best proof that Adonis was a deity of vegetation, and especially of the corn, is furnished by the gardens of Adonis, as they were called. These were baskets or pots filled with earth, in which wheat, barley, lettuces, fennel, and various kinds of flowers were sown and tended for eight days, chiefly or exclusively by women. Fostered by the sun's heat, the plants shot up rapidly, but having no root they withered as rapidly away, and at the end of eight days were carried out with the images of the dead Adonis, and flung with them into the sea or into springs.

These gardens of Adonis are most naturally interpreted as representatives of Adonis or manifestations of his power; they represented him, true to his original nature, in vegetable form, while the images of him, with which they were carried out and cast into the water, portrayed him in his later human shape. All these Adonis ceremonies, if I am right, were originally intended as charms to promote the growth or revival of vegetation; and the principle by which they were supposed to produce this effect was homoeopathic or imitative magic. For ignorant people suppose that by mimicking the effect which they desire to produce they actually help to produce it; thus by sprinkling water they make rain, by lighting a fire they make sunshine, and so on. Similarly, by mimicking the growth of crops they hope to ensure a good harvest. The rapid growth of the wheat and barley in the gardens of Adonis was intended to make the corn shoot up; and the throwing of the gardens and of the images into the water was a charm to secure a due supply of fertilising rain. The same, I take it, was the object of throwing the effigies of Death and the Carnival into water in the corresponding ceremonies of modern Europe. Certainly the custom of drenching with water a leaf-clad person, who undoubtedly personifies vegetation, is still resorted to in Europe for the express purpose of producing rain. Similarly the custom of throwing water on the last corn cut at harvest, or on the person who brings it home (a custom observed in Germany and France, and till lately in England and Scotland), is in some places practised with the avowed intent to procure rain for the next year's crops. Thus in Wallachia and amongst the Roumanians in Transylvania, when a girl is bringing home a crown made of the last ears of corn cut at harvest, all who meet her hasten to throw water on her, and two farm-servants are placed at the door for the purpose; for they believe that if this were not done, the crops next year would perish from drought. At the spring ploughing in Prussia, when the ploughmen and sowers returned in the evening from their work in the fields, the farmer's wife and the servants used to splash water over them. The ploughmen and sowers retorted by seizing every one, throwing them into the pond, and ducking them under the water. The farmer's wife might claim exemption on payment of a forfeit, but every one else had to be ducked. By observing this custom they hoped to ensure a due supply of rain for the seed.

The opinion that the gardens of Adonis are essentially charms to promote the growth of vegetation, especially of the crops, and that they belong to the same class of customs as those spring and midsummer folk-customs of modern Europe which I have described elsewhere, does not rest for its evidence merely on the intrinsic probability of the case. Fortunately we are able to show that gardens of Adonis (if we may use the expression in a general sense) are still planted, first, by a primitive race at their sowing season, and, second, by European peasants at midsummer. Amongst the Oraons and Mundas of Bengal, when the time comes for planting out the rice which has been grown in seed-beds, a party of young people of both sexes go to the forest and cut a young Karma-tree, or the branch of one. Bearing it in triumph they return dancing, singing, and beating drums, and plant it in the middle of the village dancing-ground. A sacrifice is offered to the tree; and next morning the youth of both sexes, linked arm-in-arm, dance in a great circle round the Karma-tree, which is decked with strips of coloured cloth and sham bracelets and necklets of plaited straw. As a preparation for the festival, the daughters of the headman of the village cultivate blades of barley in a peculiar way. The seed is sown in moist, sandy soil, mixed with turmeric, and the blades sprout and unfold of a pale-yellow or primrose colour. On the day of the festival the girls take up these blades and carry them in baskets to the dancing ground, where, prostrating themselves reverentially, they place some of the plants before the Karma-tree. Finally, the Karma-tree is taken away and thrown into a stream or tank. The meaning of planting these barley blades and then presenting them to the Karma-tree is hardly open to question. Trees are supposed to exercise a quickening influence upon the growth of crops, and amongst the very people in question—the Mundas or Mundaris—"the grove deities are held responsible for the crops." Therefore, when at the season for planting out the rice the Mundas bring in a tree and treat it with so much respect, their object can only be to foster thereby the growth of the rice which is about to be planted out; and the custom of causing barley blades to sprout rapidly and then presenting them to the tree must be intended to subserve the same purpose, perhaps by reminding the tree-spirit of his duty towards the crops, and stimulating his activity by this visible example of rapid vegetable growth. The throwing of the Karma-tree into the water is to be interpreted as a rain-charm. Whether the barley blades are also thrown into the water is not said ; but if my interpretation of the custom is right, probably they are so. A distinction between this Bengal custom and the Greek rites of Adonis is that in the former the tree-spirit appears in his original form as a tree ; whereas in the Adonis worship he appears in human form, represented as a dead man, though his vegetable nature is indicated by the gardens of Adonis, which are, so to say, a secondary manifestation of his original power as a tree-spirit.

Gardens of Adonis are cultivated also by the Hindoos, with the intention apparently of ensuring the fertility both of the earth and of mankind. Thus at Oodeypoor in Rajputana a festival is held in honour of Gouri, or Isani, the goddess of abundance. The rites begin when the sun enters the sign of the Ram, the opening of the Hindoo year. An image of the goddess Gouri is made of earth, and a smaller one of her husband Iswara, and the two are placed together. A small trench is next dug, barley is sown in it, and the ground watered and heated artificially till the grain sprouts, when the women dance round it hand in hand, invoking the blessing of Gouri on their husbands. After that the young corn is taken up and distributed by the women to the men, who wear it in their turbans. In these rites the distribution of the barley shoots to the men, and the invocation of a blessing on their husbands by the wives, point clearly to the desire of offspring as one motive for observing the custom. The same motive probably explains the use of gardens of Adonis at the marriage of Brahmans in the Madras Presidency. Seeds of five or nine sorts are mixed and sown in earthen pots, which are made specially for the purpose and are filled with earth. Bride and bridegroom water the seeds both morning and evening for four days ; and on the fifth day the seedlings are thrown, like the real gardens of Adonis, into a tank or river.

In Sardinia the gardens of Adonis are still planted in connexion with the great Midsummer festival which bears the name of St. John. At the end of March or on the first of April a young man of the village presents himself to a girl, and asks her to be his *comare* (gossip or sweetheart), offering to be her *compare*. The invitation is considered as an honour by the girl's family, and is gladly accepted. At the end of May the girl makes a pot of the bark of the cork-tree, fills it with earth, and sows a handful of wheat and barley in it. The pot being placed in the sun and often watered, the corn sprouts rapidly and has a good head by Midsummer Eve (St. John's Eve, the twenty-third of June). The pot is then called *Erme* or *Nenneri*. On St. John's Day the young man and the girl, dressed in their best, accompanied by a long retinue and preceded by children gambolling and frolicking, move in procession to a church outside the village. Here they break the pot by throwing it against the door of the church. Then they sit down in a ring on the grass and eat eggs and herbs to the music of flutes. Wine is mixed in a cup and passed round, each one drinking as it passes. Then they join hands and sing "Sweethearts of St. John " (*Compare e comare di San Giovanni*) over and over again, the flutes playing the while. When they tire of singing they stand up and dance gaily in a ring till evening. This is the general Sardinian custom. As practised at Ozieri it has some special features. In May the pots are made of cork-bark and planted with corn, as already described. Then on the Eve of St. John the window-sills are draped with rich cloths, on which the pots are placed, adorned with crimson and blue silk and ribbons of various colours. On each of the pots they used formerly to place a statuette or cloth doll dressed as a woman, or a Priapus-like figure made of paste ; but this custom, rigorously forbidden by the Church, has fallen into disuse. The village swains go about in a troop to look at the pots and their decorations and to wait for the girls, who assemble on the public square to celebrate the festival. Here a great bonfire is kindled, round which they dance and make merry. Those who wish to be " Sweethearts of St. John " act as follows. The young man stands on one side of the bonfire and the girl on the other, and they, in a manner, join hands by each grasping one end of a long stick, which they pass three times backwards and forwards across the fire, thus thrusting their hands thrice rapidly into the flames. This seals their relationship to each other. Dancing and music go on till late at night. The correspondence of these Sardinian pots of grain to the gardens of Adonis seems complete, and the images formerly placed in them answer to the images of Adonis which accompanied his gardens.

Customs of the same sort are observed at the same season in Sicily. Pairs of boys and girls become gossips of St. John on St. John's Day by drawing each a hair from his or her head and performing various ceremonies over them. Thus they tie the hairs together and throw them up in the air, or exchange them over a potsherd, which they afterwards break in two, preserving each a fragment with pious care. The tie formed in the latter way is supposed to last for life. In some parts of Sicily the gossips of St. John present each other with plates of sprouting corn, lentils, and canary seed, which have been planted forty days before the festival. The one who receives the plate pulls a stalk of the young plants, binds it with a ribbon, and preserves it among his or her greatest treasures, restoring the platter to the giver. At Catania the gossips exchange pots of basil and great cucumbers ; the girls tend the basil, and the thicker it grows the more it is prized.

In these midsummer customs of Sardinia and Sicily it is possible that, as Mr. R. Wünsch supposes, St. John has replaced Adonis. We have seen that the rites of Tammuz or Adonis were commonly celebrated about midsummer ; according to Jerome, their date was June.

In Sicily gardens of Adonis are still sown in spring as well as in summer, from which we may perhaps infer that Sicily as well as Syria celebrated of old a vernal festival of the dead and risen god. At the approach of Easter, Sicilian women sow wheat, lentils, and canary-seed in plates, which they keep in the dark and water every two days. The plants soon shoot up ; the stalks are tied together with red ribbons, and the plates containing them are placed on the sepulchres which, with the effigies of the dead Christ, are made up in Catholic and Greek churches on Good Friday, just as the gardens of Adonis were placed on the grave of the dead Adonis. The practice is not confined to Sicily, for it is observed also at Cosenza in Calabria, and perhaps in other places. The whole custom—sepulchres as well as plates of sprouting grain—may be nothing but a continuation, under a different name, of the worship of Adonis.

Nor are these Sicilian and Calabrian customs the only Easter ceremonies which resemble the rites of Adonis. " During the whole of Good Friday a waxen effigy of the dead Christ is exposed to view in the middle of the Greek churches and is covered with fervent kisses by the thronging crowd, while the whole church rings with melancholy, monotonous dirges. Late in the evening, when it has grown quite dark, this waxen image is carried by the priests into the street on a bier adorned with lemons, roses, jessamine, and other flowers, and there begins a grand procession of the multitude, who move in serried ranks, with slow and solemn step, through the whole town. Every man carries his taper and breaks out into doleful lamentation. At all the houses which the procession passes there are seated women with censers to fumigate the marching host. Thus the community solemnly buries its Christ as if he had just died. At last the waxen image is again deposited in the church, and the same lugubrious chants echo anew. These lamentations, accompanied by a strict fast, continue till midnight on Saturday. As the clock strikes twelve, the bishop appears and announces the glad tidings that ' Christ is risen,' to which the crowd replies, ' He is risen indeed,' and at once the whole city bursts into an uproar of joy, which finds vent in shrieks and shouts, in the endless discharge of carronades and muskets, and the explosion of fire-works of every sort. In the very same hour people plunge from the extremity of the fast into the enjoyment of the Easter lamb and neat wine."

In like manner the Catholic Church has been accustomed to bring before its followers in a visible form the death and resurrection of the Redeemer. Such sacred dramas are well fitted to impress the lively imagination and to stir the warm feelings of a susceptible southern race, to whom the pomp and pageantry of Catholicism are more congenial than to the colder temperament of the Teutonic peoples.

When we reflect how often the Church has skilfully contrived to plant the seeds of the new faith on the old stock of paganism, we may surmise that the Easter celebration of the dead and risen Christ was grafted upon a similar celebration of the dead and risen Adonis, which, as we have seen reason to believe, was celebrated in Syria at the same season. The type, created by Greek artists, of the sorrowful goddess with her dying lover in her arms, resembles and may have been the model of the *Pietà* of Christian art, the Virgin with the dead body of her divine Son in her lap, of which the most celebrated example is the one by Michael Angelo in St. Peter's. That noble group, in which the living sorrow of the mother contrasts so wonderfully with the languor of death in the son, is one of the finest compositions in marble.   Ancient Greek art has bequeathed to us few works so beautiful, and none so pathetic.

In this connexion a well-known statement of Jerome may not be without significance.   He tells us that Bethlehem, the traditionary birthplace of the Lord, was shaded by a grove of that still older Syrian Lord, Adonis, and that where the infant Jesus had wept, the lover of Venus was bewailed.   Though he does not expressly say so, Jerome seems to have thought that the grove of Adonis had been planted by the heathen after the birth of Christ for the purpose of defiling the sacred spot.   In this he may have been mistaken.   If Adonis was indeed, as I have argued, the spirit of the corn, a more suitable name for his dwelling-place could hardly be found than Bethlehem, " the House of Bread," and he may well have been worshipped there at his House of Bread long ages before the birth of Him who said, " I am the bread of life."   Even on the hypothesis that Adonis followed rather than preceded Christ at Bethlehem, the choice of his sad figure to divert the allegiance of Christians from their Lord cannot but strike us as eminently appropriate when we remember the similarity of the rites which commemorated the death and resurrection of the two. One of the earliest seats of the worship of the new god was Antioch, and at Antioch, as we have seen, the death of the old god was annually celebrated with great solemnity.   A circumstance which attended the entrance of Julian into the city at the time of the Adonis festival may perhaps throw some light on the date of its celebration.   When the emperor drew near to the city he was received with public prayers as if he had been a god, and he marvelled at the voices of a great multitude who cried that the Star of Salvation had dawned upon them in the East.   This may doubtless have been no more than a fulsome compliment paid by an obsequious Oriental crowd to the Roman emperor.   But it is also possible that the rising of a bright star regularly gave the signal for the festival, and that as chance would have it the star emerged above the rim of the eastern horizon at the very moment of the emperor's approach.   The coincidence, if it happened, could hardly fail to strike the imagination of a superstitious and excited multitude, who might thereupon hail the great man as the deity whose coming was announced by the sign in the heavens.   Or the emperor may have mistaken for a greeting to himself the shouts which were addressed to the star.   Now Astarte, the divine mistress of Adonis, was identified with the planet Venus, and her changes from a morning to an evening star were carefully noted by the Babylonian astronomers, who drew omens from her alternate appearance and disappearance. Hence we may conjecture that the festival of Adonis was regularly timed to coincide with the appearance of Venus as the Morning or Evening Star.   But the star which the people of Antioch saluted at the festival was seen in the East ; therefore, if it was indeed Venus, it can only have been the Morning Star.   At Aphaca in Syria, where there was a famous temple of Astarte, the signal for the celebration of the rites was apparently given by the flashing of a meteor, which on a certain day fell like a star from the top of Mount Lebanon into the river Adonis. The meteor was thought to be Astarte herself, and its flight through the air might naturally be interpreted as the descent of the amorous goddess to the arms of her lover. At Antioch and elsewhere the appearance of the Morning Star on the day of the festival may in like manner have been hailed as the coming of the goddess of love to wake her dead leman from his earthy bed. If that were so, we may surmise that it was the Morning Star which guided the wise men of the East to Bethlehem, the hallowed spot which heard, in the language of Jerome, the weeping of the infant Christ and the lament for Adonis.

CHAPTER XXXIV

THE MYTH AND RITUAL OF ATTIS

ANOTHER of those gods whose supposed death and resurrection struck such deep roots into the faith and ritual of Western Asia is Attis. He was to Phrygia what Adonis was to Syria. Like Adonis, he appears to have been a god of vegetation, and his death and resurrection were annually mourned and rejoiced over at a festival in spring. The legends and rites of the two gods were so much alike that the ancients themselves sometimes identified them. Attis was said to have been a fair young shepherd or herdsman beloved by Cybele, the Mother of the Gods, a great Asiatic goddess of fertility, who had her chief home in Phrygia. Some held that Attis was her son. His birth, like that of many other heroes, is said to have been miraculous. His mother, Nana, was a virgin, who conceived by putting a ripe almond or a pomegranate in her bosom. Indeed in the Phrygian cosmogony an almond figured as the father of all things, perhaps because its delicate lilac blossom is one of the first heralds of the spring, appearing on the bare boughs before the leaves have opened. Such tales of virgin mothers are relics of an age of childish ignorance when men had not yet recognized the intercourse of the sexes as the true cause of off-spring. Two different accounts of the death of Attis were current. According to the one he was killed by a boar, like Adonis. According to the other he unmanned himself under a pine-tree, and bled to death on the spot. The latter is said to have been the local story told by the people of Pessinus, a great seat of the worship of Cybele, and the whole legend of which the story forms a part is stamped with a character of rudeness and savagery that speaks strongly for its antiquity. Both tales might claim the support of custom, or rather both were probably invented to explain certain customs observed by the worshippers. The story of the self-mutilation of Attis is clearly an attempt to account for the self-mutilation of his priests, who regularly castrated themselves on entering the service of the goddess. The story of his death by the boar may have been told to explain why his worshippers, especially the people of Pessinus, abstained from eating swine. In like manner the worshippers of Adonis abstained from pork, because a boar had killed their god. After his death Attis is said to have been changed into a pine-tree.

The worship of the Phrygian Mother of the Gods was adopted by the Romans in 204 B.C. towards the close of their long struggle with Hannibal. For their drooping spirits had been opportunely cheered by a prophecy, alleged to be drawn from that convenient farrago of nonsense, the Sibylline Books, that the foreign invader would be driven from Italy if the great Oriental goddess were brought to Rome. Accordingly ambassadors were despatched to her sacred city Pessinus in Phrygia. The small black stone which embodied the mighty divinity was entrusted to them and conveyed to Rome, where it was received with great respect and installed in the temple of Victory on the Palatine Hill. It was the middle of April when the goddess arrived, and she went to work at once. For the harvest that year was such as had not been seen for many a long day, and in the very next year Hannibal and his veterans embarked for Africa. As he looked his last on the coast of Italy, fading behind him in the distance, he could not foresee that Europe, which had repelled the arms, would yet yield to the gods, of the Orient. The vanguard of the conquerors had already encamped in the heart of Italy before the rearguard of the beaten army fell sullenly back from its shores.

We may conjecture, though we are not told, that the Mother of the Gods brought with her the worship of her youthful lover or son to her new home in the West. Certainly the Romans were familiar with the Galli, the emasculated priests of Attis, before the close of the Republic. These unsexed beings, in their Oriental costume, with little images suspended on their breasts, appear to have been a familiar sight in the streets of Rome, which they traversed in procession, carrying the image of the goddess and chanting their hymns to the music of cymbals and tambourines, flutes and horns, while the people, impressed by the fantastic show and moved by the wild strains, flung alms to them in abundance, and buried the image and its bearers under showers of roses. A further step was taken by the Emperor Claudius when he incorporated the Phrygian worship of the sacred tree, and with it probably the orgiastic rites of Attis, in the established religion of Rome. The great spring festival of Cybele and Attis is best known to us in the form in which it was celebrated at Rome ; but as we are informed that the Roman ceremonies were also Phrygian, we may assume that they differed hardly, if at all, from their Asiatic original. The order of the festival seems to have been as follows.

On the twenty-second day of March, a pine-tree was cut in the woods and brought into the sanctuary of Cybele, where it was treated as a great divinity. The duty of carrying the sacred tree was entrusted to a guild of Tree-bearers. The trunk was swathed like a corpse with woollen bands and decked with wreaths of violets, for violets were said to have sprung from the blood of Attis, as roses and anemones from the blood of Adonis ; and the effigy of a young man, doubtless Attis himself, was tied to the middle of the stem. On the second day of the festival, the twenty-third of March, the chief ceremony seems to have been a blowing of trumpets. The third day, the twenty-fourth of March, was known as the Day of Blood : the Archigallus or high-priest drew blood from his arms and presented it as an offering. Nor was he alone in making this bloody sacrifice. Stirred by the wild barbaric music of clashing cymbals, rumbling drums, droning horns, and screaming flutes, the inferior clergy whirled about in the dance with waggling heads and streaming hair, until, rapt into a frenzy of excitement and insensible to pain, they gashed their bodies with potsherds or slashed them with knives in order to bespatter the altar and the sacred tree with their flowing blood. The ghastly rite probably formed part of the mourning for Attis and may have been intended to strengthen him for the resurrection. The Australian aborigines cut themselves in like manner over the graves of their friends for the purpose, perhaps, of enabling them to be born again. Further, we may conjecture, though we are not expressly told, that it was on the same Day of Blood and for the same purpose that the novices sacrificed their virility. Wrought up to the highest pitch of religious excitement they dashed the severed portions of themselves against the image of the cruel goddess. These broken instruments of fertility were afterwards reverently wrapt up and buried in the earth or in sub-terranean chambers sacred to Cybele, where, like the offering of blood, they may have been deemed instrumental in recalling Attis to life and hastening the general resurrection of nature, which was then bursting into leaf and blossom in the vernal sunshine. Some confirma-tion of this conjecture is furnished by the savage story that the mother of Attis conceived by putting in her bosom a pomegranate sprung from the severed genitals of a man-monster named Agdestis, a sort of double of Attis.

If there is any truth in this conjectural explanation of the custom, we can readily understand why other Asiatic goddesses of fertility were served in like manner by eunuch priests. These feminine deities required to receive from their male ministers, who personated the divine lovers, the means of discharging their beneficent functions : they had themselves to be impregnated by the life-giving energy before they could transmit it to the world. Goddesses thus ministered to by eunuch priests were the great Artemis of Ephesus and the great Syrian Astarte of Hierapolis, whose sanctuary, frequented by swarms of pilgrims and enriched by the offerings of Assyria and Babylonia, of Arabia and Phoenicia, was perhaps in the days of its glory the most popular in the East. Now the unsexed priests of this Syrian goddess resembled those of Cybele so closely that some people took them to be the same. And the mode in which they dedicated themselves to the religious life was similar. The greatest festival of the year at Hierapolis fell at the beginning of spring, when multitudes thronged

to the sanctuary from Syria and the regions round about. While the
flutes played, the drums beat, and the eunuch priests slashed themselves with knives, the religious excitement gradually spread like a
wave among the crowd of onlookers, and many a one did that which
he little thought to do when he came as a holiday spectator to the
festival. For man after man, his veins throbbing with the music, his
eyes fascinated by the sight of the streaming blood, flung his garments
from him, leaped forth with a shout, and seizing one of the swords
which stood ready for the purpose, castrated himself on the spot.
Then he ran through the city, holding the bloody pieces in his hand,
till he threw them into one of the houses which he passed in his mad
career. The household thus honoured had to furnish him with a
suit of female attire and female ornaments, which he wore for the
rest of his life. When the tumult of emotion had subsided, and the
man had come to himself again, the irrevocable sacrifice must often
have been followed by passionate sorrow and lifelong regret. This
revulsion of natural human feeling after the frenzies of a fanatical
religion is powerfully depicted by Catullus in a celebrated poem.

The parallel of these Syrian devotees confirms the view that in
the similar worship of Cybele the sacrifice of virility took place on
the Day of Blood at the vernal rites of the goddess, when the violets,
supposed to spring from the red drops of her wounded lover, were in
bloom among the pines. Indeed the story that Attis unmanned
himself under a pine-tree was clearly devised to explain why his priests
did the same beside the sacred violet-wreathed tree at his festival.
At all events, we can hardly doubt that the Day of Blood witnessed
the mourning for Attis over an effigy of him which was afterwards
buried. The image thus laid in the sepulchre was probably the same
which had hung upon the tree. Throughout the period of mourning
the worshippers fasted from bread, nominally because Cybele had done
so in her grief for the death of Attis, but really perhaps for the same
reason which induced the women of Harran to abstain from eating
anything ground in a mill while they wept for Tammuz. To partake
of bread or flour at such a season might have been deemed a wanton
profanation of the bruised and broken body of the god. Or the fast
may possibly have been a preparation for a sacramental meal.

But when night had fallen, the sorrow of the worshippers was
turned to joy. For suddenly a light shone in the darkness : the tomb
was opened : the god had risen from the dead ; and as the priest
touched the lips of the weeping mourners with balm, he softly whispered
in their ears the glad tidings of salvation. The resurrection of the
god was hailed by his disciples as a promise that they too would issue
triumphant from the corruption of the grave. On the morrow, the
twenty-fifth day of March, which was reckoned the vernal equinox,
the divine resurrection was celebrated with a wild outburst of glee.
At Rome, and probably elsewhere, the celebration took the form of
a carnival. It was the Festival of Joy (*Hilaria*). A universal licence
prevailed. Every man might say and do what he pleased. People

went about the streets in disguise. No dignity was too high or too sacred for the humblest citizen to assume with impunity. In the reign of Commodus a band of conspirators thought to take advantage of the masquerade by dressing in the uniform of the Imperial Guard, and so, mingling with the crowd of merrymakers, to get within stabbing distance of the emperor. But the plot miscarried. Even the stern Alexander Severus used to relax so far on the joyous day as to admit a pheasant to his frugal board. The next day, the twenty-sixth of March, was given to repose, which must have been much needed after the varied excitements and fatigues of the preceding days. Finally, the Roman festival closed on the twenty-seventh of March with a procession to the brook Almo. The silver image of the goddess, with its face of jagged black stone, sat in a waggon drawn by oxen. Preceded by the nobles walking barefoot, it moved slowly, to the loud music of pipes and tambourines, out by the Porta Capena, and so down to the banks of the Almo, which flows into the Tiber just below the walls of Rome. There the high-priest, robed in purple, washed the waggon, the image, and the other sacred objects in the water of the stream. On returning from their bath, the wain and the oxen were strewn with fresh spring flowers. All was mirth and gaiety. No one thought of the blood that had flowed so lately. Even the eunuch priests forgot their wounds.

Such, then, appears to have been the annual solemnisation of the death and resurrection of Attis in spring. But besides these public rites, his worship is known to have comprised certain secret or mystic ceremonies, which probably aimed at bringing the worshipper, and especially the novice, into closer communication with his god. Our information as to the nature of these mysteries and the date of their celebration is unfortunately very scanty, but they seem to have included a sacramental meal and a baptism of blood. In the sacrament the novice became a partaker of the mysteries by eating out of a drum and drinking out of a cymbal, two instruments of music which figured prominently in the thrilling orchestra of Attis. The fast which accompanied the mourning for the dead god may perhaps have been designed to prepare the body of the communicant for the reception of the blessed sacrament by purging it of all that could defile by contact the sacred elements. In the baptism the devotee, crowned with gold and wreathed with fillets, descended into a pit, the mouth of which was covered with a wooden grating. A bull, adorned with garlands of flowers, its forehead glittering with gold leaf, was then driven on to the grating and there stabbed to death with a consecrated spear. Its hot reeking blood poured in torrents through the apertures, and was received with devout eagerness by the worshipper on every part of his person and garments, till he emerged from the pit, drenched, dripping, and scarlet from head to foot, to receive the homage, nay the adoration, of his fellows as one who had been born again to eternal life and had washed away his sins in the blood of the bull. For some time afterwards the fiction of a new birth was kept up by dieting him on milk like a new-born babe. The regeneration of the worshipper took place at the same time as the regeneration of his god, namely at the vernal equinox. At Rome the new birth and the remission of sins by the shedding of bull's blood appear to have been carried out above all at the sanctuary of the Phrygian goddess on the Vatican Hill, at or near the spot where the great basilica of St. Peter's now stands ; for many inscriptions relating to the rites were found when the church was being enlarged in 1608 or 1609. From the Vatican as a centre this barbarous system of superstition seems to have spread to other parts of the Roman empire. Inscriptions found in Gaul and Germany prove that provincial sanctuaries modelled their ritual on that of the Vatican. From the same source we learn that the testicles as well as the blood of the bull played an important part in the ceremonies. Probably they were regarded as a powerful charm to promote fertility and hasten the new birth.

CHAPTER XXXV

ATTIS AS A GOD OF VEGETATION

THE original character of Attis as a tree-spirit is brought out plainly by the part which the pine-tree plays in his legend, his ritual, and his monuments. The story that he was a human being transformed into a pine-tree is only one of those transparent attempts at rationalising old beliefs which meet us so frequently in mythology. The bringing in of the pine-tree from the woods, decked with violets and woollen bands, is like bringing in the May-tree or Summer-tree in modern folk-custom ; and the effigy which was attached to the pine-tree was only a duplicate representative of the tree-spirit Attis. After being fastened to the tree, the effigy was kept for a year and then burned. The same thing appears to have been sometimes done with the Maypole ; and in like manner the effigy of the corn-spirit, made at harvest, is often preserved till it is replaced by a new effigy at next year's harvest. The original intention of such customs was no doubt to maintain the spirit of vegetation in life throughout the year. Why the Phrygians should have worshipped the pine above other trees we can only guess. Perhaps the sight of its changeless, though sombre, green cresting the ridges of the high hills above the fading splendour of the autumn woods in the valleys may have seemed to their eyes to mark it out as the seat of a diviner life, of something exempt from the sad vicissitudes of the seasons, constant and eternal as the sky which stooped to meet it. For the same reason, perhaps, ivy was sacred to Attis ; at all events, we read that his eunuch priests were tattooed with a pattern of ivy leaves. Another reason for the sanctity of the pine may have been its usefulness. The cones of the stone-pine contain edible nut-like seeds, which have been used as food since antiquity, and are still eaten, for example, by the poorer classes in Rome. Moreover, a wine was brewed from these seeds, and this may partly account for the orgiastic nature of the rites of Cybele, which the ancients compared to those of Dionysus. Further, pine-cones were regarded as symbols or rather instruments of fertility. Hence at the festival of the Thesmophoria they were thrown, along with pigs and other agents or emblems of fecundity, into the sacred vaults of Demeter for the purpose of quickening the ground and the wombs of women.

Like tree-spirits in general, Attis was apparently thought to wield power over the fruits of the earth or even to be identical with the corn. One of his epithets was " very fruitful " : he was addressed as the " reaped green (or yellow) ear of corn " ; and the story of his sufferings, death, and resurrection was interpreted as the ripe grain wounded by the reaper, buried in the granary, and coming to life again when it is sown in the ground. A statue of him in the Lateran Museum at Rome clearly indicates his relation to the fruits of the earth, and particularly to the corn ; for it represents him with a bunch of ears of corn and fruit in his hand, and a wreath of pine-cones, pomegranates, and other fruits on his head, while from the top of his Phrygian cap ears of corn are sprouting. On a stone urn, which contained the ashes of an Archigallus or high-priest of Attis, the same idea is expressed in a slightly different way. The top of the urn is adorned with ears of corn carved in relief, and it is surmounted by the figure of a cock, whose tail consists of ears of corn. Cybele in like manner was conceived as a goddess of fertility who could make or mar the fruits of the earth ; for the people of Augustodunum (Autun) in Gaul used to cart her image about in a waggon for the good of the fields and vineyards, while they danced and sang before it, and we have seen that in Italy an unusually fine harvest was attributed to the recent arrival of the Great Mother. The bathing of the image of the goddess in a river may well have been a rain-charm to ensure an abundant supply of moisture for the crops.

CHAPTER XXXVI

HUMAN REPRESENTATIVES OF ATTIS

FROM inscriptions it appears that both at Pessinus and Rome the high-priest of Cybele regularly bore the name of Attis. It is therefore a reasonable conjecture that he played the part of his namesake, the legendary Attis, at the annual festival. We have seen that on the Day of Blood he drew blood from his arms, and this may have been an imitation of the self-inflicted death of Attis under the pine-tree. It is not inconsistent with this supposition that Attis was also represented at these ceremonies by an effigy ; for instances can be shown in which the divine being is first represented by a living person and

2 A

afterwards by an effigy, which is then burned or otherwise destroyed. Perhaps we may go a step farther and conjecture that this mimic killing of the priest, accompanied by a real effusion of his blood, was in Phrygia, as it has been elsewhere, a substitute for a human sacrifice which in earlier times was actually offered.

A reminiscence of the manner in which these old representatives of the deity were put to death is perhaps preserved in the famous story of Marsyas. He was said to be a Phrygian satyr or Silenus, according to others a shepherd or herdsman, who played sweetly on the flute. A friend of Cybele, he roamed the country with the disconsolate goddess to soothe her grief for the death of Attis. The composition of the Mother's Air, a tune played on the flute in honour of the Great Mother Goddess, was attributed to him by the people of Celaenae in Phrygia. Vain of his skill, he challenged Apollo to a musical contest, he to play on the flute and Apollo on the lyre. Being vanquished, Marsyas was tied up to a pine-tree and flayed or cut limb from limb either by the victorious Apollo or by a Scythian slave. His skin was shown at Celaenae in historical times. It hung at the foot of the citadel in a cave from which the river Marsyas rushed with an impetuous and noisy tide to join the Maeander. So the Adonis bursts full-born from the precipices of the Lebanon ; so the blue river of Ibreez leaps in a crystal jet from the red rocks of the Taurus ; so the stream, which now rumbles deep underground, used to gleam for a moment on its passage from darkness to darkness in the dim light of the Corycian cave. In all these copious fountains, with their glad promise of fertility and life, men of old saw the hand of God and worshipped him beside the rushing river with the music of its tumbling waters in their ears. At Celaenae, if we can trust tradition, the piper Marsyas, hanging in his cave, had a soul for harmony even in death ; for it is said that at the sound of his native Phrygian melodies the skin of the dead satyr used to thrill, but that if the musician struck up an air in praise of Apollo it remained deaf and motionless.

In this Phrygian satyr, shepherd, or herdsman who enjoyed the friendship of Cybele, practised the music so characteristic of her rites, and died a violent death on her sacred tree, the pine, may we not detect a close resemblance to Attis, the favourite shepherd or herdsman of the goddess, who is himself described as a piper, is said to have perished under a pine-tree, and was annually represented by an effigy hung, like Marsyas, upon a pine ? We may conjecture that in old days the priest who bore the name and played the part of Attis at the spring festival of Cybele was regularly hanged or otherwise slain upon the sacred tree, and that this barbarous custom was afterwards mitigated into the form in which it is known to us in later times, when the priest merely drew blood from his body under the tree and attached an effigy instead of himself to its trunk. In the holy grove at Upsala men and animals were sacrificed by being hanged upon the sacred trees. The human victims dedicated to Odin were regularly put to death by hanging or by a combination of hanging and stabbing, the man being strung up to a tree or a gallows and then wounded with a spear.   Hence Odin was called the Lord of the Gallows or the God of the Hanged, and he is represented sitting under a gallows tree.   Indeed he is said to have been sacrificed to himself in the ordinary way, as we learn from the weird verses of the *Havamal*, in which the god describes how he acquired his divine power by learning the magic runes :

> " *I know that I hung on the windy tree*
> *For nine whole nights,*
> *Wounded with the spear, dedicated to Odin,*
> *Myself to myself.*"

The Bagobos of Mindanao, one of the Philippine Islands, used annually to sacrifice human victims for the good of the crops in a similar way. Early in December, when the constellation Orion appeared at seven o'clock in the evening, the people knew that the time had come to clear their fields for sowing and to sacrifice a slave.   The sacrifice was presented to certain powerful spirits as payment for the good year which the people had enjoyed, and to ensure the favour of the spirits for the coming season.   The victim was led to a great tree in the forest ; there he was tied with his back to the tree and his arms stretched high above his head, in the attitude in which ancient artists portrayed Marsyas hanging on the fatal tree.   While he thus hung by the arms, he was slain by a spear thrust through his body at the level of the armpits.   Afterwards the body was cut clean through the middle at the waist, and the upper part was apparently allowed to dangle for a little from the tree, while the under part wallowed in blood on the ground.   The two portions were finally cast into a shallow trench beside the tree.   Before this was done, anybody who wished might cut off a piece of flesh or a lock of hair from the corpse and carry it to the grave of some relation whose body was being consumed by a ghoul.   Attracted by the fresh corpse, the ghoul would leave the mouldering old body in peace.   These sacrifices have been offered by men now living.

In Greece the great goddess Artemis herself appears to have been annually hanged in effigy in her sacred grove of Condylea among the Arcadian hills, and there accordingly she went by the name of the Hanged One.   Indeed a trace of a similar rite may perhaps be detected even at Ephesus, the most famous of her sanctuaries, in the legend of a woman who hanged herself and was thereupon dressed by the compassionate goddess in her own divine garb and called by the name of Hecate.   Similarly, at Melite in Phthia, a story **was** told of a girl named Aspalis who hanged herself, but who appears to have been merely a form of Artemis.   For after her death her body could not be found, but an image of her was discovered standing beside the image of Artemis, and the people bestowed on it the title of Hecaerge or Far-shooter, one of the regular epithets of the goddess.   Every year the virgins sacrificed a young goat to the image by hanging it, because Aspalis was said to have hanged herself. The sacrifice may have been a substitute for hanging an image or a human representative of Artemis. Again, in Rhodes the fair Helen was worshipped under the title of Helen of the Tree, because the queen of the island had caused her handmaids, disguised as Furies, to string her up to a bough. That the Asiatic Greeks sacrificed animals in this fashion is proved by coins of Ilium, which represent an ox or cow hanging on a tree and stabbed with a knife by a man, who sits among the branches or on the animal's back. At Hierapolis also the victims were hung on trees before they were burnt. With these Greek and Scandinavian parallels before us we can hardly dismiss as wholly improbable the conjecture that in Phrygia a man-god may have hung year by year on the sacred but fatal tree.

CHAPTER XXXVII

ORIENTAL RELIGIONS IN THE WEST

THE worship of the Great Mother of the Gods and her lover or son was very popular under the Roman Empire. Inscriptions prove that the two received divine honours, separately or conjointly, not only in Italy, and especially at Rome, but also in the provinces, particularly in Africa, Spain, Portugal, France, Germany, and Bulgaria. Their worship survived the establishment of Christianity by Constantine ; for Symmachus records the recurrence of the festival of the Great Mother, and in the days of Augustine her effeminate priests still paraded the streets and squares of Carthage with whitened faces, scented hair, and mincing gait, while, like the mendicant friars of the Middle Ages, they begged alms from the passers-by. In Greece, on the other hand, the bloody orgies of the Asiatic goddess and her consort appear to have found little favour. The barbarous and cruel character of the worship, with its frantic excesses, was doubtless repugnant to the good taste and humanity of the Greeks, who seem to have preferred the kindred but gentler rites of Adonis. Yet the same features which shocked and repelled the Greeks may have positively attracted the less refined Romans and barbarians of the West. The ecstatic frenzies, which were mistaken for divine inspiration, the mangling of the body, the theory of a new birth and the remission of sins through the shedding of blood, have all their origin in savagery, and they naturally appealed to peoples in whom the savage instincts were still strong. Their true character was indeed often disguised under a decent veil of allegorical or philosophical interpretation, which probably sufficed to impose upon the rapt and enthusiastic worshippers, reconciling even the more cultivated of them to things which otherwise must have filled them with horror and disgust.

The religion of the Great Mother, with its curious blending of crude savagery with spiritual aspirations, was only one of a multitude of similar Oriental faiths which in the later days of paganism spread over the Roman Empire, and by saturating the European peoples with alien ideals of life gradually undermined the whole fabric of ancient civilisation.   Greek and Roman society was built on the conception of the subordination of the individual to the community, of the citizen to the state ; it set the safety of the commonwealth, as the supreme aim of conduct, above the safety of the individual whether in this world or in a world to come.   Trained from infancy in this unselfish ideal, the citizens devoted their lives to the public service and were ready to lay them down for the common good ; or if they shrank from the supreme sacrifice, it never occurred to them that they acted otherwise than basely in preferring their personal existence to the interests of their country.   All this was changed by the spread of Oriental religions which inculcated the communion of the soul with God and its eternal salvation as the only objects worth living for, objects in comparison with which the prosperity and even the existence of the state sank into insignificance.   The inevitable result of this selfish and immoral doctrine was to withdraw the devotee more and more from the public service, to concentrate his thoughts on his own spiritual emotions, and to breed in him a contempt for the present life which he regarded merely as a probation for a better and an eternal.   The saint and the recluse, disdainful of earth and rapt in ecstatic contemplation of heaven, became in popular opinion the highest ideal of humanity, displacing the old ideal of the patriot and hero who, forgetful of self, lives and is ready to die for the good of his country.   The earthly city seemed poor and contemptible to men whose eyes beheld the City of God coming in the clouds of heaven.   Thus the centre of gravity, so to say, was shifted from the present to a future life, and however much the other world may have gained, there can be little doubt that this one lost heavily by the change.   A general disintegration of the body politic set in.   The ties of the state and the family were loosened : the structure of society tended to resolve itself into its individual elements and thereby to relapse into barbarism ; for civilisation is only possible through the active co-operation of the citizens and their willingness to subordinate their private interests to the common good. Men refused to defend their country and even to continue their kind. In their anxiety to save their own souls and the souls of others, they were content to leave the material world, which they identified with the principle of evil, to perish around them.   This obsession lasted for a thousand years.   The revival of Roman law, of the Aristotelian philosophy, of ancient art and literature at the close of the Middle Ages, marked the return of Europe to native ideals of life and conduct, to saner, manlier views of the world.   The long halt in the march of civilisation was over.   The tide of Oriental invasion had turned at last.   It is ebbing still.

Among the gods of eastern origin who in the decline of the ancient world competed against each other for the allegiance of the West was the old Persian deity Mithra. The immense popularity of his worship is attested by the monuments illustrative of it which have been found scattered in profusion all over the Roman Empire. In respect both of doctrines and of rites the cult of Mithra appears to have presented many points of resemblance not only to the religion of the Mother of the Gods but also to Christianity. The similarity struck the Christian doctors themselves and was explained by them as a work of the devil, who sought to seduce the souls of men from the true faith by a false and insidious imitation of it. So to the Spanish conquerors of Mexico and Peru many of the native heathen rites appeared to be diabolical counterfeits of the Christian sacraments. With more probability the modern student of comparative religion traces such resemblances to the similar and independent workings of the mind of man in his sincere, if crude, attempts to fathom the secret of the universe, and to adjust his little life to its awful mysteries. However that may be, there can be no doubt that the Mithraic religion proved a formidable rival to Christianity, combining as it did a solemn ritual with aspirations after moral purity and a hope of immortality. Indeed the issue of the conflict between the two faiths appears for a time to have hung in the balance. An instructive relic of the long struggle is preserved in our festival of Christmas, which the Church seems to have borrowed directly from its heathen rival. In the Julian calendar the twenty-fifth of December was reckoned the winter solstice, and it was regarded as the Nativity of the Sun, because the day begins to lengthen and the power of the sun to increase from that turning-point of the year. The ritual of the nativity, as it appears to have been celebrated in Syria and Egypt, was remarkable. The celebrants retired into certain inner shrines, from which at midnight they issued with a loud cry, " The Virgin has brought forth ! The light is waxing ! " The Egyptians even represented the new-born sun by the image of an infant which on his birthday, the winter solstice, they brought forth and exhibited to his worshippers. No doubt the Virgin who thus conceived and bore a son on the twenty-fifth of December was the great Oriental goddess whom the Semites called the Heavenly Virgin or simply the Heavenly Goddess ; in Semitic lands she was a form of Astarte. Now Mithra was regularly identified by his worshippers with the Sun, the Unconquered Sun, as they called him ; hence his nativity also fell on the twenty-fifth of December. The Gospels say nothing as to the day of Christ's birth, and accordingly the early Church did not celebrate it. In time, however, the Christians of Egypt came to regard the sixth of January as the date of the Nativity, and the custom of commemorating the birth of the Saviour on that day gradually spread until by the fourth century it was universally established in the East. But at the end of the third or the beginning of the fourth century the Western Church, which had never recognised the sixth of January as the day of the Nativity, adopted the twenty-fifth of December as the true date, and in time its decision was accepted also by the Eastern Church. At Antioch the change was not introduced till about the year 375 A.D.

What considerations led the ecclesiastical authorities to institute the festival of Christmas ? The motives for the innovation are stated with great frankness by a Syrian writer, himself a Christian. " The reason," he tells us, " why the fathers transferred the celebration of the sixth of January to the twenty-fifth of December was this. It was a custom of the heathen to celebrate on the same twenty-fifth of December the birthday of the Sun, at which they kindled lights in token of festivity. In these solemnities and festivities the Christians also took part. Accordingly when the doctors of the Church perceived that the Christians had a leaning to this festival, they took counsel and resolved that the true Nativity should be solemnised on that day and the festival of the Epiphany on the sixth of January. Accordingly, along with this custom, the practice has prevailed of kindling fires till the sixth." The heathen origin of Christmas is plainly hinted at, if not tacitly admitted, by Augustine when he exhorts his Christian brethren not to celebrate that solemn day like the heathen on account of the sun, but on account of him who made the sun. In like manner Leo the Great rebuked the pestilent belief that Christmas was solemnised because of the birth of the new sun, as it was called, and not because of the nativity of Christ.

Thus it appears that the Christian Church chose to celebrate the birthday of its Founder on the twenty-fifth of December in order to transfer the devotion of the heathen from the Sun to him who was called the Sun of Righteousness. If that was so, there can be no intrinsic improbability in the conjecture that motives of the same sort may have led the ecclesiastical authorities to assimilate the Easter festival of the death and resurrection of their Lord to the festival of the death and resurrection of another Asiatic god which fell at the same season. Now the Easter rites still observed in Greece, Sicily, and southern Italy bear in some respects a striking resemblance to the rites of Adonis, and I have suggested that the Church may have consciously adapted the new festival to its heathen predecessor for the sake of winning souls to Christ. But this adaptation probably took place in the Greek-speaking rather than in the Latin-speaking parts of the ancient world ; for the worship of Adonis, while it flourished among the Greeks, appears to have made little impression on Rome and the West. Certainly it never formed part of the official Roman religion. The place which it might have taken in the affections of the vulgar was already occupied by the similar but more barbarous worship of Attis and the Great Mother. Now the death and resurrection of Attis were officially celebrated at Rome on the twenty-fourth and twenty-fifth of March, the latter being regarded as the spring equinox, and therefore as the most appropriate day for the revival of a god of vegetation who had been dead or sleeping throughout the winter. But according to an ancient and widespread tradition Christ suffered on the twenty-fifth of March, and accordingly some Christians regularly celebrated the Crucifixion on that day without any regard to the state of the moon. This custom was certainly observed in

Phrygia, Cappadocia, and Gaul, and there seem to be grounds for thinking that at one time it was followed also in Rome. Thus the tradition which placed the death of Christ on the twenty-fifth of March was ancient and deeply rooted. It is all the more remarkable because astronomical considerations prove that it can have had no historical foundation. The inference appears to be inevitable that the passion of Christ must have been arbitrarily referred to that date in order to harmonise with an older festival of the spring equinox. This is the view of the learned ecclesiastical historian Mgr. Duchesne, who points out that the death of the Saviour was thus made to fall upon the very day on which, according to a widespread belief, the world had been created. But the resurrection of Attis, who combined in himself the characters of the divine Father and the divine Son, was officially celebrated at Rome on the same day. When we remember that the festival of St. George in April has replaced the ancient pagan festival of the Parilia; that the festival of St. John the Baptist in June has succeeded to a heathen Midsummer festival of water; that the festival of the Assumption of the Virgin in August has ousted the festival of Diana; that the feast of All Souls in November is a continuation of an old heathen feast of the dead; and that the Nativity of Christ himself was assigned to the winter solstice in December because that day was deemed the Nativity of the Sun; we can hardly be thought rash or unreasonable in conjecturing that the other cardinal festival of the Christian church—the solemnisation of Easter—may have been in like manner, and from like motives of edification, adapted to a similar celebration of the Phrygian god Attis at the vernal equinox.

At least it is a remarkable coincidence, if it is nothing more, that the Christian and the heathen festivals of the divine death and resurrection should have been solemnised at the same season and in the same places. For the places which celebrated the death of Christ at the spring equinox were Phrygia, Gaul, and apparently Rome, that is, the very regions in which the worship of Attis either originated or struck deepest root. It is difficult to regard the coincidence as purely accidental. If the vernal equinox, the season at which in the temperate regions the whole face of nature testifies to a fresh outburst of vital energy, had been viewed from of old as the time when the world was annually created afresh in the resurrection of a god, nothing could be more natural than to place the resurrection of the new deity at the same cardinal point of the year. Only it is to be observed that if the death of Christ was dated on the twenty-fifth of March, his resurrection, according to Christian tradition, must have happened on the twenty-seventh of March, which is just two days later than the vernal equinox of the Julian calendar and the resurrection of Attis. A similar displacement of two days in the adjustment of Christian to heathen celebrations occurs in the festivals of St. George and the Assumption of the Virgin. However, another Christian tradition, followed by Lactantius and perhaps by the practice of the

Church in Gaul, placed the death of Christ on the twenty-third and his resurrection on the twenty-fifth of March. If that was so, his resurrection coincided exactly with the resurrection of Attis.

In point of fact it appears from the testimony of an anonymous Christian, who wrote in the fourth century of our era, that Christians and pagans alike were struck by the remarkable coincidence between the death and resurrection of their respective deities, and that the coincidence formed a theme of bitter controversy between the adherents of the rival religions, the pagans contending that the resurrection of Christ was a spurious imitation of the resurrection of Attis, and the Christians asserting with equal warmth that the resurrection of Attis was a diabolical counterfeit of the resurrection of Christ. In these unseemly bickerings the heathen took what to a superficial observer might seem strong ground by arguing that their god was the older and therefore presumably the original, not the counterfeit, since as a general rule an original is older than its copy. This feeble argument the Christians easily rebutted. They admitted, indeed, that in point of time Christ was the junior deity, but they triumphantly demonstrated his real seniority by falling back on the subtlety of Satan, who on so important an occasion had surpassed himself by inverting the usual order of nature.

Taken altogether, the coincidences of the Christian with the heathen festivals are too close and too numerous to be accidental. They mark the compromise which the Church in the hour of its triumph was compelled to make with its vanquished yet still dangerous rivals. The inflexible Protestantism of the primitive missionaries, with their fiery denunciations of heathendom, had been exchanged for the supple policy, the easy tolerance, the comprehensive charity of shrewd ecclesiastics, who clearly perceived that if Christianity was to conquer the world it could do so only by relaxing the too rigid principles of its Founder, by widening a little the narrow gate which leads to salvation. In this respect an instructive parallel might be drawn between the history of Christianity and the history of Buddhism. Both systems were in their origin essentially ethical reforms born of the generous ardour, the lofty aspirations, the tender compassion of their noble Founders, two of those beautiful spirits who appear at rare intervals on earth like beings come from a better world to support and guide our weak and erring nature. Both preached moral virtue as the means of accomplishing what they regarded as the supreme object of life, the eternal salvation of the individual soul, though by a curious antithesis the one sought that salvation in a blissful eternity, the other in a final release from suffering, in annihilation. But the austere ideals of sanctity which they inculcated were too deeply opposed not only to the frailties but to the natural instincts of humanity ever to be carried out in practice by more than a small number of disciples, who consistently renounced the ties of the family and the state in order to work out their own salvation in the still seclusion of the cloister. If such faiths were to be nominally accepted by whole

nations or even by the world, it was essential that they should first
be modified or transformed so as to accord in some measure with the
prejudices, the passions, the superstitions of the vulgar. This process
of accommodation was carried out in after ages by followers who,
made of less ethereal stuff than their masters, were for that reason
the better fitted to mediate between them and the common herd.
Thus as time went on, the two religions, in exact proportion to their
growing popularity, absorbed more and more of those baser elements
which they had been instituted for the very purpose of suppressing.
Such spiritual decadences are inevitable. The world cannot live
at the level of its great men. Yet it would be unfair to the generality
of our kind to ascribe wholly to their intellectual and moral weakness
the gradual divergence of Buddhism and Christianity from their
primitive patterns. For it should never be forgotten that by their
glorification of poverty and celibacy both these religions struck straight
at the root not merely of civil society but of human existence. The
blow was parried by the wisdom or the folly of the vast majority of
mankind, who refused to purchase a chance of saving their souls with
the certainty of extinguishing the species.

CHAPTER XXXVIII

THE MYTH OF OSIRIS

In ancient Egypt the god whose death and resurrection were annually
celebrated with alternate sorrow and joy was Osiris, the most popular
of all Egyptian deities ; and there are good grounds for classing him
in one of his aspects with Adonis and Attis as a personification of the
great yearly vicissitudes of nature, especially of the corn. But the
immense vogue which he enjoyed for many ages induced his devoted
worshippers to heap upon him the attributes and powers of many
other gods ; so that it is not always easy to strip him, so to say, of
his borrowed plumes and to restore them to their proper owners.

The story of Osiris is told in a connected form only by Plutarch,
whose narrative has been confirmed and to some extent amplified in
modern times by the evidence of the monuments.

Osiris was the offspring of an intrigue between the earth-god Seb
(Keb or Geb, as the name is sometimes transliterated) and the sky-
goddess Nut. The Greeks identified his parents with their own
deities Cronus and Rhea. When the sun-god Ra perceived that his
wife Nut had been unfaithful to him, he declared with a curse that she
should be delivered of the child in no month and no year. But the
goddess had another lover, the god Thoth or Hermes, as the Greeks
called him, and he playing at draughts with the moon won from her
a seventy-second part of every day, and having compounded five
whole days out of these parts he added them to the Egyptian year

of three hundred and sixty days. This was the mythical origin of the five supplementary days which the Egyptians annually inserted at the end of every year in order to establish a harmony between lunar and solar time. On these five days, regarded as outside the year of twelve months, the curse of the sun-god did not rest, and accordingly Osiris was born on the first of them. At his nativity a voice rang out proclaiming that the Lord of All had come into the world. Some say that a certain Pamyles heard a voice from the temple at Thebes bidding him announce with a shout that a great king, the beneficent Osiris, was born. But Osiris was not the only child of his mother. On the second of the supplementary days she gave birth to the elder Horus, on the third to the god Set, whom the Greeks called Typhon, on the fourth to the goddess Isis, and on the fifth to the goddess Nephthys. Afterwards Set married his sister Nephthys, and Osiris married his sister Isis.

Reigning as a king on earth, Osiris reclaimed the Egyptians from savagery, gave them laws, and taught them to worship the gods. Before his time the Egyptians had been cannibals. But Isis, the sister and wife of Osiris, discovered wheat and barley growing wild, and Osiris introduced the cultivation of these grains amongst his people, who forthwith abandoned cannibalism and took kindly to a corn diet. Moreover, Osiris is said to have been the first to gather fruit from trees, to train the vine to poles, and to tread the grapes. Eager to communicate these beneficent discoveries to all mankind, he committed the whole government of Egypt to his wife Isis, and travelled over the world, diffusing the blessings of civilisation and agriculture wherever he went. In countries where a harsh climate or niggardly soil forbade the cultivation of the vine, he taught the inhabitants to console themselves for the want of wine by brewing beer from barley. Loaded with the wealth that had been showered upon him by grateful nations, he returned to Egypt, and on account of the benefits he had conferred on mankind he was unanimously hailed and worshipped as a deity. But his brother Set (whom the Greeks called Typhon) with seventy-two others plotted against him. Having taken the measure of his good brother's body by stealth, the bad brother Typhon fashioned and highly decorated a coffer of the same size, and once when they were all drinking and making merry he brought in the coffer and jestingly promised to give it to the one whom it should fit exactly. Well, they all tried one after the other, but it fitted none of them. Last of all Osiris stepped into it and lay down. On that the conspirators ran and slammed the lid down on him, nailed it fast, soldered it with molten lead, and flung the coffer into the Nile. This happened on the seventeenth day of the month Athyr, when the sun is in the sign of the Scorpion, and in the eight-and-twentieth year of the reign or the life of Osiris. When Isis heard of it she sheared off a lock of her hair, put on mourning attire, and wandered disconsolately up and down, seeking the body.

By the advice of the god of wisdom she took refuge in the papyrus swamps of the Delta. Seven scorpions accompanied her in her flight. One evening when she was weary she came to the house of a woman, who, alarmed at the sight of the scorpions, shut the door in her face. Then one of the scorpions crept under the door and stung the child of the woman that he died. But when Isis heard the mother's lamentation, her heart was touched, and she laid her hands on the child and uttered her powerful spells; so the poison was driven out of the child and he lived. Afterwards Isis herself gave birth to a son in the swamps. She had conceived him while she fluttered in the form of a hawk over the corpse of her dead husband. The infant was the younger Horus, who in his youth bore the name of Harpocrates, that is, the child Horus. Him Buto, the goddess of the north, hid from the wrath of his wicked uncle Set. Yet she could not guard him from all mishap; for one day when Isis came to her little son's hiding-place she found him stretched lifeless and rigid on the ground: a scorpion had stung him. Then Isis prayed to the sun-god Ra for help. The god hearkened to her and staid his bark in the sky, and sent down Thoth to teach her the spell by which she might restore her son to life. She uttered the words of power, and straightway the poison flowed from the body of Horus, air passed into him, and he lived. Then Thoth ascended up into the sky and took his place once more in the bark of the sun, and the bright pomp passed onward jubilant.

Meantime the coffer containing the body of Osiris had floated down the river and away out to sea, till at last it drifted ashore at Byblus, on the coast of Syria. Here a fine *erica*-tree shot up suddenly and enclosed the chest in its trunk. The king of the country, admiring the growth of the tree, had it cut down and made into a pillar of his house; but he did not know that the coffer with the dead Osiris was in it. Word of this came to Isis and she journeyed to Byblus, and sat down by the well, in humble guise, her face wet with tears. To none would she speak till the king's handmaidens came, and them she greeted kindly, and braided their hair, and breathed on them from her own divine body a wondrous perfume. But when the queen beheld the braids of her handmaidens' hair and smelt the sweet smell that emanated from them, she sent for the stranger woman and took her into her house and made her the nurse of her child. But Isis gave the babe her finger instead of her breast to suck, and at night she began to burn all that was mortal of him away, while she herself in the likeness of a swallow fluttered round the pillar that contained her dead brother, twittering mournfully. But the queen spied what she was doing and shrieked out when she saw her child in flames, and thereby she hindered him from becoming immortal. Then the goddess revealed herself and begged for the pillar of the roof, and they gave it her, and she cut the coffer out of it, and fell upon it and embraced it and lamented so loud that the younger of the king's children died of fright on the spot. But the trunk of the tree she wrapped in fine linen, and poured ointment on it, and gave it to the king and queen, and the wood stands in a temple of Isis and is worshipped by the people of Byblus to this day. And Isis put the coffer in a boat and took the eldest of the king's children with her and sailed away. As soon as they were alone, she opened the chest, and laying her face on the face of her brother she kissed him and wept. But the child came behind her softly and saw what she was about, and she turned and looked at him in anger, and the child could not bear her look and died ; but some say that it was not so, but that he fell into the sea and was drowned. It is he whom the Egyptians sing of at their banquets under the name of Maneros.

But Isis put the coffer by and went to see her son Horus at the city of Buto, and Typhon found the coffer as he was hunting a boar one night by the light of a full moon. And he knew the body, and rent it into fourteen pieces, and scattered them abroad. But Isis sailed up and down the marshes in a shallop made of papyrus, looking for the pieces ; and that is why when people sail in shallops made of papyrus, the crocodiles do not hurt them, for they fear or respect the goddess. And that is the reason, too, why there are many graves of Osiris in Egypt, for she buried each limb as she found it. But others will have it that she buried an image of him in every city, pretending it was his body, in order that Osiris might be worshipped in many places, and that if Typhon searched for the real grave he might not be able to find it. However, the genital member of Osiris had been eaten by the fishes, so Isis made an image of it instead, and the image is used by the Egyptians at their festivals to this day. " Isis," writes the historian Diodorus Siculus, " recovered all the parts of the body except the genitals ; and because she wished that her husband's grave should be unknown and honoured by all who dwell in the land of Egypt, she resorted to the following device. She moulded human images out of wax and spices, corresponding to the stature of Osiris, round each one of the parts of his body. Then she called in the priests according to their families and took an oath of them all that they would reveal to no man the trust she was about to repose in them. So to each of them privately she said that to them alone she entrusted the burial of the body, and reminding them of the benefits they had received she exhorted them to bury the body in their own land and to honour Osiris as a god. She also besought them to dedicate one of the animals of their country, whichever they chose, and to honour it in life as they had formerly honoured Osiris, and when it died to grant it obsequies like his. And because she would encourage the priests in their own interest to bestow the aforesaid honours, she gave them a third part of the land to be used by them in the service and worship of the gods. Accordingly it is said that the priests, mindful of the benefits of Osiris, desirous of gratifying the queen, and moved by the prospect of gain, carried out all the injunctions of Isis. Wherefore to this day each of the priests imagines that Osiris is buried in his country, and they honour the beasts that were consecrated in the beginning, and when the animals die the priests renew at their burial the mourning for Osiris. But the sacred bulls, the one called Apis and the other

Mnevis, were dedicated to Osiris, and it was ordained that they should be worshipped as gods in common by all the Egyptians, since these animals above all others had helped the discoverers of corn in sowing the seed and procuring the universal benefits of agriculture.''

Such is the myth or legend of Osiris, as told by Greek writers and eked out by more or less fragmentary notices or allusions in native Egyptian literature. A long inscription in the temple at Denderah has preserved a list of the god's graves, and other texts mention the parts of his body which were treasured as holy relics in each of the sanctuaries. Thus his heart was at Athribis, his backbone at Busiris, his neck at Letopolis, and his head at Memphis. As often happens in such cases, some of his divine limbs were miraculously multiplied. His head, for example, was at Abydos as well as at Memphis, and his legs, which were remarkably numerous, would have sufficed for several ordinary mortals. In this respect, however, Osiris was nothing to St. Denys, of whom no less than seven heads, all equally genuine, are extant.

According to native Egyptian accounts, which supplement that of Plutarch, when Isis had found the corpse of her husband Osiris, she and her sister Nephthys sat down beside it and uttered a lament which in after ages became the type of all Egyptian lamentations for the dead. " Come to thy house," they wailed, " Come to thy house. O god On ! come to thy house, thou who hast no foes. O fair youth, come to thy house, that thou mayest see me. I am thy sister, whom thou lovest ; thou shalt not part from me. O fair boy, come to thy house. . . . I see thee not, yet doth my heart yearn after thee and mine eyes desire thee. Come to her who loves thee, who loves thee, Unnefer, thou blessed one ! Come to thy sister, come to thy wife, to thy wife, thou whose heart stands still. Come to thy housewife. I am thy sister by the same mother, thou shalt not be far from me. Gods and men have turned their faces towards thee and weep for thee together. . . . I call after thee and weep, so that my cry is heard to heaven, but thou hearest not my voice ; yet am I thy sister, whom thou didst love on earth ; thou didst love none but me, my brother ! my brother ! " This lament for the fair youth cut off in his prime reminds us of the laments for Adonis. The title of Unnefer or " the Good Being " bestowed on him marks the beneficence which tradition universally ascribed to Osiris ; it was at once his commonest title and one of his names as king.

The lamentations of the two sad sisters were not in vain. In pity for her sorrow the sun-god Ra sent down from heaven the jackal-headed god Anubis, who, with the aid of Isis and Nephthys, of Thoth and Horus, pieced together the broken body of the murdered god, swathed it in linen bandages, and observed all the other rites which the Egyptians were wont to perform over the bodies of the departed. Then Isis fanned the cold clay with her wings : Osiris revived, and thenceforth reigned as king over the dead in the other world. There he bore the titles of Lord of the Underworld, Lord of Eternity, Ruler

of the Dead.   There, too, in the great Hall of the Two Truths, assisted
by forty-two assessors, one from each of the principal districts of
Egypt, he presided as judge at the trial of the souls of the departed,
who made their solemn confession before him, and, their heart having
been weighed in the balance of justice, received the reward of virtue
in a life eternal or the appropriate punishment of their sins.

In the resurrection of Osiris the Egyptians saw the pledge of a
life everlasting for themselves beyond the grave.   They believed that
every man would live eternally in the other world if only his surviving
friends did for his body what the gods had done for the body of Osiris.
Hence the ceremonies observed by the Egyptians over the human
dead were an exact copy of those which Anubis, Horus, and the rest
had performed over the dead god.   " At every burial there was
enacted a representation of the divine mystery which had been performed of old over Osiris, when his son, his sisters, his friends were
gathered round his mangled remains and succeeded by their spells
and manipulations in converting his broken body into the first mummy,
which they afterwards reanimated and furnished with the means of
entering on a new individual life beyond the grave.   The mummy of
the deceased was Osiris ; the professional female mourners were his
two sisters Isis and Nephthys ; Anubis, Horus, all the gods of the
Osirian legend gathered about the corpse."   In this way every dead
Egyptian was identified with Osiris and bore his name.   From the
Middle Kingdom onwards it was the regular practice to address the
deceased as " Osiris So-and-So," as if he were the god himself, and to
add the standing epithet " true of speech," because true speech was
characteristic of Osiris.   The thousands of inscribed and pictured
tombs that have been opened in the valley of the Nile prove that
the mystery of the resurrection was performed for the benefit of every
dead Egyptian ; as Osiris died and rose again from the dead, so all
men hoped to arise like him from death to life eternal.

Thus according to what seems to have been the general native
tradition Osiris was a good and beloved king of Egypt, who suffered
a violent death but rose from the dead and was henceforth worshipped
as a deity.   In harmony with this tradition he was regularly represented by sculptors and painters in human and regal form as a dead
king, swathed in the wrappings of a mummy, but wearing on his head
a kingly crown and grasping in one of his hands, which were left free
from the bandages, a kingly sceptre.   Two cities above all others were
associated with his myth or memory.   One of them was Busiris in
Lower Egypt, which claimed to possess his backbone ; the other was
Abydos in Upper Egypt, which gloried in the possession of his head.
Encircled by the nimbus of the dead yet living god, Abydos, originally
an obscure place, became from the end of the Old Kingdom the holiest
spot in Egypt ; his tomb there would seem to have been to the
Egyptians what the Church of the Holy Sepulchre at Jerusalem is to
Christians.   It was the wish of every pious man that his dead body
should rest in hallowed earth near the grave of the glorified Osiris.

Few indeed were rich enough to enjoy this inestimable privilege ; for, apart from the cost of a tomb in the sacred city, the mere transport of mummies from great distances was both difficult and expensive. Yet so eager were many to absorb in death the blessed influence which radiated from the holy sepulchre that they caused their surviving friends to convey their mortal remains to Abydos, there to tarry for a short time, and then to be brought back by river and interred in the tombs which had been made ready for them in their native land. Others had cenotaphs built or memorial tablets erected for themselves near the tomb of their dead and risen Lord, that they might share with him the bliss of a joyful resurrection.

CHAPTER XXXIX

THE RITUAL OF OSIRIS

§ 1. *The Popular Rites.* —A useful clue to the original nature of a god or goddess is often furnished by the season at which his or her festival is celebrated. Thus, if the festival falls at the new or the full moon, there is a certain presumption that the deity thus honoured either is the moon or at least has lunar affinities. If the festival is held at the winter or summer solstice, we naturally surmise that the god is the sun, or at all events that he stands in some close relation to that luminary. Again, if the festival coincides with the time of sowing or harvest, we are inclined to infer that the divinity is an embodiment of the earth or of the corn. These presumptions or inferences, taken by themselves, are by no means conclusive ; but if they happen to be confirmed by other indications, the evidence may be regarded as fairly strong.

Unfortunately, in dealing with the Egyptian gods we are in a great measure precluded from making use of this clue. The reason is not that the dates of the festivals are always unknown, but that they shifted from year to year, until after a long interval they had revolved through the whole course of the seasons. This gradual revolution of the festal Egyptian cycle resulted from the employment of a calendar year which neither corresponded exactly to the solar year nor was periodically corrected by intercalation.

If the Egyptian farmer of the olden time could get no help, except at the rarest intervals, from the official or sacerdotal calendar, he must have been compelled to observe for himself those natural signals which marked the times for the various operations of husbandry. In all ages of which we possess any records the Egyptians have been an agricultural people, dependent for their subsistence on the growth of the corn. The cereals which they cultivated were wheat, barley, and apparently sorghum (*Holcus sorghum*, Linnaeus), the *doora* of the modern fellaheen. Then as now the whole country, with the exception of a fringe on the coast of the Mediterranean, was almost rainless, and owed its immense fertility entirely to the annual inundation of the Nile, which, regulated by an elaborate system of dams and canals, was distributed over the fields, renewing the soil year by year with a fresh deposit of mud washed down from the great equatorial lakes and the mountains of Abyssinia. Hence the rise of the river has always been watched by the inhabitants with the utmost anxiety; for if it either falls short of or exceeds a certain height, dearth and famine are the inevitable consequences. The water begins to rise early in June, but it is not until the latter half of July that it swells to a mighty tide. By the end of September the inundation is at its greatest height. The country is now submerged, and presents the appearance of a sea of turbid water, from which the towns and villages, built on higher ground, rise like islands. For about a month the flood remains nearly stationary, then sinks more and more rapidly, till by December or January the river has returned to its ordinary bed. With the approach of summer the level of the water continues to fall. In the early days of June the Nile is reduced to half its ordinary breadth; and Egypt, scorched by the sun, blasted by the wind that has blown from the Sahara for many days, seems a mere continuation of the desert. The trees are choked with a thick layer of grey dust. A few meagre patches of vegetables, watered with difficulty, struggle painfully for existence in the immediate neighbourhood of the villages. Some appearance of verdure lingers beside the canals and in the hollows from which the moisture has not wholly evaporated. The plain appears to pant in the pitiless sunshine, bare, dusty, ash-coloured, cracked and seamed as far as the eye can see with a network of fissures. From the middle of April till the middle of June the land of Egypt is but half alive, waiting for the new Nile.

For countless ages this cycle of natural events has determined the annual labours of the Egyptian husbandman. The first work of the agricultural year is the cutting of the dams which have hitherto prevented the swollen river from flooding the canals and the fields. This is done, and the pent-up waters released on their beneficent mission, in the first half of August. In November, when the inundation has subsided, wheat, barley, and sorghum are sown. The time of harvest varies with the district, falling about a month later in the north than in the south. In Upper or Southern Egypt barley is reaped at the beginning of March, wheat at the beginning of April, and sorghum about the end of that month.

It is natural to suppose that the various events of the agricultural year were celebrated by the Egyptian farmer with some simple religious rites designed to secure the blessing of the gods upon his labours. These rustic ceremonies he would continue to perform year after year at the same season, while the solemn festivals of the priests continued to shift, with the shifting calendar, from summer through spring to winter, and so backward through autumn to summer. The rites of the husbandman were stable because they rested on direct observation

2 B

of nature : the rites of the priest were unstable because they were based on a false calculation. Yet many of the priestly festivals may have been nothing but the old rural festivals disguised in the course of ages by the pomp of sacerdotalism and severed, by the error of the calendar, from their roots in the natural cycle of the seasons.

These conjectures are confirmed by the little we know both of the popular and of the official Egyptian religion. Thus we are told that the Egyptians held a festival of Isis at the time when the Nile began to rise. They believed that the goddess was then mourning for the lost Osiris, and that the tears which dropped from her eyes swelled the impetuous tide of the river. Now if Osiris was in one of his aspects a god of the corn, nothing could be more natural than that he should be mourned at midsummer. For by that time the harvest was past, the fields were bare, the river ran low, life seemed to be suspended, the corn-god was dead. At such a moment people who saw the handi-work of divine beings in all the operations of nature might well trace the swelling of the sacred stream to the tears shed by the goddess at the death of the beneficent corn-god her husband.

And the sign of the rising waters on earth was accompanied by a sign in heaven. For in the early days of Egyptian history, some three or four thousand years before the beginning of our era, the splendid star of Sirius, the brightest of all the fixed stars, appeared at dawn in the east just before sunrise about the time of the summer solstice, when the Nile begins to rise. The Egyptians called it Sothis, and regarded it as the star of Isis, just as the Babylonians deemed the planet Venus the star of Astarte. To both peoples apparently the brilliant luminary in the morning sky seemed the goddess of life and love come to mourn her departed lover or spouse and to wake him from the dead. Hence the rising of Sirius marked the beginning of the sacred Egyptian year, and was regularly celebrated by a festival which did not shift with the shifting official year.

The cutting of the dams and the admission of the water into the canals and fields is a great event in the Egyptian year. At Cairo the operation generally takes place between the sixth and the sixteenth of August, and till lately was attended by ceremonies which deserve to be noticed, because they were probably handed down from antiquity. An ancient canal, known by the name of the Khalíj, formerly passed through the native town of Cairo. Near its entrance the canal was crossed by a dam of earth, very broad at the bottom and diminishing in breadth upwards, which used to be constructed before or soon after the Nile began to rise. In front of the dam, on the side of the river, was reared a truncated cone of earth called the 'arooseh or " bride," on the top of which a little maize or millet was generally sown. This " bride " was commonly washed down by the rising tide a week or a fortnight before the cutting of the dam. Tradition runs that the old custom was to deck a young virgin in gay apparel and throw her into the river as a sacrifice to obtain a plentiful inundation. Whether that was so or not, the intention of the practice appears to have been to marry the river, conceived as a male power, to his bride the cornland, which was so soon to be fertilised by his water. The ceremony was therefore a charm to ensure the growth of the crops. In modern times money used to be thrown into the canal on this occasion, and the populace dived into the water after it. This practice also would seem to have been ancient, for Seneca tells us that at a place called the Veins of the Nile, not far from Philae, the priests used to cast money and offerings of gold into the river at a festival which apparently took place at the rising of the water.

The next great operation of the agricultural year in Egypt is the sowing of the seed in November, when the water of the inundation has retreated from the fields. With the Egyptians, as with many peoples of antiquity, the committing of the seed to the earth assumed the character of a solemn and mournful rite. On this subject I will let Plutarch speak for himself. " What," he asks, " are we to make of the gloomy, joyless, and mournful sacrifices, if it is wrong either to omit the established rites or to confuse and disturb our conceptions of the gods by absurd suspicions ? For the Greeks also perform many rites which resemble those of the Egyptians and are observed about the same time. Thus at the festival of the Thesmophoria in Athens women sit on the ground and fast. And the Boeotians open the vaults of the Sorrowful One, naming that festival sorrowful because Demeter is sorrowing for the descent of the Maiden. The month is the month of sowing about the setting of the Pleiades. The Egyptians call it Athyr, the Athenians Pyanepsion, the Boeotians the month of Demeter. . . . For it was that time of year when they saw some of the fruits vanishing and failing from the trees, while they sowed others grudgingly and with difficulty, scraping the earth with their hands and huddling it up again, on the uncertain chance that what they deposited in the ground would ever ripen and come to maturity. Thus they did in many respects like those who bury and mourn their dead."

The Egyptian harvest, as we have seen, falls not in autumn but in spring, in the months of March, April, and May. To the husband-man the time of harvest, at least in a good year, must necessarily be a season of joy : in bringing home his sheaves he is requited for his long and anxious labours. Yet if the old Egyptian farmer felt a secret joy at reaping and garnering the grain, it was essential that he should conceal the natural emotion under an air of profound dejection. For was he not severing the body of the corn-god with his sickle and trampling it to pieces under the hoofs of his cattle on the threshing-floor ? Accordingly we are told that it was an ancient custom of the Egyptian corn-reapers to beat their breasts and lament over the first sheaf cut, while at the same time they called upon Isis. The invoca-tion seems to have taken the form of a melancholy chant, to which the Greeks gave the name of Maneros. Similar plaintive strains were chanted by corn-reapers in Phoenicia and other parts of Western Asia. Probably all these doleful ditties were lamentations for the

corn-god killed by the sickles of the reapers. In Egypt the slain
deity was Osiris, and the name *Maneros*, applied to the dirge, appears
to be derived from certain words meaning "Come to thy house,"
which often occur in the lamentations for the dead god.

Ceremonies of the same sort have been observed by other peoples,
probably for the same purpose. Thus we are told that among all
vegetables corn, by which is apparently meant maize, holds the first
place in the household economy and the ceremonial observance of
the Cherokee Indians, who invoke it under the name of "the Old
Woman" in allusion to a myth that it sprang from the blood of
an old woman killed by her disobedient sons. After the last working
of the crop a priest and his assistant went into the field and sang songs
of invocation to the spirit of the corn. After that a loud rustling
would be heard, which was thought to be caused by the Old Woman
bringing the corn into the field. A clean trail was always kept from
the field to the house, "so that the corn might be encouraged to stay
at home and not go wandering elsewhere."   "Another curious ceremony, of which even the memory is now almost forgotten, was enacted
after the first working of the corn, when the owner or priest stood in
succession at each of the four corners of the field and wept and wailed
loudly. Even the priests are now unable to give a reason for this
performance, which may have been a lament for the bloody death of
Selu," the Old Woman of the Corn. In these Cherokee practices the
lamentations and the invocations of the Old Woman of the Corn
resemble the ancient Egyptian customs of lamenting over the first
corn cut and calling upon Isis, herself probably in one of her aspects
an Old Woman of the Corn. Further, the Cherokee precaution of
leaving a clear path from the field to the house resembles the Egyptian
invitation to Osiris, "Come to thy house." So in the East Indies to
this day people observe elaborate ceremonies for the purpose of bringing back the Soul of the Rice from the fields to the barn. The Nandi
of East Africa perform a ceremony in September when the eleusine
grain is ripening. Every woman who owns a plantation goes out
with her daughters into the cornfields and makes a bonfire of the
branches and leaves of certain trees. After that they pluck some
of the eleusine, and each of them puts one grain in her necklace,
chews another and rubs it on her forehead, throat, and breast.
"No joy is shown by the womenfolk on this occasion, and they
sorrowfully cut a basketful of the corn which they take home with
them and place in the loft to dry."

The conception of the corn-spirit as old and dead at harvest is
very clearly embodied in a custom observed by the Arabs of Moab.
When the harvesters have nearly finished their task and only a small
corner of the field remains to be reaped, the owner takes a handful
of wheat tied up in a sheaf. A hole is dug in the form of a grave,
and two stones are set upright, one at the head and the other at the
foot, just as in an ordinary burial. Then the sheaf of wheat is laid
at the bottom of the grave, and the sheikh pronounces these words,

" The old man is dead." Earth is afterwards thrown in to cover the sheaf, with a prayer, " May Allah bring us back the wheat of the dead."

§ 2. *The Official Rites.*—Such, then, were the principal events of the farmer's calendar in ancient Egypt, and such the simple religious rites by which he celebrated them. But we have still to consider the Osirian festivals of the official calendar, so far as these are described by Greek writers or recorded on the monuments. In examining them it is necessary to bear in mind that on account of the movable year of the old Egyptian calendar the true or astronomical dates of the official festivals must have varied from year to year, at least until the adoption of the fixed Alexandrian year in 30 B.C. From that time onward, apparently, the dates of the festivals were determined by the new calendar, and so ceased to rotate throughout the length of the solar year. At all events Plutarch, writing about the end of the first century, implies that they were then fixed, not movable ; for though he does not mention the Alexandrian calendar, he clearly dates the festivals by it. Moreover, the long festal calendar of Esne, an important document of the Imperial age, is obviously based on the fixed Alexandrian year ; for it assigns the mark for New Year's Day to the day which corresponds to the twenty-ninth of August, which was the first day of the Alexandrian year, and its references to the rising of the Nile, the position of the sun, and the operations of agriculture are all in harmony with this supposition. Thus we may take it as fairly certain that from 30 B.C. onwards the Egyptian festivals were stationary in the solar year.

Herodotus tells us that the grave of Osiris was at Sais in Lower Egypt, and that there was a lake there upon which the sufferings of the god were displayed as a mystery by night. This commemoration of the divine passion was held once a year : the people mourned and beat their breasts at it to testify their sorrow for the death of the god ; and an image of a cow, made of gilt wood with a golden sun between its horns, was carried out of the chamber in which it stood the rest of the year. The cow no doubt represented Isis herself, for cows were sacred to her, and she was regularly depicted with the horns of a cow on her head, or even as a woman with the head of a cow. It is probable that the carrying out of her cow-shaped image symbolised the goddess searching for the dead body of Osiris ; for this was the native Egyptian interpretation of a similar ceremony observed in Plutarch's time about the winter solstice, when the gilt cow was carried seven times round the temple. A great feature of the festival was the nocturnal illumination. People fastened rows of oil-lamps to the outside of their houses, and the lamps burned all night long. The custom was not confined to Sais, but was observed throughout the whole of Egypt.

This universal illumination of the houses on one night of the year suggests that the festival may have been a commemoration not merely of the dead Osiris but of the dead in general, in other words, that it may have been a night of All Souls. For it is a widespread belief that the souls of the dead revisit their old homes on one night of the year ; and on that solemn occasion people prepare for the reception of the ghosts by laying out food for them to eat, and lighting lamps to guide them on their dark road from and to the grave. Herodotus, who briefly describes the festival, omits to mention its date, but we can determine it with some probability from other sources. Thus Plutarch tells us that Osiris was murdered on the seventeenth of the month Athyr, and that the Egyptians accordingly observed mournful rites for four days from the seventeenth of Athyr. Now in the Alexandrian calendar, which Plutarch used, these four days corresponded to the thirteenth, fourteenth, fifteenth, and sixteenth of November, and this date answers exactly to the other indications given by Plutarch, who says that at the time of the festival the Nile was sinking, the north winds dying away, the nights lengthening, and the leaves falling from the trees. During these four days a gilt cow swathed in a black pall was exhibited as an image of Isis. This, no doubt, was the image mentioned by Herodotus in his account of the festival. On the nineteenth day of the month the people went down to the sea, the priests carrying a shrine which contained a golden casket. Into this casket they poured fresh water, and thereupon the spectators raised a shout that Osiris was found. After that they took some vegetable mould, moistened it with water, mixed it with precious spices and incense, and moulded the paste into a small moon-shaped image, which was then robed and ornamented. Thus it appears that the purpose of the ceremonies described by Plutarch was to represent dramatically, first, the search for the dead body of Osiris, and, second, its joyful discovery, followed by the resurrection of the dead god who came to life again in the new image of vegetable mould and spices. Lactantius tells us how on these occasions the priests, with their shaven bodies, beat their breasts and lamented, imitating the sorrowful search of Isis for her lost son Osiris, and how afterwards their sorrow was turned to joy when the jackal-headed god Anubis, or rather a mummer in his stead, produced a small boy, the living representative of the god who was lost and was found. Thus Lactantius regarded Osiris as the son instead of the husband of Isis, and he makes no mention of the image of vegetable mould. It is probable that the boy who figured in the sacred drama played the part, not of Osiris, but of his son Horus ; but as the death and resurrection of the god were celebrated in many cities of Egypt, it is also possible that in some places the part of the god come to life was played by a living actor instead of by an image. Another Christian writer describes how the Egyptians, with shorn heads, annually lamented over a buried idol of Osiris, smiting their breasts, slashing their shoulders, ripping open their old wounds, until, after several days of mourning, they professed to find the mangled remains of the god, at which they rejoiced. However the details of the ceremony may have varied in different places, the pretence of finding the god's body, and probably of restoring it to life, was a great event in the festal year of the Egyptians. The shouts of joy which greeted it are described or alluded to by many ancient writers.

The funeral rites of Osiris, as they were observed at his great festival in the sixteen provinces of Egypt, are described in a long inscription of the Ptolemaic period, which is engraved on the walls of the god's temple at Denderah, the Tentyra of the Greeks, a town of Upper Egypt situated on the western bank of the Nile about forty miles north of Thebes. Unfortunately, while the information thus furnished is remarkably full and minute on many points, the arrangement adopted in the inscription is so confused and the expression often so obscure that a clear and consistent account of the ceremonies as a whole can hardly be extracted from it. Moreover, we learn from the document that the ceremonies varied somewhat in the several cities, the ritual of Abydos, for example, differing from that of Busiris. Without attempting to trace all the particularities of local usage I shall briefly indicate what seem to have been the leading features of the festival, so far as these can be ascertained with tolerable certainty.

The rites lasted eighteen days, from the twelfth to the thirtieth of the month Khoiak, and set forth the nature of Osiris in his triple aspect as dead, dismembered, and finally reconstituted by the union of his scattered limbs. In the first of these aspects he was called Chent-Ament (Khenti-Amenti), in the second Osiris-Sep, and in the third Sokari (Seker). Small images of the god were moulded of sand or vegetable earth and corn, to which incense was sometimes added ; his face was painted yellow and his cheek-bones green. These images were cast in a mould of pure gold, which represented the god in the form of a mummy, with the white crown of Egypt on his head. The festival opened on the twelfth day of Khoiak with a ceremony of ploughing and sowing. Two black cows were yoked to the plough, which was made of tamarisk wood, while the share was of black copper. A boy scattered the seed. One end of the field was sown with barley, the other with spelt, and the middle with flax. During the operation the chief celebrant recited the ritual chapter of " the sowing of the fields." At Busiris on the twentieth of Khoiak sand and barley were put in the god's " garden," which appears to have been a sort of large flower-pot. This was done in the presence of the cow-goddess Shenty, represented seemingly by the image of a cow made of gilt sycamore wood with a headless human image in its inside. " Then fresh inundation water was poured out of a golden vase over both the goddess and the ' garden,' and the barley was allowed to grow as the emblem of the resurrection of the god after his burial in the earth, ' for the growth of the garden is the growth of the divine substance.' " On the twenty-second of Khoiak, at the eighth hour, the images of Osiris, attended by thirty-four images of deities, performed a mysterious voyage in thirty-four tiny boats made of papyrus, which were illuminated by three hundred and sixty-five lights. On the twenty-fourth of Khoiak, after sunset, the effigy of Osiris in a coffin of mulberry wood was laid in the grave, and at the ninth hour of the night the effigy which had been made and deposited the year before was removed and placed upon boughs of sycamore. Lastly, on the thirtieth day of Khoiak they repaired to the holy sepulchre, a subterranean chamber over which appears to have grown a clump of Persea-trees. Entering the vault by the western door, they laid the coffined effigy of the dead god reverently on a bed of sand in the chamber. So they left him to his rest, and departed from the sepulchre by the eastern door. Thus ended the ceremonies in the month of Khoiak.

In the foregoing account of the festival, drawn from the great inscription of Denderah, the burial of Osiris figures prominently, while his resurrection is implied rather than expressed. This defect of the document, however, is amply compensated by a remarkable series of bas-reliefs which accompany and illustrate the inscription. These exhibit in a series of scenes the dead god lying swathed as a mummy on his bier, then gradually raising himself up higher and higher, until at last he has entirely quitted the bier and is seen erect between the guardian wings of the faithful Isis, who stands behind him, while a male figure holds up before his eyes the *crux ansata*, the Egyptian symbol of life. The resurrection of the god could hardly be portrayed more graphically. Even more instructive, however, is another representation of the same event in a chamber dedicated to Osiris in the great temple of Isis at Philae. Here we see the dead body of Osiris with stalks of corn springing from it, while a priest waters the stalks from a pitcher which he holds in his hand. The accompanying inscription sets forth that " this is the form of him whom one may not name, Osiris of the mysteries, who springs from the returning waters." Taken together, the picture and the words seem to leave no doubt that Osiris was here conceived and represented as a personification of the corn which springs from the fields after they have been fertilised by the inundation. This, according to the inscription, was the kernel of the mysteries, the innermost secret revealed to the initiated. So in the rites of Demeter at Eleusis a reaped ear of corn was exhibited to the worshippers as the central mystery of their religion. We can now fully understand why at the great festival of sowing in the month of Khoiak the priests used to bury effigies of Osiris made of earth and corn. When these effigies were taken up again at the end of a year or of a shorter interval, the corn would be found to have sprouted from the body of Osiris, and this sprouting of the grain would be hailed as an omen, or rather as the cause, of the growth of the crops. The corn-god produced the corn from himself : he gave his own body to feed the people ; he died that they might live.

And from the death and resurrection of their great god the Egyptians drew not only their support and sustenance in this life, but also their hope of a life eternal beyond the grave. This hope is indicated in the clearest manner by the very remarkable effigies of Osiris which have come to light in Egyptian cemeteries. Thus in the Valley of the Kings at Thebes there was found the tomb of a royal fan-bearer who lived about 1500 B.C. Among the rich contents of the tomb there was a bier on which rested a mattress of reeds covered with three layers of linen. On the upper side of the linen was painted a life-size figure of Osiris ; and the interior of the figure, which was waterproof, contained a mixture of vegetable mould, barley, and a sticky fluid. The barley had sprouted and sent out shoots two or three inches long. Again, in the cemetery at Cynopolis " were numerous burials of Osiris figures. These were made of grain wrapped up in cloth and roughly shaped like an Osiris, and placed inside a bricked-up recess at the side of the tomb, sometimes in small pottery coffins, sometimes in wooden coffins in the form of a hawk-mummy, sometimes without any coffins at all." These corn-stuffed figures were bandaged like mummies with patches of gilding here and there, as if in imitation of the golden mould in which the similar figures of Osiris were cast at the festival of sowing. Again, effigies of Osiris, with faces of green wax and their interior full of grain, were found buried near the necropolis of Thebes. Finally, we are told by Professor Erman that between the legs of mummies " there sometimes lies a figure of Osiris made of slime ; it is filled with grains of corn, the sprouting of which is intended to signify the resurrection of the god." We cannot doubt that, just as the burial of corn-stuffed images of Osiris in the earth at the festival of sowing was designed to quicken the seed, so the burial of similar images in the grave was meant to quicken the dead, in other words, to ensure their spiritual immortality.

CHAPTER XL

THE NATURE OF OSIRIS

§ 1. *Osiris a Corn-god.*—The foregoing survey of the myth and ritual of Osiris may suffice to prove that in one of his aspects the god was a personification of the corn, which may be said to die and come to life again every year. Through all the pomp and glamour with which in later times the priests had invested his worship, the conception of him as the corn-god comes clearly out in the festival of his death and resurrection, which was celebrated in the month of Khoiak and at a later period in the month of Athyr. That festival appears to have been essentially a festival of sowing, which properly fell at the time when the husbandman actually committed the seed to the earth. On that occasion an effigy of the corn-god, moulded of earth and corn, was buried with funeral rites in the ground in order that, dying there, he might come to life again with the new crops. The ceremony was, in fact, a charm to ensure the growth of the corn by sympathetic magic, and we may conjecture that as such it was practised in a simple form by every Egyptian farmer on his fields long before it was adopted and transfigured by the priests in the stately ritual of the temple. In the modern, but doubtless ancient, Arab custom of burying "the Old Man," namely, a sheaf of wheat, in the harvest-field and praying that he may return from the dead, we see the germ out of which the worship of the corn-god Osiris was probably developed.

The details of his myth fit in well with this interpretation of the god. He was said to be the offspring of Sky and Earth. What more appropriate parentage could be invented for the corn which springs from the ground that has been fertilised by the water of heaven? It is true that the land of Egypt owed its fertility directly to the Nile and not to showers; but the inhabitants must have known or guessed that the great river in its turn was fed by the rains which fell in the far interior. Again, the legend that Osiris was the first to teach men the use of corn would be most naturally told of the corn-god himself. Further, the story that his mangled remains were scattered up and down the land and buried in different places may be a mythical way of expressing either the sowing or the winnowing of the grain. The latter interpretation is supported by the tale that Isis placed the severed limbs of Osiris on a corn-sieve. Or more probably the legend may be a reminiscence of a custom of slaying a human victim, perhaps a representative of the corn-spirit and distributing his flesh or scattering his ashes over the fields to fertilise them. In modern Europe the figure of Death is sometimes torn in pieces, and the fragments are then buried in the ground to make the crops grow well, and in other parts of the world human victims are treated in the same way. With regard to the ancient Egyptians we have it on the authority of Manetho that they used to burn red-haired men and scatter their ashes with winnowing fans, and it is highly significant that this barbarous sacrifice was offered by the kings at the grave of Osiris. We may conjecture that the victims represented Osiris himself, who was annually slain, dismembered, and buried in their persons that he might quicken the seed in the earth.

Possibly in prehistoric times the kings themselves played the part of the god and were slain and dismembered in that character. Set as well as Osiris is said to have been torn in pieces after a reign of eighteen days, which was commemorated by an annual festival of the same length. According to one story Romulus, the first king of Rome, was cut in pieces by the senators, who buried the fragments of him in the ground; and the traditional day of his death, the seventh of July, was celebrated with certain curious rites, which were apparently connected with the artificial fertilisation of the fig. Again, Greek legend told how Pentheus, king of Thebes, and Lycurgus, king of the Thracian Edonians, opposed the vine-god Dionysus, and how the impious monarchs were rent in pieces, the one by the frenzied Bacchanals, the other by horses. These Greek traditions may well be distorted reminiscences of a custom of sacrificing human beings, and especially divine kings, in the character of Dionysus, a god who resembled Osiris in many points and was said like him to have been torn limb from limb. We are told that in Chios men were rent in pieces as a sacrifice to Dionysus ; and since they died the same death as their god, it is reasonable to suppose that they personated him. The story that the Thracian Orpheus was similarly torn limb from limb by the Bacchanals seems to indicate that he too perished in the character of the god whose death he died. It is significant that the Thracian Lycurgus, king of the Edonians, is said to have been put to death in order that the ground, which had ceased to be fruitful, might regain its fertility.

Further, we read of a Norwegian king, Halfdan the Black, whose body was cut up and buried in different parts of his kingdom for the sake of ensuring the fruitfulness of the earth. He is said to have been drowned at the age of forty through the breaking of the ice in spring. What followed his death is thus related by the old Norse historian Snorri Sturluson : " He had been the most prosperous (literally, blessed with abundance) of all kings. So greatly did men value him that when the news came that he was dead and his body removed to Hringariki and intended for burial there, the chief men from Raumariki and Westfold and Heithmörk came and all requested that they might take his body with them and bury it in their various provinces ; they thought that it would bring abundance to those who obtained it. Eventually it was settled that the body was distributed in four places. The head was laid in a barrow at Steinn in Hringariki, and each party took away their own share and buried it. All these barrows are called Halfdan's barrows." It should be remembered that this Halfdan belonged to the family of the Ynglings, who traced their descent from Frey, the great Scandinavian god of fertility.

The natives of Kiwai, an island lying off the mouth of the Fly River in British New Guinea, tell of a certain magician named Segera, who had sago for his totem. When Segera was old and ill, he told the people that he would soon die, but that, nevertheless, he would cause their gardens to thrive. Accordingly, he instructed them that when he was dead they should cut him up and place pieces of his flesh in their gardens, but his head was to be buried in his own garden. Of him it is said that he outlived the ordinary age, and that no man knew his father, but that he made the sago good and no one was hungry any more. Old men who were alive some years ago affirmed that they had known Segera in their youth, and the general opinion of the Kiwai people seems to be that Segera died not more than two generations ago.

Taken all together, these legends point to a widespread practice of dismembering the body of a king or magician and burying the pieces in different parts of the country in order to ensure the fertility of the ground and probably also the fecundity of man and beast.

To return to the human victims whose ashes the Egyptians scattered with winnowing-fans, the red hair of these unfortunates was probably significant.   For in Egypt the oxen which were sacrificed had also to be red ; a single black or white hair found on the beast would have disqualified it for the sacrifice.   If, as I conjecture, these human sacrifices were intended to promote the growth of the crops— and the winnowing of their ashes seems to support this view—red-haired victims were perhaps selected as best fitted to personate the spirit of the ruddy grain.   For when a god is represented by a living person, it is natural that the human representative should be chosen on the ground of his supposed resemblance to the divine original. Hence the ancient Mexicans, conceiving the maize as a personal being who went through the whole course of life between seed-time and harvest, sacrificed new-born babes when the maize was sown, older children when it had sprouted, and so on till it was fully ripe, when they sacrificed old men.   A name for Osiris was the " crop " or " harvest "; and the ancients sometimes explained him as a personification of the corn.

§ 2. *Osiris a Tree-spirit.*—But Osiris was more than a spirit of the corn ; he was also a tree-spirit, and this may perhaps have been his primitive character, since the worship of trees is naturally older in the history òf religion than the worship of the cereals.   The character of Osiris as a tree-spirit was represented very graphically in a ceremony described by Firmicus Maternus.   A pine-tree having been cut down, the centre was hollowed out, and with the wood thus excavated an image of Osiris was made, which was then buried like a corpse in the hollow of the tree.   It is hard to imagine how the conception of a tree as tenanted by a personal being could be more plainly expressed. The image of Osiris thus made was kept for a year and then burned, exactly as was done with the image of Attis which was attached to the pine-tree.   The ceremony of cutting the tree, as described by Firmicus Maternus, appears to be alluded to by Plutarch.   It was probably the ritual counterpart of the mythical discovery of the body of Osiris enclosed in the *erica*-tree.   In the hall of Osiris at Denderah the coffin containing the hawk-headed mummy of the god is clearly depicted as enclosed within a tree, apparently a conifer, the trunk and branches of which are seen above and below the coffin.   The scene thus corresponds closely both to the myth and to the ceremony described by Firmicus Maternus.

It accords with the character of Osiris as a tree-spirit that his worshippers were forbidden to injure fruit-trees, and with his character as a god of vegetation in general that they were not allowed to stop up wells of water, which are so important for the irrigation of hot southern lands.   According to one legend, he taught men to train the vine to poles, to prune its superfluous foliage, and to extract the juice of the grape.   In the papyrus of Nebseni, written about 1550 B.C., Osiris is depicted sitting in a shrine, from the roof of which hang clusters of grapes ; and in the papyrus of the royal scribe Nekht we see the god enthroned in front of a pool, from the banks of which a luxuriant vine, with many bunches of grapes, grows towards the green face of the seated deity. The ivy was sacred to him, and was called his plant because it is always green.

§ 3. *Osiris a God of Fertility.*—As a god of vegetation Osiris was naturally conceived as a god of creative energy in general, since men at a certain stage of evolution fail to distinguish between the reproductive powers of animals and of plants. Hence a striking feature in his worship was the coarse but expressive symbolism by which this aspect of his nature was presented to the eye not merely of the initiated but of the multitude. At his festival women used to go about the villages singing songs in his praise and carrying obscene images of him which they set in motion by means of strings. The custom was probably a charm to ensure the growth of the crops. A similar image of him, decked with all the fruits of the earth, is said to have stood in a temple before a figure of Isis, and in the chambers dedicated to him at Philae the dead god is portrayed lying on his bier in an attitude which indicates in the plainest way that even in death his generative virtue was not extinct but only suspended, ready to prove a source of life and fertility to the world when the opportunity should offer. Hymns addressed to Osiris contain allusions to this important side of his nature. In one of them it is said that the world waxes green in triumph through him ; and another declares, " Thou art the father and mother of mankind, they live on thy breath, they subsist on the flesh of thy body." We may conjecture that in this paternal aspect he was supposed, like other gods of fertility, to bless men and women with offspring, and that the processions at his festival were intended to promote this object as well as to quicken the seed in the ground. It would be to misjudge ancient religion to denounce as lewd and profligate the emblems and the ceremonies which the Egyptians employed for the purpose of giving effect to this conception of the divine power. The ends which they proposed to themselves in these rites were natural and laudable ; only the means they adopted to compass them were mistaken. A similar fallacy induced the Greeks to adopt a like symbolism in their Dionysiac festivals, and the superficial but striking resemblance thus produced between the two religions has perhaps more than anything else misled enquirers, both ancient and modern, into identifying worships which, though certainly akin in nature, are perfectly distinct and independent in origin.

§ 4. *Osiris a God of the Dead.*—We have seen that in one of his aspects Osiris was the ruler and judge of the dead. To a people like the Egyptians, who not only believed in a life beyond the grave but actually spent much of their time, labour, and money in preparing for it, this office of the god must have appeared hardly, if at all, less important than his function of making the earth to bring forth its fruits in due season. We may assume that in the faith of his worshippers the two provinces of the god were intimately connected. In laying their dead in the grave they committed them to his keeping who could raise them from the dust to life eternal, even as he caused the seed to spring from the ground. Of that faith the corn-stuffed effigies of Osiris found in Egyptian tombs furnish an eloquent and un-equivocal testimony. They were at once an emblem and an instru-ment of resurrection. Thus from the sprouting of the grain the ancient Egyptians drew an augury of human immortality. They are not the only people who have built the same lofty hopes on the same slender foundation.

A god who thus fed his people with his own broken body in this life, and who held out to them a promise of a blissful eternity in a better world hereafter, naturally reigned supreme in their affections. We need not wonder, therefore, that in Egypt the worship of the other gods was overshadowed by that of Osiris, and that while they were revered each in his own district, he and his divine partner Isis were adored in all.

CHAPTER XLI

ISIS

THE original meaning of the goddess Isis is still more difficult to determine than that of her brother and husband Osiris. Her attributes and epithets were so numerous that in the hieroglyphics she is called " the many-named," " the thousand-named," and in Greek inscriptions " the myriad-named." Yet in her complex nature it is perhaps still possible to detect the original nucleus round which by a slow process of accretion the other elements gathered. For if her brother and husband Osiris was in one of his aspects the corn-god, as we have seen reason to believe, she must surely have been the corn-goddess. There are at least some grounds for thinking so. For if we may trust Dio-dorus Siculus, whose authority appears to have been the Egyptian historian Manetho, the discovery of wheat and barley was attributed to Isis, and at her festivals stalks of these grains were carried in pro-cession to commemorate the boon she had conferred on men. A further detail is added by Augustine. He says that Isis made the discovery of barley at the moment when she was sacrificing to the common ancestors of her husband and herself, all of whom had been kings, and that she showed the newly discovered ears of barley to Osiris and his councillor Thoth or Mercury, as Roman writers called him. That is why, adds Augustine, they identify Isis with Ceres. Further, at harvest-time, when the Egyptian reapers had cut the first stalks, they laid them down and beat their breasts, wailing and calling upon Isis. The custom has been already explained as a lament for the corn-spirit slain under the sickle. Amongst the epithets by which Isis is designated in the inscriptions are " Creatress of green things," " Green goddess, whose green colour is like unto the greenness of the earth," " Lady of Bread," " Lady of Beer," " Lady of Abundance." According to Brugsch she is " not only the creatress of the fresh verdure of vegetation which covers the earth, but is actually the green corn-field itself, which is personified as a goddess." This is confirmed by her epithet *Sochit* or *Sochet*, meaning " a corn-field," a sense which the word still retains in Coptic. The Greeks conceived of Isis as a corn-goddess, for they identified her with Demeter. In a Greek epigram she is described as " she who has given birth to the fruits of the earth," and " the mother of the ears of corn " ; and in a hymn composed in her honour she speaks of herself as " queen of the wheat-field," and is described as " charged with the care of the fruitful furrow's wheat-rich path." Accordingly, Greek or Roman artists often represented her with ears of corn on her head or in her hand.

Such, we may suppose, was Isis in the olden time, a rustic Corn-Mother adored with uncouth rites by Egyptian swains. But the homely features of the clownish goddess could hardly be traced in the refined, the saintly form which, spiritualised by ages of religious evolution, she presented to her worshippers of after days as the true wife, the tender mother, the beneficent queen of nature, encircled with the nimbus of moral purity, of immemorial and mysterious sanctity. Thus chastened and transfigured she won many hearts far beyond the boundaries of her native land. In that welter of religions which accompanied the decline of national life in antiquity her worship was one of the most popular at Rome and throughout the empire. Some of the Roman emperors themselves were openly addicted to it. And however the religion of Isis may, like any other, have been often worn as a cloak by men and women of loose life, her rites appear on the whole to have been honourably distinguished by a dignity and com-posure, a solemnity and decorum well fitted to soothe the troubled mind, to ease the burdened heart. They appealed therefore to gentle spirits, and above all to women, whom the bloody and licentious rites of other Oriental goddesses only shocked and repelled. We need not wonder, then, that in a period of decadence, when traditional faiths were shaken, when systems clashed, when men's minds were dis-quieted, when the fabric of empire itself, once deemed eternal, began to show ominous rents and fissures, the serene figure of Isis with her spiritual calm, her gracious promise of immortality, should have appeared to many like a star in a stormy sky, and should have roused in their breasts a rapture of devotion not unlike that which was paid in the Middle Ages to the Virgin Mary. Indeed her stately ritual, with its shaven and tonsured priests, its matins and vespers, its tinkling music, its baptism and aspersions of holy water, its solemn processions, its jewelled images of the Mother of God, presented many points of similarity to the pomps and ceremonies of Catholicism. The re-semblance need not be purely accidental. Ancient Egypt may have contributed its share to the gorgeous symbolism of the Catholic Church as well as to the pale abstractions of her theology. Certainly in art the figure of Isis suckling the infant Horus is so like that of the Madonna and child that it has sometimes received the adoration of ignorant Christians. And to Isis in her later character of patroness of mariners the Virgin Mary perhaps owes her beautiful epithet of *Stella Maris*.

" Star of the Sea," under which she is adored by tempest-tossed sailors The attributes of a marine deity may have been bestowed on Isis by the sea-faring Greeks of Alexandria. They are quite foreign to her original character and to the habits of the Egyptians, who had no love of the sea. On this hypothesis Sirius, the bright star of Isis, which on July mornings rises from the glassy waves of the eastern Mediterranean, a harbinger of halcyon weather to mariners, was the true *Stella Maris*, " the Star of the Sea."

CHAPTER XLII

OSIRIS AND THE SUN

OSIRIS has been sometimes interpreted as the sun-god, and in modern times this view has been held by so many distinguished writers that it deserves a brief examination. If we enquire on what evidence Osiris has been identified with the sun or the sun-god, it will be found on analysis to be minute in quantity and dubious, where it is not absolutely worthless, in quality. The diligent Jablonski, the first modern scholar to collect and sift the testimony of classical writers on Egyptian religion, says that it can be shown in many ways that Osiris is the sun, and that he could produce a cloud of witnesses to prove it, but that it is needless to do so, since no learned man is ignorant of the fact. Of the ancient writers whom he condescends to quote, the only two who expressly identify Osiris with the sun are Diodorus and Macrobius. But little weight can be attached to their evidence ; for the statement of Diodorus is vague and rhetorical, and the reasons which Macrobius, one of the fathers of solar mythology, assigns for the identification are exceedingly slight.

The ground upon which some modern writers seem chiefly to rely for the identification of Osiris with the sun is that the story of his death fits better with the solar phenomena than with any other in nature. It may readily be admitted that the daily appearance and disappearance of the sun might very naturally be expressed by a myth of his death and resurrection ; and writers who regard Osiris as the sun are careful to indicate that it is the diurnal, and not the annual, course of the sun to which they understand the myth to apply. Thus Renouf, who identified Osiris with the sun, admitted that the Egyptian sun could not with any show of reason be described as dead in winter. But if his daily death was the theme of the legend, why was it celebrated by an annual ceremony ? This fact alone seems fatal to the interpretation of the myth as descriptive of sunset and sunrise. Again, though the sun may be said to die daily, in what sense can he be said to be torn in pieces ?

In the course of our enquiry it has, I trust, been made clear that there is another natural phenomenon to which the conception of death and resurrection is as applicable as to sunset and sunrise, and which, as a matter of fact, has been so conceived and represented in folk-custom. That phenomenon is the annual growth and decay of vegetation. A strong reason for interpreting the death of Osiris as the decay of vegetation rather than as the sunset is to be found in the general, though not unanimous, voice of antiquity, which classed together the worship and myths of Osiris, Adonis, Attis, Dionysus, and Demeter, as religions of essentially the same type. The consensus of ancient opinion on this subject seems too great to be rejected as a mere fancy. So closely did the rites of Osiris resemble those of Adonis at Byblus that some of the people of Byblus themselves maintained that it was Osiris and not Adonis whose death was mourned by them. Such a view could certainly not have been held if the rituals of the two gods had not been so alike as to be almost indistinguishable. Herodotus found the similarity between the rites of Osiris and Dionysus so great. that he thought it impossible the latter could have arisen independently; they must, he supposed, have been recently borrowed, with slight alterations, by the Greeks from the Egyptians. Again, Plutarch, a very keen student of comparative religion, insists upon the detailed resemblance of the rites of Osiris to those of Dionysus. We cannot reject the evidence of such intelligent and trustworthy witnesses on plain matters of fact which fell under their own cognizance. Their explanations of the worships it is indeed possible to reject, for the meaning of religious cults is often open to question ; but resemblances of ritual are matters of observation. Therefore, those who explain Osiris as the sun are driven to the alternative of either dismissing as mistaken the testimony of antiquity to the similarity of the rites of Osiris, Adonis, Attis, Dionysus, and Demeter, or of interpreting all these rites as sun-worship. No modern scholar has fairly faced and accepted either side of this alternative. To accept the former would be to affirm that we know the rites of these deities better than the men who practised, or at least who witnessed them. To accept the latter would involve a wrenching, clipping, mangling, and distorting of myth and ritual from which even Macrobius shrank. On the other hand, the view that the essence of all these rites was the mimic death and revival of vegetation, explains them separately and collectively in an easy and natural way, and harmonises with the general testimony borne by the ancients to their substantial similarity.

CHAPTER XLIII

DIONYSUS

In the preceding chapters we saw that in antiquity the civilised nations of Western Asia and Egypt pictured to themselves the changes of the seasons, and particularly the annual growth and decay of vegetation, as episodes in the life of gods, whose mournful death and happy resurrection they celebrated with dramatic rites of alternate lamentation and rejoicing. But if the celebration was in form dramatic, it was in substance magical; that is to say, it was intended, on the principles of sympathetic magic, to ensure the vernal regeneration of plants and the multiplication of animals, which had seemed to be menaced by the inroads of winter. In the ancient world, however, such ideas and such rites were by no means confined to the Oriental peoples of Babylon and Syria, of Phrygia and Egypt; they were not a product peculiar to the religious mysticism of the dreamy East, but were shared by the races of livelier fancy and more mercurial temperament who inhabited the shores and islands of the Aegean. We need not, with some enquirers in ancient and modern times, suppose that these Western peoples borrowed from the older civilisation of the Orient the conception of the Dying and Reviving God, together with the solemn ritual, in which that conception was dramatically set forth before the eyes of the worshippers. More probably the resemblance which may be traced in this respect between the religions of the East and the West is no more than what we commonly, though incorrectly, call a fortuitous coincidence, the effect of similar causes acting alike on the similar constitution of the human mind in different countries and under different skies. The Greek had no need to journey into far countries to learn the vicissitudes of the seasons, to mark the fleeting beauty of the damask rose, the transient glory of the golden corn, the passing splendour of the purple grapes. Year by year in his own beautiful land he beheld, with natural regret, the bright pomp of summer fading into the gloom and stagnation of winter, and year by year he hailed with natural delight the outburst of fresh life in spring. Accustomed to personify the forces of nature, to tinge her cold abstractions with the warm hues of imagination, to clothe her naked realities with the gorgeous drapery of a mythic fancy, he fashioned for himself a train of gods and goddesses, of spirits and elves, out of the shifting panorama of the seasons, and followed the annual fluctuations of their fortunes with alternate emotions of cheerfulness and dejection, of gladness and sorrow, which found their natural expression in alternate rites of rejoicing and lamentation, of revelry and mourning. A consideration of some of the Greek divinities who thus died and rose again from the dead may furnish us with a series of companion pictures to set side by side with the sad figures of Adonis, Attis, and Osiris. We begin with Dionysus.

The god Dionysus or Bacchus is best known to us as a personification of the vine and of the exhilaration produced by the juice of the grape. His ecstatic worship, characterised by wild dances, thrilling music, and tipsy excess, appears to have originated among the rude tribes of Thrace, who were notoriously addicted to drunkenness. Its mystic doctrines and extravagant rites were essentially foreign to the clear intelligence and sober temperament of the Greek race. Yet appealing as it did to that love of mystery and that proneness to revert to savagery which seem to be innate in most men, the religion spread like wildfire through Greece until the god whom Homer hardly deigned to notice had become the most popular figure of the pantheon. The resemblance which his story and his ceremonies present to those of Osiris have led some enquirers both in ancient and modern times to hold that Dionysus was merely a disguised Osiris, imported directly from Egypt into Greece. But the great preponderance of evidence points to his Thracian origin, and the similarity of the two worships is sufficiently explained by the similarity of the ideas and customs on which they were founded.

While the vine with its clusters was the most characteristic manifestation of Dionysus, he was also a god of trees in general. Thus we are told that almost all the Greeks sacrificed to " Dionysus of the tree." In Boeotia one of his titles was " Dionysus in the tree." His image was often merely an upright post, without arms, but draped in a mantle, with a bearded mask to represent the head, and with leafy boughs projecting from the head or body to show the nature of the deity. On a vase his rude effigy is depicted appearing out of a low tree or bush. At Magnesia on the Maeander an image of Dionysus is said to have been found in a plane-tree, which had been broken by the wind. He was the patron of cultivated trees : prayers were offered to him that he would make the trees grow ; and he was especially honoured by husbandmen, chiefly fruit-growers, who set up an image of him, in the shape of a natural tree-stump, in their orchards. He was said to have discovered all tree-fruits, amongst which apples and figs are particularly mentioned ; and he was referred to as " wellfruited," " he of the green fruit," and " making the fruit to grow." One of his titles was " teeming " or " bursting " (as of sap or blossoms) ; and there was a Flowery Dionysus in Attica and at Patrae in Achaia. The Athenians sacrificed to him for the prosperity of the fruits of the land. Amongst the trees particularly sacred to him, in addition to the vine, was the pine-tree. The Delphic oracle commanded the Corinthians to worship a particular pine-tree " equally with the god," so they made two images of Dionysus out of it, with red faces and gilt bodies. In art a wand, tipped with a pine-cone, is commonly carried by the god or his worshippers. Again, the ivy and the fig-tree were especially associated with him. In the Attic township of Acharnae there was a Dionysus Ivy ; at Lacedaemon there was a Fig Dionysus ; and in Naxos, where figs were called *meilicha*, there was a Dionysus Meilichios, the face of whose image was made of fig-wood.

Further, there are indications, few but significant, that Dionysus was conceived as a deity of agriculture and the corn. He is spoken of as himself doing the work of a husbandman : he is reported to have been the first to yoke oxen to the plough, which before had been dragged by hand alone ; and some people found in this tradition the clue to the bovine shape in which, as we shall see, the god was often supposed to present himself to his worshippers. Thus guiding the ploughshare and scattering the seed as he went, Dionysus is said to have eased the labour of the husbandman. Further, we are told that in the land of the Bisaltae, a Thracian tribe, there was a great and fair sanctuary of Dionysus, where at his festival a bright light shone forth at night as a token of an abundant harvest vouchsafed by the deity ; but if the crops were to fail that year, the mystic light was not seen, darkness brooded over the sanctuary as at other times. Moreover, among the emblems of Dionysus was the winnowing-fan, that is the large open shovel-shaped basket, which down to modern times has been used by farmers to separate the grain from the chaff by tossing the corn in the air. This simple agricultural instrument figured in the mystic rites of Dionysus ; indeed the god is traditionally said to have been placed at birth in a winnowing-fan as in a cradle : in art he is represented as an infant so cradled ; and from these traditions and representations he derived the epithet of *Liknites*, that is, " He of the Winnowing-fan."

Like other gods of vegetation Dionysus was believed to have died a violent death, but to have been brought to life again ; and his sufferings, death, and resurrection were enacted in his sacred rites. His tragic story is thus told by the poet Nonnus. Zeus in the form of a serpent visited Persephone, and she bore him Zagreus, that is, Dionysus, a horned infant. Scarcely was he born, when the babe mounted the throne of his father Zeus and mimicked the great god by brandishing the lightning in his tiny hand. But he did not occupy the throne long ; for the treacherous Titans, their faces whitened with chalk, attacked him with knives while he was looking at himself in a mirror. For a time he evaded their assaults by turning himself into various shapes, assuming the likeness successively of Zeus and Cronus, of a young man, of a lion, a horse, and a serpent. Finally, in the form of a bull, he was cut to pieces by the murderous knives of his enemies. His Cretan myth, as related by Firmicus Maternus, ran thus. He was said to have been the bastard son of Jupiter, a Cretan king. Going abroad, Jupiter transferred the throne and sceptre to the youthful Dionysus, but, knowing that his wife Juno cherished a jealous dislike of the child, he entrusted Dionysus to the care of guards upon whose fidelity he believed he could rely. Juno, however, bribed the guards, and amusing the child with rattles and a cunningly-wrought looking-glass lured him into an ambush, where her satellites, the Titans, rushed upon him, cut him limb from limb, boiled his body with various herbs, and ate it. But his sister Minerva, who had shared in the deed, kept his heart and gave it to Jupiter on his return, revealing to him the whole history of the crime. In his rage, Jupiter put the Titans to death by torture, and, to soothe his grief for the loss of his son, made an image in which he enclosed the child's heart, and then built a temple in his honour. In this version a Euhemeristic turn has been given to the myth by representing Jupiter and Juno (Zeus and Hera) as a king and queen of Crete. The guards referred to are the mythical Curetes who danced a war-dance round the infant Dionysus, as they

are said to have done round the infant Zeus.   Very noteworthy is the
legend, recorded both by Nonnus and Firmicus, that in his infancy
Dionysus occupied for a short time the throne of his father Zeus.
So Proclus tells us that " Dionysus was the last king of the gods
appointed by Zeus.   For his father set him on the kingly throne,
and placed in his hand the sceptre, and made him king of all the
gods of the world."   Such traditions point to a custom of temporarily
investing the king's son with the royal dignity as a preliminary to
sacrificing him instead of his father.   Pomegranates were supposed
to have sprung from the blood of Dionysus, as anemones from the
blood of Adonis and violets from the blood of Attis : hence women
refrained from eating seeds of pomegranates at the festival of the
Thesmophoria.   According to some, the severed limbs of Dionysus
were pieced together, at the command of Zeus, by Apollo, who buried
them on Parnassus.   The grave of Dionysus was shown in the Delphic
temple beside a golden statue of Apollo.   However, according to
another account, the grave of Dionysus was at Thebes, where he is
said to have been torn in pieces.   Thus far the resurrection of the
slain god is not mentioned, but in other versions of the myth it is
variously related.   According to one version, which represented
Dionysus as a son of Zeus and Demeter, his mother pieced together
his mangled limbs and made him young again.   In others it is simply
said that shortly after his burial he rose from the dead and ascended
up to heaven ; or that Zeus raised him up as he lay mortally wounded ;
or that Zeus swallowed the heart of Dionysus and then begat him
afresh by Semele, who in the common legend figures as mother of
Dionysus.   Or, again, the heart was pounded up and given in a potion
to Semele, who thereby conceived him.

Turning from the myth to the ritual, we find that the Cretans
celebrated a biennial festival at which the passion of Dionysus was
represented in every detail.   All that he had done or suffered in his
last moments was enacted before the eyes of his worshippers, who
tore a live bull to pieces with their teeth and roamed the woods with
frantic shouts.   In front of them was carried a casket supposed to
contain the sacred heart of Dionysus, and to the wild music of flutes
and cymbals they mimicked the rattles by which the infant god
had been lured to his doom.   Where the resurrection formed part of
the myth, it also was acted at the rites, and it even appears that a
general doctrine of resurrection, or at least of immortality, was
inculcated on the worshippers ; for Plutarch, writing to console his
wife on the death of their infant daughter, comforts her with the
thought of the immortality of the soul as taught by tradition and
revealed in the mysteries of Dionysus.   A different form of the myth
of the death and resurrection of Dionysus is that he descended into
Hades to bring up his mother Semele from the dead.   The local Argive
tradition was that he went down through the Alcyonian lake ; and his
return from the lower world, in other words his resurrection, was
annually celebrated on the spot by the Argives, who summoned him

from the water by trumpet blasts, while they threw a lamb into the lake as an offering to the warder of the dead. Whether this was a spring festival does not appear, but the Lydians certainly celebrated the advent of Dionysus in spring ; the god was supposed to bring the season with him. Deities of vegetation, who are believed to pass a certain portion of each year underground, naturally come to be regarded as gods of the lower world or of the dead. Both Dionysus and Osiris were so conceived.

A feature in the mythical character of Dionysus, which at first sight appears inconsistent with his nature as a deity of vegetation, is that he was often conceived and represented in animal shape, especially in the form, or at least with the horns, of a bull. Thus he is spoken of as " cow-born," " bull," " bull-shaped," " bull-faced," " bull-browed," " bull-horned," " horn-bearing," " two-horned," " horned." He was believed to appear, at least occasionally, as a bull. His images were often, as at Cyzicus, made in bull shape, or with bull horns ; and he was painted with horns. Types of the horned Dionysus are found amongst the surviving monuments of antiquity. On one statuette he appears clad in a bull's hide, the head, horns, and hoofs hanging down behind. Again, he is represented as a child with clusters of grapes round his brow, and a calf's head, with sprouting horns, attached to the back of his head. On a red-figured vase the god is portrayed as a calf-headed child seated on a woman's lap. The people of Cynaetha held a festival of Dionysus in winter, when men, who had greased their bodies with oil for the occasion, used to pick out a bull from the herd and carry it to the sanctuary of the god. Dionysus was supposed to inspire their choice of the particular bull, which probably represented the deity himself ; for at his festivals he was believed to appear in bull form. The women of Elis hailed him as a bull, and prayed him to come with his bull's foot. They sang, " Come hither, Dionysus, to thy holy temple by the sea ; come with the Graces to thy temple, rushing with thy bull's foot, O goodly bull, O goodly bull ! " The Bacchanals of Thrace wore horns in imitation of their god. According to the myth, it was in the shape of a bull that he was torn to pieces by the Titans ; and the Cretans, when they acted the sufferings and death of Dionysus, tore a live bull to pieces with their teeth. Indeed, the rending and devouring of live bulls and calves appear to have been a regular feature of the Dionysiac rites. When we consider the practice of portraying the god as a bull or with some of the features of the animal, the belief that he appeared in bull form to his worshippers at the sacred rites, and the legend that in bull form he had been torn in pieces, we cannot doubt that in rending and devouring a live bull at his festival the worshippers of Dionysus believed themselves to be killing the god, eating his flesh, and drinking his blood.

Another animal whose form Dionysus assumed was the goat. One of his names was " Kid." At Athens and at Hermion he was worshipped under the title of " the one of the Black Goatskin," and a

legend ran that on a certain occasion he had appeared clad in the skin
from which he took the title. In the wine-growing district of Phlius,
where in autumn the plain is still thickly mantled with the red and
golden foliage of the fading vines, there stood of old a bronze image of
a goat, which the husbandmen plastered with gold-leaf as a means of
protecting their vines against blight. The image probably represented
the vine-god himself. To save him from the wrath of Hera, his father
Zeus changed the youthful Dionysus into a kid ; and when the gods
fled to Egypt to escape the fury of Typhon, Dionysus was turned into
a goat. Hence when his worshippers rent in pieces a live goat and
devoured it raw, they must have believed that they were eating the
body and blood of the god. The custom of tearing in pieces the bodies
of animals and of men and then devouring them raw has been practised
as a religious rite by savages in modern times. We need not therefore
dismiss as a fable the testimony of antiquity to the observance of
similar rites among the frenzied worshippers of Bacchus.

The custom of killing a god in animal form, which we shall examine
more in detail further on, belongs to a very early stage of human
culture, and is apt in later times to be misunderstood. The advance
of thought tends to strip the old animal and plant gods of their bestial
and vegetable husk, and to leave their human attributes (which are
always the kernel of the conception) as the final and sole residuum.
In other words, animal and plant gods tend to become purely anthropomorphic. When they have become wholly or nearly so, the animals
and plants which were at first the deities themselves, still retain a
vague and ill-understood connexion with the anthropomorphic gods
who have been developed out of them. The origin of the relationship
between the deity and the animal or plant having been forgotten,
various stories are invented to explain it. These explanations may
follow one of two lines according as they are based on the habitual or
on the exceptional treatment of the sacred animal or plant. The
sacred animal was habitually spared, and only exceptionally slain ;
and accordingly the myth might be devised to explain either why it
was spared or why it was killed. Devised for the former purpose, the
myth would tell of some service rendered to the deity by the animal ;
devised for the latter purpose, the myth would tell of some injury
inflicted by the animal on the god. The reason given for sacrificing
goats to Dionysus exemplifies a myth of the latter sort. They were
sacrificed to him, it was said, because they injured the vine. Now
the goat, as we have seen, was originally an embodiment of the god
himself. But when the god had divested himself of his animal character and had become essentially anthropomorphic, the killing of the
goat in his worship came to be regarded no longer as a slaying of the
deity himself, but as a sacrifice offered to him ; and since some reason
had to be assigned why the goat in particular should be sacrificed, it
was alleged that this was a punishment inflicted on the goat for injuring the vine, the object of the god's especial care. Thus we have the
strange spectacle of a god sacrificed to himself on the ground that he

is his own enemy. And as the deity is supposed to partake of the victim offered to him, it follows that, when the victim is the god's old self, the god eats of his own flesh. Hence the goat-god Dionysus is represented as eating raw goat's blood ; and the bull-god Dionysus is called " eater of bulls." On the analogy of these instances we may conjecture that wherever a deity is described as the eater of a particular animal, the animal in question was originally nothing but the deity himself. Later on we shall find that some savages propitiate dead bears and whales by offering them portions of their own bodies.

All this, however, does not explain why a deity of vegetation should appear in animal form. But the consideration of that point had better be deferred till we have discussed the character and attributes of Demeter. Meantime it remains to mention that in some places, instead of an animal, a human being was torn in pieces at the rites of Dionysus. This was the practice in Chios and Tenedos ; and at Potniae in Boeotia the tradition ran that it had been formerly the custom to sacrifice to the goat-smiting Dionysus a child, for whom a goat was afterwards substituted. At Orchomenus, as we have seen, the human victim was taken from the women of an old royal family. As the slain bull or goat represented the slain god, so, we may suppose, the human victim also represented him.

The legends of the deaths of Pentheus and Lycurgus, two kings who are said to have been torn to pieces, the one by Bacchanals, the other by horses, for their opposition to the rites of Dionysus, may be, as I have already suggested, distorted reminiscences of a custom of sacrificing divine kings in the character of Dionysus and of dispersing the fragments of their broken bodies over the fields for the purpose of fertilising them. It is probably no mere coincidence that Dionysus himself is said to have been torn in pieces at Thebes, the very place where according to legend the same fate befell King Pentheus at the hands of the frenzied votaries of the vine-god.

However, a tradition of human sacrifice may sometimes have been a mere misinterpretation of a sacrificial ritual in which an animal victim was treated as a human being. For example, at Tenedos the new-born calf sacrificed to Dionysus was shod in buskins, and the mother cow was tended like a woman in child-bed. At Rome a she-goat was sacrificed to Vedijovis as if it were a human victim. Yet on the other hand it is equally possible, and perhaps more probable, that these curious rites were themselves mitigations of an older and ruder custom of sacrificing human beings, and that the later pretence of treating the sacrificial victims as if they were human beings was merely part of a pious and merciful fraud, which palmed off on the deity less precious victims than living men and women. This interpretation is supported by many undoubted cases in which animals have been substituted for human victims.

1.Sympathetic magic: an Irish Celtic druid with some bronze-age
artefacts and a mystical snake

2. *Worship of the sacred tree of life, Assyria, eighth century* BC

3. *Raising the maypole, Britain, early eighteenth century*

4. Crow Eagle medicine bundle, USA. When a bird or animal appeared in a vision as a messenger of the gods, its skin was used as a medium for power in scacred rituals. Here, the bird's body has been wrapped in cloth

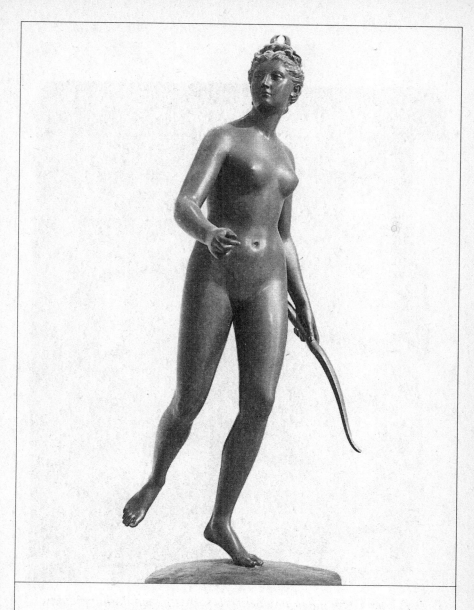

5. *Diana the Huntress, by Houdon, late eighteenth century*

6. *A board from a hut in which girls were isolated during puberty, showing a scene from future life. The woman (left) is giving birth, while her husband (right) lies beside her. Jokwe Tribe, probably early twentieth century*

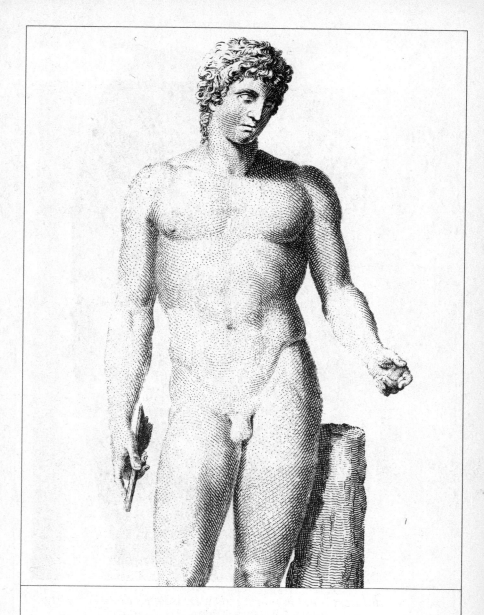

7. Statue of Adonis, the Vatican, Rome

8. Osiris with lotus blossom, Thebes, 1200 BC

9. Dionysus holding a wine cup, black figure vase,
Ancient Greece

10. *Abduction of Persephone by Hades on a unicorn, from an engraving by Albrecht Dürer*

11. Demeter (or Ceres) holding a sheaf of corn

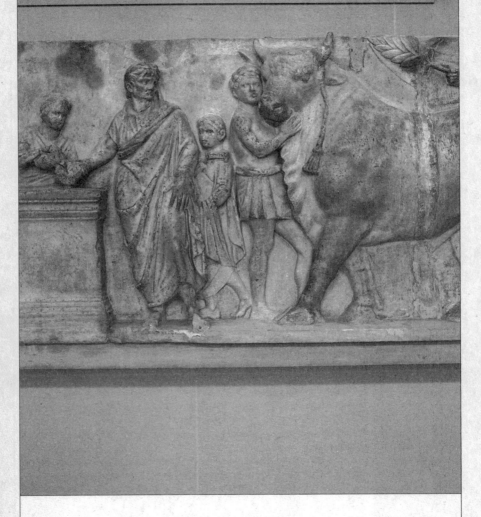

12. *Killing the Divine Animal: sacrifice frieze to Mars, Temple of Neptune, Rome, Republican era*

13. *Demon leaving the body of a possessed woman, sixteenth century*

14. *Chasing the scapegoat, Israel*

15. *Zoroastrian fire altar, coin of Hormized II, fourth century* AD

16. The King of the Wood: 'The Green Man',
Switzerland, fifteenth century

CHAPTER XLIV

DEMETER AND PERSEPHONE

DIONYSUS was not the only Greek deity whose tragic story and ritual appear to reflect the decay and revival of vegetation. In another form and with a different application the old tale reappears in the myth of Demeter and Persephone. Substantially their myth is identical with the Syrian one of Aphrodite (Astarte) and Adonis, the Phrygian one of Cybele and Attis, and the Egyptian one of Isis and Osiris. In the Greek fable, as in its Asiatic and Egyptian counterparts, a goddess mourns the loss of a loved one, who personifies the vegetation, more especially the corn, which dies in winter to revive in spring; only whereas the Oriental imagination figured the loved and lost one as a dead lover or a dead husband lamented by his leman or his wife, Greek fancy embodied the same idea in the tenderer and purer form of a dead daughter bewailed by her sorrowing mother.

The oldest literary document which narrates the myth of Demeter and Persephone is the beautiful Homeric *Hymn to Demeter*, which critics assign to the seventh century before our era. The object of the poem is to explain the origin of the Eleusinian mysteries, and the complete silence of the poet as to Athens and the Athenians, who in after ages took a conspicuous part in the festival, renders it probable that the hymn was composed in the far-off time when Eleusis was still a petty independent state, and before the stately procession of the Mysteries had begun to defile, in bright September days, over the low chain of barren rocky hills which divides the flat Eleusinian corn-land from the more spacious olive-clad expanse of the Athenian plain. Be that as it may, the hymn reveals to us the conception which the writer entertained of the character and functions of the two goddesses : their natural shapes stand out sharply enough under the thin veil of poetical imagery. The youthful Persephone, so runs the tale, was gathering roses and lilies, crocuses and violets, hyacinths and narcissuses in a lush meadow, when the earth gaped and Pluto, lord of the Dead, issuing from the abyss carried her off on his golden car to be his bride and queen in the gloomy subterranean world. Her sorrowing mother Demeter, with her yellow tresses veiled in a dark mourning mantle, sought her over land and sea, and learning from the Sun her daughter's fate she withdrew in high dudgeon from the gods and took up her abode at Eleusis, where she presented herself to the king's daughters in the guise of an old woman, sitting sadly under the shadow of an olive tree beside the Maiden's Well, to which the damsels had come to draw water in bronze pitchers for their father's house. In her wrath at her bereavement the goddess suffered not the seed to grow in the earth but kept it hidden under ground, and she vowed that never would she set foot on Olympus and never would she let the corn sprout till her lost daughter should be restored to her.

Vainly the oxen dragged the ploughs to and fro in the fields ; vainly
the sower dropped the barley seed in the brown furrows ; nothing
came up from the parched and crumbling soil.   Even the Rarian plain
near Eleusis, which was wont to wave with yellow harvests, lay bare
and fallow.   Mankind would have perished of hunger and ·the gods
would have been robbed of the sacrifices which were their due, if Zeus
in alarm had not commanded Pluto to disgorge his prey, to restore
his bride Persephone to her mother Demeter.   The grim lord of the
Dead smiled and obeyed, but before he sent back his queen to the
upper air on a golden car, he gave her the seed of a pomegranate to
eat, which ensured that she would return to him.   But Zeus stipulated
that henceforth Persephone should spend two-thirds of every year
with her mother and the gods in the upper world and one-third of the
year with her husband in the nether world, from which she was to
return year by year when the earth was gay with spring flowers.
Gladly the daughter then returned to the sunshine, gladly her mother
received her and fell upon her neck ; and in her joy at recovering the
lost one Demeter made the corn to sprout from the clods of the
ploughed fields and all the broad earth to be heavy with leaves and
blossoms.   And straightway she went and showed this happy sight to
the princes of Eleusis, to Triptolemus, Eumolpus, Diocles, and to the
king Celeus himself, and moreover she revealed to them her sacred
rites and mysteries.   Blessed, says the poet, is the mortal man who
has seen these things, but he who has had no share of them in life will
never be happy in death when he has descended into the darkness of
the grave.   So the two goddesses departed to dwell in bliss with the
gods on Olympus ; and the bard ends the hymn with a pious prayer
to Demeter and Persephone that they would be pleased to grant him
a livelihood in return for his song.

It has been generally recognised, and indeed it seems scarcely open
to doubt, that the main theme which the poet set before himself in
composing this hymn was to describe the traditional foundation of
the Eleusinian mysteries by the goddess Demeter.   The whole poem
leads up to the transformation scene in which the bare leafless expanse
of the Eleusinian plain is suddenly turned, at the will of the goddess,
into a vast sheet of ruddy corn ; the beneficent deity takes the
princes of Eleusis, shows them what she has done, teaches them her
mystic rites, and vanishes with her daughter to heaven.   The revelation of the mysteries is the triumphal close of the piece.   This conclusion is confirmed by a more minute examination of the poem,
which proves that the poet has given, not merely a general account of
the foundation of the mysteries, but also in more or less veiled language
mythical explanations of the origin of particular rites which we have
good reason to believe formed essential features of the festival.
Amongst the rites as to which the poet thus drops significant hints are
the preliminary fast of the candidates for initiation, the torchlight
procession, the all-night vigil, the sitting of the candidates, veiled and
in silence, on stools covered with sheepskins, the use of scurrilous

language, the breaking of ribald jests, and the solemn communion with the divinity by participation in a draught of barley-water from a holy chalice.

But there is yet another and a deeper secret of the mysteries which the author of the poem appears to have divulged under cover of his narrative. He tells us how, as soon as she had transformed the barren brown expanse of the Eleusinian plain into a field of golden grain, she gladdened the eyes of Triptolemus and the other Eleusinian princes by showing them the growing or standing corn. When we compare this part of the story with the statement of a Christian writer of the second century, Hippolytus, that the very heart of the mysteries consisted in showing to the initiated a reaped ear of corn, we can hardly doubt that the poet of the hymn was well acquainted with this solemn rite, and that he deliberately intended to explain its origin in precisely the same way as he explained other rites of the mysteries, namely by representing Demeter as having set the example of performing the ceremony in her own person. Thus myth and ritual mutually explain and confirm each other. The poet of the seventh century before our era gives us the myth—he could not without sacrilege have revealed the ritual : the Christian father reveals the ritual, and his revelation accords perfectly with the veiled hint of the old poet. On the whole, then, we may, with many modern scholars, confidently accept the statement of the learned Christian father Clement of Alexandria, that the myth of Demeter and Persephone was acted as a sacred drama in the mysteries of Eleusis.

But if the myth was acted as a part, perhaps as the principal part, of the most famous and solemn religious rites of ancient Greece, we have still to enquire, What was, after all, stripped of later accretions, the original kernel of the myth which appears to later ages surrounded and transfigured by an aureole of awe and mystery, lit up by some of the most brilliant rays of Grecian literature and art ? If we follow the indications given by our oldest literary authority on the subject, the author of the Homeric hymn to Demeter, the riddle is not hard to read ; the figures of the two goddesses, the mother and the daughter, resolve themselves into personifications of the corn. At least this appears to be fairly certain for the daughter Persephone. The goddess who spends three or, according to another version of the myth, six months of every year with the dead under ground and the remainder of the year with the living above ground ; in whose absence the barley seed is hidden in the earth and the fields lie bare and fallow ; on whose return in spring to the upper world the corn shoots up from the clods and the earth is heavy with leaves and blossoms—this goddess can surely be nothing else than a mythical embodiment of the vegetation, and particularly of the corn, which is buried under the soil for some months of every winter and comes to life again, as from the grave, in the sprouting cornstalks and the opening flowers and foliage of every spring. No other reasonable and probable explanation of Persephone seems possible. And if the daughter goddess was a personification of the young corn of the present year, may not the mother goddess be a personification of the old corn of last year, which has given birth to the new crops? The only alternative to this view of Demeter would seem to be to suppose that she is a personification of the earth, from whose broad bosom the corn and all other plants spring up, and of which accordingly they may appropriately enough be regarded as the daughters. This view of the original nature of Demeter has indeed been taken by some writers, both ancient and modern, and it is one which can be reasonably maintained. But it appears to have been rejected by the author of the Homeric hymn to Demeter, for he not only distinguishes Demeter from the personified Earth but places the two in the sharpest opposition to each other. He tells us that it was Earth who, in accordance with the will of Zeus and to please Pluto, lured Persephone to her doom by causing the narcissuses to grow which tempted the young goddess to stray far beyond the reach of help in the lush meadow. Thus Demeter of the hymn, far from being identical with the Earth-goddess, must have regarded that divinity as her worst enemy, since it was to her insidious wiles that she owed the loss of her daughter. But if the Demeter of the hymn cannot have been a personification of the earth, the only alternative apparently is to conclude that she was a personification of the corn.

The conclusion is confirmed by the monuments ; for in ancient art Demeter and Persephone are alike characterised as goddesses of the corn by the crowns of corn which they wear on their heads and by the stalks of corn which they hold in their hands. Again, it was Demeter who first revealed to the Athenians the secret of the corn and diffused the beneficent discovery far and wide through the agency of Triptolemus, whom she sent forth as an itinerant missionary to communicate the boon to all mankind. On monuments of art, especially in vase-paintings, he is constantly represented along with Demeter in this capacity, holding corn-stalks in his hand and sitting in his car, which is sometimes winged and sometimes drawn by dragons, and from which he is said to have sowed the seed down on the whole world as he sped through the air. In gratitude for the priceless boon many Greek cities long continued to send the first-fruits of their barley and wheat harvests as thank-offerings to the Two Goddesses, Demeter and Persephone, at Eleusis, where subterranean granaries were built to store the overflowing contributions. Theocritus tells how in the island of Cos, in the sweet-scented summer time, the farmer brought the first-fruits of the harvest to Demeter who had filled his threshing-floor with barley, and whose rustic image held sheaves and poppies in her hands. Many of the epithets bestowed by the ancients on Demeter mark her intimate association with the corn in the clearest manner.

How deeply implanted in the mind of the ancient Greeks was this faith in Demeter as goddess of the corn may be judged by the circumstance that the faith actually persisted among their Christian descendants

at her old sanctuary of Eleusis down to the beginning of the nineteenth
century. For when the English traveller Dodwell revisited Eleusis,
the inhabitants lamented to him the loss of a colossal image of Demeter,
which was carried off by Clarke in 1802 and presented to the University
of Cambridge, where it still remains.   " In my first journey to Greece,"
says Dodwell, " this protecting deity was in its full glory, situated in
the centre of a threshing-floor, amongst the ruins of her temple.   The
villagers were impressed with a persuasion that their rich harvests
were the effect of her bounty, and since her removal, their abundance,
as they assured me, has disappeared."   Thus we see the Corn Goddess
Demeter standing on the threshing-floor of Eleusis and dispensing
corn to her worshippers in the nineteenth century of the Christian
era, precisely as her image stood and dispensed corn to her worshippers
on the threshing-floor of Cos in the days of Theocritus.   And just as the
people of Eleusis in the nineteenth century attributed the diminution
of their harvests to the loss of the image of Demeter, so in antiquity
the Sicilians, a corn-growing people devoted to the worship of the two
Corn Goddesses, lamented that the crops of many towns had perished
because the unscrupulous Roman governor Verres had impiously
carried off the image of Demeter from her famous temple at Henna.
Could we ask for a clearer proof that Demeter was indeed the goddess
of the corn than this belief, held by the Greeks down to modern times,
that the corn-crops depended on her presence and bounty and perished
when her image was removed ?

On the whole, then, if, ignoring theories, we adhere to the evidence
of the ancients themselves in regard to the rites of Eleusis, we shall
probably incline to agree with the most learned of ancient antiquaries,
the Roman Varro, who, to quote Augustine's report of his opinion,
" interpreted the whole of the Eleusinian mysteries as relating to the
corn which Ceres (Demeter) had discovered, and to Proserpine (Persephone), whom Pluto had carried off from her.   And Proserpine herself,
he said, signifies the fecundity of the seeds, the failure of which at a
certain time had caused the earth to mourn for barrenness, and therefore had given rise to the opinion that the daughter of Ceres, that
is, fecundity itself, had been ravished by Pluto and detained in the
nether world ; and when the dearth had been publicly mourned and
fecundity had returned once more, there was gladness at the return
of Proserpine and solemn rites were instituted accordingly.   After
that he says," continues Augustine, reporting Varro, " that many
things were taught in her mysteries which had no reference but to
the discovery of the corn."

Thus far I have for the most part assumed an identity of nature
between Demeter and Persephone, the divine mother and daughter
personifying the corn in its double aspect of the seed-corn of last
year and the ripe ears of this, and this view of the substantial unity
of mother and daughter is borne out by their portraits in Greek art,
which are often so alike as to be indistinguishable. Such a close
resemblance between the artistic types of Demeter and Persephone

militates decidedly against the view that the two goddesses are mythical
embodiments of two things so different and so easily distinguishable
from each other as the earth and the vegetation which springs from
it. Had Greek artists accepted that view of Demeter and Persephone,
they could surely have devised types of them which would have
brought out the deep distinction between the goddesses. And if
Demeter did not personify the earth, can there be any reasonable
doubt that, like her daughter, she personified the corn which was so
commonly called by her name from the time of Homer downwards?
The essential identity of mother and daughter is suggested, not only
by the close resemblance of their artistic types, but also by the official
title of " the Two Goddesses " which was regularly applied to them
in the great sanctuary at Eleusis without any specification of their
individual attributes and titles, as if their separate individualities
had almost merged in a single divine substance.

Surveying the evidence as a whole, we are fairly entitled to conclude that in the mind of the ordinary Greek the two goddesses were
essentially personifications of the corn, and that in this germ the whole
efflorescence of their religion finds implicitly its explanation. But to
maintain this is not to deny that in the long course of religious evolution high moral and spiritual conceptions were grafted on this simple
original stock and blossomed out into fairer flowers than the bloom of
the barley and the wheat. Above all, the thought of the seed buried
in the earth in order to spring up to new and higher life readily suggested a comparison with human destiny, and strengthened the hope
that for man too the grave may be but the beginning of a better and
happier existence in some brighter world unknown. This simple and
natural reflection seems perfectly sufficient to explain the association
of the Corn Goddess at Eleusis with the mystery of death and the
hope of a blissful immortality. For that the ancients regarded initiation in the Eleusinian mysteries as a key to unlock the gates of Paradise
appears to be proved by the allusions which well-informed writers
among them drop to the happiness in store for the initiated hereafter.
No doubt it is easy for us to discern the flimsiness of the logical foundation on which such high hopes were built. But drowning men clutch
at straws, and we need not wonder that the Greeks, like ourselves,
with death before them and a great love of life in their hearts, should
not have stopped to weigh with too nice a hand the arguments that
told for and against the prospect of human immortality. The reasoning that satisfied Saint Paul and has brought comfort to untold
thousands of sorrowing Christians, standing by the deathbed or the
open grave of their loved ones, was good enough to pass muster with
ancient pagans, when they too bowed their heads under the burden
of grief, and, with the taper of life burning low in the socket, looked
forward into the darkness of the unknown. Therefore we do no
indignity to the myth of Demeter and Persephone—one of the few
myths in which the sunshine and clarity of the Greek genius are
crossed by the shadow and mystery of death—when we trace its

origin to some of the most familiar, yet eternally affecting aspects of nature, to the melancholy gloom and decay of autumn and to the freshness, the brightness, and the verdure of spring.

CHAPTER XLV

THE CORN-MOTHER AND THE CORN-MAIDEN IN NORTHERN EUROPE

IT has been argued by W. Mannhardt that the first part of Demeter's name is derived from an alleged Cretan word *deai*, " barley," and that accordingly Demeter means neither more nor less than " Barley-mother " or " Corn-mother " ; for the root of the word seems to have been applied to different kinds of grain by different branches of the Aryans. As Crete appears to have been one of the most ancient seats of the worship of Demeter, it would not be surprising if her name were of Cretan origin. But the etymology is open to serious objections, and it is safer therefore to lay no stress on it. Be that as it may, we have found independent reasons for identifying Demeter as the Corn-mother, and of the two species of corn associated with her in Greek religion, namely barley and wheat, the barley has perhaps the better claim to be her original element ; for not only would it seem to have been the staple food of the Greeks in the Homeric age, but there are grounds for believing that it is one of the oldest, if not the very oldest, cereal cultivated by the Aryan race. Certainly the use of barley in the religious ritual of the ancient Hindoos as well as of the ancient Greeks furnishes a strong argument in favour of the great antiquity of its cultivation, which is known to have been practised by the lake-dwellers of the Stone Age in Europe.

Analogies to the Corn-mother or Barley-mother of ancient Greece have been collected in great abundance by W. Mannhardt from the folk-lore of modern Europe. The following may serve as specimens.

In Germany the corn is very commonly personified under the name of the Corn-mother. Thus in spring, when the corn waves in the wind, the peasants say, " There comes the Corn-mother," or " The Corn-mother is running over the field," or " The Corn-mother is going through the corn." When children wish to go into the fields to pull the blue corn-flowers or the red poppies, they are told not to do so, because the Corn-mother is sitting in the corn and will catch them. Or again she is called, according to the crop, the Rye-mother or the Pea-mother, and children are warned against straying in the rye or among the peas by threats of the Rye-mother or the Pea-mother. Again the Corn-mother is believed to make the crop grow. Thus in the neighbourhood of Magdeburg it is sometimes said, " It will be a good year for flax ; the Flax-mother has been seen." In a village of Styria it is said that the Corn-mother, in the shape of a female puppet made out of the last sheaf of corn and dressed in white, may be seen at midnight in the corn-fields, which she fertilises by passing through them ; but if she is angry with a farmer, she withers up all his corn.

Further, the Corn-mother plays an important part in harvest customs. She is believed to be present in the handful of corn which is left standing last on the field ; and with the cutting of this last handful she is caught, or driven away, or killed. In the first of these cases, the last sheaf is carried joyfully home and honoured as a divine being. It is placed in the barn, and at threshing the corn-spirit appears again. In the Hanoverian district of Hadeln the reapers stand round the last sheaf and beat it with sticks in order to drive the Corn-mother out of it. They call to each other, "There she is ! hit her ! Take care she doesn't catch you !" The beating goes on till the grain is completely threshed out ; then the Corn-mother is believed to be driven away. In the neighbourhood of Danzig the person who cuts the last ears of corn makes them into a doll, which is called the Corn-mother or the Old Woman and is brought home on the last waggon. In some parts of Holstein the last sheaf is dressed in woman's clothes and called the Corn-mother. It is carried home on the last waggon, and then thoroughly drenched with water. The drenching with water is doubtless a rain-charm. In the district of Bruck in Styria the last sheaf, called the Corn-mother, is made up into the shape of a woman by the oldest married woman in the village, of an age from fifty to fifty-five years. The finest ears are plucked out of it and made into a wreath, which, twined with flowers, is carried on her head by the prettiest girl of the village to the farmer or squire, while the Corn-mother is laid down in the barn to keep off the mice. In other villages of the same district the Corn-mother, at the close of harvest, is carried by two lads at the top of a pole. They march behind the girl who wears the wreath to the squire's house, and while he receives the wreath and hangs it up in the hall, the Corn-mother is placed on the top of a pile of wood, where she is the centre of the harvest supper and dance. Afterwards she is hung up in the barn and remains there till the threshing is over. The man who gives the last stroke at threshing is called the son of the Corn-mother ; he is tied up in the Corn-mother, beaten, and carried through the village. The wreath is dedicated in church on the following Sunday ; and on Easter Eve the grain is rubbed out of it by a seven-year-old girl and scattered amongst the young corn. At Christmas the straw of the wreath is placed in the manger to make the cattle thrive. Here the fertilising power of the Corn-mother is plainly brought out by scattering the seed taken from her body (for the wreath is made out of the Corn-mother) among the new corn ; and her influence over animal life is indicated by placing the straw in the manger. Amongst the Slavs also the last sheaf is known as the Rye-mother, the Wheat-mother, the Oats-mother, the Barley-mother, and so on, according to the crop. In the district of Tarnow, Galicia, the wreath made out of the last stalks is called the Wheat-mother, Rye-mother, or Pea-mother. It is placed on a girl's head and kept till spring, when some of the

grain is mixed with the seed-corn.   Here again the fertilising power of
the Corn-mother is indicated.   In France, also, in the neighbourhood
of Auxerre, the last sheaf goes by the name of the Mother of the
Wheat, Mother of the Barley, Mother of the Rye, or Mother of the
Oats.   They leave it standing in the field till the last waggon is about
to wend homewards.   Then they make a puppet out of it, dress it
with clothes belonging to the farmer, and adorn it with a crown and
a blue or white scarf.   A branch of a tree is stuck in the breast of the
puppet, which is now called the Ceres.   At the dance in the evening
the Ceres is set in the middle of the floor, and the reaper who reaped
fastest dances round it with the prettiest girl for his partner.   After
the dance a pyre is made.   All the girls, each wearing a wreath, strip
the puppet, pull it to pieces, and place it on the pyre, along with
the flowers with which it was adorned.   Then the girl who was the
first to finish reaping sets fire to the pile, and all pray that Ceres may
give a fruitful year.   Here, as Mannhardt observes, the old custom
has remained intact, though the name Ceres is a bit of schoolmaster's
learning.   In Upper Brittany the last sheaf is always made into
human shape ; but if the farmer is a married man, it is made double
and consists of a little corn-puppet placed inside of a large one.   This
is called the Mother-sheaf.   It is delivered to the farmer's wife, who
unties it and gives drink-money in return.

Sometimes the last sheaf is called, not the Corn-mother, but the
Harvest-mother or the Great Mother.   In the province of Osnabrück,
Hanover, it is called the Harvest-mother ; it is made up in female
form, and then the reapers dance about with it.   In some parts of
Westphalia the last sheaf at the rye-harvest is made especially heavy
by fastening stones in it.   They bring it home on the last waggon
and call it the Great Mother, though they do not fashion it into any
special shape.   In the district of Erfurt a very heavy sheaf, not
necessarily the last, is called the Great Mother, and is carried on the last
waggon to the barn, where all hands lift it down amid a fire of jokes.

Sometimes again the last sheaf is called the Grandmother, and is
adorned with flowers, ribbons, and a woman's apron.   In East Prussia,
at the rye or wheat harvest, the reapers call out to the woman who
binds the last sheaf, " You are getting the Old Grandmother."   In the
neighbourhood of Magdeburg the men and women servants strive
who shall get the last sheaf, called the Grandmother.   Whoever gets
it will be married in the next year, but his or her spouse will be old ;
if a girl gets it, she will marry a widower ; if a man gets it, he will
marry an old crone.   In Silesia the Grandmother—a huge bundle
made up of three or four sheaves by the person who tied the last
sheaf—was formerly fashioned into a rude likeness of the human
form.   In the neighbourhood of Belfast the last sheaf sometimes
goes by the name of the Granny.   It is not cut in the usual way, but all
the reapers throw their sickles at it and try to bring it down.   It is
plaited and kept till the (next ?) autumn.   Whoever gets it will marry
in the course of the year.

Often the last sheaf is called the Old Woman or the Old Man. In Germany it is frequently shaped and dressed as a woman, and the person who cuts it or binds it is said to " get the Old Woman." At Altisheim, in Swabia, when all the corn of a farm has been cut except a single strip, all the reapers stand in a row before the strip ; each cuts his share rapidly, and he who gives the last cut " has the Old Woman." When the sheaves are being set up in heaps, the person who gets hold of the Old Woman, which is the largest and thickest of all the sheaves, is jeered at by the rest, who call out to him, " He has the Old Woman and must keep her." The woman who binds the last sheaf is sometimes herself called the Old Woman, and it is said that she will be married in the next year. In Neusaass, West Prussia, both the last sheaf—which is dressed up in jacket, hat, and ribbons— and the woman who binds it are called the Old Woman. Together they are brought home on the last waggon and are drenched with water. In various parts of North Germany the last sheaf at harvest is made up into a human effigy and called " the Old Man " ; and the woman who bound it is said " to have the Old Man."

In West Prussia, when the last rye is being raked together, the women and girls hurry with the work, for none of them likes to be the last and to get " the Old Man," that is, a puppet made out of the last sheaf, which must be carried before the other reapers by the person who was the last to finish. In Silesia the last sheaf is called the Old Woman or the Old Man and is the theme of many jests ; it is made unusually large and is sometimes weighted with a stone. Among the Wends the man or woman who binds the last sheaf at wheat harvest is said to " have the Old Man." A puppet is made out of the wheaten straw and ears in the likeness of a man and decked with flowers. The person who bound the last sheaf must carry the Old Man home, while the rest laugh and jeer at him. The puppet is hung up in the farmhouse and remains till a new Old Man is made at the next harvest.

In some of these customs, as Mannhardt has remarked, the person who is called by the same name as the last sheaf and sits beside it on the last waggon is obviously identified with it ; he or she represents the corn-spirit which has been caught in the last sheaf ; in other words, the corn-spirit is represented in duplicate, by a human being and by a sheaf. The identification of the person with the sheaf is made still clearer by the custom of wrapping up in the last sheaf the person who cuts or binds it. Thus at Hermsdorf in Silesia it used to be the regular practice to tie up in the last sheaf the woman who had bound it. At Weiden, in Bavaria, it is the cutter, not the binder, of the last sheaf who is tied up in it. Here the person wrapt up in the corn represents the corn-spirit, exactly as a person wrapt in branches or leaves represents the tree-spirit.

The last sheaf, designated as the Old Woman, is often distinguished from the other sheaves by its size and weight. Thus in some villages of West Prussia the Old Woman is made twice as long and thick as a common sheaf, and a stone is fastened in the middle of it.   Sometimes it is made so heavy that a man can barely lift it.   At Alt-Pillau, in Samland, eight or nine sheaves are often tied together to make the Old Woman, and the man who sets it up grumbles at its weight.   At Itzgrund, in Saxe-Coburg, the last sheaf, called the Old Woman, is made large with the express intention of thereby securing a good crop next year.   Thus the custom of making the last sheaf unusually large or heavy is a charm, working by sympathetic magic, to ensure a large and heavy crop at the following harvest.

In Scotland, when the last corn was cut after Hallowmas, the female figure made out of it was sometimes called the Carlin or Carline, that is, the Old Woman.   But if cut before Hallowmas, it was called the Maiden ; if cut after sunset, it was called the Witch, being supposed to bring bad luck.   Among the Highlanders of Scotland the last corn cut at harvest is known either as the Old Wife (*Cailleach*) or as the Maiden ; on the whole the former name seems to prevail in the western and the latter in the central and eastern districts.   Of the Maiden we shall speak presently ; here we are dealing with the Old Wife. The following general account of the custom is given by a careful and well-informed enquirer, the Rev. J. G. Campbell, minister of the remote Hebridean island of Tiree : " The Harvest Old Wife (*a Chailleach*).—In harvest, there was a struggle to escape from being the last done with the shearing, and when tillage in common existed, instances were known of a ridge being left unshorn (no person would claim it) because of it being behind the rest.   The fear entertained was that of having the ' famine of the farm ' (*gort a bhaile*), in the shape of an imaginary old woman (*cailleach*), to feed till next harvest.   Much emulation and amusement arose from the fear of this old woman. . . . The first done made a doll of some blades of corn, which was called the ' old wife,' and sent it to his nearest neighbour.   He in turn, when ready, passed it to another still less expeditious, and the person it last remained with had ' the old woman ' to keep for that year."

In the island of Islay the last corn cut goes by the name of the Old Wife (*Cailleach*), and when she has done her duty at harvest she is hung up on the wall and stays there till the time comes to plough the fields for the next year's crop.   Then she is taken down, and on the first day when the men go to plough she is divided among them by the mistress of the house.   They take her in their pockets and give her to the horses to eat when they reach the field.   This is supposed to secure good luck for the next harvest, and is under-stood to be the proper end of the Old Wife.

Usages of the same sort are reported from Wales.   Thus in north Pembrokeshire a tuft of the last corn cut, from six to twelve inches long, is plaited and goes by the name of the Hag (*wrach*) ; and quaint old customs used to be practised with it within the memory of many persons still alive.   Great was the excitement among the reapers when the last patch of standing corn was reached.   All in turn threw their sickles at it, and the one who succeeded in cutting it received a jug of home-brewed ale. The Hag (*wrach*) was then hurriedly made and taken to a neighbouring farm, where the reapers were still busy at their work. This was generally done by the ploughman ; but he had to be very careful not to be observed by his neighbours, for if they saw him coming and had the least suspicion of his errand they would soon make him retrace his steps. Creeping stealthily up behind a fence he waited till the foreman of his neighbour's reapers was just opposite him and within easy reach. Then he suddenly threw the Hag over the fence and, if possible, upon the foreman's sickle. On that he took to his heels and made off as fast as he could run, and he was a lucky man if he escaped without being caught or cut by the flying sickles which the infuriated reapers hurled after him. In other cases the Hag was brought home to the farmhouse by one of the reapers. He did his best to bring it home dry and without being observed ; but he was apt to be roughly handled by the people of the house, if they suspected his errand. Sometimes they stripped him of most of his clothes, sometimes they would drench him with water which had been carefully stored in buckets and pans for the purpose. If, however, he succeeded in bringing the Hag in dry and unobserved, the master of the house had to pay him a small fine ; or sometimes a jug of beer " from the cask next to the wall," which seems to have commonly held the best beer, would be demanded by the bearer. The Hag was then carefully hung on a nail in the hall or elsewhere and kept there all the year. The custom of bringing in the Hag (*wrach*) into the house and hanging it up still exists in some farms of north Pembrokeshire, but the ancient ceremonies which have just been described are now discontinued.

In County Antrim, down to some years ago, when the sickle was finally expelled by the reaping machine, the few stalks of corn left standing last on the field were plaited together ; then the reapers, blindfolded, threw their sickles at the plaited corn, and whoever happened to cut it through took it home with him and put it over his door. This bunch of corn was called the Carley—probably the same word as Carlin.

Similar customs are observed by Slavonic peoples. Thus in Poland the last sheaf is commonly called the Baba, that is, the Old Woman. " In the last sheaf," it is said, " sits the Baba." The sheaf itself is also called the Baba, and is sometimes composed of twelve smaller sheaves lashed together. In some parts of Bohemia the Baba, made out of the last sheaf, has the figure of a woman with a great straw hat. It is carried home on the last harvest-waggon and delivered, along with a garland, to the farmer by two girls. In binding the sheaves the women strive not to be last, for she who binds the last sheaf will have a child next year. Sometimes the harvesters call out to the woman who binds the last sheaf, " She has the Baba," or " She is the Baba." In the district of Cracow, when a man binds the last sheaf, they say, " The Grandfather is sitting in it " ; when a woman binds it, they say, " The Baba is sitting in it," and the woman

herself is wrapt up in the sheaf, so that only her head projects out
of it.   Thus encased in the sheaf, she is carried on the last harvest-
waggon to the house, where she is drenched with water by the whole
family.   She remains in the sheaf till the dance is over, and for a year
she retains the name of Baba.

In Lithuania the name for the last sheaf is Boba (Old Woman),
answering to the Polish name Baba.   The Boba is said to sit in the
corn which is left standing last.   The person who binds the last
sheaf or digs the last potato is the subject of much banter, and receives
and long retains the name of the Old Rye-woman or the Old Potato-
woman.   The last sheaf—the Boba—is made into the form of a woman,
carried solemnly through the village on the last harvest-waggon,
and drenched with water at the farmer's house ; then every one
dances with it.

In Russia also the last sheaf is often shaped and dressed as a
woman, and carried with dance and song to the farmhouse.   Out of
the last sheaf the Bulgarians make a doll which they call the Corn-
queen or Corn-mother ; it is dressed in a woman's shirt, carried
round the village, and then thrown into the river in order to secure
plenty of rain and dew for the next year's crop.   Or it is burned and
the ashes strewn on the fields, doubtless to fertilise them.   The name
Queen, as applied to the last sheaf, has its analogies in Central and
Northern Europe.   Thus, in the Salzburg district of Austria, at the
end of the harvest a great procession takes place, in which a Queen
of the Corn-ears (*Ährenkönigin*) is drawn along in a little carriage by
young fellows.   The custom of the Harvest Queen appears to have
been common in England.   Milton must have been familiar with it,
for in *Paradise Lost* he says :

> "*Adam the while*
> *Waiting desirous her return, had wove*
> *Of choicest flow'rs a garland to adorn*
> *Her tresses, and her rural labours crown,*
> *As reapers oft are wont their harvest-queen.*"

Often customs of this sort are practised, not on the harvest-field
but on the threshing-floor.   The spirit of the corn, fleeing before the
reapers as they cut down the ripe grain, quits the reaped corn and
takes refuge in the barn, where it appears in the last sheaf threshed,
either to perish under the blows of the flail or to flee thence to the still
unthreshed corn of a neighbouring farm.   Thus the last corn to be
threshed is called the Mother-Corn or the Old Woman.   Sometimes
the person who gives the last stroke with the flail is called the Old
Woman, and is wrapt in the straw of the last sheaf, or has a bundle
of straw fastened on his back.   Whether wrapt in the straw or carrying
it on his back, he is carted through the village amid general laughter.
In some districts of Bavaria, Thüringen, and elsewhere, the man
who threshes the last sheaf is said to have the Old Woman or the
Old Corn-woman ; he is tied up in straw, carried or carted about the

village, and set down at last on the dunghill, or taken to the threshing-floor of a neighbouring farmer who has not finished his threshing. In Poland the man who gives the last stroke at threshing is called Baba (Old Woman) ; he is wrapt in corn and wheeled through the village. Sometimes in Lithuania the last sheaf is not threshed, but is fashioned into female shape and carried to the barn of a neighbour who has not finished his threshing.

In some parts of Sweden, when a stranger woman appears on the threshing-floor, a flail is put round her body, stalks of corn are wound round her neck, a crown of ears is placed on her head, and the threshers call out, " Behold the Corn-woman." Here the stranger woman, thus suddenly appearing, is taken to be the corn-spirit who has just been expelled by the flails from the corn-stalks. In other cases the farmer's wife represents the corn-spirit. Thus in the Commune of Saligné (Vendée), the farmer's wife, along with the last sheaf, is tied up in a sheet, placed on a litter, and carried to the threshing machine, under which she is shoved. Then the woman is drawn out and the sheaf is threshed by itself, but the woman is tossed in the sheet, as if she were being winnowed. It would be impossible to express more clearly the identification of the woman with the corn than by this graphic imitation of threshing and winnowing her.

In these customs the spirit of the ripe corn is regarded as old, or at least as of mature age. Hence the names of Mother, Grandmother Old Woman, and so forth. But in other cases the corn-spirit is conceived as young. Thus at Saldern, near Wolfenbuttel, when the rye has been reaped, three sheaves are tied together with a rope so as to make a puppet with the corn ears for a head. This puppet is called the Maiden or the Corn-maiden. Sometimes the corn-spirit is conceived as a child who is separated from its mother by the stroke of the sickle. This last view appears in the Polish custom of calling out to the man who cuts the last handful of corn, " You have cut the navel-string." In some districts of West Prussia the figure made out of the last sheaf is called the Bastard, and a boy is wrapt up in it. The woman who binds the last sheaf and represents the Corn-mother is told that she is about to be brought to bed ; she cries like a woman in travail, and an old woman in the character of grandmother acts as midwife. At last a cry is raised that the child is born ; whereupon the boy who is tied up in the sheaf whimpers and squalls like an infant. The grandmother wraps a sack, in imitation of swaddling bands, round the pretended baby, who is carried joyfully to the barn, lest he should catch cold in the open air. In other parts of North Germany the last sheaf, or the puppet made out of it, is called the Child, the Harvest-Child, and so on, and they call out to the woman who binds the last sheaf, " You are getting the child."

In some parts of Scotland, as well as in the north of England, the last handful of corn cut on the harvest-field was called the *kirn*, and the person who carried it off was said " to win the kirn." It was then dressed up like a child's doll and went by the name of the kirn-baby, the kirn-doll, or the Maiden. In Berwickshire down to about the middle of the nineteenth century there was an eager competition among the reapers to cut the last bunch of standing corn. They gathered round it at a little distance and threw their sickles in turn at it, and the man who succeeded in cutting it through gave it to the girl he preferred. She made the corn so cut into a kirn-dolly and dressed it, and the doll was then taken to the farm-house and hung up there till the next harvest, when its place was taken by the new kirn-dolly. At Spottiswoode in Berwickshire the reaping of the last corn at harvest was called " cutting the Queen " almost as often as " cutting the kirn." The mode of cutting it was not by throwing sickles. One of the reapers consented to be blind-folded, and having been given a sickle in his hand and turned twice or thrice about by his fellows, he was bidden to go and cut the kirn. His groping about and making wild strokes in the air with his sickle excited much hilarity. When he had tired himself out in vain and given up the task as hopeless, another reaper was blindfolded and pursued the quest, and so on, one after the other, till at last the kirn was cut. The successful reaper was tossed up in the air with three cheers by his brother harvesters. To decorate the room in which the kirn-supper was held at Spottiswoode as well as the granary, where the dancing took place, two women made kirn-dollies or Queens every year ; and many of these rustic effigies of the corn-spirit might be seen hanging up together.

In some parts of the Highlands of Scotland the last handful of corn that is cut by the reapers on any particular farm is called the Maiden, or in Gaelic *Maidhdeanbuain*, literally " the shorn Maiden." Superstitions attach to the winning of the Maiden. If it is got by a young person, they think it an omen that he or she will be married before another harvest. For that or other reasons there is a strife between the reapers as to who shall get the Maiden, and they resort to various stratagems for the purpose of securing it. One of them, for example, will often leave a handful of corn uncut and cover it up with earth to hide it from the other reapers, till all the rest of the corn on the field is cut down. Several may try to play the same trick, and the one who is coolest and holds out longest obtains the coveted distinction. When it has been cut, the Maiden is dressed with ribbons into a sort of doll and affixed to a wall of the farmhouse. In the north of Scotland the Maiden is carefully preserved till Yule morning, when it is divided among the cattle " to make them thrive all the year round." In the neighbourhood of Balquhidder, Perth-shire, the last handful of corn is cut by the youngest girl on the field, and is made into the rude form of a female doll, clad in a paper dress, and decked with ribbons. It is called the Maiden, and is kept in the farmhouse, generally above the chimney, for a good while, some-times till the Maiden of the next year is brought in. The writer of this book witnessed the ceremony of cutting the Maiden at Balquhidder in September 1888. A lady friend informed me that as a young girl she cut the Maiden several times at the request of the reapers in the neighbourhood of Perth. The name of the Maiden was given to the last handful of standing corn ; a reaper held the top of the bunch while she cut it. Afterwards the bunch was plaited, decked with ribbons, and hung up in a conspicuous place on the wall of the kitchen till the next Maiden was brought in. The harvest-supper in this neighbourhood was also called the Maiden ; the reapers danced at it.

On some farms on the Gareloch, in Dumbartonshire, about the year 1830, the last handful of standing corn was called the Maiden. It was divided in two, plaited, and then cut with the sickle by a girl, who, it was thought, would be lucky and would soon be married. When it was cut the reapers gathered together and threw their sickles in the air. The Maiden was dressed with ribbons and hung in the kitchen near the roof, where it was kept for several years with the date attached. Sometimes five or six Maidens might be seen hanging at once on hooks. The harvest-supper was called the Kirn. In other farms on the Gareloch the last handful of corn was called the Maidenhead or the Head ; it was neatly plaited, sometimes decked with ribbons, and hung in the kitchen for a year, when the grain was given to the poultry.

In Aberdeenshire " the last sheaf cut, or ' Maiden,' is carried home in merry procession by the harvesters. It is then presented to the mistress of the house, who dresses it up to be preserved till the first mare foals. The Maiden is then taken down and presented to the mare as its first food. The neglect of this would have untoward effects upon the foal, and disastrous consequences upon farm operations generally for the season." In the north-east of Aberdeenshire the last sheaf is commonly called the *clyack* sheaf. It used to be cut by the youngest girl present and was dressed as a woman. Being brought home in triumph, it was kept till Christmas morning, and then given to a mare in foal, if there was one on the farm, or, if there was not, to the oldest cow in calf. Elsewhere the sheaf was divided between all the cows and their calves or between all the horses and the cattle of the farm. In Fifeshire the last handful of corn, known as the Maiden, is cut by a young girl and made into the rude figure of a doll, tied with ribbons, by which it is hung on the wall of the farm-kitchen till the next spring. The custom of cutting the Maiden at harvest was also observed in Inverness-shire and Sutherlandshire.

A somewhat maturer but still youthful age is assigned to the corn-spirit by the appellations of Bride, Oats-bride, and Wheat-bride, which in Germany are sometimes bestowed both on the last sheaf and on the woman who binds it. At wheat-harvest near Müglitz, in Moravia, a small portion of the wheat is left standing after all the rest has been reaped. This remnant is then cut, amid the rejoicing of the reapers, by a young girl who wears a wreath of wheaten ears on her head and goes by the name of the Wheat-bride. It is supposed that she will be a real bride that same year. Near Roslin and Stonehaven, in Scotland, the last handful of corn cut " got the name of ' the bride,' and she was placed over the *bress* or chimney-piece ; she had a ribbon tied below her numerous *ears*, and another round her waist."

Sometimes the idea implied by the name of Bride is worked out more fully by representing the productive powers of vegetation as bride and bridegroom. Thus in the Vorharz an Oats-man and an Oats-woman, swathed in straw, dance at the harvest feast. In South Saxony an Oats-bridegroom and an Oats-bride figure together at the harvest celebration. The Oats-bridegroom is a man completely wrapt in oats-straw ; the Oats-bride is a man dressed in woman's clothes, but not wrapt in straw. They are drawn in a waggon to the ale-house, where the dance takes place. At the beginning of the dance the dancers pluck the bunches of oats one by one from the Oats-bridegroom, while he struggles to keep them, till at last he is completely stript of them and stands bare, exposed to the laughter and jests of the company. In Austrian Silesia the ceremony of " the Wheat-bride " is celebrated by the young people at the end of the harvest. The woman who bound the last sheaf plays the part of the Wheat-bride, wearing the harvest-crown of wheat ears and flowers on her head. Thus adorned, standing beside her Bridegroom in a waggon and attended by brides-maids, she is drawn by a pair of oxen, in full imitation of a marriage procession, to the tavern, where the dancing is kept up till morning. Somewhat later in the season the wedding of the Oats-bride is celebrated with the like rustic pomp. About Neisse, in Silesia, an Oats-king and an Oats-queen, dressed up quaintly as a bridal pair, are seated on a harrow and drawn by oxen into the village.

In these last instances the corn-spirit is personified in double form as male and female. But sometimes the spirit appears in a double female form as both old and young, corresponding exactly to the Greek Demeter and Persephone, if my interpretation of these goddesses is right. We have seen that in Scotland, especially among the Gaelic-speaking population, the last corn cut is sometimes called the Old Wife and sometimes the Maiden. Now there are parts of Scotland in which both an Old Wife (*Cailleach*) and a Maiden are cut at harvest. The accounts of this custom are not quite clear and consistent, but the general rule seems to be that, where both a Maiden and an Old Wife (*Cailleach*) are fashioned out of the reaped corn at harvest, the Maiden is made out of the last stalks left standing, and is kept by the farmer on whose land it was cut ; while the Old Wife is made out of other stalks, sometimes out of the first stalks cut, and is regularly passed on to a laggard farmer who happens to be still reaping after his brisker neighbour has cut all his corn. Thus while each farmer keeps his own Maiden, as the embodiment of the young and fruitful spirit of the corn, he passes on the Old Wife as soon as he can to a neighbour, and so the old lady may make the round of all the farms in the district before she finds a place in which to lay her venerable head. The farmer with whom she finally takes up her abode is of course the one who has been the last of all the countryside to finish reaping his crops, and thus the distinction of entertaining her is rather an invidious one. He is

thought to be doomed to poverty or to be under the obligation of
" providing for the dearth of the township " in the ensuing season.
Similarly we saw that in Pembrokeshire, where the last corn cut is
called, not the Maiden, but the Hag, she is passed on hastily to a
neighbour who is still at work in his fields and who receives his aged
visitor with anything but a transport of joy.   If the Old Wife represents the corn-spirit of the past year, as she probably does wherever
she is contrasted with and opposed to a Maiden, it is natural enough
that her faded charms should have less attractions for the husbandman
than the buxom form of her daughter, who may be expected to become
in her turn the mother of the golden grain when the revolving year has
brought round another autumn.   The same desire to get rid of the
effete Mother of the Corn by palming her off on other people comes
out clearly in some of the customs observed at the close of threshing,
particularly in the practice of passing on a hideous straw puppet to a
neighbour farmer who is still threshing his corn.

The harvest customs just described are strikingly analogous to the
spring customs which we reviewed in an earlier part of this work.
(1) As in the spring customs the tree-spirit is represented both by a tree
and by a person, so in the harvest customs the corn-spirit is represented
both by the last sheaf and by the person who cuts or binds or threshes
it.   The equivalence of the person to the sheaf is shown by giving him
or her the same name as the sheaf ; by wrapping him or her in it ; and
by the rule observed in some places, that when the sheaf is called the
Mother, it must be made up into human shape by the oldest married
woman, but that when it is called the Maiden, it must be cut by the
youngest girl.   Here the age of the personal representative of the
corn-spirit corresponds with that of the supposed age of the corn-
spirit, just as the human victims offered by the Mexicans to promote
the growth of the maize varied with the age of the maize.   For in the
Mexican, as in the European, custom the human beings were probably
representatives of the corn-spirit rather than victims offered to it.
(2) Again, the same fertilising influence which the tree-spirit is supposed
to exert over vegetation, cattle, and even women is ascribed to the
corn-spirit.   Thus, its supposed influence on vegetation is shown by
the practice of taking some of the grain of the last sheaf (in which the
corn-spirit is regularly supposed to be present) and scattering it among
the young corn in spring or mixing it with the seed-corn.   Its influence
on animals is shown by giving the last sheaf to a mare in foal, to a cow
in calf, and to horses at the first ploughing.   Lastly, its influence on
women is indicated by the custom of delivering the Mother-sheaf,
made into the likeness of a pregnant woman, to the farmer's wife ;
by the belief that the woman who binds the last sheaf will have a
child next year ; perhaps, too, by the idea that the person who gets
it will soon be married.

Plainly, therefore, these spring and harvest customs are based on
the same ancient modes of thought, and form parts of the same primitive
heathendom, which was doubtless practised by our forefathers long

before the dawn of history.   Amongst the marks of a primitive ritual
we may note the following :

1. No special class of persons is set apart for the performance of
the rites ; in other words, there are no priests.   The rites may be
performed by any one, as occasion demands.

2. No special places are set apart for the performance of the rites ;
in other words, there are no temples.   The rites may be performed
anywhere, as occasion demands.

3. Spirits, not gods, are recognised.   (a) As distinguished from
gods, spirits are restricted in their operations to definite departments
of nature.   Their names are general, not proper.   Their attributes are
generic, rather than individual ; in other words, there is an indefinite
number of spirits of each class, and the individuals of a class are all
much alike ; they have no definitely marked individuality ; no
accepted traditions are current as to their origin, life, adventures, and
character.   (b) On the other hand gods, as distinguished from spirits,
are not restricted to definite departments of nature.   It is true that
there is generally some one department over which they preside as
their special province ; but they are not rigorously confined to it ;
they can exert their power for good or evil in many other spheres of
nature and life.   Again, they bear individual or proper names, such
as Demeter, Persephone, Dionysus ; and their individual characters
and histories are fixed by current myths and the representations of art.

4. The rites are magical rather than propitiatory.   In other words,
the desired objects are attained, not by propitiating the favour of
divine beings through sacrifice, prayer, and praise, but by ceremonies
which, as I have already explained, are believed to influence the course
of nature directly through a physical sympathy or resemblance between
the rite and the effect which it is the intention of the rite to produce.

Judged by these tests, the spring and harvest customs of our
European peasantry deserve to rank as primitive.   For no special
class of persons and no special places are set exclusively apart for their
performance ; they may be performed by any one, master or man,
mistress or maid, boy or girl ; they are practised, not in temples or
churches, but in the woods and meadows, beside brooks, in barns, on
harvest fields and cottage floors.   The supernatural beings whose
existence is taken for granted in them are spirits rather than deities :
their functions are limited to certain well-defined departments of
nature : their names are general, like the Barley-mother, the Old
Woman, the Maiden, not proper names like Demeter, Persephone,
Dionysus.   Their generic attributes are known, but their individual
histories and characters are not the subject of myths.   For they exist
in classes rather than as individuals, and the members of each class
are indistinguishable.   For example, every farm has its Corn-mother,
or its Old Woman, or its Maiden ; but every Corn-mother is much
like every other Corn-mother, and so with the Old Women and Maidens.
Lastly, in these harvest, as in the spring customs, the ritual is magical
rather than propitiatory.   This is shown by throwing the Corn-mother

into the river in order to secure rain and dew for the crops ; by making the Old Woman heavy in order to get a heavy crop next year ; by strewing grain from the last sheaf amongst the young crops in spring ; and by giving the last sheaf to the cattle to make them thrive.

CHAPTER XLVI

THE CORN-MOTHER IN MANY LANDS

§ 1. *The Corn-mother in America.*—European peoples, ancient and modern, have not been singular in personifying the corn as a mother goddess. The same simple idea has suggested itself to other agricultural races in distant parts of the world, and has been applied by them to other indigenous cereals than barley and wheat. If Europe has its Wheat-mother and its Barley-mother, America has its Maize-mother and the East Indies their Rice-mother. These personifications I will now illustrate, beginning with the American personification of the maize.

We have seen that among European peoples it is a common custom to keep the plaited corn-stalks of the last sheaf, or the puppet which is formed out of them, in the farm-house from harvest to harvest. The intention no doubt is, or rather originally was, by preserving the representative of the corn-spirit to maintain the spirit itself in life and activity throughout the year, in order that the corn may grow and the crops be good. This interpretation of the custom is at all events rendered highly probable by a similar custom observed by the ancient Peruvians, and thus described by the old Spanish historian Acosta : " They take a certain portion of the most fruitful of the maize that grows in their farms, the which they put in a certain granary which they do call *Pirua*, with certain ceremonies, watching three nights ; they put this maize in the richest garments they have, and being thus wrapped and dressed, they worship this *Pirua*, and hold it in great veneration, saying it is the mother of the maize of their inheritances, and that by this means the maize augments and is preserved. In this month [the sixth month, answering to May] they make a particular sacrifice, and the witches demand of this *Pirua* if it hath strength sufficient to continue until the next year ; and if it answers no, then they carry this maize to the farm to burn, whence they brought it, according to every man's power ; then they make another *Pirua*, with the same ceremonies, saying that they renew it, to the end the seed of maize may not perish, and if it answers that it hath force sufficient to last longer, they leave it until the next year. This foolish vanity continueth to this day, and it is very common amongst the Indians to have these *Piruas*."

In this description of the custom there seems to be some error. Probably it was the dressed-up bunch of maize, not the granary

(*Pirua*), which was worshipped by the Peruvians and regarded as the Mother of the Maize. This is confirmed by what we know of the Peruvian custom from another source. The Peruvians, we are told, believed all useful plants to be animated by a divine being who causes their growth. According to the particular plant, these divine beings were called the Maize-mother (*Zara-mama*), the Quinoa-mother (*Quinoa-mama*), the Coca-mother (*Coca-mama*), and the Potato-mother (*Axo-mama*). Figures of these divine mothers were made respectively of ears of maize and leaves of the quinoa and coca plants ; they were dressed in women's clothes and worshipped. Thus the Maize-mother was represented by a puppet made of stalks of maize dressed in full female attire ; and the Indians believed that " as mother, it had the power of producing and giving birth to much maize." Probably, therefore, Acosta misunderstood his informant, and the Mother of the Maize which he describes was not the granary (*Pirua*), but the bunch of maize dressed in rich vestments. The Peruvian Mother of the Maize, like the harvest-Maiden at Balquhidder, was kept for a year in order that by her means the corn might grow and multiply. But lest her strength might not suffice to last till the next harvest, she was asked in the course of the year how she felt, and if she answered that she felt weak, she was burned and a fresh Mother of the Maize made, " to the end the seed of maize may not perish." Here, it may be observed, we have a strong confirmation of the explanation already given of the custom of killing the god, both periodically and occasionally. The Mother of the Maize was allowed, as a rule, to live through a year, that being the period during which her strength might reasonably be supposed to last unimpaired ; but on any symptom of her strength failing she was put to death, and a fresh and vigorous Mother of the Maize took her place, lest the maize which depended on her for its existence should languish and decay.

§ 2. *The Rice-mother in the East Indies.*—If the reader still feels any doubts as to the meaning of the harvest customs which have been practised within living memory by European peasants, these doubts may perhaps be dispelled by comparing the customs observed at the rice-harvest by the Malays and Dyaks of the East Indies. For these Eastern peoples have not, like our peasantry, advanced beyond the intellectual stage at which the customs originated ; their theory and their practice are still in unison ; for them the quaint rites which in Europe have long dwindled into mere fossils, the pastime of clowns and the puzzle of the learned, are still living realities of which they can render an intelligible and truthful account. Hence a study of their beliefs and usages concerning the rice may throw some light on the true meaning of the ritual of the corn in ancient Greece and modern Europe.

Now the whole of the ritual which the Malays and Dyaks observe in connexion with the rice is founded on the simple conception of the rice as animated by a soul like that which these people attribute to mankind. They explain the phenomena of reproduction, growth, decay, and death in the rice on the same principles on which they explain the corresponding phenomena in human beings. They imagine that in the fibres of the plant, as in the body of a man, there is a certain vital element, which is so far independent of the plant that it may for a time be completely separated from it without fatal effects, though if its absence be prolonged beyond certain limits the plant will wither and die. This vital yet separable element is what, for the want of a better word, we must call the soul of a plant, just as a similar vital and separable element is commonly supposed to constitute the soul of man ; and on this theory or myth of the plant-soul is built the whole worship of the cereals, just as on the theory or myth of the human soul is built the whole worship of the dead,—a towering superstructure reared on a slender and precarious foundation.

Believing the rice to be animated by a soul like that of a man, the Indonesians naturally treat it with the deference and the consideration which they show to their fellows. Thus they behave towards the rice in bloom as they behave towards a pregnant woman ; they abstain from firing guns or making loud noises in the field, lest they should so frighten the soul of the rice that it would miscarry and bear no grain ; and for the same reason they will not talk of corpses or demons in the rice-fields. Moreover, they feed the blooming rice with foods of various kinds which are believed to be wholesome for women with child ; but when the rice-ears are just beginning to form, they are looked upon as infants, and women go through the fields feeding them with rice-pap as if they were human babes. In such natural and obvious comparisons of the breeding plant to a breeding woman, and of the young grain to a young child, is to be sought the origin of the kindred Greek conception of the Corn-mother and the Corn-daughter, Demeter and Persephone. But if the timorous feminine soul of the rice can be frightened into a miscarriage even by loud noises, it is easy to imagine what her feelings must be at harvest, when people are under the sad necessity of cutting down the rice with the knife. At so critical a season every precaution must be used to render the necessary surgical operation of reaping as inconspicuous and as painless as possible. For that reason the reaping of the seed-rice is done with knives of a peculiar pattern, such that the blades are hidden in the reapers' hands and do not frighten the rice-spirit till the very last moment, when her head is swept off almost before she is aware ; and from a like delicate motive the reapers at work in the fields employ a special form of speech, which the rice-spirit cannot be expected to understand, so that she has no warning or inkling of what is going forward till the heads of rice are safely deposited in the basket.

Among the Indonesian peoples who thus personify the rice we may take the Kayans or Bahaus of Central Borneo as typical. In order to secure and detain the volatile soul of the rice the Kayans resort to a number of devices. Among the instruments employed for this purpose are a miniature ladder, a spatula, and a basket containing hooks, thorns, and cords. With the spatula the priestess strokes the soul of the rice down the little ladder into the basket, where it is naturally held fast by the hooks, the thorn, and the cord ; and having thus captured and imprisoned the soul she conveys it into the rice-granary. Sometimes a bamboo box and a net are used for the same purpose. And in order to ensure a good harvest for the following year it is necessary not only to detain the soul of all the grains of rice which are safely stored in the granary, but also to attract and recover the soul of all the rice that has been lost through falling to the earth or being eaten by deer, apes, and pigs. For this purpose instruments of various sorts have been invented by the priests. One, for example, is a bamboo vessel provided with four hooks made from the wood of a fruit-tree, by means of which the absent rice-soul may be hooked and drawn back into the vessel, which is then hung up in the house. Sometimes two hands carved out of the wood of a fruit-tree are used for the same purpose. And every time that a Kayan housewife fetches rice from the granary for the use of her household, she must propitiate the souls of the rice in the granary, lest they should be angry at being robbed of their substance.

The same need of securing the soul of the rice, if the crop is to thrive, is keenly felt by the Karens of Burma. When a rice-field does not flourish, they suppose that the soul (*kelah*) of the rice is in some way detained from the rice. If the soul cannot be called back, the crop will fail. The following formula is used in recalling the *kelah* (soul) of the rice : " O come, rice-*kelah*, come ! Come to the field. Come to the rice. With seed of each gender, come. Come from the river Kho, come from the river Kaw ; from the place where they meet, come. Come from the West, come from the East. From the throat of the bird, from the maw of the ape, from the throat of the elephant. Come from the sources of rivers and their mouths. Come from the country of the Shan and Burman. From the distant kingdoms come. From all granaries come. O rice-*kelah*, come to the rice."

The Corn-mother of our European peasants has her match in the Rice-mother of the Minangkabauers of Sumatra. The Minangkabauers definitely attribute a soul to rice, and will sometimes assert that rice pounded in the usual way tastes better than rice ground in a mill, because in the mill the body of the rice was so bruised and battered that the soul has fled from it. Like the Javanese they think that the rice is under the special guardianship of a female spirit called Saning Sari, who is conceived as so closely knit up with the plant that the rice often goes by her name, as with the Romans the corn might be called Ceres. In particular Saning Sari is represented by certain stalks or grains called *indoea padi*, that is, literally, " Mother of Rice," a name that is often given to the guardian spirit herself. This so-called Mother of Rice is the occasion of a number of ceremonies observed at the planting and harvesting of the rice as well as during its preservation in the barn. When the seed of the rice is about to be sown in the nursery or bedding-out ground, where under the wet system of cultivation it is regularly allowed to sprout before being transplanted to the fields, the best grains are picked out to form the Rice-mother. These are then sown in the middle of the bed, and the common seed is planted round about them. The state of the Rice-mother is supposed to exert the greatest influence on the growth of the rice ; if she droops or pines away, the harvest will be bad in consequence. The woman who sows the Rice-mother in the nursery lets her hair hang loose and afterwards bathes, as a means of ensuring an abundant harvest. When the time comes to transplant the rice from the nursery to the field, the Rice-mother receives a special place either in the middle or in a corner of the field, and a prayer or charm is uttered as follows : " Saning Sari, may a measure of rice come from a stalk of rice and a basketful from a root ; may you be frightened neither by lightning nor by passers-by ! Sunshine make you glad ; with the storm may you be at peace ; and may rain serve to wash your face ! " While the rice is growing, the particular plant which was thus treated as the Rice-mother is lost sight of ; but before harvest another Rice-mother is found. When the crop is ripe for cutting, the oldest woman of the family or a sorcerer goes out to look for her. The first stalks seen to bend under a passing breeze are the Rice-mother, and they are tied together but not cut until the first-fruits of the field have been carried home to serve as a festal meal for the family and their friends, nay even for the domestic animals ; since it is Saning Sari's pleasure that the beasts also should partake of her good gifts. After the meal has been eaten, the Rice-mother is fetched home by persons in gay attire, who carry her very carefully under an umbrella in a neatly worked bag to the barn, where a place in the middle is assigned to her. Every one believes that she takes care of the rice in the barn and even multiplies it not uncommonly.

When the Tomori of Central Celebes are about to plant the rice, they bury in the field some betel as an offering to the spirits who cause the rice to grow. The rice that is planted round this spot is the last to be reaped at harvest. At the commencement of the reaping the stalks of this patch of rice are tied together into a sheaf, which is called " the Mother of the Rice " (*ineno pae*), and offerings in the shape of rice, fowl's liver, eggs, and other things are laid down before it. When all the rest of the rice in the field has been reaped, " the Mother of the Rice " is cut down and carried with due honour to the rice-barn, where it is laid on the floor, and all the other sheaves are piled upon it. The Tomori, we are told, regard the Mother of the Rice as a special offering made to the rice-spirit Omonga, who dwells in the moon. If that spirit is not treated with proper respect, for example if the people who fetch rice from the barn are not decently clad, he is angry and punishes the offenders by eating up twice as much rice in the barn as they have taken out of it ; some people have heard him smacking his lips in the barn, as he devoured the rice. On the other hand the Toradjas of Central Celebes, who also practise the custom of the Rice-mother at harvest, regard her as the actual mother of the whole harvest, and therefore keep her carefully, lest in her absence the garnered store of rice should all melt away and disappear.

Again, just as in Scotland the old and the young spirit of the corn are represented as an Old Wife (*Cailleach*) and a Maiden respectively, so in the Malay Peninsula we find both the Rice-mother and her child represented by different sheaves or bundles of ears on the harvest-field. The ceremony of cutting and bringing home the Soul of the Rice was witnessed by Mr. W. W. Skeat at Chodoi in Selangor on the twenty-eighth of January 1897. The particular bunch or sheaf which was to serve as the Mother of the Rice-soul had previously been sought and identified by means of the markings or shape of the ears. From this sheaf an aged sorceress, with much solemnity, cut a little bundle of seven ears, anointed them with oil, tied them round with parti-coloured thread, fumigated them with incense, and having wrapt them in a white cloth deposited them in a little oval-shaped basket. These seven ears were the infant Soul of the Rice and the little basket was its cradle. It was carried home to the farmer's house by another woman, who held up an umbrella to screen the tender infant from the hot rays of the sun. Arrived at the house the Rice-child was welcomed by the women of the family, and laid, cradle and all, on a new sleeping-mat with pillows at the head. After that the farmer's wife was instructed to observe certain rules of taboo for three days, the rules being in many respect identical with those which have to be observed for three days after the birth of a real child. Something of the same tender care which is thus bestowed on the newly-born Rice-child is naturally extended also to its parent, the sheaf from whose body it was taken. This sheaf, which remains standing in the field after the Rice-soul has been carried home and put to bed, is treated as a newly-made mother; that is to say, young shoots of trees are pounded together and scattered broadcast every evening for three successive days, and when the three days are up you take the pulp of a coco-nut and what are called " goat-flowers," mix them up, eat them with a little sugar, and spit some of the mixture out among the rice. So after a real birth the young shoots of the jack-fruit, the rose-apple, certain kinds of banana, and the thin pulp of young coco-nuts are mixed with dried fish, salt, acid, prawn-condiment, and the like dainties to form a sort of salad, which is administered to mother and child for three successive days. The last sheaf is reaped by the farmer's wife, who carries it back to the house, where it is threshed and mixed with the Rice-soul. The farmer then takes the Rice-soul and its basket and deposits it, together with the product of the last sheaf, in the big circular rice-bin used by the Malays. Some grains from the Rice-soul are mixed with the seed which is to be sown in the following year. In this Rice-mother and Rice-child of the Malay Peninsula we may see the counterpart and in a sense the prototype of the Demeter and Persephone of ancient Greece.

Once more, the European custom of representing the corn-spirit in the double form of bride and bridegroom has its parallel in a ceremony observed at the rice-harvest in Java. Before the reapers begin to cut the rice, the priest or sorcerer picks out a number of ears of rice, which are tied together, smeared with ointment, and adorned with flowers. Thus decked out, the ears are called the *padi-pĕngantèn*, that is, the Rice-bride and the Rice-bridegroom ; their wedding feast is celebrated, and the cutting of the rice begins immediately afterwards. Later on, when the rice is being got in, a bridal chamber is partitioned off in the barn, and furnished with a new mat, a lamp, and all kinds of toilet articles. Sheaves of rice, to represent the wedding guests, are placed beside the Rice-bride and the Rice-bridegroom. Not till this has been done may the whole harvest be housed in the barn. And for the first forty days after the rice has been housed, no one may enter the barn, for fear of disturbing the newly-wedded pair.

In the islands of Bali and Lombok, when the time of harvest has come, the owner of the field himself makes a beginning by cutting " the principal rice " with his own hands and binding it into two sheaves, each composed of one hundred and eight stalks with their leaves attached to them. One of the sheaves represents a man and the other a woman, and they are called " husband and wife." The male sheaf is wound about with thread so that none of the leaves are visible, whereas the female sheaf has its leaves bent over and tied so as to resemble the roll of a woman's hair. Sometimes, for further distinction, a necklace of rice-straw is tied round the female sheaf. When the rice is brought home from the field, the two sheaves representing the husband and wife are carried by a woman on her head, and are the last of all to be deposited in the barn. There they are laid to rest on a small erection or on a cushion of rice-straw. The whole arrangement, we are informed, has for its object to induce the rice to increase and multiply in the granary, so that the owner may get more out of it than he put in. Hence when the people of Bali bring the two sheaves, the husband and wife, into the barn, they say, " Increase ye and multiply without ceasing." When all the rice in the barn has been used up, the two sheaves representing the husband and wife remain in the empty building till they have gradually disappeared or been devoured by mice. The pinch of hunger sometimes drives individuals to eat up the rice of these two sheaves, but the wretches who do so are viewed with disgust by their fellows and branded as pigs and dogs. Nobody would ever sell these holy sheaves with the rest of their profane brethren.

The same notion of the propagation of the rice by a male and female power finds expression amongst the Szis of Upper Burma. When the paddy, that is, the rice with the husks still on it, has been dried and piled in a heap for threshing, all the friends of the household are invited to the threshing-floor, and food and drink are brought out. The heap of paddy is divided and one half spread out for threshing, while the other half is left piled up. On the pile food and spirits are set; and one of the elders, addressing " the father and mother of the paddy-plant," prays for plenteous harvests in future, and begs that the seed may bear many fold.   Then the whole party eat, drink, and make merry.   This ceremony at the threshing-floor is the only occasion when these people invoke " the father and mother of the paddy."

§ 3. *The Spirit of the Corn embodied in Human Beings.*—Thus the theory which recognises in the European Corn-mother, Corn-maiden, and so forth, the embodiment in vegetable form of the animating spirit of the crops is amply confirmed by the evidence of peoples in other parts of the world, who, because they have lagged behind the European races in mental development, retain for that very reason a keener sense of the original motives for observing those rustic rites which among ourselves have sunk to the level of meaningless survivals. The reader may, however, remember that according to Mannhardt, whose theory I am expounding, the spirit of the corn manifests itself not merely in vegetable but also in human form ; the person who cuts the last sheaf or gives the last stroke at threshing passes for a temporary embodiment of the corn-spirit, just as much as the bunch of corn which he reaps or threshes.   Now in the parallels which have been hitherto adduced from the customs of peoples outside Europe the spirit of the crops appears only in vegetable form.   It remains, therefore, to prove that other races besides our European peasantry have conceived the spirit of the crops as incorporate in or represented by living men and women.   Such a proof, I may remind the reader, is germane to the theme of this book ; for the more instances we discover of human beings representing in themselves the life or animating spirit of plants, the less difficulty will be felt at classing amongst them the King of the Wood at Nemi.

The Mandans and Minnitarees of North America used to hold a festival in spring which they called the corn-medicine festival of the women.   They thought that a certain Old Woman who Never Dies made the crops to grow, and that, living somewhere in the south, she sent the migratory waterfowl in spring as her tokens and representatives.   Each sort of bird represented a special kind of crop cultivated by the Indians : the wild goose stood for the maize, the wild swan for the gourds, and the wild duck for the beans.   So when the feathered messengers of the Old Woman began to arrive in spring the Indians celebrated the corn-medicine festival of the women.   Scaffolds were set up, on which the people hung dried meat and other things by way of offerings to the Old Woman ; and on a certain day the old women of the tribe, as representatives of the Old Woman who Never Dies, assembled at the scaffolds each bearing in her hand an ear of maize fastened to a stick.   They first planted these sticks in the ground, then danced round the scaffolds, and finally took up the sticks again in their arms.   Meanwhile old men beat drums and shook rattles as a musical accompaniment to the performance of the old women.   Further, young women came and put dried flesh into the mouths of the old women, for which they received in return a grain of the consecrated

maize to eat.   Three or four grains of the holy corn were also placed
in the dishes of the young women, to be afterwards carefully mixed
with the seed-corn, which they were supposed to fertilise.   The dried
flesh hung on the scaffold belonged to the old women, because they
represented the Old Woman who Never Dies.   A similar corn-medicine
festival was held in autumn for the purpose of attracting the herds of
buffaloes and securing a supply of meat.   At that time every woman
carried in her arms an uprooted plant of maize.   They gave the name
of the Old Woman who Never Dies both to the maize and to those
birds which they regarded as symbols of the fruits of the earth, and
they prayed to them in autumn saying, " Mother, have pity on us !
send us not the bitter cold too soon, lest we have not meat enough !
let not all the game depart, that we may have something for the
winter ! "   In autumn, when the birds were flying south, the Indians
thought that they were going home to the Old Woman and taking to
her the offerings that had been hung up on the scaffolds, especially
the dried meat, which she ate.   Here then we have the spirit or divinity
of the corn conceived as an Old Woman and represented in bodily form
by old women, who in their capacity of representatives receive some at
least of the offerings which are intended for her.

In some parts of India the harvest-goddess Gauri is represented
at once by an unmarried girl and by a bundle of wild balsam plants,
which is made up into the figure of a woman and dressed as such with
mask, garments, and ornaments.   Both the human and the vegetable
representative of the goddess are worshipped, and the intention of the
whole ceremony appears to be to ensure a good crop of rice.

§ 4. *The Double Personification of the Corn as Mother and Daughter.*—
Compared with the Corn-mother of Germany and the Harvest-maiden
of Scotland, the Demeter and Persephone of Greece are late products
of religious growth.   Yet as members of the Aryan family the Greeks
must at one time or another have observed harvest customs like those
which are still practised by Celts, Teutons, and Slavs, and which, far
beyond the limits of the Aryan world, have been practised by the
Indians of Peru and many peoples of the East Indies—a sufficient
proof that the ideas on which these customs rest are not confined to
any one race, but naturally suggest themselves to all untutored peoples
engaged in agriculture.   It is probable, therefore, that Demeter and
Persephone, those stately and beautiful figures of Greek mythology,
grew out of the same simple beliefs and practices which still prevail
among our modern peasantry, and that they were represented by rude
dolls made out of the yellow sheaves on many a harvest-field long
before their breathing images were wrought in bronze and marble by
the master hands of Phidias and Praxiteles.   A reminiscence of that
olden time—a scent, so to say, of the harvest-field—lingered to the last
in the title of the Maiden (*Kore*) by which Persephone was commonly
known.   Thus if the prototype of Demeter is the Corn-mother of
Germany, the prototype of Persephone is the Harvest-maiden, which,
autumn after autumn, is still made from the last sheaf on the Braes

of Balquhidder.   Indeed, if we knew more about the peasant-farmers
of ancient Greece, we should probably find that even in classical times
they continued annually to fashion their Corn-mothers (Demeters)
and Maidens (Persephones) out of the ripe corn on the harvest-fields.
But unfortunately the Demeter and Persephone whom we know were
the denizens of towns, the majestic inhabitants of lordly temples ; it
was for such divinities alone that the refined writers of antiquity had
eyes ; the uncouth rites performed by rustics amongst the corn were
beneath their notice.   Even if they noticed them, they probably never
dreamed of any connexion between the puppet of corn-stalks on the
sunny stubble-field and the marble divinity in the shady coolness of
the temple.   Still the writings even of these town-bred and cultured
persons afford us an occasional glimpse of a Demeter as rude as the
rudest that a remote German village can show.   Thus the story that
Iasion begat a child Plutus (" wealth," " abundance ") by Demeter
on a thrice-ploughed field, may be compared with the West Prussian
custom of the mock birth of a child on the harvest-field.   In this
Prussian custom the pretended mother represents the Corn-mother
(*Žytniamatka*) ; the pretended child represents the Corn-baby, and the
whole ceremony is a charm to ensure a crop next year.   The custom
and the legend alike point to an older practice of performing, among
the sprouting crops in spring or the stubble in autumn, one of those
real or mimic acts of procreation by which, as we have seen, primitive
man often seeks to infuse his own vigorous life into the languid or
decaying energies of nature.   Another glimpse of the savage under
the civilised Demeter will be afforded farther on, when we come to
deal with another aspect of those agricultural divinities.

The reader may have observed that in modern folk-customs the
corn-spirit is generally represented either by a Corn-mother (Old
Woman, etc.) or by a Maiden (Harvest-child, etc.), not both by a Corn-
mother and by a Maiden.   Why then did the Greeks represent the
corn both as a mother and a daughter ?

In the Breton custom the mother-sheaf—a large figure made out
of the last sheaf with a small corn-doll inside of it—clearly represents
both the Corn-mother and the Corn-daughter, the latter still unborn.
Again, in the Prussian custom just referred to, the woman who plays
the part of Corn-mother represents the ripe grain ; the child appears
to represent next year's corn, which may be regarded, naturally enough,
as the child of this year's corn, since it is from the seed of this year's
harvest that next year's crop will spring.   Further, we have seen
that among the Malays of the Peninsula and sometimes among the
Highlanders of Scotland the spirit of the grain is represented in double
female form, both as old and young, by means of ears taken alike from
the ripe crop : in Scotland the old spirit of the corn appears as the
Carline or *Cailleach*, the young spirit as the Maiden ; while among
the Malays of the Peninsula the two spirits of the rice are definitely
related to each other as mother and child.   Judged by these analogies
Demeter would be the ripe crop of this year ; Persephone would be

the seed-corn taken from it and sown in autumn, to reappear in spring. The descent of Persephone into the lower world would thus be a mythical expression for the sowing of the seed ; her reappearance in spring would signify the sprouting of the young corn.   In this way the Persephone of one year becomes the Demeter of the next, and this may very well have been the original form of the myth.   But when with the advance of religious thought the corn came to be personified, no longer as a being that went through the whole cycle of birth, growth, reproduction, and death within a year, but as an immortal goddess, consistency required that one of the two personifications, the mother or the daughter, should be sacrificed.   However, the double conception of the corn as mother and daughter may have been too old and too deeply rooted in the popular mind to be eradicated by logic, and so room had to be found in the reformed myth both for mother and daughter.   This was done by assigning to Persephone the character of the corn sown in autumn and sprouting in spring, while Demeter was left to play the somewhat vague part of the heavy mother of the corn, who laments its annual disappearance underground, and rejoices over its reappearance in spring.   Thus instead of a regular succession of divine beings, each living a year and then giving birth to her successor, the reformed myth exhibits the conception of two divine and immortal beings, one of whom annually disappears into and reappears from the ground, while the other has little to do but to weep and rejoice at the appropriate seasons.

This theory of the double personification of the corn in Greek myth assumes that both personifications (Demeter and Persephone) are original.   But if we suppose that the Greek myth started with a single personification, the aftergrowth of a second personification may perhaps be explained as follows.   On looking over the harvest customs which have been passed under review, it may be noticed that they involve two distinct conceptions of the corn-spirit.   For whereas in some of the customs the corn-spirit is treated as immanent in the corn, in others it is regarded as external to it.   Thus when a particular sheaf is called by the name of the corn-spirit, and is dressed in clothes and handled with reverence, the spirit is clearly regarded as immanent in the corn.   But when the spirit is said to make the crops grow by passing through them, or to blight the grain of those against whom she has a grudge, she is apparently conceived as distinct from, though exercising power over, the corn.   Conceived in the latter mode the corn-spirit is in a fair way to become a deity of the corn, if she has not become so already.   Of these two conceptions, that of the corn-spirit as immanent in the corn is doubtless the older, since the view of nature as animated by indwelling spirits appears to have generally preceded the view of it as controlled by external deities ; to put it shortly, animism precedes deism.   In the harvest customs of our European peasantry the corn-spirit seems to be conceived now as immanent in the corn and now as external to it.   In Greek mythology, on the other hand, Demeter is viewed rather as the deity of the corn than as the spirit immanent in it. The process of thought which leads to the change from the one mode of conception to the other is anthropomorphism, or the gradual investment of the immanent spirits with more and more of the attributes of humanity. As men emerge from savagery the tendency to humanise their divinities gains strength ; and the more human these become the wider is the breach which severs them from the natural objects of which they were at first merely the animating spirits or souls. But in the progress upwards from savagery men of the same generation do not march abreast ; and though the new anthropomorphic gods may satisfy the religious wants of the more developed intelligences, the backward members of the community will cling by preference to the old animistic notions. Now when the spirit of any natural object such as the corn has been invested with human qualities, detached from the object, and converted into a deity controlling it, the object itself is, by the withdrawal of its spirit, left inanimate ; it becomes, so to say, a spiritual vacuum. But the popular fancy, intolerant of such a vacuum, in other words, unable to conceive anything as inanimate, immediately creates a fresh mythical being, with which it peoples the vacant object. Thus the same natural object comes to be represented in mythology by two distinct beings : first by the old spirit now separated from it and raised to the rank of a deity ; second, by the new spirit, freshly created by the popular fancy to supply the place vacated by the old spirit on its elevation to a higher sphere. In such cases the problem for mythology is, having got two distinct personifications of the same object, what to do with them ? How are their relations to each other to be adjusted, and room found for both in the mythological system ? When the old spirit or new deity is conceived as creating or producing the object in question, the problem is easily solved. Since the object is believed to be produced by the old spirit, and animated by the new one, the latter, as the soul of the object, must also owe its existence to the former ; thus the old spirit will stand to the new one as producer to produced, that is, in mythology, as parent to child, and if both spirits are conceived as female, their relation will be that of mother and daughter. In this way, starting from a single personification of the corn as female, mythic fancy might in time reach a double personification of it as mother and daughter. It would be very rash to affirm that this was the way in which the myth of Demeter and Persephone actually took shape ; but it seems a legitimate conjecture that the reduplication of deities, of which Demeter and Persephone furnish an example, may sometimes have arisen in the way indicated. For example, among the pairs of deities dealt with in a former part of this work, it has been shown that there are grounds for regarding both Isis and her companion god Osiris as personifications of the corn. On the hypothesis just suggested, Isis would be the old corn-spirit, and Osiris would be the newer one, whose relationship to the old spirit was variously explained as that of brother, husband, and son ; for of course mythology would always be free to account for the coexistence of the two divinities in more ways than one. It must not, however, be forgotten that this proposed explanation of such pairs of deities as Demeter and Persephone or Isis and Osiris is purely conjectural, and is only given for what it is worth.

CHAPTER XLVII

LITYERSES

§ 1. *Songs of the Corn-reapers.*—In the preceding pages an attempt has been made to show that in the Corn-mother and Harvest-maiden of Northern Europe we have the prototypes of Demeter and Persephone. But an essential feature is still wanting to complete the resemblance. A leading incident in the Greek myth is the death and resurrection of Persephone ; it is this incident which, coupled with the nature of the goddess as a deity of vegetation, links the myth with the cults of Adonis, Attis, Osiris, and Dionysus ; and it is in virtue of this incident that the myth finds a place in our discussion of the Dying God. It remains, therefore, to see whether the conception of the annual death and resurrection of a god, which figures so prominently in these great Greek and Oriental worships, has not also its origin or its analogy in the rustic rites observed by reapers and vine-dressers amongst the corn-shocks and the vines.

Our general ignorance of the popular superstitions and customs of the ancients has already been confessed. But the obscurity which thus hangs over the first beginnings of ancient religion is fortunately dissipated to some extent in the present case. The worships of Osiris, Adonis, and Attis had their respective seats, as we have seen, in Egypt, Syria, and Phrygia ; and in each of these countries certain harvest and vintage customs are known to have been observed, the resemblance of which to each other and to the national rites struck the ancients themselves, and, compared with the harvest customs of modern peasants and barbarians, seems to throw some light on the origin of the rites in question.

It has been already mentioned, on the authority of Diodorus, that in ancient Egypt the reapers were wont to lament over the first sheaf cut, invoking Isis as the goddess to whom they owed the dis-covery of corn. To the plaintive song or cry sung or uttered by Egyptian reapers the Greeks gave the name of Maneros, and explained the name by a story that Maneros, the only son of the first Egyptian king, invented agriculture, and, dying an untimely death, was thus lamented by the people. It appears, however, that the name Maneros is due to a misunderstanding of the formula *mââ-ne-hra*, " Come to the house," which has been discovered in various Egyptian writings, for example in the dirge of Isis in the Book of the Dead. Hence we may suppose that the cry *mââ-ne-hra* was chanted by the reapers over the cut corn as a dirge for the death of the corn-spirit (Isis or Osiris) and a prayer for its return. As the cry was raised over the first ears reaped, it would seem that the corn-spirit was believed by the Egyptians to be present in the first corn cut and to die under the sickle. We have seen that in the Malay Peninsula and Java the first ears of rice are taken to represent either the Soul of the Rice or the Rice-bride and the Rice-bridegroom. In parts of Russia the first sheaf is treated much in the same way that the last sheaf is treated elsewhere. It is reaped by the mistress herself, taken home and set in the place of honour near the holy pictures ; afterwards it is threshed separately, and some of its grain is mixed with the next year's seed-corn. In Aberdeenshire, while the last corn cut was generally used to make the *clyack* sheaf, it was sometimes, though rarely, the first corn cut that was dressed up as a woman and carried home with ceremony.

In Phoenicia and Western Asia a plaintive song, like that chanted by the Egyptian corn-reapers, was sung at the vintage and probably (to judge by analogy) also at harvest. This Phoenician song was called by the Greeks Linus or Ailinus and explained, like Maneros, as a lament for the death of a youth named Linus. According to one story Linus was brought up by a shepherd, but torn to pieces by his dogs. But, like Maneros, the name Linus or Ailinus appears to have originated in a verbal misunderstanding, and to be nothing more than the cry *ai lanu*, that is " Woe to us," which the Phoenicians probably uttered in mourning for Adonis ; at least Sappho seems to have regarded Adonis and Linus as equivalent.

In Bithynia a like mournful ditty, called Bormus or Borimus, was chanted by Mariandynian reapers. Bormus was said to have been a handsome youth, the son of King Upias or of a wealthy and distinguished man. One summer day, watching the reapers at work in his fields, he went to fetch them a drink of water and was never heard of more. So the reapers sought for him, calling him in plaintive strains, which they continued to chant at harvest ever afterwards.

§ 2. *Killing the Corn-spirit.*—In Phrygia the corresponding song, sung by harvesters both at reaping and at threshing, was called Lityerses. According to one story, Lityerses was a bastard son of Midas, King of Phrygia, and dwelt at Celaenae. He used to reap the corn, and had an enormous appetite. When a stranger happened to enter the corn-field or to pass by it, Lityerses gave him plenty to eat and drink, then took him to the corn-fields on the banks of the Maeander and compelled him to reap along with him. Lastly, it was his custom to wrap the stranger in a sheaf, cut off his head with a sickle, and carry away his body, swathed in the corn-stalks. But at last Hercules undertook to reap with him, cut off his head with the sickle, and threw his body into the river. As Hercules is reported to have slain Lityerses in the same way that Lityerses slew others, we may infer that Lityerses used to throw the bodies of his victims into the river. According to another version of the story, Lityerses, a son of Midas, was wont to challenge people to a reaping match with him, and if he vanquished them he used to thrash them ; but one day he met with a stronger reaper, who slew him.

There are some grounds for supposing that in these stories of Lityerses we have the description of a Phrygian harvest custom in accordance with which certain persons, especially strangers passing the harvest field, were regularly regarded as embodiments of the corn-spirit, and as such were seized by the reapers, wrapt in sheaves, and beheaded, their bodies, bound up in the corn-stalks, being afterwards thrown into water as a rain-charm. The grounds for this supposition are, first, the resemblance of the Lityerses story to the harvest customs of European peasantry, and, second, the frequency of human sacrifices offered by savage races to promote the fertility of the fields. We will examine these grounds successively, beginning with the former.

In comparing the story with the harvest customs of Europe, three points deserve special attention, namely : I. the reaping match and the binding of persons in the sheaves ; II. the killing of the corn-spirit or his representatives ; III. the treatment of visitors to the harvest field or of strangers passing it.

I. In regard to the first head, we have seen that in modern Europe the person who cuts or binds or threshes the last sheaf is often exposed to rough treatment at the hands of his fellow-labourers. For example, he is bound up in the last sheaf, and, thus encased, is carried or carted about, beaten, drenched with water, thrown on a dunghill, and so forth. Or, if he is spared this horseplay, he is at least the subject of ridicule or is thought to be destined to suffer some misfortune in the course of the year. Hence the harvesters are naturally reluctant to give the last cut at reaping or the last stroke at threshing or to bind the last sheaf, and towards the close of the work this reluctance produces an emulation among the labourers, each striving to finish his task as fast as possible, in order that he may escape the invidious distinction of being last. For example, in the Mittelmark district of Prussia, when the rye has been reaped, and the last sheaves are about to be tied up, the binders stand in two rows facing each other, every woman with her sheaf and her straw rope before her. At a given signal they all tie up their sheaves, and the one who is the last to finish is ridiculed by the rest. Not only so, but her sheaf is made up into human shape and called the Old Man, and she must carry it home to the farmyard, where the harvesters dance in a circle round her and it. Then they take the Old Man to the farmer and deliver it to him with the words, " We bring the Old Man to the Master. He may keep him till he gets a new one." After that the Old Man is set up against a tree, where he remains for a long time, the butt of many jests. At Aschbach in Bavaria, when the reaping is nearly finished, the reapers say, " Now, we will drive out the Old Man." Each of them sets himself to reap a patch of corn as fast as he can ;

he who cuts the last handful or the last stalk is greeted by the rest with an exulting cry, " You have the Old Man." Sometimes a black mask is fastened on the reaper's face and he is dressed in woman's clothes ; or if the reaper is a woman, she is dressed in man's clothes. A dance follows. At the supper the Old Man gets twice as large a portion of the food as the others. The proceedings are similar at threshing ; the person who gives the last stroke is said to have the Old Man. At the supper given to the threshers he has to eat out of the cream-ladle and to drink a great deal. Moreover, he is quizzed and teased in all sorts of ways till he frees himself from further annoyance by treating the others to brandy or beer.

These examples illustrate the contests in reaping, threshing, and binding which take place amongst the harvesters, from their un-willingness to suffer the ridicule and discomfort incurred by the one who happens to finish his work last. It will be remembered that the person who is last at reaping, binding, or threshing, is regarded as the representative of the corn-spirit, and this idea is more fully expressed by binding him or her in corn-stalks. The latter custom has been already illustrated, but a few more instances may be added. At Kloxin, near Stettin, the harvesters call out to the woman who binds the last sheaf, " You have the Old Man, and must keep him." As late as the first half of the nineteenth century the custom was to tie up the woman herself in pease-straw, and bring her with music to the farmhouse, where the harvesters danced with her till the pease-straw fell off. In other villages round Stettin, when the last harvest-waggon is being loaded, there is a regular race amongst the women, each striving not to be last. For she who places the last sheaf on the waggon is called the Old Man, and is completely swathed in corn-stalks ; she is also decked with flowers, and flowers and a helmet of straw are placed on her head. In solemn procession she carries the harvest-crown to the squire, over whose head she holds it while she utters a string of good wishes. At the dance which follows, the Old Man has the right to choose his, or rather her, partner ; it is an honour to dance with him. At Gommern, near Magdeburg, the reaper who cuts the last ears of corn is often wrapt up in corn-stalks so completely that it is hard to see whether there is a man in the bundle or not. Thus wrapt up he is taken by another stalwart reaper on his back, and carried round the field amidst the joyous cries of the harvesters. At Neuhausen, near Merseburg, the person who binds the last sheaf is wrapt in ears of oats and saluted as the Oatsman, whereupon the others dance round him. At Brie, Isle de France, the farmer himself is tied up in the *first* sheaf. At Dingelstedt, in the district of Erfurt, down to the first half of the nineteenth century it was the custom to tie up a man in the last sheaf. He was called the Old Man, and was brought home on the last waggon, amid huzzas and music. On reaching the farmyard he was rolled round the barn and drenched with water. At Nördlingen in Bavaria the man who gives the last stroke at threshing is wrapt in straw and rolled on the threshing-floor. In some parts of Oberpfalz, Bavaria, he is said to "get the Old Man," is wrapt in straw, and carried to a neighbour who has not yet finished his threshing. In Silesia the woman who binds the last sheaf has to submit to a good deal of horse-play. She is pushed, knocked down, and tied up in the sheaf, after which she is called the corn-puppet (*Kornpopel*).

"In all these cases the idea is that the spirit of the corn—the Old Man of vegetation—is driven out of the corn last cut or last threshed, and lives in the barn during the winter. At sowing-time he goes out again to the fields to resume his activity as animating force among the sprouting corn."

II. Passing to the second point of comparison between the Lityerses story and European harvest customs, we have now to see that in the latter the corn-spirit is often believed to be killed at reaping or threshing. In the Romsdal and other parts of Norway, when the haymaking is over, the people say that "the Old Hay-man has been killed." In some parts of Bavaria the man who gives the last stroke at threshing is said to have killed the Corn-man, the Oats-man, or the Wheat-man, according to the crop. In the Canton of Tillot, in Lorraine, at threshing the last corn the men keep time with their flails, calling out as they thresh, "We are killing the Old Woman! We are killing the Old Woman!" If there is an old woman in the house she is warned to save herself, or she will be struck dead. Near Ragnit, in Lithuania, the last handful of corn is left standing by itself, with the words, "The Old Woman (*Boba*) is sitting in there." Then a young reaper whets his scythe and, with a strong sweep, cuts down the handful. It is now said of him that "he has cut off the Boba's head"; and he receives a gratuity from the farmer and a jugful of water over his head from the farmer's wife. According to another account, every Lithuanian reaper makes haste to finish his task; for the Old Rye-woman lives in the last stalks, and whoever cuts the last stalks kills the Old Rye-woman, and by killing her he brings trouble on himself. In Wilkischken, in the district of Tilsit, the man who cuts the last corn goes by the name of "the killer of the Rye-woman." In Lithuania, again, the corn-spirit is believed to be killed at threshing as well as at reaping. When only a single pile of corn remains to be threshed, all the threshers suddenly step back a few paces, as if at the word of command. Then they fall to work, plying their flails with the utmost rapidity and vehemence, till they come to the last bundle. Upon this they fling themselves with almost frantic fury, straining every nerve, and raining blows on it till the word "Halt!" rings out sharply from the leader. The man whose flail is the last to fall after the command to stop has been given is immediately surrounded by all the rest, crying out that "he has struck the Old Rye-woman dead." He has to expiate the deed by treating them to brandy; and, like the man who cuts the last corn, he is known as "the killer of the Old Rye-woman." Sometimes in Lithuania the slain corn-spirit was represented by a puppet. Thus a female figure was made out of corn-stalks, dressed in clothes, and placed on the threshing-floor, under the heap of corn which was to be threshed last. Whoever thereafter gave the last stroke at threshing " struck the Old Woman dead." We have already met with examples of burning the figure which represents the corn-spirit. In the East Riding of Yorkshire a custom called " burning the Old Witch " is observed on the last day of harvest. A small sheaf of corn is burnt on the field in a fire of stubble ; peas are parched at the fire and eaten with a liberal allowance of ale ; and the lads and lasses romp about the flames and amuse themselves by blackening each other's faces. Sometimes, again, the corn-spirit is represented by a man, who lies down under the last corn ; it is threshed upon his body, and the people say that " the Old Man is being beaten to death." We saw that sometimes the farmer's wife is thrust, together with the last sheaf, under the threshing-machine, as if to thresh her, and that afterwards a pretence is made of winnowing her. At Volders, in the Tyrol, husks of corn are stuck behind the neck of the man who gives the last stroke at threshing, and he is throttled with a straw garland. If he is tall, it is believed that the corn will be tall next year. Then he is tied on a bundle and flung into the river. In Carinthia, the thresher who gave the last stroke, and the person who untied the last sheaf on the threshing-floor, are bound hand and foot with straw bands, and crowns of straw are placed on their heads. Then they are tied, face to face, on a sledge, dragged through the village, and flung into a brook. The custom of throwing the representative of the corn-spirit into a stream, like that of drenching him with water, is, as usual, a rain-charm.

III. Thus far the representatives of the corn-spirit have generally been the man or woman who cuts, binds, or threshes the last corn. We now come to the cases in which the corn-spirit is represented either by a stranger passing the harvest-field (as in the Lityerses tale), or by a visitor entering it for the first time. All over Germany it is customary for the reapers or threshers to lay hold of passing strangers and bind them with a rope made of corn-stalks, till they pay a forfeit ; and when the farmer himself or one of his guests enters the field or the threshing-floor for the first time, he is treated in the same way. Sometimes the rope is only tied round his arm or his feet or his neck. But sometimes he is regularly swathed in corn. Thus at Solör in Norway, whoever enters the field, be he the master or a stranger, is tied up in a sheaf and must pay a ransom. In the neighbourhood of Soest, when the farmer visits the flax-pullers for the first time, he is completely enveloped in flax. Passers-by are also surrounded by the women, tied up in flax, and compelled to stand brandy. At Nördlingen strangers are caught with straw ropes and tied up in a sheaf till they pay a forfeit. Among the Germans of Haselberg, in West Bohemia, as soon as a farmer had given the last corn to be threshed on the threshing-floor, he was swathed in it and had to redeem himself by a present of cakes. In the canton of Putanges, in Normandy, a pretence of tying up the owner of the land in the last sheaf of wheat is still practised, or at least was still practised some quarter of a century ago. The task falls to the women alone. They throw themselves on the proprietor, seize him by the arms, the legs, and the body, throw him to the ground, and stretch him on the last sheaf. Then a show is made of binding him, and the conditions to be observed at the harvest-supper are dictated to him. When he has accepted them, he is released and allowed to get up. At Brie, Isle de France, when any one who does not belong to the farm passes by the harvest-field, the reapers give chase. If they catch him, they bind him in a sheaf and bite him, one after the other, in the forehead, crying, " You shall carry the key of the field." " To have the key " is an expression used by harvesters elsewhere in the sense of to cut or bind or thresh the last sheaf ; hence, it is equivalent to the phrases " You have the Old Man," " You are the Old Man," which are addressed to the cutter, binder, or thresher of the last sheaf. Therefore, when a stranger, as at Brie, is tied up in a sheaf and told that he will " carry the key of the field," it is as much as to say that he is the Old Man, that is, an embodiment of the corn-spirit. In hop-picking, if a well-dressed stranger passes the hop-yard, he is seized by the women, tumbled into the bin, covered with leaves, and not released till he has paid a fine.

Thus, like the ancient Lityerses, modern European reapers have been wont to lay hold of a passing stranger and tie him up in a sheaf. It is not to be expected that they should complete the parallel by cutting off his head ; but if they do not take such a strong step, their language and gestures are at least indicative of a desire to do so. For instance, in Mecklenburg on the first day of reaping, if the master or mistress or a stranger enters the field, or merely passes by it, all the mowers face towards him and sharpen their scythes, clashing their whet-stones against them in unison, as if they were making ready to mow. Then the woman who leads the mowers steps up to him and ties a band round his left arm. He must ransom himself by payment of a forfeit. Near Ratzeburg, when the master or other person of mark enters the field or passes by it, all the harvesters stop work and march towards him in a body, the men with their scythes in front. On meeting him they form up in line, men and women. The men stick the poles of their scythes in the ground, as they do in whetting them ; then they take off their caps and hang them on the scythes, while their leader stands forward and makes a speech. When he has done, they all whet their scythes in measured time very loudly, after which they put on their caps. Two of the women binders then come forward ; one of them ties the master or stranger (as the case may be) with corn-ears or with a silken band ; the other delivers a rhyming address. The following are specimens of the speeches made by the reaper on these occasions. In some parts of Pomerania every passer-by is stopped, his way being barred with a corn-rope. The reapers form a circle round him and sharpen their scythes, while their leader says :

> " *The men are ready,*
> *The scythes are bent,*
>
> *The corn is great and small,*
> *The gentleman must be mowed."*

Then the process of whetting the scythes is repeated. At Ramin, in the district of Stettin, the stranger, standing encircled by the reapers, is thus addressed :

> " *We'll stroke the gentleman*
> *With our naked sword,*
> *Wherewith we shear meadows and*
> *   fields.*
> *We shear princes and lords.*
> *Labourers are often athirst ;*
>
> *If the gentleman will stand beer*
> *   and brandy*
> *The joke will soon be over.*
> *But, if our prayer he does not like,*
> *The sword has a right to strike."*

On the threshing-floor strangers are also regarded as embodiments of the corn-spirit, and are treated accordingly. At Wiedingharde in Schleswig when a stranger comes to the threshing-floor he is asked, " Shall I teach you the flail-dance ? " If he says yes, they put the arms of the threshing-flail round his neck as if he were a sheaf of corn, and press them together so tight that he is nearly choked. In some parishes of Wermland (Sweden), when a stranger enters the threshing-floor where the threshers are at work, they say that " they will teach him the threshing-song." Then they put a flail round his neck and a straw rope about his body. Also, as we have seen, if a stranger woman enters the threshing-floor, the threshers put a flail round her body and a wreath of corn-stalks round her neck, and call out, " See the Corn-woman ! See ! that is how the Corn-maiden looks ! "

Thus in these harvest-customs of modern Europe the person who cuts, binds, or threshes the last corn is treated as an embodiment of the corn-spirit by being wrapt up in sheaves, killed in mimicry by agricultural implements, and thrown into the water. These coincidences with the Lityerses story seem to prove that the latter is a genuine description of an old Phrygian harvest-custom. But since in the modern parallels the killing of the personal representative of the corn-spirit is necessarily omitted or at most enacted only in mimicry, it is desirable to show that in rude society human beings have been commonly killed as an agricultural ceremony to promote the fertility of the fields. The following examples will make this plain.

§ 3. *Human Sacrifices for the Crops.*—The Indians of Guayaquil, in Ecuador, used to sacrifice human blood and the hearts of men when they sowed their fields. The people of Cañar (now Cuenca in Ecuador) used to sacrifice a hundred children annually at harvest. The kings of Quito, the Incas of Peru, and for a long time the Spaniards were unable to suppress the bloody rite. At a Mexican harvest-festival, when the first-fruits of the season were offered to the sun, a criminal was placed between two immense stones, balanced opposite each other, and was crushed by them as they fell together. His remains were buried, and a feast and dance followed. This sacrifice was known as " the meeting of the stones." We have seen that the ancient Mexicans also sacrificed human beings at all the various stages in the growth of the maize, the age of the victims corresponding to the age of the corn ; for they sacrificed new-born babes at sowing, older children when the grain had sprouted, and so on till it was fully ripe, when they sacrificed old men. No doubt the correspondence between the ages of the victims and the state of the corn was supposed to enhance the efficacy of the sacrifice.

The Pawnees annually sacrificed a human victim in spring when they sowed their fields. The sacrifice was believed to have been enjoined on them by the Morning Star, or by a certain bird which the Morning Star had sent to them as its messenger. The bird was stuffed and preserved as a powerful talisman. They thought that an omission of this sacrifice would be followed by the total failure of the crops of maize, beans, and pumpkins. The victim was a captive of either sex. He was clad in the gayest and most costly attire, was fattened on the choicest food, and carefully kept in ignorance of his doom. When he was fat enough, they bound him to a cross in the presence of the multitude, danced a solemn dance, then cleft his head with a tomahawk and shot him with arrows. According to one trader, the squaws then cut pieces of flesh from the victim's body, with which they greased their hoes ; but this was denied by another trader who had been present at the ceremony. Immediately after the sacrifice the people proceeded to plant their fields. A particular account has been preserved of the sacrifice of a Sioux girl by the Pawnees in April 1837 or 1838. The girl was fourteen or fifteen years old and had been kept for six months and well treated. Two days before the sacrifice she was led from wigwam to wigwam, accompanied by the whole council of chiefs and warriors. At each lodge she received a small billet of wood and a little paint, which she handed to the warrior next to her. In this way she called at every wigwam, receiving at each the same present of wood and paint. On the twenty-second of April she was taken out to be sacrificed, attended by the warriors, each of whom carried two pieces of wood which he had received from her hands. Her body having been painted half red and half black, she was attached to a sort of gibbet and roasted for some time over a slow fire, then shot to death with arrows. The chief sacrificer next tore out her heart and devoured it. While her flesh was still warm it was cut in small pieces from the bones, put in little baskets, and taken to a neighbouring corn-field. There the head chief took a piece of the flesh from a basket and squeezed a drop of blood upon the newly-deposited grains of corn. His example was followed by the rest, till all the seed had been sprinkled with the blood ; it was then covered up with earth. According to one account the body of the victim was reduced to a kind of paste, which was rubbed or sprinkled not only on the maize but also on the potatoes, the beans, and other seeds to fertilise them. By this sacrifice they hoped to obtain plentiful crops.

A West African queen used to sacrifice a man and woman in the month of March. They were killed with spades and hoes, and their bodies buried in the middle of a field which had just been tilled. At Lagos in Guinea it was the custom annually to impale a young girl alive soon after the spring equinox in order to secure good crops. Along with her were sacrificed sheep and goats, which, with yams, heads of maize, and plantains, were hung on stakes on each side of her. The victims were bred up for the purpose in the king's seraglio, and their minds had been so powerfully wrought upon by the fetish men that they went cheerfully to their fate. A similar sacrifice used to be annually offered at Benin, in Guinea. The Marimos, a Bechuana tribe, sacrifice a human being for the crops. The victim chosen is generally a short, stout man. He is seized by violence or intoxicated and taken to the fields, where he is killed amongst the wheat to serve as " seed " (so they phrase it). After his blood has coagulated in the sun, it is burned along with the frontal bone, the flesh attached to it, and the brain ; the ashes are then scattered over the ground to fertilise it. The rest of the body is eaten.

The Bagobos of Mindanao, one of the Philippine Islands, offer a human sacrifice before they sow their rice. The victim is a slave, who is hewn to pieces in the forest. The natives of Bontoc in the interior of Luzon, one of the Philippine Islands, are passionate head-hunters. Their principal seasons for head-hunting are the times of planting and reaping the rice. In order that the crop may turn out well, every farm must get at least one human head at planting and one at sowing. The head-hunters go out in twos or threes, lie in wait for the victim, whether man or woman, cut off his or her head, hands, and feet, and bring them back in haste to the village, where they are received with great rejoicings. The skulls are at first exposed on the branches of two or three dead trees which stand in an open space of every village surrounded by large stones which serve as seats. The people then dance round them and feast and get drunk. When the flesh has decayed from the head, the man who cut it off takes it home and preserves it as a relic, while his companions do the same with the hands and the feet. Similar customs are observed by the Apoyaos, another tribe in the interior of Luzon.

Among the Lhota Naga, one of the many savage tribes who inhabit the deep rugged labyrinthine glens which wind into the mountains from the rich valley of Brahmapootra, it used to be a common custom to chop off the heads, hands, and feet of people they met with, and then to stick up the severed extremities in their fields to ensure a good crop of grain. They bore no ill-will whatever to the persons upon whom they operated in this unceremonious fashion. Once they flayed a boy alive, carved him in pieces, and distributed the flesh among all the villagers, who put it into their corn-bins to avert bad luck and ensure plentiful crops of grain. The Gonds of India, a Dravidian race, kidnapped Brahman boys, and kept them as victims to be sacrificed on various occasions. At sowing and reaping, after a triumphal procession, one of the lads was slain by being punctured with a poisoned arrow. His blood was then sprinkled over the ploughed field or the ripe crop, and his flesh was devoured. The Oraons or Uraons of Chota Nagpur worship a goddess called Anna Kuari, who can give good crops and make a man rich, but to induce her to do so it is necessary to offer human sacrifices. In spite of the vigilance of the British Government these sacrifices are said to be still secretly perpetrated. The victims are poor waifs and strays whose disappearance attracts no notice. April and May are the months when the catchpoles are out on the prowl. At that time strangers will not go about the country alone, and parents will not let their children enter the jungle or herd the cattle. When a catchpole has found a victim, he cuts his throat and carries away the upper part of the ring finger and the nose. The goddess takes up her abode in the house of any man who has offered her a sacrifice, and from that time his fields yield a double harvest. The form she assumes in the house is that of a small child. When the householder brings in his unhusked rice, he takes the goddess and rolls her over the heap to double its size. But she soon grows restless and can only be pacified with the blood of fresh human victims.

But the best known case of human sacrifices, systematically offered to ensure good crops, is supplied by the Khonds or Kandhs, another Dravidian race in Bengal. Our knowledge of them is derived from the accounts written by British officers who, about the middle of the nineteenth century, were engaged in putting them down. The sacrifices were offered to the Earth Goddess, Tari Pennu or Bera Pennu, and were believed to ensure good crops and immunity from all disease and accidents. In particular, they were considered necessary in the cultivation of turmeric, the Khonds arguing that the turmeric could not have a deep red colour without the shedding of blood. The victim or Meriah, as he was called, was acceptable to the goddess only if he had been purchased, or had been born a victim—that is, the son of a victim father, or had been devoted as a child by his father or guardian. Khonds in distress often sold their children for victims, " considering the beatification of their souls certain, and their death, for the benefit of mankind, the most honourable possible." A man of the Panua tribe was once seen to load a Khond with curses, and finally to spit in his face, because the Khond had sold for a victim his own child, whom the Panua had wished to marry. A party of Khonds, who saw this, immediately pressed forward to comfort the seller of his child, saying, " Your child has died that all the world may live, and the Earth Goddess herself will wipe that spittle from your face." The victims were often kept for years before they were sacrificed. Being regarded as consecrated beings, they were treated with extreme affection, mingled with deference, and were welcomed wherever they went. A Meriah youth, on attaining maturity, was generally given a wife, who was herself usually a Meriah or victim ; and with her he received a portion of land and farm-stock. Their offspring were

also victims.   Human sacrifices were offered to the Earth Goddess
by tribes, branches of tribes, or villages, both at periodical festivals
and   on   extraordinary   occasions.   The   periodical   sacrifices   were
generally so arranged by tribes and divisions of tribes that each head
of a family was enabled, at least once a year, to procure a shred of
flesh for his fields, generally about the time when his chief crop was
laid down.

The mode of performing these tribal sacrifices was as follows.
Ten or twelve days before the sacrifice, the victim was devoted by
cutting off his hair, which, until then, had been kept unshorn.   Crowds
of men and women assembled to witness the sacrifice ; none might
be excluded, since the sacrifice was declared to be for all mankind.
It was preceded by several days of wild revelry and gross debauchery.
On the day before the sacrifice the victim, dressed in a new garment,
was led forth from the village in solemn procession, with music and
dancing, to the Meriah grove, a clump of high forest trees standing
a little way from the village and untouched by the axe.   There they
tied him to a post, which was sometimes placed between two plants
of the sankissar shrub.   He was then anointed with oil, ghee, and
turmeric, and adorned with flowers ; and " a species of reverence,
which it is not easy to distinguish from adoration," was paid to him
throughout the day.   A great struggle now arose to obtain the smallest
relic from his person ; a particle of the turmeric paste with which
he was smeared, or a drop of his spittle, was esteemed of sovereign
virtue, especially by the women.   The crowd danced round the post
to music, and, addressing the earth, said, " O God, we offer this sacrifice
to you ; give us good crops, seasons, and health " ; then speaking to the
victim they said, " We bought you with a price, and did not seize you ;
now we sacrifice you according to custom, and no sin rests with us."

On the last morning the orgies, which had been scarcely interrupted
during the night, were resumed, and continued till noon, when they
ceased, and the assembly proceeded to consummate the sacrifice.
The victim was again anointed with oil, and each person touched
the anointed part, and wiped the oil on his own head.   In some places
they took the victim in procession round the village, from door to
door, where some plucked hair from his head, and others begged for
a drop of his spittle, with which they anointed their heads.   As the
victim might not be bound nor make any show of resistance, the bones
of his arms and, if necessary, his legs were broken ; but often this
precaution was rendered unnecessary by stupefying him with opium.
The mode of putting him to death varied in different places.   One
of the commonest modes seems to have been strangulation, or squeezing to death.   The branch of a green tree was cleft several feet down
the middle ; the victim's neck (in other places, his chest) was inserted
in the cleft, which the priest, aided by his assistants, strove with all
his force to close.   Then he wounded the victim slightly with his
axe, whereupon the crowd rushed at the wretch and hewed the flesh
from the bones, leaving the head and bowels untouched.   Sometimes

he was cut up alive.   In Chinna Kimedy he was dragged along the fields, surrounded by the crowd, who, avoiding his head and intestines, hacked the flesh from his body with their knives till he died.   Another very common mode of sacrifice in the same district was to fasten the victim to the proboscis of a wooden elephant, which revolved on a stout post, and, as it whirled round, the crowd cut the flesh from the victim while life remained.   In some villages Major Campbell found as many as fourteen of these wooden elephants, which had been used at sacrifices.   In one district the victim was put to death slowly by fire.   A low stage was formed, sloping on either side like a roof ; upon it they laid the victim, his limbs wound round with cords to confine his struggles.   Fires were then lighted and hot brands applied, to make him roll up and down the slopes of the stage as long as possible ; for the more tears he shed the more abundant would be the supply of rain.   Next day the body was cut to pieces.

The flesh cut from the victim was instantly taken home by the persons who had been deputed by each village to bring it.   To secure its rapid arrival, it was sometimes forwarded by relays of men, and conveyed with postal fleetness fifty or sixty miles.   In each village all who stayed at home fasted rigidly until the flesh arrived.   The bearer deposited it in the place of public assembly, where it was received by the priest and the heads of families.   The priest divided it into two portions, one of which he offered to the Earth Goddess by burying it in a hole in the ground with his back turned, and without looking.   Then each man added a little earth to bury it, and the priest poured water on the spot from a hill gourd.   The other portion of flesh he divided into as many shares as there were heads of houses present.   Each head of a house rolled his shred of flesh in leaves, and buried it in his favourite field, placing it in the earth behind his back without looking.   In some places each man carried his portion of flesh to the stream which watered his fields, and there hung it on a pole.   For three days thereafter no house was swept ; and, in one district, strict silence was observed, no fire might be given out, no wood cut, and no strangers received.   The remains of the human victim (namely, the head, bowels, and bones) were watched by strong parties the night after the sacrifice ; and next morning they were burned, along with a whole sheep, on a funeral pile.   The ashes were scattered over the fields, laid as paste over the houses and granaries, or mixed with the new corn to preserve it from insects.   Sometimes, however, the head and bones were buried, not burnt.   After the suppression of the human sacrifices, inferior victims were substituted in some places ; for instance, in the capital of Chinna Kimedy a goat took the place of a human victim.   Others sacrifice a buffalo.   They tie it to a wooden post in a sacred grove, dance wildly round it with brandished knives, then, falling on the living animal, hack it to shreds and tatters in a few minutes, fighting and struggling with each other for every particle of flesh.   As soon as a man has secured a piece he makes off with it at full speed to bury it in his fields, according to ancient custom, before the sun has set, and as some of them have far to go they must run very fast.   All the women throw clods of earth at the rapidly retreating figures of the men, some of them taking very good aim.   Soon the sacred grove, so lately a scene of tumult, is silent and deserted except for a few people who remain to guard all that is left of the buffalo, to wit, the head, the bones, and the stomach, which are burned with ceremony at the foot of the stake.

In these Khond sacrifices the Meriahs are represented by our authorities as victims offered to propitiate the Earth Goddess.   But from the treatment of the victims both before and after death it appears that the custom cannot be explained as merely a propitiatory sacrifice. A part of the flesh certainly was offered to the Earth Goddess, but the rest was buried by each householder in his fields, and the ashes of the other parts of the body were scattered over the fields, laid as paste on the granaries, or mixed with the new corn.   These latter customs imply that to the body of the Meriah there was ascribed a direct or intrinsic power of making the crops to grow, quite independent of the indirect efficacy which it might have as an offering to secure the good-will of the deity.   In other words, the flesh and ashes of the victim were believed to be endowed with a magical or physical power of fertilising the land.   The same intrinsic power was ascribed to the blood and tears of the Meriah, his blood causing the redness of the turmeric and his tears producing rain ; for it can hardly be doubted that, originally at least, the tears were supposed to bring down the rain, not merely to prognosticate it.   Similarly the custom of pouring water on the buried flesh of the Meriah was no doubt a rain-charm.   Again, magical power as an attribute of the Meriah appears in the sovereign virtue believed to reside in anything that came from his person, as his hair or spittle.   The ascription of such power to the Meriah indicates that he was much more than a mere man sacrificed to propitiate a deity.   Once more, the extreme reverence paid him points to the same conclusion.   Major Campbell speaks of the Meriah as " being regarded as something more than mortal," and Major Macpherson says, " A species of reverence, which it is not easy to distinguish from adoration, is paid to him."   In short, the Meriah seems to have been regarded as divine.   As such, he may originally have represented the Earth Goddess or, perhaps, a deity of vegetation ; though in later times he came to be regarded rather as a victim offered to a deity than as himself an incarnate god.   This later view of the Meriah as a victim rather than a divinity may perhaps have received undue emphasis from the European writers who have described the Khond religion.   Habituated to the later idea of sacrifice as an offering made to a god for the purpose of conciliating his favour, European observers are apt to interpret all religious slaughter in this sense, and to suppose that wherever such slaughter takes place, there must necessarily be a deity to whom the carnage is believed by the slayers to be acceptable.   Thus their preconceived ideas may unconsciously colour and warp their descriptions of savage rites.

The same custom of killing the representative of a god, of which strong traces appear in the Khond sacrifices, may perhaps be detected in some of the other human sacrifices described above. Thus the ashes of the slaughtered Marimo were scattered over the fields ; the blood of the Brahman lad was put on the crop and field ; the flesh of the slain Naga was stowed in the corn-bin ; and the blood of the Sioux girl was allowed to trickle on the seed. Again, the identification of the victim with the corn, in other words, the view that he is an embodiment or spirit of the corn, is brought out in the pains which seem to be taken to secure a physical correspondence between him and the natural object which he embodies or represents. Thus the Mexicans killed young victims for the young corn and old ones for the ripe corn ; the Marimos sacrifice, as " seed," a short, fat man, the shortness of his stature corresponding to that of the young corn, his fatness to the condition which it is desired that the crops may attain ; and the Pawnees fattened their victims probably with the same view. Again, the identification of the victim with the corn comes out in the African custom of killing him with spades and hoes, and the Mexican custom of grinding him, like corn, between two stones.

One more point in these savage customs deserves to be noted. The Pawnee chief devoured the heart of the Sioux girl, and the Marimos and Gonds ate the victim's flesh. If, as we suppose, the victim was regarded as divine, it follows that in eating his flesh his worshippers believed themselves to be partaking of the body of their god.

§ 4. *The Corn-spirit slain in his Human Representatives.*—The barbarous rites just described offer analogies to the harvest customs of Europe. Thus the fertilising virtue ascribed to the corn-spirit is shown equally in the savage custom of mixing the victim's blood or ashes with the seed-corn and the European custom of mixing the grain from the last sheaf with the young corn in spring. Again, the identification of the person with the corn appears alike in the savage custom of adapting the age and stature of the victim to the age and stature, whether actual or expected, of the crop ; in the Scotch and Styrian rules that when the corn-spirit is conceived as the Maiden the last corn shall be cut by a young maiden, but when it is conceived as the Corn-mother it shall be cut by an old woman ; in the warning given to old women in Lorraine to save themselves when the Old Woman is being killed, that is, when the last corn is being threshed ; and in the Tyrolese expectation that if the man who gives the last stroke at threshing is tall, the next year's corn will be tall also. Further, the same identification is implied in the savage custom of killing the representative of the corn-spirit with hoes or spades or by grinding him between stones, and in the European custom of pretending to kill him with the scythe or the flail. Once more the Khond custom of pouring water on the buried flesh of the victim is parallel to the European customs of pouring water on the personal representative of the corn-spirit or plunging him into a stream. Both the Khond and the European customs are rain-charms.

To return now to the Lityerses story.   It has been shown that in rude society human beings have been commonly killed to promote the growth of the crops.   There is therefore no improbability in the supposition that they may once have been killed for a like purpose in Phrygia and Europe ; and when Phrygian legend and European folk-custom, closely agreeing with each other, point to the conclusion that men were so slain, we are bound, provisionally at least, to accept the conclusion.   Further, both the Lityerses story and European harvest-customs agree in indicating that the victim was put to death as a representative of the corn-spirit, and this indication is in harmony with the view which some savages appear to take of the victim slain to make the crops flourish.   On the whole, then, we may fairly suppose that both in Phrygia and in Europe the representative of the corn-spirit was annually killed upon the harvest-field.   Grounds have been already shown for believing that similarly in Europe the representative of the tree-spirit was annually slain.   The proofs of these two remarkable and closely analogous customs are entirely independent of each other.   Their coincidence seems to furnish fresh presumption in favour of both.

To the question, How was the representative of the corn-spirit chosen ? one answer has been already given.   Both the Lityerses story and European folk-custom show that passing strangers were regarded as manifestations of the corn-spirit escaping from the cut or threshed corn, and as such were seized and slain.   But this is not the only answer which the evidence suggests.   According to the Phrygian legend the victims of Lityerses were not simply passing strangers. but persons whom he had vanquished in a reaping contest and afterwards wrapt up in corn-sheaves and beheaded.   This suggests that the representative of the corn-spirit may have been selected by means of a competition on the harvest-field, in which the vanquished competitor was compelled to accept the fatal honour.   The supposition is countenanced by European harvest-customs.   We have seen that in Europe there is sometimes a contest amongst the reapers to avoid being last, and that the person who is vanquished in this competition, that is, who cuts the last corn, is often roughly handled. It is true we have not found that a pretence is made of killing him ; but on the other hand we have found that a pretence is made of killing the man who gives the last stroke at threshing, that is, who is vanquished in the threshing contest.   Now, since it is in the character of representative of the corn-spirit that the thresher of the last corn is slain in mimicry, and since the same representative character attaches (as we have seen) to the cutter and binder as well as to the thresher of the last corn, and since the same repugnance is evinced by harvesters to be last in any one of these labours, we may conjecture that a pretence has been commonly made of killing the reaper and binder as well as the thresher of the last corn, and that in ancient times this killing was actually carried out.   This conjecture is corroborated by the common superstition that whoever cuts the last corn must die soon. Sometimes it is thought that the person who binds the last sheaf on the field will die in the course of next year. The reason for fixing on the reaper, binder, or thresher of the last corn as the representative of the corn-spirit may be this. The corn-spirit is supposed to lurk as long as he can in the corn, retreating before the reapers, the binders, and the threshers at their work. But when he is forcibly expelled from his refuge in the last corn cut or the last sheaf bound or the last grain threshed, he necessarily assumes some other form than that of the corn-stalks, which had hitherto been his garment or body. And what form can the expelled corn-spirit assume more naturally than that of the person who stands nearest to the corn from which he (the corn-spirit) has just been expelled ? But the person in question is necessarily the reaper, binder, or thresher of the last corn. He or she, therefore, is seized and treated as the corn-spirit himself.

Thus the person who was killed on the harvest-field as the representative of the corn-spirit may have been either a passing stranger or the harvester who was last at reaping, binding, or threshing. But there is a third possibility, to which ancient legend and modern folk-custom alike point. Lityerses not only put strangers to death ; he was himself slain, and apparently in the same way as he had slain others, namely, by being wrapt in a corn-sheaf, beheaded, and cast into the river ; and it is implied that this happened to Lityerses on his own land. Similarly in modern harvest-customs the pretence of killing appears to be carried out quite as often on the person of the master (farmer or squire) as on that of strangers. Now when we remember that Lityerses was said to have been a son of the King of Phrygia, and that in one account he is himself called a king, and when we combine with this the tradition that he was put to death, apparently as a representative of the corn-spirit, we are led to conjecture that we have here another trace of the custom of annually slaying one of those divine or priestly kings who are known to have held ghostly sway in many parts of Western Asia and particularly in Phrygia. The custom appears, as we have seen, to have been so far modified in places that the king's son was slain in the king's stead. Of the custom thus modified the story of Lityerses would be, in one version at least, a reminiscence.

Turning now to the relation of the Phrygian Lityerses to the Phrygian Attis, it may be remembered that at Pessinus—the seat of a priestly kingship—the high-priest appears to have been annually slain in the character of Attis, a god of vegetation, and that Attis was described by an ancient authority as " a reaped ear of corn." Thus Attis, as an embodiment of the corn-spirit, annually slain in the person of his representative, might be thought to be ultimately identical with Lityerses, the latter being simply the rustic prototype out of which the state religion of Attis was developed. It may have been so ; but, on the other hand, the analogy of European folk-custom warns us that amongst the same people two distinct deities of vegetation may have their separate personal representatives, both of whom are slain in the character of gods at different times of the year. For in Europe, as we have seen, it appears that one man was commonly slain in the character of the tree-spirit in spring, and another in the character of the corn-spirit in autumn. It may have been so in Phrygia also. Attis was especially a tree-god, and his connexion with corn may have been only such an extension of the power of a tree-spirit as is indicated in customs like the Harvest-May. Again, the representative of Attis appears to have been slain in spring ; whereas Lityerses must have been slain in summer or autumn, according to the time of the harvest in Phrygia. On the whole, then, while we are not justified in regarding Lityerses as the prototype of Attis, the two may be regarded as parallel products of the same religious idea, and may have stood to each other as in Europe the Old Man of harvest stands to the Wild Man, the Leaf Man, and so forth, of spring. Both were spirits or deities of vegetation, and the personal representatives of both were annually slain. But whereas the Attis worship became elevated into the dignity of a state religion and spread to Italy, the rites of Lityerses seem never to have passed the limits of their native Phrygia, and always retained their character of rustic ceremonies performed by peasants on the harvest-field. At most a few villages may have clubbed together, as amongst the Khonds, to procure a human victim to be slain as representative of the corn-spirit for their common benefit. Such victims may have been drawn from the families of priestly kings or kinglets, which would account for the legendary character of Lityerses as the son of a Phrygian king or as himself a king. When villages did not so club together, each village or farm may have procured its own representative of the corn-spirit by dooming to death either a passing stranger or the harvester who cut, bound, or threshed the last sheaf. Perhaps in the olden time the practice of head-hunting as a means of promoting the growth of the corn may have been as common among the rude inhabitants of Europe and Western Asia as it still is, or was till lately, among the primitive agricultural tribes of Assam, Burma, the Philippine Islands, and the Indian Archipelago. It is hardly necessary to add that in Phrygia, as in Europe, the old barbarous custom of killing a man on the harvest-field or the threshing-floor had doubtless passed into a mere pretence long before the classical era, and was probably regarded by the reapers and threshers themselves as no more than a rough jest which the license of a harvest-home permitted them to play off on a passing stranger, a comrade, or even on their master himself.

I have dwelt on the Lityerses song at length because it affords so many points of comparison with European and savage folk-custom. The other harvest songs of Western Asia and Egypt, to which attention has been called above, may now be dismissed much more briefly. The similarity of the Bithynian Bormus to the Phrygian Lityerses helps to bear out the interpretation which has been given of the latter.

Bormus, whose death or rather disappearance was annually mourned by the reapers in a plaintive song, was, like Lityerses, a king's son or at least the son of a wealthy and distinguished man. The reapers whom he watched were at work on his own fields, and he disappeared in going to fetch water for them ; according to one version of the story he was carried off by the nymphs, doubtless the nymphs of the spring or pool or river whither he went to draw water. Viewed in the light of the Lityerses story and of European folk-custom, this disappearance of Bormus may be a reminiscence of the custom of binding the farmer himself in a corn-sheaf and throwing him into the water. The mournful strain which the reapers sang was probably a lamentation over the death of the corn-spirit, slain either in the cut corn or in the person of a human representative ; and the call which they addressed to him may have been a prayer that he might return in fresh vigour next year.

The Phoenician Linus song was sung at the vintage, at least in the west of Asia Minor, as we learn from Homer ; and this, combined with the legend of Syleus, suggests that in ancient times passing strangers were handled by vintagers and vine-diggers in much the same way as they are said to have been handled by the reaper Lityerses. The Lydian Syleus, so ran the legend, compelled passers-by to dig for him in his vineyard, till Hercules came and killed him and dug up his vines by the roots. This seems to be the outline of a legend like that of Lityerses ; but neither ancient writers nor modern folk-custom enable us to fill in the details. But, further, the Linus song was probably sung also by Phoenician reapers, for Herodotus compares it to the Maneros song, which, as we have seen, was a lament raised by Egyptian reapers over the cut corn. Further, Linus was identified with Adonis, and Adonis has some claims to be regarded as especially a corn-deity. Thus the Linus lament, as sung at harvest, would be identical with the Adonis lament ; each would be the lamentation raised by reapers over the dead spirit of the corn. But whereas Adonis, like Attis, grew into a stately figure of mythology, adored and mourned in splendid cities far beyond the limits of his Phoenician home, Linus appears to have remained a simple ditty sung by reapers and vintagers among the corn-sheaves and the vines. The analogy of Lityerses and of folk-custom, both European and savage, suggests that in Phoenicia the slain corn-spirit—the dead Adonis—may formerly have been represented by a human victim ; and this suggestion is possibly supported by the Harran legend that Tammuz (Adonis) was slain by his cruel lord, who ground his bones in a mill and scattered them to the wind. For in Mexico, as we have seen, the human victim at harvest was crushed between two stones ; and both in Africa and India the ashes or other remains of the victim were scattered over the fields. But the Harran legend may be only a mythical way of expressing the grinding of corn in the mill and the scattering of the seed. It seems worth suggesting that the mock king who was annually killed at the Babylonian festival of the Sacaea on the sixteenth day of the month Lous may have represented Tammuz himself. For the historian Berosus, who records the festival and its date, probably used the Macedonian calendar, since he dedicated his history to Antiochus Soter; and in his day the Macedonian month Lous appears to have corresponded to the Babylonian month Tammuz. If this conjecture is right, the view that the mock king at the Sacaea was slain in the character of a god would be established.

There is a good deal more evidence that in Egypt the slain corn-spirit—the dead Osiris—was represented by a human victim, whom the reapers slew on the harvest-field, mourning his death in a dirge, to which the Greeks, through a verbal misunderstanding, gave the name of Maneros. For the legend of Busiris seems to preserve a reminiscence of human sacrifices once offered by the Egyptians in connexion with the worship of Osiris. Busiris was said to have been an Egyptian king who sacrificed all strangers on the altar of Zeus. The origin of the custom was traced to a dearth which afflicted the land of Egypt for nine years. A Cyprian seer informed Busiris that the dearth would cease if a man were annually sacrificed to Zeus. So Busiris instituted the sacrifice. But when Hercules came to Egypt, and was being dragged to the altar to be sacrificed, he burst his bonds and slew Busiris and his son. Here then is a legend that in Egypt a human victim was annually sacrificed to prevent the failure of the crops, and a belief is implied that an omission of the sacrifice would have entailed a recurrence of that infertility which it was the object of the sacrifice to prevent. So the Pawnees, as we have seen, believed that an omission of the human sacrifice at planting would have been followed by a total failure of their crops. The name Busiris was in reality the name of a city, *pe-Asar*, " the house of Osiris," the city being so called because it contained the grave of Osiris. Indeed some high modern authorities believe that Busiris was the original home of Osiris, from which his worship spread to other parts of Egypt. The human sacrifices were said to have been offered at his grave, and the victims were red-haired men, whose ashes were scattered abroad by means of winnowing-fans. This tradition of human sacrifices offered at the tomb of Osiris is confirmed by the evidence of the monuments.

In the light of the foregoing discussion the Egyptian tradition of Busiris admits of a consistent and fairly probable explanation. Osiris, the corn-spirit, was annually represented at harvest by a stranger, whose red hair made him a suitable representative of the ripe corn. This man, in his representative character, was slain on the harvest-field, and mourned by the reapers, who prayed at the same time that the corn-spirit might revive and return (*mââ-ne-rha*, Maneros) with renewed vigour in the following year. Finally, the victim, or some part of him, was burned, and the ashes scattered by winnowing-fans over the fields to fertilise them. Here the choice of the victim on the ground of his resemblance to the corn which he was to represent agrees with the Mexican and African customs already described. Similarly the woman who died in the character of the Corn-mother at the Mexican

midsummer sacrifice had her face painted red and yellow in token of
the colours of the corn, and she wore a pasteboard mitre surmounted
by waving plumes in imitation of the tassel of the maize. On the
other hand, at the festival of the Goddess of the White Maize the
Mexicans sacrificed lepers. The Romans sacrificed red-haired puppies
in spring to avert the supposed blighting influence of the Dog-star,
believing that the crops would thus grow ripe and ruddy. The heathen
of Harran offered to the sun, moon, and planets human victims who
were chosen on the ground of their supposed resemblance to the
heavenly bodies to which they were sacrificed; for example, the
priests, clothed in red and smeared with blood, offered a red-haired,
red-cheeked man to " the red planet Mars " in a temple which was
painted red and draped with red hangings. These and the like cases
of assimilating the victim to the god, or to the natural phenomenon
which he represents, are based ultimately on the principle of homoeopathic or imitative magic, the notion being that the object aimed at
will be most readily attained by means of a sacrifice which resembles
the effect that it is designed to bring about.

The story that the fragments of Osiris's body were scattered up
and down the land, and buried by Isis on the spots where they lay,
may very well be a reminiscence of a custom, like that observed by the
Khonds, of dividing the human victim in pieces and burying the pieces,
often at intervals of many miles from each other, in the fields.

Thus, if I am right, the key to the mysteries of Osiris is furnished
by the melancholy cry of the Egyptian reapers, which down to Roman
times could be heard year after year sounding across the fields, announcing the death of the corn-spirit, the rustic prototype of Osiris. Similar
cries, as we have seen, were also heard on all the harvest-fields of
Western Asia. By the ancients they are spoken of as songs; but to
judge from the analysis of the names Linus and Maneros, they probably
consisted only of a few words uttered in a prolonged musical note
which could be heard at a great distance. Such sonorous and long-
drawn cries, raised by a number of strong voices in concert, must have
had a striking effect, and could hardly fail to arrest the attention of
any wayfarer who happened to be within hearing. The sounds,
repeated again and again, could probably be distinguished with
tolerable ease even at a distance; but to a Greek traveller in Asia or
Egypt the foreign words would commonly convey no meaning, and he
might take them, not unnaturally, for the name of some one (Maneros,
Linus, Lityerses, Bormus) upon whom the reapers were calling. And
if his journey led him through more countries than one, as Bithynia
and Phrygia, or Phoenicia and Egypt, while the corn was being reaped,
he would have an opportunity of comparing the various harvest cries
of the different peoples. Thus we can readily understand why these
harvest cries were so often noted and compared with each other by
the Greeks. Whereas, if they had been regular songs, they could not
have been heard at such distances, and therefore could not have
attracted the attention of so many travellers; and, moreover, even if

the wayfarer were within hearing of them, he could not so easily have picked out the words.

Down to recent times Devonshire reapers uttered cries of the same sort, and performed on the field a ceremony exactly analogous to that in which, if I am not mistaken, the rites of Osiris originated. The cry and the ceremony are thus described by an observer who wrote in the first half of the nineteenth century. " After the wheat is all cut, on most farms in the north of Devon, the harvest people have a custom of ' crying the neck.' I believe that this practice is seldom omitted on any large farm in that part of the country. It is done in this way. An old man, or some one else well acquainted with the ceremonies used on the occasion (when the labourers are reaping the last field of wheat), goes round to the shocks and sheaves, and picks out a little bundle of all the best ears he can find ; this bundle he ties up very neat and trim, and plats and arranges the straws very tastefully. This is called ' the neck ' of wheat, or wheaten-ears. After the field is cut out, and the pitcher once more circulated, the reapers, binders, and the women stand round in a circle. The person with ' the neck ' stands in the centre, grasping it with both his hands. He first stoops and holds it near the ground, and all the men forming the ring take off their hats, stooping and holding them with both hands towards the ground. They then all begin at once in a very prolonged and harmonious tone to cry ' The neck ! ' at the same time slowly raising themselves up-right, and elevating their arms and hats above their heads ; the person with ' the neck ' also raising it on high. This is done three times. They then change their cry to ' Wee yen ! '—' Way yen ! '—which they sound in the same prolonged and slow manner as before, with singular harmony and effect, three times. This last cry is accompanied by the same movements of the body and arms as in crying ' the neck.' . . . After having thus repeated ' the neck ' three times, and ' wee yen ' or ' way yen ' as often, they all burst out into a kind of loud and joyous laugh, flinging up their hats and caps into the air, capering about and perhaps kissing the girls. One of them then gets ' the neck ' and runs as hard as he can down to the farmhouse, where the dairymaid, or one of the young female domestics, stands at the door prepared with a pail of water. If he who holds ' the neck ' can manage to get into the house, in any way unseen, or openly, by any other way than the door at which the girl stands with the pail of water, then he may lawfully kiss her ; but, if otherwise, he is regularly soused with the contents of the bucket. On a fine still autumn evening the ' crying of the neck ' has a wonderful effect at a distance, far finer than that of the Turkish muezzin, which Lord Byron eulogises so much, and which he says is preferable to all the bells in Christendom. I have once or twice heard upwards of twenty men cry it, and sometimes joined by an equal number of female voices. About three years back, on some high grounds, where our people were harvesting, I heard six or seven ' necks ' cried in one night, although I know that some of them were four miles off. They are heard through the quiet evening air at a considerable distance sometimes." Again, Mrs. Bray tells how, travelling in Devonshire, " she saw a party of reapers standing in a circle on a rising ground, holding their sickles aloft. One in the middle held up some ears of corn tied together with flowers, and the party shouted three times (what she writes as) ' Arnack, arnack, arnack, we *haven*, we *haven*, we *haven*.' They went home, accompanied by women and children carrying boughs of flowers, shouting and singing. The manservant who attended Mrs. Bray said ' it was only the people making their games, as they always did, *to the spirit of harvest*.' " Here, as Miss Burne remarks, " ' arnack, we haven ! ' is obviously in the Devon dialect, ' a neck (or nack) ! we have un ! ' "

Another account of this old custom, written at Truro in 1839, runs thus : " Now, when all the corn was cut at Heligan, the farming men and maidens come in front of the house, and bring with them a small sheaf of corn, the last that has been cut, and this is adorned with ribbons and flowers, and one part is tied quite tight, so as to look like a neck. Then they cry out ' Our (my) side, my side,' as loud as they can ; then the dairymaid gives the neck to the head farming-man. He takes it, and says, very loudly three times, ' I have him, I have him, I have him.' Then another farming-man shouts very loudly, ' What have ye ? what have ye ? what have ye ? ' Then the first says, ' A neck, a neck, a neck.' And when he has said this, all the people make a very great shouting. This they do three times, and after one famous shout go away and eat supper, and dance, and sing songs." According to another account, " all went out to the field when the last corn was cut, the ' neck ' was tied with ribbons and plaited, and they danced round it, and carried it to the great kitchen, where by-and-by the supper was. The words were as given in the previous account, and ' Hip, hip, hack, heck, I have 'ee, I have 'ee, I have 'ee.' It was hung up in the hall." Another account relates that one of the men rushed from the field with the last sheaf, while the rest pursued him with vessels of water, which they tried to throw over the sheaf before it could be brought into the barn.

In the foregoing customs a particular bunch of ears, generally the last left standing, is conceived as the neck of the corn-spirit, who is consequently beheaded when the bunch is cut down. Similarly in Shropshire the name " neck," or " the gander's neck," used to be commonly given to the last handful of ears left standing in the middle of the field when all the rest of the corn was cut. It was plaited together, and the reapers, standing ten or twenty paces off, threw their sickles at it. Whoever cut it through was said to have cut off the gander's neck. The " neck " was taken to the farmer's wife, who was supposed to keep it in the house for good luck till the next harvest came round. Near Trèves, the man who reaps the last standing corn " cuts the goat's neck off." At Faslane, on the Gareloch (Dumbarton-shire), the last handful of standing corn was sometimes called the " head." At Aurich, in East Friesland, the man who reaps the last corn " cuts the hare's tail off." In mowing down the last corner of a field French reapers sometimes call out, " We have the cat by the tail." In Bresse (Bourgogne) the last sheaf represented the fox. Beside it a score of ears were left standing to form the tail, and each reaper, going back some paces, threw his sickle at it. He who succeeded in severing it " cut off the fox's tail," and a cry of " *You cou cou !* " was raised in his honour. These examples leave no room to doubt the meaning of the Devonshire and Cornish expression " the neck," as applied to the last sheaf. The corn-spirit is conceived in human or animal form, and the last standing corn is part of its body— its neck, its head, or its tail. Sometimes, as we have seen, the last corn is regarded as the navel-string. Lastly, the Devonshire custom of drenching with water the person who brings in " the neck " is a rain-charm, such as we have had many examples of. Its parallel in the mysteries of Osiris was the custom of pouring water on the image of Osiris or on the person who represented him.

CHAPTER XLVIII

THE CORN-SPIRIT AS AN ANIMAL

§ 1. *Animal Embodiments of the Corn-spirit.* —In some of the examples which I have cited to establish the meaning of the term " neck " as applied to the last sheaf, the corn-spirit appears in animal form as a gander, a goat, a hare, a cat, and a fox. This introduces us to a new aspect of the corn-spirit, which we must now examine. By doing so we shall not only have fresh examples of killing the god, but may hope also to clear up some points which remain obscure in the myths and worship of Adonis, Attis, Osiris, Dionysus, Demeter, and Virbius.

Amongst the many animals whose forms the corn-spirit is supposed to take are the wolf, dog, hare, fox, cock, goose, quail, cat, goat, cow (ox, bull), pig, and horse. In one or other of these shapes the corn-spirit is often believed to be present in the corn, and to be caught or killed in the last sheaf. As the corn is being cut the animal flees before the reapers, and if a reaper is taken ill on the field, he is supposed to have stumbled unwittingly on the corn-spirit, who has thus punished the profane intruder. It is said " The Rye-wolf has got hold of him," " The Harvest-goat has given him a push." The person who cuts the last corn or binds the last sheaf gets the name of the animal, as the Rye-wolf, the Rye-sow, the Oats-goat, and so forth, and retains the name sometimes for a year. Also the animal is frequently represented by a puppet made out of the last sheaf or of wood, flowers, and so on, which is carried home amid rejoicings on the last harvest-waggon. Even where the last sheaf is not made up in animal shape, it is often called the Rye-wolf, the Hare, Goat, and so forth. Generally each kind of crop is supposed to have its special animal, which is caught in the last sheaf, and called the Rye-wolf, the Barley-wolf, the Oats-wolf, the Pea-wolf, or the Potato-wolf, according to the crop ; but sometimes the figure of the animal is only made up once for all at getting in the last crop of the whole harvest. Sometimes the creature is believed to be killed by the last stroke of the sickle or scythe. But oftener it is thought to live so long as there is corn still unthreshed, and to be caught in the last sheaf threshed. Hence the man who gives the last stroke with the flail is told that he has got the Corn-sow, the Threshing-dog, or the like. When the threshing is finished, a puppet is made in the form of the animal, and this is carried by the thresher of the last sheaf to a neighbouring farm, where the threshing is still going on. This again shows that the corn-spirit is believed to live wherever the corn is still being threshed. Sometimes the thresher of the last sheaf himself represents the animal ; and if the people of the next farm, who are still threshing, catch him, they treat him like the animal he represents, by shutting him up in the pig-sty, calling him with the cries commonly addressed to pigs, and so forth. These general statements will now be illustrated by examples.

§ 2. *The Corn-spirit as a Wolf or a Dog.*—We begin with the corn-spirit conceived as a wolf or a dog. This conception is common in France, Germany, and Slavonic countries. Thus, when the wind sets the corn in wave-like motion the peasants often say, " The Wolf is going over, or through, the corn," " The Rye-wolf is rushing over the field," " The Wolf is in the corn," " The mad Dog is in the corn," " The big Dog is there." When children wish to go into the corn-fields to pluck ears or gather the blue corn-flowers, they are warned not to do so, for " The big Dog sits in the corn," or " The Wolf sits in the corn, and will tear you in pieces," " The Wolf will eat you." The wolf against whom the children are warned is not a common wolf, for he is often spoken of as the Corn-wolf, Rye-wolf, or the like ; thus they say, " The Rye-wolf will come and eat you up, children," " The Rye-wolf will carry you off," and so forth. Still he has all the outward appearance of a wolf. For in the neighbourhood of Feilenhof (East Prussia), when a wolf was seen running through a field, the peasants used to watch whether he carried his tail in the air or dragged it on the ground. If he dragged it on the ground, they went after him, and thanked him for bringing them a blessing, and even set tit-bits before him. But if he carried his tail high, they cursed him and tried to kill him. Here the wolf is the corn-spirit whose fertilising power is in his tail.

Both dog and wolf appear as embodiments of the corn-spirit in harvest-customs. Thus in some parts of Silesia the person who cuts or binds the last sheaf is called the Wheat-dog or the Peas-pug. But it is in the harvest-customs of the north-east of France that the idea of the Corn-dog comes out most clearly. Thus when a harvester, through sickness, weariness, or laziness, cannot or will not keep up with the reaper in front of him, they say, " The White Dog passed near him," " He has the White Bitch," or " The White Bitch has bitten him." In the Vosges the Harvest-May is called the "Dog of the harvest," and the person who cuts the last handful of hay or wheat is said to "kill the Dog." About Lons-le-Saulnier, in the Jura, the last sheaf is called the Bitch. In the neighbourhood of Verdun the regular expression for finishing the reaping is, "They are going to kill the Dog"; and at Epinal they say, according to the crop, "We will kill the Wheat-dog, or the Rye-dog, or the Potato-dog." In Lorraine it is said of the man who cuts the last corn, "He is killing the Dog of the harvest." At Dux, in the Tyrol, the man who gives the last stroke at threshing is said to "strike down the Dog"; and at Ahnebergen, near Stade, he is called, according to the crop, Corn-pug, Rye-pug, Wheat-pug.

So with the wolf. In Silesia, when the reapers gather round the last patch of standing corn to reap it they are said to be about "to catch the Wolf." In various parts of Mecklenburg, where the belief in the Corn-wolf is particularly prevalent, every one fears to cut the last corn, because they say that the Wolf is sitting in it; hence every reaper exerts himself to the utmost in order not to be the last, and every woman similarly fears to bind the last sheaf because "the Wolf is in it." So both among the reapers and the binders there is a competition not to be the last to finish. And in Germany generally it appears to be a common saying that "the Wolf sits in the last sheaf." In some places they call out to the reaper, "Beware of the Wolf"; or they say, "He is chasing the Wolf out of the corn." In Mecklenburg the last bunch of standing corn is itself commonly called the Wolf, and the man who reaps it "has the Wolf," the animal being described as the Rye-wolf, the Wheat-wolf, the Barley-wolf, and so on according to the particular crop. The reaper of the last corn is himself called Wolf or the Rye-wolf, if the crop is rye, and in many parts of Mecklenburg he has to support the character by pretending to bite the other harvesters or by howling like a wolf. The last sheaf of corn is also called the Wolf or the Rye-wolf or the Oats-wolf according to the crop, and of the woman who binds it they say, "The Wolf is biting her," "She has the Wolf," "She must fetch the Wolf" (out of the corn). Moreover, she herself is called Wolf; they cry out to her, "Thou art the Wolf," and she has to bear the name for a whole year; sometimes, according to the crop, she is called the Rye-wolf or the Potato-wolf. In the island of Rügen not only is the woman who binds the last sheaf called Wolf, but when she comes home she bites the lady of the house and the stewardess, for which she receives a large piece of meat. Yet nobody likes to be the Wolf. The same woman may be Rye-wolf, Wheat-wolf, and Oats-wolf, if she happens to bind the last sheaf of rye, wheat, and oats. At Buir, in the district of Cologne, it was formerly the custom to give to the last sheaf the shape of a wolf. It was kept in the barn till all the corn was threshed. Then it was brought to the farmer and he had to sprinkle it with beer or brandy. At Brunshaupten in Mecklenburg the young woman who bound the last sheaf of wheat used to take a handful of stalks out of it and make " the Wheat-wolf " with them ; it was the figure of a wolf about two feet long and half a foot high, the legs of the animal being represented by stiff stalks and its tail and mane by wheat-ears. This Wheat-wolf she carried back at the head of the harvesters to the village, where it was set up on a high place in the parlour of the farm and remained there for a long time. In many places the sheaf called the Wolf is made up in human form and dressed in clothes. This indicates a confusion of ideas between the corn-spirit conceived in human and in animal form. Generally the Wolf is brought home on the last waggon with joyful cries. Hence the last waggon-load itself receives the name of the Wolf.

Again, the Wolf is supposed to hide himself amongst the cut corn in the granary, until he is driven out of the last bundle by the strokes of the flail. Hence at Wanzleben, near Magdeburg, after the threshing the peasants go in procession, leading by a chain a man who is enveloped in the threshed-out straw and is called the Wolf. He represents the corn-spirit who has been caught escaping from the threshed corn. In the district of Treves it is believed that the Corn-wolf is killed at threshing. The men thresh the last sheaf till it is reduced to chopped straw. In this way they think that the Corn-wolf, who was lurking in the last sheaf, has been certainly killed.

In France also the Corn-wolf appears at harvest. Thus they call out to the reaper of the last corn, " You will catch the Wolf." Near Chambéry they form a ring round the last standing corn, and cry, " The Wolf is in there." In Finisterre, when the reaping draws near an end, the harvesters cry, " There is the Wolf ; we will catch him." Each takes a swath to reap, and he who finishes first calls out, " I've caught the Wolf." In Guyenne, when the last corn has been reaped, they lead a wether all round the field. It is called " the Wolf of the field." Its horns are decked with a wreath of flowers and corn-ears, and its neck and body are also encircled with garlands and ribbons. All the reapers march, singing, behind it. Then it is killed on the field. In this part of France the last sheaf is called the *coujou-lage*, which, in the patois, means a wether. Hence the killing of the wether represents the death of the corn-spirit, considered as present in the last sheaf ; but two different conceptions of the corn-spirit— as a wolf and as a wether—are mixed up together.

Sometimes it appears to be thought that the Wolf, caught in the last corn, lives during the winter in the farmhouse, ready to renew his activity as corn-spirit in the spring. Hence at midwinter, when the lengthening days begin to herald the approach of spring, the Wolf makes his appearance once more. In Poland a man, with a wolf's skin thrown over his head, is led about at Christmas ; or a stuffed wolf is carried about by persons who collect money. There are facts which point to an old custom of leading about a man enveloped in leaves and called the Wolf, while his conductors collected money.

§ 3. *The Corn-spirit as a Cock.*—Another form which the corn-

spirit often assumes is that of a cock.   In Austria children are warned
against straying in the corn-fields, because the Corn-cock sits there,
and will peck their eyes out.   In North Germany they say that " the
Cock sits in the last sheaf " ; and at cutting the last corn the reapers
cry, " Now we will chase out the Cock."   When it is cut they say,
" We have caught the Cock."   At Braller, in Transylvania, when the
reapers come to the last patch of corn, they cry, " Here we shall catch
the Cock."   At Fürstenwalde, when the last sheaf is about to be
bound, the master releases a cock, which he has brought in a basket,
and lets it run over the field.   All the harvesters chase it till they
catch it.   Elsewhere the harvesters all try to seize the last corn cut ;
he who succeeds in grasping it must crow, and is called Cock.   Among
the Wends it is or used to be customary for the farmer to hide a live
cock under the last sheaf as it lay on the field ; and when the corn
was being gathered up, the harvester who lighted upon this sheaf
had a right to keep the cock, provided he could catch it.   This formed
the close of the harvest-festival and was known as " the Cock-catching,"
and the beer which was served out to the reapers at this time went
by the name of " Cock-beer."   The last sheaf is called Cock, Cock-
sheaf, Harvest-cock, Harvest-hen, Autumn-hen.   A distinction is
made between a Wheat-cock, Bean-cock, and so on, according to the
crop.   At Wünschensuhl, in Thüringen, the last sheaf is made into
the shape of a cock, and called the Harvest-cock.   A figure of a cock,
made of wood, pasteboard, ears of corn, or flowers, is borne in front of
the harvest-waggon, especially in Westphalia, where the cock carries
in his beak fruits of the earth of all kinds.   Sometimes the image of
the cock is fastened to the top of a May-tree on the last harvest-waggon.
Elsewhere a live cock, or a figure of one, is attached to a harvest-
crown and carried on a pole.   In Galicia and elsewhere this live cock
is fastened to the garland of corn-ears or flowers, which the leader
of the women-reapers carries on her head as she marches in front
of the harvest procession.   In Silesia a live cock is presented to the
master on a plate.   The harvest-supper is called Harvest-cock,
Stubble-cock, etc., and a chief dish at it, at least in some places, is a
cock.   If a waggoner upsets a harvest-waggon, it is said that " he has
spilt the Harvest cock," and he loses the cock, that is, the harvest-
supper.   The harvest-waggon, with the figure of the cock on it, is
driven round the farmhouse before it is taken to the barn.   Then the
cock is nailed over or at the side of the house-door, or on the gable,
and remains there till next harvest.   In East Friesland the person
who gives the last stroke at threshing is called the Clucking-hen, and
grain is strewed before him as if he were a hen.

   Again, the corn-spirit is killed in the form of a cock.   In parts
of Germany, Hungary, Poland, and Picardy the reapers place a live
cock in the corn which is to be cut last, and chase it over the field,
or bury it up to the neck in the ground ; afterwards they strike off
its head with a sickle or scythe.   In many parts of Westphalia, when
the harvesters bring the wooden cock to the farmer, he gives them a

live cock, which they kill with whips or sticks, or behead with an old
sword, or throw into the barn to the girls, or give to the mistress to
cook. If the harvest-cock has not been spilt—that is, if no waggon
has been upset—the harvesters have the right to kill the farmyard
cock by throwing stones at it or beheading it. Where this custom
has fallen into disuse, it is still common for the farmer's wife to make
cockie-leekie for the harvesters, and to show them the head of the
cock which has been killed for the soup. In the neighbourhood of
Klausenburg, Transylvania, a cock is buried on the harvest-field in
the earth, so that only its head appears. A young man then takes a
scythe and cuts off the cock's head at a single sweep. If he fails to
do this, he is called the Red Cock for a whole year, and people fear
that next year's crop will be bad. Near Udvarhely, in Transylvania,
a live cock is bound up in the last sheaf and killed with a spit. It is
then skinned. The flesh is thrown away, but the skin and feathers
are kept till next year ; and in spring the grain from the last sheaf is
mixed with the feathers of the cock and scattered on the field which
is to be tilled. Nothing could set in a clearer light the identification
of the cock with the spirit of the corn. By being tied up in the last
sheaf and killed, the cock is identified with the corn, and its death
with the cutting of the corn. By keeping its feathers till spring,
then mixing them with the seed-corn taken from the very sheaf in
which the bird had been bound, and scattering the feathers together
with the seed over the field, the identity of the bird with the corn
is again emphasised, and its quickening and fertilising power, as an
embodiment of the corn-spirit, is intimated in the plainest manner.
Thus the corn-spirit, in the form of a cock, is killed at harvest, but rises
to fresh life and activity in spring. Again, the equivalence of the
cock to the corn is expressed, hardly less plainly, in the custom of
burying the bird in the ground, and cutting off its head (like the ears
of corn) with the scythe.

§ 4. *The Corn-spirit as a Hare.*—Another common embodiment
of the corn-spirit is the hare. In Galloway the reaping of the last
standing corn is called " cutting the Hare." The mode of cutting it
is as follows. When the rest of the corn has been reaped, a handful is
left standing to form the Hare. It is divided into three parts and
plaited, and the ears are tied in a knot. The reapers then retire a
few yards and each throws his or her sickle in turn at the Hare to cut
it down. It must be cut below the knot, and the reapers continue
to throw their sickles at it, one after the other, until one of them
succeeds in severing the stalks below the knot. The Hare is then
carried home and given to a maidservant in the kitchen, who places
it over the kitchen-door on the inside. Sometimes the Hare used to
be thus kept till the next harvest. In the parish of Minnigaff, when the
Hare was cut, the unmarried reapers ran home with all speed, and the
one who arrived first was the first to be married. In Germany also
one of the names for the last sheaf is the Hare. Thus in some parts
of Anhalt, when the corn has been reaped and only a few stalks are

left standing, they say, " The Hare will soon come," or the reapers cry to each other, " Look how the Hare comes jumping out." In East Prussia they say that the Hare sits in the last patch of standing corn, and must be chased out by the last reaper. The reapers hurry with their work, each being anxious not to have " to chase out the Hare " ; for the man who does so, that is, who cuts the last corn, is much laughed at. At Aurich, as we have seen, an expression for cutting the last corn is " to cut off the Hare's tail." " He is killing the Hare " is commonly said of the man who cuts the last corn in Germany, Sweden, Holland, France, and Italy. In Norway the man who is thus said to " kill the Hare " must give " hare's blood " in the form of brandy to his fellows to drink. In Lesbos, when the reapers are at work in two neighbouring fields, each party tries to finish first in order to drive the Hare into their neighbour's field ; the reapers who succeed in doing so believe that next year the crop will be better. A small sheaf of corn is made up and kept beside the holy picture till next harvest.

§ 5. *The Corn-spirit as a Cat.*—Again, the corn-spirit sometimes takes the form of a cat. Near Kiel children are warned not to go into the corn-fields because " the Cat sits there." In the Eisenach Oberland they are told " The Corn-cat will come and fetch you," " The Corn-cat goes in the corn." In some parts of Silesia at mowing the last corn they say, " The Cat is caught " ; and at threshing, the man who gives the last stroke is called the Cat. In the neighbourhood of Lyons the last sheaf and the harvest-supper are both called the Cat. About Vesoul when they cut the last corn they say, " We have the Cat by the tail." At Briançon, in Dauphiné, at the beginning of reaping, a cat is decked out with ribbons, flowers, and ears of corn. It is called the Cat of the ball-skin (*le chat de peau de balle*). If a reaper is wounded at his work, they make the cat lick the wound. At the close of the reaping the cat is again decked out with ribbons and ears of corn ; then they dance and make merry. When the dance is over the girls solemnly strip the cat of its finery. At Grüneberg, in Silesia, the reaper who cuts the last corn goes by the name of the Tom-cat. He is enveloped in rye-stalks and green withes, and is furnished with a long plaited tail. Sometimes as a companion he has a man similarly dressed, who is called the (female) Cat. Their duty is to run after people whom they see and to beat them with a long stick. Near Amiens the expression for finishing the harvest is, " They are going to kill the Cat " ; and when the last corn is cut they kill a cat in the farmyard. At threshing, in some parts of France, a live cat is placed under the last bundle of corn to be threshed, and is struck dead with the flails. Then on Sunday it is roasted and eaten as a holiday dish. In the Vosges Mountains the close of haymaking or harvest is called " catching the cat," " killing the dog," or more rarely " catching the hare." The cat, the dog, or the hare is said to be fat or lean according as the crop is good or bad. The man who cuts the last handful of hay or of wheat is said to catch the cat or the hare or to kill the dog.

§ 6. *The Corn-spirit as a Goat.*—Further, the corn-spirit often appears in the form of a goat. In some parts of Prussia, when the corn bends before the wind, they say, " The Goats are chasing each other," " The wind is driving the Goats through the corn," " The Goats are browsing there," and they expect a very good harvest. Again they say, " The Oats-goat is sitting in the oats-field," " The Corn-goat is sitting in the rye-field." Children are warned not to go into the corn-fields to pluck the blue corn-flowers, or amongst the beans to pluck pods, because the Rye-goat, the Corn-goat, the Oats-goat, or the Bean-goat is sitting or lying there, and will carry them away or kill them. When a harvester is taken sick or lags behind his fellows at their work, they call out, " The Harvest-goat has pushed him," " He has been pushed by the Corn-goat." In the neighbourhood of Braunsberg (East Prussia) at binding the oats every harvester makes haste " lest the Corn-goat push him." At Oefoten, in Norway, each reaper has his allotted patch to reap. When a reaper in the middle has not finished reaping his piece after his neighbours have finished theirs, they say of him, " He remains on the island." And if the laggard is a man, they imitate the cry with which they call a he-goat ; if a woman, the cry with which they call a she-goat. Near Straubing, in Lower Bavaria, it is said of the man who cuts the last corn that " he has the Corn-goat, or the Wheat-goat, or the Oats-goat," according to the crop. Moreover, two horns are set up on the last heap of corn, and it is called " the horned Goat." At Kreutzburg, East Prussia, they call out to the woman who is binding the last sheaf, " The Goat is sitting in the sheaf." At Gablingen, in Swabia, when the last field of oats upon a farm is being reaped, the reapers carve a goat out of wood. Ears of oats are inserted in its nostrils and mouth, and it is adorned with garlands of flowers. It is set up on the field and called the Oats-goat. When the reaping approaches an end, each reaper hastens to finish his piece first ; he who is the last to finish gets the Oats-goat. Again, the last sheaf is itself called the Goat. Thus, in the valley of the Wiesent, Bavaria, the last sheaf bound on the field is called the Goat, and they have a proverb, " The field must bear a goat." At Spachbrücken, in Hesse, the last handful of corn which is cut is called the Goat, and the man who cuts it is much ridiculed. At Dürrenbüchig and about Mosbach in Baden the last sheaf is also called the Goat. Sometimes the last sheaf is made up in the form of a goat, and they say, " The Goat is sitting in it." Again, the person who cuts or binds the last sheaf is called the Goat. Thus, in parts of Mecklenburg they call out to the woman who binds the last sheaf, " You are the Harvest-goat." Near Uelzen, in Hanover, the harvest festival begins with " the bringing of the Harvest-goat " ; that is, the woman who bound the last sheaf is wrapt in straw, crowned with a harvest-wreath, and brought in a wheel-barrow to the village, where a round dance takes place. About Luneburg, also, the woman who binds the last corn is decked with a crown of corn-ears and is called the Corn-goat. At Münzesheim in Baden the reaper who cuts the last handful

of corn or oats is called the Corn-goat or the Oats-goat.   In the Canton
St. Gall, Switzerland, the person who cuts the last handful of corn on
the field, or drives the last harvest-waggon to the barn, is called the
Corn-goat or the Rye-goat, or simply the Goat.   In the Canton Thurgau
he is called Corn-goat ; like a goat he has a bell hung round his neck,
is led in triumph, and drenched with liquor.   In parts of Styria, also,
the man who cuts the last corn is called Corn-goat, Oats-goat, or the
like.   As a rule, the man who thus gets the name of Corn-goat has to
bear it a whole year till the next harvest.

According to one view, the corn-spirit, who has been caught in the
form of a goat or otherwise, lives in the farmhouse or barn over winter.
Thus, each farm has its own embodiment of the corn-spirit.   But,
according to another view, the corn-spirit is the genius or deity, not
of the corn of one farm only, but of all the corn.   Hence when the
corn on one farm is all cut, he flees to another where there is still corn
left standing.   This idea is brought out in a harvest-custom which was
formerly observed in Skye.   The farmer who first finished reaping
sent a man or woman with a sheaf to a neighbouring farmer who had
not finished ; the latter in his turn, when he had finished, sent on the
sheaf to his neighbour who was still reaping ; and so the sheaf made
the round of the farms till all the corn was cut.   The sheaf was called
the *goabbir bhacagh*, that is, the Cripple Goat.   The custom appears
not to be extinct at the present day, for it was reported from Skye
not very many years ago.   The corn-spirit was probably thus represented as lame because he had been crippled by the cutting of the
corn.   Sometimes the old woman who brings home the last sheaf must
limp on one foot.

But sometimes the corn-spirit, in the form of a goat, is believed to
be slain on the harvest-field by the sickle or scythe.   Thus, in the
neighbourhood of Bernkastel, on the Moselle, the reapers determine
by lot the order in which they shall follow each other.   The first is
called the fore-reaper, the last the tail-bearer.   If a reaper overtakes
the man in front he reaps past him, bending round so as to leave the
slower reaper in a patch by himself.   This patch is called the Goat ;
and the man for whom " the Goat is cut " in this way, is laughed and
jeered at by his fellows for the rest of the day.   When the tail-bearer
cuts the last ears of corn, it is said, " He is cutting the Goat's neck off."
In the neighbourhood of Grenoble, before the end of the reaping, a
live goat is adorned with flowers and ribbons and allowed to run about
the field.   The reapers chase it and try to catch it.   When it is caught,
the farmer's wife holds it fast while the farmer cuts off its head.   The
goat's flesh serves to furnish the harvest-supper.   A piece of the flesh
is pickled and kept till the next harvest, when another goat is killed.
Then all the harvesters eat of the flesh.   On the same day the skin of
the goat is made into a cloak, which the farmer, who works with his
men, must always wear at harvest-time if rain or bad weather sets in.
But if a reaper gets pains in his back, the farmer gives him the goat-
skin to wear.   The reason for this seems to be that the pains in the

back, being inflicted by the corn-spirit, can also be healed by it. Similarly, we saw that elsewhere, when a reaper is wounded at reaping, a cat, as the representative of the corn-spirit, is made to lick the wound. Esthonian reapers in the island of Mon think that the man who cuts the first ears of corn at harvest will get pains in his back, probably because the corn-spirit is believed to resent especially the first wound ; and, in order to escape pains in the back, Saxon reapers in Transylvania gird their loins with the first handful of ears which they cut. Here, again, the corn-spirit is applied to for healing or protection, but in his original vegetable form, not in the form of a goat or a cat.

Further, the corn-spirit under the form of a goat is sometimes conceived as lurking among the cut corn in the barn, till he is driven from it by the threshing-flail. Thus in Baden the last sheaf to be threshed is called the Corn-goat, the Spelt-goat, or the Oats-goat according to the kind of grain. Again, near Marktl, in Upper Bavaria, the sheaves are called Straw-goats or simply Goats. They are laid in a great heap on the open field and threshed by two rows of men standing opposite each other, who, as they ply their flails, sing a song in which they say that they see the Straw-goat amongst the corn-stalks. The last Goat, that is, the last sheaf, is adorned with a wreath of violets and other flowers and with cakes strung together. It is placed right in the middle of the heap. Some of the threshers rush at it and tear the best of it out ; others lay on with their flails so recklessly that heads are sometimes broken. At Oberinntal, in the Tyrol, the last thresher is called Goat. So at Haselberg, in West Bohemia, the man who gives the last stroke at threshing oats is called the Oats-goat. At Tettnang, in Würtemburg, the thresher who gives the last stroke to the last bundle of corn before it is turned goes by the name of the He-goat, and it is said, " He has driven the He-goat away." The person who, after the bundle has been turned, gives the last stroke of all, is called the She-goat. In this custom it is implied that the corn is inhabited by a pair of corn-spirits, male and female.

Further, the corn-spirit, captured in the form of a goat at threshing, is passed on to a neighbour whose threshing is not yet finished. In Franche Comté, as soon as the threshing is over, the young people set up a straw figure of a goat on the farmyard of a neighbour who is still threshing. He must give them wine or money in return. At Ellwangen, in Würtemburg, the effigy of a goat is made out of the last bundle of corn at threshing ; four sticks form its legs, and two its horns. The man who gives the last stroke with the flail must carry the Goat to the barn of a neighbour who is still threshing and throw it down on the floor ; if he is caught in the act, they tie the Goat on his back. A similar custom is observed at Indersdorf, in Upper Bavaria ; the man who throws the straw Goat into the neighbour's barn imitates the bleating of a goat ; if they catch him, they blacken his face and tie the Goat on his back. At Saverne, in Alsace, when a farmer is a week or more behind his neighbours with his threshing, they set a real stuffed goat or fox before his door.

Sometimes the spirit of the corn in goat form is believed to be killed at threshing. In the district of Traunstein, Upper Bavaria, they think that the Oats-goat is in the last sheaf of oats. He is represented by an old rake set up on end, with an old pot for a head. The children are then told to kill the Oats-goat.

§ 7. *The Corn-spirit as a Bull, Cow, or Ox.*—Another form which the corn-spirit often assumes is that of a bull, cow, or ox. When the wind sweeps over the corn they say at Conitz, in West Prussia, " The Steer is running in the corn " ; when the corn is thick and strong in one spot, they say in some parts of East Prussia, " The Bull is lying in the corn." When a harvester has overstrained and lamed himself, they say in the Graudenz district of West Prussia, " The Bull pushed him " ; in Lorraine they say, " He has the Bull." The meaning of both expressions is that he has unwittingly lighted upon the divine corn-spirit, who has punished the profane intruder with lameness. So near Chambéry when a reaper wounds himself with his sickle, it is said that he has " the wound of the Ox." In the district of Bunzlau (Silesia) the last sheaf is sometimes made into the shape of a horned ox, stuffed with tow and wrapt in corn-ears. This figure is called the Old Man. In some parts of Bohemia the last sheaf is made up in human form and called the Buffalo-bull. These cases show a confusion of the human with the animal shape of the corn-spirit. The confusion is like that of killing a wether under the name of a wolf. All over Swabia the last bundle of corn on the field is called the Cow ; the man who cuts the last ears " has the Cow," and is himself called Cow or Barley-cow or Oats-cow, according to the crop ; at the harvest-supper he gets a nosegay of flowers and corn-ears and a more liberal allowance of drink than the rest. But he is teased and laughed at ; so no one likes to be the Cow. The Cow was sometimes represented by the figure of a woman made out of ears of corn and corn-flowers. It was carried to the farmhouse by the man who had cut the last handful of corn. The children ran after him and the neighbours turned out to laugh at him, till the farmer took the Cow from him. Here again the confusion between the human and the animal form of the corn-spirit is apparent. In various parts of Switzerland the reaper who cuts the last ears of corn is called Wheat-cow, Corn-cow, Oats-cow, or Corn-steer, and is the butt of many a joke. On the other hand, in the district of Rosenheim, Upper Bavaria, when a farmer is later of getting in his harvest than his neighbours, they set up on his land a Straw-bull, as it is called. This is a gigantic figure of a bull made of stubble on a framework of wood and adorned with flowers and leaves. Attached to it is a label on which are scrawled doggerel verses in ridicule of the man on whose land the Straw-bull is set up.

Again, the corn-spirit in the form of a bull or ox is killed on the harvest-field at the close of the reaping. At Pouilly, near Dijon,

when the last ears of corn are about to be cut, an ox adorned with
ribbons, flowers, and ears of corn is led all round the field, followed
by the whole troop of reapers dancing. Then a man disguised as
the Devil cuts the last ears of corn and immediately slaughters the
ox. Part of the flesh of the animal is eaten at the harvest-supper ;
part is pickled and kept till the first day of sowing in spring. At
Pont à Mousson and elsewhere on the evening of the last day of reaping,
a calf adorned with flowers and ears of corn is led thrice round the
farmyard, being allured by a bait or driven by men with sticks, or
conducted by the farmer's wife with a rope. The calf chosen for
this ceremony is the calf which was born first on the farm in the spring
of the year. It is followed by all the reapers with their tools. Then
it is allowed to run free ; the reapers chase it, and whoever catches
it is called King of the Calf. Lastly, it is solemnly killed ; at Luné-
ville the man who acts as butcher is the Jewish merchant of the village.

Sometimes again the corn-spirit hides himself amongst the cut
corn in the barn to reappear in bull or cow form at threshing. Thus
at Wurmlingen, in Thüringen, the man who gives the last stroke at
threshing is called the Cow, or rather the Barley-cow, Oats-cow,
Peas-cow, or the like, according to the crop. He is entirely enveloped
in straw ; his head is surmounted by sticks in imitation of horns,
and two lads lead him by ropes to the well to drink. On the way
thither he must low like a cow, and for a long time afterwards he
goes by the name of the Cow. At Obermedlingen, in Swabia, when
the threshing draws near an end, each man is careful to avoid giving
the last stroke. He who does give it " gets the Cow," which is a
straw figure dressed in an old ragged petticoat, hood, and stockings.
It is tied on his back with a straw-rope ; his face is blackened, and
being bound with straw-ropes to a wheelbarrow he is wheeled round
the village. Here, again, we meet with that confusion between the
human and animal shape of the corn-spirit which we have noted in
other customs. In Canton Schaffhausen the man who threshes the
last corn is called the Cow ; in Canton Thurgau, the Corn-bull ; in
Canton Zurich, the Thresher-cow. In the last-mentioned district he
is wrapt in straw and bound to one of the trees in the orchard. At
Arad, in Hungary, the man who gives the last stroke at threshing is
enveloped in straw and a cow's hide with the horns attached to it.
At Pessnitz, in the district of Dresden, the man who gives the last
stroke with the flail is called Bull. He must make a straw-man and
set it up before a neighbour's window. Here, apparently, as in so
many cases, the corn-spirit is passed on to a neighbour who has not
finished threshing. So at Herbrechtingen, in Thüringen, the effigy
of a ragged old woman is flung into the barn of the farmer who is last
with his threshing. The man who throws it in cries, " There is the
Cow for you." If the threshers catch him they detain him over
night and punish him by keeping him from the harvest-supper. In
these latter customs the confusion between the human and the animal
shape of the corn-spirit meets us again.

Further, the corn-spirit in bull form is sometimes believed to be killed at threshing. At Auxerre, in threshing the last bundle of corn, they call out twelve times, " We are killing the Bull." In the neighbourhood of Bordeaux, where a butcher kills an ox on the field immediately after the close of the reaping, it is said of the man who gives the last stroke at threshing that " he has killed the Bull." At Chambéry the last sheaf is called the sheaf of the Young Ox, and a race takes place to it in which all the reapers join. When the last stroke is given at threshing they say that " the Ox is killed " ; and immediately thereupon a real ox is slaughtered by the reaper who cut the last corn. The flesh of the ox is eaten by the threshers at supper.

We have seen that sometimes the young corn-spirit, whose task it is to quicken the corn of the coming year, is believed to be born as a Corn-baby on the harvest-field. Similarly in Berry the young corn-spirit is sometimes supposed to be born on the field in calf form ; for when a binder has not rope enough to bind all the corn in sheaves, he puts aside the wheat that remains over and imitates the lowing of a cow. The meaning is that " the sheaf has given birth to a calf." In Puy-de-Dôme when a binder cannot keep up with the reaper whom he or she follows, they say " He (or she) is giving birth to the Calf." In some parts of Prussia, in similar circumstances, they call out to the woman, " The Bull is coming," and imitate the bellowing of a bull. In these cases the woman is conceived as the Corn-cow or old corn-spirit, while the supposed calf is the Corn-calf or young corn-spirit. In some parts of Austria a mythical calf (*Muhkälbchen*) is believed to be seen amongst the sprouting corn in spring and to push the children ; when the corn waves in the wind they say, " The Calf is going about." Clearly, as Mannhardt observes, this calf of the spring-time is the same animal which is afterwards believed to be killed at reaping.

§ 8. *The Corn-spirit as a Horse or Mare.*—Sometimes the corn-spirit appears in the shape of a horse or mare. Between Kalw and Stuttgart, when the corn bends before the wind, they say, " There runs the Horse." At Bohlingen, near Radolfzell in Baden, the last sheaf of oats is called the Oats-stallion. In Hertfordshire, at the end of the reaping, there is or used to be observed a ceremony called " crying the Mare." The last blades of corn left standing on the field are tied together and called the Mare. The reapers stand at a distance and throw their sickles at it ; he who cuts it through " has the prize, with acclamations and good cheer." After it is cut the reapers cry thrice with a loud voice, " I have her ! " Others answer thrice, " What have you ? " —" A Mare ! a Mare ! a Mare ! "—" Whose is she ? " is next asked thrice. " A. B.'s," naming the owner thrice. " Whither will you send her ? "—" To C. D.," naming some neighbour who has not reaped all his corn. In this custom the corn-spirit in the form of a mare is passed on from a farm where the corn is all cut to another farm where it is still standing, and where therefore the corn-spirit may be supposed naturally to take refuge. In Shropshire the custom is similar. The farmer who finishes his harvest last, and who therefore cannot send the Mare to any one else, is said " to keep her all winter." The mocking offer of the Mare to a laggard neighbour was sometimes responded to by a mocking acceptance of her help. Thus an old man told an inquirer, " While we wun at supper, a mon cumm'd wi' a autar [halter] to fatch her away." At one place a real mare used to be sent, but the man who rode her was subjected to some rough treatment at the farmhouse to which he paid his unwelcome visit.

In the neighbourhood of Lille the idea of the corn-spirit in horse form is clearly preserved. When a harvester grows weary at his work, it is said, " He has the fatigue of the Horse." The first sheaf, called the " Cross of the Horse," is placed on a cross of boxwood in the barn, and the youngest horse on the farm must tread on it. The reapers dance round the last blades of corn, crying, " See the remains of the Horse.": The sheaf made out of these last blades is given to the youngest horse of the parish (commune) to eat. This youngest horse of the parish clearly represents, as Mannhardt says, the corn-spirit of the following year, the Corn-foal, which absorbs the spirit of the old Corn-horse by eating the last corn cut ; for, as usual, the old corn-spirit takes his final refuge in the last sheaf. The thresher of the last sheaf is said to " beat the Horse."

§ 9. *The Corn-spirit as a Pig* (*Boar or Sow*).—The last animal embodiment of the corn-spirit which we shall notice is the pig (boar or sow). In Thüringen, when the wind sets the young corn in motion, they sometimes say, " The Boar is rushing through the corn." Amongst the Esthonians of the island of Oesel the last sheaf is called the Rye-boar, and the man who gets it is saluted with a cry of " You have the Rye-boar on your back ! " In reply he strikes up a song, in which he prays for plenty. At Kohlerwinkel, near Augsburg, at the close of the harvest, the last bunch of standing corn is cut down, stalk by stalk, by all the reapers in turn. He who cuts the last stalk " gets the Sow," and is laughed at. In other Swabian villages also the man who cuts the last corn " has the Sow," or " has the Rye-sow." At Bohlingen, near Radolfzell in Baden, the last sheaf is called the Rye-sow or the Wheat-sow, according to the crop ; and at Röhrenbach in Baden the person who brings the last armful for the last sheaf is called the Corn-sow or the Oats-sow. At Friedingen, in Swabia, the thresher who gives the last stroke is called Sow—Barley-sow, Corn-sow, or the like, according to the crop. At Onstmettingen the man who gives the last stroke at threshing " has the Sow " ; he is often bound up in a sheaf and dragged by a rope along the ground. And, generally, in Swabia the man who gives the last stroke with the flail is called Sow. He may, however, rid himself of this invidious distinction by passing on to a neighbour the straw-rope, which is the badge of his position as Sow. So he goes to a house and throws the straw-rope into it, crying, " There, I bring you the Sow." All the inmates give chase ; and if they catch him they beat him, shut him up for several hours in the pig-sty, and oblige him to take the " Sow " away again.   In various parts of Upper Bavaria the man who gives the last stroke at threshing must " carry the Pig "—that is, either a straw effigy of a pig or merely a bundle of straw-ropes.   This he carries to a neighbouring farm where the threshing is not finished, and throws it into the barn.   If the threshers catch him they handle him roughly, beating him, blackening or dirtying his face, throwing him into filth, binding the Sow on his back, and so on ; if the bearer of the Sow is a woman they cut off her hair.   At the harvest supper or dinner the man who " carried the Pig " gets one or more dumplings made in the form of pigs.   When the dumplings are served up by the maid-servant, all the people at table cry " Süz, süz, süz ! " that being the cry used in calling pigs.   Sometimes after dinner the man who " carried the Pig " has his face blackened, and is set on a cart and drawn round the village by his fellows, followed by a crowd crying " Süz, süz, süz ! " as if they were calling swine.   Sometimes, after being wheeled round the village, he is flung on the dunghill.

Again, the corn-spirit in the form of a pig plays his part at sowing-time as well as at harvest.   At Neuautz, in Courland, when barley is sown for the first time in the year, the farmer's wife boils the chine of a pig along with the tail, and brings it to the sower on the field. He eats of it, but cuts off the tail and sticks it in the field ; it is believed that the ears of corn will then grow as long as the tail.   Here the pig is the corn-spirit, whose fertilising power is sometimes supposed to lie especially in his tail.   As a pig he is put in the ground at sowing-time, and as a pig he reappears amongst the ripe corn at harvest. For amongst the neighbouring Esthonians, as we have seen, the last sheaf is called the Rye-boar.   Somewhat similar customs are observed in Germany.   In the Salza district, near Meiningen, a certain bone in the pig is called " the Jew on the winnowing-fan."   The flesh of this bone is boiled on Shrove Tuesday, but the bone is put amongst the ashes which the neighbours exchange as presents on St. Peter's Day (the twenty-second of February), and then mix with the seed-corn.   In the whole of Hesse, Meiningen, and other districts, people eat pea-soup with dried pig-ribs on Ash Wednesday or Candlemas. The ribs are then collected and hung in the room till sowing-time, when they are inserted in the sown field or in the seed-bag amongst the flax seed.   This is thought to be an infallible specific against earth-fleas and moles, and to cause the flax to grow well and tall.

But the idea of the corn-spirit as embodied in pig form is nowhere more clearly expressed than in the Scandinavian custom of the Yule Boar.   In Sweden and Denmark at Yule (Christmas) it is the custom to bake a loaf in the form of a boar-pig.   This is called the Yule Boar.   The corn of the last sheaf is often used to make it.   All through Yule the Yule Boar stands on the table.   Often it is kept till the sowing-time in spring, when part of it is mixed with the seed-corn and part given to the ploughman and plough-horses or plough-oxen to eat, in the expectation of a good harvest.   In this custom the corn-spirit, immanent in the last sheaf, appears at midwinter in the form of a boar made from the corn of the last sheaf ; and his quickening influence on the corn is shown by mixing part of the Yule Boar with the seed-corn, and giving part of it to the ploughman and his cattle to eat. Similarly we saw that the Corn-wolf makes his appearance at mid-winter, the time when the year begins to verge towards spring. Formerly a real boar was sacrificed at Christmas, and apparently also a man in the character of the Yule Boar. This, at least, may perhaps be inferred from a Christmas custom still observed in Sweden. A man is wrapt up in a skin, and carries a wisp of straw in his mouth, so that the projecting straws look like the bristles of a boar. A knife is brought, and an old woman, with her face blackened, pretends to sacrifice him.

On Christmas Eve in some parts of the Esthonian island of Oesel they bake a long cake with the two ends turned up. It is called the Christmas Boar, and stands on the table till the morning of New Year's Day, when it is distributed among the cattle. In other parts of the island the Christmas Boar is not a cake but a little pig born in March, which the housewife fattens secretly, often without the know-ledge of the other members of the family. On Christmas Eve the little pig is secretly killed, then roasted in the oven, and set on the table standing on all-fours, where it remains in this posture for several days. In other parts of the island, again, though the Christmas cake has neither the name nor the shape of a boar, it is kept till the New Year, when half of it is divided among all the members and all the quadrupeds of the family. The other half of the cake is kept till sowing-time comes round, when it is similarly distributed in the morning among human beings and beasts. In other parts of Esthonia, again, the Christmas Boar, as it is called, is baked of the first rye cut at harvest ; it has a conical shape and a cross is impressed on it with a pig's bone or a key, or three dints are made in it with a buckle or a piece of charcoal. It stands with a light beside it on the table all through the festal season. On New Year's Day and Epiphany, before sunrise, a little of the cake is crumbled with salt and given to the cattle. The rest is kept till the day when the cattle are driven out to pasture for the first time in spring. It is then put in the herdsman's bag, and at evening is divided among the cattle to guard them from magic and harm. In some places the Christmas Boar is partaken of by farm-servants and cattle at the time of the barley sowing, for the purpose of thereby producing a heavier crop.

§ 10. *On the Animal Embodiments of the Corn-spirit.*—So much for the animal embodiments of the corn-spirit as they are presented to us in the folk-customs of Northern Europe. These customs bring out clearly the sacramental character of the harvest-supper. The corn-spirit is conceived as embodied in an animal ; this divine animal is slain, and its flesh and blood are partaken of by the harvesters. Thus, the cock, the hare, the cat, the goat, and the ox are eaten sacramentally by the harvesters, and the pig is eaten sacramentally by ploughmen in spring. Again, as a substitute for the real flesh of the divine being, bread or dumplings are made in his image and eaten sacramentally ; thus, pig-shaped dumplings are eaten by the harvesters, and loaves made in boar-shape (the Yule Boar) are eaten in spring by the ploughman and his cattle.

The reader has probably remarked the complete parallelism between the conceptions of the corn-spirit in human and in animal form. The parallel may be here briefly resumed. When the corn waves in the wind it is said either that the Corn-mother or that the Corn-wolf, etc., is passing through the corn. Children are warned against straying in corn-fields either because the Corn-mother or because the Corn-wolf, etc., is there. In the last corn cut or the last sheaf threshed either the Corn-mother or the Corn-wolf, etc., is supposed to be present. The last sheaf is itself called either the Corn-mother or the Corn-wolf, etc., and is made up in the shape either of a woman or of a wolf, etc. The person who cuts, binds, or threshes the last sheaf is called either the Old Woman or the Wolf, etc., according to the name bestowed on the sheaf itself. As in some places a sheaf made in human form and called the Maiden, the Mother of the Maize, etc., is kept from one harvest to the next in order to secure a continuance of the corn-spirit's blessing, so in some places the Harvest-cock and in others the flesh of the goat is kept for a similar purpose from one harvest to the next. As in some places the grain taken from the Corn-mother is mixed with the seed-corn in spring to make the crop abundant, so in some places the feathers of the cock, and in Sweden the Yule Boar, are kept till spring and mixed with the seed-corn for a like purpose. As part of the Corn-mother or Maiden is given to the cattle at Christmas or to the horses at the first plough-ing, so part of the Yule Boar is given to the ploughing horses or oxen in spring. Lastly, the death of the corn-spirit is represented by killing or pretending to kill either his human or his animal representa-tive ; and the worshippers partake sacramentally either of the actual body and blood of the representative of the divinity, or of bread made in his likeness.

Other animal forms assumed by the corn-spirit are the fox, stag, roe, sheep, bear, ass, mouse, quail, stork, swan, and kite. If it is asked why the corn-spirit should be thought to appear in the form of an animal and of so many different animals, we may reply that to primitive man the simple appearance of an animal or bird among the corn is probably enough to suggest a mysterious link between the creature and the corn ; and when we remember that in the old days, before fields were fenced in, all kinds of animals must have been free to roam over them, we need not wonder that the corn-spirit should have been identified even with large animals like the horse and cow, which nowa-days could not, except by a rare accident, be found straying in an English corn-field. This explanation applies with peculiar force to the very common case in which the animal embodiment of the corn-spirit is believed to lurk in the last standing corn. For at harvest a number of wild animals, such as hares, rabbits, and partridges, are commonly driven by the progress of the reaping into the last patch of standing corn, and make their escape from it as it is being cut down. So regularly does this happen that reapers and others often stand round the last patch of corn armed with sticks or guns, with which they kill the animals as they dart out of their last refuge among the stalks. Now, primitive man, to whom magical changes of shape seem perfectly credible, finds it most natural that the spirit of the corn, driven from his home in the ripe grain, should make his escape in the form of the animal which is seen to rush out of the last patch of corn as it falls under the scythe of the reaper. Thus the identification of the corn-spirit with an animal is analogous to the identification of him with a passing stranger. As the sudden appearance of a stranger near the harvest-field or threshing-floor is, to the primitive mind, enough to identify him as the spirit of the corn escaping from the cut or threshed corn, so the sudden appearance of an animal issuing from the cut corn is enough to identify it with the corn-spirit escaping from his ruined home. The two identifications are so analogous that they can hardly be dissociated in any attempt to explain them. Those who look to some other principle than the one here suggested for the explanation of the latter identification are bound to show that their theory covers the former identification also.

CHAPTER XLIX

ANCIENT DEITIES OF VEGETATION AS ANIMALS

§ 1. *Dionysus, the Goat and the Bull.*—However we may explain it, the fact remains that in peasant folk-lore the corn-spirit is very commonly conceived and represented in animal form. May not this fact explain the relation in which certain animals stood to the ancient deities of vegetation, Dionysus, Demeter, Adonis, Attis, and Osiris ?

To begin with Dionysus. We have seen that he was represented sometimes as a goat and sometimes as a bull. As a goat he can hardly be separated from the minor divinities, the Pans, Satyrs, and Silenuses, all of whom are closely associated with him and are represented more or less completely in the form of goats. Thus, Pan was regularly portrayed in sculpture and painting with the face and legs of a goat. The Satyrs were depicted with pointed goat-ears, and sometimes with sprouting horns and short tails. They were sometimes spoken of simply as goats ; and in the drama their parts were played by men dressed in goatskins. Silenus is represented in art clad in a goatskin. Further, the Fauns, the Italian counterpart of the Greek Pans and Satyrs, are described as being half goats, with goat-feet and goat-horns. Again, all these minor goat-formed divinities partake more or less clearly of the character of woodland deities. Thus, Pan was called by the Arcadians the Lord of the Wood. The Silenuses kept company with the tree-nymphs. The Fauns are expressly designated as woodland deities ; and their character as such is still further brought out by their association, or even identification, with Silvanus and the Silvanuses, who, as their name of itself indicates, are spirits of the woods. Lastly, the association of the Satyrs with the Silenuses, Fauns, and Silvanuses proves that the Satyrs also were woodland deities. These goat-formed spirits of the woods have their counterparts in the folk-lore of Northern Europe. Thus, the Russian wood-spirits, called *Ljeschie* (from *ljes*, " wood "), are believed to appear partly in human shape, but with the horns, ears, and legs of goats. The *Ljeschi* can alter his stature at pleasure ; when he walks in the wood he is as tall as the trees ; when he walks in the meadows he is no higher than the grass. Some of the *Ljeschie* are spirits of the corn as well as of the wood ; before harvest they are as tall as the corn-stalks, but after it they shrink to the height of the stubble. This brings out—what we have remarked before—the close connexion between tree-spirits and corn-spirits, and shows how easily the former may melt into the latter. Similarly the Fauns, though wood-spirits, were believed to foster the growth of the crops. We have already seen how often the corn-spirit is represented in folk-custom as a goat. On the whole, then, as Mannhardt argues, the Pans, Satyrs, and Fauns perhaps belong to a widely diffused class of wood-spirits conceived in goat-form. The fondness of goats for straying in woods and nibbling the bark of trees, to which indeed they are most destructive, is an obvious and perhaps sufficient reason why wood-spirits should so often be supposed to take the form of goats. The inconsistency of a god of vegetation subsisting upon the vegetation which he personifies is not one to strike the primitive mind. Such inconsistencies arise when the deity, ceasing to be immanent in the vegetation, comes to be regarded as its owner or lord ; for the idea of owning the vegetation naturally leads to that of subsisting on it. Sometimes the corn-spirit, originally conceived as immanent in the corn, afterwards comes to be regarded as its owner, who lives on it and is reduced to poverty and want by being deprived of it. Hence he is often known as " the Poor Man " or " the Poor Woman." Occasionally the last sheaf is left standing on the field for " the Poor Old Woman " or for " the Old Rye-woman."

Thus the representation of wood-spirits in the form of goats appears to be both widespread and, to the primitive mind, natural. Therefore when we find, as we have done, that Dionysus—a tree-god—is sometimes represented in goat-form, we can hardly avoid concluding that this representation is simply a part of his proper character as a tree-god and is not to be explained by the fusion of two distinct and independent worships, in one of which he originally appeared as a tree-god and in the other as a goat.

Dionysus was also figured, as we have seen, in the shape of a bull. After what has gone before we are naturally led to expect that his bull form must have been only another expression for his character as a deity of vegetation, especially as the bull is a common embodiment of the corn-spirit in Northern Europe ; and the close association of Dionysus with Demeter and Persephone in the mysteries of Eleusis shows that he had at least strong agricultural affinities.

The probability of this view will be somewhat increased if it can be shown that in other rites than those of Dionysus the ancients slew an ox as a representative of the spirit of vegetation. This they appear to have done in the Athenian sacrifice known as " the murder of the ox " (*bouphonia*). It took place about the end of June or beginning of July, that is, about the time when the threshing is nearly over in Attica. According to tradition the sacrifice was instituted to procure a cessation of drought and dearth which had afflicted the land. The ritual was as follows. Barley mixed with wheat, or cakes made of them, were laid upon the bronze altar of Zeus Polieus on the Acropolis. Oxen were driven round the altar, and the ox which went up to the altar and ate the offering on it was sacrificed. The axe and knife with which the beast was slain had been previously wetted with water brought by maidens called " water-carriers." The weapons were then sharpened and handed to the butchers, one of whom felled the ox with the axe and another cut its throat with the knife. As soon as he had felled the ox, the former threw the axe from him and fled ; and the man who cut the beast's throat apparently imitated his example. Meantime the ox was skinned and all present partook of its flesh. Then the hide was stuffed with straw and sewed up ; next the stuffed animal was set on its feet and yoked to a plough as if it were ploughing. A trial then took place in an ancient law-court presided over by the King (as he was called) to determine who had murdered the ox. The maidens who had brought the water accused the men who had sharpened the axe and knife ; the men who had sharpened the axe and knife blamed the men who had handed these implements to the butchers ; the men who had handed the implements to the butchers blamed the butchers ; and the butchers laid the blame on the axe and knife, which were accordingly found guilty, condemned, and cast into the sea.

The name of this sacrifice,—" the *murder* of the ox,"—the pains taken by each person who had a hand in the slaughter to lay the blame on some one else, together with the formal trial and punishment of the axe or knife or both, prove that the ox was here regarded not merely as a victim offered to a god, but as itself a sacred creature, the slaughter of which was sacrilege or murder. This is borne out by a statement of Varro that to kill an ox was formerly a capital crime in Attica. The mode of selecting the victim suggests that the ox which tasted the corn was viewed as the corn-deity taking possession of his own. This interpretation is supported by the following custom. In Beauce, in the district of Orleans, on the twenty-fourth or twenty-fifth of April they make a straw man called " the great *mondard*." For they say that the old *mondard* is now dead and it is necessary to make a new

one.   The straw man is carried in solemn procession up and down
the village and at last is placed upon the oldest apple-tree.   There he
remains till the apples are gathered, when he is taken down and thrown
into the water, or he is burned and his ashes cast into water.   But the
person who plucks the first fruit from the tree succeeds to the title of
" the great *mondard.*"   Here the straw figure, called " the great
mondard " and placed on the oldest apple-tree in spring, represents the
spirit of the tree, who, dead in winter, revives when the apple-blossoms
appear on the boughs.   Thus the person who plucks the first fruit
from the tree and thereby receives the name of " the great *mondard* "
must be regarded as a representative of the tree-spirit.   Primitive
peoples are usually reluctant to taste the annual first-fruits of any
crop, until some ceremony has been performed which makes it safe
and pious for them to do so.   The reason of this reluctance appears
to be a belief that the first-fruits either belong to or actually contain a
divinity.   Therefore when a man or animal is seen boldly to appropriate
the sacred first-fruits, he or it is naturally regarded as the divinity
himself in human or animal form taking possession of his own.   The
time of the Athenian sacrifice, which fell about the close of the threshing,
suggests that the wheat and barley laid upon the altar were a harvest
offering ;   and the sacramental character of the subsequent repast—
all partaking of the flesh of the divine animal—would make it parallel
to the harvest-suppers of modern Europe, in which, as we have seen,
the flesh of the animal which stands for the corn-spirit is eaten by the
harvesters.   Again, the tradition that the sacrifice was instituted in
order to put an end to drought and famine is in favour of taking it as
a harvest festival.   The resurrection of the corn-spirit, enacted by
setting up the stuffed ox and yoking it to the plough, may be compared
with the resurrection of the tree-spirit in the person of his representative, the Wild Man.

The ox appears as a representative of the corn-spirit in other parts
of the world.   At Great Bassam, in Guinea, two oxen are slain annually
to procure a good harvest.   If the sacrifice is to be effectual, it is
necessary that the oxen should weep.   So all the women of the village
sit in front of the beasts, chanting, " The ox will weep ; yes, he will
weep ! "   From time to time one of the women walks round the beasts,
throwing manioc meal or palm wine upon them, especially into their
eyes.   When tears roll down from the eyes of the oxen, the people
dance, singing, " The ox weeps ! the ox weeps ! "   Then two men
seize the tails of the beasts and cut them off at one blow.   It is believed
that a great misfortune will happen in the course of the year if the
tails are not severed at one blow.   The oxen are afterwards killed,
and their flesh is eaten by the chiefs.   Here the tears of the oxen, like
those of the human victims amongst the Khonds and the Aztecs, are
probably a rain-charm.   We have already seen that the virtue of the
corn-spirit, embodied in animal form, is sometimes supposed to reside
in the tail, and that the last handful of corn is sometimes conceived
as the tail of the corn-spirit.   In the Mithraic religion this conception

is graphically set forth in some of the numerous sculptures which represent Mithras kneeling on the back of a bull and plunging a knife into its flank ; for on certain of these monuments the tail of the bull ends in three stalks of corn, and in one of them corn-stalks instead of blood are seen issuing from the wound inflicted by the knife. Such representations certainly suggest that the bull, whose sacrifice appears to have formed a leading feature in the Mithraic ritual, was conceived, in one at least of its aspects, as an incarnation of the corn-spirit.

Still more clearly does the ox appear as a personification of the corn-spirit in a ceremony which is observed in all the provinces and districts of China to welcome the approach of spring. On the first day of spring, usually on the third or fourth of February, which is also the beginning of the Chinese New Year, the governor or prefect of the city goes in procession to the east gate of the city, and sacrifices to the Divine Husbandman, who is represented with a bull's head on the body of a man. A large effigy of an ox, cow, or buffalo has been prepared for the occasion, and stands outside of the east gate, with agricultural implements beside it. The figure is made of differently-coloured pieces of paper pasted on a framework either by a blind man or according to the directions of a necromancer. The colours of the paper prognosticate the character of the coming year ; if red prevails, there will be many fires ; if white, there will be floods and rain ; and so with the other colours. The mandarins walk slowly round the ox, beating it severely at each step with rods of various hues. It is filled with five kinds of grain, which pour forth when the effigy is broken by the blows of the rods. The paper fragments are then set on fire, and a scramble takes place for the burning fragments, because the people believe that whoever gets one of them is sure to be fortunate throughout the year. A live buffalo is next killed, and its flesh is divided among the mandarins. According to one account, the effigy of the ox is made of clay, and, after being beaten by the governor, is stoned by the people till they break it in pieces, " from which they expect an abundant year." Here the corn-spirit appears to be plainly represented by the corn-filled ox, whose fragments may therefore be supposed to bring fertility with them.

On the whole we may perhaps conclude that both as a goat and as a bull Dionysus was essentially a god of vegetation. The Chinese and European customs which I have cited may perhaps shed light on the custom of rending a live bull or goat at the rites of Dionysus. The animal was torn in fragments, as the Khond victim was cut in pieces, in order that the worshippers might each secure a portion of the life-giving and fertilising influence of the god. The flesh was eaten raw as a sacrament, and we may conjecture that some of it was taken home to be buried in the fields, or otherwise employed so as to convey to the fruits of the earth the quickening influence of the god of vegetation. The resurrection of Dionysus, related in his myth, may have been enacted in his rites by stuffing and setting up the slain ox, as was done at the Athenian *bouphonia*.

§ 2. *Demeter, the Pig and the Horse.*—Passing next to the corn-goddess Demeter, and remembering that in European folk-lore the pig is a common embodiment of the corn-spirit, we may now ask whether the pig, which was so closely associated with Demeter, may not have been originally the goddess herself in animal form ? The pig was sacred to her ; in art she was portrayed carrying or accompanied by a pig ; and the pig was regularly sacrificed in her mysteries, the reason assigned being that the pig injures the corn and is therefore an enemy of the goddess. But after an animal has been conceived as a god, or a god as an animal, it sometimes happens, as we have seen, that the god sloughs off his animal form and becomes purely anthropomorphic ; and that then the animal, which at first had been slain in the character of the god, comes to be viewed as a victim offered to the god on the ground of its hostility to the deity ; in short, the god is sacrificed to himself on the ground that he is his own enemy. This happened to Dionysus, and it may have happened to Demeter also. And in fact the rites of one of her festivals, the Thesmophoria, bear out the view that originally the pig was an embodiment of the corn-goddess herself, either Demeter or her daughter and double Persephone. The Attic Thesmophoria was an autumn festival, celebrated by women alone in October, and appears to have represented with mourning rites the descent of Persephone (or Demeter) into the lower world, and with joy her return from the dead. Hence the name Descent or Ascent variously applied to the first, and the name *Kalligeneia* (fair-born) applied to the third day of the festival. Now it was customary at the Thesmophoria to throw pigs, cakes of dough, and branches of pine-trees into " the chasms of Demeter and Persephone," which appear to have been sacred caverns or vaults. In these caverns or vaults there were said to be serpents, which guarded the caverns and con-sumed most of the flesh of the pigs and dough-cakes which were thrown in. Afterwards—apparently at the next annual festival—the decayed remains of the pigs, the cakes, and the pine-branches were fetched by women called " drawers," who, after observing rules of ceremonial purity for three days, descended into the caverns, and, frightening away the serpents by clapping their hands, brought up the remains and placed them on the altar. Whoever got a piece of the decayed flesh and cakes, and sowed it with the seed-corn in his field, was believed to be sure of a good crop.

To explain the rude and ancient ritual of the Thesmophoria the following legend was told. At the moment when Pluto carried off Persephóne, a swineherd called Eubuleus chanced to be herding his swine on the spot, and his herd was engulfed in the chasm down which Pluto vanished with Persephone. Accordingly at the Thesmo-phoria pigs were annually thrown into caverns to commemorate the disappearance of the swine of Eubuleus. It follows from this that the casting of the pigs into the vaults at the Thesmophoria formed part of the dramatic representation of Persephone's descent into the lower world ; and as no image of Persephone appears to have been thrown in, we may infer that the descent of the pigs was not so much an accompaniment of her descent as the descent itself, in short, that the pigs were Persephone. Afterwards when Persephone or Demeter (for the two are equivalent) took on human form, a reason had to be found for the custom of throwing pigs into caverns at her festival; and this was done by saying that when Pluto carried off Persephone there happened to be some swine browsing near, which were swallowed up along with her. The story is obviously a forced and awkward attempt to bridge over the gulf between the old conception of the corn-spirit as a pig and the new conception of her as an anthropo-morphic goddess. A trace of the older conception survived in the legend that when the sad mother was searching for traces of the vanished Persephone the footprints of the lost one were obliterated by the footprints of a pig; originally, we may conjecture, the foot-prints of the pig were the footprints of Persephone and of Demeter herself. A consciousness of the intimate connexion of the pig with the corn lurks in the legend that the swineherd Eubuleus was a brother of Triptolemus, to whom Demeter first imparted the secret of the corn. Indeed, according to one version of the story, Eubuleus himself received, jointly with his brother Triptolemus, the gift of the corn from Demeter as a reward for revealing to her the fate of Persephone. Further, it is to be noted that at the Thesmophoria the women appear to have eaten swine's flesh. The meal, if I am right, must have been a solemn sacrament or communion, the worshippers partaking of the body of the god.

As thus explained, the Thesmophoria has its analogies in the folk-customs of Northern Europe which have been already described. Just as at the Thesmophoria—an autumn festival in honour of the corn-goddess—swine's flesh was partly eaten, partly kept in caverns till the following year, when it was taken up to be sown with the seed-corn in the fields for the purpose of securing a good crop; so in the neighbourhood of Grenoble the goat killed on the harvest-field is partly eaten at the harvest-supper, partly pickled and kept till the next harvest; so at Pouilly the ox killed on the harvest-field is partly eaten by the harvesters, partly pickled and kept till the first day of sowing in spring, probably to be then mixed with the seed, or eaten by the ploughmen, or both; so at Udvarhely the feathers of the cock which is killed in the last sheaf at harvest are kept till spring, and then sown with the seed on the field; so in Hesse and Meiningen the flesh of pigs is eaten on Ash Wednesday or Candlemas, and the bones are kept till sowing-time, when they are put into the field sown or mixed with the seed in the bag; so, lastly, the corn from the last sheaf is kept till Christmas, made into the Yule Boar, and afterwards broken and mixed with the seed-corn at sowing in spring. Thus, to put it generally, the corn-spirit is killed in animal form in autumn; part of his flesh is eaten as a sacrament by his worshippers; and part of it is kept till next sowing-time or harvest as a pledge and security for the continuance or renewal of the corn-spirit's energies.

If persons of fastidious taste should object that the Greeks never could have conceived Demeter and Persephone to be embodied in the form of pigs, it may be answered that in the cave of Phigalia in Arcadia the Black Demeter was portrayed with the head and mane of a horse on the body of a woman. Between the portrait of a goddess as a pig, and the portrait of her as a woman with a horse's head, there is little to choose in respect of barbarism. The legend told of the Phigalian Demeter indicates that the horse was one of the animal forms assumed in ancient Greece, as in modern Europe, by the corn-spirit. It was said that in her search for her daughter, Demeter assumed the form of a mare to escape the addresses of Poseidon, and that, offended at his importunity, she withdrew in dudgeon to a cave not far from Phigalia in the highlands of Western Arcadia. There, robed in black, she tarried so long that the fruits of the earth were perishing, and mankind would have died of famine if Pan had not soothed the angry goddess and persuaded her to quit the cave. In memory of this event, the Phigalians set up an image of the Black Demeter in the cave ; it represented a woman dressed in a long robe, with the head and mane of a horse. The Black Demeter, in whose absence the fruits of the earth perish, is plainly a mythical expression for the bare wintry earth stripped of its summer mantle of green.

§ 3. *Attis, Adonis, and the Pig.*—Passing now to Attis and Adonis, we may note a few facts which seem to show that these deities of vegetation had also, like other deities of the same class, their animal embodiments. The worshippers of Attis abstained from eating the flesh of swine. This appears to indicate that the pig was regarded as an embodiment of Attis. And the legend that Attis was killed by a boar points in the same direction. For after the examples of the goat Dionysus and the pig Demeter it may almost be laid down as a rule that an animal which is said to have injured a god was originally the god himself. Perhaps the cry of " Hyes Attes ! Hyes Attes ! " which was raised by the worshippers of Attis may be neither more nor less than " Pig Attis ! Pig Attis ! "—*hyes* being possibly a Phrygian form of the Greek *hȳs*, " a pig."

In regard to Adonis, his connexion with the boar was not always explained by the story that he had been killed by the animal. According to another story, a boar rent with his tusk the bark of the tree in which the infant Adonis was born. According to yet another story, he perished at the hands of Hephaestus on Mount Lebanon while he was hunting wild boars. These variations in the legend serve to show that, while the connexion of the boar with Adonis was certain, the reason of the connexion was not understood, and that consequently different stories were devised to explain it. Certainly the pig ranked as a sacred animal among the Syrians. At the great religious metropolis of Hierapolis on the Euphrates pigs were neither sacrificed nor eaten, and if a man touched a pig he was unclean for the rest of the day. Some people said this was because the pigs were unclean ; others said it was because the pigs were sacred. This difference of opinion points to a hazy state of religious thought in which the ideas of sanctity and uncleanness are not yet sharply distinguished, both being blent in a sort of vaporous solution to which we give the name of taboo. It is quite consistent with this that the pig should have been held to be an embodiment of the divine Adonis, and the analogies of Dionysus and Demeter make it probable that the story of the hostility of the animal to the god was only a late misapprehension of the old view of the god as embodied in a pig. The rule that pigs were not sacrificed or eaten by worshippers of Attis and presumably of Adonis does not exclude the possibility that in these rituals the pig was slain on solemn occasions as a representative of the god and consumed sacramentally by the worshippers. Indeed, the sacramental killing and eating of an animal implies that the animal is sacred, and that, as a general rule, it is spared.

The attitude of the Jews to the pig was as ambiguous as that of the heathen Syrians towards the same animal. The Greeks could not decide whether the Jews worshipped swine or abominated them. On the one hand they might not eat swine ; but on the other hand they might not kill them. And if the former rule speaks for the uncleanness, the latter speaks still more strongly for the sanctity of the animal. For whereas both rules may, and one rule must, be explained on the supposition that the pig was sacred ; neither rule must, and one rule cannot, be explained on the supposition that the pig was unclean. If, therefore, we prefer the former supposition, we must conclude that, originally at least, the pig was revered rather than abhorred by the Israelites. We are confirmed in this opinion by observing that down to the time of Isaiah some of the Jews used to meet secretly in gardens to eat the flesh of swine and mice as a religious rite. Doubtless this was a very ancient ceremony, dating from a time when both the pig and the mouse were venerated as divine, and when their flesh was partaken of sacramentally on rare and solemn occasions as the body and blood of gods. And in general it may perhaps be said that all so-called unclean animals were originally sacred ; the reason for not eating them was that they were divine.

§ 4. *Osiris, the Pig and the Bull.*—In ancient Egypt, within historical times, the pig occupied the same dubious position as in Syria and Palestine, though at first sight its uncleanness is more prominent than its sanctity. The Egyptians are generally said by Greek writers to have abhorred the pig as a foul and loathsome animal. If a man so much as touched a pig in passing, he stepped into the river with all his clothes on, to wash off the taint. To drink pig's milk was believed to cause leprosy to the drinker. Swineherds, though natives of Egypt, were forbidden to enter any temple, and they were the only men who were thus excluded. No one would give his daughter in marriage to a swineherd, or marry a swineherd's daughter ; the swineherds married among themselves. Yet once a year the Egyptians sacrificed pigs to the moon and to Osiris, and not only sacrificed them, but ate of their flesh, though on any other day of the year they would neither sacrifice them nor taste of their flesh. Those who were too poor to offer a pig on this day baked cakes of dough, and offered them instead. This can hardly be explained except by the supposition that the pig was a sacred animal which was eaten sacramentally by his worshippers once a year.

The view that in Egypt the pig was sacred is borne out by the very facts which, to moderns, might seem to prove the contrary. Thus the Egyptians thought, as we have seen, that to drink pig's milk produced leprosy. But exactly analogous views are held by savages about the animals and plants which they deem most sacred. Thus in the island of Wetar (between New Guinea and Celebes) people believe themselves to be variously descended from wild pigs, serpents, crocodiles, turtles, dogs, and eels ; a man may not eat an animal of the kind from which he is descended ; if he does so, he will become a leper, and go mad. Amongst the Omaha Indians of North America men whose totem is the elk believe that if they ate the flesh of the male elk they would break out in boils and white spots in different parts of their bodies. In the same tribe men whose totem is the red maize think that if they ate red maize they would have running sores all round their mouths. The Bush negroes of Surinam, who practise totemism, believe that if they ate the *capiaï* (an animal like a pig) it would give them leprosy ; perhaps the *capiaï* is one of their totems. The Syrians, in antiquity, who esteemed fish sacred, thought that if they ate fish their bodies would break out in ulcers, and their feet and stomach would swell up. The Chasas of Orissa believe that if they were to injure their totemic animal they would be attacked by leprosy and their line would die out. These examples prove that the eating of a sacred animal is often believed to produce leprosy or other skin-diseases ; so far, therefore, they support the view that the pig must have been sacred in Egypt, since the effect of drinking its milk was believed to be leprosy.

Again, the rule that, after touching a pig, a man had to wash himself and his clothes, also favours the view of the sanctity of the pig. For it is a common belief that the effect of contact with a sacred object must be removed, by washing or otherwise, before a man is free to mingle with his fellows. Thus the Jews wash their hands after reading the sacred scriptures. Before coming forth from the tabernacle after the sin-offering the high priest had to wash himself, and put off the garments which he had worn in the holy place. It was a rule of Greek ritual that, in offering an expiatory sacrifice, the sacrificer should not touch the sacrifice, and that, after the offering was made, he must wash his body and his clothes in a river or spring before he could enter a city or his own house. The Polynesians felt strongly the need of ridding themselves of the sacred contagion, if it may be so called, which they caught by touching sacred objects. Various ceremonies were performed for the purpose of removing this contagion. We have seen, for example, how in Tonga a man who happened to touch a sacred chief, or anything personally belonging to him, had to perform a certain ceremony before he could feed himself with his hands ;

otherwise it was believed that he would swell up and die, or at least be afflicted with scrofula or some other disease. We have seen, too, what fatal effects are supposed to follow, and do actually follow, from contact with a sacred object in New Zealand. In short, primitive man believes that what is sacred is dangerous ; it is pervaded by a sort of electrical sanctity which communicates a shock to, even if it does not kill, whatever comes in contact with it. Hence the savage is unwilling to touch or even to see that which he deems peculiarly holy. Thus Bechuanas, of the Crocodile clan, think it " hateful and unlucky " to meet or see a crocodile ; the sight is thought to cause inflammation of the eyes. Yet the crocodile is their most sacred object ; they call it their father, swear by it, and celebrate it in their festivals. The goat is the sacred animal of the Madenassana Bushmen ; yet " to look upon it would be to render the man for the time impure, as well as to cause him undefined uneasiness." The Elk clan, among the Omaha Indians, believe that even to touch the male elk would be followed by an eruption of boils and white spots on the body. Members of the Reptile clan in the same tribe think that if one of them touches or smells a snake it will make his hair white. In Samoa people whose god was a butterfly believed that if they caught a butterfly it would strike them dead. Again, in Samoa the reddish-seared leaves of the banana-tree were commonly used as plates for handing food ; but if any member of the Wild Pigeon family had used banana leaves for this purpose, it was supposed that he would suffer from rheumatic swellings or an eruption all over the body like chicken-pox. The Mori clan of the Bhils in Central India worship the peacock as their totem and make offerings of grain to it ; yet members of the clan believe that were they even to set foot on the tracks of a peacock they would afterwards suffer from some disease, and if a woman sees a peacock she must veil her face and look away. Thus the primitive mind seems to conceive of holiness as a sort of dangerous virus, which a prudent man will shun as far as possible, and of which, if he should chance to be infected by it, he will carefully disinfect himself by some form of ceremonial purification.

In the light of these parallels the beliefs and customs of the Egyptians touching the pig are probably to be explained as based upon an opinion of the extreme sanctity rather than of the extreme un-cleanness of the animal ; or rather, to put it more correctly, they imply that the animal was looked on, not simply as a filthy and dis-gusting creature, but as a being endowed with high supernatural powers, and that as such it was regarded with that primitive sentiment of religious awe and fear in which the feelings of reverence and abhor-rence are almost equally blended. The ancients themselves seem to have been aware that there was another side to the horror with which swine seemed to inspire the Egyptians. For the Greek astronomer and mathematician Eudoxus, who resided fourteen months in Egypt and conversed with the priests, was of opinion that the Egyptians spared the pig, not out of abhorrence, but from a regard to its utility in agriculture; for, according to him, when the Nile had subsided, herds of swine were turned loose over the fields to tread the seed down into the moist earth. But when a being is thus the object of mixed and implicitly contradictory feelings, he may be said to occupy a position of unstable equilibrium. In course of time one of the contradictory feelings is likely to prevail over the other, and according as the feeling which finally predominates is that of reverence or abhorrence, the being who is the object of it will rise into a god or sink into a devil. The latter, on the whole, was the fate of the pig in Egypt. For in historical times the fear and horror of the pig seem certainly to have outweighed the reverence and worship of which he may once have been the object, and of which, even in his fallen state, he never quite lost trace. He came to be looked on as an embodiment of Set or Typhon, the Egyptian devil and enemy of Osiris. For it was in the shape of a black pig that Typhon injured the eye of the god Horus, who burned him and instituted the sacrifice of the pig, the sun-god Ra having declared the beast abominable. Again, the story that Typhon was hunting a boar when he discovered and mangled the body of Osiris, and that this was the reason why pigs were sacrificed once a year, is clearly a modernised version of an older story that Osiris, like Adonis and Attis, was slain or mangled by a boar, or by Typhon in the form of a boar. Thus, the annual sacrifice of a pig to Osiris might naturally be interpreted as vengeance inflicted on the hostile animal that had slain or mangled the god. But, in the first place, when an animal is thus killed as a solemn sacrifice once and once only in the year, it generally or always means that the animal is divine, that he is spared and respected the rest of the year as a god and slain, when he is slain, also in the character of a god. In the second place, the examples of Dionysus and Demeter, if not of Attis and Adonis, have taught us that the animal which is sacrificed to a god on the ground that he is the god's enemy may have been, and probably was, originally the god himself. Therefore, the annual sacrifice of a pig to Osiris, coupled with the alleged hostility of the animal to the god, tends to show, first, that originally the pig was a god, and, second, that he was Osiris. At a later age, when Osiris became anthropomorphic and his original relation to the pig had been forgotten, the animal was first distinguished from him, and afterwards opposed as an enemy to him by mythologists who could think of no reason for killing a beast in connexion with the worship of a god except that the beast was the god's enemy; or, as Plutarch puts it, not that which is dear to the gods, but that which is the contrary, is fit to be sacrificed. At this later stage the havoc which a wild boar notoriously makes amongst the corn would supply a plausible reason for regarding him as the foe of the corn-spirit, though originally, if I am right, the very freedom with which the boar ranged at will through the corn led people to identify him with the corn-spirit, to whom he was afterwards opposed as an enemy.

The view which identifies the pig with Osiris derives not a little support from the sacrifice of pigs to him on the very day on which, according to tradition, Osiris himself was killed ; for thus the killing of the pig was the annual representation of the killing of Osiris, just as the throwing of the pigs into the caverns at the Thesmophoria was an annual representation of the descent of Persephone into the lower world ; and both customs are parallel to the European practice of killing a goat, cock, and so forth, at harvest as a representative of the corn-spirit.

Again, the theory that the pig, originally Osiris himself, afterwards came to be regarded as an embodiment of his enemy Typhon, is supported by the similar relation of red-haired men and red oxen to Typhon. For in regard to the red-haired men who were burned and whose ashes were scattered with winnowing-fans, we have seen fair grounds for believing that originally, like the red-haired puppies killed at Rome in spring, they were representatives of the corn-spirit himself, that is, of Osiris, and were slain for the express purpose of making the corn turn red or golden. Yet at a later time these men were explained to be representatives, not of Osiris, but of his enemy Typhon, and the killing of them was regarded as an act of vengeance inflicted on the enemy of the god. Similarly, the red oxen sacrificed by the Egyptians were said to be offered on the ground of their resemblance to Typhon ; though it is more likely that originally they were slain on the ground of their resemblance to the corn-spirit Osiris. We have seen that the ox is a common representative of the corn-spirit and is slain as such on the harvest-field.

Osiris was regularly identified with the bull Apis of Memphis and the bull Mnevis of Heliopolis. But it is hard to say whether these bulls were embodiments of him as the corn-spirit, as the red oxen appear to have been, or whether they were not in origin entirely distinct deities who came to be fused with Osiris at a later time. The universality of the worship of these two bulls seems to put them on a different footing from the ordinary sacred animals whose worships were purely local. But whatever the original relation of Apis to Osiris may have been, there is one fact about the former which ought not to be passed over in a disquisition on the custom of killing a god. Although the bull Apis was worshipped as a god with much pomp and profound reverence, he was not suffered to live beyond a certain length of time which was prescribed by the sacred books, and on the expiry of which he was drowned in a holy spring. The limit, according to Plutarch, was twenty-five years ; but it cannot always have been enforced, for the tombs of the Apis bulls have been discovered in modern times, and from the inscriptions on them it appears that in the twenty-second dynasty two of the holy steers lived more than twenty-six years.

§ 5. *Virbius and the Horse.*—We are now in a position to hazard a conjecture as to the meaning of the tradition that Virbius, the first of the divine Kings of the Wood at Aricia, had been killed in the character of Hippolytus by horses. Having found, first, that spirits of the corn are not infrequently represented in the form of horses ; and, second, that the animal which in later legends is said to have injured the god was sometimes originally the god himself, we may conjecture that the horses by which Virbius or Hippolytus was said to have been slain were really embodiments of him as a deity of vegetation. The myth that he had been killed by horses was probably invented to explain certain features in his worship, amongst others the custom of excluding horses from his sacred grove. For myth changes while custom remains constant ; men continue to do what their fathers did before them, though the reasons on which their fathers acted have been long forgotten. The history of religion is a long attempt to reconcile old custom with new reason, to find a sound theory for an absurd practice. In the case before us we may be sure that the myth is more modern than the custom and by no means represents the original reason for excluding horses from the grove. From their exclusion it might be inferred that horses could not be the sacred animals or embodiments of the god of the grove. But the inference would be rash. The goat was at one time a sacred animal or embodiment of Athena, as may be inferred from the practice of representing the goddess clad in a goat-skin (*aegis*). Yet the goat was neither sacrificed to her as a rule, nor allowed to enter her great sanctuary, the Acropolis at Athens. The reason alleged for this was that the goat injured the olive, the sacred tree of Athena. So far, therefore, the relation of the goat to Athena is parallel to the relation of the horse to Virbius, both animals being excluded from the sanctuary on the ground of injury done by them to the god. But from Varro we learn that there was an exception to the rule which excluded the goat from the Acropolis. Once a year, he says, the goat was driven on to the Acropolis for a necessary sacrifice. Now, as has been remarked before, when an animal is sacrificed once and once only in the year, it is probably slain, not as a victim offered to the god, but as a representative of the god himself. Therefore we may infer that if a goat was sacrificed on the Acropolis once a year, it was sacrificed in the character of Athena herself ; and it may be conjectured that the skin of the sacrificed animal was placed on the statue of the goddess and formed the *aegis*, which would thus be renewed annually. Similarly at Thebes in Egypt rams were sacred and were not sacrificed. But on one day in the year a ram was killed, and its skin was placed on the statue of the god Ammon. Now, if we knew the ritual of the Arician grove better, we might find that the rule of excluding horses from it, like the rule of excluding goats from the Acropolis at Athens, was subject to an annual exception, a horse being once a year taken into the grove and sacrificed as an embodiment of the god Virbius. By the usual misunderstanding the horse thus killed would come in time to be regarded as an enemy offered up in sacrifice to the god whom he had injured, like the pig which was sacrificed to Demeter and Osiris or the goat which was sacrificed to Dionysus, and possibly to Athena. It is so easy for a writer to record a rule without noticing an exception that we need not wonder at finding the rule of the Arician grove recorded without any mention of an exception such as I suppose. If we had had only the statements of Athenaeus and Pliny, we should have known only the rule which forbade the sacrifice of goats to Athena and excluded them from the Acropolis, without being aware of the important exception which the fortunate preservation of Varro's work has revealed to us.

The conjecture that once a year a horse may have been sacrificed in the Arician grove as a representative of the deity of the grove derives some support from the similar sacrifice of a horse which took place once a year at Rome. On the fifteenth of October in each year a chariot-race was run on the Field of Mars. Stabbed with a spear, the right-hand horse of the victorious team was then sacrificed to Mars for the purpose of ensuring good crops, and its head was cut off and adorned with a string of loaves. Thereupon the inhabitants of two wards—the Sacred Way and the Subura—contended with each other who should get the head. If the people of the Sacred Way got it, they fastened it to a wall of the king's house ; if the people of the Subura got it, they fastened it to the Mamilian tower. The horse's tail was cut off and carried to the king's house with such speed that the blood dripped on the hearth of the house. Further, it appears that the blood of the horse was caught and preserved till the twenty-first of April, when the Vestal Virgins mixed it with the blood of the unborn calves which had been sacrificed six days before. The mixture was then distributed to shepherds, and used by them for fumigating their flocks.

In this ceremony the decoration of the horse's head with a string of loaves, and the alleged object of the sacrifice, namely, to procure a good harvest, seem to indicate that the horse was killed as one of those animal representatives of the corn-spirit of which we have found so many examples. The custom of cutting off the horse's tail is like the African custom of cutting off the tails of the oxen and sacrificing them to obtain a good crop. In both the Roman and the African custom the animal apparently stands for the corn-spirit, and its fructifying power is supposed to reside especially in its tail. The latter idea occurs, as we have seen, in European folk-lore. Again, the practice of fumigating the cattle in spring with the blood of the horse may be compared with the practice of giving the Old Wife, the Maiden, or the *clyack* sheaf as fodder to the horses in spring or the cattle at Christmas, and giving the Yule Boar to the ploughing oxen or horses to eat in spring. All these usages aim at ensuring the blessing of the corn-spirit on the homestead and its inmates and storing it up for another year.

The Roman sacrifice of the October horse, as it was called, carries us back to the early days when the Subura, afterwards a low and squalid quarter of the great metropolis, was still a separate village, whose inhabitants engaged in a friendly contest on the harvest-field with their neighbours of Rome, then a little rural town. The Field of Mars on which the ceremony took place lay beside the Tiber, and formed part of the king's domain down to the abolition of the monarchy. For tradition ran that at the time when the last of the kings was driven from Rome the corn stood ripe for the sickle on the crown lands beside the river ; but no one would eat the accursed grain and it was flung into the river in such heaps that, the water being low with the summer heat, it formed the nucleus of an island. The horse sacrifice was thus an old autumn custom observed upon the king's corn-fields at the end of the harvest. The tail and blood of the horse, as the chief parts of the corn-spirit's representative, were taken to the king's house and kept there ; just as in Germany the harvest-cock is nailed on the gable or over the door of the farmhouse ; and as the last sheaf, in the form of the Maiden, is carried home and kept over the fireplace in the Highlands of Scotland. Thus the blessing of the corn-spirit was brought to the king's house and hearth and, through them, to the community of which he was the head. Similarly in the spring and autumn customs of Northern Europe the Maypole is sometimes set up in front of the house of the mayor or burgomaster, and the last sheaf at harvest is brought to him as the head of the village. But while the tail and blood fell to the king, the neighbouring village of the Subura, which no doubt once had a similar ceremony of its own, was gratified by being allowed to compete for the prize of the horse's head. The Mamilian tower, to which the Suburans nailed the horse's head when they succeeded in carrying it off, appears to have been a peel-tower or keep of the old Mamilian family, the magnates of the village. The ceremony thus performed on the king's fields and at his house on behalf of the whole town and of the neighbouring village presupposes a time when each township performed a similar ceremony on its own fields. In the rural districts of Latium the villages may have continued to observe the custom, each on its own land, long after the Roman hamlets had merged their separate harvest-homes in the common celebration on the king's lands. There is no intrinsic improbability in the supposition that the sacred grove of Aricia, like the Field of Mars at Rome, may have been the scene of a common harvest celebration, at which a horse was sacrificed with the same rude rites on behalf of the neighbouring villages. The horse would represent the fructifying spirit both of the tree and of the corn, for the two ideas melt into each other, as we see in customs like the Harvest-May.

CHAPTER L

EATING THE GOD

§ 1. *The Sacrament of First-Fruits.*—We have now seen that the corn-spirit is represented sometimes in human, sometimes in animal form, and that in both cases he is killed in the person of his repre-

sentative and eaten sacramentally. To find examples of actually
killing the human representative of the corn-spirit we had naturally
to go to savage races ; but the harvest-suppers of our European
peasants have furnished unmistakable examples of the sacramental
eating of animals as representatives of the corn-spirit. But further,
as might have been anticipated, the new corn is itself eaten sacramentally, that is, as the body of the corn-spirit. In Wermland,
Sweden, the farmer's wife uses the grain of the last sheaf to bake a
loaf in the shape of a little girl ; this loaf is divided amongst the whole
household and eaten by them. Here the loaf represents the corn-
spirit conceived as a maiden ; just as in Scotland the corn-spirit is
similarly conceived and represented by the last sheaf made up in the
form of a woman and bearing the name of the Maiden. As usual, the
corn-spirit is believed to reside in the last sheaf ; and to eat a loaf
made from the last sheaf is, therefore, to eat the corn-spirit itself.
Similarly at La Palisse, in France, a man made of dough is hung upon
the fir-tree which is carried on the last harvest-waggon. The tree
and the dough-man are taken to the mayor's house and kept there till
the vintage is over. Then the close of the harvest is celebrated by a
feast at which the mayor breaks the dough-man in pieces and gives
the pieces to the people to eat.

In these examples the corn-spirit is represented and eaten in human
shape. In other cases, though the new corn is not baked in loaves of
human shape, still the solemn ceremonies with which it is eaten suffice
to indicate that it is partaken of sacramentally, that is, as the body
of the corn-spirit. For example, the following ceremonies used to be
observed by Lithuanian peasants at eating the new corn. About the
time of the autumn sowing, when all the corn had been got in and the
threshing had begun, each farmer held a festival called Sabarios, that
is, " the mixing or throwing together." He took nine good handfuls
of each kind of crop—wheat, barley, oats, flax, beans, lentils, and the
rest ; and each handful he divided into three parts. The twenty-
seven portions of each grain were then thrown on a heap and all mixed
up together. The grain used had to be that which was first threshed
and winnowed and which had been set aside and kept for this purpose.
A part of the grain thus mixed was employed to bake little loaves,
one for each of the household ; the rest was mixed with more barley
or oats and made into beer. The first beer brewed from this mixture
was for the drinking of the farmer, his wife, and children ; the second
brew was for the servants. The beer being ready, the farmer chose
an evening when no stranger was expected. Then he knelt down
before the barrel of beer, drew a jugful of the liquor and poured it on
the bung of the barrel, saying, " O fruitful earth, make rye and barley
and all kinds of corn to flourish." Next he took the jug to the parlour,
where his wife and children awaited him. On the floor of the parlour
lay bound a black or white or speckled (not a red) cock and a hen of
the same colour and of the same brood, which must have been hatched
within the year. Then the farmer knelt down, with the jug in his

hand, and thanked God for the harvest and prayed for a good crop next year. Next all lifted up their hands and said, " O God, and thou, O earth, we give you this cock and hen as a free-will offering." With that the farmer killed the fowls with the blows of a wooden spoon, for he might not cut their heads off. After the first prayer and after killing each of the birds he poured out a third of the beer. Then his wife boiled the fowls in a new pot which had never been used before. After that, a bushel was set, bottom upwards, on the floor, and on it were placed the little loaves mentioned above and the boiled fowls. Next the new beer was fetched, together with a ladle and three mugs, none of which was used except on this occasion. When the farmer had ladled the beer into the mugs, the family knelt down round the bushel. The father then uttered a prayer and drank off the three mugs of beer. The rest followed his example. Then the loaves and the flesh of the fowls were eaten, after which the beer went round again, till every one had emptied each of the three mugs nine times. None of the food should remain over ; but if anything did happen to be left, it was consumed next morning with the same ceremonies. The bones were given to the dog to eat ; if he did not eat them all up, the remains were buried under the dung in the cattle-stall. This ceremony was observed at the beginning of December. On the day on which it took place no bad word might be spoken.

Such was the custom about two hundred years or more ago. At the present day in Lithuania, when new potatoes or loaves made from the new corn are being eaten, all the people at table pull each other's hair. The meaning of this last custom is obscure, but a similar custom was certainly observed by the heathen Lithuanians at their solemn sacrifices. Many of the Esthonians of the island of Oesel will not eat bread baked of the new corn till they have first taken a bite at a piece of iron. The iron is here plainly a charm, intended to render harmless the spirit that is in the corn. In Sutherlandshire at the present day, when the new potatoes are dug all the family must taste them, other- wise " the spirits in them [the potatoes] take offence, and the potatoes would not keep." In one part of Yorkshire it is still customary for the clergyman to cut the first corn ; and my informant believes that the corn so cut is used to make the communion bread. If the latter part of the custom is correctly reported (and analogy is all in its favour), it shows how the Christian communion has absorbed within itself a sacrament which is doubtless far older than Christianity.

The Aino or Ainu of Japan are said to distinguish various kinds of millet as male and female respectively, and these kinds, taken together, are called " the divine husband and wife cereal " (*Umurek haru kamui*). " Therefore before millet is pounded and made into cakes for general eating, the old men have a few made for themselves first to worship. When they are ready they pray to them very earnestly and say : ' O thou cereal deity, we worship thee. Thou hast grown very well this year, and thy flavour will be sweet. Thou art good. The goddess of fire will be glad, and we also shall rejoice greatly. O thou god, O thou divine cereal, do thou nourish the people. I now partake of thee. I worship thee and give thee thanks.' After having thus prayed, they, the worshippers, take a cake and eat it, and from this time the people may all partake of the new millet. And so with many gestures of homage and words of prayer this kind of food is dedicated to the well-being of the Ainu. No doubt the cereal offering is regarded as a tribute paid to god, but that god is no other than the seed itself; and it is only a god in so far as it is beneficial to the human body."

At the close of the rice harvest in the East Indian island of Buru, each clan meets at a common sacramental meal, to which every member of the clan is bound to contribute a little of the new rice. This meal is called "eating the soul of the rice," a name which clearly indicates the sacramental character of the repast. Some of the rice is also set apart and offered to the spirits. Amongst the Alfoors of Minahassa, in Celebes, the priest sows the first rice-seed and plucks the first ripe rice in each field. This rice he roasts and grinds into meal, and gives some of it to each of the household. Shortly before the rice-harvest in Bolang Mongondo, another district of Celebes, an offering is made of a small pig or a fowl. Then the priest plucks a little rice, first on his own field and next on those of his neighbours. All the rice thus plucked by him he dries along with his own, and then gives it back to the re-spective owners, who have it ground and boiled. When it is boiled the women take it back, with an egg, to the priest, who offers the egg in sacrifice and returns the rice to the women. Of this rice every member of the family, down to the youngest child, must partake. After this ceremony every one is free to get in his rice.

Amongst the Burghers or Badagas, a tribe of the Neilgherry Hills in Southern India, the first handful of seed is sown and the first sheaf reaped by a Curumbar, a man of a different tribe, the members of which the Burghers regard as sorcerers. The grain contained in the first sheaf "is that day reduced to meal, made into cakes, and, being offered as a first-fruit oblation, is, together with the remainder of the sacrificed animal, partaken of by the Burgher and the whole of his family, as the meat of a federal offering and sacrifice." Among the Hindoos of Southern India the eating of the new rice is the occasion of a family festival called Pongol. The new rice is boiled in a new pot on a fire which is kindled at noon on the day when, according to Hindoo astrologers, the sun enters the tropic of Capricorn. The boiling of the pot is watched with great anxiety by the whole family, for as the milk boils, so will the coming year be. If the milk boils rapidly, the year will be prosperous; but it will be the reverse if the milk boils slowly. Some of the new boiled rice is offered to the image of Ganesa; then every one partakes of it. In some parts of Northern India the festival of the new crop is known as *Navan*, that is, "new grain." When the crop is ripe, the owner takes the omens, goes to the field, plucks five or six ears of barley in the spring crop and one of the millets in the autumn harvest. This is brought home, parched, and mixed with coarse sugar, butter, and curds. Some of it is thrown on the fire in the name of the village gods and deceased ancestors; the rest is eaten by the family.

The ceremony of eating the new yams at Onitsha, on the Niger, is thus described: " Each headman brought out six yams, and cut down young branches of palm-leaves and placed them before his gate, roasted three of the yams, and got some kola-nuts and fish. After the yam is roasted, the *Libia*, or country doctor, takes the yam, scrapes it into a sort of meal, and divides it into halves; he then takes one piece, and places it on the lips of the person who is going to eat the new yam. The eater then blows up the steam from the hot yam, and afterwards pokes the whole into his mouth, and says, ' I thank God for being permitted to eat the new yam '; he then begins to chew it heartily, with fish likewise."

Among the Nandi of British East Africa, when the eleusine grain is ripening in autumn, every woman who owns a cornfield goes out into it with her daughters, and they all pluck some of the ripe grain. Each of the women then fixes one grain in her necklace and chews another, which she rubs on her forehead, throat, and breast. No mark of joy escapes them; sorrowfully they cut a basketful of the new corn, and carrying it home place it in the loft to dry. As the ceiling is of wickerwork, a good deal of the grain drops through the crevices and falls into the fire, where it explodes with a crackling noise. The people make no attempt to prevent this waste; for they regard the crackling of the grain in the fire as a sign that the souls of the dead are partaking of it. A few days later porridge is made from the new grain and served up with milk at the evening meal. All the members of the family take some of the porridge and dab it on the walls and roofs of the huts; also they put a little in their mouths and spit it out towards the east and on the outside of the huts. Then, holding up some of the grain in his hand, the head of the family prays to God for health and strength, and likewise for milk, and everybody present repeats the words of the prayer after him.

Amongst the Caffres of Natal and Zululand, no one may eat of the new fruits till after a festival which marks the beginning of the Caffre year and falls at the end of December or the beginning of January. All the people assemble at the king's kraal, where they feast and dance. Before they separate the " dedication of the people " takes place. Various fruits of the earth, as corn, mealies, and pumpkins, mixed with the flesh of a sacrificed animal and with " medicine," are boiled in great pots, and a little of this food is placed in each man's mouth by the king himself. After thus partaking of the sanctified fruits, a man is himself sanctified for the whole year, and may immediately get in his crops. It is believed that if any man were to partake of the new fruits before the festival, he would die; if he were detected, he would be put to death, or at least all his cattle would be taken from him. The holiness of the new fruits is well marked by the rule that they must be cooked in a special pot which is used only for this purpose, and on a new fire kindled by a magician through the friction of two sticks which are called " husband and wife."

Among the Bechuanas it is a rule that before they partake of the new crops they must purify themselves. The purification takes place at the commencement of the new year on a day in January which is fixed by the chief. It begins in the great kraal of the tribe, where all the adult males assemble. Each of them takes in his hand leaves of a gourd called by the natives *lerotse* (described as something between a pumpkin and a vegetable marrow) ; and having crushed the leaves he anoints with the expressed juice his big toes and his navel ; many people indeed apply the juice to all the joints of their body, but the better-informed say that this is a vulgar departure from ancient custom. After this ceremony in the great kraal every man goes home to his own kraal, assembles all the members of his family, men, women, and children, and smears them all with the juice of the *lerotse* leaves. Some of the leaves are also pounded, mixed with milk in a large wooden dish, and given to the dogs to lap up. Then the porridge plate of each member of the family is rubbed with the *lerotse* leaves. When this purification has been completed, but not before, the people are free to eat of the new crops.

The Bororo Indians of Brazil think that it would be certain death to eat the new maize before it has been blessed by the medicine-man. The ceremony of blessing it is as follows. The half-ripe husk is washed and placed before the medicine-man, who by dancing and singing for several hours, and by incessant smoking, works himself up into a state of ecstasy, whereupon he bites into the husk, trembling in every limb and uttering shrieks from time to time. A similar ceremony is performed whenever a large animal or a large fish is killed. The Bororo are firmly persuaded that were any man to touch unconsecrated maize or meat, before the ceremony had been completed, he and his whole tribe would perish.

Amongst the Creek Indians of North America, the *busk* or festival of first-fruits was the chief ceremony of the year. It was held in July or August, when the corn was ripe, and marked the end of the old year and the beginning of the new one. Before it took place, none of the Indians would eat or even handle any part of the new harvest. Sometimes each town had its own busk ; sometimes several towns united to hold one in common. Before celebrating the busk, the people provided themselves with new clothes and new household utensils and furniture ; they collected their old clothes and rubbish, together with all the remaining grain and other old provisions, cast them together in one common heap, and consumed them with fire. As a preparation for the ceremony, all the fires in the village were extinguished, and the ashes swept clean away. In particular, the hearth or altar of the temple was dug up and the ashes carried out. Then the chief priest put some roots of the button-snake plant, with some green tobacco leaves and a little of the new fruits, at the bottom

of the fireplace, which he afterwards commanded to be covered up
with white clay, and wetted over with clean water. A thick arbour
of green branches of young trees was then made over the altar.
Meanwhile the women at home were cleaning out their houses,
renewing the old hearths, and scouring all the cooking vessels that
they might be ready to receive the new fire and the new fruits. The
public or sacred square was carefully swept of even the smallest
crumbs of previous feasts, " for fear of polluting the first-fruit offerings."
Also every vessel that had contained or had been used about any
food during the expiring year was removed from the temple before
sunset. Then all the men who were not known to have violated
the law of the first-fruit offering and that of marriage during the
year were summoned by a crier to enter the holy square and observe
a solemn fast. But the women (except six old ones), the children,
and all who had not attained the rank of warriors were forbidden
to enter the square. Sentinels were also posted at the corners of the
square to keep out all persons deemed impure and all animals. A
strict fast was then observed for two nights and a day, the devotees
drinking a bitter decoction of button-snake root " in order to vomit
and purge their sinful bodies." That the people outside the square
might also be purified, one of the old men laid down a quantity of
green tobacco at a corner of the square ; this was carried off by an
old woman and distributed to the people without, who chewed and
swallowed it " in order to afflict their souls." During this general
fast, the women, children, and men of weak constitution were allowed
to eat after mid-day, but not before. On the morning when the
fast ended, the women brought a quantity of the old year's food to
the outside of the sacred square. These provisions were then fetched
in and set before the famished multitude, but all traces of them had
to be removed before noon. When the sun was declining from the
meridian, all the people were commanded by the voice of a crier to
stay within doors, to do no bad act, and to be sure to extinguish and
throw away every spark of the old fire. Universal silence now reigned.
Then the high priest made the new fire by the friction of two pieces
of wood, and placed it on the altar under the green arbour. This
new fire was believed to atone for all past crimes except murder.
Next a basket of new fruits was brought ; the high priest took out
a little of each sort of fruit, rubbed it with bear's oil, and offered it,
together with some flesh, " to the bountiful holy spirit of fire, as a
first-fruit offering, and an annual oblation for sin." He also consecrated the sacred emetics (the button-snake root and the cassina or
black-drink) by pouring a little of them into the fire. The persons
who had remained outside now approached, without entering, the
sacred square ; and the chief priest thereupon made a speech, exhorting
the people to observe their old rites and customs, announcing that the
new divine fire had purged away the sins of the past year, and earnestly
warning the women that, if any of them had not extinguished the
old fire, or had contracted any impurity, they must forthwith depart,

" lest the divine fire should spoil both them and the people." Some of the new fire was then set down outside the holy square ; the women carried it home joyfully, and laid it on their unpolluted hearths. When several towns had united to celebrate the festival, the new fire might thus be carried for several miles. The new fruits were then dressed on the new fires and eaten with bear's oil, which was deemed indispensable. At one point of the festival the men rubbed the new corn between their hands, then on their faces and breasts. During the festival which followed, the warriors, dressed in their wild martial array, their heads covered with white down and carrying white feathers in their hands, danced round the sacred arbour, under which burned the new fire. The ceremonies lasted eight days, during which the strictest continence was practised. Towards the conclusion of the festival the warriors fought a mock battle ; then the men and women together, in three circles, danced round the sacred fire. Lastly, all the people smeared themselves with white clay and bathed in running water. They came out of the water believing that no evil could now befall them for what they had done amiss in the past. So they departed in joy and peace.

To this day, also, the remnant of the Seminole Indians of Florida, a people of the same stock as the Creeks, hold an annual purification and festival called the Green Corn Dance, at which the new corn is eaten. On the evening of the first day of the festival they quaff a nauseous " Black Drink," as it is called, which acts both as an emetic and a purgative ; they believe that he who does not drink of this liquor cannot safely eat the new green corn, and besides that he will be sick at some time in the year. While the liquor is being drunk, the dancing begins, and the medicine-men join in it. Next day they eat of the green corn ; the following day they fast, probably from fear of polluting the sacred food in their stomachs by contact with common food ; but the third day they hold a great feast.

Even tribes which do not till the ground sometimes observe analogous ceremonies when they gather the first wild fruits or dig the first roots of the season. Thus among the Salish and Tinneh Indians of North-West America, " before the young people eat the first berries or roots of the season, they always addressed the fruit or plant, and begged for its favour and aid. In some tribes regular First-fruit ceremonies were annually held at the time of picking the wild fruit or gathering the roots, and also among the salmon-eating tribes when the run of the ' sockeye ' salmon began. These ceremonies were not so much thanksgivings, as performances to ensure a plentiful crop or supply of the particular object desired, for if they were not properly and reverently carried out there was danger of giving offence to the ' spirits ' of the objects, and being deprived of them." For example, these Indians are fond of the young shoots or suckers of the wild raspberry, and they observe a solemn ceremony at eating the first of them in season. The shoots are cooked in a new pot : the people assemble and stand in a great circle with closed eyes, while the presiding chief or medicine-man invokes the spirit of the plant, begging that it will be propitious to them and grant them a good supply of suckers. After this part of the ceremony is over the cooked suckers are handed to the presiding officer in a newly carved dish, and a small portion is given to each person present, who reverently and decorously eats it.

The Thompson Indians of British Columbia cook and eat the sunflower root (*Balsamorrhiza sagittata*, Nutt.), but they used to regard it as a mysterious being, and observed a number of taboos in connexion with it ; for example, women who were engaged in digging or cooking the root must practise continence, and no man might come near the oven where the women were baking the root. When young people ate the first berries, roots, or other products of the season, they addressed a prayer to the Sunflower-Root as follows : " I inform thee that I intend to eat thee. Mayest thou always help me to ascend, so that I may always be able to reach the tops of mountains, and may I never be clumsy ! I ask this from thee, Sunflower-Root. Thou art the greatest of all in mystery." To omit this prayer would make the eater lazy and cause him to sleep long in the morning.

These customs of the Thompson and other Indian tribes of North-West America are instructive, because they clearly indicate the motive, or at least one of the motives, which underlies the ceremonies observed at eating the first fruits of the season. That motive in the case of these Indians is simply a belief that the plant itself is animated by a conscious and more or less powerful spirit, who must be propitiated before the people can safely partake of the fruits or roots which are supposed to be part of his body. Now if this is true of wild fruits and roots, we may infer with some probability that it is also true of cultivated fruits and roots, such as yams, and in particular that it holds good of the cereals, such as wheat, barley, oats, rice, and maize. In all cases it seems reasonable to infer that the scruples which savages manifest at eating the first fruits of any crop, and the ceremonies which they observe before they overcome their scruples, are due at least in large measure to a notion that the plant or tree is animated by a spirit or even a deity, whose leave must be obtained, or whose favour must be sought, before it is possible to partake with safety of the new crop. This indeed is plainly affirmed of the Aino : they call the millet " the divine cereal," " the cereal deity," and they pray to and worship him before they will eat of the cakes made from the new millet. And even where the indwelling divinity of the first fruits is not expressly affirmed, it appears to be implied both by the solemn preparations made for eating them and by the danger supposed to be incurred by persons who venture to partake of them without observing the prescribed ritual. In all such cases, accordingly, we may not improperly describe the eating of the new fruits as a sacrament or communion with a deity, or at all events with a powerful spirit.

Among the usages which point to this conclusion are the custom of employing either new or specially reserved vessels to hold the new fruits, and the practice of purifying the persons of the communicants before it is lawful to engage in the solemn act of communion with the divinity. Of all the modes of purification adopted on these occasions none perhaps brings out the sacramental virtue of the rite so clearly as the Creek and Seminole practice of taking a purgative before swallowing the new corn. The intention is thereby to prevent the sacred food from being polluted by contact with common food in the stomach of the eater. For the same reason Catholics partake of the Eucharist fasting ; and among the pastoral Masai of Eastern Africa the young warriors, who live on meat and milk exclusively, are obliged to eat nothing but milk for so many days and then nothing but meat for so many more, and before they pass from the one food to the other they must make sure that none of the old food remains in their stomachs ; this they do by swallowing a very powerful purgative and emetic.

In some of the festivals which we have examined, the sacrament of first-fruits is combined with a sacrifice or presentation of them to gods or spirits, and in course of time the sacrifice of first-fruits tends to throw the sacrament into the shade, if not to supersede it. The mere fact of offering the first-fruits to the gods or spirits comes now to be thought a sufficient preparation for eating the new corn ; the higher powers having received their share, man is free to enjoy the rest. This mode of viewing the new fruits implies that they are regarded no longer as themselves instinct with divine life, but merely as a gift bestowed by the gods upon man, who is bound to express his gratitude and homage to his divine benefactors by returning to them a portion of their bounty.

§ 2. *Eating the God among the Aztecs.*—The custom of eating bread sacramentally as the body of a god was practised by the Aztecs before the discovery and conquest of Mexico by the Spaniards. Twice a year, in May and December, an image of the great Mexican god Huitzilo-pochtli or Vitzilipuztli was made of dough, then broken in pieces, and solemnly eaten by his worshippers. The May ceremony is thus described by the historian Acosta : " The Mexicans in the month of May made their principal feast to their god Vitzilipuztli, and two days before this feast, the virgins whereof I have spoken (the which were shut up and secluded in the same temple and were as it were religious women) did mingle a quantity of the seed of beets with roasted maize, and then they did mould it with honey, making an idol of that paste in bigness like to that of wood, putting instead of eyes grains of green glass, of blue or white ; and for teeth grains of maize set forth with all the ornament and furniture that I have said. This being finished, all the noblemen came and brought it an exquisite and rich garment, like unto that of the idol, wherewith they did attire it. Being thus clad and deckt, they did set it in an azured chair and in a litter to carry it on their shoulders. The morning of this feast being come, an hour before day all the maidens came forth attired in white, with new ornaments, the which that day were called the Sisters of their god

Vitzilipuztli, they came crowned with garlands of maize roasted and parched, being like unto azahar or the flower of orange ; and about their necks they had great chains of the same, which went bauldrick-wise under their left arm. Their cheeks were dyed with vermilion, their arms from the elbow to the wrist were covered with red parrots' feathers." Young men, dressed in red robes and crowned like the virgins with maize, then carried the idol in its litter to the foot of the great pyramid-shaped temple, up the steep and narrow steps of which it was drawn to the music of flutes, trumpets, cornets, and drums. " While they mounted up the idol all the people stood in the court with much reverence and fear. Being mounted to the top, and that they had placed it in a little lodge of roses which they held ready, presently came the young men, which strewed many flowers of sundry kinds, wherewith they filled the temple both within and without. This done, all the virgins came out of their convent, bringing pieces of paste compounded of beets and roasted maize, which was of the same paste whereof their idol was made and compounded, and they were of the fashion of great bones. They delivered them to the young men, who carried them up and laid them at the idol's feet, wherewith they filled the whole place that it could receive no more. They called these morsels of paste the flesh and bones of Vitzilipuztli. Having laid abroad these bones, presently came all the ancients of the temple, priests, Levites, and all the rest of the ministers, according to their dignities and antiquities (for herein there was a strict order amongst them) one after another, with their veils of diverse colours and works, every one according to his dignity and office, having garlands upon their heads and chains of flowers about their necks ; after them came their gods and goddesses whom they worshipped, of diverse figures, attired in the same livery ; then putting themselves in order about those morsels and pieces of paste, they used certain ceremonies with singing and dancing. By means whereof they were blessed and con-secrated for the flesh and bones of this idol. This ceremony and blessing (whereby they were taken for the flesh and bones of the idol) being ended, they honoured those pieces in the same sort as their god. . . . All the city came to this goodly spectacle, and there was a command-ment very strictly observed throughout all the land, that the day of the feast of the idol of Vitzilipuztli they should eat no other meat but this paste, with honey, whereof the idol was made. And this should be eaten at the point of day, and they should drink no water nor any other thing till after noon : they held it for an ill sign, yea, for sacrilege to do the contrary : but after the ceremonies ended, it was lawful for them to eat anything. During the time of this ceremony they hid the water from their little children, admonishing all such as had the use of reason not to drink any water ; which, if they did, the anger of God would come upon them, and they should die, which they did observe very carefully and strictly. The ceremonies, dancing, and sacrifice ended, they went to unclothe themselves, and the priests and superiors of the temple took the idol of paste, which they spoiled of all the ornaments it had, and made many pieces, as well of the idol itself as of the truncheons which they consecrated, and then they gave them to the people in manner of a communion, beginning with the greater, and continuing unto the rest, both men, women, and little children, who received it with such tears, fear, and reverence as it was an admirable thing, saying that they did eat the flesh and bones of God, wherewith they were grieved. Such as had any sick folks demanded thereof for them, and carried it with great reverence and veneration."

From this interesting passage we learn that the ancient Mexicans, even before the arrival of Christian missionaries, were fully acquainted with the doctrine of transubstantiation and acted upon it in the solemn rites of their religion. They believed that by consecrating bread their priests could turn it into the very body of their god, so that all who thereupon partook of the consecrated bread entered into a mystic communion with the deity by receiving a portion of his divine substance into themselves. The doctrine of transubstantiation, or the magical conversion of bread into flesh, was also familiar to the Aryans of ancient India long before the spread and even the rise of Christianity. The Brahmans taught that the rice-cakes offered in sacrifice were substitutes for human beings, and that they were actually converted into the real bodies of men by the manipulation of the priest. We read that " when it (the rice-cake) still consists of rice-meal, it is the hair. When he pours water on it, it becomes skin. When he mixes it, it becomes flesh : for then it becomes consistent ; and consistent also is the flesh. When it is baked, it becomes bone : for then it becomes somewhat hard ; and hard is the bone. And when he is about to take it off (the fire) and sprinkles it with butter, he changes it into marrow. This is the completeness which they call the fivefold animal sacrifice."

Now, too, we can perfectly understand why on the day of their solemn communion with the deity the Mexicans refused to eat any other food than the consecrated bread which they revered as the very flesh and bones of their God, and why up till noon they might drink nothing at all, not even water. They feared no doubt to defile the portion of God in their stomachs by contact with common things. A similar pious fear led the Creek and Seminole Indians, as we saw, to adopt the more thoroughgoing expedient of rinsing out their bodies by a strong purgative before they dared to partake of the sacrament of first-fruits.

At the festival of the winter solstice in December the Aztecs killed their god Huitzilopochtli in effigy first and ate him afterwards. As a preparation for this solemn ceremony an image of the deity in the likeness of a man was fashioned out of seeds of various sorts, which were kneaded into a dough with the blood of children. The bones of the god were represented by pieces of acacia wood. This image was placed on the chief altar of the temple, and on the day of the festival the king offered incense to it. Early next day it was taken down and set on its feet in a great hall. Then a priest, who bore the name and acted the part of the god Quetzalcoatl, took a flint-tipped dart and hurled it into the breast of the dough-image, piercing it through and through.   This was called " killing the god Huitzilopochtli so that his body might be eaten."   One of the priests cut out the heart of the image and gave it to the king to eat.   The rest of the image was divided into minute pieces, of which every man great and small, down to the male children in the cradle, receive one to eat.   But no woman might taste a morsel.   The ceremony was called *teoqualo*, that is, " god is eaten."

At another festival the Mexicans made little images like men, which stood for the cloud-capped mountains.   These images were moulded of a paste of various seeds and were dressed in paper ornaments.   Some people fashioned five, others ten, others as many as fifteen of them.   Having been made, they were placed in the oratory of each house and worshipped.   Four times in the course of the night offerings of food were brought to them in tiny vessels ; and people sang and played the flute before them through all the hours of darkness.   At break of day the priests stabbed the images with a weaver's instrument, cut off their heads, and tore out their hearts, which they presented to the master of the house on a green saucer.   The bodies of the images were then eaten by all the family, especially by the servants, " in order that by eating them they might be preserved from certain distempers, to which those persons who were negligent of worship to those deities conceived themselves to be subject."

§ 3. *Many Manii at Aricia.*—We are now able to suggest an explanation of the proverb " There are many Manii at Aricia."   Certain loaves made in the shape of men were called by the Romans *maniae*, and it appears that this kind of loaf was especially made at Aricia. Now, Mania, the name of one of these loaves, was also the name of the Mother or Grandmother of Ghosts, to whom woollen effigies of men and women were dedicated at the festival of the Compitalia. These effigies were hung at the doors of all the houses in Rome ; one effigy was hung up for every free person in the house, and one effigy, of a different kind, for every slave.   The reason was that on this day the ghosts of the dead were believed to be going about, and it was hoped that, either out of good nature or through simple inadvertence, they would carry off the effigies at the door instead of the living people in the house.   According to tradition, these woollen figures were substitutes for a former custom of sacrificing human beings.   Upon data so fragmentary and uncertain, it is impossible to build with confidence ; but it seems worth suggesting that the loaves in human form, which appear to have been baked at Aricia, were sacramental bread, and that in the old days, when the divine King of the Wood was annually slain, loaves were made in his image, like the paste figures of the gods in Mexico, and were eaten sacramentally by his worshippers.   The Mexican sacraments in honour of Huitzilopochtli were also accompanied by the sacrifice of human victims.   The tradition that the founder of the sacred grove at Aricia was a man named Manius, from whom many Manii were descended, would thus be an etymological myth invented to explain the name *maniae* as applied to these sacramental loaves. A dim recollection of the original connexion of the loaves with human sacrifices may perhaps be traced in the story that the effigies dedicated to Mania at the Compitalia were substitutes for human victims. The story itself, however, is probably devoid of foundation, since the practice of putting up dummies to divert the attention of ghosts or demons from living people is not uncommon.

For example, the Tibetans stand in fear of innumerable earth-demons, all of whom are under the authority of Old Mother Khön-ma. This goddess, who may be compared to the Roman Mania, the Mother or Grandmother of Ghosts, is dressed in golden-yellow robes, holds a golden noose in her hand, and rides on a ram. In order to bar the dwelling-house against the foul fiends, of whom Old Mother Khön-ma is mistress, an elaborate structure somewhat resembling a chandelier is fixed above the door on the outside of the house. It contains a ram's skull, a variety of precious objects such as gold-leaf, silver, and turquoise, also some dry food, such as rice, wheat, and pulse, and finally images or pictures of a man, a woman, and a house. " The object of these figures of a man, wife, and house is to deceive the demons should they still come in spite of this offering, and to mislead them into the belief that the foregoing pictures are the inmates of the house, so that they may wreak their wrath on these bits of wood and so save the real human occupants." When all is ready, a priest prays to Old Mother Khön-ma that she would be pleased to accept these dainty offerings and to close the open doors of the earth, in order that the demons may not come forth to infest and injure the household.

Again, effigies are often employed as a means of preventing or curing sickness ; the demons of disease either mistake the effigies for living people or are persuaded or compelled to enter them, leaving the real men and women well and whole. Thus the Alfoors of Minahassa, in Celebes, will sometimes transport a sick man to another house, while they leave on his bed a dummy made up of a pillow and clothes. This dummy the demon is supposed to mistake for the sick man, who consequently recovers. Cure or prevention of this sort seems to find especial favour with the natives of Borneo. Thus, when an epidemic is raging among them, the Dyaks of the Katoengouw river set up wooden images at their doors in the hope that the demons of the plague may be deluded into carrying off the effigies instead of the people. Among the Oloh Ngadju of Borneo, when a sick man is supposed to be suffering from the assaults of a ghost, puppets of dough or rice-meal are made and thrown under the house as substitutes for the patient, who thus rids himself of the ghost. In certain of the western districts of Borneo if a man is taken suddenly and violently sick, the physician, who in this part of the world is generally an old woman, fashions a wooden image and brings it seven times into contact with the sufferer's head, while she says : " This image serves to take the place of the sick man ;

sickness, pass over into the image." Then, with some rice, salt, and tobacco in a little basket, the substitute is carried to the spot where the evil spirit is supposed to have entered into the man. There it is set upright on the ground, after the physician has invoked the spirit as follows : " O devil, here is an image which stands instead of the sick man. Release the soul of the sick man and plague the image, for it is indeed prettier and better than he." Batak magicians can conjure the demon of disease out of the patient's body into an image made out of a banana-tree with a human face and wrapt up in magic herbs ; the image is then hurriedly removed and thrown away or buried beyond the boundaries of the village. Sometimes the image, dressed as a man or a woman according to the sex of the patient, is deposited at a cross-road or other thoroughfare, in the hope that some passer-by, seeing it, may start and cry out, " Ah ! So-and-So is dead " ; for such an ex-clamation is supposed to delude the demon of disease into a belief that he has accomplished his fell purpose, so he takes himself off and leaves the sufferer to get well. The Mai Darat, a Sakai tribe of the Malay Peninsula, attribute all kinds of diseases to the agency of spirits which they call *nyani* ; fortunately, however, the magician can induce these maleficent beings to come out of the sick person and take up their abode in rude figures of grass, which are hung up outside the houses in little bell-shaped shrines decorated with peeled sticks. During an epidemic of small-pox the Ewe negroes will sometimes clear a space outside of the town, where they erect a number of low mounds and cover them with as many little clay figures as there are people in the place. Pots of food and water are also set out for the refreshment of the spirit of small-pox, who, it is hoped, will take the clay figures and spare the living folk ; and to make assurance doubly sure the road into the town is barricaded against him.

With these examples before us we may surmise that the woollen effigies, which at the festival of the Compitalia might be seen hanging at the doors of all the houses in ancient Rome, were not substitutes for human victims who had formerly been sacrificed at this season, but rather vicarious offerings presented to the Mother or Grandmother of Ghosts, in the hope that on her rounds through the city she would accept or mistake the effigies for the inmates of the house and so spare the living for another year. It is possible that the puppets made of rushes, which in the month of May the pontiffs and Vestal Virgins annually threw into the Tiber from the old Sublician bridge at Rome, had originally the same significance ; that is, they may have been designed to purge the city from demoniac influence by diverting the attention of the demons from human beings to the puppets and then toppling the whole uncanny crew, neck and crop, into the river, which would soon sweep them far out to sea. In precisely the same way the natives of Old Calabar used periodically to rid their town of the devils which infested it by luring the unwary demons into a number of lamentable scarecrows, which they afterwards flung into the river. This interpretation of the Roman custom is supported to some extent by the evidence of Plutarch, who speaks of the ceremony as " the greatest of purifications."

CHAPTER LI

HOMOEOPATHIC MAGIC OF A FLESH DIET

THE practice of killing a god has now been traced amongst peoples who have reached the agricultural stage of society. We have seen that the spirit of the corn, or of other cultivated plants, is commonly represented either in human or in animal form, and that in some places a custom has prevailed of killing annually either the human or the animal representative of the god. One reason for thus killing the corn-spirit in the person of his representative has been given implicitly in an earlier part of this work : we may suppose that the intention was to guard him or her (for the corn-spirit is often feminine) from the enfeeblement of old age by transferring the spirit, while still hale and hearty, to the person of a youthful and vigorous successor. Apart from the desirability of renewing his divine energies, the death of the corn-spirit may have been deemed inevitable under the sickles or the knives of the reapers, and his worshippers may accordingly have felt bound to acquiesce in the sad necessity. But, further, we have found a widespread custom of eating the god sacramentally, either in the shape of the man or animal who represents the god, or in the shape of bread made in human or animal form. The reasons for thus partaking of the body of the god are, from the primitive standpoint, simple enough. The savage commonly believes that by eating the flesh of an animal or man he acquires not only the physical, but even the moral and intellectual qualities which were characteristic of that animal or man ; so when the creature is deemed divine, our simple savage naturally expects to absorb a portion of its divinity along with its material substance. It may be well to illustrate by instances this common faith in the acquisition of virtues or vices of many kinds through the medium of animal food, even when there is no pretence that the viands consist of the body or blood of a god. The doctrine forms part of the widely ramified system of sympathetic or homoeo-pathic magic.

Thus, for example, the Creeks, Cherokee, and kindred tribes of North American Indians " believe that nature is possest of such a property, as to transfuse into men and animals the qualities, either of the food they use, or of those objects that are presented to their senses ; he who feeds on venison is, according to their physical system, swifter and more sagacious than the man who lives on the flesh of the clumsy bear, or helpless dunghill fowls, the slow-footed tame cattle, or the heavy wallowing swine. This is the reason that several of their old men recommend, and say, that formerly their greatest chieftains observed a constant rule in their diet, and seldom ate of any animal of a gross quality, or heavy motion of body, fancying it conveyed a dullness through the whole system, and disabled them from exerting themselves with proper vigour in their martial, civil, and religious duties." The Zaparo Indians of Ecuador " will, unless from necessity, in most cases not eat any heavy meats, such as tapir and peccary, but confine themselves to birds, monkeys, deer, fish, etc., principally because they argue that the heavier meats make them unwieldy, like the animals who supply the flesh, impeding their agility, and unfitting them for the chase." Similarly some of the Brazilian Indians would eat no beast, bird, or fish that ran, flew, or swam slowly, lest by partaking of its flesh they should lose their agility and be unable to escape from their enemies. The Caribs abstained from the flesh of pigs lest it should cause them to have small eyes like pigs ; and they refused to partake of tortoises from a fear that if they did so they would become heavy and stupid like the animal. Among the Fans of West Africa men in the prime of life never eat tortoises for a similar reason ; they imagine that if they did so, their vigour and fleetness of foot would be gone. But old men may eat tortoises freely, because having already lost the power of running they can take no harm from the flesh of the slow-footed creature.

While many savages thus fear to eat the flesh of slow-footed animals lest they should themselves become slow-footed, the Bushmen of South Africa purposely ate the flesh of such creatures, and the reason which they gave for doing so exhibits a curious refinement of savage philosophy. They imagined that the game which they pursued would be influenced sympathetically by the food in the body of the hunter, so that if he had eaten of swift-footed animals, the quarry would be swift-footed also and would escape him ; whereas if he had eaten of slow-footed animals, the quarry would also be slow-footed, and he would be able to overtake and kill it. For that reason hunters of gemsbok particularly avoided eating the flesh of the swift and agile springbok ; indeed they would not even touch it with their hands, because they believed the springbok to be a very lively creature which did not go to sleep at night, and they thought that if they ate spring-bok, the gemsbok which they hunted would likewise not be willing to go to sleep, even at night. How, then, could they catch it ?

The Namaquas abstain from eating the flesh of hares, because they think it would make them faint-hearted as a hare. But they eat the flesh of the lion, or drink the blood of the leopard or lion, to get the courage and strength of these beasts. The Bushmen will not give their children a jackal's heart to eat, lest it should make them timid like the jackal ; but they give them a leopard's heart to eat to make them brave like the leopard. When a Wagogo man of East Africa kills a lion, he eats the heart in order to become brave like a lion ; but he thinks that to eat the heart of a hen would make him timid. When a serious disease has attacked a Zulu kraal, the medicine-man takes the bone of a very old dog, or the bone of an old cow, bull, or other very old animal, and administers it to the healthy as well as to the sick people, in order that they may live to be as old as the animal of whose bone they have partaken. So to restore the aged Aeson to youth, the witch Medea infused into his veins a decoction of the liver of the long-lived deer and the head of a crow that had outlived nine generations of men.

Among the Dyaks of North-West Borneo young men and warriors may not eat venison, because it would make them as timid as deer ; but the women and very old men are free to eat it. However, among the Kayans of the same region, who share the same view as to the ill effect of eating venison, men will partake of the dangerous viand provided it is cooked in the open air, for then the timid spirit of the animal is supposed to escape at once into the jungle and not to enter into the eater. The Aino believe that the heart of the water-ousel is exceedingly wise, and that in speech the bird is most eloquent. Therefore whenever he is killed, he should be at once torn open and his heart wrenched out and swallowed before it has time to grow cold or suffer damage of any kind. If a man swallows it thus, he will become very fluent and wise, and will be able to argue down all his adversaries. In Northern India people fancy that if you eat the eyeballs of an owl you will be able like an owl to see in the dark.

When the Kansas Indians were going to war, a feast used to be held in the chief's hut, and the principal dish was dog's flesh, because, said the Indians, the animal who is so brave that he will let himself be cut in pieces in defence of his master, must needs inspire valour. Men of the Buru and Aru Islands, East Indies, eat the flesh of dogs in order to be bold and nimble in war. Amongst the Papuans of the Port Moresby and Motumotu districts, New Guinea, young lads eat strong pig, wallaby, and large fish, in order to acquire the strength of the animal or fish. Some of the natives of Northern Australia fancy that by eating the flesh of the kangaroo or emu they are enabled to jump or run faster than before. The Miris of Assam prize tiger's flesh as food for men ; it gives them strength and courage. But " it is not suited for women ; it would make them too strong-minded." In Corea the bones of tigers fetch a higher price than those of leopards as a means of inspiring courage. A Chinaman in Seoul bought and ate a whole tiger to make himself brave and fierce. In Norse legend, Ingiald, son of King Aunund, was timid in his youth, but after eating the heart of a wolf he became very bold ; Hialto gained strength and courage by eating the heart of a bear and drinking its blood.

In Morocco lethargic patients are given ants to swallow, and to eat lion's flesh will make a coward brave ; but people abstain from eating the hearts of fowls, lest thereby they should be rendered timid. When a child is late in learning to speak, the Turks of Central Asia will give it the tongues of certain birds to eat. A North American Indian thought that brandy must be a decoction of hearts and tongues, " because," said he, " after drinking it I fear nothing, and I talk wonderfully." In Java there is a tiny earthworm which now and then utters a shrill sound like that of the alarum of a small clock.

Hence when a public dancing girl has screamed herself hoarse in the exercise of her calling, the leader of the troop makes her eat some of these worms, in the belief that thus she will regain her voice and will, after swallowing them, be able to scream as shrilly as ever. The people of Darfur, in Central Africa, think that the liver is the seat of the soul, and that a man may enlarge his soul by eating the liver of an animal. " Whenever an animal is killed its liver is taken out and eaten, but the people are most careful not to touch it with their hands, as it is considered sacred ; it is cut up in small pieces and eaten raw, the bits being conveyed to the mouth on the point of a knife, or the sharp point of a stick. Any one who may accidentally touch the liver is strictly forbidden to partake of it, which prohibition is regarded as a great misfortune for him." Women are not allowed to eat liver, because they have no soul.

Again, the flesh and blood of dead men are commonly eaten and drunk to inspire bravery, wisdom, or other qualities for which the men themselves were remarkable, or which are supposed to have their special seat in the particular part eaten. Thus among the mountain tribes of South-eastern Africa there are ceremonies by which the youths are formed into guilds or lodges, and among the rites of initiation there is one which is intended to infuse courage, intelligence, and other qualities into the novices. Whenever an enemy who has behaved with conspicuous bravery is killed, his liver, which is considered the seat of valour ; his ears, which are supposed to be the seat of intelligence ; the skin of his forehead, which is regarded as the seat of perseverance ; his testicles, which are held to be the seat of strength ; and other members, which are viewed as the seat of other virtues, are cut from his body and baked to cinders. The ashes are carefully kept in the horn of a bull, and, during the ceremonies observed at circumcision, are mixed with other ingredients into a kind of paste, which is administered by the tribal priest to the youths. By this means the strength, valour, intelligence, and other virtues of the slain are believed to be imparted to the eaters. When Basutos of the mountains have killed a very brave foe, they immediately cut out his heart and eat it, because this is supposed to give them his courage and strength in battle. When Sir Charles M'Carthy was killed by the Ashantees in 1824, it is said that his heart was devoured by the chiefs of the Ashantee army, who hoped by this means to imbibe his courage. His flesh was dried and parcelled out among the lower officers for the same purpose, and his bones were long kept at Coomassie as national fetishes. The Nauras Indians of New Granada ate the hearts of Spaniards when they had the opportunity, hoping thereby to make themselves as dauntless as the dreaded Castilian chivalry. The Sioux Indians used to reduce to powder the heart of a valiant enemy and swallow the powder, hoping thus to appropriate the dead man's valour.

But while the human heart is thus commonly eaten for the sake of imbuing the eater with the qualities of its original owner, it is not, as we have already seen, the only part of the body which is consumed for this purpose. Thus warriors of the Theddora and Ngarigo tribes of South-eastern Australia used to eat the hands and feet of their slain enemies, believing that in this way they acquired some of the qualities and courage of the dead. The Kamilaroi of New South Wales ate the liver as well as the heart of a brave man to get his courage. In Tonquin also there is a popular superstition that the liver of a brave man makes brave any who partake of it. With a like intent the Chinese swallow the bile of notorious bandits who have been executed. The Dyaks of Sarawak used to eat the palms of the hands and the flesh of the knees of the slain in order to steady their own hands and strengthen their own knees. The Tolalaki, notorious head-hunters of Central Celebes, drink the blood and eat the brains of their victims that they may become brave. The Italones of the Philippine Islands drink the blood of their slain enemies, and eat part of the back of their heads and of their entrails raw to acquire their courage. For the same reason the Efugaos, another tribe of the Philippines, suck the brains of their foes. In like manner the Kai of German New Guinea eat the brains of the enemies they kill in order to acquire their strength. Among the Kimbunda of Western Africa, when a new king succeeds to the throne, a brave prisoner of war is killed in order that the king and nobles may eat his flesh, and so acquire his strength and courage. The notorious Zulu chief Matuana drank the gall of thirty chiefs, whose people he had destroyed, in the belief that it would make him strong. It is a Zulu fancy that by eating the centre of the forehead and the eyebrow of an enemy they acquire the power of looking steadfastly at a foe. Before every warlike expedition the people of Minahassa in Celebes used to take the locks of hair of a slain foe and dabble them in boiling water to extract the courage ; this infusion of bravery was then drunk by the warriors. In New Zealand " the chief was an *atua* [god], but there were powerful and powerless gods ; each naturally sought to make himself one of the former ; the plan therefore adopted was to incorporate the spirits of others with their own ; thus, when a warrior slew a chief, he immediately gouged out his eyes and swallowed them, the *atua tonga*, or divinity, being supposed to reside in that organ ; thus he not only killed the body, but also possessed himself of the soul of his enemy, and consequently the more chiefs he slew the greater did his divinity become."

It is now easy to understand why a savage should desire to partake of the flesh of an animal or man whom he regards as divine. By eating the body of the god he shares in the god's attributes and powers. And when the god is a corn-god, the corn is his proper body ; when he is a vine-god, the juice of the grape is his blood ; and so by eating the bread and drinking the wine the worshipper partakes of the real body and blood of his god. Thus the drinking of wine in the rites of a vine-god like Dionysus is not an act of revelry, it is a solemn sacrament. Yet a time comes when reasonable men find it hard to understand how any one in his senses can suppose that by eating bread or drinking wine he consumes the body or blood of a deity. "When we call corn Ceres and wine Bacchus," says Cicero, "we use a common figure of speech; but do you imagine that anybody is so insane as to believe that the thing he feeds upon is a god?"

CHAPTER LII

KILLING THE DIVINE ANIMAL

§ 1. *Killing the Sacred Buzzard.*—In the preceding chapters we saw that many communities which have progressed so far as to subsist mainly by agriculture have been in the habit of killing and eating their farinaceous deities either in their proper form of corn, rice, and so forth, or in the borrowed shapes of animals and men. It remains to show that hunting and pastoral tribes, as well as agricultural peoples, have been in the habit of killing the beings whom they worship. Among the worshipful beings or gods, if indeed they deserve to be dignified by that name, whom hunters and shepherds adore and kill are animals pure and simple, not animals regarded as embodiments of other supernatural beings. Our first example is drawn from the Indians of California, who living in a fertile country under a serene and temperate sky, nevertheless rank near the bottom of the savage scale. The Acagchemem tribe adored the great buzzard, and once a year they celebrated a great festival called *Panes* or bird-feast in its honour. The day selected for the festival was made known to the public on the evening before its celebration and preparations were at once made for the erection of a special temple (*vanquech*), which seems to have been a circular or oval enclosure of stakes with the stuffed skin of a coyote or prairie-wolf set up on a hurdle to represent the god Chinigchinich. When the temple was ready, the bird was carried into it in solemn procession and laid on an altar erected for the purpose. Then all the young women, whether married or single, began to run to and fro, as if distracted, some in one direction and some in another, while the elders of both sexes remained silent spectators of the scene, and the captains, tricked out in paint and feathers, danced round their adored bird. These ceremonies being concluded, they seized upon the bird and carried it to the principal temple, all the assembly uniting in the grand display, and the captains dancing and singing at the head of the procession. Arrived at the temple, they killed the bird without losing a drop of its blood. The skin was removed entire and preserved with the feathers as a relic or for the purpose of making the festal garment or *paelt*. The carcase was buried in a hole in the temple, and the old women gathered round the grave weeping and moaning bitterly, while they threw various kinds of seeds or pieces of food on it, crying out, "Why did you run

away ? Would you not have been better with us ? you would have
made *pinole* (a kind of gruel) as we do, and if you had not run away,
you would not have become a *Panes*," and so on. When this ceremony was concluded, the dancing was resumed and kept up for three
days and nights. They said that the *Panes* was a woman who had
run off to the mountains and there been changed into a bird by the
god Chinigchinich. They believed that though they sacrificed the
bird annually, she came to life again and returned to her home in
the mountains. Moreover they thought that " as often as the bird
was killed, it became multiplied ; because every year all the different
Capitanes celebrated the same feast of *Panes*, and were firm in the
opinion that the birds sacrificed were but one and the same female."

The unity in multiplicity thus postulated by the Californians is
very noticeable and helps to explain their motive for killing the divine
bird. The notion of the life of a species as distinct from that of an
individual, easy and obvious as it seems to us, appears to be one which
the Californian savage cannot grasp. He is unable to conceive the
life of the species otherwise than as an individual life, and therefore
as exposed to the same dangers and calamities which menace and
finally destroy the life of the individual. Apparently he imagines
that a species left to itself will grow old and die like an individual,
and that therefore some step must be taken to save from extinction
the particular species which he regards as divine. The only means
he can think of to avert the catastrophe is to kill a member of the
species in whose veins the tide of life is still running strong and has
not yet stagnated among the fens of old age. The life thus diverted
from one channel will flow, he fancies, more freshly and freely in a
new one ; in other words, the slain animal will revive and enter on
a new term of life with all the spring and energy of youth. To us
this reasoning is transparently absurd, but so too is the custom. A
similar confusion, it may be noted, between the individual life and the
life of the species was made by the Samoans. Each family had for
its god a particular species of animal ; yet the death of one of these
animals, for example an owl, was not the death of the god, " he was
supposed to be yet alive, and incarnate in all the owls in existence."

§ 2. *Killing the Sacred Ram.*—The rude Californian rite which we
have just considered has a close parallel in the religion of ancient
Egypt. The Thebans and all other Egyptians who worshipped the
Theban god Ammon held rams to be sacred, and would not sacrifice
them. But once a year at the festival of Ammon they killed a ram,
skinned it, and clothed the image of the god in the skin. Then they
mourned over the ram and buried it in a sacred tomb. The custom
was explained by a story that Zeus had once exhibited himself to
Hercules clad in the fleece and wearing the head of a ram. Of course
the ram in this case was simply the beast-god of Thebes, as the wolf
was the beast-god of Lycopolis, and the goat was the beast-god of
Mendes. In other words, the ram was Ammon himself. On the
monuments, it is true, Ammon appears in semi-human form with

the body of a man and the head of a ram. But this only shows that he was in the usual chrysalis state through which beast-gods regularly pass before they emerge as full-blown anthropomorphic gods. The ram, therefore, was killed, not as a sacrifice to Ammon, but as the god himself, whose identity with the beast is plainly shown by the custom of clothing his image in the skin of the slain ram. The reason for thus killing the ram-god annually may have been that which I have assigned for the general custom of killing a god and for the special Californian custom of killing the divine buzzard. As applied to Egypt, this explanation is supported by the analogy of the bull-god Apis, who was not suffered to outlive a certain term of years. The intention of thus putting a limit to the life of the human god was, as I have argued, to secure him from the weakness and frailty of age. The same reasoning would explain the custom—probably an older one—of putting the beast-god to death annually, as was done with the ram of Thebes.

One point in the Theban ritual—the application of the skin to the image of the god—deserves particular attention. If the god was at first the living ram, his representation by an image must have originated later. But how did it originate? One answer to this question is perhaps furnished by the practice of preserving the skin of the animal which is slain as divine. The Californians, as we have seen, preserved the skin of the buzzard; and the skin of the goat, which is killed on the harvest-field as a representative of the corn-spirit, is kept for various superstitious purposes. The skin in fact was kept as a token or memorial of the god, or rather as containing in it a part of the divine life, and it had only to be stuffed or stretched upon a frame to become a regular image of him. At first an image of this kind would be renewed annually, the new image being provided by the skin of the slain animal. But from annual images to permanent images the transition is easy. We have seen that the older custom of cutting a new May-tree every year was superseded by the practice of maintaining a permanent Maypole, which was, however, annually decked with fresh leaves and flowers, and even surmounted each year by a fresh young tree. Similarly when the stuffed skin, as a representative of the god, was replaced by a permanent image of him in wood, stone, or metal, the permanent image was annually clad in the fresh skin of the slain animal. When this stage had been reached, the custom of killing the ram came naturally to be interpreted as a sacrifice offered to the image, and was explained by a story like that of Ammon and Hercules.

§ 3. *Killing the Sacred Serpent.*—West Africa appears to furnish another example of the annual killing of a sacred animal and the preservation of its skin. The negroes of Issapoo, in the island of Fernando Po, regard the cobra-capella as their guardian deity, who can do them good or ill, bestow riches or inflict disease and death. The skin of one of these reptiles is hung tail downwards from a branch of the highest tree in the public square, and the placing of it on the tree is an annual ceremony. As soon as the ceremony is over, all children born within the past year are carried out and their hands made to touch the tail of the serpent's skin. The latter custom is clearly a way of placing the infants under the protection of the tribal god. Similarly in Senegambia a python is expected to visit every child of the Python clan within eight days after birth ; and the Psylli, a Snake clan of ancient Africa, used to expose their infants to snakes in the belief that the snakes would not harm true-born children of the clan.

§ 4. *Killing the Sacred Turtles.*—In the Californian, Egyptian, and Fernando Po customs the worship of the animal seems to have no relation to agriculture, and may therefore be presumed to date from the hunting or pastoral stage of society. The same may be said of the following custom, though the Zuni Indians of New Mexico, who practise it, are now settled in walled villages or towns of a peculiar type, and practise agriculture and the arts of pottery and weaving. But the Zuni custom is marked by certain features which appear to place it in a somewhat different class from the preceding cases. It may be well therefore to describe it at full length in the words of an eye-witness.

"With midsummer the heat became intense. My brother [*i.e.* adopted Indian brother] and I sat, day after day, in the cool under-rooms of our house,—the latter [*sic*] busy with his quaint forge and crude appliances, working Mexican coins over into bangles, girdles, ear-rings, buttons, and what not, for savage ornament. Though his tools were wonderfully rude, the work he turned out by dint of combined patience and ingenuity was remarkably beautiful. One day as I sat watching him, a procession of fifty men went hastily down the hill, and off westward over the plain. They were solemnly led by a painted and shell-bedecked priest, and followed by the torch-bearing Shu-lu-wit-si or God of Fire. After they had vanished, I asked old brother what it all meant.

" ' They are going,' said he, ' to the city of the Ka-ka and the home of our others.'

" Four days after, towards sunset, costumed and masked in the beautiful paraphernalia of the Ka-k'ok-shi, or ' Good Dance,' they returned in file up the same pathway, each bearing in his arms a basket filled with living, squirming turtles, which he regarded and carried as tenderly as a mother would her infant. Some of the wretched reptiles were carefully wrapped in soft blankets, their heads and forefeet protruding,—and, mounted on the backs of the plume-bedecked pilgrims, made ludicrous but solemn caricatures of little children in the same position. While I was at supper upstairs that evening, the governor's brother-in-law came in. He was welcomed by the family as if a messenger from heaven. He bore in his tremulous fingers one of the much-abused and rebellious turtles. Paint still adhered to his hands and bare feet, which led me to infer that he had formed one of the sacred embassy.

" ' So you went to Ka-thlu-el-lon, did you ? ' I asked.

" ' E'e,' replied the weary man, in a voice husky with long chanting, as he sank, almost exhausted, on a roll of skins which had been placed for him, and tenderly laid the turtle on the floor. No sooner did the creature find itself at liberty than it made off as fast as its lame legs would take it. Of one accord, the family forsook dish, spoon, and drinking-cup, and grabbing from a sacred meal-bowl whole handfuls of the contents, hurriedly followed the turtle about the room, into dark corners, around water-jars, behind the grinding-troughs, and out into the middle of the floor again, praying and scattering meal on its back as they went. At last, strange to say, it approached the foot-sore man who had brought it.

" ' Ha ! ' he exclaimed with emotion ; ' see it comes to me again ; ah, what great favours the fathers of all grant me this day,' and, passing his hand gently over the sprawling animal, he inhaled from his palm deeply and long, at the same time invoking the favour of the gods. Then he leaned his chin upon his hand, and with large, wistful eyes regarded his ugly captive as it sprawled about, blinking its meal-bedimmed eyes, and clawing the smooth floor in memory of its native element. At this juncture I ventured a question :

" ' Why do you not let him go, or give him some water ? '

" Slowly the man turned his eyes toward me, an odd mixture of pain, indignation, and pity on his face, while the worshipful family stared at me with holy horror.

" ' Poor younger brother ! ' he said at last, ' know you not how precious it is ? It die ? It will *not* die ; I tell you, it cannot die.'

" ' But it will die if you don't feed it and give it water.'

" ' I tell you it *cannot* die ; it will only change houses to-morrow, and go back to the home of its brothers. Ah, well ! How should *you* know ? ' he mused. Turning to the blinded turtle again : ' Ah ! my poor dear lost child or parent, my sister or brother to have been ! Who knows which ? Maybe my own great-grandfather or mother ! ' And with this he fell to weeping most pathetically, and, tremulous with sobs, which were echoed by the women and children, he buried his face in his hands. Filled with sympathy for his grief, however mistaken, I raised the turtle to my lips and kissed its cold shell ; then depositing it on the floor, hastily left the grief-stricken family to their sorrows. Next day, with prayers and tender beseechings, plumes, and offerings, the poor turtle was killed, and its flesh and bones were removed and deposited in the little river, that it might ' return once more to eternal life among its comrades in the dark waters of the lake of the dead.' The shell, carefully scraped and dried, was made into a dance-rattle, and, covered by a piece of buckskin, it still hangs from the smoke-stained rafters of my brother's house. Once a Navajo tried to buy it for a ladle ; loaded with indignant reproaches, he was turned out of the house. Were any one to venture the suggestion that the turtle no longer lived, his remark would cause a flood of tears, and he would be reminded that it had only ' changed houses and gone to live for ever in the home of " our lost others." ' "

In this custom we find expressed in the clearest way a belief in the transmigration of human souls into the bodies of turtles. The theory of transmigration is held by the Moqui Indians, who belong to the same race as the Zunis. The Moquis are divided into totem clans— the Bear clan, Deer clan, Wolf clan, Hare clan, and so on ; they believe that the ancestors of the clans were bears, deer, wolves, hares, and so forth ; and that at death the members of each clan become bears, deer, and so on according to the particular clan to which they belonged. The Zuni are also divided into clans, the totems of which agree closely with those of the Moquis, and one of their totems is the turtle. Thus their belief in transmigration into the turtle is probably one of the regular articles of their totem faith. What then is the meaning of killing a turtle in which the soul of a kinsman is believed to be present ? Apparently the object is to keep up a communication with the other world in which the souls of the departed are believed to be assembled in the form of turtles. It is a common belief that the spirits of the dead return occasionally to their old homes ; and accordingly the unseen visitors are welcomed and feasted by the living, and then sent upon their way. In the Zuni ceremony the dead are fetched home in the form of turtles, and the killing of the turtles is the way of sending back the souls to the spirit-land. Thus the general explanation given above of the custom of killing a god seems inapplicable to the Zuni custom, the true meaning of which is somewhat obscure. Nor is the obscurity which hangs over the subject entirely dissipated by a later and fuller account which we possess of the ceremony. From it we learn that the ceremony forms part of the elaborate ritual which these Indians observe at the midsummer solstice for the purpose of ensuring an abundant supply of rain for the crops. Envoys are despatched to bring " their otherselves, the tortoises," from the sacred lake Kothlu-walawa, to which the souls of the dead are believed to repair. When the creatures have thus been solemnly brought to Zuni, they are placed in a bowl of water and dances are performed beside them by men in costume, who personate gods and goddesses. " After the ceremonial the tortoises are taken home by those who caught them and are hung by their necks to the rafters till morning, when they are thrown into pots of boiling water. The eggs are considered a great delicacy. The meat is seldom touched except as a medicine, which is curative for cutaneous diseases. Part of the meat is deposited in the river with *kóhakwa* (white shell beads) and turquoise beads as offerings to Council of the Gods." This account at all events confirms the inference that the tortoises are supposed to be reincarnations of the human dead, for they are called the " otherselves " of the Zuni ; indeed, what else should they be than the souls of the dead in the bodies of tortoises seeing that they come from the haunted lake ? As the principal object of the prayers uttered and of the dances performed at these midsummer ceremonies appears to be to procure rain for the crops, it may be that the intention of bringing the tortoises to Zuni and dancing before them is to intercede with the ancestral spirits, incarnate in the animals, that they may be pleased to exert their power over the waters of heaven for the benefit of their living descendants.

§ 5. *Killing the Sacred Bear.*—Doubt also hangs at first sight over the meaning of the bear-sacrifice offered by the Aino or Ainu, a primitive people who are found in the Japanese island of Yezo or Yesso, as well as in Saghalien and the southern of the Kurile Islands. It is not quite easy to define the attitude of the Aino towards the bear. On the one hand they give it the name of *kamui* or " god " ; but as they apply the same word to strangers, it may mean no more than a being supposed to be endowed with superhuman, or at all events extraordinary, powers. Again, it is said that " the bear is their chief divinity " ; " in the religion of the Aino the bear plays a chief part " ; " amongst the animals it is especially the bear which receives an idolatrous veneration " ; " they worship it after their fashion " ; " there is no doubt that this wild beast inspires more of the feeling which prompts worship than the inanimate forces of nature, and the Aino may be distinguished as bear-worshippers." Yet, on the other hand, they kill the bear whenever they can ; " in bygone years the Ainu considered bear-hunting the most manly and useful way in which a person could possibly spend his time " ; " the men spend the autumn, winter, and spring in hunting deer and bears. Part of their tribute or taxes is paid in skins, and they subsist on the dried meat " ; bear's flesh is indeed one of their staple foods ; they eat it both fresh and salted ; and the skins of bears furnish them with clothing. In fact, the worship of which writers on this subject speak appears to be paid chiefly to the dead animal. Thus, although they kill a bear whenever they can, " in the process of dissecting the carcass they endeavour to conciliate the deity, whose representative they have slain, by making elaborate obeisances and deprecatory salutations " ; " when a bear has been killed the Ainu sit down and admire it, make their salaams to it, worship it, and offer presents of *inao* " ; " when a bear is trapped or wounded by an arrow, the hunters go through an apologetic or propitiatory ceremony." The skulls of slain bears receive a place of honour in their huts, or are set up on sacred posts outside the huts, and are treated with much respect : libations of millet beer, and of *sake*, an intoxicating liquor, are offered to them ; and they are addressed as " divine preservers " or " precious divinities." The skulls of foxes are also fastened to the sacred posts outside the huts ; they are regarded as charms against evil spirits, and are consulted as oracles. Yet it is expressly said, " The live fox is revered just as little as the bear ; rather they avoid it as much as possible, considering it a wily animal." The bear can hardly, therefore, be described as a sacred animal of the Aino, nor yet as a totem ; for they do not call themselves bears, and they kill and eat the animal freely. However, they have a legend of a woman who had a son by a bear ; and many of them who dwell in the mountains pride themselves on being descended from a bear. Such people are called " Descendants of the bear " (*Kimun Kamui sanikiri*), and in the pride of their heart they will say, " As for me, I am a child of the god of the mountains ; I am descended from the divine one who rules in the mountains," meaning by " the god of the mountains " no other than the bear. It is therefore possible that, as our principal authority, the Rev. J. Batchelor, believes, the bear may have been the totem of an Aino clan ; but even if that were so it would not explain the respect shown for the animal by the whole Aino people.

But it is the bear-festival of the Aino which concerns us here. Towards the end of winter a bear cub is caught and brought into the village. If it is very small, it is suckled by an Aino woman, but should there be no woman able to suckle it, the little animal is fed from the hand or the mouth. During the day it plays about in the hut with the children and is treated with great affection. But when the cub grows big enough to pain people by hugging or scratching them, he is shut up in a strong wooden cage, where he stays generally for two or three years, fed on fish and millet porridge, till it is time for him to be killed and eaten. But " it is a peculiarly striking fact that the young bear is not kept merely to furnish a good meal ; rather he is regarded and honoured as a fetish, or even as a sort of higher being." In Yezo the festival is generally celebrated in September or October. Before it takes place the Aino apologise to their gods, alleging that they have treated the bear kindly as long as they could, now they can feed him no longer, and are obliged to kill him. A man who gives a bear-feast invites his relations and friends ; in a small village nearly the whole community takes part in the feast ; indeed, guests from distant villages are invited and generally come, allured by the prospect of getting drunk for nothing. The form of invitation runs somewhat as follows : " I, so and so, am about to sacrifice the dear little divine thing who resides among the mountains. My friends and masters, come ye to the feast ; we will then unite in the great pleasure of sending the god away. Come." When all the people are assembled in front of the cage, an orator chosen for the purpose addresses the bear and tells it that they are about to send it forth to its ancestors. He craves pardon for what they are about to do to it, hopes it will not be angry, and comforts it by assuring the animal that many of the sacred whittled sticks (*inao*) and plenty of cakes and wine will be sent with it on the long journey. One speech of this sort which Mr. Batchelor heard ran as follows : " O thou divine one, thou wast sent into the world for us to hunt. O thou precious little divinity, we worship thee ; pray hear our prayer. We have nourished thee and brought thee up with a deal of pains and trouble, all because we love thee so. Now, as thou hast grown big, we are about to send thee to thy father and mother. When thou comest to them please speak well of us, and tell them how kind we have been ; please come to us again and we will sacrifice thee." Having been secured with ropes, the bear is then let out of the cage and assailed with a shower of blunt arrows in order to rouse it to fury. When it has spent itself in vain struggles, it is tied up to a stake, gagged and strangled, its neck being placed between two poles, which are then violently compressed, all the people eagerly helping to squeeze the animal to death. An arrow is also discharged into the beast's heart by a good marksman, but so as not to shed blood, for they think that it would be very unlucky if any of the blood were to drip on the ground. However, the men sometimes drink the warm blood of the bear " that the courage and other virtues it possesses may pass into them " ; and sometimes they besmear themselves and their clothes with the blood in order to ensure success in hunting. When the animal has been strangled to death, it is skinned and its head is cut off and set in the east window of the house, where a piece of its own flesh is placed under its snout, together with a cup of its own meat boiled, some millet dumplings, and dried fish. Prayers are then addressed to the dead animal ; amongst other things it is sometimes invited, after going away to its father and mother, to return into the world in order that it may again be reared for sacrifice. When the bear is supposed to have finished eating its own flesh, the man who presides at the feast takes the cup containing the boiled meat, salutes it, and divides the contents between all the company present : every person, young and old alike, must taste a little. The cup is called " the cup of offering " because it has just been offered to the dead bear. When the rest of the flesh has been cooked, it is shared out in like manner among all the people, everybody partaking of at least a morsel ; not to partake of the feast would be equivalent to excommunication, it would be to place the recreant outside the pale of Aino fellowship. Formerly every particle of the bear, except the bones, had to be eaten up at the banquet, but this rule is now relaxed. The head, on being detached from the skin, is set up on a long pole beside the sacred wands (*inao*) outside of the house, where it remains till nothing but the bare white skull is left. Skulls so set up are worshipped not only at the time of the festival, but very often as long as they last. The Aino assured Mr. Batchelor that they really do believe the spirits of the worshipful animals to reside in the skulls ; that is why they address them as " divine preservers " and " precious divinities."

The ceremony of killing the bear was witnessed by Dr. B. Scheube on the tenth of August at Kunnui, which is a village on Volcano Bay in the island of Yezo or Yesso. As his description of the rite contains some interesting particulars not mentioned in the foregoing account, it may be worth while to summarise it.

On entering the hut he found about thirty Aino present, men, women, and children, all dressed in their best. The master of the house first offered a libation on the fireplace to the god of the fire, and the guests followed his example. Then a libation was offered to the house-god in his sacred corner of the hut. Meanwhile the house-wife, who had nursed the bear, sat by herself, silent and sad, bursting now and then into tears. Her grief was obviously unaffected, and it deepened as the festival went on. Next, the master of the house and some of the guests went out of the hut and offered libations before the bear's cage. A few drops were presented to the bear in a saucer, which he at once upset. Then the women and girls danced round the cage, their faces turned towards it, their knees slightly bent, rising and hopping on their toes. As they danced they clapped their hands and sang a monotonous song. The housewife and a few old women, who might have nursed many bears, danced tearfully, stretching out their arms to the bear, and addressing it in terms of endearment. The young folks were less affected ; they laughed as well as sang. Disturbed by the noise, the bear began to rush about his cage and howl lamentably. Next libations were offered at the *inao* (*inabos*) or sacred wands which stand outside of an Aino hut. These wands are about a couple of feet high, and are whittled at the top into spiral shavings. Five new wands with bamboo leaves attached to them had been set up for the festival. This is regularly done when a bear is killed ; the leaves mean that the animal may come to life again. Then the bear was let out of his cage, a rope was thrown round his neck, and he was led about in the neighbourhood of the hut. While this was being done the men, headed by a chief, shot at the beast with arrows tipped with wooden buttons. Dr. Scheube had to do so also. Then the bear was taken before the sacred wands, a stick was put in his mouth, nine men knelt on him and pressed his neck against a beam. In five minutes the animal had expired without uttering a sound. Meantime the women and girls had taken post behind the men, where they danced, lamenting, and beating the men who were killing the bear. The bear's carcase was next placed on the mat before the sacred wands ; and a sword and quiver, taken from the wands, were hung round the beast's neck. Being a she-bear, it was also adorned with a necklace and ear-rings. Then food and drink were offered to it, in the shape of millet-broth, millet-cakes, and a pot of *sake*. The men now sat down on mats before the dead bear, offered libations to it, and drank deep. Meanwhile the women and girls had laid aside all marks of sorrow, and danced merrily, none more merrily than the old women. When the mirth was at its height two young Aino, who had let the bear out of his cage, mounted the roof of the hut and threw cakes of millet among the company, who all scrambled for them without distinction of age or sex. The bear was next skinned and disembowelled, and the trunk severed from the head, to which the skin was left hanging. The blood, caught in cups, was eagerly swallowed by the men. None of the women or children appeared to drink the blood, though custom did not forbid them to do so. The liver was cut in small pieces and eaten raw, with salt, the women and children getting their share. The flesh and the rest of the vitals were taken into the house to be kept till the next day but one, and then to be divided among the persons who had been present at the feast. Blood and liver were offered to Dr. Scheube. While the bear was being disembowelled, the women and girls danced the same dance which they had danced at the beginning— not, however, round the cage, but in front of the sacred wands. At this dance the old women, who had been merry a moment before, again shed tears freely. After the brain had been extracted from the bear's head and swallowed with salt, the skull, detached from the skin, was hung on a pole beside the sacred wands. The stick with which the bear had been gagged was also fastened to the pole, and so were the sword and quiver which had been hung on the carcase. The latter were removed in about an hour, but the rest remained standing. The whole company, men and women, danced noisily before the pole ; and another drinking-bout, in which the women joined, closed the festival.

Perhaps the first published account of the bear-feast of the Aino is one which was given to the world by a Japanese writer in 1652. It has been translated into French and runs thus : " When they find a young bear, they bring it home, and the wife suckles it. When it is grown they feed it with fish and fowl and kill it in winter for the sake of the liver, which they esteem an antidote to poison, the worms, colic, and disorders of the stomach. It is of a very bitter taste, and is good for nothing if the bear has been killed in summer. This butchery begins in the first Japanese month. For this purpose they put the animal's head between two long poles, which are squeezed together by fifty or sixty people, both men and women. When the bear is dead they eat his flesh, keep the liver as a medicine, and sell the skin, which is black and commonly six feet long, but the longest measure twelve feet. As soon as he is skinned, the persons who nourished the beast begin to bewail him ; afterwards they make little cakes to regale those who helped them."

The Aino of Saghalien rear bear cubs and kill them with similar ceremonies. We are told that they do not look upon the bear as a god but only as a messenger whom they despatch with various commissions to the god of the forest. The animal is kept for about two years in a cage, and then killed at a festival, which always takes place in winter and at night. The day before the sacrifice is devoted to lamentation, old women relieving each other in the duty of weeping and groaning in front of the bear's cage. Then about the middle of the night or very early in the morning an orator makes a long speech to the beast, reminding him how they have taken care of him, and fed him well, and bathed him in the river, and made him warm and comfortable. " Now," he proceeds, " we are holding a great festival in your honour. Be not afraid. We will not hurt you. We will only kill you and send you to the god of the forest who loves you. We are about to offer you a good dinner, the best you have ever eaten among us, and we will all weep for you together. The Aino who will kill you is the best shot among us. There he is, he weeps and asks your forgiveness ; you will feel almost nothing, it will be done so quickly. We cannot feed you always, as you will understand. We have done enough for you ; it is now your turn to sacrifice yourself for us. You will ask God to send us, for the winter, plenty of otters and sables, and for the summer, seals and fish in abundance. Do not forget our messages, we love you much, and our children will never forget you." When the bear has partaken of his last meal amid the general emotion of the spectators, the old women weeping afresh and the men uttering stifled cries, he is strapped, not without difficulty and danger, and being let out of the cage is led on leash or dragged, according to the state of his temper, thrice round his cage, then round his master's house, and lastly round the house of the orator. Thereupon he is tied up to a tree, which is decked with sacred whittled sticks (*inao*) of the usual sort ; and the orator again addresses him in a long harangue, which sometimes lasts till the day is beginning to break. " Remember," he cries, " remember ! I remind you of your whole life and of the services we have rendered you. It is now for you to do your duty. Do not forget what I have asked of you. You will tell the gods to give us riches, that our hunters may return from the forest laden with rare furs and animals good to eat ; that our fishers may find troops of seals on the shore and in the sea, and that their nets may crack under the weight of the fish. We have no hope but in you. The evil spirits laugh at us, and too often they are unfavourable and malignant to us, but they will bow before you. We have given you food and joy and health ; now we kill you in order that you may in return send riches to us and to our children." To this discourse the bear, more and more surly and agitated, listens without conviction ; round and round the tree he paces and howls lamentably, till, just as the first beams of the rising sun light up the scene, an archer speeds an arrow to his heart. No sooner has he done so, than the marksman throws away his bow and flings himself on the ground, and the old men and women do the same, weeping and sobbing. Then they offer the dead beast a repast of rice and wild potatoes, and having spoken to him in terms of pity and thanked him for what he has done and suffered, they cut off his head and paws and keep them as sacred things. A banquet on the flesh and blood of the bear follows. Women were formerly excluded from it, but now they share with the men. The blood is drunk warm by all present ; the flesh is boiled, custom forbids it to be roasted. And as the relics of the bear may not enter the house by the door, and Aino houses in Saghalien have no windows, a man gets up on the roof and lets the flesh, the head, and the skin down through the smoke-hole. Rice and wild potatoes are then offered to the head, and a pipe, tobacco, and matches are considerately placed beside it. Custom requires that the guests should eat up the whole animal before they depart : the use of salt and pepper at the meal is forbidden ; and no morsel of the flesh may be given to the dogs. When the banquet is over, the head is carried away into the depth of the forest and deposited on a heap of bears' skulls, the bleached and mouldering relics of similar festivals in the past.

The Gilyaks, a Tunguzian people of Eastern Siberia, hold a bear-festival of the same sort once a year in January. " The bear is the object of the most refined solicitude of an entire village and plays the chief part in their religious ceremonies." An old she-bear is shot and her cub is reared, but not suckled, in the village. When the bear is big enough he is taken from his cage and dragged through the village. But first they lead him to the bank of the river, for this is believed to ensure abundance of fish to each family. He is then taken into every house in the village, where fish, brandy, and so forth are offered to him. Some people prostrate themselves before the beast. His entrance into a house is supposed to bring a blessing; and if he snuffs at the food offered to him, this also is a blessing. Nevertheless they tease and worry, poke and tickle the animal continually, so that he is surly and snappish. After being thus taken to every house, he is tied to a peg and shot dead with arrows. His head is then cut off, decked with shavings, and placed on the table where the feast is set out. Here they beg pardon of the beast and worship him. Then his flesh is roasted and eaten in special vessels of wood finely carved. They do not eat the flesh raw nor drink the blood, as the Aino do. The brain and entrails are eaten last; and the skull, still decked with shavings, is placed on a tree near the house. Then the people sing and both sexes dance in ranks, as bears.

One of these bear-festivals was witnessed by the Russian traveller L. von Schrenck and his companions at the Gilyak village of Tebach in January 1856. From his detailed report of the ceremony we may gather some particulars which are not noticed in the briefer accounts which I have just summarised. The bear, he tells us, plays a great part in the life of all the peoples inhabiting the region of the Amoor and Siberia as far as Kamtchatka, but among none of them is his importance greater than among the Gilyaks. The immense size which the animal attains in the valley of the Amoor, his ferocity whetted by hunger, and the frequency of his appearance, all combine to make him the most dreaded beast of prey in the country. No wonder, therefore, that the fancy of the Gilyaks is busied with him and surrounds him, both in life and in death, with a sort of halo of superstitious fear. Thus, for example, it is thought that if a Gilyak falls in combat with a bear, his soul transmigrates into the body of the beast. Nevertheless his flesh has an irresistible attraction for the Gilyak palate, especially when the animal has been kept in captivity for some time and fattened on fish, which gives the flesh, in the opinion of the Gilyaks, a peculiarly delicious flavour. But in order to enjoy this dainty with impunity they deem it needful to perform a long series of ceremonies, of which the intention is to delude the living bear by a show of respect, and to appease the anger of the dead animal by the homage paid to his departed spirit. The marks of respect begin as soon as the beast is captured. He is brought home in triumph and kept in a cage, where all the villagers take it in turns to feed him. For although he may have been captured or purchased by one man, he belongs in a manner to the whole village. His flesh will furnish a common feast, and hence all must contribute to support him in his life. The length of time he is kept in captivity depends on his age. Old bears are kept only a few months; cubs are kept till they are full-grown. A thick layer of fat on the captive bear gives the signal for the festival, which is always held in winter, generally in December but sometimes in January or February. At the festival witnessed by the Russian travellers, which lasted a good many days, three bears were killed and eaten. More than once the animals were led about in procession and compelled to enter every house in the village, where they were fed as a mark of honour, and to show that they were welcome guests. But before the beasts set out on this round of visits, the Gilyaks played at skipping-rope in presence, and perhaps, as L. von Schrenck inclined to believe, in honour of the animals. The night before they were killed, the three bears were led by moonlight a long way on the ice of the frozen river. That night no one in the village might sleep. Next day, after the animals had been again led down the steep bank to the river, and conducted thrice round the hole in the ice from which the women of the village drew their water, they were taken to an appointed place not far from the village and shot to death with arrows. The place of sacrifice or execution was marked as holy by being surrounded with whittled sticks, from the tops of which shavings hung in curls. Such sticks are with the Gilyaks, as with the Aino, the regular symbols that accompany all religious ceremonies.

When the house has been arranged and decorated for their reception, the skins of the bears, with their heads attached to them, are brought into it, not however by the door, but through a window, and then hung on a sort of scaffold opposite the hearth on which the flesh is to be cooked. The boiling of the bears' flesh among the Gilyaks is done only by the oldest men, whose high privilege it is ; women and children, young men and boys have no part in it. The task is performed slowly and deliberately, with a certain solemnity. On the occasion described by the Russian travellers the kettle was first of all surrounded with a thick wreath of shavings, and then filled with snow, for the use of water to cook bear's flesh is forbidden. Meanwhile a large wooden trough, richly adorned with arabesques and carvings of all sorts, was hung immediately under the snouts of the bears ; on one side of the trough was carved in relief a bear, on the other side a toad. When the carcases were being cut up, each leg was laid on the ground in front of the bears, as if to ask their leave, before being placed in the kettle ; and the boiled flesh was fished out of the kettle with an iron hook, and set in the trough before the bears, in order that they might be the first to taste of their own flesh. As fast, too, as the fat was cut in strips it was hung up in front of the bears, and afterwards laid in a small wooden trough on the ground before them. Last of all the inner organs of the beasts were cut up and placed in small vessels. At the same time the women made bandages out of parti-coloured rags, and after sunset these bandages were tied round the bears' snouts just below the eyes " in order to dry the tears that flowed from them."

As soon as the ceremony of wiping away poor bruin's tears had been performed, the assembled Gilyaks set to work in earnest to devour his flesh. The broth obtained by boiling the meat had already been partaken of. The wooden bowls, platters, and spoons out of which the Gilyaks eat the broth and flesh of the bears on these occasions are always made specially for the purpose at the festival and only then ; they are elaborately ornamented with carved figures of bears and other devices that refer to the animal or the festival, and the people have a strong superstitious scruple against parting with them. After the bones had been picked clean they were put back in the kettle in which the flesh had been boiled. And when the festal meal was over, an old man took his stand at the door of the house with a branch of fir in his hand, with which, as the people passed out, he gave a light blow to every one who had eaten of the bear's flesh or fat, perhaps as a punishment for their treatment of the worshipful animal. In the afternoon the women performed a strange dance. Only one woman danced at a time, throwing the upper part of her body into the oddest postures, while she held in her hands a branch of fir or a kind of wooden castanets. The other women meanwhile played an accompaniment by drumming on the beams of the house with clubs. Von Schrenk believed that after the flesh of the bear has been eaten the bones and the skull are solemnly carried out by the oldest people to a place in the forest not far from the village. There all the bones except the skull are buried. After that a young tree is felled a few inches above the ground, its stump cleft, and the skull wedged into the cleft. When the grass grows over the spot, the skull disappears from view, and that is the end of the bear.

Another description of the bear-festivals of the Gilyaks has been given us by Mr. Leo Sternberg. It agrees substantially with the foregoing accounts, but a few particulars in it may be noted. According to Mr. Sternberg, the festival is usually held in honour of a deceased relation : the next of kin either buys or catches a bear cub and nurtures it for two or three years till it is ready for the sacrifice. Only certain distinguished guests (*Narch-en*) are privileged to partake of the bear's flesh, but the host and members of his clan eat a broth made from the flesh ; great quantities of this broth are prepared and consumed on the occasion. The guests of honour (*Narch-en*) must belong to the clan into which the host's daughters and the other women of his clan are married : one of these guests, usually the host's son-in-law, is entrusted with the duty of shooting the bear dead with an arrow. The skin, head, and flesh of the slain bear are brought into the house not through the door but through the smoke-hole ; a quiver full of arrows is laid under the head and beside it are deposited tobacco, sugar, and other food. The soul of the bear is supposed to carry off the souls of these things with it on the far journey. A special vessel is used for cooking the bear's flesh, and the fire must be kindled by a sacred apparatus of flint and steel, which belongs to the clan and is handed down from generation to generation, but which is never used to light fires except on these solemn occasions. Of all the many viands cooked for the consumption of the assembled people a portion is placed in a special vessel and set before the bear's head : this is called " feeding the head."   After the bear has been killed, dogs are sacrificed in couples of male and female.   Before being throttled, they are fed and invited to go to their lord on the highest mountain, to change their skins, and to return next year in the form of bears.   The soul of the dead bear departs to the same lord, who is also lord of the primaeval forest ; it goes away laden with the offerings that have been made to it, and attended by the souls of the dogs and also by the souls of the sacred whittled sticks, which figure prominently at the festival.

The Goldi, neighbours of the Gilyaks, treat the bear in much the same way.   They hunt and kill it ; but sometimes they capture a live bear and keep him in a cage, feeding him well and calling him their son and brother.   Then at a great festival he is taken from his cage, paraded about with marked consideration, and afterwards killed and eaten.   " The skull, jaw-bones, and ears are then suspended on a tree, as an antidote against evil spirits ; but the flesh is eaten and much relished, for they believe that all who partake of it acquire a zest for the chase, and become courageous."

The Orotchis, another Tunguzian people of the region of the Amoor, hold bear-festivals of the same general character.   Any one who catches a bear cub considers it his bounden duty to rear it in a cage for about three years, in order at the end of that time to kill it publicly and eat the flesh with his friends.   The feasts being public, though organised by individuals, the people try to have one in each Orotchi village every year in turn.   When the bear is taken out of his cage, he is led about by means of ropes to all the huts, accompanied by people armed with lances, bows, and arrows.   At each hut the bear and bear-leaders are treated to something good to eat and drink. This goes on for several days until all the huts, not only in that village but also in the next, have been visited.   The days are given up to sport and noisy jollity.   Then the bear is tied to a tree or wooden pillar and shot to death by the arrows of the crowd, after which its flesh is roasted and eaten.   Among the Orotchis of the Tundja River women take part in the bear-feasts, while among the Orotchis of the River Vi the women will not even touch bear's flesh.

In the treatment of the captive bear by these tribes there are features which can hardly be distinguished from worship.   Such, for example, are the prayers offered to it both alive and dead ; the offerings of food, including portions of its own flesh, laid before the animal's skull ; and the Gilyak custom of leading the living beast to the river in order to ensure a supply of fish, and of conducting him from house to house in order that every family may receive his blessing, just as in Europe a May-tree or a personal representative of the tree-spirit used to be taken from door to door in spring for the sake of diffusing among all and sundry the fresh energies of reviving nature.   Again, the solemn participation in his flesh and blood, and particularly the Aino custom of sharing the contents of the cup which had been consecrated by being set before the dead beast, are strongly suggestive of a sacrament, and the suggestion is confirmed by the Gilyak practice of reserving special vessels to hold the flesh and cooking it on a fire kindled by a sacred apparatus which is never employed except on these religious occasions. Indeed our principal authority on Aino religion, the Rev. John Batchelor, frankly describes as worship the ceremonious respect which the Aino pay to the bear, and he affirms that the animal is undoubtedly one of their gods. Certainly the Aino appear to apply their name for god (*kamui*) freely to the bear ; but, as Mr. Batchelor himself points out, that word is used with many different shades of meaning and is applied to a great variety of objects, so that from its application to the bear we cannot safely argue that the animal is actually regarded as a deity. Indeed we are expressly told that the Aino of Saghalien do not consider the bear to be a god but only a messenger to the gods, and the message with which they charge the animal at its death bears out the statement. Apparently the Gilyaks also look on the bear in the light of an envoy despatched with presents to the Lord of the Mountain, on whom the welfare of the people depends. At the same time they treat the animal as a being of a higher order than man, in fact as a minor deity, whose presence in the village, so long as he is kept and fed, diffuses blessings, especially by keeping at bay the swarms of evil spirits who are constantly lying in wait for people, stealing their goods and destroying their bodies by sickness and disease. Moreover, by partaking of the flesh, blood, or broth of the bear, the Gilyaks, the Aino, and the Goldi are all of opinion that they acquire some portion of the animal's mighty powers, particularly his courage and strength. No wonder, therefore, that they should treat so great a benefactor with marks of the highest respect and affection.

Some light may be thrown on the ambiguous attitude of the Aino to bears by comparing the similar treatment which they accord to other creatures. For example, they regard the eagle-owl as a good deity who by his hooting warns men of threatened evil and defends them against it ; hence he is loved, trusted, and devoutly worshipped as a divine mediator between men and the Creator. The various names applied to him are significant both of his divinity and of his mediatorship. Whenever an opportunity offers, one of these divine birds is captured and kept in a cage, where he is greeted with the endearing titles of " Beloved god " and " Dear little divinity." Nevertheless the time comes when the dear little divinity is throttled and sent away in his capacity of mediator to take a message to the superior gods or to the Creator himself. The following is the form of prayer addressed to the eagle-owl when it is about to be sacrificed : " Beloved deity, we have brought you up because we loved you, and now we are about to send you to your father. We herewith offer you food, *inao*, wine, and cakes ; take them to your parent, and he will be very pleased. When you come to him say, ' I have lived a long time among the Ainu, where an Ainu father and an Ainu mother reared me. I now come to thee. I have brought a variety of good things. I saw while living in Ainu-land a great deal of distress. I observed that some of the people were possessed by demons, some were wounded by wild animals, some were hurt by landslides, others suffered shipwreck, and many were attacked by disease. The people are in great straits. My father, hear me, and hasten to look upon the Ainu and help them.' If you do this, your father will help us."

Again, the Aino keep eagles in cages, worship them as divinities, and ask them to defend the people from evil. Yet they offer the bird in sacrifice, and when they are about to do so they pray to him, saying : " O precious divinity, O thou divine bird, pray listen to my words. Thou dost not belong to this world, for thy home is with the Creator and his golden eagles. This being so, I present thee with these *inao* and cakes and other precious things. Do thou ride upon the *inao* and ascend to thy home in the glorious heavens. When thou arrivest, assemble the deities of thy own kind together and thank them for us for having governed the world. Do thou come again, I beseech thee, and rule over us. O my precious one, go thou quietly." Once more, the Aino revere hawks, keep them in cages, and offer them in sacrifice. At the time of killing one of them the following prayer should be addressed to the bird : " O divine hawk, thou art an expert hunter, please cause thy cleverness to descend on me." If a hawk is well treated in captivity and prayed to after this fashion when he is about to be killed, he will surely send help to the hunter.

Thus the Aino hopes to profit in various ways by slaughtering the creatures, which, nevertheless, he treats as divine. He expects them to carry messages for him to their kindred or to the gods in the upper world ; he hopes to partake of their virtues by swallowing parts of their bodies or in other ways ; and apparently he looks forward to their bodily resurrection in this world, which will enable him again to catch and kill them, and again to reap all the benefits which he has already derived from their slaughter. For in the prayers addressed to the worshipful bear and the worshipful eagle before they are knocked on the head the creatures are invited to come again, which seems clearly to point to a faith in their future resurrection. If any doubt could exist on this head, it would be dispelled by the evidence of Mr. Batchelor, who tells us that the Aino " are firmly convinced that the spirits of birds and animals killed in hunting or offered in sacrifice come and live again upon the earth clothed with a body ; and they believe, further, that they appear here for the special benefit of men, particularly Ainu hunters." The Aino, Mr. Batchelor tells us, " confessedly slays and eats the beast that another may come in its place and be treated in like manner " ; and at the time of sacrificing the creatures " prayers are said to them which form a request that they will come again and furnish viands for another feast, as if it were an honour to them to be thus killed and eaten, and a pleasure as well. Indeed such is the people's idea." These last observations, as the context shows, refer especially to the sacrifice of bears.

Thus among the benefits which the Aino anticipates from the

slaughter of the worshipful animals not the least substantial is that of gorging himself on their flesh and blood, both on the present and on many a similar occasion hereafter; and that pleasing prospect again is derived from his firm faith in the spiritual immortality and bodily resurrection of the dead animals. A like faith is shared by many savage hunters in many parts of the world and has given rise to a variety of quaint customs, some of which will be described presently. Meantime it is not unimportant to observe that the solemn festivals at which the Aino, the Gilyaks, and other tribes slaughter the tame caged bears with demonstrations of respect and sorrow, are probably nothing but an extension or glorification of similar rites which the hunter performs over any wild bear which he chances to kill in the forest. Indeed with regard to the Gilyaks we are expressly informed that this is the case. If we would understand the meaning of the Gilyak ritual, says Mr. Sternberg, " we must above all remember that the bear-festivals are not, as is usually but falsely assumed, celebrated only at the killing of a house-bear but are held on every occasion when a Gilyak succeeds in slaughtering a bear in the chase. It is true that in such cases the festival assumes less imposing dimensions, but in its essence it remains the same. When the head and skin of a bear killed in the forest are brought into the village, they are accorded a triumphal reception with music and solemn ceremonial. The head is laid on a consecrated scaffold, fed, and treated with offerings, just as at the killing of a house-bear; and the guests of honour (*Narch-en*) are also assembled. So, too, dogs are sacrificed, and the bones of the bear are preserved in the same place and with the same marks of respect as the bones of a house-bear. Hence the great winter festival is only an extension of the rite which is observed at the slaughter of every bear."

Thus the apparent contradiction in the practice of these tribes, who venerate and almost deify the animals which they habitually hunt, kill, and eat, is not so flagrant as at first sight it appears to us: the people have reasons, and some very practical reasons, for acting as they do. For the savage is by no means so illogical and unpractical as to superficial observers he is apt to seem; he has thought deeply on the questions which immediately concern him, he reasons about them, and though his conclusions often diverge very widely from ours, we ought not to deny him the credit of patient and prolonged meditation on some fundamental problems of human existence. In the present case, if he treats bears in general as creatures wholly subservient to human needs and yet singles out certain individuals of the species for homage which almost amounts to deification, we must not hastily set him down as irrational and inconsistent, but must endeavour to place ourselves at his point of view, to see things as he sees them, and to divest ourselves of the prepossessions which tinge so deeply our own views of the world. If we do so, we shall probably discover that, however absurd his conduct may appear to us, the savage nevertheless generally acts on a train of reasoning which seems to him in harmony with the facts of his limited experience. This I propose to illustrate in the following chapter, where I shall attempt to show that the solemn ceremonial of the bear-festival among the Ainos and other tribes of North-eastern Asia is only a particularly striking example of the respect which on the principles of his rude philosophy the savage habitually pays to the animals which he kills and eats.

CHAPTER LIII

THE PROPITIATION OF WILD ANIMALS BY HUNTERS

THE explanation of life by the theory of an indwelling and practically immortal soul is one which the savage does not confine to human beings but extends to the animate creation in general. In so doing he is more liberal and perhaps more logical than the civilised man, who commonly denies to animals that privilege of immortality which he claims for himself. The savage is not so proud ; he commonly believes that animals are endowed with feelings and intelligence like those of men, and that, like men, they possess souls which survive the death of their bodies either to wander about as disembodied spirits or to be born again in animal form.

Thus to the savage, who regards all living creatures as practically on a footing of equality with man, the act of killing and eating an animal must wear a very different aspect from that which the same act presents to us, who regard the intelligence of animals as far inferior to our own and deny them the possession of immortal souls. Hence on the principles of his rude philosophy the primitive hunter who slays an animal believes himself exposed to the vengeance either of its disembodied spirit or of all the other animals of the same species, whom he considers as knit together, like men, by the ties of kin and the obligations of the blood feud, and therefore as bound to resent the injury done to one of their number. Accordingly the savage makes it a rule to spare the life of those animals which he has no pressing motive for killing, at least such fierce and dangerous animals as are likely to exact a bloody vengeance for the slaughter of one of their kind. Crocodiles are animals of this sort. They are only found in hot countries, where, as a rule, food is abundant and primitive man has therefore little reason to kill them for the sake of their tough and unpalatable flesh. Hence it is a custom with some savages to spare crocodiles, or rather only to kill them in obedience to the law of blood feud, that is, as a retaliation for the slaughter of men by crocodiles. For example, the Dyaks of Borneo will not kill a crocodile unless a crocodile has first killed a man. " For why, say they, should they commit an act of aggression, when he and his kindred can so easily repay them ? But should the alligator take a human life, revenge becomes a sacred duty of the living relatives, who will trap the man-eater in the spirit of an officer of justice pursuing a criminal. Others, even then, hang back, reluctant to embroil themselves in a quarrel which does not concern them. The man-eating alligator is supposed to be pursued by a righteous Nemesis ; and whenever one is caught they have a profound conviction that it must be the guilty one, or his accomplice."

Like the Dyaks, the natives of Madagascar never kill a crocodile " except in retaliation for one of their friends who has been destroyed by a crocodile. They believe that the wanton destruction of one of these reptiles will be followed by the loss of human life, in accordance with the principle of *lex talionis*." The people who live near the lake Itasy in Madagascar make a yearly proclamation to the crocodiles, announcing that they will revenge the death of some of their friends by killing as many crocodiles in return, and warning all well-disposed crocodiles to keep out of the way, as they have no quarrel with them, but only with their evil-minded relations who have taken human life. Various tribes of Madagascar believe themselves to be descended from crocodiles, and accordingly they view the scaly reptile as, to all intents and purposes, a man and a brother. If one of the animals should so far forget himself as to devour one of his human kinsfolk, the chief of the tribe, or in his absence an old man familiar with the tribal customs, repairs at the head of the people to the edge of the water, and summons the family of the culprit to deliver him up to the arm of justice. A hook is then baited and cast into the river or lake. Next day the guilty brother, or one of his family, is dragged ashore, and after his crime has been clearly brought home to him by a strict interrogation, he is sentenced to death and executed. The claims of justice being thus satisfied and the majesty of the law fully vindicated, the deceased crocodile is lamented and buried like a kinsman ; a mound is raised over his relics and a stone marks the place of his head.

Again, the tiger is another of those dangerous beasts whom the savage prefers to leave alone, lest by killing one of the species he should excite the hostility of the rest. No consideration will induce a Sumatran to catch or wound a tiger except in self-defence or immediately after a tiger has destroyed a friend or relation. When a European has set traps for tigers, the people of the neighbourhood have been known to go by night to the place and explain to the animals that the traps are not set by them nor with their consent. The inhabitants of the hills near Rajamahall, in Bengal, are very averse to killing a tiger, unless one of their kinsfolk has been carried off by one of the beasts. In that case they go out for the purpose of hunting and slaying a tiger ; and when they have succeeded they lay their bows and arrows on the carcase and invoke God, declaring that they slew the animal in retaliation for the loss of a kinsman. Vengeance having been thus taken, they swear not to attack another tiger except under similar provocation.

The Indians of Carolina would not molest snakes when they came upon them, but would pass by on the other side of the path, believing that if they were to kill a serpent the reptile's kindred would destroy some of their brethren, friends, or relations in return. So the Seminole Indians spared the rattlesnake, because they feared that the soul of the dead rattlesnake would incite its kinsfolk to take vengeance. The Cherokee regard the rattlesnake as the chief of the snake tribe and fear and respect him accordingly. Few Cherokee will venture to kill a rattlesnake, unless they cannot help it, and even then they must atone for the crime by craving pardon of the snake's ghost either in their own person or through the mediation of a priest, according to a set formula. If these precautions are neglected, the kinsfolk of the dead snake will send one of their number as an avenger of blood, who will track down the murderer and sting him to death. No ordinary Cherokee dares to kill a wolf, if he can possibly help it; for he believes that the kindred of the slain beast would surely avenge its death, and that the weapon with which the deed had been done would be quite useless for the future, unless it were cleaned and exorcised by a medicine-man. However, certain persons who know the proper rites of atonement for such a crime can kill wolves with impunity, and they are sometimes hired to do so by people who have suffered from the raids of the wolves on their cattle or fish-traps. In Jebel-Nuba, a district of the Eastern Sudan, it is forbidden to touch the nests or remove the young of a species of black birds, resembling our blackbirds, because the people believe that the parent birds would avenge the wrong by causing a stormy wind to blow, which would destroy the harvest.

But the savage clearly cannot afford to spare all animals. He must either eat some of them or starve, and when the question thus comes to be whether he or the animal must perish, he is forced to overcome his superstitious scruples and take the life of the beast. At the same time he does all he can to appease his victims and their kinsfolk. Even in the act of killing them he testifies his respect for them, endeavours to excuse or even conceal his share in procuring their death, and promises that their remains will be honourably treated. By thus robbing death of its terrors he hopes to reconcile his victims to their fate and to induce their fellows to come and be killed also. For example, it was a principle with the Kamtchatkans never to kill a land or sea animal without first making excuses to it and begging that the animal would not take it ill. Also they offered it cedar-nuts and so forth, to make it think that it was not a victim but a guest at a feast. They believed that this hindered other animals of the same species from growing shy. For instance, after they had killed a bear and feasted on its flesh, the host would bring the bear's head before the company, wrap it in grass, and present it with a variety of trifles. Then he would lay the blame of the bear's death on the Russians, and bid the beast wreak his wrath upon them. Also he would ask the bear to inform the other bears how well he had been treated, that they too might come without fear. Seals, sea-lions, and other animals were treated by the Kamtchatkans with the same ceremonious respect. Moreover, they used to insert sprigs of a plant resembling bear's wort in the mouths of the animals they killed ; after which they would exhort the grinning skulls to have no fear but to go and tell it to their fellows, that they also might come and be caught and so partake of this splendid hospitality. When the Ostiaks have hunted and killed a bear, they cut off its head and hang it on a tree. Then they gather round in a circle and pay it divine honours. Next they run towards the carcase uttering lamentations and saying, " Who killed you ? It was the Russians. Who cut off your head ? It was a Russian axe. Who skinned you ? It was a knife made by a Russian." They explain, too, that the feathers which sped the arrow on its flight came from the wing of a strange bird, and that they did nothing but let the arrow go. They do all this because they believe that the wandering ghost of the slain bear would attack them on the first opportunity, if they did not thus appease it. Or they stuff the skin of the slain bear with hay ; and after celebrating their victory with songs of mockery and insult, after spitting on and kicking it, they set it up on its hind legs, " and then, for a considerable time, they bestow on it all the veneration due to a guardian god." When a party of Koryak have killed a bear or a wolf, they skin the beast and dress one of themselves in the skin. Then they dance round the skin-clad man, saying that it was not they who killed the animal, but some one else, generally a Russian. When they kill a fox they skin it, wrap the body in grass, and bid him go tell his companions how hospitably he has been received, and how he has received a new cloak instead of his old one. A fuller account of the Koryak ceremonies is given by a more recent writer. He tells us that when a dead bear is brought to the house, the women come out to meet it, dancing with firebrands. The bear-skin is taken off along with the head ; and one of the women puts on the skin, dances in it, and entreats the bear not to be angry, but to be kind to the people. At the same time they offer meat on a wooden platter to the dead beast, saying, " Eat, friend." Afterwards a ceremony is performed for the purpose of sending the dead bear, or rather his spirit, away back to his home. He is provided with provisions for the journey in the shape of puddings or reindeer-flesh packed in a grass bag. His skin is stuffed with grass and carried round the house, after which he is supposed to depart towards the rising sun. The intention of the ceremonies is to protect the people from the wrath of the slain bear and his kinsfolk, and so to ensure success in future bear-hunts. The Finns used to try to persuade a slain bear that he had not been killed by them, but had fallen from a tree, or met his death in some other way ; moreover, they held a funeral festival in his honour, at the close of which bards expatiated on the homage that had been paid to him, urging him to report to the other bears the high consideration with which he had been treated, in order that they also, following his example, might come and be slain. When the Lapps had succeeded in killing a bear with impunity, they thanked him for not hurting them and for not breaking the clubs and spears which had given him his death wounds ; and they prayed that he would not visit his death upon them by sending storms or in any other way. His flesh then furnished a feast.

The reverence of hunters for the bear whom they regularly kill and eat may thus be traced all along the northern region of the Old World, from Bering's Straits to Lappland. It reappears in similar forms in North America. With the American Indians a bear hunt was an important event for which they prepared by long fasts and purgations. Before setting out they offered expiatory sacrifices to the souls of bears slain in previous hunts, and besought them to be favourable to the hunters. When a bear was killed the hunter lit his pipe, and putting the mouth of it between the bear's lips, blew into the bowl, filling the beast's mouth with smoke. Then he begged the bear not to be angry at having been killed, and not to thwart him afterwards in the chase. The carcase was roasted whole and eaten ; not a morsel of the flesh might be left over. The head, painted red and blue, was hung on a post and addressed by orators, who heaped praise on the dead beast. When men of the Bear clan in the Otawa tribe killed a bear, they made him a feast of his own flesh, and addressed him thus : " Cherish us no grudge because we have killed you. You have sense ; you see that our children are hungry. They love you and wish to take you into their bodies. Is it not glorious to be eaten by the children of a chief ? " Amongst the Nootka Indians of British Columbia, when a bear had been killed, it was brought in and seated before the head chief in an upright posture, with a chief's bonnet, wrought in figures, on its head, and its fur powdered over with white down. A tray of provisions was then set before it, and it was invited by words and gestures to eat. After that the animal was skinned, boiled, and eaten.

A like respect is testified for other dangerous creatures by the hunters who regularly trap and kill them. When Caffre hunters are in the act of showering spears on an elephant, they call out, " Don't kill us, great captain ; don't strike or tread upon us, mighty chief." When he is dead they make their excuses to him, pretending that his death was a pure accident. As a mark of respect they bury his trunk with much solemn ceremony ; for they say that " the elephant is a great lord ; his trunk is his hand." Before the Amaxosa Caffres attack an elephant they shout to the animal and beg him to pardon them for the slaughter they are about to perpetrate, professing great submission to his person and explaining clearly the need they have of his tusks to enable them to procure beads and supply their wants. When they have killed him they bury in the ground, along with the end of his trunk, a few of the articles they have obtained for the ivory, thus hoping to avert some mishap that would otherwise befall them. Amongst some tribes of Eastern Africa, when a lion is killed, the carcase is brought before the king, who does homage to it by prostrating himself on the ground and rubbing his face on the muzzle of the beast. In some parts of Western Africa if a negro kills a leopard he is bound fast and brought before the chiefs for having killed one of their peers. The man defends himself on the plea that the leopard is chief of the forest and therefore a stranger. He is then set at liberty and rewarded. But the dead leopard, adorned with a chief's bonnet, is set up in the village, where nightly dances are held in its honour. The Baganda greatly fear the ghosts of buffaloes which they have killed, and they always appease these dangerous spirits. On no account will they bring the head of a slain buffalo into a village or into a garden of plantains: they always eat the flesh of the head in the open country. Afterwards they place the skull in a small hut built for the purpose, where they pour out beer as an offering and pray to the ghost to stay where he is and not to harm them.

Another formidable beast whose life the savage hunter takes with joy, yet with fear and trembling, is the whale. After the slaughter of a whale the maritime Koryak of North-eastern Siberia hold a communal festival, the essential part of which " is based on the conception that the whale killed has come on a visit to the village ; that it is staying for some time, during which it is treated with great respect ; that it then returns to the sea to repeat its visit the following year ; that it will induce its relatives to come along, telling them of the hospitable reception that has been accorded to it. According to the Koryak ideas, the whales, like all other animals, constitute one tribe, or rather family, of related individuals, who live in villages like the Koryak. They avenge the murder of one of their number, and are grateful for kindnesses that they may have received." When the inhabitants of the Isle of St. Mary, to the north of Madagascar, go a-whaling, they single out the young whales for attack and "humbly beg the mother's pardon, stating the necessity that drives them to kill her progeny, and requesting that she will be pleased to go below while the deed is doing, that her maternal feelings may not be outraged by witnessing what must cause her so much uneasiness." An Ajumba hunter having killed a female hippopotamus on Lake Azyingo in West Africa, the animal was decapitated and its quarters and bowels removed. Then the hunter, naked, stepped into the hollow of the ribs, and kneeling down in the bloody pool washed his whole body with the blood and excretions of the animal, while he prayed to the soul of the hippopotamus not to bear him a grudge for having killed her and so blighted her hopes of future maternity ; and he further entreated the ghost not to stir up other hippopotamuses to avenge her death by butting at and capsizing his canoe.

The ounce, a leopard-like creature, is dreaded for its depredations by the Indians of Brazil. When they have caught one of these animals in a snare, they kill it and carry the body home to the village. There the women deck the carcase with feathers of many colours, put bracelets on its legs, and weep over it, saying, " I pray thee not to take vengeance on our little ones for having been caught and killed through thine own ignorance. For it was not we who deceived thee, it was thyself. Our husbands only set the trap to catch animals that are good to eat : they never thought to take thee in it. Therefore, let not thy soul counsel thy fellows to avenge thy death on our little ones ! " When a Blackfoot Indian has caught eagles in a trap and killed them, he takes them home to a special lodge, called the eagles' lodge, which has been prepared for their reception outside of the camp. Here he sets the birds in a row on the ground, and propping up their heads on a stick, puts a piece of dried meat in each of their mouths in order that the spirits of the dead eagles may go and tell the other eagles how well they are being treated by the Indians. So when Indian hunters of the Orinoco region have killed an animal, they open its mouth and pour into it a few drops of the liquor they generally carry with them, in order that the soul of the dead beast may inform its fellows of the welcome it has met with, and that they too, cheered by the prospect of the same kind reception, may come with alacrity to be killed. When a Teton Indian is on a journey and he meets a grey spider or a spider with yellow legs, he kills it, because some evil would befall him if he did not. But he is very careful not to let the spider know that he kills it, for if the spider knew, his soul would go and tell the other spiders, and one of them would be sure to avenge the death of his relation. So in crushing the insect, the Indian says, " O Grandfather Spider, the Thunder-beings kill you." And the spider is crushed at once and believes what is told him. His soul probably runs and tells the other spiders that the Thunder-beings have killed him ; but no harm comes of that. For what can grey or yellow-legged spiders do to the Thunder-beings ?

But it is not merely dangerous creatures with whom the savage desires to keep on good terms. It is true that the respect which he pays to wild beasts is in some measure proportioned to their strength and ferocity. Thus the savage Stiens of Cambodia, believing that all animals have souls which roam about after their death, beg an animal's pardon when they kill it, lest its soul should come and torment them. Also they offer it sacrifices, but these sacrifices are proportioned to the size and strength of the animal. The ceremonies which they observe at the death of an elephant are conducted with much pomp and last seven days. Similar distinctions are drawn by North American Indians. " The bear, the buffalo, and the beaver are manidos [divinities] which furnish food. The bear is formidable, and good to eat. They render ceremonies to him, begging him to allow himself to be eaten, although they know he has no fancy for it. We kill you, but you are not annihilated. His head and paws are objects of homage. . . . Other animals are treated similarly from similar reasons. . . . Many of the animal manidos, not being dangerous, are often treated with contempt —the terrapin, the weasel, polecat, etc." The distinction is instructive. Animals which are feared, or are good to eat, or both, are treated with ceremonious respect ; those which are neither formidable nor good to eat are despised. We have had examples of reverence paid to animals which are both feared and eaten. It remains to prove that similar respect is shown to animals which, without being feared, are either eaten or valued for their skins.

When Siberian sable-hunters have caught a sable, no one is allowed to see it, and they think that if good or evil be spoken of the captured sable no more sables will be caught. A hunter has been known to express his belief that the sables could hear what was said of them as far off as Moscow. He said that the chief reason why the sable hunt was now so unproductive was that some live sables had been sent to Moscow. There they had been viewed with astonishment as strange animals, and the sables cannot abide that. Another, though minor, cause of the diminished take of sables was, he alleged, that the world is now much worse than it used to be, so that nowadays a hunter will sometimes hide the sable which he has got instead of putting it into the common stock. This also, said he, the sables cannot abide. Alaskan hunters preserve the bones of sables and beavers out of reach of the dogs for a year and then bury them carefully, " lest the spirits who look after the beavers and sables should consider that they are regarded with contempt, and hence no more should be killed or trapped." The Canadian Indians were equally particular not to let their dogs gnaw the bones, or at least certain of the bones, of beavers. They took the greatest pains to collect and preserve these bones, and, when the beaver had been caught in a net, they threw them into the river. To a Jesuit who argued that the beavers could not possibly know what became of their bones, the Indians replied, " You know nothing about catching beavers and yet you will be prating about it. Before the beaver is stone dead, his soul takes a turn in the hut of the man who is killing him and makes a careful note of what is done with his bones. If the bones are given to the dogs, the other beavers would get word of it and would not let themselves be caught. Whereas, if their bones are thrown into the fire or a river, they are quite satisfied ; and it is particularly gratifying to the net which caught them." Before hunting the beaver they offered a solemn prayer to the Great Beaver, and presented him with tobacco ; and when the chase was over, an orator pronounced a funeral oration over the dead beavers. He praised their spirit and wisdom. " You will hear no more," said he, " the voice of the chieftains who commanded you and whom you chose from among all the warrior beavers to give you laws. Your language, which the medicine-men understand perfectly, will be heard no more at the bottom of the lake. You will fight no more battles with the otters, your cruel foes. No, beavers ! But your skins shall serve to buy arms ; we will carry your smoked hams to our children ; we will keep the dogs from eating your bones, which are so hard."

The elan, deer, and elk were treated by the American Indians with the same punctilious respect, and for the same reason. Their bones might not be given to the dogs nor thrown into the fire, nor might their fat be dropped upon the fire, because the souls of the dead animals were believed to see what was done to their bodies and to tell it to the other beasts, living and dead. Hence, if their bodies were ill-used, the animals of that species would not allow themselves to be taken, neither in this world nor in the world to come. Among the Chiquites of Paraguay a sick man would be asked by the medicine-man whether he had not thrown away some of the flesh of the deer or turtle, and if he answered yes, the medicine-man would say, " That is what is killing you. The soul of the deer or turtle has entered into your body to avenge the wrong you did it." The Canadian Indians would not eat the embryos of the elk, unless at the close of the hunting season ; otherwise the mother-elks would be shy and refuse to be caught.

In the Timor-laut islands of the Indian Archipelago the skulls of all the turtles which a fisherman has caught are hung up under his house. Before he goes out to catch another, he addresses himself to the skull of the last turtle that he killed, and having inserted betel between its jaws, he prays the spirit of the dead animal to entice its kinsfolk in the sea to come and be caught. In the Poso district of Central Celebes hunters keep the jawbones of deer and wild pigs which they have killed and hang them up in their houses near the fire. Then they say to the jawbones, " Ye cry after your comrades, that your grandfathers, or nephews, or children may not go away." Their notion is that the souls of the dead deer and pigs tarry near their jawbones and attract the souls of living deer and pigs, which are thus drawn into the toils of the hunter. Thus the wily savage employs dead animals as decoys to lure living animals to their doom.

The Lengua Indians of the Gran Chaco love to hunt the ostrich, but when they have killed one of these birds and are bringing home the carcase to the village, they take steps to outwit the resentful ghost of their victim. They think that when the first natural shock of death is passed, the ghost of the ostrich pulls himself together and makes after his body. Acting on this sage calculation, the Indians pluck feathers from the breast of the bird and strew them at intervals along the track. At every bunch of feathers the ghost stops to con-sider, " Is this the whole of my body or only a part of it ? " The doubt gives him pause, and when at last he has made up his mind fully at all the bunches, and has further wasted valuable time by the zigzag course which he invariably pursues in going from one to another, the hunters are safe at home, and the bilked ghost may stalk in vain round about the village, which he is too timid to enter.

The Esquimaux about Bering Strait believe that the souls of dead sea-beasts, such as seals, walrus, and whales, remain attached to their bladders, and that by returning the bladders to the sea they can cause the souls to be reincarnated in fresh bodies and so multiply the game which the hunters pursue and kill. Acting on this belief every hunter carefully removes and preserves the bladders of all the sea-beasts that he kills ; and at a solemn festival held once a year in winter these bladders, containing the souls of all the sea-beasts that have been killed throughout the year, are honoured with dances and offerings of food in the public assembly-room, after which they are taken out on the ice and thrust through holes into the water; for the simple Esquimaux imagine that the souls of the animals, in high good humour at the kind treatment they have experienced, will thereafter be born again as seals, walrus, and whales, and in that form will flock willingly to be again speared, harpooned, or otherwise done to death by the hunters.

For like reasons, a tribe which depends for its subsistence, chiefly or in part, upon fishing is careful to treat the fish with every mark of honour and respect. The Indians of Peru " adored the fish that they caught in greatest abundance; for they said that the first fish that was made in the world above (for so they named Heaven) gave birth to all other fish of that species, and took care to send them plenty of its children to sustain their tribe. For this reason they worshipped sardines in one region, where they killed more of them than of any other fish; in others, the skate; in others, the dogfish; in others, the golden fish for its beauty; in others, the crawfish; in others, for want of larger gods, the crabs, where they had no other fish, or where they knew not how to catch and kill them. In short, they had whatever fish was most serviceable to them as their gods." The Kwakiutl Indians of British Columbia think that when a salmon is killed its soul returns to the salmon country. Hence they take care to throw the bones and offal into the sea, in order that the soul may reanimate them at the resurrection of the salmon. Whereas if they burned the bones the soul would be lost, and so it would be quite impossible for that salmon to rise from the dead. In like manner the Otawa Indians of Canada, believing that the souls of dead fish passed into other bodies of fish, never burned fish bones, for fear of displeasing the souls of the fish, who would come no more to the nets. The Hurons also refrained from throwing fish bones into the fire, lest the souls of the fish should go and warn the other fish not to let themselves be caught, since the Hurons would burn their bones. Moreover, they had men who preached to the fish and persuaded them to come and be caught. A good preacher was much sought after, for they thought that the exhortations of a clever man had a great effect in drawing the fish to the nets. In the Huron fishing village where the French missionary Sagard stayed, the preacher to the fish prided himself very much on his eloquence, which was of a florid order. Every evening after supper, having seen that all the people were in their places and that a strict silence was observed, he preached to the fish. His text was that the Hurons did not burn fish bones. " Then enlarging on this theme with extraordinary unction, he exhorted and conjured and invited and implored the fish to come and be caught and to be of good courage and to fear nothing, for it was all to serve their friends who honoured them and did not burn their bones." The natives of the Duke of York Island annually decorate a canoe with flowers and ferns, lade it, or are supposed to lade it, with shell-money, and set it adrift to compensate the fish for their fellows who have been caught and eaten. It is especially necessary to treat the first fish caught with consideration in order to conciliate the rest of the fish, whose conduct may be supposed to be influenced by the reception given to those of their kind which were the first to be taken. Accordingly the Maoris always put back into the sea the first fish caught, " with a prayer that it may tempt other fish to come and be caught."

Still more stringent are the precautions taken when the fish are the first of the season. On salmon rivers, when the fish begin to run up the stream in spring, they are received with much deference by tribes who, like the Indians of the Pacific Coast of North America, subsist largely upon a fish diet. In British Columbia the Indians used to go out to meet the first fish as they came up the river : " They paid court to them, and would address them thus : ' You fish, you fish ; you are all chiefs, you are ; you are all chiefs.' " Amongst the Tlingit of Alaska the first halibut of the season is carefully handled and addressed as a chief, and a festival is given in his honour, after which the fishing goes on. In spring, when the winds blow soft from the south and the salmon begin to run up the Klamath river, the Karoks of California dance for salmon, to ensure a good catch. One of the Indians, called the Kareya or God-man, retires to the mountains and fasts for ten days. On his return the people flee, while he goes to the river, takes the first salmon of the catch, eats some of it, and with the rest kindles the sacred fire in the sweating-house. " No Indian may take a salmon before this dance is held, nor for ten days after it, even if his family are starving." The Karoks also believe that a fisherman will take no salmon if the poles of which his spearing-booth is made were gathered on the river-side, where the salmon might have seen them. The poles must be brought from the top of the highest mountain. The fisherman will also labour in vain if he uses the same poles a second year in booths or weirs, " because the old salmon will have told the young ones about them." There is a favourite fish of the Aino which appears in their rivers about May and June. They prepare for the fishing by observing rules of ceremonial purity, and when they have gone out to fish, the women at home must keep strict silence or the fish would hear them and disappear. When the first fish is caught he is brought home and passed through a small opening at the end of the hut, but not through the door ; for if he were passed through the door, " the other fish would certainly see him and disappear." This may partly explain the custom observed by other savages of bringing game in certain cases into their huts, not by the door, but by the window, the smoke-hole, or by a special opening at the back of the hut.

With some savages a special reason for respecting the bones of game, and generally of the animals which they eat, is a belief that, if the bones are preserved, they will in course of time be reclothed with flesh, and thus the animal will come to life again. It is, therefore, clearly for the interest of the hunter to leave the bones intact, since to destroy them would be to diminish the future supply of game. Many of the Minnetaree Indians " believe that the bones of those bisons which they have slain and divested of flesh rise again clothed with renewed flesh, and quickened with life, and become fat, and fit for slaughter the succeeding June." Hence on the western prairies of America the skulls of buffaloes may be seen arranged in circles and symmetrical piles, awaiting the resurrection. After feasting on a dog, the Dacotas carefully collect the bones, scrape, wash, and bury them, " partly, as it is said, to testify to the dog-species, that in feasting upon one of their number no disrespect was meant to the species itself, and partly also from a belief that the bones of the animal will rise and reproduce another." In sacrificing an animal the Lapps regularly put aside the bones, eyes, ears, heart, lungs, sexual parts (if the animal was a male), and a morsel of flesh from each limb. Then, after eating the remainder of the flesh, they laid the bones and the rest in anatomical order in a coffin and buried them with the usual rites, believing that the god to whom the animal was sacrificed would reclothe the bones with flesh and restore the animal to life in Jabme-Aimo, the subterranean world of the dead. Sometimes, as after feasting on a bear, they seem to have contented themselves with thus burying the bones. Thus the Lapps expected the resurrection of the slain animal to take place in another world, resembling in this respect the Kamtchatkans, who believed that every creature, down to the smallest fly, would rise from the dead and live underground. On the other hand, the North American Indians looked for the resurrection of the animals in the present world. The habit, observed especially by Mongolian peoples, of stuffing the skin of a sacrificed animal, or stretching it on a framework, points rather to a belief in a resurrection of the latter sort. The objection commonly entertained by primitive peoples to break the bones of the animals which they have eaten or sacrificed may be based either on a belief in the resurrection of the animals, or on a fear of intimidating other creatures of the same species and offending the ghosts of the slain animals. The reluctance of North American Indians and Esquimaux to let dogs gnaw the bones of animals is perhaps only a precaution to prevent the bones from being broken.

But after all the resurrection of dead game may have its inconveniences, and accordingly some hunters take steps to prevent it by hamstringing the animal so as to prevent it or its ghost from getting up and running away. This is the motive alleged for the practice by Koui hunters in Laos ; they think that the spells which they utter in the chase may lose their magical virtue, and that the slaughtered animal may consequently come to life again and escape. To prevent that catastrophe they therefore hamstring the beast as soon as they have butchered it. When an Esquimau of Alaska has killed a fox, he carefully cuts the tendons of all the animal's legs in order to prevent the ghost from reanimating the body and walking about. But hamstringing the carcase is not the only measure which the prudent savage adopts for the sake of disabling the ghost of his victim. In old days, when the Aino went out hunting and killed a fox first, they took care to tie its mouth up tightly in order to prevent the ghost of the animal from sallying forth and warning its fellows against the approach of the hunter. The Gilyaks of the Amoor River put out the eyes of the seals they have killed, lest the ghosts of the slain animals should know their slayers and avenge their death by spoiling the seal-hunt.

Besides the animals which primitive man dreads for their strength and ferocity, and those which he reveres on account of the benefits which he expects from them, there is another class of creatures which he sometimes deems it necessary to conciliate by worship and sacrifice. These are the vermin that infest his crops and his cattle. To rid himself of these deadly foes the farmer has recourse to many superstitious devices, of which, though some are meant to destroy or intimidate the vermin, others aim at propitiating them and persuading them by fair means to spare the fruits of the earth and the herds. Thus Esthonian peasants, in the island of Oesel, stand in great awe of the weevil, an insect which is exceedingly destructive to the grain. They give it a fine name, and if a child is about to kill a weevil they say, " Don't do it ; the more we hurt him, the more he hurts us." If they find a weevil they bury it in the earth instead of killing it. Some even put the weevil under a stone in the field and offer corn to it. They think that thus it is appeased and does less harm. Amongst the Saxons of Transylvania, in order to keep sparrows from the corn, the sower begins by throwing the first handful of seed backwards over his head, saying, " That is for you, sparrows." To guard the corn against the attacks of leaf-flies he shuts his eyes and scatters three handful of oats in different directions. Having made this offering to the leaf-flies he feels sure that they will spare the corn. A Transylvanian way of securing the crops against all birds, beasts, and insects, is this : after he has finished sowing, the sower goes once more from end to end of the field imitating the gesture of sowing, but with an empty hand. As he does so he says, " I sow this for the animals ; I sow it for everything that flies and creeps, that walks and stands, that sings and springs, in the name of God the Father, etc." The following is a German way of freeing a garden from caterpillars. After sunset or at midnight the mistress of the house, or another female member of the family, walks all round the garden dragging a broom after her. She may not look behind her, and must keep murmuring, " Good evening, Mother Caterpillar, you shall come with your husband to church." The garden gate is left open till the following morning.

Sometimes in dealing with vermin the farmer aims at hitting a happy mean between excessive rigour on the one hand and weak indulgence on the other ; kind but firm, he tempers severity with mercy. An ancient Greek treatise on farming advises the husbandman who would rid his lands of mice to act thus : " Take a sheet of paper and write on it as follows : ' I adjure you, ye mice here present, that ye neither injure me nor suffer another mouse to do so. I give you yonder field ' (here you specify the field) ; ' but if ever I catch you here again, by the Mother of the Gods I will rend you in seven pieces.' Write this, and stick the paper on an unhewn stone in the field before sunrise, taking care to keep the written side up." In the Ardennes they say that to get rid of rats you should repeat the following words : " *Erat verbum, apud Deum vestrum.* Male rats and female rats, I conjure you, by the great God, to go out of my house, out of all my habitations, and to betake yourselves to such and such a place, there to end your days. *Decretis, reversis et desembarassis virgo potens, clemens, justitiae.*" Then write the same words on pieces of paper, fold them up, and place one of them under the door by which the rats are to go forth, and the other on the road which they are to take. This exorcism should be performed at sunrise. Some years ago an American farmer was reported to have written a civil letter to the rats, telling them that his crops were short, that he could not afford to keep them through the winter, that he had been very kind to them, and that for their own good he thought they had better leave him and go to some of his neighbours who had more grain. This document he pinned to a post in his barn for the rats to read.

Sometimes the desired object is supposed to be attained by treating with high distinction one or two chosen individuals of the obnoxious species, while the rest are pursued with relentless rigour. In the East Indian island of Bali, the mice which ravage the rice-fields are caught in great numbers, and burned in the same way that corpses are burned. But two of the captured mice are allowed to live, and receive a little packet of white linen. Then the people bow down before them, as before gods, and let them go. When the farms of the Sea Dyaks or Ibans of Sarawak are much pestered by birds and insects, they catch a specimen of each kind of vermin (one sparrow, one grasshopper, and so on), put them in a tiny boat of bark well-stocked with provisions, and then allow the little vessel with its obnoxious passengers to float down the river. If that does not drive the pests away, the Dyaks resort to what they deem a more effectual mode of accomplishing the same purpose. They make a clay crocodile as large as life and set it up in the fields, where they offer it food, rice-spirit, and cloth, and sacrifice a fowl and a pig before it. Mollified by these attentions, the ferocious animal very soon gobbles up all the creatures that devour the crops. In Albania, if the fields or vineyards are ravaged by locusts or beetles, some of the women will assemble with dishevelled hair, catch a few of the insects, and march with them in a funeral procession to a spring or stream, in which they drown the creatures. Then one of the women sings, " O locusts and beetles who have left us bereaved," and the dirge is taken up and repeated by all the women in chorus. Thus by celebrating the obsequies of a few locusts and beetles, they hope to bring about the death of them all. When caterpillars invaded a vineyard or field in Syria, the virgins were gathered, and one of the caterpillars was taken and a girl made its mother. Then they bewailed and buried it. Thereafter they conducted the " mother " to the place where the caterpillars were, consoling her, in order that all the caterpillars might leave the garden.

CHAPTER LIV

TYPES OF ANIMAL SACRAMENT

§ I. *The Egyptian and the Aino Types of Sacrament.*—We are now perhaps in a position to understand the ambiguous behaviour of the Aino and Gilyaks towards the bear. It has been shown that the sharp line of demarcation which we draw between mankind and the lower animals does not exist for the savage. To him many of the other animals appear as his equals or even his superiors, not merely in brute force but in intelligence ; and if choice or necessity leads him to take their lives, he feels bound, out of regard to his own safety, to do it in a way which will be as inoffensive as possible not merely to the living animal, but to its departed spirit and to all the other animals of the same species, which would resent an affront put upon one of their kind much as a tribe of savages would revenge an injury or insult offered to a tribesman. We have seen that among the many devices by which the savage seeks to atone for the wrong done by him to his animal victims one is to show marked deference to a few chosen individuals of the species, for such behaviour is apparently regarded as entitling him to exterminate with impunity all the rest of the species upon which he can lay hands. This principle perhaps explains the attitude, at first sight puzzling and contradictory, of the Aino towards the bear. The flesh and skin of the bear regularly afford them food and clothing ; but since the bear is an intelligent and powerful animal, it is necessary to offer some satisfaction or atonement to the bear species for the loss which it sustains in the death of so many of its members. This satisfaction or atonement is made by rearing young bears, treating them, so long as they live, with respect, and killing them with extraordinary marks of sorrow and devotion. So the other bears are appeased, and do not resent the slaughter of their kind by attacking the slayers or deserting the country, which would deprive the Ainó of one of their means of subsistence.

Thus the primitive worship of animals conforms to two types, which are in some respects the converse of each other. On the one hand, animals are worshipped, and are therefore neither killed nor eaten. On the other hand, animals are worshipped because they are habitually killed and eaten. In both types of worship the animal is revered on account of some benefit, positive or negative, which the savage hopes to receive from it. In the former worship the benefit comes either in the positive shape of protection, advice, and help which the animal affords the man, or in the negative shape of abstinence from injuries which it is in the power of the animal to inflict. In the latter worship the benefit takes the material form of the animal's flesh and skin. The two types of worship are in some measure antithetical : in the one, the animal is not eaten because it is revered ; in the other, it is revered because it is eaten. But both may be practised by the same people, as we see in the case of the North American Indians, who, while they apparently revere and spare their totem animals, also revere the animals and fish upon which they subsist. The aborigines of Australia have totemism in the most primitive form known to us ; but there is no clear evidence that they attempt, like the North American Indians, to conciliate the animals which they kill and eat. The means which the Australians adopt to secure a plentiful supply of game appear to be primarily based, not on conciliation, but on sympathetic magic, a principle to which the North American Indians also resort for the same purpose. Hence, as the Australians undoubtedly represent a ruder and earlier stage of human progress than the American Indians, it would seem that before hunters think of worshipping the game as a means of ensuring an abundant supply of it, they seek to attain the same end by sympathetic magic. This, again, would show—what there is good reason for believing— that sympathetic magic is one of the earliest means by which man endeavours to adapt the agencies of nature to his needs.

Corresponding to the two distinct types of animal worship, there are two distinct types of the custom of killing the animal god. On the one hand, when the revered animal is habitually spared, it is nevertheless killed—and sometimes eaten—on rare and solemn occasions. Examples of this custom have been already given and an explanation of them offered. On the other hand, when the revered animal is habitually killed, the slaughter of any one of the species involves the killing of the god, and is atoned for on the spot by apologies and sacrifices, especially when the animal is a powerful and dangerous one ; and, in addition to this ordinary and everyday atonement, there is a special annual atonement, at which a select individual of the species is slain with extraordinary marks of respect and devotion. Clearly the two types of sacramental killing—the Egyptian and the Aino types, as we may call them for distinction—are liable to be confounded by an observer ; and, before we can say to which type any particular example belongs, it is necessary to ascertain whether the animal sacramentally slain belongs to a species which is habitually spared, or to one which is habitually killed by the tribe. In the former case the example belongs to the Egyptian type of sacrament, in the latter to the Aino type.

The practice of pastoral tribes appears to furnish examples of both types of sacrament. " Pastoral tribes," says Adolf Bastian, " being sometimes obliged to sell their herds to strangers who may handle the bones disrespectfully, seek to avert the danger which such a sacrilege would entail by consecrating one of the herd as an object of worship, eating it sacramentally in the family circle with closed doors, and afterwards treating the bones with all the ceremonious respect which, strictly speaking, should be accorded to every head of cattle, but which, being punctually paid to the representative animal, is deemed to be paid to all. Such family meals are found among various peoples, especially those of the Caucasus. When amongst the Abchases the shepherds in spring eat their common meal with their loins girt and their staves in their hands, this may be looked upon both as a sacrament and as an oath of mutual help and support. For the strongest of all oaths is that which is accompanied with the eating of a sacred substance, since the perjured person cannot possibly escape the avenging god whom he has taken into his body and assimilated." This kind of sacrament is of the Aino or expiatory type, since it is meant to atone to the species for the possible ill-usage of individuals. An expiation, similar in principle but different in details, is offered by the Kalmucks to the sheep, whose flesh is one of their staple foods. Rich Kalmucks are in the habit of consecrating a white ram under the title of " the ram of heaven " or " the ram of the spirit." The animal is never shorn and never sold ; but when it grows old and its owner wishes to consecrate a new one, the old ram must be killed and eaten at a feast to which the neighbours are invited. On a lucky day, generally in autumn when the sheep are fat, a sorcerer kills the old ram, after sprinkling it with milk. Its flesh is eaten ; the skeleton, with a portion of the fat, is burned on a turf altar ; and the skin, with the head and feet, is hung up.

An example of a sacrament of the Egyptian type is furnished by the Todas, a pastoral people of Southern India, who subsist largely upon the milk of their buffaloes. Amongst them " the buffalo is to a certain degree held sacred " and " is treated with great kindness, even with a degree of adoration, by the people." They never eat the flesh of the cow buffalo, and as a rule abstain from the flesh of the male. But to the latter rule there is a single exception. Once a year all the adult males of the village join in the ceremony of killing and eating a very young male calf—seemingly under a month old. They take the animal into the dark recesses of the village wood, where it is killed with a club made from the sacred tree of the Todas (the *Millingtonia*). A sacred fire having been made by the rubbing of sticks, the flesh of the calf is roasted on the embers of certain trees, and is eaten by the men alone, women being excluded from the assembly. This is the only occasion on which the Todas eat buffalo flesh. The Madi or Moru tribe of Central Africa, whose chief wealth is their cattle, though they also practise agriculture, appear to kill a lamb sacramentally on certain solemn occasions. The custom is thus described by Dr. Felkin : " A remarkable custom is observed at stated times—once a year, I am led to believe. I have not been able to ascertain what exact meaning is attached to it. It appears, however, to relieve the people's minds, for beforehand they evince much sadness, and seem very joyful when the ceremony is duly accomplished. The following is what takes place : A large concourse of people of all ages assemble, and sit down round a circle of stones, which is erected by the side of a road (really a narrow path). A very choice lamb is then fetched by a boy, who leads it four times round the assembled people. As it passes they pluck off little bits of its fleece and place them in their hair, or on to some other part of their body. The lamb is then led up to the stones, and there killed by a man belonging to a kind of priestly order, who takes some of the blood and sprinkles it four times over the people. He then applies it individually. On the children he makes a small ring of blood over the lower end of the breast bone, on women and girls he makes a mark above the breasts, and the men he touches on each shoulder. He then proceeds to explain the ceremony, and to exhort the people to show kindness. . . . When this discourse, which is at times of great length, is over, the people rise, each places a leaf on or by the circle of stones, and then they depart with signs of great joy. The lamb's skull is hung on a tree near the stones, and its flesh is eaten by the poor. This ceremony is observed on a small scale at other times. If a family is in any great trouble, through illness or bereavement, their friends and neighbours come together and a lamb is killed ; this is thought to avert further evil. The same custom prevails at the grave of departed friends, and also on joyful occasions, such as the return of a son home after a very prolonged absence." The sorrow thus manifested by the people at the annual slaughter of the lamb seems to show that the lamb slain is a sacred or divine animal, whose death is mourned by his worshippers, just as the death of the sacred buzzard was mourned by the Californians and the death of the Theban ram by the Egyptians. The smearing each of the worshippers with the blood of the lamb is a form of communion with the divinity ; the vehicle of the divine life is applied externally instead of being taken internally, as when the blood is drunk or the flesh eaten.

§ 2. *Processions with Sacred Animals.*—The form of communion in which the sacred animal is taken from house to house, that all may enjoy a share of its divine influence, has been exemplified by the Gilyak custom of promenading the bear through the village before it is slain. A similar form of communion with the sacred snake is observed by a Snake tribe in the Punjaub. Once a year in the month of September the snake is worshipped by all castes and religions for nine days only. At the end of August the Mirasans, especially those of the Snake tribe, make a snake of dough which they paint black and red, and place on a winnowing basket. This basket they carry round the village, and on entering any house they say : " God be with you all ! May every ill be far ! May our patron's (Gugga's) word thrive ! " Then they present the basket with the snake, saying : " A small cake of flour : a little bit of butter : if you obey the snake, you and yours shall thrive ! " Strictly speaking, a cake and butter should be given, but it is seldom done. Every one, however, gives something, generally a handful of dough or some corn. In houses where there is a new bride or whence a bride has gone, or where a son has been born, it is usual to give a rupee and a quarter, or some cloth. Some-times the bearers of the snake also sing :

" *Give the snake a piece of cloth, and he will send a lively bride !* "

When every house has been thus visited, the dough snake is buried and a small grave is erected over it. Thither during the nine days of September the women come to worship. They bring a basin of curds, a small portion of which they offer at the snake's grave, kneeling on the ground and touching the earth with their foreheads. Then they go home and divide the rest of the curds among the children. Here the dough snake is clearly a substitute for a real snake. Indeed, in districts where snakes abound the worship is offered, not at the grave of the dough snake, but in the jungles where snakes are known to be. Besides this yearly worship, performed by all the people, the members of the Snake tribe worship in the same way every morning after a new moon. The Snake tribe is not uncommon in the Punjaub. Members of it will not kill a snake, and they say that its bite does not hurt them. If they find a dead snake, they put clothes on it and give it a regular funeral.

Ceremonies closely analogous to this Indian worship of the snake have survived in Europe into recent times, and doubtless date from a very primitive paganism. The best-known example is the " hunting of the wren." By many European peoples—the ancient Greeks and Romans, the modern Italians, Spaniards, French, Germans, Dutch, Danes, Swedes, English, and Welsh—the wren has been designated the king, the little king, the king of birds, the hedge king, and so forth, and has been reckoned amongst those birds which it is extremely unlucky to kill. In England it is supposed that if any one kills a wren or harries its nest he will infallibly break a bone or meet with some dreadful misfortune within the year ; sometimes it is thought that the cows will give bloody milk. In Scotland the wren is called " the Lady of Heaven's hen," and boys say :

> " Malisons, malisons, mair than ten,
> That harry the Ladye of Heaven's hen ! "

At Saint Donan, in Brittany, people believe that if children touch the young wrens in the nest they will suffer from the fire of St. Lawrence, that is, from pimples on the face, legs, and so on. In other parts of France it is thought that if a person kills a wren or harries its nest his house will be struck by lightning, or that the fingers with which he did the deed will shrivel up and drop off, or at least be maimed, or that his cattle will suffer in their feet.

Notwithstanding such beliefs, the custom of annually killing the wren has prevailed widely both in this country and in France. In the Isle of Man down to the eighteenth century the custom was observed on Christmas Eve, or rather Christmas morning. On the twenty-fourth of December, towards evening, all the servants got a holiday ; they did not go to bed all night, but rambled about till the bells rang in all the churches at midnight. When prayers were over, they went to hunt the wren, and having found one of these birds they killed it and fastened it to the top of a long pole with its wings extended. Thus they carried it in procession to every house, chanting the following rhyme :

> " *We hunted the wren for Robin the Bobbin,*
> *We hunted the wren for Jack of the Can,*
> *We hunted the wren for Robin the Bobbin,*
> *We hunted the wren for every one.*"

When they had gone from house to house and collected all the money they could, they laid the wren on a bier and carried it in procession to the parish churchyard, where they made a grave and buried it " with the utmost solemnity, singing dirges over her in the Manks language, which they call her knell ; after which Christmas begins." The burial over, the company outside the churchyard formed a circle and danced to music.

A writer of the eighteenth century says that in Ireland the wren " is still hunted and killed by the peasants on Christmas Day, and on the following (St. Stephen's Day) he is carried about, hung by the leg, in the centre of two hoops, crossing each other at right angles, and a procession made in every village, of men, women, and children, singing an Irish catch, importing him to be the king of all birds." Down to the present time the " hunting of the wren " still takes place in parts of Leinster and Connaught. On Christmas Day or St. Stephen's Day the boys hunt and kill the wren, fasten it in the middle of a mass of holly and ivy on the top of a broomstick, and on St. Stephen's Day go about with it from house to house, singing :

> " *The wren, the wren, the king of all birds,*
> *St. Stephen's Day was caught in the furze :*
> *Although he is little, his family 's great,*
> *I pray you, good landlady, give us a treat.*"

Money or food (bread, butter, eggs, etc.) were given them, upon which they feasted in the evening.

In the first half of the nineteenth century similar customs were still observed in various parts of the south of France. Thus at Carcassone, every year on the first Sunday of December the young people of the street Saint Jean used to go out of the town armed with sticks, with which they beat the bushes, looking for wrens. The first to strike down one of these birds was proclaimed King. Then they returned to the town in procession, headed by the King, who carried the wren on a pole. On the evening of the last day of the year the King and all who had hunted the wren marched through the streets of the town to the light of torches, with drums beating and fifes playing in front of them. At the door of every house they stopped, and one of them wrote with chalk on the door *vive le roi !* with the number of the year which was about to begin. On the morning of Twelfth Day the King again marched in procession with great pomp, wearing a crown and a blue mantle and carrying a sceptre. In front of him was borne the wren fastened to the top of a pole, which was adorned with a verdant wreath of olive, of oak, and sometimes of mistletoe grown on an oak.

After hearing high mass in the parish church of St. Vincent, surrounded by his officers and guards, the King visited the bishop, the mayor, the magistrates, and the chief inhabitants, collecting money to defray the expenses of the royal banquet which took place in the evening and wound up with a dance.

The parallelism between this custom of " hunting the wren " and some of those which we have considered, especially the Gilyak procession with the bear, and the Indian one with the snake, seems too close to allow us to doubt that they all belong to the same circle of ideas. The worshipful animal is killed with special solemnity once a year ; and before or immediately after death he is promenaded from door to door, that each of his worshippers may receive a portion of the divine virtues that are supposed to emanate from the dead or dying god. Religious processions of this sort must have had a great place in the ritual of European peoples in prehistoric times, if we may judge from the numerous traces of them which have survived in folk-custom. For example, on the last day of the year, or Hogmanay as it was called, it used to be customary in the Highlands of Scotland for a man to dress himself up in a cow's hide and thus attired to go from house to house, attended by young fellows, each of them armed with a staff, to which a bit of raw hide was tied. Round every house the hide-clad man used to run thrice *deiseal*, that is, according to the course of the sun, so as to keep the house on his right hand; while the others pursued him, beating the hide with their staves and thereby making a loud noise like the beating of a drum. In this disorderly procession they also struck the walls of the house. On being admitted, one of the party, standing within the threshold, pronounced a blessing on the family in these words : " May God bless the house and all that belongs to it, cattle, stones, and timber ! In plenty of meat, of bed and body clothes, and health of men may it ever abound ! " Then each of the party singed in the fire a little bit of the hide which was tied to his staff ; and having done so he applied the singed hide to the nose of every person and of every domestic animal belonging to the house. This was imagined to secure them from diseases and other misfortunes, particularly from witchcraft, throughout the ensuing year. The whole ceremony was called *calluinn* because of the great noise made in beating the hide. It was observed in the Hebrides, including St. Kilda, down to the second half of the eighteenth century at least, and it seems to have survived well into the nineteenth century.

CHAPTER LV

THE TRANSFERENCE OF EVIL

§ 1. *The Transference to Inanimate Objects.*—We have now traced the practice of killing a god among peoples in the hunting, pastoral, and agricultural stages of society ; and I have attempted to explain the motives which led men to adopt so curious a custom.   One aspect of the custom still remains to be noticed.   The accumulated misfortunes and sins of the whole people are sometimes laid upon the dying god, who is supposed to bear them away for ever, leaving the people innocent and happy.   The notion that we can transfer our guilt and sufferings to some other being who will bear them for us is familiar to the savage mind.   It arises from a very obvious confusion between the physical and the mental, between the material and the immaterial.   Because it is possible to shift a load of wood, stones, or what not, from our own back to the back of another, the savage fancies that it is equally possible to shift the burden of his pains and sorrows to another, who will suffer them in his stead.   Upon this idea he acts, and the result is an endless number of very unamiable devices for palming off upon some one else the trouble which a man shrinks from bearing himself.   In short, the principle of vicarious suffering is commonly understood and practised by races who stand on a low level of social and intellectual culture.   In the following pages I shall illustrate the theory and the practice as they are found among savages in all their naked simplicity, undisguised by the refinements of metaphysics and the subtleties of theology.

The devices to which the cunning and selfish savage resorts for the sake of easing himself at the expense of his neighbour are manifold ; only a few typical examples out of a multitude can be cited.   At the outset it is to be observed that the evil of which a man seeks to rid himself need not be transferred to a person ; it may equally well be transferred to an animal or a thing, though in the last case the thing is often only a vehicle to convey the trouble to the first person who touches it.   In some of the East Indian islands they think that epilepsy can be cured by striking the patient on the face with the leaves of certain trees and then throwing them away.   The disease is believed to have passed into the leaves, and to have been thrown away with them.   To cure toothache some of the Australian blacks apply a heated spear-thrower to the cheek.   The spear-thrower is then cast away, and the toothache goes with it in the shape of a black stone called *karriitch*. Stones of this kind are found in old mounds and sandhills.   They are carefully collected and thrown in the direction of enemies in order to give them toothache.   The Bahima, a pastoral people of Uganda, often suffer from deep-seated abscesses : " their cure for this is to transfer the disease to some other person by obtaining herbs from the medicine-man, rubbing them over the place where the swelling is, and burying them in the road where people continually pass ; the first person who steps over these buried herbs contracts the disease, and the original patient recovers."

Sometimes in case of sickness the malady is transferred to an effigy as a preliminary to passing it on to a human being.   Thus among the Baganda the medicine-man would sometimes make a model of his patient in clay ; then a relative of the sick man would rub the image over the sufferer's body and either bury it in the road or hide it in the grass by the wayside. The first person who stepped over the image or passed by it would catch the disease. Sometimes the effigy was made out of a plantain-flower tied up so as to look like a person ; it was used in the same way as the clay figure. But the use of images for this maleficent purpose was a capital crime ; any person caught in the act of burying one of them in the public road would surely have been put to death.

In the western district of the island of Timor, when men or women are making long and tiring journeys, they fan themselves with leafy branches, which they afterwards throw away on particular spots where their forefathers did the same before them. The fatigue which they felt is thus supposed to have passed into the leaves and to be left behind. Others use stones instead of leaves. Similarly in the Babar Archipelago tired people will strike themselves with stones, believing that they thus transfer to the stones the weariness which they felt in their own bodies. They then throw away the stones in places which are specially set apart for the purpose. A like belief and practice in many distant parts of the world have given rise to those cairns or heaps of sticks and leaves which travellers often observe beside the path, and to which every passing native adds his contribution in the shape of a stone, or stick, or leaf. Thus in the Solomon and Banks' Islands the natives are wont to throw sticks, stones, or leaves upon a heap at a place of steep descent, or where a difficult path begins, saying, " There goes my fatigue." The act is not a religious rite, for the thing thrown on the heap is not an offering to spiritual powers, and the words which accompany the act are not a prayer. It is nothing but a magical ceremony for getting rid of fatigue, which the simple savage fancies he can embody in a stick, leaf, or stone, and so cast it from him.

§ 2. *The Transference to Animals.*—Animals are often employed as a vehicle for carrying away or transferring the evil. When a Moor has a headache he will sometimes take a lamb or a goat and beat it till it falls down, believing that the headache will thus be transferred to the animal. In Morocco most wealthy Moors keep a wild boar in their stables, in order that the jinn and evil spirits may be diverted from the horses and enter into the boar. Amongst the Caffres of South Africa, when other remedies have failed, " natives sometimes adopt the custom of taking a goat into the presence of a sick man, and confess the sins of the kraal over the animal. Sometimes a few drops of blood from the sick man are allowed to fall on the head of the goat, which is turned out into an uninhabited part of the veldt. The sickness is supposed to be transferred to the animal, and to become lost in the desert." In Arabia, when the plague is raging, the people will sometimes lead a camel through all the quarters of the town in order that the animal may take the pestilence on itself. Then they strangle it in a sacred place and imagine that they have rid themselves of the camel and of the plague at one blow. It is said that when smallpox is raging the savages of Formosa will drive the demon of disease into a sow, then cut off the animal's ears and burn them or it, believing that in this way they rid themselves of the plague.

Amongst the Malagasy the vehicle for carrying away evils is called a *faditra*. " The faditra is anything selected by the sikidy [divining board] for the purpose of taking away any hurtful evils or diseases that might prove injurious to an individual's happiness, peace, or prosperity. The faditra may be either ashes, cut money, a sheep, a pumpkin, or anything else the sikidy may choose to direct. After the particular article is appointed, the priest counts upon it all the evils that may prove injurious to the person for whom it is made, and which he then charges the faditra to take away for ever. If the faditra be ashes, it is blown, to be carried away by the wind. If it be cut money, it is thrown to the bottom of deep water, or where it can never be found. If it be a sheep, it is carried away to a distance on the shoulders of a man, who runs with all his might, mumbling as he goes, as if in the greatest rage against the faditra, for the evils it is bearing away. If it be a pumpkin, it is carried on the shoulders to a little distance, and there dashed upon the ground with every appearance of fury and indignation." A Malagasy was informed by a diviner that he was doomed to a bloody death, but that possibly he might avert his fate by performing a certain rite. Carrying a small vessel full of blood upon his head, he was to mount upon the back of a bullock; while thus mounted, he was to spill the blood upon the bullock's head, and then send the animal away into the wilderness, whence it might never return.

The Bataks of Sumatra have a ceremony which they call " making the curse to fly away." When a woman is childless, a sacrifice is offered to the gods of three grasshoppers, representing a head of cattle, a buffalo, and a horse. Then a swallow is set free, with a prayer that the curse may fall upon the bird and fly away with it. " The entrance into a house of an animal which does not generally seek to share the abode of man is regarded by the Malays as ominous of misfortune. If a wild bird flies into a house, it must be carefully caught and smeared with oil, and must then be released in the open air, a formula being recited in which it is bidden to fly away with all the ill-luck and misfortunes of the occupier." In antiquity Greek women seem to have done the same with swallows which they caught in the house : they poured oil on them and let them fly away, apparently for the purpose of removing ill-luck from the household. The Huzuls of the Carpathians imagine that they can transfer freckles to the first swallow they see in spring by washing their face in flowing water and saying, " Swallow, swallow, take my freckles, and give me rosy cheeks."

Among the Badagas of the Neilgherry Hills in Southern India, when a death has taken place, the sins of the deceased are laid upon a buffalo calf. For this purpose the people gather round the corpse and carry it outside of the village. There an elder of the tribe, standing at the head of the corpse, recites or chants a long list of sins such as any Badaga may commit, and the people repeat the last words of each line after him. The confession of sins is thrice repeated. "By a conventional mode of expression, the sum total of sins a man may do is said to be thirteen hundred. Admitting that the deceased has committed them all, the performer cries aloud, ' Stay not their flight to God's pure feet.' As he closes, the whole assembly chants aloud ' Stay not their flight.' Again the performer enters into details, and cries, ' He killed the crawling snake. It is a sin.' In a moment the last word is caught up, and all the people cry ' It is a sin.' As they shout, the performer lays his hand upon the calf. The sin is transferred to the calf. Thus the whole catalogue is gone through in this impressive way. But this is not enough. As the last shout ' Let all be well ' dies away, the performer gives place to another, and again confession is made, and all the people shout ' It is a sin.' A third time it is done. Then, still in solemn silence, the calf is let loose. Like the Jewish scapegoat, it may never be used for secular work." At a Badaga funeral witnessed by the Rev. A. C. Clayton the buffalo calf was led thrice round the bier, and the dead man's hand was laid on its head. " By this act, the calf was supposed to receive all the sins of the deceased. It was then driven away to a great distance, that it might contaminate no one, and it was said that it would never be sold, but looked on as a dedicated sacred animal." " The idea of this ceremony is, that the sins of the deceased enter the calf, or that the task of his absolution is laid on it. They say that the calf very soon disappears, and that it is never after heard of."

§ 3. *The Transference to Men.*—Again, men sometimes play the part of scapegoat by diverting to themselves the evils that threaten others. When a Cingalese is dangerously ill, and the physicians can do nothing, a devil-dancer is called in, who by making offerings to the devils, and dancing in the masks appropriate to them, conjures these demons of disease, one after the other, out of the sick man's body and into his own. Having thus successfully extracted the cause of the malady, the artful dancer lies down on a bier, and shamming death is carried to an open place outside the village. Here, being left to himself, he soon comes to life again, and hastens back to claim his reward. In 1590 a Scotch witch of the name of Agnes Sampson was convicted of curing a certain Robert Kers of a disease " laid upon him by a westland warlock when he was at Dumfries, whilk sickness she took upon herself, and kept the same with great groaning and torment till the morn, at whilk time there was a great din heard in the house." The noise was made by the witch in her efforts to shift the disease, by means of clothes, from herself to a cat or dog. Unfortunately the attempt partly miscarried. The disease missed the animal and hit Alexander Douglas of Dalkeith, who dwined and died of it, while the original patient, Robert Kers, was made whole.

" In one part of New Zealand an expiation for sin was felt to be necessary ; a service was performed over an individual, by which all the sins of the tribe were supposed to be transferred to him, a fern stalk was previously tied to his person, with which he jumped into the river, and there unbinding, allowed it to float away to the sea, bearing their sins with it." In great emergencies the sins of the Rajah of Manipur used to be transferred to somebody else, usually to a criminal, who earned his pardon by his vicarious sufferings. To effect the transference the Rajah and his wife, clad in fine robes, bathed on a scaffold erected in the bazaar, while the criminal crouched beneath it. With the water which dripped from them on him their sins also were washed away and fell on the human scapegoat. To complete the transference the Rajah and his wife made over their fine robes to their substitute, while they themselves, clad in new raiment, mixed with the people till evening. In Travancore, when a Rajah is near his end, they seek out a holy Brahman, who consents to take upon himself the sins of the dying man in consideration of the sum of ten thousand rupees. Thus prepared to immolate himself on the altar of duty, the saint is introduced into the chamber of death, and closely embraces the dying Rajah, saying to him, "O King, I undertake to bear all your sins and diseases. May your Highness live long and reign happily." Having thus taken to himself the sins of the sufferer, he is sent away from the country and never more allowed to return. At Utch Kurgan in Turkestan Mr. Schuyler saw an old man who was said to get his living by taking on himself the sins of the dead, and thenceforth devoting his life to prayer for their souls.

In Uganda, when an army had returned from war, and the gods warned the king by their oracles that some evil had attached itself to the soldiers, it was customary to pick out a woman slave from the captives, together with a cow, a goat, a fowl, and a dog from the booty, and to send them back under a strong guard to the borders of the country from which they had come. There their limbs were broken and they were left to die ; for they were too crippled to crawl back to Uganda. In order to ensure the transference of the evil to these substitutes, bunches of grass were rubbed over the people and cattle and then tied to the victims. After that the army was pronounced clean and was allowed to return to the capital. So on his accession a new king of Uganda used to wound a man and send him away as a scapegoat to Bunyoro to carry away any uncleanness that might attach to the king or queen.

§ 4. *The Transference of Evil in Europe.*—The examples of the transference of evil hitherto adduced have been mostly drawn from the customs of savage or barbarous peoples. But similar attempts to shift the burden of disease, misfortune, and sin from one's self to another person, or to an animal or thing, have been common also among the civilised nations of Europe, both in ancient and modern times. A Roman cure for fever was to pare the patient's nails, and stick the parings with wax on a neighbour's door before sunrise ; the fever then passed from the sick man to his neighbour. Similar devices must have been resorted to by the Greeks ; for in laying down laws for his ideal state, Plato thinks it too much to expect that

men should not be alarmed at finding certain wax figures adhering
to their doors or to the tombstones of their parents, or lying at cross-
roads.   In the fourth century of our era Marcellus of Bordeaux prescribed a cure for warts, which has still a great vogue among the
superstitious in various parts of Europe.   You are to touch your
warts with as many little stones as you have warts ;   then wrap
the stones in an ivy leaf, and throw them away in a thoroughfare.
Whoever picks them up will get the warts, and you will be rid of
them.   People in the Orkney Islands will sometimes wash a sick man,
and then throw the water down at a gateway, in the belief that the
sickness will leave the patient and be transferred to the first person
who passes through the gate.   A Bavarian cure for fever is to write
upon a piece of paper, " Fever, stay away, I am not at home," and
to put the paper in somebody's pocket.   The latter then catches the
fever, and the patient is rid of it.   A Bohemian prescription for the
same malady is this.   Take an empty pot, go with it to a cross-road,
throw it down, and run away.   The first person who kicks against
the pot will catch your fever, and you will be cured.

Often in Europe, as among savages, an attempt is made to transfer
a pain or malady from a man to an animal.   Grave writers of antiquity
recommended that, if a man be stung by a scorpion, he should
sit upon an ass with his face to the tail, or whisper in the animal's
ear, " A scorpion has stung me " ;   in either case, they thought, the
pain would be transferred from the man to the ass.   Many cures of
this sort are recorded by Marcellus.   For example, he tells us that
the following is a remedy for toothache.   Standing booted under the
open sky on the ground, you catch a frog by the head, spit into its
mouth, ask it to carry away the ache, and then let it go.   But the
ceremony must be performed on a lucky day and at a lucky hour.
In Cheshire the ailment known as aphtha or thrush, which affects
the mouth or throat of infants, is not uncommonly treated in much
the same manner.   A young frog is held for a few moments with its
head inside the mouth of the sufferer, whom it is supposed to relieve
by taking the malady to itself.   " I assure you," said an old woman
who had often superintended such a cure, " we used to hear the poor
frog whooping and coughing, mortal bad, for days after ;   it would
have made your heart ache to hear the poor creature coughing as it
did about the garden."   A Northamptonshire, Devonshire, and Welsh
cure for a cough is to put a hair of the patient's head between two
slices of buttered bread and give the sandwich to a dog.   The animal
will thereupon catch the cough and the patient will lose it.   Sometimes an ailment is transferred to an animal by sharing food with it.
Thus in Oldenburg, if you are sick of a fever you set a bowl of sweet
milk before a dog and say, " Good luck, you hound !   may you be
sick and I be sound ! "   Then when the dog has lapped some of the
milk, you take a swig at the bowl ;   and then the dog must lap again,
and then you must swig again ;   and when you and the dog have
done it the third time, he will have the fever and you will be quit of it.

A Bohemian cure for fever is to go out into the forest before the sun is up and look for a snipe's nest. When you have found it, take out one of the young birds and keep it beside you for three days. Then go back into the wood and set the snipe free. The fever will leave you at once. The snipe has taken it away. So in Vedic times the Hindoos of old sent consumption away with a blue jay. They said, " O consumption, fly away, fly away with the blue jay ! With the wild rush of the storm and the whirlwind, oh, vanish away ! " In the village of Llandegla in Wales there is a church dedicated to the virgin martyr St. Tecla, where the falling sickness is, or used to be, cured by being transferred to a fowl. The patient first washed his limbs in a sacred well hard by, dropped fourpence into it as an offering, walked thrice round the well, and thrice repeated the Lord's prayer. Then the fowl, which was a cock or a hen according as the patient was a man or a woman, was put into a basket and carried round first the well and afterwards the church. Next the sufferer entered the church and lay down under the communion table till break of day. After that he offered sixpence and departed, leaving the fowl in the church. If the bird died, the sickness was supposed to have been transferred to it from the man or woman, who was now rid of the disorder. As late as 1855 the old parish clerk of the village remembered quite well to have seen the birds staggering about from the effects of the fits which had been transferred to them.

Often the sufferer seeks to shift his burden of sickness or ill-luck to some inanimate object. In Athens there is a little chapel of St. John the Baptist built against an ancient column. Fever patients resort thither, and by attaching a waxed thread to the inner side of the column believe that they transfer the fever from themselves to the pillar. In the Mark of Brandenburg they say that if you suffer from giddiness you should strip yourself naked and run thrice round a flax-field after sunset ; in that way the flax will get the giddiness and you will be rid of it.

But perhaps the thing most commonly employed in Europe as a receptacle for sickness and trouble of all sorts is a tree or bush. A Bulgarian cure for fever is to run thrice round a willow-tree at sunrise, crying, " The fever shall shake thee, and the sun shall warm me." In the Greek island of Karpathos the priest ties a red thread round the neck of a sick person. Next morning the friends of the patient remove the thread and go out to the hillside, where they tie the thread to a tree, thinking that they thus transfer the sickness to the tree. Italians attempt to cure fever in like manner by tethering it to a tree. The sufferer ties a thread round his left wrist at night, and hangs the thread on a tree next morning. The fever is thus believed to be tied up to the tree, and the patient to be rid of it ; but he must be careful not to pass by that tree again, otherwise the fever would break loose from its bonds and attack him afresh. A Flemish cure for the ague is to go early in the morning to an old willow, tie three knots in one of its branches, say, " Good-morrow, Old One, I give thee the cold; good-morrow, Old One," then turn and run away without looking round. In Sonnenberg, if you would rid yourself of gout you should go to a young fir-tree and tie a knot in one of its twigs, saying, "God greet thee, noble fir. I bring thee my gout. Here will I tie a knot and bind my gout into it. In the name," etc.

Another way of transferring gout from a man to a tree is this. Pare the nails of the sufferer's fingers and clip some hairs from his legs. Bore a hole in an oak, stuff the nails and hair in the hole, stop up the hole again, and smear it with cow's dung. If, for three months thereafter, the patient is free of gout, you may be sure the oak has it in his stead. In Cheshire if you would be rid of warts, you have only to rub them with a piece of bacon, cut a slit in the bark of an ash-tree, and slip the bacon under the bark. Soon the warts will disappear from your hand, only however to reappear in the shape of rough excrescences or knobs on the bark of the tree. At Berkhampstead, in Hertfordshire, there used to be certain oak-trees which were long celebrated for the cure of ague. The transference of the malady to the tree was simple but painful. A lock of the sufferer's hair was pegged into an oak; then by a sudden wrench he left his hair and his ague behind him in the tree.

CHAPTER LVI

THE PUBLIC EXPULSION OF EVILS

§ 1. *The Omnipresence of Demons.*—In the foregoing chapter the primitive principle of the transference of ills to another person, animal, or thing was explained and illustrated. But similar means have been adopted to free a whole community from diverse evils that afflict it. Such attempts to dismiss at once the accumulated sorrows of a people are by no means rare or exceptional; on the contrary they have been made in many lands, and from being occasional they tend to become periodic and annual.

It needs some effort on our part to realise the frame of mind which prompts these attempts. Bred in a philosophy which strips nature of personality and reduces it to the unknown cause of an orderly series of impressions on our senses, we find it hard to put ourselves in the place of the savage, to whom the same impressions appear in the guise of spirits or the handiwork of spirits. For ages the army of spirits, once so near, has been receding farther and farther from us, banished by the magic wand of science from hearth and home, from ruined cell and ivied tower, from haunted glade and lonely mere, from the riven murky cloud that belches forth the lightning, and from those fairer clouds that pillow the silver moon or fret with flakes of burning red the golden eve. The spirits are gone even from their last stronghold in the sky, whose blue arch no longer passes, except with children, for the screen that hides from mortal eyes the glories of the celestial world.   Only in poets' dreams or impassioned flights of oratory is it given to catch a glimpse of the last flutter of the standards of the retreating host, to hear the beat of their invisible wings, the sound of their mocking laughter, or the swell of angel music dying away in the distance.   Far otherwise is it with the savage.   To his imagination the world still teems with those motley beings whom a more sober philosophy has discarded. Fairies and goblins, ghosts and demons, still hover about him both waking and sleeping.   They dog his footsteps, dazzle his senses, enter into him, harass and deceive and torment him in a thousand freakish and mischievous ways.   The mishaps that befall him, the losses he sustains, the pains he has to endure, he commonly sets down, if not to the magic of his enemies, to the spite or anger or caprice of the spirits.   Their constant presence wearies him, their sleepless malignity exasperates him ; he longs with an unspeakable longing to be rid of them altogether, and from time to time, driven to bay, his patience utterly exhausted, he turns fiercely on his persecutors and makes a desperate effort to chase the whole pack of them from the land, to clear the air of their swarming multitudes, that he may breathe more freely and go on his way unmolested, at least for a time.   Thus it comes about that the endeavour of primitive people to make a clean sweep of all their troubles generally takes the form of a grand hunting out and expulsion of devils or ghosts.   They think that if they can only shake off these their accursed tormentors, they will make a fresh start in life, happy and innocent ; the tales of Eden and the old poetic golden age will come true again.

§ 2. *The Occasional Expulsion of Evils.*—We can therefore understand why those general clearances of evil, to which from time to time the savage resorts, should commonly take the form of a forcible expulsion of devils.   In these evil spirits primitive man sees the cause of many if not of most of his troubles, and he fancies that if he can only deliver himself from them, things will go better with him.   The public attempts to expel the accumulated ills of a whole community may be divided into two classes, according as the expelled evils are immaterial and invisible or are embodied in a material vehicle or scapegoat.   The former may be called the direct or immediate expulsion of evils ; the latter the indirect or mediate expulsion, or the expulsion by scapegoat.   We begin with examples of the former.

In the island of Rook, between New Guinea and New Britain, when any misfortune has happened, all the people run together, scream, curse, howl, and beat the air with sticks to drive away the devil, who is supposed to be the author of the mishap.   From the spot where the mishap took place they drive him step by step to the sea, and on reaching the shore they redouble their shouts and blows in order to expel him from the island.   He generally retires to the sea or to the island of Lottin.   The natives of New Britain ascribe sickness, drought, the failure of crops, and in short all misfortunes, to the influence of wicked spirits. So at times when many people sicken and die, as at the beginning of the rainy season, all the inhabitants of a district, armed with branches and clubs, go out by moonlight to the fields, where they beat and stamp on the ground with wild howls till morning, believing that this drives away the devils ; and for the same purpose they rush through the village with burning torches. The natives of New Caledonia are said to believe that all evils are caused by a powerful and malignant spirit ; hence in order to rid themselves of him they will from time to time dig a great pit, round which the whole tribe gathers. After cursing the demon, they fill up the pit with earth, and trample on the top with loud shouts. This they call burying the evil spirit. Among the Dieri tribe of Central Australia, when a serious illness occurs, the medicine-men expel Cootchie or the devil by beating the ground in and outside of the camp with the stuffed tail of a kangaroo, until they have chased the demon away to some distance from the camp.

When a village has been visited by a series of disasters or a severe epidemic, the inhabitants of Minahassa in Celebes lay the blame upon the devils who are infesting the village and who must be expelled from it. Accordingly, early one morning all the people, men, women, and children, quit their homes, carrying their household goods with them, and take up their quarters in temporary huts which have been erected outside the village. Here they spend several days, offering sacrifices and preparing for the final ceremony. At last the men, some wearing masks, others with their faces blackened, and so on, but all armed with swords, guns, pikes, or brooms, steal cautiously and silently back to the deserted village. Then, at a signal from the priest, they rush furiously up and down the streets and into and under the houses (which are raised on piles above the ground), yelling and striking on walls, doors, and windows, to drive away the devils. Next, the priests and the rest of the people come with the holy fire and march nine times round each house and thrice round the ladder that leads up to it, carrying the fire with them. Then they take the fire into the kitchen, where it must burn for three days continuously. The devils are now driven away, and great and general is the joy.

The Alfoors of Halmahera attribute epidemics to the devil who comes from other villages to carry them off. So, in order to rid the village of the disease, the sorcerer drives away the devil. From all the villagers he receives a costly garment and places it on four vessels, which he takes to the forest and leaves at the spot where the devil is supposed to be. Then with mocking words he bids the demon abandon the place. In the Kei Islands to the south-west of New Guinea, the evil spirits, who are quite distinct from the souls of the dead, form a mighty host. Almost every tree and every cave is the lodging-place of one of these fiends, who are moreover extremely irascible and apt to fly out on the smallest provocation. They manifest their displeasure by sending sickness and other calamities. Hence in times of public misfortune, as when an epidemic is raging, and all other remedies have failed, the whole population go forth with the priest at their head to a place at some distance from the village. Here at sunset they erect a couple of poles with a cross-bar between them, to which they attach bags of rice, wooden models of pivot-guns, gongs, bracelets, and so on. Then, when everybody has taken his place at the poles and a death-like silence reigns, the priest lifts up his voice and addresses the spirits in their own language as follows : " Ho ! ho ! ho ! ye evil spirits who dwell in the trees, ye evil spirits who live in the grottoes, ye evil spirits who lodge in the earth, we give you these pivot-guns, these gongs, etc. Let the sickness cease and not so many people die of it." Then everybody runs home as fast as their legs can carry them.

In the island of Nias, when a man is seriously ill and other remedies have been tried in vain, the sorcerer proceeds to exorcise the devil who is causing the illness. A pole is set up in front of the house, and from the top of the pole a rope of palm-leaves is stretched to the roof of the house. Then the sorcerer mounts the roof with a pig, which he kills and allows to roll from the roof to the ground. The devil, anxious to get the pig, lets himself down hastily from the roof by the rope of palm-leaves, and a good spirit, invoked by the sorcerer, prevents him from climbing up again. If this remedy fails, it is believed that other devils must still be lurking in the house. So a general hunt is made after them. All the doors and windows in the house are closed, except a single dormer-window in the roof. The men, shut up in the house, hew and slash with their swords right and left to the clash of gongs and the rub-a-dub of drums. Terrified at this onslaught, the devils escape by the dormer-window, and sliding down the rope of palm-leaves take themselves off. As all the doors and windows, except the one in the roof, are shut, the devils cannot get into the house again. In the case of an epidemic, the proceedings are similar. All the gates of the village, except one, are closed ; every voice is raised, every gong and drum beaten, every sword brandished. Thus the devils are driven out and the last gate is shut behind them. For eight days thereafter the village is in a state of siege, no one being allowed to enter it.

When cholera has broken out in a Burmese village the able-bodied men scramble on the roofs and lay about them with bamboos and billets of wood, while all the rest of the population, old and young, stand below and thump drums, blow trumpets, yell, scream, beat floors, walls, tin pans, everything to make a din. This uproar, repeated on three successive nights, is thought to be very effective in driving away the cholera demons. When smallpox first appeared amongst the Kumis of South-eastern India, they thought it was a devil come from Aracan. The villages were placed in a state of siege, no one being allowed to leave or enter them. A monkey was killed by being dashed on the ground, and its body was hung at the village gate. Its blood, mixed with small river pebbles, was sprinkled on the houses, the threshold of every house was swept with the monkey's tail, and the fiend was adjured to depart.

When an epidemic is raging on the Gold Coast of West Africa, the people will sometimes turn out, armed with clubs and torches, to drive the evil spirits away. At a given signal the whole population begin with frightful yells to beat in every corner of the houses, then rush like mad into the streets waving torches and striking frantically in the empty air. The uproar goes on till somebody reports that the cowed and daunted demons have made good their escape by a gate of the town or village ; the people stream out after them, pursue them for some distance into the forest, and warn them never to return. The expulsion of the devils is followed by a general massacre of all the cocks in the village or town, lest by their unseasonable crowing they should betray to the banished demons the direction they must take to return to their old homes. When sickness was prevalent in a Huron village, and all other remedies had been tried in vain, the Indians had recourse to the ceremony called *Lonouyroya*, " which is the principal invention and most proper means, so they say, to expel from the town or village the devils and evil spirits which cause, induce, and import all the maladies and infirmities which they suffer in body and mind." Accordingly, one evening the men would begin to rush like madmen about the village, breaking and upsetting whatever they came across in the wigwams. They threw fire and burning brands about the streets, and all night long they ran howling and singing without cessation. Then they all dreamed of something, a knife, dog, skin, or whatever it might be, and when morning came they went from wigwam to wigwam asking for presents. These they received silently, till the particular thing was given them which they had dreamed about. On receiving it they uttered a cry of joy and rushed from the hut, amid the congratulations of all present. The health of those who received what they had dreamed of was believed to be assured ; whereas those who did not get what they had set their hearts upon regarded their fate as sealed.

Sometimes, instead of chasing the demon of disease from their homes, savages prefer to leave him in peaceable possession, while they themselves take to flight and attempt to prevent him from following in their tracks. Thus when the Patagonians were attacked by small-pox, which they attributed to the machinations of an evil spirit, they used to abandon their sick and flee, slashing the air with their weapons and throwing water about in order to keep off the dreadful pursuer ; and when after several days' march they reached a place where they hoped to be beyond his reach, they used by way of precaution to plant all their cutting weapons with the sharp edges turned towards the quarter from which they had come, as if they were repelling a charge of cavalry. Similarly, when the Lules or Tonocotes Indians of the Gran Chaco were attacked by an epidemic, they regularly sought to evade it by flight, but in so doing they always followed a sinuous, not a straight, course ; because they said that when the disease made after them he would be so exhausted by the turnings and windings of the route that he would never be able to come up with them.   When the Indians of New Mexico were decimated by smallpox or other infectious disease, they used to shift their quarters every day, retreating into the most sequestered parts of the mountains and choosing the thorniest thickets they could find, in the hope that the smallpox would be too afraid of scratching himself on the thorns to follow them.   When some Chins on a visit to Rangoon were attacked by cholera, they went about with drawn swords to scare away the demon, and they spent the day hiding under bushes so that he might not be able to find them.

§ 3. *The Periodic Expulsion of Evils.*—The expulsion of evils, from being occasional, tends to become periodic.   It comes to be thought desirable to have a general riddance of evil spirits at fixed times, usually once a year, in order that the people may make a fresh start in life, freed from all the malignant influences which have been long accumulating about them.   Some of the Australian blacks annually expelled the ghosts of the dead from their territory.   The ceremony was witnessed by the Rev. W. Ridley on the banks of the River Barwan. " A chorus of twenty, old and young, were singing and beating time with boomerangs. . . . Suddenly, from under a sheet of bark darted a man with his body whitened by pipeclay, his head and face coloured with lines of red and yellow, and a tuft of feathers fixed by means of a stick two feet above the crown of his head.   He stood twenty minutes perfectly still, gazing upwards.   An aboriginal who stood by told me he was looking for the ghosts of dead men.   At last he began to move very slowly, and soon rushed to and fro at full speed, flourishing a branch as if to drive away some foes invisible to us.   When I thought this pantomime must be almost over, ten more, similarly adorned, suddenly appeared from behind the trees, and the whole party joined in a brisk conflict with their mysterious assailants. . . . At last, after some rapid evolutions in which they put forth all their strength, they rested from the exciting toil which they had kept up all night and for some hours after sunrise ; they seemed satisfied that the ghosts were driven away for twelve months.   They were performing the same ceremony at every station along the river, and I am told it is an annual custom."

Certain seasons of the year mark themselves naturally out as appropriate moments for a general expulsion of devils.   Such a moment occurs towards the close of an Arctic winter, when the sun reappears on the horizon after an absence of weeks or months.   Accordingly, at Point Barrow, the most northerly extremity of Alaska, and nearly of America, the Esquimaux choose the moment of the sun's reappearance to hunt the mischievous spirit Tuña from every house. The ceremony was witnessed by the members of the United States Polar Expedition, who wintered at Point Barrow.   A fire was built in front of the council-house, and an old woman was posted at the entrance to every house.   The men gathered round the council-house, while the young women and girls drove the spirit out of every house with their knives, stabbing viciously under the bunk and deer-skins, and calling upon Tuña to be gone. When they thought he had been driven out of every hole and corner, they thrust him down through the hole in the floor and chased him into the open air with loud cries and frantic gestures. Meanwhile the old woman at the entrance of the house made passes with a long knife in the air to keep him from returning. Each party drove the spirit towards the fire and invited him to go into it. All were by this time drawn up in a semicircle round the fire, when several of the leading men made specific charges against the spirit ; and each after his speech brushed his clothes violently, calling on the spirit to leave him and go into the fire. Two men now stepped forward with rifles loaded with blank cartridges, while a third brought a vessel of urine and flung it on the flames. At the same time one of the men fired a shot into the fire ; and as the cloud of steam rose it received the other shot, which was supposed to finish Tuña for the time being.

In late autumn, when storms rage over the land and break the icy fetters by which the frozen sea is as yet but slightly bound, when the loosened floes are driven against each other and break with loud crashes, and when the cakes of ice are piled in wild disorder one upon another, the Esquimaux of Baffin Land fancy they hear the voices of the spirits who people the mischief-laden air. Then the ghosts of the dead knock wildly at the huts, which they cannot enter, and woe to the hapless wight whom they catch ; he soon sickens and dies. Then the phantom of a huge hairless dog pursues the real dogs, which expire in convulsions and cramps at sight of him. All the countless spirits of evil are abroad, striving to bring sickness and death, foul weather and failure in hunting on the Esquimaux. Most dreaded of all these spectral visitants are Sedna, mistress of the nether world, and her father, to whose share dead Esquimaux fall. While the other spirits fill the air and the water, she rises from under ground. It is then a busy season for the wizards. In every house you may hear them singing and praying, while they conjure the spirits, seated in a mystic gloom at the back of the hut, which is dimly lit by a lamp burning low. The hardest task of all is to drive away Sedna, and this is reserved for the most powerful enchanter. A rope is coiled on the floor of a large hut in such a way as to leave a small opening at the top, which represents the breathing hole of a seal. Two enchanters stand beside it, one of them grasping a spear as if he were watching a seal-hole in winter, the other holding the harpoon-line. A third sorcerer sits at the back of the hut chanting a magic song to lure Sedna to the spot. Now she is heard approaching under the floor of the hut, breathing heavily ; now she emerges at the hole ; now she is harpooned and sinks away in angry haste, dragging the harpoon with her, while the two men hold on to the line with all their might. The struggle is severe, but at last by a desperate wrench she tears herself away and returns to her dwelling in Adlivun. When the harpoon is drawn up out of the hole it is found to be splashed with blood, which the enchanters proudly exhibit as a proof of their prowess. Thus Sedna and the other evil spirits are at last driven away, and next day a great festival is celebrated by old and young in honour of the event. But they must still be cautious, for the wounded Sedna is furious and will seize any one she may find outside of his hut ; so they all wear amulets on the top of their hoods to protect themselves against her. These amulets consist of pieces of the first garments that they wore after birth.

The Iroquois inaugurated the new year in January, February, or March (the time varied) with a " festival of dreams " like that which the Hurons observed on special occasions. The whole ceremonies lasted several days, or even weeks, and formed a kind of saturnalia. Men and women, variously disguised, went from wigwam to wigwam smashing and throwing down whatever they came across. It was a time of general license ; the people were supposed to be out of their senses, and therefore not to be responsible for what they did. Accordingly, many seized the opportunity of paying off old scores by belabouring obnoxious persons, drenching them with ice-cold water, and covering them with filth or hot ashes. Others seized burning brands or coals and flung them at the heads of the first persons they met. The only way of escaping from these persecutors was to guess what they had dreamed of. On one day of the festival the ceremony of driving away evil spirits from the village took place. Men clothed in the skins of wild beasts, their faces covered with hideous masks, and their hands with the shell of the tortoise, went from hut to hut making frightful noises ; in every hut they took the fuel from the fire and scattered the embers and ashes about the floor with their hands. The general confession of sins which preceded the festival was probably a preparation for the public expulsion of evil influences ; it was a way of stripping the people of their moral burdens, that these might be collected and cast out.

In September the Incas of Peru celebrated a festival called Situa, the object of which was to banish from the capital and its vicinity all disease and trouble. The festival fell in September because the rains begin about this time, and with the first rains there was generally much sickness. As a preparation for the festival the people fasted on the first day of the moon after the autumnal equinox. Having fasted during the day, and the night being come, they baked a coarse paste of maize. This paste was made of two sorts. One was kneaded with the blood of children aged from five to ten years, the blood being obtained by bleeding the children between the eyebrows. These two kinds of paste were baked separately, because they were for different uses. Each family assembled at the house of the eldest brother to celebrate the feast ; and those who had no elder brother went to the house of their next relation of greater age. On the same night all who had fasted during the day washed their bodies, and taking a little of the blood-kneaded paste, rubbed it over their head, face, breast, shoulders, arms, and legs. They did this in order that the paste might take away all their infirmities. After this the head of the family anointed the threshold with the same paste, and left it there as a token that the inmates of the house had performed their ablutions and cleansed their bodies. Meantime the High Priest performed the same ceremonies in the temple of the Sun. As soon as the Sun rose, all the people worshipped and besought him to drive all evils out of the city, and then they broke their fast with the paste that had been kneaded without blood. When they had paid their worship and broken their fast, which they did at a stated hour, in order that all might adore the Sun as one man, an Inca of the blood royal came forth from the fortress, as a messenger of the Sun, richly dressed, with his mantle girded round his body, and a lance in his hand. The lance was decked with feathers of many hues, extending from the blade to the socket, and fastened with rings of gold. He ran down the hill from the fortress brandishing his lance, till he reached the centre of the great square, where stood the golden urn, like a fountain, that was used for the sacrifice of the fermented juice of the maize. Here four other Incas of the blood royal awaited him, each with a lance in his hand, and his mantle girded up to run. The messenger touched their four lances with his lance, and told them that the Sun bade them, as his messengers, drive the evils out of the city. The four Incas then separated and ran down the four royal roads which led out of the city to the four quarters of the world. While they ran, all the people, great and small, came to the doors of their houses, and with great shouts of joy and gladness shook their clothes, as if they were shaking off dust, while they cried, " Let the evils be gone. How greatly desired has this festival been by us. O Creator of all things, permit us to reach another year, that we may see another feast like this." After they had shaken their clothes, they passed their hands over their heads, faces, arms, and legs, as if in the act of washing. All this was done to drive the evils out of their houses, that the messengers of the Sun might banish them from the city ; and it was done not only in the streets through which the Incas ran, but generally in all quarters of the city. Moreover, they all danced, the Inca himself amongst them, and bathed in the rivers and fountains, saying that their maladies would come out of them. Then they took great torches of straw, bound round with cords. These they lighted, and passed from one to the other, striking each other with them, and saying, " Let all harm go away." Meanwhile the runners ran with their lances for a quarter of a league outside the city, where they found four other Incas ready, who received the lances from their hands and ran with them. Thus the lances were carried by relays of runners for a distance of five or six leagues, at the end of which the runners washed themselves and their weapons in rivers, and set up the lances, in sign of a boundary within which the banished evils might not return.

The negroes of Guinea annually banish the devil from all their towns with much ceremony at a time set apart for the purpose. At Axim, on the Gold Coast, this annual expulsion is preceded by a feast of eight days, during which mirth and jollity, skipping, dancing, and singing prevail, and " a perfect lampooning liberty is allowed, and scandal so highly exalted, that they may freely sing of all the faults, villanies, and frauds of their superiors as well as inferiors, without punishment, or so much as the least interruption." On the eighth day they hunt out the devil with a dismal cry, running after him and pelting him with sticks, stones, and whatever comes to hand. When they have driven him far enough out of the town, they all return. In this way he is expelled from more than a hundred towns at the same time. To make sure that he does not return to their houses, the women wash and scour all their wooden and earthen vessels, " to free them from all uncleanness and the devil."

At Cape Coast Castle, on the Gold Coast, the ceremony was witnessed on the ninth of October 1844 by an Englishman, who has described it as follows : " To-night the annual custom of driving the evil spirit, Abonsam, out of the town has taken place. As soon as the eight o'clock gun fired in the fort the people began firing muskets in their houses, turning all their furniture out of doors, beating about in every corner of the rooms with sticks, etc., and screaming as loudly as possible, in order to frighten the devil. Being driven out of the houses, as they imagine, they sallied forth into the streets, throwing lighted torches about, shouting, screaming, beating sticks together, rattling old pans, making the most horrid noise, in order to drive him out of the town into the sea. The custom is preceded by four weeks' dead silence ; no gun is allowed to be fired, no drum to be beaten, no palaver to be made between man and man. If, during these weeks, two natives should disagree and make a noise in the town, they are immediately taken before the king and fined heavily. If a dog or pig, sheep or goat be found at large in the street, it may be killed, or taken by anyone, the former owner not being allowed to demand any compensation. This silence is designed to deceive Abonsam, that, being off his guard, he may be taken by surprise, and frightened out of the place. If anyone die during the silence, his relatives are not allowed to weep until the four weeks have been completed."

Sometimes the date of the annual expulsion of devils is fixed with reference to the agricultural seasons. Thus among the Hos of Togoland, in West Africa, the expulsion is performed annually before the people partake of the new yams. The chiefs summon the priests and magicians and tell them that the people are now to eat the new yams and be merry, therefore they must cleanse the town and remove the evils. Accordingly the evil spirits, witches, and all the ills that infest the people are conjured into bundles of leaves and creepers, fastened to poles, which are carried away and set up in the earth on various roads outside the town. During the following night no fire may be lit and no food eaten. Next morning the women sweep out their hearths and houses, and deposit the sweepings on broken wooden plates. Then the people pray, saying, " All ye sicknesses that are in our body and plague us, we are come to-day to throw you out." Thereupon they run as fast as they can in the direction of Mount Adaklu, smiting their mouths and screaming, "Out to-day! Out to-day! That which kills anybody, out to-day! Ye evil spirits, out to-day! and all that causes our heads to ache, out to-day! Anlo and Adaklu are the places whither all ill shall betake itself!" When they have come to a certain tree on Mount Adaklu, they throw everything away and return home.

At Kiriwina, in South-eastern New Guinea, when the new yams had been harvested, the people feasted and danced for many days, and a great deal of property, such as armlets, native money, and so forth, was displayed conspicuously on a platform erected for the purpose. When the festivities were over, all the people gathered together and expelled the spirits from the village by shouting, beating the posts of the houses, and overturning everything under which a wily spirit might be supposed to lurk. The explanation which the people gave to a missionary was that they had entertained and feasted the spirits and provided them with riches, and it was now time for them to take their departure. Had they not seen the dances, and heard the songs, and gorged themselves on the souls of the yams, and appropriated the souls of the money and all the other fine things set out on the platform? What more could the spirits want? So out they must go.

Among the Hos of North-eastern India the great festival of the year is the harvest home, held in January, when the granaries are full of grain, and the people, to use their own expression, are full of devilry. "They have a strange notion that at this period, men and women are so overcharged with vicious propensities, that it is absolutely necessary for the safety of the person to let off steam by allowing for a time full vent to the passions." The ceremonies open with a sacrifice to the village god of three fowls, a cock and two hens, one of which must be black. Along with them are offered flowers of the Palas tree (*Butea frondosa*), bread made from rice-flour, and sesamum seeds. These offerings are presented by the village priest, who prays that during the year about to begin they and their children may be preserved from all misfortune and sickness, and that they may have seasonable rain and good crops. Prayer is also made in some places for the souls of the dead. At this time an evil spirit is supposed to infest the place, and to get rid of it men, women, and children go in procession round and through every part of the village with sticks in their hands, as if beating for game, singing a wild chant, and shouting vociferously, till they feel assured that the evil spirit must have fled. Then they give themselves up to feasting and drinking rice-beer, till they are in a fit state for the wild debauch which follows. The festival now "becomes a saturnale, during which servants forget their duty to their masters, children their reverence for parents, men their respect for women, and women all notions of modesty, delicacy, and gentleness; they become raging bacchantes." Usually the Hos are quiet and reserved in manner, decorous and gentle to women. But during this festival "their natures appear to undergo a temporary change. Sons and daughters revile their parents in gross language, and parents their children ; men and women become almost like animals in the indulgence of their amorous propensities.'' The Mundaris, kinsmen and neighbours of the Hos, keep the festival in much the same manner. " The resemblance to a Saturnale is very complete, as at this festival the farm labourers are feasted by their masters, and allowed the utmost freedom of speech in addressing them.   It is the festival of the harvest home ; the termination of one year's toil, and a slight respite from it before they commence again.''

Amongst some of the Hindoo Koosh tribes, as among the Hos and Mundaris, the expulsion of devils takes place after harvest.   When the last crop of autumn has been got in, it is thought necessary to drive away evil spirits from the granaries.   A kind of porridge is eaten, and the head of the family takes his matchlock and fires it into the floor.   Then, going outside, he sets to work loading and firing till his powder-horn is exhausted, while all his neighbours are similarly employed.   The next day is spent in rejoicings.   In Chitral this festival is called " devil-driving.''   On the other hand the Khonds of India expel the devils at seed-time instead of at harvest.   At this time they worship Pitteri Pennu, the god of increase and of gain in every shape.   On the first day of the festival a rude car is made of a basket set upon a few sticks, tied upon bamboo rollers for wheels. The priest takes this car first to the house of the lineal head of the tribe, to whom precedence is given in all ceremonies connected with agriculture.   Here he receives a little of each kind of seed and some feathers.   He then takes the car to all the other houses in the village, each of which contributes the same things.   Lastly, the car is conducted to a field without the village, attended by all the young men, who beat each other and strike the air violently with long sticks. The seed thus carried out is called the share of the " evil spirits, spoilers of the seed.''   " These are considered to be driven out with the car ; and when it and its contents are abandoned to them, they are held to have no excuse for interfering with the rest of the seed-corn.''

The people of Bali, an island to the east of Java, have periodical expulsions of devils upon a great scale.   Generally the time chosen for the expulsion is the day of the " dark moon '' in the ninth month. When the demons have been long unmolested the country is said to be " warm,'' and the priest issues orders to expel them by force, lest the whole of Bali should be rendered uninhabitable.   On the day appointed the people of the village or district assemble at the principal temple. Here at a cross-road offerings are set out for the devils.   After prayers have been recited by the priests, the blast of a horn summons the devils to partake of the meal which has been prepared for them.   At the same time a number of men step forward and light their torches at the holy lamp which burns before the chief priest.   Immediately afterwards, followed by the bystanders, they spread in all directions and march through the streets and lanes crying, " Depart ! go away ! '' Wherever they pass, the people who have stayed at home hasten, by a deafening clatter on doors, beams, rice-blocks, and so forth, to take their share in the expulsion of devils. Thus chased from the houses, the fiends flee to the banquet which has been set out for them ; but here the priest receives them with curses which finally drive them from the district. When the last devil has taken his departure, the uproar is succeeded by a dead silence, which lasts during the next day also. The devils, it is thought, are anxious to return to their old homes, and in order to make them think that Bali is not Bali but some desert island, no one may stir from his own abode for twenty-four hours. Even ordinary household work, including cooking, is discontinued. Only the watchmen may show themselves in the streets. Wreaths of thorns and leaves are hung at all the entrances to warn strangers from entering. Not till the third day is this state of siege raised, and even then it is forbidden to work at the rice-fields or to buy and sell in the market. Most people still stay at home, whiling away the time with cards and dice.

In Tonquin a *theckydaw* or general expulsion of malevolent spirits commonly took place once a year, especially if there was a great mortality amongst men, the elephants or horses of the general's stable, or the cattle of the country, " the cause of which they attribute to the malicious spirits of such men as have been put to death for treason, rebellion, and conspiring the death of the king, general, or princes, and that in revenge of the punishment they have suffered, they are bent to destroy everything and commit horrible violence. To prevent which their superstition has suggested to them the institution of this *theckydaw*, as a proper means to drive the devil away, and purge the country of evil spirits." The day appointed for the ceremony was generally the twenty-fifth of February, one month after the beginning of the new year, which fell on the twenty-fifth of January. The intermediate month was a season of feasting, merry-making of all kinds, and general license. During the whole month the great seal was kept shut up in a box, face downwards, and the law was, as it were, laid asleep. All courts of justice were closed ; debtors could not be seized ; small crimes, such as petty larceny, fighting, and assault, escaped with impunity ; only treason and murder were taken account of and the malefactors detained till the great seal should come into operation again. At the close of the saturnalia the wicked spirits were driven away. Great masses of troops and artillery having been drawn up with flying colours and all the pomp of war, " the general beginneth then to offer meat offerings to the criminal devils and malevolent spirits (for it is usual and customary likewise amongst them to feast the condemned before their execution), inviting them to eat and drink, when presently he accuses them in a strange language, by characters and figures, etc., of many offences and crimes committed by them, as to their having disquieted the land, killed his elephants and horses, etc., for all which they justly deserve to be chastised and banished the country. Whereupon three great guns are fired as the last signal ; upon which all the artillery and musquets are discharged, that, by their most terrible noise the devils may be driven away ; and they are so blind as to believe for certain, that they really and effectually put them to flight."

In Cambodia the expulsion of evil spirits took place in March. Bits of broken statues and stones, considered as the abode of the demons, were collected and brought to the capital. Here as many elephants were collected as could be got together. On the evening of the full moon volleys of musketry were fired and the elephants charged furiously to put the devils to flight. The ceremony was performed on three successive days. In Siam the banishment of demons is annually carried into effect on the last day of the old year. A signal gun is fired from the palace ; it is answered from the next station, and so on from station to station, till the firing has reached the outer gate of the city. Thus the demons are driven out step by step. As soon as this is done a consecrated rope is fastened round the circuit of the city walls to prevent the banished demons from returning. The rope is made of tough couch-grass and is painted in alternate stripes of red, yellow, and blue.

Annual expulsions of demons, witches, or evil influences appear to have been common among the heathen of Europe, if we may judge from the relics of such customs among their descendants at the present day. Thus among the heathen Wotyaks, a Finnish people of Eastern Russia, all the young girls of the village assemble on the last day of the year or on New Year's Day, armed with sticks, the ends of which are split in nine places. With these they beat every corner of the house and yard, saying, " We are driving Satan out of the village." Afterwards the sticks are thrown into the river below the village, and as they float down stream Satan goes with them to the next village, from which he must be driven out in turn. In some villages the expulsion is managed otherwise. The unmarried men receive from every house in the village groats, flesh, and brandy. These they take to the fields, light a fire under a fir-tree, boil the groats, and eat of the food they have brought with them, after pronouncing the words, " Go away into the wilderness, come not into the house." Then they return to the village and enter every house where there are young women. They take hold of the young women and throw them into the snow, saying, " May the spirits of disease leave you." The remains of the groats and the other food are then distributed among all the houses in proportion to the amount that each con-tributed, and each family consumes its share. According to a Wotyak of the Malmyz district the young men throw into the snow whomever they find in the houses, and this is called " driving out Satan " ; moreover, some of the boiled groats are cast into the fire with the words, " O god, afflict us not with sickness and pestilence, give us not up as a prey to the spirits of the wood." But the most antique form of the ceremony is that observed by the Wotyaks of the Kasan Government. First of all a sacrifice is offered to the Devil at noon. Then all the men assemble on horseback in the centre of the village, and decide with which house they shall begin. When this question, which often gives rise to hot disputes, is settled, they tether their horses to the paling, and arm themselves with whips, clubs of lime-wood, and bundles of lighted twigs. The lighted twigs are believed to have the greatest terrors for Satan. Thus armed, they proceed with frightful cries to beat every corner of the house and yard, then shut the door, and spit at the ejected fiend. So they go from house to house, till the Devil has been driven from every one. Then they mount their horses and ride out of the village, yelling wildly and brandishing their clubs in every direction. Outside of the village they fling away the clubs and spit once more at the Devil. The Cheremiss, another Finnish people of Eastern Russia, chase Satan from their dwellings by beating the walls with cudgels of lime-wood. For the same purpose they fire guns, stab the ground with knives, and insert burning chips of wood in the crevices. Also they leap over bonfires, shaking out their garments as they do so ; and in some districts they blow on long trumpets of lime-tree bark to frighten him away. When he has fled to the wood, they pelt the trees with some of the cheese-cakes and eggs which furnished the feast.

In Christian Europe the old heathen custom of expelling the powers of evil at certain times of the year has survived to modern times. Thus in some villages of Calabria the month of March is inaugurated with the expulsion of the witches. It takes place at night to the sound of the church bells, the people running about the streets and crying, " March is come." They say that the witches roam about in March, and the ceremony is repeated every Friday evening during the month. Often, as might have been anticipated, the ancient pagan rite has attached itself to church festivals. In Albania on Easter Eve the young people light torches of resinous wood and march in procession, swinging them, through the village. At last they throw the torches into the river, crying, " Ha, Kore ! we throw you into the river, like these torches, that you may never return." Silesian peasants believe that on Good Friday the witches go their rounds and have great power for mischief. Hence about Oels, near Strehlitz, the people on that day arm themselves with old brooms and drive the witches from house and home, from farmyard and cattle-stall, making a great uproar and clatter as they do so.

In Central Europe the favourite time for expelling the witches is, or was, Walpurgis Night, the Eve of May Day, when the baleful powers of these mischievous beings were supposed to be at their height. In the Tyrol, for example, as in other places, the expulsion of the powers of evil at this season goes by the name of " Burning out the Witches." It takes place on May Day, but people have been busy with their preparations for days before. On a Thursday at midnight bundles are made up of resinous splinters, black and red spotted hemlock, caperspurge, rosemary, and twigs of the sloe. These are kept and burned on May Day by men who must first have received plenary absolution from the Church. On the last three days of April all the houses are cleansed and fumigated with juniper berries and rue. On May Day, when the evening bell has rung and the twilight is falling, the ceremony of " Burning out the Witches " begins. Men and boys make a racket with whips, bells, pots, and pans ; the women carry censers ; the dogs are unchained and run barking and yelping about. As soon as the church bells begin to ring, the bundles of twigs, fastened on poles, are set on fire and the incense is ignited. Then all the house-bells and dinner-bells are rung, pots and pans are clashed, dogs bark, every one must make a noise. And amid this hubbub all scream at the pitch of their voices :

> " *Witch flee, flee from here, or it will go ill with thee.*"

Then they run seven times round the houses, the yards, and the village. So the witches are smoked out of their lurking-places and driven away. The custom of expelling the witches on Walpurgis Night is still, or was down to recent years, observed in many parts of Bavaria and among the Germans of Bohemia. Thus in the Böhmerwald Mountains all the young fellows of the village assemble after sunset on some height, especially at a cross-road, and crack whips for a while in unison with all their strength. This drives away the witches ; for so far as the sound of the whips is heard, these maleficent beings can do no harm. In some places, while the young men are cracking their whips, the herdsmen wind their horns, and the long-drawn notes, heard far off in the silence of night, are very effectual for banning the witches.

Another witching time is the period of twelve days between Christmas and Epiphany. Hence in some parts of Silesia the people burn pine-resin all night long between Christmas and the New Year in order that the pungent smoke may drive witches and evil spirits far away from house and homestead ; and on Christmas Eve and New Year's Eve they fire shots over fields and meadows, into shrubs and trees, and wrap straw round the fruit-trees, to prevent the spirits from doing them harm. On New Year's Eve, which is Saint Sylvester's Day, Bohemian lads, armed with guns, form themselves into circles and fire thrice into the air. This is called " Shooting the Witches " and is supposed to frighten the witches away. The last of the mystic twelve days is Epiphany or Twelfth Night, and it has been selected as a proper season for the expulsion of the powers of evil in various parts of Europe. Thus at Brunnen, on the Lake of Lucerne, boys go about in procession on Twelfth Night carrying torches and making a great noise with horns, bells, whips, and so forth to frighten away two female spirits of the wood, Strudeli and Strätteli. The people think that if they do not make enough noise there will be little fruit that year. Again, in Labruguière, a canton of southern France, on the eve of Twelfth Day the people run through the streets, jangling bells, clattering kettles, and doing everything to make a discordant noise. Then by the light of torches and blazing faggots they set up a prodigious hue and cry, an ear-splitting uproar, hoping thereby to chase all the wandering ghosts and devils from the town.

CHAPTER LVII

PUBLIC SCAPEGOATS

§ 1. *The Expulsion of Embodied Evils.*—Thus far we have dealt with that class of the general expulsion of evils which I have called direct or immediate. In this class the evils are invisible, at least to common eyes, and the mode of deliverance consists for the most part in beating the empty air and raising such a hubbub as may scare the mischievous spirits and put them to flight. It remains to illustrate the second class of expulsions, in which the evil influences are embodied in a visible form or are at least supposed to be loaded upon a material medium, which acts as a vehicle to draw them off from the people, village, or town.

The Pomos of California celebrate an expulsion of devils every seven years, at which the devils are represented by disguised men. " Twenty or thirty men array themselves in harlequin rig and barbaric paint, and put vessels of pitch on their heads ; then they secretly go out into the surrounding mountains. These are to personify the devils. A herald goes up to the top of the assembly-house, and makes a speech to the multitude. At a signal agreed upon in the evening the masqueraders come in from the mountains, with the vessels of pitch flaming on their heads, and with all the frightful accessories of noise, motion, and costume which the savage mind can devise in representation of demons. The terrified women and children flee for life, the men huddle them inside a circle, and, on the principle of fighting the devil with fire, they swing blazing firebrands in the air, yell, whoop, and make frantic dashes at the marauding and bloodthirsty devils, so creating a terrific spectacle, and striking great fear into the hearts of the assembled hundreds of women, who are screaming and fainting and clinging to their valorous protectors. Finally the devils succeed in getting into the assembly-house, and the bravest of the men enter and hold a parley with them. As a conclusion of the whole farce, the men summon courage, the devils are expelled from the assembly-house, and with a prodigious row and racket of sham fighting are chased away into the mountains." In spring, as soon as the willow-leaves were full grown on the banks of the river, the Mandan Indians celebrated their great annual festival, one of the features of which was the expulsion of the devil. A man, painted black to represent the devil, entered the village from the prairie, chased and frightened the women, and acted the part of a buffalo bull in the buffalo dance, the object of which was to ensure a plentiful supply of buffaloes during the ensuing year. Finally he was chased from the village, the women pursuing him with hisses and gibes, beating him with sticks, and pelting him with dirt.

Some of the native tribes of Central Queensland believe in a noxious being called Molonga, who prowls unseen and would kill men and violate women if certain ceremonies were not performed. These ceremonies last for five nights and consist of dances, in which only men, fantastically painted and adorned, take part. On the fifth night Molonga himself, personified by a man tricked out with red ochre and feathers and carrying a long feather-tipped spear, rushes forth from the darkness at the spectators and makes as if he would run them through. Great is the excitement, loud are the shrieks and shouts, but after another feigned attack the demon vanishes in the gloom. On the last night of the year the palace of the Kings of Cambodia is purged of devils. Men painted as fiends are chased by elephants about the palace courts. When they have been expelled, a consecrated thread of cotton is stretched round the palace to keep them out. In Munzerabad, a district of Mysore in Southern India, when cholera or smallpox has broken out in a parish, the inhabitants assemble and conjure the demon of the disease into a wooden image, which they carry, generally at midnight, into the next parish. The inhabitants of that parish in like manner pass the image on to their neighbours, and thus the demon is expelled from one village after another, until he comes to the bank of a river into which he is finally thrown.

Oftener, however, the expelled demons are not represented at all, but are understood to be present invisibly in the material and visible vehicle which conveys them away. . Here, again, it will be convenient to distinguish between occasional and periodical expulsions. We begin with the former.

§ 2. *The Occasional Expulsion of Evils in a Material Vehicle.*— The vehicle which conveys away the demons may be of various kinds. A common one is a little ship or boat. Thus, in the southern district of the island of Ceram, when a whole village suffers from sickness, a small ship is made and filled with rice, tobacco, eggs, and so forth, which have been contributed by all the people. A little sail is hoisted on the ship. When all is ready, a man calls out in a very loud voice, " O all ye sicknesses, ye smallpoxes, agues, measles, etc., who have visited us so long and wasted us so sorely, but who now cease to plague us, we have made ready this ship for you, and we have furnished you with provender sufficient for the voyage. Ye shall have no lack of food nor of betel-leaves nor of areca nuts nor of tobacco. Depart, and sail away from us directly ; never come near us again ; but go to a land which is far from here. Let all the tides and winds waft you speedily thither, and so convey you thither that for the time to come we may live sound and well, and that we may never see the sun rise on you again." Then ten or twelve men carry the vessel to the shore, and let it drift away with the land-breeze, feeling convinced that they are free from sickness for ever, or at least till the next time. If sickness attacks them again, they are sure it is not the same sickness, but a different one, which in due time they dismiss in the same manner. When the demon-laden bark is lost to sight, the bearers return to the village, whereupon a man cries out, " The sicknesses are now gone, vanished, expelled, and sailed away." At this all the people come running out of their houses, passing the word from one to the other with great joy, beating on gongs and on tinkling instruments.

Similar ceremonies are commonly resorted to in other East Indian islands. Thus in Timor-laut, to mislead the demons who are causing sickness, a small proa, containing the image of a man and provisioned for a long voyage, is allowed to drift away with wind and tide. As it is being launched, the people cry, " O sickness, go from here ; turn back ; what do you here in this poor land ? " Three days after this ceremony a pig is killed, and part of the flesh is offered to Dudilaa, who lives in the sun. One of the oldest men says, " Old sir, I beseech you make well the grand-children, children, women, and men, that we may be able to eat pork and rice and to drink palm-wine. I will keep my promise. Eat your share, and make all the people in the village well." If the proa is stranded at any inhabited spot, the sickness will break out there. Hence a stranded proa excites much alarm amongst the coast population, and they immediately burn it, because demons fly from fire. In the island of Buru the proa which carries away the demons of disease is about twenty feet long, rigged out with sails, oars, anchor, and so on, and well stocked with provisions. For a day and a night the people beat gongs and drums, and rush about to frighten the demons. Next morning ten stalwart young men strike the people with branches, which have been pre-viously dipped in an earthen pot of water. As soon as they have done so, they run down to the beach, put the branches on board the proa, launch another boat in great haste, and tow the disease-burdened bark far out to sea. There they cast it off, and one of them calls out, " Grandfather Smallpox, go away—go willingly away—go visit another land ; we have made you food ready for the voyage, we have now nothing more to give." When they have landed, all the people bathe together in the sea. In this ceremony the reason for striking the people with the branches is clearly to rid them of the disease-demons, which are then supposed to be transferred to the branches. Hence the haste with which the branches are deposited in the proa and towed away to sea. So in the inland districts of Ceram, when smallpox or other sickness is raging, the priest strikes all the houses with consecrated branches, which are then thrown into the river, to be carried down to the sea : exactly as amongst the Wotyaks of Russia the sticks which have been used for expelling the devils from the village are thrown into the river, that the current may sweep the baleful burden away. The plan of putting puppets in the boat to represent sick persons, in order to lure the demons after them, is not uncommon. For example, most of the pagan tribes on the coast of Borneo seek to drive away epidemic disease as follows. They carve one or more rough human images from the pith of the sago palm and place them on a small raft or boat or full-rigged Malay ship together with rice and other food. The boat is decked with blossoms of the areca palm and with ribbons made from its leaves, and thus adorned the little craft is allowed to float out to sea with the ebb-tide, bearing, as the people fondly think or hope, the sickness away with it.

Often the vehicle which carries away the collected demons or ills of a whole community is an animal or scapegoat. In the Central Provinces of India, when cholera breaks out in a village, every one retires after sunset to his house. The priests then parade the streets, taking from the roof of each house a straw, which is burnt with an offering of rice, ghee, and turmeric, at some shrine to the east of the village. Chickens daubed with vermilion are driven away in the direction of the smoke, and are believed to carry the disease with them. If they fail, goats are tried, and last of all pigs. When cholera rages among the Bhars, Mallans, and Kurmis of India, they take a goat or a buffalo—in either case the animal must be a female, and as black as possible—then having tied some grain, cloves, and red lead in a yellow cloth on its back they turn it out of the village. The animal is conducted beyond the boundary and not allowed to return. Sometimes the buffalo is marked with a red pigment and driven to the next village, where he carries the plague with him.

Amongst the Dinkas, a pastoral people of the White Nile, each family possesses a sacred cow. When the country is threatened with war, famine, or any other public calamity, the chiefs of the village require a particular family to surrender their sacred cow to serve as a scapegoat. The animal is driven by the women to the brink of the river and across it to the other bank, there to wander in the wilderness and fall a prey to ravening beasts. Then the women return in silence and without looking behind them; were they to cast a backward glance, they imagine that the ceremony would have no effect. In 1857, when the Aymara Indians of Bolivia and Peru were suffering from a plague, they loaded a black llama with the clothes of the plague-stricken people, sprinkled brandy on the clothes, and then turned the animal loose on the mountains, hoping that it would carry the pest away with it.

Occasionally the scapegoat is a man. For example, from time to time the gods used to warn the King of Uganda that his foes the Banyoro were working magic against him and his people to make them die of disease. To avert such a catastrophe the king would send a scapegoat to the frontier of Bunyoro, the land of the enemy. The scapegoat consisted of either a man and a boy or a woman and her child, chosen because of some mark or bodily defect, which the gods had noted and by which the victims were to be recognised. With the human victims were sent a cow, a goat, a fowl, and a dog; and a strong guard escorted them to the land which the god had indicated. There the limbs of the victims were broken and they were left to die a lingering death in the enemy's country, being too crippled to crawl back to Uganda. The disease or plague was thought to have been thus transferred to the victims and to have been conveyed back in their persons to the land from which it came.

Some of the aboriginal tribes of China, as a protection against pestilence, select a man of great muscular strength to act the part of scapegoat. Having besmeared his face with paint, he performs many antics with the view of enticing all pestilential and noxious influences to attach themselves to him only. He is assisted by a priest. Finally the scapegoat, hotly pursued by men and women beating gongs and tom-toms, is driven with great haste out of the town or village. In the Punjaub a cure for the murrain is to hire a man of the Chamar caste, turn his face away from the village, brand him with a red-hot sickle, and let him go out into the jungle taking the murrain with him. He must not look back.

§ 3. *The Periodic Expulsion of Evils in a Material Vehicle.*—The mediate expulsion of evils by means of a scapegoat or other material vehicle, like the immediate expulsion of them in invisible form, tends to become periodic, and for a like reason. Thus every year, generally in March, the people of Leti, Moa, and Lakor, islands of the Indian Archipelago, send away all their diseases to sea. They make a proa about six feet long, rig it with sails, oars, rudder, and other gear, and every family deposits in it some rice, fruit, a fowl, two eggs, insects that ravage the fields, and so on. Then they let it drift away to sea, saying, " Take away from here all kinds of sickness, take them to other islands, to other lands, distribute them in places that lie eastward, where the sun rises." The Biajas of Borneo annually send to sea a little bark laden with the sins and misfortunes of the people. The crew of any ship that falls in with the ill-omened bark at sea will suffer all the sorrows with which it is laden. A like custom is annually observed by the Dusuns of the Tuaran district in British North Borneo. The ceremony is the most important of the whole year. Its aim is to bring good luck to the village during the ensuing year by solemnly expelling all the evil spirits that may have collected in or about the houses throughout the last twelve months. The task of routing out the demons and banishing them devolves chiefly on women. Dressed in their finest array, they go in procession through the village. One of them carries a small sucking pig in a basket on her back ; and all of them bear wands, with which they belabour the little pig at the appropriate moment ; its squeals help to attract the vagrant spirits. At every house the women dance and sing, clashing castanets or cymbals of brass and jingling bunches of little brass bells in both hands. When the performance has been repeated at every house in the village, the procession defiles down to the river, and all the evil spirits, which the performers have chased from the houses, follow them to the edge of the water. There a raft has been made ready and moored to the bank. It contains offerings of food, cloth, cooking-pots, and swords ; and the deck is crowded with figures of men, women, animals, and birds, all made out of the leaves of the sago palm. The evil spirits now embark on the raft, and when they are all aboard, it is pushed off and allowed to float down with the current, carrying the demons with it. Should the raft run aground near the village, it is shoved off with all speed, lest the invisible passengers should seize the opportunity of landing and returning to the village. Finally, the sufferings of the little pig, whose squeals served to decoy the demons from their lurking-places, are terminated by death, for it is killed and its carcase thrown away.

Every year, at the beginning of the dry season, the Nicobar Islanders carry the model of a ship through their villages. The devils are chased out of the huts, and driven on board the little ship, which is then launched and suffered to sail away with the wind. The ceremony has been described by a catechist, who witnessed it at Car Nicobar in July 1897. For three days the people were busy preparing two very large floating cars, shaped like canoes, fitted with sails, and loaded with certain leaves, which possessed the valuable property of expelling devils. While the young people were thus engaged, the exorcists and the elders sat in a house singing songs by turns ; but often they would come forth, pace the beach armed with rods, and forbid the devil to enter the village. The fourth day of the solemnity bore a name which means " Expelling the Devil by Sails." In the evening all the villagers assembled, the women bringing baskets of ashes and bunches of devil-expelling leaves. These leaves were then distributed to everybody, old and young. When all was ready, a band of robust men, attended by a guard of exorcists, carried one of the cars down to the sea on the right side of the village graveyard, and set it floating in the water. As soon as they had returned, another band of men carried the other car to the beach and floated it similarly in the sea to the left of the graveyard. The demon-laden barks being now launched, the women threw ashes from the shore, and the whole crowd shouted, saying, " Fly away, devil, fly away, never come again ! " The wind and the tide being favourable, the canoes sailed quickly away ; and that night all the people feasted together with great joy, because the devil had departed in the direction of Chowra. A similar expulsion of devils takes place once a year in other Nicobar villages ; but the ceremonies are held at different times in different places.

Amongst many of the aboriginal tribes of China, a great festival is celebrated in the third month of every year. It is held by way of a general rejoicing over what the people believe to be a total annihilation of the ills of the past twelve months. The destruction is supposed to be effected in the following way. A large earthenware jar filled with gunpowder, stones, and bits of iron is buried in the earth. A train of gunpowder, communicating with the jar, is then laid ; and a match being applied, the jar and its contents are blown up. The stones and bits of iron represent the ills and disasters of the past year, and the dispersion of them by the explosion is believed to remove the ills and disasters themselves. The festival is attended with much revelling and drunkenness.

At Old Calabar on the coast of Guinea, the devils and ghosts are, or used to be, publicly expelled once in two years. Among the spirits thus driven from their haunts are the souls of all the people who died since the last lustration of the town. About three weeks or a month before the expulsion, which according to one account takes place in the month of November, rude effigies representing men and animals, such as crocodiles, leopards, elephants, bullocks, and birds, are made of wicker-work or wood, and being hung with strips of cloth and bedizened with gew-gaws, are set before the door of every house. About three o'clock in the morning of the day appointed for the ceremony the whole population turns out into the streets, and proceeds with a deafening uproar and in a state of the wildest excitement to drive all lurking devils and ghosts into the effigies, in order that they may be banished with them from the abodes of men. For this purpose bands of people roam through the streets knocking on doors, firing guns, beating drums, blowing on horns, ringing bells, clattering pots and pans, shouting and hallooing with might and main, in short making all the noise it is possible for them to raise. The hubbub goes on till the approach of dawn, when it gradually subsides and ceases altogether at sunrise. By this time the houses have been thoroughly swept, and all the frightened spirits are supposed to have huddled into the effigies or their fluttering drapery. In these wicker figures are also deposited the sweepings of the houses and the ashes of yesterday's fires. Then the demon-laden images are hastily snatched up, carried in tumultuous procession down to the brink of the river, and thrown into the water to the tuck of drums. The ebb-tide bears them away seaward, and thus the town is swept clean of ghosts and devils for another two years.

Similar annual expulsions of embodied evils are not unknown in Europe. On the evening of Easter Sunday the gypsies of Southern Europe take a wooden vessel like a band-box, which rests cradle-wise on two cross pieces of wood. In this they place herbs and simples, together with the dried carcase of a snake, or lizard, which every person present must first have touched with his fingers. The vessel is then wrapt in white and red wool, carried by the oldest man from tent to tent, and finally thrown into running water, not, however, before every member of the band has spat into it once, and the sorceress has uttered some spells over it. They believe that by performing this ceremony they dispel all the illnesses that would otherwise have afflicted them in the course of the year; and that if any one finds the vessel and opens it out of curiosity, he and his will be visited by all the maladies which the others have escaped.

The scapegoat by means of which the accumulated ills of a whole year are publicly expelled is sometimes an animal. For example, among the Garos of Assam, " besides the sacrifices for individual cases of illness, there are certain ceremonies which are observed once a year by a whole community or village, and are intended to safe-guard its members from dangers of the forest, and from sickness and mishap during the coming twelve months. The principal of these is the Asongtata ceremony. Close to the outskirts of every big village a number of stones may be noticed stuck into the ground, apparently without order or method. These are known by the name of *asong*, and on them is offered the sacrifice which the Asongtata demands. The sacrifice of a goat takes place, and a month later, that of a *langur* (*Entellus* monkey) or a bamboo-rat is considered necessary. The animal chosen has a rope fastened round its neck and is led by two men, one on each side of it, to every house in the village. It is taken inside each house in turn, the assembled villagers, meanwhile, beating the walls from the outside, to frighten and drive out any evil spirits which may have taken up their residence within. The round of the village having been made in this manner, the monkey or rat is led to the outskirts of the village, killed by a blow of a *dao*, which disembowels it, and then crucified on bamboos set up in the ground. Round the crucified animal long, sharp bamboo stakes are placed, which form *chevaux de frise* round about it. These commemorate the days when such defences surrounded the villages on all sides to keep off human enemies, and they are now a symbol to ward off sickness and dangers to life from the wild animals of the forest. The *langur* required for the purpose is hunted down some days before, but should it be found impossible to catch one, a brown monkey may take its place ; a hulock may not be used." Here the crucified ape or rat is the public scapegoat, which by its vicarious sufferings and death relieves the people from all sickness and mishap in the coming year.

Again, on one day of the year the Bhotiyas of Juhar, in the Western Himalayas, take a dog, intoxicate him with spirits and bhang or hemp, and having fed him with sweetmeats, lead him round the village and let him loose. They then chase and kill him with sticks and stones, and believe that, when they have done so, no disease or misfortune will visit the village during the year. In some parts of Breadalbane it was formerly the custom on New Year's Day to take a dog to the door, give him a bit of bread, and drive him out, saying, " Get away, you dog ! Whatever death of men or loss of cattle would happen in this house to the end of the present year, may it all light on your head ! " On the Day of Atonement, which was the tenth day of the seventh month, the Jewish high-priest laid both his hands on the head of a live goat, confessed over it all the iniquities of the Children of Israel, and, having thereby transferred the sins of the people to the beast, sent it away into the wilderness.

The scapegoat upon whom the sins of the people are periodically laid, may also be a human being. At Onitsha, on the Niger, two human beings used to be annually sacrificed to take away the sins of the land. The victims were purchased by public subscription. All persons who, during the past year, had fallen into gross sins, such as incendiarism, theft, adultery, witchcraft, and so forth, were expected to contribute 28 *ngugas*, or a little over £2. The money thus collected was taken into the interior of the country and expended in the purchase of two sickly persons " to be offered as a sacrifice for all these abominable crimes—one for the land and one for the river." A man from a neighbouring town was hired to put them to death. On the twenty-seventh of February 1858 the Rev. J. C. Taylor witnessed the sacrifice of one of these victims. The sufferer was a woman, about nineteen or twenty years of age. They dragged her alive along the ground, face downwards, from the king's house to the river, a distance of two miles, the crowds who accompanied her crying, " Wickedness ! wickedness ! " The intention was " to take away the iniquities of the land. The body was dragged along in a merciless manner, as if the weight of all their wickedness was thus carried away." Similar customs are said to be still secretly practised every year by many tribes in the delta of the Niger in spite of the vigilance of the British Government. Among the Yoruba negroes of West Africa " the human victim chosen for sacrifice, and who may be either a freeborn or a slave, a person of noble or wealthy parentage, or one of humble birth, is, after he has been chosen and marked out for the purpose, called an *Oluwo*. He is always well fed and nourished and supplied with whatever he should desire during the period of his confinement. When the occasion arrives for him to be sacrificed and offered up, he is commonly led about and paraded through the streets of the town or city of the Sovereign who would sacrifice him for the well-being of his government and of every family and individual under it, in order that he might carry off the sin, guilt, misfortune and death of all without exception. Ashes and chalk would be employed to hide his identity by the one being freely thrown over his head, and his face painted with the latter, whilst individuals would often rush out of their houses to lay their hands upon him that they might thus transfer to him their sin, guilt, trouble, and death." This parade over, he is taken to an inner sanctuary and beheaded. His last words or dying groans are the signal for an outburst of joy among the people assembled outside, who believe that the sacrifice has been accepted and the divine wrath appeased.

In Siam it used to be the custom on one day of the year to single out a woman broken down by debauchery, and carry her on a litter through all the streets to the music of drums and hautboys. The mob insulted her and pelted her with dirt ; and after having carried her through the whole city, they threw her on a dunghill or a hedge of thorns outside the ramparts, forbidding her ever to enter the walls again. They believed that the woman thus drew upon herself all the malign influences of the air and of evil spirits. The Bataks of Sumatra offer either a red horse or a buffalo as a public sacrifice to purify the land and obtain the favour of the gods. Formerly, it is said, a man was bound to the same stake as the buffalo, and when they killed the animal, the man was driven away ; no one might receive him, converse with him, or give him food. Doubtless he was supposed to carry away the sins and misfortunes of the people.

Sometimes the scapegoat is a divine animal. The people of Malabar share the Hindoo reverence for the cow, to kill and eat which

LVII THE PERIODIC EXPULSION OF EVILS

" they esteem to be a crime as heinous as homicide or wilful murder."
Nevertheless the " Bramans transfer the sins of the people into one
or more Cows, which are then carry'd away, both the Cows and the
Sins wherewith these Beasts are charged, to what place the Braman
shall appoint." When the ancient Egyptians sacrificed a bull, they
invoked upon its head all the evils that might otherwise befall themselves and the land of Egypt, and thereupon they either sold the bull's
head to the Greeks or cast it into the river. Now, it cannot be said
that in the times known to us the Egyptians worshipped bulls in
general, for they seem to have commonly killed and eaten them.
But a good many circumstances point to the conclusion that originally
all cattle, bulls as well as cows, were held sacred by the Egyptians.
For not only were all cows esteemed holy by them and never sacrificed,
but even bulls might not be sacrificed unless they had certain natural
marks ; a priest examined every bull before it was sacrificed ; if it
had the proper·marks, he put his seal on the animal in token that it
might be sacrificed ; and if a man sacrificed a bull which had not been
sealed, he was put to death. Moreover, the worship of the black bulls
Apis and Mnevis, especially the former, played an important part
in Egyptian religion ; all bulls that died a natural death were carefully
buried in the suburbs of the cities, and their bones were afterwards
collected from all parts of Egypt and interred in a single spot ; and
at the sacrifice of a bull in the great rites of Isis all the worshippers
beat their breasts and mourned. On the whole, then, we are perhaps
entitled to infer that bulls were originally, as cows were always,
esteemed sacred by the Egyptians, and that the slain bull upon whose
head they laid the misfortunes of the people was once a divine scapegoat. It seems not improbable that the lamb annually slain by the
Madis of Central Africa is a divine scapegoat, and the same supposition
may partly explain the Zuni sacrifice of the turtle.

Lastly, the scapegoat may be a divine man. Thus, in November
the Gonds of India worship Ghansyam Deo, the protector of the crops,
and at the festival the god himself is said to descend on the head of
one of the worshippers, who is suddenly seized with a kind of fit and,
after staggering about, rushes off into the jungle, where it is believed
that, if left to himself, he would die mad. However, they bring him
back, but he does not recover his senses for one or two days. The
people think that one man is thus singled out as a scapegoat for the
sins of the rest of the village. In the temple of the Moon the Albanians
of the Eastern Caucasus kept a number of sacred slaves, of whom
many were inspired and prophesied. When one of these men exhibited
more than usual symptoms of inspiration or insanity, and wandered
solitary up and down the woods, like the Gond in the jungle, the
high priest had him bound with a sacred chain and maintained him
in luxury for a year. At the end of the year he was anointed with
unguents and led forth to be sacrificed. A man whose business it
was to slay these human victims, and to whom practice had given
dexterity, advanced from the crowd and thrust a sacred spear into

the victim's side, piercing his heart. From the manner in which
the slain man fell, omens were drawn as to the welfare of the commonwealth.   Then the body was carried to a certain spot where all the
people stood upon it as a purificatory ceremony.   This last circumstance clearly indicates that the sins of the people were transferred
to the victim, just as the Jewish priest transferred the sins of the
people to the scapegoat by laying his hands on the animal's head ;
and since the man was believed to be possessed by the divine spirit,
we have here an undoubted example of a man-god slain to take away
the sins and misfortunes of the people.

In Tibet the ceremony of the scapegoat presents some remarkable
features. The Tibetan new year begins with the new moon which
appears about the fifteenth of February. For twenty-three days
afterwards the government of Lhasa, the capital, is taken out of the
hands of the ordinary rulers and entrusted to the monk of the Debang
monastery who offers to pay the highest sum for the privilege. The
successful bidder is called the Jalno, and he announces his accession
to power in person, going through the streets of Lhasa with a silver
stick in his hand. Monks from all the neighbouring monasteries and
temples assemble to pay him homage. The Jalno exercises his
authority in the most arbitrary manner for his own benefit, as all the
fines which he exacts are his by purchase. The profit he makes is
about ten times the amount of the purchase money. His men go
about the streets in order to discover any conduct on the part of the
inhabitants that can be found fault with. Every house in Lhasa is
taxed at this time, and the slightest offence is punished with unsparing
rigour by fines. This severity of the Jalno drives all working classes
out of the city till the twenty-three days are over. But if the laity
go out, the clergy come in. All the Buddhist monasteries of the
country for miles round about open their gates and disgorge their
inmates. All the roads that lead down into Lhasa from the neighbouring mountains are full of monks hurrying to the capital, some on foot,
some on horseback, some riding asses or lowing oxen, all carrying their
prayer-books and culinary utensils. In such multitudes do they come
that the streets and squares of the city are encumbered with their
swarms, and incarnadined with their red cloaks. The disorder and
confusion are indescribable. Bands of the holy men traverse the
streets chanting prayers or uttering wild cries. They meet, they
jostle, they quarrel, they fight ; bloody noses, black eyes, and broken
heads are freely given and received. All day long, too, from before
the peep of dawn till after darkness has fallen, these red-cloaked monks
hold services in the dim incense-laden air of the great Machindranath
temple, the cathedral of Lhasa ; and thither they crowd thrice a day
to receive their doles of tea and soup and money. The cathedral is a
vast building, standing in the centre of the city, and surrounded by
bazaars and shops. The idols in it are richly inlaid with gold and
precious stones.

Twenty-four days after the Jalno has ceased to have authority, he assumes it again, and for ten days acts in the same arbitrary manner as before. On the first of the ten days the priests again assemble at the cathedral, pray to the gods to prevent sickness and other evils among the people, " and, as a peace-offering, sacrifice one man. The man is not killed purposely, but the ceremony he undergoes often proves fatal. Grain is thrown against his head, and his face is painted half white, half black." Thus grotesquely disguised, and carrying a coat of skin on his arm, he is called the King of the Years, and sits daily in the market-place, where he helps himself to whatever he likes and goes about shaking a black yak's tail over the people, who thus transfer their bad luck to him. On the tenth day, all the troops in Lhasa march to the great temple and form in line before it. The King of the Years is brought forth from the temple and receives small donations from the assembled multitude. He then ridicules the Jalno, saying to him, " What we perceive through the five senses is no illusion. All you teach is untrue," and the like. The Jalno, who represents the Grand Lama for the time being, contests these heretical opinions ; the dispute waxes warm, and at last both agree to decide the questions at issue by a cast of the dice, the Jalno offering to change places with the scapegoat should the throw be against him. If the King of the Years wins, much evil is prognosticated ; but if the Jalno wins, there is great rejoicing, for it proves that his adversary has been accepted by the gods as a victim to bear all the sins of the people of Lhasa. Fortune, however, always favours the Jalno, who throws sixes with unvarying success, while his opponent turns up only ones. Nor is this so extraordinary as at first sight it might appear ; for the Jalno's dice are marked with nothing but sixes and his adversary's with nothing but ones. When he sees the finger of Providence thus plainly pointed against him, the King of the Years is terrified and flees away upon a white horse, with a white dog, a white bird, salt, and so forth, which have all been provided for him by the government. His face is still painted half white and half black, and he still wears his leathern coat. The whole populace pursues him, hooting, yelling, and firing blank shots in volleys after him. Thus driven out of the city, he is detained for seven days in the great chamber of horrors at the Samyas monastery, surrounded by monstrous and terrific images of devils and skins of huge serpents and wild beasts. Thence he goes away into the mountains of Chetang, where he has to remain an outcast for several months or a year in a narrow den. If he dies before the time is out, the people say it is an auspicious omen ; but if he survives, he may return to Lhasa and play the part of scapegoat over again the following year.

This quaint ceremonial, still annually observed in the secluded capital of Buddhism—the Rome of Asia—is interesting because it exhibits, in a clearly marked religious stratification, a series of divine redeemers themselves redeemed, of vicarious sacrifices vicariously atoned for, of gods undergoing a process of fossilisation, who, while they retain the privileges, have disburdened themselves of the pains and penalties of divinity. In the Jalno we may without undue straining discern a successor of those temporary kings, those mortal gods, who purchase a short lease of power and glory at the price of their lives. That he is the temporary substitute of the Grand Lama is certain ; that he is, or was once, liable to act as scapegoat for the people is made nearly certain by his offer to change places with the real scapegoat—the King of the Years—if the arbitrament of the dice should go against him. It is true that the conditions under which the question is now put to the hazard have reduced the offer to an idle form. But such forms are no mere mushroom growths, springing up of themselves in a night. If they are now lifeless formalities, empty husks devoid of significance, we may be sure that they once had a life and a meaning ; if at the present day they are blind alleys leading nowhere, we may be certain that in former days they were paths that led somewhere, if only to death. That death was the goal to which of old the Tibetan scapegoat passed after his brief period of license in the market-place, is a conjecture that has much to commend it. Analogy suggests it ; the blank shots fired after him, the statement that the ceremony often proves fatal, the belief that his death is a happy omen, all confirm it. We need not wonder then that the Jalno, after paying so dear to act as deputy-deity for a few weeks, should have preferred to die by deputy rather than in his own person when his time was up. The painful but necessary duty was accordingly laid on some poor devil, some social outcast, some wretch with whom the world had gone hard, who readily agreed to throw away his life at the end of a few days if only he might have his fling in the meantime. For observe that while the time allowed to the original deputy—the Jalno—was measured by weeks, the time allowed to the deputy's deputy was cut down to days, ten days according to one authority, seven days according to another. So short a rope was doubtless thought a long enough tether for so black or sickly a sheep ; so few sands in the hour-glass, slipping so fast away, sufficed for one who had wasted so many precious years. Hence in the jack-pudding who now masquerades with motley countenance in the market-place of Lhasa, sweeping up misfortune with a black yak's tail, we may fairly see the substitute of a substitute, the vicar of a vicar, the proxy on whose back the heavy burden was laid when it had been lifted from nobler shoulders. But the clue, if we have followed it aright, does not stop at the Jalno ; it leads straight back to the pope of Lhasa himself, the Grand Lama, of whom the Jalno is merely the temporary vicar. The analogy of many customs in many lands points to the conclusion that, if this human divinity stoops to resign his ghostly power for a time into the hands of a substitute, it is, or rather was once, for no other reason than that the substitute might die in his stead. Thus through the mist of ages unillumined by the lamp of history, the tragic figure of the pope of Buddhism—God's vicar on earth for Asia—looms dim and sad as the man-god who bore his people's sorrows, the Good Shepherd who laid down his life for the sheep.

§ 4. *On Scapegoats in General.*—The foregoing survey of the custom of publicly expelling the accumulated evils of a village or town or country suggests a few general observations.

In the first place, it will not be disputed that what I have called the immediate and the mediate expulsions of evil are identical in intention ; in other words, that whether the evils are conceived of as invisible or as embodied in a material form, is a circumstance entirely subordinate to the main object of the ceremony, which is simply to effect a total clearance of all the ills that have been infesting a people. If any link were wanting to connect the two kinds of expulsion, it would be furnished by such a practice as that of sending the evils away in a litter or a boat. For here, on the one hand, the evils are invisible and intangible ; and, on the other hand, there is a visible and tangible vehicle to convey them away. And a scapegoat is nothing more than such a vehicle.

In the second place, when a general clearance of evils is resorted to periodically, the interval between the celebrations of the ceremony is commonly a year, and the time of year when the ceremony takes place usually coincides with some well-marked change of season, such as the beginning or end of winter in the arctic and temperate zones, and the beginning or end of the rainy season in the tropics. The increased mortality which such climatic changes are apt to produce, especially amongst ill-fed, ill-clothed, and ill-housed savages, is set down by primitive man to the agency of demons, who must accordingly be expelled. Hence, in the tropical regions of New Britain and Peru, the devils are or were driven out at the beginning of the rainy season ; hence, on the dreary coasts of Baffin Land, they are banished at the approach of the bitter arctic winter. When a tribe has taken to husbandry, the time for the general expulsion of devils is naturally made to agree with one of the great epochs of the agricultural year, as sowing, or harvest ; but, as these epochs themselves naturally coincide with changes of season, it does not follow that the transition from the hunting or pastoral to the agricultural life involves any alteration in the time of celebrating this great annual rite. Some of the agricultural communities of India and the Hindoo Koosh, as we have seen, hold their general clearance of demons at harvest, others at sowing-time. But, at whatever season of the year it is held, the general expulsion of devils commonly marks the beginning of the new year. For, before entering on a new year, people are anxious to rid themselves of the troubles that have harassed them in the past ; hence it comes about that in so many communities the beginning of the new year is inaugurated with a solemn and public banishment of evil spirits.

In the third place, it is to be observed that this public and periodic expulsion of devils is commonly preceded or followed by a period of general license, during which the ordinary restraints of society are thrown aside, and all offences, short of the gravest, are allowed to pass unpunished. In Guinea and Tonquin the period of license precedes the public expulsion of demons ; and the suspension of the ordinary government in Lhasa previous to the expulsion of the scape-goat is perhaps a relic of a similar period of universal license. Amongst the Hos of India the period of license follows the expulsion of the devil. Amongst the Iroquois it hardly appears whether it preceded or followed the banishment of evils. In any case, the extraordinary relaxation of all ordinary rules of conduct on such occasions is doubtless to be explained by the general clearance of evils which precedes or follows it. On the one hand, when a general riddance of evil and absolution from all sin is in immediate prospect, men are encouraged to give the rein to their passions, trusting that the coming ceremony will wipe out the score which they are running up so fast. On the other hand, when the ceremony has just taken place, men's minds are freed from the oppressive sense, under which they generally labour, of an atmosphere surcharged with devils ; and in the first revulsion of joy they overleap the limits commonly imposed by custom and morality. When the ceremony takes place at harvest-time, the elation of feeling which it excites is further stimulated by the state of physical wellbeing produced by an abundant supply of food.

Fourthly, the employment of a divine man or animal as a scapegoat is especially to be noted ; indeed, we are here directly concerned with the custom of banishing evils only in so far as these evils are believed to be transferred to a god who is afterwards slain. It may be suspected that the custom of employing a divine man or animal as a public scape-goat is much more widely diffused than appears from the examples cited. For, as has already been pointed out, the custom of killing a god dates from so early a period of human history that in later ages, even when the custom continues to be practised, it is liable to be mis-interpreted. The divine character of the animal or man is forgotten, and he comes to be regarded merely as an ordinary victim. This is especially likely to be the case when it is a divine man who is killed. For when a nation becomes civilised, if it does not drop human sacrifices altogether, it at least selects as victims only such wretches as would be put to death at any rate. Thus the killing of a god may sometimes come to be confounded with the execution of a criminal.

If we ask why a dying god should be chosen to take upon himself and carry away the sins and sorrows of the people, it may be suggested that in the practice of using the divinity as a scapegoat we have a combination of two customs which were at one time distinct and independent. On the one hand we have seen that it has been customary to kill the human or animal god in order to save his divine life from being weakened by the inroads of age. On the other hand we have seen that it has been customary to have a general expulsion of evils and sins once a year. Now, if it occurred to people to combine these two customs, the result would be the employment of the dying god as a scapegoat. He was killed, not originally to take away sin, but to save the divine life from the degeneracy of old age ; but, since he had to be killed at any rate, people may have thought that they might as well seize the opportunity to lay upon him the burden of their sufferings and sins, in order that he might bear it away with him to the unknown world beyond the grave.

The use of the divinity as a scapegoat clears up the ambiguity which, as we saw, appears to hang about the European folk-custom of " carrying out Death." Grounds have been shown for believing that in this ceremony the so-called Death was originally the spirit of vegetation, who was annually slain in spring, in order that he might come to life again with all the vigour of youth. But, as I pointed out, there are certain features in the ceremony which are not explicable on this hypothesis alone. Such are the marks of joy with which the effigy of Death is carried out to be buried or burnt, and the fear and abhorrence of it manifested by the bearers. But these features become at once intelligible if we suppose that the Death was not merely the dying god of vegetation, but also a public scapegoat, upon whom were laid all the evils that had afflicted the people during the past year. Joy on such an occasion is natural and appropriate ; and if the dying god appears to be the object of that fear and abhorrence which are properly due not to himself, but to the sins and misfortunes with which he is laden, this arises merely from the difficulty of distinguishing, or at least of marking the distinction, between the bearer and the burden. When the burden is of a baleful character, the bearer of it will be feared and shunned just as much as if he were himself instinct with those dangerous properties of which, as it happens, he is only the vehicle. Similarly we have seen that disease-laden and sin-laden boats are dreaded and shunned by East Indian peoples. Again, the view that in these popular customs the Death is a scapegoat as well as a representative of the divine spirit of vegetation derives some support from the circumstance that its expulsion is always celebrated in spring and chiefly by Slavonic peoples. For the Slavonic year began in spring ; and thus, in one of its aspects, the ceremony of " carrying out Death " would be an example of the widespread custom of expelling the accumulated evils of the old year before entering on a new one.

CHAPTER LVIII

HUMAN SCAPEGOATS IN CLASSICAL ANTIQUITY

§ 1. *The Human Scapegoat in Ancient Rome.*—We are now prepared to notice the use of the human scapegoat in classical antiquity. Every year on the fourteenth of March a man clad in skins was led in procession through the streets of Rome, beaten with long white rods, and driven out of the city. He was called Mamurius Veturius, that is, " the old Mars," and as the ceremony took place on the day preceding the first full moon of the old Roman year (which began on the first of March), the skin-clad man must have represented the Mars of the past year, who was driven out at the beginning of a new one. Now Mars was

2 P

originally not a god of war but of vegetation. For it was to Mars that the Roman husbandman prayed for the prosperity of his corn and his vines, his fruit-trees and his copses ; it was to Mars that the priestly college of the Arval Brothers, whose business it was to sacrifice for the growth of the crops, addressed their petitions almost exclusively ; and it was to Mars, as we saw, that a horse was sacrificed in October to secure an abundant harvest.   Moreover, it was to Mars, under his title of " Mars of the woods " (*Mars Silvanus*), that farmers offered sacrifice for the welfare of their cattle. We have already seen that cattle are commonly supposed to be under the special patronage ot tree-gods.   Once more, the consecration of the vernal month of March to Mars seems to point him out as the deity of the sprouting vegetation. Thus the Roman custom of expelling the old Mars at the beginning of the new year in spring is identical with the Slavonic custom of " carrying out Death," if the view here taken of the latter custom is correct.   The similarity of the Roman and Slavonic customs has been already remarked by scholars, who appear, however, to have taken Mamurius Veturius and the corresponding figures in the Slavonic ceremonies to be representatives of the old year rather than of the old god of vegetation.   It is possible that ceremonies of this kind may have come to be thus interpreted in later times even by the people who practised them. But the personification of a period of time is too abstract an idea to be primitive. However, in the Roman, as in the Slavonic, ceremony, the representative of the god appears to have been treated not only as a deity of vegetation but also as a scapegoat.   His expulsion implies this ; for there is no reason why the god of vegetation, as such, should be expelled the city. But it is otherwise if he is also a scapegoat ; it then becomes necessary to drive him beyond the boundaries, that he may carry his sorrowful burden away to other lands.   And, in fact, Mamurius Veturius appears to have been driven away to the land of the Oscans, the enemies of Rome.

§ 2. *The Human Scapegoat in Ancient Greece.*—The ancient Greeks were also familiar with the use of a human scapegoat. In Plutarch's native town of Chaeronea a ceremony of this kind was performed by the chief magistrate at the Town Hall, and by each householder at his own home. It was called the " expulsion of hunger." A slave was beaten with rods of the *agnus castus*, and turned out of doors with the words, " Out with hunger, and in with wealth and health." When Plutarch held the office of chief magistrate of his native town he per-formed this ceremony at the Town Hall, and he has recorded the discussion to which the custom afterwards gave rise.

But in civilised Greece the custom of the scapegoat took darker forms than the innocent rite over which the amiable and pious Plutarch presided. Whenever Marseilles, one of the busiest and most brilliant of Greek colonies, was ravaged by a plague, a man of the poorer classes used to offer himself as a scapegoat. For a whole year he was main-tained at the public expense, being fed on choice and pure food. At the expiry of the year he was dressed in sacred garments, decked with holy branches, and led through the whole city, while prayers were uttered that all the evils of the people might fall on his head. He was then cast out of the city or stoned to death by the people outside of the walls. The Athenians regularly maintained a number of degraded and useless beings at the public expense ; and when any calamity, such as plague, drought, or famine, befell the city, they sacrificed two of these outcasts as scapegoats. One of the victims was sacrificed for the men and the other for the women. The former wore round his neck a string of black, the latter a string of white figs. Sometimes, it seems, the victim slain on behalf of the women was a woman. They were led about the city and then sacrificed, apparently by being stoned to death outside the city. But such sacrifices were not confined to extraordinary occasions of public calamity ; it appears that every year, at the festival of the Thargelia in May, two victims, one for the men and one for the women, were led out of Athens and stoned to death. The city of Abdera in Thrace was publicly purified once a year, and one of the burghers, set apart for the purpose, was stoned to death as a scapegoat or vicarious sacrifice for the life of all the others ; six days before his execution he was excommunicated, " in order that he alone might bear the sins of all the people."

From the Lover's Leap, a white bluff at the southern end of their island, the Leucadians used annually to hurl a criminal into the sea as a scapegoat. But to lighten his fall they fastened live birds and feathers to him, and a flotilla of small boats waited below to catch him and convey him beyond the boundary. Probably these humane precautions were a mitigation of an earlier custom of flinging the scapegoat into the sea to drown. The Leucadian ceremony took place at the time of a sacrifice to Apollo, who had a temple or sanctuary on the spot. Elsewhere it was customary to cast a young man every year into the sea, with the prayer, " Be thou our offscouring." This ceremony was supposed to rid the people of the evils by which they were beset, or according to a somewhat different interpretation it redeemed them by paying the debt they owed to the sea-god. As practised by the Greeks of Asia Minor in the sixth century before our era, the custom of the scapegoat was as follows. When a city suffered from plague, famine, or other public calamity, an ugly or deformed person was chosen to take upon himself all the evils which afflicted the community. He was brought to a suitable place, where dried figs, a barley loaf, and cheese were put into his hand. These he ate. Then he was beaten seven times upon his genital organs with squills and branches of the wild fig and other wild trees, while the flutes played a particular tune. Afterwards he was burned on a pyre built of the wood of forest trees ; and his ashes were cast into the sea. A similar custom appears to have been annually celebrated by the Asiatic Greeks at the harvest festival of the Thargelia.

In the ritual just described the scourging of the victim with squills, branches of the wild fig, and so forth, cannot have been intended to aggravate his sufferings, otherwise any stick would have been good

enough to beat him with. The true meaning of this part of the ceremony has been explained by W. Mannhardt. He points out that the
ancients attributed to squills a magical power of averting evil influences,
and that accordingly they hung them up at the doors of their houses
and made use of them in purificatory rites. Hence the Arcadian
custom of whipping the image of Pan with squills at a festival, or
whenever the hunters returned empty-handed, must have been meant,
not to punish the god, but to purify him from the harmful influences
which were impeding him in the exercise of his divine functions as a
god who should supply the hunter with game. Similarly the object
of beating the human scapegoat on the genital organs with squills and
so on must have been to release his reproductive energies from any
restraint or spell under which they might be laid by demoniacal or other
malignant agency ; and as the Thargelia at which he was annually
sacrificed was an early harvest festival celebrated in May, we must
recognise in him a representative of the creative and fertilising god of
vegetation. The representative of the god was annually slain for the
purpose I have indicated, that of maintaining the divine life in perpetual vigour, untainted by the weakness of age ; and before he was
put to death it was not unnatural to stimulate his reproductive powers
in order that these might be transmitted in full activity to his successor,
the new god or new embodiment of the old god, who was doubtless
supposed immediately to take the place of the one slain. Similar
reasoning would lead to a similar treatment of the scapegoat on special
occasions, such as drought or famine. If the crops did not answer to
the expectation of the husbandman, this would be attributed to some
failure in the generative powers of the god whose function it was to
produce the fruits of the earth. It might be thought that he was under
a spell or was growing old and feeble. Accordingly he was slain in the
person of his representative, with all the ceremonies already described,
in order that, born young again, he might infuse his own youthful
vigour into the stagnant energies of nature. On the same principle
we can understand why Mamurius Veturius was beaten with rods, why
the slave at the Chaeronean ceremony was beaten with the *agnus castus*
(a tree to which magical properties were ascribed), why the effigy of
Death in some parts of Europe is assailed with sticks and stones, and
why at Babylon the criminal who played the god was scourged before
he was crucified. The purpose of the scourging was not to intensify
the agony of the divine sufferer, but on the contrary to dispel any
malignant influences by which at the supreme moment he might con-
ceivably be beset.

Thus far I have assumed that the human victims at the Thargelia
represented the spirits of vegetation in general, but it has been well
remarked by Mr. W. R. Paton that these poor wretches seem to have
masqueraded as the spirits of fig-trees in particular. He points out
that the process of caprification, as it is called, that is, the artificial
fertilisation of the cultivated fig-trees by hanging strings of wild figs
among the boughs, takes place in Greece and Asia Minor in June about

a month after the date of the Thargelia, and he suggests that the hanging of the black and white figs round the necks of the two human victims, one of whom represented the men and the other the women, may have been a direct imitation of the process of caprification designed, on the principle of imitative magic, to assist the fertilisation of the fig-trees.   And since caprification is in fact a marriage of the male fig-tree with the female fig-tree, Mr. Paton further supposes that the loves of the trees may, on the same principle of imitative magic, have been simulated by a mock or even a real marriage between the two human victims, one of whom appears sometimes to have been a woman. On this view the practice of beating the human victims on their genitals with branches of wild fig-trees and with squills was a charm intended to stimulate the generative powers of the man and woman who for the time being personated the male and the female fig-trees respectively, and who by their union in marriage, whether real or pretended, were believed to help the trees to bear fruit.

The interpretation which I have adopted of the custom of beating the human scapegoat with certain plants is supported by many analogies.   Thus among the Kai of German New Guinea, when a man wishes to make his banana shoots bear fruit quickly, he beats them with a stick cut from a banana-tree which has already borne fruit. Here it is obvious that fruitfulness is believed to inhere in a stick cut from a fruitful tree and to be imparted by contact to the young banana plants.   Similarly in New Caledonia a man will beat his taro plants lightly with a branch, saying as he does so, " I beat this taro that it may grow," after which he plants the branch in the ground at the end of the field.   Among the Indians of Brazil at the mouth of the Amazon, when a man wishes to increase the size of his generative organ, he strikes it with the fruit of a white aquatic plant called an *aninga*, which grows luxuriantly on the banks of the river.   The fruit, which is inedible, resembles a banana, and is clearly chosen for this purpose on account of its shape.   The ceremony should be performed three days before or after the new moon.   In the county of Bekes, in Hungary, barren women are fertilised by being struck with a stick which has first been used to separate pairing dogs.   Here a fertilising virtue is clearly supposed to be inherent in the stick and to be conveyed by contact to the women.   The Toradjas of Central Celebes think that the plant *Dracaena terminalis* has a strong soul, because when it is lopped it soon grows up again.   Hence when a man is ill, his friends will sometimes beat him on the crown of the head with *Dracaena* leaves in order to strengthen his weak soul with the strong soul of the plant.

These analogies, accordingly, support the interpretation which, following my predecessors W. Mannhardt and Mr. W. R. Paton, I have given of the beating inflicted on the human victims at the Greek harvest festival of the Thargelia.   That beating, being administered to the generative organs of the victims by fresh green plants and branches, is most naturally explained as a charm to increase the reproductive energies of the men or women either by communicating to them the fruitfulness of the plants and branches, or by ridding them of maleficent influences ; and this interpretation is confirmed by the observation that the two victims represented the two sexes, one of them standing for the men in general and the other for the women. The season of the year when the ceremony was performed, namely the time of the corn harvest, tallies well with the theory that the rite had an agricultural significance. Further, that it was above all intended to fertilise the fig-trees is strongly suggested by the strings of black and white figs which were hung round the necks of the victims, as well as by the blows which were given their genital organs with the branches of a wild fig-tree ; since this procedure closely resembles the procedure which ancient and modern husbandmen in Greek lands have regularly resorted to for the purpose of actually fertilising their fig-trees. When we remember what an important part the artificial fertilisation of the date palm-tree appears to have played of old not only in the husbandry but in the religion of Meso-potamia, there seems no reason to doubt that the artificial fertilisation of the fig-tree may in like manner have vindicated for itself a place in the solemn ritual of Greek religion.

If these considerations are just, we must apparently conclude that while the human victims at the Thargelia certainly appear in later classical times to have figured chiefly as public scapegoats, who carried away with them the sins, misfortunes, and sorrows of the whole people, at an earlier time they may have been looked on as embodiments of vegetation, perhaps of the corn but particularly of the fig-trees ; and that the beating which they received and the death which they died were intended primarily to brace and refresh the powers of vegetation then beginning to droop and languish under the torrid heat of the Greek summer.

The view here taken of the Greek scapegoat, if it is correct, obviates an objection which might otherwise be brought against the main argument of this book. To the theory that the priest of Aricia was slain as a representative of the spirit of the grove, it might have been objected that such a custom has no analogy in classical antiquity. But reasons have now been given for believing that the human being periodically and occasionally slain by the Asiatic Greeks was regularly treated as an embodiment of a divinity of vegetation. Probably the persons whom the Athenians kept to be sacrificed were similarly treated as divine. That they were social outcasts did not matter. On the primitive view a man is not chosen to be the mouth-piece or embodiment of a god on account of his high moral qualities or social rank. The divine afflatus descends equally on the good and the bad, the lofty and the lowly. If then the civilised Greeks of Asia and Athens habitually sacrificed men whom they regarded as incarnate gods, there can be no inherent improbability in the supposition that at the dawn of history a similar custom was observed by the semi-barbarous Latins in the Arician Grove.

But to clinch the argument, it is clearly desirable to prove that the custom of putting to death a human representative of a god was known and practised in ancient Italy elsewhere than in the Arician Grove. This proof I now propose to adduce.

§ 3. *The Roman Saturnalia.*—We have seen that many peoples have been used to observe an annual period of license, when the customary restraints of law and morality are thrown aside, when the whole population give themselves up to extravagant mirth and jollity, and when the darker passions find a vent which would never be allowed them in the more staid and sober course of ordinary life. Such outbursts of the pent-up forces of human nature, too often degenerating into wild orgies of lust and crime, occur most commonly at the end of the year, and are frequently associated, as I have had occasion to point out, with one or other of the agricultural seasons, especially with the time of sowing or of harvest. Now, of all these periods of license the one which is best known and which in modern language has given its name to the rest is the Saturnalia. This famous festival fell in December, the last month of the Roman year, and was popularly supposed to commemorate the merry reign of Saturn, the god of sowing and of husbandry, who lived on earth long ago as a righteous and beneficent king of Italy, drew the rude and scattered dwellers on the mountains together, taught them to till the ground, gave them laws, and ruled in peace. His reign was the fabled Golden Age : the earth brought forth abundantly : no sound of war or discord troubled the happy world : no baleful love of lucre worked like poison in the blood of the industrious and contented peasantry. Slavery and private property were alike unknown : all men had all things in common. At last the good god, the kindly king, vanished suddenly ; but his memory was cherished to distant ages, shrines were reared in his honour, and many hills and high places in Italy bore his name. Yet the bright tradition of his reign was crossed by a dark shadow : his altars are said to have been stained with the blood of human victims, for whom a more merciful age afterwards substituted effigies. Of this gloomy side of the god's religion there is little or no trace in the descriptions which ancient writers have left us of the Saturnalia. Feasting and revelry and all the mad pursuit of pleasure are the features that seem to have especially marked this carnival of antiquity, as it went on for seven days in the streets and public squares and houses of ancient Rome from the seventeenth to the twenty-third of December.

But no feature of the festival is more remarkable, nothing in it seems to have struck the ancients themselves more than the license granted to slaves at this time. The distinction between the free and the servile classes was temporarily abolished. The slave might rail at his master, intoxicate himself like his betters, sit down at table with them, and not even a word of reproof would be administered to him for conduct which at any other season might have been punished with stripes, imprisonment, or death. Nay, more, masters actually changed places with their slaves and waited on them at table ; and not till the serf had done eating and drinking was the board cleared and dinner set for his master. So far was this inversion of ranks carried, that each household became for a time a mimic republic in which the high offices of state were discharged by the slaves, who gave their orders and·laid down the law as if they were indeed invested with all the dignity of the consulship, the praetorship, and the bench. Like the pale reflection of power thus accorded to bondsmen at the Saturnalia was the mock kingship for which freemen cast lots at the same season. The person on whom the lot fell enjoyed the title of king, and issued commands of a playful and ludicrous nature to his temporary subjects. One of them he might order to mix the wine, another to drink, another to sing, another to dance, another to speak in his own dispraise, another to carry a flute-girl on his back round the house.

Now, when we remember that the liberty allowed to slaves at this festive season was supposed to be an imitation of the state of society in Saturn's time, and that in general the Saturnalia passed for nothing more or less than a temporary revival or restoration of the reign of that merry monarch, we are tempted to surmise that the mock king who presided over the revels may have originally represented Saturn himself. The conjecture is strongly confirmed, if not established, by a very curious and interesting account of the way in which the Saturnalia was celebrated by the Roman soldiers stationed on the Danube in the reign of Maximian and Diocletian. The account is preserved in a narrative of the martyrdom of St. Dasius, which was unearthed from a Greek manuscript in the Paris library, and published by Professor Franz Cumont of Ghent. Two briefer descriptions of the event and of the custom are contained in manuscripts at Milan and Berlin ; one of them had already seen the light in an obscure volume printed at Urbino in 1727, but its importance for the history of the Roman religion, both ancient and modern, appears to have been overlooked until Professor Cumont drew the attention of scholars to all three narratives by publishing them together some years ago. According to these narratives, which have all the appearance of being authentic, and of which the longest is probably based on official documents, the Roman soldiers at Durostorum in Lower Moesia celebrated the Saturnalia year by year in the following manner. Thirty days before the festival they chose by lot from amongst themselves a young and handsome man, who was then clothed in royal attire to resemble Saturn. Thus arrayed and attended by a multitude of soldiers he went about in public with full license to indulge his passions and to taste of every pleasure, however base and shameful. But if his reign was merry, it was short and ended tragically ; for when the thirty days were up and the festival of Saturn had come, he cut his own throat on the altar of the god whom he personated. In the year A.D. 303 the lot fell upon the Christian soldier Dasius, but he refused to play the part of the heathen god and soil his last days by debauchery. The threats and arguments of his commanding officer Bassus failed to shake his constancy, and accordingly he was beheaded, as the Christian martyrologist records with minute accuracy, at Durostorum by the soldier John on Friday the twentieth day of November, being the twenty-fourth day of the moon, at the fourth hour.

Since this narrative was published by Professor Cumont, its historical character, which had been doubted or denied, has received strong confirmation from an interesting discovery. In the crypt of the cathedral which crowns the promontory of Ancona there is preserved, among other remarkable antiquities, a white marble sarcophagus bearing a Greek inscription, in characters of the age of Justinian, to the following effect : " Here lies the holy martyr Dasius, brought from Durostorum." The sarcophagus was transferred to the crypt of the cathedral in 1848 from the church of San Pellegrino, under the high altar of which, as we learn from a Latin inscription let into the masonry, the martyr's bones still repose with those of two other saints. How long the sarcophagus was deposited in the church of San Pellegrino, we do not know ; but it is recorded to have been there in the year 1650. We may suppose that the saint's relics were transferred for safety to Ancona at some time in the troubled centuries which followed his martyrdom, when Moesia was occupied and ravaged by successive hordes of barbarian invaders. At all events it appears certain from the independent and mutually confirmatory evidence of the martyrology and the monuments that Dasius was no mythical saint, but a real man, who suffered death for his faith at Durostorum in one of the early centuries of the Christian era. Finding the narrative of the nameless martyrologist thus established as to the principal fact recorded, namely, the martyrdom of St. Dasius, we may reasonably accept his testimony as to the manner and cause of the martyrdom, all the more because his narrative is precise, circumstantial, and entirely free from the miraculous element. Accordingly I conclude that the account which he gives of the celebration of the Saturnalia among the Roman soldiers is trustworthy.

This account sets in a new and lurid light the office of the King of the Saturnalia, the ancient Lord of Misrule, who presided over the winter revels at Rome in the time of Horace and of Tacitus. It seems to prove that his business had not always been that of a mere harlequin or merry-andrew whose only care was that the revelry should run high and the fun grow fast and furious, while the fire blazed and crackled on the hearth, while the streets swarmed with festive crowds, and through the clear frosty air, far away to the north, Soracte showed his coronal of snow. When we compare this comic monarch of the gay, the civilised metropolis with his grim counterpart of the rude camp on the Danube, and when we remember the long array of similar figures, ludicrous yet tragic, who in other ages and in other lands, wearing mock crowns and wrapped in sceptred palls, have played their little pranks for a few brief hours or days, then passed before their

time to a violent death, we can hardly doubt that in the King of the
Saturnalia at Rome, as he is depicted by classical writers, we see only
a feeble emasculated copy of that original, whose strong features have
been fortunately preserved for us by the obscure author of the *Martyrdom of St. Dasius.* In other words, the martyrologist's account of the
Saturnalia agrees so closely with the accounts of similar rites elsewhere,
which could not possibly have been known to him, that the substantial
accuracy of his description may be regarded as established; and
further, since the custom of putting a mock king to death as a representative of a god cannot have grown out of a practice of appointing
him to preside over a holiday revel, whereas the reverse may very well
have happened, we are justified in assuming that in an earlier and more
barbarous age it was the universal practice in ancient Italy, wherever
the worship of Saturn prevailed, to choose a man who played the part
and enjoyed all the traditionary privileges of Saturn for a season,
and then died, whether by his own or another's hand, whether by the
knife or the fire or on the gallows-tree, in the character of the good
god who gave his life for the world. In Rome itself and other great
towns the growth of civilization had probably mitigated this cruel
custom long before the Augustan age, and transformed it into the
innocent shape it wears in the writings of the few classical writers who
bestow a passing notice on the holiday King of the Saturnalia. But
in remoter districts the older and sterner practice may long have
survived; and even if after the unification of Italy the barbarous
usage was suppressed by the Roman government, the memory of it
would be handed down by the peasants and would tend from time to
time, as still happens with the lowest forms of superstition among
ourselves, to lead to a recrudescence of the practice, especially among
the rude soldiery on the outskirts of the empire over whom the once
iron hand of Rome was beginning to relax its grasp.

The resemblance between the Saturnalia of ancient and the Carnival
of modern Italy has often been remarked; but in the light of all the
facts that have come before us, we may well ask whether the resemblance does not amount to identity. We have seen that in Italy,
Spain, and France, that is, in the countries where the influence of Rome
has been deepest and most lasting, a conspicuous feature of the Carnival
is a burlesque figure personifying the festive season, which after a short
career of glory and dissipation is publicly shot, burnt, or otherwise
destroyed, to the feigned grief or genuine delight of the populace. If
the view here suggested of the Carnival is correct, this grotesque
personage is no other than a direct successor of the old King of the
Saturnalia, the master of the revels, the real man who personated
Saturn and, when the revels were over, suffered a real death in his
assumed character. The King of the Bean on Twelfth Night and the
mediaeval Bishop of Fools, Abbot of Unreason, or Lord of Misrule are
figures of the same sort and may perhaps have had a similar origin.
Whether that was so or not, we may conclude with a fair degree of
probability that if the King of the Wood at Aricia lived and died as

an incarnation of a sylvan deity, he had of old a parallel at Rome in the men who, year by year, were slain in the character of King Saturn, the god of the sown and sprouting seed.

CHAPTER LIX

KILLING THE GOD IN MEXICO

By no people does the custom of sacrificing the human representative of a god appear to have been observed so commonly and with so much solemnity as by the Aztecs of ancient Mexico. With the ritual of these remarkable sacrifices we are well acquainted, for it has been fully described by the Spaniards who conquered Mexico in the sixteenth century, and whose curiosity was naturally excited by the discovery in this distant region of a barbarous and cruel religion which presented many curious points of analogy to the doctrine and ritual of their own church. " They took a captive," says the Jesuit Acosta, " such as they thought good ; and afore they did sacrifice him unto their idols, they gave him the name of the idol, to whom he should be sacrificed, and apparelled him with the same ornaments like their idol, saying, that he did represent the same idol. And during the time that this representation lasted, which was for a year in some feasts, in others six months, and in others less, they reverenced and worshipped him in the same manner as the proper idol ; and in the meantime he did eat, drink, and was merry. When he went through the streets, the people came forth to worship him, and every one brought him an alms, with children and sick folks, that he might cure them, and bless them, suffering him to do all things at his pleasure, only he was accompanied with ten or twelve men lest he should fly. And he (to the end he might be reverenced as he passed) sometimes sounded upon a small flute, that the people might prepare to worship him. The feast being come, and he grown fat, they killed him, opened him, and ate him, making a solemn sacrifice of him."

This general description of the custom may now be illustrated by particular examples. Thus at the festival called Toxcatl, the greatest festival of the Mexican year, a young man was annually sacrificed in the character of Tezcatlipoca, " the god of gods," after having been maintained and worshipped as that great deity in person for a whole year. According to the old Franciscan monk Sahagun, our best authority on the Aztec religion, the sacrifice of the human god fell at Easter or a few days later, so that, if he is right, it would correspond in date as well as in character to the Christian festival of the death and resurrection of the Redeemer. More exactly he tells us that the sacrifice took place on the first day of the fifth Aztec month, which according to him began on the twenty-third or twenty-seventh day of April.

At this festival the great god died in the person of one human representative and came to life again in the person of another, who was destined to enjoy the fatal honour of divinity for a year and to perish, like all his predecessors, at the end of it. The young man singled out for this high dignity was carefully chosen from among the captives on the ground of his personal beauty. He had to be of unblemished body, slim as a reed and straight as a pillar, neither too tall nor too short. If through high living he grew too fat, he was obliged to reduce himself by drinking salt water. And in order that he might behave in his lofty station with becoming grace and dignity he was carefully trained to comport himself like a gentleman of the first quality, to speak correctly and elegantly, to play the flute, to smoke cigars and to snuff at flowers with a dandified air. He was honourably lodged in the temple, where the nobles waited on him and paid him homage, bringing him meat and serving him like a prince. The king himself saw to it that he was apparelled in gorgeous attire, " for already he esteemed him as a god." Eagle down was gummed to his head and white cock's feathers were stuck in his hair, which drooped to his girdle. A wreath of flowers like roasted maize crowned his brows, and a garland of the same flowers passed over his shoulders and under his armpits. Golden ornaments hung from his nose, golden armlets adorned his arms, golden bells jingled on his legs at every step he took ; earrings of turquoise dangled from his ears, bracelets of turquoise bedecked his wrists ; necklaces of shells encircled his neck and depended on his breast ; he wore a mantle of network, and round his middle a rich waistcloth. When this bejewelled exquisite lounged through the streets playing on his flute, puffing at a cigar, and smelling at a nosegay, the people whom he met threw themselves on the earth before him and prayed to him with sighs and tears, taking up the dust in their hands and putting it in their mouths in token of the deepest humiliation and subjection. Women came forth with children in their arms and presented them to him, saluting him as a god. For " he passed for our Lord God ; the people acknowledged him as the Lord." All who thus worshipped him on his passage he saluted gravely and courteously. Lest he should flee, he was everywhere attended by a guard of eight pages in the royal livery, four of them with shaven crowns like the palace-slaves, and four of them with the flowing locks of warriors ; and if he contrived to escape, the captain of the guard had to take his place as the representative of the god and to die in his stead. Twenty days before he was to die, his costume was changed, and four damsels delicately nurtured and bearing the names of four goddesses—the Goddess of Flowers, the Goddess of the Young Maize, the Goddess " Our Mother among the Water," and the Goddess of Salt—were given him to be his brides, and with them he consorted. During the last five days divine honours were showered on the destined victim. The king remained in his palace while the whole court went after the human god. Solemn banquets and dances followed each other in regular succession and at appointed places. On the last day the young

man, attended by his wives and pages, embarked in a canoe covered
with a royal canopy and was ferried across the lake to a spot where a
little hill rose from the edge of the water.   It was called the Mountain
of Parting, because there his wives bade him a last farewell.   Then,
accompanied only by his pages, he repaired to a small and lonely
temple by the wayside.   Like the Mexican temples in general, it was
built in the form of a pyramid ; and as the young man ascended the
stairs he broke at every step one of the flutes on which he had played
in the days of his glory.   On reaching the summit he was seized and
held down by the priests on his back upon a block of stone, while one
of them cut open his breast, thrust his hand into the wound, and
wrenching out his heart held it up in sacrifice to the sun.   The body
of the dead god was not, like the bodies of common victims, sent
rolling down the steps of the temple, but was carried down to the foot,
where the head was cut off and spitted on a pike.   Such was the regular
end of the man who personated the greatest god of the Mexican
pantheon.

The honour of living for a short time in the character of a god and
dying a violent death in the same capacity was not restricted to men
in Mexico ; women were allowed, or rather compelled, to enjoy the
glory and to share the doom as representatives of goddesses.   Thus
at a great festival in September, which was preceded by a strict
fast of seven days, they sanctified a young slave girl of twelve or
thirteen years, the prettiest they could find, to represent the Maize
Goddess Chicomecohuatl.   They invested her with the ornaments
of the goddess, putting a mitre on her head and maize-cobs round
her neck and in her hands, and fastening a green feather upright
on the crown of her head to imitate an ear of maize.   This they did,
we are told, in order to signify that the maize was almost ripe at the
time of the festival, but because it was still tender they chose a girl
of tender years to play the part of the Maize Goddess.   The whole
long day they led the poor child in all her finery, with the green plume
nodding on her head, from house to house dancing merrily to cheer
people after the dulness and privations of the fast.

In the evening all the people assembled at the temple, the courts
of which they lit up by a multitude of lanterns and candles.   There
they passed the night without sleeping, and at midnight, while the
trumpets, flutes, and horns discoursed solemn music, a portable
framework or palanquin was brought forth, bedecked with festoons of
maize-cobs and peppers and filled with seeds of all sorts.   This the
bearers set down at the door of the chamber in which the wooden
image of the goddess stood.   Now the chamber was adorned and
wreathed, both outside and inside, with wreaths of maize-cobs, peppers,
pumpkins, roses, and seeds of every kind, a wonder to behold ;   the
whole floor was covered deep with these verdant offerings of the pious.
When the music ceased, a solemn procession came forth of priests and
dignitaries, with flaring lights and smoking censers, leading in their
midst the girl who played the part of the goddess.   Then they made

her mount the framework, where she stood upright on the maize and peppers and pumpkins with which it was strewed, her hands resting on two banisters to keep her from falling. Then the priests swung the smoking censers round her; the music struck up again, and while it played, a great dignitary of the temple suddenly stepped up to her with a razor in his hand and adroitly shore off the green feather she wore on her head, together with the hair in which it was fastened, snipping the lock off by the root. The feather and the hair he then presented to the wooden image of the goddess with great solemnity and elaborate ceremonies, weeping and giving her thanks for the fruits of the earth and the abundant crops which she had bestowed on the people that year; and as he wept and prayed, all the people, standing in the courts of the temple, wept and prayed with him. When that ceremony was over, the girl descended from the framework and was escorted to the place where she was to spend the rest of the night. But all the people kept watch in the courts of the temple by the light of torches till break of day.

The morning being come, and the courts of the temple being still crowded by the multitude, who would have deemed it sacrilege to quit the precincts, the priests again brought forth the damsel attired in the costume of the goddess, with the mitre on her head and the cobs of maize about her neck. Again she mounted the portable framework or palanquin and stood on it, supporting herself by her hands on the banisters. Then the elders of the temple lifted it on their shoulders, and while some swung burning censers and others played on instruments or sang, they carried it in procession through the great courtyard to the hall of the god Huitzilopochtli and then back to the chamber, where stood the wooden image of the Maize Goddess, whom the girl personated. There they caused the damsel to descend from the palanquin and to stand on the heaps of corn and vegetables that had been spread in profusion on the floor of the sacred chamber. While she stood there all the elders and nobles came in a line, one behind the other, carrying saucers full of dry and clotted blood which they had drawn from their ears by way of penance during the seven days' fast. One by one they squatted on their haunches before her, which was the equivalent of falling on their knees with us, and scraping the crust of blood from the saucer cast it down before her as an offering in return for the benefits which she, as the embodiment of the Maize Goddess, had conferred upon them. When the men had thus humbly offered their blood to the human representative of the goddess, the women, forming a long line, did so likewise, each of them dropping on her hams before the girl and scraping her blood from the saucer. The ceremony lasted a long time, for great and small, young and old, all without exception had to pass before the incarnate deity and make their offering. When it was over, the people returned home with glad hearts to feast on flesh and viands of every sort as merrily, we are told, as good Christians at Easter partake of meat and other carnal mercies after the long abstinence of Lent. And when they had eaten and drunk their fill and rested after the night watch, they returned quite refreshed to the temple to see the end of the festival.   And the end of the festival was this.   The multitude being assembled, the priests solemnly incensed the girl who personated the goddess ; then they threw her on her back on the heap of corn and seeds, cut off her head, caught the gushing blood in a tub, and sprinkled the blood on the wooden image of the goddess, the walls of the chamber, and the offerings of corn, peppers, pumpkins, seeds, and vegetables which cumbered the floor.   After that they flayed the headless trunk, and one of the priests made shift to squeeze himself into the bloody skin.   Having done so they clad him in all the robes which the girl had worn ; they put the mitre on his head, the necklace of golden maize-cobs about his neck, the maize-cobs of feathers and gold in his hands ; and thus arrayed they led him forth in public, all of them dancing to the tuck of drum, while he acted as fugleman, skipping and posturing at the head of the procession as briskly as he could be expected to do, incommoded as he was by the tight and clammy skin of the girl and by her clothes, which must have been much too small for a grown man.

In the foregoing custom the identification of the young girl with the Maize Goddess appears to be complete.   The golden maize-cobs which she wore round her neck, the artificial maize-cobs which she carried in her hands, the green feather which was stuck in her hair in imitation (we are told) of a green ear of maize, all set her forth as a personification of the corn-spirit ; and we are expressly informed that she·was specially chosen as a young girl to represent the young maize, which at the time of the festival had not yet fully ripened.   Further, her identification with the corn and the corn-goddess was clearly announced by making her stand on the heaps of maize and there receive the homage and blood-offerings of the whole people, who thereby returned her thanks for the benefits which in her character of a divinity she was supposed to have conferred upon them.   Once more, the practice of beheading her on a heap of corn and seeds and sprinkling her blood, not only on the image of the Maize Goddess, but on the piles of maize, peppers, pumpkins, seeds, and vegetables, can seemingly have had no other object but to quicken and strengthen the crops of corn and the fruits of the earth in general by infusing into their representatives the blood of the Corn Goddess herself.   The analogy of this Mexican sacrifice, the meaning of which appears to be indisputable, may be allowed to strengthen the interpretation which I have given of other human sacrifices offered for the crops.   If the Mexican girl, whose blood was sprinkled on the maize, indeed personated the Maize Goddess, it becomes more than ever probable that the girl whose blood the Pawnees similarly sprinkled on the seed corn personated in like manner the female Spirit of the Corn ; and so with the other human beings whom other races have slaughtered for the sake of promoting the growth of the crops.

Lastly, the concluding act of the sacred drama, in which the body of the dead Maize Goddess was flayed and her skin worn, together with all her sacred insignia, by a man who danced before the people in this grim attire, seems to be best explained on the hypothesis that it was intended to ensure that the divine death should be immediately followed by the divine resurrection.   If that was so, we may infer with some degree of probability that the practice of killing a human representative of a deity has commonly, perhaps always, been regarded merely as a means of perpetuating the divine energies in the fulness of youthful vigour, untainted by the weakness and frailty of age, from which they must have suffered if the deity had been allowed to die a natural death.

These Mexican rites suffice to prove that human sacrifices of the sort I suppose to have prevailed at Aricia were, as a matter of fact, regularly offered by a people whose level of culture was probably not inferior, if indeed it was not distinctly superior, to that occupied by the Italian races at the early period to which the origin of the Arician priesthood must be referred.   The positive and indubitable evidence of the prevalence of such sacrifices in one part of the world may reasonably be allowed to strengthen the probability of their prevalence in places for which the evidence is less full and trustworthy.   Taken all together, the facts which we have passed in review seem to show that the custom of killing men whom their worshippers regard as divine has prevailed in many parts of the world.

CHAPTER LX

BETWEEN HEAVEN AND EARTH

§ 1. *Not to touch the Earth.*—At the outset of this book two questions were proposed for answer : Why had the priest of Aricia to slay his predecessor ?   And why, before doing so, had he to pluck the Golden Bough ?   Of these two questions the first has now been answered. The priest of Aricia, if I am right, was one of those sacred kings or human divinities on whose life the welfare of the community and even the course of nature in general are believed to be intimately dependent. It does not appear that the subjects or worshippers of such a spiritual potentate form to themselves any very clear notion of the exact relationship in which they stand to him ; probably their ideas on the point are vague and fluctuating, and we should err if we attempted to define the relationship with logical precision.   All that the people know, or rather imagine, is that somehow they themselves, their cattle, and their crops are mysteriously bound up with their divine king, so that according as he is well or ill the community is healthy or sickly, the flocks and herds thrive or languish with disease, and the fields yield an abundant or a scanty harvest.   The worst evil which they can conceive of is the natural death of their ruler, whether he succumb to sickness or old age, for in the opinion of his followers such a death would entail the most disastrous consequences on themselves and their possessions ; fatal epidemics would sweep away man and beast, the earth would refuse her increase, nay, the very frame of nature itself might be dissolved.   To guard against these catastrophes it is necessary to put the king to death while he is still in the full bloom of his divine manhood, in order that his sacred life, transmitted in unabated force to his successor, may renew its youth, and thus by successive trans-missions through a perpetual line of vigorous incarnations may remain eternally fresh and young, a pledge and security that men and animals shall in like manner renew their youth by a perpetual succession of generations, and that seedtime and harvest, and summer and winter, and rain and sunshine shall never fail.   That, if my conjecture is right, was why the priest of Aricia, the King of the Wood at Nemi, had regularly to perish by the sword of his successor.

But we have still to ask, What was the Golden Bough ? and why had each candidate for the Arician priesthood to pluck it before he could slay the priest ?   These questions I will now try to answer.

It will be well to begin by noticing two of those rules or taboos by which, as we have seen, the life of divine kings or priests is regulated. The first of the rules to which I would call the reader's attention is that the divine personage may not touch the ground with his foot. This rule was observed by the supreme pontiff of the Zapotecs in Mexico ; he profaned his sanctity if he so much as touched the ground with his foot.   Montezuma, emperor of Mexico, never set foot on the ground ; he was always carried on the shoulders of noblemen, and if he lighted anywhere they laid rich tapestry for him to walk upon. For the Mikado of Japan to touch the ground with his foot was a shameful degradation ; indeed, in the sixteenth century, it was enough to deprive him of his office.   Outside his palace he was carried on men's shoulders ; within it he walked on exquisitely wrought mats. The king and queen of Tahiti might not touch the ground anywhere but within their hereditary domains ; for the ground on which they trod became sacred.   In travelling from place to place they were carried on the shoulders of sacred men.   They were always accom-panied by several pairs of these sanctified attendants ; and when it became necessary to change their bearers, the king and queen vaulted on to the shoulders of their new bearers without letting their feet touch the ground.   It was an evil omen if the king of Dosuma touched the ground, and he had to perform an expiatory ceremony.   Within his palace the king of Persia walked on carpets on which no one else might tread ; outside of it he was never seen on foot but only in a chariot or on horseback.   In old days the king of Siam never set foot upon the earth, but was carried on a throne of gold from place to place. Formerly neither the kings of Uganda, nor their mothers, nor their queens might walk on foot outside of the spacious enclosures in which they lived.   Whenever they went forth they were carried on the shoulders of men of the Buffalo clan, several of whom accompanied any of these royal personages on a journey and took it in turn to bear the burden. The king sat astride the bearer's neck with a leg over each shoulder and his feet tucked under the bearer's arms. When one of these royal carriers grew tired he shot the king on to the shoulders of a second man without allowing the royal feet to touch the ground. In this way they went at a great pace and travelled long distances in a day, when the king was on a journey. The bearers had a special hut in the king's enclosure in order to be at hand the moment they were wanted. Among the Bakuba, or rather Bushongo, a nation in the southern region of the Congo, down to a few years ago persons of the royal blood were forbidden to touch the ground; they must sit on a hide, a chair, or the back of a slave, who crouched on hands and feet; their feet rested on the feet of others. When they travelled they were carried on the backs of men; but the king journeyed in a litter supported on shafts. Among the Ibo people about Awka, in Southern Nigeria, the priest of the Earth has to observe many taboos; for example, he may not see a corpse, and if he meets one on the road he must hide his eyes with his wristlet. He must abstain from many foods, such as eggs, birds of all sorts, mutton, dog, bush-buck, and so forth. He may neither wear nor touch a mask, and no masked man may enter his house. If a dog enters his house, it is killed and thrown out. As priest of the Earth he may not sit on the bare ground, nor eat things that have fallen on the ground, nor may earth be thrown at him. According to ancient Brahmanic ritual a king at his inauguration trod on a tiger's skin and a golden plate; he was shod with shoes of boar's skin, and so long as he lived thereafter he might not stand on the earth with his bare feet.

But besides persons who are permanently sacred or tabooed and are therefore permanently forbidden to touch the ground with their feet, there are others who enjoy the character of sanctity or taboo only on certain occasions, and to whom accordingly the prohibition in question only applies at the definite seasons during which they exhale the odour of sanctity. Thus among the Kayans or Bahaus of Central Borneo, while the priestesses are engaged in the performance of certain rites they may not step on the ground, and boards are laid for them to tread on. Warriors, again, on the war-path are surrounded, so to say, by an atmosphere of taboo; hence some Indians of North America might not sit on the bare ground the whole time they were out on a warlike expedition. In Laos the hunting of elephants gives rise to many taboos; one of them is that the chief hunter may not touch the earth with his foot. Accordingly, when he alights from his elephant, the others spread a carpet of leaves for him to step upon.

Apparently holiness, magical virtue, taboo, or whatever we may call that mysterious quality which is supposed to pervade sacred or tabooed persons, is conceived by the primitive philosopher as a physical substance or fluid, with which the sacred man is charged just as a Leyden jar is charged with electricity; and exactly as the electricity in the jar can be discharged by contact with a good conductor, so the holiness or magical virtue in the man can be discharged and drained away by contact with the earth, which on this theory serves as an excellent conductor for the magical fluid. Hence in order to preserve the charge from running to waste, the sacred or tabooed personage must be carefully prevented from touching the ground ; in electrical language he must be insulated, if he is not to be emptied of the precious substance or fluid with which he, as a vial, is filled to the brim. And in many cases apparently the insulation of the tabooed person is recommended as a precaution not merely for his own sake but for the sake of others ; for since the virtue of holiness or taboo is, so to say, a powerful explosive which the smallest touch may detonate, it is necessary in the interest of the general safety to keep it within narrow bounds, lest breaking out it should blast, blight, and destroy whatever it comes into contact with.

§ 2. *Not to see the Sun.*—The second rule to be here noted is that the sun may not shine upon the divine person. This rule was observed both by the Mikado and by the pontiff of the Zapotecs. The latter " was looked upon as a god whom the earth was not worthy to hold, nor the sun to shine upon." The Japanese would not allow that the Mikado should expose his sacred person to the open air, and the sun was not thought worthy to shine on his head. The Indians of Granada, in South America, " kept those who were to be rulers or commanders, whether men or women, locked up for several years when they were children, some of them seven years, and this so close that they were not to see the sun, for if they should happen to see it they forfeited their lordship, eating certain sorts of food appointed ; and those who were their keepers at certain times went into their retreat or prison and scourged them severely." Thus, for example, the heir to the throne of Bogota, who was not the son but the sister's son of the king, had to undergo a rigorous training from his infancy : he lived in complete retirement in a temple, where he might not see the sun nor eat salt nor converse with a woman : he was surrounded by guards who observed his conduct and noted all his actions : if he broke a single one of the rules laid down for him, he was deemed infamous and forfeited all his rights to the throne. So, too, the heir to the kingdom of Sogamoso, before succeeding to the crown, had to fast for seven years in the temple, being shut up in the dark and not allowed to see the sun or light. The prince who was to become Inca of Peru had to fast for a month without seeing light.

§ 3. *The Seclusion of Girls at Puberty.*—Now it is remarkable that the foregoing two rules—not to touch the ground and not to see the sun—are observed either separately or conjointly by girls at puberty in many parts of the world. Thus amongst the negroes of Loango girls at puberty are confined in separate huts, and they may not touch the ground with any part of their bare body. Among the Zulus and kindred tribes of South Africa, when the first signs of puberty show themselves " while a girl is walking, gathering wood, or working in the field, she runs to the river and hides herself among the reeds for the day, so as not to be seen by men. She covers her head carefully with her blanket that the sun may not shine on it and shrivel ner up into a withered skeleton, as would result from exposure to the sun's beams. After dark she returns to her home and is secluded " in a hut for some time. With the Awa-nkonde, a tribe at the northern end of Lake Nyassa, it is a rule that after her first menstruation a girl must be kept apart, with a few companions of her own sex, in a darkened house. The floor is covered with dry banana leaves, but no fire may be lit in the house, which is called " the house of the Awasungu," that is, " of maidens who have no hearts."

In New Ireland girls are confined for four or five years in small cages, being kept in the dark and not allowed to set foot on the ground. The custom has been thus described by an eye-witness. " I heard from a teacher about some strange custom connected with some of the young girls here, so I asked the chief to take me to the house where they were. The house was about twenty-five feet in length, and stood in a reed and bamboo enclosure, across the entrance to which a bundle of dried grass was suspended to show that it was strictly ' tabu.' Inside the house were three conical structures about seven or eight feet in height, and about ten or twelve feet in circumference at the bottom, and for about four feet from the ground, at which point they tapered off to a point at the top. These cages were made of the broad leaves of the pandanus-tree, sewn quite close together so that no light and little or no air could enter. On one side of each is an opening which is closed by a double door of plaited cocoa-nut tree and pandanus-tree leaves. About three feet from the ground there is a stage of bamboos which forms the floor. In each of these cages we were told there was a young woman confined, each of whom had to remain for at least four or five years, without ever being allowed to go outside the house. I could scarcely credit the story when I heard it ; the whole thing seemed too horrible to be true. I spoke to the chief, and told him that I wished to see the inside of the cages, and also to see the girls that I might make them a present of a few beads. He told me that it was ' tabu,' forbidden for any men but their own relations to look at them ; but I suppose the promised beads acted as an inducement, and so he sent away for some old lady who had charge, and who alone is allowed to open the doors. While we were waiting we could hear the girls talking to the chief in a querulous way as if objecting to something or expressing their fears. The old woman came at length and certainly she did not seem a very pleasant jailor or guardian ; nor did she seem to favour the request of the chief to allow us to see the girls, as she regarded us with anything but pleasant looks. However, she had to undo the door when the chief told her to do so, and then the girls peeped out at us, and, when told to do so, they held out their hands for the beads. I, however, purposely sat at some distance away and merely held out the beads to them, as I wished to draw them quite outside, that I might inspect the inside of the cages. This desire of mine gave rise to another difficulty, as these girls were not allowed to put their feet to the ground all the time they were confined in these places. However, they wished to get the beads, and so the old lady had to go outside and collect a lot of pieces of wood and bamboo, which she placed on the ground, and then going to one of the girls, she helped her down and held her hand as she stepped from one piece of wood to another until she came near enough to get the beads I held out to her. I then went to inspect the inside of the cage out of which she had come, but could scarcely put my head inside of it, the atmosphere was so hot and stifling. It was clean and contained nothing but a few short lengths of bamboo for holding water. There was only room for the girl to sit or lie down in a crouched position on the bamboo platform, and when the doors are shut it must be nearly or quite dark inside. The girls are never allowed to come out except once a day to bathe in a dish or wooden bowl placed close to each cage. They say that they perspire profusely. They are placed in these stifling cages when quite young, and must remain there until they are young women, when they are taken out and have each a great marriage feast provided for them. One of them was about fourteen or fifteen years old, and the chief told us that she had been there for five years, but would soon be taken out now. The other two were about eight and ten years old, and they have to stay there for several years longer."

In Kabadi, a district of British New Guinea, " daughters of chiefs, when they are about twelve or thirteen years of age, are kept indoors for two or three years, never being allowed, under any pretence, to descend from the house, and the house is so shaded that the sun cannot shine on them." Among the Yabim and Bukaua, two neighbouring and kindred tribes on the coast of Northern New Guinea, a girl at puberty is secluded for some five or six weeks in an inner part of the house ; but she may not sit on the floor, lest her uncleanness should cleave to it, so a log of wood is placed for her to squat on. Moreover, she may not touch the ground with her feet ; hence if she is obliged to quit the house for a short time, she is muffled up in mats and walks on two halves of a coco-nut shell, which are fastened like sandals to her feet by creeping plants. Among the Ot Danoms of Borneo girls at the age of eight or ten years are shut up in a little room or cell of the house, and cut off from all intercourse with the world for a long time. The cell, like the rest of the house, is raised on piles above the ground, and is lit by a single small window opening on a lonely place, so that the girl is in almost total darkness. She may not leave the room on any pretext whatever, not even for the most necessary purposes. None of her family may see her all the time she is shut up, but a single slave woman is appointed to wait on her. During her lonely confinement, which often lasts seven years, the girl occupies herself in weaving mats or with other handiwork. Her bodily growth is stunted by the long want of exercise, and when, on attaining womanhood, she is brought out, her complexion is pale and wax-like. She is now shown the sun, the earth, the water, the trees, and the flowers, as if she were newly born. Then a great feast is made, a slave is killed, and the girl is smeared with his blood. In Ceram girls at puberty were formerly shut up by themselves in a hut which was kept dark. In Yap, one of the Caroline Islands, should a girl be overtaken by her first menstruation on the public road, she may not sit down on the earth, but must beg for a coco-nut shell to put under her. She is shut up for several days in a small hut at a distance from her parents' house, and afterwards she is bound to sleep for a hundred days in one of the special houses which are provided for the use of menstruous women.

In the island of Mabuiag, Torres Straits, when the signs of puberty appear on a girl, a circle of bushes is made in a dark corner of the house. Here, decked with shoulder-belts, armlets, leglets just below the knees, and anklets, wearing a chaplet on her head, and shell ornaments in her ears, on her chest, and on her back, she squats in the midst of the bushes, which are piled so high round about her that only her head is visible. In this state of seclusion she must remain for three months. All this time the sun may not shine upon her, but at night she is allowed to slip out of the hut, and the bushes that hedge her in are then changed. She may not feed herself or handle food, but is fed by one or two old women, her maternal aunts, who are especially appointed to look after her. One of these women cooks food for her at a special fire in the forest. The girl is forbidden to eat turtle or turtle eggs during the season when the turtles are breeding ; but no vegetable food is refused her. No man, not even her own father, may come into the house while her seclusion lasts ; for if her father saw her at this time he would certainly have bad luck in his fishing, and would probably smash his canoe the very next time he went out in it. At the end of the three months she is carried down to a fresh-water creek by her attendants, hanging on to their shoulders in such a way that her feet do not touch the ground, while the women of the tribe form a ring round her, and thus escort her to the beach. Arrived at the shore, she is stripped of her ornaments, and the bearers stagger with her into the creek, where they immerse her, and all the other women join in splashing water over both the girl and her bearers. When they come out of the water one of the two attendants makes a heap of grass for her charge to squat upon. The other runs to the reef, catches a small crab, tears off its claws, and hastens back with them to the creek. Here in the meantime a fire has been kindled, and the claws are roasted at it. The girl is then fed by her attendants with the roasted claws. After that she is freshly decorated, and the whole party marches back to the village in a single rank, the girl walking in the centre between her two old aunts, who hold her by the wrists. The husbands of her aunts now receive her and lead her into the house of one of them, where all partake of food, and the girl is allowed once more to feed herself in the usual manner. A dance follows, in which the girl takes a prominent part, dancing between the husbands of the two aunts who had charge of her in her retirement.

Among the Yaraikanna tribe of Cape York Peninsula, in Northern Queensland, a girl at puberty is said to live by herself for a month or six weeks ; no man may see her, though any woman may. She stays in a hut or shelter specially made for her, on the floor of which she lies supine. She may not see the sun, and towards sunset she must keep her eyes shut until the sun has gone down, otherwise it is thought that her nose will be diseased. During her seclusion she may eat nothing that lives in salt water, or a snake would kill her. An old woman waits upon her and supplies her with roots, yams, and water. Some Australian tribes are wont to bury their girls at such seasons more or less deeply in the ground, perhaps in order to hide them from the light of the sun.

Among the Indians of California a girl at her first menstruation " was thought to be possessed of a particular degree of supernatural power, and this was not always regarded as entirely defiling or malevolent. Often, however, there was a strong feeling of the power of evil inherent in her condition. Not only was she secluded from her family and the community, but an attempt was made to seclude the world from her. One of the injunctions most strongly laid upon her was not to look about her. She kept her head bowed and was forbidden to see the world and the sun. Some tribes covered her with a blanket. Many of the customs in this connexion resembled those of the North Pacific Coast most strongly, such as the prohibition to the girl to touch or scratch her head with her hand, a special implement being furnished her for the purpose. Sometimes she could eat only when fed and in other cases fasted altogether."

Among the Chinook Indians who inhabited the coast of Washington State, when a chief's daughter attained to puberty, she was hidden for five days from the view of the people ; she might not look at them nor at the sky, nor might she pick berries. It was believed that if she were to look at the sky, the weather would be bad ; that if she picked berries, it would rain ; and that when she hung her towel of cedar-bark on a spruce-tree, the tree withered up at once. She went out of the house by a separate door and bathed in a creek far from the village. She fasted for some days, and for many days more she might not eat fresh food.

Amongst the Aht or Nootka Indians of Vancouver Island, when girls reach puberty they are placed in a sort of gallery in the house " and are there surrounded completely with mats, so that neither the sun nor any fire can be seen. In this cage they remain for several days. Water is given them, but no food. The longer a girl remains in this retirement the greater honour is it to the parents ; but she is disgraced for life if it is known that she has seen fire or the sun during this initiatory ordeal." Pictures of the mythical thunder-bird are painted on the screens behind which she hides. During her seclusion she may neither move nor lie down, but must always sit in a squatting posture. She may not touch her hair with her hands, but is allowed to scratch her head with a comb or a piece of bone provided for the purpose. To scratch her body is also forbidden, as it is believed that every scratch would leave a scar. For eight months after reaching maturity she may not eat any fresh food, particularly salmon ; moreover, she must eat by herself, and use a cup and dish of her own.

In the Tsetsaut tribe of British Columbia a girl at puberty wears a large hat of skin which comes down over her face and screens it from the sun. It is believed that if she were to expose her face to the sun or to the sky, rain would fall. The hat protects her face also against the fire, which ought not to strike her skin ; to shield her hands she wears mittens. In her mouth she carries the tooth of an animal to prevent her own teeth from becoming hollow. For a whole year she may not see blood unless her face is blackened ; otherwise she would grow blind. For two years she wears the hat and lives in a hut by herself, although she is allowed to see other people. At the end of two years a man takes the hat from her head and throws it away. In the Bilqula or Bella Coola tribe of British Columbia, when a girl attains puberty she must stay in the shed which serves as her bedroom, where she has a separate fireplace. She is not allowed to descend to the main part of the house, and may not sit by the fire of the family. For four days she is bound to remain motionless in a sitting posture. She fasts during the day, but is allowed a little food and drink very early in the morning. After the four days' seclusion she may leave her room, but only through a separate opening cut in the floor, for the houses are raised on piles. She may not yet come into the chief room. In leaving the house she wears a large hat which protects her face against the rays of the sun. It is believed that if the sun were to shine on her face her eyes would suffer. She may pick berries on the hills, but may not come near the river or sea for a whole year. Were she to eat fresh salmon she would lose her senses, or her mouth would be changed into a long beak.

Amongst the Tlingit (Thlinkeet) or Kolosh Indians of Alaska, when a girl showed signs of womanhood she used to be confined to a little hut or cage, which was completely blocked up with the exception of a small air-hole. In this dark and filthy abode she had to remain a year, without fire, exercise, or associates. Only her mother and a female slave might supply her with nourishment. Her food was put in at the little window ; she had to drink out of the wing-bone of a white-headed eagle. The time of her seclusion was afterwards reduced in some places to six or three months or even less. She had to wear a sort of hat with long flaps, that her gaze might not pollute the sky ; for she was thought unfit for the sun to shine upon, and it was imagined that her look would destroy the luck of a hunter, fisher, or gambler, turn things to stone, and do other mischief. At the end of her confinement her old clothes were burnt, new ones were made, and a feast was given, at which a slit was cut in her under lip parallel to the mouth, and a piece of wood or shell was inserted to keep the aperture open. Among the Koniags, an Esquimau people of Alaska, a girl at puberty was placed in a small hut in which she had to remain on her hands and feet for six months ; then the hut was enlarged a little so as to allow her to straighten her back, but in this posture she had to remain for six months more. All this time she was regarded as an unclean being with whom no one might hold intercourse.

When symptoms of puberty appeared on a girl for the first time, the Guaranis of Southern Brazil, on the borders of Paraguay, used to sew her up in her hammock, leaving only a small opening in it to allow her to breathe. In this condition, wrapt up and shrouded like a corpse, she was kept for two or three days or so long as the symptoms lasted, and during this time she had to observe a most rigorous fast. After that she was entrusted to a matron, who cut the girl's hair and enjoined her to abstain most strictly from eating flesh of any kind until her hair should be grown long enough to hide her ears. In similar circumstances the Chiriguanos of South-eastern Bolivia hoisted the girl in her hammock to the roof, where she stayed for a month : the second month the hammock was let half-way down from the roof ; and in the third month old women, armed with sticks, entered the hut and ran about striking everything they met, saying they were hunting the snake that had wounded the girl.

Among the Matacos or Mataguayos, an Indian tribe of the Gran Chaco, a girl at puberty has to remain in seclusion for some time. She lies covered up with branches or other things in a corner of the hut, seeing no one and speaking to no one, and during this time she may eat neither flesh nor fish. Meantime a man beats a drum in front of the house. Among the Yuracares, an Indian tribe of Eastern Bolivia, when a girl perceives the signs of puberty, her father constructs a little hut of palm leaves near the house. In this cabin he shuts up his daughter so that she cannot see the light, and there she remains fasting rigorously for four days.

Amongst the Macusis of British Guiana, when a girl shows the first signs of puberty, she is hung in a hammock at the highest point of the hut. For the first few days she may not leave the hammock by day, but at night she must come down, light a fire, and spend the night beside it, else she would break out in sores on her neck, throat, and other parts of her body. So long as the symptoms are at their height, she must fast rigorously. When they have abated, she may come down and take up her abode in a little compartment that is made for her in the darkest corner of the hut. In the morning she may cook her food, but it must be at a separate fire and in a vessel of her own. After about ten days the magician comes and undoes the spell by muttering charms and breathing on her and on the more valuable of the things with which she has come in contact. The pots and drinking-vessels which she used are broken and the fragments buried. After her first bath, the girl must submit to be beaten by her mother with thin rods without uttering a cry. At the end of the second period she is again beaten, but not afterwards. She is now " clean," and can mix again with people. Other Indians of Guiana, after keeping the girl in her hammock at the top of the hut for a month, expose her to certain large ants, whose bite is very painful. Sometimes, in addition to being stung with ants, the sufferer has to fast day and night so long as she remains slung up on high in her hammock, so that when she comes down she is reduced to a skeleton.

When a Hindoo maiden reaches maturity she is kept in a dark room for four days, and is forbidden to see the sun. She is regarded as unclean ; no one may touch her. Her diet is restricted to boiled rice, milk, sugar, curd, and tamarind without salt. On the morning of the fifth day she goes to a neighbouring tank, accompanied by five women whose husbands are alive. Smeared with turmeric water, they all bathe and return home, throwing away the mat and other things that were in the room. The Rarhi Brahmans of Bengal compel a girl at puberty to live alone, and do not allow her to see the face of any male. For three days she remains shut up in a dark room, and has to undergo certain penances. Fish, flesh, and sweetmeats are forbidden her ; she must live upon rice and ghee. Among the Tiyans of Malabar a girl is thought to be polluted for four days from the beginning of her first menstruation. During this time she must keep to the north side of the house, where she sleeps on a grass mat of a particular kind, in a room festooned with garlands of young coco-nut leaves. Another girl keeps her company and sleeps with her, but she may not touch any other person, tree or plant. Further, she may not see the sky, and woe betide her if she catches sight of a crow or a cat ! Her diet must be strictly vegetarian, without salt, tamarinds, or chillies. She is armed against evil spirits by a knife, which is placed on the mat or carried on her person.

In Cambodia a girl at puberty is put to bed under a mosquito curtain, where she should stay a hundred days. Usually, however, four, five, ten, or twenty days are thought enough ; and even this, in a hot climate and under the close meshes of the curtain, is sufficiently trying. According to another account, a Cambodian maiden at puberty is said to " enter into the shade." During her retirement, which, according to the rank and position of her family, may last any time from a few days to several years, she has to observe a number of rules, such as not to be seen by a strange man, not to eat flesh or fish, and so on. She goes nowhere, not even to the pagoda. But this state of seclusion is discontinued during eclipses ; at such times she goes forth and pays her devotions to the monster who is supposed to cause eclipses by catching the heavenly bodies between his teeth. This permission to break her rule of retirement and appear abroad during an eclipse seems to show how literally the injunction is interpreted which forbids maidens entering on womanhood to look upon the sun.

A superstition so widely diffused as this might be expected to leave traces in legends and folk-tales. And it has done so. The old Greek story of Danae, who was confined by her father in a subterranean chamber or a brazen tower, but impregnated by Zeus, who reached her in the shape of a shower of gold, perhaps belongs to this class of tales. It has its counterpart in the legend which the Kirghiz of Siberia tell of their ancestry. A certain Khan had a fair daughter, whom he kept in a dark iron house, that no man might see her. An old woman tended her ; and when the girl was grown

to maidenhood she asked the old woman, " Where do you go so often ? "
" My child," said the old dame, " there is a bright world. In that
bright world your father and mother live, and all sorts of people
live there. That is where I go." The maiden said, " Good mother,
I will tell nobody, but show me that bright world." So the old woman
took the girl out of the iron house. But when she saw the bright
world, the girl tottered and fainted ; and the eye of God fell upon
her, and she conceived. Her angry father put her in a golden chest
and sent her floating away (fairy gold can float in fairyland) over the
wide sea. The shower of gold in the Greek story, and the eye of God
in the Kirghiz legend, probably stand for sunlight and the sun. The
idea that women may be impregnated by the sun is not uncommon
in legends, and there are even traces of it in marriage customs.

§ 4. *Reasons for the Seclusion of Girls at Puberty.*—The motive
for the restraints so commonly imposed on girls at puberty is the
deeply engrained dread which primitive man universally entertains
of menstruous blood. He fears it at all times but especially on its
first appearance ; hence the restrictions under which women lie at
their first menstruation are usually more stringent than those which
they have to observe at any subsequent recurrence of the mysterious
flow. Some evidence of the fear and of the customs based on it has
been cited in an earlier part of this work ; but as the terror, for it is
nothing less, which the phenomenon periodically strikes into the
mind of the savage has deeply influenced his life and institutions, it
may be well to illustrate the subject with some further examples.

Thus in the Encounter Bay tribe of South Australia there is, or
used to be, a " superstition which obliges a woman to separate
herself from the camp at the time of her monthly illness, when, if a
young man or boy should approach, she calls out, and he immediately
makes a circuit to avoid her. If she is neglectful upon this point,
she exposes herself to scolding, and sometimes to severe beating by
her husband or nearest relation, because the boys are told from their
infancy that if they see the blood they will early become grey-headed,
and their strength will fail prematurely." The Dieri of Central
Australia believe that if women at these times were to eat fish or
bathe in a river the fish would all die and the water would dry up.
The Arunta of the same region forbid menstruous women to gather
the *irriakura* bulbs, which form a staple article of diet for both men
and women. They think that were a woman to break this rule, the
supply of bulbs would fail.

In some Australian tribes the seclusion of menstruous women
was even more rigid, and was enforced by severer penalties than a
scolding or a beating. Thus " there is a regulation relating to camps
in the Wakelbura tribe which forbids the women coming into the
encampment by the same path as the men. Any violation of this
rule would in a large camp be punished with death. The reason
for this is the dread with which they regard the menstrual period of
women. During such a time, a woman is kept entirely away from

the camp, half a mile at least. A woman in such a condition has boughs of some tree of her totem tied round her loins, and is constantly watched and guarded, for it is thought that should any male be so unfortunate as to see a woman in such a condition, he would die. If such a woman were to let herself be seen by a man, she would probably be put to death. When the woman has recovered, she is painted red and white, her head covered with feathers, and returns to the camp."

In Muralug, one of the Torres Straits Islands, a menstruous woman may not eat anything that lives in the sea, else the natives believe that the fisheries would fail. In Galela, to the west of New Guinea, women at their monthly periods may not enter a tobacco-field, or the plants would be attacked by disease. The Minangka-bauers of Sumatra are persuaded that if a woman in her unclean state were to go near a rice-field the crop would be spoiled.

The Bushmen of South Africa think that, by a glance of a girl's eye at the time when she ought to be kept in strict retirement, men become fixed in whatever position they happen to occupy, with whatever they were holding in their hands, and are changed into trees that talk. Cattle-rearing tribes of South Africa hold that their cattle would die if the milk were drunk by a menstruous woman; and they fear the same disaster if a drop of her blood were to fall on the ground and the oxen were to pass over it. To prevent such a calamity women in general, not menstruous women only, are forbidden to enter the cattle enclosure; and more than that, they may not use the ordinary paths in entering the village or in passing from one hut to another. They are obliged to make circuitous tracks at the back of the huts in order to avoid the ground in the middle of the village where the cattle stand or lie down. These women's tracks may be seen at every Caffre village. Among the Baganda, in like manner, no menstruous woman might drink milk or come into contact with any milk-vessel; and she might not touch anything that belonged to her husband, nor sit on his mat, nor cook his food. If she touched anything of his at such a time it was deemed equivalent to wishing him dead or to actually working magic for his destruction. Were she to handle any article of his, he would surely fall ill; were she to touch his weapons, he would certainly be killed in the next battle. Further, the Baganda would not suffer a menstruous woman to visit a well; if she did so, they feared that the water would dry up, and that she herself would fall sick and die, unless she confessed her fault and the medicine-man made atonement for her. Among the Akikuyu of British East Africa, if a new hut is built in a village and the wife chances to menstruate in it on the day she lights the first fire there, the hut must be broken down and demolished the very next day. The woman may on no account sleep a second night in it; there is a curse both on her and on it.

According to the Talmud, if a woman at the beginning of her period passes between two men, she thereby kills one of them. Peasants of the Lebanon think that menstruous women are the cause of many misfortunes ; their shadow causes flowers to wither and trees to perish, it even arrests the movements of serpents ; if one of them mounts a horse, the animal might die or at least be disabled for a long time.

The Guayquiries of the Orinoco believe that when a woman has her courses, everything upon which she steps will die, and that if a man treads on the place where she has passed, his legs will immediately swell up. Among the Bri-bri Indians of Costa Rica a married woman at her periods uses for plates only banana leaves, which, when she has done with them, she throws away in a sequestered spot ; for should a cow find and eat them, the animal would waste away and perish. Also she drinks only out of a special vessel, because any person who should afterwards drink out of the same vessel would infallibly pine away and die.

Among most tribes of North American Indians the custom was that women in their courses retired from the camp or the village and lived during the time of their uncleanness in special huts or shelters which were appropriated to their use. There they dwelt apart, eating and sleeping by themselves, warming themselves at their own fires, and strictly abstaining from all communications with men, who shunned them just as if they were stricken with the plague.

Thus, to take examples, the Creek and kindred Indians of the United States compelled women at menstruation to live in separate huts at some distance from the village. There the women had to stay, at the risk of being surprised and cut off by enemies. It was thought " a most horrid and dangerous pollution " to go near the women at such times ; and the danger extended to enemies who, if they slew the women, had to cleanse themselves from the pollution by means of certain sacred herbs and roots. The Stseelis Indians of British Columbia imagined that if a menstruous woman were to step over a bundle of arrows, the arrows would thereby be rendered useless and might even cause the death of their owner ; and similarly that if she passed in front of a hunter who carried a gun, the weapon would never shoot straight again. Among the Chippeways and other Indians of the Hudson Bay Territory, menstruous women are excluded from the camp, and take up their abode in huts of branches. They wear long hoods, which effectually conceal the head and breast. They may not touch the household furniture nor any objects used by men ; for their touch " is supposed to defile them, so that their subsequent use would be followed by certain mischief or misfortune," such as disease or death. They must drink out of a swan's bone. They may not walk on the common paths nor cross the tracks of animals. They " are never permitted to walk on the ice of rivers or lakes, or near the part where the men are hunting beaver, or where a fishing-net is set, for fear of averting their success. They are also prohibited at those times from partaking of the head of any animal, and even from walking in or crossing the track where the head of a deer, moose, beaver, and many other animals have lately been carried, either on a sledge or on the back.   To be guilty of a violation of this custom is considered as of the greatest importance ; because they firmly believe that it would be a means of preventing the hunter from having an equal success in his future excursions." So the Lapps forbid women at menstruation to walk on that part of the shore where the fishers are in the habit of setting out their fish ; and the Esquimaux of Bering Strait believe that if hunters were to come near women in their courses they would catch no game.   For a like reason the Carrier Indians will not suffer a menstruous woman to cross the tracks of animals ; if need be, she is carried over them.   They think that if she waded in a stream or a lake, the fish would die.

Amongst the civilised nations of Europe the superstitions which cluster round this mysterious aspect of woman's nature are not less extravagant than those which prevail among savages.   In the oldest existing cyclopaedia—the *Natural History* of Pliny—the list of dangers apprehended from menstruation is longer than any furnished by mere barbarians.   According to Pliny, the touch of a menstruous woman turned wine to vinegar, blighted crops, killed seedlings, blasted gardens, brought down the fruit from trees, dimmed mirrors, blunted razors, rusted iron and brass (especially at the waning of the moon), killed bees, or at least drove them from their hives, caused mares to miscarry, and so forth.   Similarly, in various parts of Europe, it is still believed that if a woman in her courses enters a brewery the beer will turn sour ; if she touches beer, wine, vinegar, or milk, it will go bad ; if she makes jam, it will not keep ; if she mounts a mare, it will miscarry ; if she touches buds, they will wither ; if she climbs a cherry tree, it will die.   In Brunswick people think that if a menstruous woman assists at the killing of a pig the pork will putrefy. In the Greek island of Calymnos a woman at such times may not go to the well to draw water, nor cross a running stream, nor enter the sea.   Her presence in a boat is said to raise storms.

Thus the object of secluding women at menstruation is to neutralise the dangerous influences which are supposed to emanate from them at such times.   That the danger is believed to be especially great at the first menstruation appears from the unusual precautions taken to isolate girls at this crisis.   Two of these precautions have been illustrated above, namely, the rules that the girl may not touch the ground nor see the sun.   The general effect of these rules is to keep her suspended, so to say, between heaven and earth.   Whether enveloped in her hammock and slung up to the roof, as in South America, or raised above the ground in a dark and narrow cage, as in New Ireland, she may be considered to be out of the way of doing mischief, since, being shut off both from the earth and from the sun, she can poison neither of these great sources of life by her deadly contagion.   In short, she is rendered harmless by being, in electrical language, insulated.   But the precautions thus taken to isolate or insulate the girl are dictated by a regard for her own safety as well as for the safety of others.   For it is thought that she herself would suffer if she were to neglect the prescribed regimen. Thus Zulu girls, as we have seen, believe that they would shrivel to skeletons if the sun were to shine on them at puberty, and the Macusis imagine that, if a young woman were to transgress the rules, she would suffer from sores on various parts of her body. In short, the girl is viewed as charged with a powerful force which, if not kept within bounds, may prove destructive both to herself and to all with whom she comes in contact. To repress this force within the limits necessary for the safety of all concerned is the object of the taboos in question.

The same explanation applies to the observance of the same rules by divine kings and priests. The uncleanness, as it is called, of girls at puberty and the sanctity of holy men do not, to the primitive mind, differ materially from each other. They are only different manifestations of the same mysterious energy which, like energy in general, is in itself neither good nor bad, but becomes beneficent or maleficent according to its application. Accordingly, if, like girls at puberty, divine personages may neither touch the ground nor see the sun, the reason is, on the one hand, a fear lest their divinity might, at contact with earth or heaven, discharge itself with fatal violence on either ; and, on the other hand, an apprehension that the divine being, thus drained of his ethereal virtue, might thereby be incapacitated for the future performance of those magical functions, upon the proper discharge of which the safety of the people and even of the world is believed to hang. Thus the rules in question fall under the head of the taboos which we examined in an earlier part of this book ; they are intended to preserve the life of the divine person and with it the life of his subjects and worshippers. Nowhere, it is thought, can his precious yet dangerous life be at once so safe and so harmless as when it is neither in heaven nor on earth, but, as far as possible, suspended between the two.

CHAPTER LXI

THE MYTH OF BALDER

A DEITY whose life might in a sense be said to be neither in heaven nor on earth but between the two was the Norse Balder, the good and beautiful god, the son of the great god Odin, and himself the wisest mildest, best beloved of all the immortals. The story of his death, as it is told in the younger or prose *Edda*, runs thus. Once on a time Balder dreamed heavy dreams which seemed to forebode his death. Thereupon the gods held a council and resolved to make him secure against every danger. So the goddess Frigg took an oath from fire and water, iron and all metals, stones and earth, from trees, sicknesses and poisons, and from all four-footed beasts, birds, and creeping things, that they would not hurt Balder. When this was done Balder was deemed invulnerable ; so the gods amused themselves by setting him in their midst, while some shot at him, others hewed at him, and others threw stones at him. But whatever they did, nothing could hurt him ; and at this they were all glad. Only Loki, the mischief-maker, was displeased, and he went in the guise of an old woman to Frigg, who told him that the weapons of the gods could not wound Balder, since she had made them all swear not to hurt him. Then Loki asked, " Have all things sworn to spare Balder ? " She answered, " East of Walhalla grows a plant called mistletoe ; it seemed to me too young to swear." So Loki went and pulled the mistletoe and took it to the assembly of the gods. There he found the blind god Hother standing at the outside of the circle. Loki asked him, " Why do you not shoot at Balder ? " Hother answered, " Because I do not see where he stands ; besides I have no weapon." Then said Loki, " Do like the rest and show Balder honour, as they all do. I will show you where he stands, and do you shoot at him with this twig." Hother took the mistletoe and threw it at Balder, as Loki directed him. The mistletoe struck Balder and pierced him through and through, and he fell down dead. And that was the greatest misfortune that ever befell gods and men. For a while the gods stood speechless, then they lifted up their voices and wept bitterly. They took Balder's body and brought it to the sea-shore. There stood Balder's ship ; it was called Ringhorn, and was the hugest of all ships. The gods wished to launch the ship and to burn Balder's body on it, but the ship would not stir. So they sent for a giantess called Hyrrockin. She came riding on a wolf and gave the ship such a push that fire flashed from the rollers and all the earth shook. Then Balder's body was taken and placed on the funeral pile upon his ship. When his wife Nanna saw that, her heart burst for sorrow and she died. So she was laid on the funeral pile with her husband, and fire was put to it. Balder's horse, too, with all its trappings, was burned on the pile.

Whether he was a real or merely a mythical personage, Balder was worshipped in Norway. On one of the bays of the beautiful Sogne Fiord, which penetrates far into the depths of the solemn Norwegian mountains, with their sombre pine-forests and their lofty cascades dissolving into spray before they reach the dark water of the fiord far below, Balder had a great sanctuary. It was called Balder's Grove. A palisade enclosed the hallowed ground, and within it stood a spacious temple with the images of many gods, but none of them was worshipped with such devotion as Balder. So great was the awe with which the heathen regarded the place that no man might harm another there, nor steal his cattle, nor defile himself with women. But women cared for the images of the gods in the temple ; they warmed them at the fire, anointed them with oil, and dried them with cloths.

Whatever may be thought of an historical kernel underlying a mythical husk in the legend of Balder, the details of the story suggest that it belongs to that class of myths which have been dramatised in ritual, or, to put it otherwise, which have been performed as magical ceremonies for the sake of producing those natural effects which they describe in figurative language. A myth is never so graphic and precise in its details as when it is, so to speak, the book of the words which are spoken and acted by the performers of the sacred rite. That the Norse story of Balder was a myth of this sort will become probable if we can prove that ceremonies resembling the incidents in the tale have been performed by Norsemen and other European peoples. Now the main incidents in the tale are two—first, the pulling of the mistletoe, and second, the death and burning of the god ; and both of them may perhaps be found to have had their counterparts in yearly rites observed, whether separately or conjointly, by people in various parts of Europe. These rites will be described and discussed in the following chapters. We shall begin with the annual festivals of fire and shall reserve the pulling of the mistletoe for consideration later on.

CHAPTER LXII

THE FIRE-FESTIVALS OF EUROPE

§ 1. *The Fire-festivals in general.*—All over Europe the peasants have been accustomed from time immemorial to kindle bonfires on certain days of the year, and to dance round or leap over them. Customs of this kind can be traced back on historical evidence to the Middle Ages, and their analogy to similar customs observed in antiquity goes with strong internal evidence to prove that their origin must be sought in a period long prior to the spread of Christianity. Indeed the earliest proof of their observance in Northern Europe is furnished by the attempts made by Christian synods in the eighth century to put them down as heathenish rites. Not uncommonly effigies are burned in these fires, or a pretence is made of burning a living person in them ; and there are grounds for believing that anciently human beings were actually burned on these occasions. A brief view of the customs in question will bring out the traces of human sacrifice, and will serve at the same time to throw light on their meaning.

The seasons of the year when these bonfires are most commonly lit are spring and midsummer ; but in some places they are kindled also at the end of autumn or during the course of the winter, particularly on Hallow E'en (the thirty-first of October), Christmas Day, and the Eve of Twelfth Day. Space forbids me to describe all these festivals at length ; a few specimens must serve to illustrate their general character. We shall begin with the fire-festivals of spring, which usually fall on the first Sunday of Lent (*Quadragesima* or *Invocavit*), Easter Eve, and May Day.

§ 2. *The Lenten Fires.*—The custom of kindling bonfires on the first Sunday in Lent has prevailed in Belgium, the north of France, and many parts of Germany. Thus in the Belgian Ardennes for a week

2 R

or a fortnight before the " day of the great fire," as it is called, children go about from farm to farm collecting fuel. At Grand Halleux any one who refuses their request is pursued next day by the children, who try to blacken his face with the ashes of the extinct fire. When the day has come, they cut down bushes, especially juniper and broom, and in the evening great bonfires blaze on all the heights. It is a common saying that seven bonfires should be seen if the village is to be safe from conflagrations. If the Meuse happens to be frozen hard at the time, bonfires are lit also on the ice. At Grand Halleux they set up a pole called *makral*, or " the witch," in the midst of the pile, and the fire is kindled by the man who was last married in the village. In the neighbourhood of Morlanwelz a straw man is burnt in the fire. Young people and children dance and sing round the bonfires, and leap over the embers to secure good crops or a happy marriage within the year, or as a means of guarding themselves against colic. In Brabant on the same Sunday, down to the beginning of the nineteenth century, women and men disguised in female attire used to go with burning torches to the fields, where they danced and sang comic songs for the purpose, as they alleged, of driving away " the wicked sower," who is mentioned in the Gospel for the day. At Pâturages, in the province of Hainaut, down to about 1840 the custom was observed under the name of *Escouvion* or *Scouvion*. Every year on the first Sunday of Lent, which was called the Day of the Little Scouvion, young folks and children used to run with lighted torches through the gardens and orchards. As they ran they cried at the pitch of their voices :

> *" Bear apples, bear pears, and cherries all black*
> *To Scouvion ! "*

At these words the torch-bearer whirled his blazing brand and hurled it among the branches of the apple-trees, the pear-trees, and the cherry-trees. The next Sunday was called the Day of the Great Scouvion, and the same race with lighted torches among the trees of the orchards was repeated in the afternoon till darkness fell.

In the French department of the Ardennes the whole village used to dance and sing round the bonfires which were lighted on the first Sunday in Lent. Here, too, it was the person last married, sometimes a man and sometimes a woman, who put the match to the fire. The custom is still kept up very commonly in the district. Cats used to be burnt in the fire or roasted to death by being held over it ; and while they were burning the shepherds drove their flocks through the smoke and flames as a sure means of guarding them against sickness and witchcraft. In some communes it was believed that the livelier the dance round the fire, the better would be the crops that year.

In the French province of Franche-Comté, to the west of the Jura Mountains, the first Sunday of Lent is known as the Sunday of the Firebrands (*Brandons*), on account of the fires which it is customary to kindle on that day. On the Saturday or the Sunday the village lads harness themselves to a cart and drag it about the streets, stopping at the doors of the houses where there are girls and begging for a faggot. When they have got enough, they cart the fuel to a spot at some little distance from the village, pile it up, and set it on fire. All the people of the parish come out to see the bonfire. In some villages, when the bells have rung the Angelus, the signal for the observance is given by cries of, " To the fire ! to the fire ! " Lads, lasses, and children dance round the blaze, and when the flames have died down they vie with each other in leaping over the red embers. He or she who does so without singeing his or her garments will be married within the year. Young folk also carry lighted torches about the streets or the fields, and when they pass an orchard they cry out, " More fruit than leaves ! " Down to recent years at Laviron, in the department of Doubs, it was the young married couples of the year who had charge of the bonfires. In the midst of the bonfire a pole was planted with a wooden figure of a cock fastened to the top. Then there were races, and the winner received the cock as a prize.

In Auvergne fires are everywhere kindled on the evening of the first Sunday in Lent. Every village, every hamlet, even every ward, every isolated farm has its bonfire or *figo*, as it is called, which blazes up as the shades of night are falling. The fires may be seen flaring on the heights and in the plains ; the people dance and sing round about them and leap through the flames. Then they proceed to the ceremony of the *Grannas-mias*. A *granno-mio* is a torch of straw fastened to the top of a pole. When the pyre is half consumed, the bystanders kindle the torches at the expiring flames and carry them into the neighbouring orchards, fields, and gardens, wherever there are fruit-trees. As they march they sing at the top of their voices, " Granno my friend, Granno my father, Granno my mother." Then they pass the burning torches under the branches of every tree, singing :

" Brando, brandounci tsaque brantso, in plan panei ! "

that is, " Firebrand burn ; every branch a basketful ! " In some villages the people also run across the sown fields and shake the ashes of the torches on the ground ; also they put some of the ashes in the fowls' nests, in order that the hens may lay plenty of eggs throughout the year. When all these ceremonies have been performed, everybody goes home and feasts ; the special dishes of the evening are fritters and pancakes. Here the application of the fire to the fruit-trees, to the sown fields, and to the nests of the poultry is clearly a charm intended to ensure fertility ; and the Granno to whom the invocations are addressed, and who gives his name to the torches, may possibly be, as Dr. Pommerol suggests, no other than the ancient Celtic god Grannus, whom the Romans identified with Apollo, and whose worship is attested by inscriptions found not only in France but in Scotland and on the Danube.

The custom of carrying lighted torches of straw (*brandons*) about the orchards and fields to fertilise them on the first Sunday of Lent seems to have been common in France, whether it was accompanied with the practice of kindling bonfires or not. Thus in the province of Picardy " on the first Sunday of Lent people carried torches through the fields, exorcising the field-mice, the darnel, and the smut. They imagined that they did much good to the gardens and caused the onions to grow large. Children ran about the fields, torch in hand, to make the land more fertile." At Verges, a village between the Jura and the Combe d'Ain, the torches at this season were kindled on the top of a mountain, and the bearers went to every house in the village, demanding roasted peas and obliging all couples who had been married within the year to dance. In Berry, a district of Central France, it appears that bonfires are not lighted on this day, but when the sun has set the whole population of the villages, armed with blazing torches of straw, disperse over the country and scour the fields, the vineyards, and the orchards. Seen from afar, the multitude of moving lights, twinkling in the darkness, appear like will-o'-the-wisps chasing each other across the plains, along the hillsides, and down the valleys. While the men wave their flambeaus about the branches of the fruit-trees, the women and children tie bands of wheaten-straw round the tree-trunks. The effect of the ceremony is supposed to be to avert the various plagues from which the fruits of the earth are apt to suffer ; and the bands of straw fastened round the stems of the trees are believed to render them fruitful.

In Germany, Austria, and Switzerland at the same season similar customs have prevailed. Thus in the Eifel Mountains, Rhenish Prussia, on the first Sunday in Lent young people used to collect straw and brushwood from house to house. These they carried to an eminence and piled up round a tall, slim beech-tree, to which a piece of wood was fastened at right angles to form a cross. The structure was known as the " hut " or " castle." Fire was set to it and the young people marched round the blazing " castle " bare-headed, each carrying a lighted torch and praying aloud. Sometimes a straw-man was burned in the " hut." People observed the direction in which the smoke blew from the fire. If it blew towards the corn-fields, it was a sign that the harvest would be abundant. On the same day, in some parts of the Eifel, a great wheel was made of straw and dragged by three horses to the top of a hill. Thither the village boys marched at nightfall, set fire to the wheel, and sent it rolling down the slope. At Oberstattfeld the wheel had to be provided by the young man who was last married. About Echternach in Luxemburg the same ceremony is called " burning the witch." At Voralberg in the Tyrol, on the first Sunday in Lent, a slender young fir-tree is surrounded with a pile of straw and firewood. To the top of the tree is fastened a human figure called the " witch," made of old clothes and stuffed with gunpowder. At night the whole is set on fire and boys and girls dance round it, swinging torches and singing rhymes in which the words " corn in the winnowing-basket, the plough in the earth " may be distinguished. In Swabia on the first Sunday in Lent a figure

called the " witch " or the " old wife " or " winter's grandmother "
is made up of clothes and fastened to a pole. This is stuck in the
middle of a pile of wood, to which fire is applied.   While the " witch "
is burning, the young people throw blazing discs into the air.   The
discs are thin round pieces of wood, a few inches in diameter, with
notched edges to imitate the rays of the sun or stars.   They have a
hole in the middle, by which they are attached to the end of a wand.
Before the disc is thrown it is set on fire, the wand is swung to and
fro, and the impetus thus communicated to the disc is augmented
by dashing the rod sharply against a sloping board.   The burning
disc is thus thrown off, and mounting high into the air, describes a
long fiery curve before it reaches the ground.   The charred embers
of the burned " witch " and discs are taken home and planted in the
flax-fields the same night, in the belief that they will keep vermin
from the fields.   In the Rhön Mountains, situated on the borders
of Hesse and Bavaria, the people used to march to the top of a hill
or eminence on the first Sunday in Lent.   Children and lads carried
torches, brooms daubed with tar, and poles swathed in straw. A
wheel, wrapt in combustibles, was kindled and rolled down the hill ;
and the young people rushed about the fields with their burning
torches and brooms, till at last they flung them in a heap, and standing
round them, struck up a hymn or a popular song.   The object of
running about the fields with the blazing torches was to " drive away
the wicked sower."   Or it was done in honour of the Virgin, that
she might preserve the fruits of the earth throughout the year and
bless them.   In neighbouring villages of Hesse, between the Rhön
and the Vogel Mountains, it is thought that wherever the burning
wheels roll, the fields will be safe from hail and storm.

In Switzerland, also, it is or used to be customary to kindle bonfires
on high places on the evening of the first Sunday in Lent, and the day
is therefore popularly known as Spark Sunday.   The custom prevailed,
for example, throughout the canton of Lucerne.   Boys went about
from house to house begging for wood and straw, then piled the fuel
on a conspicuous mountain or hill round about a pole, which bore a
straw effigy called " the witch."   At nightfall the pile was set on fire,
and the young folks danced wildly round it, some of them cracking
whips or ringing bells ; and when the fire burned low enough, they
leaped over it.   This was called " burning the witch."   In some
parts of the canton also they used to wrap old wheels in straw and
thorns, put a light to them, and send them rolling and blazing down
hill.   The more bonfires could be seen sparkling and flaring in the
darkness, the more fruitful was the year expected to be ; and the
higher the dancers leaped beside or over the fire, the higher, it was
thought, would grow the flax.   In some districts it was the last married
man or woman who must kindle the bonfire.

It seems hardly possible to separate from these bonfires, kindled
on the first Sunday in Lent, the fires in which, about the same season,
the effigy called Death is burned as part of the ceremony of " carrying

out Death." We have seen that at Spachendorf, in Austrian Silesia, on the morning of Rupert's Day (Shrove Tuesday ?), a straw-man, dressed in a fur coat and a fur cap, is laid in a hole outside the village and there burned, and that while it is blazing every one seeks to snatch a fragment of it, which he fastens to a branch of the highest tree in his garden or buries in his field, believing that this will make the crops to grow better. The ceremony is known as the " burying of Death." Even when the straw-man is not designated as Death, the meaning of the observance is probably the same ; for the name Death, as I have tried to show, does not express the original intention of the ceremony. At Cobern in the Eifel Mountains the lads make up a straw-man on Shrove Tuesday. The effigy is formally tried and accused of having perpetrated all the thefts that have been com-mitted in the neighbourhood throughout the year. Being condemned to death, the straw-man is led through the village, shot, and burned upon a pyre. They dance round the blazing pile, and the last bride must leap over it. In Oldenburg on the evening of Shrove Tuesday people used to make long bundles of straw, which they set on fire, and then ran about the fields waving them, shrieking, and singing wild songs. Finally they burned a straw-man on the field. In the district of Düsseldorf the straw-man burned on Shrove Tuesday was made of an unthreshed sheaf of corn. On the first Monday after the spring equinox the urchins of Zurich drag a straw-man on a little cart through the streets, while at the same time the girls carry about a May-tree. When vespers ring, the straw-man is burned. In the district of Aachen on Ash Wednesday a man used to be encased in peas-straw and taken to an appointed place. Here he slipped quietly out of his straw casing, which was then burned, the children thinking that it was the man who was being burned. In the Val di Ledro (Tyrol) on the last day of the Carnival a figure is made up of straw and brushwood and then burned. The figure is called the Old Woman, and the ceremony " burning the Old Woman."

§ 3. *The Easter Fires.*—Another occasion on which these fire-festivals are held is Easter Eve, the Saturday before Easter Sunday. On that day it has been customary in Catholic countries to extinguish all the lights in the churches, and then to make a new fire, sometimes with flint and steel, sometimes with a burning-glass. At this fire is lit the great Paschal or Easter candle, which is then used to rekindle all the extinguished lights in the church. In many parts of Germany a bonfire is also kindled, by means of the new fire, on some open space near the church. It is consecrated, and the people bring sticks of oak, walnut, and beech, which they char in the fire, and then take home with them. Some of these charred sticks are thereupon burned at home in a newly-kindled fire, with a prayer that God will preserve the homestead from fire, lightning, and hail. Thus every house receives " new fire." Some of the sticks are kept throughout the year and laid on the hearth-fire during heavy thunder-storms to prevent the house from being struck by lightning, or they are inserted in the roof with the like intention. Others are placed in the fields, gardens, and meadows, with a prayer that God will keep them from blight and hail. Such fields and gardens are thought to thrive more than others ; the corn and the plants that grow in them are not beaten down by hail, nor devoured by mice, vermin, and beetles ; no witch harms them, and the ears of corn stand close and full. The charred sticks are also applied to the plough. The ashes of the Easter bonfire, together with the ashes of the consecrated palm-branches, are mixed with the seed at sowing. A wooden figure called Judas is sometimes burned in the consecrated bonfire, and even where this custom has been abolished the bonfire itself in some places goes by the name of " the burning of Judas."

The essentially pagan character of the Easter fire festival appears plainly both from the mode in which it is celebrated by the peasants and from the superstitious beliefs which they associate with it. All over Northern and Central Germany, from Altmark and Anhalt on the east, through Brunswick, Hanover, Oldenburg, the Harz district, and Hesse to Westphalia the Easter bonfires still blaze simultaneously on the hill-tops. As many as forty may sometimes be counted within sight at once. Long before Easter the young people have been busy collecting firewood ; every farmer contributes, and tar-barrels, petroleum cases, and so forth go to swell the pile. Neighbouring villages vie with each other as to which shall send up the greatest blaze. The fires are always kindled, year after year, on the same hill, which accordingly often takes the name of Easter Mountain. It is a fine spectacle to watch from some eminence the bonfires flaring up one after another on the neighbouring heights. As far as their light reaches, so far, in the belief of the peasants, the fields will be fruitful, and the houses on which they shine will be safe from conflagration or sickness. At Volkmarsen and other places in Hesse the people used to observe which way the wind blew the flames, and then they sowed flax seed in that direction, confident that it would grow well. Brands taken from the bonfires preserve houses from being struck by lightning ; and the ashes increase the fertility of the fields, protect them from mice, and mixed with the drinking-water of cattle make the animals thrive and ensure them against plague. As the flames die down, young and old leap over them, and cattle are sometimes driven through the smouldering embers. In some places tar-barrels or wheels wrapt in straw used to be set on fire, and then sent rolling down the hillside. In others the boys light torches and wisps of straw at the bonfires and rush about brandishing them in their hands.

In Münsterland these Easter fires are always kindled upon certain definite hills, which are hence known as Easter or Paschal Mountains. The whole community assembles about the fire. The young men and maidens, singing Easter hymns, march round and round the fire, till the blaze dies down. Then the girls jump over the fire in a line, one after the other, each supported by two young men who hold her hands and run beside her. In the twilight boys with blazing bundles of straw

run over the fields to make them fruitful. At Delmenhorst, in Oldenburg, it used to be the custom to cut down two trees, plant them in the
ground side by side, and pile twelve tar-barrels against each. Brushwood was then heaped about the trees, and on the evening of Easter
Saturday the boys, after rushing about with blazing bean-poles in their
hands, set fire to the whole. At the end of the ceremony the urchins
tried to blacken each other and the clothes of grown-up people. In
the Altmark it is believed that as far as the blaze of the Easter bonfire
is visible, the corn will grow well throughout the year, and no conflagration will break out. At Braunröde, in the Harz Mountains, it
was the custom to burn squirrels in the Easter bonfire. In the Altmark, bones were burned in it.

Near Forchheim, in Upper Franken, a straw-man called the Judas
used to be burned in the churchyards on Easter Saturday. The whole
village contributed wood to the pyre on which he perished, and the
charred sticks were afterwards kept and planted in the fields on
Walpurgis Day (the first of May) to preserve the wheat from blight and
mildew. About a hundred years ago or more the custom at Althenne-
berg, in Upper Bavaria, used to be as follows. On the afternoon of
Easter Saturday the lads collected wood, which they piled in a corn-
field, while in the middle of the pile they set up a tall wooden cross all
swathed in straw. After the evening service they lighted their lanterns
at the consecrated candle in the church, and ran with them at full
speed to the pyre, each striving to get there first. The first to arrive
set fire to the heap. No woman or girl might come near the bonfire,
but they were allowed to watch it from a distance. As the flames
rose the men and lads rejoiced and made merry, shouting, " We are
burning the Judas ! " The man who had been the first to reach the
pyre and to kindle it was rewarded on Easter Sunday by the women,
who gave him coloured eggs at the church door. The object of the
whole ceremony was to keep off the hail. At other villages of Upper
Bavaria the ceremony, which took place between nine and ten at night
on Easter Saturday, was called " burning the Easter Man." On a
height about a mile from the village the young fellows set up a tall
cross enveloped in straw, so that it looked like a man with his arms
stretched out. This was the Easter Man. No lad under eighteen
years of age might take part in the ceremony. One of the young men
stationed himself beside the Easter Man, holding in his hand a consecrated taper which he had brought from the church and lighted.
The rest stood at equal intervals in a great circle round the cross.
At a given signal they raced thrice round the circle, and then at a
second signal ran straight at the cross and at the lad with the lighted
taper beside it ; the one who reached the goal first had the right
of setting fire to the Easter Man. Great was the jubilation while he
was burning. When he had been consumed in the flames, three
lads were chosen from among the rest, and each of the three drew a
circle on the ground with a stick thrice round the ashes. Then they
all left the spot. On Easter Monday the villagers gathered the ashes

and strewed them on their fields ; also they planted in the fields palm-branches which had been consecrated on Palm Sunday, and sticks which had been charred and hallowed on Good Friday, all for the purpose of protecting their fields against showers of hail. In some parts of Swabia the Easter fires might not be kindled with iron or steel or flint, but only by the friction of wood.

The custom of the Easter fires appears to have prevailed all over Central and Western Germany from north to south. We find it also in Holland, where the fires were kindled on the highest eminences, and the people danced round them and leaped through the flames or over the glowing embers. Here too, as often in Germany, the materials for the bonfire were collected by the young folk from door to door. In many parts of Sweden firearms are discharged in all directions on Easter Eve, and huge bonfires are lighted on hills and eminences. Some people think that the intention is to keep off the Troll and other evil spirits who are especially active at this season.

§ 4. *The Beltane Fires.*—In the Central Highlands of Scotland bonfires, known as the Beltane fires, were formerly kindled with great ceremony on the first of May, and the traces of human sacrifices at them were particularly clear and unequivocal. The custom of lighting the bonfires lasted in various places far into the eighteenth century, and the descriptions of the ceremony by writers of that period present such a curious and interesting picture of ancient heathendom surviving in our own country that I will reproduce them in the words of their authors. The fullest of the descriptions is the one bequeathed to us by John Ramsay, laird of Ochtertyre, near Crieff, the patron of Burns and the friend of Sir Walter Scott. He says : " But the most considerable of the Druidical festivals is that of Beltane, or May-day, which was lately observed in some parts of the Highlands with extraordinary ceremonies. . . . Like the other public worship of the Druids, the Beltane feast seems to have been performed on hills or eminences. They thought it degrading to him whose temple is the universe, to suppose that he would dwell in any house made with hands. Their sacrifices were therefore offered in the open air, frequently upon the tops of hills, where they were presented with the grandest views of nature, and were nearest the seat of warmth and order. And, according to tradition, such was the manner of celebrating this festival in the Highlands within the last hundred years. But since the decline of superstition, it has been celebrated by the people of each hamlet on some hill or rising ground around which their cattle were pasturing. Thither the young folks repaired in the morning, and cut a trench, on the summit of which a seat of turf was formed for the company. And in the middle a pile of wood or other fuel was placed, which of old they kindled with *tein-eigin—i.e.,* forced-fire or *need-fire.* Although, for many years past, they have been contented with common fire, yet we shall now describe the process, because it will hereafter appear that recourse is still had to the *tein-eigin* upon extraordinary emergencies.

" The night before, all the fires in the country were carefully extinguished, and next morning the materials for exciting this sacred fire were prepared. The most primitive method seems to be that which was used in the islands of Skye, Mull, and Tiree   A well-seasoned plank of oak was procured, in the midst of which a hole was bored.   A wimble of the same timber was then applied, the end of which they fitted to the hole.   But in some parts of the mainland the machinery was different.   They used a frame of green wood, of a square form, in the centre of which was an axle-tree.   In some places three times three persons, in others three times nine, were required for turning round by turns the axle-tree or wimble.   If any of them had been guilty of murder, adultery, theft, or other atrocious crime, it was imagined either that the fire would not kindle, or that it would be devoid of its usual virtue.   So soon as any sparks were emitted by means of the violent friction, they applied a species of agaric which grows on old birch-trees, and is very combustible.   This fire had the appearance of being immediately derived from heaven, and manifold were the virtues ascribed to it.   They esteemed it a preservative against witch-craft, and a sovereign remedy against malignant diseases, both in the human species and in cattle ; and by it the strongest poisons were supposed to have their nature changed.

" After kindling the bonfire with the *tein-eigin* the company prepared their victuals.   And as soon as they had finished their meal, they amused themselves a while in singing and dancing round the fire. Towards the close of the entertainment, the person who officiated as master of the feast produced a large cake baked with eggs and scalloped round the edge, called *am bonnach beal-tine—i.e.*, the Beltane cake. It was divided into a number of pieces, and distributed in great form to the company.   There was one particular piece which whoever got was called *cailleach beal-tine—i.e.*, the Beltane *carline*, a term of great reproach.   Upon his being known, part of the company laid hold of him and made a show of putting him into the fire ; but the majority interposing, he was rescued.   And in some places they laid him flat on the ground, making as if they would quarter him.   Afterwards, he was pelted with egg-shells, and retained the odious appellation during the whole year.   And while the feast was fresh in people's memory, they affected to speak of the *cailleach beal-tine* as dead."

In the parish of Callander, a beautiful district of western Perthshire, the Beltane custom was still in vogue towards the end of the eighteenth century.   It has been described as follows by the parish minister of the time : " Upon the first day of May, which is called *Beltan*, or *Bal-tein* day, all the boys in a township or hamlet meet in the moors.   They cut a table in the green sod, of a round figure, by casting a trench in the ground, of such circumference as to hold the whole company. They kindle a fire, and dress a repast of eggs and milk in the con-sistence of a custard.   They knead a cake of oatmeal, which is toasted at the embers against a stone.   After the custard is eaten up, they divide the cake into so many portions, as similar as possible to one

another in size and shape, as there are persons in the company. They
daub one of these portions all over with charcoal, until it be perfectly
black. They put all the bits of the cake into a bonnet. Every one,
blindfold, draws out a portion. He who holds the bonnet is entitled
to the last bit. Whoever draws the black bit is the *devoted* person who
is to be sacrificed to *Baal*, whose favour they mean to implore, in
rendering the year productive of the sustenance of man and beast.
There is little doubt of these inhuman sacrifices having been once
offered in this country, as well as in the east, although they now pass
from the act of sacrificing, and only compel the *devoted* person to leap
three times through the flames ; with which the ceremonies of this
festival are closed."

Thomas Pennant, who travelled in Perthshire in the year 1769,
tells us that " on the first of May, the herdsmen of every village hold
their Bel-tien, a rural sacrifice. They cut a square trench on the
ground, leaving the turf in the middle ; on that they make a fire of
wood, on which they dress a large caudle of eggs, butter, oatmeal and
milk ; and bring besides the ingredients of the caudle, plenty of
beer and whisky ; for each of the company must contribute something.
The rites begin with spilling some of the caudle on the ground, by way
of libation : on that every one takes a cake of oatmeal, upon which
are raised nine square knobs, each dedicated to some particular being,
the supposed preserver of their flocks and herds, or to some particular
animal, the real destroyer of them : each person then turns his face to
the fire, breaks off a knob, and flinging it over his shoulders, says,
' This I give to thee, preserve thou my horses ; this to thee, preserve
thou my sheep ; and so on.' After that, they use the same ceremony
to the noxious animals : ' This I give to thee, O fox ! spare thou my
lambs ; this to thee, O hooded crow ! this to thee, O eagle ! ' When
the ceremony is over, they dine on the caudle ; and after the feast is
finished, what is left is hid by two persons deputed for that purpose ;
but on the next Sunday they reassemble, and finish the reliques of the
first entertainment."

Another writer of the eighteenth century has described the Beltane
festival as it was held in the parish of Logierait in Perthshire. He
says : " On the first of May, O.S., a festival called *Beltan* is annually
held here. It is chiefly celebrated by the cow-herds, who assemble by
scores in the fields, to dress a dinner for themselves, of boiled milk
and eggs. These dishes they eat with a sort of cakes baked for the
occasion, and having small lumps in the form of *nipples*, raised all over
the surface." In this last account no mention is made of bonfires, but
they were probably lighted, for a contemporary writer informs us that
in the parish of Kirkmichael, which adjoins the parish of Logierait
on the east, the custom of lighting a fire in the fields and baking a
consecrated cake on the first of May was not quite obsolete in his
time. We may conjecture that the cake with knobs was formerly
used for the purpose of determining who should be the " Beltane
carline " or victim doomed to the flames. A trace of this custom

survived, perhaps, in the custom of baking oatmeal cakes of a special kind and rolling them down hill about noon on the first of May ; for it was thought that the person whose cake broke as it rolled would die or be unfortunate within the year. These cakes, or bannocks as we call them in Scotland, were baked in the usual way, but they were washed over with a thin batter composed of whipped egg, milk or cream, and a little oatmeal. This custom appears to have prevailed at or near Kingussie in Inverness-shire.

In the north-east of Scotland the Beltane fires were still kindled in the latter half of the eighteenth century ; the herdsmen of several farms used to gather dry wood, kindle it, and dance three times " southways " about the burning pile. But in this region, according to a later authority, the Beltane fires were lit not on the first but on the second of May, Old Style. They were called bone-fires. The people believed that on that evening and night the witches were abroad and busy casting spells on cattle and stealing cows' milk. To counteract their machinations, pieces of rowan-tree and woodbine, but especially of rowan-tree, were placed over the doors of the cow-houses, and fires were kindled by every farmer and cottar. Old thatch, straw, furze, or broom was piled in a heap and set on fire a little after sunset. While some of the bystanders kept tossing the blazing mass, others hoisted portions of it on pitchforks or poles and ran hither and thither, holding them as high as they could. Meantime the young people danced round the fire or ran through the smoke shouting, " Fire ! blaze and burn the witches ; fire ! fire ! burn the witches." In some districts a large round cake of oat or barley meal was rolled through the ashes. When all the fuel was consumed, the people scattered the ashes far and wide, and till the night grew quite dark they continued to run through them, crying, " Fire ! burn the witches."

In the Hebrides " the Beltane bannock is smaller than that made at St. Michael's, but is made in the same way ; it is no longer made in Uist, but Father Allan remembers seeing his grandmother make one about twenty-five years ago. There was also a cheese made, generally on the first of May, which was kept to the next Beltane as a sort of charm against the bewitching of milk-produce. The Beltane customs seem to have been the same as elsewhere. Every fire was put out and a large one lit on the top of the hill, and the cattle driven round it sunwards (*dessil*), to keep off murrain all the year. Each man would take home fire wherewith to kindle his own."

In Wales also the custom of lighting Beltane fires at the beginning of May used to be observed, but the day on which they were kindled varied from the eve of May Day to the third of May. The flame was sometimes elicited by the friction of two pieces of oak, as appears from the following description. " The fire was done in this way. Nine men would turn their pockets inside out, and see that every piece of money and all metals were off their persons. Then the men went into the nearest woods, and collected sticks of nine different kinds of trees. These were carried to the spot where the fire had to be built. There a circle was cut in the sod, and the sticks were set crosswise. All around the circle the people stood and watched the proceedings. One of the men would then take two bits of oak, and rub them together until a flame was kindled. This was applied to the sticks, and soon a large fire was made. Sometimes two fires were set up side by side. These fires, whether one or two, were called *coelcerth* or bonfire. Round cakes of oatmeal and brown meal were split in four, and placed in a small flour-bag, and everybody present had to pick out a portion. The last bit in the bag fell to the lot of the bag-holder. Each person who chanced to pick up a piece of brown-meal cake was compelled to leap three times over the flames, or to run thrice between the two fires, by which means the people thought they were sure of a plentiful harvest. Shouts and screams of those who had to face the ordeal could be heard ever so far, and those who chanced to pick the oatmeal portions sang and danced and clapped their hands in approval, as the holders of the brown bits leaped three times over the flames, or ran three times between the two fires."

The belief of the people that by leaping thrice over the bonfires or running thrice between them they ensured a plentiful harvest is worthy of note. The mode in which this result was supposed to be brought about is indicated by another writer on Welsh folk-lore, according to whom it used to be held that "the bonfires lighted in May or Midsummer protected the lands from sorcery, so that good crops would follow. The ashes were also considered valuable as charms." Hence it appears that the heat of the fires was thought to fertilise the fields, not directly by quickening the seeds in the ground, but indirectly by counteracting the baleful influence of witchcraft or perhaps by burning up the persons of the witches.

The Beltane fires seem to have been kindled also in Ireland, for Cormac, "or somebody in his name, says that *belltaine*, May-day, was so called from the 'lucky fire,' or the 'two fires,' which the druids of Erin used to make on that day with great incantations; and cattle, he adds, used to be brought to those fires, or to be driven between them, as a safeguard against the diseases of the year." The custom of driving cattle through or between fires on May Day or the eve of May Day persisted in Ireland down to a time within living memory.

The first of May is a great popular festival in the more midland and southern parts of Sweden. On the eve of the festival huge bonfires, which should be lighted by striking two flints together, blaze on all the hills and knolls. Every large hamlet has its own fire, round which the young people dance in a ring. The old folk notice whether the flames incline to the north or to the south. In the former case, the spring will be cold and backward; in the latter, it will be mild and genial. In Bohemia, on the eve of May Day, young people kindle fires on hills and eminences, at crossways, and in pastures, and dance round them. They leap over the glowing embers or even through the flames. The ceremony is called "burning the witches." In some places an effigy representing a witch used to be burnt in the bonfire. We have to remember that the eve of May Day is the notorious Walpurgis Night, when the witches are everywhere speeding unseen through the air on their hellish errands. On this witching night children in Voigtland also light bonfires on the heights and leap over them. Moreover, they wave burning brooms or toss them into the air. So far as the light of the bonfire reaches, so far will a blessing rest on the fields. The kindling of the fires on Walpurgis Night is called " driving away the witches." The custom of kindling fires on the eve of May Day (Walpurgis Night) for the purpose of burning the witches is, or used to be, widespread in the Tyrol, Moravia, Saxony and Silesia.

§ 5. *The Midsummer Fires.*—But the season at which these fire-festivals have been mostly generally held all over Europe is the summer solstice, that is Midsummer Eve (the twenty-third of June) or Mid-summer Day (the twenty-fourth of June). A faint tinge of Christianity has been given to them by naming Midsummer Day after St. John the Baptist, but we cannot doubt that the celebration dates from a time long before the beginning of our era. The summer solstice, or Midsummer Day, is the great turning-point in the sun's career, when, after climbing higher and higher day by day in the sky, the luminary stops and thenceforth retraces his steps down the heavenly road. Such a moment could not but be regarded with anxiety by primitive man so soon as he began to observe and ponder the courses of the great lights across the celestial vault ; and having still to learn his own powerlessness in face of the vast cyclic changes of nature, he may have fancied that he could help the sun in his seeming decline— could prop his failing steps and rekindle the sinking flame of the red lamp in his feeble hand. In some such thoughts as these the mid-summer festivals of our European peasantry may perhaps have taken their rise. Whatever their origin, they have prevailed all over this quarter of the globe, from Ireland on the west to Russia on the east, and from Norway and Sweden on the north to Spain and Greece on the south. According to a mediæval writer, the three great features of the midsummer celebration were the bonfires, the procession with torches round the fields, and the custom of rolling a wheel. He tells us that boys burned bones and filth of various kinds to make a foul smoke, and that the smoke drove away certain noxious dragons which at this time, excited by the summer heat, copulated in the air and poisoned the wells and rivers by dropping their seed into them ; and he explains the custom of trundling a wheel to mean that the sun, having now reached the highest point in the ecliptic, begins thence-forward to descend.

The main features of the midsummer fire-festival resemble those which we have found to characterise the vernal festivals of fire. The similarity of the two sets of ceremonies will plainly appear from the following examples.

A writer of the first half of the sixteenth century informs us that in almost every village and town of Germany public bonfires were kindled on the Eve of St. John, and young and old, of both sexes, gathered about them and passed the time in dancing and singing. People on this occasion wore chaplets of mugwort and vervain, and they looked at the fire through bunches of larkspur which they held in their hands, believing that this would preserve their eyes in a healthy state throughout the year. As each departed, he threw the mugwort and vervain into the fire, saying, "May all my ill-luck depart and be burnt up with these." At Lower Konz, a village situated on a hillside overlooking the Moselle, the midsummer festival used to be celebrated as follows. A quantity of straw was collected on the top of the steep Stromberg Hill. Every inhabitant, or at least every householder, had to contribute his share of straw to the pile. At nightfall the whole male population, men and boys, mustered on the top of the hill; the women and girls were not allowed to join them, but had to take up their position at a certain spring half-way down the slope. On the summit stood a huge wheel completely encased in some of the straw which had been jointly contributed by the villagers; the rest of the straw was made into torches. From each side of the wheel the axle-tree projected about three feet, thus furnishing handles to the lads who were to guide it in its descent. The mayor of the neighbouring town of Sierck, who always received a basket of cherries for his services, gave the signal; a lighted torch was applied to the wheel, and as it burst into flame, two young fellows, strong-limbed and swift of foot, seized the handles and began running with it down the slope. A great shout went up. Every man and boy waved a blazing torch in the air, and took care to keep it alight so long as the wheel was trundling down the hill. The great object of the young men who guided the wheel was to plunge it blazing into the water of the Moselle; but they rarely succeeded in their efforts, for the vineyards which cover the greater part of the declivity impeded their progress, and the wheel was often burned out before it reached the river. As it rolled past the women and girls at the spring, they raised cries of joy which were answered by the men on the top of the mountain; and the shouts were echoed by the inhabitants of neighbouring villages who watched the spectacle from their hills on the opposite bank of the Moselle. If the fiery wheel was successfully conveyed to the bank of the river and extinguished in the water, the people looked for an abundant vintage that year, and the inhabitants of Konz had the right to exact a waggon-load of white wine from the surrounding vineyards. On the other hand, they believed that, if they neglected to perform the ceremony, the cattle would be attacked by giddiness and convulsions and would dance in their stalls.

Down at least to the middle of the nineteenth century the midsummer fires used to blaze all over Upper Bavaria. They were kindled especially on the mountains, but also far and wide in the lowlands, and we are told that in the darkness and stillness of night the moving groups, lit up by the flickering glow of the flames, presented an impressive spectacle. Cattle were driven through the fire to cure the sick animals and to guard such as were sound against plague and harm of every kind throughout the year. Many a householder on that day put out the fire on the domestic hearth and rekindled it by means of a brand taken from the midsummer bonfire. The people judged of the height to which the flax would grow in the year by the height to which the flames of the bonfire rose ; and whoever leaped over the burning pile was sure not to suffer from backache in reaping the corn at harvest. In many parts of Bavaria it was believed that the flax would grow as high as the young people leaped over the fire. In others the old folk used to plant three charred sticks from the bonfire in the fields, believing that this would make the flax grow tall. Elsewhere an extinguished brand was put in the roof of the house to protect it against fire. In the towns about Würzburg the bonfires used to be kindled in the market-places, and the young people who jumped over them wore garlands of flowers, especially of mugwort and vervain, and carried sprigs of larkspur in their hands. They thought that such as looked at the fire holding a bit of larkspur before their face would be troubled by no malady of the eyes throughout the year. Further, it was customary at Würzburg, in the sixteenth century, for the bishop's followers to throw burning discs of wood into the air from a mountain which overhangs the town. The discs were discharged by means of flexible rods, and in their flight through the darkness presented the appearance of fiery dragons.

Similarly in Swabia, lads and lasses, hand in hand, leap over the midsummer bonfire, praying that the hemp may grow three ells high, and they set fire to wheels of straw and send them rolling down the hill. Sometimes, as the people sprang over the midsummer bonfire they cried out, " Flax, flax ! may the flax this year grow seven ells high ! " At Rottenburg a rude effigy in human form, called the Angelman, used to be enveloped in flowers and then burnt in the midsummer fire by boys, who afterwards leaped over the glowing embers.

So in Baden the children collected fuel from house to house for the midsummer bonfire on St. John's Day ; and lads and lasses leaped over the fire in couples. Here, as elsewhere, a close connexion was traced between these bonfires and the harvest. In some places it was thought that those who leaped over the fires would not suffer from backache at reaping. Sometimes, as the young folk sprang over the flames, they cried, " Grow, that the hemp may be three ells high ! " This notion that the hemp or the corn would grow as high as the flames blazed or as the people jumped over them seems to have been widespread in Baden. It was held that the parents of the young people who bounded highest over the fire would have the most abundant harvest ; and on the other hand, if a man contributed nothing to the bonfire, it was imagined that there would be no blessing on his crops, and that his hemp in particular would never grow. At Edersleben, near Sangerhausen, a high pole was planted in the ground and a tar-barrel was hung from it by a chain which reached to the ground.   The barrel was then set on fire and swung round the pole amid shouts of joy.

In Denmark and Norway also midsummer fires were kindled on St. John's Eve on roads, open spaces, and hills.   People in Norway thought that the fires banished sickness from among the cattle.   Even yet the fires are said to be lighted all over Norway on Midsummer Eve. They are kindled in order to keep off the witches, who are said to be flying from all parts that night to the Blocksberg, where the big witch lives.   In Sweden the Eve of St. John (St. Hans) is the most joyous night of the whole year.   Throughout some parts of the country, especially in the provinces of Bohus and Scania and in districts border-ing on Norway, it is celebrated by the frequent discharge of firearms and by huge bonfires, formerly called Balder's Balefires (*Balder's Bălar*), which are kindled at dusk on hills and eminences and throw a glare of light over the surrounding landscape.   The people dance round the fires and leap over or through them.   In parts of Norrland on St. John's Eve the bonfires are lit at the cross-roads.   The fuel consists of nine different sorts of wood, and the spectators cast into the flames a kind of toad-stool (*Băran*) in order to counteract the power of the Trolls and other evil spirits, who are believed to be abroad that night ; for at that mystic season the mountains open and from their cavernous depths the uncanny crew pours forth to dance and disport themselves for a time.   The peasants believe that should any of the Trolls be in the vicinity they will show themselves ; and if an animal, for example a he or she goat, happens to be seen near the blazing, crackling pile, the peasants are firmly persuaded that it is no other than the Evil One in person.   Further, it deserves to be remarked that in Sweden St. John's Eve is a festival of water as well as of fire ; for certain holy springs are then supposed to be endowed with wonderful medicinal virtues, and many sick people resort to them for the healing of their infirmities.

In Austria the midsummer customs and superstitions resemble those of Germany.   Thus in some parts of the Tyrol bonfires are kindled and burning discs hurled into the air.   In the lower valley of the Inn a tatterdemalion effigy is carted about the village on Midsummer Day and then burned.   He is called the *Lotter*, which has been corrupted into Luther.   At Ambras, one of the villages where Martin Luther is thus burned in effigy, they say that if you go through the village between eleven and twelve on St. John's Night and wash yourself in three wells you will see all who are to die in the following year. At Gratz on St. John's Eve (the twenty-third of June) the common people used to make a puppet called the *Tatermann*, which they dragged to the bleaching ground, and pelted with burning besoms till it took fire.   At Reutte, in the Tyrol, people believed that the flax would grow as high as they leaped over the midsummer bonfire, and they took pieces of charred wood from the fire and stuck them in their flax-fields the same night, leaving them there till the flax harvest had been got in.   In Lower Austria bonfires are kindled on the heights, and the boys caper round them, brandishing lighted torches drenched in pitch. Whoever jumps thrice across the fire will not suffer from fever within the year. Cart-wheels are often smeared with pitch, ignited, and sent rolling and blazing down the hillsides.

All over Bohemia bonfires still burn on Midsummer Eve. In the afternoon boys go about with handcarts from house to house collecting fuel and threatening with evil consequences the curmudgeons who refuse them a dole. Sometimes the young men fell a tall straight fir in the woods and set it up on a height, where the girls deck it with nosegays, wreaths of leaves, and red ribbons. Then brushwood is piled about it, and at nightfall the whole is set on fire. While the flames break out, the young men climb the tree and fetch down the wreaths which the girls had placed on it. After that lads and lasses stand on opposite sides of the fire and look at one another through the wreaths to see whether they will be true to each other and marry within the year. Also the girls throw the wreaths across the flames to the men, and woe to the awkward swain who fails to catch the wreath thrown him by his sweetheart. When the blaze has died down, each couple takes hands and leaps thrice across the fire. He or she who does so will be free from ague throughout the year, and the flax will grow as high as the young folks leap. A girl who sees nine bonfires on Midsummer Eve will marry before the year is out. The singed wreaths are carried home and carefully preserved throughout the year. During thunderstorms a bit of the wreath is burned on the hearth with a prayer ; some of it is given to kine that are sick or calving, and some of it serves to fumigate house and cattle-stall, that man and beast may keep hale and well. Sometimes an old cart-wheel is smeared with resin, ignited, and sent rolling down the hill. Often the boys collect all the worn-out besoms they can get hold of, dip them in pitch, and having set them on fire wave them about or throw them high into the air. Or they rush down the hillside in troops, brandishing the flaming brooms and shouting. The stumps of the brooms and embers from the fire are preserved and stuck in cabbage gardens to protect the cabbages from caterpillars and gnats. Some people insert charred sticks and ashes from the midsummer bonfire in their sown fields and meadows, in their gardens and the roofs of their houses, as a talisman against lightning and foul weather ; or they fancy that the ashes placed in the roof will prevent any fire from breaking out in the house. In some districts they crown or gird themselves with mugwort while the midsummer fire is burning, for this is supposed to be a protection against ghosts, witches, and sickness ; in particular, a wreath of mugwort is a sure preventive of sore eyes. Sometimes the girls look at the bonfires through garlands of wild flowers, praying the fire to strengthen their eyes and eyelids. She who does this thrice will have no sore eyes all that year. In some parts of Bohemia they used to drive the cows through the midsummer fire to guard them against witchcraft.

In Slavonic countries, also, the midsummer festival is celebrated with similar rites. We have already seen that in Russia on the Eve of St. John young men and maidens jump over a bonfire in couples carrying a straw effigy of Kupalo in their arms. In some parts of Russia an image of Kupalo is burnt or thrown into a stream on St. John's Night. Again, in some districts of Russia the young folk wear garlands of flowers and girdles of holy herbs when they spring through the smoke or flames; and sometimes they drive the cattle also through the fire in order to protect the animals against wizards and witches, who are then ravenous after milk. In Little Russia a stake is driven into the ground on St. John's Night, wrapt in straw, and set on fire. As the flames rise the peasant women throw birchen boughs into them, saying, " May my flax be as tall as this bough ! " In Ruthenia the bonfires are lighted by a flame procured by the friction of wood. While the elders of the party are engaged in thus " churning " the fire, the rest maintain a respectful silence; but when the flame bursts from the wood, they break forth into joyous songs. As soon as the bonfires are kindled, the young people take hands and leap in pairs through the smoke, if not through the flames; and after that the cattle in their turn are driven through the fire.

In many parts of Prussia and Lithuania great fires are kindled on Midsummer Eve. All the heights are ablaze with them, as far as the eye can see. The fires are supposed to be a protection against witch-craft, thunder, hail, and cattle disease, especially if next morning the cattle are driven over the places where the fires burned. Above all, the bonfires ensure the farmer against the arts of witches, who try to steal the milk from his cows by charms and spells. That is why next morning you may see the young fellows who lit the bonfire going from house to house and receiving jugfuls of milk. And for the same reason they stick burs and mugwort on the gate or the hedge through which the cows go to pasture, because that is supposed to be a preserva-tive against witchcraft. In Masuren, a district of Eastern Prussia inhabited by a branch of the Polish family, it is the custom on the evening of Midsummer Day to put out all the fires in the village. Then an oaken stake is driven into the ground and a wheel is fixed on it as on an axle. This wheel the villagers, working by relays, cause to revolve with great rapidity till fire is produced by friction. Every one takes home a lighted brand from the new fire and with it rekindles the fire on the domestic hearth. In Serbia on Midsummer Eve herdsmen light torches of birch bark and march round the sheepfolds and cattle-stalls; then they climb the hills and there allow the torches to burn out.

Among the Magyars in Hungary the midsummer fire-festival is marked by the same features that meet us in so many parts of Europe. On Midsummer Eve in many places it is customary to kindle bonfires on heights and to leap over them, and from the manner in which the young people leap the bystanders predict whether they will marry soon. On this day also many Hungarian swineherds make fire by rotating a wheel round a wooden axle wrapt in hemp, and through the fire thus made they drive their pigs to preserve them from sickness.

The Esthonians of Russia, who, like the Magyars, belong to the great Turanian family of mankind, also celebrate the summer solstice in the usual way. They think that the St. John's fire keeps witches from the cattle, and they say that he who does not come to it will have his barley full of thistles and his oats full of weeds. In the Esthonian island of Oesel, while they throw fuel into the midsummer fire, they call out, " Weeds to the fire, flax to the field," or they fling three billets into the flames, saying, " Flax grow long ! " And they take charred sticks from the bonfire home with them and keep them to make the cattle thrive. In some parts of the island the bonfire is formed by piling brushwood and other combustibles round a tree, at the top of which a flag flies. Whoever succeeds in knocking down the flag with a pole before it begins to burn will have good luck. Formerly the festivities lasted till daybreak, and ended in scenes of debauchery which looked doubly hideous by the growing light of a summer morning.

When we pass from the east to the west of Europe we still find the summer solstice celebrated with rites of the same general character. Down to about the middle of the nineteenth century the custom of lighting bonfires at midsummer prevailed so commonly in France that there was hardly a town or a village, we are told, where they were not kindled. People danced round and leaped over them, and took charred sticks from the bonfire home with them to protect the houses against lightning, conflagrations, and spells.

In Brittany, apparently, the custom of the midsummer bonfires is kept up to this day. When the flames have died down, the whole assembly kneels round about the bonfire and an old man prays aloud. Then they all rise and march thrice round the fire ; at the third turn they stop and every one picks up a pebble and throws it on the burning pile. After that they disperse. In Brittany and Berry it is believed that a girl who dances round nine midsummer bonfires will marry within the year. In the valley of the Orne the custom was to kindle the bonfire just at the moment when the sun was about to dip below the horizon ; and the peasants drove their cattle through the fires to protect them against witchcraft, especially against the spells of witches and wizards who attempted to steal the milk and butter. At Jumièges in Normandy, down to the first half of the nineteenth century, the midsummer festival was marked by certain singular features which bore the stamp of a very high antiquity. Every year, on the twenty-third of June, the Eve of St. John, the Brotherhood of the Green Wolf chose a new chief or master, who had always to be taken from the hamlet of Conihout. On being elected, the new head of the brotherhood assumed the title of the Green Wolf, and donned a peculiar costume consisting of a long green mantle and a very tall green hat of a conical shape and without a brim. Thus arrayed he stalked solemnly at the head of the brothers, chanting the hymn of St. John, the crucifix and holy banner leading the way, to a place called Chouquet. Here the procession was met by the priest, precentors, and choir, who conducted the brotherhood to the

parish church. After hearing mass the company adjourned to the
house of the Green Wolf, where a simple repast was served up to them.
At night a bonfire was kindled to the sound of hand-bells by a young
man and a young woman, both decked with flowers. Then the Green
Wolf and his brothers, with their hoods down on their shoulders
and holding each other by the hand, ran round the fire after the man
who had been chosen to be the Green Wolf of the following year.
Though only the first and the last man of the chain had a hand free,
their business was to surround and seize thrice the future Green
Wolf, who in his efforts to escape belaboured the brothers with a
long wand which he carried. When at last they succeeded in catching him they carried him to the burning pile and made as if they
would throw him on it. This ceremony over, they returned to the
house of the Green Wolf, where a supper, still of the most meagre fare,
was set before them. Up till midnight a sort of religious solemnity
prevailed. But at the stroke of twelve all this was changed. Constraint gave way to license ; pious hymns were replaced by Bac-
chanalian ditties, and the shrill quavering notes of the village fiddle
hardly rose above the roar of voices that went up from the merry
brotherhood of the Green Wolf. Next day, the twenty-fourth of June
or Midsummer Day, was celebrated by the same personages with the
same noisy gaiety. One of the ceremonies consisted in parading, to
the sound of musketry, an enormous loaf of consecrated bread, which,
rising in tiers, was surmounted by a pyramid of verdure adorned with
ribbons. After that the holy hand-bells, deposited on the step of the
altar, were entrusted as insignia of office to the man who was to be the
Green Wolf next year.

At Château-Thierry, in the department of Aisne, the custom of
lighting bonfires and dancing round them at the midsummer festival
of St. John lasted down to about 1850 ; the fires were kindled especially
when June had been rainy, and the people thought that the lighting
of the bonfires would cause the rain to cease. In the Vosges it is still
customary to kindle bonfires upon the hill-tops on Midsummer Eve ;
the people believe that the fires help to preserve the fruits of the earth
and ensure good crops.

Bonfires were lit in almost all the hamlets of Poitou on the Eve
of St. John. People marched round them thrice, carrying a branch
of walnut in their hand. Shepherdesses and children passed sprigs of
mullein (*verbascum*) and nuts across the flames ; the nuts were supposed
to cure toothache, and the mullein to protect the cattle from sickness
and sorcery. When the fire died down people took some of the ashes
home with them, either to keep them in the house as a preservative
against thunder or to scatter them on the fields for the purpose of
destroying corn-cockles and darnel. In Poitou also it used to be
customary on the Eve of St. John to trundle a blazing wheel wrapt
in straw over the fields to fertilise them.

In the mountainous part of Comminges, a province of Southern
France, the midsummer fire is made by splitting open the trunk of a

tall tree, stuffing the crevice with shavings, and igniting the whole. A garland of flowers is fastened to the top of the tree, and at the moment when the fire is lighted the man who was last married has to climb up a ladder and bring the flowers down. In the flat parts of the same district the materials of the midsummer bonfires consist of fuel piled in the usual way; but they must be put together by men who have been married since the last midsummer festival, and each of these benedicts is obliged to lay a wreath of flowers on the top of the pile.

In Provence the midsummer fires are still popular. Children go from door to door begging for fuel, and they are seldom sent empty away. Formerly the priest, the mayor, and the aldermen used to walk in procession to the bonfire, and even deigned to light it; after which the assembly marched thrice round the burning pile. At Aix a nominal king, chosen from among the youth for his skill in shooting at a popinjay, presided over the midsummer festival. He selected his own officers, and escorted by a brilliant train marched to the bonfire, kindled it, and was the first to dance round it. Next day he distributed largesse to his followers. His reign lasted a year, during which he enjoyed certain privileges. He was allowed to attend the mass celebrated by the commander of the Knights of St. John on St. John's Day; the right of hunting was accorded to him, and soldiers might not be quartered in his house. At Marseilles also on this day one of the guilds chose a king of the *badache* or double axe; but it does not appear that he kindled the bonfire, which is said to have been lighted with great ceremony by the préfet and other authorities.

In Belgium the custom of kindling the midsummer bonfires has long disappeared from the great cities, but it is still kept up in rural districts and small towns. In that country the Eve of St. Peter's Day (the twenty-ninth of June) is celebrated by bonfires and dances exactly like those which commemorate St. John's Eve. Some people say that the fires of St. Peter, like those of St. John, are lighted in order to drive away dragons. In French Flanders down to 1789 a straw figure representing a man was always burned in the midsummer bonfire, and the figure of a woman was burned on St. Peter's Day, the twenty-ninth of June. In Belgium people jump over the midsummer bonfires as a preventive of colic, and they keep the ashes at home to hinder fire from breaking out.

The custom of lighting bonfires at midsummer has been observed in many parts of our own country, and as usual people danced round and leaped over them. In Wales three or nine different kinds of wood and charred faggots carefully preserved from the last midsummer were deemed necessary to build the bonfire, which was generally done on rising ground. In the Vale of Glamorgan a cart-wheel swathed in straw used to be ignited and sent rolling down the hill. If it kept alight all the way down and blazed for a long time, an abundant harvest was expected. On Midsummer Eve people in the Isle of Man were wont to light fires to the windward of every field, so that the smoke might pass over the corn; and they folded their cattle and carried blazing furze or gorse round them several times. In Ireland cattle, especially barren cattle, were driven through the midsummer fires, and the ashes were thrown on the fields to fertilise them, or live coals were carried into them to prevent blight. In Scotland the traces of midsummer fires are few ; but at that season in the highlands of Perthshire cowherds used to go round their folds thrice, in the direction of the sun, with lighted torches. This they did to purify the flocks and herds and to keep them from falling sick.

The practice of lighting bonfires on Midsummer Eve and dancing or leaping over them is, or was till recently, common all over Spain and in some parts of Italy and Sicily. In Malta great fires are kindled in the streets and squares of the towns and villages on the Eve of St. John (Midsummer Eve) ; formerly the Grand Master of the Order of St. John used on that evening to set fire to a heap of pitch barrels placed in front of the sacred Hospital. In Greece, too, the custom of kindling fires on St. John's Eve and jumping over them is said to be still universal. One reason assigned for it is a wish to escape from the fleas. According to another account, the women cry out, as they leap over the fire, " I leave my sins behind me." In Lesbos the fires on St. John's Eve are usually lighted by threes, and the people spring thrice over them, each with a stone on his head, saying, " I jump the hare's fire, my head a stone ! " In Calymnos the midsummer fire is supposed to ensure abundance in the coming year as well as deliverance from fleas. The people dance round the fires singing, with stones on their heads, and then jump over the blaze or the glowing embers. When the fire is burning low, they throw the stones into it ; and when it is nearly out, they make crosses on their legs and then go straightway and bathe in the sea.

The custom of kindling bonfires on Midsummer Day or on Midsummer Eve is widely spread among the Mohammedan peoples of North Africa, particularly in Morocco and Algeria ; it is common both to the Berbers and to many of the Arabs or Arabic-speaking tribes. In these countries Midsummer Day (the twenty-fourth of June, Old Style) is called *l'ánṣăra*. The fires are lit in the courtyards, at crossroads, in the fields, and sometimes on the threshing-floors. Plants which in burning give out a thick smoke and an aromatic smell are much sought after for fuel on these occasions ; among the plants used for the purpose are giant-fennel, thyme, rue, chervil-seed, camomile, geranium, and penny-royal. People expose themselves, and especially their children, to the smoke, and drive it towards the orchards and the crops. Also they leap across the fires ; in some places everybody ought to repeat the leap seven times. Moreover they take burning brands from the fires and carry them through the houses in order to fumigate them. They pass things through the fire, and bring the sick into contact with it, while they utter prayers for their recovery. The ashes of the bonfires are also reputed to possess beneficial properties ; hence in some places people rub their hair or their bodies with them. In some places they think that by leaping over the fires they rid themselves of all misfortune, and that childless couples thereby obtain offspring. Berbers of the Rif province, in Northern Morocco, make great use of fires at midsummer for the good of themselves, their cattle, and their fruit-trees. They jump over the bonfires in the belief that this will preserve them in good health, and they light fires under fruit-trees to keep the fruit from falling untimely. And they imagine that by rubbing a paste of the ashes on their hair they prevent the hair from falling off their heads. In all these Moroccan customs, we are told, the beneficial effect is attributed wholly to the smoke, which is supposed to be endued with a magical quality that removes misfortune from men, animals, fruit-trees, and crops.

The celebration of a midsummer festival by Mohammedan peoples is particularly remarkable, because the Mohammedan calendar, being purely lunar and uncorrected by intercalation, necessarily takes no note of festivals which occupy fixed points in the solar year ; all strictly Mohammedan feasts, being pinned to the moon, slide gradually with that luminary through the whole period of the earth's revolution about the sun. This fact of itself seems to prove that among the Mohammedan peoples of Northern Africa, as among the Christian peoples of Europe, the midsummer festival is quite independent of the religion which the people publicly profess, and is a relic of a far older paganism.

§ 6. *The Hallowe'en Fires.*—From the foregoing survey we may infer that among the heathen forefathers of the European peoples the most popular and widespread fire-festival of the year was the great celebration of Midsummer Eve or Midsummer Day. The coincidence of the festival with the summer solstice can hardly be accidental. Rather we must suppose that our pagan ancestors purposely timed the ceremony of fire on earth to coincide with the arrival of the sun at the highest point of his course in the sky. If that was so, it follows that the old founders of the midsummer rites had observed the solstices or turning-points of the sun's apparent path in the sky, and that they accordingly regulated their festal calendar to some extent by astronomical considerations.

But while this may be regarded as fairly certain for what we may call the aborigines throughout a large part of the continent, it appears not to have been true of the Celtic peoples who inhabited the Land's End of Europe, the islands and promontories that stretch out into the Atlantic Ocean on the north-west. The principal fire-festivals of the Celts, which have survived, though in a restricted area and with diminished pomp, to modern times and even to our own day, were seemingly timed without any reference to the position of the sun in the heaven. They were two in number, and fell at an interval of six months, one being celebrated on the eve of May Day and the other on Allhallow Even or Hallowe'en, as it is now commonly called, that is, on the thirty-first of October, the day preceding All Saints' or Allhallows' Day. These dates coincide with none of the four great hinges on which the solar year revolves, to wit, the solstices and the equinoxes. Nor do they agree with the principal seasons of the agricultural year, the sowing in spring and the reaping in autumn. For when May Day comes, the seed has long been committed to the earth ; and when November opens, the harvest has long been reaped and garnered, the fields lie bare, the fruit-trees are stripped, and even the yellow leaves are fast fluttering to the ground. Yet the first of May and the first of November mark turning-points of the year in Europe ; the one ushers in the genial heat and the rich vegetation of summer, the other heralds, if it does not share, the cold and barrenness of winter. Now these particular points of the year, as has been well pointed out by a learned and ingenious writer, while they are of comparatively little moment to the European husbandman, do deeply concern the European herdsman ; for it is on the approach of summer that he drives his cattle out into the open to crop the fresh grass, and it is on the approach of winter that he leads them back to the safety and shelter of the stall. Accordingly it seems not improbable that the Celtic bisection of the year into two halves at the beginning of May and the beginning of November dates from a time when the Celts were mainly a pastoral people, dependent for their subsistence on their herds, and when accordingly the great epochs of the year for them were the days on which the cattle went forth from the homestead in early summer and returned to it again in early winter. Even in Central Europe, remote from the region now occupied by the Celts, a similar bisection of the year may be clearly traced in the great popularity, on the one hand, of May Day and its Eve (Walpurgis Night), and, on the other hand, of the Feast of All Souls at the beginning of November, which under a thin Christian cloak conceals an ancient pagan festival of the dead. Hence we may conjecture that everywhere throughout Europe the celestial division of the year according to the solstices was preceded by what we may call a terrestrial division of the year according to the beginning of summer and the beginning of winter.

Be that as it may, the two great Celtic festivals of May Day and the first of November, or, to be more accurate, the Eves of these two days, closely resemble each other in the manner of their celebration and in the superstitions associated with them, and alike, by the antique character impressed upon both, betray a remote and purely pagan origin. The festival of May Day or Beltane, as the Celts called it, which ushered in summer, has already been described ; it remains to give some account of the corresponding festival of Hallowe'en, which announced the arrival of winter.

Of the two feasts Hallowe'en was perhaps of old the more important, since the Celts would seem to have dated the beginning of the year from it rather than from Beltane. In the Isle of Man, one of the fortresses in which the Celtic language and lore longest held out against the siege of the Saxon invaders, the first of November, Old Style, has been regarded as New Year's Day down to recent times. Thus Manx mummers used to go round on Hallowe'en (Old Style), singing, in the

Manx language, a sort of Hogmanay song which began " To-night is New Year's Night, *Hogunnaa* ! " In ancient Ireland, a new fire used to be kindled every year on Hallowe'en or the Eve of Samhain, and from this sacred flame all the fires in Ireland were rekindled. Such a custom points strongly to Samhain or All Saints' Day (the first of November) as New Year's Day ; since the annual kindling of a new fire takes place most naturally at the beginning of the year, in order that the blessed influence of the fresh fire may last throughout the whole period of twelve months. Another confirmation of the view that the Celts dated their year from the first of November is furnished by the manifold modes of divination which were commonly resorted to by Celtic peoples on Hallowe'en for the purpose of ascertaining their destiny, especially their fortune in the coming year ; for when could these devices for prying into the future be more reasonably put in practice than at the beginning of the year ? As a season of omens and auguries Hallowe'en seems to have far surpassed Beltane in the imagination of the Celts ; from which we may with some probability infer that they reckoned their year from Hallowe'en rather than Beltane. Another circumstance of great moment which points to the same conclusion is the association of the dead with Hallowe'en. Not only among the Celts but throughout Europe, Hallowe'en, the night which marks the transition from autumn to winter, seems to have been of old the time of year when the souls of the departed were supposed to revisit their old homes in order to warm themselves by the fire and to comfort themselves with the good cheer provided for them in the kitchen or the parlour by their affectionate kinsfolk. It was, perhaps, a natural thought that the approach of winter should drive the poor shivering hungry ghosts from the bare fields and the leafless woodlands to the shelter of the cottage with its familiar fireside. Did not the lowing kine then troop back from the summer pastures in the forests and on the hills to be fed and cared for in the stalls, while the bleak winds whistled among the swaying boughs and the snow-drifts deepened in the hollows ? and could the good-man and the good-wife deny to the spirits of their dead the welcome which they gave to the cows ?

But it is not only the souls of the departed who are supposed to be hovering unseen on the day " when autumn to winter resigns the pale year." Witches then speed on their errands of mischief, some sweeping through the air on besoms, others galloping along the roads on tabby-cats, which for that evening are turned into coal-black steeds. The fairies, too, are all let loose, and hobgoblins of every sort roam freely about.

Yet while a glamour of mystery and awe has always clung to Hallowe'en in the minds of the Celtic peasantry, the popular celebration of the festival has been, at least in modern times, by no means of a prevailingly gloomy cast ; on the contrary it has been attended by picturesque features and merry pastimes, which rendered it the gayest night of all the year. Amongst the things which in the Highlands of Scotland contributed to invest the festival with a romantic beauty were the bonfires which used to blaze at frequent intervals on the heights. " On the last day of autumn children gathered ferns, tar-barrels, the long thin stalks called *gàinisg*, and everything suitable for a bonfire. These were placed in a heap on some eminence near the house, and in the evening set fire to. The fires were called *Samhnagan*. There was one for each house, and it was an object of ambition who should have the biggest. Whole districts were brilliant with bonfires, and their glare across a Highland loch, and from many eminences, formed an exceedingly picturesque scene." Like the Beltane fires on the first of May, the Hallowe'en bonfires seem to have been kindled most commonly in the Perthshire Highlands. In the parish of Callander they still blazed down to near the end of the eighteenth century. When the fire had died down, the ashes were carefully collected in the form of a circle, and a stone was put in, near the circumference, for every person of the several families interested in the bonfire. Next morning, if any of these stones was found to be displaced or injured, the people made sure that the person represented by it was *fey* or devoted, and that he could not live twelve months from that day. At Balquhidder down to the latter part of the nineteenth century each household kindled its bonfire at Hallowe'en, but the custom was chiefly observed by children. The fires were lighted on any high knoll near the house ; there was no dancing round them. Hallowe'en fires were also lighted in some districts of the north-east of Scotland, such as Buchan. Villagers and farmers alike must have their fire. In the villages the boys went from house to house and begged a peat from each householder, usually with the words, " Ge's a peat t' burn the witches." When they had collected enough peats, they piled them in a heap, together with straw, furze, and other combustible materials, and set the whole on fire. Then each of the youths, one after another, laid himself down on the ground as near to the fire as he could without being scorched, and thus lying allowed the smoke to roll over him. The others ran through the smoke and jumped over their prostrate comrade. When the heap was burned down, they scattered the ashes, vying with each other who should scatter them most.

In the northern part of Wales it used to be customary for every family to make a great bonfire called *Coel Coeth* on Hallowe'en. The fire was kindled on the most conspicuous spot near the house ; and when it had nearly gone out every one threw into the ashes a white stone, which he had first marked. Then having said their prayers round the fire, they went to bed. Next morning, as soon as they were up, they came to search out the stones, and if any one of them was found to be missing, they had a notion that the person who threw it would die before he saw another Hallowe'en. According to Sir John Rhys, the habit of celebrating Hallowe'en by lighting bonfires on the hills is perhaps not yet extinct in Wales, and men still living can remember how the people who assisted at the bonfires would wait till the last spark was out and then would suddenly take to their heels, shouting at the top of their voices, " The cropped black sow seize the hindmost ! " The saying, as Sir John Rhys justly remarks, implies that originally one of the company became a victim in dead earnest. Down to the present time the saying is current in Carnarvonshire, where allusions to the cutty black sow are still occasionally made to frighten children. We can now understand why in Lower Brittany every person throws a pebble into the midsummer bonfire. Doubtless there, as in Wales and the Highlands of Scotland, omens of life and death have at one time or other been drawn from the position and state of the pebbles on the morning of All Saints' Day. The custom, thus found among three separate branches of the Celtic stock, probably dates from a period before their dispersion, or at least from a time when alien races had not yet driven home the wedges of separation between them.

In the Isle of Man also, another Celtic country, Hallowe'en was celebrated down to modern times by the kindling of fires, accompanied with all the usual ceremonies designed to prevent the baneful influence of fairies and witches.

§ 7. *The Midwinter Fires.*—If the heathen of ancient Europe celebrated, as we have good reason to believe, the season of Midsummer with a great festival of fire, of which the traces have survived in many places down to our own time, it is natural to suppose that they should have observed with similar rites the corresponding season of Midwinter ; for Midsummer and Midwinter, or, in more technical language, the summer solstice and the winter solstice, are the two great turning-points in the sun's apparent course through the sky, and from the standpoint of primitive man nothing might seem more appropriate than to kindle fires on earth at the two moments when the fire and heat of the great luminary in heaven begin to wane or to wax.

In modern Christendom the ancient fire-festival of the winter solstice appears to survive, or to have survived down to recent years, in the old custom of the Yule log, clog, or block, as it was variously called in England. The custom was widespread in Europe, but seems to have flourished especially in England, France, and among the South Slavs ; at least the fullest accounts of the custom come from these quarters. That the Yule log was only the winter counterpart of the midsummer bonfire, kindled within doors instead of in the open air on account of the cold and inclement weather of the season, was pointed out long ago by our English antiquary John Brand ; and the view is supported by the many quaint superstitions attaching to the Yule log, superstitions which have no apparent connexion with Christianity but carry their heathen origin plainly stamped upon them. But while the two solstitial celebrations were both festivals of fire, the necessity or desirability of holding the winter celebration within doors lent it the character of a private or domestic festivity, which contrasts strongly with the publicity of the summer celebration, at which the people gathered on some open space or conspicuous height, kindled a huge bonfire in common, and danced and made merry round it together.

Down to about the middle of the nineteenth century the old rite of the Yule log was kept up in some parts of Central Germany. Thus in the valleys of the Sieg and Lahn the Yule log, a heavy block of oak, was fitted into the floor of the hearth, where, though it glowed under the fire, it was hardly reduced to ashes within a year. When the new log was laid next year, the remains of the old one were ground to powder and strewed over the fields during the Twelve Nights, which was supposed to promote the growth of the crops. In some villages of Westphalia the practice was to withdraw the Yule log (*Christbrand*) from the fire so soon as it was slightly charred; it was then kept carefully to be replaced on the fire whenever a thunderstorm broke, because the people believed that lightning would not strike a house in which the Yule log was smouldering. In other villages of Westphalia the old custom was to tie up the Yule log in the last sheaf cut at harvest.

In several provinces of France, and particularly in Provence, the custom of the Yule log or *tréfoir*, as it was called in many places, was long observed. A French writer of the seventeenth century denounces as superstitious " the belief that a log called the *tréfoir* or Christmas brand, which you put on the fire for the first time on Christmas Eve and continue to put on the fire for a little while every day till Twelfth Night, can, if kept under the bed, protect the house for a whole year from fire and thunder; that it can prevent the inmates from having chilblains on their heels in winter; that it can cure the cattle of many maladies; that if a piece of it be steeped in the water which cows drink it helps them to calve; and lastly that if the ashes of the log be strewn on the fields it can save the wheat from mildew."

In some parts of Flanders and France the remains of the Yule log were regularly kept in the house under a bed as a protection against thunder and lightning; in Berry, when thunder was heard, a member of the family used to take a piece of the log and throw it on the fire, which was believed to avert the lightning. Again, in Perigord, the charcoal and ashes are carefully collected and kept for healing swollen glands; the part of the trunk which has not been burnt in the fire is used by ploughmen to make the wedge for their plough, because they allege that it causes the seeds to thrive better; and the women keep pieces of it till Twelfth Night for the sake of their chickens. Some people imagine that they will have as many chickens as there are sparks that fly out of the brands of the log when they shake them; and others place the extinct brands under the bed to drive away vermin. In various parts of France the charred log is thought to guard the house against sorcery as well as against lightning.

In England the customs and beliefs concerning the Yule log used to be similar. On the night of Christmas Eve, says the antiquary John Brand, " our ancestors were wont to light up candles of an uncommon size, called Christmas Candles, and lay a log of wood upon the fire, called a Yule-clog or Christmas-block, to illuminate the house, and, as it were, to turn night into day." The old custom was to light the Yule log with a fragment of its predecessor, which had been kept throughout the year for the purpose ; where it was so kept, the fiend could do no mischief. The remains of the log were also supposed to guard the house against fire and lightning.

To this day the ritual of bringing in the Yule log is observed with much solemnity among the Southern Slavs, especially the Serbians. The log is usually a block of oak, but sometimes of olive or beech. They seem to think that they will have as many calves, lambs, pigs, and kids as they strike sparks out of the burning log. Some people carry a piece of the log out to the fields to protect them against hail. In Albania down to recent years it was a common custom to burn a Yule log at Christmas, and the ashes of the fire were scattered on the fields to make them fertile. The Huzuls, a Slavonic people of the Carpathians, kindle fire by the friction of wood on Christmas Eve (Old Style, the fifth of January) and keep it burning till Twelfth Night.

It is remarkable how common the belief appears to have been that the remains of the Yule log, if kept throughout the year, had power to protect the house against fire and especially against lightning. As the Yule log was frequently of oak, it seems possible that this belief may be a relic of the old Aryan creed which associated the oak-tree with the god of thunder. Whether the curative and fertilising virtues ascribed to the ashes of the Yule log, which are supposed to heal cattle as well as men, to enable cows to calve, and to promote the fruitfulness of the earth, may not be derived from the same ancient source, is a question which deserves to be considered.

§ 8. *The Need-fire.*—The fire-festivals hitherto described are all celebrated periodically at certain stated times of the year. But besides these regularly recurring celebrations the peasants in many parts of Europe have been wont from time immemorial to resort to a ritual of fire at irregular intervals in seasons of distress and calamity, above all when their cattle were attacked by epidemic disease. No account of the popular European fire-festivals would be complete without some notice of these remarkable rites, which have all the greater claim on our attention because they may perhaps be regarded as the source and origin of all the other fire-festivals ; certainly they must date from a very remote antiquity. The general name by which they are known among the Teutonic peoples is need-fire. Sometimes the need-fire was known as " wild fire," to distinguish it no doubt from the tame fire produced by more ordinary methods. Among Slavonic peoples it is called " living fire."

The history of the custom can be traced from the early Middle Ages, when it was denounced by the Church as a heathen superstition, down to the first half of the nineteenth century, when it was still occasionally practised in various parts of Germany, England, Scotland, and Ireland. Among Slavonic peoples it appears to have lingered even longer. The usual occasion for performing the rite was an outbreak of plague or cattle-disease, for which the need-fire was believed to be an infallible remedy. The animals which were subjected to it included cows, pigs, horses, and sometimes geese. As a necessary preliminary to the kindling of the need-fire all other fires and lights in the neighbourhood were extinguished, so that not so much as a spark remained alight ; for so long as even a night-light burned in a house, it was imagined that the need-fire could not kindle. Sometimes it was deemed enough to put out all the fires in the village ; but sometimes the extinction extended to neighbouring villages or to a whole parish. In some parts of the Highlands of Scotland the rule was that all householders who dwelt within the two nearest running streams should put out their lights and fires on the day appointed. Usually the need-fire was made in the open air, but in some parts of Serbia it was kindled in a dark room ; sometimes the place was a cross-way or a hollow in a road. In the Highlands of Scotland the proper places for performing the rite seem to have been knolls or small islands in rivers.

The regular method of producing the need-fire was by the friction of two pieces of wood ; it might not be struck by flint and steel. Very exceptionally among some South Slavs we read of a practice of kindling a need-fire by striking a piece of iron on an anvil. Where the wood to be employed is specified, it is generally said to be oak ; but on the Lower Rhine the fire was kindled by the friction of oak-wood or fir-wood. In Slavonic countries we hear of poplar, pear, and cornel wood being used for the purpose. Often the material is simply described as two pieces of dry wood. Sometimes nine different kinds of wood were deemed necessary, but rather perhaps to be burned in the bonfire than to be rubbed together for the production of the need-fire. The particular mode of kindling the need-fire varied in different districts ; a very common one was this. Two poles were driven into the ground about a foot and a half from each other. Each pole had in the side facing the other a socket into which a smooth cross-piece or roller was fitted. The sockets were stuffed with linen, and the two ends of the roller were rammed tightly into the sockets. To make it more inflammable the roller was often coated with tar. A rope was then wound round the roller, and the free ends at both sides were gripped by two or more persons, who by pulling the rope to and fro caused the roller to revolve rapidly, till through the friction the linen in the sockets took fire. The sparks were immediately caught in tow or oakum and waved about in a circle until they burst into a bright glow, when straw was applied to it, and the blazing straw used to kindle the fuel that had been stacked to make the bonfire. Often a wheel, sometimes a cart-wheel or even a spinning-wheel, formed part of the mechanism ; in Aberdeenshire it was called " the muckle wheel " ; in the island of Mull the wheel was turned from east to west over nine spindles of oak-wood. Sometimes we are merely told that two wooden planks were rubbed together. Sometimes it was prescribed that the cart-wheel used for fire-making and the axle on which it turned should both be new. Similarly it was said that the rope which turned the roller should be new ; if possible it should be woven of strands taken from a gallows rope with which people had been hanged, but this was a counsel of perfection rather than a strict necessity.

Various rules were also laid down as to the kind of persons who might or should make the need-fire. Sometimes it was said that the two persons who pulled the rope which twirled the roller should always be brothers or at least bear the same baptismal name ; sometimes it was deemed sufficient if they were both chaste young men. In some villages of Brunswick people thought that if everybody who lent a hand in kindling the need-fire did not bear the same Christian name, they would labour in vain. In Silesia the tree employed to produce the need-fire used to be felled by a pair of twin brothers. In the western islands of Scotland the fire was kindled by eighty-one married men, who rubbed two great planks against each other, working in relays of nine ; in North Uist the nine times nine who made the fire were all first-begotten sons, but we are not told whether they were married or single. Among the Serbians the need-fire is sometimes kindled by a boy and girl between eleven and fourteen years of age, who work stark naked in a dark room ; sometimes it is made by an old man and an old woman also in the dark. In Bulgaria, too, the makers of need-fire strip themselves of their clothes ; in Caithness they divested themselves of all kinds of metal. If after long rubbing of the wood no fire was elicited they concluded that some fire must still be burning in the village ; so a strict search was made from house to house, any fire that might be found was put out, and the negligent householder punished or upbraided ; indeed a heavy fine might be inflicted on him.

When the need-fire was at last kindled, the bonfire was lit from it, and as soon as the blaze had somewhat died down, the sick animals were driven over the glowing embers, sometimes in a regular order of precedence, first the pigs, next the cows, and last of all the horses. Sometimes they were driven twice or thrice through the smoke and flames, so that occasionally some of them were scorched to death. As soon as all the beasts were through, the young folk would rush wildly at the ashes and cinders, sprinkling and blackening each other with them ; those who were most blackened would march in triumph behind the cattle into the village and would not wash themselves for a long time. From the bonfire people carried live embers home and used them to rekindle the fires in their houses. These brands, after being extinguished in water, they sometimes put in the mangers at which the cattle fed, and kept them there for a while. Ashes from the need-fire were also strewed on the fields to protect the crops against vermin ; sometimes they were taken home to be employed as remedies in sickness, being sprinkled on the ailing part or mixed in water and drunk by the patient. In the western islands of Scotland and on the adjoining mainland, as soon as the fire on the domestic hearth had been rekindled from the need-fire, a pot full of water was set on it, and the water thus heated was afterwards sprinkled upon the people infected with the plague or upon the cattle that were tainted by the murrain. Special virtue was attributed to the smoke of the bonfire ; in Sweden fruit-trees and nets were fumigated with it, in order that the trees might bear fruit and the nets catch fish. In the Highlands of Scotland the need-fire was accounted a sovereign remedy for witchcraft. In the island of Mull, when the fire was kindled as a cure for the murrain, we hear of the rite being accompanied by the sacrifice of a sick heifer, which was cut in pieces and burnt. Slavonian and Bulgarian peasants conceive cattle-plague as a foul fiend or vampyre which can be kept at bay by interposing a barrier of fire between it and the herds. A similar conception may perhaps have originally everywhere underlain the use of the need-fire as a remedy for the murrain. It appears that in some parts of Germany the people did not wait for an outbreak of cattle-plague, but, taking time by the forelock, kindled a need-fire annually to prevent the calamity. Similarly in Poland the peasants are said to kindle fires in the village streets every year on St. Rochus's day and to drive the cattle thrice through them in order to protect the beasts against the murrain. We have seen that in the Hebrides the cattle were in like manner driven annually round the Beltane fires for the same purpose. In some cantons of Switzerland children still kindle a need-fire by the friction of wood for the sake of dispelling a mist.

CHAPTER LXIII

THE INTERPRETATION OF THE FIRE-FESTIVALS

§ 1. *On the Fire-festivals in general.*—The foregoing survey of the popular fire-festivals of Europe suggests some general observations. In the first place we can hardly help being struck by the resemblance which the ceremonies bear to each other, at whatever time of the year and in whatever part of Europe they are celebrated. The custom of kindling great bonfires, leaping over them, and driving cattle through or round them would seem to have been practically universal throughout Europe, and the same may be said of the processions or races with blazing torches round fields, orchards, pastures, or cattle-stalls. Less widespread are the customs of hurling lighted discs into the air and trundling a burning wheel down hill. The ceremonial of the Yule log is distinguished from that of the other fire-festivals by the privacy and domesticity which characterise it ; but this distinction may well be due simply to the rough weather of midwinter, which is apt not only to render a public assembly in the open air disagreeable, but also at any moment to defeat the object of the assembly by extinguishing the all-important fire under a downpour of rain or a fall of snow. Apart from these local or seasonal differences, the general resemblance between the fire-festivals at all times of the year and in all places is tolerably close. And as the ceremonies themselves resemble each other, so do the benefits which the people expect to reap from them. Whether applied in the form of bonfires blazing at fixed points, or of torches carried about from place to place, or of embers and ashes taken from the smouldering heap of fuel, the fire is believed to promote the growth of the crops and the welfare of man and beast, either positively by stimulating them, or negatively by averting the dangers and calamities which threaten them from such causes as thunder and lightning, conflagration, blight, mildew, vermin, sterility, disease, and not least of all witchcraft.

But we naturally ask, How did it come about that benefits so great and manifold were supposed to be attained by means so simple ? In what way did people imagine that they could procure so many goods or avoid so many ills by the application of fire and smoke, of embers and ashes ? Two different explanations of the fire-festivals have been given by modern enquirers. On the one hand it has been held that they are sun-charms or magical ceremonies intended, on the principle of imitative magic, to ensure a needful supply of sunshine for men, animals, and plants by kindling fires which mimic on earth the great source of light and heat in the sky. This was the view of Wilhelm Mannhardt. It may be called the solar theory. On the other hand it has been maintained that the ceremonial fires have no necessary reference to the sun but are simply purificatory in intention, being designed to burn up and destroy all harmful influences, whether these are conceived in a personal form as witches, demons, and monsters, or in an impersonal form as a sort of pervading taint or corruption of the air. This is the view of Dr. Edward Westermarck and apparently of Professor Eugen Mogk. It may be called the purificatory theory. Obviously the two theories postulate two very different conceptions of the fire which plays the principal part in the rites. On the one view, the fire, like sunshine in our latitude, is a genial creative power which fosters the growth of plants and the development of all that makes for health and happiness ; on the other view, the fire is a fierce destructive power which blasts and consumes all the noxious elements, whether spiritual or material, that menace the life of men, of animals, and of plants. According to the one theory the fire is a stimulant, according to the other it is a disinfectant ; on the one view its virtue is positive, on the other it is negative.

Yet the two explanations, different as they are in the character which they attribute to the fire, are perhaps not wholly irreconcilable. If we assume that the fires kindled at these festivals were primarily intended to imitate the sun's light and heat, may we not regard the purificatory and disinfecting qualities, which popular opinion certainly appears to have ascribed to them, as attributes derived directly from the purificatory and disinfecting qualities of sunshine ? In this way we might conclude that, while the imitation of sunshine in these ceremonies was primary and original, the purification attributed to them was secondary and derivative. Such a conclusion, occupying an intermediate position between the two opposing theories and recognising an element of truth in both of them, was adopted by me in earlier editions of this work ; but in the meantime Dr. Wester-marck has argued powerfully in favour of the purificatory theory alone, and I am bound to say that his arguments carry great weight, and that on a fuller review of the facts the balance of evidence seems to me to incline decidedly in his favour. However, the case is not so clear as to justify us in dismissing the solar theory without discussion, and accordingly I propose to adduce the considerations which tell for it before proceeding to notice those which tell against it. A theory which had the support of so learned and sagacious an investigator as W. Mannhardt is entitled to a respectful hearing.

§ 2. *The Solar Theory of the Fire-festivals.*—In an earlier part of this work we saw that savages resort to charms for making sunshine, and it would be no wonder if primitive man in Europe did the same. Indeed, when we consider the cold and cloudy climate of Europe during a great part of the year, we shall find it natural that sun-charms should have played a much more prominent part among the super-stitious practices of European peoples than among those of savages who live nearer the equator and who consequently are apt to get in the course of nature more sunshine than they want. This view of the festivals may be supported by various arguments drawn partly from their dates, partly from the nature of the rites, and partly from the influence which they are believed to exert upon the weather and on vegetation.

First, in regard to the dates of the festivals it can be no mere accident that two of the most important and widely spread of the festivals are timed to coincide more or less exactly with the summer and winter solstices, that is, with the two turning-points in the sun's apparent course in the sky when he reaches respectively his highest and his lowest elevation at noon. Indeed with respect to the mid-winter celebration of Christmas we are not left to conjecture ; we know from the express testimony of the ancients that it was instituted by the church to supersede an old heathen festival of the birth of the sun, which was apparently conceived to be born again on the shortest day of the year, after which his light and heat were seen to grow till they attained their full maturity at midsummer. Therefore it is no very far-fetched conjecture to suppose that the Yule log, which figures so prominently in the popular celebration of Christmas, was originally designed to help the labouring sun of midwinter to rekindle his seemingly expiring light.

Not only the date of some of the festivals but the manner of their celebration suggests a conscious imitation of the sun. The custom of rolling a burning wheel down a hill, which is often observed at these ceremonies, might well pass for an imitation of the sun's course in the sky, and the imitation would be especially appropriate on Midsummer Day when the sun's annual declension begins. Indeed the custom has been thus interpreted by some of those who have recorded it. Not less graphic, it may be said, is the mimicry of his apparent revolution by swinging a burning tar-barrel round a pole. Again, the common practice of throwing fiery discs, sometimes expressly said to be shaped like suns, into the air at the festivals may well be a piece of imitative magic. In these, as in so many cases, the magic force may be supposed to take effect through mimicry or sympathy : by imitating the desired result you actually produce it : by counterfeiting the sun's progress through the heavens you really help the luminary to pursue his celestial journey with punctuality and despatch. The name " fire of heaven," by which the midsummer fire is sometimes popularly known, clearly implies a consciousness of a connexion between the earthly and the heavenly flame.

Again, the manner in which the fire appears to have been originally kindled on these occasions has been alleged in support of the view that it was intended to be a mock-sun. As some scholars have perceived, it is highly probable that at the periodic festivals in former times fire was universally obtained by the friction of two pieces of wood. It is still so procured in some places both at the Easter and the Midsummer festivals, and it is expressly said to have been formerly so procured at the Beltane celebration both in Scotland and Wales. But what makes it nearly certain that this was once the invariable mode of kindling the fire at these periodic festivals is the analogy of the need-fire, which has almost always been produced by the friction of wood, and sometimes by the revolution of a wheel. It is a plausible conjecture that the wheel employed for this purpose represents the sun, and if the fires at the regularly recurring celebrations were formerly produced in the same way, it might be regarded as a confirmation of the view that they were originally sun-charms. In point of fact there is, as Kuhn has indicated, some evidence to show that the midsummer fire was originally thus produced. We have seen that many Hungarian swine-herds make fire on Midsummer Eve by rotating a wheel round a wooden axle wrapt in hemp, and that they drive their pigs through the fire thus made. At Obermedlingen, in Swabia, the " fire of heaven," as it was called, was made on St. Vitus's Day (the fifteenth of June) by igniting a cart-wheel, which, smeared with pitch and plaited with straw, was fastened on a pole twelve feet high, the top of the pole being inserted in the nave of the wheel. This fire was made on the summit of a mountain, and as the flame ascended, the people uttered a set form of words, with eyes and arms directed heavenward. Here the fixing of a wheel on a pole and igniting it suggests that originally the fire was produced, as in the case of the need-fire, by the revolution of a wheel. The day on which the ceremony takes place (the fifteenth of June) is near midsummer ; and we have seen that in Masuren fire is, or used to be, actually made on Midsummer Day by turning a wheel rapidly about an oaken pole, though it is not said that the new fire so obtained is used to light a bonfire. However, we must bear in mind that in all such cases the use of a wheel may be merely a mechanical device to facilitate the operation of fire-making by increasing the friction ; it need not have any symbolical significance.

Further, the influence which these fires, whether periodic or occasional, are supposed to exert on the weather and vegetation may be cited in support of the view that they are sun-charms, since the effects ascribed to them resemble those of sunshine.   Thus, the French belief that in a rainy June the lighting of the midsummer bonfires will cause the rain to cease appears to assume that they can disperse the dark clouds and make the sun to break out in radiant glory, drying the wet earth and dripping trees.   Similarly the use of the need-fire by Swiss children on foggy days for the purpose of clearing away the mist may very naturally be interpreted as a sun-charm.   In the Vosges Mountains the people believe that the midsummer fires help to preserve the fruits of the earth and ensure good crops.   In Sweden the warmth or cold of the coming season is inferred from the direction in which the flames of the May Day bonfire are blown ; if they blow to the south, it will be warm, if to the north, cold.   No doubt at present the direction of the flames is regarded merely as an augury of the weather, not as a mode of influencing it.   But we may be pretty sure that this is one of the cases in which magic has dwindled into divination.   So in the Eifel Mountains, when the smoke blows towards the corn-fields, this is an omen that the harvest will be abundant.   But the older view may have been not merely that the smoke and flames prognosticated, but that they actually produced an abundant harvest, the heat of the flames acting like sunshine on the corn.   Perhaps it was with this view that people in the Isle of Man lit fires to windward of their fields in order that the smoke might blow over them.   So in South Africa, about the month of April, the Matabeles light huge fires to the windward of their gardens, " their idea being that the smoke, by passing over the crops, will assist the ripening of them."   Among the Zulus also " medicine is burned on a fire placed to windward of the garden, the fumigation which the plants in consequence receive being held to improve the crop."   Again, the idea of our European peasants that the corn will grow well as far as the blaze of the bonfire is visible, may be interpreted as a remnant of the belief in the quickening and fertilising power of the bonfires.   The same belief, it may be argued, reappears in the notion that embers taken from the bonfires and inserted in the fields will promote the growth of the crops, and it may be thought to underlie the customs of sowing flax-seed in the direction in which the flames blow, of mixing the ashes of the bonfire with the seed-corn at sowing, of scattering the ashes by themselves over the field to fertilise it, and of incorporating a piece of the Yule log in the plough to make the seeds thrive.   The opinion that the flax or hemp will grow as high as the flames rise or the people leap over them belongs clearly to the same class of ideas.   Again, at Konz, on the banks of the Moselle, if the blazing wheel which was trundled down the hillside reached the river without being extinguished, this was hailed as a proof that the vintage would be abundant.   So firmly was this belief held that the successful performance of the ceremony entitled the villagers to levy a tax upon the owners of the neighbouring vineyards. Here the unextinguished wheel might be taken to represent an unclouded sun, which in turn would portend an abundant vintage. So the waggon-load of white wine which the villagers received from the vineyards round about might pass for a payment for the sunshine which they had procured for the grapes. Similarly in the Vale of Glamorgan a blazing wheel used to be trundled down hill on Midsummer Day, and if the fire were extinguished before the wheel reached the foot of the hill, the people expected a bad harvest; whereas if the wheel kept alight all the way down and continued to blaze for a long time, the farmers looked forward to heavy crops that summer. Here, again, it is natural to suppose that the rustic mind traced a direct connexion between the fire of the wheel and the fire of the sun, on which the crops are dependent.

But in popular belief the quickening and fertilising influence of the bonfires is not limited to the vegetable world; it extends also to animals. This plainly appears from the Irish custom of driving barren cattle through the midsummer fires, from the French belief that the Yule log steeped in water helps cows to calve, from the French and Serbian notion that there will be as many chickens, calves, lambs, and kids as there are sparks struck out of the Yule log, from the French custom of putting the ashes of the bonfires in the fowls' nests to make the hens lay eggs, and from the German practice of mixing the ashes of the bonfires with the drink of cattle in order to make the animals thrive. Further, there are clear indications that even human fecundity is supposed to be promoted by the genial heat of the fires. In Morocco the people think that childless couples can obtain offspring by leaping over the midsummer bonfire. It is an Irish belief that a girl who jumps thrice over the midsummer bonfire will soon marry and become the mother of many children; in Flanders women leap over the midsummer fires to ensure an easy delivery; in various parts of France they think that if a girl dances round nine fires she will be sure to marry within the year, and in Bohemia they fancy that she will do so if she merely sees nine of the bonfires. On the other hand, in Lechrain people say that if a young man and woman, leaping over the midsummer fire together, escaped unsmirched, the young woman will not become a mother within twelve months: the flames have not touched and fertilised her. In parts of Switzerland and France the lighting of the Yule log is accompanied by a prayer that the women may bear children, the she-goats bring forth kids, and the ewes drop lambs. The rule observed in some places that the bonfires should be kindled by the person who was last married seems to belong to the same class of ideas, whether it be that such a person is supposed to receive from, or to impart to, the fire a generative and fertilising influence. The common practice of lovers leaping over the fires hand in hand may very well have originated in a notion that thereby their marriage would be blessed with offspring; and the like motive would explain the custom which obliges couples married within the year to dance to the light of torches. And the scenes of profligacy which appear to have marked the midsummer celebration among the Esthonians, as they once marked the celebration of May Day among ourselves, may have sprung, not from the mere licence of holiday-makers, but from a crude notion that such orgies were justified, if not required, by some mysterious bond which linked the life of man to the courses of the heavens at this turning-point of the year.

At the festivals which we are considering the custom of kindling bonfires is commonly associated with a custom of carrying lighted torches about the fields, the orchards, the pastures, the flocks and the herds ; and we can hardly doubt that the two customs are only two different ways of attaining the same object, namely, the benefits which are believed to flow from the fire, whether it be stationary or portable. Accordingly if we accept the solar theory of the bonfires, we seem bound to apply it also to the torches ; we must suppose that the practice of marching or running with blazing torches about the country is simply a means of diffusing far and wide the genial influence of the sunshine, of which these flickering flames are a feeble imitation. In favour of this view it may be said that sometimes the torches are carried about the fields for the express purpose of fertilising them, and with the same intention live coals from the bonfires are sometimes placed in the fields to prevent blight. On the eve of Twelfth Day in Normandy men, women, and children run wildly through the fields and orchards with lighted torches, which they wave about the branches and dash against the trunks of the fruit-trees for the sake of burning the moss and driving away the moles and field-mice. " They believe that the ceremony fulfils the double object of exorcising the vermin whose multiplication would be a real calamity, and of imparting fecundity to the trees, the fields, and even the cattle " ; and they imagine that the more the ceremony is prolonged, the greater will be the crop of fruit next autumn. In Bohemia they say that the corn will grow as high as they fling the blazing besoms into the air. Nor are such notions confined to Europe. In Corea, a few days before the New Year festival, the eunuchs of the palace swing burning torches, chanting invocations the while, and this is supposed to ensure bountiful crops for the next season. The custom of trundling a burning wheel over the fields, which used to be observed in Poitou for the express purpose of fertilising them, may be thought to embody the same idea in a still more graphic form ; since in this way the mock-sun itself, not merely its light and heat represented by torches, is made actually to pass over the ground which is to receive its quickening and kindly influence. Once more, the custom of carrying lighted brands round cattle is plainly equivalent to driving the animals through the bonfire ; and if the bonfire is a sun-charm, the torches must be so also.

§ 3. *The Purificatory Theory of the Fire-festivals.*—Thus far we have considered what may be said for the theory that at the European fire-festivals the fire is kindled as a charm to ensure an abundant supply of sunshine for man and beast, for corn and fruits. It remains to consider what may be said against this theory and in favour of the view that in these rites fire is employed not as a creative but as a cleansing agent, which purifies men, animals, and plants by burning up and consuming the noxious elements, whether material or spiritual, which menace all living things with disease and death.

First, then, it is to be observed that the people who practise the fire-customs appear never to allege the solar theory in explanation of them, while on the contrary they do frequently and emphatically put forward the purificatory theory. This is a strong argument in favour of the purificatory and against the solar theory ; for the popular explanation of a popular custom is never to be rejected except for grave cause. And in the present case there seems to be no adequate reason for rejecting it. The conception of fire as a destructive agent, which can be turned to account for the consumption of evil things, is so simple and obvious that it could hardly escape the minds even of the rude peasantry with whom these festivals originated. On the other hand the conception of fire as an emanation of the sun, or at all events as linked to it by a bond of physical sympathy, is far less simple and obvious ; and though the use of fire as a charm to produce sunshine appears to be undeniable, nevertheless in attempting to explain popular customs we should never have recourse to a more recondite idea when a simpler one lies to hand and is supported by the explicit testimony of the people themselves. Now in the case of the fire-festivals the destructive aspect of fire is one upon which the people dwell again and again ; and it is highly significant that the great evil against which the fire is directed appears to be witchcraft. Again and again we are told that the fires are intended to burn or repel the witches ; and the intention is sometimes graphically expressed by burning an effigy of a witch in the fire. Hence, when we remember the great hold which the dread of witchcraft has had on the popular European mind in all ages, we may suspect that the primary intention of all these fire-festivals was simply to destroy or at all events get rid of the witches, who were regarded as the causes of nearly all the misfortunes and calamities that befall men, their cattle, and their crops.

This suspicion is confirmed when we examine the evils for which the bonfires and torches were supposed to provide a remedy. Foremost, perhaps, among these evils we may reckon the diseases of cattle ; and of all the ills that witches are believed to work there is probably none which is so constantly insisted on as the harm they do to the herds, particularly by stealing the milk from the cows. Now it is significant that the need-fire, which may perhaps be regarded as the parent of the periodic fire-festivals, is kindled above all as a remedy for a murrain or other disease of cattle ; and the circumstance suggests, what on general grounds seems probable, that the custom of kindling the need-fire goes back to a time when the ancestors of the European peoples subsisted chiefly on the products of their herds, and when agriculture as yet played a subordinate part in their lives. Witches and wolves are the two great foes still dreaded by the herdsman in many parts of Europe ; and we need not wonder that he should resort to fire as a powerful means of banning them both. Among Slavonic peoples it appears that the foes whom the need-fire is designed to combat are not so much living witches as vampyres and other evil spirits, and the ceremony aims rather at repelling these baleful beings than at actually consuming them in the flames. But for our present purpose these distinctions are immaterial. The important thing to observe is that among the Slavs the need-fire, which is probably the original of all the ceremonial fires now under consideration, is not a sun-charm, but clearly and unmistakably nothing but a means of protecting man and beast against the attacks of maleficent creatures, whom the peasant thinks to burn or scare by the heat of the fire, just as he might burn or scare wild animals.

Again, the bonfires are often supposed to protect the fields against hail and the homestead against thunder and lightning. But both hail and thunderstorms are frequently thought to be caused by witches ; hence the fire which bans the witches necessarily serves at the same time as a talisman against hail, thunder, and lightning. Further, brands taken from the bonfires are commonly kept in the houses to guard them against conflagration ; and though this may perhaps be done on the principle of homoeopathic magic, one fire being thought to act as a preventive of another, it is also possible that the intention may be to keep witch-incendiaries at bay. Again, people leap over the bonfires as a preventive of colic, and look at the flames steadily in order to preserve their eyes in good health ; and both colic and sore eyes are in Germany, and probably elsewhere, set down to the machinations of witches. Once more, to leap over the midsummer fires or to circumambulate them is thought to prevent a person from feeling pains in his back at reaping ; and in Germany such pains are called " witch-shots " and ascribed to witchcraft.

But if the bonfires and torches of the fire-festivals are to be regarded primarily as weapons directed against witches and wizards, it becomes probable that the same explanation applies not only to the flaming discs which are hurled into the air, but also to the burning wheels which are rolled down hill on these occasions ; discs and wheels, we may suppose, are alike intended to burn the witches who hover invisible in the air or haunt unseen the fields, the orchards, and the vineyards on the hillside. Certainly witches are constantly thought to ride through the air on broomsticks or other equally convenient vehicles ; and if they do so, how can you get at them so effectually as by hurling lighted missiles, whether discs, torches, or besoms, after them as they flit past overhead in the gloom ? The South Slavonian peasant believes that witches ride in the dark hail-clouds ; so he shoots at the clouds to bring down the hags, while he curses them, saying, " Curse, curse Herodias, thy mother is a heathen, damned of God and fettered through the Redeemer's blood." Also he brings out a pot of glowing charcoal on which he has thrown holy oil, laurel leaves, and wormwood to make a smoke. The fumes are supposed to ascend to the clouds and stupefy the witches, so that they tumble down to earth. And in order that they may not fall soft, but may hurt themselves very much, the yokel hastily brings out a chair and tilts it bottom up so that the witch in falling may break her legs on the legs of the chair. Worse than that, he cruelly lays scythes, bill-hooks, and other formidable weapons edge upwards so as to cut and mangle the poor wretches when they drop plump upon them from the clouds.

On this view the fertility supposed to follow the application of fire in the form of bonfires, torches, discs, rolling wheels, and so forth, is not conceived as resulting directly from an increase of solar heat which the fire has magically generated ; it is merely an indirect result obtained by freeing the reproductive powers of plants and animals from the fatal obstruction of witchcraft. And what is true of the reproduction of plants and animals may hold good also of the fertility of the human sexes. The bonfires are supposed to promote marriage and to procure offspring for childless couples. This happy effect need not flow directly from any quickening or fertilising energy in the fire ; it may follow indirectly from the power of the fire to remove those obstacles which the spells of witches and wizards notoriously present to the union of man and wife.

On the whole, then, the theory of the purificatory virtue of the ceremonial fires appears more probable and more in accordance with the evidence than the opposing theory of their connexion with the sun.

CHAPTER LXIV

THE BURNING OF HUMAN BEINGS IN THE FIRES

§ 1. *The Burning of Effigies in the Fires.*—We have still to ask, What is the meaning of burning effigies in the fire at these festivals ? After the preceding investigation the answer to the question seems obvious. As the fires are often alleged to be kindled for the purpose of burning the witches, and as the effigy burnt in them is sometimes called " the Witch," we might naturally be disposed to conclude that all the effigies consumed in the flames on these occasions represent witches or warlocks, and that the custom of burning them is merely a substitute for burning the wicked men and women themselves, since on the principle of homoeopathic or imitative magic you practically destroy the witch herself in destroying her effigy. On the whole this explanation of the burning of straw figures in human shape at the festivals is perhaps the most probable.

Yet it may be that this explanation does not apply to all the cases, and that certain of them may admit and even require another interpretation. For the effigies so burned, as I have already remarked, can hardly be separated from the effigies of Death which are burned or otherwise destroyed in spring ; and grounds have been already given for regarding the so-called effigies of Death as really representatives of the tree-spirit or spirit of vegetation. Are the other effigies, which are burned in the spring and midsummer bonfires, susceptible of the same explanation ? It would seem so. For just as the fragments of the so-called Death are stuck in the fields to make the crops grow, so the charred embers of the figure burned in the spring bonfires are sometimes laid on the fields in the belief that they will keep vermin from the crop. Again, the rule that the last married bride must leap over the fire in which the straw-man is burned on Shrove Tuesday, is probably intended to make her fruitful. But, as we have seen, the power of blessing women with offspring is a special attribute of tree-spirits ; it is therefore a fair presumption that the burning effigy over which the bride must leap is a representative of the fertilising tree-spirit or spirit of vegetation. This character of the effigy, as representative of the spirit of vegetation, is almost unmistakable when the figure is composed of an unthreshed sheaf of corn or is covered from head to foot with flowers. Again, it is to be noted that, instead of a puppet, trees, either living or felled, are sometimes burned both in the spring and midsummer bonfires. Now, considering the frequency with which the tree-spirit is represented in human shape, it is hardly rash to suppose that when sometimes a tree and sometimes an effigy is burned in these fires, the effigy and the tree are regarded as equivalent to each other, each being a representative of the tree-spirit. This, again, is confirmed by observing, first, that sometimes the effigy which is to be burned is carried about simultaneously with a May-tree, the former being carried by the boys, the latter by the girls ; and, second, that the effigy is sometimes tied to a living tree and burned with it. In these cases, we can scarcely doubt, the tree-spirit is represented, as we have found it represented before, in duplicate, both by the tree and by the effigy. That the true character of the effigy as a representative of the beneficent spirit of vegetation should sometimes be forgotten, is natural. The custom of burning a beneficent god is too foreign to later modes of thought to escape misinterpretation. Naturally enough the people who continued to burn his image came in time to identify it as the effigy of persons, whom, on various grounds, they regarded with aversion, such as Judas Iscariot, Luther, and a witch.

The general reasons for killing a god or his representative have been examined in a preceding chapter. But when the god happens to be a deity of vegetation, there are special reasons why he should die by fire. For light and heat are necessary to vegetable growth ; and, on the principle of sympathetic magic, by subjecting the personal representative of vegetation to their influence, you secure a supply of these necessaries for trees and crops. In other words, by burning the spirit of vegetation in a fire which represents the sun, you make sure that, for a time at least, vegetation shall have plenty of sun. It may be objected that, if the intention is simply to secure enough sunshine for vegetation, this end would be better attained, on the principles of sympathetic magic, by merely passing the representative of vegetation through the fire instead of burning him. In point of fact this is sometimes done. In Russia, as we have seen, the straw figure of Kupalo is not burned in the midsummer fire, but merely carried backwards and forwards across it. But, for the reasons already given, it is necessary that the god should die ; so next day Kupalo is stripped of her ornaments and thrown into a stream. In this Russian custom the passage of the image through the fire, if it is not simply a purification, may possibly be a sun-charm ; the killing of the god is a separate act, and the mode of killing him—by drowning —is probably a rain-charm. But usually people have not thought it necessary to draw this fine distinction ; for the various reasons already assigned, it is advantageous, they think, to expose the god of vegetation to a considerable degree of heat, and it is also advantageous to kill him, and they combine these advantages in a rough-and-ready way by burning him.

§ 2. *The Burning of Men and Animals in the Fires.*—In the popular customs connected with the fire-festivals of Europe there are certain features which appear to point to a former practice of human sacrifice. We have seen reasons for believing that in Europe living persons have often acted as representatives of the tree-spirit and corn-spirit and have suffered death as such. There is no reason, therefore, why they should not have been burned, if any special advantages were likely to be attained by putting them to death in that way. The consideration of human suffering is not one which enters into the calculations of primitive man. Now, in the fire-festivals which we are discussing, the pretence of burning people is sometimes carried so far that it seems reasonable to regard it as a mitigated survival of an older custom of actually burning them. Thus in Aachen, as we saw, the man clad in peas-straw acts so cleverly that the children really believe he is being burned. At Jumièges in Normandy the man clad all in green, who bore the title of the Green Wolf, was pursued by his comrades, and when they caught him they feigned to fling him upon the midsummer bonfire. Similarly at the Beltane fires in Scotland the pretended victim was seized, and a show made of throwing him into the flames, and for some time afterwards people affected to speak of him as dead. Again, in the Hallowe'en bonfires of North-eastern Scotland we may perhaps detect a similar pretence in the custom observed by a lad of lying down as close to the fire as possible and allowing the other lads to leap over him. The titular king at Aix, who reigned for a year and danced the first dance round the midsummer bonfire, may perhaps in days of old have discharged the less agreeable duty of serving as fuel for that fire which in later times he only kindled. In the following customs Mannhardt is probably right in recognising traces of an old custom of burning a leaf-clad representative of the spirit of vegetation. At Wolfeck, in Austria, on Midsummer Day, a boy completely clad in green fir branches goes from house to house, accompanied by a noisy crew, collecting wood for the bonfire.   As he gets the wood he sings :

" Forest trees I want,   *But beer and wine,*
No sour milk for me,   *So can the wood-man be jolly and gay."*

In some parts of Bavaria, also, the boys who go from house to house collecting fuel for the midsummer bonfire envelop one of their number from head to foot in green branches of firs, and lead him by a rope through the whole village.   At Moosheim, in Wurtemberg, the festival of St. John's Fire usually lasted for fourteen days, ending on the second Sunday after Midsummer Day.   On this last day the bonfire was left in charge of the children, while the older people retired to a wood.   Here they encased a young fellow in leaves and twigs, who, thus disguised, went to the fire, scattered it, and trod it out. All the people present fled at the sight of him.

But it seems possible to go farther than this.   Of human sacrifices offered on these occasions the most unequivocal traces, as we have seen, are those which, about a hundred years ago, still lingered at the Beltane fires in the Highlands of Scotland, that is, among a Celtic people who, situated in a remote corner of Europe and almost completely isolated from foreign influence, had till then conserved their old heathenism better perhaps than any other people in the West of Europe.   It is significant, therefore, that human sacrifices by fire are known, on unquestionable evidence, to have been systematically practised by the Celts.   The earliest description of these sacrifices has been bequeathed to us by Julius Caesar.   As conqueror of the hitherto independent Celts of Gaul, Caesar had ample opportunity of observing the national Celtic religion and manners, while these were still fresh and crisp from the native mint and had not yet been fused in the melting-pot of Roman civilisation.   With his own notes Caesar appears to have incorporated the observations of a Greek explorer, by name Posidonius, who travelled in Gaul about fifty years before Caesar carried the Roman arms to the English Channel.   The Greek geographer Strabo and the historian Diodorus seem also to have derived their descriptions of the Celtic sacrifices from the work of Posidonius, but independently of each other, and of Caesar, for each of the three derivative accounts contains some details which are not to be found in either of the others.   By combining them, therefore, we can restore the original account of Posidonius with some probability, and thus obtain a picture of the sacrifices offered by the Celts of Gaul at the close of the second century before our era.   The following seem to have been the main outlines of the custom.   Condemned criminals were reserved by the Celts in order to be sacrificed to the gods at a great festival which took place once in every five years. The more there were of such victims, the greater was believed to be the fertility of the land.   If there were not enough criminals to furnish victims, captives taken in war were immolated to supply the deficiency. When the time came the victims were sacrificed by the Druids or priests. Some they shot down with arrows, some they impaled, and some they burned alive in the following manner. Colossal images of wicker-work or of wood and grass were constructed ; these were filled with live men, cattle, and animals of other kinds ; fire was then applied to the images, and they were burned with their living contents.

Such were the great festivals held once every five years. But besides these quinquennial festivals, celebrated on so grand a scale, and with, apparently, so large an expenditure of human life, it seems reasonable to suppose that festivals of the same sort, only on a lesser scale, were held annually, and that from these annual festivals are lineally descended some at least of the fire-festivals which, with their traces of human sacrifices, are still celebrated year by year in many parts of Europe. The gigantic images constructed of osiers or covered with grass in which the Druids enclosed their victims remind us of the leafy framework in which the human representative of the tree-spirit is still so often encased. Hence, seeing that the fertility of the land was apparently supposed to depend upon the due performance of these sacrifices, Mannhardt interpreted the Celtic victims, cased in osiers and grass, as representatives of the tree - spirit or spirit of vegetation.

These wicker giants of the Druids seem to have had till lately, if not down to the present time, their representatives at the spring and midsummer festivals of modern Europe. At Douay, down at least to the early part of the nineteenth century, a procession took place annually on the Sunday nearest to the seventh of July. The great feature of the procession was a colossal figure, some twenty or thirty feet high, made of osiers, and called " the giant," which was moved through the streets by means of rollers and ropes worked by men who were enclosed within the effigy. The figure was armed as a knight with lance and sword, helmet and shield. Behind him marched his wife and his three children, all constructed of osiers on the same principle, but on a smaller scale. At Dunkirk the procession of the giants took place on Midsummer Day, the twenty-fourth of June. The festival, which was known as the Follies of Dunkirk, attracted multitudes of spectators. The giant was a huge figure of wicker-work, occasionally as much as forty-five feet high, dressed in a long blue robe with gold stripes, which reached to his feet, concealing the dozen or more men who made it dance and bob its head to the spectators. This colossal effigy went by the name of Papa Reuss, and carried in its pocket a bouncing infant of Brobdingnagian proportions. The rear was brought up by the daughter of the giant, constructed, like her sire, of wicker-work, and little, if at all, inferior to him in size. Most towns and even villages of Brabant and Flanders have, or used to have, similar wicker giants which were annually led about to the delight of the populace, who loved these grotesque figures, spoke of them with patriotic enthusiasm, and never wearied of gazing at them. At Antwerp the giant was so big that no gate in the city was large enough to let him go through ; hence he could not visit his brother giants in neighbouring towns, as the other Belgian giants used to do on solemn occasions.

In England artificial giants seem to have been a standing feature of the midsummer festival. A writer of the sixteenth century speaks of " Midsommer pageants in London, where to make the people wonder, are set forth great and uglie gyants marching as if they were alive, and armed at all points, but within they are stuffed full of browne paper and tow, which the shrewd boyes, underpeering, do guilefully discover, and turne to a greate derision." At Chester the annual pageant on Midsummer Eve included the effigies of four giants, with animals, hobby-horses, and other figures. At Coventry it appears that the giant's wife figured beside the giant. At Burford, in Oxfordshire, Midsummer Eve used to be celebrated with great jollity by the carrying of a giant and a dragon up and down the town. The last survivor of these perambulating English giants lingered at Salisbury, where an antiquary found him mouldering to decay in the neglected hall of the Tailors' Company about the year 1844. His bodily framework was of lath and hoop, like the one which used to be worn by Jack-in-the-Green on May Day.

In these cases the giants merely figured in the processions. But sometimes they were burned in the summer bonfires. Thus the people of the Rue aux Ours in Paris used annually to make a great wickerwork figure, dressed as a soldier, which they promenaded up and down the streets for several days, and solemnly burned on the third of July, the crowd of spectators singing *Salve Regina*. A personage who bore the title of king presided over the ceremony with a lighted torch in his hand. The burning fragments of the image were scattered among the people, who eagerly scrambled for them. The custom was abolished in 1743. In Brie, Isle de France, a wicker-work giant, eighteen feet high, was annually burned on Midsummer Eve.

Again, the Druidical custom of burning live animals, enclosed in wicker-work, has its counterpart at the spring and midsummer festivals. At Luchon in the Pyrenees on Midsummer Eve " a hollow column, composed of strong wickerwork, is raised to the height of about sixty feet in the centre of the principal suburb, and interlaced with green foliage up to the very top ; while the most beautiful flowers and shrubs procurable are artistically arranged in groups below, so as to form a sort of background to the scene. The column is then filled with combustible materials, ready for ignition. At an appointed hour—about 8 P.M.—a grand procession, composed of the clergy, followed by young men and maidens in holiday attire, pour forth from the town chanting hymns, and take up their position around the column. Meanwhile, bonfires are lit, with beautiful effect, in the surrounding hills. As many living serpents as could be collected are now thrown into the column, which is set on fire at the base by means of torches, armed with which about fifty boys and men dance around with frantic gestures. The serpents, to avoid the flames, wriggle their way to the top, whence they are seen lashing out laterally until finally obliged to drop, their struggles for life giving rise to enthusiastic delight among the surrounding spectators. This is a favourite annual ceremony for the inhabitants of Luchon and its neighbourhood, and local tradition assigns it to a heathen origin." In the midsummer fires formerly kindled on the Place de Grève at Paris it was the custom to burn a basket, barrel, or sack full of live cats, which was hung from a tall mast in the midst of the bonfire ; sometimes a fox was burned. The people collected the embers and ashes of the fire and took them home, believing that they brought good luck. The French kings often witnessed these spectacles and even lit the bonfire with their own hands. In 1648 Louis the Fourteenth, crowned with a wreath of roses and carrying a bunch of roses in his hand, kindled the fire, danced at it and partook of the banquet afterwards in the town hall. But this was the last occasion when a monarch presided at the midsummer bonfire in Paris. At Metz midsummer fires were lighted with great pomp on the esplanade, and a dozen cats, enclosed in wicker cages, were burned alive in them, to the amusement of the people. Similarly at Gap, in the department of the High Alps, cats used to be roasted over the midsummer bonfire. In Russia a white cock was sometimes burned in the midsummer bonfire ; in Meissen or Thuringia a horse's head used to be thrown into it. Sometimes animals are burned in the spring bonfires. In the Vosges cats were burned on Shrove Tuesday ; in Alsace they were thrown into the Easter bonfire. In the department of the Ardennes cats were flung into the bonfires kindled on the first Sunday in Lent ; sometimes, by a refinement of cruelty, they were hung over the fire from the end of a pole and roasted alive. " The cat, which represented the devil, could never suffer enough." While the creatures were perishing in the flames, the shepherds guarded their flocks and forced them to leap over the fire, esteeming this an infallible means of preserving them from disease and witchcraft. We have seen that squirrels were sometimes burned in the Easter fire.

Thus it appears that the sacrificial rites of the Celts of ancient Gaul can be traced in the popular festivals of modern Europe. Naturally it is in France, or rather in the wider area comprised within the limits of ancient Gaul, that these rites have left the clearest traces in the customs of burning giants of wicker-work and animals enclosed in wicker-work or baskets. These customs, it will have been remarked, are generally observed at or about midsummer. From this we may infer that the original rites of which these are the degenerate successors were solemnised at midsummer. This inference harmonises with the conclusion suggested by a general survey of European folk-custom, that the midsummer festival must on the whole have been the most widely diffused and the most solemn of all the yearly festivals celebrated by the primitive Aryans in Europe. At the same time we must bear in mind that among the British Celts the chief fire-festivals of the year appear certainly to have been those of Beltane (May Day) and Hallowe'en (the last day of October) ; and this suggests a doubt whether the Celts of Gaul also may not have celebrated their principal rites of fire, including their burnt sacrifices of men and animals, at the beginning of May or the beginning of November rather than at Midsummer.

We have still to ask, What is the meaning of such sacrifices? Why were men and animals burnt to death at these festivals? If we are right in interpreting the modern European fire-festivals as attempts to break the power of witchcraft by burning or banning the witches and warlocks, it seems to follow that we must explain the human sacrifices of the Celts in the same manner; that is, we must suppose that the men whom the Druids burnt in wicker-work images were condemned to death on the ground that they were witches or wizards, and that the mode of execution by fire was chosen because burning alive is deemed the surest mode of getting rid of these noxious and dangerous beings. The same explanation would apply to the cattle and wild animals of many kinds which the Celts burned along with the men. They, too, we may conjecture, were supposed to be either under the spell of witchcraft or actually to be the witches and wizards, who had transformed themselves into animals for the purpose of prosecuting their infernal plots against the welfare of their fellow-creatures. This conjecture is confirmed by the observation that the victims most commonly burned in modern bonfires have been cats, and that cats are precisely the animals into which, with the possible exception of hares, witches were most usually supposed to transform themselves. Again, we have seen that serpents and foxes used sometimes to be burnt in the midsummer fires; and Welsh and German witches are reported to have assumed the form both of foxes and serpents. In short, when we remember the great variety of animals whose forms witches can assume at pleasure, it seems easy on this hypothesis to account for the variety of living creatures that have been burnt at festivals both in ancient Gaul and modern Europe; all these victims, we may surmise, were doomed to the flames, not because they were animals, but because they were believed to be witches who had taken the shape of animals for their nefarious purposes. One advantage of explaining the ancient Celtic sacrifices in this way is that it introduces, as it were, a harmony and consistency into the treatment which Europe has meted out to witches from the earliest times down to about two centuries ago, when the growing influence of rationalism discredited the belief in witchcraft and put a stop to the custom of burning witches. Be that as it may, we can now perhaps understand why the Druids believed that the more persons they sentenced to death, the greater would be the fertility of the land. To a modern reader the connexion at first sight may not be obvious between the activity of the hangman and the productivity of the earth. But a little reflection may satisfy him that when the criminals who perish at the stake or on the gallows are witches, whose delight it is to blight the crops of the farmer or to lay them low under storms of hail, the execution of these wretches is really calculated to ensure an abundant harvest by removing one of the principal causes which paralyse the efforts and blast the hopes of the husbandman.

The Druidical sacrifices which we are considering were explained in a different way by W. Mannhardt. He supposed that the men whom the Druids burned in wicker-work images represented the spirits of vegetation, and accordingly that the custom of burning them was a magical ceremony intended to secure the necessary sunshine for the crops. Similarly, he seems to have inclined to the view that the animals which used to be burnt in the bonfires represented the corn-spirit, which, as we saw in an earlier part of this work, is often supposed to assume the shape of an animal. This theory is no doubt tenable, and the great authority of W. Mannhardt entitles it to careful consideration. I adopted it in former editions of this book ; but on reconsideration it seems to me on the whole to be less probable than the theory that the men and animals burnt in the fires perished in the character of witches. This latter view is strongly supported by the testimony of the people who celebrate the fire-festivals, since a popular name for the custom of kindling the fires is " burning the witches," effigies of witches are sometimes consumed in the flames, and the fires, their embers, or their ashes are supposed to furnish protection against witchcraft. On the other hand there is little to show that the effigies or the animals burnt in the fires are regarded by the people as representatives of the vegetation-spirit, and that the bonfires are sun-charms. With regard to serpents in particular, which used to be burnt in the midsummer fire at Luchon, I am not aware of any certain evidence that in Europe snakes have been regarded as embodiments of the tree-spirit or corn-spirit, though in other parts of the world the conception appears to be not unknown. Whereas the popular faith in the transformation of witches into animals is so general and deeply rooted, and the fear of these uncanny beings is so strong, that it seems safer to suppose that the cats and other animals which were burnt in the fire suffered death as embodiments of witches than that they perished as representatives of vegetation-spirits.

CHAPTER LXV

BALDER AND THE MISTLETOE

THE reader may remember that the preceding account of the popular fire-festivals of Europe was suggested by the myth of the Norse god Balder, who is said to have been slain by a branch of mistletoe and burnt in a great fire. We have now to enquire how far the customs which have been passed in review help to shed light on the myth. In this enquiry it may be convenient to begin with the mistletoe, the instrument of Balder's death.

From time immemorial the mistletoe has been the object of superstitious veneration in Europe. It was worshipped by the Druids, as we learn from a famous passage of Pliny. After enumerating the different kinds of mistletoe, he proceeds : " In treating of this subject, the admiration in which the mistletoe is held throughout Gaul ought not to pass unnoticed. The Druids, for so they call their wizards, esteem nothing more sacred than the mistletoe and the tree on which it grows, provided only that the tree is an oak. But apart from this they choose oak-woods for their sacred groves and perform no sacred rites without oak-leaves ; so that the very name of Druids may be regarded as a Greek appellation derived from their worship of the oak. For they believe that whatever grows on these trees is sent from heaven, and is a sign that the tree has been chosen by the god himself. The mistletoe is very rarely to be met with ; but when it is found, they gather it with solemn ceremony. This they do above all on the sixth day of the moon, from whence they date the beginnings of their months, of their years, and of their thirty years' cycle, because by the sixth day the moon has plenty of vigour and has not run half its course. After due preparations have been made for a sacrifice and a feast under the tree, they hail it as the universal healer and bring to the spot two white bulls, whose horns have never been bound before. A priest clad in a white robe climbs the tree and with a golden sickle cuts the mistletoe, which is caught in a white cloth. Then they sacrifice the victims, praying that God may make his own gift to prosper with those upon whom he has bestowed it. They believe that a potion prepared from mistletoe will make barren animals to bring forth, and that the plant is a remedy against all poison."

In another passage Pliny tells us that in medicine the mistletoe which grows on an oak was esteemed the most efficacious, and that its efficacy was by some superstitious people supposed to be increased if the plant was gathered on the first day of the moon without the use of iron, and if when gathered it was not allowed to touch the earth ; oak-mistletoe thus obtained was deemed a cure for epilepsy ; carried about by women it assisted them to conceive ; and it healed ulcers most effectually, if only the sufferer chewed a piece of the plant and laid another piece on the sore. Yet again, he says that mistletoe was supposed, like vinegar and an egg, to be an excellent means of extinguishing a fire.

If in these latter passages Pliny refers, as he apparently does, to the beliefs current among his contemporaries in Italy, it will follow that the Druids and the Italians were to some extent agreed as to the valuable properties possessed by mistletoe which grows on an oak ; both of them deemed it an effectual remedy for a number of ailments, and both of them ascribed to it a quickening virtue, the Druids believing that a potion prepared from mistletoe would fertilise barren cattle, and the Italians holding that a piece of mistletoe carried about by a woman would help her to conceive a child. Further, both peoples thought that if the plant were to exert its medicinal properties it must be gathered in a certain way and at a certain time. It might not be cut with iron, hence the Druids cut it with gold ; and it might not touch the earth, hence the Druids caught it in a white cloth. In choosing the time for gathering the plant, both peoples were determined by observation of the moon ; only they differed as to the particular day of the moon, the Italians preferring the first, and the Druids the sixth.

With these beliefs of the ancient Gauls and Italians as to the wonderful medicinal properties of mistletoe we may compare the similar beliefs of the modern Aino of Japan. We read that they, " like many nations of the Northern origin, hold the mistletoe in peculiar veneration. They look upon it as a medicine, good in almost every disease, and it is sometimes taken in food and at others separately as a decoction. The leaves are used in preference to the berries, the latter being of too sticky a nature for general purposes. . . . But many, too, suppose this plant to have the power of making the gardens bear plentifully. When used for this purpose, the leaves are cut up into fine pieces, and, after having been prayed over, are sown with the millet and other seeds, a little also being eaten with the food. Barren women have also been known to eat the mistletoe, in order to be made to bear children. That mistletoe which grows upon the willow is supposed to have the greatest efficacy. This is because the willow is looked upon by them as being an especially sacred tree."

Thus the Aino agree with the Druids in regarding mistletoe as a cure for almost every disease, and they agree with the ancient Italians that applied to women it helps them to bear children. Again, the Druidical notion that the mistletoe was an " all-healer " or panacea may be compared with a notion entertained by the Walos of Senegambia. These people " have much veneration for a sort of mistletoe, which they call *tob* ; they carry leaves of it on their persons when they go to war as a preservative against wounds, just as if the leaves were real talismans (*gris-gris*)." The French writer who records this practice adds : " Is it not very curious that the mistletoe should be in this part of Africa what it was in the superstitions of the Gauls ? This prejudice, common to the two countries, may have the same origin ; blacks and whites will doubtless have seen, each of them for themselves, something supernatural in a plant which grows and flourishes without having roots in the earth. May they not have believed, in fact, that it was a plant fallen from the sky, a gift of the divinity ? "

This suggestion as to the origin of the superstition is strongly confirmed by the Druidical belief, reported by Pliny, that whatever grew on an oak was sent from heaven and was a sign that the tree had been chosen by the god himself. Such a belief explains why the Druids cut the mistletoe, not with a common knife, but with a golden sickle, and why, when cut, it was not suffered to touch the earth ; probably they thought that the celestial plant would have been profaned and its marvellous virtue lost by contact with the ground. With the ritual observed by the Druids in cutting the mistletoe we may compare the ritual which in Cambodia is prescribed in a similar case. They say that when you see an orchid growing as a parasite on a tamarind tree, you should dress in white, take a new earthenware pot, then climb the tree at noon, break off the plant, put it in the pot and let the pot fall to the ground. After that you make in the pot a decoction which confers the gift of invulnerability. Thus just as in Africa the leaves of one parasitic plant are supposed to render the wearer invulnerable, so in Cambodia a decoction made from another parasitic plant is considered to render the same service to such as make use of it, whether by drinking or washing. We may conjecture that in both places the notion of invulnerability is suggested by the position of the plant, which, occupying a place of comparative security above the ground, appears to promise to its fortunate possessor a similar security from some of the ills that beset the life of man on earth. We have already met with examples of the store which the primitive mind sets on such vantage grounds.

Whatever may be the origin of these beliefs and practices concerning the mistletoe, certain it is that some of them have their analogies in the folk-lore of modern European peasants. For example, it is laid down as a rule in various parts of Europe that mistletoe may not be cut in the ordinary way but must be shot or knocked down with stones from the tree on which it is growing. Thus, in the Swiss canton of Aargau " all parasitic plants are esteemed in a certain sense holy by the country folk, but most particularly so the mistletoe growing on an oak. They ascribe great powers to it, but shrink from cutting it off in the usual manner. Instead of that they procure it in the following manner. When the sun is in Sagittarius and the moon is on the wane, on the first, third, or fourth day before the new moon, one ought to shoot down with an arrow the mistletoe of an oak and to catch it with the left hand as it falls. Such mistletoe is a remedy for every ailment of children." Here among the Swiss peasants, as among the Druids of old, special virtue is ascribed to mistletoe which grows on an oak : it may not be cut in the usual way : it must be caught as it falls to the ground ; and it is esteemed a panacea for all diseases, at least of children. In Sweden, also, it is a popular superstition that if mistletoe is to possess its peculiar virtue, it must either be shot down out of the oak or knocked down with stones. Similarly, " so late as the early part of the nineteenth century, people in Wales believed that for the mistletoe to have any power, it must be shot or struck down with stones off the tree where it grew."

Again, in respect of the healing virtues of mistletoe the opinion of modern peasants, and even of the learned, has to some extent agreed with that of the ancients. The Druids appear to have called the plant, or perhaps the oak on which it grew, the " all-healer " ; and " all-healer " is said to be still a name of the mistletoe in the modern Celtic speech of Brittany, Wales, Ireland, and Scotland. On St. John's morning (Midsummer morning) peasants of Piedmont and Lombardy go out to search the oak-leaves for the " oil of St. John," which is supposed to heal all wounds made with cutting instruments.

Originally, perhaps, the " oil of St. John " was simply the mistletoe, or a decoction made from it.   For in Holstein the mistletoe, especially oak-mistletoe, is still regarded as a panacea for green wounds and as a sure charm to secure success in hunting ; and at Lacaune, in the south of France, the old Druidical belief in the mistletoe as an antidote to all poisons still survives among the peasantry ; they apply the plant to the stomach of the sufferer or give him a decoction of it to drink. Again, the ancient belief that mistletoe is a cure for epilepsy has survived in modern times not only among the ignorant but among the learned.   Thus in Sweden persons afflicted with the falling sickness think they can ward off attacks of the malady by carrying about with them a knife which has a handle of oak mistletoe ; and in Germany for a similar purpose pieces of mistletoe used to be hung round the necks of children.   In the French province of Bourbonnais a popular remedy for epilepsy is a decoction of mistletoe which has been gathered on an oak on St. John's Day and boiled with rye-flour.   So at Bottesford in Lincolnshire a decoction of mistletoe is supposed to be a palliative for this terrible disease.   Indeed mistletoe was recommended as a remedy for the falling sickness by high medical authorities in England and Holland down to the eighteenth century.

However, the opinion of the medical profession as to the curative virtues of mistletoe has undergone a radical alteration.   Whereas the Druids thought that mistletoe cured everything, modern doctors appear to think that it cures nothing.   If they are right, we must conclude that the ancient and widespread faith in the medicinal virtue of mistletoe is a pure superstition based on nothing better than the fanciful inferences which ignorance has drawn from the parasitic nature of the plant, its position high up on the branch of a tree seeming to protect it from the dangers to which plants and animals are subject on the surface of the ground.   From this point of view we can perhaps understand why mistletoe has so long and so persistently been pre-scribed as a cure for the falling sickness.   As mistletoe cannot fall to the ground because it is rooted on the branch of a tree high above the earth, it seems to follow as a necessary consequence that an epileptic patient cannot possibly fall down in a fit so long as he carries a piece of mistletoe in his pocket or a decoction of mistletoe in his stomach. Such a train of reasoning would probably be regarded even now as cogent by a large portion of the human species.

Again the ancient Italian opinion that mistletoe extinguishes fire appears to be shared by Swedish peasants, who hang up bunches of oak-mistletoe on the ceilings of their rooms as a protection against harm in general and conflagration in particular.   A hint as to the way in which mistletoe comes to be possessed of this property is furnished by the epithet " thunder-besom," which people of the Aargau canton in Switzerland apply to the plant.   For a thunder-besom is a shaggy, bushy excrescence on branches of trees, which is popularly believed to be produced by a flash of lightning ; hence in Bohemia a thunder-besom burnt in the fire protects the house against being struck by a thunder-bolt.   Being itself a product of lightning it naturally serves, on homoeopathic principles, as a protection against lightning, in fact as a kind of lightning-conductor.   Hence the fire which mistletoe in Sweden is designed especially to avert from houses may be fire kindled by lightning ; though no doubt the plant is equally effective against conflagration in general.

Again, mistletoe acts as a master-key as well as a lightning-con-ductor ; for it is said to open all locks.   But perhaps the most precious of all the virtues of mistletoe is that it affords efficient protection against sorcery and witchcraft.   That, no doubt, is the reason why in Austria a twig of mistletoe is laid on the threshold as a preventive of night-mare ; and it may be the reason why in the north of England they say that if you wish your dairy to thrive you should give your bunch of mistletoe to the first cow that calves after New Year's Day, for it is well known that nothing is so fatal to milk and butter as witchcraft. Similarly in Wales, for the sake of ensuring good luck to the dairy, people used to give a branch of mistletoe to the first cow that gave birth to a calf after the first hour of the New Year ; and in rural districts of Wales, where mistletoe abounded, there was always a profusion of it in the farmhouses.   When mistletoe was scarce, Welsh farmers used to say, " No mistletoe, no luck " ; but if there was a fine crop of mistletoe, they expected a fine crop of corn.   In Sweden mistletoe is diligently sought after on St. John's Eve, the people " believing it to be, in a high degree, possessed of mystic qualities ; and that if a sprig of it be attached to the ceiling of the dwelling-house, the horse's stall, or the cow's crib, the Troll will then be powerless to injure either man or beast."

With regard to the time when the mistletoe should be gathered opinions have varied.   The Druids gathered it above all on the sixth day of the moon, the ancient Italians apparently on the first day of the moon.   In modern times some have preferred the full moon of March and others the waning moon of winter when the sun is in Sagit-tarius.   But the favourite time would seem to be Midsummer Eve or Midsummer Day.   We have seen that both in France and Sweden special virtues are ascribed to mistletoe gathered at Midsummer. The rule in Sweden is that " mistletoe must be cut on the night of Midsummer Eve when sun and moon stand in the sign of their might." Again, in Wales it was believed that a sprig of mistletoe gathered on St. John's Eve (Midsummer Eve), or at any time before the berries appeared, would induce dreams of omen, both good and bad, if it were placed under the pillow of the sleeper.   Thus mistletoe is one of the many plants whose magical or medicinal virtues are believed to culminate with the culmination of the sun on the longest day of the year.   Hence it seems reasonable to conjecture that in the eyes of the Druids, also, who revered the plant so highly, the sacred mistletoe may have acquired a double portion of its mystic qualities at the solstice in June, and that accordingly they may have regularly cut it with solemn ceremony on Midsummer Eve.

Be that as it may, certain it is that the mistletoe, the instrument of Balder's death, has been regularly gathered for the sake of its mystic qualities on Midsummer Eve in Scandinavia, Balder's home. The plant is found commonly growing on pear-trees, oaks, and other trees in thick damp woods throughout the more temperate parts of Sweden. Thus one of the two main incidents of Balder's myth is reproduced in the great midsummer festival of Scandinavia. But the other main incident of the myth, the burning of Balder's body on a pyre, has also its counterpart in the bonfires which still blaze, or blazed till lately, in Denmark, Norway, and Sweden on Midsummer Eve. It does not appear, indeed, that any effigy is burned in these bonfires ; but the burning of an effigy is a feature which might easily drop out after its meaning was forgotten. And the name of Balder's balefires (*Balder's Bälar*), by which these midsummer fires were formerly known in Sweden, puts their connexion with Balder beyond the reach of doubt, and makes it probable that in former times either a living representative or an effigy of Balder was annually burned in them. Midsummer was the season sacred to Balder, and the Swedish poet Tegner, in placing the burning of Balder at midsummer, may very well have followed an old tradition that the summer solstice was the time when the good god came to his untimely end.

Thus it has been shown that the leading incidents of the Balder myth have their counterparts in those fire-festivals of our European peasantry which undoubtedly date from a time long prior to the introduction of Christianity. The pretence of throwing the victim chosen by lot into the Beltane fire, and the similar treatment of the man, the future Green Wolf, at the midsummer bonfire in Normandy, may naturally be interpreted as traces of an older custom of actually burning human beings on these occasions ; and the green dress of the Green Wolf, coupled with the leafy envelope of the young fellow who trod out the midsummer fire at Moosheim, seems to hint that the persons who perished at these festivals did so in the character of tree-spirits or deities of vegetation. From all this we may reasonably infer that in the Balder myth on the one hand, and the fire-festivals and custom of gathering mistletoe on the other hand, we have, as it were, the two broken and dissevered halves of an original whole. In other words, we may assume with some degree of probability that the myth of Balder's death was not merely a myth, that is, a description of physical phenomena in imagery borrowed from human life, but that it was at the same time the story which people told to explain why they annually burned a human representative of the god and cut the mistletoe with solemn ceremony. If I am right, the story of Balder's tragic end formed, so to say, the text of the sacred drama which was acted year by year as a magical rite to cause the sun to shine, trees to grow, crops to thrive, and to guard man and beast from the baleful arts of fairies and trolls, of witches and warlocks. The tale belonged, in short, to that class of nature myths which are meant to be supplemented by ritual ; here, as so often, myth stood to magic in the relation of theory to practice.

But if the victims—the human Balders—who died by fire, whether in spring or at midsummer, were put to death as living embodiments of tree-spirits or deities of vegetation, it would seem that Balder himself must have been a tree-spirit or deity of vegetation.   It becomes desirable, therefore, to determine, if we can, the particular kind of tree or trees, of which a personal representative was burned at the fire-festivals.   For we may be quite sure that it was not as a representative of vegetation in general that the victim suffered death. The idea of vegetation in general is too abstract to be primitive. Most probably the victim at first represented a particular kind of sacred tree.   But of all European trees none has such claims as the oak to be considered as pre-eminently the sacred tree of the Aryans. We have seen that its worship is attested for all the great branches of the Aryan stock in Europe ; hence we may certainly conclude that the tree was venerated by the Aryans in common before the dispersion, and that their primitive home must have lain in a land which was clothed with forests of oak.

Now, considering the primitive character and remarkable similarity of the fire-festivals observed by all the branches of the Aryan race in Europe, we may infer that these festivals form part of the common stock of religious observances which the various peoples carried with them in their wanderings from their old home.   But, if I am right, an essential feature of those primitive fire-festivals was the burning of a man who represented the tree-spirit.   In view, then, of the place occupied by the oak in the religion of the Aryans, the presumption is that the tree so represented at the fire-festivals must originally have been the oak.   So far as the Celts and Lithuanians are concerned, this conclusion will perhaps hardly be contested.   But both for them and for the Germans it is confirmed by a remarkable piece of religious conservatism.   The most primitive method known to man of producing fire is by rubbing two pieces of wood against each other till they ignite ;   and we have seen that this method is still used in Europe for kindling sacred fires such as the need-fire, and that most probably it was formerly resorted to at all the fire-festivals under discussion. Now it is sometimes required that the need-fire, or other sacred fire, should be made by the friction of a particular kind of wood ;   and when the kind of wood is prescribed, whether among Celts, Germans, or Slavs, that wood appears to be generally the oak.   But if the sacred fire was regularly kindled by the friction of oak-wood, we may infer that originally the fire was also fed with the same material. In point of fact, it appears that the perpetual fire of Vesta at Rome was fed with oak-wood, and that oak-wood was the fuel consumed in the perpetual fire which burned under the sacred oak at the great Lithuanian sanctuary of Romove.   Further, that oak-wood was formerly the fuel burned in the midsummer fires may perhaps be inferred from the custom, said to be still observed by peasants in many mountain districts of Germany, of making up the cottage fire on Midsummer Day with a heavy block of oak-wood.   The block

is so arranged that it smoulders slowly and is not finally reduced
to charcoal till the expiry of a year. Then upon next Midsummer
Day the charred embers of the old log are removed to make room
for the new one, and are mixed with the seed-corn or scattered about
the garden. This is believed to guard the food cooked on the hearth
from witchcraft, to preserve the luck of the house, to promote the
growth of the crops, and to keep them from blight and vermin.
Thus the custom is almost exactly parallel to that of the Yule-log,
which in parts of Germany, France, England, Serbia, and other Slavonic
lands was commonly of oak-wood. The general conclusion is, that
at those periodic or occasional ceremonies the ancient Aryans both
kindled and fed the fire with the sacred oak-wood.

But if at these solemn rites the fire was regularly made of oak-
wood, it follows that any man who was burned in it as a personification
of the tree-spirit could have represented no tree but the oak. The
sacred oak was thus burned in duplicate ; the wood of the tree was
consumed in the fire, and along with it was consumed a living man,
as a personification of the oak-spirit. The conclusion thus drawn for
the European Aryans in general is confirmed in its special application
to the Scandinavians by the relation in which amongst them the
mistletoe appears to have stood to the burning of the victim in the
midsummer fire. We have seen that among Scandinavians it has
been customary to gather the mistletoe at midsummer. But so far
as appears on the face of this custom, there is nothing to connect it
with the midsummer fires in which human victims or effigies of them
were burned. Even if the fire, as seems probable, was originally
always made with oak-wood, why should it have been necessary to
pull the mistletoe ? The last link between the midsummer customs
of gathering the mistletoe and lighting the bonfires is supplied by
Balder's myth, which can hardly be disjoined from the customs in
question. The myth suggests that a vital connexion may once have
been believed to subsist between the mistletoe and the human representative of the oak who was burned in the fire. According to the
myth, Balder could be killed by nothing in heaven or earth except
the mistletoe ; and so long as the mistletoe remained on the oak,
he was not only immortal but invulnerable. Now, if we suppose
that Balder was the oak, the origin of the myth becomes intelligible.
The mistletoe was viewed as the seat of life of the oak, and so long
as it was uninjured nothing could kill or even wound the oak. The
conception of the mistletoe as the seat of life of the oak would naturally
be suggested to primitive people by the observation that while the
oak is deciduous, the mistletoe which grows on it is evergreen. In
winter the sight of its fresh foliage among the bare branches must
have been hailed by the worshippers of the tree as a sign that the
divine life which had ceased to animate the branches yet survived
in the mistletoe, as the heart of a sleeper still beats when his body
is motionless. Hence when the god had to be killed—when the sacred
tree had to be burnt—it was necessary to begin by breaking off the

mistletoe. For so long as the mistletoe remained intact, the oak (so people might think) was invulnerable ; all the blows of their knives and axes would glance harmless from its surface. But once tear from the oak its sacred heart—the mistletoe—and the tree nodded to its fall. And when in later times the spirit of the oak came to be represented by a living man, it was logically necessary to suppose that, like the tree he personated, he could neither be killed nor wounded so long as the mistletoe remained uninjured. The pulling of the mistletoe was thus at once the signal and the cause of his death.

On this view the invulnerable Balder is neither more nor less than a personification of a mistletoe-bearing oak. The interpretation is confirmed by what seems to have been an ancient Italian belief, that the mistletoe can be destroyed neither by fire nor water ; for if the parasite is thus deemed indestructible, it might easily be supposed to communicate its own indestructibility to the tree on which it grows, so long as the two remain in conjunction. Or, to put the same idea in mythical form, we might tell how the kindly god of the oak had his life securely deposited in the imperishable mistletoe which grew among the branches ; how accordingly so long as the mistletoe kept its place there, the deity himself remained invulnerable ; and how at last a cunning foe, let into the secret of the god's invulnerability, tore the mistletoe from the oak, thereby killing the oak-god and afterwards burning his body in a fire which could have made no impression on him so long as the incombustible parasite retained its seat among the boughs.

But since the idea of a being whose life is thus, in a sense, outside himself, must be strange to many readers, and has, indeed, not yet been recognised in its full bearing on primitive superstition, it will be worth while to illustrate it by examples drawn both from story and custom. The result will be to show that, in assuming this idea as the explanation of Balder's relation to the mistletoe, I assume a principle which is deeply engraved on the mind of primitive man.

CHAPTER LXVI

THE EXTERNAL SOUL IN FOLK-TALES

In a former part of this work we saw that, in the opinion of primitive people, the soul may temporarily absent itself from the body without causing death. Such temporary absences of the soul are often believed to involve considerable risk, since the wandering soul is liable to a variety of mishaps at the hands of enemies, and so forth. But there is another aspect to this power of disengaging the soul from the body. If only the safety of the soul can be ensured during its absence, there is no reason why the soul should not continue absent for an indefinite time ; indeed a man may, on a pure calculation of personal safety, desire that his soul should never return to his body. Unable to conceive of life abstractly as a " permanent possibility of sensation " or a " continuous adjustment of internal arrangements to external relations," the savage thinks of it as a concrete material thing of a definite bulk, capable of being seen and handled, kept in a box or jar, and liable to be bruised, fractured, or smashed in pieces. It is not needful that the life, so conceived, should be in the man ; it may be absent from his body and still continue to animate him by virtue of a sort of sympathy or action at a distance. So long as this object which he calls his life or soul remains unharmed, the man is well ; if it is injured, he suffers ; if it is destroyed, he dies. Or, to put it otherwise, when a man is ill or dies, the fact is explained by saying that the material object called his life or soul, whether it be in his body or out of it, has either sustained injury or been destroyed. But there may be circumstances in which, if the life or soul remains in the man, it stands a greater chance of sustaining injury than if it were stowed away in some safe and secret place. Accordingly, in such circumstances, primitive man takes his soul out of his body and deposits it for security in some snug spot, intending to replace it in his body when the danger is past. Or if he should discover some place of absolute security, he may be content to leave his soul there permanently. The advantage of this is that, so long as the soul remains unharmed in the place where he has deposited it, the man himself is immortal ; nothing can kill his body, since his life is not in it.

Evidence of this primitive belief is furnished by a class of folk-tales of which the Norse story of " The giant who had no heart in his body " is perhaps the best-known example. Stories of this kind are widely diffused over the world, and from their number and the variety of incident and of details in which the leading idea is embodied we may infer that the conception of an external soul is one which has had a powerful hold on the minds of men at an early stage of history. For folk-tales are a faithful reflection of the world as it appeared to the primitive mind ; and we may be sure that any idea which commonly occurs in them, however absurd it may seem to us, must once have been an ordinary article of belief. This assurance, so far as it concerns the supposed power of disengaging the soul from the body for a longer or shorter time, is amply corroborated by a comparison of the folk-tales in question with the actual beliefs and practices of savages. To this we shall return after some specimens of the tales have been given. The specimens will be selected with a view of illustrating both the characteristic features and the wide diffusion of this class of tales.

In the first place, the story of the external soul is told, in various forms, by all Aryan peoples from Hindoostan to the Hebrides. A very common form of it is this : A warlock, giant, or other fairyland being is invulnerable and immortal because he keeps his soul hidden far away in some secret place ; but a fair princess, whom he holds enthralled in his enchanted castle, wiles his secret from him and reveals it to the hero, who seeks out the warlock's soul, heart, life, or death (as it is variously called), and by destroying it, simultaneously kills the warlock. Thus a Hindoo story tells how a magician called Punchkin held a queen captive for twelve years, and would fain marry her, but she would not have him. At last the queen's son came to rescue her, and the two plotted together to kill Punchkin. So the queen spoke the magician fair, and pretended that she had at last made up her mind to marry him. " And do tell me," she said, " are you quite immortal ? Can death never touch you ? And are you too great an enchanter ever to feel human suffering ? " " It is true," he said, " that I am not as others. Far, far away, hundreds of thousands of miles from this, there lies a desolate country covered with thick jungle. In the midst of the jungle grows a circle of palm trees, and in the centre of the circle stand six chattees full of water, piled one above another : below the sixth chattee is a small cage, which contains a little green parrot ;—on the life of the parrot depends my life ;— and if the parrot is killed I must die. It is, however," he added, " impossible that the parrot should sustain any injury, both on account of the inaccessibility of the country, and because, by my appointment, many thousand genii surround the palm trees, and kill all who approach the place." But the queen's young son overcame all difficulties, and got possession of the parrot. He brought it to the door of the magician's palace, and began playing with it. Punchkin, the magician, saw him, and, coming out, tried to persuade the boy to give him the parrot. " Give me my parrot ! " cried Punchkin. Then the boy took hold of the parrot and tore off one of his wings ; and as he did so the magician's right arm fell off. Punchkin then stretched out his left arm, crying, " Give me my parrot ! " The prince pulled off the parrot's second wing, and the magician's left arm tumbled off. " Give me my parrot ! " cried he, and fell on his knees. The prince pulled off the parrot's right leg, the magician's right leg fell off ; the prince pulled off the parrot's left leg, down fell the magician's left. Nothing remained of him except the trunk and the head ; but still he rolled his eyes, and cried, " Give me my parrot ! " " Take your parrot, then," cried the boy ; and with that he wrung the bird's neck, and threw it at the magician ; and, as he did so, Punchkin's head twisted round, and, with a fearful groan, he died ! In another Hindoo tale an ogre is asked by his daughter, " Papa, where do you keep your soul ? " " Sixteen miles away from this place," he said, " is a tree. Round the tree are tigers, and bears, and scorpions, and snakes ; on the top of the tree is a very great fat snake ; on his head is a little cage ; in the cage is a bird ; and my soul is in that bird." The end of the ogre is like that of the magician in the previous tale. As the bird's wings and legs are torn off, the ogre's arms and legs drop off ; and when its neck is wrung he falls down dead. In a Bengalee story it is said that all the ogres dwell in Ceylon, and that all their lives are in a single lemon. A boy cuts the lemon in pieces, and all the ogres die.

In a Siamese or Cambodian story, probably derived from India, we are told that Thossakan or Ravana, the King of Ceylon, was able by magic art to take his soul out of his body and leave it in a box at home, while he went to the wars. Thus he was invulnerable in battle. When he was about to give battle to Rama, he deposited his soul with a hermit called Fire-eye, who was to keep it safe for him. So in the fight Rama was astounded to see that his arrows struck the king without wounding him. But one of Rama's allies, knowing the secret of the king's invulnerability, transformed himself by magic into the likeness of the king, and going to the hermit asked back his soul. On receiving it he soared up into the air and flew to Rama, brandishing the box and squeezing it so hard that all the breath left the King of Ceylon's body, and he died. In a Bengalee story a prince going into a far country planted with his own hands a tree in the court-yard of his father's palace, and said to his parents, " This tree is my life. When you see the tree green and fresh, then know that it is well with me ; when you see the tree fade in some parts, then know that I am in an ill case ; and when you see the whole tree fade, then know that I am dead and gone." In another Indian tale a prince, setting forth on his travels, left behind him a barley plant, with instructions that it should be carefully tended and watched ; for if it flourished, he would be alive and well, but if it drooped, then some mischance was about to happen to him. And so it fell out. For the prince was beheaded, and as his head rolled off, the barley plant snapped in two and the ear of barley fell to the ground.

In Greek tales, ancient and modern, the idea of an external soul is not uncommon. When Meleager was seven days old, the Fates appeared to his mother and told her that Meleager would die when the brand which was blazing on the hearth had burnt down. So his mother snatched the brand from the fire and kept it in a box. But in after-years, being enraged at her son for slaying her brothers, she burnt the brand in the fire and Meleager expired in agonies, as if flames were preying on his vitals. Again, Nisus King of Megara had a purple or golden hair on the middle of his head, and it was fated that whenever the hair was pulled out the king should die. When Megara was besieged by the Cretans, the king's daughter Scylla fell in love with Minos, their king, and pulled out the fatal hair from her father's head. So he died. In a modern Greek folk-tale a man's strength lies in three golden hairs on his head. When his mother pulls them out, he grows weak and timid and is slain by his enemies. In another modern Greek story the life of an enchanter is bound up with three doves which are in the belly of a wild boar. When the first dove is killed, the magician grows sick ; when the second is killed, he grows very sick ; and when the third is killed, he dies. In another Greek story of the same sort an ogre's strength is in three singing birds which are in a wild boar. The hero kills two of the birds, and then coming to the ogre's house finds him lying on the ground in great pain. He shows the third bird to the ogre, who begs that the hero will either let it fly away or give it to him to eat. But the hero wrings the bird's neck, and the ogre dies on the spot.

In a modern Roman version of " Aladdin and the Wonderful Lamp " the magician tells the princess, whom he holds captive in a floating rock in mid-ocean, that he will never die.   The princess reports this to the prince her husband, who has come to rescue her.   The prince replies, " It is impossible but that there should be some one thing or other that is fatal to him ; ask him what that one fatal thing is."   So the princess asked the magician, and he told her that in the wood was a hydra with seven heads ; in the middle head of the hydra was a leveret, in the head of the leveret was a bird, in the bird's head was a precious stone, and if this stone were put under his pillow he would die.   The prince procured the stone, and the princess laid it under the magician's pillow.   No sooner did the enchanter lay his head on the pillow than he gave three terrible yells, turned himself round and round three times, and died.

Stories of the same sort are current among Slavonic peoples. Thus a Russian story tells how a warlock called Koshchei the Deathless carried off a princess and kept her prisoner in his golden castle.   However, a prince made up to her one day as she was walking alone and disconsolate in the castle garden, and cheered by the prospect of escaping with him she went to the warlock and coaxed him with false and flattering words, saying, " My dearest friend, tell me, I pray you, will you never die ? "   " Certainly not," says he.   " Well," says she, " and where is your death ? is it in your dwelling ? "   " To be sure it is," says he, " it is in the broom under the threshold."   Thereupon the princess seized the broom and threw it on the fire, but although the broom burned, the deathless Koshchei remained alive ; indeed not so much as a hair of him was singed.   Balked in her first attempt, the artful hussy pouted and said, " You do not love me true, for you have not told me where your death is ; yet I am not angry, but love you with all my heart."   With these fawning words she besought the warlock to tell her truly where his death was.   So he laughed and said, " Why do you wish to know ?   Well then, out of love I will tell you where it lies.   In a certain field there stand three green oaks, and under the roots of the largest oak is a worm, and if ever this worm is found and crushed, that instant I shall die." When the princess heard these words, she went straight to her lover and told him all ; and he searched till he found the oaks and dug up the worm and crushed it.   Then he hurried to the warlock's castle, but only to learn from the princess that the warlock was still alive.   Then she fell to wheedling and coaxing Koshchei once more, and this time, overcome by her wiles, he opened his heart to her and told her the truth. " My death," said he, " is far from here and hard to find, on the wide ocean.   In that sea is an island, and on the island there grows a green oak, and beneath the oak is an iron chest, and in the chest is a small basket, and in the basket is a hare, and in the hare is a duck, and in the duck is an egg ; and he who finds the egg and breaks it, kills me at the same time."   The prince naturally procured the fateful egg and with it in his hands he confronted the deathless warlock.   The monster would have killed him, but the prince began to squeeze the egg. At that the warlock shrieked with pain, and turning to the false princess, who stood by smirking and smiling, " Was it not out of love for you," said he, " that I told you where my death was ? And is this the return you make to me ? " With that he grabbed at his sword, which hung from a peg on the wall ; but before he could reach it, the prince had crushed the egg, and sure enough the deathless warlock found his death at the same moment. " In one of the descriptions of Koshchei's death, he is said to be killed by a blow on the forehead inflicted by the mysterious egg—that last link in the magic chain by which his life is darkly bound. In another version of the same story, but told of a snake, the fatal blow is struck by a small stone found in the yolk of an egg, which is inside a duck, which is inside a hare, which is inside a stone, which is on an island."

Amongst peoples of the Teutonic stock stories of the external soul are not wanting. In a tale told by the Saxons of Transylvania it is said that a young man shot at a witch again and again. The bullets went clean through her but did her no harm, and she only laughed and mocked at him. " Silly earthworm," she cried, " shoot as much as you like. It does me no harm. For know that my life resides not in me but far, far away. In a mountain is a pond, on the pond swims a duck, in the duck is an egg, in the egg burns a light, that light is my life. If you could put out that light, my life would be at an end. But that can never, never be." However, the young man got hold of the egg, smashed it, and put out the light, and with it the witch's life went out also. In a German story a cannibal called Body without Soul or Soulless keeps his soul in a box, which stands on a rock in the middle of the Red Sea. A soldier gets possession of the box and goes with it to Soulless, who begs the soldier to give him back his soul. But the soldier opens the box, takes out the soul, and flings it backward over his head. At the same moment the cannibal drops dead to the ground.

In another German story an old warlock lives with a damsel all alone in the midst of a vast and gloomy wood. She fears that being old he may die and leave her alone in the forest. But he reassures her. " Dear child," he said, " I cannot die, and I have no heart in my breast." But she importuned him to tell her where his heart was. So he said, " Far, far from here in an unknown and lonesome land stands a great church. The church is well secured with iron doors, and round about it flows a broad deep moat. In the church flies a bird and in the bird is my heart. So long as the bird lives, I live. It cannot die of itself, and no one can catch it ; therefore I cannot die, and you need have no anxiety." However the young man, whose bride the damsel was to have been before the warlock spirited her away, contrived to reach the church and catch the bird. He brought it to the damsel, who stowed him and it away under the warlock's bed. Soon the old warlock came home. He was ailing, and said so. The girl wept and said, " Alas, daddy is dying ; he has a heart in his breast after all." " Child," replied the warlock, " hold your tongue. I *can't* die. It will soon pass over." At that the young man under the bed gave the bird a gentle squeeze ; and as he did so, the old warlock felt very unwell and sat down. Then the young man gripped the bird tighter, and the warlock fell senseless from his chair. " Now squeeze him dead," cried the damsel. Her lover obeyed, and when the bird was dead, the old warlock also lay dead on the floor.

In the Norse tale of " the giant who had no heart in his body," the giant tells the captive princess, " Far, far away in a lake lies an island, on that island stands a church, in that church is a well, in that well swims a duck, in that duck there is an egg, and in that egg there lies my heart." The hero of the tale, with the help of some animals to whom he had been kind, obtains the egg and squeezes it, at which the giant screams piteously and begs for his life. But the hero breaks the egg in pieces and the giant at once bursts. In another Norse story a hill-ogre tells the captive princess that she will never be able to return home unless she finds the grain of sand which lies under the ninth tongue of the ninth head of a certain dragon ; but if that grain of sand were to come over the rock in which the ogres live, they would all burst " and the rock itself would become a gilded palace, and the lake green meadows." The hero finds the grain of sand and takes it to the top of the high rock in which the ogres live. So all the ogres burst and the rest falls out as one of the ogres had foretold.

In a Celtic tale, recorded in the West Highlands of Scotland, a giant is questioned by a captive queen as to where he keeps his soul. At last, after deceiving her several times, he confides to her the fatal secret : " There is a great flagstone under the threshold. There is a wether under the flag. There is a duck in the wether's belly, and an egg in the belly of the duck, and it is in the egg that my soul is." On the morrow when the giant was gone, the queen contrived to get possession of the egg and crushed it in her hands, and at that very moment the giant, who was coming home in the dusk, fell down dead. In another Celtic tale, a sea beast has carried off a king's daughter, and an old smith declares that there is no way of killing the beast but one. " In the island that is in the midst of the loch is Eillid Chaisfhion —the white-footed hind, of the slenderest legs, and the swiftest step, and though she should be caught, there would spring a hoodie out of her, and though the hoodie should be caught, there would spring a trout out of her, but there is an egg in the mouth of the trout, and the soul of the beast is in the egg, and if the egg breaks, the beast is dead." As usual the egg is broken and the beast dies.

In an Irish story we read how a giant kept a beautiful damsel a prisoner in his castle on the top of a hill, which was white with the bones of the champions who had tried in vain to rescue the fair captive. At last the hero, after hewing and slashing at the giant all to no purpose, discovered that the only way to kill him was to rub a mole on the giant's right breast with a certain egg, which was in a duck, which was in a chest, which lay locked and bound at the bottom of the sea.

With the help of some obliging animals, the hero made himself master of the precious egg and slew the giant by merely striking it against the mole on his right breast. Similarly in a Breton story there figures a giant whom neither fire nor water nor steel can harm. He tells his seventh wife, whom he has just married after murdering all her predecessors, " I am immortal, and no one can hurt me unless he crushes on my breast an egg, which is in a pigeon, which is in the belly of a hare ; this hare is in the belly of a wolf, and this wolf is in the belly of my brother, who dwells a thousand leagues from here. So I am quite easy on that score." A soldier contrived to obtain the egg and crush it on the breast of the giant, who immediately expired. In another Breton tale the life of a giant resides in an old box-tree which grows in his castle garden ; and to kill him it is necessary to sever the tap-root of the tree at a single blow of an axe without injuring any of the lesser roots. This task the hero, as usual, successfully accomplishes, and at the same moment the giant drops dead.

The notion of an external soul has now been traced in folk-tales told by Aryan peoples from India to Ireland. We have still to show that the same idea occurs commonly in the popular stories of peoples who do not belong to the Aryan stock. In the ancient Egyptian tale of " The Two Brothers," which was written down in the reign of Rameses II., about 1300 B.C., we read how one of the brothers enchanted his heart and placed it in the flower of an acacia tree, and how, when the flower was cut at the instigation of his wife, he immediately fell down dead, but revived when his brother found the lost heart in the berry of the acacia and threw it into a cup of fresh water.

In the story of Seyf el-Mulook in the *Arabian Nights* the jinnee tells the captive daughter of the King of India, " When I was born, the astrologers declared that the destruction of my soul would be effected by the hand of one of the sons of the human kings. I therefore took my soul, and put it into the crop of a sparrow, and I imprisoned the sparrow in a little box, and put this into another small box, and this I put within seven other small boxes, and I put these within seven chests, and the chests I put into a coffer of marble within the verge of this circumambient ocean ; for this part is remote from the countries of mankind, and none of mankind can gain access to it." But Seyf el-Mulook got possession of the sparrow and strangled it, and the jinnee fell upon the ground a heap of black ashes. In a Kabyle story an ogre declares that his fate is far away in an egg, which is in a pigeon, which is in a camel, which is in the sea. The hero procures the egg and crushes it between his hands, and the ogre dies. In a Magyar folk-tale, an old witch detains a young prince called Ambrose in the bowels of the earth. At last she confided to him that she kept a wild boar in a silken meadow,and if it were killed, they would find a hare inside, and inside the hare a pigeon, and inside the pigeon a small box, and inside the box one black and one shining beetle : the shining beetle held her life, and the black one held her power ; if these two beetles died, then her life would come to an end also. When the old hag went out, Ambrose killed the wild boar, and took out the hare ; from the hare he took the pigeon, from the pigeon the box, and from the box the two beetles ; he killed the black beetle, but kept the shining one alive. So the witch's power left her immediately, and when she came home, she had to take to her bed. Having learned from her how to escape from his prison to the upper air, Ambrose killed the shining beetle, and the old hag's spirit left her at once. In a Kalmuck tale we read how a certain khan challenged a wise man to show his skill by stealing a precious stone on which the khan's life depended. The sage contrived to purloin the talisman while the khan and his guards slept ; but not content with this he gave a further proof of his dexterity by bonneting the slumbering potentate with a bladder. This was too much for the khan. Next morning he informed the sage that he could overlook everything else, but that the indignity of being bonneted with a bladder was more than he could bear ; and he ordered his facetious friend to instant execution. Pained at this exhibition of royal ingratitude, the sage dashed to the ground the talisman which he still held in his hand ; and at the same instant blood flowed from the nostrils of the khan, and he gave up the ghost.

In a Tartar poem two heroes named Ak Molot and Bulat engage in mortal combat. Ak Molot pierces his foe through and through with an arrow, grapples with him, and dashes him to the ground, but all in vain, Bulat could not die. At last when the combat has lasted three years, a friend of Ak Molot sees a golden casket hanging by a white thread from the sky, and bethinks him that perhaps this casket contains Bulat's soul. So he shot through the white thread with an arrow, and down fell the casket. He opened it, and in the casket sat ten white birds, and one of the birds was Bulat's soul. Bulat wept when he saw that his soul was found in the casket. But one after the other the birds were killed, and then Ak Molot easily slew his foe. In another Tartar poem, two brothers going to fight two other brothers take out their souls and hide them in the form of a white herb with six stalks in a deep pit. But one of their foes sees them doing so and digs up their souls, which he puts into a golden ram's horn, and then sticks the ram's horn in his quiver. The two warriors whose souls have thus been stolen know that they have no chance of victory, and accordingly make peace with their enemies. In another Tartar poem a terrible demon sets all the gods and heroes at defiance. At last a valiant youth fights the demon, binds him hand and foot, and slices him with his sword. But still the demon is not slain. So the youth asked him, " Tell me, where is your soul hidden ? For if your soul had been hidden in your body, you must have been dead long ago." The demon replied, " On the saddle of my horse is a bag. In the bag is a serpent with twelve heads. In the serpent is my soul. When you have killed the serpent, you have killed me also." So the youth took the saddle-bag from the horse and killed the twelve-headed serpent, whereupon the demon expired. In another Tartar poem a hero called Kök Chan deposits with a maiden a golden ring, in which is half his strength. Afterwards when Kök Chan is wrestling long with a hero and cannot kill him, a woman drops into his mouth the ring which contains half his strength. Thus inspired with fresh force he slays his enemy.

In a Mongolian story the hero Joro gets the better of his enemy the lama Tschoridong in the following way. The lama, who is an enchanter, sends out his soul in the form of a wasp to sting Joro's eyes. But Joro catches the wasp in his hand, and by alternately shutting and opening his hand he causes the lama alternately to lose and recover consciousness. In a Tartar poem two youths cut open the body of an old witch and tear out her bowels, but all to no purpose, she still lives. On being asked where her soul is, she answers that it is in the middle of her shoe-sole in the form of a seven-headed speckled snake. So one of the youths slices her shoe-sole with his sword, takes out the speckled snake, and cuts off its seven heads. Then the witch dies. Another Tartar poem describes how the hero Kartaga grappled with the Swan-woman. Long they wrestled. Moons waxed and waned and still they wrestled; years came and went, and still the struggle went on. But the piebald horse and the black horse knew that the Swan-woman's soul was not in her. Under the black earth flow nine seas; where the seas meet and form one, the sea comes to the surface of the earth. At the mouth of the nine seas rises a rock of copper; it rises to the surface of the ground, it rises up between heaven and earth, this rock of copper. At the foot of the copper rock is a black chest, in the black chest is a golden casket, and in the golden casket is the soul of the Swan-woman. Seven little birds are the soul of the Swan-woman; if the birds are killed the Swan-woman will die straightway. So the horses ran to the foot of the copper rock, opened the black chest, and brought back the golden casket. Then the piebald horse turned himself into a bald-headed man, opened the golden casket, and cut off the heads of the seven birds. So the Swan-woman died. In another Tartar poem the hero, pursuing his sister who has driven away his cattle, is warned to desist from the pursuit because his sister has carried away his soul in a golden sword and a golden arrow, and if he pursues her she will kill him by throwing the golden sword or shooting the golden arrow at him.

A Malay poem relates how once upon a time in the city of Indra-poora there was a certain merchant who was rich and prosperous, but he had no children. One day as he walked with his wife by the river they found a baby girl, fair as an angel. So they adopted the child and called her Bidasari. The merchant caused a golden fish to be made, and into this fish he transferred the soul of his adopted daughter. Then he put the golden fish in a golden box full of water, and hid it in a pond in the midst of his garden. In time the girl grew to be a lovely woman. Now the King of Indrapoora had a fair young queen, who lived in fear that the king might take to himself a second wife. So, hearing of the charms of Bidasari, the queen resolved to put her out of the way. She lured the girl to the palace and tortured her cruelly ; but Bidasari could not die, because her soul was not in her. At last she could stand the torture no longer and said to the queen, " If you wish me to die, you must bring the box which is in the pond in my father's garden." So the box was brought and opened, and there was the golden fish in the water. The girl said, " My soul is in that fish. In the morning you must take the fish out of the water, and in the evening you must put it back into the water. Do not let the fish lie about, but bind it round your neck. If you do this, I shall soon die." So the queen took the fish out of the box and fastened it round her neck ; and no sooner had she done so than Bidasari fell into a swoon. But in the evening, when the fish was put back into the water, Bidasari came to herself again. Seeing that she thus had the girl in her power, the queen sent her home to her adopted parents. To save her from further persecution her parents resolved to remove their daughter from the city. So in a lonely and desolate spot they built a house and brought Bidasari thither. There she dwelt alone, undergoing vicissitudes that corresponded with the vicissitudes of the golden fish in which was her soul. All day long, while the fish was out of the water, she remained unconscious ; but in the evening, when the fish was put into the water, she revived. One day the king was out hunting, and coming to the house where Bidasari lay unconscious, was smitten with her beauty. He tried to waken her, but in vain. Next day, towards evening, he repeated his visit, but still found her unconscious. However, when darkness fell, she came to herself and told the king the secret of her life. So the king returned to the palace, took the fish from the queen, and put it in water. Immediately Bidasari revived, and the king took her to wife.

Another story of an external soul comes from Nias, an island to the west of Sumatra. Once on a time a chief was captured by his enemies, who tried to put him to death but failed. Water would not drown him nor fire burn him nor steel pierce him. At last his wife revealed the secret. On his head he had a hair as hard as a copper wire ; and with this wire his life was bound up. So the hair was plucked out, and with it his spirit fled.

A West African story from Southern Nigeria relates how a king kept his soul in a little brown bird, which perched on a tall tree beside the gate of the palace. The king's life was so bound up with that of the bird that whoever should kill the bird would simultaneously kill the king and succeed to the kingdom. The secret was betrayed by the queen to her lover, who shot the bird with an arrow and thereby slew the king and ascended the vacant throne. A tale told by the Ba-Ronga of South Africa sets forth how the lives of a whole family were contained in one cat. When a girl of the family, named Titishan, married a husband, she begged her parents to let her take the precious cat with her to her new home. But they refused, saying, " You know that our life is attached to it " ; and they offered to give her an antelope or even an elephant instead of it. But nothing would satisfy her but the cat. So at last she carried it off with her and shut it up in a place where nobody saw it ; even her husband knew nothing about it. One day, when she went to work in the fields, the cat escaped from its place of concealment, entered the hut, put on the warlike trappings of the husband, and danced and sang. Some children, attracted by the noise, discovered the cat at its antics, and when they expressed their astonishment, the animal only capered the more and insulted them besides. So they went to the owner and said, " There is somebody dancing in your house, and he insulted us." " Hold your tongues," said he, " I'll soon put a stop to your lies." So he went and hid behind the door and peeped in, and there sure enough was the cat prancing about and singing. He fired at it, and the animal dropped down dead. At the same moment his wife fell to the ground in the field where she was at work ; said she, " I have been killed at home." But she had strength enough left to ask her husband to go with her to her parents' village, taking with him the dead cat wrapt up in a mat. All her relatives assembled, and bitterly they reproached her for having insisted on taking the animal with her to her husband's village. As soon as the mat was unrolled and they saw the dead cat, they all fell down lifeless one after the other. So the Clan of the Cat was destroyed ; and the bereaved husband closed the gate of the village with a branch, and returned home, and told his friends how in killing the cat he had killed the whole clan, because their lives depended on the life of the cat.

Ideas of the same sort meet us in stories told by the North American Indians. Thus the Navajoes tell of a certain mythical being called " the Maiden that becomes a Bear," who learned the art of turning herself into a bear from the prairie wolf. She was a great warrior and quite invulnerable ; for when she went to war she took out her vital organs and hid them, so that no one could kill her ; and when the battle was over she put the organs back in their places again. The Kwakiutl Indians of British Columbia tell of an ogress, who could not be killed because her life was in a hemlock branch. A brave boy met her in the woods, smashed her head with a stone, scattered her brains, broke her bones, and threw them into the water. Then, thinking he had disposed of the ogress, he went into her house. There he saw a woman rooted to the floor, who warned him, saying, " Now do not stay long. I know that you have tried to kill the ogress. It is the fourth time that somebody has tried to kill her. She never dies ; she has nearly come to life. There in that covered hemlock branch is her life. Go there, and as soon as you see her enter, shoot her life. Then she will be dead." Hardly had she finished speaking when sure enough in came the ogress, singing as she walked. But the boy shot at her life, and she fell dead to the floor.

CHAPTER LXVII

THE EXTERNAL SOUL IN FOLK-CUSTOM

§ 1. *The External Soul in Inanimate Things.*—Thus the idea that the soul may be deposited for a longer or shorter time in some place of security outside the body, or at all events in the hair, is found in the popular tales of many races. It remains to show that the idea is not a mere figment devised to adorn a tale, but is a real article of primitive faith, which has given rise to a corresponding set of customs.

We have seen that in the tales the hero, as a preparation for battle, sometimes removes his soul from his body, in order that his body may be invulnerable and immortal in the combat. With a like intention the savage removes his soul from his body on various occasions of real or imaginary peril. Thus among the people of Minahassa in Celebes, when a family moves into a new house, a priest collects the souls of the whole family in a bag, and afterwards restores them to their owners, because the moment of entering a new house is supposed to be fraught with supernatural danger. In Southern Celebes, when a woman is brought to bed, the messenger who fetches the doctor or the midwife always carries with him something made of iron, such as a chopping-knife, which he delivers to the doctor. The doctor must keep the thing in his house till the confinement is over, when he gives it back, receiving a fixed sum of money for doing so. The chopping-knife, or whatever it is, represents the woman's soul, which at this critical time is believed to be safer out of her body than in it. Hence the doctor must take great care of the object ; for were it lost, the woman's soul would assuredly, they think, be lost with it.

Among the Dyaks of Pinoeh, a district of South-eastern Borneo, when a child is born, a medicine-man is sent for, who conjures the soul of the infant into half a coco-nut, which he thereupon covers with a cloth and places on a square platter or charger suspended by cords from the roof. This ceremony he repeats at every new moon for a year. The intention of the ceremony is not explained by the writer who describes it, but we may conjecture that it is to place the soul of the child in a safer place than its own frail little body. This conjecture is confirmed by the reason assigned for a similar custom observed elsewhere in the Indian Archipelago. In the Kei Islands, when there is a newly-born child in a house, an empty coco-nut, split and spliced together again, may sometimes be seen hanging beside a rough wooden image of an ancestor. The soul of the infant is believed to be temporarily deposited in the coco-nut in order that it may be safe from the attacks of evil spirits ; but when the child grows bigger and stronger, the soul will take up its permanent abode in its own body. Similarly among the Esquimaux of Alaska, when a child is sick, the medicine-man will sometimes extract its soul from its body and place it for safe-keeping in an amulet, which for further security he deposits in his own medicine-bag. It seems probable that many amulets have been similarly regarded as soul-boxes, that is, as safes in which the souls of the owners are kept for greater security. An old Mang'anje woman in the West Shire district of British Central Africa used to wear round her neck an ivory ornament, hollow, and about three inches long, which she called her life or soul. Naturally, she would not part with it ; a planter tried to buy it of her, but in vain. When Mr. James Macdonald was one day sitting in the house of a Hlubi chief, awaiting the appearance of that great man, who was busy decorating his person, a native pointed to a pair of magnificent ox-horns, and said, " Ntame has his soul in these horns." The horns were those of an animal which had been sacrificed, and they were held sacred. A magician had fastened them to the roof to protect the house and its inmates from the thunder-bolt.   " The idea," adds Mr. Macdonald, " is in no way foreign to South African thought. A man's soul there may dwell in the roof of his house, in a tree, by a spring of water, or on some mountain scaur." Among the natives of the Gazelle Peninsula in New Britain there is a secret society which goes by the name of Ingniet or Ingiet. On his entrance into it every man receives a stone in the shape either of a human being or of an animal, and henceforth his soul is believed to be knit up in a manner with the stone. If it breaks, it is an evil omen for him ; they say that the thunder has struck the stone and that he who owns it will soon die. If nevertheless the man survives the breaking of his soul-stone, they say that it was not a proper soul-stone and he gets a new one instead. The emperor Romanus Lecapenus was once informed by an astronomer that the life of Simeon, prince of Bulgaria, was bound up with a certain column in Constantinople, so that if the capital of the column were removed, Simeon would immediately die. The emperor took the hint and removed the capital, and at the same hour, as the emperor learned by enquiry, Simeon died of heart disease in Bulgaria.

Again, we have seen that in folk-tales a man's soul or strength is sometimes represented as bound up with his hair, and that when his hair is cut off he dies or grows weak. So the natives of Amboyna used to think that their strength was in their hair and would desert them if it were shorn. A criminal under torture in a Dutch Court of that island persisted in denying his guilt till his hair was cut off, when he immediately confessed. One man, who was tried for murder, endured without flinching the utmost ingenuity of his torturers till he saw the surgeon standing with a pair of shears. On asking what this was for, and being told that it was to cut his hair, he begged they would not do it, and made a clean breast. In subsequent cases, when torture failed to wring a confession from a prisoner, the Dutch authorities made a practice of cutting off his hair.

Here in Europe it used to be thought that the maleficent powers of witches and wizards resided in their hair, and that nothing could make any impression on these miscreants so long as they kept their hair on. Hence in France it was customary to shave the whole bodies of persons charged with sorcery before handing them over to the torturer. Millaeus witnessed the torture of some persons at Toulouse, from whom no confession could be wrung until they were stripped and completely shaven, when they readily acknowledged the truth of the charge.   A woman also, who apparently led a pious life, was put to the torture on suspicion of witchcraft, and bore her agonies with incredible constancy, until complete depilation drove her to admit her guilt.   The noted inquisitor Sprenger contented himself with shaving the head of the suspected witch or wizard ; but his more thoroughgoing colleague Cumanus shaved the whole bodies of forty-seven women before committing them all to the flames.   He had high authority for this rigorous scrutiny, since Satan himself, in a sermon preached from the pulpit of North Berwick church, comforted his many servants by assuring them that no harm could befall them " sa lang as their hair wes on, and sould newir latt ane teir fall fra thair ene."   Similarly in Bastar, a province of India, " if a man is adjudged guilty of witchcraft, he is beaten by the crowd, his hair is shaved, the hair being supposed to constitute his power of mischief, his front teeth are knocked out, in order, it is said, to prevent him from muttering incantations. . . . Women suspected of sorcery have to undergo the same ordeal ; if found guilty, the same punishment is awarded, and after being shaved, their hair is attached to a tree in some public place."   So among the Bhils of India, when a woman was convicted of witchcraft and had been subjected to various forms of persuasion, such as hanging head downwards from a tree and having pepper put into her eyes, a lock of hair was cut from her head and buried in the ground, " that the last link between her and her former powers of mischief might be broken." In like manner among the Aztecs of Mexico, when wizards and witches " had done their evil deeds, and the time came to put an end to their detestable life, some one laid hold of them and cropped the hair on the crown of their heads, which took from them all their power of sorcery and enchantment, and then it was that by death they put an end to their odious existence."

§ 2. *The External Soul in Plants.*—Further it has been shown that in folk-tales the life of a person is sometimes so bound up with the life of a plant that the withering of the plant will immediately follow or be followed by the death of the person.   Among the M'Bengas in Western Africa, about the Gaboon, when two children are born on the same day, the people plant two trees of the same kind and dance round them. The life of each of the children is believed to be bound up with the life of one of the trees ; and if the tree dies or is thrown down, they are sure that the child will soon die.   In the Cameroons, also, the life of a person is believed to be sympathetically bound up with that of a tree.   The chief of Old Town in Calabar kept his soul in a sacred grove near a spring of water.   When some Europeans, in frolic or ignorance, cut down part of the grove, the spirit was most indignant and threatened the perpetrators of the deed, according to the king, with all manner of evil.

Some of the Papuans unite the life of a new-born babe sympathetically with that of a tree by driving a pebble into the bark of the tree. This is supposed to give them complete mastery over the child's life ; if the tree is cut down, the child will die. After a birth the Maoris used to bury the navel-string in a sacred place and plant a young sapling over it. As the tree grew, it was a *tohu oranga* or sign of life for the child ; if it flourished, the child would prosper ; if it withered and died, the parents augured the worst for the little one. In some parts of Fiji the navel-string of a male infant is planted together with a coco-nut or the slip of a breadfruit-tree, and the child's life is supposed to be intimately connected with that of the tree. Amongst the Dyaks of Landak and Tajan, districts of Dutch Borneo, it is customary to plant a fruit-tree for a baby, and henceforth in the popular belief the fate of the child is bound up with that of the tree. If the tree shoots up rapidly, it will go well with the child ; but if the tree is dwarfed or shrivelled, nothing but misfortune can be expected for its human counterpart.

It is said that there are still families in Russia, Germany, England, France, and Italy who are accustomed to plant a tree at the birth of a child. The tree, it is hoped, will grow with the child, and it is tended with special care. The custom is still pretty general in the canton of Aargau in Switzerland ; an apple-tree is planted for a boy and a pear-tree for a girl, and the people think that the child will flourish or dwindle with the tree. In Mecklenburg the afterbirth is thrown out at the foot of a young tree, and the child is then believed to grow with the tree. Near the Castle of Dalhousie, not far from Edinburgh, there grows an oak-tree, called the Edgewell Tree, which is popularly believed to be linked to the fate of the family by a mysterious tie ; for they say that when one of the family dies, or is about to die, a branch falls from the Edgewell Tree. Thus, on seeing a great bough drop from the tree on a quiet, still day in July 1874, an old forester exclaimed, " The laird's deid noo ! " and soon after news came that Fox Maule, eleventh Earl of Dalhousie, was dead.

In England children are sometimes passed through a cleft ash-tree as a cure for rupture or rickets, and thenceforward a sympathetic connexion is supposed to exist between them and the tree. An ash-tree which had been used for this purpose grew at the edge of Shirley Heath, on the road from Hockly House to Birmingham. " Thomas Chillingworth, son of the owner of an adjoining farm, now about thirty-four, was, when an infant of a year old, passed through a similar tree, now perfectly sound, which he preserves with so much care that he will not suffer a single branch to be touched, for it is believed the life of the patient depends on the life of the tree, and the moment that is cut down, be the patient ever so distant, the rupture returns, and a mortification ensues, and terminates in death, as was the case in a man driving a waggon on the very road in question." " It is not uncommon, however," adds the writer, " for persons to survive for a time the felling of the tree." The ordinary mode of effecting the cure is to split a young ash-sapling longitudinally for a few feet and pass the child, naked, either three times or three times three through the fissure at sunrise.   In the West of England it is said that the passage should be " against the sun."   As soon as the ceremony has been performed, the tree is bound tightly up and the fissure plastered over with mud or clay.   The belief is that just as the cleft in the tree closes up, so the rupture in the child's body will be healed ; but that if the rift in the tree remains open, the rupture in the child will remain too, and if the tree were to die, the death of the child would surely follow.

A similar cure for various diseases, but especially for rupture and rickets, has been commonly practised in other parts of Europe, as Germany, France, Denmark, and Sweden ; but in these countries the tree employed for the purpose is usually not an ash but an oak ; sometimes a willow-tree is allowed or even prescribed instead.   In Mecklenburg, as in England, the sympathetic relation thus established between the tree and the child is believed to be so close that if the tree is cut down the child will die.

§ 3. *The External Soul in Animals.*—But in practice, as in folk-tales, it is not merely with inanimate objects and plants that a person is occasionally believed to be united by a bond of physical sympathy. The same bond, it is supposed, may exist between a man and an animal, so that the welfare of the one depends on the welfare of the other, and when the animal dies the man dies also.   The analogy between the custom and the tales is all the closer because in both of them the power of thus removing the soul from the body and stowing it away in an animal is often a special privilege of wizards and witches. Thus the Yakuts of Siberia believe that every shaman or wizard keeps his soul, or one of his souls, incarnate in an animal which is carefully concealed from all the world.   " Nobody can find my external soul," said one famous wizard, " it lies hidden far away in the stony mountains of Edzhigansk."   Only once a year, when the last snows melt and the earth turns black, do these external souls of wizards appear in the shape of animals among the dwellings of men.   They wander everywhere, yet none but wizards can see them.   The strong ones sweep roaring and noisily along, the weak steal about quietly and furtively. Often they fight, and then the wizard whose external soul is beaten falls ill or dies.   The weakest and most cowardly wizards are they whose souls are incarnate in the shape of dogs, for the dog gives his human double no peace, but gnaws his heart and tears his body.   The most powerful wizards are they whose external souls have the shape of stallions, elks, black bears, eagles, or boars.   Again, the Samoyeds of the Turukhinsk region hold that every shaman has a familiar spirit in the shape of a boar, which he leads about by a magic belt.   On the death of the boar the shaman himself dies ; and stories are told of battles between wizards, who send their spirits to fight before they encounter each other in person.   The Malays believe that " the soul of a person may pass into another person or into an animal, or rather that such a mysterious relation can arise between the two that the fate of the one is wholly dependent on that of the other."

Among the Melanesians of Mota, one of the New Hebrides islands, the conception of an external soul is carried out in the practice of daily life. In the Mota language the word *tamaniu* signifies "something animate or inanimate which a man has come to believe to have an existence intimately connected with his own. . . . It was not every one in Mota who had his *tamaniu*; only some men fancied that they had this relation to a lizard, a snake, or it might be a stone; sometimes the thing was sought for and found by drinking the infusion of certain leaves and heaping together the dregs; then whatever living thing was first seen in or upon the heap was the *tamaniu*. It was watched but not fed or worshipped; the natives believed that it came at call, and that the life of the man was bound up with the life of his *tamaniu*, if a living thing, or with its safety; should it die, or if not living get broken or be lost, the man would die. Hence in case of sickness they would send to see if the *tamaniu* was safe and well."

The theory of an external soul deposited in an animal appears to be very prevalent in West Africa, particularly in Nigeria, the Cameroons, and the Gaboon. Among the Fans of the Gaboon every wizard is believed at initiation to unite his life with that of some particular wild animal by a rite of blood-brotherhood; he draws blood from the ear of the animal and from his own arm, and inoculates the animal with his own blood, and himself with the blood of the beast. Henceforth such an intimate union is established between the two that the death of the one entails the death of the other. The alliance is thought to bring to the wizard or sorcerer a great accession of power, which he can turn to his advantage in various ways. In the first place, like the warlock in the fairy tales who has deposited his life outside of himself in some safe place, the Fan wizard now deems himself invulnerable. Moreover, the animal with which he has exchanged blood has become his familiar, and will obey any orders he may choose to give it; so he makes use of it to injure and kill his enemies. For that reason the creature with whom he establishes the relation of blood-brotherhood is never a tame or domestic animal, but always a ferocious and dangerous wild beast, such as a leopard, a black serpent, a crocodile, a hippopotamus, a wild boar, or a vulture. Of all these creatures the leopard is by far the commonest familiar of Fan wizards, and next to it comes the black serpent; the vulture is the rarest. Witches as well as wizards have their familiars; but the animals with which the lives of women are thus bound up generally differ from those to which men commit their external souls. A witch never has a panther for her familiar, but often a venomous species of serpent, sometimes a horned viper, sometimes a black serpent, sometimes a green one that lives in banana-trees; or it may be a vulture, an owl, or other bird of night. In every case the beast or bird with which the witch or wizard has contracted this mystic alliance is an individual, never a species; and when the individual animal dies the alliance is naturally at an end, since the death of the animal is supposed to entail the death of the man.

Similar beliefs are held by the natives of the Cross River valley within the provinces of the Cameroons. Groups of people, generally the inhabitants of a village, have chosen various animals, with which they believe themselves to stand on a footing of intimate friendship or relationship. Amongst such animals are hippopotamuses, elephants, leopards, crocodiles, gorillas, fish, and serpents, all of them creatures which are either very strong or can easily hide themselves in the water or a thicket. This power of concealing themselves is said to be an indispensable condition of the choice of animal familiars, since the animal friend or helper is expected to injure his owner's enemy by stealth ; for example, if he is a hippopotamus, he will bob up suddenly out of the water and capsize the enemy's canoe. Between the animals and their human friends or kinsfolk such a sympathetic relation is supposed to exist that the moment the animal dies the man dies also, and similarly the instant the man perishes so does the beast. From this it follows that the animal kinsfolk may never be shot at or molested for fear of injuring or killing the persons whose lives are knit up with the lives of the brutes. This does not, however, prevent the people of a village, who have elephants for their animal friends, from hunting elephants. For they do not respect the whole species but merely certain individuals of it, which stand in an intimate relation to certain individual men and women ; and they imagine that they can always distinguish these brother elephants from the common herd of elephants which are mere elephants and nothing more. The recognition indeed is said to be mutual. When a hunter, who has an elephant for his friend, meets a human elephant, as we may call it, the noble animal lifts up a paw and holds it before his face, as much as to say, " Don't shoot." Were the hunter so inhuman as to fire on and wound such an elephant, the person whose life was bound up with the elephant would fall ill.

The Balong of the Cameroons think that every man has several souls, of which one is in his body and another in an animal, such as an elephant, a wild pig, a leopard, and so forth. When a man comes home, feeling ill, and says, " I shall soon die," and dies accordingly, the people aver that one of his souls has been killed in a wild pig or a leopard, and that the death of the external soul has caused the death of the soul in his body. A similar belief in the external souls of living people is entertained by the Ibos, an important tribe of the Niger delta. They think that a man's spirit can quit his body for a time during life and take up its abode in an animal. A man who wishes to acquire this power procures a certain drug from a wise man and mixes it with his food. After that his soul goes out and enters into an animal. If it should happen that the animal is killed while the man's soul is lodged in it, the man dies ; and if the animal be wounded, the man's body will presently be covered with boils. This belief instigates to many deeds of darkness ; for a sly rogue will sometimes surreptitiously administer the magical drug to his enemy in his food, and having thus smuggled the other's soul into an animal will destroy the creature, and with it the man whose soul is lodged in it.

The negroes of Calabar, at the mouth of the Niger, believe that every person has four souls, one of which always lives outside of his or her body in the form of a wild beast in the forest. This external soul, or bush soul, as Miss Kingsley calls it, may be almost any animal, for example, a leopard, a fish, or a tortoise ; but it is never a domestic animal and never a plant. Unless he is gifted with second sight, a man cannot see his own bush soul, but a diviner will often tell him what sort of creature his bush soul is, and after that the man will be careful not to kill any animal of that species, and will strongly object to any one else doing so. A man and his sons have usually the same sort of animals for their bush souls, and so with a mother and her daughters. But sometimes all the children of a family take after the bush soul of their father ; for example, if his external soul is a leopard, all his sons and daughters will have leopards for their external souls. And on the other hand, sometimes they all take after their mother ; for instance, if her external soul is a tortoise, all the external souls of her sons and daughters will be tortoises too. So intimately bound up is the life of the man with that of the animal which he regards as his external or bush soul, that the death or injury of the animal necessarily entails the death or injury of the man. And, conversely, when the man dies, his bush soul can no longer find a place of rest, but goes mad and rushes into the fire or charges people and is knocked on the head, and that is an end of it.

Near Eket in North Calabar there is a sacred lake, the fish of which are carefully preserved because the people believe that their own souls are lodged in the fish, and that with every fish killed a human life would be simultaneously extinguished. In the Calabar River not very many years ago there used to be a huge old crocodile, popularly supposed to contain the external soul of a chief who resided in the flesh at Duke Town. Sporting vice-consuls used from time to time to hunt the animal, and once an officer contrived to hit it. Forthwith the chief was laid up with a wound in his leg. He gave out that a dog had bitten him, but no doubt the wise shook their heads and refused to be put off with so flimsy a pretext. Again, among several tribes on the banks of the Niger between Lokoja and the delta there prevails " a belief in the possibility of a man possessing an *alter ego* in the form of some animal such as a crocodile or a hippopotamus. It is believed that such a person's life is bound up with that of the animal to such an extent that whatever affects the one produces a corresponding impression upon the other, and that if one dies the other must speedily do so too. It happened not very long ago that an Englishman shot a hippopotamus close to a native village ; the friends of a woman who died the same night in the village demanded and eventually obtained five pounds as compensation for the murder of the woman."

Amongst the Zapotecs of Central America, when a woman was about to be confined, her relations assembled in the hut, and began to draw on the floor figures of different animals, rubbing each one out as soon as it was completed. This went on till the moment of birth, and the figure that then remained sketched upon the ground was called the child's *tona* or second self. " When the child grew old enough, he procured the animal that represented him and took care of it, as it was believed that health and existence were bound up with that of the animal's, in fact that the death of both would occur simultaneously," or rather that when the animal died the man would die too. Among the Indians of Guatemala and Honduras the *nagual* or *naual* is " that animate or inanimate object, generally an animal, which stands in a parallel relation to a particular man, so that the weal and woe of the man depend on the fate of the *nagual.*" According to an old writer, many Indians of Guatemala " are deluded by the devil to believe that their life dependeth upon the life of such and such a beast (which they take unto them as their familiar spirit), and think that when that beast dieth they must die ; when he is chased, ·their hearts pant ; when he is faint, they are faint ; nay, it happeneth that by the devil's delusion they appear in the shape of that beast (which commonly by their choice is a buck, or doe, a lion, or tigre, or dog, or eagle) and in that shape have been shot at and wounded." The Indians were persuaded that the death of their *nagual* would entail their own. Legend affirms that in the first battles with the Spaniards on the plateau of Quetzaltenango the *naguals* of the Indian chiefs fought in the form of serpents. The *nagual* of the highest chief was especially conspicuous, because it had the form of a great bird, resplendent in green plumage. The Spanish general Pedro de Alvarado killed the bird with his lance, and at the same moment the Indian chief fell dead to the ground.

In many tribes of South-eastern Australia each sex used to regard a particular species of animals in the same way that a Central American Indian regarded his *nagual*, but with this difference, that whereas the Indian apparently knew the individual animal with which his life was bound up, the Australians only knew that each of their lives was bound up with some one animal of the species, but they could not say with which. The result naturally was that every man spared and protected all the animals of the species with which the lives of the men were bound up ; and every woman spared and protected all the animals of the species with which the lives of the women were bound up ; because no one knew but that the death of any animal of the respective species might entail his or her own ; just as the killing of the green bird was immediately followed by the death of the Indian chief, and the killing of the parrot by the death of Punchkin in the fairy tale. Thus, for example, the Wotjobaluk tribe of South-eastern Australia " held that ' the life of Ngŭnŭngŭnŭt (the Bat) is the life of a man, and the life of Yártatgŭrk (the Nightjar) is the life of a woman,' and that when either of these creatures is killed the life of some man or of some woman is shortened. In such a case every man or every woman in the camp feared that he or she might be the victim, and from this cause great fights arose in this tribe. I learn that in these fights, men on one side and women on the other, it was not at all certain which would be victorious, for at times the women gave the men a severe drubbing with their yamsticks, while often women were injured or killed by spears." The Wotjobaluk said that the bat was the man's " brother " and that the nightjar was his " wife." The particular species of animals with which the lives of the sexes were believed to be respectively bound up varied somewhat from tribe to tribe. Thus whereas among the Wotjobaluk the bat was the animal of the men, at Gunbower Creek on the Lower Murray the bat seems to have been the animal of the women, for the natives would not kill it for the reason that " if it was killed, one of their lubras [women] would be sure to die in consequence." But whatever the particular sorts of creature with which the lives of men and women were believed to be bound up, the belief itself and the fights to which it gave rise are known to have prevailed over a large part of South-eastern Australia, and probably they extended much farther. The belief was a very serious one, and so consequently were the fights which sprang from it. Thus among some tribes of Victoria " the common bat belongs to the men, who protect it against injury, even to the half-killing of their wives for its sake. The fern owl, or large goatsucker, belongs to the women, and, although a bird of evil omen, creating terror at night by its cry, it is jealously protected by them. If a man kills one, they are as much enraged as if it was one of their children, and will strike him with their long poles."

The jealous protection thus afforded by Australian men and women to bats and owls respectively (for bats and owls seem to be the creatures usually allotted to the two sexes) is not based upon purely selfish considerations. For each man believes that not only his own life but the lives of his father, brothers, sons, and so on are bound up with the lives of particular bats, and that therefore in protecting the bat species he is protecting the lives of all his male relations as well as his own. Similarly, each woman believes that the lives of her mother, sisters, daughters, and so forth, equally with her own, are bound up with the lives of particular owls, and that in guarding the owl species she is guarding the lives of all her female relations besides her own. Now, when men's lives are thus supposed to be contained in certain animals, it is obvious that the animals can hardly be distinguished from the men, or the men from the animals. If my brother John's life is in a bat, then, on the one hand, the bat is my brother as well as John ; and, on the other hand, John is in a sense a bat, since his life is in a bat. Similarly, if my sister Mary's life is in an owl, then the owl is my sister and Mary is an owl. This is a natural enough con-clusion, and the Australians have not failed to draw it. When the bat is the man's animal, it is called his brother ; and when the owl is the woman's animal, it is called her sister. And conversely a man

addresses a woman as an owl, and she addresses him as a bat. So
with the other animals allotted to the sexes respectively in other tribes.
For example, among the Kurnai all emu-wrens were " brothers " of
the men, and all the men were emu-wrens ; all superb warblers were
" sisters " of the women, and all the women were superb warblers.

But when a savage names himself after an animal, calls it his
brother, and refuses to kill it, the animal is said to be his totem.   Accordingly in the tribes of South-eastern Australia which we have
been considering the bat and the owl, the emu-wren and the superb
warbler may properly be described as totems of the sexes.   But the
assignation of a totem to a sex is comparatively rare, and has hitherto
been discovered nowhere but in Australia.   Far more commonly the
totem is appropriated not to a sex, but to a clan, and is hereditary
either in the male or female line.   The relation of an individual to
the clan totem does not differ in kind from his relation to the sex
totem ; he will not kill it, he speaks of it as his brother, and he calls
himself by its name.   Now if the relations are similar, the explanation
which holds good of the one ought equally to hold good of the other.
Therefore the reason why a clan revere a particular species of animals
or plants (for the clan totem may be a plant) and call themselves after
it, would seem to be a belief that the life of each individual of the clan
is bound up with some one animal or plant of the species, and that
his or her death would be the consequence of killing that particular
animal or destroying that particular plant.   This explanation of
totemism squares very well with Sir George Grey's definition of a
totem or *kobong* in Western Australia.   He says : " A certain mysterious connexion exists between a family and its *kobong*, so that a
member of the family will never kill an animal of the species to which
his *kobong* belongs, should he find it asleep ; indeed he always kills it
reluctantly, and never without affording it a chance to escape.   This
arises from the family belief that some one individual of the species
is their nearest friend, to kill whom would be a great crime, and to
be carefully avoided.   Similarly, a native who has a vegetable for his
kobong may not gather it under certain circumstances, and at a
particular period of the year."   Here it will be observed that though
each man spares all the animals or plants of the species, they are not
all equally precious to him ; far from it, out of the whole species there
is only one which is specially dear to him ; but as he does not know
which the dear one is, he is obliged to spare them all from fear of injuring the one.   Again, this explanation of the clan totem harmonises
with the supposed effect of killing one of the totem species.   " One
day one of the blacks killed a crow.   Three or four days afterwards
a Boortwa (crow) [*i.e.* a man of the Crow clan] named Larry died.
He had been ailing for some days, but the killing of his *wingong* [totem]
hastened his death."   Here the killing of the crow caused the death
of a man of the Crow clan, exactly as, in the case of the sex-totems,
the killing of a bat causes the death of a Bat-man or the killing of an
owl causes the death of an Owl-woman.   Similarly, the killing of his

nagual causes the death of a Central American Indian, the killing of his bush soul causes the death of a Calabar negro, the killing of his *tamaṇiu* causes the death of a Banks Islander, and the killing of the animal in which his life is stowed away causes the death of the giant or warlock in the fairy tale.

Thus it appears that the story of " The giant who had no heart in his body " may perhaps furnish the key to the relation which is supposed to subsist between a man and his totem. The totem, on this theory, is simply the receptacle in which a man keeps his life, as Punchkin kept his life in a parrot, and Bidasari kept her soul in a golden fish. It is no valid objection to this view that when a savage has both a sex totem and a clan totem his life must be bound up with two different animals, the death of either of which would entail his own. If a man has more vital places than one in his body, why, the savage may think, should he not have more vital places than one outside it ? Why, since he can put his life outside himself, should he not transfer one portion of it to one animal and another to another ? The divisibility of life, or, to put it otherwise, the plurality of souls, is an idea suggested by many familiar facts, and has commended itself to philosophers like Plato, as well as to savages. It is only when the notion of a soul, from being a quasi-scientific hypothesis, becomes a theological dogma that its unity and indivisibility are insisted upon as essential. The savage, unshackled by dogma, is free to explain the facts of life by the assumption of as many souls as he thinks necessary. Hence, for example, the Caribs supposed that there was one soul in the head, another in the heart, and other souls at all the places where an artery is felt pulsating. Some of the Hidatsa Indians explain the phenomena of gradual death, when the extremities appear dead first, by supposing that man has four souls, and that they quit the body, not simultaneously, but one after the other, dissolution being only complete when all four have departed. Some of the Dyaks of Borneo and the Malays of the Peninsula believe that every man has seven souls. The Alfoors of Poso in Celebes are of opinion that he has three. The natives of Laos suppose that the body is the seat of thirty spirits, which reside in the hands, the feet, the mouth, the eyes, and so on. Hence, from the primitive point of view, it is perfectly possible that a savage should have one soul in his sex totem and another in his clan totem. However, as I have observed, sex totems have been found nowhere but in Australia ; so that as a rule the savage who practises totemism need not have more than one soul out of his body at a time.

If this explanation of the totem as a receptacle in which a man keeps his soul or one of his souls is correct, we should expect to find some totemic people of whom it is expressly said that every man amongst them is believed to keep at least one soul permanently out of his body, and that the destruction of this external soul is supposed to entail the death of its owner. Such a people are the Bataks of Sumatra. The Bataks are divided into exogamous clans (*margas*) with descent in the male line ; and each clan is forbidden to eat the flesh of a particular animal.   One clan may not eat the tiger, another the ape, another the crocodile, another the dog, another the cat, another the dove, another the white buffalo, and another the locust. The reason given by members of a clan for abstaining from the flesh of the particular animal is either that they are descended from animals of that species, and that their souls after death may transmigrate into the animals, or that they or their forefathers have been under certain obligations to the creatures.   Sometimes, but not always, the clan bears the name of the animal.   Thus the Bataks have totemism in full.   But, further, each Batak believes that he has seven or, on a more moderate computation, three souls.   One of these souls is always outside the body, but nevertheless whenever it dies, however far away it may be at the time, that same moment the man dies also.   The writer who mentions this belief says nothing about the Batak totems ; but on the analogy of the Australian, Central American, and African evidence we may conjecture that the external soul, whose death entails the death of the man, is housed in the totemic animal or plant.

Against this view it can hardly be thought to militate that the Batak does not in set terms affirm his external soul to be in his totem, but alleges other grounds for respecting the sacred animal or plant of his clan.   For if a savage seriously believes that his life is bound up with an external object, it is in the last degree unlikely that he will let any stranger into the secret.   In all that touches his inmost life and beliefs the savage is exceedingly suspicious and reserved ; Europeans have resided among savages for years without discovering some of their capital articles of faith, and in the end the discovery has often been the result of accident.   Above all, the savage lives in an intense and perpetual dread of assassination by sorcery ;   the most trifling relics of his person—the clippings of his hair and nails, his spittle, the remnants of his food, his very name—all these may, he fancies, be turned by the sorcerer to his destruction, and he is therefore anxiously careful to conceal or destroy them.   But if in matters such as these, which are but the outposts and outworks of his life, he is so shy and secretive, how close must be the concealment, how impenetrable the reserve in which he enshrouds the inner keep and citadel of his being ! When the princess in the fairy tale asks the giant where he keeps his soul, he often gives false or evasive answers, and it is only after much coaxing and wheedling that the secret is at last wrung from him.   In his jealous reticence the giant resembles the timid and furtive savage ; but whereas the exigencies of the story demand that the giant should at last reveal his secret, no such obligation is laid on the savage ; and no inducement that can be offered is likely to tempt him to imperil his soul by revealing its hiding-place to a stranger.   It is therefore no matter for surprise that the central mystery of the savage's life should so long have remained a secret, and that we should be left to piece it together from scattered hints and fragments and from the recollections of it which linger in fairy tales.

§ 4. *The Ritual of Death and Resurrection.*—This view of totemism throws light on a class of religious rites of which no adequate explanation, so far as I am aware, has yet been offered. Amongst many savage tribes, especially such as are known to practise totemism, it is customary for lads at puberty to undergo certain initiatory rites, of which one of the commonest is a pretence of killing the lad and bringing him to life again. Such rites become intelligible if we suppose that their substance consists in extracting the youth's soul in order to transfer it to his totem. For the extraction of his soul would naturally be supposed to kill the youth or at least to throw him into a death-like trance, which the savage hardly distinguishes from death. His recovery would then be attributed either to the gradual recovery of his system from the violent shock which it had received, or, more probably, to the infusion into him of fresh life drawn from the totem. Thus the essence of these initiatory rites, so far as they consist in a simulation of death and resurrection, would be an exchange of life or souls between the man and his totem. The primitive belief in the possibility of such an exchange of souls comes clearly out in a story of a Basque hunter who affirmed that he had been killed by a bear, but that the bear had, after killing him, breathed its own soul into him, so that the bear's body was now dead, but he himself was a bear, being animated by the bear's soul. This revival of the dead hunter as a bear is exactly analogous to what, on the theory here suggested, is supposed to take place in the ceremony of killing a lad at puberty and bringing him to life again. The lad dies as a man and comes to life again as an animal ; the animal's soul is now in him, and his human soul is in the animal. With good right, therefore, does he call himself a Bear or a Wolf, etc., according to his totem ; and with good right does he treat the bears or the wolves, etc., as his brethren, since in these animals are lodged the souls of himself and his kindred.

Examples of this supposed death and resurrection at initiation are as follows. In the Wonghi or Wonghibon tribe of New South Wales the youths on approaching manhood are initiated at a secret ceremony, which none but initiated men may witness. Part of the proceedings consists in knocking out a tooth and giving a new name to the novice, indicative of the change from youth to manhood. While the teeth are being knocked out an instrument known as a bull-roarer, which consists of a flat piece of wood with serrated edges tied to the end of a string, is swung round so as to produce a loud humming noise. The uninitiated are not allowed to see this instrument. Women are forbidden to witness the ceremonies under pain of death. It is given out that the youths are each met in turn by a mythical being called Thuremlin (more commonly known as Daramulun), who takes the youth to a distance, kills him, and in some instances cuts him up, after which he restores him to life and knocks out a tooth. Their belief in the power of Thuremlin is said to be undoubted.

The Ualaroi of the Upper Darling River said that at initiation the boy met a ghost, who killed him and brought him to life again as a young man. Among the natives on the Lower Lachlan and Murray Rivers it was Thrumalun (Daramulun) who was thought to slay and resuscitate the novices. In the Unmatjera tribe of Central Australia women and children believe that a spirit called Twanyirika kills the youth and afterwards brings him to life again during the period of initiation. The rites of initiation in this tribe, as in the other Central tribes, comprise the operations of circumcision and sub-incision ; and as soon as the second of these has been performed on him, the young man receives from his father a sacred stick (*churinga*), with which, he is told, his spirit was associated in the remotest past. While he is out in the bush recovering from his wounds, he must swing the bull-roarer, or a being who lives up in the sky will swoop down and carry him off. In the Binbinga tribe, on the western coast of the Gulf of Carpentaria, the women and children believe that the noise of the bull-roarer at initiation is made by a spirit named Katajalina, who lives in an ant-hill and comes out and eats up the boy, afterwards restoring him to life. Similarly among their neighbours the Anula the women imagine that the droning sound of the bull-roarer is produced by a spirit called Gnabaia, who swallows the lads at initiation and afterwards disgorges them in the form of initiated men.

Among the tribes settled on the southern coast of New South Wales, of which the Coast Murring tribe may be regarded as typical, the drama of resurrection from the dead was exhibited in a graphic form to the novices at initiation. The ceremony has been described for us by an eye-witness. A man, disguised with stringy bark fibre, lay down in a grave and was lightly covered up with sticks and earth. In his hand he held a small bush, which appeared to be growing in the soil, and other bushes were stuck in the ground to heighten the effect. Then the novices were brought and placed beside the grave. Next, a procession of men, disguised in stringy bark fibre, drew near. They represented a party of medicine-men, guided by two reverend seniors, who had come on pilgrimage to the grave of a brother medicine-man, who lay buried there. When the little procession, chanting an invocation to Daramulun, had defiled from among the rocks and trees into the open, it drew up on the side of the grave opposite to the novices, the two old men taking up a position in the rear of the dancers. For some time the dance and song went on till the tree that seemed to grow from the grave began to quiver. " Look there ! " cried the men to the novices, pointing to the trembling leaves. As they looked, the tree quivered more and more, then was violently agitated and fell to the ground, while amid the excited dancing of the dancers and the chanting of the choir the supposed dead man spurned from him the superincumbent mass of sticks and leaves, and springing to his feet danced his magic dance in the grave itself, and exhibited in his mouth the magic sub-stances which he was supposed to have received from Daramulun in person.

Some tribes of Northern New Guinea—the Yabim, Bukaua, Kai, and Tami—like many Australian tribes, require every male member of the tribe to be circumcised before he ranks as a full-grown man ; and the tribal initiation, of which circumcision is the central feature, is conceived by them, as by some Australian tribes, as a process of being swallowed and disgorged by a mythical monster, whose voice is heard in the humming sound of the bull-roarer. Indeed the New Guinea tribes not only impress this belief on the minds of women and children, but enact it in a dramatic form at the actual rites of initiation, at which no woman or uninitiated person may be present. For this purpose a hut about a hundred feet long is erected either in the village or in a lonely part of the forest. It is modelled in the shape of the mythical monster ; at the end which represents his head it is high, and it tapers away at the other end. A betel-palm, grubbed up with the roots, stands for the backbone of the great being and its clustering fibres for his hair ; and to complete the resemblance the butt end of the building is adorned by a native artist with a pair of goggle eyes and a gaping mouth. When after a tearful parting from their mothers and women folk, who believe or pretend to believe in the monster that swallows their dear ones, the awe-struck novices are brought face to face with this imposing structure, the huge creature emits a sullen growl, which is in fact no other than the humming note of bull-roarers swung by men concealed in the monster's belly. The actual process of deglutition is variously enacted. Among the Tami it is represented by causing the candidates to defile past a row of men who hold bull-roarers over their heads ; among the Kai it is more graphically set forth by making them pass under a scaffold on which stands a man, who makes a gesture of swallowing and takes in fact a gulp of water as each trembling novice passes beneath him. But the present of a pig, opportunely offered for the redemption of the youth, induces the monster to relent and disgorge his victim ; the man who represents the monster accepts the gift vicariously, a gurgling sound is heard, and the water which had just been swallowed descends in a jet on the novice. This signifies that the young man has been released from the monster's belly. However, he has now to undergo the more painful and dangerous operation of circumcision. It follows immediately, and the cut made by the knife of the operator is explained to be a bite or scratch which the monster inflicted on the novice in spewing him out of his capacious maw. While the operation is proceeding, a prodigious noise is made by the swinging of bull-roarers to represent the roar of the dreadful being who is in the act of swallowing the young men.

When, as sometimes happens, a lad dies from the effect of the operation, he is buried secretly in the forest, and his sorrowing mother is told that the monster has a pig's stomach as well as a human stomach, and that unfortunately her son slipped into the wrong stomach, from which it was impossible to extricate him. After they have been circumcised the lads must remain for some months in seclusion, shunning all contact with women and even the sight of them. They live in the long hut which represents the monster's belly. When at last the lads, now ranking as initiated men, are brought back with great pomp and ceremony to the village, they are received with sobs and tears of joy by the women, as if the grave had given up its dead. At first the young men keep their eyes rigidly closed or even sealed with a plaster of chalk, and they appear not to understand the words of command which are given them by an elder. Gradually, however, they come to themselves as if awaking from a stupor, and next day they bathe and wash off the crust of white chalk with which their bodies had been coated.

It is highly significant that all these tribes of New Guinea apply the same word to the bull-roarer and to the monster, who is supposed to swallow the novices at circumcision, and whose fearful roar is represented by the hum of the harmless wooden instruments. Further, it deserves to be noted that in three languages out of the four the same word which is applied to the bull-roarer and to the monster means also a ghost or spirit of the dead, while in the fourth language (the Kai) it signifies " grandfather." From this it seems to follow that the being who swallows and disgorges the novices at initiation is believed to be a powerful ghost or ancestral spirit, and that the bull-roarer, which bears his name, is his material representative. That would explain the jealous secrecy with which the sacred implement is kept from the sight of women. While they are not in use, the bull-roarers are stowed away in the men's club-houses, which no woman may enter ; indeed no woman or uninitiated person may set eyes on a bull-roarer under pain of death. Similarly among the Tugeri or Kaya-Kaya, a large Papuan tribe on the south coast of Dutch New Guinea, the name of the bull-roarer, which they call *sosom*, is given to a mythical giant, who is supposed to appear every year with the south-east monsoon. When he comes, a festival is held in his honour and bull-roarers are swung. Boys are presented to the giant, and he kills them, but considerately brings them to life again.

In certain districts of Viti Levu, the largest of the Fijian Islands, the drama of death and resurrection used to be acted with much solemnity before the eyes of young men at initiation. In a sacred enclosure they were shown a row of dead or seemingly dead men lying on the ground, their bodies cut open and covered with blood, their entrails protruding. But at a yell from the high priest the counterfeit dead men started to their feet and ran down to the river to cleanse themselves from the blood and guts of pigs with which they were beslobbered. Soon they marched back to the sacred enclosure as if come to life, clean, fresh, and garlanded, swaying their bodies in time to the music of a solemn hymn, and took their places in front of the novices. Such was the drama of death and resurrection.

The people of Rook, an island between New Guinea and New Britain, hold festivals at which one or two disguised men, their heads covered with wooden masks, go dancing through the village, followed by all the other men. They demand that the circumcised boys who have not yet been swallowed by Marsaba (the devil) shall be given up to them. The boys, trembling and shrieking, are delivered to them, and must creep between the legs of the disguised men. Then the procession moves through the village again, and announces that Marsaba has eaten up the boys, and will not disgorge them till he receives a present of pigs, taro, and so forth. So all the villagers, according to their means, contribute provisions, which are then consumed in the name of Marsaba.

In the west of Ceram boys at puberty are admitted to the Kakian association. Modern writers have commonly regarded this association as primarily a political league instituted to resist foreign domination. In reality its objects are purely religious and social, though it is possible that the priests may have occasionally used their powerful influence for political ends. The society is in fact merely one of those widely-diffused primitive institutions of which a chief object is the initiation of young men. In recent years the true nature of the association has been duly recognised by the distinguished Dutch ethnologist, J. G. F. Riedel. The Kakian house is an oblong wooden shed, situated under the darkest trees in the depth of the forest, and is built to admit so little light that it is impossible to see what goes on in it. Every village has such a house. Thither the boys who are to be initiated are conducted blindfold, followed by their parents and relations. Each boy is led by the hand by two men, who act as his sponsors or guardians, looking after him during the period of initiation. When all are assembled before the shed, the high priest calls aloud upon the devils. Immediately a hideous uproar is heard to proceed from the shed. It is made by men with bamboo trumpets, who have been secretly introduced into the building by a back door, but the women and children think it is made by the devils, and are much terrified. Then the priests enter the shed, followed by the boys, one at a time. As soon as each boy has disappeared within the precincts, a dull chopping sound is heard, a fearful cry rings out, and a sword or spear, dripping with blood, is thrust through the roof of the shed. This is a token that the boy's head has been cut off, and that the devil has carried him away to the other world, there to regenerate and transform him. So at sight of the bloody sword the mothers weep and wail, crying that the devil has murdered their children. In some places, it would seem, the boys are pushed through an opening made in the shape of a crocodile's jaws or a cassowary's beak, and it is then said that the devil has swallowed them. The boys remain in the shed for five or nine days. Sitting in the dark, they hear the blast of the bamboo trumpets, and from time to time the sound of musket shots and the clash of swords. Every day they bathe, and their faces and bodies are smeared with a yellow dye, to give them the appearance of having been swallowed by the devil. During his stay in the Kakian house each boy has one or two crosses tattooed with thorns on his breast or arm. When they are not sleeping, the lads must sit in a crouching posture without moving a muscle. As they sit in a row cross-legged, with their hands stretched out, the chief takes his trumpet, and placing the mouth of it on the hands of each lad, speaks through it in strange tones, imitating the voice of the spirits. He warns the lads, under pain of death, to observe the rules of the Kakian society, and never to reveal what has passed in the Kakian house. The novices are also told by the priests to behave well to their blood relations, and are taught the traditions and secrets of the tribe.

Meantime the mothers and sisters of the lads have gone home to weep and mourn. But in a day or two the men who acted as guardians or sponsors to the novices return to the village with the glad tidings that the devil, at the intercession of the priests, has restored the lads to life. The men who bring this news come in a fainting state and daubed with mud, like messengers freshly arrived from the nether world. Before leaving the Kakian house, each lad receives from the priest a stick adorned at both ends with cock's or cassowary's feathers. The sticks are supposed to have been given to the lads by the devil at the time when he restored them to life, and they serve as a token that the youths have been in the spirit land. When they return to their homes they totter in their walk, and enter the house backward, as if they had forgotten how to walk properly ; or they enter the house by the back door. If a plate of food is given to them, they hold it upside down. They remain dumb, indicating their wants by signs only. All this is to show that they are still under the influence of the devil or the spirits. Their sponsors have to teach them all the common acts of life, as if they were new-born children. Further, upon leaving the Kakian house the boys are strictly forbidden to eat of certain fruits until the next celebration of the rites has taken place. And for twenty or thirty days their hair may not be combed by their mothers or sisters. At the end of that time the high priest takes them to a lonely place in the forest, and cuts off a lock of hair from the crown of each of their heads. After these initiatory rites the lads are deemed men, and may marry ; it would be a scandal if they married before.

In the region of the Lower Congo a simulation of death and resurrection is, or rather used to be, practised by the members of a guild or secret society called *ndembo*. " In the practice of Ndembo the initiating doctors get some one to fall down in a pretended fit, and in that state he is carried away to an enclosed place outside the town. This is called ' dying Ndembo.' Others follow suit, generally boys and girls, but often young men and women. . . . They are supposed to have died. But the parents and friends supply food, and after a period varying, according to custom, from three months to three years, it is arranged that the doctor shall bring them to life again. . . . When the doctor's fee has been paid, and money (goods) saved for a feast, the *Ndembo* people are brought to life. At first they pretend to know no one and nothing ; they do not even know how to masticate food, and friends have to perform that office for them. They want everything nice that any one uninitiated may have, and beat them if it is not granted, or even strangle and kill people. They do not get into trouble for this, because it is thought that they do not know better. Sometimes they carry on the pretence of talking gibberish, and behaving as if they had returned from the spirit-world. After this they are known by another name, peculiar to those who have ' died Ndembo.' . . . We hear of the custom far along on the upper river, as well as in the cataract region."

Among some of the Indian tribes of North America there exist certain religious associations which are only open to candidates who have gone through a pretence of being killed and brought to life again. In 1766 or 1767 Captain Jonathan Carver witnessed the admission of a candidate to an association called " the friendly society of the Spirit " (*Wakon-Kitchewah*) among the Naudowessies, a Siouan or Dacotan tribe in the region of the great lakes. The candidate knelt before the chief, who told him that " he himself was now agitated by the same spirit which he should in a few moments communicate to him ; that it would strike him dead, but that he would instantly be restored again to life ; to this he added, that the communication, however terrifying, was a necessary introduction to the advantages enjoyed by the community into which he was on the point of being admitted. As he spoke this, he appeared to be greatly agitated ; till at last his emotions became so violent, that his countenance was distorted, and his whole frame convulsed. At this juncture he threw something that appeared both in shape and colour like a small bean, at the young man, which seemed to enter his mouth, and he instantly fell as motionless as if he had been shot." For a time the man lay like dead; but under a shower of blows he showed signs of consciousness, and finally, discharging from his mouth the bean, or whatever it was that the chief had thrown at him, he came to life. In other tribes, for example, the Ojebways, Winnebagoes, and Dacotas or Sioux, the instrument by which the candidate is apparently slain is the medicine-bag. The bag is made of the skin of an animal (such as the otter, wild cat, serpent, bear, raccoon, wolf, owl, weasel), of which it roughly preserves the shape. Each member of the society has one of these bags, in which he keeps the odds and ends that make up his " medicine " or charms. " They believe that from the miscellaneous contents in the belly of the skin bag or animal there issues a spirit or breath, which has the power, not only to knock down and kill a man, but also to set him up and restore him to life." The mode of killing a man with one of these medicine-bags is to thrust it at him ; he falls like dead, but a second thrust of the bag restores him to life.

A ceremony witnessed by the castaway John R. Jewitt during his captivity among the Indians of Nootka Sound doubtless belongs to this class of customs. The Indian king or chief " discharged a pistol close to his son's ear, who immediately fell down as if killed, upon which all the women of the house set up a most lamentable cry, tearing handfuls of hair from their heads, and exclaiming that the prince was dead ; at the same time a great number of the inhabitants rushed into the house armed with their daggers, muskets, etc., enquiring the cause of their outcry.   These were immediately followed by two others dressed in wolf skins, with masks over their faces representing the head of that animal.   The latter came in on their hands and feet in the manner of a beast, and taking up the prince, carried him off upon their backs, retiring in the same manner they entered." In another place Jewitt mentions that the young prince—a lad of about eleven years of age—wore a mask in imitation of a wolf's head. Now, as the Indians of this part of America are divided into totem clans, of which the Wolf clan is one of the principal, and as the members of each clan are in the habit of wearing some portion of the totem animal about their person, it is probable that the prince belonged to the Wolf clan, and that the ceremony described by Jewitt represented the killing of the lad in order that he might be born anew as a wolf, much in the same way that the Basque hunter supposed himself to have been killed and to have come to life again as a bear.

This conjectural explanation of the ceremony has, since it was first put forward, been to some extent confirmed by the researches of Dr. Franz Boas among these Indians ; though it would seem that the community to which the chief's son thus obtained admission was not so much a totem clan as a secret society called Tlokoala, whose members imitated wolves.   Every new member of the society must be initiated by the wolves.   At night a pack of wolves, personated by Indians dressed in wolf-skins and wearing wolf-masks, make their appearance, seize the novice, and carry him into the woods.   When the wolves are heard outside the village, coming to fetch away the novice, all the members of the society blacken their faces and sing, " Among all the tribes is great excitement, because I am Tlokoala."   Next day the wolves bring back the novice dead, and the members of the society have to revive him.   The wolves are supposed to have put a magic stone into his body, which must be removed before he can come to life.   Till this is done the pretended corpse is left lying outside the house.   Two wizards go and remove the stone, which appears to be quartz, and then the novice is resuscitated.   Among the Niska Indians of British Columbia, who are divided into four principal clans with the raven, the wolf, the eagle, and the bear for their respective totems, the novice at initiation is always brought back by an artificial totem animal.   Thus when a man was about to be initiated into a secret society called Olala, his friends drew their knives and pretended to kill him.   In reality they let him slip away, while they cut off the head of a dummy which had been adroitly substituted for him.   Then they laid the decapitated dummy down and covered it over, and the women began to mourn and wail.   His relations gave a funeral banquet and solemnly burnt the effigy.   In short, they held a regular funeral. For a whole year the novice remained absent and was seen by none but members of the secret society.   But at the end of that time he came back alive, carried by an artificial animal which represented his totem.

In these ceremonies the essence of the rite appears to be the killing of the novice in his character of a man and his restoration to life in the form of the animal which is thenceforward to be, if not his guardian spirit, at least linked to him in a peculiarly intimate relation. It is to be remembered that the Indians of Guatemala, whose life was bound up with an animal, were supposed to have the power of appearing in the shape of the particular creature with which they were thus sympathetically united. Hence it seems not unreasonable to conjecture that in like manner the Indians of British Columbia may imagine that their life depends on the life of some one of that species of creature to which they assimilate themselves by their costume. At least if that is not an article of belief with the Columbian Indians of the present day, it may very well have been so with their ancestors in the past, and thus may have helped to mould the rites and ceremonies both of the totem clans and of the secret societies. For though these two sorts of communities differ in respect of the mode in which membership of them is obtained—a man being born into his totem clan but admitted into a secret society later in life—we can hardly doubt that they are near akin and have their root in the same mode of thought. That thought, if I am right, is the possibility of establishing a sympathetic relation with an animal, a spirit, or other mighty being, with whom a man deposits for safe-keeping his soul or some part of it, and from whom he receives in return a gift of magical powers.

Thus, on the theory here suggested, wherever totemism is found, and wherever a pretence is made of killing and bringing to life again the novice at initiation, there may exist or have existed not only a belief in the possibility of permanently depositing the soul in some external object—animal, plant, or what not—but an actual intention of so doing. If the question is put, why do men desire to deposit their life outside their bodies ? the answer can only be that, like the giant in the fairy tale, they think it safer to do so than to carry it about with them, just as people deposit their money with a banker rather than carry it on their persons. We have seen that at critical periods the life or soul is sometimes temporarily stowed away in a safe place till the danger is past. But institutions like totemism are not resorted to merely on special occasions of danger ; they are systems into which every one, or at least every male, is obliged to be initiated at a certain period of life. Now the period of life at which initiation takes place is regularly puberty ; and this fact suggests that the special danger which totemism and systems like it are intended to obviate is supposed not to arise till sexual maturity has been attained, in fact, that the danger apprehended is believed to attend the relation of the sexes to each other. It would be easy to prove by a long array of facts that the sexual relation is associated in the primitive mind with many serious perils ; but the exact nature of the danger apprehended is still obscure. We may hope that a more exact acquaintance with savage modes of thought will in time disclose this central mystery of primitive society, and will thereby furnish the clue, not only to totemism, but to the origin of the marriage system.

CHAPTER LXVIII

THE GOLDEN BOUGH

THUS the view that Balder's life was in the mistletoe is entirely in harmony with primitive modes of thought. It may indeed sound like a contradiction that, if his life was in the mistletoe, he should neverthe- less have been killed by a blow from the plant. But when a person's life is conceived as embodied in a particular object, with the existence of which his own existence is inseparably bound up, and the destruction of which involves his own, the object in question may be regarded and spoken of indifferently as his life or his death, as happens in the fairy tales. Hence if a man's death is in an object, it is perfectly natural that he should be killed by a blow from it. In the fairy tales Koshchei the Deathless is killed by a blow from the egg or the stone in which his life or death is secreted; the ogres burst when a certain grain of sand—doubtless containing their life or death—is carried over their heads; the magician dies when the stone in which his life or death is contained is put under his pillow; and the Tartar hero is warned that he may be killed by the golden arrow or golden sword in which his soul has been stowed away.

The idea that the life of the oak was in the mistletoe was probably suggested, as I have said, by the observation that in winter the mistletoe growing on the oak remains green while the oak itself is leafless. But the position of the plant—growing not from the ground but from the trunk or branches of the tree—might confirm this idea. Primitive man might think that, like himself, the oak-spirit had sought to deposit his life in some safe place, and for this purpose had pitched on the mistletoe, which, being in a sense neither on earth nor in heaven, might be supposed to be fairly out of harm's way. In a former chapter we saw that primitive man seeks to preserve the life of his human divinities by keeping them poised between earth and heaven, as the place where they are least likely to be assailed by the dangers that encompass the life of man on earth. We can therefore understand why it has been a rule both of ancient and of modern folk-medicine that the mistletoe should not be allowed to touch the ground; were it to touch the ground, its healing virtue would be gone. This may be a survival of the old superstition that the plant in which the life of the sacred tree was concentrated should not be exposed to the risk incurred by contact with the earth. In an Indian legend, which offers a parallel to the Balder myth, Indra swore to the demon Namuci that he would slay him neither by day nor by night, neither with staff nor with bow, neither with the palm of the hand nor with the fist, neither with the wet nor with the dry. But he killed him in the morning twilight by sprinkling over him the foam of the sea. The foam of the sea is just such an object as a savage might choose to put his life in, because it occupies that sort of intermediate or nondescript position between earth and sky or sea and sky in which primitive man sees safety. It is therefore not surprising that the foam of the river should be the totem of a clan in India.

Again, the view that the mistletoe owes its mystic character partly to its not growing on the ground is confirmed by a parallel superstition about the mountain-ash or rowan-tree. In Jutland a rowan that is found growing out of the top of another tree is esteemed " exceedingly effective against witchcraft : since it does not grow on the ground witches have no power over it ; if it is to have its full effect it must be cut on Ascension Day." Hence it is placed over doors to prevent the ingress of witches. In Sweden and Norway, also, magical properties are ascribed to a " flying-rowan " (*flögrönn*), that is to a rowan which is found growing not in the ordinary fashion on the ground but on another tree, or on a roof, or in a cleft of the rock, where it has sprouted from seed scattered by birds. They say that a man who is out in the dark should have a bit of " flying-rowan " with him to chew ; else he runs a risk of being bewitched and of being unable to stir from the spot. Just as in Scandinavia the parasitic rowan is deemed a countercharm to sorcery, so in Germany the parasitic mistletoe is still commonly considered a protection against witch-craft, and in Sweden, as we saw, the mistletoe which is gathered on Midsummer Eve is attached to the ceiling of the house, the horse's stall or the cow's crib, in the belief that this renders the Troll power-less to injure man or beast.

The view that the mistletoe was not merely the instrument of Balder's death, but that it contained his life, is countenanced by the analogy of a Scottish superstition. Tradition ran that the fate of the Hays of Errol, an estate in Perthshire, near the Firth of Tay, was bound up with the mistletoe that grew on a certain great oak. A member of the Hay family has recorded the old belief as follows : " Among the low country families the badges are now almost generally forgotten ; but it appears by an ancient MS. and the tradition of a few old people in Perthshire, that the badge of the Hays was the mistletoe. There was formerly in the neighbourhood of Errol, and not far from the Falcon stone, a vast oak of an unknown age, and upon which grew a profusion of the plant : many charms and legends were considered to be connected with the tree, and the duration of the family of Hay was said to be united with its existence. It was believed that a sprig of the mistletoe cut by a Hay on Allhallow-mas eve, with a new dirk, and after surrounding the tree three times sunwise, and pronouncing a certain spell, was a sure charm against all glamour or witchery, and an infallible guard in the day of battle. A spray gathered in the same manner was placed in the cradle of infants, and thought to defend them from being changed for elf-bairns by the fairies. Finally, it was affirmed, that when the root of the oak had perished, ' the grass should grow in the hearth of Errol, and a raven should sit in the falcon's nest.' The two most unlucky deeds which could be done by one of the name of Hay was, to kill a white falcon, and to cut down a limb from the oak of Errol. When the old tree was destroyed I could never learn. The estate has been sold out of the family of Hay, and of course it is said that the fatal oak was cut down a short time before." The old superstition is recorded in verses which are traditionally ascribed to Thomas the Rhymer :

> *While the mistletoe bats on Errol's aik,*
> *And that aik stands fast,*
> *The Hays shall flourish, and their good grey hawk*
> *Shall nocht flinch before the blast.*

> *But when the root of the aik decays,*
> *And the mistletoe dwines on its withered breast,*
> *The grass shall grow on Errol's hearthstane,*
> *And the corbie roup in the falcon's nest.*

It is not a new opinion that the Golden Bough was the mistletoe. True, Virgil does not identify but only compares it with mistletoe. But this may be only a poetical device to cast a mystic glamour over the humble plant. Or, more probably, his description was based on a popular superstition that at certain times the mistletoe blazed out into a supernatural golden glory. The poet tells how two doves, guiding Aeneas to the gloomy vale in whose depth grew the Golden Bough, alighted upon a tree, " whence shone a flickering gleam of gold. As in the woods in winter cold the mistletoe—a plant not native to its tree—is green with fresh leaves and twines its yellow berries about the boles ; such seemed upon the shady holm-oak the leafy gold, so rustled in the gentle breeze the golden leaf." Here Virgil definitely describes the Golden Bough as growing on a holm-oak, and compares it with the mistletoe. The inference is almost inevitable that the Golden Bough was nothing but the mistletoe seen through the haze of poetry or of popular superstition.

Now grounds have been shown for believing that the priest of the Arician grove—the King of the Wood—personified the tree on which grew the Golden Bough. Hence if that tree was the oak, the King of the Wood must have been a personification of the oak-spirit. It is, therefore, easy to understand why, before he could be slain, it was necessary to break the Golden Bough. As an oak-spirit, his life or death was in the mistletoe on the oak, and so long as the mistletoe remained intact, he, like Balder, could not die. To slay him, therefore, it was necessary to break the mistletoe, and probably, as in the case of Balder, to throw it at him. And to complete the parallel, it is only necessary to suppose that the King of the Wood was formerly burned, dead or alive, at the midsummer fire festival which, as we have seen, was annually celebrated in the Arician grove. The perpetual fire which burned in the grove, like the perpetual fire which burned in the temple of Vesta at Rome and under the oak at Romove, was probably fed with the sacred oak-wood ; and thus it would be in a great fire of oak that the King of the Wood formerly met his end. At a later time, as I have suggested, his annual tenure of office was lengthened or shortened, as the case might be, by the rule which allowed him to live so long as he could prove his divine right by the strong hand. But he only escaped the fire to fall by the sword.

Thus it seems that at a remote age in the heart of Italy, beside the sweet Lake of Nemi, the same fiery tragedy was annually enacted which Italian merchants and soldiers were afterwards to witness among their rude kindred, the Celts of Gaul, and which, if the Roman eagles had ever swooped on Norway, might have been found repeated with little difference among the barbarous Aryans of the North. The rite was probably an essential feature in the ancient Aryan worship of the oak.

It only remains to ask, Why was the mistletoe called the Golden Bough ? The whitish-yellow of the mistletoe berries is hardly enough to account for the name, for Virgil says that the bough was altogether golden, stem as well as leaves. Perhaps the name may be derived from the rich golden yellow which a bough of mistletoe assumes when it has been cut and kept for some months ; the bright tint is not confined to the leaves, but spreads to the stalks as well, so that the whole branch appears to be indeed a Golden Bough. Breton peasants hang up great bunches of mistletoe in front of their cottages, and in the month of June these bunches are conspicuous for the bright golden tinge of their foliage. In some parts of Brittany, especially about Morbihan, branches of mistletoe are hung over the doors of stables and byres to protect the horses and cattle, probably against witchcraft.

The yellow colour of the withered bough may partly explain why the mistletoe has been sometimes supposed to possess the property of disclosing treasures in the earth ; for on the principles of homoeopathic magic there is a natural affinity between a yellow bough and yellow gold. This suggestion is confirmed by the analogy of the marvellous properties popularly ascribed to the mythical fern-seed, which is popularly supposed to bloom like gold or fire on Midsummer Eve. Thus in Bohemia it is said that " on St. John's Day fern-seed blooms with golden blossoms that gleam like fire." Now it is a property of this mythical fern-seed that whoever has it, or will ascend a mountain holding it in his hand on Midsummer Eve, will discover a vein of gold or will see the treasures of the earth shining with a bluish flame. In Russia they say that if you succeed in catching the wondrous bloom of the fern at midnight on Midsummer Eve you have only to throw it up into the air, and it will fall like a star on the very spot where a treasure lies hidden.   In Brittany treasure-seekers gather fern-seed at midnight on Midsummer Eve, and keep it till Palm Sunday of the following year ; then they strew the seed on the ground where they think a treasure is concealed.   Tyrolese peasants imagine that hidden treasures can be seen glowing like flame on Midsummer Eve, and that fern-seed, gathered at this mystic season, with the usual precautions, will help to bring the buried gold to the surface.   In the Swiss canton of Freiburg people used to watch beside a fern on St. John's night in the hope of winning a treasure, which the devil himself sometimes brought to them.   In Bohemia they say that he who procures the golden bloom of the fern at this season has thereby the key to all hidden treasures ; and that if maidens will spread a cloth under the fast-fading bloom, red gold will drop into it.   And in the Tyrol and Bohemia if you place fern-seed among money, the money will never decrease, however much of it you spend.   Sometimes the fern-seed is supposed to bloom on Christmas night, and whoever catches it will become very rich.   In Styria they say that by gathering fern-seed on Christmas night you can force the devil to bring you a bag of money.

Thus, on the principle of like by like, fern-seed is supposed to discover gold because it is itself golden ; and for a similar reason it enriches its possessor with an unfailing supply of gold.   But while the fern-seed is described as golden, it is equally described as glowing and fiery.   Hence, when we consider that two great days for gathering the fabulous seed are Midsummer Eve and Christmas—that is, the two solstices (for Christmas is nothing but an old heathen celebration of the winter solstice)—we are led to regard the fiery aspect of the fern-seed as primary, and its golden aspect as secondary and derivative. Fern-seed, in fact, would seem to be an emanation of the sun's fire at the two turning-points of its course, the summer and winter solstices. This view is confirmed by a German story in which a hunter is said to have procured fern-seed by shooting at the sun on Midsummer Day at noon ; three drops of blood fell down, which he caught in a white cloth, and these blood-drops were the fern-seed.   Here the blood is clearly the blood of the sun, from which the fern-seed is thus directly derived.   Thus it may be taken as probable that fern-seed is golden, because it is believed to be an emanation of the sun's golden fire.

Now, like fern-seed, the mistletoe is gathered either at Midsummer or at Christmas—that is, either at the summer or at the winter solstice— and, like fern-seed, it is supposed to possess the power of revealing treasures in the earth.   On Midsummer Eve people in Sweden make divining-rods of mistletoe, or of four different kinds of wood one of which must be mistletoe.   The treasure-seeker places the rod on the ground after sundown, and when it rests directly over treasure, the rod begins to move as if it were alive.   Now, if the mistletoe discovers gold, it must be in its character of the Golden Bough ; and if it is gathered at the solstices, must not the Golden Bough, like the golden fern-seed, be an emanation of the sun's fire ?   The question cannot be answered with a simple affirmative. We have seen that the old Aryans perhaps kindled the solstitial and other ceremonial fires in part as sun-charms, that is, with the intention of supplying the sun with fresh fire ; and as these fires were usually made by the friction or combustion of oak-wood, it may have appeared to the ancient Aryan that the sun was periodically recruited from the fire which resided in the sacred oak. In other words, the oak may have seemed to him the original storehouse or reservoir of the fire which was from time to time drawn out to feed the sun. But if the life of the oak was conceived to be in the mistletoe, the mistletoe must on that view have contained the seed or germ of the fire which was elicited by friction from the wood of the oak. Thus, instead of saying that the mistletoe was an emanation of the sun's fire, it might be more correct to say that the sun's fire was regarded as an emanation of the mistletoe. No wonder, then, that the mistletoe shone with a golden splendour, and was called the Golden Bough. Probably, however, like fern-seed, it was thought to assume its golden aspect only at those stated times, especially midsummer, when fire was drawn from the oak to light up the sun. At Pulverbatch, in Shropshire, it was believed within living memory that the oak-tree blooms on Midsummer Eve and the blossom withers before daylight. A maiden who wishes to know her lot in marriage should spread a white cloth under the tree at night, and in the morning she will find a little dust, which is all that remains of the flower. She should place the pinch of dust under her pillow, and then her future husband will appear to her in her dreams. This fleeting bloom of the oak, if I am right, was probably the mistletoe in its character of the Golden Bough. The conjecture is confirmed by the observation that in Wales a real sprig of mistletoe gathered on Midsummer Eve is similarly placed under the pillow to induce prophetic dreams ; and further the mode of catching the imaginary bloom of the oak in a white cloth is exactly that which was employed by the Druids to catch the real mistletoe when it dropped from the bough of the oak, severed by the golden sickle. As Shropshire borders on Wales, the belief that the oak blooms on Midsummer Eve may be Welsh in its immediate origin, though probably the belief is a fragment of the primitive Aryan creed. In some parts of Italy, as we saw, peasants still go out on Midsummer morning to search the oak-trees for the " oil of St. John," which, like the mistletoe, heals all wounds, and is, perhaps, the mistletoe itself in its glorified aspect. Thus it is easy to understand how a title like the Golden Bough, so little descriptive of its usual appearance on the tree, should have been applied to the seemingly insignificant parasite. Further, we can perhaps see why in antiquity mistletoe was believed to possess the remarkable property of extinguishing fire, and why in Sweden it is still kept in houses as a safeguard against conflagration. Its fiery nature marks it out, on homoeopathic principles, as the best possible cure or preventive of injury by fire.

These considerations may partially explain why Virgil makes Aeneas carry a glorified bough of mistletoe with him on his descent

into the gloomy subterranean world.   The poet describes how at the
very gates of hell there stretched a vast and gloomy wood, and how
the hero, following the flight of two doves that lured him on, wandered
into the depths of the immemorial forest till he saw afar off through
the shadows of the trees the flickering light of the Golden Bough
illuminating the matted boughs overhead.   If the mistletoe, as a
yellow withered bough in the sad autumn woods, was conceived to
contain the seed of fire, what better companion could a forlorn wanderer
in the nether shades take with him than a bough that would be a
lamp to his feet as well as a rod and staff to his hands ?   Armed with
it he might boldly confront the dreadful spectres that would cross his
path on his adventurous journey.   Hence when Aeneas, emerging
from the forest, comes to the banks of Styx, winding slow with
sluggish stream through the infernal marsh, and the surly ferryman
refuses him passage in his boat, he has but to draw the Golden Bough
from his bosom and hold it up, and straightway the blusterer quails
at the sight and meekly receives the hero into his crazy bark, which
sinks deep in the water under the unusual weight of the living man.
Even in recent times, as we have seen, mistletoe has been deemed a
protection against witches and trolls, and the ancients may well have
credited it with the same magical virtue.   And if the parasite can, as
some of our peasants believe, open all locks, why should it not have
served as an " open Sesame " in the hands of Aeneas to unlock the
gates of death ?

     Now, too, we can conjecture why Virbius at Nemi came to be
confounded with the sun.   If Virbius was, as I have tried to show,
a tree-spirit, he must have been the spirit of the oak on which grew
the Golden Bough ; for tradition represented him as the first of the
Kings of the Wood.   As an oak-spirit he must have been supposed
periodically to rekindle the sun's fire, and might therefore easily be
confounded with the sun itself.   Similarly we can explain why Balder,
an oak-spirit, was described as " so fair of face and so shining that
a light went forth from him," and why he should have been so often
taken to be the sun.   And in general we may say that in primitive
society, when the only known way of making fire is by the friction
of wood, the savage must necessarily conceive of fire as a property
stored away, like sap or juice, in trees, from which he has laboriously
to extract it.   The Senal Indians of California " profess to believe
that the whole world was once a globe of fire, whence that element
passed up into the trees, and now comes out whenever two pieces
of wood are rubbed together."   Similarly the Maidu Indians of California hold that " the earth was primarily a globe of molten matter,
and from that the principle of fire ascended through the roots into
the trunk and branches of trees, whence the Indians can extract it
by means of their drill."   In Namoluk, one of the Caroline Islands,
they say that the art of making fire was taught men by the gods.
Olofaet, the cunning master of flames, gave fire to the bird *mwi* and
bade him carry it to earth in his bill.   So the bird flew from tree to

tree and stored away the slumbering force of the fire in the wood, from which men can elicit it by friction. In the ancient Vedic hymns of India the fire-god Agni " is spoken of as born in wood, as the embryo of plants, or as distributed in plants. He is also said to have entered into all plants or to strive after them. When he is called the embryo of trees or of trees as well as plants, there may be a side-glance at the fire produced in forests by the friction of the boughs of trees."

A tree which has been struck by lightning is naturally regarded by the savage as charged with a double or triple portion of fire ; for has he not seen the mighty flash enter into the trunk with his own eyes ? Hence perhaps we may explain some of the many superstitious beliefs concerning trees that have been struck by lightning. When the Thompson Indians of British Columbia wished to set fire to the houses of their enemies, they shot at them arrows which were either made from a tree that had been struck by lightning or had splinters of such wood attached to them. Wendish peasants of Saxony refuse to burn in their stoves the wood of trees that have been struck by lightning ; they say that with such fuel the house would be burnt down. In like manner the Thonga of South Africa will not use such wood as fuel nor warm themselves at a fire which has been kindled with it. On the contrary, when lightning sets fire to a tree, the Winamwanga of Northern Rhodesia put out all the fires in the village and plaster the fireplaces afresh, while the head men convey the lightning-kindled fire to the chief, who prays over it. The chief then sends out the new fire to all his villages, and the villagers reward his messengers for the boon. This shows that they look upon fire kindled by lightning with reverence, and the reverence is intelligible, for they speak of thunder and lightning as God himself coming down to earth. Similarly the Maidu Indians of California believe that a Great Man created the world and all its inhabitants, and that lightning is nothing but the Great Man himself descending swiftly out of heaven and rending the trees with his flaming arm.

It is a plausible theory that the reverence which the ancient peoples of Europe paid to the oak, and the connexion which they traced between the tree and their sky-god, were derived from the much greater frequency with which the oak appears to be struck by lightning than any other tree of our European forests. This peculiarity of the tree has seemingly been established by a series of observations instituted within recent years by scientific enquirers who have no mythological theory to maintain. However we may explain it, whether by the easier passage of electricity through oakwood than through any other timber, or in some other way, the fact itself may well have attracted the notice of our rude forefathers, who dwelt in the vast forests which then covered a large part of Europe ; and they might naturally account for it in their simple religious way by supposing that the great sky-god, whom they worshipped and whose awful voice they heard in the roll of thunder, loved the oak above all the trees of the wood and often descended into it from the murky cloud in a flash of lightning, leaving a token of his presence or of his passage in the riven and blackened trunk and the blasted foliage. Such trees would thenceforth be encircled by a nimbus of glory as the visible seats of the thundering sky-god. Certain it is that, like some savages, both Greeks and Romans identified their great god of the sky and of the oak with the lightning flash which struck the ground ; and they regularly enclosed such a stricken spot and treated it thereafter as sacred. It is not rash to suppose that the ancestors of the Celts and Germans in the forests of Central Europe paid a like respect for like reasons to a blasted oak.

This explanation of the Aryan reverence for the oak and of the association of the tree with the great god of the thunder and the sky, was suggested or implied long ago by Jacob Grimm, and has been in recent years powerfully reinforced by Mr. W. Warde Fowler. It appears to be simpler and more probable than the explanation which I formerly adopted, namely, that the oak was worshipped primarily for the many benefits which our rude forefathers derived from the tree, particularly for the fire which they drew by friction from its wood ; and that the connexion of the oak with the sky was an after-thought based on the belief that the flash of lightning was nothing but the spark which the sky-god up aloft elicited by rubbing two pieces of oak wood against each other, just as his savage worshipper kindled fire in the forest on earth. On that theory the god of the thunder and the sky was derived from the original god of the oak ; on the present theory, which I now prefer, the god of the sky and the thunder was the great original deity of our Aryan ancestors, and his association with the oak was merely an inference based on the frequency with which the oak was seen to be struck by lightning. If the Aryans, as some think, roamed the wide steppes of Russia or Central Asia with their flocks and herds before they plunged into the gloom of the European forests, they may have worshipped the god of the blue or cloudy firmament and the flashing thunderbolt long before they thought of associating him with the blasted oaks in their new home.

Perhaps the new theory has the further advantage of throwing light on the special sanctity ascribed to mistletoe which grows on an oak. The mere rarity of such a growth on an oak hardly suffices to explain the extent and the persistence of the superstition. A hint of its real origin is possibly furnished by the statement of Pliny that the Druids worshipped the plant because they believed it to have fallen from heaven and to be a token that the tree on which it grew was chosen by the god himself. Can they have thought that the mistletoe dropped on the oak in a flash of lightning ? The conjecture is confirmed by the name thunder-besom which is applied to mistletoe in the Swiss canton of Aargau, for the epithet clearly implies a close connexion between the parasite and the thunder ; indeed " thunder-besom " is a popular name in Germany for any bushy nest-like excrescence growing on a branch, because such a parasitic growth is actually believed by the ignorant to be a product of lightning.

If there is any truth in this conjecture, the real reason why the Druids worshipped a mistletoe-bearing oak above all other trees of the forest was a belief that every such oak had not only been struck by lightning but bore among its branches a visible emanation of the celestial fire ; so that in cutting the mistletoe with mystic rites they were securing for themselves all the magical properties of a thunder-bolt. If that was so, we must apparently conclude that the mistletoe was deemed an emanation of the lightning rather than, as I have thus far argued, of the midsummer sun. Perhaps, indeed, we might combine the two seemingly divergent views by supposing that in the old Aryan creed the mistletoe descended from the sun on Midsummer Day in a flash of lightning. But such a combination is artificial and unsupported, so far as I know, by any positive evidence. Whether on mythical principles the two interpretations can really be reconciled with each other or not, I will not presume to say ; but even should they prove to be discrepant, the inconsistency need not have prevented our rude forefathers from embracing both of them at the same time with an equal fervour of conviction ; for like the great majority of mankind the savage is above being hidebound by the trammels of a pedantic logic. In attempting to track his devious thought through the jungle of crass ignorance and blind fear, we must always remember that we are treading enchanted ground, and must beware of taking for solid realities the cloudy shapes that cross our path or hover and gibber at us through the gloom. We can never completely replace ourselves at the standpoint of primitive man, see things with his eyes, and feel our hearts beat with the emotions that stirred his. All our theories concerning him and his ways must therefore fall far short of certainty ; the utmost we can aspire to in such matters is a reasonable degree of probability.

To conclude these enquiries we may say that if Balder was indeed, as I have conjectured, a personification of a mistletoe-bearing oak, his death by a blow of the mistletoe might on the new theory be explained as a death by a stroke of lightning. So long as the mistletoe, in which the flame of the lightning smouldered, was suffered to remain among the boughs, so long no harm could befall the good and kindly god of the oak, who kept his life stowed away for safety between earth and heaven in the mysterious parasite ; but when once that seat of his life, or of his death, was torn from the branch and hurled at the trunk, the tree fell—the god died—smitten by a thunderbolt.

And what we have said of Balder in the oak forests of Scandinavia may perhaps, with all due diffidence in a question so obscure and uncertain, be applied to the priest of Diana, the King of the Wood, at Aricia in the oak forests of Italy. He may have personated in flesh and blood the great Italian god of the sky, Jupiter, who had kindly come down from heaven in the lightning flash to dwell among men in the mistletoe—the thunder-besom—the Golden Bough—growing on the sacred oak in the dells of Nemi. If that was so, we need not wonder that the priest guarded with drawn sword the mystic bough which contained the god's life and his own. The goddess whom he served and married was herself, if I am right, no other than the Queen of Heaven, the true wife of the sky-god. For she, too, loved the solitude of the woods and the lonely hills, and sailing overhead on clear nights in the likeness of the silver moon looked down with pleasure on her own fair image reflected on the calm, the burnished surface of the lake, Diana's Mirror.

CHAPTER LXIX

FAREWELL TO NEMI

WE are at the end of our enquiry, but as often happens in the search after truth, if we have answered one question, we have raised many more ; if we have followed one track home, we have had to pass by others that opened off it and led, or seemed to lead, to far other goals than the sacred grove at Nemi. Some of these paths we have followed a little way ; others, if fortune should be kind, the writer and the reader may one day pursue together. For the present we have journeyed far enough together, and it is time to part. Yet before we do so, we may well ask ourselves whether there is not some more general conclusion, some lesson, if possible, of hope and encouragement, to be drawn from the melancholy record of human error and folly which has engaged our attention in this book.

If then we consider, on the one hand, the essential similarity of man's chief wants everywhere and at all times, and on the other hand, the wide difference between the means he has adopted to satisfy them in different ages, we shall perhaps be disposed to conclude that the movement of the higher thought, so far as we can trace it, has on the whole been from magic through religion to science. In magic man depends on his own strength to meet the difficulties and dangers that beset him on every side. He believes in a certain established order of nature on which he can surely count, and which he can manipulate for his own ends. When he discovers his mistake, when he recognises sadly that both the order of nature which he had assumed and the control which he had believed himself to exercise over it were purely imaginary, he ceases to rely on his own intelligence and his own unaided efforts, and throws himself humbly on the mercy of certain great invisible beings behind the veil of nature, to whom he now ascribes all those far-reaching powers which he once arrogated to himself. Thus in the acuter minds magic is gradually superseded by religion, which explains the succession of natural phenomena as regulated by the will, the passion, or the caprice of spiritual beings like man in kind, though vastly superior to him in power.

But as time goes on this explanation in its turn proves to be unsatisfactory. For it assumes that the succession of natural events is not determined by immutable laws, but is to some extent variable and irregular, and this assumption is not borne out by closer observation. On the contrary, the more we scrutinise that succession the more we are struck by the rigid uniformity, the punctual precision with which, wherever we can follow them, the operations of nature are carried on. Every great advance in knowledge has extended the sphere of order and correspondingly restricted the sphere of apparent disorder in the world, till now we are ready to anticipate that even in regions where chance and confusion appear still to reign, a fuller knowledge would everywhere reduce the seeming chaos to cosmos. Thus the keener minds, still pressing forward to a deeper solution of the mysteries of the universe, come to reject the religious theory of nature as inadequate, and to revert in a measure to the older standpoint of magic by postulating explicitly, what in magic had only been implicitly assumed, to wit, an inflexible regularity in the order of natural events, which, if carefully observed, enables us to foresee their course with certainty and to act accordingly. In short, religion, regarded as an explanation of nature, is displaced by science.

But while science has this much in common with magic that both rest on a faith in order as the underlying principle of all things, readers of this work will hardly need to be reminded that the order presupposed by magic differs widely from that which forms the basis of science. The difference flows naturally from the different modes in which the two orders have been reached. For whereas the order on which magic reckons is merely an extension, by false analogy, of the order in which ideas present themselves to our minds, the order laid down by science is derived from patient and exact observation of the phenomena themselves. The abundance, the solidity, and the splendour of the results already achieved by science are well fitted to inspire us with a cheerful confidence in the soundness of its method. Here at last, after groping about in the dark for countless ages, man has hit upon a clue to the labyrinth, a golden key that opens many locks in the treasury of nature. It is probably not too much to say that the hope of progress —moral and intellectual as well as material—in the future is bound up with the fortunes of science, and that every obstacle placed in the way of scientific discovery is a wrong to humanity.

Yet the history of thought should warn us against concluding that because the scientific theory of the world is the best that has yet been formulated, it is necessarily complete and final. We must remember that at bottom the generalisations of science or, in common parlance, the laws of nature are merely hypotheses devised to explain that ever-shifting phantasmagoria of thought which we dignify with the high-sounding names of the world and the universe. In the last analysis magic, religion, and science are nothing but theories of thought ; and as science has supplanted its predecessors, so it may hereafter be itself superseded by some more perfect hypothesis, perhaps by some totally different way of looking at the phenomena—of registering the shadows on the screen—of which we in this generation can form no idea. The

advance of knowledge is an infinite progression towards a goal that for
ever recedes.   We need not murmur at the endless pursuit :

> *Fatti non foste a viver come bruti*
> *Ma per seguir virtute e conoscenza.*

Great things will come of that pursuit, though we may not enjoy them.
Brighter stars will rise on some voyager of the future—some great
Ulysses of the realms of thought—than shine on us.   The dreams of
magic may one day be the waking realities of science.   But a dark
shadow lies athwart the far end of this fair prospect.   For however vast
the increase of knowledge and of power which the future may have in
store for man, he can scarcely hope to stay the sweep of those great
forces which seem to be making silently but relentlessly for the destruction of all this starry universe in which our earth swims as a speck or
mote.   In the ages to come man may be able to predict, perhaps even
to control, the wayward courses of the winds and clouds, but hardly
will his puny hands have strength to speed afresh our slackening
planet in its orbit or rekindle the dying fire of the sun.   Yet the
philosopher who trembles at the idea of such distant catastrophes may
console himself by reflecting that these gloomy apprehensions, like the
earth and the sun themselves, are only parts of that unsubstantial
world which thought has conjured up out of the void, and that the
phantoms which the subtle enchantress has evoked to-day she may
ban to-morrow.   They too, like so much that to common eyes seems
solid, may melt into air, into thin air.

Without dipping so far into the future, we may illustrate the course
which thought has hitherto run by likening it to a web woven of three
different threads—the black thread of magic, the red thread of religion,
and the white thread of science, if under science we may include those
simple truths, drawn from observation of nature, of which men in all
ages have possessed a store.   Could we then survey the web of thought
from the beginning, we should probably perceive it to be at first a
chequer of black and white, a patchwork of true and false notions,
hardly tinged as yet by the red thread of religion.   But carry your
eye farther along the fabric and you will remark that, while the black
and white chequer still runs through it, there rests on the middle
portion of the web, where religion has entered most deeply into its
texture, a dark crimson stain, which shades off insensibly into a lighter
tint as the white thread of science is woven more and more into the
tissue.   To a web thus chequered and stained, thus shot with threads
of diverse hues, but gradually changing colour the farther it is unrolled,
the state of modern thought, with all its divergent aims and conflicting
tendencies, may be compared.   Will the great movement which for
centuries has been slowly altering the complexion of thought be continued in the near future ? or will a reaction set in which may arrest
progress and even undo much that has been done ?   To keep up our
parable, what will be the colour of the web which the Fates are now
weaving on the humming loom of time ? will it be white or red ?   We

cannot tell.   A faint glimmering light illumines the backward portion of the web.   Clouds and thick darkness hide the other end.

Our long voyage of discovery is over and our bark has drooped her weary sails in port at last.   Once more we take the road to Nemi. It is evening, and as we climb the long slope of the Appian Way up to the Alban Hills, we look back and see the sky aflame with sunset, its golden glory resting like the aureole of a dying saint over Rome and touching with a crest of fire the dome of St. Peter's.   The sight once seen can never be forgotten, but we turn from it and pursue our way darkling along the mountain side, till we come to Nemi and look down on the lake in its deep hollow, now fast disappearing in the evening shadows.   The place has changed but little since Diana received the homage of her worshippers in the sacred grove.   The temple of the sylvan goddess, indeed, has vanished and the King of the Wood no longer stands sentinel over the Golden Bough.   But Nemi's woods are still green, and as the sunset fades above them in the west, there comes to us, borne on the swell of the wind, the sound of the church bells of Aricia ringing the Angelus.   *Ave Maria!* Sweet and solemn they chime out from the distant town and die lingeringly away across the wide Campagnan marshes.   *Le roi est mort, vive le roi!* *Ave Maria!*

INDEX

Abbas the Great, Shah of Persia, 289
Abbot of Unreason, 586
Abchases of the Caucasus, 534
Abduction of souls by demons, 186
Absence and recall of the soul, 180
Abstinence, 136, 138
Abydos, 366; specially associated with Osiris, 367
Abeokuta, the Alake of, 295
Abipones of Paraguay, 254
Abonsam, an evil spirit, 555
Abruzzi, the Carnival in the, 303
Abscesses, cure for, 539
Abyssinia, rain-making in, 66; rain-making priests on the borders of, 107
Acagchemem tribe of California, 499
Acaill, Book of, 273
Acosta, J. de, 587
Acts, tabooed, 194-202
Adam of Bremen, 160
Adon, a Semitic title, 325
Adonis, and Aphrodite (Venus), 7, 8, 328; the myth of, 324-7; in Syria, 327-9; in Cyprus, 329-35; ritual of, 335-41; the gardens of, 341-7; in relation to the pig, 471
Adonis, the river, 328, 336
Adoption, pretence of birth at, 14
Adultery of wife thought to spoil the luck of absent husband, 23, 24
Aegira, priestess of Earth at, 94
Aegis, Athena and the, 477
Aeneas, and the Golden Bough, 3, 163, 703, 706, 707; his vision of the glories of Rome, 149
Aeolus, King of the Winds, 81
Aesculapius, 5, 111, 301
Afghanistan, ceremony at the reception of strangers in, 196
Africa, magicians, especially rain-makers, as chiefs and kings in, 84-6; human gods in, 98; rules of life or taboos observed by kings in, 169-72; reluctance of people to tell their own names in, 247; seclusion of girls at puberty in, 595; dread and seclusion of menstruous women in, 604; birth-trees in, 681

Africa, British Central, heart of lion eaten to make eater brave in, 495
——, East, seclusion and purification of man-slayers in, 214; infanticide in, 293; propitiation of dead lions in, 522
——, North, charms to render bridegroom impotent in, 241; Midsummer fires in, 631
——, South, rat's hair as a charm in, 31; continence in war in, 211; seclusion of man-slayers in, 214; disposal of cut hair and nails in, 235; magic use of spittle in, 237; personal names tabooed in, 247; rites of initiation in, 497; seclusion of girls at puberty in, 595; dread of menstruous women in, 604; story of the external soul in, 677
——, West, magical functions of chiefs in, 85; reverence for silk-cotton trees in, 112; kings forced to accept office in, 176; fetish kings in, 177; traps set for souls in, 187; purification after a journey in, 197; custom as to blood shed on the ground, 229; rain-charms, 234; negroes of, 236; human sacrifices in, 433, 570; propitiation of dead leopard in, 523; the external soul in, 684; ritual of death and resurrection in, 697
Afterbirth, contagious magic of, 39-41
Agar Dinka, the, 270
Agaric, superstitions as to, 618
Agdestis, a man-monster, 349
Age of magic, 55, 56
Agni, Indian fire-god, 708
Agricultural year, expulsion of demons timed to coincide with seasons of the, 575
Agrionia, festival at Orchomenus, 291
Agu, Mount, in Togo, wind-fetish on, 81; fetish priest on, 169
Ague, cure for, 545, 546
Aht or Nootka Indians, 599
Ainos, 481, 496, 515, 528, 530, 532; of Japan, 252, 505, 506, 660; of Saghalien, 20, 509
Akikuyu of British East Africa, 145, 604

Buddha, images of, drenched as a rain-charm, 77 ; the Footprint of, 235
Buddhas, living, 102
Buddhism, 112 ; and Christianity, 361
Buffalo, sacrificed for human victim, 436 ; a Batak totem, 691
Buffalo-bull, last sheaf called, 457
Buffaloes, propitiation of dead, 523 ; the resurrection of, 529 ; revered by the Todas, 534 ; as scapegoats, 565
Buginese of Celebes, 33
Building, continence during, 220
Bukaua of New Guinea, 597, 694
Bulgaria, 15 ; charms in, 30, 31 ; peasants threaten fruit trees to make them bear, 114 ; superstitions in, 240 ; harvest customs in, 405 ; cure for fever in, 545 ; need-fire in, 640
Bull, in relation to Dionysus, 389, 390 ; corn-spirit as, 457, 465 ; at threshing, 458, 459
Bull's blood, bath of, in rites of Attis, 351
Bull-roarers, 692-5
Bullets, magical treatment of, 19 ; magical modes of averting, 26
Bullocks as scapegoats, 541
Bulls, sacred, of Ancient Egypt, 476
Bunyoro, king of, 199, 270
Burghers or Badagas. See Badagas
Burglars, charms employed by, 30
Burial customs, 35, 175, 185, 190
Burma, priestly king in, 226, 227 ; king's name tabooed in, 257 ; custom of threshing in, 418 ; expulsion of demons in, 549
Burne, Miss C. S., 446
Buru, East Indian island, girl sacrificed to crocodile in, 145 ; eating the soul of the rice in, 482 ; dog's flesh eaten in, 496
Burying the Carnival, 301-7
Bush negroes of Surinam, 166, 473
Bushmen of South Africa, 495, 604
Busiris, backbone of Osiris at, 367 ; ritual of Osiris at, 375 ; " the house of Osiris," 443
Busiris, king of Egypt, 443
Butter, time for making, 35
Buzzard, killing the sacred, 499
Byblus, Adonis at, 327 ; Osiris and Isis at, 364

Cacongo, king of, 199
Cactus, the sacred, 23
Cadiz, death at low tide at, 35
Caesar, Julius, 46, 653
Caffres, the, 222, 235, 247-9, 522 ; of Sofala, 33 ; of Natal and Zululand, 483
Cailleach (Old Wife), name given to last corn cut, 403, 409
Cairo, ceremony of cutting the dams at, 370
Cajaboneros Indians, the, 138
Calabar, expulsion of demons at Old, 492, 567 ; soul of chief in sacred grove at, 681 ; belief of negroes regarding external souls, 686

Calabashes, souls shut up in, 188
Calabria, Easter custom in, 345 ; annual expulsion of witches in, 560
Calendar, the ancient Greek, 279 ; regulation of the early, an affair of religion, 280 ; the Egyptian, 368 ; the Alexandrian, 373 ; of Esne, 373 ; the Mohammedan, 632
Calf, killed at harvest, 458 ; mythical, in the corn, 459
Calicut, rule of succession observed by the kings of, 275-7, 296
California, the shaman in, 88 ; killing the sacred buzzard in, 499 ; Indians of, 599, 707
Caligula and the priest of Nemi, 3
Cambodia, homoeopathic magic used by hunters in, 18 ; human incarnation of god in, 95 ; kings of, 108, 167, 224, 266, 284, 289 ; superstitions regarding the head in, 230 ; annual expulsion of demons in, 559 ; palace purged of demons, 563 ; seclusion of girls at puberty, 602 ; ritual at cutting a parasitic orchid in, 660, 661
Cambodian story of the external soul, 668
Camel, plague transferred to, 540
Cameroons, the external soul in the, 681 ; theory of, 685
Camomile, burnt in Midsummer fire, 631
Camp shifted after a death, 252
Campbell, Major-General John, 436, 437
——, Rev. J. G., 403
Camphor, 21, 24
Canadian Indians, 525, 526
Candlemas, 134, 461
Candles, 3 ; magical, 30 ; of human tallow, 56
Cannibal feast, legendary, at the Boeotian Orchomenus, 292
Cannibalism, 233, 391, 497
Caprification, 580
Car Nicobar, expulsion of devils in, 567
Caramantran, death of, 304
Caribs, the, 27, 495, 690
Carinthia, Green George in, 126 ; ceremony at the installation of a prince of, 287 ; custom at threshing in, 429
Carlin or Carline, " the Old Woman," in Scotland, 403
Carnival, dances at the, 28 ; burying the, 298, 301-7 ; the burial and resurrection of the, 315 ; at Rome in the rites of Attis, 350 ; in relation to the Saturnalia, 586 ; effigy burnt at end of, 614
Carolina, Indians of, 519
Caroline Islands, 40, 218 ; traditionary origin of fire in the, 707
Carpathus, laying out of corpses in, 243
Carrier Indians of North-West America, 18, 219, 606
" Carrying out Death," 125, 302, 307-16, 577, 613, 614
Carthage, Christians worshipping each other at, 101 ; the effeminate priests of the Great Mother at, 356

3 A

Masks worn by devil-dancers, 542 ; at expulsion of demons, 548, 553 ; by members of a secret Wolf society, 699

Maspero, Sir Gaston, 53

" Mass of the Holy Spirit," 53

Mass of Saint Sécaire, 54

Massagetae sacrifice horses to the sun, 79

Masset, in Queen Charlotte Islands, dances of Haida women at, 27

Matabele, the, 72, 645

Matacos or Mataguayos, the, 601

Matiamvo, a potentate in Angola, 271

Matuana, Zulu chief, 498

May, King of, 129, 130, 299 ; King and Queen of, 157, 320 ; Queen of, 129, 131

May Bride, 135, 317, 320 ; Bridegroom, 133 ; Lady, in Cambridge, 127 ; Rose, the Little, 125

—— Day, celebration of, 119-35, 316, 621 ; " Burning out of the Witches " on, 560 ; bonfires on, 617-22

May-bushes, 119, 129, 130, 132 ; -garlands, 121 ; -poles, 119, 120, 122-4, 132, 479 ; -trees, 119-21, 123, 124, 297, 299, 311, 314, 614, 651

Mbaya Indians, the, 293

M'Bengas of the Gaboon, 681

Mecca, pilgrims to, 238

Mecklenburg, magic in, 44 ; locks unlocked at childbirth in, 239 ; harvest customs in, 430, 449, 454 ; treatment of the after-birth in, 682

Medea and Aeson, 496

Medicine bag, at initiation, 698

—— men, 64, 85, 87, 88, 92, 105, 180, 183-7, 484, 520, 679, 693

Melanesia, homoeopathic magic of stones in, 33 ; contagious magic of wounds in, 41 ; confusion of magic and religion in, 52 ; supernatural power of chiefs in, 84 ; continence while yam vines are being trained in, 138 ; malignant spirits in, 192 ; disposal of cut hair and nails in, 235 ; names of relations by marriage tabooed in, 251 ; conception of the external soul in, 684

Melanesians, 52, 246

Melicertes, son of King Athamas, 290, 291

Melos, milk-stones in, 34

Memphis, head of Osiris at, 366

Men, evil transferred to, 542 ; disguised as demons, 562, 563 ; as scapegoats, 565 ; divine, as scapegoats, 571, 576 ; disguised as women, 610

Menedemus, sacrifices to, 224

Menelik, Emperor of Abyssinia, 66

Menstruation, women tabooed at, 207 ; seclusion of girls at, 595 ; reasons for secluding women at, 606

Meriahs, human victims sacrificed among the Khonds, 434, 437

Merlin, the wizard, 76

Meroe, Ethiopian kings of, 266

Mesopotamia, artificial fertilisation of the date-palm in, 582

Messiah, pretended, in America, 102

Metsik, a forest-spirit, 315

Mexican kings, their oath, 87, 104 ; sacraments, 488 ; temples, 589

Mexicans, the ancient, 79, 380, 432

Mexico, ancient, festival in honour of the goddess of maize, 28 ; treatment of the navel-string in, 40 ; human sacrifices in, 380, 431, 432 ; killing the god in, 587-92

Micah, the prophet, 51

Mice, in magic, 39 ; eaten by the Jews as a religious rite, 472 ; superstitious precautions of farmers against, 530, 531

Midsummer, death of the spirit of vegetation celebrated at, 319 ; bonfire at, called " fire of heaven," 644 ; procession of giants at, 654 ; sacred to Balder, 664

Midsummer bonfires, 122, 622. See also Midsummer fires

—— Bride and Bridegroom, 133

—— Day, ancient Roman festival of, 153. See also St. John's Day

—— Eve, in Sweden, 122 ; in Russia, 318 ; trolls and evil spirits abroad on, 625 ; oak thought to bloom on, 706. See also St. John's Eve

—— festival, in Europe, 153, 622 ; named after St. John, 343 ; the most important of the year among the primitive Aryans of Europe, 656

—— fires, 622-32 ; animals burnt in, 655

Midwinter fires, 636

Mikado of Japan, 168, 169, 176, 202, 593, 595

Miklucho-Maclay, Baron, 197

Milk, women's, promoted by milk-stones, 34 ; of cows, thought to be promoted by green boughs, 119 ; customs observed when the king of Bunyoro drinks, 199 ; of pig thought to cause leprosy, 472, 473 ; omens from boiling, 482 ; taboos referring to, 488 ; not to be drunk by menstruous women, 604 ; stolen by witches from cows, 620, 627, 628, 648

Milk-stones, magical, 34

Milkmen of the Todas sacred or divine, 100 ; taboos of, 175

Millet, homoeopathic magic of, 29 ; the deity of, 481

Minangkabauers of Sumatra, 180, 183, 415, 604

Minahassa, inspired priests in, 95 ; ceremony at house-warming in, 186, 679 ; names of parents-in-law tabooed in, 250 ; sowing and plucking the new rice in, 482 ; dummies to deceive demons in, 492 ; hair of slain foe used to impart courage in, 498 ; expulsion of devils in, 548

Minnetaree Indians, 419, 529

Minos, king of Cnossus, 280

3 C

with Persephone, 388 ; said to have transferred the sceptre to young Dionysus, 388 ; father of Dionysus by Demeter, 389 ; his appearance to Hercules in the shape of a ram, 500 ; and Danae, 602

Zeus, the Descender, places struck by lightning consecrated to, 159 ; Heavenly, at Sparta, 9 ; Lacedaemon, at Sparta, 9 ; Laphystian, 290-92 ; Lightning, sacrificial hearth of, 159 ; Polieus in Cos, 466

Zimbas, or Muzimbas, of South-east Africa, 97

Zoganes, temporary king at Babylon, put to death after a reign of five days, 282

Zoilus, priest of Dionysus at Orchomenus, 291

Zulu language, its diversity, 258

Zululand, rain-making by means of a "heaven-bird" in, 75 ; children buried to the neck as a rain-charm in, 75 ; names of chiefs and kings tabooed in, 257 ; kings put to death in, 272 ; festival of first-fruits in, 483 ; seclusion of girls at puberty in, 595 ; gardens fumigated with medicated smoke in, 645

Zulus, 192, 495, 498

Zuni Indians of New Mexico, 502, 504, 571

Żytniamatka, the Corn-mother, 421

THE END

Printed in Great Britain by R. & R. CLARK, LIMITED, *Edinburgh.*